Fifth Edition

Strategic Management and Business Policy

Thomas L. Wheelen
University of South Florida

J. David Hunger
Iowa State University

Addison-Wesley Publishing Company
Reading, Massachusetts / Menlo Park, California
New York / Don Mills, Ontario / Wokingham, England
Amsterdam / Bonn / Sydney / Singapore
Tokyo / Madrid / San Juan / Milan / Paris

Executive Editor: Michael Payne
Senior Sponsoring Editor: Beth Toland
Development Editor: Janice Jutras
Managing Editor: Kazia Navas
Senior Production Supervisor: Loren Hilgenhurst Stevens
Senior Production Coordinator: Beth F. Houston
Production Services: Nancy Benjamin
Copy Editor: Gerry Moore
Design Director: Karen Rappaport
Art Development Editor: Abrams & La Brecque Design
Prepress Buying Manager: Sarah McCracken
Technical Art Buyer: Joseph Vetere
Art Editor: Susan London-Payne
Illustrator: Network Graphics
Text Design: Richard Hollant, Winston Ford Design
Cover Design Director: Peter M. Blaiwas
Cover Design and Illustration: Leslie Haimes
Senior Marketing Manager: David Theisen
Marketing Manager: Craig Bleyer
Senior Manufacturing Manager: Roy Logan
Compositor: Compset, Inc.
Printer: R. R. Donnelley & Sons Company

Library of Congress Cataloging-in-Publication Data

Wheelen, Thomas L.
Strategic management and business policy / by Thomas L. Wheelen, J. David Hunger. — 5th ed.
p. cm.
Includes bibliographical references and index.
ISBN 0-201-56388-6
1. Strategic planning. I. Hunger, J. David, 1941– II. Title.
HD30.28.W43 1995 95-6030
658.4'012—dc20 CIP

ISBN 0-201-56388-6
2345678910—DOC—979695

DEDICATED TO

Kathy, Tom, Richard

Betty, Kari, Suzi, Lori, Merry, and Smokey

Special Dedication by Tom Wheelen:

Kathryn Elizabeth McGrath Wheelen (1895–1972)
My mother was born April 23, 1895, in Fitchburg, Massachusetts, to William E. McGrath (1865–1939) and Catherine McCarthy (1867–1932). Both parents were born in Ireland. She had two sisters, Mary and Margaret. The year 1995 would mark her 100th birthday. She graduated from Fitchburg High School in 1913. She worked for Webber Lumber Company as a clerk. She married Thomas L. Wheelen in 1933 and became President of Thomas Wheelen Company (circa 1879) in 1938 when her husband died. She had excellent business acumen, true concern for others, and many true friends of all ages. She had a strong and underlying belief system that allowed her to survive many years of serious illnesses. She always remained positive and very grateful for her life. The births of her three grandchildren, Kathryn, Thomas, and Richard, were true highlights and joys of her life. She never gave up and enjoyed life.
Tá grá thú.

The corporate world is becoming a very different place. Mergers and acquisitions have transformed the landscape. International boundaries are fading in importance as businesses take on a more global perspective, and the technology of the Information Age is telescoping the time it takes to communicate and make decisions. Strategic management takes a panoramic view of this changing corporate terrain and dares to ask why.

As a capstone course, strategic management and business policy unites the various departments, majors, and subdisciplines usually found in a business school. Other courses deal in depth with procedures and activities that are designed to answer how corporations exist. Because strategic management itself is in a constant state of flux, and because the course takes a holistic approach, business policy is often a difficult course to teach and to take. Consequently, this book is organized around a strategic management model that prefaces each chapter and provides a structure for content and complex case analyses by students.

Both the text and the cases have been class-tested in policy courses and revised on the basis of feedback from students, reviewers, and instructors. In response to comments, we have emphasized primarily those concepts that have proved to be most useful in understanding strategic decision making and in conducting case analysis. Our goal was to make the text as comprehensive as possible without getting bogged down in any one area. Endnote references are provided for those who wish to learn more about any particular topic. As in previous editions, *all the cases are about actual corporations.* The firms range in size and maturity from large, established multinationals to small, entrepreneurial ventures and cover a broad range of issues and questions.

Objectives

This book focuses on the following objectives, which are typically found in most strategic management and business policy courses:

- To develop conceptual skills so that a student is able to integrate previously learned aspects of corporations.
- To develop a framework of analysis to enable a student to identify central issues and problems in complex, comprehensive cases; to suggest alternative courses of action; and to present well-supported recommendations for future action.
- To develop an understanding of strategic management concepts, research, and theories.
- To develop an understanding of the roles and responsibilities of the Board of Directors, Chief Executive Officer, and other key managers in strategic management positions.
- To develop the ability to analyze and evaluate, both quantitatively and qualitatively, the performance of the people who are responsible for strategic decisions.
- To bridge the gap between theory and practice by developing an understanding of when and how to apply concepts and techniques learned in earlier courses on marketing, accounting, finance, management, production, and information systems.

- To improve research capabilities necessary to gather and interpret key environmental data.
- To develop a better understanding of the present and future environments in which corporations must function.
- To develop and refine analytical and decision-making skills for dealing with complex conceptual problems in an ethical manner.
- To develop an understanding of the emerging world economy and its potential impact on business activities in any location.

This book achieves these objectives by presenting and explaining concepts and theories that are useful in understanding the strategic management process. It critically analyzes studies in the field of strategy to acquaint the student with the literature of this area and to help develop the student's research capabilities. It also describes the people who manage strategically and suggests a model of strategic management. It recommends the strategic audit as one approach to the systematic analysis of complex, organizationwide issues. Through a series of comprehensive cases, it provides the student with an opportunity to apply concepts, skills, and techniques to real-world corporate problems. The book focuses on the business corporation because of its crucial position in the economic system of the world and in the material development of any society.

Time-Tested Features

This edition includes many of the same features and content that helped to make previous editions successful. Some of these are the following:

- A **strategic management model** runs throughout the entire book as a unifying concept (all chapters).
- The **strategic audit,** a way to operationalize the strategic decision-making process, serves as a checklist in case analysis (Chapter 2).
- Internal and external strategic factors are emphasized through the use of specially designed External Factor Analysis Summary (**EFAS**) and Internal Factor Analysis Summary (**IFAS**) **tables** (Chapters 4 and 5).
- **Top management** and the **Board of Directors** are examined in detail in their roles as strategic managers (Chapter 2).
- **Suggestions for in-depth case analysis** provide a complete listing of financial ratios, recommendations for oral and written analysis, and ideas for further research (Chapter 15).
- Special chapters deal with strategic issues in **multinational corporations, entrepreneurial ventures and small businesses,** and **not-for-profit organizations** (Chapters 11, 13, 14, respectively).
- A chapter on **social responsibility and ethics** deals with these increasingly salient concerns in strategic decision making (Chapter 3).
- Equal emphasis is placed on **environmental scanning** of the societal environment as well as on industry strategic factors. Topics include forecasting and Miles and Snow's typology in addition to Porter's industry analysis (Chapter 4).
- **Company Spotlight Maytag Corporation** boxes illustrate the issues in each chapter and serve to integrate the material (Chapters 1–15).

- **Corporate strategy** is explained for the single business firm in an easy-to-understand model using growth, stability, and retrenchment strategies and then presented for the multibusiness firm in terms of portfolio analysis and the SWOT (TOWS) matrix (Chapter 6).
- **Business** (competitive) and **functional strategies** as well as **competitive tactics** are explained and evaluated in a separate chapter (Chapter 7).
- Two chapters deal with issues in **strategy implementation,** such as organizational and job design plus strategy-manager fit, action planning, and corporate culture (Chapters 8 and 9).
- A separate chapter on **evaluation and control** explains the importance of measurement and incentives to organizational performance (Chapter 10).
- **Timely, well-researched, and class-tested cases** deal with interesting companies and industries. Many of the cases are about well-known, publicly held corporations—ideal subjects for further research by students who wish to "update" the cases.
- **An Industry Note for Use in Industry Analysis** of the major home appliance industry in 1993 is included for use by itself or with the Maytag and Whirlpool cases. A second industry note on the retailing industry is included in the accompanying CASE Instructor's Manual, to be used either on its own or in conjunction with the cases on Nordstrom, Kmart, Wal-Mart, and Blockbuster Video.

New Features For This Edition

In addition to updating and fine-tuning of time-tested features, other additions and changes to both the chapters and the cases make the book more useful to students and professors and more representative of the rapidly growing field of strategic management and business policy.

New Chapter

Strategic Issues in Managing Technology and Innovation (Chapter 12)

This is the first strategic management textbook to provide a chapter on these topics. This new chapter emphasizes the importance of technology and innovation to strategic managers. Cases such as those on Microsoft, Maytag, and Invacare enable readers to apply these concepts to actual situations.

New Topics

New Concepts and Approaches in Strategic Management

- Resource-based view of the firm (Chapter 5)
- Reengineering (Chapter 8)
- Total quality management (Chapter 8)
- Benchmarking (Chapter 10)
- Economic value-added measures (Chapter 10)
- International transfer pricing (Chapter 11)

New Features

Key Theory Capsules

Boxed inserts highlight and explain key theories underlying strategic management. This feature adds emphasis to the theories without interrupting the flow of the text material.

- *Agency theory* (corporate governance, Chapter 2)
- *Transaction cost economics* (vertical integration versus outsourcing, Chapter 6)
- *Population ecology, resource dependence,* and *institution theory* (organization change, Chapter 8)
- *Absolute and comparative advantage* (international trade, Chapter 11)

Introductory Vignettes and In Conclusion . . .

Brief descriptions of current situations in actual organizations introduce and conclude chapter material to add life to the concepts that are explained in each chapter.

Points to Remember

- Summary sentences end each chapter and add emphasis to key concepts.
- Brief bulleted sentences help the reader to better remember chapter essentials. Key points are more memorable than the usual summary and conclusion paragraph.

New Methodologies

Strategic Factor Analysis Summary (Chapter 6)

This Strategic Factor Analysis Summary (SFAS) table is designed to integrate previously identified external (EFAS) and internal (IFAS) factors into a combined list of strategic factors facing a corporation.

Integrated SWOT (TOWS) Analysis (Chapter 6)

This table connects EFAS and IFAS factors with the development of a SWOT/TOWS analysis. This illustrates how an analysis of strategic factors can help to generate possible alternative strategies.

Strategic Audit Worksheet (Chapter 15)

This worksheet is based on the time-tested strategic audit and is designed to help students *organize* and *structure* daily case preparation in a brief period of time. The worksheet works exceedingly well for checking the level of daily student case preparation, especially for open class discussions of cases. Examples are shown in Part B of the Instructor's Manual.

Strategy Cases

Thirty-three Cases New to This Edition

All 37 cases are current (1991–1993), high-quality cases of actual corporations and industries that are in the midst of strategic change. Thirty-three are new to this edition. The case authors graciously allowed us to edit their cases for this book. Many of these cases have been critiqued by expert referees of the North American Case Research Association, the Society for Case Research, and the World Association for Case Method Research and Application and appear in the *Case Research Journal, Journal of Business Cases, International Journal of Case Studies and Research,* and *Annual Advances in Business Cases.*

Twenty-six Comprehensive Strategy Cases Grouped by Industry

Twenty-six comprehensive, multi-issue strategy cases are grouped into the nine industries of (1) Grocery/Merchandising, (2) Fast Food Restaurants, (3) Major Home Appliances, (4) Computers/Software, (5) Beverages/Food, (6) Mass Merchandising/Retailing, (7) Athletic Shoes, (8) Health Care Industry, and (9) Commercial Aircraft. The firms profiled in these cases range from entrepreneurial small businesses to large multinational corporations. This is useful to the instructor who wishes to assign a series of cases in one industry.

Six Special Issues Cases

Six cases are categorized into the specific topic areas of Strategic Managers, Environmental Issues, and Not-for-Profit. These cases are somewhat shorter than the more comprehensive, multi-issue strategic management cases. They help an instructor to emphasize the particular topics of corporate governance, social responsibility and ethics, and the not-for-profit organization.

Five Special International Cases

Five cases deal specifically with strategic issues in Eastern Europe, the European Community, and the North American Trade Zone. Although most of the multi-issue comprehensive cases in the book have some multinational aspects, these cases focus on international issues to help an instructor put special emphasis on this area.

Videos

Videos to Accompany Cases and Chapters

A video consisting of eight segments is available to adopters of this edition for use with various chapters and cases.

Supplements

Instructor's Manuals

Two comprehensive Instructor's Manuals have been carefully constructed to accompany this book. The first one accompanies the text chapters. The second one accompanies the cases.

TEXT Instructor's Manual

To aid in discussing the 15 chapters dealing with strategic management concepts, the TEXT Instructor's Manual includes the following:

1. *Suggestions for teaching strategic management:* discusses various teaching methods and includes suggested course syllabi.
2. *Video guide:* presents summaries of free videos and suggestions for classroom use.
3. *Chapter notes:* includes summaries of each chapter, lists of key concepts and terms, and suggested answers to discussion questions.
4. *Multiple-choice test bank questions:* contains approximately 50 questions for each of the 15 chapters summing to over 700 questions from which to choose.
5. *Transparency masters:* includes over 170 transparency masters of figures and tables in the text as well as other exhibits.

CASE Instructor's Manual

To aid in case method teaching, the CASE Instructor's Manual includes detailed suggestions for use, teaching objectives, and examples of student analyses for each of the 37 cases. A standardized format is provided for each case:

1. *Case abstract.*
2. *Case issues and subjects.*
3. *Steps covered in the strategic decision-making process.*
4. *Case objectives.*
5. *Suggested classroom approaches.*
6. *Discussion questions.*
7. *Case author's teaching note.*
8. *Student-written strategic audit or paper.*
9. *EFAS, IFAS, and SFAS exhibits.*
10. *Financial analysis* (ratios and common-size income statements).

This is the most comprehensive Instructor's Manual in strategic management. The CASE Instructor's Manual also includes the industry note *Retailing 1993: Emerging from the Chaos*. This note can be used independently for industry analysis or with the cases on Nordstrom, Kmart, Wal-Mart, and Blockbuster Video. This industry note can be copied from the Instructor's Manual by book adopters and disseminated to students at no charge and without the need for additional copyright permissions.

Computerized Test Bank–Test Generator

Multiple-choice questions are available free to adopters of this textbook in a computerized test bank on a 3½" diskette for IBM-compatible personal computers. These questions are the same ones listed in the test bank portion of the TEXT Instructor's Manual and cover all 15 chapters of the book with over 700 questions. This Test Generator allows instructors to personalize exams and easily add, edit, or delete questions from the test bank. The order of questions may be scrambled, and multiple versions of the test may be prepared. Answer sheets are generated for each test designed.

Videos

A videotape cassette containing eight segments featuring company and industry vignettes for use with various chapters and cases is available free to adopters of this textbook. One of the videos features Maytag Corporation (Case 13). The video was presented at Maytag Corporation's 1993 annual shareholders meeting (as mentioned in the case) on the consolidation of the Jenn-Air and Magic Chef product lines into one sales/marketing organization. Other videos examine issues in various industries and companies, such as The Body Shop's view of social responsibility, drug prices (which can be used with Case 3, "Burroughs Wellcome and AZT," Coca-Cola's global marketing, technology transfer in VCRs, the successful use of focused differentiation competitive strategy in local breweries, strategy implementation at Au Bon Pain fast food restaurants, and Chrysler's use of platform teams and concurrent engineering to improve its strategy implementation. These videos can accompany various chapters in the text to provide examples of strategic management issues and concepts.

Transparency Acetates

A collection of over 170 acetates of the transparency masters from the TEXT Instructor's Manual are available free to adopters of the text.

Recommended Software

In conjunction with the fifth edition of *Strategic Management and Business Policy,* Addison-Wesley recommends utilizing the fisCAL business analysis software for IBM computers and its companion handbook, *Profiting from Financial Statements,* available from the Halcyon Group. Upon adoption, instructors will receive a copy of the software free of charge, as well as a diskette containing all of the financial data from the Wheelen/Hunger cases. Bookstore orders for students should be directed to Halcyon by contacting Thomas J. Bullock at the Halcyon Group, One Halcyon Place, P.O. Box 1249, Folly Beach, South Carolina, 29439. Any and all technical support for instructors using this software should also be directed to Halcyon.

Acknowledgments

We are grateful to the people who reviewed this edition for their constructive comments and suggestions. Their thought and effort have resulted in a book that is far superior to our original manuscript. The reviewers who worked directly on all 15 chapters have asterisks next to their names and are especially acknowledged. Special thanks to Stan Mendenhall for suggesting the Index of Sustainable Growth.

Ernest R. Archer, Winthrop University

Kimberly B. Boal, Texas Tech University*

Robert DeFillippi, Suffolk University*

Charles Gowen, Northern Illinois University

Robert Hopley, University of Massachusetts at Amherst

William R. LaFollette, Ball State University

Fred R. Landrum, Florida Atlantic University

Richard Linowes, American University

Stan Mendenhall, Eastern Montana College

Michael J. Merenda, University of New Hampshire

Ken Smith, Syracuse University*

Walt Tymon, Villanova University*

Daniel L. White, Drexel University

Our thanks go to Janice Jutras of Addison-Wesley Publishing Company for her help in the development of this Fifth Edition—in particular for her work with the reviewers. Beth Toland was the editor for this edition and should be thanked for her strong support of the resource-based view of the firm. We are especially grateful to Nancy Benjamin for her patience, expertise, and even disposition during the copyediting and production process. Nancy is a true professional; we enjoyed our continued relationship with her and her staff.

Thanks are due to Michael Potter of Iowa State University for his analysis of the resource-based view of the firm and for his energetic work on the complicated indexes. We are also very grateful to Kathy Wheelen for her first-rate administrative support. We are thankful to the many students who tried out the cases we chose to include in this book. Their comments helped us find any flaws in the cases before the book went to the printer.

In addition, we express our appreciation to Dr. David Shrock, Dean, and Dr. Brad Shrader, Management Department Chair, of Iowa State University's College of Business for their support and provision of the resources so necessary to produce a textbook. We also thank Dr. Robert Anderson, Chairman and Associate Dean of the College of Business and Don Quartermane (for his development of case materials), both of the University of South Florida. Both of us acknowledge our debt to Dr. William Shenkir and Dr. Frank S. Kaulback, former Deans of the McIntire School of Commerce of the University of Virginia, for the provision of a work climate that was most supportive of the original development of this book.

Finally, to the many strategy/policy instructors and students who have moaned to us about their problems with the strategy/policy course: We have tried to respond to your problems and concerns as best we could by providing a comprehensive yet usable text coupled with recent and complex cases. To you, the people who work hard in the strategy/policy trenches, we acknowledge our debt. This book is yours.

Tampa, Florida T. L. W.
Ames, Iowa J. D. H.

Part One Introduction to Strategic Management and Business Policy

Part Two Scanning the Environment

Part Three Strategy Formulation

Strategy Implementation and Control

Chapter 8 Strategy Implementation: Organizing for Action 220

Chapter 9 Strategy Implementation: Staffing and Directing 254

Chapter 10 Evaluation and Control 280

Other Strategic Issues

Introduction to Case Analysis

Cases in Strategic Management

Section C Issues in Strategic Management 458

ABOUT THE CONTRIBUTORS

Moustafa H. Abdelsamad, D.B.A. (George Washington University), is Dean of the College of Business Administration at Texas A&M University–Corpus Christi. He previously served as Dean of the College of Business and Industry at Southeastern Massachusetts University and as Professor of Finance and Associate Dean of Graduate Studies in Business at Virginia Commonwealth University. He is Editor-in-Chief of *SAM Advanced Management Journal* and past International President of the Society for the Advancement of Management. He is the author of *A Guide to Capital Expenditure Analysis* and two chapters in the *Dow Jones–Irwin Capital Budgeting Handbook*. He is the author or coauthor of numerous articles in various publications.

Sexton Adams, Ph.D., is Professor of Management at North Texas State University. He has taught at Texas Tech University and has been an adjunct professor at several institutions, including the University of Northern Colorado and Pepperdine University. He is actively engaged as a consultant to various organizations in strategic planning and management development. He is the author of *Administrative Policy and Strategy* and *Personnel Management* and is coauthor of *The Corporate Promotables* and *Modern Personnel Management.* He has published business policy cases in over 20 case books.

A. J. Almaney, Ph.D. (Indiana University), is Professor of Strategic Management at DePaul University. He is the author of *Strategic Management: The Process of Gaining a Competitive Advantage* and *Strategic Management: A Framework for Decision Making and Problem Solving.* His articles and cases have appeared in numerous journals and textbooks.

Stephen E. Barndt, Ph.D. (The Ohio State University), is Professor of Management at the School of Business, Pacific Lutheran University. Formerly, he was head of a department in the Graduate Education Division of the Air Force Institute of Technology's School of Systems and Logistics and taught at Central Michigan University. He has over 15 years of line and staff experience in operations and research and development. He has coauthored two fundamentals texts, *Managing by Project Management* and *Operations Management Concepts and Practices,* and has authored or coauthored numerous papers, articles, chapters, and cases addressing such subjects as organizational communication, project management, and strategic management. He is Director of Pacific Lutheran University's Small Business Institute and serves on the Editorial Review Board of the *Business Case Journal.*

Julius S. Brown, Ph.D. (University of California, Berkeley), is Professor of Management, Emeritus, at Loyola Marymount University. His primary research interest has been in the field of decision making in the economic area of uncertainty. He has published in the *Administrative Science Quarterly, Journal of Industrial Relations, The Harvard Business School Bulletin,* and the *California Monthly.* He has held management positions in the C.N.A. Financial Corp., Penn Mutual Life Insurance Co., and the U.S. Army. Dr. Brown's consulting work has been primarily with professional corporations. He is currently administrator of the Robert W. Zinn Memorial Scholarship.

James W. Camerius, M.S. (University of North Dakota), is Professor of Marketing, Northern Michigan University. He is a member of the Board of Directors of the Society for Case Research, a member of the North American Case Research Association, and a member of the World Association for Case Method Research and Application. His cases have appeared in over 30 management, marketing, and retailing textbooks, in addition to *Annual Advances in Business Cases.* He is an award and grant recipient of the Direct Selling Education Foundation, Washington, D.C., and was among those chosen to attend an academic symposium on "Retailing in the Year 2000" at the University of Texas IC2 Institute. His case studies have been presented and discussed at conferences, workshops, and symposia in the United States and Europe. He is listed in *Who's Who in the Midwest.*

Roy A. Cook, D.B.A. (Mississippi State University), is Associate Professor of Management, Fort Lewis College, Durango, Colorado. He has written and published numerous articles, cases, and papers based on his extensive experience in the hospitality industry and research interests in the areas of small business management, strategy, human relations, and communications. He is a member of the Small Business Institute Directors Association, the Academy of Management, and the Society for Case Research. He currently serves on the Board of Directors of the Society for Case Research, as well as the Editorial Review Boards of the *Business Case Journal* and the *Journal of Business Strategies.*

Richard A. Cosier, Ph.D. (University of Iowa), is Dean and the Fred E. Brown Chair of Business Administration at the University of Oklahoma. Previously, he served as Associate Dean and as Chair of the Management Department at Indiana University. He was formerly a planning engineer with the Western Electric Company and instructor of Management and Quantitative Methods at the University of Notre Dame. He has published in *Behavioral Science, Academy of Management Journal, Academy of Management Review, Organizational Behavior and Human Performance, Management Science, Strategic Management Journal, Business Horizons, Decisions Sciences, Personnel Psychology, Journal of Creative Behavior, International Journal of Management, Business Quarterly, Public Administration Quarterly, Human Relations,* and other journals. In addition, Professor Cosier has presented numerous papers at professional meetings, has coauthored a management textbook, and has a chapter on conflict in a popular management text. He has been active in many executive development programs and has acted as a management education consultant for several organizations. He belongs to the Institute of Management Consultants, Inc., Beta Gamma Sigma, the Academy of Management, Sigma Iota Epsilon, and the Decision Sciences Institute.

David B. Croll, Ph.D. (Pennsylvania State University), is Associate Professor of Accounting at the McIntire School of Commerce, University of Virginia. He was Visiting Professor at the University of Michigan. He is coauthor of *Behavioral Accounting—A Reader.* His cases have appeared in over ten management and accounting textbooks as well as in the *Journal of Management Case Studies.* He is currently consultant to the U.S. Navy, the Institute of Textile Technology, and the Institute of Chartered Financial Analysts.

Dan R. Dalton, Ph.D. (University of California, Irvine), is Professor of Management and Director of Graduate Programs, Graduate School of Business, Indiana University. He was formerly with General Telephone & Electronics for 13 years. He has been widely published in business and psychology periodicals; his articles have appeared in the *Academy of Management Journal, Journal of Applied Psychology, Personnel Psychology, Journal of Business Strategy, Academy of Management Review, Strategic Management Journal, Personnel Administrator,* and *Strategy and Executive Action,* as well as many others. He is coauthor of *Applied Readings in Personnel and Human Resource Management* and *Case Problems in Management.*

Michael De Luz, M.B.A. (Boston University), is a doctoral student at Florida International University. His research interests lie in blending strategic management concepts with exporting success factors, as well as entrepreneurship for American minorities. He has worked in management positions for the U.S. Marine Corps and the University of Florida. He has authored several articles in the *Journal of Global Marketing, Organizational Dynamics,* and the *Business Association of Latin American Studies* (BALAS) *Conference Proceedings.* He is currently the strategic planner/export manager of Native American Crafts, Inc. of Dartmouth, Massachusetts, and a member of the faculty at Bristol Community College of Fall River, Massachusetts.

John Dunkelberg, Ph.D. (University of South Carolina), is Associate Professor of Finance at Wake Forest University. His research interests lie in efficient markets and small business management. He has worked in management positions for South Carolina Electric and Gas Company, Ralston Purina, and the U.S. Army. He has published over a dozen cases in strategic management, small business management, and entrepreneurship textbooks. He has coauthored four textbooks.

Brentt Eads, M.B.A. (Loyola Marymount University), was recipient of the Robert W. Zinn Memorial Scholarship while earning his graduate degree. He is Marketing Director of *Cal-Hi Sports Magazine.*

Cathy A. Enz, Ph.D. (Ohio State University), is Associate Professor of Management at Cornell University. She served on the Board of Directors or the Organizational Behavior Teaching Society and the Executive Committee of the Midwest Academy of Management. Dr. Enz is currently Associate Editor of the *Journal of Management Education.* She serves on the Editorial Review Boards of the *International Journal of Value-Based Management, The Journal of Management Issues,* and the *Case Research Journal.* She is a member of the Academic Advisory Board for Institut de Management Hôtelier International in Paris. She has published numerous articles and a book on value sharing, organizational culture, and social influence.

Patricia Feltes, Ph.D. (University of Nebraska–Lincoln), is Assistant Professor of Management at Southwest Missouri State University. Her research interests are in international strategic management, women in management, and selection and recruitment of expatriate managers. She is currently the newsletter editor for the Southwest Academy of Management. She has recently published in the *Business Case Journal, Business Forum,* and *Journal of Business Strategies.*

Frank J. Fish III, M.B.A. (Saint Peter's College), is National Marketing Manager with Panasonic's Business Systems Telephone Division, a subsidiary of Matsushita Electric Corporation of America. He had over 15 years of sales/marketing experience with IBM and AT&T in the computer and telecommunications industries before joining Panasonic in the fall of 1992. He is a member of the Society for Case Research. He looks forward to teaching evening undergraduate business courses as an adjunct instructor.

Donna M. Gallo, is a graduate student in Business Administration at Boston College. She is conducting research at The United Way of Massachusetts Bay. She is a member of the Board of Trustees of the Natick Visiting Nurse Association, a nonprofit organization in the health care industry.

Thomas S. Goho, Ph.D. (University of North Carolina at Chapel Hill), is Associate Professor of Business at the School of Business and Accountancy of Wake Forest University. He was previously with New Mexico State University and the Babcock Graduate School of Management of Wake Forest University. He has worked for Mellon Bank, as well as serving as a training consultant for a number of banks in the Southeast. In addition, he has conducted more than 100 seminars on pension management for medical, dental, legal, and accounting organizations. He currently serves on the Boards of Directors of Overland Express, Stagecoach, and the Wellsfund families of mutual funds. His research and publications focus on case writing in finance and strategic management.

Pradeep Gopalakrishna, Ph.D. (University of North Texas), is Assistant Professor of Marketing and International Business at Hofstra University. His articles have appeared in the *International Journal of Advertising, Journal of Ambulatory Care Marketing, Management International Review, Journal of Health Care Marketing, Journal of Teaching in International Business,* and several national and regional conference *Proceedings.* He has also coedited a consumer behavior readings book for use at Hofstra University. His research interests are in the areas of health care marketing, customer satisfaction, consumer behavior, and cross-cultural marketing.

Barbara Gottfried, Ph.D. (University of California, Santa Cruz), is Assistant Professor of English at Bentley College in Waltham, Massachusetts. She previously taught at the University of Hawaii at Manoa. She is a feminist teacher and critic; her scholarly interests include nineteenth and twentieth century fiction, gender studies, film, semiotics, and advertising. She coauthored *Understanding Philip Roth* with Murray Baumgarten of the University of California, Santa Cruz, and has published articles on such diverse writers as Chaucer and Dickens and on gender and advertising. Collaborations with her colleague, Alan Hoffman, and Donna Gallo on the Boston YWCA and Rykä cases are the beginning of what she hopes will be an ongoing and fruitful cross-curricular endeavor.

Peter Goulet, Ph.D. (Ohio State University), is Professor of Management at the University of Northern Iowa. Although he concentrates on strategic planning, he has also taught numerous courses in finance, real estate, and statistics. While at the University of Northern Iowa, he has also served as M.B.A. Director, Head of the Management Department, Head of the Finance Department, and Chair of the University Strategic Planning Committee. His articles have appeared in the *Journal of Finance, Journal of Portfolio Management,* and *Journal of Financial Education.* More than 20 of his cases have appeared in over two dozen texts, as well as *Annual Advances in Business Cases* and several electronic databases, including *Primis.* He is the author of *Real Estate: A Value Approach* (Glencoe, 1979). He has also served as a director of the Society for Case Research. In addition to his academic work, he serves as a corporate director and is active as a strategic planning consultant for manufacturing firms, financial institutions, nonprofit corporations, and governments. He formerly served as a top manager for ILC Products Company, an aluminum products producer.

Walter E. Greene, Ph.D. (University of Arkansas), is a Professor of Business Policy in the Department of Management and Computer Information Systems and Administrative Information Systems at the University of Texas–Pan American. He was formerly a commissioned officer in the U.S. Air Force and worked with industry before entering the teaching profession. He has written several articles, and his cases have appeared in more than 20 textbooks. He has served on the boards of directors of SWDSI, SWSBI, and SWFAD and is currently President of SWCRA. Dr. Greene has served as acting Chair and Area Coordinator of the Management and Marketing Department, Assistant Dean and Director of the M.B.A. Program, acting Dean, and Director of the Small Business Institute.

Adelaide Griffin, Ph.D. (University of North Texas), is Professor of Management at Texas Woman's University. She has published numerous business policy cases and articles on strategic planning in the health care industry. She has been interviewed in the broadcast and print media about her published research concerning the problems and successful strategies of women executives. Currently, her research interests focus on crisis management planning for business organizations, with a particular emphasis on terrorism. She is a research fellow with the Mosher Institute for Defense Studies.

Rolf Hackmann, Dr. rer. pol. (Graz University, Austria), is Assistant Professor in the Marketing, Finance, and Transportation Departments of Western Illinois University. His special fields of interest are international business and marketing, sales management, and general management. He worked for 20 years in the pharmaceutical and consumer goods industry in Europe and the United States. His business experience includes the Western European free market system and that of the socialist societies of Eastern Europe. His special field of research interest is the effect of private direct foreign investment made by U.S. and other national companies and industries.

Alan N. Hoffman, D.B.A. (Indiana University, Bloomington), is Associate Professor of Management at Bentley College in Waltham, Massachusetts. He previously taught at the University of Connecticut. Dr. Hoffman has written numerous articles and cases that have appeared in the *Academy of Management Journal, Human Relations, Journal of Business Research, Business Horizons,* and the *Journal of Managerial Issues*. Dr. Hoffman and Hugh O'Neill are coauthors of *The Strategic Management Casebook and Skill Builder*.

J. David Hunger, Ph.D. (Ohio State University), is Professor of Strategic Management at Iowa State University. He previously taught at George Mason University and the University of Virginia. His research interests lie in strategic management, conflict management, and leadership. He has worked in management positions for Procter & Gamble, Lazarus Department Store, and the U.S. Army. He has been active as consultant and trainer to business corporations, as well as to state and federal government agencies. He has written numerous articles and cases that have appeared in the *Academy of Management Journal, Journal of Management, Case Research Journal, International Journal of Management, Journal of Business Strategies, Journal of Management Case Studies, Human Resource Management, SAM Advanced Management Journal, Annual Advances in Business Cases, Business Case Journal,* and *Handbook of Business Strategy,* among others. Dr. Hunger is a member of the Academy of Management, Society for Case Research, North American Case Research Association, World Association for Case Method Research and Application, and Strategic Management Society. He is past President of the Society for Case Research and has served on the Executive Board of the Midwest Academy of Management. He is currently serving on the Board of Directors of the Iowa State University Press (as President), the Society for Case Research, the North American Case Research Association, and the Midwest Management Society, as well as on the Editorial Review Boards of *SAM Advanced Management Journal* and *Journal of Business Strategies.* He is coauthor of *Strategic Management, Cases in Strategic Management,* and *Strategic Management Cases (PIC: Preferred Individualized Cases).*

Penko K. Ivanov, B.A., M.B.A. (University of South Florida), is currently an accountant with Ernst & Young in Munich, Germany. He served for five semesters as a teaching assistant in strategic management.

George A. Johnson, Ph.D. (University of Oregon), is Professor of Management and M.B.A. Director at Idaho State University. He is the author of numerous papers, articles, and cases. He has been active in developing educational software and has authored a production simulation entitled *COPE: A Computerized Production Environment.*

Kim Jursa, M.B.A. (University of South Florida), has served as a teaching assistant in strategic management.

Jim Kendall, M.B.A (Southwest Missouri State University), is Manager of Customer Service for City Utilities of Springfield, Missouri. Before joining City Utilities, he was with Central Illinois Public Service Company and Price Waterhouse & Company.

John A. Kilpatrick, Ph.D. (University of Iowa), is Associate Professor of Management, Idaho State University. He is coauthor of *Issues for Managers: An International Perspective* and *International Business: A Resource Guide* and is author of *The Labor Content of U.S. Foreign Trade.* He has published in the *Journal of Business Ethics, Journal of International Business Studies,* and *Case Research Journal.* He is also Director of the Small Business Institute at Idaho State University.

Suk H. Kim, M.B.A. (Pepperdine University), Ph.D. (St. Louis University), is Research Professor of Finance and Program Coordinator of Finance at the University of Detroit, Mercy. Dr. Kim has published 11 finance textbooks and over 60 articles in various academic journals. His latest book is *Global Corporate Finance: Text and Cases* (Kolb Publishing). His articles have appeared in *Journal of International Business Studies (JIBS), Columbia Journal of World Business, Multinational Business Review, Financial Practice and Education, Engineering Economist,* and several other journals. According to an article by Morrison and Inkpen (*JIBS,* 1st Quarter, 1991), Dr. Kim was among the top 25 international business researchers in the 1980s. He is the editor of *Multinational Business Review* and serves on the Editorial Review Boards of several academic journals.

Daniel G. Kopp, Ph.D. (Virginia Tech), is Associate Professor of Management, Southwest Missouri State University. He has written articles and cases that have appeared in the *Academy of Management Journal, Academy of Management Review,* and *Journal of Management Case Studies.* His current focus is on case writing and research in the health care field.

Thomas Ladd, C.P.A., M.A.C. (University of South Florida), has served as a graduate assistant in strategic management and is now employed as a C.P.A.

Bryan McDonald, C.P.A., M.A.C. (University of South Florida), has served as a graduate teaching assistant in strategic management. He is on the staff of Arthur Andersen.

Marie McKendall, Ph.D. (Michigan State University), is Associate Professor of Management at the F. E. Seidman School of Business at Grand Valley State University. Her research interests are in the areas of corporate crime, ethics, and multicultural issues. Her articles and cases have appeared in a number of management journals.

Charles E. Michaels, Jr., Ph.D. (University of South Florida), is Associate Professor of Management at the University of South Florida, Sarasota. He has served on the Editorial Review Board of *SAM Advanced Management Journal* and has authored articles appearing in the *Journal of Applied Psychology, Journal of Retail Banking,* and *Journal of Occupational Psychology,* as well as papers in the fields of business management and industrial psychology.

Janice S. Miller, M.A. (University of Missouri, Kansas City), is a doctoral candidate in the Department of Management at Arizona State University. Her area of concentration is human resource management. Current research interests include performance appraisal, executive compensation, and product loyalty among concurrent engineering teams in high-technology industries.

Charles H. Noble, M.B.A. (Babson College), is a doctoral candidate in the Department of Marketing at Arizona State University. His current research interests lie in the areas of managerial cognitions, strategic groupings, and strategy development, all primarily within a retailing context. He has worked in strategic planning and analysis for Waban, Inc. and Lechmere, Inc., both major Northeastern retailers, and has consulted for Woolworths Ltd. in Sydney, Australia.

Lawrence C. Pettit, Jr., D.B.A. (University of Virginia), is Professor of Commerce at the McIntire School of Commerce, University of Virginia, where he specializes in corporate financing and banking. He was Associate Director of the Virginia-Maryland School of Bank Management and the originator of the National Banking School for the AICPA, and he teaches in the Virginia Bankers School, Stonier Graduate School of Banking, and Consumer Bankers School of Retail Bank Management. He has been Visiting Professor at Washington and Lee University, the University of Texas at Austin, and Emory University and has taught at Virginia Polytechnic Institute and the University of Southwestern Louisiana. He has a special publishing interest in the valuation of the middle market firm and commercial banking. His articles have appeared in various banking and financial publications, including The *Bankers Magazine, Financial Review, The Southern Banker,* the *Journal of Financial Education,* and the *Journal of Bank Accounting & Auditing.*

Phanos Pitiris, B.S. (Iowa State University), is President of ELLI Corporation, a computer hardware and software development company.

Valerie J. Porciello, M.B.A. (Bentley College), is currently a business planning and organization consultant at Digital Equipment Corporation.

Allen Rappaport, Ph.D. (University of Texas at Austin), is Professor of Finance at the University of Northern Iowa. He is Executive Director of the North American Economics and Finance Association and a former Managing Editor of the *North American Journal of Economics and Finance.* He has published in a broad variety of journals, including the *Journal of Psychology, Systems Research, Small Business Economics, Multivariate Clinical Experimental Research,* and the *Journal of Business Ethics.*

William G. Shenkir, Ph.D. (University of Texas), is the William Stamps Farish Professor of Free Enterprise at the McIntire School of Commerce, University of Virginia, where he previously served as Dean. He has served as project director with the Financial Accounting Standards Board and as a visiting professor at the New York University Graduate School of Business. He also served as President of the American Assembly of Collegiate Schools of Business (AACSB) during 1990–1991 and as Vice-President of the American Accounting Association during 1986–1988. He is currently a member of the AICPA Council, the AICPA's Professional Education Executive Committee, and the Accounting Education Change Commission (as Vice-Chairman). He was a member of the Board of Directors of Dominion Bankshares Corporation and currently serves on the board of First Union National Bank of Virginia. He has published numerous articles in professional journals, has edited two books, and has served on the Editorial Board of two accounting journals.

Lois M. Shufeldt, Ph.D. (New Mexico State University), is Professor of Computer Information Systems at Southwest Missouri State University. Before her teaching career, she worked for Allyn and Bacon, Inc., and with a center for business research. She has authored several articles in professional and academic journals and in the *Proceedings* of various professional conferences.

Laurence J. Stybel, Ed.D. (Harvard University), is President of Stybel, Peabody & Associates, a Lincolnshire Company. He was previously a management consultant with Hay Associates in the area of executive compensation and Assistant Professor of Management at Babson College. His areas of expertise include outplacement, evaluation of management potential, and management succession planning.

Ram Subramanian, Ph.D. (University of North Texas), is Assistant Professor of Management at the F. E. Seidman School of Business at Grand Valley State University. His research interests are in strategic management and multicultural issues in international business. His articles and cases have appeared in the *Journal of Business Strategies, Mid-Atlantic Journal of Business, Management International Review, Annual Advances in Case Research,* and *Journal of Business Communication,* among others.

Arieh A. Ullmann, Ph.D. (St. Gall University, Switzerland), is Associate Professor of Strategic Management and International Business at the State University of New York in Binghamton. Previously, he was with the Science Center, Berlin, Germany. His research interests lie in strategic management and international business. He spent a year in Israel as a Fulbright Fellow. Currently, he is involved in several projects assisting businesses, universities, and local governments in Central Europe. He has been active as a consultant to large and small companies and nonprofit organizations in the United States and Europe. He has published four books. His articles have appeared in the *Academy of Management Review, California Management Review, Journal of General Management, Case Research Journal,* and *Zeitschrift für Betriebswirtschaft,* among others.

Robert P. Vichas, Ph.D. (University of Florida), is Professor of International Business at Texas A&M International University and visiting scholar at Kannas Technological University at Panevėžys, Lithuania. He was formerly at the University of Connecticut, Florida Atlantic University, and Old Dominion University. He studied in the United States, Mexico, and Switzerland; was Fulbright-Hayes Senior Lecturer at Universidad José Simeón Cañas in El Salvador and at Kannas Technological University at Panevėžys; and held visiting professorships in Puerto Rico at the Interamerican

University in San Germán and Catholic University in Ponce. He was Executive Secretary of the Business Association of Latin American Studies and currently heads the foundation of that organization. He has been active in the North American Case Research Association as reviewer, presenter, discussant, and session chair and on the Editorial Board of NACRA's *Proceedings.* He has written eight books, including the best-selling *Handbook of Financial Mathematics, Formulas, and Tables,* published by Prentice Hall. His numerous articles and cases have appeared in such publications as the *Case Research Journal, Long Range Planning, Managerial and Decision Economics, Journal of Management Studies, International Journal of Management,* and others.

Kathryn E. Wheelen, B.A. (University of Tampa), has worked as an administrative assistant for case and textbook development. She is also employed by Thomas Wheelen Company (circa 1879).

Richard D. Wheelen, A.A. (Hillsborough Community College), is a student at University of South Florida. He has worked as a case research assistant.

Thomas L. Wheelen, D.B.A., M.B.A., B.S., Cum Laude (George Washington University, Babson College, and Boston College, respectively), is Professor of Strategic Management, University of South Florida, and was formerly the Ralph A. Beeton Professor of Free Enterprise at the McIntire School of Commerce, University of Virginia. He was Visiting Professor at both the University of Arizona and Northeastern University. He has worked in management positions for General Electric and the U.S. Navy and has been active as a consultant and trainer to business corporations, as well as to federal and state government agencies. He served on the Board of Directors of Lazer Surgical Software, Inc. and on the Editorial Boards of the *Journal of Management* and *Journal of Management Case Studies.* He currently serves on the Editorial Boards of *SAM Advanced Management Journal* and *Case Research Journal.* He is the Associate Editor of *SAM Advanced Management Journal.* He is coauthor of *Strategic Management* and *Cases in Strategic Management* and *Strategic Management Cases (PIC: Preferred Individualized Cases)* as well as coeditor of *Developments in Management Information Systems and Collective Bargaining in the Public Sector* and codeveloper of *Financial Analyzer (FAN)* and *Strategic Financial Analyzer (ST. FAN)* software. He has authored 40 articles that have appeared in such journals as the *Journal of Management, Business Quarterly, Personnel Journal, SAM Advanced Management Journal, Journal of Retailing, International Journal of Management,* and the *Handbook of Business Strategy.* His cases have appeared in 50 text and case books, as well as the *Journal of Management Case Studies, Case Research Journal,* and *International Journal of Case Studies and Research.* He has served on the Board of Directors of the Southern Management Association, as Vice-President-at-large and Vice-President of Strategic Management for the Society for the Advancement of Management, and as President of the North American Case Research Association. He is a member of the Academy of Management, Beta Gamma Sigma, Southern Management Association, North American Case Research Association, Society for Advancement of Management, Society for Case Research, Strategic Management Association, and World Association for Case Method Research and Application. He is listed in *Who's Who in Finance and Industry, Who's Who in the South and Southwest,* and *Who's Who in American Education.*

Thomas L. Wheelen II, B.A. (Boston College), is a graduate student at the University of Colorado in Telecommunications. He has worked as a case research assistant.

Joseph Wolfe, Ph.D. (New York University), is Professor of Management, University of Tulsa. He has been a Fulbright Lecturer in Strategic Management at the International Management Center, Budapest, Hungary, as well as a consultant to such organizations as Cook County (Illinois) Hospital, ServiceMaster, International Harvester, the Planned Parenthood Association of Chicago, and the Jewel Foods Company. He is on the Editorial Board of Simulation & Gaming and has published in the *Academy of Management Journal,* the *Academy of Management Review, Decision Science,* the *Journal of Management, Simulation & Gaming,* and *Management Science,* among others. His cases have appeared in numerous textbooks, and he is past President of the Association for Business Simulation and Experiential Learning, as well as past Chair of the Academy of Management's Management Education and Development Division.

Other Contributing Author:

Gamewell Gantt

1 Introduction

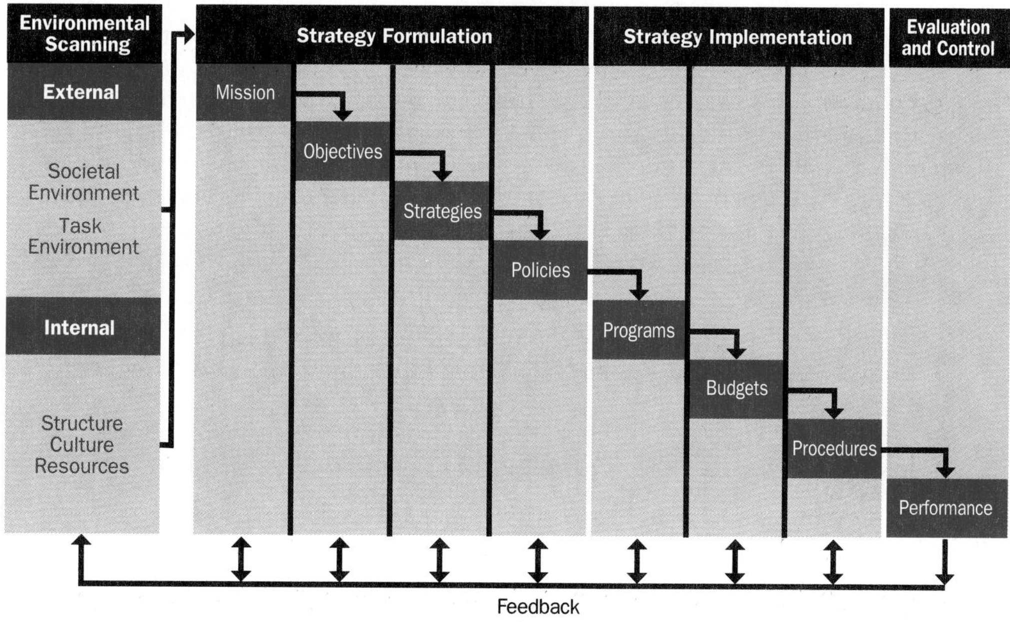

> *The reason why firms succeed or fail is perhaps the central question in strategy.*[1]
> [Michael Porter]

During the 1950s and 1960s, no bicycle manufacturer was as successful in the United States as Schwinn Bicycle Company. Schwinn "bikes" dominated the world of paper routes and after-school street races. "We used to ride Schwinns anywhere and everywhere," remembered one ex-rider wistfully. "We rode them with kids from the neighborhood to school and to baseball practice and when they got old we'd repaint them."

Founded in 1895 by the German immigrant Ignaz Schwinn, the firm led the U.S. bicycle market for many years. In the 1960s, one of every four bikes sold in the United States was a Schwinn. Toward the end of the 1980s, however, the company seemed to fall apart. Sales dropped from 1 million bikes in 1987 to 500,000 in 1991. Market share declined from 10% in 1983 to less than 4% in 1992. "Schwinn used to be the only bike I'd look at," offered one biking enthusiast. "[Now] I don't even know where a Schwinn bike store is."

Between 1989 and 1992, the company lost some $50 million. Top management looked for an outside partner to save the company, but President Edward Schwinn, great-grandson of the founder, was reluctant to give up control. By 1992, the Schwinn Bicycle Company had filed for Chapter 11 bankruptcy. The end was in sight for one of the most renowned brand names in the United States.

What went wrong? How could such a successful company fall on such hard times? "Schwinn never spent the money on research and development or planned for the long-term. . . . And they never took their competition seriously," explained one custom bicycle dealer. "Except for their name, they really have nothing to sell."[2] Once, when asked about the company's competition, Schwinn's management reportedly responded, "We don't have competition. We're Schwinn."[3]

These comments suggest why the managers of today's business corporations must manage firms strategically. They cannot make decisions based on long-standing rules, historical policies, or simple extrapolations of current trends. Instead, they must look to the future as they plan organizationwide objectives, initiate strategy, and set policies. They must rise above their training and experience in functional and operational areas such as accounting, marketing, production, or finance, and grasp the overall picture. They must be willing to ask **three key strategic questions.**

1. Where is the organization now? (Not where do we hope it is!)
2. If no changes are made, where will the organization be in one year; two years; five years; ten years? Are the answers acceptable?
3. If the answers are not acceptable, what specific actions should management undertake? What are the risks and payoffs involved?

In the 1960s and 1970s, Schwinn sold quality bicycles to a market composed mostly of school-age children. Preferring to sell its products through dealers, the company allowed Huffy and Murray to take over the low-end, mass-merchandise market (in which over 70% of today's bikes are now sold). Management seemed unaware of changing consumer tastes and did not take aggressive new rivals seriously. Newcomers Trek USA and Specialized Bicycle Components attracted biking enthusiasts with lighter, sleeker models in the early 1980s. Considering mountain bikes to be just a temporary fad, Schwinn continued to crank out its durable, but bulky standbys. Trying to reduce costs, it began making its bikes overseas using cheaper foreign labor. This shift led to quality problems that began to erode the brand's image. By the end of the 1980s, management's inability to manage the company strategically resulted in a crisis. Schwinn's management had failed to realize the environmental changes that had altered the rules for success. A poor job of environmental scanning had resulted in poor strategic planning.

This example shows how a leading company can quickly become an also-ran because of its failure to adapt to change or, even worse, its failure to create change. Current predictions are that the environment will become even more complex and turbulent in the years ahead. A report prepared by the American Assembly of Collegiate Schools of Business and the European Foundation for Management Development states, "Living with uncertainty is likely to be management's biggest challenge."[4]

Strategic management is a rapidly developing field of study that has emerged in response to increasing environmental turbulence. This field of study looks at managing the corporation as a whole and attempts to explain why some firms develop and thrive while others stagnate and go bankrupt. The distinguishing characteristic of strategic management is its emphasis on strategic decision making.[5] Unlike many other decisions, strategic decisions deal with the long-run future of the entire organization and have three characteristics.

1. **Rare:** strategic decisions are unusual and typically have no precedent to follow.
2. **Consequential:** strategic decisions commit substantial resources and demand a great deal of commitment.
3. **Directive:** strategic decisions set precedents for lesser decisions and future actions throughout the organization.[6]

Because strategic decisions have these characteristics, the stakes can be very high. For instance, Sears, Roebuck and Company's strategic decision after World War II to expand from catalog sales into retail stores and insurance yielded many years of successful profits. Similarly, Sears' decision in the early 1980s to diversify into financial services (instead of bolstering its retail outlets to compete better with the growing number of discount operations and specialty stores) by acquiring Coldwell Bankers and Dean Witter led to an eventual decline in profits. The company's retail stores floundered while management's attention seemed to be sidetracked by the success of its financial units. By 1993, under significant pressure from its shareholders, top management had spun off Dean Witter, the Discover card, and Coldwell Banker Real Estate as separate units. These decisions meant that the company would live or die by the success of its retail stores and Allstate Insurance. A new turnaround strategy for the crucial merchandise division included (1) focusing on women customers and increasing apparel offerings, (2) closing the money-losing catalogue operations and cutting 34,000 part-time and 16,000 full-time employees, (3) recruiting outsiders to bring in new ideas, (4) spending $4 billion to renovate stores, and (5) training salespeople to improve service—long a sore spot for Sears' customers. Some analysts were not sure that this new strategy would ensure the company's future; however, all agreed that it was a risky, but worthwhile decision.[7]

1.1 The Study of Strategic Management and Business Policy

Strategic management is that set of managerial decisions and actions that determines the long-run performance of a corporation. It includes environmental scanning, strategy formulation (strategic or long-range planning), strategy implementation, and evaluation and control. The study of strategic management therefore emphasizes monitoring and evaluating environmental opportunities and threats in light of a corporation's strengths and weaknesses. Originally called business policy, strategic management encompasses long-range planning and strategy. **Business policy,** in contrast, had a general management orientation and tended primarily to look inward with its concern for properly integrating the corporation's many functional activities. By focusing on the efficient utilization of a corporation's assets, it thus emphasized the formulation of general guidelines that would better accomplish a firm's mission and objectives. *Strategic management, as* *a field of study, incorporates the integrative concerns of business policy with a heavier environmental and strategic emphasis.* Hence *strategic management* generally has replaced *business policy* as the preferred name of the field of study.

Evolution of Strategic Management

Many of the concepts and techniques dealing with long-range (now called strategic) planning and strategic management have been developed and used successfully by business corporations such as General Electric and the Boston Consulting Group, among others. Not all organizations use these tools or even attempt to manage strategically, even though many succeed for a while with unstated objectives and intuitive strategies. American Hospital Supply Corporation (AHS) was one such organization until Karl Bays became Chief Executive Officer and introduced strategic planning to a sales-dominated management. Previously, the company's idea of long-range planning was "Maybe in December we should look at next year's budget," recalled a former AHS executive.[8]

From his extensive work in this field, Bruce Henderson of the Boston Consulting Group concluded that intuitive strategies cannot be continued successfully if (1) the corporation becomes large, (2) the layers of management increase, or (3) the environment changes substantially.[9] Research suggests that the increasing risks of error, costly mistakes, and even economic ruin are causing today's professional managers to take strategic management seriously in order to keep their companies competitive in an increasingly volatile environment.[10] Research by Gluck, Kaufman, and Walleck proposes that, as top managers attempt to deal with their changing worlds, strategic management within a firm evolves through four sequential phases.

- **Phase 1.** **Basic financial planning:** seeking better operational control through the meeting of budgets.
- **Phase 2.** **Forecast-based planning:** seeking more effective planning for growth by trying to predict the future beyond the next year.
- **Phase 3.** **Externally oriented planning (strategic planning):** seeking increased responsiveness to markets and competition by trying to think strategically.
- **Phase 4.** **Strategic management:** seeking to manage all resources to develop competitive advantage and to help create a successful future.[11]

Phase 4 in the evolution of strategic management includes a consideration of strategy implementation and evaluation and control, in addition to Phase 3's emphasis on strategic planning.

General Electric, one of the pioneers of strategic planning, led the transition from strategic planning to strategic management during the 1980s. By the 1990s, most large corporations around the world had begun the conversion to strategic management. Emphasizing that strategy formulation and implementation are now considered equally important and interdependent (a key concept of strategic management), F. A. Maljers, Chairman of the Board of Unilever, stated: "The largest companies in the world all have to take strategic management seriously."[12]

William Rothschild, staff executive for business development and strategy at General Electric, notes the current trend to push strategic management duties down the organizational hierarchy to operating line managers. He observes that, at GE, "over half of our managers are strategic thinkers. Another 20 percent to 25 percent lean that way. The rest don't understand it, and if they're fortunate enough to be in the right business where there is a stable environment, it doesn't matter too much."[13]

Impact of Strategic Management on Performance

Researchers have conducted many studies to determine whether organizations that engage in strategic management outperform those that do not. In general, the research revealed that strategic management leads to improved performance far more often than it results in no change or in even poorer performance.[14] For example, in a review of 28 studies of manufacturing firms, 20 studies revealed better performance with formal planning, 5 studies revealed no difference, and 3 studies revealed planning to be detrimental to performance.[15] Although many of the firms studied were fairly large, other studies showed that the use of strategic management by medium-sized firms improved performance. For example, a study of 200 medium-sized Dutch companies showed that profitability was directly related to each company's position in Gluck, Kaufman, and Walleck's phases of development (that is, companies tend to be more profitable in the fourth phase, strategic management, than in the three earlier phases).[16]

Research further revealed that the attainment of an appropriate match or "fit" between an organization's environment and its strategy, structure, and processes has positive effects on the organization's performance.[17] For example, a study of the impact of deregulation on U.S. railroads found that railroads that changed strategies as their environment changed outperformed those that did not change theirs.[18]

Nevertheless, strategic management needn't always be a formal process to be effective. Studies of the planning practices of actual organizations suggest that the real value of strategic planning may be more in the future orientation of the planning process itself than in any resulting written strategic plan.[19] Small companies, in particular, may plan informally and irregularly. The president and a handful of top managers might get together casually to resolve strategic issues and plan their next steps. As we discuss in Chapter 13, Strategic Issues in Entrepreneurial Ventures and Small Businesses, they need no formal, elaborate planning system because the number of key executives is small enough that they can meet relatively often to discuss the company's future.

In large, multidivisional corporations, however, the planning of strategy can become complex. A study of strategic decisions made in 30 large organizations in the United Kingdom revealed that the average amount of time that elapsed from the beginning of situation assessment to final decision was a little over 12 months.[20] Because of the relatively large number of people affected by a strategic decision in such a firm, a formalized, more sophisticated system is needed to ensure that strategic planning leads to successful performance. Otherwise, top management becomes isolated from developments in the divisions and lower level managers lose sight of the corporate mission.

From this evidence we conclude that a knowledge of strategic management is essential to effective business performance in a changing environment. The use of strategic planning and the selection of alternative courses of action based on an assessment of important external and internal factors are becoming essential parts of a manager's job.

1.2 Initiation of Strategic Change

After much research, Henry Mintzberg discovered that strategy formulation typically is not a regular, continuous process: "It is most often an irregular, discontinuous process, proceeding in fits and starts. There are periods of stability in strategy development, but also there are periods of flux, of groping, of piecemeal change, and of global change."[21] This view of strategy formulation as an irregular process reflects an understanding of the human tendency to continue on a particular course of action until something goes wrong or a person is forced to question his or her actions. This period of "strategic drift" may simply result from inertia on the part of the organization or may simply reflect management's belief that the current strategy is still valid and needs only some fine-tuning. Research does indicate that most large organizations tend to follow a particular strategic orientation for about 15 to 20 years before they make a significant change in direction.[22] After this rather long period of fine-tuning an existing strategy, some sort of shock to the system is needed to motivate management to reassess the corporation's situation.

The stimulus for a strategic change usually lies in one or more triggering events. Some possible triggering events (or triggers) are

- New CEO;
- Intervention by an external institution, such as a bank;
- Threat of a change in ownership, that is, a takeover; and
- Recognition by management of a performance gap.[23]

One act that is likely to serve as a triggering event is the emergence of a new chief executive officer. By asking a series of embarrassing questions, the new CEO cuts through the veil of complacency and forces people to question the very reason for the corporation's existence—a frightening and threatening situation for most long-term employees.

A similar stimulus is a bank's sudden refusal to make a new loan or suddenly call for payment in full of an old one. The bank may no longer be willing to underwrite what it perceives as a developing weakness in the company. The ensuing panic and need to arrange new financing may trigger initiation of a complete strategic review of the company. The threat of a takeover, of course, can have the same result.

Another trigger is a **performance gap,** that is, when corporate performance does not meet expectations. A typical performance gap occurs when sales and profits decline or when sales and profits stagnate while those of competitors rise. If management chooses to confront the problem (not always the case), the formulation process begins in earnest. Top management urges employees at all levels to question present objectives, strategies, and policies. Even the company's mission may be questioned. Are we aiming too high? Do our strategies make sense? Environmental scanning of both internal and external variables begins. What went wrong? Why? Questions such as these prompt top management to review the corporation's current position and to initiate strategic change. Work begins in earnest to revitalize the corporation's process of strategic management. As described in the Strategy in Action on page 8, Texas Instruments used a deteriorating situation to stimulate a strategic review.

1.3 Model of Strategic Management

The process of strategic management involves four basic elements: (1) **environmental scanning,** (2) **strategy formulation,** (3) **strategy implementation,** and (4) **evaluation and control.** Figure 1.1 shows how these four elements interact. At the corporate level, the strategic management process includes activities that range from environmental scanning to performance evaluation. Management scans both the external environment for opportunities and threats and the internal environment for strengths and weaknesses. The factors that are most important to the corporation's future are referred to as **strategic factors** and are summarized with the acronym **S.W.O.T.,** standing for Strengths, Weaknesses, Opportunities, and Threats. After identifying these strategic factors, management evaluates their interaction and determines the appropriateness of the corporate mission. The first step in the formulation of strategy is a statement of mission, which leads to a determination of corporate objectives, strategies, and policies. Corporations implement these strategies and policies through programs, budgets, and procedures. Finally, performance evaluation and feedback ensure adequate control of organizational activities. The strategic management model in Fig. 1.2 depicts this process as continuous. It is an expansion of the basic model presented in Fig. 1.1. As a *normative* model, it attempts to indicate how strategic management should be done rather than describes what is actually done in many organizations.

Environmental Scanning

External Analysis

The **external environment** consists of variables (Opportunities and Threats) that are outside the organization and not typically within the short-run control of top management. These variables form the context within which the corporation exists. The external environment has two parts: Task environment and Societal environment. The **Task Environment** includes those elements or groups that directly affect and are affected by an organization's major operations. Some of these elements are shareholders, governments, suppliers, local communities, competitors, customers, creditors, labor unions, special interest groups, and trade associations. A corporation's task environment often is referred to as its *industry*. The **Societal Environment** includes more general forces—those that do not directly touch the short-run activities of the organization but that can, and often do, influence its long-run decisions. Figure 1.3 depicts these economic, sociocultural, technological, and political–legal forces in relation to a firm's total environment. (We discuss these external variables in more detail in Chapters 3 and 4.)

THE PERFORMANCE GAP: A TRIGGERING EVENT AT TEXAS INSTRUMENTS

Strategy in Action

When Texas Instruments' Chief Executive Officer Jerry Junkins initiated a week-long strategic planning meeting called *TI 2000* in June 1989, most of the 20 invited executives assumed that this was going to be just another now-routine exercise. Instead, Junkins began the meeting by suggesting that Texas Instruments (TI) was in danger of becoming the dinosaur of the semiconductor industry. "We've been infected by mediocrity, and we're not the company we thought we were," announced Junkins. The stunned executives were forced to acknowledge that even though TI had invented the integrated circuit in 1958, it had failed to keep pace with technological change. TI had long felt that its chip expertise was the best in the business and paid little attention to outside technology. This was its undoing. The company's share of the computer chip market had plunged from 30% (first in the industry) to 5% (seventh in the industry) during the 1980s. Even worse, TI was in the process of going into the red with a loss of $39 million in 1989. "We were so successful in the 1950s and 1960s that we became a real arrogant bunch of young SOBs," admitted TI's former CEO Mark Shepherd.

The TI 2000 meeting forced top management to redefine its business and to change the tightly controlled culture that had prevailed at Texas Instruments. The emphasis changed from making commodity chips sold mostly through catalogues to making specially designed chips in partnership with key customers. Shifting from a "go it alone" strategy to a series of joint ventures and partnerships, TI worked to become a leading chip supplier for Sun Microsystems, Sony, General Motors, and Ericsson, the Swedish telecommunications giant. Even though losses continued through 1991, the company invested $1.7 billion in new plants in order to make specialty chips. By 1993, the new strategy appeared to be a resounding success. TI was earning almost 50% of its revenues from high-margin microprocessors and customized chips as compared to just 25% in 1988. Profits were at record levels. The new partnership approach was working. According to Mel Friedman, purchasing vice president for Sun Microsystems, "TI really understands how to form these partnerships and make them grow." The two companies were even making joint sales calls to market the chips and exploring ways to share distribution channels—a significant change from those dinosaur days in 1989!

Source: P. Burrows and J. B. Levine, "TI Is Moving Up in the World," *Business Week* (August 2, 1993), pp. 46–47.

FIGURE 1.1 Basic Elements of the Strategic Management Process

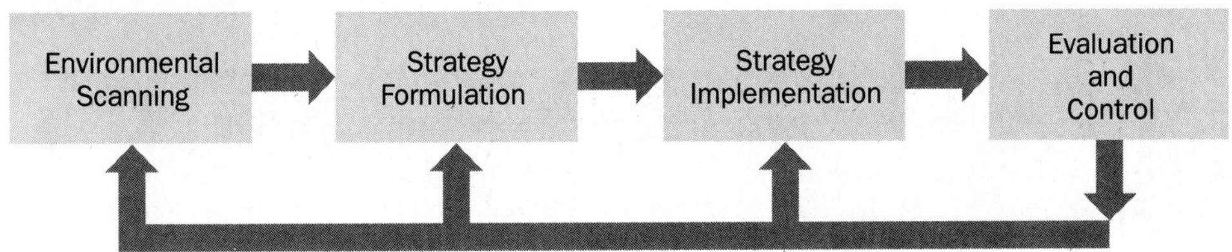

Internal Analysis

The **internal environment** consists of variables (Strengths and Weaknesses) that are within the organization itself but not usually within the short-run control of top management. These variables form the context in which work is done. They include the corporation's structure, culture, and resources. **Structure** is the way a corporation is organized in terms of communication, authority, and workflow. Often it is referred to as the *chain of command* and is graphically described in an organization chart. **Culture** is that pattern of beliefs, expectations, and values shared by the corporation's members. Organizational norms typically emerge and define the acceptable behavior of members from top management to operative employees. **Resources** are the assets that constitute the raw materials for the organization's production of goods or services. These assets include people's skills, abilities, and managerial talents, as well as financial assets and plant facilities within functional areas. A primary goal in strategic management is to combine these internal corporate variables to give the firm a *distinctive competence,* enabling it to attain a sustainable competitive advantage—and thus generate profits. (We discuss these internal variables in a firm's environment in more detail in Chapter 5.)

Strategy Formulation

Strategy formulation is the development of long-range plans for the effective management of environmental opportunities and threats, in light of corporate strengths and weaknesses. It includes defining the corporate mission, specifying achievable objectives, developing strategies, and setting policy guidelines.[24]

Mission

An organization's **mission** is the purpose of or reason for the organization's existence. A well-conceived mission statement defines the fundamental, unique purpose that sets a company apart from other firms of its type and identifies the scope of the company's operations in terms of products offered and markets served. It promotes a sense of shared expectations in employees and communicates a public image to important stakeholder groups in the company's task environment. It tells *who we are and what we do.* Surveys of large North American and European corporations reveal that approximately 60%–75% of them have formal, written

FIGURE 1.2 **Strategic Management Model**

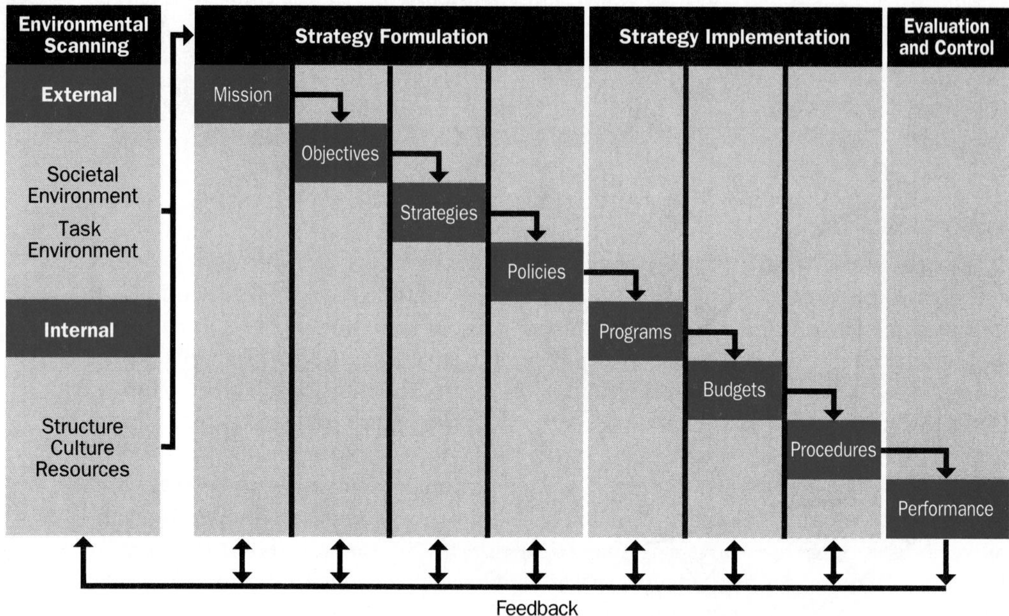

statements of mission. A high percentage of the rest have an unwritten, informal mission.[25]

A mission may be defined narrowly or broadly. For example, a narrowly defined mission of a savings and loan association or community bank might be to provide mortgage money to people within the local community. This type of a **narrow mission** statement clearly defines the organization's primary business, but it also clearly limits the scope of the firm's activities in terms of the products or services offered, the technology used, and the market served. It might even restrict opportunities for growth. In contrast, a **broad mission** widens the scope of the organization's activities to include many types of products or services, markets, and technologies. A more broadly defined mission of the same community bank might be to offer financial services to anyone, regardless of location. The problem with such a broad statement of mission is that it does not clearly identify which aspect of financial services the bank wants to emphasize and might confuse employees and customers. Other examples of narrow and broad missions include the following.

Narrow Scope	**Broad Scope**
Railroads	Transportation
Insurance	Financial services
Computers	Office equipment
Television	Telecommunications

FIGURE 1.3 **Environmental Variables**

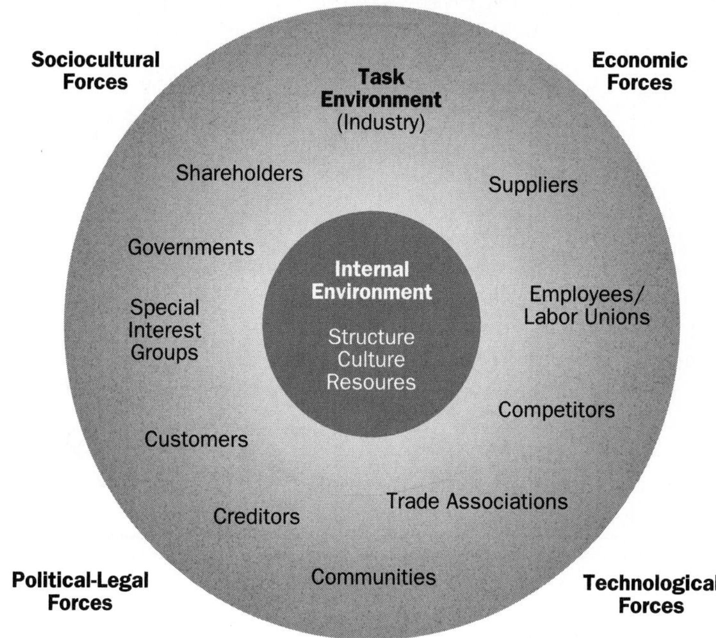

The concept of a corporate mission implies that a **common thread** or unifying theme should run through a corporation's many activities and that corporations with such a common thread are better able to direct and administer their many activities.[26] In acquiring new firms or in developing new products, such corporations try to ensure that the new activities will mesh with present activities to increase the firms' overall effectiveness and efficiency. A common thread may be common distribution channels or similar customers, warehousing economies or the mutual use of R&D, better use of managerial talent, or any of several possible synergistic effects.

Andy Grove, CEO of Intel Corporation, the world's largest semiconductor company, emphasizes the importance of an appropriate and challenging mission:

> Our corporate mission is to be the preeminent supplier of building blocks to the new computing community. If we develop the right building blocks, we'll win. If we are wrong, we'll fail. There's no competitor around who can do as much damage to us as we can do to ourselves.[27]

Objectives

Objectives are the end results of planned activity. They state **what** is to be accomplished by **when** and should be **quantified** if possible. The achievement of corporate objectives should result in fulfillment of the corporate mission. A community bank, for example, might set a one-year objective of earning a 10% rate of return on its investment portfolio.

The term goal is often confused with the term objective. In contrast to an objective, a **goal** is an open-ended statement of what one wishes to accomplish with no quantification of what is to be achieved and no time horizon for completion.[28] For example, a community bank's goal might be to increase its rate of return—a rather vague statement.

Some of the areas in which a corporation might establish its goals and objectives are:

- Profitability (net profits);
- Efficiency (low costs, etc.);
- Growth (increase in total assets, sales, etc.);
- Shareholder wealth (dividends plus stock price appreciation);
- Utilization of resources (ROE or ROI);
- Reputation (being considered a "top" firm);
- Contributions to employees (employment security, wages);
- Contributions to society (taxes paid, participation in charities, providing a needed product or service);
- Market leadership (market share);
- Technological leadership (innovations, creativity);
- Survival (avoiding bankruptcy); and/or
- Personal needs of top management (using the firm for personal purposes, such as providing jobs for relatives).

The top management of most large, publicly traded U.S. corporations like to announce their long-term objectives for the company—partially because that sets challenging measurable goals to work toward and partially because they hope to impress shareholders and financial analysts. For example, Rubbermaid, Inc., a maker of housewares, toys, outdoor furniture, and office products, established the objective that its sales and earnings should increase by 15% annually. To emphasize the importance of developing new products in this highly competitive market, it also set the objective that 30% of its yearly revenue come from products launched in the past five years.[29]

Strategies

A corporation's **strategy** forms a comprehensive plan stating how the corporation will achieve its mission and objectives. It maximizes competitive advantage and minimizes competitive disadvantage. For example, to achieve its objective of a 10% rate of return, a community bank could increase mortgage demand by offering special terms to a particular market segment, such as young professional people who can't meet standard down-payment requirements. In order to increase the amount of money deposited in savings accounts that fund the mortgages, the bank might offer large depositors special privileges and interest rates not available from other financial institutions. A different strategy to reach the same objective might be to offer other kinds of financial services, such as credit cards, so that the bank's income would become less dependent on mortgages.

Just as many firms have no formal objectives, many CEOs have unstated, incremental, or intuitive strategies that have never been articulated or analyzed. If pressured, these executives might state that they are following a certain strategy. This stated or *explicit* strategy is one with which few could quarrel, such as the development and acquisition of new product lines. Further investigation, however, might reveal the existence of a very different *implicit* strategy. Managers at all levels might realize that the company described in the official strategic plan and the one they work for are significantly different, but few would dare admit it.

Often the only way to spot a corporation's implicit strategies is to look not at what management says but at what it does. Implicit strategies can be derived from corporation policies, programs approved (and disapproved), and authorized budgets. Programs and divisions favored by budget increases and staffed by managers who are considered to be on the fast promotion track reveal where the corporation is putting its money and its energy.[30]

Policies

Flowing from strategy, **policies** provide broad guidance for decision making throughout the organization. They are **broad guidelines** that link strategy formulation and implementation. In attempting to increase the amount of mortgage loans, and the amount of deposits available for mortgages, a community bank might set policies of always evaluating a mortgage candidate on the basis of potential rather than current or historical income and of developing creative incentives for savings depositors.

Corporate policies are broad guidelines for divisions to follow in compliance with corporate strategy. These policies are interpreted and implemented through each division's own objectives and strategies. Divisions may then develop their own policies that will be guidelines for their functional areas to follow. At General Electric, for example, Chairman Jack Welch insists that GE be Number One or Number Two wherever it competes. This corporate policy provides a guideline for the acquisition and divestiture of product lines. If a proposed or current product or service doesn't have the potential to dominate its market, efforts must thus be shifted elsewhere. At Walt Disney Corporation, the policy emphasis is on the constant effort to find and create whatever is both *unique* and *compatible* with the well-defined Disney culture. Disney CEO Michael Eisner continually challenges his management team with questions such as "Where's the Disney difference?" and "What makes it Disney?"[31] Policies like these provide clear guidance to managers throughout the organization. (We discuss strategy formulation in greater detail in Chapters 6 and 7.)

Strategy Implementation

Strategy implementation is the process by which management translates strategies and policies into action through the development of programs, budgets, and procedures. This process might involve changes within the overall culture, structure, and/or management system of the entire organization. Except when such drastic corporationwide changes are needed, middle and lower level managers typically implement strategy, with review by top management. Sometimes referred to as operational planning, strategy implementation often involves day-to-day decisions in resource allocation.

Programs

A **program** is a statement of the activities or steps needed to accomplish a single-use plan, making the strategy action-oriented. It may involve restructuring the corporation, changing the company's internal culture, or beginning a new research effort. For example, when Hewlett-Packard CEO John Young asked some managers to look into the future of personal computing, they foresaw a world of portable and specialized devices communicating through wireless networks. Unfortunately, nothing like that was being developed within the company. As a result, H-P established a series of R&D programs to generate new "information appliances," such as a hand-held computer and a wireless interactive device for use with television sets.[32]

Implementation might also include a series of advertising and promotional programs to boost customer interest in the company's products or services. For instance, to implement its strategy and policies, a community bank might initiate a local advertising program, develop close ties with the local realtors' association, and offer free silverware with every $1,000 savings deposit.

Budgets

A **budget** is a statement of a corporation's programs in dollar terms, listing in detail the cost of each program, that management uses in both planning and control. Many corporations demand a certain percentage return on investment, often called a *hurdle rate,* before management will approve a new program. This demand ensures that the new program will significantly add to the corporation's profit performance and thus build shareholder value. The budget thus not only serves as a detailed plan of the new strategy in action, but it also specifies through pro-forma financial statements the expected impact on the firm's financial condition. For example, in approving a group of three programs—advertising, public relations, and customer service—management of the community bank probably would draw up and approve separate budgets for each.

Procedures

Sometimes termed Standard Operating Procedures (SOPs), **procedures** are a system of sequential steps or techniques that describe in detail how a particular task or job is to be done. They typically detail the various activities that must be carried out for completion of the corporation's programs. The community bank, for example, might develop procedures for the placement of ads in newspapers and on TV and radio. The procedures might list persons to contact, techniques for the writing of acceptable copy (with samples), and details about payment. It also might establish detailed procedures concerning eligibility requirements for silverware premiums. (We discuss strategy implementation in more detail in Chapters 8 and 9.)

EVALUATION AND CONTROL AT ANN TAYLOR STORES

Strategy in Action

When Sally Frame Kasaks left her position as CEO of The Limited's Abercrombie & Fitch to assume the top position at Ann Taylor Stores in 1991, it was because she couldn't resist the challenge of turning the company around. She knew that she had to first alter the company's product offerings if she was to turn Ann Taylor's losses into profits. Disgruntled customers were complaining about the poor quality of the stores' offerings. Others no longer shopped at the stores because they wanted a broader assortment than just the Ann Taylor traditional career-woman look. An investigation revealed that the company's outside suppliers had been providing clothing made from shoddy cloth with poorly-attached buttons. To put quality under her close control so that she could reduce costs and boost quality, CEO Kasaks entered into a joint manufacturing venture with a key supplier. She worked to introduce a broader assortment of elegant, updated working and weekend wear. As a result, the company earned $5.9 million in 1992 and was looking forward to $18 million in earnings during 1993. Thankfully, the complaints also stopped. The rewards seemed to be worth the effort. Looking at her mail, Kasaks set aside a stack that made her smile. "You see these?" she beamed, waving the letters in the air. "These are thank-you letters for bringing Ann Taylor back."

Source: S. W. Bhargava, "Ann Retaylored," *Business Week* (May 17, 1993), pp. 70–72.

Evaluation and Control

Evaluation and control is the process by which corporate activities and performance results are monitored and actual performance compared with desired performance. Managers at all levels use the resulting information to take corrective action and resolve problems. Although evaluation and control is the final major element of strategic management, it also can pinpoint weaknesses in previously implemented strategic plans and thus stimulate the entire process to begin again.

For evaluation and control to be effective, managers must obtain clear, prompt, and unbiased feedback from the people below them in the corporation's hierarchy. The strategic management model in Fig. 1.2 indicates how feedback in the forms of performance data and activity reports runs through the entire management process. Using this feedback, managers compare what is actually happening with what was originally planned in the formulation stage.

For example, the management of the community bank would probably ask its internal information systems people to keep track of both the number of mortgages being granted and the level of deposits at the end of each week for each

COMPANY SPOTLIGHT

MAYTAG Corporation

Strategic Management Process

Maytag Corporation is a successful full-line manufacturer of major home appliances. Beginning with its successful high-quality washers and dryers, it branched out through acquisitions into cooking appliances (Magic Chef, Hardwick, and Jenn-Air), refrigerators (Admiral), and vacuum cleaners (Hoover). Until 1978, however, the corporation (then known simply as Maytag Company) was strictly a laundry appliances manufacturer. Its only experience with any sort of strategic planning was in preparing the next year's budget!

In 1978, Daniel Krumm, Maytag's CEO, asked Leonard Hadley (at that time the company's Assistant Controller in charge of preparing the annual budget) and two others (from manufacturing and marketing) to serve as a strategic planning task force. Krumm posed to these three people the question: *"If we keep doing what we're now doing, what will the Maytag Company look like in five years?"* The question was a challenge to answer, especially considering that the company had never done financial modeling and none of the three knew much about strategic planning. Hadley worked with a programmer in his MIS section to develop "what if" scenarios. The task force presented its conclusion to the board of directors: A large part of Maytag's profits (the company at that time had the best profit margin in the industry) was coming from products and services with no future: repair parts, portable washers and dryers, and wringer washing machines.

This report triggered Maytag's interest in strategic change. After engaging in a series of acquisitions to broaden its product line, the corporation was poised in 1993 to become a global power in the home appliance industry. Its 1988 purchase of Hoover gave Maytag not only a firm with worldwide strength in floor-care appliances, but also Hoover's strong laundry, cooking, and refrigeration appliance business in the United Kingdom and Australia. The trend toward the unification of Europe and rapid economic development in the Far East meant that Maytag could no longer survive simply as a specialty appliance manufacturer serving only North America.

(continued)

branch office. It might also develop special rewards for loan officers who increase their mortgage lending. The Strategy in Action on page 15 describes the application of evaluation and control at Ann Taylor Stores. (We discuss evaluation and control in more detail in Chapter 10.)

Performance evaluation and control completes the strategic management model. Based on performance results, management may need to adjust either strategy formulation or implementation, or both. The Company Spotlight: Maytag Corporation feature on pages 16–18 presents an example of one company's strategic management process.

(continued)

Updated every year, the corporation's current strategic plan usually has a three-year time horizon. Although the latest plan does not list explicitly the corporation's mission, objectives, strategies, policies, and the like, the following can be inferred from the statements of top management and from corporate activities in mid 1993.

STRATEGY FORMULATION

Mission

Broad: Serve the best interests of shareholders, customers, and employees.

Narrow: Become a full-line globally oriented major home appliance manufacturer and marketer.

Objectives

1. Increased profitability. (Maytag had lost money in 1992.)
2. Be number one in total customer satisfaction.
3. Grow in the North American appliance business and become the third largest appliance manufacturer (in unit sales) in North America.

Strategies

1. Grow horizontally in those major home appliance product lines and geographic areas (such as Europe and Asia) where the corporation is not yet well represented, through external acquisitions or joint ventures.
2. Grow horizontally internally by improving efficiency and quality of acquired companies and by using one business unit's expertise in one area to introduce quality products to a business unit in another area.

Policies

1. No cost reduction proposal will be approved if it reduces product quality in any way.
2. Every product, from the least expensive to the highest priced, should be superior to the competition in overall quality and performance.
3. The corporation must not emphasize market share at the expense of profitability.
4. Business units must be managed for synergies while simultaneously allowing the specialized expertise among those units to flourish.

STRATEGY IMPLEMENTATION

Programs

1. Work with Bosch-Siemens to develop joint marketing and supplier agreements to reduce costs and to increase

(continued)

1.4 Hierarchy of Strategy

The typical large, multidivisional business firm has three levels of strategy: (1) corporate, (2) business, and (3) functional.[33] **Corporate strategy** describes a company's overall direction in terms of its general attitude toward growth and the management of its various businesses and product lines to achieve a balanced portfolio of products and services. Additionally, it is (a) the pattern of decisions regarding the types of businesses in which a firm should be involved, (b) the flow of financial and other resources to and from its divisions, and (c) the relationship of

(continued)

sales of Hoover major home appliances in Europe.

2. Initiate a program to analyze and develop the Asian market—growing probably through current distributors and licensees and possibly through a joint venture partner.
3. Develop new major home appliances for continental Europe.
4. Develop television advertising for Jenn-Aire and Magic Chef to ensure distribution of these brands by all "power dealers."
5. Develop plans to consolidate eventually into two large modern dedicated plants the manufacture of washing machines and clothes dryers currently being done separately by each of the U.S. business units.

Budgets

Prepare budgets showing a cost–benefit analysis of each planned program and a statement of how much the corporation can afford to spend for each program.

Procedures

1. Develop procedures for joint purchasing and the possible joint marketing of Bosch-Siemens with Hoover major home appliances in Europe.
2. Coordinate the marketing, manufacturing, and purchasing activities of the business units through corporation-wide planning committees chaired by representatives from the corporate planning staff.
3. Research and development activities for each major product line take place in the business unit where they are housed but in coordination with experts specialized in that area from other parts of the corporation. For example, because Hoover is the corporation's expert in front-loading washers, other units wanting to produce a front-loader should call on Hoover for assistance in developing it.
4. Consolidate all advertising under one agency but establish internal advertising directors for each brand category, who will interact with each other to ensure that the advertising and promotions among the various brands achieve their objectives but do not clash.

EVALUATION AND CONTROL

1. Require all business units to provide monthly status reports on sales and costs by product line and trends in expenses.
2. Require all business units to provide annual reports giving operating revenues, costs, and expenses, identifiable assets in dollars, and property additions and deletions.
3. Require all business units to provide quarterly assessments of competitive activity and overall trends affecting each of their product lines.
4. Require all business units to inform corporate headquarters before they proceed on any financially risky plan.

the corporation to key groups in its environment. Corporate strategy may be one of *stability, growth,* or *retrenchment.*

Business strategy, sometimes called **competitive strategy,** usually is developed at the divisional level, and emphasizes improvement of the competitive position of a corporation's products or services in the specific industry or market segment served by that division. A division's business strategy probably would stress increasing its profit margin in the production and sales of its products and services. Business strategies also should integrate various functional activities to achieve divisional objectives. Business (competitive) strategy may be one of *overall cost leadership* or *differentiation*.

Functional strategy is concerned primarily with maximizing resource productivity.[34] Within the constraints of the corporate and business strategies around them, functional departments develop strategies to pull together their various activities and competencies to improve performance. For example, a typical strategy of a marketing department might center on developing ways to increase the current year's sales over those of the previous year. Under a *market development* functional strategy, the department would attempt to sell current products to different customers in the current market or to new customers in a new geographical area. Examples of R&D functional strategies are *technological followership* (imitate the products of other companies) and *technological leadership* (pioneer an innovation).

The three levels of strategy—corporate, business, and functional—form a hierarchy of strategy within a large corporation. They interact closely and constantly and must be well integrated for corporate success. The model presented in Fig. 1.2 reflects the strategic management process at each level within an organization. Figure 1.4 shows how each level of strategy forms the strategic environment of the next level in the corporation. A division's external environment, for example, includes not only those task and societal variables of special importance to the division, but also the corporate mission, objectives, strategies, and policies. Similarly, both corporate and divisional constraints form a large part of the external environment of a functional department. Therefore the strategic plan for each lower level is constrained by the strategic plan(s) of the next higher level(s).

The specific operation of the hierarchy of strategy may vary from one corporation to another. The one described in the Company Spotlight: Maytag Corporation feature is an example of **top-down strategic planning.** Corporate-level management initiates the strategy formulation process and calls on divisions and functional units to formulate their own strategies as ways of implementing corporate-level strategies. Another approach is **bottom-up strategic planning,** in which the strategic proposals from divisional or functional units initiate the strategy formulation process. Strategy formulation leads from the functional level to the divisional level and from the divisional to the corporate level. Bechtel Group, the largest construction and engineering company in the United States, uses bottom-up strategic planning because it uses autonomous divisions as independent profit centers. A third means of strategic planning, the **interactive approach,** emphasizes the fact that in most companies the origin of the strategy formulation process isn't as important as the resultant interaction between levels.[35] This approach involves a lot of negotiation between levels in the hierarchy so that the various objectives, strategies, policies, programs, budgets, and procedures fit and reinforce each other. It represents a continuous process of adjustment between the formulation and implementation of each level of strategy.

FIGURE 1.4 **Hierarchy of Strategy***

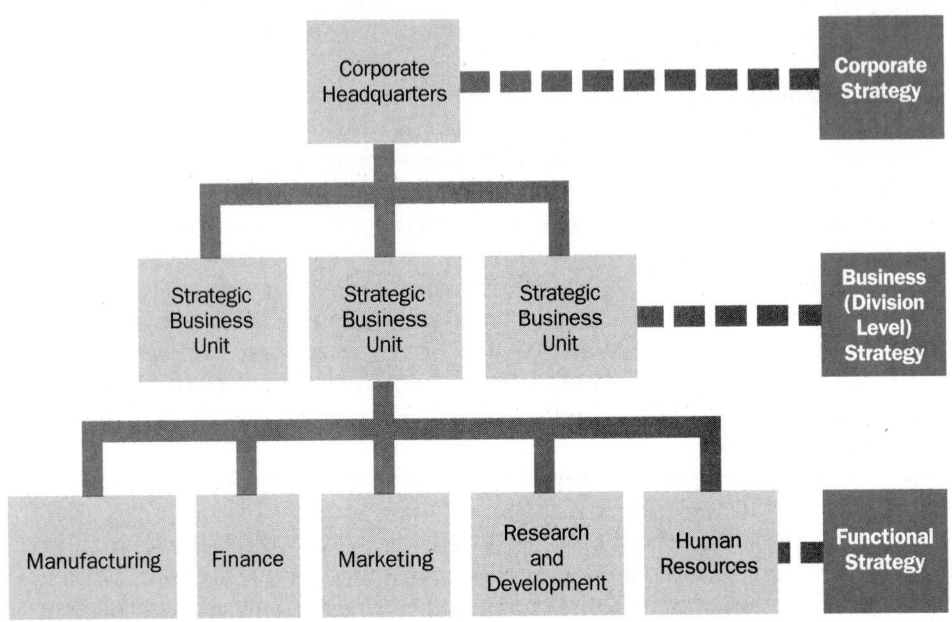

*Strategic management may be initiated at any or all of these hierarchical levels of an organization.

F. A. Maljers, Chairman of the Board of Unilever, points out the necessity for an integrated hierarchy of strategy:

> If a global company is to function successfully, strategies at different levels need to inter-relate. The strategy at corporate level must build upon the strategies at lower levels in the hierarchy (the bottom-up element of strategy). However, at the same time, all parts of the business have to work to accommodate the overriding corporate goals (the top-down approach).[36]

In Conclusion . . .

Schwinn is back! In January 1993 a group of investors acquired Schwinn for $43 million. They immediately invested $7 million more in a new downsized bicycle and moved the company from Chicago to Boulder, Colorado. Schwinn's new slogan was "Established 1895. Re-established 1994." To attract bike enthusiasts, Schwinn doubled its advertising budget to $10 million and sponsored a three-member professional mountain-bike team that placed in the top 15 among 74 racers at the World Cup in Vail, Colorado, in the summer of 1993. "We're telling the world we've reestablished Schwinn," announced Ralph Murray, President and CEO.[37]

Points to Remember

- Strategic managers must be willing to ask three key questions: (1) Where is the organization now? (2) If no changes are made, where will the organization be in a few years? (3) If the answers are not acceptable, what specific actions should management undertake?
- Unlike other decisions, strategic decisions deal with the long-run future of the entire organization and are rare, consequential, and directive. Because of these characteristics, the stakes of these decisions usually are high.
- Strategic management is the set of managerial decisions and actions that determines the long-run performance of a corporation. It includes environmental scanning, strategy formulation, strategy implementation, and evaluation and control. It therefore emphasizes the monitoring and evaluating of environmental Opportunities and Threats in light of the corporation's Strengths and Weaknesses. The internal and external variables that are most important to the corporation's future are called strategic factors and are identified through SWOT analysis.
- Strategic management in many organizations tends to evolve in four phases from basic financial planning to forecast-based planning to what people refer to as strategic planning (strategy formulation only) to full-blown strategic management (including implementation and evaluation and control).
- Research reveals that companies engaging in strategic management tend to outperform organizations that don't. In many organizations, however, significant strategic decisions occur only under the impetus of a triggering event after a prolonged period of strategic drift.
- The strategic management model proceeds from environmental scanning to strategy formulation (including establishing mission, objectives, strategies, and policies) to strategy implantation (including developing programs, budgets, and procedures) to evaluation and control.
- A large corporation tends to have three levels of strategy (corporate, business, and functional), which form a hierarchy of strategy. These strategies interact and must be well integrated for corporate success.

Discussion Questions

1. What differentiates strategic decisions from other types of decisions?
2. How does strategic management typically evolve in a corporation? Why?
3. What is meant by the hierarchy of strategy?
4. Does every business firm have business strategies? Explain.
5. What information is needed for the proper formulation of strategy? Why?
6. What are the pros and cons of bottom-up as contrasted with top-down strategic planning?

Notes

1. Michael Porter in M. E. Porter, "Toward a Dynamic Theory of Strategy," *Strategic Management Journal* (Winter 1991), p. 95. Reprinted by permission of John Wiley & Sons, Ltd.
2. T. L. O'Brien, "Beleaguered Schwinn Seeks Partner to Regain Its Luster," *Wall Street Journal* (May 20, 1992), p. B2.
3. S. D. Atchison, "Pump, Pump, Pump at Schwinn," *Business Week* (August 23, 1993), p. 79.
4. J. Robertson, "The Changing Expectations of Society in the Next Thirty Years," in *Management for the XXI Century,* edited by the AACSB and EFMD (Boston/The Hague/London: Kluwer-Nijhoff Publishing, 1982), p. 5.
5. H. Mintzberg, "Strategy Formulation: Schools of Thought," in *Perspectives on Strategic Management,* edited by J. W. Fredrickson (New York: HarperCollins, 1990), p. 179.
6. D. J. Hickson, R. J. Butler, D. Cray, G. R. Mallory, and D. C. Wilson, *Top Decisions: Strategic Decision-Making in Organizations* (San Francisco: Jossey-Bass, 1986), pp. 26–42.
7. K. Kelly, "The Big Store May Be on a Big Roll," *Business Week* (August 30, 1993), pp. 82–85.
8. B. Lancaster, "American Hospital's Marketing Program Places Company Atop a Troubled Industry," *Wall Street Journal* (August 24, 1984), p. 19.
9. B. D. Henderson, *Henderson on Corporate Strategy* (Cambridge, Mass.: Abt Books, 1979), p. 33.
10. R. Lamb, *Advances in Strategic Management,* Vol. 2 (Greenwich, Conn.: JAI Press, 1983), p. x.
11. F. W. Gluck, S. P. Kaufman, and A. S. Walleck, "The Four Phases of Strategic Management," *Journal of Business Strategy* (Winter 1982), pp. 9–21.
12. F. A. Maljers, "Strategic Planning and Intuition at Unilever," *Long Range Planning* (April 1990), p. 63.
13. P. Pascarella, "Strategy Comes Down to Earth," *Industry Week* (January 9, 1984), p. 51.
14. T. C. Powell, "Strategic Planning as Competitive Advantage," *Strategic Management Journal* (October 1992), pp. 551–558.
15. J. S. Armstrong, "Strategic Planning Improves Manufacturing Performance," *Long Range Planning* (August 1991), pp. 127–129.
16. P. Waalewijn and P. Segaar, "Strategic Management: The Key to Profitability in Small Companies," *Long Range Planning* (April 1993), pp. 24–30.
17. J. L. Naman and D. P. Slevin, "Entrepreneurship and the Concept of Fit: A Model and Empirical Tests," *Strategic Management Journal* (February 1993), pp. 137–153; N. Venkatraman and J. E. Prescott, "Environment–Strategy Coalignment: An Empirical Test of Its Performance Implications," *Strategic Management Journal* (January 1990), pp. 1–23.
18. K. G. Smith and C. M. Grimm, "Environmental Variation, Strategic Change and Firm Performance: A Study of Railroad Deregulation," *Strategic Management Journal* (July–August 1987), pp. 363–376.
19. J. M. Bryson and P. Bromiley, "Critical Factors Affecting the Planning and Implementation of Major Projects," *Strategic Management Journal* (July 1993), pp. 319–337; R. Veliyath, "Strategic Planning: Balancing Short-Run Performance and Longer Term Prospects," *Long Range Planning* (June 1992), pp. 86–97.
20. Hickson et al., pp. 100–101.
21. H. Mintzberg, "Planning on the Left Side and Managing on the Right," *Harvard Business Review* (July–August 1976), p. 56.
22. D. Miller and P. H. Friesen, "Momentum and Revolution in Organizational Adaptation," *Academy of Management Journal* (December 1980), pp. 600–601; H. Mintzberg and A. McHugh, "Strategy Formulation in an Adhocracy," *Administrative Science Quarterly* (June 1985), p. 190; G. Johnson, "Managing Strategic Change—Strategy, Culture and Action," *Long Range Planning* (February 1992), pp. 33–34.
23. P. Grinzer and P. McKiernan, "Generating Major Change in Stagnating Companies," *Strategic Management Journal* (Summer 1990), pp. 131–146; T. K. Lant and F. J. Milliken, "The Role of Managerial Learning and Interpretation in Strategic Persistence and Reorientation: An Empirical Exploration," *Strategic Management Journal* (November 1992), pp. 585–608.

24. Although some theorists propose that both objective setting and the consideration of competitive methods are a part of strategy, we agree with those who contend that objectives and strategy are separate means and ends considerations. See G. G. Dess, "Consensus on Strategy Formulation and Organizational Performance: Competitors in a Fragmented Industry," *Strategic Management Journal* (May–June 1987), pp. 259–260.
25. M. Klemm, S. Sanderson, and G. Luffman, "Mission Statements: Selling Corporate Values to Employees," *Long Range Planning* (June 1991), pp. 73–78; J. A. Pearce and F. David, "Corporate Mission Statements: The Bottom Line," *Academy of Management Executive* (May 1987), pp. 109–115; L. L. Byars and T. C. Neil, "Organizational Philosophy and Mission Statements," *Planning Review* (July–August 1987), pp. 32–35.
26. H. I. Ansoff, *The New Corporate Strategy* (New York: John Wiley & Sons, 1988), pp. 75–77.
27. S. Sherman, "Andy Grove: How Intel Makes Spending Pay Off," *Fortune* (February 22, 1993), pp. 60–61.
28. M. D. Richards, *Setting Strategic Goals and Objectives,* 2nd ed. (St. Paul, Minn.: West, 1987), p. 12.
29. V. Reitman, "Rubbermaid Turns Up Plenty of Profit in the Mundane," *Wall Street Journal* (March 27, 1992), p. B3.
30. K. R. Andrews, *The Concept of Corporate Strategy,* 2nd ed. (Homewood, Ill.: Irwin, 1987), p. 18.
31. R. Johnson, "A Strategy for Service—Disney Style," *Journal of Business Strategy* (September/October 1991), pp. 38–43.
32. R. D. Hof, "Information Appliances Turn HP On," *Business Week* (March 23, 1992), p. 89.
33. Some theorists propose a fourth level of strategy called "enterprise," which seeks to position an organization within its broader environment. See R. E. Freeman and P. Lorange, "Theory Building in Strategic Management," in *Advances in Strategic Management,* Vol. 3, edited by R. Lamb and P. Shrivastava (Greenwich, Conn.: JAI Press, 1985), p. 20. We chose, however, to include these broad environmental concerns with other factors considered in the development of corporate-level strategy. See Andrews, p. 13.
34. Of the three, functional strategies have been discussed the least. One of the earliest and best descriptions of functional strategy is C. W. Hofer and D. Schendel, *Strategy Formulation: Analytical Concepts* (St. Paul, Minn.: West, 1978), p. 29.
35. I. A. Marquardt, "Strategists Confront Planning Challenges," *Journal of Business Strategy* (May/June 1990), p. 6.
36. Maljers, p. 63.
37. Atchison, p. 79.

2

Strategic Decision Makers: Strategic Managers and the Strategic Audit

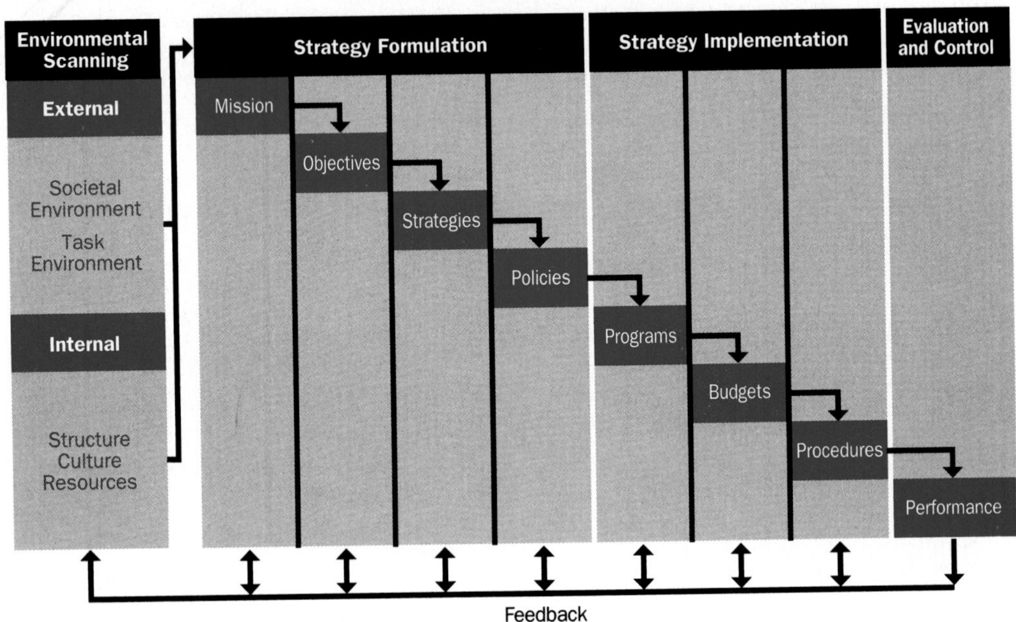

> *When they are falling down saying "Gee, I can't do it anymore," you've got to pick them up and say, "Yes, you can, and here's why." It's getting them to dream the dream.*[1]
> [Linda Wachner, CEO, Warnaco Corporation]

Strategic decision makers are the people in a corporation who are directly involved in the strategic management process. They are the strategic managers who (with some assistance from staff) scan the internal and external environments, formulate and implement objectives, strategies, and policies, and evaluate and control the results. The people with direct responsibility for this process are the board of directors and top management. The chief executive officer (CEO), the chief operations officer (COO) or president, the executive vice-president(s), and the vice-presidents in charge of operating divisions and functional areas typically form the top management group. Traditionally, boards of directors have engaged in strategic management only to the extent that they passively approved proposals from top management and hired and fired their CEOs. Their role, however, is changing dramatically. The strategic management process, therefore, is also changing.

2.1 Corporate Board of Directors

Over the past decade, shareholders and various interest groups have seriously questioned the role of the board of directors in corporate governance. A survey by the National Association of Corporate Directors, for example, revealed that almost half the shareholders polled believed that directors ignore shareholder interests when considering a merger.[2] Some also were concerned that outside board members lack sufficient knowledge, involvement, and enthusiasm to provide adequate guidance to top management. For example, when officials of the California Public Employees' Retirement System—a key shareholder group—criticized IBM's board of directors for not doing more to prevent the company's recent nosedive in earnings, the four outside members of the board's executive committee admitted that they did not know enough about the company's business to properly evaluate management. Like IBM's top management, they had missed the trend away from main-frame computers and toward personal computers. Board members actually admitted in the meeting that none of them felt comfortable using a personal computer. According to one director, "Not one of us has a PC in our home or office."[3]

The general public not only has become more aware and more critical of many boards' apparent lack of responsibility for corporate activities, but it also has begun to push government to demand accountability. For example, the Federal Home Loan Bank Board, concerned that the savings and loan (S&L) industry had become riddled with unscrupulous practices and unwise lending policies during the 1980s, sued the directors of 135 failed S&Ls for not properly supervising top management. It felt that board members were expected to monitor closely the actions of management and to intervene actively when necessary.[4] The board as a rubber stamp of the CEO or as a bastion of the "old-boy" selection system is being replaced by more active, more professional boards.

Responsibilities of the Board

Laws and standards defining the accountability or responsibilities of boards of directors vary from country to country. For example, board members in Ontario, Canada, operate under more than 100 provincial and federal laws governing director liability.[5] In the United States, however, no clear national standards or federal laws address director liability. Specific requirements of directors vary, depending on the state in which the corporate charter is issued. Nevertheless, a worldwide consensus concerning the major responsibilities of a board is developing. Interviews with 200 directors from eight countries (Canada, France, Germany, Finland, Switzerland, the Netherlands, the United Kingdom, and Venezuela) revealed strong agreement on the following five board of director responsibilities, listed in order of importance:

1. Setting corporate strategy, overall direction, mission or vision;
2. Succession—hiring and firing the CEO and top management;
3. Controlling, monitoring, or supervising top management;
4. Reviewing and approving the use of resources; and
5. Caring for shareholder interests.[6]

A study of U.S. directors by Ernst & Young presented a similar list of primary responsibilities.[7] Directors in the United States must make certain that, in addition to the preceding list of duties, the corporation is managed in accordance with the laws of the state in which it is incorporated. They must also ensure management's adherence to laws and regulations, such as those dealing with the issuance of securities, insider trading, and other conflict-of-interest situations. They must also be aware of the needs and demands of diverse constituent groups so that they can balance the interests of these groups while ensuring the continued functioning of the corporation.

In a legal sense, the board is required to direct the affairs of the corporation but not to manage them. It is charged by law to act with *due care* (sometimes called *due diligence*). As Bacon and Brown state in their classic study of boards, "Directors must act with that degree of diligence, care and skill which ordinarily prudent [people] would exercise under similar circumstances in like positions."[8] If a director or the board as a whole fails to act with due care and, as a result, the corporation is in some way harmed, the careless director or directors can be held personally liable for the harm done. For example, the Delaware Supreme Court fined directors of Trans Union Corporation, a railcar-leasing company, for negligence in connection with the sale of the company. It held the members of the board personally liable for the difference between the offer they accepted and the supposed value of the company. As a result of this and other court decisions, most members of today's boards of directors are concerned that they might be held personally liable not only for their own actions but also for the actions of the corporation as a whole. This concern is reinforced by the requirement of the U. S. Securities and Exchange Commission (SEC) that a majority of directors must sign the *Annual Form 10-K Report.*

Role of the Board in Strategic Management

How does a board of directors fulfill these many responsibilities? In terms of strategic management, a board of directors can do so by carrying out three basic tasks.[9]

- **Monitor:** By acting through its committees, a board can stay abreast of developments both inside and outside the corporation. It can thus bring to management's attention developments that management might have overlooked. At a minimum, a board should carry out this task.
- **Evaluate and influence:** A board can examine management's proposals, decisions, and actions; agree or disagree with them; give advice and offer suggestions; and outline alternatives. More active boards do so in addition to monitoring management's activities.
- **Initiate and determine:** A board can delineate a corporation's mission and specify strategic options to its management. Only the most active boards take on this task in addition to the previous two.

Even though every board will be composed of people with varying degrees of commitment to the corporation, we can generalize about a board of directors as a whole, in its attempt to fulfill these three basic tasks. We can characterize a board as being at a specific point on a continuum, on the basis of its degree of involvement in corporate strategic affairs. As types, boards range from phantom boards with no real involvement to catalyst boards with a high degree of involvement. A study of corporate boards (ranging from hospitals to Fortune 500 firms) supports the existence of this continuum. The study revealed that 30% of the boards actively worked with management to develop strategic direction (active participation/catalyst), 30% worked to revise, as well as ratify, management's proposals (minimal review/nominal participation), and 40% merely ratified management's strategic proposals (phantom/rubber stamp).[10]

Highly involved boards tend to be very active. They take their tasks of monitoring, evaluating and influencing, and initiating very seriously; they provide advice when necessary and keep management alert. As Fig. 2.1 shows, boards may be deeply involved in the strategic management process. For example, Control Data Corporation's Board of Directors spends the day before the official board meeting studying a business sector, such as computer peripherals, or an issue, such as efforts to improve quality. Other corporations with actively participating boards are Mead Corporation, Rolm and Haas, Whirlpool Corporation, Westinghouse, Dayton-Hudson, and General Motors. (GM's board was very passive until 1992 when it took control of the company and reorganized top management.) Research suggests that board involvement in strategic management is positively related to corporate financial performance.[11]

As a board becomes less involved in the affairs of the corporation, it moves farther to the left on the continuum (see Fig. 2.1). On the far left are passive boards that typically never initiate or determine strategy unless a crisis occurs. Lee Iacocca described how such a situation existed at the Ford Motor Company under Henry Ford II:

> The Ford Motor Company had gone public in 1956, but Henry never really accepted the change. As he saw it, he was like his grandfather, the rightful owner—Henry Ford, Prop. (Proprietor)—and the company was his to do with as he pleased. When it came to the board, he, more than most CEOs, believed in the mushroom treatment—throw manure on them and keep them in the dark. That attitude, of course, was fostered by the fact that Henry and his family, with only 12% of the stock, held on to 40% of the voting rights.[12]

Generally, the smaller the corporation, the less active is its board of directors. The board tends to be dominated by directors who are also owner–managers of the company. Other directors usually are friends or family members. As the corporation grows and goes public, however, boards generally become more active in terms of roles and responsibilities.

Most large, publicly owned corporations probably have boards that operate at some point between nominal and active participation. The few corporations that have catalyst boards, are those with major problems (pending bankruptcies, mergers, or acquisitions). Nevertheless, a recent survey of 450 publicly held companies in 24 industries indicated that 55% of the boards were holding special meetings devoted to strategic planning. Even though the directors agreed that strategic planning was the most important issue that boards must face today and in the near future, only 23% of the directors in this study reported having a strong influence in this area.[13]

FIGURE 2.1 **Board of Directors Continuum**

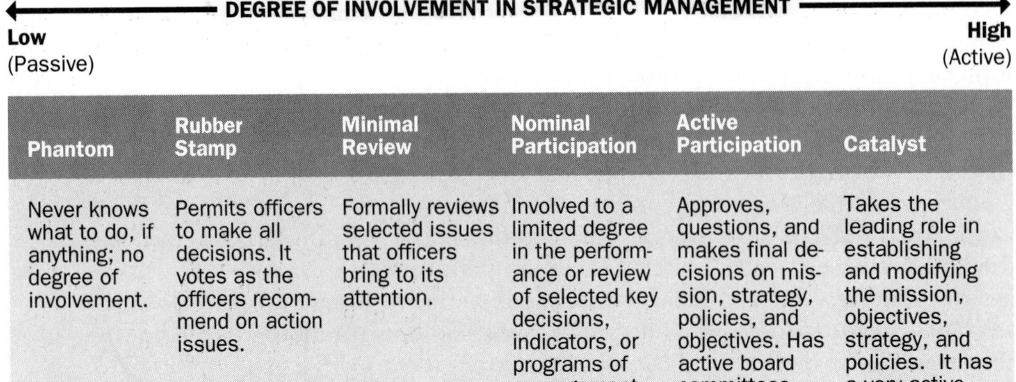

← DEGREE OF INVOLVEMENT IN STRATEGIC MANAGEMENT →

Low (Passive) — High (Active)

Phantom	Rubber Stamp	Minimal Review	Nominal Participation	Active Participation	Catalyst
Never knows what to do, if anything; no degree of involvement.	Permits officers to make all decisions. It votes as the officers recommend on action issues.	Formally reviews selected issues that officers bring to its attention.	Involved to a limited degree in the performance or review of selected key decisions, indicators, or programs of management.	Approves, questions, and makes final decisions on mission, strategy, policies, and objectives. Has active board committees. Performs fiscal and management audits.	Takes the leading role in establishing and modifying the mission, objectives, strategy, and policies. It has a very active strategy committee.

Source: T. L. Wheelen and J. D. Hunger, "Board of Directors Continuum." Copyright © 1994 by Wheelen and Hunger Associates. Reprinted by permission.

Board Membership

The boards of most publicly owned corporations are composed of both inside and outside directors. Inside directors (sometimes called management directors) typically are officers or executives employed by the corporation. Outside directors may be executives of other firms and are not employees of the board's corporation. Recent surveys of large U.S. corporations revealed that outsiders form an increasing percentage of board membership. They now account for 74%–75% of board members.[14] A survey of small companies showed that, although the number of outsiders on these boards may also be increasing, they constitute only 40% of the average board.[15]

This trend toward having a larger proportion of outsiders on a board is in line with guidelines proposed by the Securities and Exchange Commission, New York Stock Exchange, American Stock Exchange, National Association of Securities Dealers, and American Law Institute. For example, the New York Stock Exchange requires that all companies listed on the exchange have an audit committee composed entirely of independent, outside members. These groups apparently take the view that outside directors are less biased and more likely to evaluate management's performance objectively than are inside directors. This view agrees with **agency theory,** which holds that problems arise in corporations because the agents (top management) are not willing to bear responsibility for their decisions unless they own a substantial amount of stock in the corporation. The theory suggests that a majority of a board needs to be from outside the firm, so that top management is prevented from acting selfishly to the detriment of the stockholders. (See the Key Theory capsule on page 30.) However, S. C. Vance, an authority on boards of directors, contends that outside directors are less effective than insiders because the outsiders have "questionable interest, availability, or competency."[16] Sometimes, directors may serve on so many boards that they spread their time and interests too thinly. Current evidence is mixed regarding the relationship between the proportion of outside and inside directors and a corporation's financial performance.[17]

The majority of outside directors are active or retired CEOs and COOs of other corporations. Others are academicians, attorneys, consultants, former government officials, major shareholders, and bankers.[18] A 1992 survey of 327 large U.S. corporations by Korn/Ferry International found that 60% of the boards had at least one woman director—up from 11% twenty years earlier. Minority representation increased from 9% in 1973 to 46% of board membership in 1992. Outside directors serving on the boards of large U.S. corporations earned on average $34,276 in 1992.[19] Directors serving on the boards of small companies usually received less than $10,000 annually.

The vast majority of inside directors includes the chief executive officer, chief operating officer, and presidents or vice-presidents of key operating divisions or functional units. Few if any inside directors receive extra compensation for performing this extra duty. Very rarely does a U.S. board include any lower level operating employees.

Codetermination

Codetermination, or the inclusion of a corporation's workers on its board, began only recently in the United States. Corporations such as Chrysler, Northwest Airlines, and Wheeling-Pittsburgh Steel have added employee representatives to their boards as part of union agreements. Critics raise the issue of conflict of interest. Can a member of the board, who is privy to confidential managerial information, function, for example, as a union leader whose primary duty is to fight for the best benefits for the union's members? Research in 14 U.S. firms with workers on the board found that "worker board representation is no guarantee that workers will have an effective role in the governance of the organization."[20] The need to work for the corporation as a whole and at the same time to represent the workers creates role conflict and stress among the worker directors, thus reducing their effectiveness.

Although the movement to place employees on the boards of directors of U.S. companies shows little likelihood of increasing, European experience reveals an increasing acceptance of worker participation on corporate boards. The Federal Republic of Germany pioneered the practice. Most other Western European countries have either passed similar codetermination legislation or use worker councils to work closely with management.[21]

Interlocking Directorates

Boards composed primarily of outside directors will not necessarily be more objective than those composed primarily of insiders. CEOs nominate chief executives

Application of Agency Theory to Corporate Governance

Managers of large, publicly held corporations typically are not the owners these days. In fact, most top managers own only nominal amounts of stock in the corporation they manage. The real owners (shareholders) elect boards of directors who hire managers as their agents to run the day-to-day activities of the firm. As suggested in the classic study by Berle and Means, top managers, in effect, are "hired hands" who may be more interested in their personal welfare than that of the shareholders. For example, management might emphasize strategies, such as acquisitions, that increase the size of the firm (in order to become more powerful and to demand increased pay and benefits) or that diversify the firm into unrelated businesses (in order to reduce short-term risk and to allow them to put less effort into a core product line that may be facing difficulty) but that result in reduced dividends and/or stock price.

Agency theory is concerned with analyzing and attempting to resolve two problems that occur in relationships between principals (owners) and their agents (top management). The first is the *agency problem* that arises when (a) the desires or objectives of the owners and the agents conflict, or (b) verifying what the agent actually is doing is difficult or expensive for the owners. The second is the *problem of risk sharing* that arises when owners and agents have different attitudes toward risk. The likelihood of these problems increases when stock is widely held (no one shareholder owns more than a small percentage of the total common shares), when the board of directors is composed of people who know little of the company or who are personal friends of top management, and when a high percentage of board membership are inside (management) directors. Agency theory therefore suggests that, in order to better align the interests of the agents with those of the owners and to increase the corporation's overall performance, top management should have a significant degree of ownership in the firm and/or have a strong financial stake in its long-term performance.

Source: For a good summary of agency theory as applied to corporate governance, see J. P. Walsh and J. K. Seward, "On the Efficiency of Internal and External Corporate Control Mechanisms," *Academy of Management Review* (July 1990), pp. 421–458; K. M. Eisenhardt, "Agency Theory: An Assessment and Review," *Academy of Management Review* (January 1989), pp. 57–74; S. L. Oswald and J. S. Jahera, Jr., "The Influence of Ownership on Performance: An Empirical Study," *Strategic Management Journal* (May 1991), pp. 321–326. For background, see also A. A. Berle, Jr., and G. C. Means, *The Modern Corporation and Private Property* (New York: Macmillan, 1932).

from other firms to membership on their boards for the exchange of important information and a guarantee of the stability of key marketplace relationships. A *direct* **interlocking directorate** occurs when two firms share a director or when an executive of one firm sits on the board of a second firm. An *indirect* interlock occurs when two corporations have directors who also serve on the board of a third firm, such as a bank.[22]

Although the Clayton Act and the Banking Act of 1933 prohibit interlocking directorates by U.S. companies competing in the same industry, interlocking continues to occur in almost all corporations, especially large ones.[23] Research shows that the larger the firm, the greater are the number of corporations represented on its board of directors. Interlocking occurs because large firms have a significant impact on other corporations; these other corporations, in turn, have some control over the firm's inputs and marketplace. Interlocking directorates also are a useful method of gaining both inside information about an uncertain environment and objective expertise about potential strategies and tactics.[24] Family-owned corporations are less likely to have interlocking directorates than are corporations with highly dispersed stock ownership, probably because families don't like to dilute their control by adding outsiders to boardroom discussions.[25] Nevertheless, the evidence indicates that well-interlocked corporations are better able to survive in a highly competitive environment than those with no interlocking.[26]

Nomination and Election of Board Members

Traditionally, the CEO of the corporation decided whom to invite to board membership and merely asked the shareholders for approval. The main criteria used by most CEOs in nominating board members were that they be compatible with the CEO and that they bring some prestige to the board. Allowing the CEO free rein in nominating directors may be dangerous, however. The CEO might select only board members who, in the CEO's opinion, will not question or disturb the company's policies and operations. Moreover, directors selected by the CEO often feel that they should go along with any proposals made by the CEO. Thus board members find themselves accountable to the very management they are charged to oversee. As a result, increasingly the tendency is for a special board committee to nominate new outside board members for election by the shareholders. A 1992 survey by Korn/Ferry International revealed that 61% of large U.S. corporations use nominating committees to identify potential directors (in contrast to only 23% in 1973).[27]

Virtually every corporation whose directors serve terms of more than one year divides the board into classes and staggers elections so that only a portion of the board stands for election each year.[28] Arguments in favor of this practice are that it provides continuity by reducing the chance of an abrupt turnover in its membership and that it reduces the likelihood of people unfriendly to management (who might be interested in a hostile takeover) being elected through cumulative voting.

Organization of the Board

The corporation's charter and bylaws, in compliance with state laws, determine board size. Although some states require a minimum number of board members, most corporations have discretion in determining board size. According to a 1992 study by Korn/Ferry International, the average large, publicly held firm has 12 directors (three insiders and nine outsiders)—one less than five years earlier.[29] The average size of the boards of small- and medium-sized privately held companies is seven to eight members.

A fairly common practice in U.S. corporations is to have the chairman of the board also serve as the chief executive officer. The CEO concentrates on strategy, planning, external relations, and responsibility to the board. The chairman is responsible for ensuring that the board and its committees perform their functions as stated in the corporation's charter. Further, the chairman schedules board meetings and presides over the annual shareholders' meeting. Approximately 76% of the top executives of large, publicly held U.S. corporations hold the dual designation of chairman and CEO (down from 84% in 1988).[30] Some observers of corporate life believe that a CEO should not also serve as chairman because of the potential for a conflict of interest. How can the board properly oversee top management if the chairman is top management? For this reason, the chairman and CEO roles are separated by law in Germany, the Netherlands, and Finland. Similar laws are being considered in the United Kingdom and Australia. Recent research suggests that firms that separate the two positions outperform financially those firms that combine the offices.[31] Nevertheless, only 35% of surveyed CEOs of large U.S. publicly held corporations were willing to consider separating the positions.[32]

The most effective boards accomplish much of their work through committees. Although the committees do not have legal duties, unless detailed in the bylaws, most committees are granted full power to act with the authority of the board between board meetings. Typical standing committees are the executive, audit, compensation, finance, and nominating committees. The executive committee is formed from local directors who can meet between board meetings to deal with matters that must be settled quickly. This committee acts as an extension of the board and, consequently, may have almost unrestricted authority in certain areas.[33]

Trends in Corporate Governance

The board of directors is likely to play a more active role in corporate strategic management in the future. However, change probably will be more evolutionary than revolutionary. Different boards are at different levels of maturity and will not change in the same direction or at the same speed. Some present trends that are likely to continue include the following.

- Institutional investors, such as pension funds, mutual funds, and insurance companies, will put increasing pressure on top management to improve corporate performance. Institutions now own approximately 50% of the shares of public companies. Market analysts expect this percentage to continue rising.[34]
- Shareholders will demand that directors and top managers own more than token amounts of stock in the corporation. Research thus far shows mixed results, however, regarding the relationship of top management's shareholdings and corporate performance.[35]

- Outside or nonmanagement directors will continue to increase their numbers and power in publicly held corporations as CEOs loosen their grip on boards. As was the case in 1992 with General Motors, shareholders will increase pressures for the chairman of the board to be selected from the outside directors. This shift is one of the key recommendations of the United Kingdom's *Cadbury Report on the Financial Aspects of Corporate Governance*.[36]

James Worthy and Robert Neuschel aptly summarized the importance of the board of directors and its likely future in their study on corporate governance:

> Boards of directors will be importantly concerned with helping to achieve the balance (between the degree of freedom necessary for business to function profitably and the need for society to preserve other freedoms and institutions) in the years ahead. More and more, society will expect the board to provide the fine line between achieving the economic objectives of the corporation and meeting the broader needs of society.[37]

2.2 Top Management

The CEO of the corporation usually performs the top management function in coordination with the COO or president, executive vice-president, and vice-presidents of divisions and functional areas. Hence an understanding of top management is especially important to the study of strategic management. Research consistently reports that chief executive officers not only have a strong impact on the strategic direction of their firms, but they also directly affect corporate performance through their actions and statements.[38]

Responsibilities of Top Management

Top management, and especially the CEO, is responsible to the board of directors for the overall management of the corporation. Its task is to get things accomplished through and with others, in order to meet the corporation's objectives. Top management's job thus is multidimensional and is oriented toward the welfare of the total organization. Specific top management tasks vary from firm to firm and reflect an analysis of the mission, objectives, strategies, and key activities of the corporation. But, generally, effective top managers are people who see the business as a whole, who can balance the present needs of the business against future needs, and who can make sound, timely decisions.[39] The CEO, in particular, must successfully handle three responsibilities crucial to effective strategic management: (1) fulfill key roles, (2) provide executive leadership, and (3) manage the strategic planning process.

Fulfill Key Roles

From five weeks of in-depth observation of five chief executives, Henry Mintzberg concluded that the job of a top manager contains ten interrelated roles. The importance of each role and the amount of time demanded by each probably vary from one job to another.

- **Figurehead:** Acts as legal and symbolic head and performs obligatory social, ceremonial, or legal duties (hosts retirement dinners; signs contracts for corporation; represents firm at civic affairs).
- **Leader:** Motivates, develops, and guides subordinates (introduces Total Quality Management [TQM]; acts as a role model; provides a vision for the company's future).
- **Liaison:** Maintains a network of contacts and information sources with key people in the task environment (meets with shareholder groups; active in industry trade association; plays golf with other CEOs).
- **Monitor:** Seeks and obtains information needed for understanding the corporation and its environment (reads business periodicals; subscribes to data services; reviews key indicators of firm's performance).
- **Disseminator:** Transmits information to the rest of the top management team and other key people in the corporation (chairs staff meetings; communicates strategic plan; makes policy announcements).
- **Spokesperson:** Transmits information to key groups and people in the task environment (writes letter to shareholders; talks to Chamber of Commerce; participates in advertising campaign).
- **Entrepreneur:** Searches the corporation and its environment for projects to improve products, processes, procedures, and structures (reorganizes the company; originates a study of new product development; initiates search for joint venture partners).
- **Disturbance Handler:** Takes corrective action in times of trouble or crisis (personally talks with key creditors or union representatives; establishes investigative committees; replaces disruptive employees).
- **Resource Allocator:** Allocates corporate resources by making and/or approving decisions (reviews budgets; plans personnel loads; sets objectives).
- **Negotiator:** Represents the corporation in negotiating important agreements (resolves disputes between divisions; negotiates with key customers, suppliers, and creditors; reviews contracts).[40]

Provide Executive Leadership

Executive leadership is important because it sets the tone for the entire corporation. Researchers in this area believe that developing and articulating a strategic vision of the corporation's mission and objectives for all to follow is essential. Many go further by proposing that the CEO's primary job is to be a "manager of meaning," that is, to help employees make sense of the many things that are going on both inside and outside of the organization.[41]

Most middle managers look to their boss for guidance and direction and so tend to emulate the characteristics and style of successful top managers. People in an organization want to have a vision of what they are working toward—a sense of mission. Only top management is in the position to specify and communicate this sense of mission to the general work force. Top management's enthusiasm (or lack of it) about the corporation tends to be contagious.

Chief executive officers with a clear sense of mission often are perceived as dynamic and charismatic leaders. For instance, the positive attitudes of many well-known industrial leaders—such as the late Sam Walton at Wal-Mart, Mary Kay Ash at Mary Kay Cosmetics, Ted Turner at CNN, Herb Kelleher at Southwest Airlines, and Lee Iacocca at Chrysler—have energized their respective corporations. Such leaders command respect and influence strategy formulation and implementation because of three basic characteristics.

1. The CEO *articulates a transcendent goal* for the corporation. The CEO's vision of the corporation goes beyond the petty complaints and grievances of the average work day. Because this vision puts activities and conflicts in a new perspective, it gives renewed meaning to everyone's work activities and enables them to see beyond the details of their own jobs to the functioning of the total corporation. As John W. Teets, CEO and Chairman of the Greyhound Corporation, states, "Management's job is to see the company not as it is . . . but as it can become."[42]
2. The CEO *presents a role* for others to identify with and follow. The CEO sets an example in terms of behavior and dress. The leader's attitudes and values concerning the corporation's purpose and activities are clear-cut and constantly communicated in words and deeds.
3. The CEO *communicates high performance standards* but also *shows confidence in the followers' abilities* to meet these standards. No leader ever improved performance by setting easily attainable goals that provide no challenge. The CEO must be willing to follow through by coaching people.[43]

An example of executive leadership is John Welch, Jr., Chairman and CEO of General Electric Company, who transformed GE after he took office. Welch dismantled GE's sectors and groups and established 14 separate businesses reporting directly to him and his two vice-chairmen. According to Welch: "Good business leaders create a vision, articulate the vision, passionately own the vision, and relentlessly drive it to completion."[44]

Manage Strategic Planning Process

Top management must initiate and manage the strategic planning process. To specify the corporate mission, delineate corporate objectives, and formulate appropriate strategies and policies, it must take a long-range view. The ideal time horizon for management's planning varies by level in the corporate hierarchy. The president of a corporation, for example, should allocate the largest proportion of planning time to looking five or more years ahead. One reason given for the worldwide economic success of many Japanese corporations is the reputed ability of their top managers to conceptualize corporate mission and strategy even farther into the future. Mr. Ishihara, President of Nissan, has been quoted as saying, "In what I do now, I am thinking twenty or thirty years ahead."[45] A department manager, however, should devote the heaviest proportion of planning time to looking a year or two into the future. A first-line supervisor may sometimes look ahead a year or so but should spend most planning time on activities taking place within the next few weeks or months.

To accomplish its tasks, top management must use information provided by three key corporate groups: a strategic planning staff, divisional or SBU managers, and managers of functional departments. A **strategic planning staff** typically consists of a few people, headed by a senior vice-president or director of corporate planning. To generate data for strategic decisions by top management, it monitors both internal and external environments. It also suggests to top management possible changes in the corporate mission, objectives, strategies, and policies. Nearly all large corporations have a planning staff. As strategic planning responsibilities are being shifted to line managers, staff planners increasingly are being used as consultants who respond to requests for assistance.[46]

Divisional or SBU managers, with the assistance of the strategic planning staff and with input from their product managers, perform the strategic planning function for each division. These SBU managers typically initiate proposals for top management's consideration and/or respond to requests for such proposals by corporate headquarters. They may also carry out strategies and policies decided upon at the corporate level for organizationwide implementation. Division managers typically work with the heads of various functional units within the division to develop appropriate functional strategies for the implementation of planned business-level strategies.

Managers of functional departments (marketing, engineering, R&D managers, etc.) report directly either to divisional managers in a multidivision corporation or to top management if the corporation has no divisions. Although they may develop specific functional strategies, they generally do so within the framework of divisional or corporate strategies. They also respond to initiatives from above that ask for input or require them to develop strategies for the implementation of divisional plans.

Characteristics of Top Management Tasks

Top-level management tasks have two characteristics that differentiate them from other managerial tasks.[47] First, *very few of them are continuous.* Although a manager rarely works on these tasks all day, the responsibility for them always is present. And such tasks when performed are crucial, such as the selection of a person to head a new division. Supporting this, Mintzberg reports that the activities of most executives are characterized by brevity, variety, and fragmentation: "Half of the observed activities were completed in less than nine minutes and only one-tenth took more than an hour. In effect, the managers were seldom able or willing to spend much time on any one issue in any one session."[48]

The second characteristic of top management tasks is that *they require a wide range of capabilities and temperaments.* Some tasks require the capacity to analyze and carefully weigh alternative courses of action. Some require an awareness of and an interest in people. Still others call for the ability to pursue abstract ideas, concepts, and calculations.

One effect of tasks having these two characteristics is to draw top managers back into the functional work of the corporation. Because their activities are not continuous, people in top management often have unplanned free time. They tend therefore to get caught up in the day-to-day work in manufacturing, marketing, accounting, engineering, or other operations. They may find themselves constantly dealing with crises that could probably be handled better by lower level managers.

A second effect of such tasks is that top managers tend to perceive only those aspects and responsibilities of their function that are compatible with their abilities, experience, and temperaments. And, if the board of directors fails to state explicitly what it considers to be the basic responsibilities and activities of top management, the top managers are free to define their jobs themselves. Therefore important tasks can be overlooked until a crisis occurs.

Modes of Strategy Formulation

Based on his studies of chief executives, H. Mintzberg proposes that a corporation's mission, objectives, and strategies are strongly affected by top management's perception of the world.[49] This perception determines the approach or *mode* used by the CEO and staff in strategy formulation. He names three basic modes: entrepreneurial, adaptive, and planning.

- **Entrepreneurial mode:** One powerful individual formulates strategy. The focus is on opportunities, and problems are secondary. Strategy is guided by the founder's own vision of direction and is exemplified by large, bold decisions. The dominant goal is growth of the corporation. Bill Gates, founder and Chairman of Microsoft Corporation, embodies this mode of strategic planning. The company reflects his vision of the personal computer industry: Although Microsoft's clear mission—competitiveness, tenacity, and technological self-confidence which emanate from Gates—are certainly advantages of the entrepreneurial mode, its tendency to introduce products before they are ready is a significant disadvantage. "Microsoft is a very seat-of-the-pants operation," comments Michael Swavely, President of Compaq Computer's North American operations.[50]
- **Adaptive mode:** Sometimes referred to as "muddling through," this strategy formulation mode is characterized by reactive solutions to existing problems, rather than a proactive search for new opportunities. Much bargaining goes on concerning priorities of objectives. Strategy is fragmented and is developed to move the corporation forward in incremental steps. This mode is typical of most universities, many large hospitals, a large number of government agencies, and a surprising number of large corporations.
- **Planning mode:** Analysts assume major responsibilities for strategy formulation. Strategic planning includes both the proactive search for new opportunities and the reactive solution of existing problems. Systematic comprehensive analysis is used for the development of strategies that integrate the corporation's decision-making processes. As described in the Company Spotlight: Maytag Corporation feature on page 38, the current Maytag Corporation uses the planning mode in strategy formulation. After realizing how the major home appliance industry was changing in the U.S. and throughout the world, Maytag's top management deliberately chose to transform the company from a domestic high-quality niche producer of laundry appliances to a full-line global competitor.

In the *entrepreneurial mode,* top management believes that the environment is a force to be used and controlled. In the *adaptive mode,* management assumes that the environment is too complex to be comprehended completely. In the *planning*

During the lifetime of F. L. Maytag, the firm's approach to strategy formulation seemed to epitomize the *entrepreneurial mode.* As both founder and owner of the company, F. L. based key decisions on his evolving vision of the company's future. He slowly phased out the company's original line of farm equipment as sales of his new line of washing machines increased. Between 1909 and 1911, F. L. worked with the famed Duesenberg brothers to build a Maytag–Mason automobile in Waterloo, Iowa. He experimented with several marginal ventures until he decided to devote all the company's energies to the manufacture and sale of washing machines.

After F. L.'s departure from the company's management in the 1920s, the firm's approach to strategy formulation changed from an entrepreneurial to an *adaptive mode.* Family descendants and professional managers continued to follow the founder's ideas concerning washing machines and generally made strategic changes as a way of adapting to a changing environment. The innovative genius and entrepreneurial drive of the company's early years no longer existed. The firm's slowness in converting from wringer to automatic washing machines in the 1940s cost the company its leadership of the industry. Its share of the U.S. washing machine market dropped from 40%–45% during the 1920s and 1930s to 8% in 1954. Although management continued to add to and improve Maytag's product line throughout the 1950s and 1960s, the company remained primarily a high-quality niche producer of laundry appliances.

As mentioned in Chapter 1, Maytag Company's strategy formulation process changed radically in 1978. Chief Executive Officer Daniel Krumm took a hard look at Maytag's position in the industry, established a strategic planning task force, and asked its members to answer the question: "If we keep doing what we're doing now, what will the Maytag Company look like in five years?" The resulting report shook the company from top to bottom and initiated the corporation's current *planning mode* of strategy formulation.

The corporation's current strategic plan is updated every year and usually has a three-year time horizon. Maytag's top management usually begins the process by scanning the firm's external and internal environments. After much brainstorming, the strategic issues committee, which is composed of top management, generates a strategic proposal for the corporation. The committee then invites the rest of the top-level staff and the business-unit heads to an annual meeting for an open discussion to flesh out the proposal. The resulting strategic plan deals with implementation in addition to formulating a general direction for the firm as a whole.

mode, management works on the assumption that systematic scanning and analysis of the environment can provide the knowledge it needs to influence the environment to the corporation's advantage. The use of a specific planning mode reflects top management's perception of the corporation's environment. Categorizing a corporation's top management according to these three planning modes, leads to an understanding of how and why key decisions are made. Then, looking at these decisions in the light of the corporation's mission, objectives, strategies, and policies, reveals whether the dominant mode is appropriate.

In some instances, a corporation might follow an approach called **logical incrementalism,** which is a synthesis of the planning, adaptive, and to a lesser extent the entrepreneurial modes of strategy formulation. According to J. B. Quinn, top management might have a reasonably clear idea of the corporation's mission and objectives, but, in its development of strategies, chooses to use "an interactive process in which the organization probes the future, experiments and learns from a series of partial (incremental) commitments rather than through global formulations of total strategies."[51] This approach appears to be useful when the environment is changing rapidly and when building consensus and developing needed resources are important before committing the entire corporation to a specific strategy.

Importance of Conceptual Skills in Strategic Management

Top managers face a **strategic management paradox.** On the one hand, top managers are charged with maintaining organizational efficiency and internal stability in order to earn a predictable stream of profits. On the other hand, they must be able to change the organization quickly when external pressures pose new threats or opportunities. Unfortunately, those executives who succeed in getting their companies to use resources very efficiently might also be making the firms passive and ill-prepared for radical environmental shifts. In contrast, top managers who succeed in making their corporations flexible and responsive to new environmental challenges will not ensure the firm's survival if they ignore their responsibility to maintain efficient performance in the face of competitive pressures.[52] Balancing these seemingly conflicting priorities requires a mix of managerial skills.

Robert L. Katz suggests that effective management depends on a proper mix of three basic skills: technical, human, and conceptual.[53]

- **Technical skills** pertain to what is done and to working with things. They comprise a person's ability to use technology to perform an organizational task.
- **Human skills** pertain to how something is done and to working with people. They comprise a person's ability to work with people in the achievement of goals.
- **Conceptual skills** pertain to why something is done and to a person's view of the corporation as a whole. They comprise the ability to understand the complexities of the corporation as it affects and is affected by its environment.

FIGURE 2.2 **Optimal Managerial Skill Mix by Hierarchical Level**

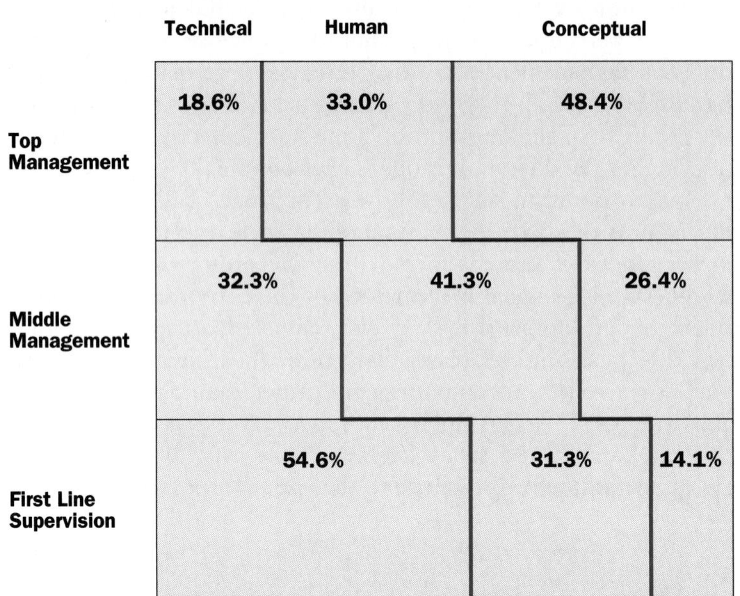

Source: T. L. Wheelen and J. D. Hunger, "Optimal Managerial Skill Mix by Hierarchical Level." Copyright © 1994 by Wheelen and Hunger Associates. Reprinted by permission.

Katz further suggests that the optimal mix of these three skills varies at the different corporate levels. Results of a survey of 300 presidents of *Fortune's* list of the top 50 banking, insurance, public utility, and retailing and 100 top industrial firms support Katz's suggestion.[54] As Fig. 2.2 shows, the need for technical skills decreases and the need for conceptual skills increases as a person moves from first-line supervision to top management. This transition from primarily technical skills to an emphasis on conceptual skills is important because the conceptual work carried out by an organization's executives is the heart of strategy making.

2.3 Strategic Audit: Aid to Strategic Decision Making

As business corporations become larger and more complex, strategic decision making becomes more complicated. Executives often need some type of checklist or guidelines to aid them in collecting the necessary data and organizing them for strategic analysis and the development of alternative strategies and programs. Consulting firms, management scholars, boards of directors, and practicing managers suggest the use of management audits of corporate activities.

The **strategic audit** is a type of management audit that takes a corporation-wide perspective and provides a comprehensive assessment of a corporation's strategic situation.[55] It covers the key aspects of the strategic management process and places them in a decision-making framework. This framework comprises eight interrelated steps:

1. **Evaluation of a corporation's current performance results** in terms of (a) return on investment, profitability, and so on, and (b) the current mission, objectives, strategies, and policies;
2. **Examination and evaluation of a corporation's strategic managers,** its board of directors and top management;
3. **A scan of the external environment** to locate strategic factors that pose Opportunities and Threats;
4. **A scan of the internal corporate environment** to determine strategic factors that are Strengths and Weaknesses;
5. **Analysis of the strategic (SWOT) factors** to (a) pinpoint problem areas, and (b) review and revise the corporate mission and objectives as necessary;
6. **Generation, evaluation, and selection of the best alternative strategy** in light of the analysis conducted in Step 5;
7. **Implementation** of selected strategies by means of programs, budgets, and procedures; and
8. **Evaluation** of the implemented strategies via feedback systems, and the control of activities to ensure their minimum deviation from plans.

Figure 2.3 depicts this strategic decision-making process, which basically reflects a rational approach to strategic decision making being used successfully by corporations such as Warner-Lambert, Dayton Hudson, Avon Products, Bechtel Group, Inc., and Taisei Corporation. Some have criticized this approach as being too prescriptive and failing to describe the more political way that managers make many strategic decisions.[56] Nevertheless, many others endorse this normative approach as an excellent way to manage strategically in an uncertain environment.[57] Monitoring strategic factors and keeping the process flexible in light of changing circumstances are essential.

The strategic audit makes the strategic decision-making process operational. The audit describes not only how objectives, strategies, and policies are formulated as strategic decisions, but also how they are implemented, evaluated, and controlled by programs, budgets, and procedures. The strategic audit, therefore, enables a manager to understand better the ways in which various functional areas are interrelated and interdependent and the manner in which they contribute to the achievement of the corporate mission. Consequently, the strategic audit is very useful to boards of directors and top management, whose jobs are to evaluate the corporation's overall performance. A person writing a business plan (see Chapter 13) can use the strategic audit questions to develop the business plan.

The appendix at the end of this chapter presents a strategic audit that may be used as a guide for analysis of complex business policy cases and strategic decision making. The questions in the audit parallel the eight steps of the strategic decision-making process shown in Fig. 2.3. It isn't an all-inclusive list, but it does present many of the critical questions needed for the strategic analysis of any business

FIGURE 2.3 **Strategic Decision-Making Process**

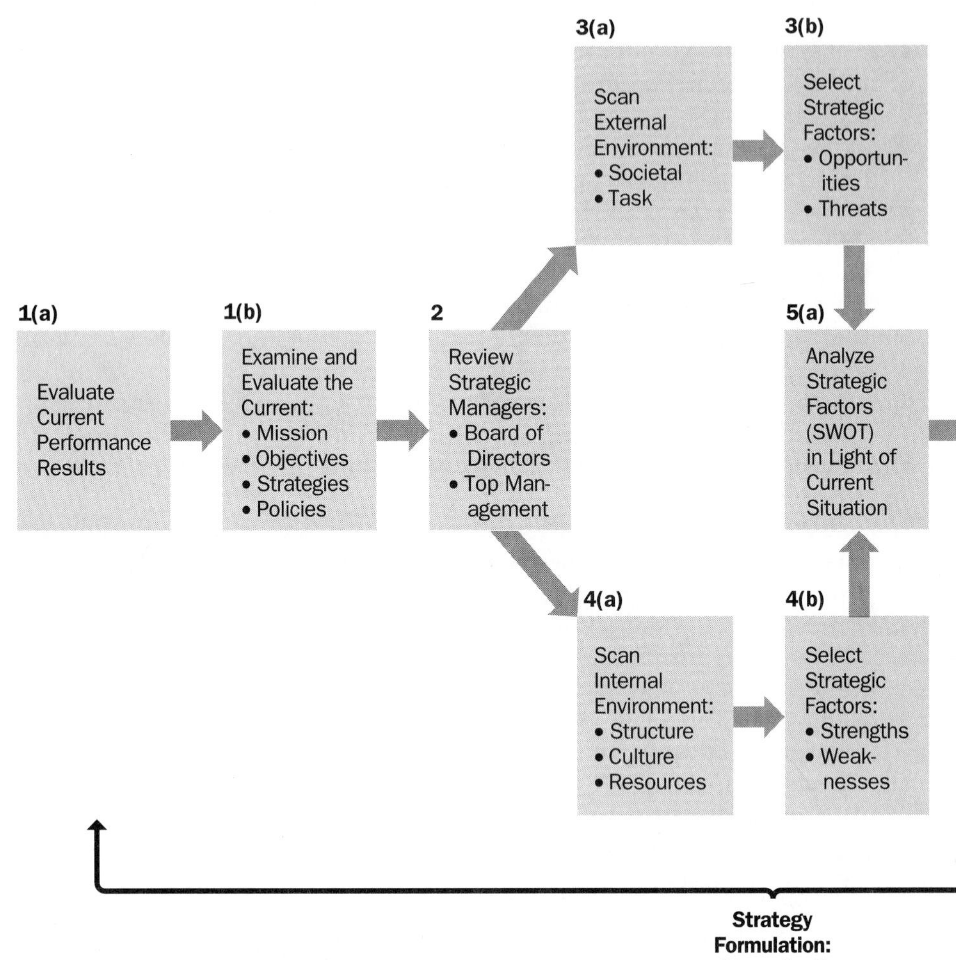

Source: T. L. Wheelen and J. D. Hunger, "Strategic Decision-Making Process." Copyright © 1994 by Wheelen and Hunger Associates. Reprinted by permission.

corporation. A person should consider the audit as a guide for analysis. Some questions or even some areas might be inappropriate for a particular situation; in other cases, the questions may be insufficient for a complete analysis. However, each question in a particular area of the strategic audit may be broken down into an additional series of subquestions. It is up to the individual to develop these subquestions when they are needed.

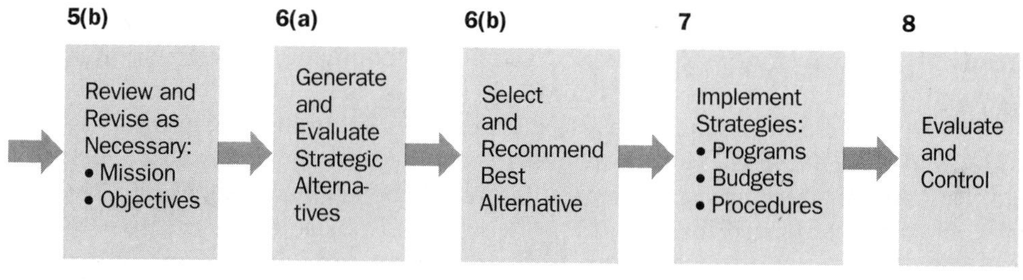

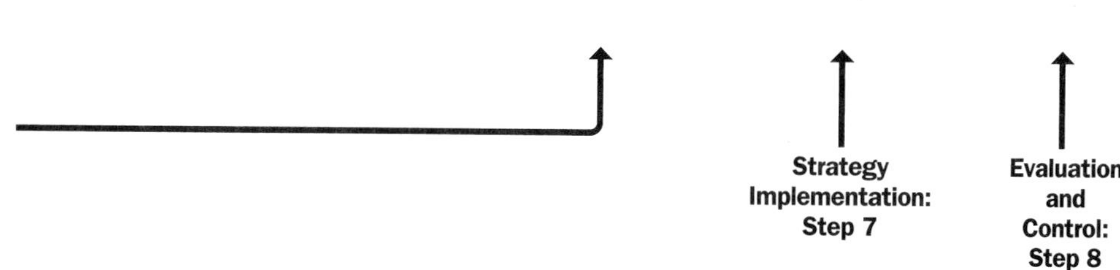

In Conclusion . . .

There is no doubt in most people's minds that strategic managers are important. They can have a huge impact on an entire corporation through their values and their vision. For example, when Kay Anderson founded the Medical Graphics Corporation in 1978 in St. Paul, Minnesota, she acted out of a desire to achieve more than just profits. Concerned with improving medical diagnostics since her father died suddenly of a heart attack when she was 13 years old, Anderson had a personal mission to help save lives. She used Medical Graphics to help achieve that mission. After doing everything from building the equipment to writing software to visiting hospitals in order to demonstrate and sell her products, sales climbed to almost $10 million annually. In her words, "I was on a crusade to save lives by inventing and perfecting a technology that would aid the early detection and diagnosis of heart and lung disease. . . . It was a crusade and I was its driving force." Nevertheless, her inability to stabilize the company financially forced her to step aside for professional managers who could keep track of the bottom line.

Serving only as chairman of the board, Anderson began to notice salespeople quitting and R&D people losing enthusiasm. Sales and profits were up, but no one seemed to care. When Anderson left the company's management team, she apparently also took away the excitement. "People and companies that abandon all ardor and passion lose their purpose in life," she explained. "Maybe I had been a little crazy, but I'd been crazy like a fox, crazy with determination, crazy about an idea and a vision. That kind of madness is a thing all companies desperately need. . . ." Anderson returned to Medical Graphics management as CEO but this time hired an experienced manager to work with and advise her. She also refocused the company on its real mission: *to prevent heart and lung disease,* the reason that originally drove her and her employees to build a successful company. She began to acknowledge openly that her purpose was to save people like her father. The excitement returned. "It turned out that all of us were in it for something more than money, . . ." concluded Anderson.[58]

Points to Remember

- The board of directors of the modern corporation is responsible not just for overseeing top management's performance and use of resources; it is increasingly needed to help set overall corporate direction.
- Boards can be placed on a continuum from passive involvement to active involvement in the strategic management process. Because of current trends in society, few boards will be able to remain passive in the future.
- Boards of directors of large, publicly held corporations are beginning to realize that top management doesn't always have the best interests of shareholders at heart in its strategic and operational decision making. In accordance with agency theory, pressure is increasing to increase the number of outside directors, demand greater stock ownership by executives (and directors), and separate the roles of chairman and CEO.
- In addition to fulfilling key roles and managing the strategic planning process, top management is responsible for providing executive leadership. As the example of Kay Anderson at Medical Graphics shows, the CEO must provide a vision for the company, lead by example, and demand that others follow the CEO's lead to achieve the company's mission and objectives.

- Top managers must use the appropriate strategy formulation mode (entrepreneurial, adaptive, or planning) and have the right mix of technical, human, and conceptual skills to lead the company.
- The strategic audit, by providing a checklist for managers and analysts, is one way to implement the strategic decision-making process so necessary for effective strategic management.

Discussion Questions

1. Does a corporation really need a board of directors? Why or why not?
2. What aspects of a corporation's environment should be represented on a board of directors?
3. What recommendations would you make to improve the effectiveness of today's boards of directors?
4. Do you agree that a chief executive officer (CEO), in order to be effective, should fulfill Mintzberg's ten roles?
5. What makes an effective top manager? What types of skills and experiences should a person have in order to become a CEO?
6. Reconcile the strategic decision-making process depicted in Fig. 2.3 with the strategic management model depicted in Fig. 1.2.
7. What are the strengths and weaknesses of the strategic audit as a technique for assessing corporate performance?

Notes

1. L. J. Wachner, "Leaders of Corporate Change," *Fortune* (December 14, 1992), p. 108. © 1992 Time Inc. All rights reserved.
2. M. L. Weidenbaum, "The Best Defense Against the Raiders," *Business Week* (September 23, 1985), p. 21. This belief is supported by research reporting that the shareholders of an acquiring firm tend to lose in the transaction. See M. Weidenbaum and S. Vogt, "Takeovers and Stockholders: Winners and Losers," *California Management Review* (Summer 1987), pp. 157–168.
3. J. H. Dobrzynski, "These Board Members Aren't IBM-Compatible," *Business Week* (August 2, 1992), p. 23.
4. J. H. Dobrzynski, M. Schroeder, G. L. Miles, and J. Weber, "Taking Charge," *Business Week* (July 3, 1989), p. 69.
5. *Wall Street Journal* (December 22, 1992), p. A1.
6. A. Demb and F. F. Neubauer, "The Corporate Board: Confronting the Paradoxes," *Long Range Planning* (June 1992), p. 13.
7. "Key Organization Issues for the Board," *Directors & Boards* (Winter 1992), p. 55.
8. J. Bacon and J. K. Brown, *Corporate Directorship Practices: Role, Selection and Legal Status of the Board* (New York: The Conference Board, Report No. 646, 1975), p. 75.
9. Ibid., p. 15.
10. W. Q. Judge, Jr. and C. P. Zeithaml, "Institutional and Strategic Choice Perspectives on Board Involvement in the Strategic Decision Process," *Academy of Management Journal* (October 1992), pp. 766–794.
11. Ibid.; J. A. Pearce II and S. A. Zahra, "Effective Power-Sharing Between the Board of Directors and the CEO," *Handbook of Business Strategy, 1992/93 Yearbook* (Boston: Warren, Gorham & Lamont, 1992), pp. 1.1–1.16.
12. L. Iacocca, *Iacocca: An Autobiography* (Toronto: Bantam Books, 1984), p. 104.
13. "Key Organization Issues for the Board," p. 54.
14. J. W. Hoft, J. D. Hunger, and C. B. Shrader, "Characteristics of Boards of Directors and

Corporate Social Responsibility: An Examination of the *Fortune* Survey," *Journal of Business Strategies* (Fall 1991), pp. 77–85; "Key Organization Issues for the Board," pp. 54–55; R. M. Ferry, *Board of Directors Twentieth Annual Study: 1993* (New York: Korn/Ferry International, 1993), p. 3.

15. R. J. Bronstein, "Good Pay on Small Boards, *Directors & Strategy* (Spring 1987), pp. 36–37.
16. S. C. Vance, *Corporate Leadership: Boards, Directors and Strategy* (New York: McGraw-Hill, 1983), p. 274.
17. J. R. Bolton, "A Second Look at Boardroom Reform," *Wall Street Journal* (June 2, 1993), p. A14; B. Boyd, "Corporate Linkages and Organizational Environment: A Test of the Resource Dependence Model," *Strategic Management Journal* (October 1990), pp. 419–430; M. H. Schellenger, D. D. Wood, and A. Tashakori, "Board of Director Composition, Shareholder Wealth, and Dividend Policy," *Journal of Management* (September 1989), pp. 457–467.
18. Outside directors elected to U.S. corporate boards during the one-year period from June 1990 through May 1991, as reported by *Directors & Boards,* were from the following: chairmen/CEOs (22%), senior managers (18%), financial (12%), academia (8%), retired (9%), consultants (11%), private investors/professional investors (14%), legal (4%), and former government officials (2%).
19. Ferry, pp. 1–2.
20. T. H. Hammer and R. N. Stern, "Worker Representation on Company Boards of Directors," *Proceedings, Academy of Management* (1983), p. 368.
21. T. O. Prenting, "Co-Determination: Its Practice and Applicability to the U.S.," *SAM Advanced Management Journal* (Spring 1992), pp. 12–16.
22. J. R. Lang and D. E. Lockhart, "Increased Environmental Uncertainty and Changes in Board Linkage Patterns," *Academy of Management Journal* (March 1990), p. 106.
23. M. H. Bazerman and F. D. Schoorman, "A Limited Rationality Model of Interlocking Directorates," *Academy of Management Review* (April 1983), pp. 206–217.
24. G. F. David, "Agents Without Principles? The Spread of the Poison Pill Through the Intercorporate Network," *Administrative Science Quarterly* (December 1991), pp. 583–613.
25. For a more in-depth discussion of this topic, see J. M. Pennings, *Interlocking Directorates* (San Francisco: Jossey-Bass, 1980), and M. S. Mizruchi, *The American Corporate Network 1904–1974* (Beverly Hills, Calif.: Sage, 1982).
26. J. A. C. Baum and C. Oliver, "Institutional Linkages and Organizational Mortality," *Administrative Science Quarterly* (June 1991) pp. 187–218.
27. Ferry, p. 3.
28. A 1991 survey by Ernst & Ernst of 450 publicly held corporations in 24 industries found that 74% of the boards used staggered elections as a takeover defense. See "Key Organization Issues for the Board," *Directors & Boards* (Winter 1992), p. 54.
29. Ferry, p. 7. This trend toward smaller boards is supported by a Spencer Stuart & Associates survey, as reported by J. Dobrzynski, "Corporate Boards May Finally Be Shaping Up," *Business Week* (August 9, 1993), p. 26.
30. Ferry, p. 7.
31. P. L. Rechner and D. R. Dalton, "CEO Duality and Organizational Performance: A Longitudinal Analysis," *Strategic Management Journal* (February 1991), pp. 155–160; P. L. Rechner and D. R. Dalton, "The Link Between Financial Performance and Board Leadership Structure," *Handbook of Business Strategy, 1992/93 Yearbook,* edited by H. E. Glass and M. A. Hovde (Boston: Warren, Gorham, and Lamont, 1992), pp. 20.1–20.7.
32. Ferry, p. 7.
33. For further information on board committees, see I. F. Kesner, "Directors' Characteristics and Committee Membership: An Investigation of Type, Occupation, Tenure, and Gender," *Academy of Management Journal* (March 1988), pp. 66–84.
34. J. Young, "Pawns or Potentates: the Reality of America's Corporate Boards—An Interview with Jay Lorsch," *Academy of Management Executive* (November 1990), p. 87.
35. S. L. Oswald and J. S. Jahera, Jr., "The Influence of Ownership on Performance: An Empirical Study," *Strategic Management Journal* (May 1991), pp. 321–326; C. M. Daily and D. R. Dalton, "Officer and Director Stock Ownership and Firm Performance in the Publicly Traded Small Corporation," *Journal of Business Strategies* (Fall 1992), pp. 101–113.

36. P. Stiles, "The Future for Boards: Self-Regulation or Legislation?" *Long Range Planning* (April 1993), pp. 119–124.
37. J. C. Worthy and R. P. Neuschel, *Emerging Issues in Corporate Governance* (Evanston, Ill.: Northwestern University Press, 1983), p. 100.
38. E. J. Zajac, "CEO Selection, Succession, Compensation and Firm Performance: A Theoretical Integration and Empirical Analysis," *Strategic Management Journal* (March–April 1990), pp. 217–230; K. M. Eisenhardt and C. B. Shoonhoven, "Organizational Growth: Linking Founding Team, Strategy, Environment and Growth Among U.S. Semiconductor Ventures, 1978–1988," *Administrative Science Quarterly* (September 1990), pp. 504–529; A. I. Murray, "Top Management Heterogeneity and Firm Performance," *Handbook of Business Strategy, 1991/92 Yearbook,* edited by H. E. Glass and M. A. Hovde (Boston: Warren, Gorham & Lamont, 1991) pp. 3.1–3.13.
39. P. F. Drucker, *Management: Tasks, Responsibilities, Practices* (New York: HarperCollins, 1974), p. 613.
40. H. Mintzberg, *The Nature of Managerial Work* (New York: HarperCollins, 1973), pp. 54–94.
41. D. A. Gioia and K. Chittipeddi, "Sensemaking and Sensegiving in Strategic Change Initiation," *Strategic Management Journal* (September 1991), pp. 433–448; H. S. Jonas III, R. Fry, and S. Srivastva, "The Office of the CEO, Understanding the Executive Experience," *Academy of Management Executive* (August 1990), pp. 36–48; J. P. Kotler, *The Leadership Factor* (New York: Free Press, 1988).
42. Advertisement in *Business Week* (October 23, 1987), pp. 118–119.
43. Adapted from R. J. House, "A 1976 Theory of Charismatic Leadership," *Leadership: The Cutting Edge,* edited by J. G. Hunt and L. L. Larson (Carbondale, Ill.: SIU Press, 1977), pp. 189–207. This view of executive leadership is also referred to as transformational leadership. See B. M. Bass, "From Transactional to Transformational Leadership: Learning to Share the Vision," *Organizational Dynamics* (Winter 1990), pp. 19–31.
44. N. Tichy and R. Charan, "Speed, Simplicity, Self-Confidence: An Interview with Jack Welch," *Harvard Business Review* (September–October 1989), p. 113.
45. M. Trevor, "Japanese Decision-making and Global Strategy," in *Strategic Management Research: A European Perspective,* edited by J. McGee and H. Thomas (Chichester, U.K.: John Wiley & Sons, 1986), p. 301.
46. M. Prete and C. Boschetti, "The Corporate Planner as Consultant," *Long Range Planning* (December 1990), pp. 23–30.
47. Drucker, pp. 615–617.
48. Mintzberg, *Managerial Work,* p. 33.
49. H. Mintzberg, "Strategy-Making in Three Modes," *California Management Review* (Winter 1973), pp. 44–53.
50. B. Schlender, "How Bill Gates Keeps the Magic Going," *Fortune* (June 18, 1990), pp. 82–89.
51. J. B. Quinn, *Strategies for Change: Logical Incrementalism* (Homewood, Ill.: Irwin, 1980), p. 58.
52. A. Ginsberg and A. Buchholtz, "Converting to For-Profit Status: Corporate Responsiveness to Radical Change," *Academy of Management Journal* (September 1990), p. 470.
53. R. L. Katz, "Skills of an Effective Administrator," *Harvard Business Review* (January–February 1955), pp. 33–42.
54. T. L. Wheelen, C. E. Michaels, Jr., and J. D. Hunger, "A Longitudinal Study of the Skills of an Effective Executive," Working Paper, 1991.
55. T. L. Wheelen and J. D. Hunger, "Using the Strategic Audit," *SAM Advanced Management Journal* (Winter 1987), pp. 4–12.
56. H. Mintzberg and J. B. Quinn, *The Strategy Process: Concepts, Contexts, and Cases,* 2nd ed. (Englewood Cliffs, N.J.: Prentice Hall, 1991); J. W. Fredrickson and A. L. Iaquinto, "Inertia and Creeping Rationality in Strategic Decision Processes," *Academy of Management Journal* (September 1989), pp. 516–542.
57. H. I. Ansoff, "Critique of Henry Mintzberg's 'The Design School: Reconsidering the Basic Premises of Strategic Management,'" *Strategic Management Journal* (September 1991), pp. 449–461; R. E. Jones, L. W. Jacobs, and R. D. Von Riesen, "Comprehensive Strategic Decision Processes in High Technology Firms," Working Paper, University of Wyoming, February 1990.
58. K. Anderson, "The Purpose at the Heart of Management," *Harvard Business Review* (May–June 1992), pp. 52–62.

Appendix 2: Strategic Audit of a Corporation

I. Current Situation

A. Performance

How is the corporation performing in terms of return on investment, overall market share, profitability trends, earnings per share, etc.?

B. Strategic Posture

What are the corporation's current mission, objectives, strategies, and policies?

1. Are they clearly stated or are they merely implied from performance?
2. **Mission:** What business(es) is (are) the corporation in? Why?
3. **Objectives:** What are the corporate, business, and functional objectives? Are they consistent with each other, with the mission, and with the internal and external environments?
4. **Strategies:** What strategy or mix of strategies is the corporation following? Are they consistent with each other, with the mission and objectives, and with the internal and external environments?
5. **Policies:** What are they? Are they consistent with each other, with the mission, objectives, and strategies and with the internal and external environments?

II. Strategic Managers

A. Board of Directors

1. Who are they? Are they internal or external?
2. Do they own significant shares of stock?
3. Is the stock privately held or publicly traded?
4. What do they contribute to the corporation in terms of knowledge, skills, background, and connections?
5. How long have they served on the board?
6. What is their level of involvement in strategic management? Do they merely rubber-stamp top management's proposals or do they actively participate and suggest future directions?

B. Top Management

1. What person or group constitutes top management?
2. What are top management's main characteristics in terms of knowledge, skills, background, and style?
3. Has top management been responsible for the corporation's performance over the past few years?
4. Has it established a systematic approach to the formulation, implementation, and evaluation and control of strategic management?
5. What is its level of involvement in the strategic management process?
6. How well does top management interact with lower level management?
7. How well does top management interact with the board of directors?
8. Is top management sufficiently skilled to cope with likely future challenges?

III. External Environment: Opportunities and Threats (SW*OT*)

A. Societal Environment

1. What general environmental factors among the sociocultural, economic, political–legal, and technological forces are currently affecting both the corporation and the industries in which it competes? Which present current or future threats? Opportunities?
2. Which of these are currently the most important (that is, are **strategic factors**) to the corporation and to the industries in which it competes? Which will be important in the future?

B. Task Environment

1. What forces in the immediate environment (that is, threat of new entrants, bargaining power of buyers, threat of substitute products or services, bargaining power of suppliers, rivalry among competing firms, and the relative power of unions, governments, etc.) are currently affecting the level of competitive intensity within the industries in which the corporation offers products or services?
2. What key factors in the immediate environment (that is, customers, competitors, suppliers, creditors, labor unions, governments, trade associations, interest groups, local communities, and stockholders) are currently affecting the corporation? Which present current or future threats? Opportunities?
3. Which of these forces and factors are the most important (that is, are strategic factors) at the present time? Which will be important in the future? *(See External Factor Analysis Summary (EFAS) in Chapter 4 on page 109. This provides a method to summarize external strategic factors by employing a weighted average.)*

IV. Internal Environment: Strengths and Weaknesses (SWOT)

A. Corporate Structure

1. How is the corporation structured at present?
   a) Is decision-making authority centralized around one group or decentralized to many groups or units?
   b) Is it organized on the basis of functions, projects, geography, or some combination of these?
2. Is the structure clearly understood by everyone in the corporation?
3. Is the present structure consistent with current corporate objectives, strategies, policies, and programs?
4. In what ways does this structure compare with those of similar corporations?

B. Corporate Culture

1. Is there a well-defined or emerging culture composed of shared beliefs, expectations, and values?
2. Is the culture consistent with current objectives, strategies, policies, and programs?
3. What is the culture's position on important issues facing the corporation (that is, on productivity, quality of performance, adaptability to changing conditions)?

C. Corporate Resources

1. Marketing
   a) What are the corporation's current marketing objectives, strategies, policies, and programs?
      i) Are they clearly stated, or merely implied from performance and/or budgets?
      ii) Are they consistent with the corporation's mission, objectives, strategies, and policies and with internal and external environments?
   b) How well is the corporation performing in terms of analysis of market position and marketing mix (that is, product, price, place, and promotion)?
      i) What trends emerge from this analysis?
      ii) What impact have these trends had on past performance and how will they probably affect future performance?
      iii) Does this analysis support the corporation's past and pending strategic decisions?
   c) How well does this corporation's marketing performance compare with those of similar corporations?
   d) Are marketing managers using accepted marketing concepts and techniques to evaluate and improve product performance? (Consider product life cycle, market segmentation, market research, and product portfolios.)
   e) What is the role of the marketing manager in the strategic management process?

2. Finance

a) What are the corporation's current financial objectives, strategies, policies, and programs?
   i) Are they clearly stated or merely implied from performance and/or budgets?
   ii) Are they consistent with the corporation's mission, objectives, strategies, and policies and with internal and external environments?

b) How well is the corporation performing in terms of financial analysis? (Consider liquidity ratios, profitability ratios, activity ratios, leverage ratios, capitalization structure, and common-size financial statements.)
   i) What trends emerge from this analysis?
   ii) Are there any significant differences when statements are calculated in constant versus reported dollars?
   iii) What impact have these trends had on past performance and how will they probably affect future performance?
   iv) Does this analysis support the corporation's past and pending strategic decisions?

c) How well does this corporation's financial performance compare with that of similar corporations?

d) Are financial managers using accepted financial concepts and techniques to evaluate and improve current corporate and divisional performance? (Consider financial leverage, capital budgeting, and ratio analysis.)

e) What is the role of the financial manager in the strategic management process?

3. Research and Development (R&D)

a) What are the corporation's current R&D objectives, strategies, policies, and programs?
   i) Are they clearly stated, or implied from performance and/or budgets?
   ii) Are they consistent with the corporation's mission, objectives, strategies, and policies and with internal and external environments?
   iii) What is the role of technology in corporate performance?
   iv) Is the mix of basic, applied, and engineering research appropriate for the corporation's mission and strategies?

b) What return is the corporation receiving from its investment in R&D?

c) Is the corporation technologically competent?

d) How well does the corporation's investment in R&D compare with the investments of similar corporations?

e) What is the role of the R&D manager in the strategic management process?

4. Operations (Manufacturing/Service)

a) What are the corporation's current manufacturing/service objectives, strategies, policies, and programs?
   i) Are they clearly stated, or merely implied from performance and/or budgets?

ii) Are they consistent with the corporation's mission, objectives, strategies, and policies and with internal and external environments?

b) What are the type and extent of operations capabilities of the corporation?

  i) If product-oriented, consider plant facilities, type of manufacturing system (continuous mass production or intermittent job shop), age and type of equipment, degree and role of automation and/or robots, plant capacities and utilization, productivity ratings, and availability and type of transportation.

  ii) If service-oriented, consider service facilities (e.g., hospital, theater, or school buildings), type of operations systems (continuous service over time to same clientele or intermittent service over time to varied clientele), age and type of supporting equipment, degree and role of automation and/or use of mass-communication devices (e.g., diagnostic machinery, videotape machines), facility capacities and utilization rates, efficiency ratings of professional/service personnel, and availability and type of transportation to bring service staff and clientele together.

c) Are manufacturing or service facilities vulnerable to natural disasters, local or national strikes, reduction or limitation of resources from suppliers, substantial cost increases of materials, or nationalization by governments?

d) Is operating leverage being used successfully with an appropriate mix of people and machines, in manufacturing firms, or of support staff to professionals, in service firms?

e) How well does the corporation perform relative to its competition? Consider costs per unit of labor, material, and overhead; downtime; inventory control management and/or scheduling of service staff; production ratings; facility utilization percentages; and number of clients successfully treated by category (if service firm), or percentage of orders shipped on time (if product firm).

  i) What trends emerge from this analysis?

  ii) What impact have these trends had on past performance and how will they probably affect future performance?

  iii) Does this analysis support the corporation's past and pending strategic decisions?

f) Are operations managers using appropriate concepts and techniques to evaluate and improve current performance? Consider cost systems, quality control and reliability systems, inventory control management, personnel scheduling, learning curves, safety programs, and engineering programs that can improve efficiency of manufacturing or of service.

g) What is the role of the operations manager in the strategic management process?

5. Human Resources Management (HRM)

a) What are the corporation's current HRM objectives, strategies, policies, and programs?

  i) Are they clearly stated, or merely implied from performance and/or budgets?

    ii) Are they consistent with the corporation's mission, objectives, strategies, and policies and with internal and external environments?

b) How well is the corporation's HRM performing in terms of improving the fit between the individual employee and the job? Consider turnover, grievances, strikes, layoffs, employee training, quality of work life.
    i) What trends emerge from this analysis?
    ii) What impact have these trends had on past performance and how will they probably affect future performance?
    iii) Does this analysis support the corporation's past and pending strategic decisions?

c) How does this corporation's HRM performance compare with that of similar corporations?

d) Are HRM managers using appropriate concepts and techniques to evaluate and improve corporate performance? Consider the job analysis program, performance appraisal system, up-to-date job descriptions, training and development programs, attitude surveys, job design programs, and quality of relationship with unions.

e) What is the role of the HRM manager in the strategic management process?

6. Information Systems (IS)

a) What are the corporation's current IS objectives, strategies, policies, and programs?
    i) Are they clearly stated, or merely implied from performance and/or budgets?
    ii) Are they consistent with the corporation's mission, objectives, strategies, and policies and with internal and external environments?

b) How well is the corporation's IS performing in terms of providing a useful database, automating routine clerical operations, assisting managers in making routine decisions, and providing information necessary for strategic decisions?
    i) What trends emerge from this analysis?
    ii) What impact have these trends had on past performance and how will they probably affect future performance?
    iii) Does this analysis support the corporation's past and pending strategic decisions?

c) How does this corporation's IS performance and stage of development compare with that of similar corporations?

d) Are IS managers using appropriate concepts and techniques to evaluate and improve corporate performance? Do they know how to build and manage a complex database, conduct system analyses, and implement interactive decision-support systems?

e) What is the role of the IS manager in the strategic management process?

(See Internal Factor Analysis Summary (IFAS) in Chapter 5 on page 136. This provides a method to summarize internal strategic factors by employing a weighted average.)

V. Analysis of Strategic Factors (SWOT)

A. What are the key internal and external factors (**Strengths, Weaknesses, Opportunities, Threats**) that strongly affect the corporation's present and future performance? (List five to ten strategic factors.)
(See Strategic Factor Analysis Summary (SFAS) in Chapter 6 on pages 174–175. This provides a means to combine both external and internal strategic factors by means of a weighted average.)

B. Are the current mission and objectives appropriate in light of the key strategic factors and problems?
1. Should the mission and objectives be changed? If so, how?
2. If changed, what will be the effects on the firm?

VI. Strategic Alternatives and Recommended Strategy

A. Strategic Alternatives

1. Can the current or revised objectives be met simply by more careful implementation of those strategies presently in use (for example, fine-tuning the current strategies)?

2. What are the primary feasible alternative strategies available to this corporation? What are the pros and cons of each? Can scenarios be developed and agreed upon?
a. Consider *stability, growth,* and *retrenchment* as corporate strategies.
b. Consider *cost leadership* and *differentiation* as business strategies.
c. Consider any functional strategic alternatives that might be needed to reinforce an important corporate or business strategic alternative.

B. Recommended Strategy

1. Specify which of the strategic alternatives you are recommending for the corporate, business, and functional levels of the corporation. Do you recommend different business or functional strategies for different units of the corporation?

2. Justify your recommendation in terms of its ability to resolve both long- and short-term problems and effectively deal with the key strategic factors.

3. What **policies** should be developed or revised to guide effective implementation?

VII. Implementation

A. What kinds of **programs** (for example, restructuring the corporation) should be developed to implement the recommended strategy?
1. Who should develop these programs?
2. Who should be in charge of these programs?

B. Are the programs financially feasible? Can pro forma **budgets** be developed and agreed upon? Are priorities and timetables appropriate to individual programs?

C. Will new standard operating **procedures** need to be developed?

VIII. Evaluation and Control

A. Is the current information system capable of providing sufficient feedback on implementation activities and performance?

  1. Can performance results be pinpointed by area, unit, project, or function?
  2. Is the information timely?

B. Are adequate control measures in place to ensure conformance with the recommended strategic plan?

  1. Are appropriate standards and measures being used?
  2. Are current reward systems capable of recognizing and rewarding good performance?

Social Responsibility and Ethics in Strategic Management

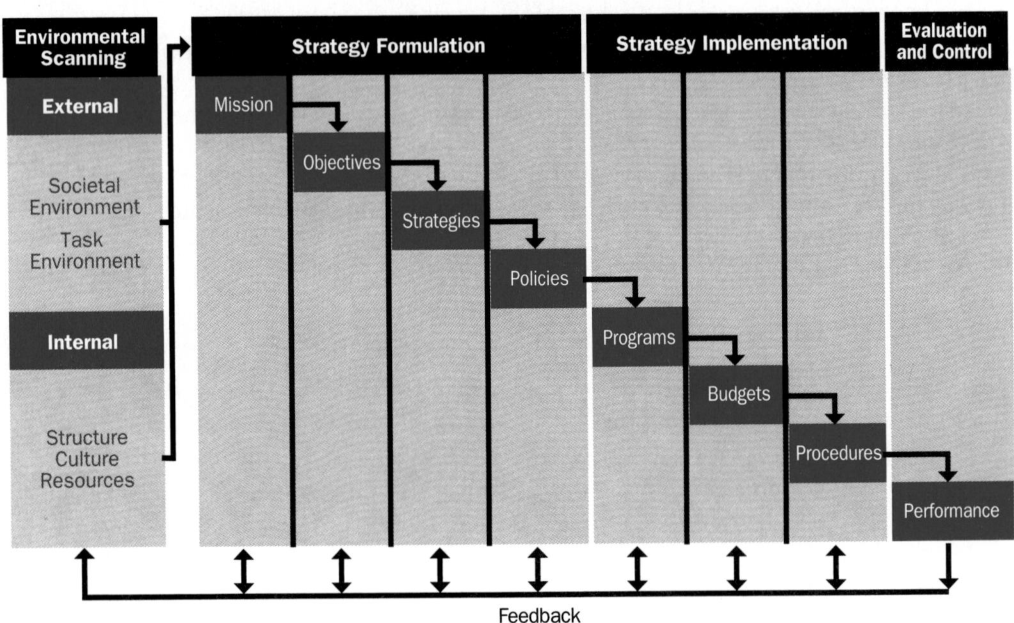

If you're going to take money out of a community, give something back.[1]
[Ray Kroc, Founder of McDonald's]

Until late 1992, Comptronix Corporation of Guntersville, Alabama, appeared to be a very successful electronics company whose main business was providing manufacturing services to original equipment manufacturers. It was thought of as a profitable "high flyer" by the financial community. Its stock price had more than quadrupled from its original offering price of $5 in 1989 when the company went public. The company's co-founders, William Hebding, chairman and CEO, and Allen Shifflett, President and COO, were perceived to be extremely effective managers. According to one financial analyst, Chairman Hebding "always came across as someone absolutely focused on his business."

In July 1992, the company reported record second quarter results and the stock price rose from $13 to $14.75 a share. Even though both CEO Hebding and COO Shifflett each sold 50,000 shares of the company's stock soon after announcing the quarterly results, few thought anything about it.

In November, however, Hebding confessed to the Comptronix Board of Directors that he, Shifflett, and Paul Medlin, controller and treasurer, had been deliberately inflating company profits since the company went public through the use of fraudulent accounting practices. The goal had been to increase both gross profits and sales. To boost profits, the three men inflated inventory and decreased the cost of sales by equal amounts each month. Periodically during the year, they shifted a portion of the amounts improperly added to inventory to the equipment line on the company's balance sheet. To document the apparent increase in the amount of equipment, they prepared fake invoices for the purchase of equipment. To increase sales, the executives recorded phony sales from the company's growing (but bogus) inventory. They also established phony accounts receivable. To show that the money owed for the fake sales (listed as accounts receivable) actually was being paid, they wrote checks for equipment that was never purchased and deposited it into the company's bank accounts. Under an unusual arrangement, if Comptronix owed money to a company that was both a supplier and a customer of Comptronix, the executives used the account to reconcile the difference. This game had apparently gone undetected for years. According to a spokesperson from KPMG Peat Marwick, the public accounting firm that had audited the company's records during that time, "These are people who knew the accounting rules inside and out and knew what documentation would be needed in a test to fool an auditor." (The accounting firm resigned as the company's auditor soon after Hebding's confession.)

In attempting to explain why these three executives "cooked the company's books," a director of the company suggested that, when the executives foresaw a less than desirable quarterly performance report, they "got in a cycle of fudging the results" rather than face criticism from the board. Others speculated that, based on Hebding and Shifflett's well-timed sales of Comptronix stock, the motive simply was greed.[2]

3.1 Business and Society: An Interactive Relationship

Organizations such as Comptronix Corporation do not exist in a social and ethical vacuum. They exist because society or a segment of it needs a particular product or service, and they can continue to exist relatively unchecked only so long as they take responsibility for their actions and acknowledge their role in the larger society. As a result, management must be aware constantly of the variables and forces in the firm's task environment and the larger societal environment (see Fig. 1.3).

These variables and forces constantly interact with each other. In the short run, societal forces affect the decisions and actions of an organization through the groups in its task environment. In the long run, however, the organization also affects these groups through its activities. For example, the decision by several U.S. business corporations to relocate their manufacturing facilities to Asia and Latin America in order to reduce labor costs increased unemployment among U.S. blue-collar workers. That in turn reduced union membership, adversely affected the country's balance of trade with other nations, and created economic depressions in

WHICH IS MORE SOCIALLY RESPONSIBLE: GIVING TO CHARITY OR PROVIDING JOBS?

Strategy in Action

The walls inside the gleaming Cambridge, Massachusetts, headquarters of Stride Rite Corporation are lined with plaques honoring the shoe company for its socially responsible actions. The awards, which were given by the National Women's Political Caucus, Northeastern University, the Northeast Human Resources Association, and Harvard University, praised Stride Rite for "improving the quality of life" in its community and the nation. Over the years, the company has donated 5% of pretax profits to a charity foundation, given scholarships to inner-city youths, sent 100,000 pairs of sneakers to war-torn Mozambique, permitted employees to tutor disadvantaged children on company time, and been a pioneer in establishing on-site day-care and elder-care facilities. While doing good, Stride Rite has also done well. It consistently earned profits. Management expected its 1993 sales to exceed $625 million, more than double its 1986 total. The company's stock price has increased six times in value since 1986, making it very popular with socially conscious investors.

Just a few miles away in Boston's rough inner-city Roxbury neighborhood, stood another Stride Rite building—a run-down red-brick building surrounded by empty lots, crumbling roads, and chain-link fences. This used to be Stride Rite's headquarters, where it employed 2,500 people making the company's Keds sneakers and Sperry Top-Sider shoes. In 1993, it was only being used as a warehouse employing 175 workers. It and another warehouse in New Bedford were scheduled to be closed the next year when the operations would be moved to Kentucky. With the lo-

those communities dependent for employment and tax revenue on the now-closed plants. The Stride Rite Corporation has received 14 public service awards during the four-year period from 1990 to 1993, even though it has closed 15 U.S. factories and moved most of its production to low-cost Asian countries, as described in the Strategy in Action on pages 58–59.

The relationship between business organizations and society, as summarized in Table 3.1, has varied over time. In ancient times, commercial activities such as trading and money-lending were regarded as necessary but distasteful and were merely tolerated. During Europe's Middle Ages, the Roman Catholic Church held business and commercial activity in disdain and placed strict rules and limitations on it. Trade itself was a dubious undertaking, and many people believed that accumulating wealth was contrary to the charitable teachings of Jesus Christ. Muslims, cal unemployment rate at nearly 30%, the soon-to-be-jobless workers were discouraged. "There is no place to go," lamented Miguel Brandao, a 46-year-old immigrant who had worked at the plant 11 years. In the past decade, Stride Rite has prospered partly because it closed 15 factories, mostly in the Northeast and several in depressed areas, and moved production to various Asian countries. Even while the company was nurturing social programs in the late 1960s, it had already begun to close plants in Maine and New Hampshire. The company's U.S. work force dropped from a peak of 6,000 to 2,500 by 1993.

Stride Rite's actions have caused people to question their understanding of social responsibility. What makes a company socially responsible? Is it sufficient to do good deeds or is something else needed, such as providing jobs in depressed areas at the expense of profits? According to Donald Gillis, executive director of Boston's Economic Development and Industrial Commission, "The most socially responsible thing a company can do is to give a person a job." Stride Rite's management contends, however, that it has been socially responsible. It must balance the demands of shareholders and society. If a company doesn't stay competitive, according to management, this could jeopardize its future survival. Asserted Chairman Ervin Shames, "Putting jobs into places where it doesn't make economic sense is a dilution of corporate and community wealth."

Source: J. Pereira, "Social Responsibility and Need for Low Cost Clash at Stride Rite," *Wall Street Journal* (May 28, 1993), pp. A1, A4.

like early Christians, believed that *usury,* the charging of interest, was wrong. However, the Renaissance and the Protestant Reformation began to change long-held values and brought a more positive view of business activities. These changes also encouraged a new spirit of individualism. Utilizing the economic concept of **mercantilism,** in which all business activity was considered an instrument of the state, governments in the West encouraged the formation of business ventures as a way to support the economic development of society.

In 1776, economist Adam Smith advanced a theory justifying **capitalism** in his book *An Inquiry into the Nature and Causes of the Wealth of Nations.* Smith argued that economic freedom would enable individuals, through self-interest, to fulfill themselves and thereby benefit the total society. Arguing against the centralized aspects of mercantilism, Smith used the term *laissez-faire* to suggest that

TABLE 3.1 **Brief History of Society's Attitudes Toward Business**

Time Period	Society's Attitude
Greek/Roman period (100 B.C.)	Tolerate Them
Middle Ages (1000 A.D.)	Restrict Them
Renaissance–Western Europe Protestant ethic Mercantilism (1500s)	Use Them
Industrial expansion Laissez-faire (1800s)	Glorify Them
Industrial domination Monopolies, cartels, sweatshops, depressions (late 1800s)	Disillusionment and Betrayal
Nationalism Battle of ideologies (early 1900s)	*Capitalism:* Restrict Them Via Laws *Socialism:* Nationalize Them Via Government Ownership *Marxist communism:* Outlaw Them
Developing global village World trade Modern mercantilism (late 1900s)	Encourage/Support Them (Capitalism, Socialism, and Communism)

government should leave business alone—that the "invisible hand" of the marketplace, through pure competition, would ensure maximum benefit to society. With changes in sociocultural values fed by the benefits of new technology and laissez-faire economics, governments in the West began not only to give developing business organizations increasing autonomy, but they also began to support and even glorify business as key to increasing the material well-being of society.

The resulting industrial revolution also had its negative side, which increasingly caused people to question the autonomy given business firms. Karl Marx, who wrote *The Communist Manifesto* with Friedrich Engels in 1848 and *Das Kapital* in 1867, rejected capitalism because of its many unsavory side effects, such as child labor, unsafe working conditions, and subsistence wages. Society's response to the development of self-centered monopolistic corporations and cartels—in terms of government action—varied from legislation restricting business autonomy to taking over (nationalizing) ownership of businesses to completely outlawing business activities. Even more recently, laws regarding air and water pollution, product safety, and employment practices, among others, increasingly have constrained business activities.

Faced with serious problems of unemployment and balance of trade problems during the 1980s and 1990s, governments around the world acted to reduce some of those constraints. The general view seemed to be that state-controlled or heavily regulated business organizations could not operate as efficiently or effectively as those given more autonomy.[3] More and more countries recognized that their people and institutions now had to compete globally. As a result, many countries began to support and encourage business activity. The view that a government should encourage business activity as a way of improving or protecting its people's standard of living was more in line with the economic philosophy of mercantilism than it was with Adam Smith's laissez-faire capitalism.

Unfortunately, this strong support of business by governments around the world was tempered by business's ever-present tendency to take advantage of and exploit the very society that supported it. Allegations of insider trading and revelations of negligence, bribery, and fraud revealed some very low ethical standards. Strategic managers in corporations began to realize that they might lose their new-found support and autonomy if they failed to show some social responsibility.

3.2 Issues in Social Responsibility and Ethics

The concept that business must be socially responsible sounds appealing until someone asks, "Responsible to whom?" As Fig. 1.3 shows, the task environment includes a large number of groups with interest in a business organization's activities. These groups are called **stakeholders** because they have a direct interest in—they affect or are affected by—the achievement of the firm's objectives.[4] Should a corporation be responsible only to some of these groups, or does it have an equal responsibility to all of them?

As pointed out in the Stride Rite example, the trend of many North American business corporations to move manufacturing activities to low-wage countries has created resentment, not only among union members but also among other employees and nonemployee stakeholders. In its haste to satisfy one group of people—say, shareholders, management may create problems with other concerned parties. The negative reactions may be especially severe if a company's foreign operations or contractors abuse workers and provide only near-starvation wages.

Increasingly, the emphasis being placed on increasing shareholder wealth as the primary objective of business activity is being criticized. In his book *Tyranny of the Bottom Line: Holding Corporations Accountable,* Ralph Estes points out that many others besides shareholders invest heavily in a business. These investors are the workers, the customers, and the taxpayers of the communities who support the corporation. Estes says, "These forgotten investors are often called stakeholders, and they are owed an accounting because they, too, invest by committing valuable resources, including not only money but their work, their careers, sometimes their lives to the corporation."[5]

Juggling Stakeholder Priorities

In any one decision the interests of one stakeholder group may conflict with another. For example, a firm's decision to use only recycled materials in its manufacturing process may have a positive effect on environmental groups but a negative effect on shareholder dividends. The Company Spotlight: Maytag Corporation feature on pages 64–65 describes the corporation's decision to move dishwasher production to a low-cost area. On the one hand, shareholders generally were pleased with the decision because it would lower costs. On the other hand, employees, local officials, and union representatives were very unhappy at what they called "community cannibalism." Which group's interests should have priority?

In a 1991 survey sponsored by the American Management Association, researchers asked 1,000 executives to rate on a seven-point scale the importance of several organizational goals. Executives listed quality, customer service, and organizational effectiveness as the most important. They rated service to the public and organizational value to the community as the least important. (Surprisingly, the respondents also rated profit maximization fairly low.) The executives then rated various stakeholder groups on the same scale. They listed customers, employees, and "myself" as the most important. They rated groups such as public officials, government bureaucrats, shareholders, and the general public as the least important. (The low ranking of shareholders isn't surprising because of the fairly low ranking of profit maximization as an objective!) Interestingly, the overall rankings of these goals and stakeholders changed little from those obtained in a similar survey ten years earlier.[6]

In another survey, when interviewers asked CEOs to rate the importance of various objectives, the lowest rated objectives were community service and dividend payout. The researchers concluded: "Perhaps social responsibility and maximizing shareholder wealth are not as important as the popular press often suggests."[7]

The wide range of interests and concerns present in any organization's task environment virtually guarantees that, at any one time, one or more groups probably will be dissatisfied with an organization's activities. For example, consider Celestial Seasonings, Inc., a maker of herb teas in Boulder, Colorado. Led by Morris "Mo" Siegel, CEO and one-time hippie, Celestial Seasonings is considered an enlightened company in terms of its values and treatment of its employees. According to Siegel, "We don't care if you're Buddhist or Baptist, straight or gay, as long as you want to make the world's best tea and draw pretty pictures." Unfortunately, this philosophy wasn't sufficient for the group *New York Boycott Colorado* (NYBC). It urged everyone to boycott Celestial because Siegel refused to take a high-profile stand against Colorado's (constitutional) Amendment 2. Approved by voters in November 1992, Amendment 2 forbade Colorado cities from designating gays as an official minority group eligible for hiring quotas or set-aside contracts. After the election, gay and lesbian groups called for a boycott of the state. At a meeting in New York, one NYBC official demanded that Celestial spend $100,000 or more on a campaign to repeal Amendment 2. According to Siegel, "They said, 'You either pay, or we'll destroy you.'" Siegel refused. NYBC called for a ban on all Colorado-made products, such as Samsonite luggage and Coors beer, but singled out Celestial for particular emphasis. "If it's their right to remain silent, it's our right to stop buying their product," explained NYBC founder Chip Druckett, who denied any extortion attempt. Because New York was Celestial's largest market, Siegel admitted that he was worried: "If they could panic the supermarkets, we could be in big trouble."[8]

Another recent controversial issue in juggling stakeholder concerns was charitable contributions. Even though corporations, like individuals, have the right to donate money to any charitable cause of their choice, some companies recently found themselves inundated by letters and phone calls from groups protesting donations to one charity in particular: Planned Parenthood. Even though well-known companies such as BP America, Dayton Hudson, and Pillsbury supported Planned Parenthood because of its prenatal care for low-income families, contraceptive research, and counseling programs to reduce unwanted pregnancies among teens, they were strongly criticized by "pro-life" groups against Planned Parenthood's advocacy of abortion. Doug Scott, Director of Public Policy at the Christian Action Council, urged consumers to boycott the products of companies supporting Planned Parenthood. He contended that opponents of abortion had a moral duty to oppose organizations that were, in his words, "antichild and antifamily." Primarily as a result of this pressure, J.C. Penney, AT&T, Pioneer Hi-Bred, and Union Pacific stopped their annual donations to Planned Parenthood. Dayton Hudson, in contrast, first canceled its contribution to Planned Parenthood and then reversed its decision after "pro-choice" groups favoring abortion as a woman's right mobilized their members to cancel their Dayton Hudson charge accounts. The Minneapolis-based department store chain entered the Christmas buying season facing a threatened boycott from either pro-life or pro-choice interest groups, depending on its final funding decision.[9]

Unethical and Illegal Behavior

The examples just mentioned indicate how easily a corporation can run into problems—even when its managers are trying to achieve the best outcome for all involved. However, some firms engage in questionable, unethical, or even illegal actions. They reveal the dark side of corporate decision making and give encouragement to those who favor more government regulation and less business autonomy. Without doubt the top management of some firms (including Comptronix) at times make decisions emphasizing short-term profitability or personal gain over long-term relations with governments, local communities, suppliers, and even customers and employees. During the 1980s, 11% of the largest U.S. firms were convicted of bribery, criminal fraud, illegal campaign contributions, tax evasion, or some sort of price fixing![10] Questionable practices that have been exposed in recent years include:

- Possible negligent construction and management practices at nuclear power, weapons, and chemical plants (for example, the nuclear plant at Three Mile Island, the weapons plant at Rocky Flats, Colorado, and Union Carbide's chemical plant in Bhopal, India);
- Denying mortgages and loans to members of minority groups simply on the basis of race (for example, denial of loans by U.S. commercial banks and S&Ls in 1991 to 23% of the highest income African-Americans but to only 9% of whites with comparable incomes[11]);
- Improper disposal of toxic wastes (for instance, Hooker Chemical at Love Canal, New York, and Shell Oil Company at a pesticide plant near Denver, Colorado);

Throughout its history, Maytag Corporation has tried to act responsibly in light of the various concerns of its many stakeholder groups. Even though the corporation has kept its headquarters in Newton, Iowa, the recent acquisitions of Magic Chef and Hoover has meant that Maytag Corporation had to view things differently from Maytag Company. The company made Maytag brand appliances in Newton, Iowa, only. The corporation now makes Maytag, Admiral, Magic Chef, Jenn-Air, Hardwick, Norge, and Hoover brand appliances, and Dixie-Narco vending machines, throughout North America and the world. Maytag Corporation's top management (most of whom came from Maytag Company) now has had to consider not only the company's responsibilities to the stakeholders of Maytag Company but also to the various stakeholders of Magic Chef, Jenn-Air, Hoover, Admiral, and Dixie-Narco and stakeholders of the corporation as a whole. This adjustment hasn't been easy.

Location Decision

Maytag tarnished its reputation as a good corporate citizen in some people's eyes when it announced at its 1990 shareholder meeting the decision to move dishwasher manufacturing from Newton, Iowa, to Jackson, Tennessee. Chairman and CEO Daniel Krumm announced that the plant would consolidate the manufacture of all the brands marketed by the corporation into one large, highly efficient plant. Krumm said:

> *Currently, the only dishwasher manufacturing operation we have is here in Newton, where we only have the ability to manufacture dishwashers for Maytag Company and some Jenn-Air models. . . . We expect to invest about $42 million in the Jackson plant, which will incorporate all new equipment, state-of-the-art technology and advanced automation, coupled with the ability and capacity to manufacture highly differentiated products.*
>
> *We are nearing the upper limits of our production capacity for Maytag brand dishwashers and there is no efficient way that our manufacturing facilities*

(continued)

- Production and sale of defective products (for example, A. H. Robbins's Dalkon Shield birth control device and Dow Corning's silicon breast implants);
- Pushing customers to purchase unneeded products or services (for example, Sears, Roebuck's recommending unnecessary auto repairs);
- Insufficient safeguarding of employees from exposure to dangerous chemicals and materials in the workplace (for instance, the asbestos problem at Johns-Manville and the overexposure of workers to lead and arsenic at Chrysler Corporation); and
- Continual instances of fraud, bribery, and price fixing at corporations of all sizes and locations (for example, aerospace companies selling defective components and overbilling, PharMor's altering of financial statements to inflate

(continued)

in Newton could accommodate the new dishwasher design, let alone provide the capacity we require to supply all corporate brands. Beyond that, phasing out dishwasher production at Maytag Company's Newton plant will provide the necessary space for extensive manufacturing revisions needed to meet anticipated demand for Maytag washers and dryers later in the 1990s.

Lonnie White, President of United Auto Workers Local 997—the bargaining unit representing Maytag Company unionized employees in Newton, Iowa—responded with dismay to top management's decision. "Where is their commitment to the community and the state of Iowa?" asked White. "They can add a facility here in Newton to do the same thing that they're doing in Jackson, Tennessee."

Pointing out that Maytag owned plenty of unused land in Newton, White contended that management could have only three reasons for moving dishwasher production to Tennessee: (1) to escape union shop requirements; (2) to reduce wage costs, and (3) to cut benefits. "The Newton dishwasher line is only running one shift. Other lines run two shifts," said White in response to the statement that the line was near capacity. He indicated that the union was not so much concerned with itself as it was with the impact on local communities and the need to avoid "community cannibalism." White argued that the area could supply sufficient workers to expand production: "When Maytag Company last had a production increase in the mid-'80s and wanted to hire around 300 new workers, the company received around 4,000 applications from all over the area."

One of White's concerns was the perceived change in the relationship between labor and management after Maytag became a large corporation. Management now seemed more formal and less flexible. Somewhat ruefully, White summed up the situation: "We're no longer dealing with Mother Maytag. Now we're dealing with a corporation."

earnings; Fiat paying bribes to Italian politicians; and Drexel Burnham Lambert's involvement in mail, wire, and securities fraud).

3.3 Ethics: A Question of Values

Such questionable practices by business corporations run counter to the values of society as a whole and are justly criticized and prosecuted. Why do executives take actions that so obviously harm important stakeholders in the organization's task environment? Are business corporations and the people who run them amoral, or are they simply ignorant of many consequences of their actions?

Cultural Differences

One reason for unethical behavior is that there is no worldwide standard of conduct for businesspeople. Cultural norms and values vary among countries and even among different geographic regions and ethnic groups within a country. One example is the use of payoffs and bribes to influence a potential customer to buy from a particular supplier. Although this practice is illegal in the United States, it is deeply entrenched in many other countries. *Dash,* or bribery, for instance, permeates Nigerian society and, although illegal, is widely accepted as a normal part of life. In Nigeria, many consider *dash* to be a lubricant for an economy of scarcity and rigid government control. The dilemma facing a manager of a multinational corporation in Nigeria is whether to pay *dash* to a customs officer to expedite shipping or run the risk that the goods will be permanently "lost." Although the U.S. Foreign Corrupt Practices Act of 1977 forbids U.S. citizens from engaging in bribery, it does not affect non–U.S. citizens.[12]

Personal Differences

Stages of Moral Development

A person's ethical behavior will be affected by his or her stage of moral development and other personality traits in addition to situational factors such as the job itself, the individual's supervisor, and the organizational culture.[13] Similar in some ways to Maslow's hierarchy of needs theory, moral development proceeds from total self-centeredness to a concern for universal values.[14] L. Kohlberg proposes that a person's individual moral development progresses through three levels.[15] The first level, **preconventional,** is characterized by a concern for self. Small children and others who have not progressed beyond this stage evaluate behaviors on the basis of personal interest—avoiding punishment or a quid pro quo. The second level, **conventional,** is characterized by considerations of society's laws and norms. People at this stage justify actions by an external code of conduct. The third level, **principled,** is characterized by a person's adherence to an internal moral code. Individuals at this stage look beyond norms or laws to find universal values or principles. Kohlberg places most people in the conventional level, with less than 20% of U.S. adults in the principled level of development.[16]

Individual Values

Another possible reason for an organization's questionable practices lies in differences in values between top management and key stakeholders in the task environment. Some businesspeople may believe that profit maximization is the primary goal of their firms, whereas concerned interest groups may have other priority goals, such as the hiring of minorities and women or the safety of their neighborhoods.

Economist Milton Friedman, in urging a return to a laissez-faire worldwide economy with a minimum of government regulation, argues against the concept of corporate social responsibility. If a businessperson acts "responsibly" by cutting the price of the firm's product to prevent inflation, making expenditures to reduce pollution, or hiring the hard-core unemployed, that person, according to Friedman, is spending shareholders' money for a general social interest. Even with shareholder permission or encouragement to do so, the businessperson is still acting from motives other than economic and may, in the long run, harm the very society the firm is trying to help. By taking on the burden of social costs, the business becomes less efficient; either prices go up to pay for the increased costs, or investment in new activities, research, and plant and equipment is postponed. These results negatively affect—perhaps fatally—the long-term efficiency of a business. Friedman thus referred to the social responsibility of business as a "fundamentally subversive doctrine" and stated that "there is one and only one social responsibility of business—to use its resources and engage in activities designed to increase its profits so long as it stays within the rules of the game, which is to say, engages in open and free competition without deception or fraud."[17]

Friedman's stand on free enterprise has been both criticized and praised. Businesspeople tend to agree with Friedman because his views are compatible not only with their own self-interests but also with their hierarchy of values. It certainly fits the rationale given by Stride Rite's CEO for moving production out of the country. Of the six values measured by the Allport-Vernon-Lindzey Study of Values test (aesthetic, economic, political, religious, social, and theoretical), both U.S. and U.K. executives score high on economic and political values and low on social and religious values. This result is similar to the value profile of Japanese, Korean, Indian, and Australian managers. In contrast, U.S. Protestant ministers score high on religious and social values and low on economic values.[18]

Imagine the controversy that would result if a group comprising ministers and executives had to decide the following issues: *Should businesses close on Sunday?* (Most liquor stores in Massachusetts in 1993 were closed by law on Sundays, thus giving stores in neighboring New Hampshire increased business.) *Should the corporation hire handicapped workers and accept the increased training costs associated with their employment?* In discussing these issues, the executives probably would be most concerned with the effects on profits, whereas the ministers probably would be concerned with the effects on society and salvation (a very different bottom line).

Overall, businesspeople seem to be concerned with the needs of various stakeholders but limit their social responsibilities to those concerns that clearly will benefit the corporation in terms of increased sales, reduced costs, or less government regulation.[19] This narrow view of businesses' responsibilities to society is bound to cause conflicts between the business corporation and certain stakeholders in its task environment.

Relativism

A serious challenge to the study of ethics and ethical behavior is the doctrine of moral relativism. Simply put, **moral relativism** claims that morality is relative to some personal, social, or cultural standard and that no standard is better than another. At one time or another, most managers probably have used one of the four types of relativism—naive, role, social group, and cultural—to justify questionable behavior.[20]

- **Naive relativism:** Based on the beliefs that all moral decisions are deeply personal and that individuals have the right to run their own lives; people should be allowed to interpret situations and act on the basis of their own moral values. Critics of naive relativism argue that tolerance is good up to a point, but that it can be taken too far. It is not a belief, but an excuse for not having a belief or is an excuse for inaction. Comptronix executives could have argued that their manipulation of the company's inventory to boost profits didn't directly hurt anyone and thus they did nothing wrong, even if it was technically illegal.
- **Role relativism:** Holds that social roles carry with them certain obligations to the role only. A manager in charge of a department, for example, must put aside personal beliefs and instead do what the role requires, that is, acting in the best interests of the department. The three top executives of Comptronix could have argued that their jobs required them to boost the company's stock price by whatever means necessary in order to attract needed capital to build the company. Besides, if they did something wrong, the auditors' job was to point it out—that's what auditors are paid for.
- **Social group relativism:** Based on the belief that morality is simply a matter of following the norms of the individual's peer group, decisions are based on accepted practices. If an action is considered accepted practice, then it appears to have some legitimacy. Echoing the often-heard teenager's refrain that "everyone is doing it" so it must be all right, Comptronix top management could have stated that they were only doing what most other firms were doing. (Hard economic times during the early 1990s did lead to a fourfold increase in inventory fraud from just five years earlier.[21]) Social group relativism is a pervasive phenomenon in the day-to-day business world. A real danger in embracing it is that the person may incorrectly believe that a certain action is commonly accepted practice in the industry when it isn't.
- **Cultural relativism:** Holds that morality is relative to a particular culture, society, or community. People should therefore "understand" the practices of other countries, but not judge them. If the norms and customs are shared by members of another country, what right does an outsider have to criticize them? The concept may be summed up as "When in Rome, do as the Romans do." This type of relativism suggests that a business corporation must be "all things to all people" and warns against moral imperialism—imposing a certain type of morality on others and judging them by standards they do not accept. Critics of this view state that it is the lazy way out of dealing with ethical problems.

Basic Approaches to Ethical Behavior

According to Von der Embse and Wagley, **ethics** is defined as the consensually accepted standards of behavior for an occupation, trade, or profession. **Morality,** in contrast, is the precepts of personal behavior, based on religious or philosophical grounds. **Law** is the formal codes that permit or forbid certain behaviors and may or may not enforce ethics or morality.[22] How can someone use these definitions to arrive at a comprehensive statement of ethics for decision making in a specific occupation, trade, or profession? A starting point for such a code of ethics is to consider the three basic approaches to ethical behavior: utilitarian, individual rights, and justice.[23]

- **Utilitarian approach:** Actions and plans should be judged by their consequences. A person should therefore behave in such a way that will produce the greatest benefit to society and produce the least harm or the lowest cost. A problem with this approach is the difficulty in recognizing all the benefits and the costs of any particular decision. Only the most obvious stakeholders are likely to be considered, whereas others may be "conveniently" forgotten.
- **Individual rights approach:** Human beings have certain fundamental rights that should be respected in all decisions. A particular decision or behavior should be avoided if it interferes with the rights of others. A problem with this approach lies in defining *fundamental rights.* The U.S. Constitution includes a Bill of Rights that may or may not be accepted throughout the world. This approach also may encourage selfish behavior when a person defines a personal need or want as a "right."
- **Justice approach:** Decision makers should be equitable, fair, and impartial in the distribution of costs and benefits to individuals and groups. It follows the principles of *distributive justice* (people with similar skill levels, productivity, job seniority, and the like should be treated in the same way) and *fairness* (liberty should be equal for all persons). The justice approach may include the concepts of retributive justice and compensatory justice. *Retributive justice* means that the punishment should fit the "crime." *Compensatory justice* means that wrongs should be compensated in proportion to the suffering caused. Issues in affirmative action (such as reverse discrimination) are examples of conflicts between distributive and compensatory justice.

Each of these three basic approaches to ethical behavior has strengths and weaknesses. Figure 3.1 shows a decision tree based on Cavanagh, Moberg, and Velasquez's proposal for incorporating all three approaches in making a decision involving ethical issues. It includes the concept of the *overwhelming factor*—a situational factor—that may, in a particular case, justify overriding one of the three ethical criteria of utilitarian outcomes, individual rights, and equal justice.[24] This is where individual judgment comes into play. Principles and approaches, not hard-and-fast rules, govern ethics. When overwhelming factors are present in a situation, one good rule of thumb to follow is the *principle of double effect.* If the alternative chosen has the intent of achieving the maximum of good with the minimum of bad effects, the person who makes the decision is likely to receive a sympathetic hearing if that decision is questioned later in a court of law.[25]

Promoting Ethical Behavior

Having a set of business ethics is one thing; protecting and upholding them in the everyday rough-and-tumble world of business competition is another thing. For example, a 1991 survey of a cross section of 1,000 American managers revealed that 44% of supervisors, 42% of middle managers, and 32% of top managers indicated that "sometimes I must compromise my personal principles to conform to

FIGURE 3.1 **Decision Tree for Incorporating Ethics into Decision Making**

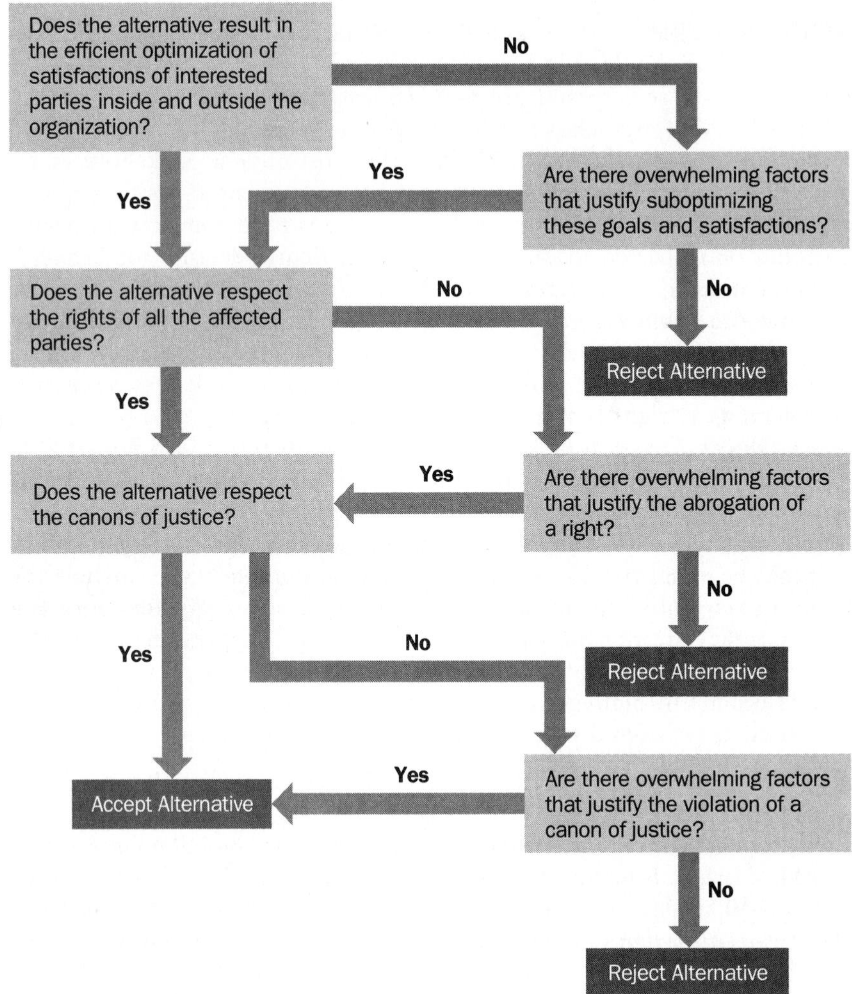

Source: Adapted from G. F. Cavanagh, D. J. Moberg, and M. Velasquez, "The Ethics of Organizational Politics," *Academy of Management Review* (July 1981), p. 368. Reprinted by permission.

my organization's expectations."[26] The same survey revealed that 40% of supervisors, 32% of middle managers, and 21% of top managers either agreed or strongly agreed to the statement, "Managers in my company often engage in behavior that I consider unethical." Human resource managers surveyed stated that the people most likely to be unethical are the 40–45-year-old middle managers who are driven by the desire to "make it before it's too late." The next group most likely to be unethical are top managers who tell subordinates to "do whatever you have to do; just don't tell me about it."[27]

Unfortunately, the problem seems to begin even before a career is launched. A study of 15,904 undergraduate students at 31 universities found that 76% of business majors said that they cheated on at least one test. (The percentage of cheating on one test by other majors ranged from 71% in engineering to 57% in education.) Nineteen percent of business majors said they cheated on four or more tests. In responding to an open-ended question about cheating as a way to get ahead, one business student wrote, "This is the Nineties. You snooze, you lose."[28]

Codes of Ethics

Developing codes of ethics can be a useful way to promote ethical behavior. About half of all U.S. corporations currently use such codes. Most managers agree that corporate codes of ethics and ethics workshops help them understand ethical issues and guide their day-to-day activities.[29] According to a report by The Business Roundtable, an association of CEOs from 200 major U.S. corporations, a code is important because it (1) clarifies company expectations of employee conduct in various situations and (2) makes clear that the company expects its people to recognize the ethical dimensions in decisions and actions.[30] Various studies indicate that a growing number of companies are developing codes of ethics and implementing ethics training workshops and seminars. About 200 U.S. corporations have appointed ethics officers.[31] The top management of a company desiring to improve the ethical behavior of its employees not only should develop a comprehensive code of ethics, but also disseminate the code in its training programs, performance appraisal system, and policies and procedures and through its own actions.

Promoting Ethical Criticism

Employees may not believe that top management is serious about ethics until they see the code in action. A study of Champion International Corporation, for example, revealed that the farther down the hierarchy they were, the greater was employee cynicism and hostility toward ethics codes. One manager reported that it is what the company does, not what it says, that counts.[32]

R. P. Nielsen proposes several alternative actions that a person can take when caught in a serious ethical dilemma.[33] Table 3.2 lists seven possible responses and pros and cons for each. Nielsen recommends building consensus for change internally (item 7) as the best approach if there is enough time and the key people in authority are reasonable. Avoidance, obeying, or leaving doesn't improve the situation. Conscientiously objecting typically doesn't work. Telling the press or government may resolve the problem but also may have many negative consequences. Nielsen recommends the following approach.

> In all but the most extreme and unusual circumstances one should first try negotiating a consensus. If that doesn't succeed, then a good move is to simultaneously conscientiously object and go public. . . . If you cooperate instead of conscientiously objecting, then you're acting just as unethically as everybody else. And if you go outside the organization secretly instead of publicly, you're not standing up for what you profess to believe in.[34]

Following Nielsen's view, it makes sense for management to promote ethical criticism. If employees are encouraged to consider ethical issues and discuss them

TABLE 3.2 **Possible Responses to Ethical Dilemmas**

Action	Pros	Cons
1. Avoid thinking about it	Avoids conflict; good team player	Prevents a solution
2. Obey orders	Avoids conflict; good performance evaluation	Become part of the problem Where draw the line?
3. Leave	Revenge on company; good feelings in short run	Lack courage to stay and fight; quickly replaced
4. Conscientiously object	Courageous feelings; encourages other people; may resolve the problem	Likely to be threatened or fired; seen as a troublemaker
5. Secretly tell the press or government	Likely to resolve the problem; safe from retaliation	Feel like a coward; must lie to keep safe
6. Publicly tell the press or government	Likely to resolve the problem; treated as a hero by public	Likely to be fired or harassed; no longer able to resolve problem internally
7. Build consensus for change internally	Resolves problem from within; encourages others to help; may become an internal hero	May take a long time; may be manipulated by others

Source: R. P. Nielsen, "Alternative Managerial Responses to Ethical Dilemmas," *Planning Review* (November 1985), pp. 24–29, 43.

openly without fear of retaliation or disapproval, a constructive, consensus-building approach to addressing ethical concerns could emerge.

3.4 Responsibilities of Business

From a strategic point of view, a business corporation needs to consider its responsibilities to the society of which it is a part. The history of business and society clearly suggests that when business ignores its responsibilities to its stakeholders, society tends to respond through government to restrict business's autonomy. Business organizations must therefore recognize all their responsibilities if they want to have the autonomy essential to effectiveness and efficiency. But what are the responsibilities of a business?

Carroll's Four Responsibilities

A. B. Carroll proposes that the managers of business organizations have four responsibilities: economic, legal, ethical, and discretionary, as illustrated in Fig. 3.2.[35] The **economic responsibilities** of a business organization's management are to produce goods and services of value to society so that the firm may repay its creditors and shareholders. **Legal responsibilities** are defined by governments in laws that management is expected to obey. Economic and legal responsibilities are

FIGURE 3.2 **Responsibilities of Business**

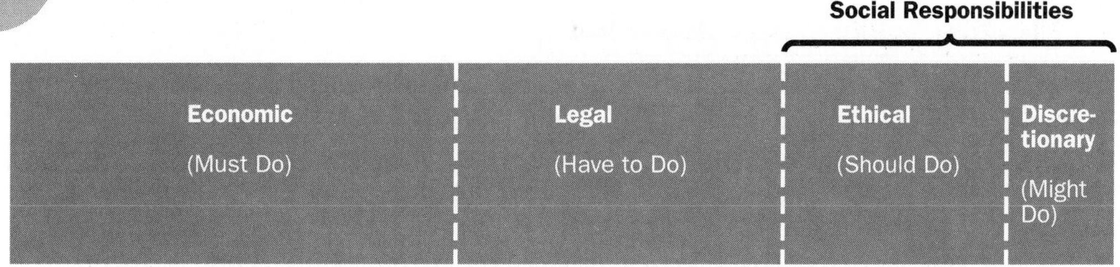

Source: Adapted from A. B. Carroll, "A Three Dimensional Conceptual Model of Corporate Performance," *Academy of Management Review* (October 1979), p. 499. Reprinted with permission.

not social responsibilities; they are merely what a business firm must do to stay in business. **Social responsibility** includes both ethical and discretionary responsibilities. **Ethical responsibilities** of an organization's management are to follow the generally held beliefs about how people should act in a society. For example, society generally expects firms to work with employees and the community in planning for layoffs, even though no law may require their doing so. The people affected may get very upset if an organization's management fails to act according to generally prevailing ethical values. **Discretionary responsibilities,** in contrast, are the purely *voluntary* obligations that a corporation assumes. Examples are philanthropic contributions, training the hard-core unemployed, and providing day-care centers. The difference between ethical and discretionary responsibilities is that few people expect an organization to fulfill discretionary responsibilities, whereas many expect an organization to fulfill ethical ones.

These four responsibilities are listed in order of priority. A business firm must first make a profit to satisfy its economic responsibilities. In order to continue to exist, it must follow laws—thus fulfilling its legal responsibilities. After these basic responsibilities have been satisfied, the firm should seek to fulfill its social responsibilities. It can then fulfill its ethical responsibilities by doing those things that society tends to value but has not yet put into law. After satisfying its ethical responsibilities, a firm can focus on discretionary responsibilities—the purely voluntary actions that society has not yet decided are important. One example of a discretionary responsibility is Volkswagen's pilot project to design cars for disassembly and recycling.[36]

The discretionary responsibilities of today may become the ethical responsibilities of tomorrow. The provision of day-care facilities, for example, is moving rapidly from a discretionary to an ethical responsibility. Carroll suggests that to the extent that business corporations fail to acknowledge discretionary or ethical responsibilities, society (through government) will act, making them legal responsibilities. Moreover, government may do so without regard to a corporation's economic responsibilities. As a result, firms may have greater difficulty in earning a profit than they would have had in assuming voluntarily some ethical and discretionary responsibilities.

Reasons Often Given for Being Socially Responsible

The arguments in favor of a business corporation's management acting in a socially responsible manner may be summarized in the following manner.

1. **Morality:** A firm should be responsible to its many stakeholders because it is the "right thing to do." Based primarily on religious values or on some personally held moral code, actions are justified on the basis of the good of society in general. This rationale is altruistic; there is no expectation of receiving anything in return. For example, Home Depot, the do-it-yourself building supplies retailer, takes its role as a "corporate citizen" very seriously. When a woman in the community lost her uninsured home and her teenaged son to fire, the company responded by providing thousands of dollars of free materials and supplies to assist in the rebuilding effort. Newman's Own, Inc., the all-natural food company founded by actor Paul Newman, donates all of its profits ($40 million since 1982) to charitable causes.
2. **Enlightened self-interest:** A firm should be responsible to its stakeholders because of "quid pro quo" considerations. Sometimes expressed in terms of "what goes around, comes around," this reason proposes that the corporation is likely to be rewarded for its responsible actions either in the short or long term. For example, Procter & Gamble found that because of its reputation for treating its employees well, the company has little difficulty hiring and keeping well-qualified people. Although there may be no direct connection with profits, this rationale implies the existence of some eventual return for responsible actions. For example, Minneapolis-based Dayton Hudson was able to use its positive relationship with its stakeholder groups throughout Minnesota to influence the state to enact a tough antitakeover law when the company was in danger of being bought out by Dart Group Corporation of Landover, Maryland.
3. **Sound investment theory:** A firm should be responsible to its stakeholders because such actions will be reflected in higher profits and in the price of its stock. This rationale proposes a direct connection between socially responsible actions and the corporation's financial performance. Unfortunately, studies have yielded mixed results.[37] They cite both highly profitable and marginally profitable companies with both poor and excellent social records. One interesting example is Control Data Corporation. Under the leadership of socially concerned William C. Norris—founder, Chairman, and CEO—Control Data had established assembly plants in ghettos and prisons and spent millions of dollars on computer systems for education and training in schools and industry. Unfortunately, corporate earnings fell and Norris was criticized for allowing his "pet businesses" to drain investment away from the company's profitable ventures. Shareholders forced him to resign from the company.

4. **Retain autonomy:** A firm should be responsible to its stakeholders in order to avoid interference in managerial decision making by groups in its task environment. This reason is similar to Carroll's argument that the failure to fulfill ethical and discretionary responsibilities will eventually result in an enlargement of a corporation's legal responsibilities to the detriment of its economic responsibilities. Even with no clear and direct connection between social responsibility and profits or stock price, the **iron law of responsibility** does apply. As Keith Davis points out, "In the long run those who do not use power in a manner that society considers responsible will tend to lose it."[38]

Stewardship and the Social Audit

Even though many examples of socially irresponsible behavior by business executives can be cited, many responsible actions continually occur. McDonald's stands out not only as one of the more socially responsible companies in the United States, but also as one of the few to make a significant impact on society. Its commitment to investing in people and in neighborhoods has resulted in 70% of McDonald's restaurant managers and 25% of the company's executives being minorities and women. Through its innovative jobs training program, nearly 7,000 disabled and handicapped people have become full McDonald's employees. According to Senior Vice-President Robert Beavers, the company's socially minded business practices have made the company stronger: "Our energy level and our understanding of the market today are much better because of the cultural diversity we have."[39]

Even though environmentalists are doing everything they can to save the tropical rain forests of South America, they are happy to support the activities of Brazilian lumber company Aracruz Celulose S.A. Instead of chopping down native trees, Aracruz cuts only eucalyptus trees that it grows in already deforested areas. New trees are then planted to replace those harvested. "It's a partnership with nature," explains Lineu Siqueira, manager of Aracruz's environmental resources department. "We are helping nature and it's helping us."[40]

These are examples of businesses that follow a managerial philosophy of **stewardship** toward the needs and wants of its many stakeholders. This approach to social responsibility takes the long view. Stewardship is more than just an extension of enlightened self-interest or the need for continued autonomy on the part of business. The quote at the beginning of this chapter by Ray Kroc, the founder of McDonald's, suggests that the company should give something back to local communities, not just because it's good for business, but also because it's the moral thing to do.

To keep track of their socially related activities, many large companies in North America and western Europe conduct social audits. The **social audit** is a process used to identify, monitor, measure, evaluate, and report the effects a business organization is having on society or on certain segments of society that are not covered in traditional financial reports.[41] It is a way to measure a company's progress toward achieving social goals such as minority employment, pollution cleanup, improved working conditions, community development, philanthropic contributions, and various consumer issues.[42] Although several different social audit approaches may be used, the five-part approach suggested by the U.S. Committee for Economic Development is as good as any. It involves preparing

- A summary of program areas, such as consumer affairs, and the reasoning for undertaking certain activities and not others;
- A report of specific programs and the priorities for each set of activities;
- A list of objectives for each priority activity and a description of how the organization is striving to reach the objectives;
- A summary report of the costs of each program area and activity to the company; and
- A summary using quantitative measures whenever possible of the extent of achievement of each social objective.[43]

Conducting a social audit of a firm is not an easy task because the list of social concerns is almost endless. Nevertheless, a line must be drawn somewhere to make social responsibility a do-able task. Measurement is even more difficult. Should measures be input-oriented (pollution control expenditures) or output-oriented (reduction of pollution)? If a company is only one of many companies dumping waste into a river, how can it pinpoint the effect of its efforts alone on water purity? Evaluation of standards is equally difficult. Should government minimum standards for pollution, for example, be accepted as the company's standard? Because pesticides and herbicides are necessary for adequate food production, how much of these poisons is acceptable in local drinking water? The lack of common measures or a common reporting format makes comparing the social performance of different companies difficult. One company that is successfully developing such measures is Niagara Mohawk Power of Syracuse, New York. It has developed an index to measure a utility's performance in the categories of waste and emissions, environmental compliance, and environmental enhancement. According to Thomas Fair, Niagara's Vice-President of Environmental Affairs, "If you can't develop some kind of measure, the plans you have are wishful thinking."[44]

Although the problems inherent in conducting a social audit are many, a company needs to take this step. Surveys by Louis Harris & Associates reveal that 58% of a sample of U.S. adults feel that business executives have only fair to poor ethical standards. With 69% agreeing that business has too much power over too many aspects of American life, business corporations need to pay more attention to how others perceive their actions.[45] Acting on these antibusiness attitudes, special interest groups are beginning to conduct their own social audits of corporations and to lobby government for more legislation. The Council on Economic Priorities, for example, publishes *Rating America's Corporate Conscience* and *Shopping for a Better World.* In the latter, the Council evaluates companies on the basis of (1) charitable contributions, (2) women's advancement, (3) minority advancement, (4) animal testing, (5) disclosure of information, (6) community outreach, (7) activities in South Africa, (8) environmental pollution, (9) family benefits, and (10) workplace issues. Evaluations are listed for consumer products such as Crest Toothpaste (P&G) or Jimmy Dean Sausage (Sara Lee).

In Conclusion . . .

A new type of company may be emerging in the world: the corporation that fulfills not only its economic and legal responsibilities, but also its ethical and even discretionary responsibilities. In a compelling book entitled *Companies with a Conscience,* Scott and Rothman contend:

> As the nineties wear on, it becomes increasingly apparent that business in general can no longer function or be judged solely on the basis of fiscal nets and grosses. A positive impact on employees, customers, and the community at large has assumed an equal or even greater significance in the overall picture. Today's bottom line encompasses more than just dollars and cents, and corporations of all sizes and philosophical orientations are beginning to recognize this.[46]

The book profiles 12 socially responsible companies from Ben & Jerry's Homemade Ice Cream and Celestial Seasonings to Esprit de Corp Clothing and The Grateful Dead. The authors identify 14 common threads running through each of these companies, as listed in Table 3.3.

TABLE 3.3 **Common Threads Running Through 12 Socially Responsible Firms**

1. Initially founded by far-sighted people who visibly set the firm's moral tone.
2. Stuck to the basics and produced only high quality goods and services for specific market niches.
3. Developed a public image that emphasized their commitment to quality and often used nontraditional means to promote it.
4. Firmly practiced the dual principles of self-management and decentralization.
5. Brought in outside people to provide needed talent and additional perspectives.
6. Encouraged all employees to become part of the shared mission through full worker participation in decisions.
7. Paid fairly and usually offered benefit packages exceeding the competition.
8. Emphasized a democratic people orientation and did without executive perks.
9. Constantly solicited feedback from customers on all manner of subjects from product direction to corporate donations.
10. Top managers possessed an extensive knowledge of current events and took a wide-ranging interest in affairs outside their business.
11. Offered donations in cash or services to people in need of help.
12. Took an active role in the operations of their local communities.
13. Deal with like-minded businesses and encourage their employees to do the same.
14. Constantly look to the future but always pay attention to the past.

Source: From *Companies with a Conscience* by Mary Scott and Howard Rothman. Copyright © 1992 by Mary Scott and Howard Rothman. Published by arrangement with Carol Publishing Group. A Birch Lane Press Book. Reprinted by permission of the authors and their agent, Richard Curtis Associates, Inc.

Points to Remember

- The history of business and society is like a pendulum. Society tends to swing between antibusiness and probusiness views. When society is antibusiness, it tends to take away business autonomy through laws and regulations, taxation, and even nationalization of industries. The best way to keep society thinking positively about business and thus allowing it significant autonomy is for business to be socially responsible.
- Strategic managers must be aware of the stakeholders within their company's task environment and be prepared to juggle priorities in order to negotiate a maze of conflicting demands.
- At times society perceives businesspeople as unethical because of cultural and personal differences. Businesspeople tend to be more concerned with economic and political values than with social and religious values. Friedman's argument that the only social responsibility of business is to increase its profits through legal means emphasizes economic values.
- Although relativism is a serious challenge to establishing a generally accepted and followed business code of ethics, strategic managers need to promote a better understanding of ethical issues through codes of ethics and ethics training.
- Even though a business has economic and legal responsibilities (in agreement with Friedman's stand), it arguably also has ethical and discretionary responsibilities. The term social responsibility includes these ethical and discretionary responsibilities.
- Many arguments may be used for corporations to engage in socially responsible actions, but the most compelling one to most businesspeople is the iron law of responsibility. It states that "in the long run those who do not use power in a manner that society considers responsible will tend to lose it."

Discussion Questions

1. Should ethics and social responsibility be essential to the study of strategic management and business policy? Why or why not?
2. How appropriate is the theory of laissez-faire in today's world?
3. Should Maytag Corporation have moved its dishwasher production from Newton, Iowa, to Jackson, Tennessee? What are the pros and cons of that decision?
4. Is there a conflict between Agency Theory (discussed in Chapter 2) and the concept of stakeholders developed in this chapter? Explain your answer.
5. Can a company priding itself on enlightened attitudes toward employees at home ignore the actions its foreign contractors who abuse their workers, employ child labor, and/or pay near-starvation wages?
6. Tobacco companies are increasing their marketing efforts in Third World countries. Faced with a decline in tobacco use in the developed countries (down 9% in the

United States and 25% in the United Kingdom between 1970 and 1985), these corporations are using their advertising expertise and political connections to open new markets in Japan, Taiwan, Thailand, and South Korea, as well as in eastern Europe. In light of the accumulating evidence regarding the link between tobacco use and cancer, should the strategic managers in these tobacco companies be criticized for taking socially irresponsible actions? Should the government declare making and selling tobacco products illegal?

7. Do you agree with economist Milton Friedman that social responsibility is a "fundamentally subversive doctrine" that will only hurt a business corporation's long-term efficiency? Why or why not?
8. Why is moral relativism a challenge to improving a strategic manager's ethical behavior?
9. Using Carroll's list of four responsibilities, should a company be concerned about discretionary responsibilities? Why or why not?
10. Is there a correlation between a corporation's level of social responsibility and its financial performance? Explain your response.

Notes

1. E. M. Reingold, "America's Hamburger Helper," *Time* (June 29, 1992), p. 67.
2. M. Brannigan and L. M. Grossman, "Comptronix Fires Its CEO But Keeps Two Other Aides," *Wall Street Journal* (December 14, 1992), p. B6; L. Berton, "Inventory Chicanery Tempts More Firms, Fools More Auditors," *Wall Street Journal* (December 14, 1992), p. A1.
3. Research by the World Bank of a dozen privatization actions in the United Kingdom, Chile, Malaysia, and Mexico revealed that, in 11 of the 12 cases, privatization raised the welfare of workers, consumers, investors, and the government sector alike. Improvements in productivity and better investments led to large gains in nine cases. Profits increased in each instance. For a summary of the report see G. S. Becker, "Surprises in a World According to Adam Smith," *Business Week* (August 17, 1992), p. 18.
4. R. E. Freeman, *Strategic Management: A Stakeholder Approach* (Boston: Pitman, 1984), p. 25.
5. R. Estes, "How to Save Corporate America," *Des Moines Register* (October 7, 1990), p. C1.
6. B. Z. Posner and W. H. Schmidt, "Values and the American Manager: An Update Updated," *California Management Review* (Spring 1992), pp. 80–94.
7. K. Roth and D. A. Ricks, "Objective Setting in International Business: An Empirical Analysis," *International Journal of Management* (March 1990), p. 16.
8. S. D. Atchison, "Herbal Teas in Hot Water," *Business Week* (March 1, 1993), pp. 42–44.
9. B. Tierney, "Planned Parenthood Didn't Plan on This," *Business Week* (July 3, 1989), p. 34; K. Kelly, "Dayton Hudson Finds There's No Graceful Way to Flip-Flop," *Business Week* (September 24, 1990), p. 50.
10. G. F. Cavanagh, *American Business Values,* 3rd ed. (Englewood Cliffs, N.J.: Prentice Hall, 1990), p. 173.
11. "The Thin Red Line," *Time* (November 9, 1992), p. 26.
12. T. Clark, "Ethical Dilemmas in International Business," *International Journal of Management* (December 1988), p. 440.
13. L. K. Trevino, "Ethical Decision Making in Organizations: A Person–Situation Interac-

tionist Model," *Academy of Management Review* (July 1986), pp. 601–617.

14. A. H. Maslow, "A Theory of Human Motivation," *Psychological Review,* Vol. 50 (1943), pp. 370–396.
15. L. Kohlberg, "Moral Stage and Moralization: The Cognitive-Development Approach," in *Moral Development and Behavior,* edited by T. Lickona (New York: Holt, Rinehart & Winston, 1976).
16. Trevino, p. 606.
17. M. Friedman, "The Social Responsibility of Business Is to Increase Its Profits," *New York Times Magazine* (September 13, 1970), pp. 30, 126–127; M. Friedman, *Capitalism and Freedom* (Chicago: University of Chicago Press, 1963), p. 133.
18. M. Gable and P. Arlow, "A Comparative Examination of the Value Orientations of British and American Executives," *International Journal of Management* (September 1986), pp. 97–106; W. D. Guth and R. Tagiuri, "Personal Values and Corporate Strategy," *Harvard Business Review* (September–October 1965), pp. 126–127; G. W. England, "Managers and Their Value Systems: A Five Country Comparative Study," *Columbia Journal of World Business* (Summer 1978), p. 35.
19. S. Vyakarnam, "Social Responsibility: What Leading Companies Do," *Long Range Planning* (October 1992), pp. 59–67.
20. Summarized from R. E. Freeman and D. R. Gilbert, Jr., *Corporate Strategy and the Search for Ethics* (Englewood Cliffs, N.J.: Prentice Hall, 1988), pp. 24–41.
21. Berton, p. A1.
22. T. J. Von der Embse and R. A. Wagley, "Managerial Ethics: Hard Decisions on Soft Criteria," *SAM Advanced Management Journal* (Winter 1988), p. 6.
23. Summarized from G. F. Cavanagh, D. J. Moberg, and M. Velasquez, "The Ethics of Organizational Politics," *Academy of Management Review* (July 1981), pp. 363–374; J. E. Smith, J. B. Forbes, and M. M. Extejt, "Ethics in the Organizational Behavior Course," *Organizational Behavior Teaching Review,* Vol. XIII, Issue 1 (1988–1989), pp. 85–95. See also G. F. Cavanagh, *American Business Values,* 3rd ed. (Englewood Cliffs, N.J.: Prentice Hall, 1990), pp. 186–199.
24. Cavanagh et al., p. 370.
25. Ibid.
26. Posner and Schmidt, pp. 87–88. The figures reported are the sum of "agree" and "strongly agree" responses to the statement given.
27. Summarized from *Personnel Journal:* P. Plawin and A. Blum, "The Young and the Ruthless," *Changing Times* (August 1988), p. 76.
28. "Business Students Cheat Most," *Fortune* (July 1, 1991), pp. 14, 18.
29. Posner and Schmidt, pp. 88–89.
30. J. Keogh, editor, *Corporate Ethics: A Prime Business Asset* (New York: The Business Roundtable, 1988), p. 5.
31. S. J. Harrington, "What Corporate America Is Teaching About Ethics," *Academy of Management Executive* (February 1991), pp. 21–30; K. Labich, "The New Crisis in Business Ethics," *Fortune* (April 20, 1992), pp. 167–176.
32. Keogh, p. 24.
33. R. P. Nielsen, "Alternative Managerial Responses to Ethical Dilemmas," *Planning Review* (November 1985), pp. 24–29, 43; R. P. Nielsen, "Changing Unethical Organizational Behavior," *Academy of Management Executive* (May 1989), pp. 123–130.
34. Nielsen, "Alternative Managerial Responses," p. 43.
35. A. B. Carroll, "A Three-Dimensional Conceptual Model of Corporate Performance," *Academy of Management Review* (October 1979), pp. 497–505. Another way of conceptualizing responsibilities was proposed by S. P. Sethi in "Dimensions of Corporate Social Responsibility," *California Management Review* (Spring 1975), pp. 58–64. Economic and legal responsibilities may be considered as social obligation; ethical responsibilities may be considered as social responsibility; discretionary responsibilities may be considered as social responsiveness. We prefer to use Carroll's conceptualization because it includes ethical and discretionary responsibilities in social responsibility.
36. S. Schmidheiny, *Changing Course* (Cambridge, Mass.: MIT Press, 1992) as reported by E. T. Smith, "Reaping the Spoils—Without Spoiling the Earth," *Business Week* (June 22, 1992), p. 12.
37. P. Rechner and K. Roth, "Social Responsibility and Financial Performance: A Structural Equation Methodology," *International Journal of Management* (Decem-

ber 1990), pp. 382–391; K. E. Aupperle, A. B. Carroll, and J. D. Hatfield, "An Empirical Examination of the Relationship Between Corporate Social Responsibility and Profitability," *Academy of Management Journal* (June 1985), p. 459. One recent study found that successful companies are more likely to be socially responsible than are less successful companies, suggesting that outstanding financial performance leads to increased social responsibility, rather than the reverse! See J. B. McGuire, A. Sundgren, and T. Schneeweis, "Corporate Social Responsibility and Firm Financial Performance," *Academy of Management Journal* (December 1988), pp. 854–872.

38. K. Davis, "The Meaning and Scope of Social Responsibility," in *Contemporary Management: Issues and Viewpoints,* edited by J. W. McGuire (Englewood Cliffs, N.J.: Prentice Hall, 1974), p. 631.
39. E. M. Reingold, pp. 66–67.
40. T. Kamm, "Brazilian Tree Harvester Sows As It Reaps," *Wall Street Journal* (May 21, 1992), p. A10.
41. R. A. Buchholz, *Business Environment and Public Policy,* 3rd ed. (Englewood Cliffs, N.J.: Prentice Hall, 1989), p. 471.
42. A. B. Carroll and G. W. Beiler, "Landmarks in the Evolution of the Social Audit," *Academy of Management Journal* (September 1975), p. 598.
43. J. J. Corson and G. A. Steiner, *Measuring Business's Performance: The Corporate Social Audit* (New York: Committee for Economic Development, 1974).
44. "Companies Try Grading Their Own Activities," *Wall Street Journal* (July 26, 1993), p. B1.
45. Surveys reported in *Business Week* (July 20, 1987), p. 71 and (May 29, 1989), p. 29.
46. M. Scott and H. Rothman, *Companies With a Conscience* (New York: Birch Lane Press, 1992), p. ix.

Environmental Scanning and Industry Analysis

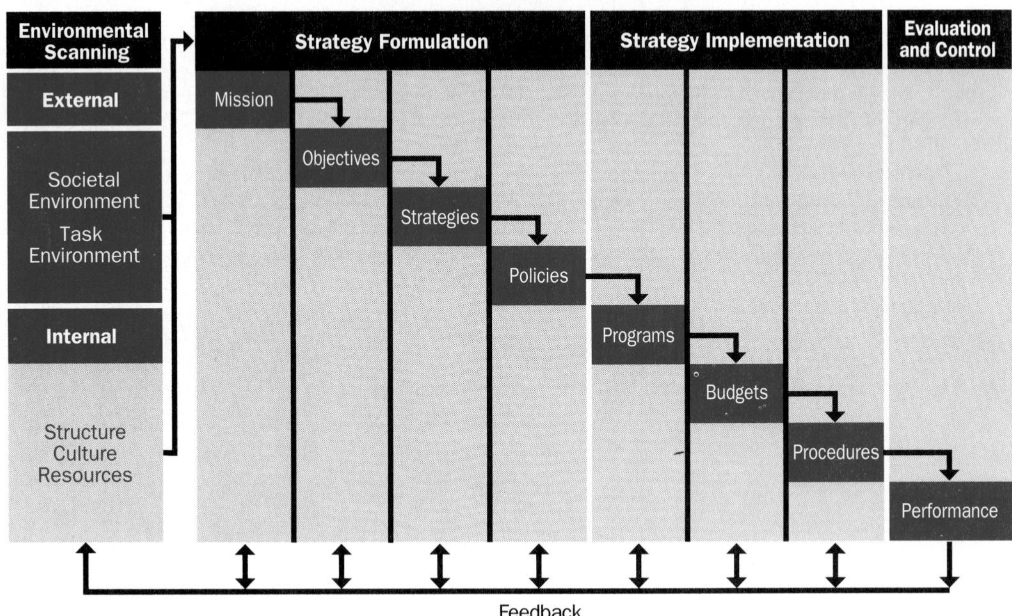

The central problem for complex organizations is one of coping with uncertainty.[1]
[J. D. Thompson]

The decades of the 1960s and 1970s were exciting days for Tupperware, the company that originated airtight, easy-to-use plastic food-storage containers. Named for Earl Tupper, the inventor of the product, sales of the novel product languished until frustrated distributors developed the idea of the Tupperware party. Housewives would gather ten at a time in each others' homes to socialize and play games. The Tupperware lady demonstrated the latest products, attendees purchased products, the hostess received a free gift; and the Tupperware lady made a few dollars. The party concept was a huge success, company sales nearly doubled every five years, and the number of Tupperware dealers increased steadily.

However, Tupperware dealers noticed that things were changing during the late 1970s and the 1980s. The inflation and divorce rates had jumped. With the exception of World War II more women than ever were working full-time. Many customers were single, childless, and working outside the home. Rubbermaid, a competitor in the food-storage container market, responded to this market change by canceling its sponsored parties and began distributing products through supermarkets. Tupperware's top managers, however, viewed market developments differently. They inaccurately believed that more women looking for work would mean more prospective dealers and customers with more money to spend. Although management concluded in 1986 that, because more women were working outside the home, two-thirds of Tupperware's potential customers weren't available for product demonstrations, the company decided against changing its marketing system. It did attempt a mail-order catalogue in 1988, but canceled it when its dealers protested.

From 1984 to 1992, Tupperware's North American sales slipped from 59% to a little over 40% of the market, even though overseas sales continued to do reasonably well. The number of dealers dropped from 32,000 to 24,000. During the same time period, Rubbermaid's market share increased from a little over 5% to nearly 40% of units sold. Tupperware's management estimated in 1992 that most U.S. women either had no idea how to find Tupperware or no desire to go to a Tupperware party. About 40% of the company's sales were to people who skipped the parties, but sent orders along with friends who attended.

Nevertheless, management still refused to change its marketing system. According to Allan Nagle, president of Tupperware Worldwide, "To wipe away our existing distribution and replace it would be a pretty traumatic exercise." Pinning his company's future on the hope that the Tupperware party would make a comeback, he predicted in 1992 that it "will become more in vogue than in the 1980s because of the greater propensity of women and families to spend more time at home." Industry analysts wondered about Nagle's prediction, and Rubbermaid and other competitors continued to grow at Tupperware's expense. Would the company's sales continue to slide or would sociocultural changes again bring growing sales to Tupperware?[2]

The preceding example shows how quickly a pioneering company can become an also-ran because of its failure to adapt to environmental change or, even worse, its failure to create change. To be successful over time, an organization must be in tune with its external environment. There must be a **strategic fit** between what the environment wants and what the corporation has to offer, as well as between what the corporation needs and what the environment can provide.[3] Current predictions are that the environment for all organizations will become even more uncertain in the coming years. **Environmental uncertainty** refers to the combination of the degree of *complexity* and the degree of *change* in an organization's external environment.[4] Environmental uncertainty is a threat to strategic managers because it hampers their ability to develop long-range plans and to make strategic decisions to keep the corporation in equilibrium with its external environment. In a July 1993 survey of 400 American executives, 79% reported that change in their companies was rapid or extremely rapid. Although 61% of the executives predicted that the pace of change would accelerate, only 47% felt that their companies would be able to cope with the change.[5] Based on their willingness

FIGURE 4.1 **Basic Orientations for Dealing with Environmental Uncertainty**

		The Environment	
		Don't Change Environment	Change Environment
The Corporation	Don't Change Corporation	**Avoid** • Ignore • Hide	**Influence** • Advertise • Lobby • Cooptation
	Change Corporation	**React** • Follow leader • Reorganize	**Anticipate** • Strategic management

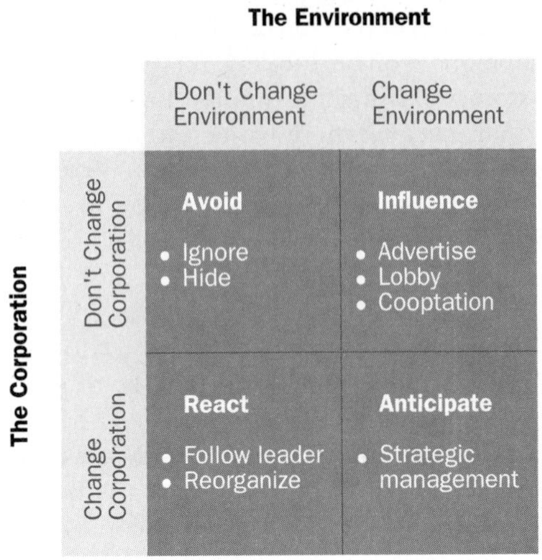

to change their corporations and/or their environments, strategic managers may adopt one of the four basic orientations for dealing with uncertainty illustrated in Fig. 4.1.

If managers do not want to change a firm's way of doing things or to change how the environment affects the firm, they may simply **avoid** change completely by either ignoring the situation until good times return or by hiding in a small, secure market niche. Avoidance appeared to be Tupperware's primary orientation for dealing with societal changes. If managers choose, in contrast, to change the environment in some way so that the firm can continue its activities unchanged, they may attempt to **influence** key groups in the firm's environment by advertising the firm's virtues, lobbying the government for favors, or co-opting antagonistic groups by inviting one of the firm's critics to join the corporation's board of directors. (These actions sometimes are called political strategies.) For example, Tupperware could lobby the federal government to establish quality and safety standards for food containers so rigorous that only Tupperware's products would be acceptable. If managers fear changing the firm's environment, they may respond to increasing environmental uncertainty by **reacting** to a new situation, either by simply imitating the actions of the industry leader or by reorganizing to cut costs. For example, Tupperware's top management might be tempted to switch to supermarket distribution because this channel worked so well for Rubbermaid. None of these three orientations, however, can be thought of as true strategic management. They simply are temporary approaches that postpone the inevitable adjustments needed to gain and keep strategic fit.

Managers who are willing to actively embrace the increasing uncertainty facing their organization in order to **anticipate** future developments engage in strategic management. To be successful, however, they must have the will not only to change the way the firm operates, but also to attempt to change or modify certain elements in its environment to help create a future more favorable to the corporation. The dilemma facing Tupperware was how to try alternative methods of marketing and distribution without antagonizing its current dealers, the *Tupperware ladies.*

4.1 Environmental Scanning

Before an organization can begin to formulate strategy, management must scan the external environment to identify possible opportunities and threats. **Environmental scanning** is the monitoring, evaluating, and disseminating of information from the external environment to key people within the corporation. It is a management tool for avoiding strategic surprise and ensuring the firm's long-term health. Research has identified a positive relationship between environmental scanning and profits.[6]

Environmental Variables

In undertaking environmental scanning, strategic managers must first be aware of the many variables within a corporation's societal and task environments. The **societal environment** includes general forces that do not directly touch on the short-run activities of the organization but that can, and often do, influence its long-run decisions. Shown previously in Fig. 3.1, they are

- **Economic forces** that regulate the exchange of materials, money, energy, and information;
- **Technological forces** that generate problem-solving inventions;
- **Political-legal forces** that allocate power and provide constraining and protecting laws and regulations; and
- **Sociocultural forces** that regulate the values, mores, and customs of society.

The **task environment** includes the elements or groups that directly affect the corporation and, in turn, are affected by it. These groups include governments, local communities, suppliers, competitors, customers, creditors, employee/labor unions, special-interest groups, and trade associations. A corporation's task environment typically is the *industry* within which it operates. Managers must monitor both the societal and task environments to detect strategic factors that are likely to have a strong impact on corporate success or failure.

Identifying External Strategic Factors

Strategic managers should engage in environmental scanning by monitoring for weak as well as strong environmental signals. As mentioned earlier, Tupperware paid little attention to sociocultural changes being reported by its dealers during the late 1970s and early 1980s. The fact that more customers were single, childless, and working outside the home was an example of a weak signal. By 1992, however, Tupperware's market share had dropped from 59% to 40%—a rather strong signal!

One way to identify and analyze developments in the societal environment is to use the matrix provided in Fig. 4.2. *First,* identify approximately three or more emerging trends for each of the four forces in the societal environment. *Second,* attempt to ascertain the likely impact, if any, of each of these trends on each of the ten elements (stakeholder groups) in the corporation's task environment. For example, if a period of rapid economic growth appears to be developing, list that as one of the economic forces in the societal environment and attempt to identify its impact on the task elements likely to be affected. This approach enables the strategic manager to estimate how future developments may affect the firm through its impact on elements in the company's task environment.

When analyzed, environmental data form a series of **strategic environmental issues,** which are the trends and developments that are likely to determine future conditions. However, insofar as strategic managers are concerned, they must further analyze these strategic environmental issues to identify their importance to the corporation's future. A corporation's **external strategic factors** are the strategic environmental issues that are judged to have a *high probability of occurrence* and a *high probability of impact on the corporation.* As Fig. 4.3 shows, managers can use an **issues priority matrix** to help them decide which strategic issues should be merely scanned (low priority) and which should be monitored as strategic factors (high priority). They can then categorize the corporation's external strategic factors as *opportunities* and *threats* and include them in strategy formulation.

Unfortunately, few firms successfully monitor all external strategic factors.[7] The personal values of a corporation's top managers and the success of current strategies are likely to bias both their perceptions of what is important to monitor in the external environment and their interpretations of what they perceive. Companies therefore often respond differently to the same environmental changes because of differences in the ability of their strategic managers to recognize and understand strategic issues and factors.[8] For example, businesses following a differentiation strategy tend to scan the environment primarily for opportunities and closely monitor customer attitudes. In contrast, firms following a cost leadership strategy tend to scan the environment primarily for threats and closely monitor competitors' activities.[9] Thus, in either case, if one such firm needs to change its strategy, it might not gather the appropriate external information required to do so successfully.

Societal Environment

The number of possible strategic factors in the societal environment is enormous. Generally speaking, each country in the world may have its own unique set of societal forces—some of which are similar to those of neighboring countries and some of which are different. For example, even though Austria and the Czech Republic share borders in Central Europe, the Czech Republic's recent history as a

FIGURE 4.2

Matrix for Environmental Trend Analysis

	Societal Forces			
	Economic	Technological	Political-Legal	Sociocultural
Task Elements	1. 2. 3.	1. 2. 3.	1. 2. 3.	1. 2. 3.
Communities				
Competitors				
Creditors				
Customers				
Employees/labor unions				
Governments				
Special-interest groups				
Shareholders				
Suppliers				
Trade associations				

Source: Suggested by J. C. Camillus, *Strategic Planning and Management Control* (Lexington, Mass.: D. C. Heath & Co., 1986), pp. 59–67.

FIGURE 4.3 **Issues Priority Matrix**

Probable Impact on Corporation

Probability of Occurrence	High	Medium	Low
High	High Priority	High Priority	Medium Priority
Medium	High Priority	Medium Priority	Low Priority
Low	Medium Priority	Low Priority	Low Priority

Source: Adapted from L. L. Lederman, "Foresight Activities in the U.S.A.: Time for a Re-Assessment?" *Long-Range Planning* (June 1984), p. 46. Copyright ©1984 by Pergamon Press, Ltd. Reprinted by permission.

communist-bloc country meant that in 1990 it had none of the commercial infrastructure to support the transition from a centrally planned to a free-market economy. Consequently, starting a business in Austria was significantly easier than in the Czech Republic where the old lethargic, state-controlled companies were neither able to produce needed supplies quickly nor to distribute products effectively. Nevertheless, excellent school systems in both countries have produced well-educated and cultured consumers and employees. (We present additional examples of various societal forces in countries around the world in Table 11.1.)

Table 4.1 shows that large corporations divide the societal environment in any one geographic region into four categories and focus their scanning in each category on trends that have relevance for the entire corporation. Obviously, trends in any one category may be important to the firms in one industry but less important to firms in other industries. Trends in the *political–legal* part of the societal environment have a significant impact on firms. For example, periods of strict enforcement of U.S. antitrust laws directly affect corporate growth strategy. As large

TABLE 4.1 Some Important Variables in the Societal Environment

Economic	Technological	Political–Legal	Sociocultural
GNP trends	Total federal spending for R&D	Antitrust regulations	Life-style changes
Interest rates	Total industry spending for R&D	Environmental protection laws	Career expectations
Money supply	Focus of technological efforts	Tax laws	Consumer activism
Inflation rates	Patent protection	Special incentives	Rate of family formation
Unemployment levels	New products	Foreign trade regulations	Growth rate of population
Wage/price controls	New developments in technology transfer from lab to marketplace	Attitudes toward foreign companies	Age distribution of population
Devaluation/revaluation	Productivity improvements through automation	Laws on hiring and promotion	Regional shifts in population
Energy availability and cost		Stability of government	Life expectancies
Disposable and discretionary income			Birth rates

companies find that acquiring another firm in the same or a related industry is becoming more difficult, they typically diversify into unrelated industries.[10]

Demographic trends are part of the *sociocultural* part of the societal environment. The demographic bulge in the U.S. population caused by the "baby boom" in the 1950s strongly affected the ski resort industry, among others. Instead of emphasizing steep down-hill slopes and the singles bar aspect of the ski lodge as they did so successfully in the 1960s and 1970s, resorts have switched to offering ski classes for children and more gentle "family slopes" in the 1990s. According to Howard Harris, president of Eagle Direct, a Denver marketing firm with ski-area clients, "Your hot-dog skier of 20 years ago is now craving white wine and chateaubriand and has two kids he's introducing to skiing. The resorts are trying to hang onto that skier longer."[11] Even now, companies are preparing for the inevitable aging of this demographic group. Maybelline is introducing a new Revitalizers line of foundations, concealers, blushes, and powders to counteract signs of aging in women. Expecting the number of men over 40 to grow by 21% from 1992 to 2000, companies are expanding their offerings of hair-coloring products such as Just For Men and Grecian Formula.[12] As the 1990s wear on, health care and financial planning are moving to center stage. Can retirement homes and adult diapers be far behind?

In the United States six sociocultural trends are helping to define the future.

1. **Increasing environmental awareness:** Recycling and conservation are becoming more than slogans. Busch Gardens, for example, eliminated the use of disposable styrofoam trays in favor of washing and reusing plastic trays.
2. **Growth of the seniors market:** As the number of people over age 55 increases, they will become an even more important market. Already, some companies

are segmenting the senior population into Young Matures, Older Matures, and the Elderly—each having a different set of attitudes and interests.

3. **New baby boomlet:** With a new interest in babies, a decline in the percentage increase in women entering the work force, and younger women showing more interest in starting families earlier than their older sisters, the signs point to a new baby boomlet. The actual number of births thus far in the decade has been significantly greater than Census Bureau projections.[13]
4. **Decline of the mass market:** Niche markets are beginning to define the marketers' environment. People want products that are adapted more to their personal needs. Johnson Products, for example, became very successful by developing hair care products specifically for members of ethnic groups. Estée Lauder's All Skin and Maybelline's Shades of You lines of cosmetic products are specifically made for African-American women.[14]
5. **Pace and location of life:** Instant communication by means of facsimile (fax) machines, car telephones, and overnight mail enhances efficiency—but increases the pressure on people. The merging of the personal computer with the communications and entertainment industries through telephone lines, satellite dishes, and cable TV gives consumers an increasing number of choices. It also means that people can leave overcrowded urban areas for small towns and *telecommute* to work via personal computers and modems.
6. **Changing household:** According the United States Census Bureau, the number of people living alone will have grown from 13% in 1960 to 26% in 2000. Only 20% of U.S. homes will have a child under 18, compared to 44% in 1960. Although the baby boomlet trend may alter this estimate, a household clearly will no longer be the same as it was once portrayed on the "Brady Bunch" or the "Cosby Show" TV programs of the 1970s and 1980s.[15]

Task Environment

To comprehend a corporation's task environment, management needs to monitor and understand what each stakeholder group wants and needs from the corporation. Each stakeholder group uses its own criteria to determine how well a corporation is performing and constantly judges management's actions in terms of their effect on the group. To the extent that a stakeholder group believes that it isn't being treated properly, it will pressure the organization to remedy the situation. Therefore all levels of management must be aware not only of the principal stakeholders in the corporation's task environment, but also of the criteria that each group uses to judge the corporation's performance. Strategic managers have the responsibility of keeping track of the concerns of important stakeholders and considering their desires when making strategic decisions.

As Fig. 4.4 illustrates, environmental scanning should include analyses of all relevant task elements. These analyses take the form of individual reports written by various people in different parts of the firm. At Procter & Gamble (P&G), for example, each quarter people from each of the brand management teams work with key people from the sales and market research departments to research and write a "competitive activity report" on each of P&G's product categories. People

FIGURE 4.4 **Scanning the External Environment**

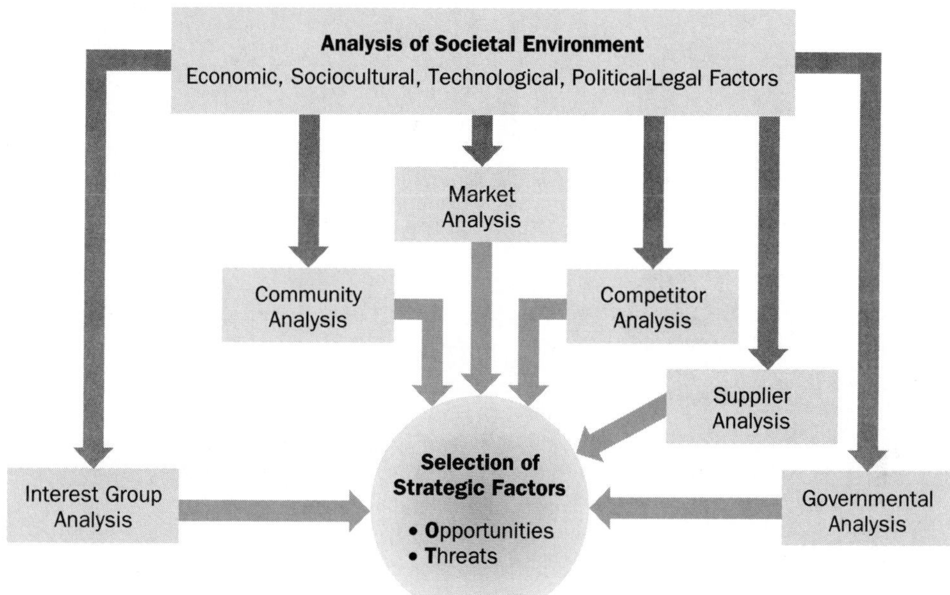

in purchasing write similar reports concerning new developments in the industries that supply P&G. These and other reports are then summarized and transmitted up the corporate hierarchy for top management to use in strategic decision making. If a new development is reported for a particular product category, top management may then send memos to people throughout the organization to watch for and report on developments in related product areas. The many reports resulting from these scanning efforts, when boiled down to their essentials, act as a detailed list of external strategic factors—the opportunities and threats facing the corporation from its task environment.

4.2 Industry Analysis

An **industry** is a group of firms producing a similar product or service, such as financial services or soft drinks. Examination of the important stakeholder groups in a particular corporation's task environment may thus be called **industry analysis.**

Competitive Analysis

M. E. Porter, an authority on competitive strategy, contends that a corporation is most concerned with the intensity of competition within its industry. Basic competitive forces, which are depicted in Fig. 4.5, determine the intensity level. "The collective strength of these forces," he contends, "determines the ultimate profit

FIGURE 4.5 **Forces Driving Industry Competition**

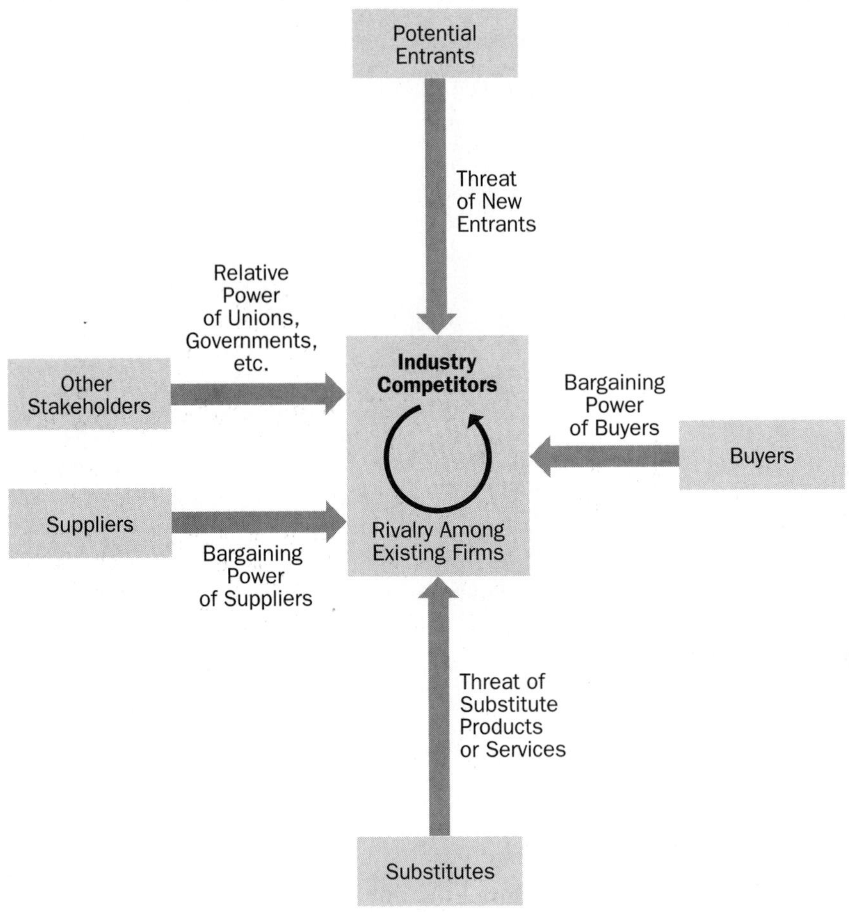

Source: Adapted/reprinted with permission of The Free Press, an imprint of Simon & Schuster, from *Competitive Strategy: Techniques for Analyzing Industries and Competitors* by Michael E. Porter. Copyright © 1980 by The Free Press.

potential in the industry, where profit potential is measured in terms of long-run return on invested capital."[16] The stronger each of these forces is, the more companies are limited in their ability to raise prices and earn greater profits. Although Porter mentions only five forces, we follow R. E. Freeman's recommendation and add a sixth—other stakeholders—to reflect the power that unions, governments, and other groups from the task environment wield over an industry's activities.

A strong force may be regarded as a threat because it is likely to reduce profits. In contrast, a weak force may be viewed as an opportunity because it may allow the company to earn greater profits. In the short run, strong forces act as constraints on a company's activities. In the long run, however, a company, through its choice of strategy, may be able to change the strength of one or more of the forces to the company's advantage.

In scanning its industry, a corporation must assess the importance to its success of the following six forces: threat of new entrants, rivalry among existing firms, threat of substitute products, bargaining power of buyers, bargaining power of suppliers, and relative power of other stakeholders.[17]

Threat of New Entrants

New entrants to an industry typically bring to it new capacity, a desire to gain market share, and substantial resources. They therefore are threats to an established corporation. The threat of entry depends on the presence of entry barriers and the reactions that can be expected from existing competitors. For example, no new domestic automobile companies have been established successfully in the United States since the 1930s because of the large amounts of capital required to build production facilities and develop a dealer distribution network. Some of the **barriers to entry** are:

- **Economies of scale:** Economies of scale are the cost advantages associated with large size. They deter new entrants by forcing them to enter the industry at a large scale (usually with high costs) and risk retaliation from existing firms, or to enter the industry at a small scale and accept a cost disadvantage. Economies of scale in the production and sale of mainframe computers, for example, gave IBM a significant advantage over any new rival.
- **Product differentiation:** Brand identification creates a barrier to entry by forcing entrants to spend heavily to overcome existing customer loyalty. Advertising, customer service, and being first with a new product foster brand identification. For example, corporations such as Procter & Gamble and General Mills, which manufacture products such as Tide and Cheerios, create high entry barriers with their substantial advertising and promotion efforts.
- **Capital requirements:** The need to invest huge financial resources in order to compete creates a significant barrier to entry, particularly if it is for unrecoverable up-front expenses such as R&D. Xerox's original decision to rent instead of sell copiers created an entry barrier for competitors. A new entrant had to have a lot of working capital to support a similar rental policy.
- **Switching costs:** Switching costs are the one-time costs facing a buyer when that buyer switches from one supplier's product to another's. If these switching costs are high, a new entrant must offer a major improvement in cost or performance to entice a potential customer to change from its current supplier. Computer software is one example of an industry with high switching costs. Once a software program such as Lotus 1-2-3 or WordPerfect becomes established in an office, office managers are very reluctant to switch to a new program because of the high training costs.
- **Access to distribution channels:** A barrier to entry can be the new entrant's need to secure distribution for its products. To the extent that appropriate distribution channels already have been served by the established firms, the new entrant must persuade those channels to accept its products through costly

promotion allowances. For example, small entrepreneurs have a difficult time obtaining supermarket shelf space for their goods because large retailers charge for space on their shelves and give priority to the established firms who can pay not only the shelf fees but also for the advertising needed to generate high customer demand.

- **Cost disadvantages independent of size:** Established companies may have cost advantages not easily imitated by new entrants. These advantages may be proprietary product knowledge protected by patents, favorable access to raw materials, favorable locations, or government subsidies. Microsoft's development of the first widely adopted operating system (MS-DOS) for IBM and IBM-compatible personal computers gave it a significant advantage over potential competitors. Its introduction of Windows helped cement that advantage. A cost advantage also may come from the effects of an *experience* (or learning) *curve.* In some industries, such as aerospace, unit costs tend to decline as the firm gains cumulative experience in making and selling the product. In such an industry, a new entrant will find competing against an established firm with a low cost position based on experience very costly. (We discuss the experience curve and its implications for strategic management in more detail in Chapter 5.)
- **Government policy:** The government can limit entry into an industry through licensing requirements and limitations on access to needed raw materials. For example, the U.S. government limits access to off-shore drilling sites for petroleum companies to reduce the likelihood of contamination of the nation's coastline.

Rivalry Among Existing Firms

In most industries, corporations are mutually dependent. A competitive move by one firm can be expected to have a noticeable effect on its competitors and thus may cause retaliation or counterefforts. For example, the entry by mail-order companies such as Dell and Gateway into a PC industry previously dominated by IBM, Apple, and Compaq increased the level of competitive activity to such an extent that any price reduction or new product introduction is now quickly followed by similar moves from other PC makers. According to Porter, intense rivalry is related to the presence of several factors.

- **Number of competitors:** Competitors are either numerous or roughly equal in size and power. When competitors are numerous, as in the case of restaurants, there is plenty of room for new strategies to be tried by one firm and copied by others. When competitors are roughly equal in size, they watch each other carefully to make sure that they can counter a move by any one of the firms.
- **Rate of industry growth:** A rapidly growing industry usually presents plenty of opportunity for many firms to grow within it. However, when industry growth slows, any one firm may not be able to continue its sales growth unless it takes sales away from a competitor. For example, any drop in passenger traffic tends to set off price wars in the airline industry.

- **Product or service characteristics:** When a product or service is basically the same regardless of the company offering it, that product or service resembles a commodity. Commodities, such as grain or petroleum, usually are graded and compete within each grade only on price and service. If switching costs are low, customers will jump from one supplier to another to reduce their costs, generating intense rivalry among suppliers. For example, people may patronize a certain videotape rental store because of its location, variety of selection, and pricing. They assume that a particular videotape from one store is the same as that offered by another store.
- **Amount of fixed costs:** To the extent that a company's fixed costs are high, it may be willing to cut prices below its total costs in order at least to cover its fixed costs. Airlines, for example, must fly their planes on a schedule regardless of the number of paying passengers for any one flight. As a result, the airlines use cheap standby or excursion fares whenever a plane has empty seats. Although these fares may not cover the complete cost of the trip, at least they contribute to the relatively fixed costs of fuel, crew salaries, and administration, which must be paid regardless of the number of tickets sold. To the extent that a product is perishable (e.g., fresh fruits or vegetables), it must be sold at whatever price can be obtained before the product deteriorates.
- **Capacity:** If the only way a company can increase manufacturing volume is to add a large increment of capacity by building a new plant, it may run that new plant at full capacity to keep its unit costs as low as possible. This possibility is especially strong if economies of scale are present in the manufacture of that product, as with computer microchips. Hence, in the short run, the company probably will produce more than market demand at the current price and may reduce its price, hoping that it can recoup its costs from a greater number of sales.
- **Height of exit barriers:** The reverse of entry barriers—exit barriers—keep a company from leaving an industry. These barriers may be specialized assets or management's loyalty to an existing business. To the extent that a firm finds exiting an industry difficult, it will continue to compete so long as it can avoid losing significant amounts of money, while management hopes for better times. In the brewing industry, for example, a low percentage of companies leave the industry because there are few uses for breweries except for making beer.
- **Diversity of rivals:** Rivals often have diverse origins, strategies, and corporate cultures. They also may have widely differing ideas of how to compete and so they are likely to cross paths often and unknowingly challenge each others' positions.

Threat of Substitute Products or Services

In effect, all corporations within an industry compete with firms in other industries that produce substitute products. **Substitute products** appear to be different but can satisfy the same need as another product. According to Porter, "Substitutes limit the potential returns of an industry by placing a ceiling on the prices firms in the industry can profitably charge."[18] To the extent that switching costs are low, substitutes may have a strong effect on an industry. Tea may be considered a substitute for coffee. If the price of coffee goes up high enough, coffee drinkers will slowly begin switching to tea. The price of tea thus puts a price ceiling on the price of coffee. Sometimes a difficult task, the identification of possible substitute products or services means searching for products or services that can perform the same function, even though they may not appear to be easily substitutable. For example, Saran-wrap (a product from the plastics industry) substituted for Reynolds-wrap (a product from the aluminum industry) when the plastics industry identified the target market as food wrap rather than simply "plastics."

Bargaining Power of Buyers

Buyers affect an industry through their ability to force down prices, bargain for higher quality or more services, and play competitors against each other. A buyer or a group of buyers is powerful if some of the following conditions hold.

- A buyer purchases a large proportion of the seller's product or service.
- A buyer has the potential to integrate backward by producing the product itself.
- Alternative suppliers are plentiful because the product is standard or undifferentiated.
- Changing suppliers costs very little.
- The purchased product represents a high percentage of a buyer's costs, thus providing an incentive to shop around for a lower price.
- A buyer earns low profits and thus is sensitive to cost and service differences.
- The purchased product is unimportant to the final quality or price of a buyer's products or services and thus can be easily substituted without affecting the final product adversely.

For example, if General Motors purchased a large percentage of Cooper Tire's total tire production, GM's purchasing department could easily make all sorts of demands on Cooper's marketing people. Such would be the case especially if GM could just as easily get its tires from Goodyear or Michelin at no extra trouble or cost. (This situation is one reason why small firms such as Cooper Tire stay out of the original equipment market.) Increasing demands by large manufacturing companies for just-in-time delivery means that, to get orders, a small supplier dependent on the large firm's business must take over the warehousing functions previously handled by the large firm.

Bargaining Power of Suppliers

Suppliers can affect an industry through their ability to raise prices or reduce the quality of purchased goods and services. A supplier or supplier group is powerful if some of the following conditions apply.

- The supplier industry is dominated by a few companies, but sells to many (e.g., petroleum industry).

- Its product or service is unique and/or it has built up switching costs (e.g., word processing software).
- Substitutes are not readily available (e.g., electricity).
- Suppliers are able to integrate forward and compete directly with their present customers (e.g., microprocessor manufacturers).
- A purchasing industry buys only a small portion of the supplier group's goods and services and is thus unimportant to the supplier (e.g., sales of lawn-mower tires are less important to the tire industry than are sales of auto tires).

Relative Power of Other Stakeholders

Freeman's addition of a sixth force to Porter's list includes a variety of stakeholder groups from the task environment.[19] These groups comprise governments, unions, local communities, creditors (if not included with suppliers), trade associations, special-interest groups, and stockholders. The importance of these stakeholders varies by industry. For example, environmental groups in Maine, Michigan, Oregon, and Iowa successfully lobbied for legislation to outlaw disposable bottles and cans; thus deposits for most drink containers are now required in those states. These actions effectively raised costs across the board, with the greatest impact on marginal producers who couldn't absorb all of these costs internally. Although Porter contends that government influences the level of competitive activity through the previously mentioned five forces, we believe that government deserves special mention because of its power to affect all industries.

Industry Evolution

Over time most industries evolve through a series of stages from growth through maturity to eventual decline.[20] The strength of each of the six forces mentioned above varies according to the stage of industry evolution. Based on the product life cycle (discussed in Chapter 5), the industry life cycle is useful for explaining and predicting the strengths of and trends among the six forces that drive industry competition. When an industry is new, people often buy the product regardless of price because it fulfills a unique need. As new competitors enter the industry, prices drop as a result of competition. Companies use the experience curve and economies of scale to reduce costs faster than the competition. Companies vertically integrate to reduce costs even further by acquiring their suppliers and distributors. Competitors try to differentiate their products from others' in order to avoid the fierce price competition common to the competitive turbulence part of the growth stage (see Fig. 5.3).

By the time an industry enters maturity, products tend to become more like commodities. As buyers become more sophisticated, they base their purchasing decisions on better information. Price becomes a dominant concern when a product meets a minimum level of quality and features. One example of this trend is the videocassette recorder industry. By the 1990s, the differences among brands of VCRs were few and mostly minor. Consumers realized that, because slight improvements cost significantly more money, paying more than the minimum for a VCR made little sense. Porter thus argues that "there is a natural force reducing

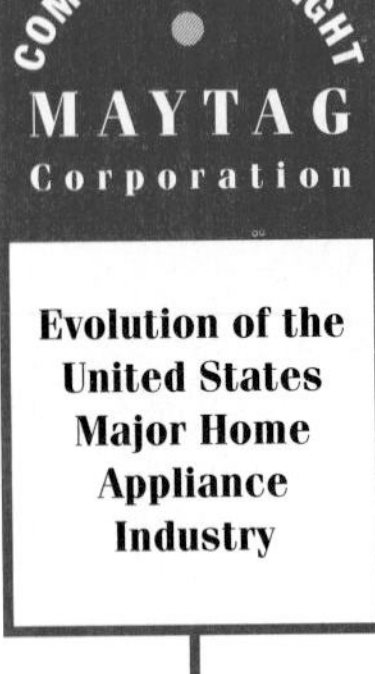

Evolution of the United States Major Home Appliance Industry

In 1945, there were approximately 300 U.S. major home appliance manufacturers in the United States. By 1993, however, the "big five" of Whirlpool, General Electric, AB Electrolux (*no* relation to Electrolux Corporation, a U.S. company selling Electrolux brand vacuum cleaners), Maytag, and Raytheon controlled almost 98% of the U.S. market. Consolidation of the industry reflected fierce domestic competition. Emphasis on quality and durability coupled with strong price competition drove the surviving firms to increased efficiencies and a strong concern for customer satisfaction.

Prior to World War II, most appliance manufacturers produced a limited line of appliances featuring one successful product. General Electric made refrigerators, Maytag focused on washing machines, and Hotpoint produced electric ranges. Each offered variations of its basic product, but not until 1945 did firms begin to offer full lines of various appliances. By 1955, the major home appliance industry began experiencing overcapacity, leading to mergers and acquisitions and a proliferation of national and private brands.

The industry almost doubled in size during the 1960s as sales of several products grew very rapidly. Dishwasher unit sales almost quadrupled, and unit sales of clothes dryers more than tripled. Product reliability improved even though real prices (adjusted for inflation) declined by about 10%. Maytag successfully expanded into clothes dryers and dishwashers and upgraded its manufacturing facilities.

Although the 1970s were a time of high inflation and high interest rates, unit sales of home appliances continued to increase. But profit margins were squeezed, and the industry continued to consolidate around fewer firms. Antitrust considerations prevented GE and Whirlpool from acquiring other appliance manufacturers. However, White was able to buy the troubled appliance divisions of all the automobile manufacturers and Westinghouse's as they were put up for sale. Maytag's emphasis on quality and durability enabled it to earn good profits during this period.

The market continued to expand in the early 1980s, thanks partially to

(continued)

product differentiation over time in an industry."[21] Supporting this tendency is the diffusion of technology from one company to another. For example, when Xerox faced strong competition from Japanese firms able to sell copiers more cheaply than Xerox, management introduced *competitive benchmarking*. In effect, the company purchased a competitor's product in order to take it apart and through reverse engineering discover how to get around patented technology to make a similar or better product. (We discuss competitive benchmarking in more detail in Chapter 12.)

(continued)

the acceptance by the U.S. consumer of the microwave oven. Seeing the importance of becoming a full-line appliance manufacturer like its major competitors GE, White, and Whirlpool, Maytag acquired Jenn-Air and Magic Chef. Nevertheless, total major home appliance sales actually began to fall in the late 1980s. By the 1990s, U.S. appliance manufacturers offered a full range of products even if they did not make some items themselves. That approach was crucial for a company to get distribution in the developing appliance *super stores*. A company would fill the gaps in its line by putting its own brand name on products it purchased from another manufacturer. For example, Caloric (Raytheon) not only made gas ranges for its in-house Amana brand but also for Whirlpool. General Electric made some microwave ovens for Caloric (Raytheon) and for Jenn-Air and Magic Chef (Maytag), as well as for its own Hotpoint and RCA brands.

In the mid 1990s the U.S. major home appliance industry faced some significant threats and opportunities. After 40 years of rising sales (both in units and dollars), the North American market had reached maturity. Future unit sales were expected to grow only 1%–2% annually on average for the foreseeable future. Operating margins had been dropping as competition forced appliance manufacturers to hold prices low, even though costs kept increasing. In western Europe, however, a market already 25% larger than the mature North American appliance market, unit sales were expected to grow 5% annually. This figure was expected to increase significantly once eastern European countries became more involved in world trade. In addition, rapid economic growth in Asia, Mexico, and South America had tremendous implications for the emerging global appliance industry.

With Whirlpool's acquisition of the appliance business of Philips (the Netherlands), GE's joint venture with GEC (the United Kingdom), AB Electrolux's (Sweden) purchase of White, and Maytag's acquisition of Hoover (vacuum cleaners worldwide and major home appliances in the U. K.), the level of competition increased dramatically in both Europe and North America. Environmental scanning and industry analysis had to be international in scope if a firm was to succeed in the 21st century.

As an industry moves through maturity into decline, the growth rates of its products' sales slow and may even begin to decline. To the extent that exit barriers are low, firms will begin converting their facilities to alternative uses or will sell them. The industry tends to consolidate around fewer but larger competitors. As in the case of the U.S. major home appliance industry—described in the Company Spotlight: Maytag Corporation feature on pages 98–99—the industry changed from a fragmented industry comprising hundreds of appliance manufacturers in the industry's early years to an oligopoly of five companies (including Maytag) controlling almost 98% of U.S. major home appliance sales. These firms then realized that they needed access to less mature European and Asian markets if they were to remain profitable in such a competitive industry.

Strategic Groups and Strategic Mapping

In the analysis of a particular industry, categorizing the various competitors within that industry into strategic groups may be useful. According to K. J. and M. L. Hatten, a **strategic group** comprises business units or firms that "pursue similar strategies with similar resources."[22] Research indicates that strategic groups are very useful to strategic managers as a way of better understanding the competitive environment.[23] Because a corporation's structure and culture tend to reflect the kinds of strategies it follows (discussed further in Chapter 8), companies or business units belonging to a particular strategic group within the same industry tend to be strong rivals and more similar to each other than to competitors in other strategic groups within the same industry. For example, although McDonald's and Olive Garden are a part of the same restaurant industry, they have different missions, objectives, and strategies, and thus belong to different strategic groups. They generally have very little in common and pay scant attention to each other when planning competitive actions. Burger King and Hardee's, however, have a great deal in common with McDonald's in terms of strategy: producing a high volume of low-priced meals targeted for sale to the average family. Consequently, they are strong rivals and are organized to operate similarly.

Strategic groups in a particular industry can be *mapped* by plotting the market positions of industry competitors on a two-dimensional graph. *First,* select two strategic variables or characteristics that differentiate the companies in an industry and use them as the vertical and horizontal axes. *Second,* plot the intersection of these two characteristics for each company. *Third,* draw a circle around the companies that are closest to one another to define strategic groups, varying the size of the circles to reflect the groups' shares of total industry sales. If needed, add a name to each strategic group in the industry (such as fast-food or buffet style service for the restaurant industry).

Figure 4.6 illustrates mapping of the restaurant chain industry using the dimensions of price and product-line breadth. Other dimensions, such as quality and degree of vertical integration, also may be used in additional graphs of the industry to indicate how the various firms in the industry compete. Keep in mind, however, that the two dimensions in each set should not be highly correlated; otherwise, the circles on the graph will simply lie along the diagonal, providing little information other than the obvious. Note that in Fig. 4.6, although product-line breadth generally seems to be correlated with price (that is, the wider the selection of offerings at a restaurant, the higher the price per offering), such isn't always the case. Long John Silver's, for example, charges more for its fish offerings than does the typical hamburger-oriented fast-food restaurant, even though its offerings are no broader than those of McDonald's.

FIGURE 4.6 **Mapping Strategic Groups in the U.S. Restaurant Chain Industry**

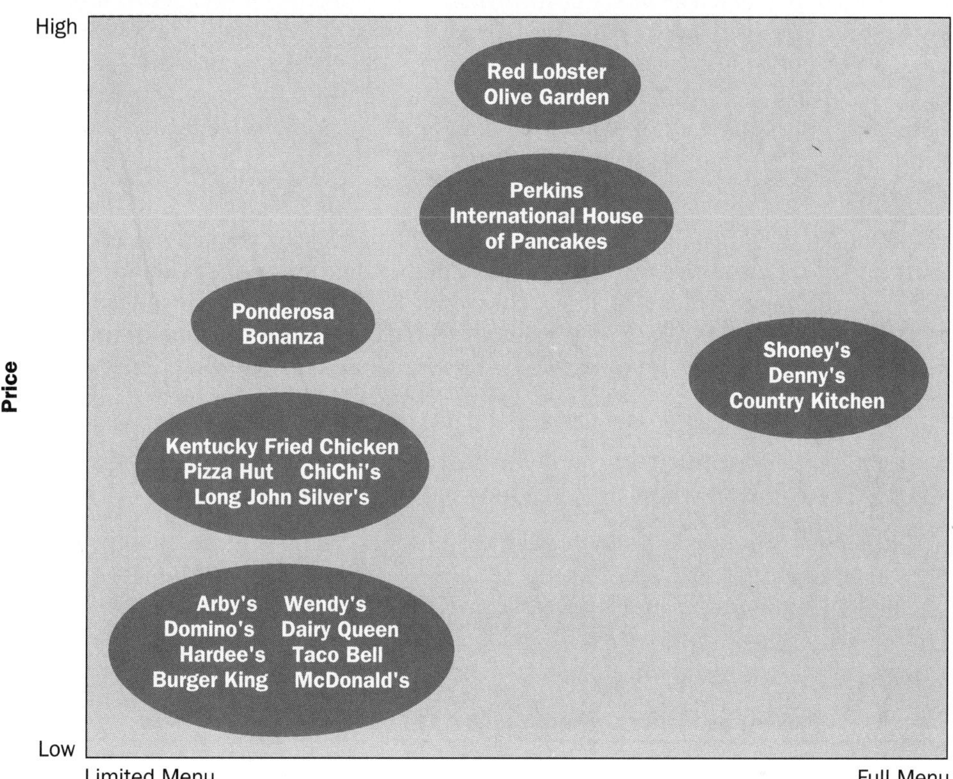

Mobility Barriers

A corporation or business unit within a particular industry or strategic group makes strategic decisions that competitors outside the group cannot easily imitate without substantial costs and a significant amount of time. These obstacles to casual imitation of a firm's strategy form entry barriers. These barriers are important to a strategic manager because their presence in an industry can either reduce or increase the likelihood of competitors in a particular market segment.

Barriers may not just protect companies in a strategic group from entry by firms outside the industry; they may also provide barriers to moving from one strategic group to another. Porter thus recommends the use of the term mobility barriers when doing strategic group analysis. According to Porter, **mobility barriers** are "factors that deter the movement of firms from one strategic position to another."[24]

The huge, vertically integrated manufacturing and distribution facilities of General Motors, Chrysler, and Ford acted as a mobility barrier in the United States for many years. The heavy costs involved in competing at even a low level in the United States acted as a mobility barrier to most foreign-based auto companies, until Volkswagen found a lucrative niche in the 1960s, which the Japanese soon explored and expanded. Table 4.2 presents some of the possible entry and mobility barriers and ways in which they can be avoided or overcome.

Strategic Types

In analyzing the level of competitive intensity within a particular industry or strategic group, characterizing the various competitors for predictive purposes is useful. According to Miles and Snow, competing firms within a single industry can be categorized on the basis of their general strategic orientation as one of four basic types.[25] Each of these types has its own favorite strategy for responding to the environment and its own combination of structure, culture, and processes consistent with that strategy. This distinction helps explain why companies facing similar situations behave differently and why they continue to do so over a long period of time. These general types have the following characteristics.

- **Defenders** are companies with a limited product line that focus on improving the efficiency of their existing operations. This cost orientation makes them unlikely to innovate in new areas. An example of such a corporation is the

TABLE 4.2 **Examples of Mobility and Entry Barriers and Ways to Avoid or Overcome Them**

Examples of Entry and Mobility Barriers in Some Industries

- High fixed asset requirement (steel industry)
- Heavy advertising expenses (beer industry)
- Scarce raw materials (petroleum industry)
- Difficult government requirements (electric utilities)
- Credit sales required (appliance industry)
- Ability to handle trade-ins (retail auto industry)
- Products protected by patents, trademarks, and trade secrets (drug industry)
- Control of key distribution channels (network television)
- Very low competitive prices (consumer electronics industry)

Ways in Which Entry and Mobility Barriers Can Be Avoided or Overcome

- Find an open niche (Neutrogena's mild soap)
- Find a substitute product (personal computers replace typewriters)
- Develop a technological improvement (P&G's low-fat cooking oil)
- Differentiate product through marketing mix (Zenith's sales of computers to colleges)
- Locate spot where competitors are weak (Toyota's emphasis on low-cost quality)
- Create process improvements (Deere's flexible manufacturing)

Adolph Coors Company, which for many years emphasized production efficiency in its one Colorado brewery and virtually ignored marketing.

- **Prospectors** are companies with fairly broad product lines that focus on product innovation and market opportunities. This sales orientation makes them somewhat inefficient. They tend to emphasize creativity over efficiency. An example is the Miller Brewing Company, which successfully promoted "light" beer and generated aggressive, innovative advertising campaigns but had to close a brand-new brewery when management overestimated market demand.
- **Analyzers** are corporations that operate in at least two different product market areas, one stable and one variable. These firms emphasize efficiency in the stable areas and innovation in the variable areas. An example is Anheuser-Busch, which can take a defender orientation to protect its massive market share in beer and a prospector orientation to generate sales in its snack foods and amusement parks.
- **Reactors** are corporations that lack a consistent strategy-structure-culture relationship. Their (often ineffective) responses to environmental pressures tend to be piecemeal strategic changes. An example is the Pabst Brewing Company, which, because of numerous takeover attempts, has been unable to generate a consistent strategy to keep its sales from dropping.

Dividing the competition into these four categories enables the strategic manager not only to monitor the effectiveness of certain strategic orientations, but also to develop scenarios of future industry developments (discussed later in this chapter). Research on the Miles and Snow model indicates that, although each of these four types can be found in any industry, the industry's characteristics will determine which of the four types will be most successful. For example, defenders tend to thrive in stable, mature, and noninnovative industries, whereas prospectors capitalize on the growth opportunities found in innovative, dynamic environments.[26]

4.3 Industry Intelligence

Studies have shown that people do much of their environmental scanning informally and individually. They obtain information from a variety of sources, such as customers, suppliers, bankers, consultants, publications, personal observations, subordinates, superiors, and peers. For example, scientists and engineers working in R&D can learn about new products and competitors' ideas at professional meetings; someone from the purchasing department, speaking with supplier representatives, may also uncover valuable bits of information about a competitor. A study of product innovation in the scientific instrument and machine tool industries reported that customers initiated 80% of all product innovations by making inquiries and complaining.[27] In these industries, the sales force and service departments must be especially vigilant.

Because people at all levels in an organization can obtain an extraordinary amount of data in a short time, top management must develop a system to get these data from those who obtained them to the people who can integrate them with other information to form a comprehensive environmental assessment.

Research indicates that less than 5% of U.S. corporations have fully developed intelligence programs. In contrast, all Japanese corporations involved in international business and over half of German and Swedish companies have active intelligence programs.[28] However, this situation is changing in the United States. At General Mills, for example, all members of the company have been trained to recognize and tap sources of competitive information. Janitors no longer simply place orders with suppliers of cleaning materials, they also ask about relevant practices at competing firms![29]

Most corporations rely on outside organizations to provide them with environmental data. Firms such as A. C. Nielsen Company provide subscribers with bimonthly data on brand share, retail prices, percentages of stores stocking an item, and percentages of stock-out stores. Management can use these data to spot regional and national trends and to assess market share. Management also can buy information on market conditions, government regulations, competitors, and new products from information brokers. Firms such as FIND/SVP, a New York licensee of the French information retrieval firm SVP, and Finsbury Data Services, owned by Reuters in London, get their data from periodicals, reference books, computer data banks, directors, and experts in the area. Other firms, such as Chase Econometrics, offer various databases and a software package that enable corporate planners to gain computer access to a large number of key indicators. Typically, the largest corporations spend from $25,000 to $30,000 per year for information services.[30] Many also have established their own in-house libraries to deal with the growing mass of available information.

Some companies, however, choose to use industrial espionage or other intelligence gathering techniques to get their information straight from their competitors. For example, Avon Products hired private investigators to retrieve from a public dumpster documents (some of them shredded) that Mary Kay Corporation had thrown away. Avon's management asserted that they wanted to learn more about Mary Kay's attempts to acquire Avon. Mary Kay executives protested in a lawsuit that Avon conspired to get trade secrets and confidential information. Until the lawsuit was settled, Mary Kay executives strengthened the firm's security. When a squirrel peered into a window at Mary Kay's Dallas headquarters, someone jokingly advised everyone to be careful: "It might be Avon's 'squirrel cam.' "[31] Even at Procter & Gamble, which defends itself like a fortress from information leaks, is vulnerable. A competitor was able to learn the precise launch date of a concentrated laundry detergent in Europe when one of its people visited a factory where machines were being made. Simply asking a few questions about what a certain machine did, to whom it was for, and when it would be delivered was all that was necessary. John Prescott, an expert on competitive intelligence, warns companies: "You can't build a competitive house unless you have intelligence as its foundation."[32]

4.4 Forecasting

After a company has collected data about its current environment, it must analyze present trends and attempt to discern whether they will continue into the future. The strategic planning horizon for many large corporations is from five to ten years in the future. A long-term planning horizon is especially necessary for large, capital-intensive corporations, such as automobile or heavy-machinery manufacturers. In these corporations, moving from an accepted proposal to a finished product requires many years. Most corporations must base their future plans on a forecast—a set of assumptions about what that future will look like. These assumptions can be derived from an entrepreneur's vision, from a head-in-the-sand hope that the future will be similar to the present, or from the opinions of experts.

Danger of Assumptions

A forecast is nothing more than a leap of faith into the future. Environmental scanning provides reasonably hard data on the present situation, but intuition and luck are needed to predict the future accurately. Faulty underlying assumptions appear to be the most frequent cause of forecasting errors.[33] Nevertheless, many managers who formulate and implement strategic plans have little or no realization that their success is based on a series of assumptions. Many long-range plans are simply based on projections of the current situation. Tupperware is an example of what can happen when corporate strategy rests on the questionable assumption that the future will simply be an extension of the present. Management not only assumed in the 1960s and 1970s that Tupperware parties would continue to be an excellent distribution channel, but its faith in this assumption also blinded it to information about changing lifestyles and their likely impact on sales. Even in 1992, when Tupperware executives realized that they could no longer justify their extrapolated sales forecasts, they merely changed their assumptions instead of working to improve their forecasting techniques.

Techniques

Forecasters use various techniques, each of which has its proponents and opponents. A study of nearly 500 of the world's largest corporations revealed trend extrapolation to be the most widely practiced form of forecasting—over 70% use this technique either occasionally or frequently.[34] Simply stated, **extrapolation** is the extension of present trends into the future. As shown in the Tupperware example, it rests on the assumption that the world is reasonably consistent and changes slowly in the short run. This type of approach includes time-series methods, which attempt to extend a series of historical events into the future. The basic problem with extrapolation is that a historical trend is based on a series of patterns or relationships among so many different variables that a change in any one can drastically alter the direction of the trend. As a rule of thumb, the further into the past that relevant data support the trend, the more confidence the forecaster can have in the prediction. Nevertheless, even experts in forecasting admit: "Forecasts that cover a period of two years or more are typically very inaccurate."[35]

Brainstorming and statistical modeling also are popular forecasting techniques. **Brainstorming** is a nonquantitative approach simply requiring the presence of people with some knowledge of the situation to be predicted. The basic ground rule is to propose ideas without first mentally screening them. No criticism is allowed, and ideas tend to build on previous ideas until a consensus is reached. This technique is a good one to use with operating managers who have more faith in "gut feelings" than quantitative "number-crunching" techniques. **Statistical modeling** is a quantitative technique that attempts to discover causal or at least explanatory factors that link two or more time series. Statistical modeling includes regression analysis and other econometric methods. Although useful in identifying trends, statistical modeling, like trend extrapolation, is based on historical data. As the patterns of relationships change, forecast accuracy deteriorates.[36] Other forecasting techniques, such as cross-impact analysis (CIA) and trend-impact analysis (TIA), are not yet utilized regularly.

Scenario writing appears to be the most widely used forecasting technique after trend extrapolation. Originated by Royal Dutch Shell, scenarios are "focused descriptions of fundamentally different futures presented in coherent script-like or narrative fashion."[37] The scenario thus may be merely a written description of some future state, in terms of principal variables and issues, or it may be generated in combination with other forecasting techniques.[38] One example is the method used by General Electric, as depicted in Fig. 4.7. It is based on a Delphi panel of anonymous experts, a trend-impact analysis, and a cross-impact analysis.

Porter strongly recommends the use of industry scenarios to conduct industry analyses. This forecasting technique utilizes variables from the societal environment and examines their effect on the main stakeholders in a corporation's task environment (industry). You may apply the process in the following manner.[39]

1. **Examine possible shifts in societal variables:** Begin with the obvious variables listed in Table 4.1 and included in Fig. 4.2 and decide which of them might be changing to create a strategic issue. To identify the issues of most importance to the corporation and/or the industry, plot these variables on an issues priority matrix (see Fig. 4.3).
2. **Identify uncertainties in each of the six forces of the task environment** (competitors, buyers, suppliers, likely substitutes, potential entrants, and other key stakeholders) as depicted in Fig. 4.5. Be sure to specify all the high-priority strategic issues identified in the first step in terms of the appropriate forces in the task environment.
3. **Make a range of plausible assumptions about future trends:** For example, if the price of oil is an important factor, make reasonable assumptions about future high, low, and most probable prices.
4. **Combine assumptions about individual trends into internally consistent scenarios:** Combine various likely trends into sets of scenarios. Because one trend may affect another, be sure that the scenarios are internally consistent. For example, if a scenario includes the assumptions of high oil prices and low inflation, that scenario is not internally consistent and should be rejected. (It is an unlikely event because high oil prices tend to drive inflation up.)
5. **Analyze the industry situation that would prevail under each scenario:** For example, if one scenario assumes that generic drugs will be more in demand than brand name drugs, the situation in the drug industry under that assumption will be quite different from that under the assumption that the demand for generic drugs will be negligible. For example, in an industry dominated by generic drugs profit margins for all firms would be low and competition

FIGURE 4.7 **Scenario Construction at General Electric**

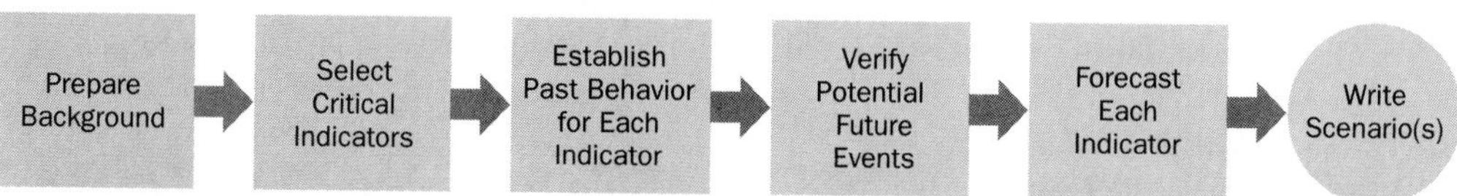

Assess overall environmental factors for the industrial sector under investigation:

- Demographic and life-style
- General business and economic
- Legislative and regulatory
- Scientific and technological

Develop crude "systems" model of the industry.

Identify the industry's key indicators (trends).

Undertake literature search to identify potential future events impacting the key trends.

Nominate Delphi panel participants whose expert opinion is credible in evaluating the industry's future.

INDICATOR
Potential future events

Experts on indicator

Establish the historical performance for each indicator.

Value
1950 1995

Enter these data into the data base of the TIA program.*

Analyze reasons for past behavior of each trend:

- Demographic and social
- Economic
- Political and legislative
- Technological

Construct Delphi panel interview artifact.

Interrogate Delphi panel:

- Evaluate past trends.
- Assess the potential impact of future events.
- Assess the probability of future events.
- Forecast future values.

Specify and document assumptions for forecasts.

Specify and document rationale for projected values.

Operate the TIA* and CIA† programs on the literature search and the Delphi output to establish the range of future values.

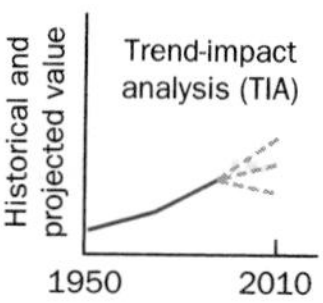

Cost-impact analysis (CIA)

Interdependence Events Most Impacted / Wild Card Events	OPEC cheating	Coal constraints	Imports > 50%	Bilateral agreements
Development of fusion	+	+		
Cost-effective oil shale	+	+		
Economic synthetics from coal	+	–	–	–
Clean combustion of coal	+	–	–	–
Conservation ethic	+			

*TIA = Trend-impact Analysis
†CIA = Cross-impact Analysis

Source: General Electric Company. Used by permission.

would be heavy. In that situation some firms would likely leave the drug industry.

6. **Determine the sources of competitive advantage under each scenario:** For example, in an industry dominated by generic drugs, the combination of low price backed by low operating costs would provide competitive advantage to a firm. If brand name drugs dominated, the combination of strong advertising, high-quality production, and heavy promotion would provide competitive advantage to a firm.
7. **Predict competitors' behavior under each scenario:** As the industry moves toward a particular scenario, each competitor will adjust. Some might leave the industry, and new competitors might enter it. Using each competitor's history and what is known about its management, estimate what each competitor is likely to do. After doing so, specify the *external strategic factors* that are necessary for success (opportunities) and those that could cause failure (threats), in a variety of future scenarios. Attaching probabilities to each of the developed scenarios can help in choosing the ones most likely to occur.[40]

4.5 Synthesis of External Strategic Factors—EFAS

After strategic managers have scanned the external societal and task environments and identified strategic factors for the corporation, they may summarize their analysis on a form such as that shown in Table 4.3, entitled External Strategic Factors Analysis Summary (EFAS). It helps managers organize external strategic factors into the generally accepted categories of opportunities and threats. It also aids in the analysis of how well management (rating) is responding to these specific factors in light of their perceived importance (weight) to the company. Use of the EFAS form involves the following steps.

First, identify and list in Column 1 about 5 to 10 opportunities and about the same number of threats. A good starting point is to use Table 4.1 and Figure 4.5 to identify key variables. *Second,* assign a **weight** in Column 2 to each factor from 1.0 (most important) to 0.0 (not important) based on that factor's probable impact on the company's current strategic position. The higher the weight, the more this factor becomes a priority for management. (All weights must sum to 1.0 regardless of the number of strategic factors.) *Third,* assign a **rating** in Column 3 to each factor from 5 (outstanding) to 1 (poor) based on management's current response to that particular factor. Each rating is a judgment about how well the analyst believes the company's management is currently dealing with each external factor.

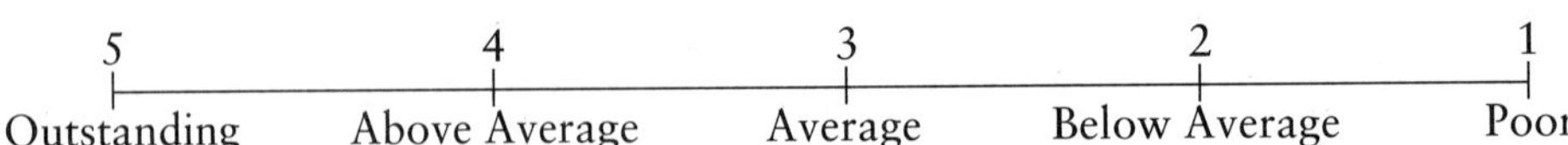

Fourth, multiply the **weight** (Column 2) for each factor by its **rating** (Column 3) to obtain that factor's **weighted score** in Column 4. *Fifth,* use Column 5 (comments) to note why a particular factor was selected and how its weight and rating

TABLE 4.3 External Strategic Factor Analysis Summary (EFAS): Maytag as Example

External Strategic Factors [1]	Weight [2]	Rating [3]	Weighted Score [4]	Comments [5]
Opportunities				
• Economic integration of European Community	.20	4	.80	Acquisition of Hoover
• Demographics favor quality appliances	.10	5	.50	Maytag quality
• Economic development of Asia	.05	1	.05	Low Maytag presence
• Opening of Eastern Europe	.05	2	.10	Will take time
• Trend to "Super Stores"	.10	2	.20	Maytag weak in this channel
Threats				
• Increasing government regulations	.10	4	.40	Well positioned
• Strong U.S. competition	.10	4	.40	Well positioned
• Whirlpool and Electrolux strong globally	.15	3	.45	Hoover weak globally
• New product advances	.05	1	.05	Questionable
• Japanese appliance companies	.10	2	.20	Only Asian presence is Australia
Total	1.00		3.15	

Notes:

1. List opportunities and threats (5–10 each) in column 1.
2. Weight each factor from 1.0 (Most Important) to 0.0 (Not Important) in Column 2 based on that factor's probable impact on the company's strategic position. **The total weights must sum to 1.00.**
3. Rate each factor from 5 (Outstanding) to 1 (Poor) in Column 3 based on the company's response to that factor.
4. Multiply each factor's weight times its rating to obtain each factor's weighted score in Column 4.
5. Use Column 5 (comments) for rationale used for each factor.
6. Add the weighted scores to obtain the total weighted score for the company in Column 4. This tells how well the company is responding to the strategic factors in its external environment.

Source: T. L. Wheelen and J. D. Hunger, "External Strategic Factors Analysis Summary (EFAS)." Copyright © 1991 by Wheelen and Hunger Associates. Reprinted by permission.

were estimated. *Sixth,* add the weighted scores for all the external factors in Column 4 to determine the total weighted score for the company. The total weighted score indicates how well the company is responding to current and expected strategic factors in its external environment. The total weighted score can range from 5.0 (outstanding) to 1.0 (poor), with 3.0 being average. This score can be used to compare that firm to other firms in its industry. In essence, the EFAS summary is your analysis of a company's management of the key external strategic factors based on a prioritized listing (using weights).

Table 4.3 shows some external strategic factors for Maytag Corporation, along with corresponding weights, ratings, and the total weighted score. If you do a similiar EFAS analysis of each company in an industry, then you are able to develop a ranking of the companies in that industry based on their management of the *external* strategic factors.

After strategic managers have completed their analysis of a firm's external strategic factors in terms of opportunities and threats, they must do the same for the corporation's internal strategic factors in terms of strengths and weaknesses. (They may then complete a form similar to that shown in Table 4.3 for an Internal Strategic Factors Analysis Summary [IFAS] in Table 5.2.) We cover this topic in Chapter 5.

In Conclusion . . .

When Wal-Mart comes to town, it isn't always appreciated. In fact, it is sometimes referred to as the "Merchant of Death." Wal-Mart earned that reputation when many small-town merchants were unable to compete with the newcomer's wide selection and low prices and went out of business. In Anamosa, Iowa, for example, the death toll was two men's clothing shops, a shoe store, a children's clothing store, a drug store, a hardware store, and a dime store. Small-town markets have been the key to Wal-Mart's expansion, but more than 80% of a Wal-Mart's business can come at the expense of other local businesses. With the arrival of Wal-Mart, sales of specialty retailers in 15 Iowa towns dropped 12.1% in a three-year period. A study by Ken Stone of Iowa State University revealed that many small-town businesses get into trouble because they fail to investigate and find lucrative market niches that Wal-Mart is unable to cover. According to Stone, the best way to compete with the giant retailer is to carry different merchandise.

Merchants in the small town of Viroqua, Wisconsin, learned Stone's lessons well. Months before the new Wal-Mart opened, Fred Nelson, then owner of Nelson Mill & Agri-Center, took six employees on a spying mission to visit the discounter 140 miles away in Anamosa, Iowa. After checking prices and service at the Wal-Mart, Nelson talked with the manager of the farm store next door to learn how he responded to the new neighbor. Nelson learned that he couldn't match Wal-Mart's prices because it buys in such large quantities but that he could focus on available niches. Returning home to Viroqua, Nelson reduced his inventories of toys and housewares and eliminated health and beauty aids entirely. He focused on clothing, tools, and giftwares and stocked better quality brands and a broader range than Wal-Mart. He expanded his repair and parts-ordering services, liberalized his returns policy, and extended his hours. He stressed his service to his main clientele—local farmers. He expanded his farm supply department and priced basics such as WD-40 at Wal-Mart levels. Thanks to his environmental scanning efforts, Fred Nelson's new strategy yielded annual sales in excess of $8 million—up from $6.8 million before Wal-Mart came to town—and profits remained stable. Soon, other Viroqua merchants were following Nelson's example. Change may seem to come slowly to small towns, but when it comes in the form of a Wal-Mart, the pace accelerates and local merchants have to be ready for it.[41]

Points to Remember

- Strategic managers must actively face uncertainty and take an active role in scanning external strategic issues for strategic factors. Firmly taking his destiny in his own hands, Fred Nelson chose to *anticipate* the arrival of Wal-Mart through environmental scanning and strategic planning.
- The societal environment is composed of sociocultural, economic, political–legal, and technological forces that do not directly touch the organization's daily activities but may influence its strategic decisions through their impact on stakeholders in the task environment. Monitoring the societal environment can provide some early warning signals before they directly impact on the firm in the form of stakeholder demands or competitive pressures.
- The task environment contains stakeholder groups that affect the organization or are greatly affected by it. Scanning these elements provides the material for industry analysis. The level of competitive intensity present in an industry is determined by (1) threat of new entrants, (2) rivalry among existing firms, (3) threat of substitute products, (4) bargaining power of buyers, (5) bargaining power of suppliers, and (6) relative power of other stakeholders.
- Strategic managers must be aware of how industries evolve in order to predict what might soon happen in their industry. They also need to consider strategic groups and strategic types as ways of better understanding their competitors.
- The key to environmental scanning is to get access to the kind of information that enables a strategic manager to better understand the forces existing in the current situation so that she/he can better predict the future. Methods of doing so range from developing a sophisticated computerized information system to personally visiting places where change is having an impact (as Fred Nelson did when he visited Anamosa's Wal-Mart).
- Although most people use trend extrapolation in forecasting, most large companies are experimenting with scenario writing to rehearse the future rather than trying to predict it. The acts of scanning and forecasting help managers gain a broader perspective of the environment.

Discussion Questions

1. Why is environmental uncertainty an important concept in strategic management?
2. Discuss how a development in a corporation's societal environment can affect the corporation through its task environment. Provide an example.
3. How can an analyst identify external strategic factors for a particular corporation?
4. What can a corporation do to ensure that information about strategic environmental factors gets to the attention of strategy makers?
5. According to Porter, what factors determine the level of competitive intensity among companies? Briefly describe each factor.
6. Describe the importance of entry and mobility barriers in an industry. Provide an example.

7. According to Miles and Snow, competing firms within a single industry may be classified as four basic types based on their generic strategy orientation. Briefly describe each of the four types.
8. Why is industrial espionage becoming an important issue in strategic management?
9. If most long-term forecasts usually are incorrect, why bother doing them?
10. Compare and contrast trend extrapolation with the writing of scenarios as forecasting techniques.

Notes

1. J. D. Thompson, *Organizations in Action* (New York: McGraw-Hill, 1967), p. 13. Copyright © 1967. Reproduced by permission of McGraw-Hill, Inc.
2. L. M. Grossman, "Families Have Changed But Tupperware Keeps Holding Its Parties," *Wall Street Journal* (July 21, 1992), pp. A1, A13.
3. T. C. Powell, "Organizational Alignment as Competitive Advantage," *Strategic Management Journal* (February 1992), pp. 119–134.
4. R. B. Duncan, "Characteristics of Organizational Environments and Perceived Environmental Uncertainty," *Administrative Science Quarterly* (September 1972), pp. 313–327.
5. K. H. Hammonds, "Changing, But Not Happy About It," *Business Week* (September 20, 1993), p. 44.
6. J. B. Thomas, S. M. Clark, and D. A. Gioia, "Strategic Sensemaking and Organizational Performance: Linkages Among Scanning, Interpretation, Action, and Outcomes," *Academy of Management Journal* (April 1993), pp. 239–270.
7. P. V. Jenster, "Using Critical Success Factors in Planning," *Long Range Planning* (August 1987), p. 108.
8. J. B. Thomas, "Interpreting Strategic Issues: Effects of Strategy and the Information-Processing Structure of Top Management Teams," *Academy of Management Journal* (June 1990), pp. 286–306; D. Miller, "The Architecture of Simplicity," *Academy of Management Review* (January 1993), 116–138.
9. D. F. Jennings and J. R. Lumpkin, "Insights Between Environmental Scanning Activities and Porter's Generic Strategies: An Empirical Analysis," *Journal of Management* (December 1992), pp. 791–803.
10. A. Shleifer and R. W. Vishny, "Takeovers in the '60s and the '80s: Evidence and Implications," *Strategic Management Journal* (Winter 1991), pp. 51–59.
11. M. Charlier, "United States Ski Resorts Stress Family Values," *Wall Street Journal* (November 20, 1992), p. B1.
12. S. L. Hwang, "To Brush Away Middle-Age Malaise, Male Baby Boomers Color Graying Hair," *Wall Street Journal* (March 2, 1993), p. B1.
13. J. Spiers, "The Baby Boomlet Is for Real," *Fortune* (February 10, 1992), pp. 101–104.
14. M. Mallory and S. Anderson, "Waking Up to a Major Market," *Business Week* (March 23, 1992), pp. 70–73.
15. D. A. Szymanski, "Six Trends That Will Drive Businesses in the 90s," *Tampa Tribune* (November 5, 1990), pp. 10D–11D.
16. M. E. Porter, *Competitive Strategy* (New York: Free Press, 1980), p. 3.
17. This summary of the forces driving competitive strategy is taken from Porter, *Competitive Strategy*, pp. 7–29.
18. Ibid., p. 23.
19. R. E. Freeman, *Strategic Management: A Stakeholder Approach* (Boston: Pitman, 1984), pp. 140–142.
20. G. Miles, C. C. Snow, and M. P. Sharfman, "Industry Variety and Performance," *Strategic Management Journal* (March 1993), pp. 163–177.
21. Porter, *Competitive Strategy*, p. 170.
22. K. J. Hatten and M. L. Hatten, "Strategic Groups, Asymmetrical Mobility Bar-

riers, and Contestability," *Strategic Management Journal* (July–August 1987), p. 329.
23. R. K. Reger and A. S. Huff, "Strategic Groups: A Cognitive Perspective," *Strategic Management Journal* (February 1993), pp. 103–124.
24. Porter, *Competitive Strategy,* pp. 133–134.
25. R. E. Miles and C. C. Snow, *Organizational Strategy, Structure, and Process* (New York: McGraw-Hill, 1978).
26. S. A. Zahra and J. A. Pearce II, "Research Evidence on the Miles–Snow Typology," *Journal of Management* (December 1990), pp. 751–768.
27. R. T. Pascale, "Perspective on Strategy: The Real Story Behind Honda's Success," *California Management Review* (Spring 1981), p. 70.
28. J. P. Herring, "Scientific and Technical Intelligence: The Key to R & D," *Journal of Business Strategy* (May/June 1993), pp. 10–12; J. P. Herring, "Business Intelligence in Japan and Sweden: Lessons for the United States," *Journal of Business Strategy* (March/April 1992), pp. 44–49.
29. D. C. Smith and J. E. Prescott, "Demystifying Competitive Analysis," *Planning Review* (September/October 1987), p. 13. For more in-depth information on the gathering of competitor intelligence, refer to the May/June 1989 issue of *Planning Review.*
30. C. Cox, "Planning in a Changing Environment: The Search for External Data," in *Handbook of Business Strategy, 1985/86 Yearbook,* edited by W. D. Guth (Boston: Warren, Gorham, and Lamont, 1985), p. 5.2.
31. J. C. Hyatt, "Avon Lady's Visit to Trash Dumpster Yields Court Accord," *Wall Street Journal* (March 19, 1991), p. A16; W. Zellner and B. Hager, "Dumpster Raids? That's Not Very Ladylike, Avon," *Business Week* (April 1, 1991), p. 32.
32. R. S. Teitelbaum, "The New Race for Intelligence," *Fortune* (November 2, 1992), p. 107.
33. S. P. Schnaars, "How to Develop and Use Scenarios," *Long Range Planning* (February 1987), p. 106.
34. H. E. Klein and R. E. Linneman, "Environmental Assessment: An International Study of Corporate Practices," *Journal of Business Strategy* (Summer 1984), p. 72.
35. S. Makridakis and S. C. Wheelwright, "Introduction to Management Forecasting," *Handbook of Forecasting* (New York: John Wiley & Sons, 1982), p. 8.
36. Ibid., p. 6.
37. P. J. H. Schoemaker, "Multiple Scenario Development: Its Conceptual and Behavioral Foundation," *Strategic Management Journal* (March 1993), p. 195.
38. For detailed information on Royal Dutch Shell's use of scenarios, see P. Schwartz, *The Art of the Long View: Planning for the Future in an Uncertain World* (Doubleday Currency, 1991). For other articles on scenario-writing, see the March/April and May/June, 1992 issues of *Planning Review.*
39. This process of scenario development is adapted from M. E. Porter, *Competitive Advantage,* (New York: Free Press, 1985), pp. 448–470.
40. For further information on forecasting, see S. Makridakis and S. C. Wheelwright, *Forecasting Methods for Management,* 5th ed. (New York: John Wiley & Sons, 1989).
41. Taken from B. Marsh, "Merchants Mobilize to Battle Wal-Mart in a Small Community," *Wall Street Journal* (June 5, 1991), pp. A1, A4; L. Pasquarella, "Study: Wal-Mart Has Varied Effects on Towns," *The (Ames, Iowa) Daily Tribune* (March 1, 1993), p. C13; R. Jost, "Wal-Mart's Early Fears of ISU Prof," *Des Moines Register* (January 7, 1991), p. 3B.

Internal Scanning and Analysis

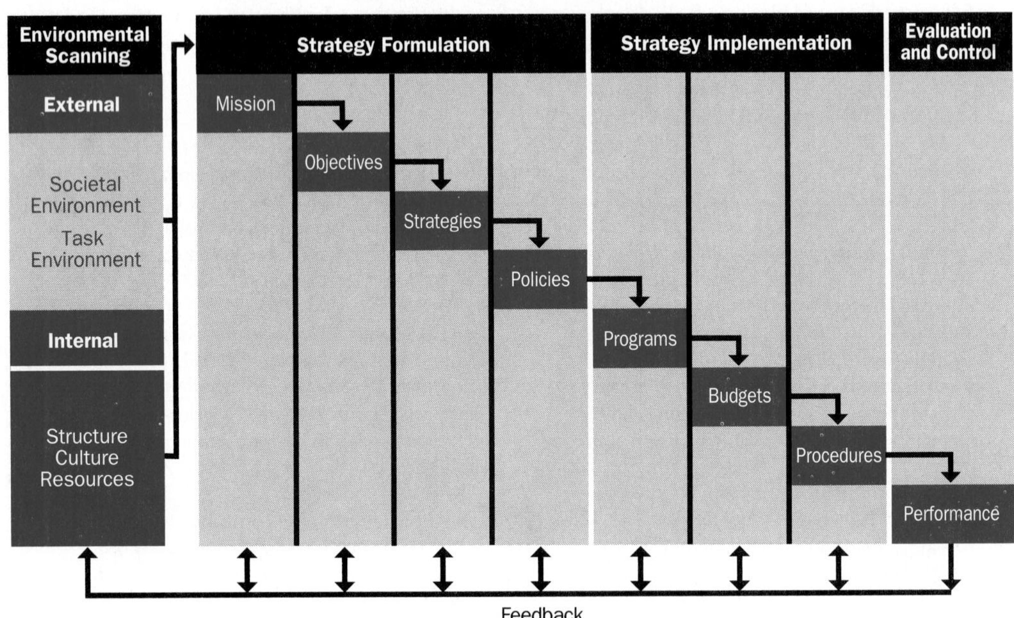

> *The study of sustained competitive advantage depends, in a critical way, on the resource endowments controlled by a firm.*[1]
> [Jay Barney]

A man stands before his mirror and, as he does several times a week, prepares to shave. After applying shaving cream, he deliberately shaves only one side of his face. He then changes razors to do the other side. He runs his fingers over his cheeks to check the closeness of the shave. "That's the only way to really compare shaves," he comments. This incident might be unusual if it weren't for the fact that the man is Alfred Zeien, Chairman and Chief Executive Officer of Gillette Company. Zeien routinely tests both his company's razors and those of his competition.

Gillette is obsessed with shaving and with making the best razors. It routinely spends large amounts of money on research and development. At any one time, Gillette is working on as many as 20 experimental razors. A promising prototype has been in process for four years and might not be ready for eight more. According to Chairman Zeien, "We're spending more than $1 million a year on that project, knowing that we can't launch till 2000 or 2001. That's assuming we'll overcome the technical barriers, and we're not sure that we can."

Why does this company spend so much time and money on a product so simple and mundane as a razor? It isn't some new electronic technology or an untested wonder drug. The answer lies in Gillette's dedication to being the best in its field. It was the leading brand in the 1920s, and it continues to be the leading brand in the 1990s. One reason is that Gillette's researchers have designed razors that are difficult for its competitors to copy. In the days of the double-edged razor, others could make blades that fit Gillette's, as well as their own, razors relatively easily. Trac II and other twin-blade razors changed things—rivals couldn't produce compatible cartridges quickly and easily. Gillette then spent ten years and $200 million to develop and perfect the hugely successful Sensor, a razor with twin blades that move independently. Since Sensor's introduction in 1989, no competitor has yet reproduced the Sensor design, partially because the manufacturing equipment needed to produce it is so expensive and complicated. Determined to sustain its competitive advantage, Gillette continues to invest in its research and development. The company is working on a Sensor II that will supersede the current Sensor. "That's one of the successes of the Japanese: They always have their next play in hand when making the current play," explained Scott Roberts, Gillette Vice-President.[2]

5.1 Resource-based View of the Firm[3]

In Chapter 4, we emphasized scanning and analyzing important variables in the corporation's external environment. Societal trends were monitored and forecasted. Important forces in the task environment were scrutinized to identify their impact on the level of competitive intensity in the firm's industry. The stages of industry evolution and the composition of strategic groups were examined so that strategic planners could better find undefended market niches that a firm could exploit with the right combination of price, quality, and service. The idea was to identify external strategic factors—opportunities and threats—that are likely to affect the future of the corporation. Although this information is essential to success, it isn't sufficient by itself to achieve that success.[4] Strategic managers must also look within the corporation to identify **internal strategic factors,** which are the strengths and weaknesses that may well determine whether the firm will be able to take advantage of opportunities while avoiding threats. Experts in the area, led by J. Barney and R. M. Grant, suggest that differences in performance among companies may be explained best, not through differences in industry structure identified by industry analysis, but through differences in corporate assets and resources and their application.[5]

Following this view that a company's sustained competitive advantage is primarily determined by its resource endowments, Grant proposes the following resource-based approach to strategy analysis (illustrated in Fig. 5.1).

FIGURE 5.1 **A Resource-Based Approach to Strategy Analysis**

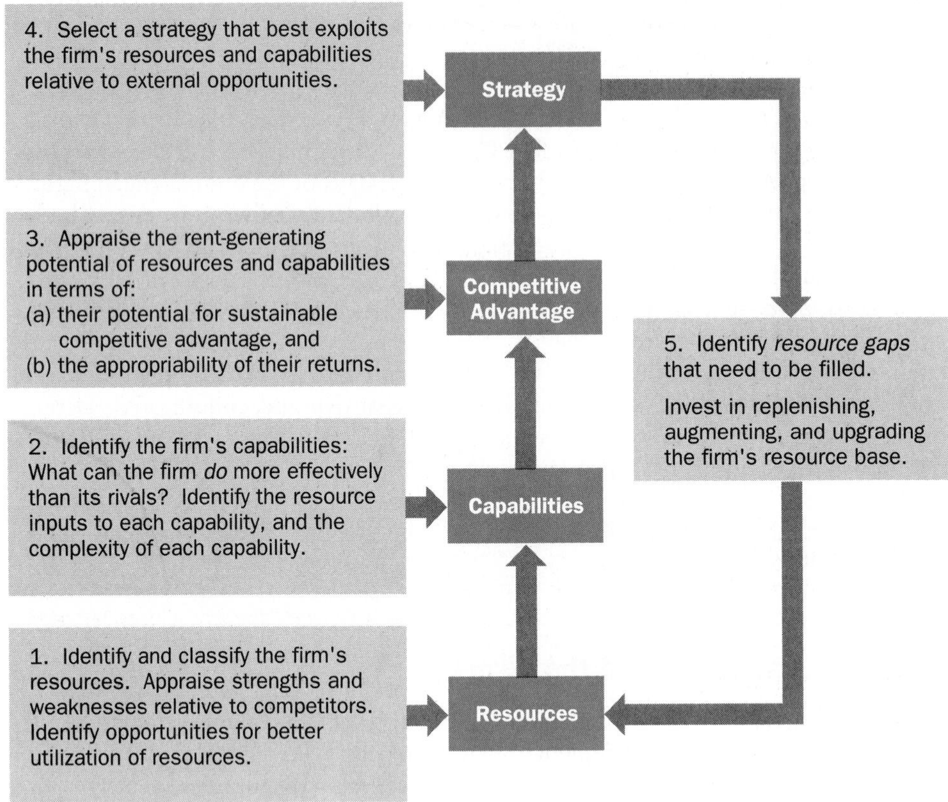

Source: R. M. Grant, "The Resource-Based Theory of Competitive Advantage: Implications for Strategy Formulation." Copyright © 1991 by The Regents of the University of California. Reprinted from the *California Management Review,* Vol. 33, No. 3. By permission of The Regents.

1. Identify and classify the firm's resources in terms of strengths and weaknesses.
2. Combine the firm's resources into specific capabilities. These are the company's **distinctive** or **core competencies** that are "the collective learning in the organization, especially how to coordinate diverse production skills and integrate multiple streams of technology."[6]
3. Appraise the rent-generating (profit) potential of these resources and capabilities in terms of their potential for sustainable competitive advantage and the appropriability of their returns (ability to harvest the profits resulting from the use of these resources and capabilities).
4. Select the strategy that best exploits the firm's resources and capabilities relative to external opportunities.
5. Identify resource gaps and invest in upgrading weaknesses.

Grant proposes in Step 2 that, when an organization's resources are combined, they form a number of capabilities. Capabilities are to the organization what skills are to the individual.[7] One example of such a capability is Procter & Gamble's development and use of the brand management concept as a way of managing its many consumer products. The concept encompasses various skills and resources that are integrated into a unique brand management capability. Although some competitors have hired brand managers from P&G, they have never been able to duplicate P&G's success with the concept. The Gillette example showed that the Gillette company has two identifiable resources: (1) the technology itself, and (2) the capability for developing and using new technological resources.

Grant further states in Step 3 that four characteristics of resources and capabilities are important in sustaining competitive advantage.

- **Durability:** The rate at which a firm's underlying resources and capabilities depreciate or become obsolete.
- **Transparency:** The speed with which other firms can understand the relationship of resources and capabilities supporting a successful firm's strategy. A capability that requires a complex pattern of various resources is more difficult to comprehend than a capability based on a single key resource.
- **Transferability:** The ability of competitors to gather the resources and capabilities necessary to support a competitive challenge. Duplicating another firm's primary resource of Rocky Mountain spring water may be difficult, especially if the imitator is located in Alabama. Some resources such as brand names may be impossible to transfer without purchasing them.
- **Replicability:** The ability of competitors to use resources and capabilities to duplicate a firm's success. As mentioned in the Procter & Gamble example, even if a competitor is able to hire brand managers away from P&G, it may still fail to duplicate P&G's success with the concept. The competitor may fail to identify less visible coordination mechanisms or fail to note that the behaviors of another company's brand managers may conflict with its own corporate culture.[8]

An organization's resources and capabilities may be placed on a continuum based on the extent to which they can be duplicated (i.e., are transparent, transferable, and replicable) by another firm. Figure 5.2 depicts this continuum. At one extreme are *slow-cycle resources,* which are durable and enduring because they are shielded by patents, geography, strong brand names, and the like. These resources and capabilities provide a sustainable competitive advantage. Gillette's Sensor razor is a good example of a product built around slow-cycle resources. At the other extreme are *fast-cycle resources,* which face tremendous imitation pressures because they are based on a concept or technology that can be easily duplicated, such as Sony's Walkman. To the extent that a company has fast-cycle resources, the primary way it can compete successfully is through increased speed from lab to marketplace. Otherwise, it has no real, sustainable competitive advantage.[9]

FIGURE 5.2 **Continuum of Resource Sustainability**

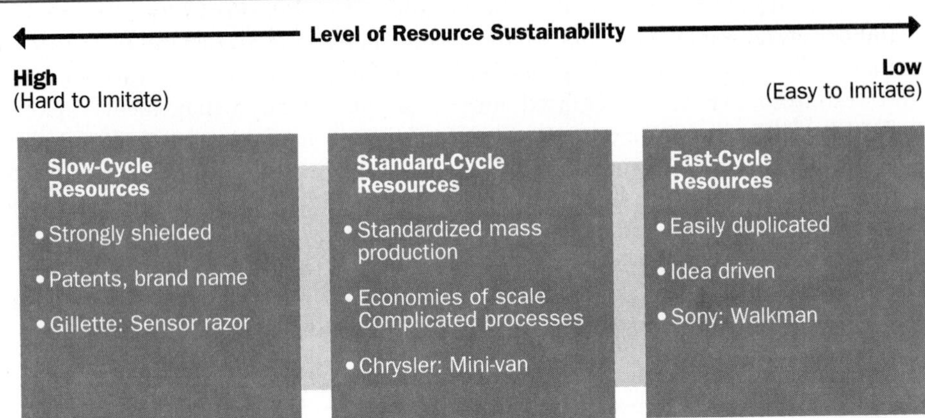

Source: Suggested by J. R. Williams, "How Sustainable Is Your Competitive Advantage?" *California Management Review* (Spring 1992), p. 33.

5.2 Approaches to Internal Scanning and Analysis

Strategic managers should identify the variables within their company that may be important strengths or weaknesses. A variable is a strength if it provides a competitive advantage. It is something the firm does or has the potential to do particularly well relative to the abilities of existing or potential competitors. A variable is a weakness if it is something the corporation does poorly or doesn't have the capacity to do although its competitors have that capacity. In evaluating the importance of these variables, management should ascertain whether they are **internal strategic factors**—a company's particular strengths and weaknesses that will help determine its future. One way of doing so is to compare measures of these variables with measures of (1) the company's past performance, (2) the company's key competitors, and (3) the industry as a whole. To the extent that a variable (such as a firm's financial situation) is significantly different from the firm's past, its key competitors, or the industry average, that variable is likely to be a strategic factor and should be considered in strategic decisions. Strategic managers can scan and analyze internal variables by following one or a combination of three distinct approaches: PIMS analysis, value chain analysis, and functional analysis.

PIMS Analysis

The Strategic Planning Institute is conducting research to help pinpoint relevant internal strategic factors for business corporations. The institute's Profit Impact of Market Strategy (PIMS) Program comprises various analyses of a data bank containing about 100 items of information on the strategic experiences of nearly 3,000 strategic business units of some 450 companies throughout North America and Europe, for periods ranging from 2 to 12 years. The research is aimed at discovering empirical "principles" that determine which strategy, under which conditions, produces what results in terms of return on investment and cash flows, regardless of the specific product or services. To date, PIMS research has identified nine major strategic factors that account for some 80% of the variation in profitability among the businesses in the database.[10] In working with these factors, the Strategic Planning Institute has prepared profiles of both high return on investment (ROI) companies and low ROI companies. They found that the companies with high rates of return had the following characteristics:

- Low investment intensity (the amount of fixed capital and working capital required to produce a dollar of sales);
- High market share;
- High relative product quality;
- High capacity utilization;
- High operating effectiveness (the ratio of actual to expected employee productivity); and
- Low direct costs per unit, relative to competition.[11]

These and other PIMS research findings are controversial. For example, PIMS research has consistently indicated that a large market share should lead to greater profitability.[12] The reason appears to be that high market share results in low unit costs because of economies of scale. Several studies have found, however, that high market share doesn't always lead to profitability. Some firms selling high-quality products (relative to the competition) are very profitable even though they do not have large market share.[13] The PIMS researchers respond that the single most important factor affecting a business unit's performance relative to its competitors' is the quality of its products or services. They also state that the market leader tends to have products of higher quality than those of its competitors and market followers.[14]

Value Chain Analysis

Value chain analysis, as proposed by Porter, is a way of examining the nature and extent of the synergies, if any, among the internal activities of a corporation. The systematic examination of individual activities can lead to a better understanding of a corporation's strengths and weaknesses. According to Porter, "Every firm is a collection of activities that are performed to design, produce, market, deliver, and support its product. All of these activities can be represented using a value chain (shown in Figure [5.3]). . . . Differences among competitor value chains are a key source of competitive advantage."[15]

First, examine the value chain of a particular product or service in terms of the various activities involved in its production or provision. As depicted in Fig. 5.3, Porter identifies five **primary activities** that usually occur in any business: (1) inbound logistics of raw materials, (2) operations, (3) outbound logistics of the finished goods, (4) marketing and sales, and (5) customer service. He also identifies four **support activities:** (1) the procurement process, (2) technology development,

FIGURE 5.3 **The Value Chain**

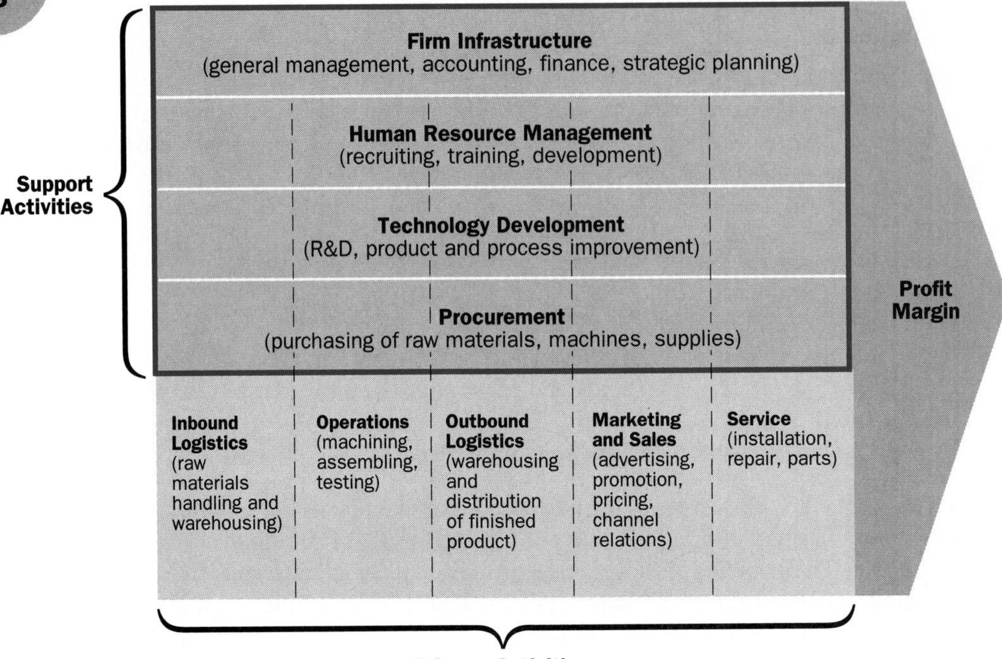

Source: Adapted/reprinted with the permission of The Free Press, an imprint of Simon & Schuster, from *Competitive Advantage: Creating and Sustaining Superior Performance* by Michael E. Porter, p. 37. Copyright © 1985 by Michael E. Porter.

(3) human resource management, and (4) the infrastructure of planning, accounting, finance, legal, government affairs, and quality management.

Second, examine the linkages among activities. **Linkages** are the connections between the way one activity is performed and the cost of performing another activity. In seeking ways to gain competitive advantage in the marketplace, a corporation can perform the same function in different ways with different results. For example, quality inspection of 100% of output by the workers themselves instead of the usual 10% by quality control inspectors might increase production costs. However, those additional costs may be more than offset by the savings obtained from the reduction in the number of repair people needed to fix defective products and the increase in the amount of salespeople's time devoted to selling instead of exchanging already sold, but defective, products.

Third, examine the potential synergies among products or business units. Not only does each value element, such as advertising or manufacturing, have an inherent economy of scale, in which activities are conducted at their lowest possible cost per unit of output, but economies of scope across elements as well. Such **economies of scope** result when the value chains of two separate products or services share activities, such as the same marketing channels or manufacturing facilities, and can be combined to reduce costs. For example, the cost of joint production of multiple products in the same plant can be less than the cost of production in separate plants. The same can be true of marketing.

Functional Analysis

One of the simplest ways to scan and analyze an organization's internal environment is through functional analysis. H. I. Ansoff, an authority on strategic management, suggests that a company's skills and resources can be organized into a *competence profile* according to the typical business functions of marketing, finance, research and development, and operations, among others.[16] Because of its simplicity and widespread use, functional analysis is a good way to begin the scanning and analysis of a corporation's internal environment.

5.3 Scanning the Internal Environment with Functional Analysis

Functional resources include not only the financial, physical, and human resources in each area of the corporation, but also the ability of the people in each area to formulate and implement—under corporate guidance—functional objectives, strategies, and policies. Thus the resources include both the knowledge of analytical concepts and procedural techniques common to each area and the ability of the people in each area to utilize them effectively. Used properly, these resources serve as strengths to support strategic decisions.

Structure

An understanding of how a particular corporation is structured is useful in strategy formulation. If the structure is compatible with a proposed change in strategy, it is a corporate strength. However, if the structure isn't compatible with either the present or proposed strategy, it is a definite corporate weakness and will keep the strategy from being implemented properly. Intel Corporation, for example, has had some problems because its successful growth strategy became incompatible with its centralized decision-making structure. The company grew too big and its markets too turbulent for the CEO, Andy Grove, to control it closely. Opportunities were in danger of being missed because of managers' dependence on Grove for guidance.

Although an almost infinite variety of structural forms are possible, certain basic types predominate in complex organizations. Figure 5.4 illustrates three basic structures. (The conglomerate structure is a variant of divisional structure and thus is not shown as a fourth structure.) Generally speaking, each structure tends to support some corporate strategies over others.[17]

- **Simple structure:** No functional or product categories; appropriate for a small, entrepreneur-dominated company with one or two product lines that operates in a reasonably small, easily identifiable market niche. Employees tend to be generalists and jacks-of-all-trades.

FIGURE 5.4 Basic Structures of Corporations

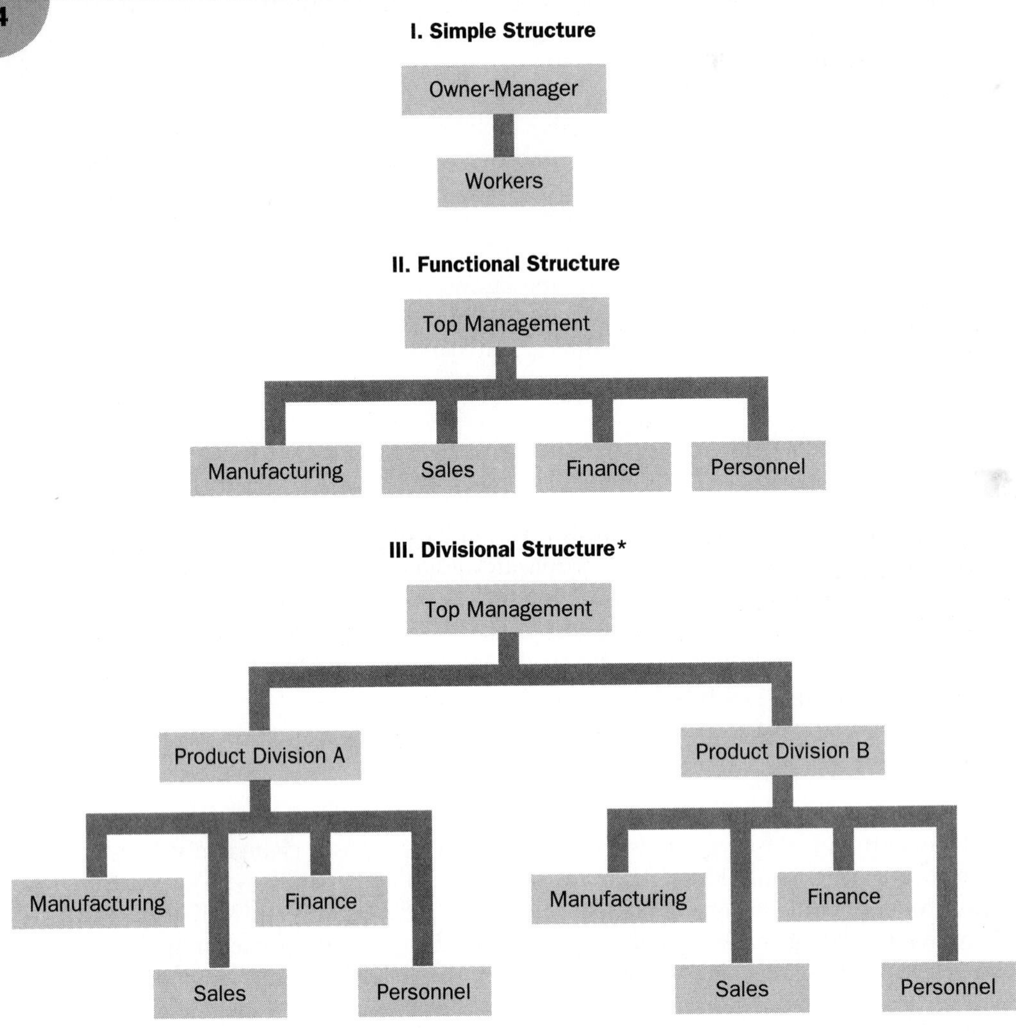

*Conglomerate structure is a variant of the divisional structure.

- **Functional structure:** Appropriate for a medium-sized firm with several product lines in one industry. Employees tend to be specialists in the business functions important to that industry, such as manufacturing, marketing, finance, and human resources.
- **Divisional structure:** Appropriate for a large corporation with many product lines in several related industries. Employees tend to be functional specialists organized according to product or market distinctions. General Motors, for

example, groups its various auto lines into the separate divisions of Chevrolet, Pontiac, Oldsmobile, Buick, and Cadillac. Management attempts to find some synergy among divisional activities through the use of committees and horizontal linkages.

- **Conglomerate structure:** Appropriate for a large corporation with many product lines in several unrelated industries. A variant of the divisional structure, the conglomerate structure (sometimes called a holding company), is typically an assemblage of legally independent firms (subsidiaries) operating under one corporate umbrella but controlled through the subsidiaries' boards of directors. The unrelated nature of the subsidiaries prevents any attempt at gaining synergy among them.

If the current structure of a corporation does not easily support a strategy under consideration, top management must decide whether the proposed strategy is feasible or whether the structure should be changed to a more complex structure such as the SBU, matrix, or network. We present additional information regarding such complex structures in Chapter 8.

Culture

Corporate culture is the collection of beliefs, expectations, and values learned and shared by a corporation's members and transmitted from one generation of employees to the next.[18] It generally reflects the values of the founder(s) and the mission of the firm. It gives a company a sense of identity: "This is who we are. This is what we do. This is what we stand for." The culture includes the dominant orientation of the company, such as research and development at Hewlett-Packard, customer service at Nordstrom, or product quality at Maytag.

Corporate culture fulfills several important functions in an organization.

1. Culture conveys a sense of identity for employees.
2. Culture helps generate employees' commitment to something greater than themselves.
3. Culture adds to the stability of the organization as a social system.
4. Culture serves as a frame of reference for employees to use to make sense out of organizational activities and to use as a guide for appropriate behavior.[19]

Corporate culture shapes the behavior of people in the corporation. Because the culture has a powerful influence on the behavior of managers at all levels, it can affect greatly a corporation's ability to shift its strategic direction. A strong culture not only should promote survival, but should also create the basis for a superior competitive position.[20] To the extent that a unique capability is embedded in an organization's culture, a competitor will be hard-pressed to duplicate it.[21] The Company Spotlight: Maytag Corporation feature on page 124 explains how corporate culture affects Maytag's strategic managers.

Thus managers' understanding of a corporation's (or division's) culture is imperative if the firm is to be managed strategically. An organization's culture can produce a **strategic myopia,** in which strategic managers fail to perceive the significance of changing external conditions because they are partially blinded by

In 1993, the Maytag Corporation still reflected the strong ideas of Maytag Company founder F. L. Maytag. The corporate headquarters were housed on the second floor of a relatively small and modest building. Built in 1961, the Newton, Iowa, building also housed Maytag Company administrative offices on the first floor. Responding to a comment from outside observers that the corporation had "spartan" offices, Leonard Hadley, then Chief Operating Officer, looked around at his rather small, windowless office and said, "See for yourself. We want to keep corporate staff to a minimum." Hadley felt that the headquarters' location, coupled with the fact that most of the corporate officers had originally been with the Maytag Company, resulted in an overall top management concern for product quality and financial conservatism.

Culture as a Key Strength

When asked to discuss specific resources that gave the corporation a competitive edge, past Chairman and CEO Daniel Krumm pointed to the firm's roots and focused on dedication to quality above corporate perquisites:

> *That, of course, has been Maytag's hallmark for as long as any of us can remember. We believe quality and reliability are, ultimately, what the consumer wants. That has been a challenge to us as we have acquired companies that may have had a different emphasis, but we have made significant recent strides in improving the quality of all our products.*

strongly held common beliefs. In this instance, a strongly held corporate culture can become a major deterrent to success at a time when the corporation most needs to change its strategic direction.[22] Such was the case at IBM during the 1980s, when the company's dedication to mainframe computers prevented managers from emphasizing personal computers.

A change in mission, objectives, strategies, or policies is not likely to be successful if it goes against the firm's accepted culture. Foot-dragging and even sabotage may result, as employees fight to resist a radical change in corporate philosophy and direction. Like structure, if an organization's culture is compatible with a new strategy, it is an internal strength. But if the corporate culture is not compatible with the proposed strategy, it is a serious weakness. (We present additional information regarding corporate culture and techniques to change it in Chapter 8).

Marketing

The major task of a marketing manager is to influence the level, timing, and character of demand in a way that will help the corporation achieve its objectives.[23] The marketing manager is the company's primary link to the customer and the competition and must therefore be especially concerned with the firm's market position and marketing mix.

TABLE 5.1 Marketing Mix Variables

Product	Place	Promotion	Price
Quality	Channels	Advertising	List price
Features	Coverage	Personal selling	Discounts
Options	Locations	Sales promotion	Allowances
Style	Inventory	Publicity	Payment periods
Brand name	Transport		Credit terms
Packaging			
Sizes			
Services			
Warranties			
Returns			

Source: Philip Kotler, *Marketing Management: Analysis, Planning, and Control,* 4th ed. (Englewood Cliffs, N.J.: Prentice-Hall, 1980), p. 89. Copyright © 1980. Reprinted by permission of Prentice-Hall, Inc.

Market Position and Segmentation

Market position answers the question, "Who are our customers?" It refers to the selection of specific areas for marketing concentration and may be expressed in terms of market, product, and geographic locations. Through market research, corporations practice **market segmentation** with various products or services to help managers discover what niches to seek, which new types of products to develop, and how to ensure that a company's many products do not directly compete with one another. The use of segmentation marketing to identify potential customers clearly improves financial performance.[24]

Marketing Mix

Marketing mix refers to the particular combination of key variables under the corporation's control that it can use to affect demand and to gain competitive advantage. These variables are *product, place, promotion,* and *price.* Each variable can be subdivided into several subvariables, listed in Table 5.1, which should be analyzed in terms of their effects on divisional and corporate performance.

Product Life Cycle

One of the most useful concepts in marketing insofar as strategic management is concerned is that of the product life cycle. As depicted in Fig. 5.5, the **product life cycle** is a graph showing time plotted against sales as a product moves from introduction through growth and maturity to decline. This concept enables a marketing manager to examine the marketing mix of a particular product or group of products in terms of its life-cycle position. Although marketing people agree that different products have different-shaped life cycles, consideration of product life cycle is an important factor in strategy formulation.[25]

FIGURE 5.5

The Product Life Cycle

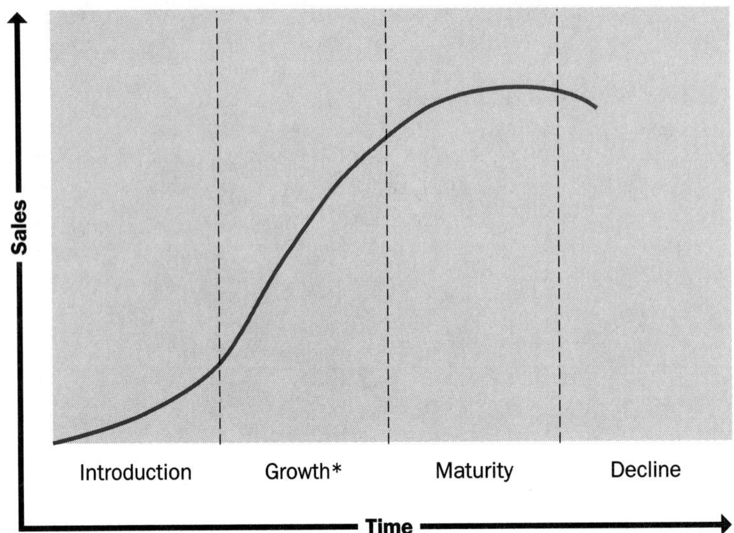

*The right end of the Growth stage is often called Competitive Turbulence because of price and distribution competition that shakes out the weaker competitors. For further information, see C. R. Wasson, *Dynamic Competitive Strategy and Product Life Cycles,* 3rd ed. (Austin, Tex.: Austin Press, 1978).

Finance

The job of the financial manager is to manage funds. The financial manager ascertains the best sources and uses of funds and controls their use. Cash must be raised from internal or external sources and allocated for different uses. The flow of funds to operations of the organization must be monitored. Benefits, in the form of returns, repayments, or products and services, must be given to the sources of outside financing. In handling these tasks, the financial manager must complement and support overall corporate strategy.

Financial Leverage

From a strategic point of view, the financial area should be analyzed to see how well it handles funds. The mix of externally generated short-term and long-term funds in relation to the amount and timing of internally generated funds should be appropriate to corporate objectives, strategies, and policies. The concept of **financial leverage** (the ratio of total debt to total assets) is useful in descriptions of the use of debt to increase the earnings available to holders of common stock.[26] Financing activities by selling bonds or notes instead of by issuing stock boosts earnings per share: the interest paid on the debt reduces taxable income, but the same number of shareholders receive the profits through higher share prices and/or dividends. However, the debt raises the firm's break-even point above what it would have been if the firm had financed internally. High leverage may therefore be perceived as a corporate strength in times of prosperity and ever-increasing sales or as a weakness in times of a recession and falling sales. The reason is that leverage magnifies the effect of an increase or decrease in dollar sales on earnings per share.

Capital Budgeting

The knowledge and use of capital budgeting techniques are important financial resources. The finance department should analyze and rank possible investments in fixed assets such as land, buildings, and equipment in terms of additional outlays required and additional receipts that will result. Then it can rank investment proposals on the basis of some accepted criterion or **hurdle rate,** which may include years to pay back investment, rate of return, or time to break-even point and make its decisions. To select acquisition candidates and to analyze the amount of risk present in a corporation's portfolio of business units, financial analysts also should be able to utilize analytical techniques such as the Capital Asset Pricing Model (CAPM) and the Arbitrage Pricing Model (APM).[27]

The financial manager must be knowledgeable of these and other more sophisticated analytical techniques if management is successfully to implement functional strategies, such as internal financing or leveraged buy outs (discussed in Chapter 7).

Research and Development

A corporation's technology helps define its market niche and the type of competition it faces.[28] The R&D manager is responsible for suggesting and implementing a company's technological strategy in light of its corporate objectives and policies. The manager's job therefore involves (1) choosing among alternative new technologies to use within the corporation, (2) developing methods of embodying the new technology in new products and processes, and (3) deploying resources so that the new technology can be successfully implemented.[29]

R&D Mix

The term research and development is used to describe a wide range of activities. In some corporations scientists conduct **basic R&D** in well-equipped laboratories, concentrating on theoretical problem areas. The best indicators of a company's capability in this area are its patents and research publications.[30] In other firms, experts conduct **product R&D,** concentrating on improving products or product packaging. The best measurements of ability in this area are the number of successful new products introduced and the percentage of total sales and profits coming from products introduced within the past five years. In still other firms, engineers conduct **engineering** or **process R&D,** concentrating on improving quality control, design specifications, and production equipment. A company's capability in this area is best measured by consistent reductions in unit manufacturing costs and product defects. Most large corporations have a mix of basic, product, and process R&D, which varies by industry, company, and product line. The balance of these types of research is known as the **R&D mix** and should be appropriate to the strategy being considered and to each product's life cycle. For example, product R&D normally dominates the early stages of a product's life cycle (when the product's optimal form and features are still being debated), whereas process R&D becomes especially important in the later stages (when the product's design has been solidified and the emphasis is on reducing costs and improving quality).[31]

Technological Competence

A company's R&D unit should be evaluated for technological competence in both the development and use of innovative technology. Not only should the corporation make a consistent research effort (as measured by reasonably constant corporate expenditures that result in usable innovations), but it also should be proficient in managing research personnel and integrating their innovations into its day-to-day operations. If a company isn't proficient in **technology transfer,** the process of taking a new technology from the laboratory to the marketplace, it will not gain much advantage from technological advances. Both American Telephone and Telegraph (AT&T) and Xerox Corporation have been criticized for their inability to translate the research, ideas, and innovations developed in their sophisticated R&D facilities (AT&T's Bell Labs and Xerox's Palo Alto Research Center) into improved products and services. The Strategy in Action on page 129 describes a problem in technology transfer at Xerox. (We discuss the impact of technology on strategic management in more detail in Chapter 12.)

Operations (Manufacturing or Service)

The primary task of the manufacturing or service manager is to develop and operate a system that will produce the required number of products or services—with a certain quality, at a given cost, and within an allotted time. Many of the same concepts and techniques popularly used in manufacturing may be applied to service businesses.[32] In general terms, manufacturing can be intermittent or continuous. In **intermittent systems** (job shops), workers normally process an item sequentially, but the work and sequence of the process vary by item. At each location, the tasks determine the details of processing and the time required for them. In contrast, **continuous systems** are those laid out as lines on which products can be continuously assembled or processed, such as an automobile assembly line.

The type of manufacturing system used determines divisional or corporate strategy. For example, planning to increase sales by saturating the market with low-priced products makes no sense if the company's manufacturing process was designed as an intermittent *job shop* system that produces one-time-only products to a customer's specifications. Conversely, planning to produce several specialty products might not be economically feasible if the manufacturing process was designed to be a mass-producing, continuous system using low-skilled labor or special purpose robots.

Operating Leverage

Continuous systems are popular because they allow a company to take advantage of manufacturing operating leverage. According to J. F. Weston and T. E.

A PROBLEM IN TECHNOLOGY TRANSFER AT XEROX CORPORATION

Strategy in Action

In the mid 1970s, Xerox Corporation's Palo Alto Research Center (PARC) had developed a new type of computer with some innovative features, called Alto. Although Alto was supposed to be a research prototype, it became so popular among PARC personnel that some researchers began to develop Alto as a commercial product. Unfortunately, this action brought PARC into direct conflict with Xerox's product development group, which at the same time was developing a rival machine called the Star. Because the Star was being worked on in accordance with the company's official product development strategy, top management ignored Alto and focused on the Star.

In 1979, Steve Jobs, co-founder of Apple Computer, Inc., made a now-legendary tour of the normally secretive PARC. Researchers demonstrated the Alto for Jobs. Unlike the computers that Apple was then building, Alto had the power of a minicomputer. Its user-friendly software generated crisp text and bright graphics. Jobs fell in love with the machine. He promptly asked Apple's engineers to duplicate the look and feel of Alto. The result was the Macintosh—a personal computer that soon revolutionized the industry.

Source: J. D. Hunger, T. L. Conquest, and W. Miller, "Xerox Corporation: Proposed Diversification," in *Cases in Strategic Management*, 3rd ed., edited by T. L. Wheelen and J. D. Hunger (Reading, Mass.: Addison-Wesley, 1990), pp. 142–143; J. W. Verity, "Rethinking the Computer," *Business Week* (November 26, 1990), p. 116.

Copeland, **operating leverage** is the impact of a specific change in sales volume on net operating income.[33] For example, a highly labor-intensive firm has little automated machinery and thus a small amount of fixed costs. It has a fairly low break-even point, but its variable cost line has a relatively steep slope. Because most of the costs associated with the product are variable (many employees earn piece-rate wages), its variable costs are higher than those of automated firms. Its advantage over other firms is that it can operate at low levels and still be profitable. When sales reach and exceed break-even, however, the high variable costs as a percentage of total costs keep the profit per unit relatively low. Its low operating leverage thus prevents the firm from gathering the large profits possible from a high volume of sales. In terms of strategy, this firm should look for a niche in the marketplace for which it can produce and sell a reasonably small quantity of goods.

In contrast, a capital-intensive firm has a lot of money in fixed investments, such as automated processes and highly sophisticated machinery. Its relatively small but highly skilled labor force, earns salaries rather than piece-rate wages.

Consequently, this firm has high fixed costs. It also has a relatively high break-even point, but its variable cost line rises slowly. When it reaches and exceeds break-even, its profits rise faster than do those of less automated firms with its high operating leverage making it extremely profitable and competitive. In terms of strategy, this firm needs to find a high-demand niche in the marketplace for which it can produce and sell a large quantity of goods. Changes in the level of sales magnify (leverage) profits. However, this type of firm is likely to suffer huge losses during a recession. During an economic downturn, the firm with less automation and thus less leverage is more likely to survive comfortably because a drop in sales primarily affects variable costs. Laying off workers often is easier than selling off specialized plants and machines.

The operations of a service business can also be continuous or intermittent. Continuous operations describe the provision of fairly similar services (such as a hospital's providing allergy shots or blood tests), whereas intermittent operations describe somewhat variable services (such as organ transplants). To benefit from operating leverage, service firms that use continuous operations might be able to substitute diagnostic machinery, videotape machines, or support workers for highly paid professional personnel.

Experience Curve

A conceptual framework that many large corporations have used successfully is the experience curve (originally called the learning curve). As it applies to manufacturing, the **experience curve** concept holds that unit production costs decline by some fixed percentage (commonly 20%–30%) each time the total accumulated volume of production (in units) doubles. The actual percentage varies by industry and is based on many variables: the amount of time for a person to learn a new task, economies of scale, product and process improvements, and lower raw materials costs, among others. For example, in an industry with an 85% experience curve, a corporation might expect a 15% reduction in costs for every doubling of volume. Hence the total costs per unit (adjusted for inflation) can be expected to drop from $100 when the total production is 10 units to $85 ($100 × 85%) when production increases to 20 units to $72.25 ($85 × 85%) when it reaches 40 units.[34] Achieving these results often means investing in R&D and fixed assets, with higher operating leverage and less flexibility. Nevertheless, the manufacturing strategy is to build capacity ahead of demand, in order to achieve the lower unit costs expected from the experience curve. Then, on the basis of some future point on the experience curve, the company could price the product or service low to preempt competition and increase market demand. The resulting high number of units sold and high market share should result in high profits, based on the low unit costs.[35] This idea of using the experience curve to price low—to gain high market share and thus high profits—underlies the Boston Consulting Group's portfolio matrix (discussed in Chapter 6).

Management commonly uses the experience curve to estimate the production costs of (1) a product never before made with existing equipment and processes or (2) current products made with newly introduced equipment or processes. The airframe industry first applied the concept which also may be applied in the service industry. Although many firms have used experience curves extensively, unquestioning acceptance of the industry norm (such as 80% for the airframe industry or 70% for integrated circuits) is risky. The experience curve of the industry as a whole might not hold true for a particular company for a variety of reasons.

Flexible Manufacturing

Recently, the use of large mass-production facilities to take advantage of experience curve economies has been criticized. The use of computer-assisted design and computer-assisted manufacturing (CAD/CAM) and robot technology means that learning times are shorter and products can be manufactured economically in small, customized batches. **Economies of scope** (in which common parts of the value chains of various products are combined to gain manufacturing economies even though small numbers of each product are made) replace **economies of scale** (in which unit costs are reduced by making large numbers of the same product) in flexible manufacturing.[36] The new flexible factories permit a low-volume output of custom-tailored products to produce a profit. Thus having both the cost advantages of continuous systems and the customer-oriented advantages of intermittent systems is possible.[37]

Human Resources

The primary task of the manager of human resources is to improve the match between individuals and jobs. The quality of this match influences job performance, employee satisfaction, and employee turnover.[38] A good HRM department should know how to use attitude surveys and other feedback devices to assess employees' satisfaction with their jobs and with the corporation as a whole. Human resource departments also should use job analysis. **Job analysis** is a means of obtaining job-description information about what needs to be accomplished by each job in terms of quality and quantity. Up-to-date job descriptions based on sound job analysis are essential for proper employee selection, appraisal, training, and development; wage and salary administration; labor negotiations, and summarizing corporationwide human resources in terms of employee-skill categories. Just as a company must know the number, type, and quality of its manufacturing facilities, it must also know the kinds of people it employs and the skills they possess. The best strategies are meaningless if employees do not have the skills to carry them out or if jobs cannot be designed to accommodate the available workers. Hewlett-Packard, for example, uses employee profiles to ensure that it has the right mix of talents for implementing its planned strategies.[39]

Use of Teams

Strategic managers are beginning to realize that the company must be flexible in utilizing employees. Human resource managers therefore need to be knowledgeable about options such as part-time work, job sharing, flextime, extended leaves, contract work, and especially the proper use of teams. About one in five U.S. companies are successfully using autonomous or self-directed work teams in which a group of people work together without a supervisor to plan, coordinate, and evaluate their own work.[40] Productivity and quality increased to such an extent at Northern Telecom that it was able to reduce the number of quality inspectors by 40%.[41]

As a way to move a product more quickly through its development stage, companies such as Motorola, Chrysler, NCR, Boeing, and General Electric have begun using cross-functional work teams. Instead of developing products in a series of steps—beginning with a request from sales and proceeding sequentially through design, engineering, and on to purchasing, and finally to manufacturing (often resulting in customer rejection of a costly product)—companies are tearing down the traditional walls separating departments so that people from each discipline can get involved in projects at the start. In a process called **concurrent engineering,** once-isolated specialists now work side by side and compare notes constantly to design cost-effective products with features customers want.[42] The Strategy in Action on page 133 indicates how Boeing utilized teams.

Union Relations

If the corporation is unionized, the HR manager should be able to work closely with the union. Although private-sector union membership in the United States has dropped to 11.9% in 1992 from 23.3% in 1977, unions still represent nearly 24% of workers in manufacturing in the United States.[43] (Government-sector union membership raises the 1992 overall total to 16.1%.) However, the average proportion of unionized workers among 17 other major industrialized nations actually increased from 48% in 1970 to 53% in 1987.[44] These developments have significant implications for the management of multinational corporations. To save jobs, U.S. unions are increasingly willing to support employee involvement programs designed to increase worker participation in decision making.[45]

Quality of Work Life

Human resource departments have found that to reduce employee dissatisfaction and unionization efforts (or, conversely, to improve employee satisfaction and existing union relations), they must consider the quality of work life (QWL) in the design of jobs.[46] Partially a reaction to the traditionally heavy emphasis on technical and economic factors in job design, QWL emphasizes the human dimension of work. In general, quality of work life is "the degree to which members of a work organization are able to satisfy important personal needs through their experiences in the organization."[47] Human resource managers therefore should be able to improve the corporation's quality of work life by (1) introducing participative problem solving, (2) restructuring work, (3) introducing innovative reward systems, and (4) improving the work environment. Such improvements should lead to a more participative corporate culture and thus higher productivity and quality products.

An organization's human resources are especially important in today's world of global communication and transportation systems. Competitors around the

USING CROSS-FUNCTIONAL WORK TEAMS AT BOEING

Strategy in Action

When Grace Robertson was selected to take on the challenge of designing and building a new version of the Boeing 767 in 33 months, she thought the task was impossible. Such a task normally took 42 months. In order to get an order for 30 planes from United Parcel Service, Boeing had been forced to guarantee early delivery *and* lower price. To meet this challenge, Robertson gathered all 400 employees who were to work on the new plane into one location and organized them into cross-functional work teams. By combining people from the design, planning, manufacturing, and tooling sectors, the teams were able to improve communication and avoid rework—thus speeding up development and cutting costs. So far, Robinson's team concept seems to be working. The development group is on schedule and on budget.

Source: D. J. Yang, "Grace Robertson: Piloting a Superfast Rollout at Boeing," *Business Week* (August 30, 1993), p. 77.

world copy advances in technology almost immediately. People, however, are not as willing to move to other companies in other countries. Porter, among others, suggests therefore that the only long-term resource advantage remaining to corporations operating in the industrialized nations lies in the area of skilled human resources.[48]

Information Systems

The primary task of the manager of information systems (IS) is to design and manage the flow of information in an organization in ways that improve productivity and decision making. Information must be collected, stored, and synthesized in such a manner that it will answer important operating and strategic questions. The importance of this function is growing rapidly.

A corporation's information system can be either a strength or a weakness in all three aspects of strategic management. It not only can aid in environmental scanning and in controlling a company's many activities, but it also can be a strategic weapon in gaining competitive advantage. For example, American Hospital Supply (AHS), a leading manufacturer and distributor of a broad line of products for doctors, laboratories, and hospitals, has developed an order-entry distribution system that directly links the majority of its customers to AHS computers. The system has been successful because it simplifies ordering processes for the customer, reduces costs for both AHS and the customer, and allows AHS to provide pricing incentives to the customer. As a result, customer loyalty is high and AHS has a dominant share of the market.

Purposes

An information system can fulfill four major purposes.

- It can provide early warning signals of problems that originate both externally and internally. An information system has a database, which, like a library, collects, categorizes, and files data for use by employees in every department.
- It can automate routine clerical operations. Payroll, inventory reports, and other records can be generated automatically from the database and thus reduce the need for file clerks.
- It can assist all levels of managers in making routine (programmed) decisions. Scheduling orders, assigning orders to machines, and reordering supplies are routine tasks that can be automated through a detailed analysis of the company's work flow.
- It can provide the information necessary for management to make strategic (nonprogrammed) decisions. Increasingly, managers are using personal computers coupled with sophisticated software to analyze large amounts of information and calculate likely payoffs from alternative strategies. The best results are obtained from decision-support systems that allow easy computer–user interaction.[49]

Phases of Development

In assessing a corporation's strengths and weaknesses, the analyst should note the level of development of the firm's information system. Research conducted by M.I.T.'s Sloan School of Management (sponsored by Arthur Anderson & Co. and others) identified four distinct phases of information system development.

In **Phase One,** companies use information systems to improve the efficiency of existing businesses through customer billing, data entry, and report writing. In this phase the IS helps companies save money but cannot yet be used for competitive advantage. For example, American Airlines first installed its Sabre computerized reservation system to keep better track of available seats on its flights.

In **Phase Two,** companies attempt to differentiate themselves from their competitors by using their installed IS to introduce new, electronically delivered products and services to *existing* customers. During this phase, American Airlines connected its Sabre system to travel agents' offices. Because this action made reservations easier for agents, American's ticket sales increased.

In **Phase Three,** companies attempt to sell new information-based products and services to *new* customers. In this phase, American Airlines opened its Sabre system to competing airlines. It not only gained revenues from processing other airlines' tickets, it further increased its own ticket sales.

In **Phase Four,** firms develop new, innovative information-based products and services on an ongoing basis. During this phase, American Airlines began selling information gathered from travel agents on Sabre. American used its database on fliers for its Advantage program by tracking their mileage and offering free flights for specific amounts of mileage on American flights. According to John Sifonis, an information technology strategist who directed Arthur Young's participation in the M.I.T. program, the fourth phase is the hardest to achieve: "Success in the fourth phase requires a continuing investment in information systems and a constant commitment to innovation in products and services."[50]

5.4 Synthesis of Internal Strategic Factors—IFAS

After scanning the internal organizational environment and identifying strategic factors for the corporation, strategic managers may summarize their analysis on a form such as the one shown in Table 5.2, entitled Internal Strategic Factors Analysis Summary (IFAS). It helps managers to organize internal strategic factors into generally accepted categories of strengths and weaknesses. It also aids in the analysis of how well management is responding to these specific factors in light of their perceived importance to the company. Use of the IFAS form involves the following steps.

First, identify and list in Column 1 about 5 to 10 strengths and about the same number of weaknesses. *Second,* assign a **weight** in Column 2 to each factor from 1.0 (most important) to 0.0 (not important) based on that factor's probable impact on the company's strategic position. (*All weights must sum to 1.0* regardless of the number of strategic factors.) *Third,* assign a **rating** in Column 3 to each factor from 5 (outstanding) to 1 (poor) based on management's current response to that particular factor. Each rating is a judgment about how well the analyst believes the company's management is currently dealing with each internal factor.

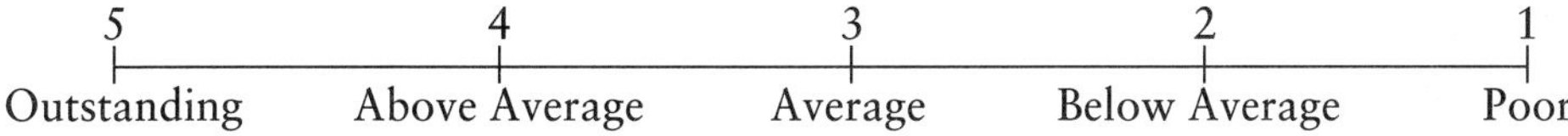

Fourth, multiply the weight (Column 2) for each factor by its rating (Column 3) to obtain that factor's **weighted score** in Column 4. *Fifth,* use Column 5 (comments) to note why a particular factor was selected and how its weight and rating were estimated. *Sixth,* add the weighted scores for all the internal factors in Column 4 to determine the total weighted score for that particular company. The **total weighted score** indicates how well the company is responding to current and expected strategic factors in its internal environment. The total weighted score can range from 5.0 (outstanding) to 1.0 (poor), with 3.0 being average. Management can use this score to compare the firm to other firms in its industry. In essence, the IFAS summary is your analysis of a company's management of the key internal strategic factors based on a prioritized listing (using weights).

Table 5.2 shows some internal strategic factors for Maytag Corporation, along with corresponding weights, ratings, and the total weighted score. Thus it is similar to Table 4.3 (EFAS) on which external strategic factors are summarized. If you do a similar IFAS analysis of each company in an industry, then you are able

TABLE 5.2 **Internal Strategic Factor Analysis Summary (IFAS): Maytag as Example**

Internal Strategic Factors (1)	Weight (2)	Rating (3)	Weighted Score (4)	Comments (5)
Strengths				
• Quality Maytag culture	.15	5	.75	Quality key to success
• Experienced top management	.05	4	.20	Know appliances
• Vertical integration	.10	4	.40	Dedicated factories
• Employee relations	.05	3	.15	Good, but deteriorating
• Hoover's international orientation	.15	3	.45	Hoover name in cleaners
Weaknesses				
• Process-oriented R&D	.05	2	.10	Slow on new products
• Distribution channels	.05	2	.10	Superstores replacing small dealers
• Financial position	.15	2	.30	High debt load
• Global positioning	.20	2	.40	Hoover weak outside the United Kingdom and Australia
• Manufacturing facilities	.05	4	.20	Investing now
Total	1.00		3.05	

Notes:

1. List strengths and weaknesses (5–10 each) in Column 1.
2. Weight each factor from 1.0 (Most Important) to 0.0 (Not Important) in Column 2 based on that factor's probable impact on the company's strategic position. **The total weights must sum to 1.00.**
3. Rate each factor from 5 (Outstanding) to 1 (Poor) in Column 3 based on the company's response to that factor.
4. Multiply each factor's weight times its rating to obtain each factor's weighted score in Column 4.
5. Use Column 5 (comments) for rationale used for each factor.
6. Add the weighted scores to obtain the total weighted score for the company in Column 4. This tells how well the company is responding to the strategic factors in its internal environment.

Source: T. L. Wheelen and J. D. Hunger, "Internal Strategic Factor Analysis Summary (IFAS)." Copyright © 1991 by Wheelen and Hunger Associates. Reprinted by permission.

to develop a ranking of the companies in that industry based on their management of the *internal* strategic factors.

After strategic managers have completed their analysis of a firm's internal strategic factors in terms of strengths and weaknesses, they must then analyze these factors in light of the corporation's previously considered external strategic factors. This overall situation analysis is the topic covered next in Chapter 6.

In Conclusion . . .

An organization's distinctive competencies may be integrated through a corporation's culture in such a way that another firm cannot easily imitate them without achieving the very dynamics underlying the culture itself—something that it is almost impossible to do. For example, the key to Walt Disney Productions' competitive advantage has always been the vision and determination of the company's founder. Walt Disney's force of personality and obsession with perfection were essential in building Walt Disney Productions and the source of its corporate culture. Even though the company expanded from simple cartoons into theme parks and hotels, Walt Disney had always pointed to animation (and especially to Mickey Mouse, his personal creation) as a principal factor in the company's success. One of his favorite expressions was, "Remember, it all started with a mouse." Others have evaluated his influence on the company as both good and bad. Some attributed his obsession with perfection as the reason the company stayed creative and original. Some viewed his dominant personality as stifling and inhibiting to those who worked for and with him.

Even in 1992, long after Walt Disney died, his vision still dominated the company. Jeffrey Katzenberg, the man in charge of Disney Studios, reaffirmed the founder's wisdom when he commented, "Animation films represent the heart and soul of the company. It's the blood that flows through this world-wide enterprise."[51]

Points to Remember

- According to the resource-based view of the firm, a company's sustained competitive advantage is determined primarily by its resources. The four characteristics of a company's resources and capabilities that determine sustainability are durability, transparency, transferability, and replicability.
- Analysts may scan and analyze a firm's resources using PIMS analysis, value chain analysis, or functional analysis. Although functional analysis is the preferred method in this book, many analysts recommend the closely related method, value chain analysis.
- In functional analysis, analysts scan an organization's internal resources and capabilities by examining the strengths and weaknesses in its structure and culture, marketing, finance, research and development, operations, human resources, and information systems. Employees in the functional areas not only should have an in-depth knowledge of analytical concepts and procedures, but they also should know how to apply them effectively to achieve competitive advantage.
- The EFAS and IFAS tables at the end of Chapters 4 and 5 help strategic managers summarize their analyses of both internal and external strategic factors and forces them to assign a priority to each factor in terms of its importance to the corporation's future. The results can be used to develop an industry profile and a comparison of each company in the industry, and thus form the basis of an industry analysis.

Discussion Questions

1. What is the relevance of the resource-based view of a firm to strategic management?
2. Compare and contrast the four approaches to scanning and analyzing a corporation's internal environment.
3. Describe Porter's value chain analysis and how it relates to strategic management.
4. In what ways may a corporation's structure and culture be internal strengths or weaknesses?
5. What types of internal factors help managers determine whether a firm should emphasize the production and sales of a large number of low-priced products or a small number of high-priced products?
6. What is the difference between operating and financial leverage? What are their implications for strategic planning?
7. What are the pros and cons of management's using the experience curve to determine strategy?
8. Why should information systems be included in the analysis of a corporation's strengths and weaknesses?

Notes

1. J. Barney, "Firm Resources and Sustained Competitive Advantage," *Journal of Management* (March 1991), p. 116. Reprinted with permission.
2. L. Ingrassia, "Gillette Holds Its Edge by Endlessly Searching for a Better Shave," *Wall Street Journal* (December 10, 1992), pp. A1, A6.
3. Much of this section was developed from an analysis by Michael Potter while he was a graduate student at Iowa State University.
4. M. J. Kiernan, "The New Strategic Architecture: Learning to Compete in the Twenty-First Century," *Academy of Management Executive* (February 1993), pp. 7–21; D. J. Collis, "A Resource-Based Analysis of Global Competition: The Case of the Bearings Industry," *Strategic Management Journal* (Summer 1991), pp. 49–68; J. T. Mahoney and J. R. Pandian, "The Resource-Based View Within the Conversation of Strategic Management," *Strategic Management Journal* (June 1992), pp. 363–380.
5. Barney, pp. 99–120; C. Carroll, P. M. Lewis, and H. Thomas, "Developing Competitive Strategies in Retailing," *Long Range Planning* (April 1992), pp. 81–88; R. M. Grant, "The Resource-Based Theory of Competitive Advantage: Implications for Strategy Formulation." *California Management Review* (Spring 1991), pp. 114–135; M. A. Peteraf, "The Cornerstone of Competitive Advantage: A Resource-Based View," *Strategic Management Journal* (March 1993), pp. 179–191.
6. C. K. Prahalad and G. Hamel, "The Core Competencies of the Corporation," *Harvard Business Review* (May/June 1990), pp. 79–91.
7. Grant, p. 122.
8. Ibid., pp. 123–128.
9. J. R. Williams, "How Sustainable Is Your Competitive Advantage?" *California Management Review* (Spring 1992), pp. 29–51.
10. S. Schoeffler, "Nine Basic Findings on Business Strategy," *The PIMSletter on Business Strategy,* No. 1 (Cambridge, Mass.: The Strategic Planning Institute, 1984), pp. 3–5.
11. G. Badler, "Strategizing for a Spectrum of Possibilities," *Planning Review* (July 1984), pp. 28–31; R. J. Allio and J. M. Patten, "The Market Share/Excellence Equation," *Planning Review* (September/October 1991), pp. 12–15, 45.
12. R. D. Buzzell and B. T. Gale, *The PIMS Principles* (New York: Free Press, 1987), pp. 8–10; M. J. Chussil, "Does Market Share

Really Matter?" *Planning Review* (September/October 1991), pp. 31–37.

13. J. Schwalbach, "Profitability and Market Share: A Reflection of the Functional Relationship," *Strategic Management Journal* (May 1991), pp. 299–306.
14. Buzzell and Gale, p. 7; B. T. Gale, "Quality Comes First When Hatching Power Brands," *Planning Review* (July/August 1992), pp. 4–9, 48.
15. M. E. Porter, *Competitive Advantage: Creating and Sustaining Superior Performance* (New York: Free Press, 1985), p. 36.
16. H. I. Ansoff, *The New Corporate Strategy* (New York: John Wiley & Sons, 1988), pp. 66–71.
17. Based on J. R. Galbraith and R. K. Kazanjian, *Strategy Implementation: Structure, Systems, and Process,* 2nd ed. (St. Paul, Minn.: West, 1986), pp. 67–68.
18. W. J. Duncan, "Organizational Culture: 'Getting a Fix' on an Elusive Concept," *Academy of Management Executive* (August 1989), p. 229.
19. L. Smircich, "Concepts of Culture and Organizational Analysis," *Administrative Science Quarterly* (September 1983), pp. 345–346.
20. H. H. Hinterhuber and W. Holleis, "Corporate Success Tomorrow: A European Perspective," *International Review of Strategic Management,* Vol. 2, No. 2, edited by D. E. Hussey (New York: John Wiley & Sons, 1991), pp. 163–178.
21. C. M. Fiol, "Managing Culture as a Competitive Resource: An Identity-Based View of Sustainable Competitive Advantage," *Journal of Management* (March 1991), pp. 191–211.
22. J. Lorsch, "Strategic Myopia: Culture as an Invisible Barrier to Change," in *Gaining Control of the Corporate Culture,* edited by R. H. Kilmann, M. J. Saxton, R. Serpa, and Associates (San Francisco: Jossey-Bass, 1985), pp. 84–102.
23. P. Kotler, *Marketing Management,* 4th ed. (Englewood Cliffs, N.J.: Prentice Hall, 1980), p. 22.
24. P. R. Nayyar, "Performance Effects of Three Foci in Service Firms," *Academy of Management Journal* (December 1992), pp. 985–1009.
25. M. Schofeld and D. Arnold, "Strategies for Mature Businesses," *Long Range Planning* (October 1988), pp. 69–76.
26. C. M. Sandberg, W. G. Lewellen, and K. L. Stanley, "Financial Strategy: Planning and Managing the Corporate Leverage Position," *Strategic Management Journal* (January–February 1987), pp. 15–24.
27. For further information on capital budgeting, discounted cash flow, CAPM, and APM Techniques, see R. G. Dyson and R. H. Berry, "Capital Investment Appraisal," in *Strategic Planning: Models and Analytical Techniques,* edited by R. G. Dyson (New York: John Wiley & Sons, 1991), pp. 217–243; R. G. Quintero, "Financial Tools for Strategy Evaluation," in *Handbook of Business Strategy,* 2nd ed., edited by H. E. Glass (Boston: Warren, Gorham & Lamont, 1991), pp. 7.1–7.62.
28. W. P. Barnett, "The Organizational Ecology of a Technological System," *Administrative Science Quarterly* (March 1990), pp. 31–60.
29. M. A. Maidique and P. Patch, "Corporate Strategy and Technological Policy" (Boston: Intercollegiate Case Clearing House, No. 9–769–033, 1978, rev., March 1980), p. 3.
30. C. Van der Eerden and F. H. Saelens, "The Use of Science and Technology Indicators in Strategic Planning," *Long Range Planning* (June 1991), pp. 18–25.
31. W. J. Abernathy and J. M. Utterback, "Innovation Over Time and in Historical Context," in *Readings in the Management of Innovation,* 2nd ed., edited by M. L. Tushman and W. L. Moore (Cambridge, Mass.: Ballinger, 1988), pp. 25–36; R. E. Gomory, "From the 'Ladder of Science' to the Product Development Cycle," *Harvard Business Review* (November–December 1989), pp. 99–103.
32. L. J. Krajewski and L. P. Ritzman, *Operations Management* (Reading, Mass.: Addison–Wesley, 1987), p. 10.
33. J. F. Weston and T. E. Copeland, *Managerial Finance,* 8th ed. (Chicago: Dryden, 1986), p. 220.
34. J. D. Camm, "A Note on Learning Curve Parameters," *Decision Sciences* (Summer 1985), pp. 325–327; A. C. Hax and N. S. Majuf, "Competitive Cost Dynamics: The Experience Curve," in *Readings on Strategic Management,* edited by A. C. Hax (Cambridge, Mass.: Ballinger, 1984), pp. 49–60.
35. B. D. Henderson, *Henderson on Corporate Strategy* (Cambridge, Mass.: Abt Books, 1979), p. 11.

36. For more information on economies of scope, see P. R. Nayyar, "Performance Effects of Information Symmetry and Economies of Scope in Diversified Service Firms," *Academy of Management Journal* (February 1993), pp. 28–57.
37. R. S. Sriram and Y. P. Gupta, "Strategic Cost Measurement for Flexible Manufacturing Systems," *Long Range Planning* (October 1991), pp. 34–40.
38. J. A. Chatman, "Matching People and Organizations: Selection and Socialization in Public Accounting Firms," *Administrative Science Quarterly* (September 1991), pp. 459–484; H. G. Heneman, D. P. Schwab, J. A. Fossum, and L. D. Dyer, *Personnel/Human Resource Management* (Homewood, Ill.: Irwin, 1986), p. 7.
39. R. J. Mirabile, "Identifying the Employee of the Future," *Journal of Business Strategy* (May/June 1991), pp. 32–36.
40. J. S. Lublin, "Trying to Increase Worker Productivity, More Employers Alter Management Style," *Wall Street Journal* (February 13, 1992), p. B1.
41. A. Versteeg, "Self-Directed Work Teams Yield Long-Term Benefits," *Journal of Business Strategy* (November/December 1990), pp. 9–12. For further information on autonomous work teams, see D. Barry, "Managing the Bossless Team: Lessons in Distributed Leadership," *Academy of Management Executive* (Summer 1991), pp. 31–47.
42. R. R. Gehani, "Concurrent Product Development for Fast-Track Corporations," *Long Range Planning* (December 1992), pp. 40–47; D. E. Carter and B. S. Baker, *Concurrent Engineering: The Product Development Environment for the 1990s* (Reading, Mass.: Addison-Wesley, 1992).
43. D. Milbank, "Unions' Woes Suggest How the Labor Force in U.S. Is Shifting," *Wall Street Journal* (May 5, 1992), pp. A1, A4.
44. G. Koretz, "Why Unions Thrive Abroad—But Wither in the U.S." *Business Week* (September 10, 1990), p. 26.
45. S. Baker and T. Buell, Jr., "Buddy-Buddy at the Steel Smelter," *Business Week* (April 5, 1993), p. 26.
46. M. W. Fields and J. W. Thacker, "Influence of Quality of Work Life on Company and Union Commitment," *Academy of Management Journal* (June 1992), pp. 439–450.
47. J. L. Suttle, "Improving Life at Work—Problems and Perspectives," in *Improving Life at Work: Behavioral Science Approaches to Organizational Change,* edited by J. R. Hackman and J. L. Suttle (Santa Monica, Calif.: Goodyear, 1976), p. 4.
48. M. E. Porter, *Competitive Advantage of Nations* (New York: Free Press, 1990), pp. 158, 582, 628; R. Hall, "The Strategic Analysis of Intangible Resources," *Strategic Management Journal* (February 1992), pp. 135–144.
49. R. G. Murdick, *MIS: Concepts and Designs* (Englewood Cliffs, N.J.: Prentice-Hall, 1980), p. 253.
50. J. G. Sifonis, "Mining for Gold in Your Information Systems," *Directors and Boards* (Summer 1989), p. 23.
51. P. E. Cole and M. Smilgis, "Aladdin's Magic," *Time* (November 1992), p. 76.

6

Strategy Formulation: Situation Analysis and Corporate Strategy

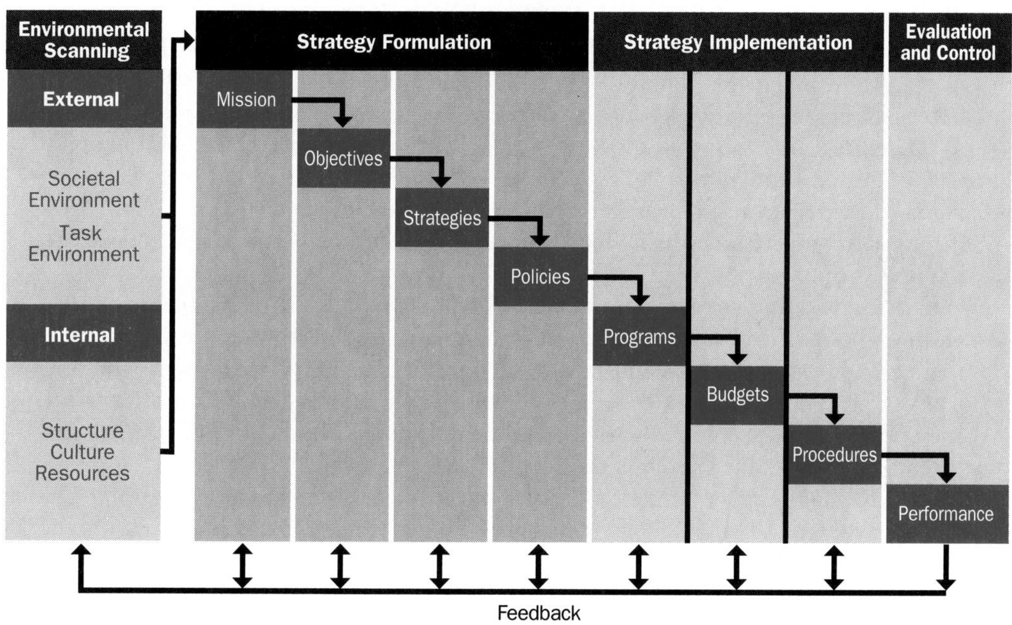

> *Everyone else is making deals with the phone company. We're starting a hockey team [the Anaheim Mighty Ducks].*[1]
>
> [Michael Eisner, Chairman, Walt Disney Company]

When Lewis Platt stepped into the job of CEO of Hewlett-Packard Company in 1992, he soon realized that the company was in danger of missing critical opportunities. Computers, communications, and consumer electronics were rapidly converging into one interrelated industry. Anything that was capable of being recorded digitally, such as TV programs, magazines, telephone calls, and pop music was capable of being distributed over cable TV, satellites, telephones, and personal computers. Unfortunately, Hewlett-Packard was not involved in the strategic alliances and acquisitions needed to take advantage of this development. What could the company do to avoid losing out?

A close look internally at Hewlett-Packard's strengths identified what HP Laboratories Director Joel Birnbaum called the company's "secret weapon"—a unique mix of core technologies that no single competitor could match. For example, HP offered a broad and well-regarded family of computers. It also was a leader in test and measurement instruments—the area in which the company began and had always dominated—and strong in computer networking. Birnbaum proposed that the company blend these three technologies to create new product categories.

Following this suggestion, Hewlett-Packard developed a diagnostic system for Ford Motor Company's dealers that combined instruments that monitor a car's internal operations with an HP computer. The system included a small "flight recorder" that plugged into the data link in most Ford cars and stored the vital signs for later analysis at the garage. Hewlett-Packard won the $63 million Ford contract over IBM because of HP's measurement expertise. According to a Ford manager, "HP's instrumentation was the key factor for us." HP also began developing other products that could take advantage of its core competencies—video servers, interactive TV devices, digital cable TV decoders, video printers, interactive notepads, health monitors, and a physician's workstation, among others.[2]

The preceding example shows how a corporation can use situational analysis to initiate the strategy formulation process. Management analyzed both Hewlett-Packard's external and internal environments in some depth to find the company's distinctive competence, which would enable it to take advantage of newly developing opportunities.

Strategy formulation is often referred to as strategic planning or long-range planning. As shown in the strategic management model beginning each chapter, the formulation process is concerned with developing a corporation's mission, objectives, strategies, and policies. In order to do this, strategy makers must analyze the corporation's strategic factors (key strengths, weaknesses, opportunities, and threats) in light of the current situation.

In this chapter, we present SWOT analysis as a systematic way of doing situation analysis, shown in Fig. 6.1 (repeated from Fig. 2.3) as Step 5(a) of the strategic decision-making process. We suggest that, before generating feasible alternative strategies, strategic managers review and revise as necessary the firm's current mission and objectives, shown as Step 5(b) in Fig. 6.1. Step 6 then involves the generation, evaluation, and selection of the best strategic alternatives. We propose a set of alternative corporate strategies as a way of helping strategic managers decide not only what industries their corporations should be in, but also what directions their firms can take to grow and develop. After deciding what industries to be in, companies also must decide how they can best compete in each of those industries. This topic is presented and discussed in the next chapter under business and functional strategies.

6.1 Situation Analysis: SWOT

Situation analysis begins the process of strategy formulation and requires that strategic managers attempt to find a strategic fit between external opportunities and internal strengths while working around external threats and internal weaknesses. Recall that SWOT is an acronym for the organization's Strengths, Weaknesses, Opportunities, and Threats that are strategic factors. Hence, SWOT analysis should identify a corporation's **distinctive competence**—the particular skills and resources a firm possesses and the superior way in which they are used.[3]

(Distinctive competence sometimes is considered a collection of **core capabilities**—capabilities that differentiate a company strategically.[4]) An appropriate use of a firm's distinctive competence (core capabilities) should give it a sustainable competitive advantage. For example, the emphasis by Urschel Laboratories on building high-quality, low-cost food processing machines provided a distinctive competence in manufacturing that enables it to dominate the industry. Management's willingness to pass savings on to customers in the form of lower prices, instead of maintaining prices and realizing more profits, has created an entry barrier for Urschel's prospective competitors. Prices are just too low to attract another company into the business!

Generating a Strategic Factors Analysis Summary (SFAS)

One way to summarize a corporation's strategic factors is to combine the **external strategic factors (EFAS)** with the **internal strategic factors (IFAS)** into a Strategic Factors Analysis Summary (SFAS), as shown in Fig. 6.2. The EFAS and IFAS examples for Maytag Corporation (Tables 4.3 and 5.2) contain a total of 20 strategic factors—five each for Strengths, Weaknesses, Opportunities, and Threats. These are too many factors for management to use effectively in strategy formulation. The Strategic Factors Analysis Summary requires the strategic manager to condense these many factors into less than 10 factors. Use of the SFAS form involves the following steps.

First, list the most important EFAS and IFAS items in the Key Strategic Factors Column; after each factor, indicate whether it is a strength (S), weakness (W), opportunity (O), or threat (T). *Second,* review the weights assigned to these factors in the EFAS and IFAS tables and adjust them as necessary so that the Weight Column for all of the internal and external strategic factors *will still sum to 1.00. Third,* enter in the Rating Column the ratings of how the company's management is responding to each factor from the EFAS and IFAS tables. *Fourth,* multiply the weight for each factor by its rating to obtain the entires for the Weighted Score Column. *Fifth,* place an X in the Duration Column to indicate whether a factor has a short-term (less than one year), intermediate-term (one to three years), or long-term (beyond three years) time horizon. *Sixth,* insert your comments for each factor from the EFAS and IFAS tables.

The resulting SFAS summarizes the firm's external and internal strategic factors on one form. The SFAS contains only the most important factors and provides the basis for strategy formulation. If you do an analysis of each company's management using EFAS and IFAS, combined into SFAS, then you can rank the management of each company within an industry according to their management of each company's strategic factors.

Finding a Propitious Niche

One desired outcome of analyzing strategic factors is identifying a propitious niche in which an organization can use its distinctive competence (unique internal strengths) to greatest advantage. A **propitious niche** is a company's specific competitive strength that is so well suited to the firm's internal and external environment that other corporations are not likely to challenge or dislodge it.[5]

FIGURE 6.1 **Strategic Decision-Making Process**

1(a) Evaluate Current Performance Results

1(b) Examine and Evaluate the Current:
- Mission
- Objectives
- Strategies
- Policies

2 Review Strategic Managers:
- Board of Directors
- Top Management

3(a) Scan External Environment:
- Societal
- Task

3(b) Select Strategic Factors:
- Opportunities
- Threats

4(a) Scan Internal Environment:
- Structure
- Culture
- Resources

4(b) Select Strategic Factors:
- Strengths
- Weaknesses

5(a) Analyze Strategic Factors (SWOT) in Light of Current Situation

Strategy Formulation: Steps 1–6

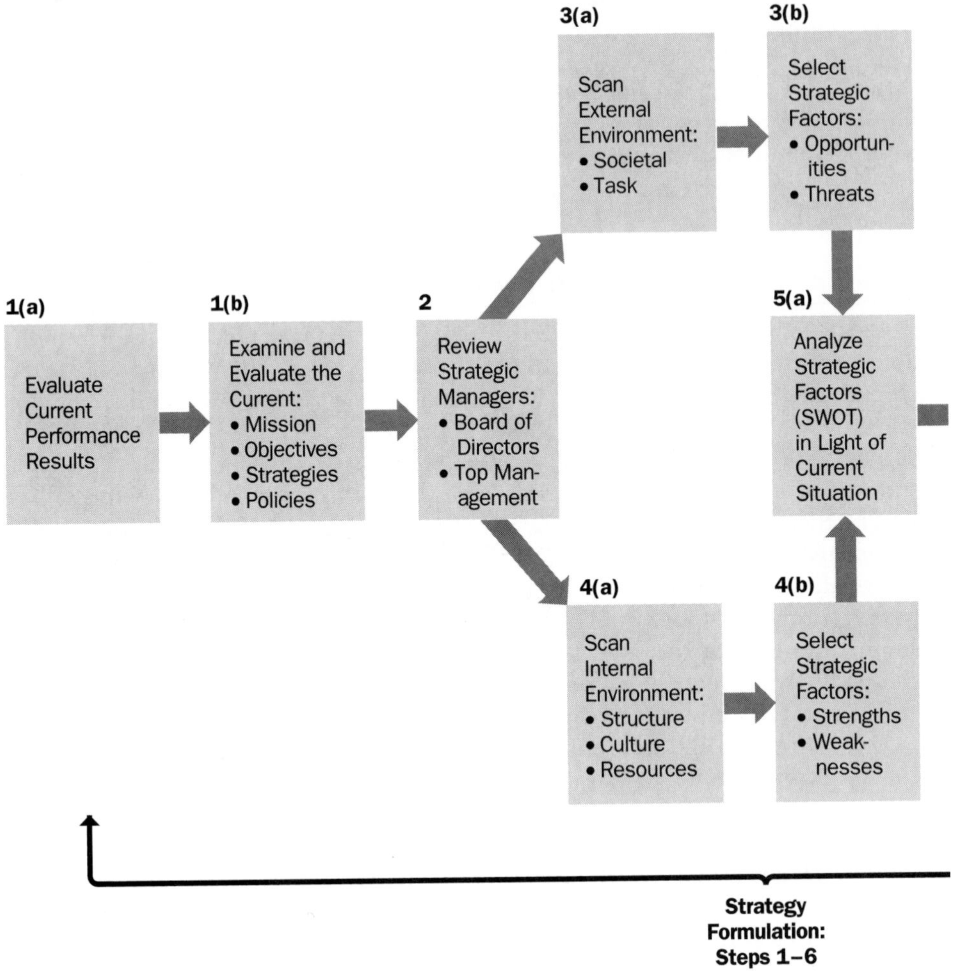

Source: T. L. Wheelen and J. D. Hunger, "Strategic Decision-Making Process." Copyright © 1994 by Wheelen and Hunger Associates. Reprinted by permission.

Finding such a niche isn't always easy. Management must always be looking for *strategic windows,* that is, unique market opportunities.[6] The first firm through the strategic window can occupy a propitious niche and discourage competition (if the firm has the required internal strengths). A company that has successfully found a propitious niche is Frank J. Zamboni & Company, manufacturer of the machines that smooth the ice at skating and hockey rinks. Frank Zamboni invented the unique tractorlike machine in 1949 and no one has come up with a substitute for what it does. Before Zamboni invented the machine, people had to clean and scrape the ice by hand to prepare a surface for skating. Now hockey fans look forward to intermissions just to watch "the Zamboni"

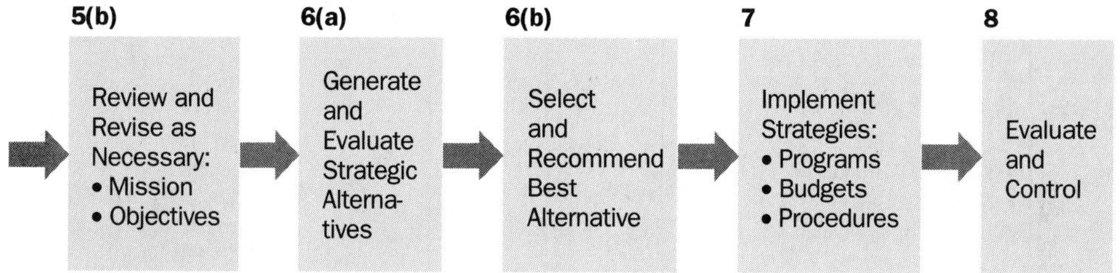

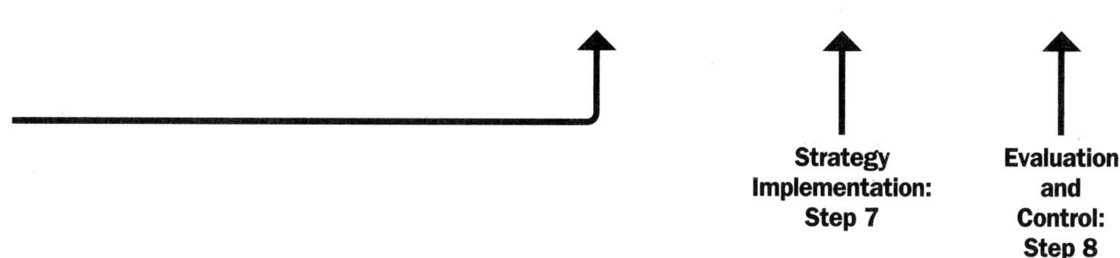

slowly drive up and down the ice rink turning rough, scraped ice into a mirror smooth surface—almost as if by magic. So long as the Zamboni company continues to produce the machines in the quantity and quality desired at a reasonable price, no other company is likely to go after Frank Zamboni & Company's propitious niche.[7]

A company may also discover in its situation analysis that it may need to invest heavily in its capabilities to keep them competitively strong in a changing niche. The Strategy in Action on pages 148–149 describes how Cummins Engine took this approach when it realized that it couldn't take advantage of a developing opportunity in the diesel engine market.

TABLE 5.2 **Internal Strategic Factor Analysis Summary (IFAS): Maytag as Example**

Internal Strategic Factors	Weight	Rating	Weighted Score	Comments
1	2	3	4	5
Strengths				
• Quality Maytag culture	.15	5	.75	Quality key to success
• Experienced top management	.05	4	.20	Know appliances
• Vertical integration	.10	4	.40	Dedicated factories
• Employee relations	.05	3	.15	Good, but deteriorating
• Hoover's international orientation	.15	3	.45	Hoover name in cleaners
Weaknesses				
• Process-oriented R&D	.05	2	.10	Slow on new products
• Distribution channels	.05	2	.10	Superstores replacing small dealers
• Financial position	.15	2	.30	High debt load
• Global positioning	.20	2	.40	Hoover weak outside the United Kingdom and Australia
• Manufacturing facilities	.05	4	.20	Investing now
Total	1.00		3.05	

TABLE 4.3 **External Strategic Factor Analysis Summary (EFAS): Maytag as Example**

External Strategic Factors	Weight	Rating	Weighted Score	Comments
1	2	3	4	5
Opportunities				
• Economic integration of European Community	.20	4	.80	Acquisition of Hoover
• Demographics favor quality appliances	.10	5	.50	Maytag quality
• Economic development of Asia	.05	1	.05	Low Maytag presence
• Opening of Eastern Europe	.05	2	.10	Will take time
• Trend to "Super Stores"	.10	2	.20	Maytag weak in this channel
Threats				
• Increasing government regulations	.10	4	.40	Well positioned
• Strong U.S. competition	.10	4	.40	Well positioned
• Whirlpool and Electrolux strong globally	.15	3	.45	Hoover weak globally
• New product advances	.05	1	.05	Questionable
• Japanese appliance companies	.10	2	.20	Only Asian presence is Australia
Total	1.00		3.15	

FIGURE 6.2

Strategic Factor Analysis Summary (SFAS)

1 **Key Strategic Factors** (Select the most important opportunies/threats from EFAS, Table 4.3 and the most important strengths and weaknesses from IFAS, Table 5.2)	2 **Weight**	3 **Rating**	4 **Weighted Score**	5 **Duration** **SHORT**	**INTERMEDIATE**	**LONG**	6 **Comments**
• Quality Maytag culture (S)	.10	5	.5			X	Quality key to success
• Hoover's international orientation (S)	.10	3	.3		X		Name recognition
• Global positioning (W)	.15	2	.3			X	Only in N.A., U.K., and Australia
• Financial position (W)	.10	2	.2		X		High debt
• Economic integration of European Community (O)	.10	4	.4			X	Acquisition of Hoover
• Demographics favor quality (O)	.10	5	.5		X		Maytag quality
• Trend to super stores (O + T)	.10	2	.2	X			Weak in this channel
• Whirlpool and Electrolux (T)	.15	3	.45	X			Dominate industry
• Japanese appliance companies (T)	.10	2	.2			X	Asian presence
Total	1.00		3.05				

Notes:

1. List each of your key strategic features developed in your IFAS and EFAS tables in Column 1.
2. Weight each factor from 1.0 (Most Important) to 0.0 (Not Important) in Column 2 based on that factor's probable impact on the company's strategic position. **The total weights must sum to 1.00.**
3. Rate each factor from 5 (Outstanding) to 1 (Poor) in Column 3 based on the company's response to that factor.
4. Multiply each factor's weight times its rating to obtain each factor's weighted score in Column 4.
5. For duration in Column 5, check appropriate column (short term—less than 1 year; intermediate—1 to 3 years; long term—over 3 years.)
6. Use Column 6 (comments) for rationale used for each factor.

Source: T. J. Wheelen and J. D. Hunger. "Strategic Factor Analysis Summary (SFAS)." Copyright © 1993 by Wheelen and Hunger Associates. Reprinted by permission.

CUMMINS ENGINE REINVESTS IN ITS DISTINCTIVE COMPETENCE

Strategy in Action

Cummins Engine, the leading U.S. manufacturer of large truck diesel engines, found itself at a crossroads in the late 1970s. By then, most trucking fleets had finished converting from gasoline to diesel engines. The demand for the large engines Cummins was expert at producing began to decline. Future demand seemed to be in the smaller diesel engines which Cummins did not then have the expertise to build. Management concluded in 1981 that the only way the company could continue to have a future would be to heavily and simultaneously invest in a smaller line of heavy-duty truck engines and in lines for medium and light-duty trucks. The investment would cost $1 billion—more than three times the market value of its stock.

Within four years, Cummins had to cut prices as much as 30% on its new products to compete with Japanese imports. Profits faded. Even though Wall Street analysts had little good to say about Cummins Engine stock, CEO Henry Schacht kept insisting that the long-term strategy would one day deliver healthy profits. Nevertheless, the company's market share dropped from more than 50% in 1988 to around 38% in 1991 after its primary competitor, Detroit Diesel, introduced electronic fuel injection.

6.2 Reviewing the Company's Mission and Objectives

Management must reexamine a corporation's current mission and objectives before it can generate and evaluate alternative strategies. B. B. Tregoe and J. W. Zimmerman emphasize the seriousness of this step:

> When making a decision, there is an almost universal tendency to concentrate on the alternatives—the action possibilities—rather than on the objectives we want to achieve. This tendency is widespread because it is much easier to deal with alternative courses of action that exist right here and now than to really think about what we want to accomplish in the future. Projecting a set of values forward is hard work. The end result is that we make choices that set our objectives for us, rather than having our choices incorporate clear objectives.[8]

Problems in performance can arise from an inappropriate statement of mission, which may be too narrow or too broad. If the mission does not provide a common thread (a unifying theme) for a corporation's businesses, managers may be unclear about where the company is heading. Objectives and strategies might

The strategy was, nevertheless, slowly beginning to pay off. Impressed that Cummins's engines surpassed stringent EPA standards, Ford Motor Company invested $100 million in Cummins in 1990 so that it would not have to develop diesel engines of its own. Others began to notice the value of Cummins's strategy.

By 1992, eager customers such as Ford and Chrysler were purchasing so many of the fuel-efficient motors for their light trucks that Cummins had to build a second plant to meet demand. Heavy-duty engine orders jumped 30% when a new fuel injector was introduced. The mid-range truck engines were also successful and in demand. In addition, 24% of sales were coming from stationary motors used to power electric generators. Even Japanese rival, Komatsu Ltd., was buying mid-range Cummins diesels for its construction equipment.

The company ended a four-year string of losses in 1992 with a $67 million profit before a one-time charge for retiree health benefits. According to CEO Schacht, the company was now "far beyond anyone else" in diesel engine volume and could now afford to pour enough into research to maintain its technological leadership. "Competence has given us an economic opportunity," explained Schacht. In retrospect, the CEO pointed out that if in 1981 the company had not chosen to invest heavily, "we would be in decline if not out of business."

conflict, with divisions competing against one another—rather than against outside competition—to the detriment of the corporation as a whole.

An example of a revision of a corporation's mission statement is that by American Telephone and Telegraph (AT&T). The revised mission was published in AT&T's *1980 Annual Report* to shareholders and had important implications for its future corporate strategy:

> No longer do we perceive that our business will be limited to telephony or, for that matter, telecommunications. Ours is the business of information handling, the knowledge business. And the market that we seek is global.

A company's objectives also may be stated inappropriately. They may either focus too much on short-term operational goals or be so general that they provide little real guidance. There may be a **planning gap** between planned and achieved objectives.[9] When such a gap occurs, management either has to change the strategies to improve performance or adjust objectives downward to be more realistic. Hence constant review of objectives is needed to ensure their usefulness. For example, in 1992 Toyota Motor Corporation's top management realized that its "Global 10" objective of aiming for 10% of the global vehicle market by the end of the century was no longer feasible. It then shifted emphasis from market share to profits. According to senior managing director Iwao Isomura, "This notion of more production and more market share is not an important principle of the company any more." Added President Shoichiro Toyoda, "The main thing is achieving mutual prosperity."[10]

6.3 Corporate Strategy

Corporate strategy specifies (1) the firm's orientation toward growth and (2) the industries or markets in which it will compete. For multibusiness corporations operating in more than one industry or market, corporate strategy also includes decisions regarding the flow of financial and other resources to and from their business units. These decisions are crucial to a corporation's future and typically involve top management and the board of directors. Corporate strategy can provide a *strategic platform,* or the ability of the organization to handle businesses in various environments with a common set of strategic capabilities.[11] All corporations, from the smallest company offering one product in only one industry to the largest conglomerate operating in many industries with many products must, at one time or another, consider the questions embedded within corporate strategy.

- Should we expand, cut back, or continue our operations unchanged?
- Should we concentrate our activities within our current industry or should we diversify into other industries?
- If we want to grow and expand, should we do so through internal development or through external acquisitions, mergers, or joint ventures?

Corporate strategy embodies three general orientations (sometimes called grand strategies): *growth, stability,* and *retrenchment.* In other words, a corporation, like a person, can move forward, stay where it is, or take a step back. After choosing the general orientation (such as growth), a company's strategic managers can select from several specific corporate strategies, such as concentration within one industry or diversification into other industries. Such strategies are useful both to corporations operating in only one industry as single business firms and to those operating in many industries as multibusiness firms. Because visualizing alternative corporate strategies from the perspective of a company with a few products operating only in one industry is somewhat easier, let's begin with the single-business firm.

Corporate Strategy in the Single-Business Firm

Assume for now that the corporation operates primarily in *one industry,* such as Caterpillar in heavy construction equipment or McDonald's in fast-food restaurants. From SWOT analysis, the strategic managers in this type of firm can consolidate the company's many external strategic factors (opportunities and threats) under the category **industry attractiveness.** They also can consolidate the company's many internal strategic factors (strengths and weaknesses) under the category **competitive position.** Strategic managers in firms operating in one industry may consider the appropriateness of several alternative corporate strategies by combining industry attractiveness with the company's competitive position into a nine-cell matrix. The resulting matrix, depicted in Fig. 6.3, may be used as a model to plot some of the alternative corporate strategies that might fit the company's situation. This model suggests which corporate strategy from 12 possible strategies may be most appropriate. The placement of strategies in the matrix generally agrees with research regarding top management's reported motives for choosing one strategy over another.[12] These aren't the only strategies that could be used but are strategies that seem reasonable to consider.

Figure 6.3 identifies nine cells containing corporate strategies that fit under the categories of growth, stability, and retrenchment. **Growth strategies** involve either concentration, that is, expansion within the firm's current industry (Cells 1, 2, and 5), or diversification, where growth is generated outside the firm's current industry (Cells 7 and 8). **Stability strategies** (Cells 4 and 5) represent a firm's choice to retain its current mission and objectives without any significant change in strategic direction. **Retrenchment strategies** (Cells 3, 6, and 9) call for reduction in scope and magnitude of the firm's efforts.

Growth Strategies

By far the most widely pursued corporate strategies are those designed to achieve growth in sales, assets, profits, or some combination. Companies that do business in dynamic environments must grow in order to survive. Continuing growth means increasing sales and a chance to take advantage of the experience curve to reduce the per unit cost of products sold, thereby increasing profits. This cost reduction becomes extremely important if a corporation's industry is growing rapidly and competitors are engaging in price wars in attempts to increase their shares of the market. Firms that have not reached *critical mass* (that is, gained the necessary economies of large-scale production) will face large losses unless they can find and fill a small, but profitable, niche where special product or service features can offset higher prices. That is why Motorola, Inc., continued to spend large sums on the development of cellular phones, pagers, and two-way radios, despite a serious drop in profits in 1990. According to Motorola's Chairman George Fisher, "What's at stake here is leadership." Even though the industry was changing rapidly, the company was working to avoid the erosion of its market share by jumping into new wireless markets as fast as possible. Continuing as the market leader in this industry would almost guarantee Motorola enormous future returns.[13]

However, growth is a very seductive strategy for two principal reasons.

- A growing firm can cover up mistakes and inefficiencies more easily than can a stable one. A growing flow of revenue into a highly leveraged corporation can

FIGURE 6.3 **Model of Corporate Strategies**

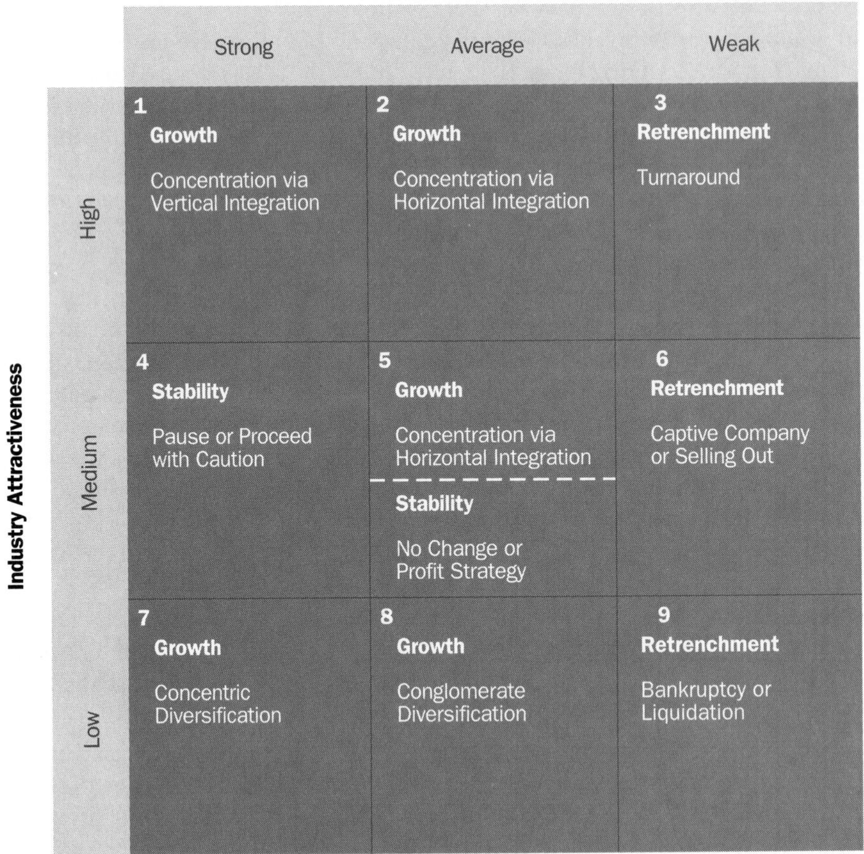

Source: J. D. Hunger, E. J. Flynn, and T. L. Wheelen, "Contingency Corporate Strategy: A Proposed Typology with Research Propositions." Paper presented to the Midwest Division of the Academy of Management, Milwaukee, Wisconsin, April 1990. Copyright © 1990 by Wheelen and Hunger Associates. Reprinted by permission.

create a large amount of "organization slack" (unused resources) that can be used to resolve problems and conflicts quickly between departments and divisions. Growth also provides a cushion in case management makes a strategic error. Large firms also have more clout than do small firms and are more likely to obtain support from their unions and local communities in case of impending bankruptcy.

- A growing firm offers many opportunities for advancement, promotion, and interesting jobs. Growth itself is exciting and ego-enhancing for CEOs. A growing corporation tends to be seen as a "winner" or "on the move" by the marketplace and by potential investors. Executive compensation tends to rise as an organization increases in size. Large firms also are more difficult to acquire than small firms; thus an executive's job is more secure.[14]

Two basic growth strategies are: concentration in one industry and diversification into other industries. If, as Fig. 6.3 shows, the current industry's growth rate and other criteria are attractive, concentration of resources in that industry makes sense as a strategy for growth. However, if the current industry isn't particularly attractive, a company probably should diversify out of that industry if it wants to pursue growth. Research indicates that high-performing firms are less likely to diversify and that low-performing firms may seek diversification in order to improve their performance.[15] If it chooses concentration, a company can grow through vertical or horizontal integration.

Concentration Through Vertical Integration (Cell 1) Growth through concentration in the firm's current industry can be achieved via **vertical integration**, that is, taking over a function previously performed by a supplier (**backward integration**) or by a distributor (**forward integration**). This strategy is logical for a corporation or business unit with a strong competitive position in a highly attractive industry.[16] The industry's attractiveness compels the firm to stay in that industry. That attractiveness, however, will likely result in more competition as new competitors enter the industry and current competitors strive to increase their sales. To keep and even improve its competitive position through backward integration, a company may act to minimize resource acquisition costs and inefficient operations; through forward integration it may gain control over quality and product distribution. In effect, the firm builds on its distinctive competence to gain greater competitive advantage.

A firm may achieve vertical integration either internally or externally. Henry Ford, for example, used internal company resources to build his River Rouge Plant outside Detroit. He integrated the manufacturing process to the point that iron ore entered one end of the long plant and finished automobiles rolled out the other end into a huge parking lot. In contrast, DuPont, the huge chemical company, chose the external route to backward vertical integration by acquiring Conoco for oil needed in the production of DuPont's synthetic fabrics.

Vertical integration is common in the oil, basic metals, automobile, and forest products industries. As pointed out in Table 6.1, its advantages include lowering costs and improving coordination and control. Vertical integration is a good way for a strong firm to increase its competitive advantage in an attractive industry. Although backward integration usually is more profitable than forward integration,[17] it may reduce a corporation's strategic flexibility: by creating an encumbrance of expensive assets that might be hard to sell, it can thus create an exit barrier if the corporation wants to leave that particular industry.[18] With sales of its autos declining, General Motors, for example, has resorted to offering outside parts suppliers the use of its idle factories and workers.[19]

TABLE 6.1 Some Advantages and Disadvantages of Vertical Integration

Advantages	Disadvantages
Internal Benefits	**Internal Costs**
Integration economics reduce costs by eliminating steps, reducing duplicate overhead, and cutting costs (technology dependent).	Need for overhead to coordinate vertical integration increases costs.
Improved coordination of activities reduces inventorying and other costs.	Burden of excess capacity from unevenly balanced minimum efficient scale plants (technology dependent).
Avoid time-consuming tasks, such as price shopping, communicating design details, or negotiating contracts.	Poorly organized vertically integrated firms do not enjoy synergies that compensate for higher costs.
Competitive Benefits	**Competitive Dangers**
Avoid foreclosure to inputs, services, or markets.	Obsolete processes may be perpetuated.
Improved marketing or technological intelligence.	Creates mobility (or exit) barriers.
Opportunity to create product differentiation (increased value added).	Links firm to sick adjacent businesses.
Superior control of firm's economic environment (market power).	Lose access to information from suppliers or distributors.
Create credibility for new products.	Synergies created through vertical integration may be overrated.
Synergies could be created by coordinating vertical activities skillfully.	Managers integrated before thinking through the most appropriate way to do so.

Source: K. R. Harrigan, "Formulating Vertical Integration Strategies," *Academy of Management Review* (October 1984), p. 639. Copyright © 1984 by the Academy of Management. Reprinted by permission.

A study by K. R. Harrigan reveals at least four types of vertical integration, ranging from full integration to long-term contracts.[20] For example, if a corporation doesn't want to have the disadvantages of full vertical integration, it may choose either taper or quasi-integration strategies. With **taper integration,** a firm produces part of its own requirements and buys the rest from outside suppliers. In the case of **quasi-integration,** a company gets most of its requirements from an outside supplier that is partially under its control. For example, by purchasing 20% of the common stock of In Focus Systems, Motorola guaranteed its access to In Focus's revolutionary technology and enabled Motorola to establish a joint venture with In Focus to manufacture flat-panel video displays.[21]

Recent events indicate movement away from full vertical integration and toward cooperative contractual relationships with suppliers and even with competitors.[22] These relationships can range from *outsourcing,* where supplies are purchased from outsiders instead of made in-house (e.g., Hewlett-Packard's buying all its laser engines from Canon for HP's laser jet printers), to *strategic alliances,* in which partnerships, technology licensing agreements, and joint ventures are used to supplement a firm's capabilities (e.g., Toshiba's strategic alliances with

GE, Siemens, Motorola, and Ericsson, among others, to become one of the world's leading electronics companies).[23] *Transaction cost economics* suggests that vertical integration is more efficient than contracting for goods and services when the transaction costs of buying goods on the open market become too great. When highly integrated firms become excessively large and bureaucratic, however, the costs of managing internal transactions may become greater than simply purchasing the needed goods externally, thus justifying outsourcing over vertical integration. The Key Theory capsule on pages 156–157 presents more information on transaction cost economics.

Concentration Through Horizontal Integration (Cells 2 and 5) Growth through concentration in the firm's current industry can be achieved via horizontal integration by expanding the firm's activities into other geographic locations and/or by increasing the range of products and services offered to current markets. Although in Cells 2 and 5 the corporation is in a highly or moderately attractive industry where it wants to remain, its competitive position is only average. Manufacturing or marketing functions may be operating satisfactorily but not providing a significant competitive advantage. A firm in this position may attempt to solidify and strengthen its presence in its current industry by working to shore up its weaknesses. When operating in a highly attractive industry (Cell 2), the firm's objectives generally are to increase its sales and profits by obtaining larger economies of scale in production and marketing and reducing current and/or potential competition for customers and supplies. When operating in a moderately attractive industry that is probably going through some consolidation (Cell 5), the firm's objectives are more defensive in nature to avoid current or future losses in sales and profits.

A company in these cells can acquire market share, production facilities, distribution outlets, or specialized technology internally through research and development or externally through acquisitions or joint ventures with another firm in the same industry.[24] For example, after purchasing Zenith's computer operations, France's Groupe Bull acquired 19.9% of Packard Bell Electronics, the largest seller of personal computers in U.S. mass-merchandise stores. Bull thus gained access to 7,000 retailers for its Zenith Data Systems subsidiary.[25] Maytag Corporation also chose acquisitions as the means to grow externally, as the Company Spotlight: Maytag Corporation feature on page 158 describes.

Concentric Diversification (Cell 7) Growth through diversification into a related industry may be an appropriate corporate strategy when a firm has a strong competitive position but industry attractiveness is low. By focusing on the characteristics that have given the company its distinctive competence, the company uses those strengths in diversifying. The emphasis in this strategy is to build on a firm's key resources and capabilities (discussed previously in Chapter 5 under the resource-based view of the firm). The firm attempts to secure strategic fit in a new industry where the firm can apply the product knowledge, manufacturing capabilities, and marketing skills it used so effectively in the original industry. The search is for **synergy**, the concept that 2 + 2 = 5, that will allow two businesses to generate more

Transaction Cost Economics Analyzes Vertical Integration

Why do corporations use vertical integration to obtain needed supplies or distribution channels when they could simply purchase them on the open market? Transaction cost economics is a branch of institutional economics that attempts to answer this question. Beginning with work by Coase and extended by Williamson, transaction cost economics proposes that vertical integration is more efficient than contracting for goods and services in the marketplace when the transaction costs of buying goods on the open market become too great. Transaction costs include the basic costs of drafting, negotiating, and safeguarding a market agreement (a contract) and the later managerial costs when the agreement is creating problems (goods aren't being delivered on time or quality is lower than needed), renegotiation costs (costs of meetings and phone calls), and the costs of settling disputes (lawyers' fees and court costs).

According to Williamson, three conditions must be met before a corporation will prefer internalizing a transaction through vertical integration over contracting for the transaction in the marketplace: (1) a high level of uncertainty must surround the transaction, (2) assets involved in the transaction must be highly specialized to the transaction, and (3) the transaction must occur frequently. If there is a high level of uncertainty, writing a contract covering all contingencies will be impossible, and the contractor is likely to act opportunistically to exploit any gaps in the written agreement, thus creating prob-

profits together than they could separately. The corporations' products possess some common thread that serves to relate them in some manner. The point of commonality may be similar technology, customer use, distribution, managerial skills, or product similarity. Companies most likely to diversify out of their current industry into a related industry are those that are the leaders in their core businesses and have the capabilities needed for success in the new industry.[26]

The firm may choose to diversify concentrically, through either internal or external means. American Airlines, for example, has diversified both internally and externally out of the increasingly unprofitable airline business into a series of related businesses run by its parent company AMR Corporation. Building on the expertise of its Sabre Travel Information Network, it built a computer reservations system for the French high-speed rail network and for the tunnel under the English Channel. Explained CEO and Chairman Robert Crandall, "Our diversification strategy has been to make the most of those things we have learned how to do in being an airline."[27]

lems and increasing costs. If the assets being contracted for are highly specialized (goods or services with few alternative uses), few alternative suppliers are likely to exist, allowing the contractor to take advantage of the situation and increase costs. The more frequent the transactions are, the more opportunity the contractor has to demand special treatment and thus increase costs further.

Vertical integration isn't always more efficient than the marketplace, however. When highly integrated firms become excessively large and bureaucratic, the costs of managing internal transactions may become greater than simply purchasing the needed goods externally, thus justifying outsourcing over vertical integration. The usually hidden management costs (excessive layers of management, endless committee meetings needed for interdepartmental coordination, and delayed decision making owing to excessively detailed rules and policies) add to the internal transaction costs, thus reducing the effectiveness as well as the efficiency of vertical integration. The decision to integrate vertically or to contract is therefore a decision based upon the particular situation surrounding the transaction and the ability of the corporation to manage the transaction internally both effectively and efficiently.

Sources: O. E. Williamson and S. G. Winter, editors, *The Nature of the Firm: Origins, Evolution, and Development* (New York: Oxford University Press, 1991); E. Mosakowski, "Organizational Boundaries and Economic Performance: An Empirical Study of Entrepreneurial Computer Firms," *Strategic Management Journal* (February 1991), pp. 115–133; P. S. Ring and A. H. Van De Ven, "Structuring Cooperative Relationships Between Organizations," *Strategic Management Journal* (October 1992), pp. 483–498.

Conglomerate Diversification (Cell 8) Growth through diversification out of an industry into an unrelated industry may be an appropriate corporate strategy when a firm's competitive position is only average and industry attractiveness is low.[28] These two factors force the firm to transfer its developmental efforts to other industries. The company probably can maintain a reasonably good level of sales and profits in its current business so long as the industry is growing and has more opportunities than threats. When its markets reach maturity, however, the performance of a company with only an average competitive position begins to decline. When management realizes that the current industry is unattractive and that the firm lacks outstanding abilities or skills that it could transfer easily to related products or services in other industries, its most likely strategy is to diversify into an unrelated industry. Such a move can be made either internally or externally. In conglomerate diversification, timing is important; early entry seems to be a key to success when established companies move into a younger industry.[29]

COMPANY SPOTLIGHT

MAYTAG Corporation

A Growth Strategy of Horizontal Integration Through External Means

Maytag management realized in 1978 that the company would be unable to continue competing effectively in the U.S. home appliance industry if it remained only a high-quality niche manufacturer of automatic washers and dryers. The industry was rapidly consolidating around appliance companies having a complete line of products at all price and quality levels in all three key lines of "white goods": laundry (washers and dryers), cooking (stoves and ovens), and cooling (refrigerators and freezers) appliances. Maytag's top management concluded that it would soon have to acquire other companies or risk being bought out itself. Because of the length of time needed to develop the technology as well as the manufacturing and marketing expertise necessary to produce and sell these other lines of appliances, Maytag chose to grow externally by acquiring Jenn-Air and Magic Chef in the mid 1980s. It thus obtained Jenn-Air's popular down-draft ranges, Magic Chef's gas stoves and other appliances, and Admiral's refrigeration facilities—products that Maytag needed to be a full-line home appliance manufacturer. Similarly, in 1989 Maytag's management concluded that the best way to ensure a global presence in major home appliances was to purchase Hoover, the well-known vacuum cleaner company with a solid position in white goods in Europe and Australia.

Rather than maintaining a common thread through the organization, strategic managers who adopt this strategy are concerned primarily with the criterion of return on investment: Will it increase profitability? The addition, however, may be justified in terms of strategic fit. The emphasis in conglomerate diversification is on financial synergy rather than on the product-market synergy common to concentric diversification. A cash-rich company with few opportunities for growth in its industry, for example, might move into another industry where opportunities are great but cash is hard to find. Another instance of conglomerate diversification might be the purchase by a company with a seasonal and therefore uneven cash flow of a firm in an unrelated industry with complementing seasonal sales that will level out the cash flow. The management of CSX Corporation (a railroad-dominated transportation company) considered the purchase of a natural gas transmission business (Texas Gas Resources) to be a good fit because most of the gas transmission revenue was realized in the winter months when railroads experience a seasonally lean period.

Conglomerate diversification through acquisitions and mergers also let established corporations move into more attractive industries without the baggage of their core businesses. U.S. Steel (now called USX), for example, began its slow movement out of the mature steel industry in which it saw little value in further investment into the still reasonably attractive petroleum industry with its purchase of Marathon Oil. Top management decided to change industries while the corporation still had the resources to support such a move.

The rationale behind conglomerate diversification aids in understanding the emphasis on external means—acquisitions and mergers. By the time a corporation's top management realizes that the company's industry is no longer attractive, it is very likely too late to change industries through internal means. However, some companies have developed a product or service in another industry strictly as a sideline to their current businesses. Maytag began as a farm implement manufacturer and added washing machines as a way to use its production facilities during slack periods. Similarly, Hoover added vacuum cleaners to its original business of horse collars and saddles.

Controversies in Growth Strategies

Many controversial issues surround the growth strategies just mentioned. We highlight two of them below.

Concentric versus Conglomerate Diversification Beginning with the classic study by R. P. Rumelt, several researchers have argued that conglomerate (unrelated) diversification into other industries is less profitable than concentric (related) diversification.[30] A recent study by P. G. Simmonds of 73 Fortune 500 firms over a ten-year period ranked diversification categories according to their financial performance from best to worst: (1) internal related, (2) external related, (3) internal unrelated, and (4) external unrelated.[31]

Supporting this conclusion are the spin-offs by conglomerates of formerly acquired units. In the past few years, Sears, ITT, RCA, Gulf & Western, Beatrice Foods, Quaker Oats, General Electric, Exxon, and R. J. Reynolds have sold or spun off major nonrelated holdings. Nevertheless, some studies reveal that both concentric (related) and conglomerate (unrelated) acquisitions create value and that one method isn't any better than the other in terms of financial performance.[32]

Most likely, concentric and conglomerate diversification are equally valuable strategies for corporate growth but are successful in different situations.[33] Figure 6.3 suggests that a company with a strong competitive position in a particular industry will do better if it diversifies concentrically into a related industry where it can most easily apply its distinctive competence. A company with only an average competitive position should thus do better by diversifying into an unrelated industry.

The real issue may not be concentric versus conglomerate diversification but the difficulty of managing an acquisition. In their review of research in the area, M. Goold and K. Luchs conclude that diversifications are likely to be successful if

1. They are limited to those businesses where synergy is likely;
2. The corporate focus is on exploiting core competencies across different businesses;
3. The new businesses fit with the *dominant logic* (the way managers conceptualize the corporation in terms of critical resource allocation decisions) of top executives and their management style.[34]

External versus Internal Growth Corporations may utilize the growth strategies of either concentration or diversification through the internal development of new products and services or through external acquisitions, mergers, and joint ventures. Although the research is not yet conclusive, firms that grow through acquisitions apparently do not perform financially as well as firms that grow through internal means.[35]

Some of the more common examples of external growth strategies are mergers, acquisitions, and joint ventures. A **merger** is a transaction involving two or more corporations in which stock is exchanged but from which only one corporation survives. Mergers usually occur between firms of somewhat similar size and are usually "friendly." The name of the new firm is likely to be derived from those of the individual firms. One example is the merging of Allied Corporation and Signal Companies to form Allied Signal.

An **acquisition** is the purchase of a company that is completely absorbed as an operating subsidiary or division of the acquiring corporation. Examples are Procter & Gamble's acquisition of Richardson-Vicks, known for its Oil of Olay and Vidal Sassoon brands, and Noxell Corporation, known for its Noxema and Cover Girl products. Acquisitions usually occur between firms of different sizes and can be either friendly or hostile. In hostile acquisitions, often called *takeovers,* the acquiring firm ignores the other firm's top management or board of directors and simply begins buying up the other firm's stock until it owns a controlling interest. The takeover target, in response, begins defensive maneuvers, such as buying up its own stock, calling in the Justice Department to initiate an antitrust suit in order to stop the acquisition, or looking for a friendly merger partner, often called a *white knight.* The Strategy in Action on page 161 presents other popular terms used in takeovers.

A **joint venture** is a "cooperative business activity, formed by two or more separate organizations for strategic purposes, that creates an independent business entity and allocates ownership, operational responsibilities, and financial risks and rewards to each member, while preserving their separate identity/autonomy."[36] Joint ventures occur because the companies involved do not want to or cannot legally merge permanently. Joint ventures provide a temporary way to meld the partners' strengths so that an outcome of value to both is achieved. For example, pharmaceutical giant Merck & Company agreed with chemical giant DuPont to form and jointly own a new company called DuPont Merck Pharmaceutical Company. Merck provided the venture its foreign marketing rights to some prescription medicines and some cash. In return, the venture got access to DuPont's experimental drugs and its small but productive research operation.

Joint ventures are one type of increasingly popular cooperative arrangements (also called *strategic alliances*) ranging from joint venture equity arrangements to nonownership cooperative agreements, R&D partnerships, and cross-licensing.[37] Extremely popular in international undertakings because of financial and political–legal constraints, joint ventures are a convenient way for a privately owned and a publicly owned (state-owned) corporation to work together. (We discuss joint ventures and other strategic alliances further in Chapter 11.)

THE WEIRD VOCABULARY OF MERGERS AND ACQUISITIONS

Strategy in Action

Slang is popular in mergers and acquisitions. For example, a *pigeon* (highly vulnerable target) or *sleeping beauty* (more desirable than a pigeon) might take a *cyanide pill* (take on a huge long-term debt on the condition that the debt falls due immediately upon the firm's acquisition) so that it can avoid being *raped* (being subjected to a forcible hostile takeover, sometimes accompanied by looting the target's profitability) by a *shark* (extremely predatory takeover artist) using *hired guns* (lawyers, merger and acquisition specialists, and certain investment bankers). To avoid takeover threats, many corporations have chosen to stagger the elections of board members, to prohibit two-tier tender offers (the offering of a higher price to stockholders who sell their shares first), to prohibit *green-mail* (the buying back of a company's stock from a "shark" at a premium price), and to require an 80% shareholder vote for approval of a takeover. The ultimate countermeasure appears to be the *poison pill,* a procedure granting present shareholders the right to acquire at a substantial discount a large equity stake in an acquiring company whose offer does not have the support of the acquired company's board of directors.

Stability Strategies

The stability category of corporate strategies probably is most appropriate for a reasonably successful company operating in an industry of medium attractiveness. The industry may be only medium in attractiveness because (1) it is facing modest growth or no growth or (2) key forces in the environment are changing and the future is uncertain. Stability strategies may be extremely useful in the short run but may be dangerous if followed too long. Some of the more popular stability strategies are pause, proceed with caution, no change, and the profit strategy. These strategies appear in Cells 4 and 5 in Fig. 6.3.

Pause or Proceed with Caution (Cell 4) A company with a strong competitive position in an industry of only moderate attractiveness may not pursue any significant change in corporate strategy. A **pause strategy** may be appropriate as a temporary strategy to enable a company to consolidate its resources after prolonged rapid growth in an industry now facing an uncertain future. Dell Computer Corporation followed this strategy in 1993 after its growth strategy had resulted in more growth than it could handle. Explained CEO Michael Dell, "We grew 285% in two years, and we're having some growing pains." Selling personal computers by mail enabled it to underprice Compaq Computer and IBM, but it couldn't keep up with the needs of the $2 billion, 5,600-employee company selling PCs in 95 countries. Dell was not giving up on its growth strategy, merely putting it temporarily in limbo until the company could hire new managers, improve its structure, and build new facilities.[38]

The situation within the industry may call for a **proceed with caution strategy.** In this case, the competitive environment is perceived as highly changeable and unpredictable. Because the external environment could soon become highly attractive with many new opportunities or unattractive with many new threats, management isn't likely to make sudden moves or take unjustified risks by investing either in or out of the industry. Ford Motor Company faced this situation when it recorded a record $2.3 billion loss in 1991. Ford didn't radically retrench, with large layoffs and plant closings. It proceeded with caution. The company had spent many years developing a lean work force and quality products. Management believed that the industry's downturn was only temporary, so it made some temporary adjustments and waited for the market to improve or worsen.[39]

No Change or Profit Strategies (Cell 5) A company may pursue a **no-change strategy** or a **profit stability strategy** when it is operating in an industry of medium attractiveness and has only an average competitive position. The relative stability created by the firm's modest competitive position in an industry facing little or no growth encourages the company to continue on its current course, making only small adjustments for inflation in its sales and profit objectives. The company faces no obvious opportunities or threats and has no significant strengths or weaknesses. Few aggressive new competitors are likely to enter such an industry. The leaders in the industry (cell 4) probably are holding off making any significant investment until the industry becomes more attractive. Weaker competitors (cell 6) are likely to retrench by cutting costs in an attempt to stay profitable or selling out. Unless the industry is undergoing consolidation, the relative comfort possessed by a company in this situation is likely to result in its following a no-change strategy in which it expects the future to continue as an extension of the present. Rarely articulated as a definite strategy, a **no change strategy's** success depends on a lack of significant change in a corporation's situation. Most small-town businesses probably follow this strategy before Wal-Mart moves into their areas. In one fell swoop, the opening of a new Wal-Mart changes the competitive position of most small-town businesses from average to weak (and thus from stability to retrenchment).

When an industry is reaching maturity and has dropped from high attractiveness to medium attractiveness (and may even be on its way to becoming unattractive), a company with only an average competitive position may find its sales and profits leveling off and perhaps even beginning to decrease. Rather than announcing this to its shareholders and the investment community at large, top management may be tempted to follow the **profit strategy.** Wanting to believe that this drop in industry attractiveness is only temporary, management defers or cuts some short-term discretionary expenses, such as R&D, maintenance, and advertising, to stabilize profits during this period. For example, many U.S. airlines were accused during the 1980s of reducing their maintenance budgets and of canceling contracts for the purchase of new planes so that they could remain profitable during a period of aggressive price competition. Obviously, the profit strategy is useful only to help a company get through a temporary difficulty when the industry's attractiveness is dropping. Unfortunately, the strategy is seductive and if continued long enough will lead to a decline in a corporation's competitive position—as several airlines discovered to their chagrin when the industry continued to be less attractive than expected and they found themselves unable to compete in any way other than price. The profit strategy thus is a passive, short-term response to the situation described in Cell 5. A more active response to this situation is horizontal growth through the acquisition of some of the weaker firms in the industry.

Retrenchment Strategies

Retrenchment strategies may be pursued when a company has a weak competitive position regardless of the industry's attractiveness. The weak competitive position typically results in poor performance—sales are down and profits may become losses. With these strategies the pressure to improve performance is great. As is the coach of a losing football team, the CEO typically is under pressure to do something quickly or be fired. In an attempt to eliminate the weaknesses that are dragging the company down, management may follow one of several retrenchment strategies. Depending on the attractiveness of the industry, managers could select from among the turnaround (Cell 3), captive company or selling out (Cell 6), and bankruptcy or liquidation (Cell 9) strategies.

Turnaround (Cell 3) The **turnaround strategy** probably is most appropriate when a corporation is in a highly attractive industry and its problems are pervasive but not yet critical. This strategy emphasizes the improvement of operational efficiency. Analogous to a diet, the two basic phases of turnaround strategy are contraction and consolidation.[40]

Contraction is the initial effort to "stop the bleeding" quickly with across-the-board cutbacks in size and costs. Consolidation is the implementation of a program to stabilize the now leaner corporation. To streamline the company, management develops plans to reduce unnecessary overhead and to justify the costs of functional activities. This time is crucial for the organization. If management doesn't conduct the consolidation phase in a positive manner, many of the company's best people will leave. However if all employees are encouraged to get involved in productivity improvements, the firm is likely to emerge from this strategic retrenchment period a much stronger and better organized company. It has improved its competitive position and is able once again to expand the business.[41] The Strategy in Action on page 164 describes the successful use of the turnaround strategy by Texaco, Inc.

Captive Company or Selling Out (Cell 6) A company with a weak competitive position in an industry of only medium (and probably declining) attractiveness may not be able to engage in a full-blown turnaround strategy. The industry isn't sufficiently attractive to justify such an effort either from the current management or

SUCCESSFUL TURNAROUND AT TEXACO, INC.

Strategy in Action

Long considered a laggard in the oil industry, Texaco ran into serious difficulty in 1986 when it was forced to file for bankruptcy. CEO James Kinnear initiated a turnaround strategy by selling marginal product lines, slashing costs, and cutting the payroll by almost one third. He expanded the company's oil exploration effort—long a weakness of the company and upgraded its refining facilities to produce cleaner fuels. The emphasis then turned to renovating its network of 14,000 gas stations. By 1993, the strategy had begun to show results. Market share increased almost 6% from 1990 to 1992, moving Texaco to fourth place in the U.S. industry. Earnings reached $1.2 billion on sales of $40 billion in 1993. The company had effectively transformed its old weaknesses into new strengths and moved from Figure 6.3's Cell 3 (retrenchment) to Cell 2 (growth via horizontal integration). The company in 1993 was busily building retail networks near each of its seven U.S. refineries to reduce costs further. Expanding internationally, Texaco opened Europe's largest gas station in the United Kingdom and was working with a partner to build a refinery in Thailand to supply the fast-growing Asian market.

Source: T. Smart, "Pumping Up at Texaco," *Business Week* (June 7, 1993), pp. 112–113.

from investors. Nevertheless, a company in this situation faces poor sales and increasing losses unless it takes some kind of action. Sometimes referred to by the chess term *endgame,* this situation of slow growth, no growth, or negative growth in an industry forms the second half of a business's life.[42] Management desperately searches for an "angel" by offering to be a **captive company** to one of its larger customers in order to guarantee the company's continued existence with a long-term contract. In this way, the corporation may be able to reduce the scope of some of its functional activities, such as marketing, thus reducing costs significantly. The weaker company gains certainty of sales and production in return for becoming heavily dependent on one firm for at least 75% of its sales. This strategy became popular during the 1980s in the moderately attractive auto parts and electronics parts industries for small firms with weak competitive positions. For example, in order to become the sole supplier of a part to General Motors, Simpson Industries of Birmingham, Michigan, agreed to have its engine parts facilities and books inspected and its employees interviewed by a special team from GM. In return, GM purchased nearly 80% of the company's production through long-term contracts.[43]

In a moderately attractive industry, economies of scale in manufacturing, marketing and distribution, and purchasing may become crucial to keeping costs down and profits up. If a corporation with a weak competitive position in this industry is unable either to pull itself up by its bootstraps or to find a customer to which it can become a captive company, it may have no choice but to sell out and leave the industry completely. The **selling out strategy** makes sense if a company doesn't see any way to build some strengths or shore up its weaknesses and management believes that the industry isn't soon likely to become more attractive. It can still obtain a good price by selling out to firms with moderately attractive positions (cell 5) that are expanding through horizontal integration. To the extent that a company with a weak competitive position in this industry can sell out at a good price for its shareholders (before things get worse), this strategy makes sense. Johnson Products, a pioneer in hair care products for African-American and other ethnic markets, over time lost its competitive position to larger cosmetics companies who had entered Johnson Products' niche. After numerous attempts to turn the company around, the Johnson family finally decided to sell out to Ivax Corporation while they could still get a decent price for the firm.

Bankruptcy or Liquidation (Cell 9) When a company finds itself in the worst possible situation with a weak competitive position in an industry of low attractiveness, management's alternatives are limited—and all are distasteful. To the extent that top management identifies with the corporation, bankruptcy or liquidation may be perceived as an admission of failure. Pride and reputation, as well as jobs and financial assets, are liquidated. Options center on getting out of the industry before continued losses drain off all assets. Because no one is interested in buying a weak company in an unattractive industry, the firm ultimately must pursue a bankruptcy or liquidation strategy.

Bankruptcy involves giving up management of the firm to the courts in return for some settlement of the corporation's obligations. Top management hopes that, after the court decides the claims, the company will be stronger and better able to compete in a more attractive industry.[44] Wang Laboratories, Inc., took this approach in 1992. Founded by An Wang, the company had been unable to make the transition from word processors to personal computers and finally collapsed after the death of its founder. It emerged from bankruptcy in 1993 under a court-supervised reorganization plan requiring the company to focus on office software. Although the new management anticipated a profitable first year, analysts had their doubts about its long-term prospects.

In contrast to bankruptcy, which seeks to perpetuate the corporation, **liquidation** terminates the firm. When the industry is unattractive and the company is too weak to be sold as a going concern, management may choose to convert as many salable assets as possible to cash, which the company then distributes to its shareholders after paying all obligations. No matter how bad the condition of some department stores or airlines, for example, real estate and airport gates usually have some value. The benefit of liquidation over bankruptcy is that the board of directors, as representatives of the shareholders, and top management make the decisions instead of turning them over to the court, which may choose to ignore the shareholders completely.

At times top management must be willing to select one of these less desirable retrenchment strategies. Unfortunately, some top managers do not like to admit that their company has serious weaknesses. From their research of companies in difficulty, Nystrom and Starbuck conclude that top managers often don't perceive that crises are developing. When they do eventually notice trouble, top managers tend to attribute problems to temporary environmental disturbances and to follow profit strategies of postponing investments, reducing maintenance, halting training, liquidating assets, denying credit to customers, and raising prices. As described in the Schwinn example in Chapter 1 on pages 1–2, management adopts a "weathering-the-storm" attitude. "A major activity becomes changing the accounting procedures in order to conceal the symptoms."[45] Even when things are going terribly wrong, top management may be tempted to avoid liquidation and hope for a miracle.[46] For this reason a corporation needs a strong board of directors that, to safeguard stockholders' interests, can tell top management when to quit.

Corporate Strategy in the Multibusiness Firm

With some slight changes, the corporate strategies presented for the single business firm—growth, stability, and retrenchment—are applicable to the multibusiness corporation. For example, the retrenchment strategy of selling out becomes one of divestment when applied to a division. However, the model presented in Fig. 6.3 for corporations operating one business in one industry is *not* applicable to the multibusiness firm. For example, a multibusiness firm cannot follow a concentration strategy unless it first goes through retrenchment to divest itself of all but its core business.

For the multibusiness corporation, a key part of corporate strategy deals with the management of its many products and business units in numerous industries. As mentioned previously in Chapter 5, this type of corporation usually is organized as a divisional or conglomerate structure, depending on whether the business units are related (divisional) or unrelated (conglomerate). Large corporations using the divisional structure often combine their divisions into strategic business units (SBUs) based on divisional similarities. (We discuss SBUs in more detail in Chapter 8.) Top management usually treats divisions or SBUs as semi-autonomous units, generally with the authority to develop their own business-level strategies within corporate objectives and strategy. The primary job of corporate headquarters is twofold: (1) to allocate financial resources among business units to encourage overall corporate growth, and (2) to promote cooperation among units to achieve some synergy and thus higher corporate profits. Exemplifying this role are the comments of Hays Watkins, past Chairman of CSX Corporation (a transportation company comprising railroads, barge lines, and trucking companies) describing the role of corporate headquarters at CSX:

> Our management strategy . . . is to leave day-to-day operations largely with our subsidiaries. We at CSX . . . concentrate on what we call the three Ps—Policy, Planning, and Policing. We provide the broad policy and program guidance, and then we make sure that guidance is carried out. We at the CSX level also ensure that proper coordination is achieved among our various subsidiaries.[47]

Corporate strategy in the multibusiness firm is especially concerned with finding the optimal mix of businesses to fit the many industries in which the corporation operates.

Portfolio Analysis

One of the most popular aids to developing corporate strategy in a multibusiness corporation is portfolio analysis. This approach places corporate headquarters in the role of an internal banker. Top management views its business units as a series of investments from which it expects to earn a profitable return. The units form a portfolio of investments that top management must constantly juggle to ensure the best return on the corporation's investments. This approach reflects the view that the essence of strategic decision making is that resources are allocated to one project and denied to another.[48] Financial techniques thus tend to dominate strategic decision making at the corporate level of a multibusiness firm. At CSX, for example, Hays Watkins reported that the financial person was "the one that the president and I work with the most . . . I guess we've had a culture around here for many years that the finance person is probably the single most important staff member of the company."[49]

Over half the Fortune 500 companies practice some form of portfolio analysis in strategy formulation.[50] The rate of use by companies located in other industrialized nations probably is similar.

Management conducts portfolio analysis with a series of two-dimensional matrixes that summarize internal and external strategic factors. One axis of the matrixes represents the business units' environments in terms of industry attractiveness; the other represents the business units' capabilities in terms of their competitive positions. Positioning these two sets of strategic factors in a matrix thus results in an easy-to-grasp graphical representation of a firm's strategic situation. There are several matrixes available to reflect the variables under consideration in a portfolio.

Four-Cell, BCG Growth-Share Matrix The simplest matrix is the growth-share matrix developed by the Boston Consulting Group (BCG), as depicted in Fig. 6.4. An analyst plots each of the corporation's product lines or business units on the matrix according to both the growth rate of the industry in which it competes and its relative market share. A unit's relative competitive position is defined as its market share in the industry divided by that of the largest other competitor. By this calculation, a relative market share above 1.0 belongs to the market leader. The business growth rate is the percentage of market growth, that is, the percentage by which sales of a particular line of products have increased. A basic assumption of this method is that, other things being equal, a growing market is an attractive one.

The line separating areas of high and low relative competitive position is set at 1.5 times. A product line or business unit must have relative strengths of at least this magnitude to ensure that it will have the dominant position needed to be a "star" or "cash cow." In contrast, a product line or unit having a relative competitive position of less than 1.0 has "dog" status.[51] Each product or unit is represented in Fig. 6.5 by a circle, the area of which represents the relative significance of each business unit or product line to the corporation in terms of assets used or sales generated.

FIGURE 6.4 **BCG Portfolio Matrix**

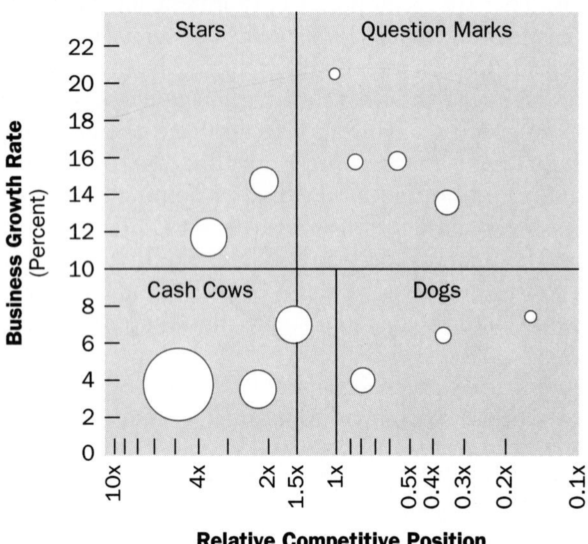

Source: B. Hedley, "Strategy and the Business Portfolio," *Long Range Planning* (February 1977), p. 12. Reprinted by permission.

The growth-share matrix has a lot in common with the product life cycle. Companies in a fast-growing industry typically introduce new products. Initially, these products are called "question marks." **Question marks** (sometimes called "problem children" or "wildcats") are new products that have potential for success but that need a lot of cash for development. If one of these products is to gain enough market share to become a market leader and thus a star, funds must be reallocated from one or more mature products to the question mark. **Stars** are market leaders typically at the peak of their product life cycle and usually generate enough cash to maintain their high share of the market. When their market growth rate slows, stars become cash cow products. **Cash cows** typically bring in far more money than needed to maintain their market share. As these products move along the decline stage of their life cycles, management "milks" them for cash to invest in new question mark products. For example, IBM's mainframe computer business had been built on a 1964 design. Even though mainframes had become a mature business by 1992, they still accounted for about 60% of the company's total profits—profits that IBM could invest in new products and developing technology.[52] Question mark products that fail to obtain a dominant market share (and thus become a star) by the time the industry growth rate inevitably slows become dogs. **Dogs** are those products with low market share that do not have the potential (because they are in an unattractive industry) to bring in much cash. According to the BCG growth-share matrix, dogs should be either sold off or managed carefully for the small amount of cash they can generate.

FIGURE 6.5 **General Electric's Business Screen**

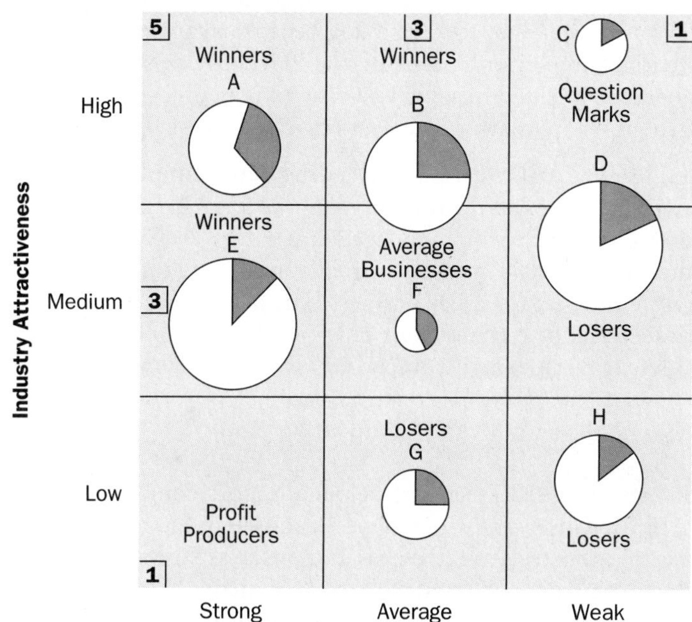

Source: Adapted from *Strategic Management in GE,* Corporate Planning and Development, General Electric Corporation. Used by permission of General Electric Company.

After plotting the current positions of a company's product lines or business units on a matrix, the analyst can project their future positions, assuming no change in strategy. Management can then use the present and projected matrixes to help identify the primary strategic issues facing the organization. The goal of any company is to maintain a balanced portfolio that allows sufficient cash flow and the ability to harvest mature products in declining industries to support new ones in growing industries.

Underlying the BCG growth-share matrix is the concept of the experience curve (discussed in Chapter 5). The key to success is assumed to be market share. Firms with the highest market share will tend to have a cost leadership position based on economies of scale, among other things. If a company uses the experience curve to its advantage, it should be able to manufacture and sell new products at a price low enough to garner early market share leadership. When a product becomes a star, it is destined to be very profitable because of its inevitable future as a cash cow.

Research into the growth-share matrix generally supports its assumptions and recommendations except for the advice that dogs should be promptly harvested or liquidated.[53] A product with a low share in a declining industry may still be profitable if the product has a niche in which market demand remains stable and predictable.[54] If enough of the competition leaves the industry, a product's market share can increase by default until the dog becomes the market leader and thus a cash cow. Some firms may choose to keep a dog because its presence creates an entry barrier for potential competitors. All in all, the BCG growth-share matrix is a popular technique because it is quantifiable and easy to use.

Nevertheless, the growth-share matrix has been criticized for several reasons.

- The use of highs and lows to make just four categories is too simplistic.
- The link between market share and profitability isn't necessarily strong. Low-share businesses can be profitable, too (and vice versa).
- Growth rate is only one aspect of industry attractiveness. High-growth markets may not always be the best for every business unit or product line.
- It considers the product line or business unit only in relation to one competitor: the market leader. It misses small competitors with fast-growing market shares.
- Market share is only one aspect of overall competitive position.[55]

Nine-Cell GE Business Screen General Electric developed a more complicated matrix with the assistance of McKinsey and Company. As shown in Fig. 6.5, its nine cells are based on long-term industry attractiveness and business strength/competitive position. Interestingly, this nine-cell matrix is almost identical to the *Directional Policy Matrix* developed by Shell Oil and used extensively by European firms. The GE business screen matrix, in contrast to the BCG growth-share matrix, includes much more data in its two principal factors than just business growth rate and comparable market share. For example, at GE, industry attractiveness includes market growth rate, industry profitability, size, and pricing practices, among possible opportunities and threats. Business strength or competitive position covers market share, technological position, profitability, and size, among possible strengths and weaknesses.[56]

The individual product lines or business units are identified by a letter and plotted as circles on the GE business screen matrix. The area of each circle is in proportion to the size of the industry in terms of sales. The pie slices within the circles depict the market share of each product line or business unit.

The following steps are recommended for the plotting of product lines or business units on the GE business screen matrix.[57]

1. Select criteria to rate the industry for each product line or business unit. Assess overall industry attactiveness for each product line or business unit on a scale from 1 (very unattractive) to 5 (very attractive).
2. Select the key factors needed for success in each product line or business unit. Assess business strength/competitive position for each product line or business unit on a scale of 1 (very weak) to 5 (very strong).
3. Plot each product line's or business unit's current position on a nine-cell matrix.
4. Plot the firm's future portfolio assuming that present corporate and business strategies remain unchanged. Is there a performance gap between projected and desired portfolios? If the answer is yes, this gap should serve as a stimulus

to serious review of the corporation's current mission, objectives, strategies, and policies.

Overall, the nine-cell GE business screen matrix is an improvement over the Boston Consulting Group growth-share matrix. The GE method considers many more variables and doesn't lead to simplistic conclusions. For example, it recognizes that many different ways may be used to assess the attractiveness of an industry (other than simply using growth rate) and thus allows users to select the criteria they believe are most appropriate to the situation.[58] Nevertheless, using this matrix can get quite complicated and cumbersome. The numerical estimates of industry attractiveness and business strength/competitive position give the appearance of objectivity but in reality are subjective judgments that may vary from person to person. Another shortcoming is that it cannot effectively show the positions of new products or business units in developing industries.

Fifteen-Cell Product/Market Evolution Matrix Developed by C.W. Hofer and based on the product life cycle, the 15-cell product/market evolution matrix (shown in Fig. 6.6) encompasses the types of developing products or business units that cannot be shown easily on the GE business screen matrix. Plotting of products or business units is by competitive position and stage of product/market evolution.[59] As in the GE matrix, the circles represent the sizes of the industries involved, and the pie wedges represent the market shares of the firm's business units or product lines. Present and future matrixes can be developed to identify strategic issues. In response to Fig. 6.6, for example, an analyst could ask why product or unit B does not have a greater share of the market, based on its strong competitive position. A limitation of this matrix is that the product life cycle doesn't always hold for every product. Many products, for example, do not inevitably decline but (like Tide detergent and Colgate toothpaste) are revitalized and put back on a growth track.[60]

Advantages and Limitations of Portfolio Analysis Strategic managers commonly use portfolio analysis in strategy formulation because it offers certain **advantages**.

- It encourages top management to evaluate each business individually and to set objectives and allocate resources for it.
- It stimulates the use of external data to supplement management's judgment.
- It raises the issue of cash flow availability for use in expansion and growth.
- Its graphic representation makes interpretation and communication easy.

However, some companies have reduced their use of portfolio analysis because of its **limitations**.[61]

- Defining product/market segments isn't easy.
- Using standard strategies may miss opportunities or be impractical.
- Providing an illusion of scientific rigor masks the reality that positions are based on subjective judgments.
- Utilizing value-laden terms such as cash cow and dog may lead to self-fulfilling prophecies. General Mills' Chief Executive H. Brewster Atwater, for example,

FIGURE 6.6 **Product/Market Evolution Portfolio Matrix**

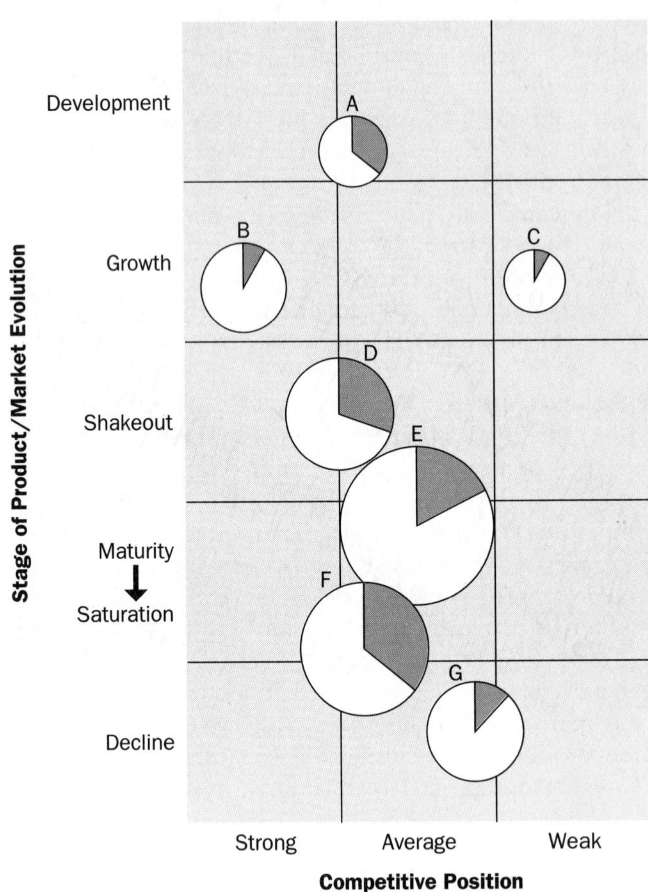

Source: C. W. Hofer and D. Schendel, *Strategy Formulation: Analytical Concepts* (St. Paul, Minn.: West, 1978), p. 34. From C. W. Hofer, "Conceptual Constructs for Formulating Corporate and Business Strategies" (Dover, Mass: Case Publishing), no. BP-0041, p. 3. Copyright © 1977 by Charles W. Hofer. Reprinted by permission.

cites his company's Bisquick brand of flour as a product that would have been written off years ago based on portfolio analysis. "This product is 57 years old. By all rights it should have been overtaken by newer products. But with the proper research to improve the product and promotion to keep customers excited, it's doing very well."[62]

- Determining what makes an industry attractive or at what stage a product is in its life cycle isn't always possible.
- Following naively the prescriptions of a portfolio method may actually reduce corporate profits if they are used inappropriately.[63]

FIGURE 6.7 **SWOT (TOWS) Matrix**

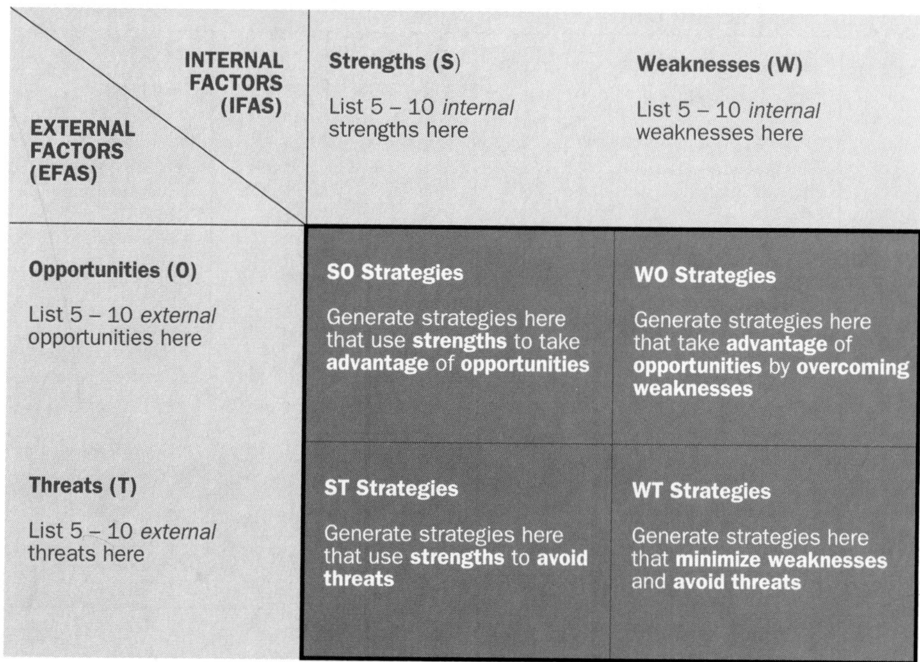

Source: Adapted from H. Weihrich, "The TOWS Matrix—A Tool for Situational Analysis," *Long Range Planning* (April 1982), p. 60. Copyright © 1982, with kind permission from Elsevier Science, Ltd., The Boulevard, Langford Lane, Kidlington OX5 1GB, UK.

Generating a SWOT (TOWS) Matrix

Thus far, we have discussed how a firm assesses its situation and have reviewed various available corporate strategies. The next task is to identify alternative ways that an organization can use its specific strengths to capitalize on opportunities or to avoid threats and to overcome its weaknesses. The SWOT (also called TOWS) matrix illustrates how management can match the external opportunities and threats facing the particular corporation with its internal strengths and weaknesses to yield in four sets of possible strategic alternatives. (See Fig. 6.7.) This method lends itself to brainstorming to create alternative strategies that management might not otherwise consider. It forces strategic managers to create both growth and retrenchment strategies. The SWOT matrix is applicable both to a single-business or a multibusiness corporation and may even be used for a business unit.

To generate a SWOT (TOWS) matrix for Maytag Corporation, for example, we used the External Strategic Factor Analysis Summary (EFAS) from Table 4.3 on page 109 and the Internal Strategic Factor Analysis Summary (IFAS) from Table 5.2 on page 136. We took the following steps to build Fig. 6.8.

TABLE 5.2 **Internal Strategic Factor Analysis Summary (IFAS): Maytag as Example**

Internal Strategic Factors (1)	Weight (2)	Rating (3)	Weighted Score (4)	Comments (5)
Strengths				
• Quality Maytag culture	.15	5	.75	Quality key to success
• Experienced top management	.05	4	.20	Know appliances
• Vertical integration	.10	4	.40	Dedicated factories
• Employee relations	.05	3	.15	Good, but deteriorating
• Hoover's international orientation	.15	3	.45	Hoover name in cleaners
Weaknesses				
• Process-oriented R&D	.05	2	.10	Slow on new products
• Distribution channels	.05	2	.10	Superstores replacing small dealers
• Financial position	.15	2	.30	High debt load
• Global positioning	.20	2	.40	Hoover weak outside the United Kingdom and Australia
• Manufacturing facilities	.05	4	.20	Investing now
Total	1.00		3.05	

TABLE 4.3 **External Strategic Factor Analysis Summary (EFAS): Maytag as Example**

External Strategic Factors (1)	Weight (2)	Rating (3)	Weighted Score (4)	Comments (5)
Opportunities				
• Economic integration of European Community	.20	4	.80	Acquisition of Hoover
• Demographics favor quality appliances	.10	5	.50	Maytag quality
• Economic development of Asia	.05	1	.05	Low Maytag presence
• Opening of Eastern Europe	.05	2	.10	Will take time
• Trend to "Super Stores"	.10	2	.20	Maytag weak in this channel
Threats				
• Increasing government regulations	.10	4	.40	Well positioned
• Strong U.S. competition	.10	4	.40	Well positioned
• Whirlpool and Electrolux strong globally	.15	3	.45	Hoover weak globally
• New product advances	.05	1	.05	Questionable
• Japanese appliance companies	.10	2	.20	Only Asian presence is Australia
Total	1.00		3.15	

FIGURE 6.8 **Generating a SWOT (TOWS) Matrix for Maytag Corporation**

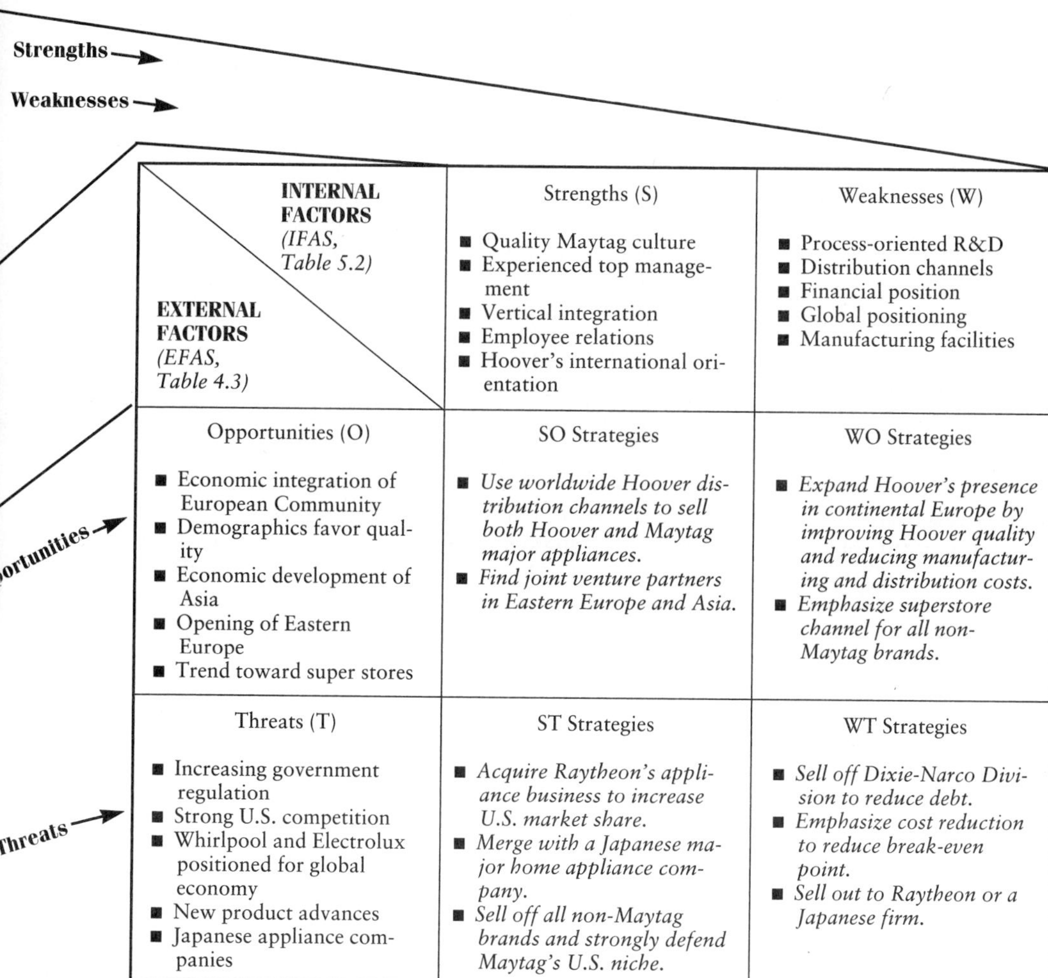

INTERNAL FACTORS *(IFAS, Table 5.2)* / **EXTERNAL FACTORS** *(EFAS, Table 4.3)*	Strengths (S)	Weaknesses (W)
	■ Quality Maytag culture ■ Experienced top management ■ Vertical integration ■ Employee relations ■ Hoover's international orientation	■ Process-oriented R&D ■ Distribution channels ■ Financial position ■ Global positioning ■ Manufacturing facilities
Opportunities (O) ■ Economic integration of European Community ■ Demographics favor quality ■ Economic development of Asia ■ Opening of Eastern Europe ■ Trend toward super stores	**SO Strategies** ■ *Use worldwide Hoover distribution channels to sell both Hoover and Maytag major appliances.* ■ *Find joint venture partners in Eastern Europe and Asia.*	**WO Strategies** ■ *Expand Hoover's presence in continental Europe by improving Hoover quality and reducing manufacturing and distribution costs.* ■ *Emphasize superstore channel for all non-Maytag brands.*
Threats (T) ■ Increasing government regulation ■ Strong U.S. competition ■ Whirlpool and Electrolux positioned for global economy ■ New product advances ■ Japanese appliance companies	**ST Strategies** ■ *Acquire Raytheon's appliance business to increase U.S. market share.* ■ *Merge with a Japanese major home appliance company.* ■ *Sell off all non-Maytag brands and strongly defend Maytag's U.S. niche.*	**WT Strategies** ■ *Sell off Dixie-Narco Division to reduce debt.* ■ *Emphasize cost reduction to reduce break-even point.* ■ *Sell out to Raytheon or a Japanese firm.*

1. In the block labeled **Opportunities,** we listed the external opportunities available in the corporation's current and future environment (EFAS, Table 4.3).
2. In the block labeled **Threats,** we listed the external threats facing the corporation now and in the future (EFAS, Table 4.3).
3. In the block labeled **Strengths,** we listed the specific areas of current and future strength for the corporation (IFAS, Table 5.2).
4. In the block labeled **Weaknesses,** we listed the specific areas of current and future weakness for the corporation (IFAS, Table 5.2).
5. We then generated a series of possible strategies for the Maytag Corporation, based on particular combinations of the four sets of strategic factors. For instance, we generated **SO Strategies** by thinking of ways that the corporation could use its strengths to take advantage of opportunities. In comparison, we considered the corporation's strengths as a way to avoid threats to obtain **ST Strategies.** We developed **WO Strategies** to take advantage of opportunities by overcoming weaknesses. We came up with the **WT Strategies** as basically defensive strategies primarily to minimize weaknesses and avoid threats.

In Conclusion . . .

KinderCare Learning Centers discovered the hard way that diversification into what seemed to be related businesses wasn't always the best route to success. KinderCare had been founded to take advantage of the increasing numbers of dual-career couples who were turning to day care centers to watch their children while they were at work. At that time, day care centers formed a fragmented, but fast-growing industry. Every neighborhood seemed to have some kind of day care center operating out of a church basement or somebody's home. The quality of care and the expertise of the staff, however, varied widely. Some centers were nothing more than baby-sitting services providing only minimal attention to the needs of the children. KinderCare changed all that. It offered pleasant surroundings staffed by well-trained personnel. Depending on the age of the child, various types of play and learning activities were offered. Soon, KinderCare had more than 1,000 centers in almost 40 states in the United States.

Not satisfied with its success, KinderCare's top management decided to take advantage of its relationship with working parents to diversify into the somewhat related businesses of banking, insurance, and retailing. Financed through junk bonds, the strategy failed to bring in enough cash to pay for its implementation. After years of losses, the company was driven to bankruptcy in the late 1980s. It emerged from bankruptcy in 1993—divested of its acquisitions and pledging to stay off the diversification bandwagon. The new CEO initiated a concentration strategy with an emphasis on horizontal integration. KinderCare opened its first center catering expressly to commuters in a renovated supermarket near the Metro line to Chicago. The company was talking to transportation authorities in New York, San Francisco, and Washington D.C. about similar sites. It was also offering to build child-care centers for big employers or running existing facilities for a fee. Management planned to open its first overseas center by the fall of 1994 in the

United Kingdom with eventual expansion into New Zealand and Australia. "We'd like to stay in countries with a common language," explained CEO Tull Gearreald. "There are enough cultural differences we'll have to work out."[64]

Points to Remember

- The basis of strategy formulation is SWOT analysis. If done well, it should lead to the identification of a corporation's distinctive competence—the particular skills and resources a firm possesses and the superior way in which it uses them. A Strategic Factors Analysis Summary (SFAS) matrix summarizes and condenses the external and internal strategic factors identified earlier as EFAS and IFAS.
- After situation analysis and before considering alternative strategies, management should take the time to review the company's current mission and objectives. If they are inappropriate, management should change them now.
- Corporate strategy for the single-business firm deals with the firm's orientation to growth and the industry in which it should compete. Strategic managers may choose among a wide variety of alternative strategies from growth to stability to retrenchment (each with a set of substrategies), depending on the attractiveness of the industry and the company's competitive position.
- Corporate strategy for the multibusiness firm considers not only the firm's orientation to growth and the industries in which it should compete, but also the management of its business units to achieve synergy. Portfolio analysis (including the BCG Matrix, GE Business Screen, and the Product/Market Evolution Matrix) is a useful technique for evaluating the contributions of various business units to corporate performance.
- The SWOT Matrix incorporates the external and internal strategic factors uncovered during environmental scanning. In the matrix, combining Opportunities and Threats with Strengths and Weaknesses yields four sets of alternative strategies for either a single-business or multibusiness corporation (or a business unit).

Discussion Questions

1. How does the Strategic Factors Analysis Summary (SFAS) aid in strategy formulation?
2. What industry forces might cause a company's propitious niche to disappear?
3. How does transaction cost economics apply to vertical integration? To concentric versus conglomerate diversification?
4. How does horizontal integration differ from vertical integration? From concentric diversification?
5. Must a corporation have a common thread running through its many activities in order to be successful? Why or why not?
6. What are the trade-offs between an internal and an external growth strategy?

7. Is stability really a strategy or is it just a term for no strategy? Explain your answer.
8. What is the value of portfolio analysis? Its dangers?
9. Compare and contrast SWOT analysis with portfolio analysis.
10. What concepts or assumptions underlie the BCG growth-share matrix? Are these concepts valid? Why or why not?
11. Is the GE Business Screen matrix just a more complicated version of the BCG growth-share matrix? Why or why not?
12. What is the value of the SWOT (TOWS) Matrix in strategy formulation? Do you agree with this way of generating strategic alternatives? Why or why not?

Notes

1. R. Turner and T. R. King, "Disney Stands Aside as Rivals Stampede to Digital Alliances," *Wall Street Journal* (September 24, 1993), p. A1.
2. R. D. Hof, "Hewlett-Packard Digs Deep For a Digital Future," *Business Week* (October 18, 1993), pp. 72–75.
3. R. Reed and R. J. DeFillipi, "Causal Ambiguity, Barriers to Imitation, and Sustainable Competitive Advantage," *Academy of Management Review* (January 1990), pp. 89–90.
4. D. Leonard-Barton, "Core Capabilities and Core Rigidities: A Paradox in Managing New Product Development," *Strategic Management Journal* (Summer 1992), pp. 111–125.
5. W. H. Newman, "Shaping the Master Strategy of Your Firm," *California Management Review,* Vol. 9, No. 3 (1967), pp. 77–88.
6. D. F. Abell, "Strategic Windows," *Journal of Marketing* (July 1978), pp. 21–26, as reported by K. R. Harrigan, "Entry Barriers in Mature Manufacturing Industries," in *Advances in Strategic Management,* Vol. 2, edited by R. Lamb (Greenwich, Conn.: JAI Press, 1983), pp. 67–97.
7. B. McLeod, "No Cold Shoulder for Zamboni: Ice Rink Fans Give Warm Reception," (Ames, Iowa) *Daily Tribune* (October 16, 1993), p. B5.
8. B. B. Tregoe and J. W. Zimmerman, "The New Strategic Manager," *Business* (May–June 1981), p. 19.
9. This phenomenon is discussed in the literature as "gap analysis." See D. E. Hussey, "Glossary of Management Techniques," *International Review of Strategic Management,* Vol. 3, edited by D. E. Hussey (New York: John Wiley & Sons, 1992), pp. 60–61; D. L. Bates and J. E. Dillard, "Desired Future Position—A Practical Tool for Planning," *Long Range Planning* (June 1991), pp. 98–99.
10. J. B. White and C. Chandler, "Pressed by All Sides, Hard-Driving Toyota Trims Back Its Goals," *Wall Street Journal* (May 19, 1992), p. A1.
11. T. S. Wurster, "Emerging Perspectives on Corporate Strategy," *International Review of Strategic Management,* Vol. 1, edited by D. E. Hussey (New York: John Wiley & Sons, 1990), pp. 69–70.
12. G. A. Walter and J. B. Barney, "Management Objectives in Mergers and Acquisitions," *Strategic Management Journal* (January 1990), pp. 79–86. This research study reported that the main objectives for engaging in the following strategies were: vertical integration—manage critical dependencies; horizontal integration—enter new businesses, economies of scale and scope, expand along product lines, and manage critical dependencies; concentric diversification—expand along product lines; conglomerate diversification—utilize financial capability and enter new businesses. These results support our rationale for placement of the four growth strategies in the particular cells depicted in Fig. 6.3.
13. L. Therrien, P. Coy, and N. Gross, "Motorola: How Much Will It Cost to Stay No.

1?" *Business Week* (October 29, 1990), pp. 96–97.
14. D. R. Dalton and I. F. Kesner, "Organizational Growth: Big Is Beautiful," *Journal of Business Strategy* (Summer 1985), pp. 38–48; D. R. Schmidt and K. L. Fowler, "Post-Acquisition Financial Performance and Executive Compensation," *Strategic Management Journal* (November–December 1990), pp. 559–569.
15. R. E. Hoskisson and M. A. Hitt, "Antecedents and Performance Outcomes of Diversification: A Review and Critique of Theoretical Perspectives," *Journal of Management* (June 1990), 461–509.
16. R. D. Buzzell, "Is Vertical Integration Profitable?" *Harvard Business Review* (January–February 1983), pp. 92–102.
17. J. Vesey, "Vertical Integration: Its Effects on Business Performance," *Managerial Planning* (May–June 1978), pp. 11–15.
18. K. R. Harrigan, "Exit Barriers and Vertical Integration," *Academy of Management Journal* (September 1985), pp. 686–697; R. A. D'Aveni and A. Y. Ilinitch, "Complex Patterns of Vertical Integration in the Forest Products Industry: Systematic and Bankruptcy Risks," *Academy of Management Journal* (August 1992), pp. 596–625.
19. N. Templin, "GM Offers Its Outside Parts Suppliers the Use of Idle Factories and Workers," *Wall Street Journal* (July 29, 1992), p. A4.
20. K. R. Harrigan, *Strategies for Vertical Integration* (Lexington, Mass.: Lexington Books, D. C. Heath, 1983), pp. 16–21.
21. L. Grant, "Partners in Profit," *U.S. News and World Report* (September 20, 1993), pp. 65–66.
22. J. A. Robins, "Organization as Strategy: Restructuring Production in the Film Industry," *Strategic Management Journal* (Summer 1993), pp. 103–118.
23. G. P. Zachary, "High-Tech Firms Find It's Good to Line Up Outside Contractors," *Wall Street Journal* (July 29, 1992), pp. A1, A5; B. R. Schlender, "How Toshiba Makes Alliances Work," *Fortune* (October 4, 1993), pp. 116–120.
24. Horizontal integration is viewed as a useful means of managing competitive uncertainty. See J. Pfeffer and G. Salancik, *The External Control of Organizations* (New York: HarperCollins, 1978).
25. L. Armstrong, "Packard Bell Discovers A Bon Ami," *Business Week* (July 5, 1993), pp. 103–106.
26. V. L. Blackburn and J. R. Lang, "Investigating the Relationship Between Pre-Merger Performance and Merger Outcomes," *International Journal of Management* (September 1990), pp. 332–342; S. Chatterjee and B. Wernerfelt, "The Link Between Resources and Type of Diversification: Theory and Practice," *Strategic Management Journal* (January 1991), pp. 33–48.
27. B. O'Brien, "Tired of Airline Losses, AMR Pushes Its Bid to Diversify Business," *Wall Street Journal* (February 8, 1993), p. A1.
28. One study reported that unrelated diversification improved the profitability of poorly performing firms. Poor performers did not do well with related diversification, however. See Blackburn and Lang, pp. 332–342.
29. C. G. Smith and A. C. Cooper, "Established Companies Diversifying into Young Industries: A Comparison of Firms with Different Levels of Performance," *Strategic Management Journal* (March–April, 1988), pp. 111–121.
30. R. P. Rumelt, *Strategy, Structure, and Economic Performance* (Cambridge, Mass.: Harvard University Press, 1974); H. Singh and C. A. Montgomery, "Corporate Acquisition Strategies and Economic Performance," *Strategic Management Journal* (July–August 1987), pp. 377–386; R. Amit and J. Livnot, "A Concept of Conglomerate Diversification," *Journal of Management* (December 1988), pp. 593–604; H. A. Haverman, "Between a Rock and a Hard Place: Organizational Change and Performance Under Conditions of Fundamental Environmental Transformation," *Administrative Science Quarterly* (March 1992), pp. 48–75.
31. P. G. Simmonds, "Using Diversification as a Tool for Effective Performance," *Handbook of Business Strategy, 1992/93 Yearbook,* edited by H. E. Glass and M. A. Hovde (Boston: Warren, Gorham and Lamont, 1992), pp. 3.1–3.7.
32. A. Seth, "Value Creation in Acquisitions: A Re-Examination of Performance Issues," *Strategic Management Journal* (February 1990), pp. 99–115; B. W. Keats, "Diversification and Business Economic Performance

Revisited: Issues of Measurement and Causality," *Journal of Management* (March 1990), pp. 61–72; V. L. Blackburn, J. R. Lang, and K. H. Johnson, "Mergers and Shareholder Returns: The Roles of Acquiring Firms' Ownership and Diversification Strategy," *Journal of Management* (December 1990), pp. 769–782.

33. S. Chatterjee and M. Lubatkin, "Corporate Mergers, Stockholder Diversification, and Changes in Systematic Risk," *Strategic Management Journal* (May–June 1990), pp. 255–268; V. Blackburn and J. R. Lang, "Toward a Market/Ownership Constrained Theory of Merger Behavior," *Journal of Management* (March 1989), pp. 77–88.
34. M. Goold and K. Luchs, "Why Diversify? Four Decades of Management Thinking," *Academy of Management Executive* (August 1993), pp. 7–25.
35. W. B. Carper, "Corporate Acquisitions and Shareholder Wealth: A Review and Exploratory Analysis," *Journal of Management* (December 1990), pp. 807–823; P. G. Simmonds, "Using Diversification as a Tool for Effective Performance," *Handbook of Business Strategy, 1992/93 Yearbook,* edited by H. E. Glass and M. A. Hovde (Boston: Warren, Gorham and Lamont, 1992), pp. 3.1–3.7; B. T. Lamont and C. A. Anderson, "Mode of Corporate Diversification and Economic Performance," *Academy of Management Journal* (December 1985), pp. 926–936.
36. R. P. Lynch, *The Practical Guide to Joint Ventures and Corporate Alliances* (New York: John Wiley & Sons, 1989), p. 7.
37. K. R. Harrigan, *Managing for Joint Venture Success* (Lexington, Mass.: Lexington Books, D. C. Heath, 1986), p. 4.
38. P. Burrows and S. Anderson, "Dell Computer Goes Into the Shop," *Business Week* (July 12, 1993), pp. 138–140.
39. E. Faltermayer, "Is This Layoff Necessary?" *Fortune* (June 1, 1992), pp. 71–86.
40. D. K. Robbins and J. A. Pearce II, "Turnaround: Retrenchment and Recovery," *Strategic Management Journal* (May 1992), pp. 287–309.
41. F. M. Zimmerman, "Managing a Successful Turnaround," *Long Range Planning* (June 1989), pp. 105–124.
42. K. R. Harrigan, *Managing Maturing Businesses* (Lexington, Mass.: Lexington Books, D. C. Heath, 1988), p. 1.
43. J. B. Treece, "U.S. Parts Makers Just Won't Say 'Uncle,'" *Business Week* (August 10, 1987), pp. 76–77.
44. D. M. Flynn and M. Farid, "The Intentional Use of Chapter XI: Lingering Versus Immediate Filing," *Strategic Management Journal* (January 1991), pp. 63–74.
45. P. C. Nystrom and W. H. Starbuck, "To Avoid Organizational Crises, Unlearn," *Organizational Dynamics* (Spring 1984), p. 55.
46. For an interesting analysis of management's persistence in attempting to save a firm characterized by sustained low performance, see M. W. Meyer and L. G. Zucker, *Permanently Failing Organizations* (Newbury Park, California: Sage, 1989).
47. J. D. Hunger, B. Ferrin, H. Felix-Gamez, and T. Goetzman, "CSX Corporation," *Cases in Strategic Management,* edited by T. L. Wheelen and J. D. Hunger (Reading, Mass.: Addison-Wesley, 1987), p. 109.
48. R. Brown, "Making the Product Portfolio a Basis for Action," *Long Range Planning* (February 1991), p. 103.
49. Hunger, Ferrin, Felix-Gamez, and Goetzman.
50. D. K. Sinha, "Strategic Planning in the Fortune 500," *Handbook of Business Strategy, 1991/92 Yearbook,* edited by H. E. Glass and M. A. Hovde (Boston: Warren, Gorham & Lamont, 1991), p. 9.6.
51. B. Hedley, "Strategy and the Business Portfolio," *Long Range Planning* (February 1977), p. 9.
52. J. W. Verity, "Twilight of the Mainframes," *Business Week* (August 17, 1992), p. 33.
53. D. C. Hambrick, I. C. MacMillan, and D. L. Day, "Strategic Attributes and Performance in the BCG Matrix—A PIMS-Based Analysis of Industrial Product Businesses," *Academy of Management Journal* (September 1982), pp. 510–531.
54. C. Y. Woo and A. C. Cooper, "The Surprising Case for Low Market Share," *Harvard Business Review* (November–December 1982), pp. 106–113; C. Carr, "Strategy Alternatives for Vehicle Component Manufacturers," *Long Range Planning* (August 1988), pp. 86–97.
55. P. McNamee, "Competitive Analysis Using Matrix Displays," *Long Range Planning* (June 1984), pp. 98–114; R. E. Walker, "Portfolio Analysis in Practice," *Long Range Planning* (June 1984), pp. 63–71; D. A. Aaker and G. S. Day, "The Perils

of High-Growth Markets," *Strategic Management Journal* (September–October 1986), pp. 409–421.

56. R. G. Hamermesh, *Making Strategy Work* (New York: John Wiley & Sons, 1986), p. 14. For a more complete list of characteristics, see McNamee, pp. 102–103.
57. C. W. Hofer and D. Schendel, *Strategy Formulation: Analytical Concepts* (St. Paul, Minn.: West, 1978), pp. 72–87.
58. B. Wernerfelt and C. A. Montgomery, "What Is an Attractive Industry?" *Management Science* (October 1986), pp. 1223–1230.
59. Similar to the Hofer model, but using 20 instead of 15 cells, is the Arthur D. Little (ADL) strategic planning matrix. For details see M. B. Coate, "Pitfalls in Portfolio Planning," *Long Range Planning* (June 1983), pp. 47–56.
60. A. Hiam, "Exposing Four Myths of Strategic Planning," *Journal of Business Strategy* (September–October 1990), pp. 27–28.
61. F. W. Gluck, "A Fresh Look at Strategic Management," *Journal of Business Strategy* (Fall 1985), pp. 4–19; D. A. Gilbert, E. Hartman, J. J. Mauriel, and R. E. Freeman, *A Logic for Strategy* (Cambridge, Mass.: Ballinger, 1988), pp. 65–74.
62. J. J. Curran, "Companies That Rob the Future," *Fortune* (July 4, 1988), p. 84.
63. S. F. Slater and T. J. Zwirlein, "Shareholder Value and Investment Strategy Using the General Portfolio Model," *Journal of Management* (December 1992), pp. 717–732.
64. S. Caminiti, "New Lessons in Customer Service," *Fortune* (September 20, 1993), pp. 79–80.

Strategy Formulation: Business and Functional Strategy

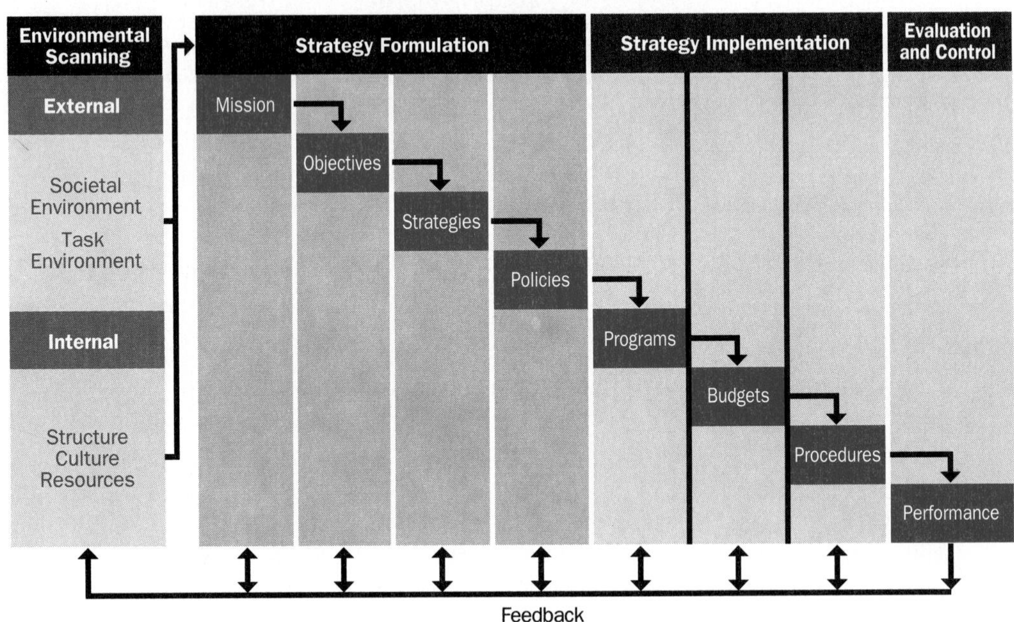

We are a Dunkin' Donuts, a Kentucky Fried Chicken, and a Pizza Hut, all rolled into one, for towns like Slater and Mitchellville.[1]
[Donald F. Lamberti, President, Casey's General Stores]

When Donald Lamberti incorporated Casey's General Stores in 1967, he formulated a strategy unknown at that time in the convenience store industry. Instead of targeting the large, growing metropolitan areas of the eastern, western, and southern United States where potential sales were high, he focused on the small towns in the agricultural heartland of the Midwest. At first, Casey's appeared to be just another imitator of the successful 7-Eleven convenience stores, offering gasoline and basic groceries.

Operating out of Des Moines, Iowa, Lamberti had noticed that many small towns in his part of the country were losing their retail businesses. Regional shopping malls with their wide selections and attractive merchandising were siphoning off customers. Even the major gasoline retailers, such as Shell Oil, were leaving the small towns of Illinois, Iowa, Nebraska, and the Dakotas. Casey's General Stores stepped into this developing retail vacuum. Contrary to all the conventional wisdom arguing against beginning a business in a declining market, Lamberti avoided direct competition with 7-Eleven and moved into these increasingly ignored small markets.

By 1993, Casey's operated 819 convenience stores (up from 653 stores in 1988) in its eight-state marketing area of Illinois, Iowa, Kansas, Minnesota, Missouri, Nebraska, South Dakota, and Wisconsin. Constantly thinking of ways to improve the offerings of his stores, Lamberti decided to expand from gasoline and basic groceries to include fast food. Casey's began offering fried chicken and pizza in its stores located in small towns without direct fast-food competition. "We want to have an exclusive," explained Lamberti. Next were in-store bakeries. In many small towns of the Midwest, Casey's was now the only retail business left. These towns were too small for even Wal-Mart to covet. Like any convenience store, prices were somewhat higher than in larger, more specialized stores in the cities. But small-town people didn't want to have to drive 10–20 miles for a loaf of bread or a pizza. At a time when other convenience stores were struggling to show a profit and avoid bankruptcy, Casey's grew and profited.

Casey's General Stores is successful because its strategic managers formulated a strategy to give it an advantage in a competitive industry. Casey's used a differentiation focus competitive strategy; that is, it focused on a particular market area and provided a differentiated product. This strategy is one of several business-level strategies discussed in this chapter as a continuation of the strategy formulation process introduced in Chapter 6. In this chapter we (1) identify and explain the range of business and functional alternative strategies available; (2) suggest criteria to use in evaluating these strategies; (3) explain how to select an optimal strategy; and (4) suggest how to translate strategy into policies.

As we described in Chapter 1, the typical large, multibusiness corporation operating in several different industries has three levels of strategy: corporate, business, and functional. In Chapter 6 we discussed alternative corporate strategies: the strategies that specify the firm's overall direction and its portfolio of businesses, that is, the industries within which the firm operates. In contrast, in this chapter we deal with the generation and selection of business and functional strategies: the strategies that determine a company's competitive advantage.

7.1 Business (Competitive) Strategy

Often called competitive strategy, **business strategy** focuses on improving the competitive position of a company's products or services within the specific industry or market segment that the company or business unit serves. Just as corporate strategy addresses **what** business(es) and industry(ies) the company should be in, business strategy addresses **how** the company or its units can compete in its businesses and industries. In addition, business strategy raises the following questions:

- Should we compete on the basis of low cost, or should we differentiate our products or services on some basis other than cost, such as quality or service?

- Should we compete head-to-head with our major competitors for the biggest but most sought-after share of the market, or should we focus on a niche in which we can satisfy a less sought-after but also profitable segment of the market?

These questions are applicable to a company operating a single business in one industry and, if a multibusiness corporation, to each of its business units.

Porter's Generic Competitive Strategies

Michael Porter proposes two "generic" competitive strategies for outperforming other corporations in a particular industry: lower cost and differentiation.[2] **Lower cost** is the ability of a company or a business unit to design, produce, and market a comparable product more efficiently than its competitors. **Differentiation,** in contrast, is the ability to provide unique and superior value to the buyer in terms of product quality, special features, or after-sale service. These strategies are called generic because any type or size of business firm—and even not-for-profit organizations—can pursue them.

Porter further proposes that a firm's competitive advantage in an industry is determined by its **competitive scope,** that is, the breadth of the company's or business unit's target market. Before using one of the two generic competitive strategies of lower cost or differentiation, the firm or unit must choose the range of product varieties it will produce, the distribution channels it will utilize, the types of buyers it will serve, the geographic areas in which it will sell, and the array of related industries in which it also will compete. These determinations should reflect an understanding of the firm's unique resources. Simply put, a company or business unit can choose a *broad target* (that is, aim at the middle of the mass market) or a *narrow target* (that is, aim at a market niche). Combining these two types of target markets with the two competitive strategies results in the four variations of generic strategies depicted in Fig. 7.1. When the lower cost and differentiation strategies have a broad mass-market target, they are simply called *cost leadership* and *differentiation.* When they are focused on a market niche (narrow target), however, they are called *cost focus* and *focused differentiation.*

Cost leadership is a low-cost competitive strategy that aims at the broad mass market and requires "aggressive construction of efficient-scale facilities, vigorous pursuit of cost reductions from experience, tight cost and overhead control, avoidance of marginal customer accounts, and cost minimization in areas like R&D, service, sales force, advertising, and so on."[3] Because of its lower costs, the cost leader is able to charge a lower price for its products than its competitors and still make a satisfactory profit. Some companies successfully following this strategy are Wal-Mart (retailing), Timex (watches), and Gateway 2000 (personal computers). Having a low-cost position also gives a company or business unit a defense against rivals. Its lower costs allow it to continue to earn profits during times of heavy competition. Its high market share gives great bargaining power with its suppliers because it buys in large quantities. Its low price serves as a barrier to entry, as few new entrants will be able to match the leader's cost advantage. As a result, cost leaders are likely to earn above average returns on investment.

FIGURE 7.1 **Porter's Generic Competitive Strategies**

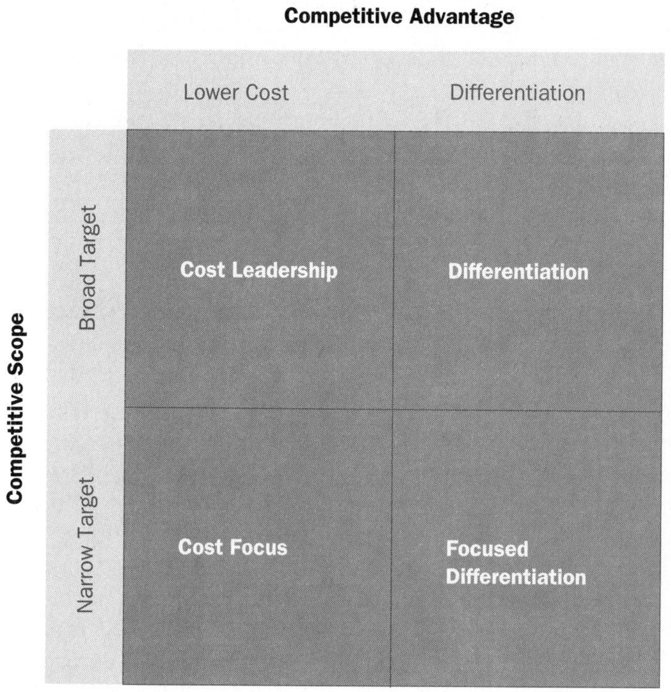

Competitive Advantage

Competitive Scope		Lower Cost	Differentiation
	Broad Target	**Cost Leadership**	**Differentiation**
	Narrow Target	**Cost Focus**	**Focused Differentiation**

Source: Reprinted with permission of The Free Press, an imprint of Simon & Schuster, from *The Competitive Advantage of Nations* by Michael E. Porter, p. 39. Copyright © 1990 by Michael E. Porter.

Dean Foods Company, for example, follows a cost leadership strategy by emphasizing a line of "copycat" private label brands it sells nationwide to supermarket chains that want good products at low prices. The company is the second-largest U.S. dairy after Borden and is the third largest in vegetable processing. As large food companies battle to build powerful national brand names, Dean Foods, located outside Chicago, satisfies supermarket demands by quickly imitating brand name products and offering them at low cost. As a result, Dean typically develops low-margin products on a shoestring budget and holds advertising costs far below the industry's average. The emphasis is on rigid cost control and close relationships with customers.

Differentiation is aimed at the broad mass market and involves the creation of a unique product or service, for which the company or business unit may charge a premium. This specialty can be associated with design or brand image, technology, features, dealer network, or customer service. Differentiation is a viable strategy for earning above average returns in a specific business because the resulting brand loyalty lowers customers' sensitivity to price. Increased costs usually can be passed

FADAL ENGINEERING PROSPERS USING A COST FOCUS STRATEGY

Strategy in Action

The machine tool industry in 1992 was not a very attractive enterprise for most U.S. companies. Led by Japanese corporations, importers were responsible for some 40% of the $4.3 billion industry. U.S. companies such as Cincinnati Milicron and Giddings & Lewis had been successful by catering to multibillion-dollar customers such as Caterpillar and Boeing, but also were threatened by foreign competition. All in all, it did not appear to be a good industry for a small, family-run business.

When Francis de Caussin, a Detroit machinist, moved his family to North Hollywood, California, in 1953, he formed a company whose name was the acronym of the first initials of the founder and his sons Adrian, David, and Larry: Fadal Engineering Company (pronounced fuh-dal). From their garage, the family built a business by making high-precision machine parts. Early in the 1980s, the family branched into the machine tool business. After considerable work, they made a no-frills vertical machining center to drill, bore, and mill metal pieces. Compared with the machine tools made for big manufacturers, Fadal's machine had fewer parts and simpler electronic controls.

The company soon expanded into other machine tools that were designed to appeal to smaller manufacturers that could not afford the more sophisticated, complex machines made by larger outfits. The machines made by Fadal were functional and durable, but far cheaper than the typical lowest priced competing machine. Since Fadal generally used

on to the buyers. Buyer loyalty also serves as an entry barrier—new firms must develop their own distinctive competence to differentiate their products in some way in order to compete successfully. Research suggests that a differentiation strategy is more likely to generate higher profits than is a low-cost strategy because differentiation creates a better entry barrier. However, a low-cost strategy is more likely to generate increases in market share.[4]

Examples of the successful use of a differentiation strategy are Walt Disney Productions (entertainment), Maytag (appliances), Mercedes-Benz (automobiles), and WordPerfect (software). Started in 1980, WordPerfect chose to compete against Wordstar and Microsoft Word for the MS-DOS, IBM-compatible word processing market. To differentiate its software from the competition, WordPerfect became the only company to offer customers a toll-free help line. At first, the company spent little on advertising, and sales grew largely through word of mouth. By 1994, WordPerfect had become one of two companies to dominate completely the word processing market. Besides the excellence of its product,

U.S.-made standard parts, repairs were usually a simple matter. Fadal's sales jumped to about $81 million in 1992 from just $12.4 million in 1985. The company controlled nearly 25% of the $300 million "vertical machining centers"—machine tools used primarily by small machine shops.

Why was a small, family-run machine toolmaker successful in a relatively unattractive industry? Its small size and the fact that existing competition was ignoring the small manufacturer's needs allowed Fadal to take advantage of an opportunity in a market niche. The company designed products with a minimum of parts and frills, making its machines inexpensive and reliable. For example, the company's toolchanger had only seven moving parts, far fewer than rival models. It kept overhead low, R&D was minimal, and only 20 of its 200 employees were salaried. Even during the downturn in the industry in the early 1990s, the company prospered. In 1992, the Fadal Engineering Company planned to introduce a new low-end machine tool. Still following the cost focus strategy that made it a success, management explained the company's policy for new products. According to Daniel de Caussin, grandson of the founder, "If it's too complicated, we throw the idea out."

Source: Z. Schiller, "Fadal's Attractions," *Business Week* (October 22, 1990), pp. 62–66; Z. Schiller, "Larry, Dave, Adrian de Caussin," *Business Week* (Reinventing American, 1992), pp. 186–188.

WordPerfect emphasizes customer service to gain competitive advantage in its battle with Microsoft.

Cost focus is a low-cost competitive strategy that focuses on a particular buyer group or geographic market and attempts to serve only this niche, to the exclusion of others. In using cost focus, the company or business unit seeks a cost advantage in its target segment. This strategy is based on the belief that a company or business unit that focuses its efforts can serve its narrow strategic target more efficiently than can its competition. However, a focus strategy does necessitate a trade-off between profitability and overall market share.

A good example of cost focus is Fadal Engineering. As described in the Strategy in Action on pages 186–187, Fadal focuses its efforts on building and selling no-frills machine tools to small manufacturers. It achieved cost focus by minimizing overhead and R&D and by focusing marketing efforts strictly on its market niche. Other examples of companies following this strategy are USAA (United Services Automobile Association), which offers low-cost insurance to active and retired military personnel, and local credit unions, which offer low-cost financial services to employees of specific organizations.

Differentiation focus, like cost focus, concentrates on a particular buyer group, product-line segment, or geographic market. Casey's General Stores, Morgan Motor Car Company (manufacturer of classic British sports cars), and local health food stores successfully follow this strategy. According to Porter, "The target segments must either have buyers with unusual needs or else the production and delivery system that best serves the target must differ from that of the other industry segments."[5] In using differentiation focus, the company or business unit seeks differentiation in its target segment. This strategy is valued because of a belief that a company or a unit that focuses its efforts can serve its narrow strategic target more effectively than can its competition.

Johnson Products, for example, successfully used a differentiation focus strategy by manufacturing and selling hair-care and cosmetic products to ethnic consumers. When the company was founded in 1955, none of the large cosmetics or hair-care companies made products tailored to the needs of African Americans. Johnson Products was the exception and worked to develop products such as Ultra Wave and Ultra Sheen to give African Americans more flexibility in hair styling. For two decades, the company dominated this market niche by capitalizing on each trend in ethnic hair fashion.

Risks in Competitive Strategies

No single competitive strategy is guaranteed to achieve success, and some companies that have successfully implemented one of Porter's competitive strategies have found that they could not sustain the strategy. In the case of Johnson Products, for example, the company did very well catering to the hair-care needs of the African-American community for two decades. Eventually, however, competitors, such as Revlon and Estée Lauder, noticed the attractiveness of this market niche and began to offer their own ethnic hair-care and cosmetic products. From a 1975 high of 80%, Johnson Products' share of the ethnic market dropped to 20% by 1990. "We got in first and opened the door for everyone," observed Eric Johnson, son of the company's founder, who went on to say, "But then somebody closed the door with our keys."[6] By 1993, the family had sold the company to a large pharmaceutical company having an ethnic cosmetics division.

As Table 7.1 shows, each of the generic strategies has its risks. For example, a company following a differentiation strategy must ensure that the higher price it charges for its higher quality is not priced too far above the competition—or else customers will not see the extra quality as worth the extra cost. This is what is meant in Table 7.1 by the term *cost proximity*.

Issues in Competitive Strategies

Porter argues that, to be successful, a company or business unit must achieve one of the generic competitive strategies. Otherwise, the company or business unit is **stuck in the middle** of the competitive marketplace with no competitive advantage

TABLE 7.1 **Risks of Generic Competitive Strategies**

Risks of Cost Leadership	Risks of Differentiation	Risks of Focus
Cost leadership is not sustained: • Competitors imitate. • Technology changes. • Other bases for cost leadership erode. Proximity in differentiation is lost.	Differentiation is not sustained: • Competitors imitate. • Bases for differentiation become less important to buyers. Cost proximity is lost.	The focus strategy is imitated: The target segment becomes structurally unattractive: • Structure erodes. • Demand disappears. Broadly targeted competitors overwhelm the segment: • The segment's differences from other segments narrow. • The advantages of a broad line increase.
Cost focusers achieve even lower cost in segments.	Differentiation focusers achieve even greater differentiation in segments.	New focusers subsegment the industry.

Source: Adapted/reprinted with permission of The Free Press, an imprint of Simon & Schuster, from *Competitive Advantage: Creating and Sustaining Superior Performance* by Michael E. Porter, p. 21. Copyright © 1985 by Michael E. Porter.

and is doomed to below average performance. An example of a company stuck in the middle was Tandy Corporation. Its strategy of selling personal computers to the average person failed to generate the amount of sales and profits top management had desired. Its computers had neither the exciting new features found on Compaq's products nor the low price of the PC clones like those sold through the mail by Dell or Gateway. Sales were stagnating. Attempting to increase its sales to business through its GRiD Systems subsidiary while keeping up its Radio Shack sales, Tandy faced the dilemma of trying to be all things to all people—and failing. Deciding at last that computers were distracting it from its primary business of consumer electronics retailing, management sold the company's computer operations to AST Research in 1993.

Research generally supports Porter's contention that a firm that fails to achieve a generic strategy is going to be stuck in the middle with no competitive advantage.[7] However, some businesses with both a low-cost and a high-differentiation position can be very successful.[8] The Japanese auto companies of Toyota, Nissan, and Honda are examples of firms that achieved both a low-cost and a high-quality position. G. S. Day refers to this result as "playing the spread" and cites the Kellogg Company as an example of a firm prospering by simultaneously lowering costs and selling at premium prices by offering superior customer value. Day contends that improving product quality can indirectly lower costs.[9] Thus Day agrees with W. Edwards Deming (the quality control expert who helped rebuild Japanese industry after World War II), who argues that quality and productivity (that is, lower cost production) are compatible. One of Deming's famous 14

FIGURE 7.2 **Combining Porter's Generic Competitive Strategies**

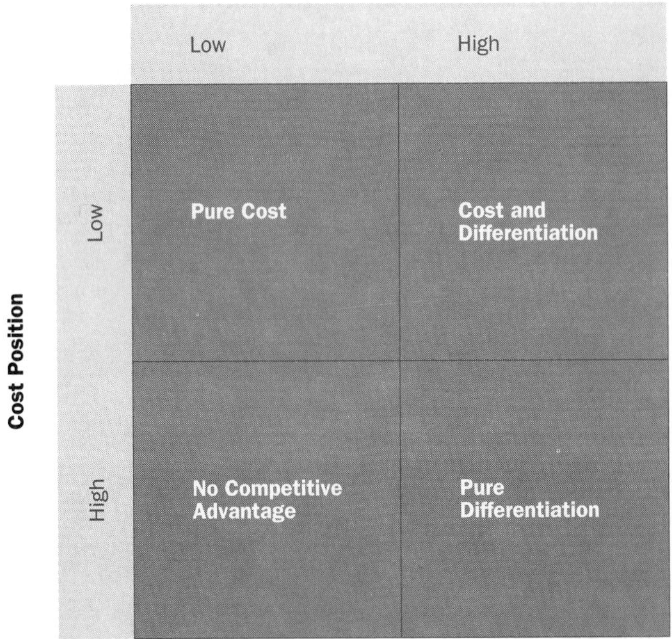

Source: R. E. White, "Generic Business Strategies, Organizational Context and Performance: An Empirical Investigation," *Strategic Management Journal* (May–June 1986), p. 226. Reprinted by permission of John Wiley & Sons, Ltd.

points for the transformation of industry states: "Improve constantly and forever the system of production and service, to improve quality and productivity, *and thus constantly decrease costs* (italics added)."[10] Instead of viewing cost leadership and differentiation as separate strategies, we can combine the two competitive strategies as shown in Fig. 7.2. Following this reasoning, Porter's stuck-in-the-middle situation actually is the cell with the high-cost and low-differentiation position labeled No Competitive Advantage.

Although Porter agrees that a company or a business unit may achieve low cost and differentiation simultaneously, he argues that this state often is temporary. "Achieving cost leadership and differentiation are also usually inconsistent, because differentiation is usually costly. . . . Eventually a competitor will choose a generic strategy and begin to implement it well, exposing the tradeoffs between cost and differentiation."[11] Porter does admit, however, that many different kinds of potentially profitable competitive strategies exist and that many variations are possible. Generally, only one company can successfully pursue the mass market cost leadership strategy (because it is so dependent on achieving dominant market share). However, others can pursue an almost unlimited number of differentiation and focus strategies (depending on the range of possible desirable features and the number of identifiable market niches).

Industry Structure and Competitive Strategy

Although Porter's generic competitive strategies are applicable to any industry, in some instances certain strategies are more likely to succeed than others. In a **fragmented industry**, for example, where many small and medium-sized local companies compete for relatively small shares of the total market, focus strategies will likely predominate. Fragmented industries are typical for businesses offering products in the early stages of their life cycles. If few economies are to be gained through size, no large firms will emerge and entry barriers will be low, allowing a stream of new entrants into the industry. If a company is able to overcome the limitations of a fragmented market, however, it can reap the benefits of a cost leadership or differentiation strategy. Until Pizza Hut used advertising to differentiate itself from local competitors, the pizza fast-food business primarily comprised locally owned pizza parlors, each offering its own distinctive product and service. Subsequently, Domino's used the cost leader strategy to achieve U.S. national market share. The same may be happening in the funeral home and cemetery industry. Service Corporation International was the largest U.S. funeral home company in 1992, owning and managing 670 funeral homes and 169 cemeteries. Even though most funeral homes were family-owned, Robert Waltrip, Service Corporation's CEO, believed that a large company could build economies of scale by consolidating many local operations. For example, embalming and transportation could be centralized to reduce costs. Because the population of those aged 75 and older should grow by 26% during the 1990s, the company's growth by acquisition strategy coupled with lower cost management may be very profitable.[12]

As an industry matures, fragmentation is overcome and the industry tends to become a **consolidated industry** dominated by a small number of large companies. Although many industries begin by being fragmented, battles for market share and creative attempts to overcome local or niche market boundaries often result in a few companies' obtaining increasingly larger market shares. When product standards have been established for minimum quality and features, competition shifts to a greater emphasis on cost and service. Slower growth combined with overcapacity and knowledgeable buyers put a premium on a firm's ability to achieve cost leadership or differentiation. Research and development shifts from product to process improvements. Overall product quality improves and costs drop significantly. In this type of industry cost leadership and differentiation tend to be combined to various degrees. A firm can no longer gain high market share simply through low price. Buyers are more sophisticated and demand a certain minimum level of quality for the price. This condition holds for firms emphasizing high quality. Either the quality must be high enough and valued by the customer enough to justify the higher price or the price must drop (by lowering costs) to compete effectively with the lower priced products. This consolidation is taking place worldwide in the automobile, airline, and home appliance industries.

When an industry begins to consolidate, distinct strategic groups emerge as competitors. Firms combine various product features in innovative ways to gain competitive advantage. New entrants into the industry are not as threatening as is the danger of a company or business unit moving from one strategic group to another (as the Japanese automakers did when they moved from low-priced dependable cars to high-priced performance cars in the late 1980s). Companies attempt to reduce the level of competitive rivalry through the use of market signals. A **market signal** is any action by a company or business unit that provides a direct or indirect indication of its intentions, motives, goals, or internal situation.[13] These signals become important in a consolidated industry that has developed some "rules of the game" and in which the potential for cutthroat competition is high and antitrust laws heavily penalize direct communication among competitors. For example, General Motors announced in 1991 that it would discontinue making the Buick Reatta and eventually switch the Reatta factory to building an electric powered vehicle. Although electric car R&D would take several years before production could begin, management announced the change both to assure workers that the Reatta factory would reopen, and to send GM's critics a message. According to GM President Lloyd Reuss, "If anyone still wonders if we are serious about producing an electric car, our announcement today should put an end to such doubts."[14]

Competitive Tactics

A **tactic** is a specific operating plan specifying *how, when* and *where* a strategy is to be implemented. Compared to strategies, tactics are narrower in scope and shorter in time horizon. Tactics may therefore be viewed (like policies) as a link between strategy formulation and implementation. Some of the tactics available to implement competitive strategies are those dealing with timing (when) and market location (where).

Timing Tactics

The first company to manufacture and sell a new product or service is called the **first mover.** Because it is a pioneer, it has certain advantages in the marketplace. According to Porter, "First mover advantages rest on the role of timing in improving a firm's position vis-à-vis sustainable sources of cost advantage or differentiation. In general terms, a first mover gets the opportunity to define the competitive rules in a variety of areas."[15] Research indicates that first movers not only tend to obtain higher market shares than do all later entrants, but that they also tend to enjoy a long-term profit advantage over their rivals. This high return is generally necessary to compensate the pioneer for its heavy investment in designing the product and developing the market.[16] Some of the advantages of being a first mover are that the company is able to establish a reputation as a leader in the industry, move down the experience curve to assume the cost leader position, and earn temporarily high profits from buyers who value the product or service very highly.

Being a first mover, however, does have disadvantages, which, conversely, are advantages enjoyed by late mover firms. **Late movers** may be able to imitate others' technological advances (and thus keep R&D costs low), minimize risks by waiting until a new market is established, and take advantage of the natural inclination of the first mover to ignore market segments.[17] M. K. Bolton proposes that imitation (late mover) may be better than innovation (first mover) in industries with (1) weak property rights, (2) interdependent technologies, (3) high technical and market uncertainty, (4) rapidly changing technology, and (5) extensive information flow.[18] In this kind of industry, a follower can watch and learn from the mistakes of the early movers and capitalize on them—much as IBM did in the early 1980s when it set the industry standard for personal computers. Another category of entrant called **early followers** may be less likely to be successful because it earns less market share than does a first mover and because later movers may be able to exploit profitable niches better.[19]

Market Location Tactics

A company or business unit can implement a competitive strategy either offensively or defensively. An offensive tactic usually takes place *away* from a company's current position in the marketplace, whereas a defensive tactic usually takes place within a company's current market position.

Offensive Tactics The following methods are some of those used to attack a competitor's position.[20]

- **Frontal assault:** The attacking firm goes head-to-head with its competitor, matching the competitor in every category from price to promotion to distribution channel. To be successful, the attacker must not only have superior resources, but it also must be willing to persevere. This tactic generally is very expensive and may serve to awaken a sleeping giant (as MCI and Sprint did to AT&T in long-distance telephone service), depressing profits for everyone in the industry.
- **Flanking maneuver:** Rather than going straight for a competitor's position of strength with a frontal assault, a firm may attack a part of the market where the competitor is weak. Cyrix Corporation followed this tactic with its 1989 entry into the microprocessor market—a market then almost totally dominated by Intel. Rather than going directly after Intel's microprocessor business, Cyrix developed a math coprocessor for Intel's 386 chip that would run 20 times faster than Intel's microprocessor. Once Cyrix earned 10% of the 386 math coprocessor market, it then aimed at Intel's 486 generation of microprocessors. To be successful, the flanker must be patient and willing to expand carefully out of the relatively undefended market niche or face retaliation by an established competitor.

- **Encirclement:** Usually evolving from a frontal assault or flanking maneuver, encirclement occurs as an attacking company or business unit encircles the competitor's position in terms of products or markets or both. The encircler has greater product variety (a complete product line ranging from low to high priced) and/or serves more markets (it dominates every secondary market). Honda successfully took this approach in motorcycles by capturing every market segment except the heavyweight segment in the United States controlled by Harley-Davidson. To be successful, the encircler must have the wide variety of abilities and resources necessary to attack multiple market segments.
- **Bypass attack:** Rather than directly attacking the established competitor frontally or on its flanks, a company or business unit may choose to change the rules of the game. This tactic attempts to cut the market out from under the established defender. The most common form of this tactic is the development of a new version of a product that will satisfy customer needs that are currently unserved by any competitor. Motorola followed this tactic when it applied its knowledge of high technology and quality manufacturing to develop a new type of electronic ballast, the transformer that runs fluorescent lighting systems. Motorola's new ballast had no irritating flicker, used only 120 watts, and weighed only 2 pounds compared to 180 watts and 8 pounds along with the annoying flicker for the standard ballast.
- **Guerrilla warfare:** Instead of a continual, extensive and resource draining attack on a competitor, a firm or business unit may choose to "hit and run." Guerrilla warfare involves small, intermittent assaults on a competitor's different market segments. Using special promotions or advertising campaigns, a firm attempts to make a series of small market share gains. In this way a new entrant or small firm can make some gains without seriously threatening a large, established competitor and evoking retaliation. To be successful, the firm or business unit conducting guerrilla warfare must be patient enough to accept small gains and avoid pushing the established competitor to the point that it must make a response or else lose face. Microbreweries, which make beer for sale to local customers, use this tactic.

Defensive Tactics According to Porter, defensive tactics aim to lower the probability of attack, divert attacks to less threatening avenues, or lessen the intensity of an attack. Instead of increasing competitive advantage per se, they make a company's or business unit's competitive advantage more sustainable by causing a challenger to conclude that an attack is unattractive. These tactics deliberately reduce short-term profitability to ensure long-term profitability.[21]

- **Raise structural barriers:** According to Porter, some of the most important actions that can be taken to block a challenger's logical avenues of attack are to (1) offer a full line of products in every profitable market segment to close off any entry points, (2) block channel access by signing exclusive agreements with distributors, (3) raise buyer switching costs by offering low-cost training to users, (4) raise the cost of gaining trial users by keeping prices low on items most likely to be purchased by new users, (5) increase economies of scale to reduce unit costs, (6) foreclose alternative technologies through patenting or licensing, (7) limit outside access to facilities and personnel, (8) tie up suppliers by obtaining exclusive contracts or purchasing key locations, (9) avoid suppliers that also serve competitors, and (10) encourage the government to raise barriers such as safety and pollution standards or favorable trade policies.

- **Increase expected retaliation:** This tactic is an action that increases the perceived threat of retaliation for an attack. For example, management may send market signals such as announced intentions to defend market share in certain product lines or plans to add capacity. Another example is by strongly defending any erosion of market share by drastically cutting prices or matching a challenger's promotion through a policy of accepting any price-reduction coupons for a competitor's product. Counterattack is especially important in those markets that are crucial to the defending company or business unit. If an attacker makes a threatening move against one of the defender's key markets, the defender must act both decisively and swiftly to signal toughness and to defend its reputation.[22] For example, when Clorox Company challenged Procter & Gamble Company in the detergent market with Clorox Super Detergent, P&G retaliated by test marketing its liquid bleach Lemon Fresh Comet in an attempt to make Clorox retreat from the detergent market. During an attack, a firm or business unit may disrupt a challenger's test or introductory markets with an exceptionally high (or exceptionally low) level of advertising and promotion. However, these actions must be tempered because—according to PIMS research—the typical new entrant doesn't represent a serious threat, and aggressive retaliation may be very costly.[23]
- **Lower the inducement for attack:** A third type of defensive tactic is to reduce a challenger's expectations of future profits in the industry. Like Southwest Airlines, a company can deliberately keep prices low and constantly invest in cost-reducing measures. Maintaining extremely low prices gives a new entrant little profit incentive. According to Southwest's CEO Herb Kelleher, "You have to be fast and tactical. And if costs ever get out of hand, we'll be vulnerable."[24] A firm can also use the media to let people know about problems facing the industry, which a challenger would have to consider in its strategic planning.[25]

Choosing a Business Strategy

Before selecting one of these generic competitive strategies (and the appropriate competitive tactic) for a company or business unit, management should assess its feasibility in terms of company or business unit resources and capabilities. Table 7.2 lists some of the commonly required skills and resources, along with organizational requirements. Because these resources usually exist within a firm's functional areas, we now examine functional strategy as a way to achieve business strategy.

TABLE 7.2 **Requirements for Generic Competitive Strategies**

Generic Strategy	Commonly Required Skills and Resources	Common Organizational Requirements
Overall Cost Leadership	Sustained capital investment and access to capital Process engineering skills Intense supervision of labor Products designed for ease of manufacture Low-cost distribution system	Tight cost control Frequent, detailed control reports Structured organization and responsibilities Incentives based on meeting strict quantitative targets
Differentiation	Strong marketing abilities Product engineering Creative flair Strong capability in basic research Corporate reputation for quality or technological leadership Long tradition in the industry or unique combination of skills drawn from other businesses Strong cooperation from channels	Strong coordination among functions in R&D, product development, and marketing Subjective measurement and incentives instead of quantitative measures Amenities to attract highly skilled labor, scientists, or creative people
Focus	Combination of the above policies directed at the particular strategic target	Combination of the above policies directed at the particular strategic target

Source: Adapted/reprinted with permission of The Free Press, an imprint of Simon & Schuster, from *Competitive Strategy: Techniques for Analyzing Industries and Competitors* by Michael E. Porter, pp. 40–41. Copyright © 1980 by The Free Press.

7.2 Functional Strategy

Functional strategy maximizes resource productivity, leading to a distinctive competence that gives a company or business unit a competitive advantage. Within the constraints of corporate and business strategies, functional strategies pull together the various activities and competencies of each function (typically housed within a department) to improve performance. For example, a manufacturing department is concerned with developing a strategy to reduce costs and improve the quality of its output. In comparison, marketing is concerned with developing strategies to increase sales. Such functional strategies need to be developed if functional managers are to implement corporate and divisional strategies properly.

Sourcing of Resources and Capabilities

One important decision deals with the question of where the function should be performed. Should it be integrated within the organization or provided by an outside contractor? Increasingly, sourcing is considered to be an important part of strategic decision making.[26] For example, DuPont contracts out project engineering and design to Morrison Knudsen, AT&T contracts its credit card processing to Total System Services, Northern Telecom its electronic-component manufacturing to Comptronix, and Eastman Kodak its computer support services to Businessland. Approximately 20% of all U.S. companies outsourced or were considering outsourcing some or all of their information technology (IT) in 1993. The percentage of Fortune 500 firms outsourcing at least some IT functions is expected to reach 80% by 1995.[27] According to J. B. Quinn, sophisticated strategists no longer are thinking just of market share or vertical integration as the keys to strategic planning:

> Instead they concentrate on identifying those few core service activities where the company has—or can develop: (1) a continuing strategic edge and (2) long term streams of new products to satisfy future customer demands. They develop these competencies in greater depth than anyone else in the world. Then they seek to eliminate, minimize, or outsource activities where the company cannot be preeminent, unless those activities are essential to support or protect the chosen areas of strategic focus.[28]

The key to outsourcing is to purchase from outside only those activities that are *not* essential to the company's distinctive competence. Otherwise, the company may give up the very core technologies and/or capabilities that made it successful in the first place—thus putting itself on the road to eventual decline as a "hollow corporation."[29] Therefore, in deciding on functional strategy, the strategic manager must (1) identify the company's or business unit's core competencies, (2) ensure that the competencies are continually being strengthened, and (3) manage the competencies in such a way that best preserves the competitive advantage they create.[30] An outsourcing decision depends on the fraction of total value added by the activity under consideration and by the amount of competitive advantage in that activity for the company or business unit. Only when the fraction of total value is small and the competitive advantage in the activity is low, should a company or business unit outsource.

Marketing Strategy

Utilizing a **market development strategy,** a company or business unit can (1) capture a larger share of an existing market for current products through market saturation and market penetration or (2) develop new markets for current products. Consumer product giants such as Procter & Gamble, Colgate-Palmolive, and Unilever are experts at using advertising and promotion to implement a market saturation or penetration strategy in order to gain the dominant market share in a product category. As seeming masters of the product life cycle, these companies extend product life almost indefinitely through "new and improved" variations of product and packaging that appeal to most market niches. These companies also follow the second market development strategy by taking a successful product that they market in one part of the world and marketing it elsewhere. Noting the success of their presoak detergents in Europe, both P&G and Colgate successfully introduced this type of laundry product to North America under the trade names of Biz and Axion.

Using the **product development strategy,** a company or business unit can (1) develop new products for *existing* markets or (2) develop new products for *new* markets. Church and Dwight has had great success following the first product development strategy by developing new products to sell to its current customers. Acknowledging the widespread appeal of its Arm & Hammer brand baking soda, the company generated new uses for its sodium bicarbonate by reformulating it as toothpaste, deodorant, and detergent. Following the same strategy, AT&T and General Motors offered VISA and Mastercard services to their current customers. Church and Dwight also successfully followed the second product development strategy by developing pollution reduction products (using sodium compounds) for sale to coal-fired electrical plants.

Numerous other marketing strategies exist in the categories of market, product line, distribution, pricing and credit, and advertising and promotion. Under advertising and promotion, for example, a company or business unit can choose between a "push" or a "pull" marketing strategy. Many large food and consumer products companies in the United States and Canada have followed a **push strategy** by spending a large amount of money on trade promotion in order to gain or hold shelf space in retail outlets. Trade promotion includes discounts and in-store special offers, and advertising allowances designed to "push" products through the distribution system. The Kellogg Company recently decided to change its emphasis from a push to a **pull strategy,** now emphasizing consumer advertising designed to pull products off the shelf by building brand awareness before shoppers enter a store.

Other marketing strategies deal with distribution and pricing. The Company Spotlight: Maytag Corporation feature on page 199 reveals the reason that the corporation chose not to sell its Maytag brand home appliances through Sears' Brand Central.

When pricing a new product, a company or business unit may follow one of two strategies. For new-product pioneers, **skim pricing** offers the opportunity to "skim the cream" from the top of the demand curve while the product is novel and competitors are few. In contrast, **penetration pricing,** attempts to hasten market development and offers the pioneer the opportunity to utilize the experience curve to gain market share and dominate the industry. Depending on corporate and business unit objectives and strategies, either of these choices may be desirable for a particular company or unit. However, research reveals that penetration pricing is more likely than skim pricing to raise a unit's operating profit in the long term.[31]

Financial Strategy

Financial strategy's goal is to provide the corporation with the appropriate financial structure and funds to achieve its overall objectives. In addition, it examines the financial implications of corporate and business-level strategic options and identifies the best financial course of action. It can also provide competitive advantage through a lower cost of funds and a flexible ability to raise capital to support

COMPANY SPOTLIGHT

MAYTAG Corporation

Maytag Supports Dealers as Part of Its Marketing Strategy

In the United States, major home appliances (white goods) such as washing machines, stoves, and refrigerators are sold by three main types of retail outlets: (1) national chain stores and mass merchandisers; (2) department, furniture, and discount stores; and (3) appliance dealers. An additional, but smaller, outlet was the commercial market, composed of laundromats and institutions such as hospitals and dormitories. Private brands promoted by the retailers usually were sold through national chain stores and mass merchandisers. For example, Whirlpool Corporation has traditionally been a heavy supplier of Sears and Kenmore brand appliances to Sears, Roebuck. Magic Chef sold similar private-brand appliances to Montgomery Ward. Traditionally, this channel sells about 30%–40% of white goods sold in the United States. Sears, Roebuck has been so strong in major home appliance sales that it alone sells one of every four home appliances in the United States.

In the late 1980s, Sears instituted its new *Brand Central* format to sell white goods. In addition to offering its own private brands, the retail giant offered nationally known brands such as General Electric, Whirlpool, Amana, Speedqueen, and Jenn-Air. Except for its Jenn-Air products, Maytag Corporation chose not to join Sears' Brand Central effort. Leonard Hadley, Chief Operating Officer of Maytag Corporation at that time, explained that the company did not want to antagonize its carefully nurtured appliance dealers who had always considered Sears their major retail competition. Maytag Company's emphasis on quality and higher price rather than market share as its business competitive strategy made the Maytag brand more dependent on appliance dealers than either GE or Whirlpool. In addition, some Maytag people feared that Sears might use the Maytag brand image to attract customers into the stores, but then persuade them to buy a less expensive Sears brand carrying a higher markup.

a business strategy.[32] Financial strategy usually attempts to maximize the financial value of the firm.

The desired level of debt versus equity versus internal long-term financing with cash flow is a principal issue in financial strategy. Many small and medium-sized companies, such as Urschel Laboratories, try to avoid all external sources of funds in order to avoid outside entanglements and to maintain family control of the company. During the 1980s, a large number of companies used long-term debt to finance a corporate strategy of growth through acquisitions. The $24.5 billion debt-financed takeover of RJR Nabisco, Inc., by Kohlberg Kravis Roberts & Co. in 1988 was one such example. The use of high-risk "junk" bonds to finance many of these acquisitions was one reason that numerous corporations were forced to declare bankruptcy. In the 1990s, however, most companies were trying to "deleverage" by reducing the amount of long-term debt on their balance sheets. According to John Lonski, Chief Economist of Moody's Investors Service, companies in the 1990s wanted less debt in order to "survive the unforeseen." With less interest payments, firms could price more competitively, invest in new technology, and pay lower rates on future borrowings.[33]

A popular financial strategy is the leveraged buyout (LBO). In a **leveraged buyout,** a company is acquired in a transaction financed largely by debt—usually obtained from a third party, such as an insurance company. Ultimately, the debt is paid with money generated from the acquired company's operations or by sales of its assets. The acquired company, in effect, pays for its own acquisition! Management of the LBO is then under tremendous pressure to keep the highly leveraged company profitable. Unfortunately, the huge amount of debt on the acquired company's books may actually cause its eventual decline. Research reveals that companies taken private in an LBO tend to reduce R&D spending in an attempt to stay profitable. Company performance tends to be better than the industry average up to three years after the buy out, but then in the period from four to seven years out is worse than the average. Management motivation, which at first is high, eventually declines and the company begins to suffer from a lack of long-term strategy. To avoid this fate, management often takes an LBO public again about three to five years after the buyout.[34]

The management of dividends to stockholders is an important part of a corporation's financial strategy. Corporations in fast-growing industries, such as computers and computer software, often do not declare dividends. They use the money they might have paid in dividends to finance rapid growth. If the company is successful, a higher stock price reflects its growth in sales and profits—eventually resulting in large capital gains when shareholders sell their common stock. Other corporations, such as electric utilities, that do not face rapid growth must support the value of their stock by offering generous and consistent dividends.

Research and Development Strategy

Corporations that depend on technology for their success are becoming increasingly concerned with the development of R&D strategies that complement business-level strategies. One of the R&D choices is to be either a leader or a follower. Porter suggests that making the decision to become a technological leader or follower may be a way to achieve either overall low cost or differentiation, as indicated in Table 7.3.

One example of an effective use of the follower R&D functional strategy to achieve a low-cost competitive advantage is Dean Foods Company. "We're able to have the customer come to us and say, 'If you can produce X, Y, and Z product for the same quality and service, but at a lower price and without that expensive label on it, you can have the business,' " says Howard Dean, company President.[35] In contrast, Nike, Inc., uses the leader R&D strategy. As detailed in the Strategy in Action on page 202, Nike spends more than most companies in the industry on R&D in order to differentiate its athletic shoes from its competitors in terms of

TABLE 7.3 **Research and Development Strategy and Competitive Advantage**

	Technological Leadership	Technological Followership
Cost Advantage	Pioneer the lowest-cost product design Be the first firm down the learning curve Create low-cost ways of performing value activities	Lower the cost of the product or value activities by learning from the leader's experience Avoid R&D costs through imitation
Differentiation	Pioneer a unique product that increases buyer value Innovate in other activities to increase buyer value	Adapt the product or delivery system more closely to buyer needs by learning from the leader's experience

Source: Adapted/reprinted with the permission of The Free Press, an imprint of Simon & Schuster, from *Competitive Advantage: Creating and Sustaining Superior Performance* by Michael E. Porter, p. 181. Copyright © 1985 by Michael E. Porter.

performance. As a result, its products have become the favorite of the serious athlete. (We present more information on the use of R&D to gain competitive advantage in Chapter 12.)

Operations Strategy

Operations strategy determines how and where a product or service is to be manufactured, the level of vertical integration needed, the deployment of physical resources required, and relationships with suppliers desired.[36] To begin with, a firm's manufacturing strategy will be affected by the product or process life cycle conceptualized by R. H. Hayes and S. C. Wheelwright.[37] This concept describes the increase in production volume ranging from lot sizes as low as 1 in a **job shop** (one-of-a-kind production using skilled labor) through **connected line batch flow** (components are standardized; each machine functions like a job shop, but is positioned in the same order as the parts are processed) to lot sizes as high as 100,000 or more per year for **flexible manufacturing systems** (parts are grouped into manufacturing families to produce a wide variety of mass-produced items) and **dedicated transfer lines** (highly automated assembly lines making one mass-produced product using little human labor). According to this concept, over time the product becomes standardized into a commodity in conjunction with increasing demand, as flexibility gives way to efficiency. Nevertheless, a company's competitive business strategy can be the main determinant of the manufacturing process. For example, Pratt & Whitney selected the connected line batch flow approach in making disks and hubs for its jet engines, whereas General Electric selected the flexible manufacturing system. General Electric was geared to the global mass market, whereas Pratt & Whitney was interested in satisfying lucrative market segments having particular needs.[38]

NIKE USES A LEADER R&D STRATEGY TO ACHIEVE DIFFERENTIATION

Strategy in Action

In an industry in which companies routinely spend tens of millions of dollars on advertising campaigns featuring superstar athletes like Michael Jordan and Bo Jackson, Nike, Inc., spends more on research and development for its athletic shoes than does any competitor except Japan's ASICS Corp. Industry analysts evaluate Nike's R&D lab as "far and away the best" in the industry. In 1979, the company introduced the air-cushioning system. In the mid-1980s, however, Nike emphasized fashion and lost market share to Reebok International Ltd. In 1987, Nike fought back with its Visible Air line of athletic shoes. Each shoe had a tiny window in the heel so consumers could see the air bag providing extra cushioning. In the two years following the Visible Air introduction, Nike surpassed Reebok in both market share (25% versus 23%) and sales. Needless to say, with Nike's return to an emphasis on performance, R&D people played a dominant role in the company's strategy making.

After the success of the Visible Air line, Bruce Kilgore, head of Nike's R&D department, wanted to develop a shoe whose entire heel was a visible air bag. Working behind a cagelike door guarded by a stuffed gorilla, ten advanced-products engineers, who called themselves APEs, labored to make Kilgore's idea a reality. Once the shoe was readied for mass production as the Nike Air 180, the company engaged 186 athletes from Alaska to the Virgin Islands to test the shoes for 90 days over all kinds of terrain. The runners' comments were then used when making the minor modifications needed to ensure that the shoe would last over 500 miles of use. The bottom of the shoe's heel held a large urethane window, bonded to the shoe by a new Nike-developed compound, that allowed a 180-degree view of a greatly expanded air bag. Nike's management reported that not only did the Nike 180 have the most cushioning of any of its running shoes, but that retailers were showing great interest. Orders were beyond expectations even before the shoes were made!

Source: D. Jones Yang and R. Buderi, "Step by Step with Nike," *Business Week* (August 13, 1990), pp. 116–117.

S. Kotha and D. Orne recommend that operations strategy have certain characteristics based on the competitive strategy of the company or business unit of which operations is a part.[39] (See Table 7.4.) The manufacturing strategy should also address the issue of vertical integration, that is, make or buy decisions. New technologies in communications, logistics, and information systems have decreased the popularity of full vertical integration in manufacturing. Quasi-

TABLE 7.4 Impact of Business Strategy on Operations Strategy

Business Competitive Strategy	Characteristics of Operations Strategy
Strong Cost Leadership Emphasis	Strong emphasis on cost reduction and control High level of process engineering skills Strong emphasis on elimination of inventories High level of production standards High level of machine pacing of material flow
Strong Differentiation Emphasis	Strong emphasis on premium-value products and services Relatively high end-product complexity Wide variety of final products High level of product engineering skills High level of production scheduling flexibility (flexible service and order lead times)

Source: Adapted from S. Kotha and D. Orne, "Generic Manufacturing Strategies: A Conceptual Synthesis," *Strategic Management Journal* (May–June 1989), p. 227. Reprinted by permission of John Wiley & Sons, Ltd.

integration, in which a company acquires partial ownership of a key supplier or distributor, is becoming more popular. Company-owned internal suppliers also are being replaced by a network of independently owned external suppliers linked by long-term contracts and close personal relationships.

Operations strategy also should deal with the optimum level of technology the firm should use in its operations processes. Advanced Manufacturing Technology (AMT) is revolutionizing operations worldwide and should continue to have a major impact as corporations integrate diverse business activities by using computer-aided design and computer-aided manufacturing (CAD/CAM) principles. The use of CAD/CAM, flexible manufacturing systems, computer numerically controlled systems, automatically guided vehicles, robotics, manufacturing resource planning (MRP II), optimized production technology, and just-in-time delivery contribute to increased flexibility, quick response time, and higher productivity. However, such methods also increase operating leverage and could cause significant problems if the company is unable to achieve economies of scale or scope.[40] (We discuss total quality management (TQM), a popular program used to improve operations, in Chapter 9.)

Human Resources and Other Functional Strategies

Strategies in human resource management (HRM), information systems (IS), and other areas of functional significance to corporations vary by industry. An **HRM strategy** needs to address the issue of whether a company or business unit should hire a large number of low-skilled employees who receive low pay, perform repetitive jobs, and most likely quit after a short time (the McDonald's restaurant strategy) or hire skilled employees who receive relatively high pay and are cross-trained

TABLE 7.5 **Some Functional Strategy Options**

Marketing

- Expand sales into new classes of customers
  1. Geographic expansion
  2. Additional related products—line extension
  3. Develop completely new products
  4. New applications for same products
  5. Develop customized products
- Increase penetration in market segments of existing customers
  1. Develop competing products—product overlap
  2. Product customization
  3. Product system concept
  4. Find pricing and service mix to give competitive edge
  5. Seek promotional techniques to drown out competitive ads
  6. Pinpoint markets by reducing variety of products and models
- Hold market share
  1. Copy, do not innovate
  2. Emphasize larger product sizes or more durable products to keep current customers out of the marketplace
  3. Increase switching costs by offering special services to current customers

Finance

- Borrow short term
  1. Credit line
  2. Bank notes
  3. Factor accounts receivable
- Borrow long term
  1. Secured debt of three to five years
  2. Bonds or debentures
  3. Commercial paper
- Equity funding
  1. Private placement
  2. Public placement
  3. Voting or nonvoting
- Refinancing
  1. Refinance long term with short term
  2. Refinance short term with long term
  3. Purchase treasury stock
  4. Split shares
  5. Liquidate debt by selling shares
- Dividend policy
  1. Begin dividend payout
  2. Increase dividend payout
  3. Reduce dividend payout
  4. Maintain present dividend payout
  5. Discontinue dividend payout

R&D and Operations

- Research and development emphasis
  1. Increase funds
  2. No change in funding
  3. Decrease funding
  4. Mix of basic and applied efforts
  5. Mix of product and process technology emphasis
- Technology
  1. Upgrade
  2. Retain
  3. Subcontract
- Operations capacity
  1. Build new capacity
  2. Maintain current capacity
  3. Expand current capacity

(continued)

in order to participate in self-managed work teams. Many companies are using increasing numbers of part-time and temporary employees and also are experimenting with leasing employees from employee leasing companies. To reduce costs and obtain increased flexibility, U.S. companies leased more than a million workers in 1993.[41] As work increases in complexity, it becomes more suited for teams. A recent survey of 476 Fortune 1000 U.S. companies revealed that, although only 7% of their work forces were organized into self-managed teams, half the companies reported that they would be relying significantly more on them in the years

TABLE 7.5 **Some Functional Strategy Options** *(continued)*

R&D and Operations *(continued)*

4. Increase size of work force
5. Add shifts
6. Reduce work force
7. Reduce inventory
8. Consolidate and centralize
9. Decentralize to smaller facilities
10. Decentralize to functional facilities

- Material and supply
  1. Obtain new domestic sources
  2. Obtain new import sources
  3. Substitute materials
  4. Negotiate lower costs
  5. Centralize procurement
  6. Decentralize procurement
- Quality/productivity
  1. Use team concept
  2. Switch to modular
  3. Superautomate with robots and computers
  4. Japanese management techniques

Human Resources

- Recruitment and training
  1. Use internal employee recruitment, selection, and placement
  2. Use external employee recruitment, selection, and placement
  3. Establish management development program
  4. Link career paths to corporate and business strategy
  5. Establish specific job skill training
  6. Establish assessment centers for selection and development
- Appraisal and benefits
  1. Link pay and benefits to corporate and business strategy
  2. Link appraisal system to corporate and business strategy
  3. Use cafeteria benefits package

Information Systems

- Hardware and software
  1. Upgrade mainframe central processor
  2. Purchase new central processor
  3. Upgrade existing distributed microprocessors
  4. Purchase new distributed microprocessors and networking system
  5. Switch from central processor to distributed system
  6. Use centralized software support system
  7. Use decentralized software support system
- Link information systems to corporate and business competitive strategy
  1. Establish and maintain environmental scanning system
  2. Automatic routine clerical operations
  3. Assist managers in making decisions
  4. Use information systems (IS) to provide improved service to customers
  5. Develop new uses of current IS that can be sold to current or new customers.

Source: Suggested by V. A. Quarstein, Old Dominion University.

ahead.[42] Approaches to management training need to be tailored to the company's or business unit's competitive strategy. For example, the more prospectorlike the business strategy, the more important is cross-functional training. In contrast, defenders will emphasize the development of skills within functional areas.[43] (Recall the discussion of prospectors and defenders as strategic types in Chapter 4 on pages 102–103.) Other HRM strategies deal with the question of promotion from within or recruitment of managers from outside the company. Table 7.5 summarizes these and other options within functional strategies.

7.3 Strategies to Avoid

Several types of corporate, business, or functional strategies are risky. Managers who have made a poor analysis or lack creativity may be trapped into considering them.

- **Follow the leader:** Imitating the strategy of a leading competitor might seem a good idea, but it ignores a firm's particular strengths and weaknesses and the possibility that the leader may be wrong. Fujitsu Ltd., the world's second-largest computer maker, was driven since the 1960s by the sole ambition of catching up to IBM. Like IBM, Fujitsu competed primarily as a mainframe computer maker. So devoted was it to catching IBM, however, it failed to notice that the mainframe business was reaching maturity and by 1993 was rapidly going into decline.[44]
- **Hit another home run:** If a company is successful because it pioneered an extremely successful product, it has a tendency to search for another super-product that will ensure growth and prosperity. Like betting on long shots at the horse races, the probability of finding a second winner is slight. Polaroid spent a lot of money developing an "instant" movie camera, but the public ignored it. Xerox introduced a revolutionary new product called "Xenith," which combined computing, scanning, faxing, and copying in an attempt to duplicate the success of its original copier.
- **Arms race:** Entering into a spirited battle with another firm for an increase in market share might increase sales revenue, but higher advertising, promotion, R&D, and manufacturing costs probably will more than offset the gain. Since the deregulation of airlines, price wars and rate "specials" have contributed to the low profit margins or bankruptcy of many major airlines, such as Eastern and Continental.
- **Do everything:** When faced with several interesting opportunities, management might tend to leap at all of them. At first, a corporation might have enough resources to develop each idea into a project, but the large infusion of resources for each project soon exhausts the available money, time, and energy.
- **Losing hand:** A corporation might have invested so much in a particular strategy that top management is unwilling to accept the fact that the strategy isn't successful. Believing that it has too much invested to quit, the corporation continues to throw "good money after bad." Pan American Corporation, for example, chose to sell its Pan Am Building and Intercontinental Hotels, the most profitable parts of the corporation, to keep its money-losing airline flying. Continuing to suffer losses, the company followed this strategy of shedding assets for cash, until it had sold off everything and went bankrupt.

7.4 Selection of the Best Strategy

After management has identified and evaluated strategic alternatives, it must select one for implementation. Because many alternatives will likely have emerged as feasible, how do managers determine which is the best strategy?

TABLE 7.6

Twenty Questions for Use in Evaluating Strategies

1. Does the strategy conform to the basic mission and purpose of the corporation? If not, a new competitive arena with which management is not familiar might be entered.
2. Is the strategy consistent with the corporation's external environment?
3. Is the strategy consistent with the internal strengths, objectives, policies, resources, and personal values of managers and employees? A strategy might not be completely in tune with all of these, but major dissonance should be avoided.
4. Does the strategy reflect the acceptance of minimum potential risk, balancing it against the maximum potential profit consistent with the corporation's resources and prospects?
5. Does the strategy fit a niche in the corporation's market not now filled by others? Is this niche likely to remain open long enough for the corporation to return capital investment plus the required level of profit? (Niches have a habit of filling up fast.)
6. Does the strategy conflict with other corporate strategies?
7. Is the strategy divided into substrategies that interrelate properly?
8. Has the strategy been tested with appropriate criteria (such as consistency with past, present, and prospective trends) and by the appropriate analytical tools (such as risk analysis, discounted cash flows, and so on)?
9. Has the strategy been tested by developing feasible implementation plans?
10. Does the strategy really fit the life cycles of the corporation's products?
11. Is the timing of the strategy correct?
12. Does the strategy pit the product against a powerful competitor? If so, reevaluate carefully.
13. Does the strategy leave the corporation vulnerable to the power of one major customer? If so, reconsider carefully.
14. Does the strategy involve the production of a new product for a new market? If so, reconsider carefully.
15. Is the corporation rushing a revolutionary product to market? If so, reconsider carefully.
16. Does the strategy imitate that of a competitor? If so, reconsider carefully.
17. Is it likely that the corporation can get to the market first with the new product or service? If so, this is a great advantage. (The second firm to market has much less chance of high returns on investment than the first.)
18. Has a really honest and accurate appraisal been made of the competition? Is the competition under- or overestimated?
19. Is the corporation trying to sell abroad something it cannot sell at home? (This is not usually a successful strategy.)
20. Is the market share likely to be sufficient to assure a required return on investment? (Market share and return on investment are generally closely related but differ from product to product and market to market.) Has this relationship of market and product been calculated?

Source: Reprinted with permission of Macmillan College Publishing Company from *Management Policy and Strategy* by George A. Steiner and John B. Miner, pp. 219–221. Copyright © 1977 by Macmillan College Publishing Company, Inc.

George Steiner and John Miner suggest that managers answer the 20 questions in Table 7.6 before selecting one strategy over another. Perhaps the most important criterion is the ability of the proposed strategy to deal with the specific strategic factors developed earlier in the SWOT analysis. If the alternative doesn't take advantage of environmental opportunities and corporate strengths—and lead away from environmental threats and corporate weaknesses—it probably will fail.

Another important consideration in the selection of a strategy is the ability of each alternative to satisfy agreed-on objectives with the least use of resources and with the fewest number of negative side effects. Developing a tentative implementation plan to address the difficulties that management is likely to face is therefore important.

Scenario Construction

Using *pro forma* (estimated future) balance sheets and income statements, management can construct detailed *scenarios* on a personal computer using spreadsheets to forecast the likely effect of each alternative strategy and its various programs on divisional and corporate return on investment. In a survey of Fortune 500 firms, 78% reported using scenarios and 84% reported using computer simulation models in strategic planning. Most of the latter were simply spreadsheet-based simulation models.[45]

The scenarios described here are simply extensions of the industry scenarios discussed in Chapter 4 on pages 106–108. For example, if industry scenarios suggest the probable emergence of a strong market demand for certain products, you can develop a series of alternative strategy scenarios. Then compare the alternative of acquiring another company having these products to the alternative of developing the products internally. Using three sets of estimated sales figures (optimistic, pessimistic, and most likely) for the new products over the next five years, evaluate the two alternatives in terms of their effect on future company performance as reflected in its probable future financial statements. Finally, generate pro forma balance sheets and income statements with spreadsheet software, such as Lotus 1-2-3 or Excel, on a personal computer.

To construct a scenario, *first* use the industry scenarios and develop a set of assumptions about the task environment. At 3M, for example, the general manager of each business unit is required annually to describe what his or her unit's industry will look like in 15 years.[46] Then list Optimistic (O), Pessimistic (P), and Most Likely (ML) assumptions for the GDP (Gross Domestic Product), CPI (Consumer Price Index), prime interest rate, and other primary external strategic factors (such as governmental regulation and industry trends) for each of the alternative scenarios to be developed.

Second, develop *common-size financial statements* (which we discuss in Chapter 15) for the company's or business unit's previous years to serve as the basis for the pro forma financial statements. Use the historical common-size percentages to obtain estimates of the level of revenues, expenses, and other categories and enter them in the pro forma statements. For each strategic alternative, develop a set of optimistic, pessimistic, and most likely assumptions about the impact of key variables on the company's future financial statements. Forecast three sets of sales and cost of goods sold figures for at least five years into the future. Look at historical data and make adjustments based on the environmental assumptions made. Do the same for other figures that can vary significantly. For the rest, assume that they will continue in their historical relationship to sales or some other determining factor. Enter expected inventory levels, accounts receivable, accounts payable, R&D expenses, advertising and promotion expenses, capital expenditures, and debt

TABLE 7.7 **Scenario Box for Use in Generating Financial Pro Forma Statements**

Factor	Last Year	Historical Average	Trend Analysis	Projections[1]									Comments
				19—			19—			19—			
				O	P	ML	O	P	ML	O	P	ML	
GDP													
CPI													
Other													
Sales units													
Dollars													
COGS													
Advertising and marketing													
Interest expense													
Plant expansion													
Dividends													
Net profits													
EPS													
ROI													
ROE													
Other													

Note 1: **O** = Optimistic; **P** = Pessimistic; **ML** = Most Likely.

Source: T. L. Wheelen and J. D. Hunger. Copyright © 1993 by Wheelen and Hunger Associates. Reprinted by permission.

payments (assuming that debt is used to finance the strategy), among others. Consider not only historical trends, but also programs that might be needed to implement each alternative strategy (such as building a new manufacturing facility or expanding the sales force). Table 7.7 presents a form to use in developing pro forma financial statements from historical averages from common-size financial statements.

Third, construct detailed pro forma financial statements for each strategic alternative. Using a spreadsheet program, list the actual figures from this year's financial statements in the left-hand column. To the right of this column, list the optimistic figures for year one, year two, year three, year four, and year five. Repeat this process for the same strategic alternative but now list the pessimistic figures for the next five years. Do the same with the most likely figures. Then develop a similar set of optimistic, pessimistic, and most likely pro forma statements for the second strategic alternative. This process will generate six different pro forma scenarios reflecting three different situations (O, P, and ML) for two strategic alternatives. Next, calculate financial ratios and common-size income statements and balance sheets to accompany the pro forma statements. To determine the feasibility of the scenarios, compare assumptions underlying the scenarios with these financial statements and ratios. For example, if cost of goods sold drops from 70% to 50% of total sales revenue in the pro forma income statements, this drop should result from a change in the production process or a shift to cheaper raw materials or labor costs rather than from a failure to keep the cost of goods sold in its usual percentage relationship to sales revenue when you developed the estimates.

The result of these detailed scenarios should be anticipated net profits, cash flow, and net working capital for each of three versions of the two alternatives for five years into the future. You might want to go further into the future if you expect the strategy to have a major impact on the company's financial statements beyond five years. The result of this work should provide sufficient information on which you can base forecasts of the likely feasibility and probable profitability of each of the strategic alternatives.

Obviously, these scenarios can quickly become very complicated, especially if three sets of acquisition price and development cost calculations are involved. Nevertheless, this sort of detailed "what if" analysis is needed for realistic comparisons of the projected outcome of each reasonable alternative strategy and its attendant programs, budgets, and procedures. Regardless of the quantifiable advantages and disadvantages of each alternative, the actual decision probably will be influenced by one or more of the following subjective factors.

Management's Attitude Toward Risk

The attractiveness of a particular strategic alternative is partially a function of the amount of risk it entails. Risk comprises not only the *probability* that the strategy will be effective, but also the *amount of assets* the corporation must allocate to that strategy and the *length of time* the assets will be unavailable for other uses. To quantify this risk, many specialists suggest the use of the **Capital Asset Pricing Model** (CAPM). It is a financial method for linking the risk involved in a particular alternative with expected returns on a company's equity.[47] Research by M. J. Stahl, however, found little evidence that corporate planners actually use the CAPM as a tool for either acquisition or divestment decisions.[48] Another proposed technique is the **Arbitrage Pricing Model** (APM), which screens acquisition candidates.[49] In response to these and other complicated approaches to risk quantification, M. D. Everett proposes a simpler approach for the assessment of the probability of success or failure for a particular strategic alternative; his approach uses a Lotus 1-2-3 spreadsheet to consider risk–return trade-offs.[50]

The greater the assets involved and the longer they are committed, the more likely top management is to demand a high probability of success. This demand might be one reason that innovations seem to occur more often in small firms than in large, established corporations.[51] Typically, the small firm managed by an entrepreneur is willing to accept greater risk than is a large firm of diversified ownership run by professional managers. Taking a chance if you are the primary shareholder and aren't concerned with periodic changes in the value of the company's common stock is one thing. It is something else if the corporation's stock is widely held and acquisition-hungry competitors or takeover artists surround the company like sharks every time the company's stock price falls below some external assessment of the firm's value!

R. H. Hayes and D. A. Garvin make the point that professional managers place too much emphasis on discounted rate of return as an aid to strategic decision making. High hurdle rates based on unrealistic assumptions often discourage investment in a firm's existing businesses whose risks are known and direct it toward acquiring businesses whose risks are less known. Over time, this results in a *disinvestment spiral,* or deferred investment in a firm's core businesses that leads to reduced profitability, which further reduces the incentive to invest. "Faced with these circumstances, top management often concludes that a division or product line is unsalvageable and purposely continues the process of disinvestment."[52] This reasoning helps explain the emphasis on growth through unrelated acquisitions during the 1970s and 1980s and the corresponding poor performance and divestment decisions in the late 1980s. The trend toward outsourcing in the 1990s may result in a similar decline in performance for those firms failing to invest in their core competencies.

Pressures from the External Environment

The attractiveness of a strategic alternative will be affected by its perceived compatibility with the principal stakeholders in a corporation's task environment. Creditors want to be paid on time, unions exert pressure for comparable wages and employment security, governments and interest groups demand social responsibility and shareholders want dividends. Management must consider all these pressures when selecting an alternative. Hicks B. Waldron, Chairman of Avon Products, argues that corporations have duties beyond maximizing value for shareholders:

> We have a number of suppliers, institutions, customers, communities. None of them have the democratic freedom as shareholders do to buy or sell their shares. They have much deeper and much more important stakes in our company than our shareholders.[53]

Strategic managers should ask four questions to assess the importance of stakeholder concerns in a particular decision: (1) Which stakeholders are most crucial for corporate success? (2) How much of what they want are they likely to get under this alternative? (3) What are they likely to do if they don't get what they want? (4) What is the probability that they will do so?

Strategic decision makers should be able to choose strategic alternatives that minimize external pressures and maximize stakeholder support. In addition, top management can utilize **political strategies** to influence stakeholders. Some of the most commonly used political strategies are constituency building, political action committee (PAC) contributions, advocacy advertising, lobbying, and coalition building.[54] For example, in response to public concerns about its disposable diapers contributing to the growing landfill problem in the United States, Procter & Gamble not only promoted the use of a new process to dispose of solid waste, but also promised to spend $20 million on R&D to develop disposable diapers that break down completely in such systems.

Pressures from the Corporate Culture

If a strategy is incompatible with the corporate culture, it probably won't succeed. Foot-dragging and even sabotage may well result, as employees fight to resist a radical change in corporate philosophy. Hence, precedent tends to restrict the kinds of objectives and strategies that management can seriously consider. The "aura" of corporations' founders may linger long past their lifetimes because they have imprinted their values on those corporations.[55]

In considering a strategic alternative, the decision makers must assess its compatibility with the corporate culture. If there is little fit, management must decide whether it should (1) take a chance on ignoring the culture, (2) manage around the culture and change the implementation plan, (3) try to change the culture to fit the strategy, or (4) change the strategy to fit the culture.[56] Further, a decision to proceed with a particular strategy without a commitment to change the culture or manage around the culture (both very tricky and time-consuming) is dangerous. Nevertheless, restricting a corporation to those strategies only that are completely compatible with its culture might eliminate from consideration the most profitable alternatives. (We discuss managing corporate culture further in Chapter 9.)

Needs and Desires of Key Managers

Even the most attractive alternative might not be selected if it runs contrary to the needs and desires of important top managers. People's egos may be tied to a particular proposal to the extent that they strongly lobby against all other alternatives. Key executives in operating divisions, for example, might be able to influence other people in top management to favor a particular alternative and ignore objections to it.

The evidence indicates a tendency to maintain the status quo, which means that decision makers are likely to hold onto existing goals and plans beyond the point when an objective observer would recommend a change in course.[57] W. S. Silver and T. R. Mitchell suggest that negative information about a particular course of action to which a person is committed may be ignored because of a desire to appear competent and because of strongly held values regarding consistency.[58] A crisis or an unlikely event may have to occur to cause strategic decision makers to consider seriously an alternative that they had previously ignored or discounted. For example, not until the CEO of ConAgra, a multinational food products company, had a heart attack did ConAgra and others started producing lines of low-fat, low-cholesterol, and low-sodium frozen-food entrees. ConAgra led the industry with its introduction of Healthy Choice—frozen dinners and boil-in-bag entrees—that consumers could eat without worrying about health and nutrition.

Strategic Choice

There is an old story at General Motors about Alfred Sloan. At a meeting with his key executives, Sloan proposed a controversial strategic decision. When asked for comments, each executive responded with supportive comments and praise. After announcing that they were all in apparent agreement, Sloan stated that they were not going to proceed with the decision. Either his executives didn't know enough to point out potential downsides of the decision, or they were agreeing to avoid upsetting the boss and disrupting the cohesion of the group. The decision was delayed until a debate could occur over the pros and cons.[59]

Although some people urge consensus in strategic decision making, research suggests that consensus is appropriate only when a company's environment is fairly stable and predictable.[60] There is mounting evidence that, when an organization faces a dynamic environment, the best strategic decisions are not unanimous—that they actually involve a certain amount of heated disagreement and even conflict.[61] Unmanaged conflict often carries a high emotional cost, so authorities in decision making propose that strategic managers use *programmed conflict* to raise different opinions, regardless of the personal feelings of the people involved. Two techniques are suggested to help strategic managers avoid the consensus trap.

The **devil's advocate** originated in the medieval Roman Catholic Church as a way of ensuring that impostors were not canonized as saints. One trusted person (the devil's advocate) was selected to find and present all the reasons why the person could not be canonized. When applied to strategic decision making, the devil's advocate (who may be an individual or a group) is assigned to identify potential pitfalls and problems with a proposed alternative strategy in a formal presentation. R. A. Cosier and C. R. Schwenk suggest that people be rotated through the devil's advocate position so that one person isn't identified as the critic on all issues. Steve Huse, Chairman and CEO of Huse Food Group, states that the devil's advocate role is an opportunity for employees to demonstrate their presentation and debating skills along with their ability to do in-depth research and to understand both sides of an issue.[62]

Dialectical philosophy can be traced back to Plato and Aristotle and more recently to Hegel. It involves combining two conflicting views—the *thesis* and the *antithesis*—into a *synthesis*. When applied to strategic decision making, dialectical inquiry requires that two proposals based on different assumptions be generated for each alternative strategy under consideration. After advocates of each position present and debate the merits of their proposals before key decision makers, either one of the alternatives or a new compromise alternative is selected as the strategy to be implemented. At Compaq Computer Corporation, for example, strategic managers followed a process of dialectical inquiry as a way to choose the best alternative, not just the one supported by the highest ranking executive in the room. To ensure that issues were thoroughly discussed, President Rod Canion took one side and Michael Swavely, President of Compaq's North American operation, or Gary Stimac, Compaq's Senior Vice President of Systems Engineering, took the other side. In theory, no one is trying to make points with the boss and there are no winners or losers. "We have to leave our egos at the door," says Swavely, "but we can put any question on the table without fear of being wrong." Once a project is approved or disapproved at Compaq, however, everyone is expected to support the decision.[63]

Research generally supports the conclusion that both the devil's advocate and dialectical inquiry are equally superior to consensus in decision making, especially when the firm's environment is dynamic. The debate itself, rather than its particular format, appears to improve the quality of decisions by formalizing and legitimizing constructive conflict and by encouraging critical evaluation. Both lead to better assumptions and recommendations and to a higher level of critical thinking among the people involved.[64]

7.5 Policy Development

The selection of the best strategic alternative isn't the end of strategy formulation. Management must now establish policies to define the ground rules for implementation. Flowing from the selected strategy, they provide guidance for decision making and actions throughout the organization. At General Electric, for example, Chairman Welch insists that GE be Number One or Number Two wherever it competes. This policy gives clear guidance to managers throughout the organization. Another example of such a policy is Casey's policy that a new service or product line may be added to its stores only when the product or service can be justified in terms of increasing store traffic.

Policies are crucial in multinational corporations where subsidiaries in different geographic areas may feel free to develop product strategies independently of the rest of the company. Concerned with the historic lack of cooperation between Ford U.S. and Ford of Europe, Ford Motor Company's top management developed a companywide policy requiring any new car design to be easily adaptable to any market in the world. Before this policy was implemented, Ford of Europe developed cars strictly for its own market, and U.S. engineers separately designed their own products. The new policy was a natural result of Ford's emphasis on manufacturing efficiency and global integration as a corporation.

Some policies will be expressions of a corporation's critical success factors (CSF). **Critical success factors** are the elements that determine a company's strategic success or failure, emphasizing its distinctive competence to ensure competitive advantage. Research indicates that organizations that possess strengths in their critical success factors outperform the competition.[65] These factors vary from company to company. For example, IBM sees customer service as its critical success factor. McDonald's CSFs are quality, cleanliness, and value. Hewlett-Packard is concerned with new product development. Dick Mahoney, Chairman and CEO of Monsanto Company, acknowledges research and development of new chemical products as the critical success factor of his company when he says, "R&D isn't part of the strategy. R&D *is* the strategy."[66] As guidelines for decision making, policies can therefore be based on a corporation's critical success factors. Nordstrom Department Stores emphasize customer service as the firm's critical success factor. Store policies state that the customer is *always* right, even if the facts show the customer to be wrong. Store management believes that even though a few people might take advantage of this policy in the short run, the stores will make up for it in the long run with goodwill and increased sales.

Policies tend to be rather long lived and may even outlast the particular strategy that created them. Interestingly, these general policies, such as "The customer is always right" or "Research and development should get first priority on all budget requests," can become, in time, part of a corporation's culture. Such policies make the implementation of specific strategies easier, but they also can restrict top management's strategic options in the future. For this reason a change in policies should quickly follow a change in strategy. Managing policy is one way to manage the corporate culture.

In Conclusion . . .

When Sheri Poe founded Rykä, Inc., she knew that to succeed she had to follow a business strategy of focused differentiation. How else was her company to compete with Nike and Reebok? Poe explained:

> Competing with billion-dollar companies is scary, but not impossible. By offering similar products and focusing on the most cost-effective ways to reach a target market, an entrepreneur can carve out a niche that the big guys have overlooked. . . .
>
> At that time [1987], women's athletic shoes were sized-down versions of men's; but a woman's body is obviously different, and when she's not wearing shoes designed for her physiology, the constant pounding of a workout will make her more likely to develop nagging injuries. . . . What Ryka developed was a fitness shoe built specifically for a woman, a patented design for better shock absorption and durability. . . .
>
> In any industry, the key is to have a strong niche; that way, if anyone copies the product, yours will still be viewed as the original. Staying a step ahead as the megabucks companies attempt to invade your niche is essential to long-term success in a crowded market.[67]

Points to Remember

- Business (often called competitive) strategy is concerned with improving the competitive position of a company's or business unit's products or services within a specific industry or market segment. Porter proposes differentiation and lower cost as the two basic competitive strategies. If the strategies are aimed at a specific market segment or niche, they are called focus strategies and designated as differentiation focus or cost focus.
- Although Porter states that a company or business unit must follow one of these two competitive strategies to be successful (or be "stuck in the middle"), some firms have been successful in following both differentiation and low cost strategies.
- A tactic is a specific operating plan specifying how, when, and where a strategy is to be implemented. The two main types are timing and market location tactics. Timing tactics involve being first, later, or last into a product line or industry. Market location tactics may be offensive or defensive and range from frontal assault to guerrilla warfare to lowering the inducement for attack.

- Functional strategy maximizes resource productivity to provide distinctive competence that gives a company or business unit a competitive advantage. An important consideration is whether the function or activity should be housed within (integrated into) the organization or purchased from an outside supplier under a long-term contract.
- Among the many types of functional strategies are marketing, financial, R&D, operations, and human resource management strategies. They can range from market or product development strategies within marketing to leader or follower strategies within research and development.
- Scenario construction is a valuable aid in choosing the best strategy from among alternatives. It often takes the form of alternative pro forma financial statements that may be calculated using a spreadsheet on a personal computer. Strategic decision makers must consider acceptable risk, stakeholders' pressure, corporate culture, and the needs and desires of key managers when selecting an alternative.
- After formulating a set of strategies, management must establish policies to define the ground rules for those charged with implementing the strategies. Policies provide guidance for operational decisions and thus link strategy formulation with implementation.

Discussion Questions

1. Is it possible for a company or business unit to follow a cost leadership strategy and a differentiation strategy simultaneously? Why or why not?
2. How can a company overcome the limitations of being in a fragmented industry?
3. What are the advantages and disadvantages of being the first mover in an industry? Give some examples of first mover and late mover firms. Were they successful?
4. How might the resource-based view (discussed in Chapter 5) influence decisions regarding seeking the advantage of being a first mover?
5. Why is penetration pricing more likely than skim pricing to raise a company's or a business unit's operating profit in the long run?
6. What are the pros and cons of R&D leadership versus R&D followership as a functional strategy?
7. What are the advantages and disadvantages of the devil's advocate, dialectical inquiry, and consensus approaches to making strategic choices?
8. What is the relationship of policies to strategies?

Notes

1. L. Collins, "Casey's Wants Exclusive Markets for Its Fried Chicken, Pizza," *Des Moines Register* (June 23, 1988), p. 5S.
2. M. E. Porter, *Competitive Strategy* (New York: Free Press, 1980), pp. 34–41, as revised in M. E. Porter, *The Competitive Ad-*

vantage of Nations (New York: Free Press, 1990), pp. 37–40. In his 1980 book, Porter originally proposed focus as a third generic competitive strategy. In his subsequent *Competitive Advantage* (1985) he introduced differentiation focus and cost focus as categories of the focus strategy. In the 1990 book Porter finally dropped focus as a separate strategy and began viewing it instead as a category of competitive scope rather than a separate competitive strategy. This modification agreed with a developing stream of research on generic competitive strategies.

3. Porter, *Competitive Strategy,* p. 35.
4. R. E. Caves and P. Ghemawat, "Identifying Mobility Barriers," *Strategic Management Journal* (January 1992), pp. 1–12.
5. Porter, *Competitive Advantage* (New York: Free Press, 1985), p. 15.
6. T. Y. Wiltz, "Johnson Products Tries to Catch a New Wave," *Business Week* (August 27, 1990), p. 56.
7. T. G. M. Van Asseldonk, "Porter Quantified," in *Handbook of Business Strategy, 1989/90 Yearbook,* edited by H. E. Glass (Boston: Warren, Gorham and Lamont, 1989), pp. 12.1–12.14; G. G. Dess and P. S. Davis, "Porter's (1980) Generic Strategies as Determinants of Strategic Group Membership and Organizational Performance," *Academy of Management Journal* (September 1984), pp. 467–488.
8. R. E. White, "Organizing to Make Business Unit Strategies Work," *Handbook of Business Strategy,* 2nd ed., edited by H. E. Glass (Boston: Warren, Gorham and Lamont, 1991), pp. 24.1–24.14; D. Miller, "The Generic Strategy Trap," *Journal of Business Strategy* (January/February 1992), pp. 37–41; S. Cappel, P. Wright, M. Kroll, and D. Wyld, "Competitive Strategies and Business Performance: An Empirical Study of Select Service Business," *International Journal of Management* (March 1992), pp. 1–11.
9. G. S. Day, "Deciding How to Compete," *Planning Review* (September–October 1989), pp. 18–23.
10. W. E. Deming, *Out of the Crisis* (Cambridge, Mass.: Massachusetts Institute of Technology, Center for Advanced Engineering Study, 1986), p. 23.
11. Porter, *Competitive Advantage,* pp. 18–19.
12. R. Jacob, "Acquisitions Done the Right Way," *Fortune* (November 16, 1992), p. 96.
13. Porter, *Competitive Strategy,* p. 75; O. Heil and T. S. Robertson, "Toward a Theory of Competitive Market Signaling: A Research Agenda," *Strategic Management Journal* (September 1991), pp. 403–418.
14. J. Mitchell, "GM to Discontinue the Buick Reatta, Citing Slow Sales," *Wall Street Journal* (March 5, 1991), p. A4.
15. Porter, *Competitive Advantage,* p. 186.
16. M. B. Lieberman and D. B. Montgomery, "Strategy of Market Entry: To Pioneer or Follow?" *Handbook of Business Strategy,* 2nd ed., edited by H. E. Glass (Boston: Warren, Gorham and Lamont, 1991), pp. 21.1–21.29; B. Mascarenkas, "Order of Entry and Performance in International Markets," *Strategic Management Journal* (October 1992), pp. 499–510; M. Lambkin, "Order of Entry and Performance in New Markets," *Strategic Management Journal* (Summer 1988), pp. 127–140.
17. Lieberman and Montgomery, pp. 21.1–21.29.
18. M. K. Bolton, "Imitation Versus Innovation: Lessons to Be Learned From the Japanese," *Organizational Dynamics* (Winter 1993), pp. 30–45.
19. Mascarenhas, pp. 499–510. For additional information on market entry, see W. T. Robinson, C. Fornell, and M. Sullivan, "Are Market Pioneers Intrinsically Stronger Than Later Entrants?" *Strategic Management Journal* (November 1992), pp. 609–624; M. M. Lele, "Selecting Strategies That Exploit Leverage," *Planning Review* (January/February 1992), pp. 15–21.
20. Summarized from various articles by L. Fahey in *The Strategic Management Reader,* edited by L. Fahey (Englewood Cliffs, N.J.: Prentice-Hall, 1989), pp. 178–205.
21. This information on defensive tactics is summarized from Porter, *Competitive Advantage,* pp. 482–512.
22. M-J. Chen and I. C. MacMillan, "Nonresponse and Delayed Response to Competitive Moves: The Roles of Competitor Dependence and Action Reversibility," *Academy of Management Journal* (August 1992), pp. 539–570.
23. W. T. Robinson, "Marketing Mix Reactions to New Business Ventures," *The PIMSletter on Business Strategy,* No. 42 (Cambridge,

Mass.: Strategic Planning Institute, 1988), p. 9.
24. R. Woodbury, "Prince of Midair," *Time* (January 25, 1993), p. 55.
25. For further information about defending against new entrants, see T. S. Robertson and H. Gatignon, "How Innovators Thwart New Entrants into Their Market," *Planning Review* (September/October 1991), pp. 4–11, 48.
26. R. A. Bettis, S. P. Bradley, and G. Hamel, "Outsourcing and Industrial Decline," *Academy of Management Executive* (February 1992), pp. 7–22.
27. D. Willey, "Who's Outsourcing What," *Journal of Business Strategy* (May/June 1993), pp. 54–55.
28. J. B. Quinn, "The Intelligent Enterprise: A New Paradigm," *Academy of Management Executive* (November 1992), pp. 48–63.
29. Bettis, Bradley, and Hamel, pp. 7–22.
30. A. V. Snyder and H. W. Ebeling, Jr., "Targeting a Company's Real Core Competencies," *Planning Review* (November/December 1992), pp. 26–32.
31. W. Redmond, "The Strategic Pricing of Innovative Products," *Handbook of Business Strategy, 1992/1993 Yearbook,* edited by H. E. Glass and M. A. Hovde (Boston: Warren, Gorham and Lamont, 1992), pp. 16.1–16.13.
32. C. J. Clarke, "Using Finance for Competitive Advantage," *Long Range Planning* (April 1988), pp. 63–64.
33. F. R. Bleakley, "A Decade of Debt Is Now Giving Way to the Age of Equity," *Wall Street Journal* (December 16, 1991), pp. A1, A8.
34. I. Fox and A. Marcus, "The Causes and Consequences of Leveraged Management Buyouts," *Academy of Management Review* (January 1992), pp. 62–85; B. Houlden, "Buy-Outs and Beyond—Motivations, Strategies and Ownership Changes," *Long Range Planning* (August 1990), pp. 73–77; S. A. Zahra and M. Fescina, "Will Leveraged Buyouts Kill U.S. Corporate Research and Development?" *Academy of Management Executive* (November 1991), pp. 7–21.
35. T. Due, "Dean Foods Thrives on Regional Off-Brand Products," *Wall Street Journal* (September 17, 1987), p. A6.
36. R. J. Mayer, "Winning Strategies for Manufacturers in Mature Industries," *Journal of Business Strategy* (Fall 1987), p. 24.
37. R. H. Hayes and S. C. Wheelwright, *Restoring Our Competitive Edge: Competing Through Manufacturing* (New York: John Wiley & Sons, 1984).
38. J. R. Williams and R. S. Novak, "Aligning CIM Strategies to Different Markets," *Long Range Planning* (February 1990), pp. 126–135.
39. S. Kotha and D. Orne, "Generic Manufacturing Strategies: A Conceptual Synthesis," *Strategic Management Journal* (May–June 1989), pp. 211–231.
40. M. Zairi, "Competitive Manufacturing: Combining Total Quality with Advanced Technology," *Long Range Planning* (June 1993), pp. 123–132.
41. "Lease, Don't Hire: Leasing Employees Becomes More Popular," in Labor Letter, *Wall Street Journal* (March 16, 1993), p. A1; D. R. Brown and G. R. Gray, "Rethinking the Contingency Workforce: Why Not Hire the Retired?" *SAM Advanced Management Journal* (Spring 1991), pp. 4–9.
42. B. Dumaine, "Who Needs a Boss?" *Fortune* (May 7, 1990), pp. 52–60.
43. D. F. Raskas and D. C. Hambrick, "Multifunctional Managerial Development: A Framework for Evaluating the Options," *Organizational Dynamics* (Autumn 1992), pp. 5–17.
44. D. P. Hamilton, "Fujitsu Readies New Products as Mainframes Wane," *Wall Street Journal* (May 27, 1993), p. B4.
45. D. K. Sinha, "Strategic Planning in the Fortune 500," *Handbook of Business Strategy, 1991/92 Yearbook,* edited by H. E. Glass and M. A. Hovde (Boston: Warren, Gorham and Lamont, 1991), pp. 9.6–9.8.
46. J. F. Bandrowski, "Taking Creative Leaps," *Planning Review* (January/February 1990), p. 35.
47. M. Hergert, "Strategic Resources Allocation Using Divisional Hurdle Rates," *Planning Review* (January/February 1987), pp. 28–32.
48. M. J. Stahl, *Strategic Executive Decisions* (New York: Quorum Books, 1989), pp. 27–55.
49. M. Kroll and S. Caples, "Managing Acquisitions of Strategic Business Units with the Aid of the Arbitrage Pricing Model," *Academy of Management Review* (October 1987), pp. 676–685.

50. M. D. Everett, "A Simplified Guide to Capital Investment Risk Analysis," *Planning Review* (July 1986), pp. 32–36.
51. H. L. Mathews and T. W. Harvey, "The Sugar Daddy Gambit: Funding Strategic Alliances with Venture Capital," *Planning Review* (November/December 1988), pp. 36–41. See also T. J. Peters and R. H. Waterman, *In Search of Excellence* (New York: HarperCollins, 1982), pp. 115–116.
52. R. H. Hayes and D. A. Garvin, "Managing as if Tomorrow Mattered," *Harvard Business Review* (May–June 1982), p. 79.
53. B. Nussbaum and J. H. Dobrzynski, "The Battle for Corporate Control," *Business Week* (May 18, 1987), p. 103.
54. For further information on stakeholder management and political strategy, see I. C. MacMillan and P. E. Jones, *Strategy Formulation: Power and Politics,* 2nd ed. (St. Paul, Minn.: West, 1986).
55. R. M. Cyert and J. G. March, "A Behavioral Theory of Organizational Objectives," in *Management Classics,* edited by M. T. Matteson and J. M. Ivancevich (Santa Monica, Calif.: Goodyear, 1977), p. 114.
56. H. Schwartz and S. M. Davis, "Matching Corporate Culture and Business Strategy," *Organizational Dynamics* (Summer 1981), p. 43.
57. P. D. Harrison and A. Harrell, "Impact of 'Adverse Selection' on Managers' Project Evaluation Decisions," *Academy of Management Journal* (June 1993), pp. 635–643.
58. W. S. Silver and T. R. Mitchell, "The Status Quo Tendency in Decision Making," *Organizational Dynamics* (Spring 1990), pp. 34–46.
59. R. A. Cosier and C. R. Schwenk, "Agreement and Thinking Alike: Ingredients for Poor Decisions," *Academy of Management Executive* (February 1990), p. 69.
60. R. L. Priem, "The Management Team Group Factors, Consensus, and Firm Performance," *Strategic Management Journal* (October 1990), pp. 469–478.
61. D. M. Schweiger, W. R. Sandberg, and P. L. Rechner, "Experiential Effects of Dialectical Inquiry, Devil's Advocacy, and Consensus Approaches to Strategic Decision Making," *Academy of Management Journal* (December 1989), pp. 745–772; K. M. Eisenhardt, "Making Fast Strategic Decisions in High-Velocity Environments," *Academy of Management Journal* (September 1989), pp. 543–576; Cosier and Schwenk, pp. 69–74.
62. Cosier and Schwenk, p. 72.
63. M. Ivey and G. Lewis, "How Compaq Gets There Firstest with the Mostest," *Business Week* (June 26, 1989), pp. 146–150.
64. Schweiger et al., pp. 745–772; G. Whyte, "Decision Failures: Why They Occur and How to Prevent Them," *Academy of Management Executive* (August 1991), pp. 23–31.
65. J. A. S. de Vasconcellos e Sa and D. C. Hambrick, "Key Success Factors: Test of a General Theory in the Mature Industrial-Product Sector," *Strategic Management Journal* (July-August 1989), pp. 367–382.
66. J. E. Ellis, "Why Monsanto Is Plunking Down Its Chips on R&D," *Business Week* (August 21, 1989), p. 66.
67. S. Poe, "To Compete with Giants, Choose Your Niche," *Nation's Business* (July 1992), p. 6.

Strategy Implementation: Organizing for Action

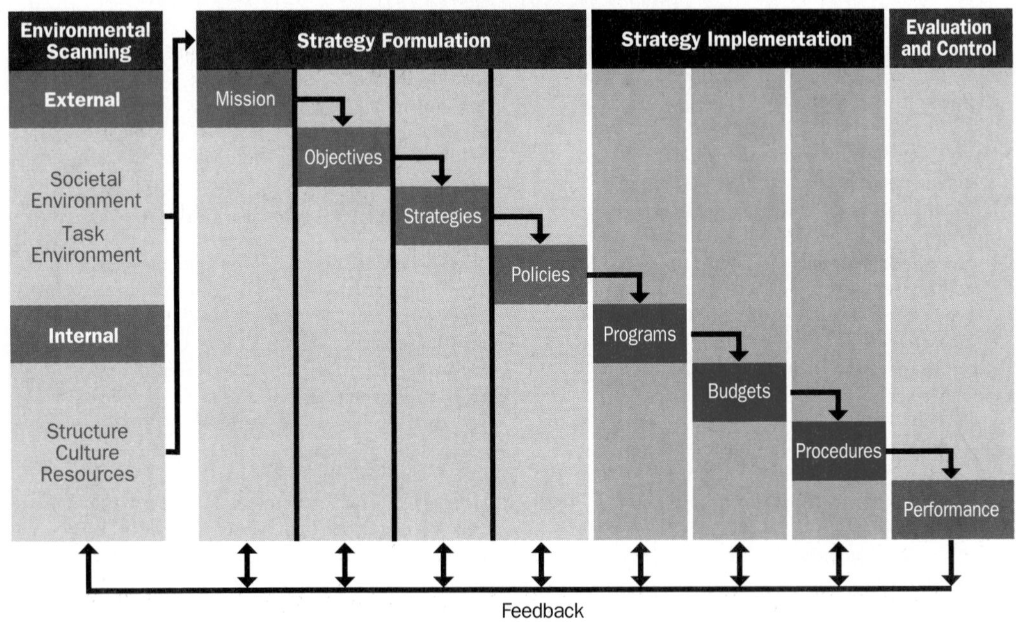

There is at least one point in the history of any company when you have to change dramatically to rise to the next performance level. Miss the moment and you start to decline.[1]
[Andrew Grove, CEO and Chairman, Intel Corporation]

Based on the huge success of its Hollywood, California, Universal Studios tour, MCA, Inc., had planned since 1969 to establish a bigger version of the studio tour in Orlando, Florida. The company bought land in central Florida, but management's reservations about the project delayed construction until the late 1980s—too late to beat Walt Disney World and its Disney–MGM Studios operation. Finally deciding to go ahead in 1989, the year the Disney–MGM studio tour opened, MCA's top management rushed to open the project well before it was ready. Everyone ignored the importance of proper implementation in the rush to meet management's deadline. Three months after the 444 acre combination studio tour and theme park opened, customers were still demanding refunds for poorly operating rides and attractions. The rides, based on Universal's movies *Jaws, Earthquake,* and *King Kong,* rarely operated as planned. One group of customers, having paid the full-price $29 admission, charged up to assembled television cameras, thrust their thumbs down, and shouted: "We're going to Disney World!" After expecting the Florida operation to add as much as $25 million a year to MCA's earnings, management revised its estimates and hoped merely to break even. Two more years passed before the studio tour began to live up to management's expectations.

Once a strategy and a set of policies have been formulated, the focus of strategic management shifts to implementation. Strategy implementation is the sum total of the activities and choices required for the execution of a strategic plan. It is the process by which strategies and policies are put into action through the development of programs, budgets, and procedures. Although implementation is usually considered after strategy has been formulated, implementation is a key part of strategic management. The Orlando Universal Tours is one example of how a good strategy can result in a disaster through poor strategy implementation. Strategy formulation and strategy implementation should thus be considered as two sides of the same coin.

To begin the implementation process, strategic managers must consider three questions.

- *Who* are the people who will carry out the strategic plan?
- *What* must be done?
- *How* are they going to do what is needed?

Management should have addressed these and similar questions initially when analyzing the pros and cons of strategic alternatives. In any event, it must address them before making implementation plans. Unless management can answer these basic questions satisfactorily, even the best-planned strategy is unlikely to yield the desired outcome.

A survey of 93 Fortune 500 firms revealed that over half the corporations experienced the following ten problems when they attempted to implement a strategic change. These problems are listed in order of frequency of occurrence.

1. Implementation slower than originally planned.
2. Unanticipated major problems.
3. Ineffective coordination of activities.
4. Competing activities and crises that distracted attention away from implementation.
5. Insufficient capabilities of the involved employees.
6. Inadequate training and instruction of lower level employees.
7. Uncontrollable external environmental factors.
8. Inadequate leadership and direction by departmental managers.
9. Poor definition of key implementation tasks and activities.
10. Inadequate monitoring of activities by the information system.[2]

Poor implementation of an appropriate strategy may cause that strategy to fail. An excellent implementation plan, however, not only will cause an appropriate strategy to succeed, but it can also rescue a questionable strategy. An increasing number of chief executives are therefore turning their attention to the problems of implementation. Now more than ever before they realize that a successful strategy depends on organization structure, resource allocation, compensation program,

SUCCESSFUL STRATEGY IMPLEMENTATION AT HEWLETT-PACKARD

Strategy in Action

The Hewlett-Packard Company (HP), often listed as one of America's best managed companies, ran into serious difficulty in 1990. Its market share in critical computer markets was declining, orders for medical equipment were falling. Earnings fell in each quarter and HP's stock price slid to an eight-year low. Even worse, the company's most important project, a series of high-speed workstations, was falling behind schedule. The company had developed sound strategies, but it no longer seemed able to implement those strategies effectively. The 1988 launch of its microcomputer, the Model 950, was late by more than a year. Its personal computer models were consistently late, high-priced copies of IBM PCs and had captured only 1.2% of the 1990 world PC market. The company spent 18 months bringing out new consumer products—far too long in this industry. An ever-expanding web of committees, which had originally been designed to foster communication between operating groups, had slowed product development and increased costs. Bob Falkenberg, General Manager of the Personal Information Products Group, dealt with at least 38 committees that decided everything from which features to include in a new software program to which city would be best for introduction of a new product. Because 70% of HP's revenues came from computer and related products, its sluggish system increasingly was putting it at a disadvantage in that fast-changing industry.

After discussions with Chairman and founder David Packard, CEO John Young reorganized the company. He eliminated two layers of man-

information system, and corporate culture, among other resources. Supporting their view is recent research on companies in 31 U.S. manufacturing industries, which revealed that performance isn't so much a result of a company's strategy but of the company's capabilities to carry out that strategy effectively.[3] The Strategy in Action on pages 222–223 gives an example of successful implementation at Hewlett-Packard Company.

8.1 Who Implements Strategy?

Those who implement strategy probably will be a much more diverse group of people than those who formulate it. In most large, multi-industry corporations, the implementers will be everyone in the organization. Vice-presidents of functional areas and directors of divisions or strategic business units (SBUs) will work with their subordinates to put together large-scale implementation plans. Plant agement and the company's committee structure. He divided the computer business into two main groups: one for personal computers, printers, and other products sold through dealers and the second for workstations and minicomputers sold directly to big customers. He replaced the single corporate sales force, giving each of the two computer units its own sales and marketing team. Instead of product designers, engineers, manufacturing managers, and marketing people working sequentially on each new product, Young put them into teams to work concurrently on a project. For example, to develop HP's new Kittyhawk match-box sized disk drive, a multi-discipline team worked on it from the start. The team produced the drive in one year, or six months less than the industry average. By 1991, some 60% of HP's orders were for products less than two years old, compared to only 45% in 1989. And in 1992, PCs turned profitable after several years of losses. According to Bob Frankenberg, who after the reorganization dealt only with three instead of 38 committees, "The results are incredible. We are doing more business and getting product out quicker with fewer people."

Source: S. K. Yoder, "A 1990 Reorganization at Hewlett-Packard Already Is Paying Off," *Wall Street Journal* (July 22, 1991), pp. A1, A10; B. Buell, R. D. Hof, and G. McWilliams, "Hewlett-Packard Rethinks Itself," *Business Week* (April 1, 1991), pp. 76–79; C. Arnst, "Now, HP Stands for Hot Products," *Business Week* (June 14, 1993), p. 36; R. D. Hof, "From Dinosaur to Gazelle," *Business Week* (Reinventing America 1992), p. 65; R. D. Hof, "Suddenly, Hewlett-Packard Is Doing Everything Right," *Business Week* (March 23, 1992), pp. 88–89.

managers, project managers, and unit heads will put together plans for their specific plants, departments, and units. Hence every operational manager down to first-line supervisors and every employee will be involved in some way in implementing corporate, business, and functional strategies.

Most of the people in the organization who are crucial to successful strategy implementation probably had little, if anything, to do with development of the corporate strategy. Therefore they might be entirely ignorant of the vast amount of data and work that went into the formulation process. Unless changes in mission, objectives, strategies, and policies and their importance to the company are communicated clearly to all operational managers, resistance and foot-dragging can result. Managers might hope to influence top management to abandon its new plans and return to its old ways. Avoiding such a situation is one reason why involving middle managers in both formulation and implementation of strategy tends to yield better organizational performance.[4]

8.2 What Must Be Done?

The managers of divisions and functional areas work with their fellow managers to develop programs, budgets, and procedures to implement strategy. They also work to achieve synergy among the divisions and functional areas in order to establish and maintain the company's distinctive competence.

Developing Programs, Budgets, and Procedures

The purpose of a program is to make the strategy action-oriented. For example, assume that Ajax Continental chose forward vertical integration as its best strategy for growth. It purchased existing retail outlets from another firm (Jones Surplus) instead of creating its own. To integrate the new stores into the company, management would now have to develop various programs, such as

1. A restructuring program to move the Jones Surplus stores into Ajax Continental's marketing chain of command so that store managers report to regional managers, who report to the merchandising manager, who reports to the vice-president in charge of marketing;
2. An advertising program ("Jones Surplus is now a part of Ajax Continental. Prices are lower. Selection is better.");
3. A training program for newly hired store managers and the Jones Surplus managers the corporation has decided to keep;
4. A reporting procedures program to integrate the Jones Surplus stores into Ajax Continental's accounting system; and
5. A modernization program for the Jones Surplus stores to prepare them for a "grand opening."

After these and other needed programs have been developed, the budget process begins. Planning a budget is the last real check that management has on the feasibility of its selected strategy. Estimates of specific implementation program costs may show an ideal strategy to be flawed or even completely impractical.

Approval of program, divisional, and corporate budgets leads to development of standard operating procedures (SOPs). They typically detail the various activities needed to complete a corporation's programs. In the case of Ajax Corporation's acquisition of Jones Surplus's retail outlets, new operating procedures must be established for in-store promotions, inventory ordering, stock selection, customer relations, credit and collections, warehouse distribution, pricing, paycheck timing, grievance handling, and raises and promotions, among other operations. These procedures ensure that day-to-day store operations will be consistent over time (i.e., next week's work activities will be the same as this week's) and consistent among stores (i.e., each store will operate in the same manner as the others). For example, to ensure that its policies are carried out explicitly in every one of its fast-food retail outlets, McDonald's has done an excellent job of developing very detailed procedures (and policing them!).

Achieving Synergy

One of the goals to be achieved in strategy implementation is synergy among functions and business units, which is why corporations commonly reorganize after an acquisition.[5] **Synergy** is said to exist for a divisional corporation if the return on investment (ROI) of each division is greater than the return would be if each division were an independent business.[6] The acquisition or development of additional product lines often is justified on the basis of achieving some advantages of scale in one or more of a company's functional areas. For example, when Ralston Purina acquired Union Carbide's Eveready and Energizer lines of batteries, Ralston's CEO argued that his company would earn better profit margins on batteries than Union Carbide would because of Ralston's expertise in developing and marketing branded consumer products. Ralston Purina felt that it could lower the battery costs by taking advantage of synergies in advertising, promotion, and distribution.

Igor Ansoff suggests the existence of four types of synergy, which often affect the success of strategy implementation.

- **Marketing synergy:** Common distribution channels, sales force, and/or warehousing create synergies. A complete line of related products increases the productivity of the sales force. Common advertising and promotions can have multiple returns for the same dollar spent.
- **Operating synergy:** The greater utilization of facilities and personnel, the spreading of overhead, and large-lot purchasing create operating synergies.
- **Investment synergy:** The joint use of plant, common raw materials inventories, transfer of R&D among products, common tooling and machinery, and increased access to sources of capital create investment synergies.
- **Management synergy:** Competent management often is a scarce commodity, so the addition of new products or businesses can enhance overall performance if management finds the new problems to be similar to the ones it has successfully overcome earlier with its current products or businesses. When acquiring another firm, for example, the acquiring firm's management knows the types of people to appoint to key jobs, the ratios to examine, and the time to intervene in activities.[7]

These synergies are not automatic. In order to achieve them, a corporation must not only encourage a supportive culture, but also develop an implementation program reorganizing and combining its operations. For example, when the tobacco company Philip Morris acquired General Foods in 1985 and Kraft Foods in 1988, top management had hoped that the food units would provide for Philip Morris's future growth. However, Philip Morris failed to develop the operating and marketing synergies needed for growth. Instead it raised prices in all food categories, a short-term move that had unfortunate consequences. The new Kraft General Foods Division began to lose market share in important categories such as cheese, processed meats, and frozen dinners. Realizing its mistake, Philip Morris cut prices and boosted advertising. It then attempted to obtain economies of scale by merging some of the activities of the two food units. By consolidating purchases and using fewer suppliers, it cut costs by 15%–20%. It consolidated the buying of media advertising and emphasized joint promotions. The company also developed a system for its many brands to exchange TV air time, allowing one brand to make use of another brand's leftover time. Philip Morris also fostered the exchange of marketing techniques among the Kraft General Foods business units.[8]

8.3 How Is Strategy to Be Implemented? Organizing for Action

Up to this point, we have discussed both strategy formulation and implementation in terms of planning. Programs, budgets, and procedures simply are more detailed plans for the eventual implementation of strategy. However, the total strategic management process also includes several types of action-oriented activities crucial to implementation: organizing, staffing, directing, and controlling. Before plans can lead to actual performance, top management must ensure that the corporation is appropriately organized, programs are adequately staffed, and activities are being directed to achieve desired objectives. In this chapter we briefly review organizing activities. We then discuss staffing, directing, and controlling activities in Chapters 9 and 10.

Fundamentals of Organizing: Mechanistic and Organic Structure

Establishing some sort of structure is the primary means of organizing the many activities and people in a large organization in order to get work done. A change in corporate strategy will likely require some sort of change in organizational structure and the skills needed in particular positions. A consensus is developing among scholars that changes in the environment affect organizational structure primarily through changes in corporate and/or business-level strategies.[9] The conclusion seems to be that strategy, structure, and the environment need to be closely aligned; otherwise, organizational performance will likely suffer.[10] Strategic managers must therefore examine closely the way their company is structured in order to decide what, if any, changes should be made in the way work is accomplished. Should activities be grouped differently? Should the authority to make key decisions be centralized at headquarters or decentralized to managers in distant locations? Should the company be managed tightly with many rules and controls, or loosely with few rules and controls? Should the corporation be organized as a tall structure with many layers of managers, each having a narrow span of control (i.e., few employees to supervise) for better control of subordinates; or should it be organized as a flat structure with fewer layers of managers, each having a wide span of control (i.e., more employees to supervise) to give more freedom to subordinates? For example, Ford has a fairly tall structure with 15 layers of managers, whereas Toyota has a relatively flat structure (for an automaker) with seven layers.[11] Is Toyota's or Ford's structure "better"? Before these and other questions can be answered, the strategic manager must understand the differences between mechanistic and organic structures.

Research by T. Burns and G. M. Stalker concluded that a **mechanistic structure,** with its emphasis on a centralization of decision making and bureaucratic rules and procedures, appears to be well suited to organizations operating in a reasonably stable environment. For example, Norfolk Southern's fairly mechanistic structure supported its very effective and efficient railroad operations when the government rigidly regulated the industry's development. In contrast, however, Burns and Stalker found that successful firms operating in a constantly changing environment, such as those in the electronics and aerospace industries, use a more **organic structure,** with decentralized decision making and flexible procedures.[12] (Once the U.S. transportation industry was deregulated, Norfolk Southern appropriately became more organic.) Studies by P. R. Lawrence and J. W. Lorsch showed that successful firms in a reasonably stable environment, such as the container industry, coordinate activities primarily through fairly centralized corporate hierarchies, which rely on direct contact by managers as well as on written directives. Successful firms in more dynamic environments, such as the plastics industry, coordinate activities through integrative departments and permanent cross-functional teams as well as through hierarchical contact and memos.[13]

The general conclusion of these studies has two parts. First, traditional mechanistic structure with few horizontal linkages and many layers of managers is most appropriate for organizations operating in a relatively certain, stable environment. Second, a looser organic structure with more horizontal linkages and fewer layers of managers is most appropriate for those organizations operating in a relatively uncertain, changing environment. This conclusion is generally supported by further research.[14]

One example of an organization becoming more organic to adjust to an uncertain environment is General Motors. Realizing that its current structure was too mechanistic to respond quickly to its changing environment, it established the completely new Saturn division with much more participative management. Created to design, build, and compete with cars built by Japanese auto companies, Saturn utilized self-managed work teams and joint decision making by labor and management. Because of the success of these programs, GM is introducing self-managed work teams and more employee participation into its Orion Township, Michigan, plant where it assembles the new Oldsmobile Aurora and the redesigned Buick Riviera. Management's new willingness to work with instead of against its unions is creating a new atmosphere of cooperation. Workers are now encouraged to stop the assembly line if a problem develops. (Previously, workers who stopped the assembly line were labeled "troublemakers.") According to the president of Orion's UAW Local 5960, "We've gone through a major change out here and our people are committed to making that change successful."[15]

Other large corporations also are trying to become more efficient and to adapt to new competitive conditions by further decentralizing decision making and by reducing the number of middle managers to obtain a flatter and more flexible structure. In order to "push decision making downward," Caterpillar, Inc., recently replaced its tall functional structure with a flatter divisional structure of highly autonomous profit centers and support divisions.

Structure Follows Strategy

In a classic study of large U.S. corporations, such as DuPont, General Motors, Sears, and Standard Oil, Alfred Chandler concluded that changes in corporate strategy lead to changes in organizational structure.[16] He also concluded that organizations evolve from one kind of structural arrangement to another as they expand. He proposed that these structural changes occur because inefficiencies caused by the old structure, by being pushed too far, have become too obviously detrimental to live with. Chandler therefore outlined the following sequence.

1. New strategy is created.
2. New administrative problems emerge.
3. Economic performance declines.
4. New appropriate structure is invented.
5. Profits return to their previous level.

Chandler found that in their early years, corporations such as DuPont tend to have a centralized functional organizational structure that is well suited to producing and selling a limited range of products. As they add new product lines, purchase their own sources of supply, and create their own distribution networks, they become too complex for highly centralized structures. In order to remain successful, this type of organization needs to shift to a decentralized structure with several semiautonomous divisions (referred to in Chapter 5 on pages 122–123 as the divisional structure). Economist O. E. Williamson calls this type of structure the M-form (for multidivisional structure).[17]

In his book *My Years with General Motors,* Alfred P. Sloan detailed how General Motors made such structural changes in the 1920s.[18] He perceived decentralization of structure as "centralized policy determination coupled with decentralized operating management." After the corporation's top management developed an overall strategy, the individual divisions (Chevrolet, Buick, etc.) were free to choose how to implement that strategy. Patterned after DuPont, GM found the decentralized multidivisional structure to be extremely effective in allowing the maximum amount of freedom for product development. Return on investment was used as a financial control. (We discuss this measure in more detail in Chapter 10.)

Research generally supports Chandler's proposition that structure follows strategy (as well as the reverse proposition from Chapter 5 that structure influences strategy).[19] As mentioned earlier, changes in the environment tend to lead to changes in a corporation's strategy and then to changes in a corporation's structure. Strategy, structure, and the environment need to be closely aligned; otherwise, organizational performance will likely suffer. For example, in one study of 110 business firms, those firms having uncertain environments reacted by divesting (selling off) business units and developing a simpler structure. They tended to sell off units having the least in common with the rest of the organization. The higher degree of relatedness among the remaining units and a simpler divisional structure made the organizations easier to manage. The top managers were able to understand markets of related products better, so environmental uncertainty decreased for them. Less divisionalization created a relatively simpler, more predictable structure.[20]

When strategies change, quick adoption of an appropriate structure may give a company a competitive advantage.[21] In support of this argument, research indicates that when companies that diversify or vertically integrate change from a functional structure to a divisional structure, their financial performance improves.[22] D. J. Teece, in particular, found that reorganization contributes approximately 1.2 percentage points to a company's return on assets.[23] Research also reveals that the fit between a business strategy and the amount of autonomy that corporate headquarters allows the business unit affects business unit performance. In particular, a business unit following a differentiation strategy needs more freedom from headquarters to be successful than does another unit following a low-cost strategy.[24]

However, a change in strategy might not necessarily result in a corresponding change in structure if the corporation has little competition. If a firm occupies a monopolistic position, with tariffs in its favor or with close ties to a government, it can raise prices to cover internal administrative inefficiencies. For these firms this path is easier than going through the pain of corporate reorganization. For example, the use of cost-plus contracts in the U.S. defense industry meant that an aerospace firm making a one-of-a-kind product could simply add increasing administrative costs to the price of the products it built.[25]

Although organizational structure should vary under different environmental conditions—which, in turn, affect an organization's strategy—authorities on organizations disagree about optimal organizational design.[26] What was appropriate for DuPont and General Motors in the 1920s might not be appropriate today. Firms in the same industry, however, do tend to organize themselves in a similar manner. For example, automobile manufacturers tend to emulate General Motors' decentralized division concept, whereas consumer goods producers tend to emulate the brand management concept (a type of matrix structure) pioneered by Procter & Gamble Company. The general conclusion seems to be that firms following similar strategies in similar industries tend to adopt similar structures.[27]

Stages of Corporate Development

A principal proposition of Chandler's was that successful corporations tend to follow a pattern of structural development as they grow and expand. Further work by D. H. Thain, B. R. Scott, and R. V. Tuason specifically delineates three distinct structural stages.[28]

Stage I: Simple Structure

Stage I is typified by the entrepreneur, who founds the company to promote an idea (product or service). The entrepreneur tends to make all the important decisions personally, and is involved in every detail and phase of the organization. The Stage I company has little formal structure, which allows the entrepreneur to supervise directly the activities of every employee (see Fig. 5.4 on page 124 for an illustration of the simple, functional, and divisional structures). Planning usually is short range or reactive. The entrepreneur usually performs the typical managerial functions of planning, organizing, directing, staffing, and controlling to a limited degree, if at all. The greatest strengths of a Stage I corporation are its flexibility and dynamism. The drive of the entrepreneur energizes the organization in its struggle for growth. Its greatest weakness is its extreme reliance on the entrepreneur for general strategies and detailed procedures. If the entrepreneur falters, the company usually flounders.

Stage I describes Oracle Corporation, the computer software firm, under the management of its co-founder and CEO Lawrence Ellison. The company developed a pioneering approach to retrieving data called structured query language (SQL). When IBM made SQL its standard, Oracle's success was assured. Unfortunately, Ellison's technical wizardry didn't carry over to management. Often working at home, he lost sight of details outside his technical interests. According to a member of Oracles' board of directors, "He didn't pay much attention to the rest of the organization, and it grew beyond him." Although the company's sales were rapidly increasing, its financial controls were so weak that management had to restate an entire year's results to rectify irregularities. In 1991, it recorded its first loss. After publicly proclaiming his errors, Ellison used executive recruiters to rebuild his top management group. In 1992, Ellison gave much of his authority to James Abrahamson, a retired general, and retreated to take charge of new products from co-founder Robert Miner.[29] This example spotlights the *crisis of leadership,* which an organization must solve before it can move into the second stage of growth.[30]

Stage II: Functional Structure

At Stage II, a team of managers who have functional specializations replaces the entrepreneur. The transition to this stage requires a substantial change in managerial style for the head of the company, especially for a Stage I entrepreneur. Otherwise, having additional staff members yields no benefits to the organization. At this juncture, the corporate strategy favors protectivism through dominance of the industry, often through vertical or horizontal integration. The greatest strength of a Stage II corporation lies in its concentration and specialization in one industry, which also is its greatest weakness.

Specialized Bicycle Components, Inc., is an example of a company that recently moved from a Stage I, freewheeling, fast-growing company founded by bike enthusiast Mike Sinyard to a Stage II firm run by professional managers. The originator of "mountain bikes," Specialized controlled 65% of the market for these fat-tired bicycles but was having difficulty managing its growth. Consequently, Sinyard hired some professional managers to bring about some order. One of these managers, Erik Eidsmo, left Citicorp to manage Specialized's marketing and sales. Eidsmo introduced the company to Management By Objectives, detailed project planning, and forecasting (see Chapter 9). According to Eidsmo, "We're finally getting—and it's been very painful—some understanding of what the company's long-term horizon should begin to look like."[31]

By concentrating on one industry while that industry remains attractive, a Stage II company, such as Specialized Bicycle Components, may be very successful. If a functionally structured firm diversifies into other products in different industries, however, the advantages of the functional structure break down. A *crisis of autonomy* can develop, in which people managing diversified product lines need more decision-making freedom than top management is willing to delegate to them.

Stage III: Divisional Structure (M-Form)

The Stage III corporation focuses on managing diverse product lines in numerous industries and decentralizes decision-making authority. These organizations grow by diversifying their product lines and expanding to cover wider geographic areas. They move to a divisional structure with a central headquarters and decentralized operating divisions—each division or business unit is a functionally organized Stage II company. They may also use a conglomerate structure if top management decides to let its Stage II subsidiaries continue to operate autonomously. Headquarters attempts to coordinate the activities of its operating divisions through performance—with results-oriented control and reporting systems—and by stressing corporate planning techniques. Top management doesn't tightly control the divisions but holds each division responsible for results. Therefore, to be effective, the company has to have a decentralized decision-making process. The greatest strength of a Stage III corporation is its almost unlimited resources. Its most significant weakness is that it is usually so large and complex that it tends to become relatively inflexible. General Electric, DuPont, and General Motors are Stage III corporations.

Research supports these descriptions of the three stages of corporate development.[32] Table 8.1 specifies the differences among the stages in more detail.

Blocks to Changing Stages

In his study, Chandler noted that the empire builder was rarely the person who created the new structure to fit the new strategy, and that, as a result, the transition from one stage to another often is a painful one.[33] Table 8.2 lists some of the possible blocks to corporate development. General Motors Corporation under the management of William Durant, Ford Motor Company under its founder, Henry Ford, Polaroid Corporation under Edwin Land, and Apple Computer under Steven Jobs all faced difficulties in moving to a new stage. These difficulties are compounded by the founder's tendency to maneuver around the need to delegate by carefully hiring, training, and grooming the management team. These managers eventually come to share the founder's beliefs and attitudes, forming and perpetuating the corporation's culture. The management team tends to maintain the founder's influence throughout the organization long after the founder is gone. Although this situation may be an organization's strength, it may also be a weakness—to the extent that the culture supports the status quo and blocks needed change.[34]

TABLE 8.1 Factors Differentiating Stage I, II, and III Companies

Function	Stage I	Stage II	Stage III
1. Sizing up: Major problems	Survival and growth dealing with short-term operating problems.	Growth, rationalization, and expansion of resources, providing for adequate attention to product problems.	Trusteeship in management and investment and control of large, increasing, and diversified resource. Also, important to diagnose and take action on problems at division level.
2. Objectives	Personal and subjective.	Profits and meeting functionally oriented budgets and performance targets.	ROI, profits, earnings per share.
3. Strategy	Implicit and personal; exploitation of immediate opportunities seen by owner-manager.	Functionally oriented moves restricted to "one product" scope; exploitation of one basic product or service field.	Growth and product diversification; exploitation of general business opportunities.
4. Organization: Major characteristic of structure	One unit, "one-man show."	One unit, functionally specialized group.	Multiunit general staff office and decentralized operating divisions.
5. (a) Measurement and control	Personal, subjective control based on simple accounting system and daily communication and observation.	Control grows beyond one person; assessment of functional operations necessary; structured control systems evolve.	Complex formal system geared to comparative assessment of performance measures, indicating problems and opportunities and assessing management ability of division managers.
5. (b) Key performance indicators	Personal criteria, relationships with owner, operating efficiency, ability to solve operating problems.	Functional and internal criteria such as sales, performance compared to budget, size of empire, status in group, personal relationships, etc.	More impersonal application of comparisons such as profits, ROI, P/E ratio, sales, market share, productivity, product leadership, personnel development, employee attitudes, public responsibility.
6. Reward–punishment system	Informal, personal, subjective; used to maintain control and divide small pool of resources to provide personal incentives for key performers.	More structured; usually based to a greater extent on agreed policies as opposed to personal opinion and relationships.	Allotment by "due process" of a wide variety of different rewards and punishments on a formal and systematic basis Companywide policies usually apply to many different classes of managers and workers with few major exceptions for individual cases.

Source: D. H. Thain, "Stages of Corporate Development," *Business Quarterly* (Winter 1969), p. 37.

TABLE 8.2 **Blocks to Development**

A) Internal Blocks

Stage I to II	Stage II to III
Lack of ambition and drive.	Unwillingness to take the risks involved.
Personal reasons of owner-manager for avoiding change in status quo.	Management resistance to change for a variety of reasons including old age, aversion to risk taking, desire to protect personal empires, etc.
Lack of operating efficiency.	Personal reasons among managers for defending the status quo.
Lack of quantity and quality of operating personnel.	Lack of control system related to appraisal of investment of decentralized operations.
Lack of resources such as borrowing power, plant and equipment, salesmen, etc.	Lack of budgetary control ability.
Product problems and weaknesses.	Organizational inflexibility.
Lack of planning and organizational ability.	Lack of management vision to see opportunities for expansion.
	Lack of management development, i.e., not enough managers to handle expansion.
	Management turnover and loss of promising young managers.
	Lack of ability to formulate and implement strategy that makes company relevant to changing conditions.
	Refusal to delegate power and authority for diversification.

B) External Blocks

Stage I to II	Stage II to III
Unfavorable economic conditions.	Unfavorable economic, political, technological, and social conditions and/or trends.
Lack of market growth.	Lack of access to financial or management resources.
Tight money or lack of an underwriter who will assist the company "to go public."	Overly conservative accountants, lawyers, investment bankers, etc.
Labor shortages in quality and quantity.	Lack of domestic markets necessary to support large diversified corporation.
Technological obsolescence of product.	"The conservative mentality," e.g., cultural contentment with the status quo and lack of desire to grow and develop.

Source: D. H. Thain, "Stages of Corporate Development," *Business Quarterly* (Winter 1969), pp. 43–44. Copyright © 1969 by *Business Quarterly*. Reprinted by permission.

Organizational Life Cycle

Instead of considering stages of development in terms of structure, the organizational life cycle approach places the primary emphasis on the dominant issue facing the corporation. The **organizational life cycle** describes how organizations grow, develop, and eventually decline.[35] The specific organizational structure

Population Ecology, Resource Dependence, and Institution Theories

The organizational life cycle is one of several theories that attempt to explain why organizations develop and change over time. The life cycle model is based on the assumption that strategic managers can change an organization to adapt it to its environment better. Not all theories of organizational change agree with the importance of strategic management in explaining organizational survival.

Population ecology is based on the concept of natural selection in biology. The essential principle is that organisms that are best suited to the environment survive; the others die. Organization theorists make two main assumptions:

1. organizations have limited capabilities to adapt to environmental change; and
2. the processes of change are controlled by the environment.

Their basic argument is that, within an industry, many organizational variations tend to develop because different strategies lead to different structures and processes. Organizations that best fit environmental constraints tend to do well, whereas others tend to fail. Those that survive tend to grow and become a dominant part of the industry. Following this line of reasoning, population ecologists are pessimistic about a specific organization's ability to change and adapt, believing that real strategic change is unlikely. They would argue that starting a new organization is easier than realigning an existing organization with its environment.

Resource dependence theorists focus on the organization's ability to acquire key resources from the environment as the determinant of the organization's sur-

is thus a secondary concern. The life cycle is one of several theories of organizational change, ranging from population ecology to resource dependence, as described in the Key Theory capsule on pages 234–235. These stages are **Birth** (Stage I), **Growth** (Stage II), **Maturity** (Stage III), **Decline** (Stage IV), and **Death** (Stage V). Table 8.3 summarizes the impact of these stages on corporate strategy and structure. Note that the first three stages of the organizational life cycle are similar to the three commonly accepted stages of corporate development mentioned previously. The only significant difference is the addition of decline and death stages to complete the cycle. Even though a company's strategy may still be sound, its aging vival. Growth and survival are easy when the environment is *munificent* (full of all the resources that an organization needs). Organizational problems develop when resources are no longer plentiful. The groups in the task environment that control needed resources then have power over an organization's decision making. To guarantee crucial resources, organizations must interact with these groups through cooperative relationships. Only those organizations that acquire continued access to resources will survive. Therefore the primary job of strategic managers is resource management. Strategic change is possible and should focus on guaranteeing continued access to resources, whether they be from customers, creditors, or donations.

The **theory of institutions** proposes that organizations adapt to a changing environment through *imitation* of other, more successful firms. It contends that organizations tend to mimic organizations in the same industry that deal with similar customers, suppliers, and regulatory agencies. Strategic managers do so because copying the practices of a successful firm not only makes sense, but it also is easier than having to develop a new, untested approach. (Note the current emphasis on competitive benchmarking as a way of imitating another company's successful products.) Top management seeks *legitimacy* (acceptance) from its stakeholders by adopting the latest management practices but doesn't want to be criticized for being too different. As a result, organizations in the same environment tend to look alike and act alike over time. When one goes into decline, the others probably will do so too.

In contrast to population ecologists, resource dependence and institution theorists believe that organizations have the ability to adapt to changing environments.

Source: V. K. Narayanan and R. Nath, *Organization Theory: A Strategic Approach* (Homewood, Ill.: Irwin, 1993), pp. 138–145.

structure, culture, and processes may prevent the strategy from being executed properly—thus the company moves into decline.

D. Miller and P. H. Friesen place a **Revival** stage between the Maturity and Decline stages, indicating that a corporation's life cycle may be extended by innovations in a manner similar to the extension of a product's life cycle. Nevertheless, we don't include revival here as a separate stage because it can occur at any time during a company's maturity stage (when a new growth strategy is implemented) or during its decline stage (when a turnaround strategy is being followed.)[36] For example, Maytag Corporation initiated the revival phase in the 1970s under the

TABLE 8.3 **Organizational Life Cycle**

	Stage I	Stage II	Stage III	Stage IV	Stage V
Dominant Issue	Birth	Growth	Maturity	Decline	Death
Popular Strategies	Concentration in a niche	Horizontal and vertical integration	Concentric and conglomerate diversification	Profit strategy followed by retrenchment	Liquidation or bankruptcy
Likely Structure	Entrepreneur-dominated	Functional management emphasized	Decentralization into profit or investment centers	Structural surgery	Dismemberment of structure

leadership of Daniel Krumm while the company was still in its mature stage of development. As pointed out in the Company Spotlight: Maytag Corporation feature on pages 238–239, the transition from aggressive growth to a rather passive and complacent maturity had left the company vulnerable to competitive advances and the possibility of being acquired.

Why do companies go into decline? According to W. Weitzel and E. Jonsson, the typical organization begins the drift into decline when management fails to notice that the company may be in serious trouble. Once decline begins, it tends to go through the five stages listed in Table 8.4.[37] In the first stage, **blinded,** management does not recognize internal or external changes that may threaten long-term survival. The company is doing a poor job of environmental scanning, and top management doesn't seem to know what is happening. The next stage, **inaction,** is a time when management does nothing despite signs of deteriorating performance. Some of the signs are consistent cash shortages, inconsistent strategies and programs, increasing management turnover, and overhead increasing as a percentage of total revenue.[38] Top management misinterprets information and views the threat as "only temporary." It blames difficulties on environmental events, such as a recession or governmental policies.[39] In the **faulty action** stage, decline is now obvious, but management responds inappropriately by focusing only on efficiencies and budget control to cope with the symptoms, such as creditor problems, instead of with the underlying causes, such as an improperly designed product.[40] An inability to deal with problems leads to a **crisis** stage when resources are too few to implement the major changes now required. Chaos, procrastination, and efforts to "get back to basics" are the result. The final stage, **dissolution,** usually is irreversible. Resources by this time are too few even to keep the organization going on a temporary basis. The end is near.

Unless a company is able to resolve the principal issues facing it in the decline stage, it is likely to move into Stage V, corporate death—also known as bankruptcy. Failure to do so sank TWA, Macy's Department Stores, Baldwin-United, Eastern Airlines, Colt Manufacturing, Orion Pictures, and Wheeling-Pittsburgh Steel, among many other firms. A study conducted by the Administrative Office of the United States Courts found that over an eight-year period only 17% of 144,000 companies actually emerged from Chapter 11 reorganizations.[41] As in the cases of Johns Manville and International Harvester, both of which went bankrupt in the 1980s, a corporation might nevertheless rise like a phoenix from its own ashes and live again (as Manville Corporation and Navistar International Corporation, respectively). The company may be reorganized or liquidated, depending on individual circumstances. In some liquidations, the corporation's name is purchased, and the purchasing corporation places that name on some or all of its products. For example, Wordtronix, a maker of stand-alone word processors, acquired the Remington Rand trademark, even though Remington Rand no longer made typewriters. Top management planned to change the Wordtronix name to Remington Rand to give its machines some name recognition in the marketplace.[42]

Few corporations will move through these five stages in sequence.[43] Some corporations, for example, might never move past Stage II. Others, such as General Motors, might go directly from Stage I to Stage III. A large number of entrepreneurial ventures will jump from Stage I into Stages IV and V. The key for management is to be able to identify when a firm is moving from one stage to another and to make the appropriate strategic and structural adjustments to maintain or even improve corporate performance.

Advanced Structures

The basic structures (simple, functional, divisional, and conglomerate) were discussed earlier in Chapter 5 and depicted in Fig. 5.4 on page 122. The previous sections described how a business corporation tends to grow and develop from a Stage I simple structure to a functional structure and finally to a Stage III divisional structure. The divisional structure isn't the last word in organization design. Advanced structures may help a company implement new strategies better so that it can avoid decline. A new strategy may require more flexible and organic characteristics than a divisional structure can offer. Under conditions of (1) increasing environmental uncertainty, (2) greater use of sophisticated technological production methods, (3) increasing size and scope of worldwide business corporations, (4) greater emphasis on multi-industry competitive strategy, and (5) better educated managers and employees, new and advanced forms of organizational structure emerged. Among the many variations and hybrid structures, three forms stand out as being real advances in organizational structure: strategic business units, matrix structure, and the network (or cluster) organization. One or a combination of these forms may become an additional stage in the development of a corporation.

Strategic Business Units

In 1971, General Electric (GE) successfully developed a method for structuring a large and complex business corporation as a variant of the divisional structure. Referred to as **strategic business units,** or SBUs, organizational groups composed of discrete, independent, product-market segments served by the firm were

Under the leadership of Lewis B. Maytag, a son of the founder, Maytag Company expanded from 1920 to 1926 into a national company. In terms of the organizational life cycle, this was Maytag Company's growth stage. The increasing demand for home laundry equipment caused the company to reduce further its production of farm implements and accessories and to concentrate all its efforts on washing machines. The company went from a $280,000 loss in 1921 to profits exceeding $6.8 million in 1926. Throughout the 1920s and 1930s, Maytag Company had an average U.S. market share of 40%–45% in washing machines. During the Great Depression of the 1930s, Maytag never suffered a loss. During World War II, the company suspended the manufacture of washers and instead produced components for military aircraft.

At the end of World War II in 1945, the Maytag Company returned to the manufacture of washing machines. Unfortunately, the innovative genius and entrepreneurial drive of the company's early years were no longer present. By then, Maytag had become the most successful washing machine company in the United States and had reached its maturity stage. Bendix, a newcomer to the industry, introduced an automatic washing machine that used an automatic spin cycle instead of a hand-cranked wringer to squeeze excess rinse water out of clothes. Maytag, however, did not immediately convert to the manufacture of automatic washers. This reluctance cost the company its leadership in the industry. Even with automatics, Maytag's share of the U.S. washer market was only 8% in 1954.

Upon the death in 1962 of CEO Fred Maytag II, professional managers took charge of the company and Maytag family members were no longer involved in company management. Until 1972, George M. Umbreit served as Chairman and CEO, and E. G.

identified and given primary responsibility and authority to manage their own functional areas. An SBU may be of any size or level, but it *must* have (1) a unique mission, (2) identifiable competitors, (3) an external market focus, and (4) control of its business functions.[44]

Recognizing that its structure of decentralized operating divisions wasn't working efficiently (massive sales growth wasn't being matched by profit growth), GE's top management decided to reorganize. It restructured nine groups and 48 divisions into 43 strategic business units, many of which crossed traditional group, divisional, and profit center lines. For example, food-preparation appliances in three separate divisions were merged into a single SBU serving the housewares market.[45] The concept thus is to decentralize on the basis of strategic elements rather than on the basis of size or span of control and to create horizontal linkages among units

Higdon served as President. These two very conservative men were concerned mainly with continuing the practices that had served the company well in the past. They strongly emphasized product quality and cost control. The company had become complacent and somewhat self-satisfied, but it continued to build on its reputation for quality. It also added related products, such as clothes dryers, to its product line. By 1969, Maytag's market shares in washers and dryers were 10% and 9%, respectively.

Taking over as company President in 1972, Daniel Krumm wasn't satisfied with Maytag's situation. Although the company had added products to its original line of washers, Krumm saw Maytag as merely a successful niche manufacturer in a maturing U.S. market and vulnerable to aggressive actions by larger competitors. Consequently, Maytag's management adopted a strategy to become a full-line manufacturer and develop a stronger position in the U.S. major home appliance industry. The company was to grow by acquisition within the appliance industry. The revival phase of Maytag's organizational life had begun.

In 1981, Maytag purchased Hardwick Stove Company, Jenn-Air a year later, and Magic Chef in 1986. Maytag Company and the Magic Chef family of companies then merged under the parent Maytag Corporation on May 30, 1986, headed by Chairman and CEO Daniel Krumm. In 1988, the top management of the new Maytag Corporation decided to extend the corporation's growth strategy by buying the Chicago Pacific Corporation to acquire the Hoover Company. In this one step Maytag Corporation moved into the international home appliance market with nine manufacturing operations in the United Kingdom, France, Australia, Mexico, Colombia, and Portugal. Maytag Corporation was now positioned as one of the "Big Five" U.S. appliance manufacturers, with a strong presence also in the developing global major home appliance industry.

previously kept separate. Following GE's lead, other firms, such as Honeywell, Mead, Eastman Kodak, Campbell Soup, Union Carbide, and Armco Steel, have implemented the concept of the strategic business unit. General Foods applied the concept by organizing certain products on the basis of menu segments: breakfast foods, beverages, main meals, desserts, and pet foods. The Strategy in Action on page 241 describes the successful beginning of a new SBU at Monsanto Company.

Even after a large corporation is organized on a divisional basis around strategic business units, too many SBUs may remain for top management to manage effectively. In this case, an additional management layer—that of group or sector executives—is added between top management and the division or SBU chiefs. The group executive is thus responsible for managing several similar SBUs, such as housewares, building materials, and auto accessories.

TABLE 8.4

Diagnosis of Stages of Organizational Decline

Stage	Situation	Questions
1. Blinded	Failure to anticipate or detect pressure toward stagnation; decline begins	Are there sufficient monitoring systems to notice long-term opportunities and threats?
2. Inaction	Failure to decide on corrective action; decline becomes noticeable	Is the information translated into trigger points to precipitate corrective action?
3. Faulty Action	Faulty actions; faulty implementation of decisions	Do decision makers use appropriate information to arrive at solutions? Does the organization have effective procedures for implementing change?
4. Crisis	Last chance for reversal in hostile environment; slow erosion in forgiving environment	Does the organization have sufficient resources and mechanisms for a major reorganization?
5. Dissolution	Rapid demise in hostile environment; slow demise in forgiving environment	Is management willing and able to manage an orderly closing or liquidation?

Source: Adapted from "Decline in Organizations: A Literature Integration and Extension," by W. Weitzel and E. Johnson, published in *Administrative Science Quarterly* (Vol. 34, March 1989) by permission of *Administrative Science Quarterly*. © 1989 Cornell University.

This type of reorganization on the basis of markets lends itself to development of a horizontal strategy based on competitive considerations that cut across divisional boundaries. The group or sector executive is responsible for developing and implementing the horizontal strategy to coordinate the various goals and strategies of related SBUs. Such a strategy can help a firm compete with multipoint competitors, that is, firms that compete with each other not only in one business unit, but in several related business units.[46] For example, Procter & Gamble, Kimberly-Clark, Scott Paper, and Johnson & Johnson compete with one another in consumer paper products, from disposable diapers to facial tissue. If (purely hypothetically) Johnson & Johnson were to develop a toilet tissue to challenge Procter & Gamble's high-share Charmin brand in a particular geographic area, it might charge a low price for its new brand to build sales quickly. Procter & Gamble might not choose to respond to this attack on its share by cutting prices on Charmin. Because of Charmin's high market share, Procter & Gamble would lose significantly more sales dollars in a price war than Johnson & Johnson would with its initially low-share brand. To retaliate, Procter & Gamble might thus challenge Johnson & Johnson's high-share baby shampoo with Procter & Gamble's own low-share brand of baby shampoo in a different geographic area. Once Johnson & Johnson had perceived Procter & Gamble's response, it might choose to stop challenging Charmin so that Procter & Gamble would stop challenging Johnson & Johnson's baby shampoo.[47]

BIRTH OF AN SBU AT MONSANTO COMPANY

Strategy in Action

The Monsanto Agricultural Company, a subsidiary of Monsanto Company, makes and sells vegetation management products primarily to industrial and agricultural customers. In 1985, one of the company's agricultural sales representatives discovered that home owners were using Roundup, an herbicide designed for farm use, to kill weeds in their lawns. After research indicated significant potential in this area, the company developed home-owner formulations of the product for sale through hardware stores, nurseries, and lawn and garden centers. The resulting sales encouraged the company to purchase the Greensweep line of lawn care products from an Ohio company. This gave the company a complete line of concentrates and ready-to-use weed killer and lawn food products. Greensweep's strength in the eastern United States helped expand the retail penetration of Roundup in that part of the country. Roundup, in turn, aided Greensweep's penetration in the western United States.

Combining these product lines created the Lawn and Garden Business Unit as an SBU within Monsanto Agricultural Company. Gardening experts recommended Roundup because of its low toxicity and its ability to break down quickly into naturally occurring substances. Five years after the SBU was established, it achieved sales in excess of $170 million and was the most profitable competitor in its category of yard care business. The new SBU is now working on more environmentally friendly products to add to its existing product lines.

Source: A. Donald, "Birth of a Business Unit," *Journal of Business Strategy* (May/June 1991), pp. 8–11.

Matrix Structure

Most organizations find that organizing around either functions (in the functional structure) or around products and geography (in the divisional structure) provides an appropriate organizational structure. The strategic business unit form is simply a more advanced version of the divisional structure pioneered by General Motors and DuPont. SBUs provide horizontal links for related product divisions so that the organization as a whole can better address changing product-market issues. In contrast, the matrix structure may be appropriate when organizations conclude that neither functional nor divisional forms, even when combined with horizontal linking mechanisms, are right for their situations. In **matrix structures**, functional and product forms are combined simultaneously at the same level of the organization, as Fig. 8.1. illustrates. Employees have two superiors: a product or project manager and a functional manager. The "home" department—engineering, manufacturing, or sales—usually is functional and reasonably permanent. People from these functional units often are assigned on a temporary basis to one or more product units or projects. Usually temporary, the product units or projects act like divisions in that they are differentiated on a product-market basis. Pioneered in the aerospace industry, the matrix structure combines the stability of the functional structure with the flexibility of the product form. The matrix structure is useful when the external environment (especially its technological and market aspects) is complex and changeable. However, it does produce conflicts revolving around duties, authority, and resource allocation. To the extent that the goals to be achieved are vague and the technology used is poorly understood, a continuous battle for power between product and functional managers is likely.[48] The matrix structure is a likely response to the following three conditions.

- Cross-fertilization of ideas across projects or products is needed.
- Resources are scarce.
- A need to improve information processing and decision making exists.[49]

Stanley Davis and Paul Lawrence, authorities on the matrix form of organization, have identified three distinct phases in the development of the matrix structure.[50] The first phase involves the use of **temporary cross-functional task forces** when a new product line is being introduced. A project manager is in charge as the key horizontal link.

If the cross-functional task forces become permanent, the project manager becomes a product or brand manager and a second phase begins. Function remains the primary organizational structure, but **product or brand managers act as the integrators of semipermanent products or brands.** Considered by many as a key to its the success, Procter & Gamble's brand management approach has been widely imitated by other consumer products firms around the world.

The third phase of matrix development involves a **true dual-authority structure.** Both the functional and product structures have become permanent. All employees are connected to both a vertical functional superior and a horizontal product manager. Functional and product managers have equal authority and must work well together to resolve disagreements over resources and priorities. The aerospace company TRW Systems is an example of a company that uses a mature matrix organizational structure.

Network (Cluster) Structure

Perhaps the newest and most radical organization design, the **network** (or cluster) **structure** (see Fig. 8.1), could be termed a nonstructure because of its virtual elimination of in-house business functions. The network structure is most useful when a firm's environment is unstable and is expected to remain so. Under such conditions, the need for innovation and quick response usually is strong.[51] Following the logic of *transaction cost economics* (see the Key Theory capsule in Chapter 6

FIGURE 8.1 **Matrix and Network Structures**

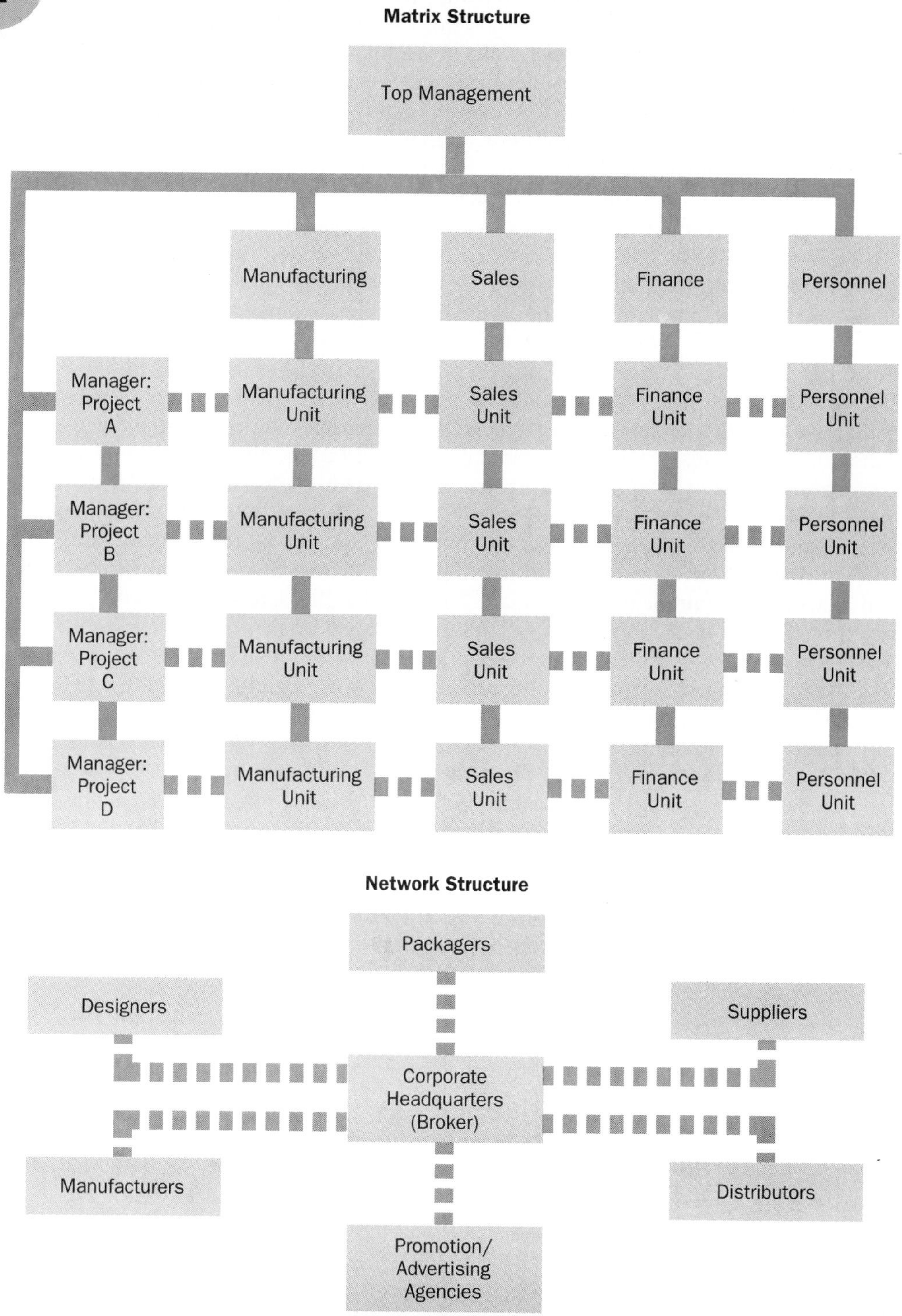

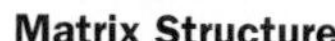

Matrix Structure
Top Management
Manufacturing
Sales
Finance
Personnel
Manager: Project A
Manufacturing Unit
Sales Unit
Finance Unit
Personnel Unit
Manager: Project B
Manufacturing Unit
Sales Unit
Finance Unit
Personnel Unit
Manager: Project C
Manufacturing Unit
Sales Unit
Finance Unit
Personnel Unit
Manager: Project D
Manufacturing Unit
Sales Unit
Finance Unit
Personnel Unit
Network Structure
Packagers
Designers
Suppliers
Corporate Headquarters (Broker)
Manufacturers
Distributors
Promotion/ Advertising Agencies

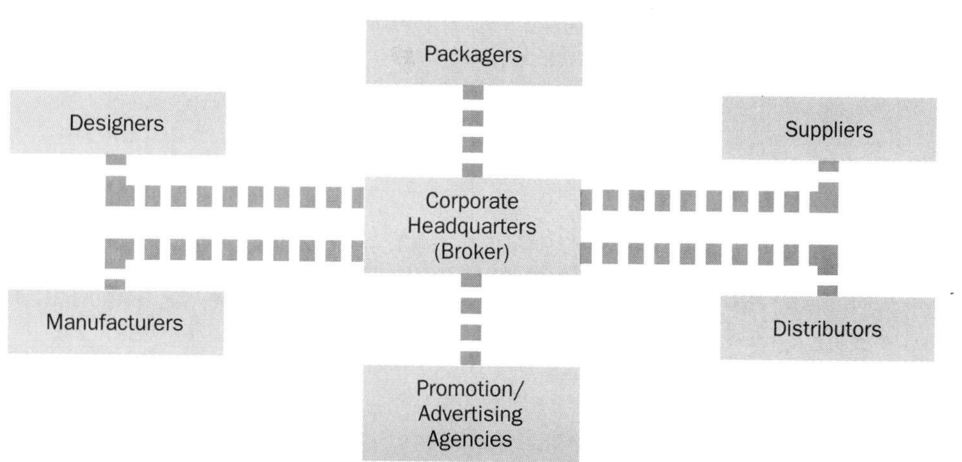

on page 156), a company enters into long-term contracts with suppliers and other strategic alliances to obtain services that the company could otherwise provide for itself through vertical integration. Electronic markets and sophisticated information systems reduce the transaction costs of the marketplace, thus justifying a *buy* over a *make* decision.[52] Rather than being located in a single building or geographic area, the organization's business functions are scattered worldwide. In effect, it is only a shell, with a small headquarters acting as a "broker," electronically connected to completely owned divisions, partially owned subsidiaries, and other independent companies.[53] In its ultimate form, the network organization is a series of independent firms or business units linked by computers in an information system that designs, produces, and markets a product or service.

Nike, the sports shoe company, has used a limited version of the network organization since the company's beginning in 1964. Nike views itself as a research, development, and marketing corporation and utilizes contract manufacturers around the world to produce its products. Another example is Benetton, which subcontracts nearly 95% of its activities in manufacturing, distribution, and sales. The company maintains what it calls an "umbilical cord" through production planning for all its subcontractors, planning their materials requirements, and providing them with bills of labor and standard prices and costs, along with technical assistance to ensure that quality meets Benetton's standards.[54] Yet another example of a complete network organization is Just Toys. The New York City company licenses manufacturers to make bendable polyvinyl chloride figures (called Bend-Ems) of characters such as Disney's Little Mermaid, Hanna-Barbera's Flintstones, and Marvel Entertainment's Spiderman. Because the characters are heavily exposed on TV and in the movies, Just Toys doesn't spend much on advertising. It thus keeps prices low and ensures large markups for stores like Toys "R" Us and Wal-Mart. All manufacturing and administrative work for Bend-Ems is contracted out, and the company has only 30 employees. If a toy isn't selling well, production can be reduced and shipments stopped almost immediately. Mattel and Hasbro would need months to react in a similar situation.[55]

The network organizational structure provides increased flexibility and adaptability for coping with rapid technological change and shifting patterns of international trade and competition. It allows a company to concentrate on its distinctive competencies while gathering efficiencies from other firms who are concentrating their efforts in their areas of expertise.[56] As Raymond Miles and Charles Snow, authorities on the network organization, point out:

> The network organization in its several variations has sought to incorporate the specialized efficiency of the functional organization, the autonomous operating effectiveness of the divisional form, and the asset-transferring capabilities of the matrix organization—all with considerable success.[57]

Increased efficiency and effectiveness are thus the basic reasons to use the network organizational structure.[58] However, the network also has some disadvantages. Miles and Snow point out that the availability of numerous potential partners is a potential source of trouble. If a particular firm overspecializes on one position in the value chain, it runs the risk of becoming a "hollow" corporation—a firm without a clearly defined essential contribution to its product or service.

Therefore firms need to occupy wide enough segments of their value chains to be able to protect and exploit their distinctive competencies.[59]

Reengineering

A new approach to strategy implementation by improving operations is reengineering. **Reengineering** is the radical redesign of business processes to achieve major gains in cost, service, or time.[60] It is not in itself a type of structure. It involves (1) a fundamental rethinking of the way work is done, (2) a structural reorganization—breaking hierarchies into cross-functional work teams, (3) a new information and measurement system, and (4) a new value system with greater emphasis on customers.[61] It is an effective way to implement a turnaround strategy. Popularized by Michael Hammer, reengineering strives to break away from the rules and procedures that have developed and become ingrained in an organization over the years and that block change. These obstacles may be a combination of policies, rules, and procedures that have never been seriously questioned since they were established years earlier. They may range from "Credit decisions are made by the credit department" to "Local inventory is needed for good customer service." Such organizational and work design rules were based on assumptions about technology, people, and organizational goals that may no longer be relevant. For example, Hammer states that the old key variables of cost, growth, and control are being rapidly replaced worldwide by quality, innovation, and service.[62] Rather than attempting to fix existing problems through minor adjustments and fine-tuning existing processes, the key to reengineering is to ask, "If this were a new company, how would we run this place?"[63]

Since the industrial revolution, most corporations have organized work as a sequence of separate tasks and have employed complex mechanisms to track its progress. Because conventional process structures are fragmented and piecemeal, they lack the integration needed to maintain quality and service. According to Hammer:

> Reengineering requires looking at the fundamental processes of the business from a cross-functional perspective. . . . Assemble a team that represents the functional units involved in the process being reengineered and all the units that depend on it. The team must analyze and scrutinize the existing processes until it really understands what the process is trying to accomplish. . . . Rather than looking for opportunities to improve the current process, the team should determine which of its steps really add value and search for new ways to achieve the results.[64]

Hammer suggests the following principles for reengineering.

- **Organize around outcomes, not tasks:** Design a person's or a department's job around an objective or outcome instead of a single task or series of tasks.
- **Have those who use the output of the process perform the process:** With computer-based information systems, processes can now be reengineered so that the people who need the result of the process can do it themselves.
- **Subsume information-processing work into the real work that produces the information:** People or departments that produce information can also process

it for use instead of just sending raw data to others in the organization to interpret.

- **Treat geographically dispersed resources as though they were centralized:** With modern information systems, companies can provide flexible service locally while keeping the actual resources in a centralized location for coordination purposes.
- **Link parallel activities instead of integrating their results:** Instead of having separate units perform different activities that must eventually come together, have them communicate while they work so that they can do the integrating.
- **Put the decision point where the work is performed, and build control into the process:** The people who do the work should make the decisions and be self-controlling.
- **Capture information once and at the source:** Instead of each unit developing its own database and information processing activities, the information can be put on a network so all can have access to the data.[65]

Several companies have had success with reengineering. Union Carbide, for example, used the concept to reduce fixed costs by $400 million over three years. GTE expected reengineering to double its revenues and cut its costs in half. Nevertheless, because reengineering is almost always accompanied by a significant amount of pain, some 50%–70% of reengineering efforts fail to achieve their goals.[66]

Designing Jobs

Organizing a company's activities and people to implement strategy involves more than simply redesigning a corporation's overall structure; it also involves redesigning the way jobs are done.[67] With the increasing emphasis on reengineering, many companies are beginning to rethink their work processes with an eye toward phasing unnecessary people and activities out of the process. Process steps that had traditionally been performed sequentially can be improved by performing them concurrently using cross-functional work teams. Harley-Davidson, for example, has managed to reduce total plant employment by 25% while reducing by 50% the time needed to build a motorcycle. Although this job-oriented form of restructuring involves some changes in an organization's structure, such as reducing the number of levels in the hierarchy, it focuses on challenging the basic assumptions and old habits concerning how to get work done. Restructuring through fewer people requires broadening the scope of jobs and encouraging teamwork—that is, moving away from job specialization, a cornerstone of the industrial revolution. It also involves reducing the time required to complete any major task. Job design and subsequent job performance increasingly are being considered as sources of competitive advantage.

Job design refers to the study of individual tasks in an attempt to make them more relevant to the company and to the employee. From the organization's point of view, jobs that are performed efficiently and effectively are optimal. From the individual's perspective, jobs should be enjoyable and motivating. The main problem with the traditional cornerstone of job design—specialization—is that people tend to find simplified and highly specialized jobs boring. Boredom results in workers not acting in the best interest of the company; they form unions, are absent, quit, and reduce the quality if not the quantity of their output.[68] Boredom has been a serious problem in manufacturing since Henry Ford invented the moving assembly line. Achieving quality took a back seat to meeting production quotas.

In an effort to minimize some of the adverse consequences of task specialization, theorists and practitioners turned to new job design techniques: **job enlargement** (combining tasks to give a worker more of the same type of duties to perform), **job rotation** (moving workers through several jobs to increase variety), and **job enrichment** (altering jobs by giving the worker more autonomy and control over activities). Although each of these methods had their adherents, none of them seemed to work in every situation.

The **job characteristics model** is an advanced approach to job enrichment based on the belief that tasks can be described in terms of certain objective characteristics and that these characteristics affect employee motivation. For the job to be motivating, (1) the worker needs to feel a sense of responsibility, feel the task to be meaningful, and receive useful feedback on performance; and (2) the job has to satisfy needs that are important to the worker.[69] The model proposes that managers follow five principles for redesigning work.

- Combine tasks to increase task variety and enable workers to identify with what they are doing.
- Form natural work units to make a worker more responsible and accountable for job performance.
- Establish client relationships so the worker will know what performance is required and why.
- Vertically load the job by giving workers increased authority and responsibility over their activities.
- Open feedback channels by providing workers information on how well they are performing.[70]

Although there are several other approaches to job design besides the job characteristics model, managers increasingly seem to follow its prescriptions as a way to improve productivity and product quality. For example, Corning, Inc., the glass manufacturer, introduced team-based production in its Blacksburg, Virginia, plant in 1989. With union approval, Corning reduced job classifications from 47 to 4 to enable production workers to rotate jobs after learning new skills. The workers were divided into 14-member teams that, in effect, managed themselves. The plant had only two levels of management: Plant Manager Robert Hoover and two line leaders who were advisors to the teams. Employees worked demanding 12½ hour shifts, alternating three-day and four-day weeks. The teams made managerial decisions and disciplined fellow workers. Workers had to learn three "skill modules" within two years or lose their jobs. As a result of this new job design, a Blacksburg team, made up of workers with interchangeable skills, can retool a line to produce a different type of filter in only ten minutes—six times faster than workers in a traditionally designed filter plant. The Blacksburg plant earned a $2 million profit in its first eight months of production, instead of losing the $2.3 million projected for the start-up period. The plant performed so well that Corning's top management began converting the company's 27 other factories to team-based production.[71]

Other corporations, such as American Express, report similar experiences. It organized its Plantation, Florida, office around work teams. After receiving about 60 hours of training in team skills, 3,500 employees were divided into work teams averaging 10 to 12 people. Instead of checking to ensure that people came to work on time, the supervisor was now a team leader who served as coach and mentor. The employees were expected to use their own judgment and to help overburdened team members as necessary. For example, letters responding to customer inquiries used to go to the quality assurance department, which checked to see that each contained a list of specific details—regardless of whether the information was relevant. If the information was missing, the employee was reprimanded. Now the employees decided on their own what to say in the letters. "We make decisions on our own," says Scott Ernst, a member of the team, adding that "we tell management what we want done." The idea was not just to create a more productive work environment, but to improve customer service. Explained Senior Vice-President Barry Murphy, who managed the Plantation office, "This is not philanthropy. It's a very self-interested investment."[72]

In Conclusion . . .

When the Nabisco Biscuit Company decided to introduce a new line of fat-free cookies, no one in management had any idea that the decision would cause the company so many problems. SnackWell's Devil's Food Cookie Cakes were introduced in 1992 as a very special type of cookie. The cookie's center was covered completely with marshmallow, then drenched with chocolate icing, followed by a chocolate glaze. Because each cookie was completely covered, it would stick to a conveyor belt and thus could not be baked using conventional methods. These cookies could be made only on equipment available in one of Nabisco's bakeries. Called a pin trolley system, the equipment had been invented in the 1920s when the original devil's food cookie was invented. After baking for six minutes, each cookie center was placed on an upright pin mounted on a trolley. A chain pulled the cookies along a mile-long track, passing through marshmallow and chocolate coating stations. Because the chocolate covering was fat-free, it could not be chilled to speed the setting process. Instead, it had to be air-dried between coats. The process took four hours compared to 30 minutes for chocolate chip cookies.

The new devil's food cookies were an immediate hit with consumers. SnackWell's had the authentic-tasting chocolate that most fat-free cookies lacked, and the marshmallow center kept the cookies moist. More than a year after the introduction of the cookie, Nabisco was still unable to meet demand. Three production lines were running overtime at the bakery and a fourth was being added in 1993. Meanwhile, the company was introducing a new SnackWell's Double Fudge Cookie Cakes containing two layers of cake with fat-free fudge in the middle. This cookie was much easier to make, but management wasn't taking any chances this time. Until Nabisco could accurately judge market demand for the new product, it was being sold only in the Northeast. Commented a company spokesperson: "We've learned our lesson."[73]

Points to Remember

- The Nabisco example illustrates two of the most common problems in the implementation of strategy: (1) more time needed than originally planned, and (2) unanticipated major problems. Investigating potential demand for the devil's food cookie in a test market might have helped prevent lost sales.
- The success of an implemented strategy may depend on uncovering one or more synergies: Marketing, operating, investment, and management synergies.
- Changes in a corporation's structure follow significant changes in strategy. As a company grows and develops, it tends to move from a Stage I simple structure to a Stage II functional structure and finally to a Stage III divisional structure.
- The organizational life cycle is one of the theories that attempt to explain why organizations develop and change over time. It is especially useful in helping explain why companies, which have successfully progressed through the stages of birth, growth, and maturity, eventually decline and die.
- Under conditions of (1) increasing environmental uncertainty, (2) greater use of sophisticated technological production methods, (3) increasing size and scope of worldwide business corporations, (4) greater emphasis on multi-industry competitive strategy, and (5) better educated managers and employees, advanced forms of organizational structure have emerged. These forms include strategic business units, matrix structure, and network (cluster) structure.
- Reengineering is a new approach to strategy implementation that may be used to improve operations. It involves (1) a fundamental rethinking of the way work gets done, (2) structural reorganization—breaking hierarchies into cross-functional work teams, (3) a new information and measurement system, and (4) a new value system with greater emphasis on customers.
- The job characteristics model of job design provides a useful way to rethink the way that work is done. Its emphasis on forming natural work units makes it compatible with the reengineering concept of cross-functional work teams.

Discussion Questions

1. What responsibilities do top managers have in strategy implementation?
2. Does structure follow strategy or does strategy follow structure? Why?
3. How should a corporation attempt to achieve synergy among functions and business units?
4. What are the advantages and disadvantages of the network structure?

5. How should an owner–manager prepare a company for its movement from Stage I to Stage II?
6. How can a corporation keep from sliding into the decline part of the organizational life cycle?
7. Is reengineering just another management fad or does it offer something of lasting value? Explain.
8. According to the job characteristics model, how should task activities be organized in order to improve product quality and productivity?

Notes

1. C. J. Loomis, "Dinosaurs?" *Fortune* (May 3, 1993), p. 39.
2. L. D. Alexander, "Strategy Implementation: Nature of the Problem," *International Review of Strategic Management,* Vol. 2, No. 1, edited by D. E. Hussey (New York: John Wiley & Sons, 1991), pp. 73–113. In an additional study of 52 federal agencies and 76 state agencies, Alexander found problems 5, 6, and 9 to be unimportant, but identified three other significant problems: employees resisted implementation because it conflicted with their personal goals; key people did not work well together; and employees did not clearly understand overall goals.
3. M. W. Lawless, D. D. Bergh, and W. D. Wilsted, "Performance Variations Among Strategic Group Members: An Examination of Individual Firm Capability," *Journal of Management* (December 1989), pp. 649–661. See also C. K. Prahalad and G. Hamel, "The Core Competence of the Corporation," *Harvard Business Review* (May–June 1990), pp. 79–91; D. A. Aaker, "Managing Assets and Skills: The Key to a Sustainable Competitive Advantage," *California Management Review* (Winter 1989), pp. 91–106.
4. B. Wooldridge and S. W. Floyd, "The Strategy Process, Middle Management Involvement, and Organizational Performance," *Strategic Management Journal* (March–April 1990), pp. 231–241.
5. A. F. de Noble, L. T. Gustafson, and M. Herger, "Planning for Post-Merger Integration: Eight Lessons for Merger Success," *Long Range Planning* (August 1988), pp. 82–85.
6. J. A. S. de Vasconcellos e Sa, "A Practical Way to Evaluate Synergy," in *Handbook of Business Strategy, 1989/90 Yearbook,* edited by H. E. Glass (Boston: Warren, Gorham and Lamont, 1989), pp. 11.1–11.19.
7. H. I. Ansoff, *The New Corporate Strategy* (New York: John Wiley & Sons, 1988), pp. 55–58; D. R. Sadtler, "The Long Road to Parenting Advantage," *Long Range Planning* (April 1993), pp. 125–127.
8. K. Deveny, "After Some Key Sales Strategies Go Sour, Kraft General Foods Gets Back to Basics," *Wall Street Journal* (March 18, 1992), pp. B1, B10.
9. D. Miller, "Relating Porter's Business Strategies to Environment and Structure: Analysis and Performance Implications," *Academy of Management Journal* (June 1988), pp. 280–308; C. Oliver, "The Collective Strategy Framework: An Application to Competing Predictors of Isomorphism," *Administrative Science Quarterly* (December 1988), pp. 543–561.
10. Miller, p. 304; R. E. Miles and C. C. Snow, "Fit, Failure and the Hall of Fame," in *Strategy and Organization: A West Coast Perspective,* edited by G. Carroll and D. Vogel (Boston: Pittman, 1984), pp. 1–19.
11. T. F. O'Boyle, "From Pyramid to Pancake," *Wall Street Journal* (June 4, 1990), p. R37.
12. T. Burns and G. M. Stalker, *The Management of Innovation* (London: Tavistock, 1961).
13. P. R. Lawrence and J. W. Lorsch, *Organization and Environment* (Homewood, Ill.: Irwin, 1969), p. 138.
14. J. G. Covin and D. P. Slevin, "Strategic Management of Small Firms in Hostile and Benign Environments," *Strategic Management Journal* (January–February 1989), pp. 75–87; P. F. Buller, "Successful Partnerships: HR and Strategic Planning at Eight Top Firms," *Organizational Dynamics* (Autumn 1988), pp. 27–43.

15. G. Gardner, "GM's Orion Plant Shows Stunning Turnaround," *Des Moines Register* (January 30, 1994), p. 10S.
16. A. D. Chandler, *Strategy and Structure* (Cambridge, Mass.: MIT Press, 1962).
17. O. E. Williamson, "The Multidivisional Structure," in *Markets and Hierarchies* (New York: Free Press, 1975), as reprinted in *Organizational Economics,* edited by J. B. Barney and W. G. Ouchi (San Francisco: Jossey-Bass, 1986), pp. 163–187.
18. A. P. Sloan, Jr., *My Years with General Motors* (Garden City, N.Y.: Doubleday, 1964).
19. H. L. Boschken, "Strategy and Structure: Reconceiving the Relationship," *Journal of Management* (March 1990), pp. 135–150.
20. B. W. Keats and M. A. Hitt, "A Causal Model of Linkages Among Environmental Dimensions, Macro Organizational Characteristics, and Performance," *Academy of Management Journal* (September 1988), pp. 570–598. See also J. R. Williams, B. L. Paez, and L. Sanders, "Conglomerates Revisited," *Strategic Management Journal* (September–October 1988), pp. 403–414.
21. J. R. Galbraith and R. K. Kazanjian, *Strategy Implementation: Structure, Systems, and Process,* 2nd ed. (St. Paul, Minn.: West Publishing Co., 1986), p. 45.
22. R. E. Hoskisson, J. S. Harrison, and D. A. Dubofsky, "Capital Market Evaluation of M-Form Implementation and Diversification Strategy," *Strategic Management Journal* (May 1991), pp. 271–279.
23. R. E. Hoskisson, "Multidivisional Structure and Performance: The Contingency of Diversification Strategy," *Academy of Management Journal* (December 1987), pp. 625–644; D. J. Teece, "Internal Organization and Economic Performance: An Empirical Analysis of the Profitability of Principal Firms," *Journal of Industrial Economics* (Vol. 30, 1981), pp. 173–199.
24. R. E. White, "Generic Business Strategies, Organizational Context and Performance: An Empirical Investigation," *Strategic Management Journal* (May–June 1986), pp. 217–231; A. K. Gupta, "SBU Strategies, Corporate-SBU Relations, and SBU Effectiveness in Strategy Implementation," *Academy of Management Journal* (September 1987), pp. 477–500.
25. Galbraith and Kazanjian, p. 24.
26. D. R. Dalton, W. D. Todor, M. J. Spendolini, G. J. Fielding, and L. W. Porter, "Organization Structure and Performance: A Critical Review," *Academy of Management Review* (January 1980), pp. 49–64.
27. L. G. Hrebiniak and W. F. Joyce, *Implementing Strategy* (New York: Macmillan, 1984), p. 70; D. A. Palmer, P. D. Jennings, X. Zhou, "Late Adoption of the Multidivisional Form by Large U.S. Corporations: Institutional, Political, and Economic Accounts," *Administrative Science Quarterly* (March 1993), pp. 100–131.
28. D. H. Thain, "Stages of Corporate Development," *The Business Quarterly* (Winter 1969), pp. 32–45; B. R. Scott, "Stages of Corporate Development" (Boston: Intercollegiate Case Clearing House, No. 9-371-294, 1971); B. R. Scott, "The Industrial State: Old Myths and New Realities," *Harvard Business Review* (March–April 1973); R. V. Tuason, "Corporate Life Cycle and the Evaluation of Corporate Strategy," *Proceedings, The Academy of Management* (August 1973), pp. 35–40.
29. G. P. Zachary, "After Fall from Grace, Oracle Gets Back on Its Feet," *Wall Street Journal* (April 15, 1993).
30. L. E. Greiner, "Evolution and Revolution as Organizations Grow," *Harvard Business Review* (July–August 1972), pp. 37–46.
31. M. Selz, "Mountain-Bike Firm Performs Tough Balancing Act," *Wall Street Journal* (October 31, 1989), p. B2.
32. F. Hoy, B. C. Vaught, and W. W. Buchanan, "Managing Managers of Firms in Transition from Stage I to Stage II," *Proceedings, Southern Management Association* (November 1982), pp. 152–153; K. Smith and T. Mitchell, "An Investigation into the Effect of Changes in Stages of Organizational Maturation on a Decision Maker's Decision Priorities," *Proceedings, Southern Management Association* (November 1983), pp. 7–9.
33. G. D. Meyer, R. M. Lenoir, and T. J. Dean, "The Executive Limit Scenario in High Technology Firms," in *Proceedings, Managing the High Technology Firm Conference,* edited by L. R. Gomez-Mejia and M. W. Lawless (Boulder: University of Colorado, January 13–15, 1988), pp. 342–349.
34. K. G. Smith and J. K. Harrison, "In Search of Excellent Leaders," in *Handbook of Business Strategy, 1986/87 Yearbook,* edited by W. D. Guth (Boston: Warren, Gorham and Lamont, 1986), p. 27.8.
35. D. Miller and P. H. Friesen, "A Longitudinal Study of the Corporate Life Cycle,"

Management Science (October 1984), pp. 1161–1183; J. R. Kimberly, R. H. Miles, and Associates, *The Organizational Life Cycle* (San Francisco: Jossey-Bass, 1980); Y. P. Gupta and D. C. W. Chin, "Organizational Life Cycle and Strategic Orientation: An Examination," *International Journal of Management* (June 1992), pp. 215–227.

36. R. D. Beatty and D. O. Ulrich, "Re-Energizing the Mature Organization," *Organizational Dynamics* (Summer 1991), pp. 16–30.
37. W. Weitzel and E. Jonsson, "Decline in Organizations: A Literature Integration and Extension," *Administrative Science Quarterly* (March 1989), pp. 91–109. See also W. Weitzel and E. Jonsson, "Reversing the Downward Spiral: Lessons Learned from W. T. Grant and Sears Roebuck," *Academy of Management Executive* (August 1991), pp. 7–22.
38. G. D. Lurie and J. M. Ahearn, "How Companies in Trouble Got There," *Journal of Business Strategy* (November/December 1990), pp. 25–29.
39. This observation is supported by research indicating that self-serving attributions in annual reports by top management are negatively related to *future* firm performance. See S. E. Clapham and C. R. Schwenk, "Self-Serving Attributions, Managerial Cognition, and Company Performance," *Strategic Management Journal* (March 1991), pp. 219–229.
40. This conclusion is supported by a study revealing that when firms are in difficulty, the ones eventually going bankrupt become increasingly concerned with creditors and internal factors—actually reducing their focus on customers—whereas the survivors decrease their emphasis on internal factors and increase their focus on critical external factors. See R. A. D'Aveni and I. C. MacMillan, "Crisis and the Content of Managerial Communications: A Study of the Focus of Attention of Top Managers in Surviving and Failing Firms," *Administrative Science Quarterly* (December 1990), pp. 634–657.
41. W. N. Moulton and H. Thomas, "Bankruptcy as a Deliberate Strategy: Theoretical Considerations and Empirical Evidence," *Strategic Management Journal* (February 1993), pp. 125–135.
42. For information on managing Chapter 11 bankruptcy, see M. Minor and K. J. Stevens-Minor, "Resuscitating the Comatose Firm: Changing Management Responsibilities Under Chapter 11," *SAM Advanced Management Journal* (Spring 1992), pp. 29–33.
43. R. Dazin and R. K. Kazanjian, "A Reanalysis of Miller and Friesen's Life Cycle Data," *Strategic Management Journal* (May–June 1990), pp. 319–325.
44. M. Leontiades, "A Diagnostic Framework for Planning," *Strategic Management Journal* (January–March 1983), p. 14.
45. W. K. Hall, "SBUs: Hot New Topic in the Management of Diversification," *Business Horizons* (February 1978), p. 19.
46. J. M. Stengrevics, "Managing the Group Executive's Job," *Organization Dynamics* (Winter 1984), p. 21.
47. For more information on the development of the Strategic Business Unit, see A. D. Chandler, "The Functions of the HQ Unit in the Multibusiness Firm," *Strategic Management Journal* (Winter 1991), pp. 31–50.
48. For a more complete listing of advantages and disadvantages of the matrix structure see R. C. Ford and W. A. Randolph, "Cross-Functional Structures: A Review and Integration of Matrix Organization and Project Management," *Journal of Management* (June 1992), pp. 267–294.
49. Hrebiniak and Joyce, pp. 85–86.
50. S. M. Davis and P. R. Lawrence, *Matrix* (Reading, Mass.: Addison-Wesley, 1977), pp. 11–24.
51. C. B. Friesen, "R & D in the Pharmaceutical Firm: Organizing for the Future," *Handbook of Business Strategy, 1992/93 Yearbook,* edited by H. E. Glass and M. A. Hovde (Boston: Warren, Gorham and Lamont, 1992), pp. 13.1–13.19.
52. T. W. Malone, J. Yates, and R. I. Benjamin, "The Logic of Electronic Markets," *Harvard Business Review* (May–June 1989), pp. 166–172.
53. R. E. Miles and C. C. Snow, "Organizations: New Concepts for New Forms," *California Management Review* (Spring 1986), pp. 62–73.
54. J. C. Jarillo and H. H. Stevenson, "Co-operative Strategies—The Payoffs and the Pitfalls," *Long Range Planning* (February 1991), pp. 64–70.
55. R. S. Teitelbaum, "Companies to Watch: Just Toys," *Fortune* (November 30, 1992), p. 87.
56. Jarillo and Stevenson, p. 67.

57. R. E. Miles and C. C. Snow, "Causes of Failure in Network Organizations," *California Management Review* (Summer 1992), p. 57.
58. J. C. Jarillo, "On Strategic Networks," *Strategic Management Journal* (January–February 1988), p. 36.
59. R. E. Miles and C. C. Snow, "Causes of Failure in Network Organizations," *California Management Review* (Summer 1992), pp. 53–72. See also C. C. Snow, R. E. Miles, and H. J. Coleman, Jr., "Managing 21st Century Network Organizations," *Organizational Dynamics* (Winter 1992), pp. 5–20.
60. T. A. Stewart, "Reengineering: The Hot New Managing Tool," *Fortune* (August 23, 1993), p. 42.
61. D. Rigby, "The Secret History of Process Reengineering," *Planning Review* (March/April 1993), pp. 24–27.
62. M. Hammer, "Reengineer Work: Don't Automate, Obliterate," *Harvard Business Review* (July–August 1990), pp. 104–112. See also M. Hammer and J. Champy, *Reengineering the Corporation: Beyond Buzzword* (New York: HarperBusiness, 1993).
63. Stewart, p. 41.
64. Hammer, p. 108.
65. Summarized from Hammer, pp. 104–112.
66. Stewart, p. 41. For details on how to implement process reengineering, see T. R. Furey, "A Six-Step Guide to Process Reengineering," *Planning Review* (March/April 1993), pp. 20–23.
67. Much of this section was suggested by J. McElroy of Iowa State University.
68. R. B. Dunham, "Job Design and Redesign," in *Organizational Behavior,* edited by S. Kerr (Columbus, Ohio: Grid, 1979), pp. 337–354.
69. J. R. Hackman and E. E. Lawler, "Employee Reactions to Job Characteristics," *Journal of Applied Psychology* (1971), pp. 259–286.
70. J. R. Hackman and G. R. Oldham, *Work Redesign* (Reading, Mass.: Addison-Wesley, 1980), pp. 135–141.
71. J. Hoerr, "Sharpening Minds for a Competitive Edge," *Business Week* (December 17, 1990), pp. 72–78.
72. L. Croghan, "American Express Revolt Places Employees in Charge," *Des Moines Register* (September 6, 1993), p. 12-B.
73. K. Deveny, "Man Walked on the Moon but Man Can't Make Enough Devil's Food Cookie Cakes," *Wall Street Journal* (September 28, 1993), pp. B1, B12.

9

Strategy Implementation: Staffing and Directing

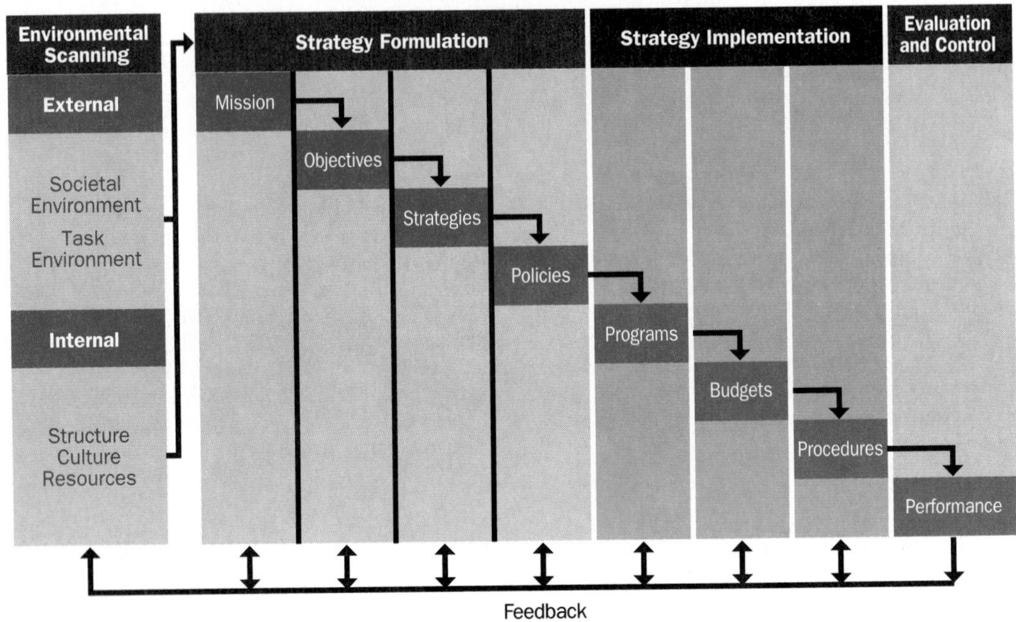

> *Communicate, communicate, communicate!*[1]
> [Sam Walton, founder, Wal-Mart]

Not long ago, Clark Equipment Company was on the brink of bankruptcy. This diversified manufacturing company realized that, in addition to other problems, its corporate office was overstaffed. When top management identified the different specialty departments within the corporate office, they found that there were enough people to operate a law firm, an accounting firm, a data processing/telecommunications company, a trucking line, and a printing and graphics business. Instead of simply firing half or more of those people, management took a more positive approach: it informed the specialty departments that they had two years to (1) develop 50% of their business outside of Clark and to (2) earn their own cost of capital. If they achieved both these objectives, they could become a Clark operating company, undertake an employee buyout of the unit, or find themselves a new owner. If they failed to attain these objectives, the choice of becoming a Clark company was no longer an option. Management also told them that after one year the operating divisions would no longer be required to use corporate staff department services and could buy the same services elsewhere. Top management also announced that the corporate personnel and purchasing departments would be phased out in one year and the responsibilities given to the operating divisions. Clark helped people transfer to an operating division or leave the company under a voluntary corporate separation plan. These programs reduced the corporate office staff from 500 to less than 100 people. Jim Rinehart, former CEO of Clark, explained why the downsizing was a success at Clark. First, the company's survival was at stake. The employees were well aware of the company's problems and the need for significant change. Second, management used a participative process. People had the chance to suggest how to save the company. Third, management presented the members of the different specialty units with choices and then gave them time to consider their options.[2]

The Clark Equipment Company example illustrates how to implement a successful retrenchment strategy with carefully considered programs. In this chapter we discuss strategy implementation in terms of staffing and directing. Staffing focuses on the selection and utilization of employees. Directing emphasizes the use of programs to align employee interests and attitudes with a new strategy.

9.1 Staffing

The implementation of new strategies and policies often calls for new human resource management priorities and a different utilization of personnel.[3] Such changes may mean hiring new people with new skills, firing people with inappropriate or substandard skills, and/or training existing employees to learn new skills.

If growth strategies are to be implemented, new people may need to be hired and trained. Experienced people with the necessary skills may need to be found for or promoted into newly created managerial positions. For example, if a manufacturing firm has decided to integrate forward by opening its own retail outlets, one key concern is the corporation's ability to find, hire, and train store managers. When a corporation follows a growth through acquisition strategy, it may need to replace some of the managers in the acquired company. Research by J. P. Walsh of 102 companies following an acquisition revealed that the percentage of the acquired company's top management team that either quit or was asked to leave was 26% after the first year and 61% after five years.[4]

If a corporation adopts a retrenchment strategy, however, a large number of people may need to be laid off or fired. Top management and divisional managers need to specify criteria for use in making these personnel decisions. Should employees be let go on the basis of low seniority or on the basis of poor performance? Sometimes corporations find that closing an entire division is easier than choosing which individuals to fire.

Staffing Follows Strategy

As with structure, staffing requirements also are likely to follow a change in strategy.

Hiring and Training Requirements Change

After a new strategy has been formulated, different types of people may be needed or current employees may need to be retrained to implement it. Recall the introduction of team-based production at Corning's filter plant mentioned in Chapter 8. Employee selection and training were crucial to the success of the new manufacturing strategy. Plant Manager Robert Hoover sorted through 8,000 job applications before hiring 150 people with good problem-solving ability and a willingness to work on a team. The majority of those selected had finished at least one year of college; they received further, extensive training in technical and interpersonal skills. During the first year of production, 25% of all hours worked were devoted to training at a cost of $750,000. The company's decision to introduce team-based production at all its plants meant that Corning's strategic managers had decided to compete in world markets on the basis of a highly skilled, well-paid work force, rather than by cutting wages or moving manufacturing to low-wage nations. As two-thirds of Corning's 20,000 employees in 1990 were either weak or seriously deficient in reading and math comprehension, they needed to receive remedial education along with job training. One of Corning's human resource objectives for the first year therefore was to devote 5% of all hours worked to classroom training—up from 4% two years earlier and far more than the 1%–2% spent on training at most companies.[5]

Training and development is one way to implement a company's corporate or business strategy and is extremely important for a differentiation strategy emphasizing quality or customer service. For example, Motorola, with annual sales of $13.3 billion, spends $120 million on employee education. The company is especially concerned with attaining the highest quality possible in all its operations. The company estimates that every $1 it spends on training delivers $30 in productivity gains within three years. Explained William Wiggenhorn, President of the company's training center, Motorola University, "When you buy a piece of equipment, you set aside a percentage for maintenance. Shouldn't you do the same for people?" Target Stores, a division of Dayton Hudson, uses training to help employees please customers better. Whenever Target opens a new store, it sets up an entertaining training course using role playing and team building conducted by a veteran manager from one of the chain's other outlets. The new training program helped reduce employee turnover (quitting) from 89% among hourly workers in 1989 to 59% in 1992. Customer service, as measured by annual surveys, has been improving steadily.

Training also is important in implementing a retrenchment strategy. As suggested earlier, successful downsizing means that the company has to invest in its remaining employees. General Electric's Aircraft Engine unit used training to maintain its share of the market even though it had cut its work force from 42,000 to 33,000 between 1991 and 1993. According to W. J. Conaty, Aircraft Engines'

Vice-President of Human Resources: "When an industry is in turmoil, productivity and people become the name of the game. That's where we get our edge."[6]

Matching the Manager to the Strategy

Several authorities suggest that the "best" or most appropriate type of general manager needed to effectively implement a new corporate or business strategy depends on the desired strategic direction of that firm or business unit.[7] That certainly was the thinking of Jan Timmer, Chairman of the Board, when he selected research-oriented Frank Carrubba to be the new CEO of the Dutch giant Philips Electronics. The Strategy in Action on pages 258–259 describes the results.

Executives with a particular mix of skills and experience may be classified as a "type" and paired with a specific corporate strategy. Figure 9.1 matches some chief executive "types" with corporate strategies in a modified form of the matrix presented earlier in Fig. 6.3. For example, a corporation following a concentration strategy emphasizing vertical or horizontal integration probably would want an aggressive new chief executive with a great deal of experience in that particular industry, i.e., a **dynamic industry expert.** A diversification strategy, in contrast, might call for someone with an analytic mind who is highly knowledgeable in other industries and can manage diverse product lines, i.e., an **analytic portfolio manager.** A corporation choosing to follow a stability strategy probably would want as its CEO a **cautious profit planner**, i.e., a person with a conservative style, a production or engineering background, and experience with controlling budgets, capital expenditures, inventories, and standardization procedures.[8] Weak companies in a relatively attractive industry tend to turn to challenge-oriented executives known as **turnaround specialists** to save them.[9] The Strategy in Action on page 261 describes one such turnaround specialist: Ronald Jackson of Fisher-Price. If a company cannot be saved, a **professional liquidator** might be called on by a bankruptcy court to close the firm and liquidate its assets.

Successful CEOs or business unit managers with a particular mix of experiences, skills, and personality factors tend to be linked with one type of strategy; those with a different mix, to a different type of strategy.[10] For example, one study of SBU executives showed that strategic business units with a *build* strategy—compared to SBUs with a *harvest* strategy—tend to be headed by managers with a greater willingness to take risks, a higher tolerance for ambiguity, and greater sales or marketing experience.[11] In addition, executives who successfully implement a differentiation business strategy tend to have a high internal locus of control; that is, they tend to view personal hard work and ability rather than some external cause as the reason for an outcome. They also tend to have more experience in R&D. Units following a low-cost business strategy tend to be run by a manager with greater experience in production.[12] Another set of studies demonstrated that the CEOs of Prospector-type firms were significantly younger, had shorter tenure in both the company and the position, and had more education than those CEOs in Defender-type firms. The CEOs of Prospector firms tended to have backgrounds in either marketing or R&D; whereas, CEOs in Defender firms tended to have backgrounds in finance, engineering, and manufacturing.[13]

PHILIPS SELECTS A NEW CEO TO MATCH ITS GROWTH STRATEGY

Strategy in Action

The Dutch giant, Philips Electronics, was in serious difficulty in 1990. The company that had pioneered the audio cassette, the compact disk, and the VCR, lost $2.2 billion. Philips either seemed to be making the wrong products or producing the right ones too late or overpriced. Research and product development were uncoordinated and failing to exploit new technology. Even after reducing employment by 70,000 people, the company found itself having to cut prices increasingly against aggressive Asian and U.S. competition.

Chairman of the Board Jan Timmer asked Frank Carrubba to become Philips's new CEO. He wanted Carrubba to reshape Philips so that it could again be known for its use of technology in developing innovative consumer products. At the time, Carrubba was director of Hewlett-Packard Company's research labs. At Hewlett-Packard (HP), Carrubba had installed rigorous project-tracking measures and brought units together to generate a series of innovative new products. According to HP's Vice-President of Research, Joel S. Birnbaum, "He has a very good intuition for which technologies will in the end work out. He can survey the scene and pick the winners." Carrubba was also known for designing "town squares" in labs where researchers could informally mingle and help solve each other's problems.

One interesting study of 173 firms over a 25-year period revealed that CEOs in these companies tended to have the same functional specialization as the former CEO, especially when the past CEO's strategy continued to be successful. The researchers concluded that the tendency is to continue with the CEO specializations that fit a successful corporate strategy and that this approach may be a pattern for successful corporations.[14] This tendency may explain why so many prosperous companies tend to recruit their top executives from one particular background. At Procter & Gamble, for example, the route to the CEO's position has always been through brand management. In other firms, the route may be through manufacturing, marketing, accounting, or finance, depending on what the corporation has always considered its principal functional areas.

Studies also show that, because priorities change over an organization's life cycle, successful corporations tend to select managers who have skills and characteristics appropriate to the organization's particular stage of development.[15] L. M. Miller suggests a different chief executive leadership style for each stage of corporate development. The styles range from the *prophet* who creates the company to the *administrator* who imposes controls to the *synergist* who unifies and continues the growth of the large, complex corporation.[16]

When Carrubba arrived at Philips, he found gaps between products being planned and the technologies they required. For example, Philips had invested heavily in its Digital Compact Cassette before considering the feasibility of a crucial component, the magnetic head. When the head cost far more to develop than planned, it created problems in the product's competition with Sony's MiniDisc. To avoid such problems, Carrubba introduced concurrent engineering to coordinate product plans. Although concurrent engineering was common in the United States and Japan, it was still rare in Europe. Carrubba also formed a committee of top executives to screen new ideas and encourage innovative projects from business units. Changing a corporation as huge as Philips probably will take quite a while. Carrubba himself noted that only about 37% of Philips' revenues came from products introduced in the past three years, compared to 72% at Hewlett-Packard when he left. Nevertheless, most agree that he seems to have the skills needed to make the company successful again.

Source: J. B. Levin and R. D. Hof, "Has Philips Found Its Wizard?" *Business Week* (September 6, 1993), pp. 82–84

Matching a manager to the strategy makes sense. To do so, however, means that the people doing the hiring must know what the strategy is or should be. But what if a corporation or SBU doesn't have a specific strategy formulated for that manager to implement? In this instance, top management or the board has no choice: it must search for a person with a proven capability to exercise initiative and leadership in the industry and hope that the person selected can lead other strategic managers in formulating and implementing an appropriate strategy.

Selection and Management Development

Selection and development are important not only to ensure that people with the right mix of skills and experience are hired initially, but also to help them grow on the job to prepare them for future promotions.

Executive Succession: Insiders versus Outsiders

The typical large U.S. corporation changes its chief executive every eight years. Hence a firm needs to plan for eventual executive succession,[17] especially if it usually promotes from within. Research indicates that firms with succession planning

FIGURE 9.1

Matching Chief Executive "Types" with Corporate Strategy

Industry Attractiveness \ Business Strength/Competitive Position	Strong	Average	Weak
High	**Growth — Concentration** Dynamic Industry Expert		**Retrenchment — Save Company** Turnaround Specialist
Medium	**Stability** Cautious Profit Planner		
Low	**Growth — Diversification** Analytical Portfolio Manager		**Retrenchment — Close Company** Professional Liquidator

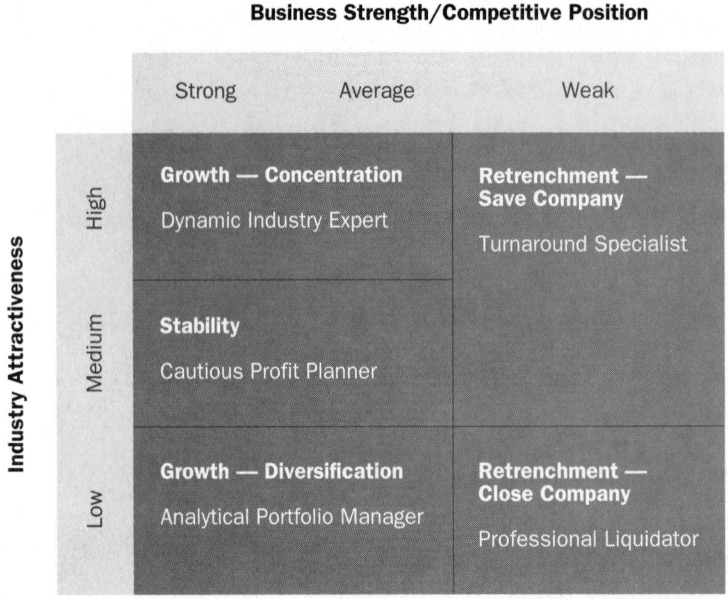

Source: Thomas L. Wheelen and J. David Hunger, "Matching Proposed Chief Executive 'Types' with Corporate Strategy." Copyright © 1991 by Wheelen and Hunger Associates. Reprinted by permission.

programs for top management have an advantage (about 15% above expected return on investment for firms in similar strategic positions) over firms that do not have formal programs.[18]

Research into the value of selecting a CEO from outside the company instead of promoting someone already with the company offers mixed conclusions. Some studies report that the top performing companies hire their CEOs from within and that insider succession improves performance.[19] However, other studies report that the percentage of CEOs hired from outside the corporation is higher for prosperous firms than for firms in decline.[20] Clearly, these results are contradictory. The data are more definite regarding firms in difficulty: such firms tend to choose outsiders to lead them. For example, in one study of 22 firms undertaking a turnaround strategy over a 13-year period, all but two companies replaced the CEO. Of 27 changes of CEO (some of the firms had more than one CEO during this period), only seven were insiders and 20 were outsiders.[21] The probability of an outsider being chosen to lead a firm in difficulty increases if there is no internal heir apparent, the last CEO was fired, and if the board of directors is composed of a large percentage of outsiders.[22]

When is the best time to replace a CEO? Based on the model proposed by Weitzel and Jonsson (see Table 8.4), the optimal time to replace a CEO appears to

RONALD JACKSON IMPLEMENTS TURNAROUND STRATEGY AT FISHER-PRICE

Strategy in Action

Ronald Jackson has earned the reputation of being a man who fixes broken toy companies. Jackson spent a year restructuring Kenner Parker Toys before Tonka Corporation purchased the company at triple its initial market value. In May 1990, Jackson accepted the head job at Fisher-Price, then a unit of Quaker Oats. At the time, Fisher-Price was losing $4 million a month. Its strategy of making toys for older children, which it had implemented in the late 1980s, had failed miserably. Jackson introduced a turnaround strategy by closing two plants, dropping most of the company's products for children over six, hiring a new management team, and consolidating operations, including product engineering and procurement. He then made sure that products could be introduced simultaneously in U.S. and foreign markets. Gross profit margins jumped to 46% in 1992 from 33% in 1990. Meanwhile, Quaker sold Fisher-Price to the public in 1991. In 1993, Mattel, Inc., purchased Fisher-Price for $1.1 billion, triple its market value. Jackson was asked to serve as a Mattel director. Industry analysts were wondering, however, how long it would take Jackson to leave Mattel for another ailing toy division.

Source: G. Smith, "The Man Who Mends Toy Companies," *Business Week* (September 13, 1993), p. 62.

be when the corporation is in the midst of stage 3 of decline, known as the faulty action stage. The CEO should not be replaced during the blinded and inaction stages of decline because of the uncertainty that decline is actually occurring. If a company waits until it enters the crisis or dissolution stages, the new CEO may not have enough resources to effect a successful turnaround.[23]

Identifying Abilities and Potential

A company can identify and prepare its people for important positions in one of several ways. One approach is to establish a sound **performance appraisal system** to identify good performers with promotion potential. A survey of 34 corporate planners and human resource executives from 24 large U.S. corporations revealed that approximately 80% made some attempt to identify managers' talents and behavioral tendencies so that they could match a manager as closely as possible with a particular strategy.[24]

Many large organizations use **assessment centers** to evaluate a person's suitability for an advanced position, including AT&T, Standard Oil, IBM, Sears, and

GE. These assessment centers are unique, with each one specifically tailored to the corporation. Methods encompass special interviews, management games, in-basket exercises, leaderless group discussions, case analyses, decision-making exercises, and oral presentations to assess the potential of employees for specific positions. Promotions into advanced positions are based not just on past performance, but on performance in the assessment center. Many assessment centers have proved to be highly predictive of subsequent job performance.[25] In his evaluation of assessment center performance, G. C. Thorton concludes:

> There is little question that a well-designed assessment center will help an organization identify individuals with a high level of potential for managerial success. In addition, the assessment of strengths and weaknesses in managerial competencies can form the basis of human resource management programs to diagnose training needs, plan developmental actions, train managers, and build effective management teams.[26]

To ensure that managers with potential for promotion have a grasp of many aspects of the company's operations other than the functional area in which they started work, many companies rotate them through different divisions and locations. Corporations that pursue related diversification strategies through internal development make greater use of interdivisional transfers of people than do companies that grow through unrelated acquisitions. Apparently, the companies that grow internally attempt to transfer important knowledge and skills throughout the corporation in order to achieve some managerial synergy.[27]

Problems in Retrenchment

Downsizing refers to the planned elimination of positions or jobs.[28] Companies commonly use this approach to implement retrenchment strategies. Because the financial community is likely to react favorably to announcements of downsizing from a company in difficulty, such a program may provide some short-term benefits (e.g., raising the company's stock price). The research indicates, however, that if not done properly, downsizing may result in less rather than in more productivity. In a study of downsizing at 30 automobile-related industrial companies in the United States, K. S. Cameron and associates concluded that management handled most of these cutbacks in personnel poorly. In about two-thirds of the cases either the wrong jobs were eliminated or blanket offers of early retirement prompted managers, even those considered invaluable, to leave. After the layoffs, the employees who were left had to do not only their work, but also the work of the people who had gone. According to Cameron, "There's a general approach of throwing a hand grenade at a bunch of employees, and whoever survives has to do all the work there was before." The survivors often don't know how to do the work of those who departed, and morale and productivity plummet.[29] Security becomes a key issue. At one manufacturing company, for example, engineers searched through the trash bins to recover the typewriter ribbon cartridge that held the list of about-to-be-dismissed employees. Even though they had been told that they would not be cut, the engineers wanted confirmation.[30]

Surveys by the Wyatt Company, the American Management Association, and the Society for Human Resource Management revealed that few firms actually benefit from downsizing. In a survey of some 400 companies that had downsized during 1992, only half reported improved earnings. Only 34% increased productivity, and only 33% improved customer service. Even worse, over half of the surveyed companies refilled positions within a year of eliminating them! These responses were similar to those gathered previously from more than 1,000 companies.[31] According to an American Management Association study, part of the reason for these poor results was that nearly half the firms were either "badly" or "not well" prepared for the dismantling.[32] In addition, cost-conscious executives tended to defer maintenance, skimp on training, delay new product introductions, and avoid risky new businesses. Referring to his previous study on downsizing, Kenneth De Meuse found that profits at large companies declined faster after layoffs than before. "Not only is a reduction in force not a quick fix, as many companies believe, but it's most likely not a fix at all," said De Meuse.[33]

A good retrenchment strategy may thus be implemented well in terms of organizing but poorly in terms of staffing. A situation may develop in which retrenchment feeds on itself and acts to further weaken instead of strengthening the company. According to a survey by Kepner–Tregoe consultants, companies that undertake cost-cutting programs are four times more likely than others to cut costs again, typically by reducing staff.[34]

The following are proposed guidelines for successful downsizing.[35]

- **Eliminate unnecessary work instead of making across-the-board cuts:** Spend the time to pinpoint where money is going and eliminate tasks, not workers, if the tasks don't add value to what the firm is producing. For example, the productivity of Colgate-Palmolive's R&D scientists increased significantly when they were freed from an excessive amount of supervising and reporting.
- **Contract out work that others can do more cheaply:** For example, Bankers Trust of New York contracts out its mail room, printing services, and some of its payroll and accounts payable activities to a division of Xerox. About 70 Bankers Trust employees were transferred to Xerox, but never left the building! According to Peter Hawes of Xerox Reproduction Centers, "Sometimes we can find efficiencies in these businesses because they are our specialty."[36]
- **Plan for long-run efficiencies:** Don't simply eliminate all postponable expenses, such as maintenance, R&D, and advertising, in the unjustifiable hope that the environment will become more supportive. (Remember when U.S. automakers predicted that Americans would soon tire of driving those small Japanese cars?) Companies such as Ford, General Electric, and Citicorp are following long-term strategies for the redeployment of their human and physical resources.
- **Communicate the reasons for actions:** Tell employees not only why the company is downsizing, but also what the company is trying to achieve. Sharpen and emphasize the mission statement. For example, Square D, a leading manufacturer of electrical equipment, had all its 19,200 employees attend a two-day program stressing the importance of quality and customer service as part of its program to improve productivity and customer satisfaction.
- **Invest in the remaining employees:** As most survivors of a corporate downsizing probably will be doing different tasks after the change, firms need to

draft new job specifications, performance standards, appraisal techniques, and compensation packages. Additional training will be needed to ensure that everyone has the proper skills to deal with expanded jobs and responsibilities. For example, after eliminating many of its supervisors, DuPont created work teams and rotated the management of each team to train its members to take responsibility for performing critical tasks.

- **Develop value-added jobs to balance out job elimination:** When no other jobs are currently available within the organization for certain remaining employees, management must consider some other staffing alternatives. For example, after a series of production improvement programs eliminated many jobs, Harley-Davidson management worked with the company's unions to find other work for surplus employees. Through an active "in-sourcing" program, in which work previously done by suppliers was moved into Harley-Davidson plants, the unions helped the company transfer people to new jobs. According to Peter Reid, author of *Well Made in America*: "This joint union–management effort has brought in 60 jobs, improved quality, and reduced costs by over $2 million. Employment security has been increased, and Harley-Davidson has been able to utilize the plant space it freed up through successful inventory reduction."[37]

9.2 Directing

Implementation also involves directing people to use their abilities and skills most effectively and efficiently to achieve organizational objectives. Without direction, people tend to do their work according to their personal view of what tasks should be done, how, and in what order. They may approach their work as they have in the past or emphasize tasks that they most enjoy—regardless of what has the highest priority for the company. Direction may take the form of leadership by management, communicated norms of behavior from the corporate culture, or agreements among workers in autonomous work groups.

To direct a new strategy effectively, top management must delegate appropriate authority and responsibility to operational managers. They should encourage employees to act in ways desired by the organization and coordinate those actions to yield effective performance. Managers should be stimulated to find creative solutions to implementation problems without getting bogged down in conflict. Sometimes this objective may be accomplished informally through a strong corporate culture, with accepted norms and values regarding teamwork and commitment to the company's objectives and strategies. It also may be accomplished more formally through action planning or through programs such as Management By Objectives and Total Quality Management.

Managing Corporate Culture

Corporate culture has two distinct attributes.[38] The first, **intensity,** is "the extent to which members of a unit agree on the norms, values, or other culture content associated with the unit." Organizations with strong norms promoting a particular value, such as quality at Maytag, have intensive cultures, whereas new firms (or those in transition) have weaker, less intensive cultures. Employees of a company with an intensive culture tend to exhibit consistency in behavior; that is, they tend to act similarly over time. The second, **integration,** is "the extent to which units within an organization share a common culture." An organization with a pervasive dominant culture may be hierarchically controlled and power-oriented, such as a military unit, and have highly integrated cultures. All its employees tend to hold the same cultural values and norms. In contrast, a diverse company that is structured by function into divisions or SBUs usually exhibits some strong subcultures (e.g., R&D versus manufacturing) and an overall weaker corporate culture.

Because an organization's culture can exert a powerful influence on the behavior of all employees, it can strongly affect a company's ability to shift its strategic direction. A problem for a strong culture is that a change in mission, objectives, strategies, or policies isn't likely to succeed if it is in opposition to the accepted culture of the company. Corporate culture has a strong tendency to resist change because its very reason for existence often rests on preserving stable relationships and patterns of behavior.[39] The Strategy in Action on pages 266–267 demonstrates how corporate culture can act as a barrier to strategic change in an auto plant.

Research indicates that there is no one best corporate culture.[40] An optimal culture is one that best supports the mission and strategy of the company of which it is a part. That is, like structure and staffing, **corporate culture should follow strategy.** Unless it is in complete agreement with the culture, a significant change in strategy should thus lead to a modification of the organization's culture. Although research indicates that corporate culture can be changed, it may take a long time and require much effort.[41] An essential job of management therefore is to (1) evaluate what a particular change in strategy will mean to the corporate culture, (2) assess whether a change in culture will be needed, and (3) decide whether an attempt to change the culture will be worth the likely costs.

Assessing Strategy–Culture Compatibility

When implementing a new strategy, management should consider the following questions regarding the corporation's culture.

1. Is the planned strategy compatible with the company's current culture?

If *yes,* proceed rapidly. Tie organizational changes to the company's culture by identifying how the new strategy will achieve the mission better than the current strategy does.

2. If the strategy isn't compatible with the current culture, can the culture be easily modified to make it more compatible with the new strategy?

If *yes,* move forward carefully by introducing a set of culture-changing activities, such as minor structural modifications, training and development activities, and/or hiring new managers who are more compatible with the new strategy. For example, Procter & Gamble's top management decided that, in order to implement the new companywide low-cost strategy, it had to change the firm's almost sacred brand management system and alter the way salespeople dealt with customers. The culture needed only slight modifications to make it compatible with the new strategy. Brand managers now reported to a "category" manager,

CORPORATE CULTURE ACTS AS A BARRIER TO THE INTRODUCTION OF STATISTICAL PROCESS CONTROL

Strategy in Action

Originally developed in the U.S. in the 1940s, statistical process control (SPC) was largely ignored until W. Edwards Deming, an M.I.T. professor, introduced it to the Japanese in 1950. **Statistical process control is a method that attempts to facilitate understanding of the critical variables in each sequence of a manufacturing process and their intercorrelation.** Following Deming's guidelines, workers in Japanese factories sampled parts as the parts moved through manufacturing processes and, with control charts, ensured that any deviations from specifications were quickly corrected. Thus SPC ensures that virtually all finished products meet or exceed specifications. In this way quality is built into the product instead of having workers correct for it after the fact by tossing out rejects—the more traditional (and more expensive) route to quality control.

An automotive company that had heard about SPC attempted to introduce it in the United States at one of its manufacturing plants. After two and a half years, the attempt had ground to a halt. There was deep pessimism about SPC's future at the plant. Members of the SPC coordination team in charge of implementing the change were considering a mass resignation. Clearly, the change had failed. Why?

The culture at the manufacturing plant contained three key values that ran counter to those values that underlie statistical process control.

- First, the plant had a norm that valued performance over learning. **Workers were paid to work, not to think.** Unfortunately, SPC goes against this value. The introduction of SPC involves not only a period of learning about SPC itself, but also a period of learning about every manufacturing process in which it is to be implemented. Managers in the plant interpreted acts through a filter of questions like "What did you do for me?" instead of "What did you learn?"

who coordinated advertising and sales to minimize the products' "cannibalizing" each other. Salespeople, long noted by retailers for their arrogance, had to pay more attention to retailers' needs and woo them with special promotions. Neither these nor other changes directly attacked any of the company's basic values. After a few years, the new system was generating significantly better performance.

3. **If the culture can't be changed easily to make it more compatible with the new strategy, is management willing and able to make major organizational changes and accept probable delays and a likely increase in costs?**

- Second, information was used only to relay expectations of future performance, report poor performance, and assign responsibility. **Information was not valued for its use in actually fixing problems, only in placing blame or assigning responsibility elsewhere.** In contrast, SPC uses information to highlight problems and help fix them. Data collection involves workers and managers together maintaining charts and graphs throughout the work area for anyone to see. Unfortunately, as time went by, management returned primarily to looking at results and assigning responsibility. People were told to fix their own problems. The feelings of the employees became, "Why make my problems visible with SPC?"
- Third, following the traditional structural concept of division of work, the plant's work was split into tiny segments parcelled out to individual operators and units in assembly-line fashion. Strong lines of demarcation existed between worker and manager, manufacturing and service, and plant and division. **There was a tendency to compartmentalize problems and information.** Statistical process control, however, takes a comprehensive approach rather than the traditional segmentalist approach. It requires thinking about the interactions of many variables in a process and managing their interdependencies. As a result, attempts to improve productivity through joint efforts among groups and departments were sabotaged by the tendency for highly paid and educated staff at division headquarters to ignore suggestions for improvement from "lowly" production employees.

Source: Summarized from G. R. Bushe, "Cultural Contradictions of Statistical Process Control in American Manufacturing Organizations," *Journal of Management* (March 1988), pp. 19–31.

If *yes,* manage around the culture by establishing a new structural unit to implement the new strategy. At General Motors, for example, top management realized that, in order to compete with Japanese automakers, the company had to change radically the way it produced cars. The corporate structure and culture were inflexible, so management decided to establish a completely new division (GM's first new division since 1918) called Saturn to build its new auto. Management and the United Auto Workers entered into an entirely new labor agreement based on decisions reached by consensus. Carefully selected employees received five days of *awareness training* to teach them how to work together in teams. They then received from 100 to 750 hours of training, including how to read financial statements, so that they would understand how much their operations affected the cost of a car. A whole new culture was built piece by piece. According to James Lewandowski, Vice-President of Human Resources, "There's a real cause here. It's been described as almost like a cult." Originally conceived in 1983, the first Saturn didn't roll off the modular assembly line in the Spring Hill, Tennessee, plant until 1990.[42]

4. If management isn't willing to make the major organizational changes required to manage around the culture, is it still committed to implementing the strategy?

If *yes,* find a joint-venture partner or contract with another company to carry out the strategy. If *no,* formulate a different strategy.

Managing Change Through Communication

Communication is crucial to the effective management of change in culture. After observing the corporate culture of more than 100 different companies, G. G. Gordon reported that the companies successfully introducing major cultural change had the following characteristics in common.

1. The CEO had a strategic vision of what the company could become.
2. The vision was translated into the key elements necessary to accomplish that vision. For example, if the vision called for the company to become a leader in quality or service, aspects of quality and service were pinpointed for improvement and appropriate measurement systems were developed to monitor them. These measures were communicated widely through contests, formal and informal recognition, and monetary rewards, among other devices.
3. The CEO and other top managers were obsessive about communicating as widely as possible to employees at all levels three key bits of information:
   a) The current state of the company in comparison with its competition plus the outlook for the future.
   b) The vision of what the company was to become and how it would achieve that vision.
   c) The progress of the company in those elements identified as important to achieve the vision.[43]

One way of communicating the new vision of the corporation is through training and development programs. At General Electric, for example, top management wanted to change the corporate culture. The old culture was built around a core set of principles based on growth in sales greater than GNP, many SBUs, reliance on financial savvy, meticulous staff work, and a domestic focus. Jack Welch, the new CEO, wanted the company to think in terms of building shareholder value in a slow-growth environment through operating competitive advantage with dynamic leadership at all levels of the organization. Top management viewed GE's management development institute (at Crotonville, New York) as an instrument for cultural change, so it drastically modified training to reflect the new emphasis on aggressive global competitiveness. Crotonville spearheaded an effort to change the way GE's middle managers operated. Its workshops emphasized radical altering of the old hierarchical bureaucracy to create a new nonhierarchical, fast-paced, flexible organization. Management development became a catalyst for mobilizing the energies of the 30,000 to 40,000 middle managers, enabling them to lead the change from the middle of the company.[44]

Managing Cultures When Growing by Acquisition

When merging with or acquiring another company, top management must give some consideration to a potential clash of cultures. Assuming that the firms can simply be integrated into the same reporting structure is dangerous. Investors are generally skeptical about mergers between companies having different cultures.[45] The greater the gap between the cultures of acquired and acquiring firms, the faster executives in the acquired firms quit their jobs and take their valuable talents elsewhere.[46] A classic example of the mismanagement of corporate cultures occurred when Exxon Corporation decided to purchase some high-tech companies. Exxon's top management decided to diversify from the declining petroleum business into the "office of the future." Buying firms from creative entrepreneurs, Exxon acquired three new word processing and printing technologies (named QWIP, QYX, and Vydec) to form Exxon Office Systems. As part of the bargain, Exxon also hired the entrepreneurs who had developed these new products. Unfortunately, the company placed the entrepreneurs—who thrived in a helter-skelter world of exciting ideas and quick, risky decisions—under the authority of Exxon's senior executives, who lived by corporate policy and procedures manuals and made decisions only after many group meetings. One by one, the creative but undisciplined "kids" left the company, with its meetings and paperwork, and started something new somewhere else. Exxon replaced them with professional managers hired from other office equipment companies such as IBM, Xerox, and Burroughs. Accustomed to large staffs and generous support, the new managers staffed these small business units as if they were the large firms they had just left. Instead of emphasizing research and innovation, they focused on advertising and promotion. The result was an estimated loss of approximately $2 billion and the eventual sale of Exxon Office Systems to Olivetti and Lanier.

After reviewing the impact of corporate cultures on the effectiveness of mergers and acquisitions, Malekzadeh and Nahavandi propose four general methods of managing disparate cultures.[47] (See Fig. 9.2.) The most appropriate method hinges on (1) how much members of the acquired firm value preservation of their own culture and (2) their perception of the attractiveness of the acquirer.

Integration involves a relatively balanced give-and-take of cultural and managerial practices between the merger partners and no strong imposition of cultural change on either company. Integration allows the two cultures to merge while preserving the separate cultures of both firms in the resulting culture. When the Seaboard and Chesapeake & Ohio railroads merged to form CSX Corporation, top executives were so concerned that both cultures be equally respected that they kept referring to the company as a "partnership of equals."

Under **assimilation,** the acquired firm surrenders its culture and adopts the culture of the acquiring company. Domination by the acquiring company isn't forced but is welcomed by members of the acquired firm, who may feel for many

FIGURE 9.2 **Methods of Managing the Culture of an Acquired Firm**

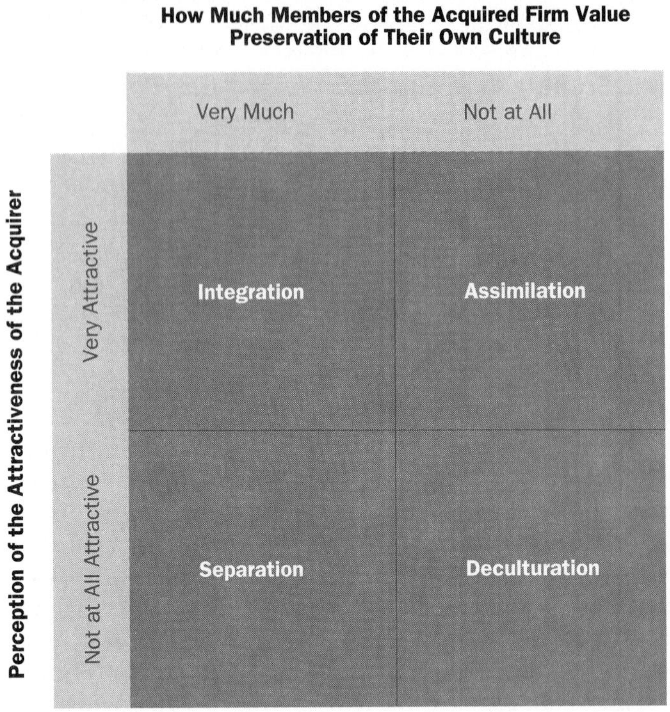

Source: A. Nahavandi and A. R. Malekzadeh, "Acculturation in Mergers and Acquisitions," *Academy of Management Review* (January 1988), p. 83. Copyright © 1988 by the Academy of Management. Reprinted by permission.

reasons that its culture and managerial practices haven't been successful. The Company Spotlight: Maytag Corporation feature on pages 272–273 describes this method of acculturation, used when Admiral, a subsidiary of Magic Chef, joined Maytag Corporation.

In the **separation** method, the two companies' cultures remain structurally separated, without any cultural exchange. In the case of the Shearson–American Express merger, both parties agreed to keep the fast-paced Shearson completely separate from the planning-oriented American Express.

Deculturation is the most common and most destructive method of dealing with two different cultures. It involves the disintegration of one company's culture resulting from unwanted and extreme pressure from the other to impose its culture and practices. This method often generates a great deal of confusion, conflict, resentment, and stress. Such a merger typically results in poor performance by the acquired company and its eventual divestment.[48]

Action Planning

As mentioned in Chapter 8, two typical problems in strategy implementation are the ineffective coordination of activities and the poor definition of essential implementation tasks and activities. Activities can be directed toward accomplishing strategic goals through action planning. At a minimum, an **action plan** identifies the actions to be taken, the people responsible for taking them, the time available for completion, and the results expected. After selecting a program to implement a particular strategy, employees should develop an action plan to put the program into effect.

Consider a company that chose forward vertical integration through the acquisition of a retailing chain as its growth strategy. After the acquisition, it must integrate the retail outlets into the company. One of the many programs it would have to develop is a new advertising campaign. The resulting action plan for this program should include the following elements.[49]

1. **Specific actions to be taken to make the program operational:** One action might be to contact three reputable ad agencies and ask them to prepare a proposal for a new radio, TV, and newspaper ad campaign based on the theme "Jones Surplus is now a part of Ajax Continental. Prices are lower. Selection is better."
2. **Dates to begin and end each action:** Time would have to be allotted not only to select and contact three agencies, but to allow them sufficient time to prepare a detailed proposal. For example, allow one week to select and contact the agencies and three months for them to prepare detailed proposals for presentation to the company's marketing director. Also allow some time to make a decision on which proposal to accept.
3. **Person (identified by name and title) responsible for carrying out each action:** Name someone—such as Jan Lewis, advertising manager—to run the program.
4. **Person responsible for monitoring the timeliness and effectiveness of each action:** Indicate that Jan Lewis is responsible for ensuring that the proposals are of good quality and are priced within the planned program budget. She will be the primary contact for the ad agencies and will report on the progress of the program once a week to the company's marketing director.
5. **Expected financial and physical consequences of each action:** Estimate when an ad campaign will be ready to show top management and how long it will take after approval to begin to air the ads. Estimate also the expected increase in store sales over the six-month period after the ads are first aired. Indicate if "recall" measures will be used to help assess the ad campaign's effectiveness and how, when, and by whom the recall data will be collected and analyzed.
6. **Contingency plans:** Indicate when another ad campaign can be ready to show top management if none of the initial proposals is acceptable.

According to J. C. Camillus, an authority on strategy implementation and control, action plans are important for several reasons. First, they serve as a link between strategy formulation and evaluation and control. Second, the action

Headquartered in Galesburg, Illinois, Admiral was the refrigeration division of Maytag Corporation. It manufactured refrigerators for the corporation's Maytag, Jenn-Air, and Magic Chef companies. Prior to Maytag's purchase of Magic Chef (and thus Admiral) in 1986, Admiral had been owned by three different corporations. In order to fit the company into the corporation better, all functional departments, except marketing, reported directly to Richard Haines, Maytag Company President. One result of Admiral's relationship with Maytag was the latter's emphasis on quality. Maytag's management had always wanted to have its own Maytag-brand refrigerator, but it was worried that Admiral might not be able to produce a quality product to Maytag's specifications.

Maytag's corporate culture had been dominated almost from the beginning of the company by the concept of quality. Maytag employees took great pride in being known as the "dependability people." Over the years, Maytag Company consistently advertised that their repairmen were "lonely" because Maytag brand products rarely, if ever, needed repair. The importance of quality to Maytag Corporation was highlighted by comments by past-Chairman and CEO Daniel Krumm regarding the specific resources that gave the corporation a competitive edge:

> *Quality, of course, has been Maytag's hallmark for as long as any of us can remember. We believe quality and reliability are, ultimately, what the consumer wants. That has been a challenge to us as we have acquired companies that may have had a different emphasis, but we have made significant recent strides in improving the quality of all our products.*

plan specifies what needs to be done differently from the way operations are currently carried out. Third, during the evaluation and control process that comes later, an action plan helps in both the appraisal of performance and in the identification of any remedial actions, as needed. In addition, the explicit assignment of responsibilities for implementing and monitoring the programs may enhance motivation.[50]

Management By Objectives (MBO)

Management By Objectives (MBO) is an organizationwide approach that can help ensure purposeful action toward desired objectives. It links organizational objectives and individual behavior. Because it is a system that links plans with performance, MBO is a powerful implementation technique.

The MBO process involves (1) establishing and communicating organizational objectives, (2) setting individual objectives (through superior–subordinate interac-

Under the direction of Leonard Hadley, while he was serving as Maytag Company President, a project was initiated to design and manufacture a Maytag brand refrigerator at the Admiral plant in Galesburg. It combined Admiral's engineering expertise in refrigeration with Maytag Company's manufacturing and quality skills. When Hadley first visited Admiral's facilities to discuss the design of a Maytag line of refrigerators, Admiral personnel asked Hadley when the name on their plant's water tower would be changed from Admiral to Maytag. Hadley (acknowledging Maytag's cultural concerns regarding quality) responded: "When you earn it."

The refrigerator resulting from the Maytag–Admiral collaboration was a huge success. The project crystallized corporate management's philosophy for forging synergies among the Maytag companies while simultaneously allowing the individual expertise of those units to flourish. Admiral's employees were willing to accept the dominance of Maytag's strong quality-oriented culture because they respected it. In turn, they expected to be treated with some respect for their tradition of skill in refrigeration technology. Daniel Krumm acknowledged the importance of respecting Admiral's culture in an interview with Appliance magazine:

> *The engineers at Admiral developed the Maytag brand refrigerator in close collaboration with R&D here in Newton. The people in Newton did not design that refrigerator, but they did make specifications. . . . We have no intention of designing refrigerators in Newton. Admiral is the expert in that area. . . . Creating these synergies is a very important element in our long-term strategy—sharing the expertise of each of our companies. As we bring all these companies together, our hope is that one-plus-one will ultimately add up to more than two.*

tion) that will help implement organizational objectives, (3) developing an action plan of activities needed to achieve the objectives, and (4) periodically (at least quarterly) reviewing performance as it relates to the objectives and including the results in the annual performance appraisal.[51] This technique also provides an opportunity to connect the objectives of people at each level to those at the next higher level.[52] Therefore MBO ties together corporate, business, and functional objectives and the strategies developed to achieve them.

Although corporate MBO programs have yielded mixed results, they generally tend to support the belief that MBO should result in higher levels of performance than would be achieved by approaches that do not include performance goals, relevant feedback, and joint supervisor–subordinate goal setting.[53]

One of the real benefits of MBO is that it can reduce the amount of internal politics in a large corporation. Political actions often cause conflict and divide the very people and groups who should be working together to implement strategy. People are less likely to jockey for position if the company's mission and objectives are clear and they know that the reward system is based not on game playing, but on achieving clearly communicated, measurable objectives.[54]

Total Quality Management (TQM)

Total Quality Management (TQM) is an operational philosophy that stresses commitment to **customer satisfaction** and **continuous improvement.** It is an umbrella term for a collection of concepts and procedures first proposed by W. Edwards Deming and built upon by Joseph Juran and Philip Crosby. Stated another way, TQM involves a commitment to quality, excellence, and being the best in all functions.[55] According to R. J. Schonberger, an expert on operations management and production engineering, TQM has four **objectives:**

1. Better, less variable quality of the product and service;
2. Quicker, less variable response in processes to customer needs;
3. Greater flexibility in adjusting to customers' shifting requirements; and
4. Lower cost through quality improvement and elimination of nonvalue-adding work.[56]

Because TQM aims to reduce costs as well as improve quality, it can be used as a program to implement both an overall low-cost or a differential business strategy.

According to TQM, faulty processes, not poorly motivated employees, are the main cause of defects in quality. Although its roots are in statistical process control (see the Strategy in Action on page 266), TQM involves a wide range of techniques, from scatter diagrams to benchmarking and cross-functional teams. The program usually involves a significant change in corporate culture, requiring strong leadership from top management, employee training, empowerment of lower level employees (giving people more control over their work), and teamwork for it to succeed.[57] The emphasis in TQM is on prevention, not correction, although inspection for quality still takes place. The emphasis is on improving the process to prevent errors and deficiencies, with quality circles or quality improvement teams identifying problems and suggesting ways to improve the processes causing problems.

The following are essential ingredients of TQM:

- **An intense focus on customer satisfaction:** Employees (not just people in the sales and marketing departments) must understand that their jobs exist only because of customer needs. Thus employees must approach their jobs in terms of how the results will affect customer satisfaction.
- **Customers are internal as well as external:** An employee in the shipping department may be the internal customer of another employee who completes assembly of a product, just as a person who buys the product is a customer of the entire company. An employee must be just as concerned with pleasing the internal customer as with pleasing the external customer.
- **Accurate measurement of every critical variable in a company's operations:** Employees have to be trained in what to measure, how to measure, and how to interpret the data. A rule of TQM is "you only improve what you measure."[58]

- **Continuous improvement of products and services:** Everyone recognizes the need to monitor operations continuously to find ways to improve products and services.
- **New work relationships based on trust and teamwork:** A key is the idea of *empowerment,* or giving employees wide latitude in how they go about achieving the company's goals.[59]

In Conclusion . . .

After hearing a speech by management expert Tom Peters, Mary Baechler, founder and President of Racing Strollers, Inc., became concerned that her company wasn't properly implementing its entrepreneurial strategy. In his speech, Peters had talked about how badly most businesses were managed and how poorly customers were being treated. Baechler tells how she used his ideas to improve her company's operations:

> Anyone in our company can stop production if he thinks there's a flaw. Any employee can send a stroller that's on order via Federal Express (at $87 a pop!) if he feels we have not met our delivery commitments. Beyond our lifetime guarantee for frames and one year guarantee on wheels, our customer service people can do whatever it takes, up to $300 per customer, to make things right for the customer (we track costs religiously, so that we can keep this up). We stay in contact after each repair, and the customer gets a postcard to send that comes directly to me and lets me know if we took care of matters to the customer's satisfaction. And we keep trying, until that customer is doing great. Those postcards are an immediate report card and the best part of my day.[60]

Points to Remember

- A change in strategy probably will require changes in staffing. If the new strategy is one of retrenchment, less people will be needed.
- The best or most appropriate type of manager needed to effectively implement a strategy depends on the desired strategic direction of the firm or business unit. Figure 9.1 suggests how a new executive could be matched with a specific strategy.
- Research into the value of selecting a CEO from outside the company instead of promoting someone already with the company has mixed results. Nevertheless, firms in trouble tend to select outsiders to implement a turnaround strategy, especially if there is no internal heir apparent, the last CEO was fired, and the board of directors contains a large percentage of outsiders.
- The chapter proposes some guidelines for successful downsizing programs. Many corporations are discovering that they may need to spend more time and money on training their employees to implement new strategies and programs. Training is needed as much for the survivors of a downsizing program as it is for a new program.
- A change in strategy also may require modification of corporate culture. Because changing the culture may take a long time, the strategic manager must

(1) evaluate what a particular change in strategy is likely to mean to the corporate culture, (2) assess whether a change in culture will be needed, and (3) decide whether an attempt to change the culture will be worth the costs.

- Action planning and Management By Objectives are two ways to implement a strategy. In particular, MBO is useful in reducing the level of internal politics in a company.
- According to Total Quality Management, faulty processes, not poorly motivated employees, cause defects in quality. TQM is an operational philosophy that emphasizes commitment to customer satisfaction and continuous improvement. Because it aims both to reduce costs and to improve quality, management can use TQM to implement either a cost leadership or a differentiation business strategy.

Discussion Questions

1. Assuming that the best person to implement a particular strategy is the one with a special mix of skills and experiences, what skills should a person have for managing a business unit using a differentiation strategy? Why? What should a company do if no one having these skills is available internally and the company has a policy of promotion only from within?
2. How might manager–strategy fit be accomplished short of firing current managers?
3. When should someone from outside the company be hired to manage the company or one of its business units?
4. What are some ways to implement a retrenchment strategy without creating a lot of resentment and conflict with labor unions?
5. Does culture follow strategy or does strategy follow culture? Why?
6. How can corporate culture be changed?
7. Compare and contrast action planning with Management By Objectives.
8. Why is internal politics a potential problem in strategy implementation? What, if anything, can management do about it?
9. What value does a Total Quality Management program have in implementing strategy?

Notes

1. From *Sam Walton: Made in America* by Sam Walton. Copyright © 1992 by Estate of Samual Moore Walton. Used by permission of Doubleday, a division of Bantam Doubleday Dell Publishing Group, Inc.
2. J. Magidson and A. E. Polcha, "Creating Market Economies Within Organizations: A Conference on 'Internal Markets,'" *Planning Review* (January/February 1992), p. 39.
3. R. S. Schuler and S. E. Jackson, "Determinants of Human Resource Management Priorities and Implications for Industrial Relations," *Journal of Management* (March 1989), pp. 89–99.
4. J. P. Walsh, "Doing a Deal: Merger and Acquisition Negotiations and Their Impact Upon Target Company Top Management Turnover," *Strategic Management Journal* (July–August 1989), pp. 307–322.

5. J. Hoerr, "Sharpening Minds for a Competitive Edge," *Business Week* (December 17, 1990), pp. 72–78.
6. R. Henkoff, "Companies That Train Best," *Fortune* (March 22, 1993), pp. 62–75.
7. A. S. Thomas, R. T. Litschert, and K. Ramaswamy, "The Performance Impact of Strategy–Manager Coalignment: An Empirical Examination," *Strategic Management Journal* (October 1991), pp. 509–522; S. F. Slater, "The Influence of Managerial Style on Business Unit Performance," *Journal of Management* (September 1989), pp. 441–455; T. T. Herbert and H. Deresky, "Should General Managers Match Their Business Strategies?" *Organizational Dynamics* (Winter 1987), pp. 40–51; R. Chaganti and R. Sambharya, "Strategic Orientation and Characteristics of Upper Management," *Strategic Management Journal* (July–August 1987), pp. 393–401.
8. Herbert and Deresky, "Should General Managers Match Their Business Strategies?" pp. 43–44.
9. G. L. Miles et al., "The Green Berets of Corporate Management," *Business Week* (September 21, 1987), pp. 110–114.
10. A. S. Thomas and K. Ramaswamy, "Top Executive Profiles, Orientation, and Organizational Performance," *International Journal of Management* (December 1992), pp. 406–416; R. M. Grant, "Competing Against Low Cost Cutlery Imports," *Long Range Planning* (October 1989), pp. 59–68; J. E. Ettlie, "What Makes A Manufacturing Firm Innovative?" *Academy of Management Executive* (November 1990), pp. 7–20.
11. A. K. Gupta and V. Govindarajan, "Business Unit Strategy, Managerial Characteristics, and Business Unit Effectiveness at Strategy Implementation," *Academy of Management Journal* (March 1984), pp. 25–41.
12. V. Govindarajan, "A Contingency Approach to Strategy Implementation at the Business-Unit Level: Integrating Administrative Mechanisms with Strategy," *Academy of Management Journal* (December 1988), pp. 828–853; V. Govindarajan, "Implementing Competitive Strategies at the Business Unit Level: Implications of Matching Managers to Strategies," *Strategic Management Journal* (May–June 1989), pp. 251–269.
13. Thomas, Litschert, and Ramaswamy, pp. 509–522; Thomas and Ramaswamy, pp. 406–416.
14. M. Smith and M. C. White, "Strategy, CEO Specialization, and Succession," *Administrative Science Quarterly* (June 1987), pp. 263–280.
15. K. G. Smith, T. R. Mitchell, and C. E. Summer, "Top Level Management Priorities in Different Stages of the Organizational Life Cycle," *Academy of Management Journal* (December 1985), pp. 799–820; G. D. Hughes, "Managing High-Tech Product Cycles," *Academy of Management Executive* (May 1990), pp. 44–55; W. E. Rothschild, "Avoid the Mismatch Between Strategy and Strategic Leaders," *Journal of Business Strategy* (January/February 1993), pp. 37–42.
16. L. M. Miller, *Barbarians to Bureaucrats* (New York: Clarkson N. Potter, 1989).
17. R. F. Vancil, *Passing the Baton* (Boston: Harvard Business School Press, 1987).
18. D. A. Hofrichter and G. J. Myszkowski, "Developing Managers Who Can Implement the Strategy: Competency-Based Succession Planning," in *Handbook of Business Strategy, 1989/90 Yearbook,* edited by H. E. Glass (Boston: Warren, Gorham and Lamont, 1989), pp. 18.1–18.12.
19. W. N. Davidson III, D. L. Worrell, and L. Cheng, "Key Executive Succession and Stockholder Wealth: The Influence of Successor's Origin, Position, and Age," *Journal of Management* (September 1990), pp. 647–664; D. R. Dalton and I. F. Kesner, "Organizational Performance as an Antecedent of Inside/Outside Chief Executive Succession: An Empirical Assessment," *Academy of Management Journal* (December 1985), pp. 749–762.
20. K. H. Chung, R. C. Rogers, M. Lubatkin, and J. E. Owers, "Do Insiders Make Better CEOs Than Outsiders?" *Academy of Management Executive* (November 1987), pp. 323–329; R. S. Schuler and S. E. Jackson, "Linking Competitive Strategies with Human Resource Management Practices," *Academy of Management Executive* (August 1987), pp. 207–219.
21. C. Gopinath, "Turnaround: Recognizing Decline and Initiation Intervention," *Long Range Planning* (December 1991), pp. 96–101.
22. K. B. Schwartz and K. Menon, "Executive Succession in Failing Firms," *Academy of Management Journal* (September 1985), pp. 680–686; A. A. Cannella, Jr., and M. Lubatkin, "Succession as a Sociopolitical Process: Internal Impediments to Outsider

Selection," *Academy of Management Journal* (August 1993), pp. 763–793; W. Boeker and J. Goodstein, "Performance and Succession Choice: The Moderating Effects of Governance and Ownership," *Academy of Management Journal* (February 1993), pp. 172–186.

23. G. J. Castrogiovanni, B. R. Baliga, and R. E. Kidwell, "Curing Sick Businesses: Changing CEOs in Turnaround Efforts," *Academy of Management Executive* (August 1992), pp. 26–41.
24. P. Lorange and D. Murphy, "Bringing Human Resources Into Strategic Planning: System Design Characteristics," in *Strategic Human Resource Management,* edited by C. J. Fombrun, N. M. Tichy, and M. A. Devanna (New York: John Wiley & Sons, 1984), pp. 281–283.
25. G. C. Thorton, *Assessment Centers in Human Resource Management* (Reading, Mass.: Addison-Wesley, 1992), pp. 189–192.
26. Thorton, p. 209.
27. R. A. Pitts, "Strategies and Structures for Diversification," *Academy of Management Journal* (June 1977), pp. 197–208.
28. W. F. Cascio, "Downsizing: What Do We Know? What Have We Learned?" *Academy of Management Executive* (February 1993), p. 96.
29. B. O'Reilly, "Is Your Company Asking Too Much?" *Fortune* (March 12, 1990), p. 41. See also K. S. Cameron, S. J. Freeman, and A. K. Miskra, "Best Practices in White-Collar Downsizing: Managing Contradictions," *Academy of Management Executive* (August 1991), pp. 57–73.
30. L. Isabella, "Downsizing: Survivor's Assessments, *Business Horizons* (May/June 1989), p. 39.
31. G. Fuchberg, "Why Shake-Ups Work for Some, Not for Others," *Wall Street Journal* (October 1, 1993), pp. B1, B10; A. Bennett, "Downsizing Doesn't Necessarily Bring an Upswing in Corporate Profitability," *Wall Street Journal* (June 6, 1991), pp. B1, B4.
32. Cascio, p. 98.
33. Fuchberg, p. B10.
34. *Wall Street Journal* (December 22, 1992), p. B1.
35. Suggested by D. A. Heenan, "The Downside of Downsizing," *Journal of Business Strategy* (November/December 1989), pp. 18–23; R. Henkoff, "Cost Cutting: How to Do It Right," *Fortune* (April 9, 1990), pp. 40–49. These suggestions agree with the more general recommendations reported by Cascio, pp. 95–104; Cameron, Freeman, and Mishra, pp. 57–73.
36. P. Truell, "Bankers Trust Transfers Departments to Xerox in Bid to Cut Costs and Staff," *Wall Street Journal* (June 17, 1988), p. A2.
37. P. C. Reid, *Well Made in America* (New York: McGraw-Hill, 1990), p. 171.
38. D. M. Rousseau, "Assessing Organizational Culture: The Case for Multiple Methods," in *Organizational Climate and Culture,* edited by B. Schneider (San Francisco: Jossey-Bass, 1990), pp. 153–192. Quotes are taken from pp. 181–182.
39. E. H. Burack, "Changing the Company Culture–The Role of Human Resource Development," *Long Range Planning* (February 1991), pp. 88–95.
40. G. Hofstede, B. Neuijen, D. D. Ohayv, and G. Sanders, "Measuring Organizational Cultures: A Qualitative and Quantitative Study Across Twenty Cases," *Administrative Science Quarterly* (June 1990), pp. 286–316; M. C. Cooper, "Managing Cultural Change to Achieve Competitive Advantage," in *Handbook of Business Strategy, 1987/1988 Yearbook,* edited by H. Babian and H. E. Glass (Boston: Warren, Gorham and Lamont, 1987), pp. 11.1–11.21.
41. D. R. Denison, *Corporate Culture and Organizational Effectiveness* (New York: John Wiley & Sons, 1990).
42. J. B. Treece, "Here Comes GM's Saturn," *Business Week* (April 9, 1990), pp. 56–62.
43. G. G. Gordon, "The Relationship of Corporate Culture to Industry Sector and Corporate Performance," in *Gaining Control of the Corporate Culture,* edited by R. H. Kilmann, M. J. Saxton, R. Serpa, and Associates (San Francisco: Jossey-Bass, 1985), p. 123.
44. N. M. Tichy, "GE's Crotonville: A Staging Ground for Corporate Revolution," *Academy of Management Executive* (May 1989), pp. 99–106.
45. S. Chatterjee, M. H. Lubatkin, D. M. Schweiger, and Y. Weber, "Cultural Differences and Shareholder Value in Related Mergers: Linking Equity and Human Capital," *Strategic Management Journal* (June 1992), pp. 319–334.

46. D. C. Hambrick and A. A. Cannella, Jr., "Relative Standing: A Framework for Understanding Departures of Acquired Executives," *Academy of Management Journal* (August 1993), pp. 733–762.
47. A. R. Malekzadeh and A. Nahavandi, "Making Mergers Work by Managing Cultures," *Journal of Business Strategy* (May/June 1990), pp. 53–57; A. Nahavandi and A. R. Malekzadeh, "Acculturation in Mergers and Acquisitions," *Academy of Management Review* (January 1988), pp. 79–90.
48. The Malekzadeh and Nahavandi model also has been applied to assessing the compatibility of joint venture partners by E. Cattaneo, "Managing Joint Venturing in Russia: Can the Problems Be Solved?" *Long Range Planning* (October 1992), pp. 68–72.
49. Suggested by J. C. Camillus, *Strategic Planning and Management Control* (Lexington, Mass.: Lexington Books, 1986), pp. 170–172.
50. Camillus, pp. 171–172.
51. S. J. Caroll, Jr., and H. L. Tosi, Jr., *Management by Objectives* (New York: Macmillan, 1973), p. 3; S. J. Caroll, Jr., "Management by Objectives: Three Decades of Research and Experience," in *Current Issues in Human Resource Management,* edited by S. L. Rynes and G. T. Milkovich (Plano, Texas: Business Publications, Inc., 1986), pp. 295–312; J. P. Muczyk and B. C. Reimann, "MBO as a Complement to Effective Leadership," *Academy of Management Executive* (May 1989), pp. 131–138.
52. M. D. Richards, *Setting Strategic Goals and Objectives,* 2nd ed. (St. Paul, Minn.: West, 1986), pp. 122–123.
53. E. J. Seyna, "MBO: The Fad That Changed Management," *Long Range Planning* (December 1986), pp. 116–123.
54. R. E. Jones, "Managing the Political Context in PMS Organizations," *European Journal of Operations Research,* in press.
55. C. Fisher, "A Primer of Total Quality Management," Working paper (New Orleans: Loyola University, 1993); G. W. Chase, "A Primer on Total Quality Management (TQM)," Working paper (Ames: Iowa State University, 1992).
56. R. J. Schonberger, "Total Quality Management Cuts a Broad Swath—Through Manufacturing and Beyond," *Organizational Dynamics* (Spring 1992), pp. 16–28.
57. Fisher.
58. R. J. Schonberger, "Is Strategy Strategic? Impact of Total Quality Management on Strategy," *Academy of Management Executive* (August 1992), p. 85.
59. M. Barrier, "Small Firms Put Quality First," *Nation's Business* (May 1992), p. 23.
60. M. Baechler, "Tom Peters Ruined My Life," *Wall Street Journal* (October 25, 1993), p. A18.

Evaluation and Control

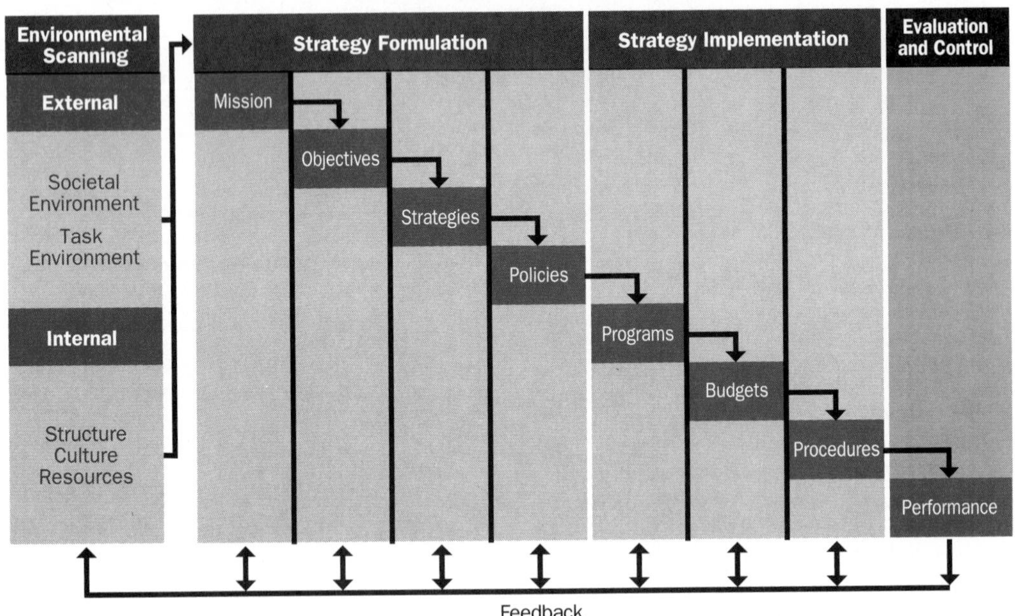

Things for which we can devise indicators can be managed; things for which we have no indicators can be out of control before we realize it.[1]
[George S. Odiorne]

During the spring of 1992, Jim Cannavino, the manager in charge of IBM's personal computer business, insisted that his was the most profitable PC business in the world. Unfortunately, his comment was based on the strange way that IBM allocated its costs to products. For example, IBM's system of accounting allocated all of a particular technology's R&D spending to the first group that used the technology; other IBM units then were able to use that technology free. As IBM began to face declining profits, it changed its cost allocation system to a more realistic one. In the fall of 1992, IBM disclosed that its PC business actually was unprofitable. Its competitors commented that the business had probably been losing money on and off for years—IBM just didn't know it![2]

The control process ensures that the company is achieving what it set out to accomplish. It compares performance with desired results and provides the feedback

FIGURE 10.1 **Evaluation and Control Process**

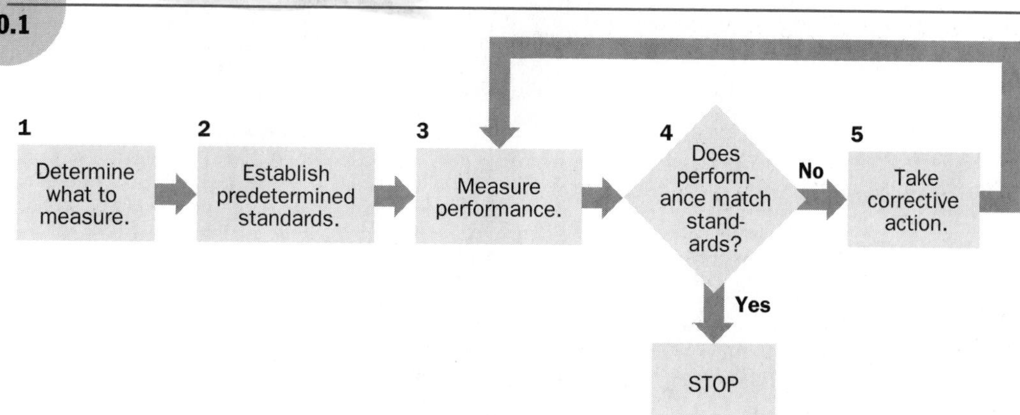

necessary for management to evaluate results and take corrective action as needed.[3] This process can be viewed as a five-step feedback model, as depicted in Fig. 10.1.

1. **Determine what to measure:** Top managers and operational managers need to specify the implementation processes and results that will be monitored and evaluated. The processes and results must be measurable in a reasonably objective and consistent manner. The focus should be on the most significant elements in a process—those that account for the highest proportion of expense or the greatest number of problems. Measurements must be found for all important areas regardless of difficulty. Because quality often is hard to measure, this step is crucial for implementing a Total Quality Management program.
2. **Establish standards of performance:** Standards used to measure performance are detailed expressions of strategic objectives. They are *measures* of acceptable performance results. Each standard usually includes a *tolerance range,* which defines acceptable deviations. Standards can be set not only for final output, but also for intermediate stages of production.
3. **Measure actual performance:** Measurements must be made at predetermined times.
4. **Compare actual performance with the standard:** If actual results are within the desired tolerance range, the measurement process stops here.
5. **Take corrective action:** If actual results fall outside the desired tolerance range, action must be taken to correct the deviation. The following must be determined:
   a. Is the deviation only a chance fluctuation?
   b. Are the processes being carried out incorrectly?
   c. Are the processes appropriate to the achievement of the desired standard? Action must be taken that will not only correct the deviation, but also will prevent its recurrence.

EVALUATION AND CONTROL AT DENNY'S AND WAL-MART

Strategy in Action

Control Problems at Denny's

During 1993, Denny's restaurants was barraged by lawsuits and accusations stating that the restaurant chain was discriminating against minority customers. Responding to complaints, CEO Jerome Richardson stated, "Our company does not tolerate discrimination of any kind." Nevertheless, a group of minority customers in San Jose, California, filed a lawsuit against Denny's charging that the restaurant demanded that 18 African-Americans not only pay a $2 cover charge before ordering food, but also prepay for their meals—even though whites at the next table had to pay neither. When asked about this event, Richardson said that he was not aware that local managers had the option of imposing the prepay policy during late night hours to avoid people leaving without paying for their meals. The company quickly agreed to cancel the policy and to expand sensitivity training for staff nationwide. Later, six African-American Secret Service agents claimed that they were denied service at an Annapolis, Maryland, Denny's because of deliberately slow service—when white colleagues were being served in the normal amount of time. In each case, the company responded that the discrimination was in direct violation of corporate policies. According to management consultants, these incidents provided yet another example of senior executives depending too heavily on policy statements instead of actively monitoring and training people to avoid discrimination complaints.

Control Success at Wal-Mart

Sam Walton, founder of Wal-Mart, set the example for his managers. Until his death in 1992, he flew his twin-engine airplane from one Wal-Mart store to another—constantly checking his people and his competition. "We couldn't have put this together without these airplanes," he explained. Walton used to boast that he personally visited every Wal-Mart store at least once a year. Admitting that it was difficult to visit 1,650 stores and 200 Sam's Clubs, he stated in 1991, "Right now there are prob-

Research indicates that top management often performs the first two steps better than the last three follow-through steps. Top management tends to establish a control system and then delegate implementation of this system to others,[4] which can have unfortunate results. The Strategy in Action on pages 282–283 presents examples of both successful and unsuccessful evaluation and control systems.

ably about 30 stores I've never been to and a bunch of others I haven't seen in more than a little while. I've got to get to 'em soon." When Walton arrived at a store, he came with no entourage and usually with little or no notice. Upon arriving at store number 950 near Memphis at 7 A.M., he tapped on the window for employees to open the locked door. A surprised expression flashed across the face of the first employee (an *associate* in Wal-Mart language) to recognize the old man in the Wal-Mart cap. Walton told the store manager: "Good morning, Doug, great to be here. I want to walk around a bit, and then we'll get everybody up front. But I'd like to get all your department heads and assistant managers up here in the snack bar, and I'd like to see your P&L and your merchandising statements, and I want to see your 30, 60, and 90 day plans. All right?" Upon being introduced to Renee, manager of the store's pet department, Walton asked her what percentage her department was of the store. "Last year it was 3.1%, but this year I'm trying for 3.3%," responded Renee. "Well, Renee, that's amazing," said Walton. "You know our average pet department only does about 2.4%. Keep up the great work."

Even after Walton's death, store visits continued to be a key part of top management's job. Every Monday morning, some 50 to 60 corporate officers, buyers, and regional officers would get into the company's fleet of 15 aircraft to visit stores across America. They visited not only the Wal-Mart stores but also local competitors to check prices and service. After an in-depth look at the local Wal-Mart store, each executive went through a Sam Walton tradition—leading the company cheer: "Give me a W! Give me an A! . . . " This cheer was followed by a solemn pledge by each associate to greet every customer within ten feet, "so help me, Sam."

Source: C. Hawkins, "Denny's: The Stain That Isn't Coming Out," *Business Week* (June 28, 1993), pp. 98–99; J. Huey, "America's MOST Successful Merchant," *Fortune* (September 23, 1991), pp. 46–59; B. Saporito, "A Week Aboard the Wal-Mart Express," *Fortune* (August 24, 1992), pp. 77–84.

10.1 Evaluation and Control in Strategic Management

The strategic management model at the beginning of each chapter shows evaluation and control information being fed back and assimilated into the entire management process. Such information consists of performance data and activity reports (gathered in Step 3 of Fig. 10.1). If undesired performance is the result of inappropriate use of strategic management processes, operational managers must know about it. They can then correct the employee activity without involving top management. However, if undesired performance results from the processes themselves, both top managers and operational managers must know about it. They must then develop new implementation programs or procedures.

Evaluation and control information must be relevant to what is being monitored. The IBM example demonstrates how the use of inappropriate data clouded the perceptions of the head of IBM's PC unit and may have led to poor strategic decisions. Evaluation and control isn't an easy process. One of the obstacles is the difficulty in developing appropriate measures of activities and outputs.

Figure 10.2 illustrates evaluation of an implemented strategy. This method gives strategic managers a series of questions to use in the evaluation. Management usually initiates such a strategy review when a *planning gap* appears between a company's financial objectives and the expected results of current activities.[5] Answering this set of questions (or a similar set), should give a manager a good idea of where the problem originated and what must be done to solve it.

P. Lorange, M. F. S. Morton, and S. Ghoshal, in their book on strategic control, identified three types of control.[6] **Strategic control** deals with the basic strategic direction of the corporation in terms of its relationship with its environment. It focuses on the organization as a whole and might emphasize long-term measures (one year or more), such as return on investment and changes in shareholder value. **Tactical control,** in contrast, deals primarily with carrying out the strategic plan. It emphasizes the implementation of programs and might use medium-range measures (considering six months to a year), such as market share in particular product categories. **Operational control** deals with near-term (considering today to six months) corporate activities and focuses on what might be going on now to achieve near- and long-term success. An example of an operational control is the use of *statistical process control,* or SPC (described in Chapter 9 on pages 266–267), to provide immediate feedback to workers to enable them to minimize defects in the production process.[7]

Lorange, Morton, and Ghoshal further suggest that there is also a **hierarchy of control.** At the *corporate level,* control focuses on maintaining a balance among the various activities of the corporation as a whole. Strategic and tactical controls are most important. Overall annual profitability is key. At the *divisional level,* control is concerned primarily with maintenance and improvement of competitive position. Tactical control dominates. Market share and unit costs are watched carefully on a monthly and quarterly basis. At the *functional level,* the role of control becomes one of developing and enhancing function-based distinctive competencies. The number of sales calls completed, the number of customer complaints, and the number of defects are watched daily and weekly. Because of their short-term time horizons, operational and tactical controls are the most important types at this level, with only slight concern for strategic control.[8]

To help achieve organizational objectives, strategic managers have an obligation to ensure that the entire hierarchy of controls are integrated and working properly. According to W. Edwards Deming, 85% of product defects are caused by the system within which the worker must perform and only 15% can be

FIGURE 10.2 **Evaluating an Implemented Strategy**

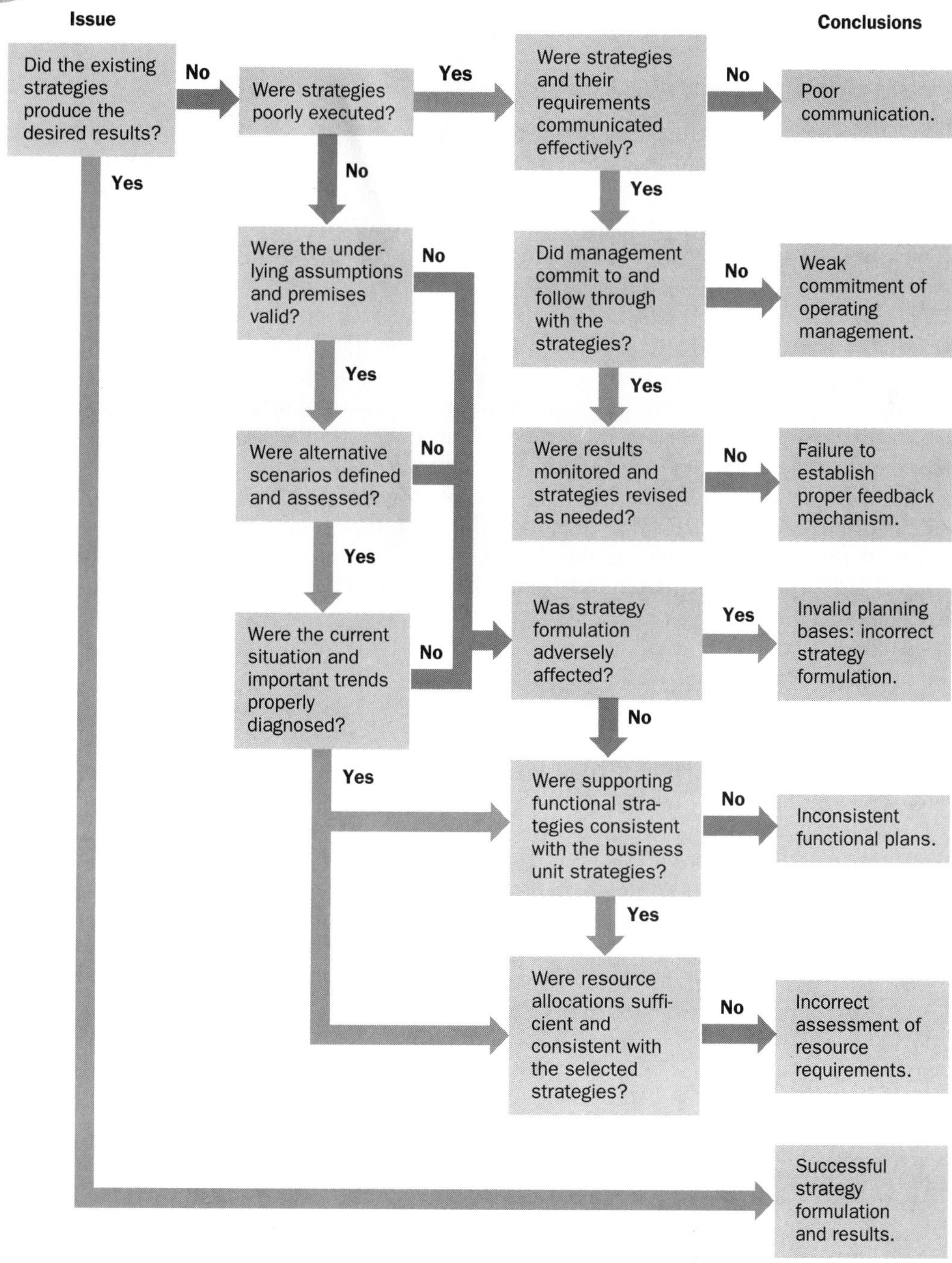

Source: Jeffrey A. Schmidt, "The Strategic Review," *Planning Review* (July/August 1988), p. 15. Copyright © 1988 by The Planning Forum, Oxford, Ohio.

directly traced to the worker.[9] Unfortunately, during the past several decades top management has almost forgotten the importance of strategic control. It often shifted control to the tactical and operational levels and led to short-term crisis management.

10.2 Measuring Performance

The measures to be used to assess performance depends on the organizational unit to be appraised and the objectives to be achieved. The objectives established in the strategy formulation stage of the strategic management process (regarding profitability, market share, and cost reduction, among others) should certainly be used to measure corporate performance during strategy implementation.

Some measures, such as return on investment (ROI), are appropriate for evaluating the corporation's or division's ability to achieve a profitability objective. This type of measure, however, is inadequate for evaluating other corporate objectives such as social responsibility or employee development. Even though profitability is the major objective for a corporation, ROI can be computed only *after* profits are totaled for a period. It tells what happened after the fact—not what *is* happening or what *will* happen. A firm therefore needs to develop measures that predict likely profitability. These are referred to as **steering** or **feed-forward controls** because they measure variables that influence future profitability.[10] One example of this type of control is the use of control charts in Statistical Process Control (SPC). In SPC, workers and managers maintain charts and graphs detailing quality and productivity on a daily basis.

Managers may establish controls to focus either on activities that generate the performance (behavior) or on actual performance results (output). **Behavior controls** specify *how* something is to be done through policies, rules, standard operating procedures, and orders from a superior. **Output controls** specify *what* is to be accomplished by focusing on the end result of the behaviors through the use of objectives and performance targets or milestones. Behavior and output controls are not interchangeable. Behavior controls (such as following company procedures, making sales calls to potential customers, and getting to work on time) are most appropriate for situations in which results are hard to measure and a clear cause–effect connection exists between activities and results. Output controls (such as sales quotas, specific cost reduction or profit objectives, and surveys of customer satisfaction) are most appropriate for situations in which there are specific agreed-upon output measures and there is no clear cause–effect connection between activities and results. Generally, output measures serve the control needs of the corporation as a whole, whereas behavior measures serve the individual manager.[11]

Measures of Corporate Performance

The most commonly used measure of corporate performance (in terms of profits) is ROI. It is simply the result of dividing net income before taxes by total assets.

TABLE 10.1 **Advantages and Limitations of Using ROI as a Measure of Corporate Performance**

Advantages

1. ROI is a single comprehensive figure influenced by everything that happens.
2. It measures how well the division manager uses the property of the company to generate profits. It is also a good way to check on the accuracy of capital investment proposals.
3. It is a common denominator that can be compared with many entities.
4. It provides an incentive to use existing assets efficiently.
5. It provides an incentive to acquire new assets only when doing so would increase the return.

Limitations

1. ROI is very sensitive to depreciation policy. Depreciation write-off variances between divisions affect ROI performance. Accelerated depreciation techniques increase ROI, conflicting with capital budgeting discounted cash-flow analysis.
2. ROI is sensitive to book value. Older plants with more depreciated assets have relatively lower investment bases than newer plants (note also the effect of inflation), thus increasing ROI. Note that asset investment may be held down or assets disposed of in order to increase ROI performance.
3. In many firms that use ROI, one division sells to another. As a result, transfer pricing must occur. Expenses incurred affect profit. Since, in theory, the transfer price should be based on the total impact on firm profit, some investment center managers are bound to suffer. Equitable transfer prices are difficult to determine.
4. If one division operates in an industry that has favorable conditions and another division operates in an industry that has unfavorable conditions, the former division will automatically "look" better than the other.
5. The time span of concern here is short range. The performance of division managers should be measured in the long run. This is top management's timespan capacity.
6. The business cycle strongly affects ROI performance, often despite managerial performance.

Source: "Advantages and Limitations of ROI as a Measure of Corporate Performance" from *Organizational Policy and Strategic Management: Text and Cases*, 2nd ed. by James M. Higgins, copyright © 1984 by The Dryden Press. Reproduced by permission of the publisher.

(This text makes no attempt to differentiate between Return on Investment and Return on Assets.) Although there are several advantages to the use of ROI, there are also several distinct limitations. (See Table 10.1.) Although ROI gives the impression of objectivity and precision, it can be easily manipulated.[12]

Other popular profit measures are earnings per share (EPS) and return on equity (ROE). Earnings per share also has several deficiencies as an evaluation of past and future performance. Because alternative accounting principles are available, EPS can have several different but equally acceptable values, depending on the principle selected for its computation. Moreover, EPS is based on accrual income—involving both the near-term and delayed conversion of income to cash—thereby ignoring the time value of money. Return on equity also has its share of limitations because it also is derived from accounting-based data. In addition, there is some evidence that EPS and ROE may be unrelated to a company's stock price.[13] Because of these and other limitations, EPS and ROE by themselves are inadequate measures of corporate performance.[14]

TABLE 10.2 A Sample Scorecard for "Keeping Score" with Stakeholders

Stakeholder Category	Possible Near-Term Measures	Possible Long-Term Measures
Customers	Sales ($ and volume) New customers Number of new customer needs met ("tries")	Growth in sales Turnover of customer base Ability to control price
Suppliers	Cost of raw material Delivery time Inventory Availability of raw material	Growth rates of: Raw material costs Delivery time Inventory New ideas from suppliers
Financial community	EPS Stock price Number of "buy" lists ROE	Ability to convince Wall Street of strategy Growth in ROE
Employees	Number of suggestions Productivity Number of grievances	Number of internal promotions Turnover
Congress	Number of new pieces of legislation that affect the firm Access to key members and staff	Number of new regulations that affect industry Ratio of "cooperative" vs. "competitive" encounters
Consumer advocate	Number of meetings Number of "hostile" encounters Number of times coalitions formed Number of legal actions	Number of changes in policy due to C.A. Number of C.A.-initiated "calls for help"
Environmentalists	Number of meetings Number of hostile encounters Number of times coalitions formed Number of EPA complaints Number of legal actions	Number of changes in policy due to environmentalists Number of environmentalist "calls for help"

Source: R. E. Freeman, *Strategic Management: A Stakeholder Approach* (Boston: Ballinger Publishing Company, 1984), p. 179. Copyright © 1984 by R. E. Freeman. Reprinted by permission.

Stakeholder Measures

Each stakeholder has its own set of criteria to determine how well the corporation is performing. These criteria typically deal with both the direct and indirect impact of corporate activities on stakeholder interests. R. E. Freeman believes that top management needs to "keep score" with these stakeholders, and as shown in Table 10.2, it should establish one or more simple measures for each stakeholder category.[15]

Value-Added Measures

Because any one measure is bound to have some shortcomings, C. W. Hofer recommends the use of value-added measures in evaluating a corporation's performance. **Value added** is the difference between dollar sales and the cost of raw materials and purchased parts. **Return on value added (ROVA)** is a measure that divides net profits before tax by value added and converts the quotient to a percentage. Hofer argues that ROVA might be a better measure of corporate performance in various industries than other measures currently in use.[16] Value added is a useful way to apply Porter's value chain concept (see Chapter 5). Unfortunately, the major disadvantage of using value added is that the necessary figures aren't readily available. In the United States, value added can't be calculated from traditional financial reports because of the allocation of direct labor costs, indirect costs, and overhead costs to the total cost of goods manufactured. Nevertheless, authorities on the subject argue that combining value-added measures with traditional performance measures creates a more complete and realistic picture of a corporation's performance.[17]

Shareholder Value

Because of the belief that accounting-based numbers such as return on investment, return on equity, and earnings per share aren't reliable indicators of a corporation's economic value, many corporations are using shareholder value as a better measure of corporate performance and strategic management effectiveness. **Shareholder value** may be defined as the present value of the anticipated future stream of cash flows from the business plus the value of the company if liquidated.[18] Based on the argument that the purpose of a company is to increase shareholder wealth, shareholder value analysis concentrates on cash flow as the primary measure of performance. The value of a corporation thus is the value of its cash flows discounted to their present value, using the cost of capital as the discount rate. So long as the returns from a business exceed its cost of capital, the business will create value and be worth more than the capital invested in it.[19]

Economic value added (EVA) has become an extremely popular shareholder value method of measuring corporate and divisional performance and may eventually replace ROI as the standard performance measure. It measures the difference between the prestrategy and poststrategy value of the business. If the difference, discounted by the cost of capital is positive, the strategy is generating value for shareholders.[20] Among the many companies using the new measure are Coca-Cola, AT&T, Quaker Oats, Briggs & Stratton, and CSX. A. Rappaport, an expert on shareholder value, states that the value generated by a particular business plan can be projected by calculating the capitalized value of the difference between operating margins and the minimum acceptable operating return on new sales.[21] Simply put, EVA is after-tax operating profit minus the total annual cost of capital. Explained by Roberto Goizueta, CEO of Coca-Cola, "We raise capital to make concentrate, and sell it at an operating profit. Then we pay the cost of that capital. Shareholders pocket the difference."[22] Unlike ROI, one of EVA's most powerful properties is its strong relationship to stock price. Managers can improve a company's or business unit's EVA by (1) earning more profit without using more capital, (2) using less capital, and (3) investing capital in high-return projects.

Evaluation of Top Management

Through its strategy, audit, and compensation committees, a board of directors may evaluate the job performance of the CEO and the top management team. Of course, the board is concerned primarily with overall profitability as measured quantitatively by return on investment, return on equity, earnings per share, and shareholder value. The absence of short-run profitability certainly is a factor contributing to the firing of any CEO, but the board also will be concerned with other factors.

Members of the compensation committees of today's boards of directors generally agree that measuring a CEO's ability to establish strategic direction, build a management team, and provide leadership is more important in the long run than are a few quantitative measures.[23] The board should evaluate top management not only on typical output-oriented quantitative measures, but also on behavioral measures—factors relating to its strategic management practices. Unfortunately, less than 30% of companies systematically evaluate their CEOs' performance.[24]

The specific measures used by a board to evaluate its top management should be based on the objectives agreed on earlier by both groups. If better relations with the local community and improved safety practices in work areas were selected as objectives for the year (or for five years), progress toward meeting them should be evaluated. In addition, other factors that tend to lead to profitability might be included, such as market share, product quality, and investment intensity.

Management Audits

Utilized by various consulting firms as a way to measure performance, audits of corporate activities are frequently suggested for use by boards of directors and by managers alike. Management audits have been developed to evaluate activities such as corporate social responsibility, functional areas such as the marketing department, and divisions such as the international division—and the corporation itself in a strategic audit (see Chapter 2, pages 48–55). To be effective, the strategic audit should parallel the corporation's strategic management process.

Measures of Divisional and Functional Performance

Companies use a variety of techniques to evaluate and control performance in divisions, SBUs, and functional areas. If a corporation is organized by SBU or division, it will use many of the same performance measures (ROI or EVA, for instance) that it uses to assess overall corporation performance. When it can isolate specific functional units, such as R&D, the corporation may develop responsibility centers. It also may use typical functional measures such as market share and sales per employee (marketing), unit costs and percentage of defects (operations), percentage of sales from new products and number of patents (R&D), and turnover and job satisfaction (HRM).

During strategy formulation and implementation, top management approves a series of programs and supporting operating budgets submitted by its business units.[25] During evaluation and control, management contrasts actual expenses with planned expenditures and assesses the degree of variance, typically each month. In addition, top management probably will require periodic statistical reports that summarize data about key factors, such as the number of new customer contracts, volume of received orders, and productivity, among others.

Control and Business Unit Strategy

The strategy chosen by an SBU should influence the type of controls chosen.[26] Research by Govindarajan and Fisher indicates that high-performing SBUs following a cost leadership competitive strategy tend to use output controls, such as piece rate or straight commission. This approach is logical because costs usually can be easily determined. In contrast, high-performing SBUs following a differentiation competitive strategy tend to use behavior controls, such as salaried compensation. Factors such as creative flair, strong R&D, and innovative product development are extremely important to this strategy but are difficult to quantify.[27]

Let's consider two computer companies as examples. Digital Equipment Corporation (DEC) follows a differentiation strategy, Data General follows a low-cost strategy, and their control systems differ accordingly. DEC's salespeople are on straight salary, but Data General's salespeople receive 50% of their pay as commissions. Product managers at DEC are evaluated primarily on the basis of the quality of their customer relationships, whereas Data General's product managers are evaluated strictly on the basis of results, that is, profits. Researchers have concluded that "for increased effectiveness, cost leadership and differentiation strategies need to be matched with output and behavior controls, respectively."[28]

Responsibility Centers

Control systems can be established to monitor specific functions, projects, or divisions. For example, budgets typically are used to control the financial indicators of performance in conjunction with responsibility centers. A **responsibility center** is a unit that can be evaluated separately from the rest of the corporation. Each responsibility center is headed by a manager who is responsible for its performance, has its own budget, and is evaluated on its use of budgeted resources. The center uses resources (measured in terms of costs or expenses) to produce a service or a product (measured in terms of volume or revenues). The type of responsibility center used is determined by the way the corporation's control system measures these resources and services or products. There are five major types of responsibility centers.[29]

1. Standard cost centers: Primarily used in manufacturing facilities, standard (or expected) costs are computed for each operation on the basis of historical data. In evaluating the center's performance, its total standard costs are multiplied by the units produced; the result is the expected cost of production, which is then compared to the actual cost of production.

2. Revenue centers: Production, usually in terms of unit or dollar sales, is measured without consideration of resource costs (e.g., salaries). The center is thus judged in terms of effectiveness rather than efficiency. The effectiveness of a sales region, for example, is determined by the comparison of its actual sales to its projected or previous year's sales. Profits are not considered because sales departments have limited influence over the cost of the products they sell.

3. Expense centers: Resources are measured in dollars without consideration of service or product costs. Thus budgets will be prepared for *engineered* expenses (costs that can be calculated) and for *discretionary* expenses (costs that can be only estimated). Typical expense centers are administrative, service, and research departments. They cost an organization money, but they contribute only indirectly to revenues.

4. Profit centers: Performance is measured in terms of the difference between revenues (which measure production) and expenditures (which measure resources). A profit center typically is established whenever an organizational unit controls both its resources and its products or services. By having such centers, a company can be organized into divisions of separate product lines. The manager of each division is given autonomy to the extent that profits remain at a satisfactory (or better) level.

Some organizational units that are not usually considered potentially autonomous can, for the purpose of profit-center evaluations, be made so. A manufacturing department, for example, may be converted from a standard cost center (or expense center) to a profit center: it is allowed to charge a **transfer price** for each product it "sells" to the sales department. The difference between the manufacturing cost per unit and the agreed-upon transfer price is the unit's "profit." Transfer pricing commonly is used in vertically integrated corporations and can work well when a price can be determined easily for a designated amount of product. Only 30%–40% of companies use market price to set the transfer price, even though most experts agree that market-based transfer prices are the best choice. (Of the rest, 50% use cost and 10%–20% use negotiation.)[30] When a price cannot be set easily, however, the relative bargaining power of the centers, rather than strategic considerations, tends to influence the agreed-upon price.[31] Top management has an obligation to make sure that political considerations do not overwhelm strategic considerations. Otherwise, profit figures for each center will be biased and will provide poor information for strategic decisions at the corporate level.

5. Investment centers: Because many divisions in large manufacturing corporations use significant assets to make their products, their asset bases should be factored into the performance evaluation. Thus focusing only on profits, as in the case of profit centers, is insufficient. An investment center's performance is measured in terms of the difference between its resources and its services or products. For example, if two divisions in a corporation make identical profits but one division has a capital investment of $3 million in a plant and the other has a capital investment of $1 million in a plant, the smaller plant obviously is more efficient: it provides shareholders with a better return on their investment.

The most widely used measure of investment center performance is return on investment (ROI). Another measure, called *residual income,* or *after-capital charge,* is obtained by subtracting an interest charge from net income. This interest charge could be based on the interest the corporation is actually paying to lenders for the assets being used. It could also be based on the amount of income that could have been earned if the assets had been invested somewhere else. Even though the residual income method is superior to ROI because it takes into account the cost of capital, it never attained ROI's popularity.[32]

Investment center performance also may be measured in terms of its contribution to shareholder value through the use of economic value added. For example, Briggs & Stratton used EVA to measure the performance of its five divisions that made engines for lawn mowers, pumps, and other products. Each division knew its EVA, and that knowledge led to the use of outsourcing to reduce costs. The company phased out production of the largest engines for pumps and generators, freeing capital that had been unprofitably used in their manufacture. It then bought premium engines elsewhere at a lower cost. When the company increased its 7.7% return on capital (the cost of capital at the time was 12%), its stock price increased from $20 to $80.[33]

Most single-business corporations, such as Apple Computer, tend to use a combination of cost, expense, and revenue centers. In these corporations, most managers are functional specialists and manage against a budget, and total profitability is integrated at the corporate level. Dominant product companies, such as Anheuser-Busch, which have diversified into a few small businesses but which still depend on a single product line for most of their revenue and income, generally use a combination of cost, expense, revenue, and profit centers. Multidivisional corporations such as General Electric tend to emphasize investment centers—although in various units throughout a corporation other types of responsibility centers also are used.[34] One problem with using responsibility centers, however, is that they sometimes complicate the calculations necessary for the kind of value chain analysis that looks for synergistic linkages among units.[35]

Benchmarking

According to Xerox Corporation, the company that pioneered this concept in the United States, **benchmarking** is "the continual process of measuring products, services, and practices against the toughest competitors or those companies recognized as industry leaders."[36] An increasingly popular program, benchmarking is based on the concept that reinventing something that someone else is already using makes no sense. It involves openly learning how others do something and imitating or perhaps even improving on their techniques. The benchmarking process usually involves the following steps.

- Identify the area or process to be examined. It should be an activity that has the potential to determine a business unit's competitive advantage.
- Find behavioral and output measures of the process and obtain measurements.
- Select an accessible set of competitors and best-in-class companies against which to benchmark. These companies may be in completely different industries but perform similar activities. For example, when Xerox wanted to improve its order fulfillment performance, it went to L. L. Bean, the successful mail order firm, to learn how it achieved excellence in this area.
- Calculate the differences among the company's performance measurements and those of the best-in-class company. Determine *why* the differences exist.
- Develop tactical programs for closing performance gaps.

- Implement the programs, measure the results, and compare the results with those of the best-in-class company.

A survey of 580 organizations in the computer, automobile, hospital, and banking industries found that 31% of U.S. corporations regularly benchmarked their products and services and that only 7% never did. Benchmarking firms include Xerox, AT&T, DuPont, Ford, IBM, Eastman Kodak, Motorola, Mellon Bank, and many smaller and less well-known businesses.[37] For example, Manco, Inc., a small Cleveland-area producer of duct tape regularly benchmarks itself against Wal-Mart, Rubbermaid, and PepsiCo to enable it to compete better with giant 3M.[38] The American Productivity & Quality Center, a Houston research group, recently established a "best practices database" of 600 leading techniques that 250 companies use.[39]

10.3 Strategic Information Systems

Before performance measures can have any impact on strategic management, they must first be communicated to the people responsible for formulating and implementing strategic plans. Strategic information systems—computer-based or manual, formal or informal—can perform this function to serve the information needs of top management.[40] One of the main reasons given for the bankruptcy of International Harvester was the inability of the corporation's top management to determine precisely its income by major class of similar products. Because of this inability, management kept trying to fix ailing businesses and was unable to respond flexibly to major changes and unexpected events.[41] In contrast, one of the key reasons for the success of Toys 'R' Us has been management's use of the company's sophisticated information system to control purchasing decisions, as described in the Strategy in Action on page 295.

Critical success factors (CSFs) are the things that must go well to ensure a corporation's success.[42] Typically, they are the 20% of the factors that determine 80% of the corporation's or business unit's performance.[43] Critical success factors should be

- Important to achieving overall corporate goals and objectives;
- Measurable and controllable by the organization to which they apply;
- Relatively few in number—not everything can be critical;
- Expressed as things that must be done;
- Applicable to all companies in the industry with similar objectives and strategies; and
- Hierarchical in nature—some CSFs will pertain to the overall corporation, whereas others will be more narrowly focused, say, in one functional area.[44]

The CSFs provide a starting point for developing an information system. Such an information system will thus pinpoint the principal areas that require a manager's attention.

At the divisional or SBU level, the information system should support, reinforce, or enlarge business-level strategy with a decision support component.[45] An

TOYS 'R' US USES INFORMATION SYSTEMS TO CONTROL PURCHASING

Strategy in Action

Since 1978, sales at Toys 'R' Us have been growing at a compounded rate of 28% annually. The company's success rests on a sophisticated information system. Cash registers in the company's 300-plus U.S. stores transmit information daily to computers at the company's headquarters in Rochelle Park, New Jersey. Consequently, managers know every morning exactly how many of each item have been sold the day before, how many have been sold so far in the year, and how this year's sales compare to last year's.

The information system allows automatic reordering by computer without any managerial input. It also allows the company to experiment with new toys without committing to big orders in advance. In effect, the system allows the customers to decide through their purchases what gets reordered. Chairman Charles Lazarus respects the information system so much that when the computer's decision conflicts with his judgment, he defers to the computer. For example, a few years ago, he personally thought that Cabbage Patch dolls were ugly and didn't think that children would want to hold them. However, the information system recognized consumer buying patterns and reordered accordingly. The system also is able to recognize drops in demand, such as when a fad like Trivial Pursuit begins to fade.

Source: S. N. Chakravarty, "Will Toys 'B' Great?" *Forbes* (February 22, 1988), pp. 37–39.

SBU pursuing a strategy of overall cost leadership could use its information system to help reduce costs either by the improvement of labor productivity or the utilization of other resources, such as inventory or machinery. Merrill Lynch took this approach when it developed PRISM software to provide its 500 U.S. retail offices quick access to financial information in order to boost the efficiency of its brokers.[46] Another SBU, in contrast, might want to pursue a differentiation strategy. It could use its information system to help add uniqueness to the product or service and contribute to quality, service, or image in its functional areas. Federal Express wanted to use superior service to gain a competitive advantage. It invested heavily in several types of information systems to track and measure the performance of its delivery service. Together, these information systems provided Federal Express the fastest error-response time in the overnight delivery business.[47]

The choice of business-level strategy will thus dictate the type of information system that the SBU needs both to implement and to control strategic activities.

The information systems will be constructed differently to monitor different activities because the two types of business-level strategies have different critical success factors.[48]

10.4 Problems in Measuring Performance

Performance measurement is crucial to evaluation and control. The lack of quantifiable objectives or performance standards and the inability of the information system to provide timely, valid information are two obvious control problems.[49] Without objective and timely measurements, making operational, let alone strategic, decisions would be extremely difficult. Nevertheless, the use of timely, quantifiable standards doesn't guarantee adequate performance. The very act of monitoring and measuring performance may cause side effects that interfere with overall corporate performance. Among the most frequent negative side effects are short-term orientation and goal displacement.

Short-Term Orientation

Hodgetts and Wortman state that in many situations top executives do not analyze *either* the long-term implications of present operations on the strategy they have adopted *or* the operational impact of a strategy on the corporate mission. They report that long-run evaluations are not conducted because executives (1) may not realize their importance, (2) may believe that short-run considerations are more important than long-run considerations, (3) may not be personally evaluated on a long-term basis, or (4) may not have the time to make a long-run analysis.[50] There is no real justification for the first and last "reasons." If executives realize the importance of long-run evaluations, they make the time to conduct those evaluations. Even though many chief executives point to immediate pressures from the investment community and to short-term incentive and promotion plans to support the second and third reasons, the evidence doesn't always support their claims.

A survey of 400 U.S. chief executives revealed that 98% of them agreed that their industries could be criticized justifiably for focusing on next quarter's earnings or tomorrow's stock price. Over half believed that institutional investors were increasingly pressuring them to improve short-term performance.[51] Research suggests, however, that this view of short-term pressure may be based more on personal interest and conventional wisdom than on actual pressures. Studies reveal that the stock market does value long-term investment and that investors (even institutional investors) place considerable value on profits that won't be earned for another five or more years.[52] Nevertheless, at times the stock market does not value a particular strategic investment. The Company Spotlight: Maytag Corporation feature on page 297 describes the investment community's response to Maytag's acquisition of Hoover (in terms of Maytag's stock price).

Many accounting-based measures do, however, encourage a short-term emphasis. Table 10.1 indicates that one of the limitations of ROI as a performance measure is its short-term nature. In theory, ROI is not limited to the short run, but in practice applying this measure to long-term performance often is difficult. Moreover, because managers can manipulate both the numerator (earnings) and

COMPANY SPOTLIGHT

MAYTAG Corporation

Stock Price Drops After Hoover Acquisition

When Maytag Corporation purchased Chicago Pacific (CP) Corporation in order to acquire one of its companies, Hoover, for its international appliance business, its debt soared to $923 million from $134 million just nine months earlier. Maytag's total outstanding shares swelled to 105 million from 75 million during the same period. Although Maytag soon reduced its debt by $200 million with the sale of CP's furniture companies, interest payments leaped to $70 million in 1989 from $20 million in 1988, and its stock price dropped from $26.50 in October 1988 to $20.00 in January 1989. This change was significant for a company that, until eight years earlier, had had no long-term debt!

By April 1993, most of the corporation's shareholders knew how much the company had changed since the days when Maytag sold washing machines as a sideline. Most appreciated management's attempts to build the company. A significant number were concerned, however, that the corporation no longer had the best profit margin in the industry. Most knowledgeable investors knew that return on equity had been a weak spot of the corporation since it first embarked on a strategy of growth through acquisitions. According to an article in *Financial World*: "Return on equity was more than 25% before the Magic Chef merger in 1986, peaked at over 30% in 1988, and was nearly halved to 18.3% in 1989 after the Chicago Pacific acquisition . . . and by 1991 Maytag was earning just 8% on equity."* For the first time since the 1920s, the *1992 Annual Report* showed a net loss.

Commenting on the corporation's poor performance at the April 1993 annual shareholders meeting, CEO Leonard Hadley explained:

> *As we've changed, I know you shareholders have suffered. Additionally, a number of employees have been displaced. In fact, in the last three years, we've reduced employment by 4,500; we've closed plants, delayed salary increases twice and reduced bonuses. . . . Also, I would add that despite disruptions brought about by change, I firmly believe that our underlying strategy is right, our management team is strong and there will be brighter days for us ahead.*

Maytag's common stock was trading in April 1993 at $13¼ per share—far lower than the $20 per share one takeover investor had concluded that Maytag's assets were worth. Some analysts were wondering if the corporation might soon be forced to sell Hoover or have to sell out to a competitor by the end of the decade.

*J. Dubashi, "Taken to the Cleaners," *Financial World* (August 4, 1992), p. 30.

the denominator (investment), an ROI figure may be meaningless. Advertising, maintenance, and research efforts may be reduced. Mergers may be undertaken that will do more for this year's earnings (and next year's paycheck) than for the division's or corporation's future profits. (Studies of 55 firms that engaged in major acquisitions revealed that, even though the firms performed poorly after the acquisition, top management still received significant increases in compensation!)[53] Expensive retooling and plant modernization may be delayed when a manager manipulates figures on production defects and absenteeism.

Efforts to compensate for these distortions tend to create a burdensome accounting control system, which stifles creativity and flexibility and leads to even more questionable "creative accounting" practices.[54] For example, the top management of Regina Corporation, a manufacturer of vacuum cleaners, admitted to the SEC that it had inflated sales, profits, and revenues by omitting from the financial statements one annoying detail—products returned by customers. Although buyers normally return approximately 5% of all vacuum cleaners sold in the United States, Regina's customers were returning 20%–25%, or more than $13 million worth, of Regina's vacuum cleaners! Other tricks to massage the "bottom line" include shipping products on the last day of the year to reduce inventory (thus flooding distributors) and extending (or contracting) years of inventory depreciation either to boost this year's profits to impress the stock market or to decrease profits in order to reduce taxes.[55]

Goal Displacement

Monitoring and measuring performance (if not carefully done) can actually result in a decline in overall corporate performance. **Goal displacement** is the confusion of means with ends and occurs when activities originally intended to help managers attain corporate objectives become ends in themselves—or are adapted to meet ends other than those for which they were intended.[56] Two types of goal displacement are behavior substitution and suboptimization.

Behavior Substitution

Managers tend to focus more of their attention on those behaviors that are clearly measurable than on those that are not.[57] Employees receive little or no reward for cooperation and initiative. However, easy-to-measure activities might have little or no relationship to the desired performance. Rational people, nevertheless, tend to work for the rewards that a system has to offer. Therefore workers will tend to substitute behaviors that are recognized and rewarded for those behaviors that are ignored, without regard to their contribution to goal accomplishment. A U.S. Navy quip sums up this situation: "What you inspect is what you get." If the evaluation and control system of an auto plant rewards the meeting of quantitative goals and pays only lip service to qualitative goals, consumers can expect to get a large number of poorly built cars.

The most frequently mentioned problem with MBO is that the measurement process partially distorts the realities of the job. Objectives are set for areas in which the measurement of accomplishments is relatively easy, such as ROI, increased sales, or reduced cost. But these might not always be the most important areas. This problem becomes crucial in professional, service, or staff activities for which quantitative measurement is difficult. For example, if a divisional manager is achieving all the quantifiable objectives set but, in so doing, alienates the work force, the result could be a long-term, significant drop in the division's performance. If promotions are based strictly on measurable short-term performance results, this manager is likely to be promoted or transferred before the employees' negative attitudes result in complaints to the personnel office, strikes, or sabotage. The law governing the effect of measurement on behavior seems to be that *quantifiable measures drive out nonquantifiable measures.*

Suboptimization

The emphasis in large corporations on developing separate responsibility centers may create some problems for the corporation as a whole. To the extent that a division or functional unit views itself as a separate entity, it might refuse to cooperate with other units or divisions if cooperation could in some way negatively affect its performance evaluation. The competition between divisions to achieve a high ROI may result in one division's refusal to share its new technology or work-process improvements. One division's attempt to optimize the accomplishment of its goals may cause other divisions to fall behind and thus negatively affect overall corporate performance. One common example of this type of suboptimization occurs when a marketing department approves an early shipment date to a customer as a means of getting an order. That commitment forces manufacturing to work overtime to get the order out, raising production costs and reducing manufacturing's overall efficiency. Although marketing might achieve its sales goal, the corporation as a whole might not achieve its expected profitability.

10.5 Guidelines for Proper Control

In designing a control system, top management needs to remember that controls should follow strategy. That is, unless controls ensure the proper use of a strategy to achieve objectives, dysfunctional side effects are likely to undermine completely the implementation of that strategy. The following guidelines are recommended.

1. **Controls should involve only the minimum amount of information** needed to give a reliable picture of events. Too many controls create confusion. Focus on that 20% of the factors that determine 80% of the results.
2. **Controls should monitor only meaningful activities and results,** regardless of measurement difficulty. If cooperation between divisions is important to corporate performance, some form of qualitative or quantitative measure should be established to monitor cooperation.
3. **Controls should be timely** so that corrective action can be taken before it is too late. *Steering controls,* or controls that monitor or measure the factors influencing performance, should be stressed so that advance notice of problems is given.
4. **Controls should be long term as well as short term** because emphasizing only short-term measures is likely to lead to a short-term managerial orientation.
5. **Controls should pinpoint exceptions,** with only those activities or results that fall outside a predetermined tolerance range being identified for attention.

6. **Controls should be used to reward meeting or exceeding standards** rather than to punish failure to meet standards. Heavy punishment of failure will typically result in goal displacement. Managers will falsify reports and lobby for lower standards.

Surprisingly, the best managed companies often have few formal objective controls. They focus on measuring critical success factors and control other factors by means of the corporate culture.[58] When the firm's culture complements and reinforces its strategic orientation, there is little need for an extensive formal control system. In their book, *In Search of Excellence,* T. J. Peters and R. H. Waterman state that "the stronger the culture and the more it was directed toward the marketplace, the less need was there for policy manuals, organization charts, or detailed procedures and rules. In these companies, people way down the line know what they are supposed to do in most situations because the handful of guiding values is crystal clear."[59]

10.6 Strategic Incentive Management

To ensure congruence between the needs of the corporation as a whole and the needs of its employees as individuals, management and the board of directors should develop an incentive program that rewards desired performance. Research confirms the conventional wisdom that, when pay is tied to performance, it motivates higher productivity, and strongly affects both absenteeism and work quality.[60] Studies of compensation plans in all types of companies—manufacturing and service, large and small, growing and declining, in stable and turbulent markets—showed that the higher the percentage of management's compensation that is linked to performance, the greater is the company's profitability.[61] Corporations therefore have developed various types of incentives for executives that range from stock options to cash bonuses. Unfortunately, research consistently reveals that CEO compensation is related more to the size of the corporation than to the size of its profits.[62] The gap between CEO compensation and corporate performance is most noticeable in those corporations with widely dispersed stock ownership and no dominant shareholder group to demand performance-based pay.[63]

However, there does appear to be a trend in U.S. executive compensation toward evaluating and rewarding long-run performance.[64] Long-term incentives made up 36% of the total annual income of CEOs of major U.S. corporations in 1990—an increase from 34% the previous year. The rest of the typical chief executive's annual compensation comprised base salary (39%) and an annual bonus (25%).[65] Although the salary portion of a CEO's compensation usually isn't related to the company's subsequent performance, the relationship between the incentive portion of a CEO's compensation and the company's subsequent ROA and ROE is strong.[66]

Incentive plans should be linked in some way to corporate and divisional strategy. For example, a survey of 600 SBUs indicates that the pay mix associated with

TABLE 10.3 **Weighted-Factor Approach to Strategic Incentive Management**

Strategic Business Unit Category	Factor	Weight
High Growth	Return on assets	10%
	Cash flow	0%
	Strategic-funds programs (developmental expenses)	45%
	Market-share increase	45%
		100%
Medium Growth	Return on assets	25%
	Cash flow	25%
	Strategic-funds programs (developmental expenses)	25%
	Market-share increase	25%
		100%
Low Growth	Return on assets	50%
	Cash flow	50%
	Strategic-funds programs (developmental expenses)	0%
	Market-share increase	0%
		100%

Source: Reprinted by permission of the publisher from "The Performance Measurement and Reward System: Critical to Strategic Management," by Paul J. Stonich, from *Organizational Dynamics* (Winter 1984), p. 51. Copyright © 1984 by American Management Association, New York. All rights reserved.

a growth strategy emphasizes bonuses and other incentives over salary and benefits, whereas the pay mix associated with a maintenance strategy has the opposite emphasis.[67] H. I. Ansoff, an authority on strategic management, proposes that one of the best ways to change corporate culture is to modify formal and informal rewards and incentives.[68] Nevertheless, in one survey of 381 investor-owned utilities, over 50% responded that the linkage between strategic planning and the compensation system was either weak or nonexistent.[69] This finding agrees with those of other studies, indicating that pay-for-performance systems are used only in slightly less than half of large corporations.[70]

The following three approaches are tailored to help match measurements and rewards with explicit strategic objectives and time frames.[71]

1. **Weighted-factor method:** This method is particularly appropriate for measuring and rewarding the performance of top SBU managers and group-level executives when performance factors and their importance vary from one SBU to another. The measurements used by one corporation might contain the following variations: the performance of high-growth SBUs measured in terms of market share, sales growth, designated future payoff, and progress on several future-oriented strategic projects; the performance of low-growth SBUs, in contrast, measured in terms of ROI and cash generation; and the performance of medium-growth SBUs measured for a combination of these factors. (See Table 10.3.)

TABLE 10.4 **Strategic-Funds Approach to an SBU's Profit-and-Loss Statement**

Sales	$12,300,000
Cost of sales	6,900,000
Gross margin	$5,400,000
General and administrative expenses	−3,700,000
Operating profit (return on sales)	$1,700,000
Strategic funds (development expenses)	−1,000,000
Pretax profit	$700,000

Source: Reprinted by permission of the publisher from "The Performance Measurement and Reward System: Critical to Strategic Management," by Paul J. Stonich, from *Organizational Dynamics* (Winter 1984), p. 51.

2. **Long-term evaluation method:** This method compensates managers for achieving objectives set over a multiyear period. An executive is promised some company stock or "performance units" (convertible into money) in amounts to be based on long-term performance. An executive committee, for example, might set a particular objective in terms of growth in earnings per share during a five-year period. Awards would be contingent on the corporation's meeting that objective within the designated time limit. Any executive who leaves the corporation before the objective is met receives nothing. The typical emphasis on stock price makes this approach more applicable to top management than to business unit managers.
3. **Strategic-funds method:** This method encourages executives to look at developmental expenses differently from current operating expenses. The accounting statement for a corporate unit enters strategic funds as a separate entry below the current ROI. Distinguishing between funds consumed in the generation of current revenues and funds invested in the future of the business therefore is possible. Hence the manager can be evaluated on both a short- and a long-term basis and has an incentive to invest strategic funds in the future. (See Table 10.4.)

According to P. J. Stonich, "An effective way to achieve the desired strategic results through a reward system is to combine the weighted-factor, long-term evaluation, and strategic-funds approaches."[72] To do so, *first,* segregate strategic funds from short-term funds, as is done in the strategic-funds method. *Second,* develop a weighted-factor chart for each SBU. *Third,* measure performance on the basis of the pretax profit indicated by the strategic-funds approach, the weighted factors, and the long-term evaluation of SBU and corporate performance. General Electric and Westinghouse are two of the firms that use a version of these measures.

In Conclusion . . .

Seitz Corporation of Torrington, Connecticut, was a family-owned company that grew from a garage-based tool shop into a major supplier of the gears and bearings that circulate paper in copiers and printers. The company provided components for all of Wang's dot-matrix printers. In 1980, employment was at 250 with annual sales of $12 million. By the mid 1980s, however, laser and ink jet printers were starting to replace dot-matrix printers. Seitz was forced to lay off all but 80 employees as sales dropped to $5 million. Facing greater losses, management used benchmarking to embark on a major overhaul. It first identified firms and activities to study and then adopted several of the practices that it had examined. Among those adopted were techniques to reduce new-product to market cycle time and just-in-time (JIT) manufacturing. The company reduced cycle time from about nine weeks to three weeks. The JIT approach cut inventories, thus increasing floor space by 30%. With these and other improvements, Seitz's sales grew by 25%–30% annually. Annual revenue reached a record $21 million in 1992 and employment climbed back to 190 people. According to Marketing Manager Sharon LeGault, "We attribute all of that to benchmarking."[73] This is an example of how benchmarking was used to improve how the company implemented its turnaround strategy.

Points to Remember

- The basic evaluation and control system comprises five steps that require the strategic manager to (1) determine what to measure, (2) establish standards for performance, (3) measure actual performance, (4) compare actual performance with the standard, and (5) take corrective action. The first step is crucial because managers tend to measure only those things that are easy to measure instead of what needs to be measured.
- Measures should relate to quantity, quality, and timing, and should be objectively verifiable.
- Strategic, tactical, and operational controls form a hierarchy of control similar to the hierarchy of strategy.
- Behavior controls are most relevant for situations in which performance results are difficult to measure and a clear cause–effect relationship exists between activities and results. Output controls are most appropriate for agreed-upon output measures and when no clear cause–effect relationship exists between activities and results.
- Among the many measures of corporate performance are stakeholder measures, value-added measures, shareholder measures (economic value added, in particular), performance objectives, and strategic audits. Business and functional units often are evaluated as responsibility centers. Benchmarking is an excellent way to compare a company's or business unit's products, services, or practices against the toughest competitors or best-in-class firms.

- Critical success factors should determine what information needs to be collected for which units as part of a strategic information system.
- Some of the negative side effects of evaluation and control are the tendency toward short-term orientation and goal displacement. A control system needs to be monitored to minimize these side effects.
- The higher the percentage of management's compensation that is linked to performance, the greater is the company's profitability. Therefore long-term incentives need to be used to reward strategic managers for effectively formulating and implementing strategy. Some of the recommended incentives are the weighted-factor, long-term evaluation, and strategic-funds methods.
- A proper evaluation and control system should complete the loop shown in the strategic management model. It should feed back information important not only to the implementation of strategy, but also to the initial formulation of strategy. In terms of the strategic decision-making process depicted in Fig. 2.3, the data coming from evaluation and control are the basis for Step 1—evaluating current performance results. Because of this feedback, evaluation and control are both the beginning and the end of the strategic management process.

Discussion Questions

1. Is Fig. 10.1 a realistic model of the evaluation and control process? Why or why not?
2. Why bother with value-added measures, shareholder value, or a stakeholder's scorecard? Isn't evaluating a corporation and its SBUs simpler if standard measures such as ROI or earnings per share are used? Why or why not?
3. What are the differences among strategic, tactical, and operational controls?
4. What are some examples of behavior controls? Output controls?
5. Is EVA an improvement over ROI, ROE, or EPS? Why or why not?
6. What is the difference between performance objectives and critical success factors?
7. What are the major types of responsibility centers? Briefly describe each type of center.
8. How much faith can a division or SBU manager place in a transfer price as a substitute for a market price in measuring a profit center's performance?
9. Is benchmarking just another fad or is it really useful for all firms? Why?
10. Why are goal displacement and short-run orientation likely side effects of the monitoring of performance? What can a corporation do to avoid them?
11. Is the evaluation and control process appropriate for a corporation that emphasizes creativity? Are control and creativity compatible? Explain.
12. What are the guidelines for proper control?

Notes

1. G. S. Odiorne, "Measuring the Unmeasurable: Setting Standards for Management Performance," *Business Horizons* (July/August 1987), p. 73. Copyright © 1987 by the Foundation for the School of Business at Indiana University. Used with permission.
2. P. B. Carroll, "The Failures of Central Planning—at IBM," *Wall Street Journal* (January 28, 1993), p. A14.
3. J. C. Camillus, *Strategic Planning and Management Control* (Lexington, Mass.: D. C. Heath, Lexington Books, 1986), p. 11.
4. E. F. Harrison, "Strategic Control at the CEO Level," *Long Range Planning* (December 1991), pp. 78–87.
5. J. A. Schmidt, "The Strategic Review," *Planning Review* (July/August 1988), pp. 14–19.
6. P. Lorange, M. F. S. Morton, and S. Ghoshal, *Strategic Control* (St. Paul, Minn.: West, 1986), pp. 11–14.
7. W. E. Deming, *Out of the Crisis* (Cambridge, Mass.: M.I.T. Center for Advanced Engineering Study, 1986).
8. Lorange, et al., p. 124.
9. J. R. Meredith, "Strategic Control of Factory Automation," *Long Range Planning* (December 1987), p. 109.
10. R. M. S. Wilson, "Corporate Strategy and Management Control," *International Review of Strategic Management,* edited by D. E. Hussey (New York: John Wiley & Sons, 1991), pp. 115–166.
11. W. G. Ouchi and M. A. Maguire, "Organizational Control: Two Functions," *Administrative Science Quarterly* (December 1975), pp. 559–569.
12. V. Cerullo, "The Appropriate Use of Return on Investment," *International Journal of Management* (June 1991), pp. 518–526.
13. B. C. Reimann reporting on a presentation by W. H. Quick to The Conference Board, "A Session For Students of Shareholder Value Creation," *Planning Review* (May/June 1990), pp. 43–44.
14. W. Mardis, "Managing for Shareholder Value," *Handbook of Business Strategy,* edited by H. E. Glass (Boston: Warren, Gorham and Lamont, 1991), pp. 3.1–3.21.
15. R. E. Freeman, *Strategic Management: A Stakeholder Approach* (Boston: Pitman, 1984), pp. 177–181.
16. C. W. Hofer, "ROVA: A New Measure for Assessing Organizational Performance," in *Advances in Strategic Management,* Vol. 2, edited by R. Lamb (Greenwich, Conn.: JAI Press, 1983), pp. 43–55.
17. J. Bryant, "Assessing Company Strength Using Added Value," *Long Range Planning* (June 1989), pp. 34–44.
18. W. Mardis, "Management for Shareholder Value," *Handbook of Business Strategy,* 2nd ed., edited by H. E. Glass (Boston: Warren, Gorham and Lamont, 1991), p. 3.7.
19. B. Reimann, *Managing for Value: A Guide to Value-Based Strategic Management* (Oxford, Ohio: The Planning Forum, 1990); F. V. McCrory and P. G. Gerstberger, "The New Math of Performance Measurement," *Journal of Business Strategy* (March/April 1992), pp. 33–38.
20. Mardis, p. 3.13.
21. A. Rappaport, "Selecting Strategies That Create Shareholder Value," *Harvard Business Review* (May/June 1981), p. 149.
22. S. Tully, "The Real Key to Creating Wealth," *Fortune* (September 20, 1993), p. 38.
23. S. J. Burchman and C. E. Schneier, "Assessing CEO Performance: It Goes Beyond the Numbers," *Directors and Boards* (Winter 1989), pp. 26–30.
24. J. S. Lublin, "Corporate Chiefs Polish Their Relations with Directors," *Wall Street Journal* (October 15, 1993), p. B1.
25. P. Lorange, "Monitoring Strategic Progress and Ad Hoc Strategy Modification," in *Strategic Management Frontiers,* edited by J. H. Grant (Greenwich, Conn.: JAI Press, 1988), pp. 261–285.
26. V. Govindarajan, "A Contingency Approach to Strategy Implementation at the Business-Unit Level: Integrating Administrative Mechanisms with Strategy," *Academy of Management Journal* (December 1988), pp. 828–853.
27. V. Govindarajan and J. Fisher, "Strategy, Control, Systems, and Resource Sharing: Effects on Business-Unit Performance," *Academy of Management Journal* (June 1990), pp. 259–285.
28. Ibid., p. 280.

29. This discussion is based on R. N. Anthony, J. Dearden, and R. F. Vancil, *Management Control Systems* (Homewood, Ill.: Irwin, 1972), pp. 200–203.
30. Z. U. Khan, S. K. Chawla, M. F. Smith, and M. F. Sharif, "Transfer Pricing Policy Issues in Europe 1992," *International Journal of Management* (September 1992), pp. 230–241.
31. Lorange, et al., p. 69. Camillus, pp. 193–195.
32. Camillus, p. 196; McCrory and Gerstberger, p. 34.
33. Tully, p. 40.
34. J. R. Galbraith and R. K. Kazanjian, *Strategy Implementation: Structure, Systems and Process* (St. Paul, Minn.: West, 1986), pp. 85–86.
35. M. Hergert and D. Morris, "Accounting Data for Value Chain Analysis," *Strategic Management Journal* (March–April 1989), pp. 175–188.
36. H. Rothman, "You Need Not Be Big to Benchmark," *Nation's Business* (December 1992), p. 64.
37. J. Main, "How to Steal the Best Ideas Around," *Fortune* (October 19, 1992), pp. 102–106.
38. O. Port and G. Smith, "Beg, Borrow, and Benchmark," *Business Week* (November 30, 1992), pp. 74–75.
39. G. Fuchsberg, "Here's Help in Finding Corporate Role Models," *Wall Street Journal* (June 1, 1993), p. B1.
40. J. A. Turner and H. C. Lucas, Jr., "Developing Strategic Information Systems," in *Handbook of Business Strategy,* edited by W. D. Guth (Boston: Warren, Gorham and Lamont, 1985), p. 21.2.
41. N. Gross, "Inquest for International Harvester," *Planning Review* (July–August 1987), p. 9.
42. J. Rockart, "Chief Executives Define Their Own Data Needs," *Harvard Business Review* (March–April 1979); P. V. Jenster, "Using Critical Success Factors in Planning," *Long Range Planning* (August 1987), pp. 102–109.
43. Vilfredo Pareto, a nineteenth-century Italian economist, originated what is sometimes called the 80–20 rule, meaning that 20% of the known variables will produce 80% of the results. Business executives have found that the rule applies to many areas of their companies. For example, Illinois Tool Works found that 80% of the business at any one plant tends to come from 20% of the customers—people who order only a handful of products but in huge quantities. Bank executives report a similar phenomenon regarding customer deposits. See R. Henkoff, "The Ultimate Nuts & Bolts Co.," *Fortune* (July 16, 1990), pp. 70–73.
44. Y. P. Freund, "Critical Success Factors," *Planning Review* (July/August 1988), p. 20.
45. W. R. King, "Strategic Management Decision Support Systems," in *Strategic Management Frontiers,* edited by J. H. Grant (Greenwich, Conn.: JAI Press, 1988) pp. 237–259.
46. E. M. Koerner, "Integrating Information Systems for Competitive Advantage at Merrill Lynch," *Long Range Planning* (April 1990), pp. 27–34.
47. T. R. Furey, "How Information Power Can Improve Service Quality," *Planning Review* (May/June 1991), pp. 24–26.
48. For other examples of the use of computerized strategic information systems to gain competitive advantage, see R. I. Benjamin, D. W. de Long, and M. F. S. Morton, "Electronic Data Interchange: How Much Competitive Advantage?" *Long Range Planning* (February 1990), pp. 29–40; B. C. Reimann, "Strategic Management in an Electronic Age: Exploiting the Power of Information Technology," *International Journal of Management* (September 1987), pp. 438–451.
49. L. G. Hrebiniak and W. F. Joyce, *Implementing Strategy* (New York: Macmillan, 1984), pp. 198–199.
50. R. M. Hodgetts and M. S. Wortman, *Administrative Policy,* 2nd ed. (New York: John Wiley & Sons, 1980), p. 128.
51. S. B. Graves and S. A. Waddock, "Institutional Ownership and Control: Implications for Long-term Corporate Strategy," *Academy of Management Executive* (February 1990), pp. 75–83.
52. J. R. Wooldridge and C. C. Snow, "Stock Market Reaction to Strategic Investment Decisions," *Strategic Management Journal* (September 1990), pp. 353–363.
53. D. R. Schmidt and K. L. Fowler, "Post-Acquisition Financial Performance and Executive Compensation," *Strategic Management Journal* (November–December 1990), pp. 559–569.

54. T. A Stewart, "Why Budgets Are Bad for Business," *Fortune* (June 4, 1990), pp. 179–190.
55. G. Hector, "Cute Tricks on the Bottom Line," *Fortune* (April 24, 1990), pp. 193–200; C. K. Bart, "Budgeting Gamesmanship," *Academy of Management Executive* (November 1988), pp. 285–294.
56. H. R. Bobbitt, Jr., R. H. Breinholt, R. H. Doktor, and J. P. McNaul, *Organizational Behavior,* 2nd ed. (Englewood Cliffs, N.J.: Prentice-Hall, 1978), p. 99.
57. J. C. Worthy and R. P. Neuschel, *Emerging Issues in Corporate Governance* (Evanston, Ill.: Northwestern University Press, 1984), p. 84.
58. Ouchi calls this "clan control." See W. Ouchi, *Theory Z* (Reading, Mass.: Addison-Wesley, 1981).
59. T. J. Peters and R. H. Waterman, *In Search of Excellence* (New York: HarperCollins, 1982), pp. 75–76.
60. E. E. Lawler III, *Strategic Pay* (San Francisco: Jossey-Bass, 1990), p. 13; R. L. Heneman, *Merit Pay* (Reading, Mass.: Addison-Wesley, 1992).
61. H. E. Glass and T. P. Flannery, "Pay for Performance at the Business Unit Level," *Handbook of Business Strategy, 1991/92 Yearbook,* edited by H. E. Glass and M. Hovde (Boston: Warren, Gorham and Lamont, 1991) pp. 20.1–20.10; H. D. Friedeck, "Changing Working Arrangements and Variable Pay: Does Pay-for-Performance Really Work?" in *Handbook of Business Strategy, 1989/1990 Yearbook* (Boston: Warren, Gorham and Lamont, 1989), pp. 20.1–20.13.
62. J. Fisher and V. Govindarajan, "Profit Center Manager Compensation: An Examination of Market, Political and Human Capital Factors," *Strategic Management Journal* (March 1992), pp. 205–217; R. A. Lambert, D. F. Larcher, and K. Weigelt, "How Sensitive Is Executive Compensation to Organization Size?" *Strategic Management Journal* (July 1991), pp. 395–402; M. C. Jensen and K. J. Murphy, "CEO Incentives—It's Not How Much You Pay, But How," *Harvard Business Review* (May–June 1990), pp. 138–153.
63. L. R. Gomez-Mejia, H. Tosi, and T. Hinkin, "Managerial Control, Performance, and Executive Compensation," *Academy of Management Journal* (March 1987), pp. 51–70.
64. R. Ferracone, "More Executive Pay Linked to Company Performance," *Journal of Business Strategy* (May/June 1990), pp. 63–64.
65. L. Barton, "This Year's Model," *Wall Street Journal* (April 17, 1991), p. R5.
66. B. Gerhart and G. T. Milkovich, "Organizational Differences in Managerial Compensation and Financial Performance," *Academy of Management Journal* (December 1990), pp. 663–691; S. Finkelstein and D. C. Hambrick, "Chief Executive Compensation: A Study of the Intersection of Markets and Political Processes," *Strategic Management Journal* (March–April 1989), pp. 121–134.
67. D. B. Balkin and L. R. Gomez-Mejia, "Matching Compensation and Organizational Strategies," *Strategic Management Journal* (February 1990), pp. 153–169.
68. H. I. Ansoff, "Strategic Management of Technology," *Journal of Business Strategy* (Winter 1987), p. 37.
69. J. Whalen and J. J. Sisson, "How To Realize the Promise of Strategic Planning," *Journal of Business Strategy* (January/February 1993), pp. 31–36.
70. "Pay-for-Performance Plans Put a Premium on Long-Term Gains," *Wall Street Journal* (September 1, 1992), p. A1.
71. P. J. Stonich, "The Performance Measurement and Reward System: Critical to Strategic Management," *Organizational Dynamics* (Winter 1984), pp. 45–57.
72. Ibid., p. 53.
73. Rothman, p. 64.

Strategic Issues in Multinational Corporations

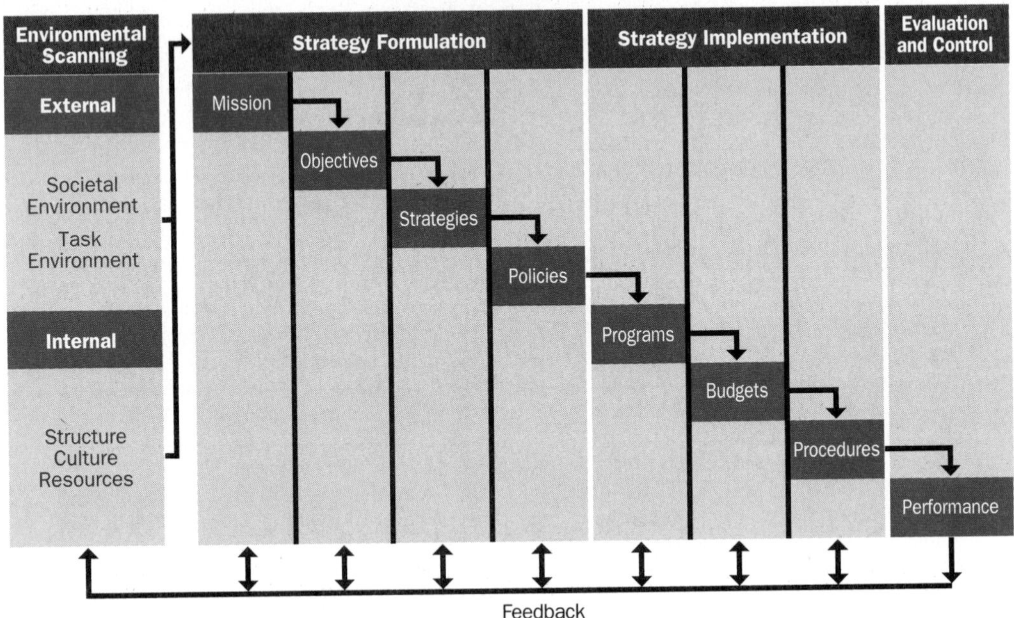

> *Think globally, act locally.*[1]
> [Harry Reid, Chairman, Ogilvy & Mather, Europe]

Half of all the citizens of Mexico are under the age of 18. To the management of the Chicago-based Dean Foods Company, this fact meant that Mexico was a potential market for milk and milk products. The country has withstood a chronic shortage of fresh milk because of government-set price ceilings, which reduced the incentive for local producers to provide the product. When trade barriers began dropping in 1991, Dean's El Paso dairy teamed with a Mexican distributor to truck milk and ice cream to border towns. By 1992, Mexico consumed one-third of that dairy's output. Dean also began purchasing broccoli and cauliflower from Mexico for its processing plants in Texas and New Mexico. The company assigned two of its corporate staff to research the Mexican market. Based on their findings, Dean Foods planned to emphasize dairy products first and then vegetables. The company would eventually like to sell products that aren't native to Mexico, such as canned sweet corn, peas, and green beans.

Although Dean Foods could buy an existing Mexican dairy or simply export products from the United States, the company decided to ask its current dairy products distributor if it would be interested in a joint venture. Dean's managers toured the distributor's facilities, and the distributor's managers toured one of Dean Foods' plants in Rockford, Illinois. Even if the joint venture became a reality, huge problems would still exist. For example, only about half of all households in Mexico had refrigerators. Instead of selling milk in gallon jugs, Dean Foods would need to use small cartons. Some supermarkets turned off their electricity overnight. Dean Foods would have to set up refrigerated cases in supermarkets and pay the stores to maintain the electricity 24 hours a day. Dairy farms were scarce in Mexico, so Dean Foods would probably have to encourage the development of new ones. The company also would probably have to establish special quality control standards, as 40% of all milk sold in the country was unpasteurized.

For Howard Dean, CEO of the company, the allure of Mexico was not in shifting plants to cut labor costs but in the market potential for his products. "We've got to move quickly. The opportunity is now," concluded the grandson of the company's founder.[2] Dean Foods isn't alone in its expansion into Mexico in cooperation with a Mexican firm. Within months of the passage of the North American Free Trade Agreement in the United States, U.S. and Mexican companies initiated dozens of joint ventures.

11.1 The Multinational Corporation (MNC)

The multinational corporation (MNC) is a special type of international firm. Any U.S. company can call itself *international* if it has a small branch office in, say, Juarez or Toronto. An international company is one that engages in any combination of activities—from exporting/importing to full-scale manufacturing—in foreign countries. In contrast, the **multinational corporation** is a highly developed international company with worldwide involvement and a global perspective in its management and decision making. A more specific definition of an MNC is suggested by W. A. Dymsza.[3]

1. Although a multinational corporation may not do business in every region of the world, its *decision makers consider opportunities globally.*
2. A *considerable portion of an MNC's assets are invested internationally.* This could occur when 20% of a company's assets are in other countries, or it could be when operations in other nations account for at least 35% of the corporation's total sales and profits.
3. The corporation *engages in international production and operates plants in several countries.* These plants may range from assembly to fully integrated facilities.
4. Managerial *decision making is based on a worldwide perspective.* The international business is no longer a sideline or segregated activity. International operations are integrated into the corporation's overall business.

FIGURE 11.1 **Continuum of International Industries**

Multidomestic ◄——	——► *Global*
Industry in which companies tailor their products to the specific needs of consumers in a particular country. • Retailing • Insurance • Banking	Industry in which companies manufacture and sell the same products, with only minor adjustments made for individual countries around the world. • Automobiles • Tires • Television sets

M. E. Porter proposes that multinationals operate in world industries that vary on a continuum from multidomestic to global, as shown in Fig. 11.1.[4] **Multidomestic industries** are specific to each country or group of countries and usually are collections of essentially domestic industries, such as retailing and insurance. The activities in an MNC's subsidiary in this type of industry essentially are independent of the activities of the MNC's subsidiaries in other countries. In each country the MNC tailors its products or services to the specific needs of those particular consumers. In contrast, **global industries** operate worldwide, with MNCs making only small adjustments for country-specific circumstances. A global industry is one in which an MNC's activities in one country are affected significantly by its activities in other countries. Multinational corporations produce products or services in various locations throughout the world and sell them all over the world, making only minor adjustments for specific country requirements. Examples of global industries are commercial aircraft, television sets, semiconductors, copiers, automobiles, watches, and tires. The largest industrial corporations in the world in terms of dollar sales, for the most part, are multinational corporations operating in global industries.

The factors that tend to determine whether an industry will be primarily multidomestic or primarily global are (1) the *pressure for coordination* within the multinational corporations operating in that industry and (2) the *pressure for local responsiveness* on the part of individual country markets. If the pressure for coordination is strong and the pressure for local responsiveness is weak for multinational corporations within a particular industry, that industry will tend to become global. But, when the pressure for local responsiveness is strong and the pressure for coordination is weak for multinational corporations in an industry, that industry will tend to be multidomestic. Between these two extremes lie many industries with varying characteristics of both multidomestic and global industries.[5]

11.2 International Trade: Competitive Advantage versus Comparative Advantage

The economic theory underlying the concept of free international trade among nations is that of comparative advantage. Recently, this concept has been challenged by the notion that it is com*pet*itive advantage, not com*par*ative advantage, that determines a nation's wealth.

Comparative Advantage of Nations

Adam Smith originally proposed the theory of **absolute advantage,** which states that, because certain countries are able to produce certain goods more efficiently than others, they should specialize in the production of those goods in which they have an advantage. A country could then use the excess of its specialized production to buy more imports than it could otherwise produce. David Ricardo expanded Smith's theory by proposing a theory of **comparative advantage.** This theory states that even if one country has an absolute advantage in producing all the products it wants, it will still gain from international trade if it specializes in those products that it can produce more efficiently than other products. The Key Theory capsule on page 312 presents examples of absolute and comparative advantage.

For comparative advantage to work, however, a country must be free to trade with any other country in the world. As a result, economists traditionally have argued that free trade (unencumbered by tariffs and other barriers) is the system most likely to provide maximum benefit to all. To encourage international free trade, the more than 100 member nations of the *General Agreement on Tariffs and Trade (GATT)* have established a basic set of rules under which trade negotiations can take place. For example, following the "most favored nation" clause means that if a member nation grants a tariff reduction for an item to one country, it must grant the same concession to all other countries of the world.[6]

Competitive Advantage of Nations

The theory of comparative advantage rests on the assumption that the factors of production are immobile between nations and thus do not influence the flow of international trade. Today, of course, people, capital, and technology are mobile, traveling the globe freely—and comparative advantage moves with them.[7] Porter suggests that **competitive advantage** is more useful than comparative advantage in explaining current international trade and development. He identifies four factors that create competitive advantage for nations (see Fig. 11.2).[8]

1. **Factor conditions:** The nation's position in the basic factors of production, such as labor or infrastructure, necessary to compete in a given industry. For example, Saudi Arabia's huge supply of high-quality oil provides its oil companies with a competitive advantage in the global petroleum industry.
2. **Demand conditions:** The nature of home demand (demand within the specific nation under consideration) for the industry's product or service. If a country's consumers are very sophisticated (like the Japanese in home electronics or Americans in software), companies operating within that country will be forced to produce advanced, high-quality, but reasonably priced products in order to succeed in the home country. Firms that are able to satisfy these demanding consumers will have a significant advantage competing in other parts of the world with MNCs not having this experience.
3. **Related and supporting industries:** The presence or absence in the nation of supplier industries and related industries that are internationally competitive. The United States currently is the leader in computers and software partially because of places such as California's "Silicon Valley" that provide domestic

Examples of Absolute and Comparative Advantage

Suppose that a country produces 1 million bushels of corn and 5 million bushels of beans each year, but its people want more corn. Should it simply plant more corn and less beans? This solution seems reasonable until we note that the soil and water are much better for growing beans than corn. Each acre planted yields twice as large a bean crop as a corn crop. The same amount of work is required, and the seeds, fertilizer, and other costs are the same for the farmers regardless of the crop planted. Suppose that a neighboring country has different soil and on every acre planted is able to produce twice as much corn as beans.

The concept of **absolute advantage** in international trade suggests that, when both countries are considered, the first country has an advantage over the second country in producing beans but that the second has an advantage over the first in producing corn. The logical conclusion is that the first country should specialize in producing beans (where it has absolute advantage) and the second should plant only corn (where it also has absolute advantage). The result would be that the first country would produce 7 million bushels of beans each year and no corn (with the 2 to 1 advantage of beans to corn, the 1 million bushels of corn would be replaced by 2 million bushels of beans). The reverse would be true in the second country. If the countries are able to trade freely with each other, both countries will be able to have more corn and beans if they each specialize in the crop that gives it the advantage, than if both countries try to produce both crops.

Therefore, in answer to the question posed earlier, if a country wants more corn but has an absolute advantage in the production of beans, it should plant more beans. The bean excess can be exported to another country in exchange for more corn than the first country could ever produce with the same resources.

What happens, however, when the first country can produce more corn and beans per acre planted than can its neighboring country? Is there any benefit to trade? According to the concept of **comparative advantage,** it still makes sense to specialize so long as the first country is able to grow more of one crop than another crop per acre planted. As an analogy, suppose that the best architect in town also happens to be the best carpenter. Would it make sense for him to build his own house? Certainly not, because he can earn more money per hour by devoting all his time to being an architect even though he has to employ a carpenter less skillful than himself to build the house. In the same manner, the first country will gain if it concentrates its resources on the production of the commodity that it can produce most efficiently. It will earn enough money from the export of that commodity to still import what it needs from its less efficient neighbor country.

FIGURE 11.2 **Determinants of National Competitive Advantage**

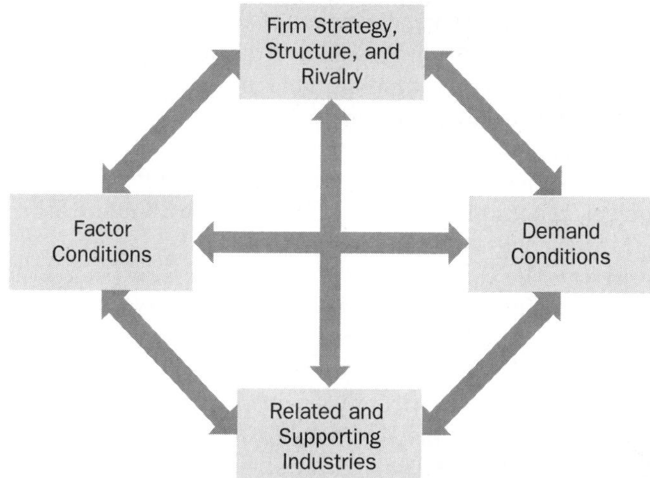

Source: Reprinted with permission of The Free Press, an imprint of Simon & Schuster, from *The Competitive Advantage of Nations* by Michael E. Porter, p. 72. Copyright © 1990 by Michael Porter.

computer companies with the kind of knowledgeable scientists and technicians and innovative components that determine computer performance.

4. **Firm strategy, structure, and rivalry:** The conditions in the nation governing how companies are created, organized, and managed and the nature of domestic rivalry. For example, state-owned enterprises are becoming privatized in most nations because governments are increasingly realizing that state-owned companies cannot successfully compete internationally if the companies are forced to follow inefficient home-country government practices and regulations regarding employment and pricing.[9]

According to Porter, "Gaining advantage in the first place requires a new approach to competing, whether it is perceiving and then exploiting a factor advantage, discovering an underserved segment, creating new product features, or changing the process by which a product is made. . . . The determinants of the 'diamond' [depicted in Fig. 11.2] and the interactions among them create the forces that shape the likelihood, direction, and speed of improvement and innovation by a nation's firms in an industry."[10]

Porter further suggests that nations evolve through **four stages of competitive development,** reflecting the sources of advantage of a nation's firms in international competition and the nature and extent of internationally successful industries.

- **Stage 1—Factor driven:** Industries within the nation draw their advantage almost solely from the basic factors of production. For example, the huge supply of cheap oil drives the success of oil companies in the Middle East. In this stage, nations that want to advance to the next stage are concerned with the process of technology transfer. Here, **international technology transfer** does not refer to the process of taking new technology from the lab to the marketplace (as defined in Chapter 5) but to the movement of sophisticated technology from an economically advanced country to a less developed country.

- **Stage 2—Investment driven:** Foreign technology and methods are not just applied (as in Stage 1) but improved on. Competitive advantages result from improving basic factor conditions and firm strategy, structure, and rivalry. Korea, for example, has invested heavily in shipbuilding to stretch well beyond its factor advantages in ocean harbors (a factor shared with many other nations) and gain worldwide competitive advantage.
- **Stage 3—Innovation driven:** The full "diamond" (Fig. 11.2) is in place in a wide range of industries that support and reinforce each other. For example, the steel, electronics, and plastics industries, among others, are needed to support the development of a successful automobile industry. Firms in this stage not only borrow and improve technology from firms in other nations, they actually create new innovations. The United Kingdom achieved this stage in the first half of the nineteenth century. The United States, Germany, and Sweden did so about the beginning of the twentieth century. Japan achieved this stage during the 1970s.
- **Stage 4—Wealth driven:** According to Porter, nations pass through the first three stages of competitive development if they are willing and able to sustain the process of upgrading national competitive advantage. In Stage 4 the driving force is the wealth accumulated in the earlier stages. This stage thus leads ultimately to economic decline as individual firms and then industries lose their competitive advantages—costs rise, quality drops, and innovation slows. The range of industries in which firms can sustain competitive advantage narrows. During the 1970s, for example, U.S. firms in the steel, auto, and electronics industries lost many of their advantages to Japanese companies. In the mid 1990s, the still-strong U.S. computer and aerospace industries faced strong competition worldwide. Even the strong financial institutions (characteristic of wealth-driven nations) of the United Kingdom and the United States were being challenged. According to Porter, Stage 4 decline isn't inevitable. Government policies supporting entrepreneurial ventures, reemphasizing societal work values, and fostering major technological advances can stop the decline of a wealth-driven economy.[11]

11.3 International Issues in Environmental Scanning

Environmental scanning, the first part of the strategic management process, is especially important when managers consider international strategies. The simplest way to begin the scanning process is to do a SWOT analysis.

Scanning for International Opportunities and Threats

The dominant consideration in the management of an organization operating internationally is the external environment. For each country or group of countries

TABLE 11.1 **Some Important Variables in International Societal Environments**

Economic	Technological	Political-Legal	Sociocultural
Economic development	Regulations on technology transfer	Form of government	Customs, norms, values
Per capita income	Energy availability/cost	Political ideology	Language
Climate	Natural resource availability	Tax laws	Demographics
GDP trends	Transportation network	Stability of government	Life expectancies
Monetary and fiscal policies	Skill level of work force	Government attitude toward foreign companies	Social institutions
Unemployment level	Patent-trademark protection	Regulations on foreign ownership of assets	Status symbols
Currency convertibility	Information-flow infrastructure	Strength of opposition groups	Life-style
Wage levels		Trade regulations	Religious beliefs
Nature of competition		Protectionist sentiment	Attitudes toward foreigners
Membership in regional economic associations		Foreign policies	Literacy level
		Terrorist activity	
		Legal system	

in which a company operates, management must confront an entirely new societal environment having different economic, technological, political–legal, and sociocultural variables. The type of relationship a multinational corporation can have with each factor in its task environment varies from one country or region to another. International societal environments vary so greatly that a corporation's internal environment and strategic management process must be very flexible. Cultural trends in Germany, for example, have resulted in the inclusion of worker representatives in corporate strategic planning. Differences in societal environments strongly affect the ways in which an MNC conducts its marketing, financial, manufacturing, and other functional activities. Table 11.1 lists some of the variables to be monitored in various international societal environments. For example, the existence of regional economic associations such as the European Community and the North American Free Trade Zone have a significant impact on the competitive "rules of the game" both for MNCs operating in and MNCs wanting to enter these areas. Note how the variables listed in Table 11.1 for an international societal environment differ from those listed earlier in Table 4.1, for a domestic societal environment.

Before a company plans its strategy for a particular international location, it must scan the societal and task environment(s) in question for opportunities and threats and compare them with its own organizational strengths and weaknesses. For example, if a company wants to operate successfully in a global industry such as automobiles, tires, electronics, or watches, it must be prepared to establish a significant presence in the three developed areas of the world known collectively as the Triad. Coined by Kenichi Ohmae, Managing Director of the Tokyo office of McKinsey & Company, Triad refers to Japan, North America, and Western

Europe, which now form a single market with common needs.[12] Arguing that consumer behavior is influenced more by their educational background and disposable income than by ethnic characteristics, Ohmae argues that strategic managers of MNCs must treat the inhabitants of the Triad as a single race of consumers with shared needs and aspirations. The decision by the members of the European Community (in conjunction with the European Free Trade Association) to allow the free movement of goods and people throughout Western Europe certainly supports Ohmae's argument.

Focusing on the Triad is essential for an MNC pursuing success in a global industry, according to Ohmae, because nearly 90% of all high-value–added, high-technology manufactured goods are produced and consumed in North America, Western Europe, and Japan. Hence international investments and strategic alliances are concentrated among the Triad countries.[13] Ideally, a company should have a significant presence in each of these regions so that it can produce and market its products simultaneously in all three areas. Otherwise, it will lose competitive advantage to Triad-oriented MNCs. No longer can an MNC develop and market a new product in one part of the world before it exports it to other developed countries.

In searching for an advantageous market or manufacturing location, a multinational corporation must gather and evaluate data on strategic factors in many countries and regions. It must be aware of the many regional economic units ranging from the European Community to the North American Free Trade Zone to the southern common market, Mercosur, composed of Argentina, Brazil, Paraguay, and Uruguay. Because of its global perspective, an MNC might use comparative advantage to its benefit by making machine parts in Brazil, assembling them as engines in Germany, installing the engines in auto bodies in Italy, and shipping completed cars to the United States for sale. This strategy reduces the risk to the MNC of operating in only one country but exposes it to a series of smaller risks in more countries. Therefore multinational corporations must be able to deal with political and economic risk in many diverse countries and regions.

Some firms, such as American Can Company and Mitsubishi Trading Company, develop elaborate information networks and computerized systems to evaluate and rank investment risks. Small companies can hire outside consultants such as Chicago's Associated Consultants International or Boston's Arthur D. Little, Inc., to provide political risk assessments. Among the many systems that exist to assess political and economic risks are the Political System Stability Index, the Business Environment Risk Index, Business International's Country Assessment Service, and Frost and Sullivan's World Political Risk Forecasts.[14] (A summary of Frost and Sullivan's risk index is published annually in either the March/April or May/June issue of *Planning Review.*) Business International provides subscribers continuously updated information on conditions in 63 countries. Boston-based International Strategies offers an *Export Hotline* (800 USA-XPORT) that faxes information to callers for only the cost of the call.[15] Regardless of the source of data, a firm must develop its own method of assessing risk. It must decide on its most important risk factors and then assign weights to each.[16]

Scanning for International Strengths and Weaknesses

Any company desiring to move into the international arena will need to assess its own strengths and weaknesses. An organization's chances for success are enhanced if it possesses or can develop the following capabilities.[17]

1. **Technological lead:** An innovative approach or a new product or a new process gives a firm a short-term monopolistic position.
2. **A strong trade name:** If a well-known product has snob appeal, a higher profit margin can cover initial entry costs.
3. **Advantage of scale:** A large corporation has the advantage of low unit costs and a financial base strong enough that it can weather setbacks.
4. **A scanning capability:** An ability to search successfully and efficiently for opportunities will take on greater importance in international dealings.
5. **An outstanding product or service:** A solid product or service is likely to have staying power in international competition.
6. **An outstanding international executive:** The presence of an executive who understands international situations and can develop a core of local executives who can work well with the home office is likely to result in the building of a strong and long-lasting international organization. The importance of such an executive is evidenced by Japanese-based NEC Corporation's decision to promote its Director of U.S. Operations to company President. According to outgoing President Tadahiro Sekimoto, "We needed someone who can make NEC an even more global company than it already is."[18]

11.4 International Issues in Strategy Formulation

Strategy formulation becomes much more complex as a company moves into the international arena. Top management must review its current mission and objectives to decide whether they are relevant to international activities. It must also consider international strategic alternatives in light of the company's strengths and weaknesses and the opportunities and threats present in the country under consideration. International portfolio analysis may help management evaluate these strategic factors.

International Portfolio Analysis

To aid international strategic planning, G. D. Harrell and R. O. Kiefer show how portfolio analysis can be applied to international markets.[19] Two factors form the axes of the matrix in Fig. 11.3. A **country's attractiveness** reflects its market size, the market rate of growth, the extent and type of government regulation, and economic and political factors. A **product's competitive strength** reflects its market share, product fit, contribution margin, and market support. Depending on where a product fits on the matrix, it should either receive more funding or be harvested for cash.

Portfolio analysis might not be useful, however, to those MNCs operating in a global industry rather than a multidomestic one. In discussing the importance of

FIGURE 11.3 Portfolio Matrix for Plotting Products by Country

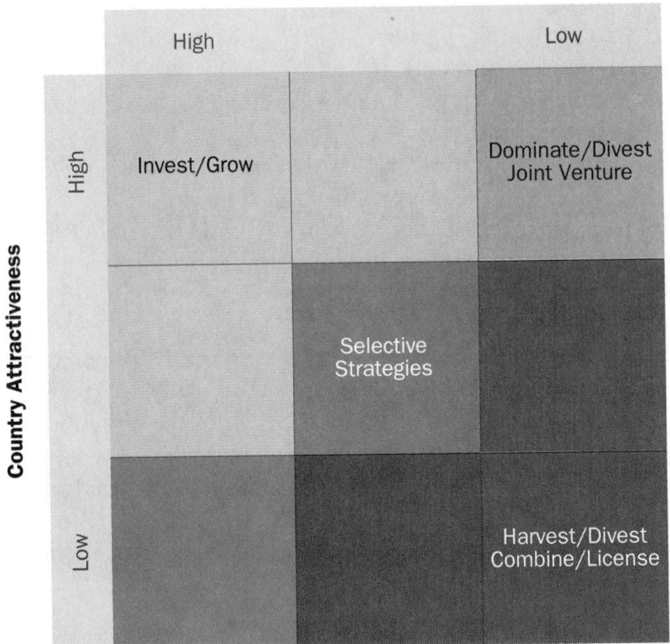

Source: G. D. Harrell and R. O. Kiefer, "Multinational Strategic Market Portfolios," *MSU Business Topics* (Winter 1981), p. 7. Reprinted by permission.

global industries, Porter argues against the use of Harrell and Kiefer's recommended portfolio analysis on a country-by-country basis:

> In a global industry . . . managing international activities like a portfolio will undermine the possibility of achieving competitive advantage. In a global industry, a firm must in some way integrate its activities on a worldwide basis to capture the linkage among countries.[20]

Popular International Strategies

Depending on its situation, its mission, and its objectives, a multinational corporation can select from several strategic options the most appropriate methods to use in entering a foreign market or establishing manufacturing facilities in another country. Such strategies can be combined with the corporate, business, and functional strategies described earlier. The following are some of the more popular international strategies.

- **Exporting:** Simply shipping goods produced in the company's home country to other countries for marketing is a good way to minimize risk and to experiment with a specific product. The company could choose to handle all critical functions itself, or it could contract these functions to an export management company. Exporting is becoming increasingly popular for small businesses because of fax machines, 800 numbers, and overnight air express services, which reduce the once formidable costs of going international.[21]

- **Licensing:** Under a licensing agreement, the licensing firm grants rights to another firm in the host country to produce and/or sell a product. The licensee pays compensation to the licensing firm in return for technical expertise. This is an especially useful strategy if the trademark or brand name is well known but the MNC doesn't have sufficient funds to finance its entering the country directly. Anheuser-Busch is using this strategy to produce and market Budweiser beer in the United Kingdom, Japan, Israel, Australia, Korea, and the Philippines. This strategy also becomes important if the country makes entry by investment either difficult or impossible. However, a licensee might develop its competence to the point that it becomes a competitor to the licensing firm. Therefore a company should never license its distinctive competence, even for some short-run advantage.
- **Joint ventures:** The rate of joint venture formation between U.S. companies and international partners has been growing 27% annually since 1985.[22] Companies often form joint ventures to combine the resources and expertise needed for the development of new products or technologies. A joint venture also enables an MNC to enter a country that restricts foreign ownership. The corporation can enter another country with less assets at stake and thus lower risk. For example, because the costs of developing a new large jet airplane were becoming too high for any one manufacturer, Boeing, Aerospatiale of France, British Aerospace, Construcciones Aeronauticas of Spain, and Deutsche Aerospace of Germany planned a joint venture to design such a plane. A joint venture may be an association between an MNC and a firm in the host country or a government agency in that country. A quick method of obtaining local management, it also reduces the risks of expropriation and harassment by host country officials. This is the approach Dean Foods used to increase its presence in Mexico. Disadvantages of joint ventures include loss of control, lower profits, probability of conflicts with partners, and the likely transfer of technological advantage to the local partner. Joint ventures often are meant to be temporary, especially by the Japanese, who view them as a way to overcome a competitive weakness until they can achieve long-term dominance in the partnership.[23]
- **Acquisitions:** A relatively quick way to move into another country is to purchase a company already operating there. Synergistic benefits can result if the MNC acquires a firm with strong complementary product lines and a good distribution network. As described in the Company Spotlight: Maytag Corporation feature on page 320, Maytag Corporation's acquisition of Hoover gave it entry into Europe through Hoover's strength in home appliances in the United Kingdom and in its vacuum cleaner distribution centers on the European continent. To expand into Central Europe, K mart purchased department stores in the Czech and Slovak Republics. In some countries,

The major home appliance industry in 1993 was on the verge of moving from a multidomestic to a global industry. The North American market had reached maturity, with sales growing only about 2% annually. The market was likely to soon increase, however, with Mexico joining Canada and the United States in a North American Free Trade Zone. In western Europe, however, a market already 25% larger than the mature North American appliance market, unit sales were expected to grow 5% annually on average. This figure was expected to increase significantly as eastern European countries opened their economies to world trade. In addition, the continuing economic integration of the 12 member countries of the European Community (EC) was providing the impetus for a series of mergers, acquisitions, and joint ventures among major home appliance manufacturers. Economies in Asia and South America were becoming more important to world trade as numerous countries moved more toward a free-market economy. Whirlpool, A.B. Electrolux, and General Electric had led the way during the 1980s by expanding internationally throughout North America and Europe. Whirlpool and GE also were involved in joint ventures in Mexico and South America. Japanese firms were in the process of dominating the Asian major home appliance market but were not yet established elsewhere.

Through its acquisition of the Hoover Company in 1988, Maytag Corporation had moved into the international home appliance market. Hoover was known worldwide for its floor care products and throughout Europe and Australia for its washers, dryers, dishwashers, microwave ovens, and refrigerators. Before the acquisition, Maytag's international revenues were too small even to report.

Unfortunately, the newly multinational Maytag Corporation was not in the best position to compete globally. It completed its acquisition of Hoover just as the major home appliance market in the United Kingdom slumped. Elsewhere in Europe, Hoover was big in vacuum cleaners, but only a minor player in major home appliances. The combination of heavy debt and low stock price prevented Maytag from using acquisitions to push deeper into Europe or even to begin expansion elsewhere in the world.

Nevertheless, Maytag formed an alliance in September 1992 with Bosch-Siemens of Germany. The companies formed a joint venture to market each others' products, consolidate distribution and service, and develop common purchasing strategies. Herbert Worner, Bosch-Siemens' Chief Managing Director, stated that his company would supply dishwashers to Hoover for sale in the United Kingdom and that he expected the companies to move jointly into markets where neither had much presence, such as South America, China, and Southeast Asia.

however, acquisitions can be difficult to arrange because of a lack of available information about potential candidates. Government restrictions on ownership, such as the U.S. requirement that limits foreign ownership of U.S. airlines to 49% of nonvoting and 25% of voting stock, also can discourage acquisitions.

- **Green-field development:** If a corporation doesn't want to obtain another firm's existing facilities through acquisition, it may choose a *green-field development,* or the building of a manufacturing facility from scratch. This approach usually is far more complicated and expensive than acquisition, but it allows the MNC more freedom in designing the plant, choosing suppliers, and hiring a work force. For example, Nissan, Honda, and Toyota built auto factories in rural areas of the United Kingdom and then hired and trained a young work force with no experience in the industry.
- **Production sharing:** Coined by Peter Drucker, the term *production sharing* means the combining of higher labor skills and technology available in developed countries with the lower cost labor available in developing countries. By locating a labor-intensive assembly plant called a *maquiladora* in Ciudad Juarez, Mexico, and a packaging plant across the border in El Paso, Texas, companies such as Hoover have been able to take advantage of Mexico's low labor costs. Companies also are moving data processing and computer programming activities "offshore" to places such as Ireland, Barbados, Jamaica, the Philippines, India, and Singapore where wages are lower, English is spoken, and telecommunications are in place.
- **Turnkey operations:** Turnkey operations typically involve contracts for the planning, design, and construction of operating facilities for a fee. The facilities are transferred to the host country or firm when they are complete. The customer usually is a government agency of, for example, a Middle Eastern country that has decreed that a particular product be produced locally and under its control. For example, Fiat built an auto plant in Russia to produce an older model of Fiat under a Russian brand name (Lada). Corporations that perform turnkey operations frequently are industrial equipment manufacturers that supply some of their own equipment for the project and also sell replacement parts and maintenance services to the host country. They thereby create customers as well as future competitors.
- **Management contracts:** A large multinational corporation is likely to have a great amount of management talent at its disposal. Management contracts offer a means through which an MNC may use part of its personnel to assist a firm in a host country for a specified fee and period of time. Such arrangements are useful when a multinational corporation builds a turnkey operation in a less developed country where people do not have the knowledge and skills needed to operate a manufacturing facility. Management contracts also are common when a host government expropriates part or all of an MNC's holdings in its country. The contracts allow the MNC to continue to earn some income from its investment and keep the operations going until it can train local management.[24]

11.5 International Issues in Strategy Implementation

To be effective, implementation of international strategies must recognize national and cultural differences. Among the many implementation considerations of an MNC, three of the most important are (1) selecting a local partner for a strategic alliance, (2) designing an appropriate organizational structure, and (3) encouraging global rather than national management practices.

International Partner Selection

Strategic alliances (joint ventures and licensing agreements) between a multinational company and a local partner in a host country are becoming increasingly popular as a way for an MNC to gain entry into other countries, especially less developed countries. Because of national policies and the complexity of the host country's market, corporations often prefer these strategies for balancing a country's attractiveness against financial risk. The key to successful implementation of these strategies is selection of the local partner. Each party needs to assess not only the strategic fit of each company's project strategy, but also the fit of each company's respective resources. A successful joint venture may require as much as two years of prior contacts between the partners. The fact that joint ventures tend to have a high rate of costly failures suggests that few multinationals use such a careful selection process.[25] Research does indicate, however, that joint ventures tend to be more successful when both partners have equal ownership in the venture and are mutually dependent upon each other for results.[26]

Multinational Organizational Design

A company's stage of development in international activities and the types of industries in which it is involved strongly influence the design of an organization's structure. The issue of centralization versus decentralization becomes especially important for a multinational corporation operating in both multidomestic and global industries. As in the case of international industries, the MNC has to deal with two conflicting pressures: one demanding adaptation to the local country for maximum effectiveness and one demanding coordination to ensure consistency within the corporation for maximum efficiency.[27]

Stages of International Development

Rarely, if ever, do multinational corporations suddenly appear full-blown as worldwide organizations. They tend to evolve through the five stages listed in Table 11.2, both in their relationships with widely dispersed geographic markets and in the manner in which they structure their operations and programs.

- **Stage 1:** The primarily domestic company exports some of its products through local dealers and distributors in the foreign countries. The impact on the organization's structure is minimal because everything is handled through an export department at corporate headquarters.

FIGURE 11.4 **Geographic Area Structure for a Multinational Corporation**

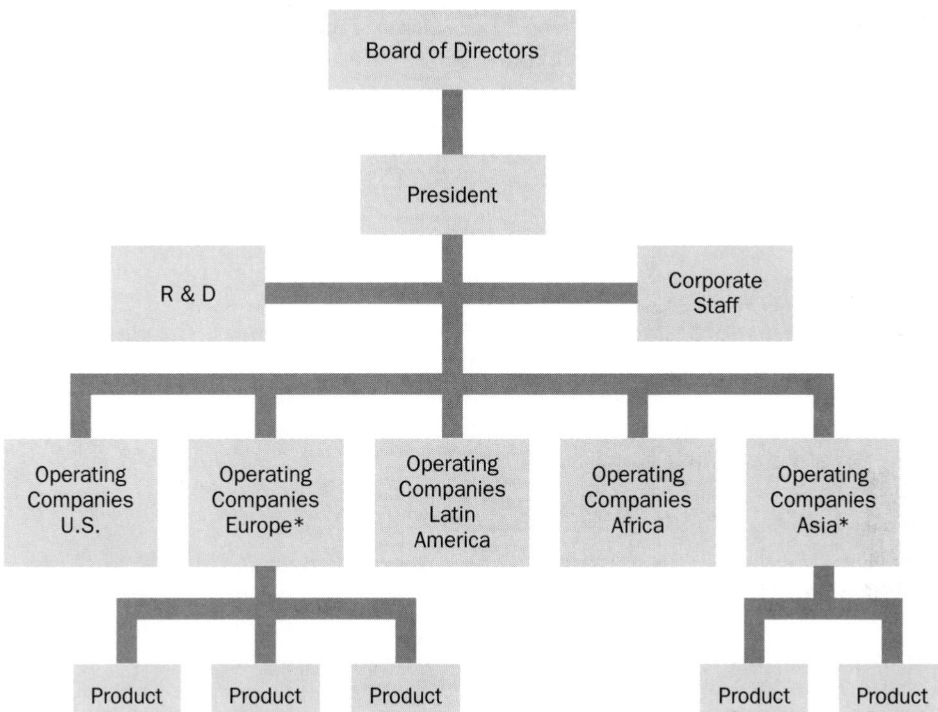

*Note: Because of space limitations, product groups for only Europe and Asia are shown here.

product lines. In contrast, the **geographic–area structure** allows a company to tailor products to regional differences, to achieve regional coordination, and to decentralize decision making to the local subsidiaries. The Dutch electronics firm NV Philips recently switched from a geographic structure, oriented to local needs, to a product structure, oriented to global needs. Philips is known for its light bulbs, for Magnavox, Sylvania, and Philco electronic products, and for Norelco shavers. The company's production facilities were small and high cost because they were designed only for regional markets. Top management believed that the switch to a product structure was crucial for Philips to compete effectively with Japanese MNCs.

A survey of 37 large, U.S.-based multinational corporations in various industries reveals that 43% use an international division; 35% are organized by product group; 14% are structured by geographic area; 5% use a functional structure; and 3% utilize the matrix structure.[31] The international division is much more commonly used by U.S.-based MNCs than European-based MNCs. One reason is the size difference between the domestic markets of the typical U.S.-based and the typical Swiss or British MNC. As the domestic operations of the U.S.-based MNC often are significantly greater than their foreign operations, all non-U.S. operations may be lumped into a single international division.[32]

Simultaneous pressures for centralization to be efficient and decentralization to be locally responsive are causing interesting structural adjustments in most large corporations. The phrase at the beginning of this chapter, "Think globally, act locally," expresses this dichotomy succinctly. Companies are attempting to decentralize those operations closest to customers—manufacturing and marketing. At the same time, the companies are consolidating less visible internal functions, such as research and development, finance, and information systems, to achieve significant economies of scale.[33]

International Management Practices and Human Resource Management

Important international issues for a multinational corporation are the universality of accepted management practices and the proper management of human resources. Are people from different countries basically the same once differences in language and race are resolved, or are they so different that each country needs a whole new style of management?

Cultural Values and Management Practices

There is no simple answer to the preceding question. People around the world are both alike and different. For example, a study of 14,644 people in eight Western countries revealed that work is a central interest for most people in all countries and that interesting work and good pay are the most important elements to jobs.[34] Another study of managers from the United Kingdom, Hungary, Japan, and the United States revealed no significant differences among the attributes preferred in jobs. All four groups ranked type of work most important, pay and opportunity for advancement next, and working conditions, benefits, and hours worked last.[35] Nevertheless, there is some evidence that the emphasis in U.S. occupations is fundamentally different from that of other countries. For example, U.S. managers tend to emphasize career over employer. In Japan, however, a manager's first loyalty is to the organization rather than to occupation or profession.[36]

Many people believe that what works well in their own society will work well anywhere. Thus someone schooled in the virtues of MBO, participative decision making, theory Y practices, job enrichment, quality circles, and management science will tend to export these practices without alteration. Unfortunately, just as products often need to be altered to appeal to a new market, so too do most management practices.

In a study of 53 different national cultures, G. Hofstede discovered that he could explain the success or failure of certain management practices on the basis of five cultural dimensions.[37] Figure 11.5 lists countries with the lowest and highest scores on each dimension, along with the scores of Canada, France, Germany, Japan, Mexico, and the United States for purposes of comparison.

1. **Power Distance (PD)** is the extent to which a society accepts an unequal distribution of power in organizations. People in those countries scoring high on this dimension tend to prefer autocratic to more participative managers.

FIGURE 11.5 **Hofstede's International Dimensions**

Highest PD Score							Lowest PD Score
Malaysia (104)	Mexico (81)	France (68)	Japan (54)	U.S. (46)	Canada (39)	Germany (35)	Austria (11)

Highest UA Score							Lowest UA Score
Greece (112)	Japan (92)	France (86)	Mexico (82)	Germany (65)	Canada (48)	U.S (46)	Singapore (8)

Highest IC Score						Lowest IC Score
U.S. (91)	Canada (80)	France (71)	Germany (67)	Japan (46)	Mexico (30)	Guatemala (6)

Highest M-F Score						Lowest M-F Score
Japan (95)	Mexico (69)	Germany (66)	U.S. (62)	Canada (52)	France (43)	Sweden (5)

Highest CD Score					Lowest CD Score
Hong Kong (96)	Japan (80)	Germany (31)	U.S. (29)	Canada (23)	Pakistan (0)

Source: Developed from G. Hofstede and M. H. Bond, "The Confucious Connection: From Cultural Roots to Economic Growth," *Organizational Dynamics* (Spring 1988), pp. 12–13. Hofstede and Bond do not state the significance of the scores for each dimension; they merely indicate that the scores are relative. The scales were chosen to allow about 100 points between the lowest and highest scores.

2. **Uncertainty Avoidance** (UA) is the extent to which a society feels threatened by uncertain and ambiguous situations. People in those nations scoring high on this dimension tend to want career stability, formal rules, and clear-cut measures of performance.
3. **Individualism–Collectivism** (IC) is the extent to which a society values individual freedom and independence of action, compared to a tight social framework and loyalty to the group. People in those nations scoring high on individualism tend to value individual success through competition, whereas people scoring low on individualism tend to value group success through collective cooperation.
4. **Masculinity–Femininity** (M–F) is the extent to which society is oriented toward money and things (which Hofstede labels masculine) or toward

people (which Hofstede labels feminine). People in those nations scoring high on masculinity tend to value clearly defined gender roles where men dominate and to emphasize performance and independence, whereas people in those nations scoring low on masculinity (and thus high on femininity) tend to value gender equality where power is shared and to emphasize the quality of life and interdependence.

5. **Confucian Dynamism** (CD) is the extent to which society follows the principles commonly ascribed to Confucius. These principles are (a) the arrangement of relationships by status and a sensitivity to social contracts; (b) the importance placed on hard work, education, and persistence; (c) the importance of thrift; and (d) the treatment of others as one would like to be treated.

Research on Hofstede's work has provided some, but not complete, support for his five dimensions.[38] Nevertheless, these dimensions of national culture may help explain why some management practices work well in some countries but not in others.[39] Management By Objectives (MBO), which originated in the United States, has succeeded in Germany, according to Hofstede, because the idea of replacing the arbitrary authority of the boss with the impersonal authority of mutually agreed-upon objectives fits the small power distance and strong uncertainty avoidance that are dimensions of the German culture. It has failed in France, however, because the French are used to large power distances—that is, to accepting orders from a highly personalized authority. This French cultural dimension runs counter to key aspects of MBO: the small power distance between superior and subordinate and impersonal, objective goal setting. This same cultural dimension explains why French managers, for whom vertical authority lines are very important, are significantly more reluctant than U.S. managers to accept the multiple authority relationships of project management or matrix structure.[40] This reluctance probably would hold for Chinese executives, who tend to value clear formal rules, lines of authority, and a high degree of control over employees.[41] Some of the difficulties experienced by U.S. companies in using Japanese-style quality circles may stem from the extremely high value that U.S. culture places on individualism.

Managerial perceptions and attitudes reflect cultural differences. Perceptions of the environment and strategic behavior differ significantly by cultural and national background. For example, one research study found that Arabian managers systematically tend to take more variables into account when making strategic decisions than do U.S. managers.[42] Another study found that Latin Europeans (contrasted to Anglo Europeans) are more likely to interpret a strategic issue as a crisis and to recommend immediate proactive strategic behavior.[43]

Hofstede and Bond believe that multinational corporations must pay attention to the many differences in cultural dimensions around the world and adjust their management practices accordingly. Cultural differences can easily go unrecognized by a headquarters staff that may interpret these differences as personality defects, whether the people in the subsidiaries are locals or expatriates. Hofstede and Bond conclude: "Whether they like it or not, the headquarters of multinationals are in the business of multicultural management."[44]

International Human Resource Management

Because of cultural differences, managerial style and human resource practices must be tailored to fit the particular situations in other countries. Most multinational corporations attempt to fill managerial positions in their subsidiaries with well-qualified citizens of the host countries. More than 95% of all managers employed by Unilever are nationals of the country in which they work.[45] IBM follows a similar policy. This policy serves to placate nationalistic governments and to better attune management practices to the host country's culture. The danger in using primarily foreign nationals to staff managerial positions in subsidiaries is the increased likelihood of suboptimization. This makes it difficult for a multinational corporation to meet its long-term, worldwide objectives. To a local national in an MNC subsidiary, the corporation as a whole is an abstraction. Communication and coordination across subsidiaries become more difficult. As it becomes harder to coordinate the activities of several international subsidiaries, an MNC will encounter serious problems operating in a global industry. The North American subsidiary of NV Philips, for example, had earned a reputation as being an independent "maverick" within the MNC. This independence may have been acceptable and even useful to the Netherlands-based MNC while it was operating in multidomestic industries. But when the industries became global, NV Philips had to take control of the North American subsidiary. It began to staff the top positions with non-Americans who could view the global situation and the MNC as a whole.

Another approach to staffing MNC managerial positions is to use people with an international orientation, regardless of their country of origin or host country assignment. This practice is widespread among continental European firms. For example, Electrolux, a Swedish firm, had a French director in its Singapore factory.[46] This approach to using third-country nationals allows more opportunities for promotion than does Unilever's policy, but it may result in a greater number of misunderstandings and conflicts with local employees and the host country's government.

Staffing foreign subsidiaries with either home-country or third-country nationals can be expensive for an MNC. Approximately 35% of expatriate managers (people from a country other than the host country) of U.S.-based MNCs fail to adjust to a particular host country's social and business environment.[47] This failure is costly in terms of management performance, operational efficiency, and customer relations. The average cost to a company of repatriating an executive and the executive's family exceeds $100,000.[48]

According to one survey, the five most important characteristics of an international executive are (1) strategic awareness, (2) adaptability to new situations, (3) sensitivity to new cultures, (4) ability to work in international teams, and (5) language skills.[49] To improve their chances of success when using expatriates, multinational corporations are emphasizing intercultural training for managers being assigned to a foreign country. This training is one of the commonly cited reasons for the lower expatriate failure rates—6% or less—for European and Japanese MNCs, compared to U.S.-based MNCs.[50] Multinational corporations that want their people to gain greater international experience must minimize the career risks for people who accept foreign assignments. Otherwise, the company may eventually find itself at a competitive disadvantage.

11.6 International Issues in Evaluation and Control

As MNCs increase the scope of their activities around the world, timely information becomes even more important for effective evaluation and control. In evaluating the activities of its international operations, an MNC should consider not only financial measures, but also the effects of its activities on the host country.

Transborder Data Flow

A multinational corporation may be viewed as a network of capital, product, and knowledge transactions among units located in different countries.[51] Thus knowledge flows constantly from the subsidiary to the rest of the world and back again. As a result, MNCs are relying increasingly on transborder data flow (TDF) and international data networks to coordinate their international operations and control their subsidiaries. TDF, the electronic movement of data across national boundaries, has been made possible by the rapid growth and convergence of new technologies, such as telecommunications and computer networks. For example, Royal Appliance Manufacturing, a maker of vacuum cleaners, tied its computers in Cleveland to those of its European subsidiaries by satellite. Each day's sales in Europe are monitored and sent back to Cleveland for analysis.

A survey of 89 MNCs concluded that these companies already depend on international data flow for their foreign operations and will do so even more in the future. Transborder data flow appears to be a major information-systems issue for multinational corporations. A study of 20 MNCs operating in Europe by A.T. Kearney, Inc. found that those companies sharing financial functions, such as accounting, on a regional rather than country basis reduced costs by 35%–45%.[52] However, more and more countries are taking steps to control the flow of data across their borders and thus handicap MNC evaluation and control functions.[53] For example, several countries argue that data should be treated like raw material and processed locally rather than internationally. Regulation of data flows is one way to ensure that a country's critical knowledge isn't given to its actual or potential enemies,[54] but it also can cripple an MNC's effectiveness.

Financial Measures

The three techniques used most to evaluate international performance are return on investment, budget analysis, and historical comparisons. In one study, 95% of the corporate officers interviewed stated that they use the same evaluation techniques for foreign and domestic operations. They mentioned rate of return as the single most important measure.[55] Return on investment can cause problems when applied to international operations: "Because of foreign currencies, different rates of inflation, different tax laws, and the use of transfer pricing, both the net income figure and the investment base may be seriously distorted."[56]

A study of 79 MNCs revealed that **international transfer pricing** from one country unit to another is primarily used *not* to evaluate performance, but to minimize taxes.[57] For example, the U.S. Internal Revenue Service contends that many Japanese firms doing business in the United States artificially inflate the value of U.S. deliveries in order to reduce profits and thus the taxes of their American subsidiaries.[58] Parts made in a subsidiary of a Japanese MNC in a low-tax country such as Singapore can be shipped to its subsidiary in a high-tax country such as the United States at such a high price that the U.S. subsidiary reports very little profit (and thus pays a small amount of tax). The Singapore subsidiary reports a very high profit (but also pays a small amount of tax because of the lower tax rate). The Japanese MNC can therefore earn more profit worldwide by reporting less profit in high-tax countries and more profit in low-tax countries. Transfer pricing is important because 56% of all trade in the Triad involves intercompany transactions.[59] Transfer pricing thus is one way to reduce taxes and move profits from a subsidiary to the parent corporation. Other common ways of transfering profits to the parent company (often referred to as *repatriating profits*) are through dividends, royalties, and management fees.[60]

Authorities in international business recommend that the control and reward systems used by a global MNC be different from those used by a multidomestic MNC.[61] The *multidomestic MNC* should use loose controls with its foreign units. The management of each geographic unit should be given considerable operational latitude but be expected to meet some performance targets. Because profit and ROI often are unreliable measures in international operations, MNC's top management should emphasize budgets and nonfinancial measures of performance, such as market share, productivity, public image, employee morale, and relations with the host country government, to name a few.[62] Multiple measures should be used to differentiate between subsidiary worth and management performance.

The *global MNC,* however, needs tight controls over its many units. In order to reduce costs and gain competitive advantage, the MNC is trying to spread the manufacturing and marketing operations of a few fairly uniform products around the world; therefore, its key strategic operational decisions must be centralized. Its environmental scanning must include research not only into each of the national markets in which the MNC competes, but also into the global arena, or the interaction between markets. Foreign units thus should be evaluated more as cost centers, revenue centers, or expense centers than as investment or profit centers because MNCs operating in a global industry often do not make the entire product in the country in which it is sold.

MNC and Host Country Relationships

As multinational corporations grow and enter various countries, those countries find themselves in a dilemma. Most, especially the less developed countries, want the benefits an MNC can bring: technology transfer, employment opportunities, tax revenues, and the opportunity for domestic firms to be built in partnership with powerful and well-connected foreign-based companies. However, these countries also fear the problems that accompany an MNC. Having welcomed an MNC with tax benefits and subsidies of various types, the host country can find itself in a double bind regarding the repatriation of profits. Either it can allow the MNC to export its profits to corporate headquarters in its home country—thereby draining the nation of potential investment capital—or it can allow the MNC to send home only a small portion of its profits—thereby making the host country unattractive to other MNCs. For example, research reveals that between 1960 and 1968, profits sent to the United States from Latin America by MNCs exceeded new investment there by $6.7 billion.[63] Host countries also note that MNCs' technology transfer to less developed countries seldom increases their exports. MNCs also have a tradition of placing business values above the cultural values of the host country.[64] For example, an MNC's need to continue manufacturing operations in order to meet a deadline dictated by the home office may conflict with a country's desire to honor a special event by declaring a national holiday that would force plant closures for a specified period. Thus MNC and host country relationships are always bound to be somewhat strained because the corporation tends to have primary allegiance to its home country.[65]

Research does suggest, however, that developing countries are beginning to revise their attitudes and policies toward multinational corporations as MNCs become more willing to contribute to rather than to exploit host countries. The number of times a host country's government has expropriated or nationalized an MNC's operations substantially decreased during the 1980s from the 1960s. Researchers concluded from their study of Latin America that "the relationship between multinational companies and the host governments seems to be shifting from confrontation to mutual understanding and cooperation."[66]

In Conclusion . . .

Toucan Sam, Tony le Tigre, and Snap, Crackle, et Pop may be European celebrities, but until recently few Europeans had heard of the Lucky Charms leprechaun or the Trix rabbit. While other American packaged-food companies became international in the 1980s, General Mills remained primarily a domestic company. With only a small snack-food business overseas, the company was in a weak position to expand internationally. Kellogg had been international for 70 years and in some countries controlled as much as 80% of the ready-to-eat cereal market. Finally deciding to expand in Europe, General Mills decided to try joint ventures. In 1990, the company joined with Nestlé to market its cereals in Europe through the joint venture Cereal Partners Worldwide (CPW). Although CPW's sales had climbed to $250 million by 1992 and in several countries passed Quaker Oats—long Europe's number two cereal marketer—the joint venture was not yet profitable. According to Rupert Gasser, the manager of CPW for Nestlé, "The break-even point will depend on the speed at which we expand." Catching up to Kellogg will, however, be a real challenge.

General Mills won European Commission approval in 1992 to merge its European snack-food business with PepsiCo, Inc., making the resulting joint venture the largest competitor in the $17 billion market. The venture, known as Snack Ventures Europe, was expected to be profitable immediately. With just 4% of a fragmented market (second in market share), the two partners saw chances to grow by using distinct product and technological capabilities. For example, General Mills was able to make products that were extruded into distinct shapes, such as its Bugles snacks, whereas PepsiCo dominated the chip business. According to Michael Dolan, CEO of the venture, "The driving force is going to be our ability to generate new products."

Industry analysts wondered how long the joint ventures would last. In an industry where brand names were very important, they questioned General Mills's willingness to allow Nestlé to put its name on all General Mills cereals outside North America. Nevertheless, General Mills and its partners vowed that they would stay together for the long term.[67] Because of the temporary nature of most joint ventures, General Mills's management might want to consider some alternative international strategies.

Points to Remember

- A multinational corporation (MNC) is an international organization that considers opportunities globally, invests a considerable portion of its assets in other countries, operates plants in several countries, and uses a worldwide perspective in decision making.
- Multinational corporations operate in world industries that vary on a continuum from multidomestic (products tailored to each country) to global (only small product adjustments for country-specific circumstances).
- Porter suggests that the concept of competitive advantage is more useful in explaining international trade and development than is comparative advantage. The reason is that the factors of production (people, capital, and technology), assumed under comparative advantage to be innate to a particular country, now travel the globe freely. According to Porter, factor conditions, demand conditions, related and supporting industries, and firm strategy, structure, and rivalry determine the competitive advantage of nations.
- To be competitive in international industries, an MNC must have a sophisticated environmental scanning system that can keep track of developments in regional economic groups and evaluate investment risks. Financial considerations, such as wage structure, tax laws, and regulations on profit repatriation are key in international strategic decisions. To be successful internationally, a company should possess or develop a capability such as a technological lead, strong trade name, advantage of scale, and outstanding product or service and have an outstanding international executive.
- Strategic managers may use international portfolio analysis to determine how they should manage their products in various countries. International strategies include exporting, licensing, joint ventures, acquisitions, green-field development, production sharing, turnkey operations, and management contracts.

- Multinational corporations tend to evolve through five stages as they become more involved internationally.
- Hofstede proposes that the success or failure of certain management practices can be explained using five cultural dimensions: power distance, uncertainty avoidance, individualism–collectivism, masculinity–femininity, and Confucian dynamism.
- Although most of the measures used to evaluate international performance are the same as those used elsewhere in a corporation, international transfer pricing can make comparisons among international subsidiaries difficult.

Discussion Questions

1. What differentiates a multidomestic from a global industry? Cite some industries that are now in the process of converting from multidomestic to global. What underlying factors are causing this change in these industries?
2. If the basic concepts of absolute and comparative advantage suggest free trade as the best route to prosperity for all nations, why do so many countries use protectionist measures to discourage imports?
3. Porter suggests that the factors of production have become internationally mobile. In contrast, the resource-based view of the firm states that companies gain competitive advantage to the extent that their key resources are *not* mobile. Reconcile these two positions.
4. What can be done to reverse the economic decline of a country that has reached the wealth-driven fourth stage of economic development? Is this a country to be avoided by a multinational corporation? Why or why not?
5. Discuss the advantages and disadvantages of using portfolio analysis in international strategic analysis.
6. What popular strategies are available to a company entering a foreign market or establishing manufacturing facilities in another country? List and describe each strategy.
7. Should MNCs be allowed to own more than half the stock of a subsidiary based in a host country? Why or why not?
8. Disadvantages of joint ventures include loss of control, lower profits, probability of conflicts with partners, the likely transfer of technological advantage to a partner, and temporary nature. So why is it such a popular strategy?
9. List and describe the stages of development of a multinational corporation.
10. What are the advantages of using a product group structure rather than a geographic area structure in a multinational corporation? The disadvantages? Which MNC structure is likely to be used increasingly in the future?
11. Based on the differences in national cultural values identified by Hofstede, how can a multinational corporation ensure the consistency and reliability of its worldwide activities (e.g., make sure a McDonald's hamburger served in Moscow is the same as one served in Akron) without ignoring local customs and traditions?

Notes

1. K. Wells, "Global Ad Campaigns, After Many Missteps, Finally Pay Dividends," *Wall Street Journal* (August 27, 1992), p. A1.
2. L. Therrein and S. Baker, "Market Share Con Leche?" *Business Week* (Reinventing America 1992 edition), p. 122.
3. W. A. Dymsza, *Multinational Business Strategy* (New York: McGraw-Hill, 1972), pp. 5–6.
4. M. E. Porter, "Changing Patterns of International Competition," *California Management Review* (Winter 1986), pp. 9–40.
5. T. Atamer, "The Single Market: Its Impact on Six Industries," *Long Range Planning* (December 1991), pp. 40–52.
6. J. D. Daniels and L. H. Radebaugh, *International Business: Environments and Operations,* 6th ed. (Reading, Mass.: Addison-Wesley, 1992), p. 186.
7. D. A. Heenan, "The Case for Convergent Capitalism," *Journal of Business Strategy* (November/December 1988), p. 55.
8. M. E. Porter, *The Competitive Advantage of Nations* (New York: Free Press, 1990), p. 71.
9. J. P. Anastassopoulos, G. Blanc, and P. Dussage, *State-Owned Multinationals* (Chicester, England: John Wiley & Sons, 1987), pp. 180–181.
10. Porter, *The Competitive Advantage of Nations,* p. 173.
11. Ibid., p. 565.
12. K. Ohmae, "The Triad World View," *Journal of Business Strategy* (Spring 1987), pp. 8–19.
13. P. Gugler, "Building Transnational Alliances to Create Competitive Advantage," *Long Range Planning* (February 1992), pp. 90–99; G. Koretz, "Where America's Bottom Line May Be Squeezed Overseas," *Business Week* (September 20, 1993), p. 22.
14. T. N. Gladwin, "Assessing the Multinational Environment for Corporate Opportunity," in *Handbook of Business Strategy,* edited by W. D. Guth (Boston: Warren, Gorham and Lamont, 1985), pp. 7.28–7.41.
15. B. Holstein, "An Export Service of Great Import," *Business Week* (September 28, 1992), p. 138.
16. For further information about international environmental scanning, see P. S. Cheng and R. T. Justis, "Using Feasibility Studies to Improve International Business Decision-Making," *International Journal of Management* (September 1992), pp. 295–303; R. Stanat, "Trends in Data Collection and Analysis: A New Approach to the Collection of Global Information," in *International Review of Strategic Management,* Vol. 3, edited by D. E. Hussey (New York: John Wiley & Sons, 1992), pp. 99–132; W. H. Davidson, "The Role of Global Scanning in Business Planning," *Organizational Dynamics* (Winter 1991), pp. 5–16; D. C. Shanks, "Multinational Strategic Planning Systems," in *Handbook of Business Strategy,* 2nd ed., edited by H. E. Glass (Boston: Warren, Gorham and Lamont, 1991), pp. 9.1–9.25.
17. Y. N. Chang and F. Campo-Flores, *Business Policy and Strategy* (Santa Monica, Calif.: Goodyear, 1980), pp. 602–604.
18. D. P. Hamilton, "Japan's NEC Picks Hiroshi Kaneko, A Global-Minded Executive, as President," *Wall Street Journal* (February 9, 1994), p. A10.
19. G. D. Harrell and R. O. Kiefer, "Multinational Strategic Market Portfolios," *MSU Business Topics* (Winter 1981), p. 5.
20. Porter, "Changing Patterns of International Competition," *California Management Review,* p. 12.
21. W. J. Holstein and K. Kelly, "Little Companies, Big Exports," *Business Week* (April 13, 1992), pp. 70–72.
22. S. Sherman, "Are Strategic Alliances Working?" *Fortune* (September 21, 1992), p. 77.
23. W. Shan and W. Hamilton, "Country-Specific Advantage and International Cooperation," *Strategic Management Journal* (September 1991), pp. 419–432; D. Lei and J. W. Slocum, Jr., "Global Strategy, Competence-Building and Strategic Alliances," *California Management Review* (Fall 1992), pp. 81–97.
24. For further information on various international entry strategies, see S. H. Akhter and R. Friedman, "International Market Entry Strategies and Level of Involvement in Marketing Activities," in *International Strategic Management,* edited by A. R. Negandhi and A. Savara (Lexington, Mass.: Lexington Books, 1989), pp. 157–172.
25. One study of 880 alliances revealed that only 45% were felt to be successful by both

parties and that 40% of the cases failed to last four years. See B. J. James, "Strategic Alliances," in *International Review of Strategic Management,* Vol. 2, No. 2, edited by D. E. Hussey (New York: John Wiley & Sons, 1992), pp. 63–72.

26. L. L. Blodgett, "Factors in the Instability of International Joint Ventures: An Event History Analysis," *Strategic Management Journal* (September 1992), pp. 475–481; J. Bleeke and D. Ernst, "The Way to Win in Cross-Border Alliances," *Harvard Business Review* (November–December 1991), pp. 127–135; J. M. Geringer, "Partner Selection Criteria for Developed Country Joint Ventures," in *International Management Behavior,* 2nd ed., edited by H. W. Lane and J. J. DiStephano (Boston: PWS-Kent, 1992), pp. 206–216.
27. P. M. Rosenzweig and J. V. Singh, "Organizational Environments and the Multinational Enterprise," *Academy of Management Review* (April 1991), pp. 340–361.
28. M. M. Habib and B. Victor, "Strategy, Structure, and Performance of U.S. Manufacturing and Services MNCs: A Comparative Analysis," *Strategic Management Journal* (November 1991), pp. 589–606.
29. L. Melin, "Internationalization as a Strategy Process," *Strategic Management Journal* (Winter 1992), p. 104.
30. C. K. Prahalad and Y. L. Doz, *The Multinational Mission* (New York: Free Press, 1987).
31. J. D. Daniels, R. A. Pitts, and M. J. Tretter, "Organizing for Dual Strategies of Product Diversity and International Expansion," *Strategic Management Journal* (July–September 1985), pp. 223–237.
32. P. S. Lewis and P. M. Fandt, "The Strategy–Structure Fit in Multinational Corporations: A Revised Model," *International Journal of Management* (June 1990), pp. 137–147.
33. G. Fuchsberg, "Decentralized Management Can Have Its Drawbacks," *Wall Street Journal* (December 9, 1992), p. B1, B8.
34. MOW International Research Team, The Meaning of Work (London: Academic Press, 1987), as reviewed by G. Akin and L. D. Loehr in *Administrative Science Quarterly* (December 1988), pp. 648–651.
35. W. S. Blumenfeld, D. C. Brenenstuhl, and L. F. Jordan, "A Comparison of the Job Attribute Preferences of British, Hungarian, Japanese, and United States Managers," *International Journal of Management* (September 1988), pp. 323–332.
36. W. A. Jones, Jr., and V. E. Johnson, "The Large Organization as a Community of Games: Another View of the 'Culture' Phenomenon," *International Journal of Management* (March 1988), pp. 74–76.
37. G. Hofstede, *Cultures and Organizations: Software of the Mind* (London: McGraw-Hill, 1991); G. Hofstede and M. H. Bond, "The Confucius Connection: From Cultural Roots to Economic Growth," *Organizational Dynamics* (Spring 1988), pp. 5–21.
38. F. L. DuBois and M. D. Oliff, "Dimensions of National Culture: A Multivariate Analysis," *International Journal of Management* (June 1992), pp. 194–200; R. H. Franke, G. Hofstede, and M. H. Bond, "Cultural Roots of Economic Performance," *Strategic Management Journal* (Summer 1991), pp. 165–173.
39. G. Hofstede, "Cultural Constraints in Management Theories," *Academy of Management Executive* (February 1993), pp. 81–94.
40. G. Inzerilli and A. Laurent, "Managerial Views of Organization Structure in France and the USA," *International Studies of Management and Organization* (Spring–Summer 1983), p. 113.
41. I. Vertinsky, D. K. Tse, D. A. Wehrung, and K. Lee, "Organizational Designs and Management Norms: A Comparative Study of Managers' Perceptions in the People's Republic of China, Hong Kong, and Canada," *Journal of Management* (December 1990), pp. 853–867.
42. A. J. Ali, A. Ali-Aali, and R. C. Camp, "A Cross-National Perspective on Strategic Behavior and Business Environment," *International Journal of Management* (June 1992), pp. 208–214.
43. S. C. Schneider and A. DeMeyer, "Interpreting and Responding to Strategic Issues: The Impact of National Culture," *Strategic Management Journal* (May 1991), pp. 307–320.
44. Hofstede and Bond, "The Confucius Connection," p. 20.
45. W. C. Kim and R. A. Mauborgne, "Cross-Cultural Strategies," *Journal of Business Strategy* (Spring 1987), p. 30.

46. M. Maruyama, "Changing Dimensions in International Business," *Academy of Management Executive* (August 1992), p. 88.
47. R. L. Tung, The New Expatriates (Cambridge, Mass.: Ballinger, 1988), as reviewed by D. J. Cohen in *Academy of Management Executive* (May 1988), pp. 171–172; G. Nunez, "Managing the Foreign Service Employee," *SAM Advanced Management Journal* (Summer 1990), pp. 25–29.
48. N. J. Adler, *International Dimensions of Organizational Behavior,* 2nd ed. (Boston: PWS/Kent, 1991), p. 257.
49. M. Osbaldeston and K. Barham, "Using Management Development for Competitive Advantage," *Long Range Planning* (December 1992), p. 21.
50. Tung, *The New Expatriates*; J. S. Black, M. Mendenhall, and G. Oddou, "Toward a Comprehensive Model of International Adjustment: An Integration of Multiple Theoretical Perspectives," *Academy of Management Review* (April 1991), pp. 291–317.
51. A. Gupta and V. Govindarajan, "Knowledge Flows and the Structure of Control Within Multinational Corporations," *Academy of Management Review* (October 1991), pp. 768–792; S. Ghoshal and C. A. Bartlett, "The Multinational Corporation as an Interorganizational Network," *Academy of Management Review* (October 1990), pp. 603–625.
52. *Wall Street Journal* (December 2, 1993), p. A1.
53. W. B. Carper, "Transborder Data Flows in the Information Age: Implications for International Management," *International Journal of Management* (December 1989), pp. 418–425; R. Chandran, A. Phatak, and R. Sambharya, "Transborder Data Flows: Implication for Multinational Corporations," *Business Horizons* (November–December 1987), pp. 74–82.
54. Y. Doz, "International Industries: Fragmentation Versus Globalization," in *Global Strategic Management: The Essentials,* 2nd ed., edited by H. Vernon-Wortzel and L. Wortzel (New York: John Wiley & Sons, 1991), pp. 18–34.
55. S. M. Robbins and R. B. Stobaugh, "The Bent Measuring Stick for Foreign Subsidiaries," *Harvard Business Review* (September–October 1973), p. 82.
56. J. D. Daniels and L. H. Radebaugh, *International Business,* 5th ed. (Reading, Mass.: Addison-Wesley, 1989), pp. 673–674.
57. W. A. Johnson and R. J. Kirsch, "International Transfer Pricing and Decision Making in United States Multinationals," *International Journal of Management* (June 1991), pp. 554–561.
58. "Fixing the Bottom Line," *Time* (November 23, 1992), p. 20.
59. T. A. Stewart, "The New Face of American Power," *Fortune* (July 26, 1993), p. 72.
60. J. M. L. Poon, R. Ainuddin, and H. Affrim, "Management Policies and Practices of American, British, European, and Japanese Subsidiaries in Malaysia: A Comparative Study," *International Journal of Management* (December 1990), pp. 467–474.
61. C. W. L. Hill, P. Hwang, and W. C. Kim, "An Eclectic Theory of the Choice of International Entry Mode," *Strategic Management Journal* (February 1990), pp. 117–128; D. Lei, J. W. Slocum, Jr., and R. W. Slater, "Global Strategy and Reward Systems: The Key Roles of Management Development and Corporate Culture," *Organizational Dynamics* (Autumn 1990), pp. 27–41; W. R. Fannin and A. F. Rodriques, "National or Global?—Control vs. Flexibility," *Long Range Planning* (October 1986), pp. 84–188.
62. A. V. Phatak, *International Dimensions of Management,* 2nd ed. (Boston: Kent, 1989), pp. 155–157.
63. K. Paul and R. Barbato, "The Multinational Corporation in the Less Developed Country: The Economic Development Model Versus the North–South Model," *Academy of Management Review* (January 1985), p. 9.
64. G. R. Bassiry, "A Third World Perspective on Western Multinational Corporations," *International Journal of Management* (December 1990), pp. 394–400.
65. Y. Hu, "Global or Stateless Corporations Are National Firms with International Operations," *California Management Review* (Winter 1992), pp. 107–126.
66. K. Fatehi-Sedeh and M. H. Safizadeh, "Sociopolitical Events and Foreign Direct Investment: American Investments in South and Central American Countries, 1950–1982," *Journal of Management* (March 1988), p. 105. For further information on

improving MNC and host country relationships including the United Nations Code of Conduct for Transnational Corporations, see G. R. Bassiry, J. Chaney, R. Motemeni, and S. Levy, "Multinationals in Economic Development: The Ethical Dimension," *International Journal of Management* (March 1992), pp. 55–61.

67. L. Therrien and C. Hoots, "Cafe Au Lait, A Croissant—and Trix," *Business Week* (August 24, 1992), pp. 50–51.

12

Strategic Issues in Managing Technology and Innovation

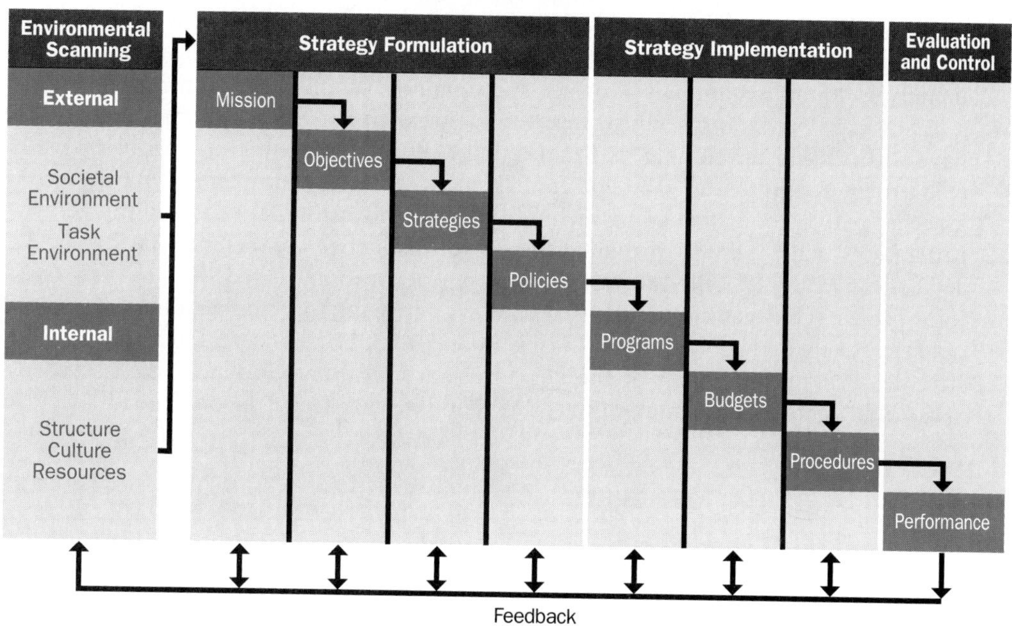

> *Historical studies indicate that as much as 40 percent of economic growth is attributable to technology.*[1]
> [J. B. Welch and P. Bolster]

The du Pont Company has long been known for its excellence in basic corporate research. In the early 1990s, for example, it led the nation's chemical companies in patents applied for and granted. The company spent more than $13 billion on chemical and related research during the 1980s, but management admitted that the company failed to develop much in the way of major innovations. "They've been like the space program: the technology is great, but where's the payoff?" asked industry analyst John Garcia. Du Pont CEO Edgar Woolard admitted that the company took too long to "convert research into products that can benefit our customers." Moreover, in major established products, the company lost ground to competitors that spent more on improving manufacturing. Customers who wanted changes in Zytel nylon-resin products often had to wait six months to get an answer. Du Pont had become a secure place to work, said Woolard, but "we have too much bureaucracy running these businesses."

According to Joseph Miller, director of du Pont's polymers research, the emphasis in R&D was to find another "big bang" like its invention of nylon (a version of the "hit another home run" strategy mentioned in Chapter 7 on page 206 as a strategy to avoid). As a result, the company introduced a series of new products—excellently designed, but rejected by the marketplace. Among them were *Kevlar,* stronger than steel, but too expensive for widespread usage; *Corfram,* a synthetic leather that didn't "breathe" and thus made shoes uncomfortable; *Qiana,* a synthetic silk that was ignored because of increasing interest in natural fibers. In addition, the company unsuccessfully spent millions on electronic imaging and pharmaceuticals. To focus "more intensity on customer needs," CEO Woolard announced that the company was shifting about 30% of its research budget (approximately $400 million annually) toward speeding new products to customers.[2]

This du Pont example illustrates how a successful, established company can have difficulty in developing and marketing new products when it fails to make technology a part of its strategic management process. Companies that aren't knowledgeable about managing technology and innovation may destroy the very capabilities that originally provided them with distinctive competence. In the late 1980s, for example, Bill Gates of Microsoft Corporation visited IBM to discuss joint projects. He was concerned that IBM was growing too cumbersome to compete effectively in the PC market. Taking a break for a bowl of cereal in an IBM office, he observed that most of the PCs in use around him were more than seven years old. "This tells me more about IBM than I've ever seen," he concluded.[3]

12.1 Role of Strategic Managers

In most industries, owing to increased competition and accelerated product development cycles, research and development is becoming crucial to corporate success. What is less obvious is how strategic managers can generate a significant return from investment in R&D. When Akio Morita, Chairman of Sony Corporation, recently visited the United Kingdom, he expressed disbelief at the number of accountants leading companies there. Uncomfortable because they lacked familiarity with science or technology, these top managers too often limited their role to approving next year's budget. Constrained by what the company could afford and guided by how much the competition was spending, they perceived R&D as a line expense item instead of as an investment in the future.[4]

The importance of technology and innovation must be emphasized by people at the very top of the corporation. If they aren't interested in these topics, neither are managers below them. When IBM began to admit its financial decline in 1993, for example, observers were astounded to discover that none of the four outside members of the board's executive committee used personal computers or knew much about them. Analysts questioned how a board of directors could direct management if key members had little or no knowledge of a crucial product area and the technology supporting it.[5]

Strategic managers have an obligation not only to encourage new product development, but also to develop a system to ensure that technology is being used most effectively with the consumer in mind. A study by Chicago consultants Kuczmarski & Associates of 11,000 new products marketed by 77 manufacturing, service, and consumer-product firms revealed that only 56% of all newly introduced products were still being sold five years later. Only one in 13 new-product ideas ever made it into test markets. Although some authorities argue that this percentage of successful new products needs to be improved, others contend that too high a percentage means that a company isn't taking the risks necessary to develop a really new product.[6]

The importance of top management's providing appropriate direction is exemplified by Chairman Morita's statement of his philosophy for Sony Corporation:

> The key to success for Sony, and to everything in business, science, and technology for that matter, is never to follow the others. . . . Our basic concept has always been this—to give new convenience, or new methods, or new benefits, to the general public with our technology.

Morita and his co-founder, Masuru Ibuka, always looked for ways to turn ideas into clear targets. Says Morita, "When Ibuka was first describing his idea for the Betamax videocassette, he gave the engineers a paperback book and said, 'Make it this size.' Those were his only instructions."[7]

12.2 Environmental Scanning

External Scanning

There is danger in focusing scanning efforts too closely on a corporation's own industry. According to N. Snyder, "History teaches that most new developments which threaten existing business practices and technologies do not come from traditional industries."[8] A new technology that can substitute for an existing technology at a lower cost and provide higher quality can change the very basis for competition in an industry. For example, with the development of the integrated circuit, electronics firms such as Texas Instruments were able to introduce high-volume, low-cost electronic digital watches. These firms' entry into the watch-making industry took well-established mechanical watchmakers by surprise. Timex, Seiko, and especially the Swiss firms found that their markets had changed overnight. These established companies were forced to spend a lot of money buying the new technology and upgrading their production facilities in order to compete with competitors using integrated circuit technology.

Motorola, a company well known for its ability to invest in profitable new technologies and manufacturing improvements, has a sophisticated scanning system. Its intelligence department monitors the latest technological developments introduced at scientific conferences, journals, and in trade gossip. This information helps it build "technology roadmaps" that assess where breakthroughs are likely to occur, when they can be incorporated into new products, how much their development will cost, and which of the developments is being worked on by the competition.[9]

Contrasted with technology research, market or customer research may not always provide useful information on new product directions. According to Sony executive Kozo Ohsone, "When you introduce products that have never been invented before, what good is market research?" Instead of standard market research, some successful companies are using speed and flexibility to gain market information. For example, Sony obtains information from the actual sales of various models and then adjusts its product mix to conform to the sales patterns. The process design of each model is based on a common core platform containing the essential technology. The platform is designed to be flexible, allowing a wide range of models to be easily built on it. The platform remains the same, but specific models change on the basis of actual sales. Seiko's only market research plan is surprisingly simple. The company introduces hundreds of new models of watches. It makes more of the models that sell; it drops those that don't.

The consulting firm Arthur D. Little found that the use of standard market research techniques has resulted in a success rate of only 8% for new cereals—92% of all new cereals fail. As a result, innovative firms, such as Keebler and the leading cereal makers, are reducing their expenditures for consumer research and working to reduce the cost of launching new products by making their manufacturing processes more flexible.[10]

Internal Scanning

As mentioned earlier in Chapter 5, external scanning is only one-half of environmental scanning (and SWOT analysis). Strategic managers also should assess a company's ability to innovate effectively by asking the following questions.

1. Has the company developed the resources needed to try new ideas?
2. Do the managers allow experimentation with new products or services?
3. Does the corporation encourage risk taking and tolerate mistakes?
4. Are people more concerned with new ideas or with defending their turf?
5. Is it easy to form autonomous project teams?[11]

In addition to answering these questions, strategic managers should assess how well company resources are allocated internally. They also should evaluate the organization's ability to develop and transfer new technology in a timely manner into the generation of innovative products and services.

Resource Allocation Issues

A company must make available the resources necessary for effective research and development. Research indicates that a company's R&D intensity (its spending on R&D as a percentage of sales revenue) is a principal means of gaining market share in global competition.[12] The amount spent on R&D often will vary by industry. For example, the computer software and drug industries spent an average of 13.2% and 11.5%, respectively, of their sales dollar for R&D in 1993. As Table 12.1 shows, other industries, such as food and containers and packaging, spent less than 1%. A good rule of thumb for R&D spending is that a corporation should spend at a "normal" rate for that particular industry. According to PIMS data, companies that spend 1% of sales more or less than the industry average

TABLE 12.1 **Research and Development Expenditures by Industry in 1993 as a Percentage of Sales**

Industry	%	Industry	%
Aerospace	4.4%	Leisure-time products	5.7%
Automotive		Manufacturing	
Cars and trucks	4.2	General manufacturing	3.3
Parts and equipment	2.4	Machine and hand tools	2.0
Tire and rubber	2.6	Special machinery	3.1
Chemicals	4.3	Textiles	1.0
Conglomerates	2.6	Metals and mining	
Consumer products		Aluminum	1.4
Appliances/home furnishings	1.9	Steel	0.8
Other consumer goods	0.7	Other metals	0.9
Personal care	2.5	Office equipment and services	
Containers and packaging	0.9	Business machines/services	2.6
Electrical and electronics		Computer communications	11.5
Electrical products	2.8	Computers	8.8
Electronics	5.8	Data processing	6.1
Instruments	5.4	Disk and tape drives	6.5
Semiconductors	9.4	Peripherals and other	5.3
Food	0.7	Software and services	13.2
Fuel		System design	10.4
Oil, gas, and coal	0.6	Paper and forest products	1.1
Petroleum services	2.9	Service industries	0.7
Health care		Telecommunications	3.1
Drugs and research	11.5		
Medical products/services	6.7		
Housing	1.8	**All-industry composite**	3.7%

Source: "R&D Scoreboard," *Business Week* (June 28, 1993), pp. 105–127.

have lower ROIs.[13] Research also indicates that consistency in R&D strategy and resource allocation across lines of business improves corporate performance by enabling the firm to better develop synergies among product lines and business units.[14]

Simply spending money on R&D or new projects does not mean that the money will produce useful results. For instance, **technology transfer,** the process of taking new technology from the laboratory to the marketplace, has become an important issue in recent decades. One study found that, although large firms spent almost twice as much per R&D patent than did smaller firms, the smaller firms utilized more of their patents. Another study revealed the maximum innovator in various industries tended to be the middle-sized firm. These firms tended to be more effective and efficient in technology transfer. From these studies, M. A. Hitt, R. E. Hoskisson, and J. S. Harrison suggest the existence of an inverted U-shaped relationship between size and innovation. According to Hitt et al., "This suggests that organizations are flexible and responsive up to some threshold size but encounter inertia after that point."[15]

Sometimes most of the firms in an entire industry can waste their R&D spending. For example, between 1950 and 1979, the U.S. steel industry spent 20% more on plant maintenance and upgrading for each ton of production capacity added or replaced than did the Japanese steel industry. Nevertheless, top management in U.S. steel firms failed to recognize and adopt two breakthroughs in steelmaking—the basic oxygen furnace and continuous casting. Their hesitancy to adopt new technology caused them to lose the world steel market.[16]

Time to Market Issues

In addition to money, another important consideration in the effective management of research and development is the time factor. A decade ago, the time from inception to profitability of a specific R&D program typically was 7 to 11 years.[17] According to Karlheinz Kaske, CEO of Siemens AG, however, the time available to complete the cycle is getting shorter. Companies no longer can assume that competitors will allow them the time needed to recoup their investment. In the past, Kaske says, "ten to fifteen years went by before old products were replaced by new ones . . . now, it takes only four or five years."[18] Time to market is an important consideration because 60% of successful patented innovations are imitated within four years at 65% of the cost of innovation.[19] In the 1980s, Japanese auto manufacturers gained incredible competitive advantage over U.S. manufacturers by reducing new products' time to market to only three years. U.S. auto companies needed five years.[20]

Andy Grove, CEO of Intel, agrees with the increasing importance of time to market as a competitive weapon by stating, "Ultimately, 'speed' is the only weapon we have." With $5 billion in annual sales, the company spends $1.2 billion a year on plant and equipment and $800 million on R&D. Intel is no longer content to introduce one or two new-generation microprocessors annually and a completely new family of computer microchips every four years. Previously, Intel would introduce a new family of chips (such as the 386) only when the current market was sufficiently saturated with one family of chips (such as the 286). The advent of lower cost microprocessor clone manufacturers, such as Cyrix and AMD, meant that Intel had to give up the 386 market prematurely to focus on the emerging 486 market in 1992. The introduction of the "Pentium" (586 chip) microprocessor followed quickly in 1993. For most of the 1990s, Intel plans to develop new chip families every two years. Grove believes that this fast developmental pace will keep chip cloners from ever catching up with Intel.[21]

Impact of Technological Discontinuity

The R&D manager must determine when to abandon present technology and when to develop or adopt new technology. Richard Foster of McKinsey and Company states that the displacement of one technology by another, called **technological discontinuity**, is a frequent and strategically important phenomenon. Such a discontinuity occurs when a new technology cannot be used simply to enhance the

FIGURE 12.1 **Technological Discontinuity**

What the S-Curves Reveal

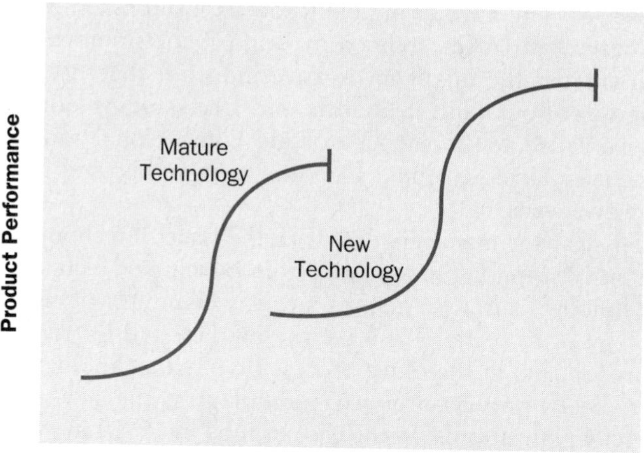

Research Effort/Expenditure

In the corporate planning process, it is generally assumed that incremental progress in technology will occur. But past developments in a given technology cannot be extrapolated into the future, because every technology has its limits. The key to competitiveness is to determine when to shift resources to a technology with more potential.

Source: P. Pascarella, "Are You Investing in the Wrong Technology?" *Industry Week* (July 25, 1983), p. 38.

current technology but actually substitutes for that technology to yield better performance. According to Foster, for each technology within a field or an industry, plotting product performance against research effort and expenditures on a graph results in an S-shaped curve. He describes the process depicted in Fig. 12.1 as follows:

> Early in the development of the technology a knowledge base is being built and progress requires a relatively large amount of effort. Later, progress comes more easily. And then, as the limits of that technology are approached, progress becomes slow and expensive. That is when R&D dollars should be allocated to technology with more potential. That is also—not so incidentally—when a competitor who has bet on a new technology can sweep away your business or topple an entire industry.[22]

The presence of a technological discontinuity in the world's steel industry during the 1960s explains why the large capital expenditures by U.S. steel companies failed to keep them competitive with Japanese firms, which adopted the new technologies. As Foster points out, "History has shown that as one technology nears the end of its S-curve, competitive leadership in a market generally changes hands."[23]

Even though many companies in various industries have invested substantially in the energy and resources needed for their conversion to leading-edge technologies and new products, relatively few have been able to do so. Established firms tend to stay with the same basic approaches, technology, and products. For example, when GE and Tappan entered the infant microwave industry, they utilized conventional product designs, such as built-in models and free-standing double ovens. Because these designs called for replacing existing conventional ranges, many of which still had long useful lives, customers ignored them and bought free-standing countertop microwave ovens.[24]

Ansoff recommends that strategic managers deal with the issue of technology substitution by (1) continuously searching for sources from which new technologies are likely; (2) as the technology surfaces, making a timely commitment either to acquire the new technology or to prepare to leave the market; and (3) reallocating resources from improvements in the older process-oriented technology to investments in the newer, typically product-oriented, technology as the new technology approaches commercial realization.[25] In the case of Intel in 1993, strategic managers had to decide when to shift from making microprocessors based on Complex Instruction Set Computing (CISC) technology to Reduced Instruction Set Computing (RISC). The company had the ability to shift to the new RISC technology, but staying with CISC enabled its microchips to handle the massive library of existing software. To deal with this strategic factor, CEO Grove depended on Intel's strength in design, production, and marketing. Intel decided to continue emphasizing CISC, but to also do some research on RISC. According to Grove, all that could derail Intel "is if we fall asleep at the switch."[26]

12.3 Strategy Formulation

Research and development strategy deals not only with the decision to be a leader or a follower in terms of technology and market entry (a topic discussed in Chapter 7 under functional strategy on page 201), but also with the source of the technology. Should a company develop its own technology or purchase it from others? The strategy also takes into account a company's particular mix of basic versus applied and product versus process R&D. The particular mix should suit the level of industry development and the firm's particular corporate and business strategies.

Product versus Process R&D

As illustrated in Fig. 12.2, the proportion of product and process R&D tend to vary as a product moves along its life cycle. In the early stages, **product innovations** are most important because the product's physical attributes and capabilities most affect financial performance. Later, **process innovations** such as improved manufacturing facilities, increasing product quality, and faster distribution become important in maintaining the product's economic returns. Generally, prod-

FIGURE 12.2 **Product and Process R&D in the Innovation Life Cycle**

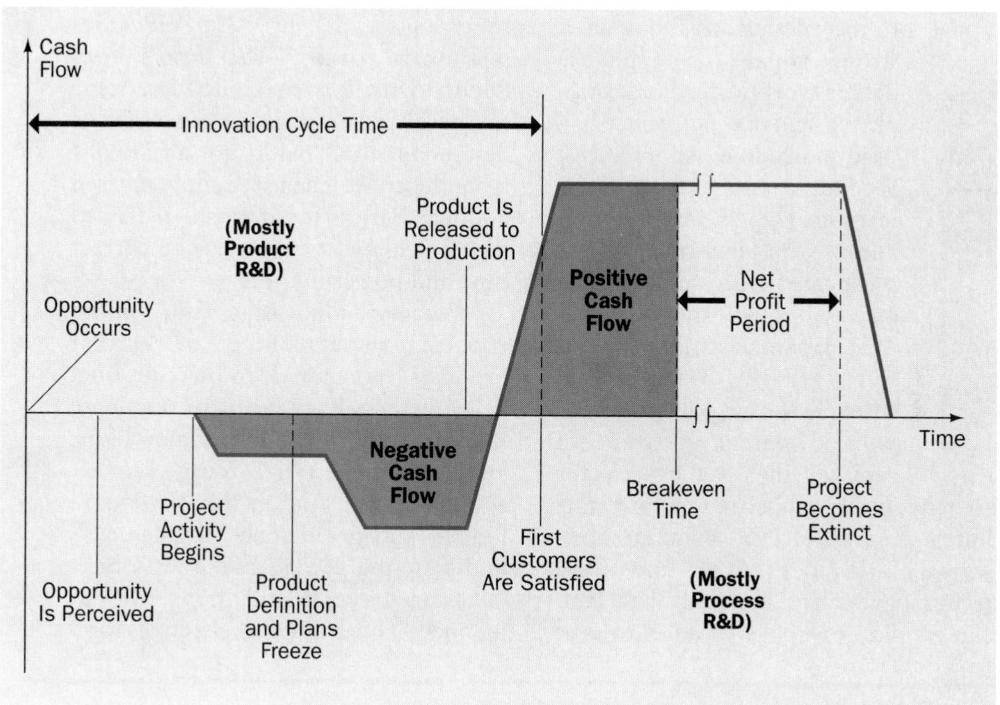

Source: Adapted from M. L. Patterson, "Lessons from the Assembly Line," *Journal of Business Strategy* (May/June 1993), p. 43. Permission granted by Faulkner & Gray, Eleven Penn Plaza, NY, NY 10001.

uct R&D has been instrumental in achieving differentiation strategies, whereas process R&D has been at the core of successful cost leadership strategies.

Historically, U.S. corporations haven't been as skillful as German and Japanese companies at process innovations. The primary reason is the amount of money invested in each form of R&D. On average, U.S. firms spend 70% of their R&D budgets on product R&D and only 30% on process R&D; German firms, 50% on each form; and Japanese firms, 30% on product and 70% on process R&D.[27] The emphasis by U.S. major home appliance manufacturers on process over product R&D may be one reason why they are starting to dominate the industry worldwide, as the Company Spotlight: Maytag Corporation feature on pages 348–349 indicates.

Technology Sourcing

The make or buy decision can be important to a firm's R&D strategy. Although in-house R&D traditionally has been an important source of technical knowledge

COMPANY SPOTLIGHT

MAYTAG Corporation

Importance of R&D in the Major Home Appliance Industry

In terms of **product innovation,** two trends were evident in the major home appliance industry. First, European visual product design was having a strong impact on appliance design worldwide. For example, Frigidaire introduced a "Euroflair" line of appliances. Second, manufacturers were introducing "smart" appliances with increasingly sophisticated electronic controls and self-diagnostic features. The Japanese firms Matsushita, Hitachi, Toshiba, and Mitsubishi introduced *fuzzy logic* computer software to replace the many selector switches on an appliance with one start button. At first, U.S. manufacturers showed little interest in the fuzzy logic technology. They believed that consumers didn't want electronics to take away completely the individual's opportunity to make choices. Nevertheless, by 1993, Whirlpool had added fuzzy logic to its successful VIP series microwave ovens. The firm's new "Sixth Sense" oven could determine the necessary settings for reheating or defrosting food with no guesswork from the cook. The user simply pressed a single button for defrost—the oven then calculated on its own the correct time and power output.

Process innovation for more efficient manufacturing of current products (compared to new-product development) has tended to dominate R&D efforts in the U.S. major home appliance industry. A refrigerator or a washing machine in the 1990s still looked and acted much the same as it did in the 1950s, but it was built in a far different and more efficient manner. The basis for effective com-

for companies, firms also can tap the R&D capabilities of competitors, suppliers, and other organizations through contractual agreements such as licensing, R&D agreements, and joint ventures. When technological cycles were longer, a company was more likely to choose an independent R&D strategy, not only because it gave the firm a longer lead time before competitors copied it, but also because it was more profitable in the long run. In today's world of shorter innovation life cycles and global competition, a company may no longer have the luxury of waiting to reap a long-term profit.[28]

During a time of technological discontinuity in an industry, a company may have no choice but to purchase the new technology from others if it desires to remain competitive. For example, Ford Motor Company paid $100 million for 10.8% of the common stock of Cummins Engine Company, an expert in diesel engine technology. In return for its money, Ford got exclusive access to Cummins's truck-engine technology. This move allowed Ford to forgo the $300 million expense of designing a new engine on its own to meet U.S. emission standards.[29]

petition in the future is likely to be in producing the fewest basic components necessary in the most efficient manufacturing facilities. Although individual designs might vary, the components inside the appliances would become more universal and would be produced in highly automated plants using computer integrated manufacturing processes. An example of this emphasis on product simplification was Maytag's "Dependable Drive" washer transmission, which was designed to have 40.6% fewer parts than the transmission it replaced. Fewer parts meant simplified manufacturing, less chance of a breakdown, lower manufacturing costs, and higher product quality.

Most industry analysts agreed that continual process improvements had kept U.S. major home appliance manufacturers dominant in their industry. The emphasis on quality and durability, coupled with a reluctance to make major design changes simply for the sake of change, resulted in products with an average life expectancy of 20 years for refrigerators and 15 years for washers and dryers. This emphasis was one compelling reason why the Japanese manufacturers had been less successful in entering the U.S. home appliance market as contrasted with their success in automobiles. Another reason was a constant unrelenting pressure to reduce costs or be driven from the marketplace. Even though quality had improved significantly over the past 20 years, the average washer, dryer, and refrigerator cost no more than they did 20 years ago and yet lasted almost twice as long. If only the same could be said of the American and European automobile industry!

Firms that are unable to finance the huge costs of developing a new technology alone may coordinate their R&D with other firms through a **strategic alliance.** By 1990, more than 150 cooperative alliances involving 1,000 companies were operating in the United States and many more were operating throughout Europe and Asia.[30] These alliances may be (1) joint programs or contracts to cooperate in developing a new technology, (2) joint ventures establishing a separate company to take a new product to market, or (3) minority investments in innovative firms giving the innovator needed capital and the investor access to valuable research. For example, General Motors, Procter & Gamble, and six other companies purchased $20 million of equity in a small artificial intelligence company called Teknowledge. GM hoped that Teknowledge's expert systems software would help it design cars and prepare factory schedules. Increasingly referred to as strategic partnerships, these cooperative alliances also may be viewed as a form of quasi-vertical integration or even as a type of network organization design. In such arrangements, identifying where one firm begins and the other leaves off often is difficult.

When should a company buy or license technology from others instead of developing it internally? According to the resource-based view of the firm discussed previously in Chapter 5 on pages 115–117, a company should *buy* technologies that are commonly available but *make* (and protect) those that are rare, valuable, hard to imitate, and have no close substitutes. In addition, outsourcing technology may be appropriate when

- The technology is of little significance to competitive advantage;
- The supplier has proprietary technology;
- The supplier's technology is better and/or cheaper and reasonably easy to integrate into the current system;
- The company's strategy is based on system design, marketing, distribution, and service—not on development and manufacturing;
- The technology development process requires special expertise; and
- The technology development process requires new people and new resources.[31]

Importance of Technological Competence

Research suggests that companies must have at least a minimal R&D capability if they are to assess correctly the value of technology developed by others. Research and development creates a capacity to assimilate and exploit new knowledge. Called a company's *absorptive capacity,* it is a valuable by-product of routine in-house R&D activity.[32]

Corporations that do purchase an innovative technology must have the **technological competence** to use it effectively. Unfortunately, some managers who introduce the latest technology have not adequately assessed the organization's competence to handle it. For example, a survey conducted in the United Kingdom found that 44% of all companies that introduced robots met with initial failure and that 22% of those firms abandoned their use altogether, mainly because of inadequate technological knowledge and skills.[33] One U.S. company built a new plant and equipped it with computer-integrated manufacturing and statistical process controls, but the employees couldn't operate the equipment because 25% of them were illiterate.[34]

12.4 Strategy Implementation

If a corporation decides to develop innovations internally, it must make sure that its corporate system and culture are suitable for such a strategy. It must ensure that its R&D operations are managed appropriately. If—like most large corporations—the culture is too bureaucratic and rigid to support entrepreneurial projects, top management must reorganize itself to allow innovative projects the freedom to develop.

Developing an Innovative Entrepreneurial Culture

To create a more innovative corporation, top management must develop an entrepreneurial culture—one that is open to the transfer of new technology into company activities and products and services. The company should be flexible, be able to accept change, and be willing to live with some product failures on the way to success. The 3M Corporation and Texas Instruments, among others, have such cultures. Research and development in these companies is managed quite differently from traditional methods. *First, employees are dedicated to a particular project outcome rather than to innovation in general. Second, employees often are responsible for all functional activities and for all phases of the innovation process.* They are allowed to take time from regular duties and spend it on innovative ideas. If the ideas are feasible, employees are temporarily reassigned to help develop them. They may become project "champions" who fight for resources to make the project a success. Management often separates these internal ventures from the rest of the company to provide them with greater independence, freedom from short-term pressures, different rewards, improved visibility, and access to key decision makers.[35]

Companies are finding that one way to overcome the barriers to successful product innovation is to use multifunctional teams that have significant autonomy and are dedicated to a project. In a survey of 701 European, U.S., and Japanese companies, 85% of the respondents stated that they have used this approach, with 62% rating it as successful.[36] Chrysler Corporation reduced the development time for new vehicles by 40% by using cross-functional teams and developing a partnership approach to new projects.[37] International Specialty Products, a maker of polymers, used "product express" teams of chemists and representatives from manufacturing and engineering to cut development time in half. Explained John Tancredi, Vice-President for R&D, "Instead of passing a baton, we bring everyone into the commercialization process at the same time. We are moving laterally, like rugby players, instead of like runners in a relay race."[38]

Organizing for Innovation: Corporate Entrepreneurship

W. D. Guth and A. Ginsberg defined **corporate entrepreneurship** (also called *intrapreneurship*) as "the birth of new businesses within existing organizations, i.e., internal innovation or venturing; and the transformation of organizations through renewal of the key ideas on which they are built, i.e., strategic renewal."[39] A large corporation that wants to encourage innovation and creativity must give the new business unit a certain amount of freedom while maintaining some degree of headquarters control.

Burgelman proposes (see Fig. 12.3) that the use of a particular organizational design should be determined by (1) the *strategic importance of the new business* to the corporation and (2) the *relatedness of the unit's operations* to those of the corporation.[40] The combination of these two factors results in nine possible organizational designs for corporate entrepreneurship.

1. **Direct integration:** If the new business has a great deal of strategic importance and operational relatedness, it must be a part of the corporation's mainstream. Product *champions*—people who are respected by others in the corporation and who know how to work the system—are needed to manage these

FIGURE 12.3 **Organizational Designs for Corporate Entrepreneurship**

Strategic Importance

Operational Relatedness	Very Important	Uncertain	Not Important
Unrelated	3 Special Business Units	6 Independent Business Units	9 Complete Spin-Off
Partly Related	2 New Product Business Department	5 New Venture Division	8 Contracting
Strongly Related	1 Direct Integration	4 Micro New Ventures Department	7 Nurturing and Contracting

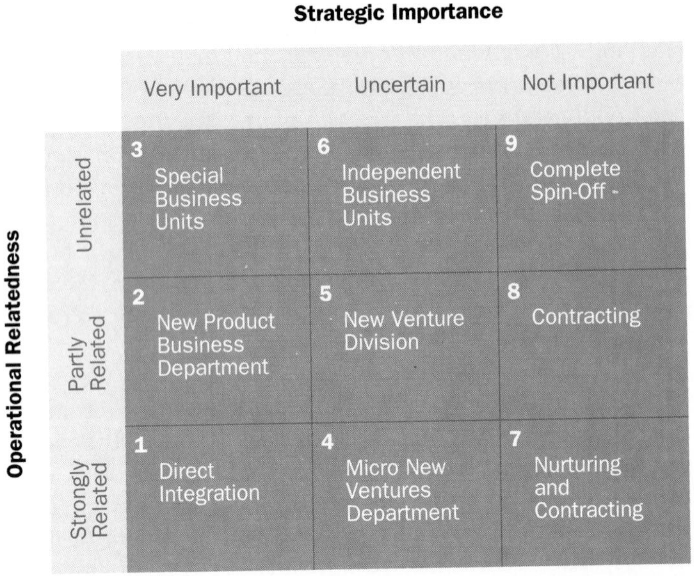

Source: Reprinted from R. A. Burgelman, "Designs for Corporate Entrepreneurship in Established Firms." Copyright © 1984 by the Regents of the University of California. Reprinted/condensed from *California Management Review*, Vol. 26, No. 3, p. 161. By permission of The Regents.

projects. When he was with Ford Motor Company, Lee Iacocca championed the Mustang.

2. **New product business department:** If the new business has a great deal of strategic importance and partial operational relatedness, it should be a separate department, organized around an entrepreneurial project in the division where skills and capabilities can be shared. Maytag Corporation built a new plant near its current Maytag Company plant to manufacture a wholly new line of energy- and water-efficient front-loading dishwashers.
3. **Special business units:** If the new business has a great deal of strategic importance and low operational relatedness, it should be a special new business unit with specific objectives and time horizons. General Motors set up an entirely new management, manufacturing, and marketing system to make the Saturn.
4. **Micro new ventures department:** If the new business has uncertain strategic importance and high operational relatedness, it is a peripheral project that is likely to emerge continuously in the operating divisions. Each division thus has its own new ventures department. Xerox Corporation uses its SBUs to generate and nurture new ideas. Small product synthesis teams in each SBU

test the feasibility of new ideas. Concepts receiving a "go" are managed by an SBU product delivery team, headed by a chief engineer, that takes the prototype from development through manufacturing.

5. **New venture division:** When the new business has uncertain strategic importance and is only partly related to present corporate operations, it belongs in a new venture division. It brings together projects that either exist in various parts of the corporation or can be acquired externally; sizable new businesses are built. R. J. Reynolds Industries established a separate company, R. J. Reynolds Development, to evaluate new business concepts with growth potential. The development company nurtures and develops businesses that might have the potential to become one of RJR's core businesses.
6. **Independent business units:** Uncertain strategic importance coupled with no relationship to present corporate activities make external arrangements attractive. IBM originally established personal computers as an independent business unit because in the early 1980s management was unsure of the PC's future.
7. **Nurturing and contracting:** When an entrepreneurial proposal might not be important strategically to the corporation but is strongly related to present operations, top management might help the entrepreneurial unit to spin off from the corporation. This approach allows a friendly competitor, instead of one of the corporation's major rivals, to capture a small niche. Techtronix has used this approach extensively. Related spin-offs tend to be poorer performers than nonrelated spin-offs (presumably owing to the loss of benefits enjoyed with a larger company), so the parent company should continue to support development of the spun-off unit.[41]
8. **Contracting:** As the required capabilities and skills of the new business are less related to those of the corporation, the parent corporation may spin off the strategically unimportant unit yet keep some relationship through a contractual arrangement with the new firm. The connection is useful in case the new firm eventually develops something of value to the corporation. For example, B. F. Goodrich offered manufacturing rights and a long-term purchasing agreement to a couple of its managers for a specific material Goodrich still used (in declining quantities) in its production process but no longer wanted to manufacture internally.
9. **Complete spin-off:** If both the strategic importance and the operational relatedness of the new business are negligible, the corporation is likely to sell off the business to another firm or to the present employees in some form of ESOP (Employee Stock Ownership Plan). Or the corporation may sell off the unit through a leveraged buyout (executives of the unit buy the unit from the parent company with money from a third source, to be repaid from the unit's anticipated earnings). Because AMF (known for its industrial and leisure products) was unwilling to invest the large amount of money in its Harley-Davidson subsidiary to effectively counter growing Japanese competition in motorcycles, it sold the subsidiary to a group of Harley-Davidson managers in a leveraged buyout.

Organizing for innovation is especially important for corporations that want to become more innovative but that are highly bureaucratic, with a culture that discourages creative thinking, because of their age and size. These new structural designs for corporate entrepreneurship cannot work by themselves, however. The entrepreneurial units must have the support of management, sufficient resources, and a modified corporate culture that encourages new ventures. They must also have employees who are risk takers willing to purchase an ownership interest in the new venture.

12.5 Evaluation and Control

Many companies want high R&D productivity, meaning fast conversion from research and development to sales. But how does management measure the effectiveness or efficiency of a company's R&D? Part of the problem is that authorities contend that a company shouldn't expect more than 1 in 20 product ideas from basic research to make it to the marketplace. Some companies measure the proportion of their sales attributable to new products. At Hewlett-Packard, for example, 72% of its revenue comes from products introduced in the past three years.[42] Bell-Core, the research part of seven regional Bell telephone companies, measures the effectiveness of its basic research by how often the lab's research is cited in other scientists' work. This measure is compiled and published by the Institute for Scientific Information. Other companies judge the quality of research by the number of patents filed annually. *Business Week* publishes a *Patent Scorecard* each August, listing the number of patents for each major company and how often the patents are cited in other patents and in scientific publications.[43]

Pittiglio Rabin Todd McGrath (PRTM), a high-tech consulting firm, proposes an *Index of R&D Effectiveness*. The index is calculated by dividing the percentage of total revenue spent on R&D into new product profitability, which is also expressed as a percentage. When they applied this measure to 45 large electronics manufacturers, only 9 companies scored 1.0 or higher, indicating that only 20% received a positive payback from their spending on R&D. The top companies held spending on marginal products to a minimum by running frequent checks on product versus market opportunities and canceling questionable products quickly. They also moved new products to market in half the time of the others. As a result, revenue growth among the top 20% of the companies was double the average of all 45 companies.[44]

A study of 15 multinational companies with successful R&D operations focused on three measures of R&D success: (1) improving technology transfer from R&D to business units, (2) accelerating time-to-market for new products and processes, and (3) institutionalizing cross-functional participation in R&D. The companies participated in basic, applied, and developmental research activities. The study revealed 13 *best practices* that all the companies followed.[45] Listed in Table 12.2, they provide a benchmark against which a strategic manager can compare a company's R&D activities.

TABLE 12.2 **Thirteen "Best Practices" for Improving R&D**

1. Corporate and business unit strategies are well defined and clearly communicated.
2. Core technologies are defined and communicated to R&D.
3. Investments are made in developing multinational R&D capabilities to tap ideas throughout the world.
4. Funding for basic research comes from corporate sources to ensure a long-term focus; funding for development comes from business units to ensure accountability.
5. Basic and applied research are performed either at a central facility or at a small number of labs, each focused on a particular discipline of science or technology. Development work is usually performed at business unit sites.
6. Formal, cross-functional teams are created for basic, applied, and developmental projects.
7. Formal mechanisms exist for regular interaction among scientists, and between R&D and other functions.
8. Analytical tools are used for selecting projects as well as for on-going project evaluation.
9. The transfer of technology to business units is the most important measure of R&D performance.
10. Effective measures of career development are in place at all levels of R&D.
11. Recruiting of new people is from diverse universities and from other companies when specific experience or skills are required that would take long to develop internally.
12. Some basic research is performed internally, but there are also many university and third-party relationships.
13. Formal mechanisms are used for monitoring external technological developments.

Source: I. Krause and J. Liu, "Benchmarking R&D Productivity." This article is reprinted from *Planning Review,* Jan/Feb 1993, with permission from The Planning Forum, The International Society for Strategic Management and Planning.

In Conclusion . . .

When CEO Edgar Woolard pointed out the failure of du Pont to convert research into successful new products, the company began to change the way it conducted its R&D. To speed up the new-product process, departments created small, interdisciplinary teams to deal with all new-product ideas. These teams had just two weeks to make a go or no go decision. If they decided to go ahead with the concept, they were given two more weeks to form another team to begin the project. This cut the time needed to move from idea to prototype stage to just two months.

The company also started working more closely with its customers in handling their requests. For example, Fluorware, Inc., wanted du Pont to make a purer version of a Teflon basket that Fluorware used to hold silicon wafers during production. The two companies formed a joint team to find a solution. Later, du Pont brought out a commercial version of the product to sell to other companies. According to John Goodman, Fluorware's Senior Director for Corporate Technology, the Fluorware–du Pont team continues to hold regular meetings, "which we hope will lead to breakthroughs in materials science."[46]

Points to Remember

- Top management must emphasize the importance of technology and innovation. Strategic managers have an obligation not only to encourage new product development, but also to develop a system to ensure that technology is being used most effectively with the consumer in mind.
- Although a company must develop an environmental scanning system capable of monitoring the latest developments in process and product technology, it must carefully decide whether market research should be part of its new-product development efforts. Flexibility in design and manufacturing may be better than endless interviews and market tests—particularly if time-to-market is essential to success in the industry. To do accurate market research for a product that doesn't currently exist is more difficult than to improve a current product.
- Companies should spend a consistent and meaningful amount of money on R&D, but should be prepared for technological discontinuities, that is, when one technology replaces another.
- As a product moves along the innovation life cycle, the proportion of product and process R&D changes, requiring less investment in product design and more investment in manufacturing efficiency.
- Shortening cycle times and global competition are forcing many companies to coordinate their R&D efforts with other firms in the hope of reducing the payback time for the use of a new technology.
- To create an innovative corporation, strategic managers must develop a culture and a system compatible with in-house entrepreneurial ventures. They can choose from a number of organizational designs to provide the new venture an appropriate amount of freedom combined with a minimum amount of corporate control.
- Techniques suggested to measure the effectiveness of R&D range from how often a lab's research is cited by others to the number of patents applied for to an index of R&D effectiveness.

Discussion Questions

1. What is the role of top management and the board of directors in managing technology and innovation?
2. How should a corporation scan the external environment for new technological developments? Who should be responsible for scanning? Why?
3. What is technology transfer and why is it important?
4. Explain the importance to strategic management of time to market.
5. How can management's knowledge of technological discontinuity help to improve a corporation's performance?
6. How might a firm's management decide whether it should continue to invest in current known technology or in new, but untested, technology? What factors might

encourage or discourage such a shift?

7. What is the importance of product and process R&D to competitive strategy?
8. What factors help determine whether a company should outsource a technology?
9. What is meant by a company's technological competence and its absorptive capacity?
10. How can a company develop an entrepreneurial culture?
11. What two factors, according to Burgelman, determine the use of a particular design for corporate entrepreneurship? Why?
12. How might a firm measure the effectiveness and efficiency of its investment in R&D?

Notes

1. Adapted from *Long Range Planning,* December 1992, J. B. Welch and P. Bolster, "Corporate Raiders Don't Cut Investment in R&D," p. 72. Copyright 1992, with kind permission from Elsevier Science Ltd., The Boulevard, Langford Lane, Kidlington OX5 IGB, UK.
2. S. McMurray, "Du Pont Tries to Make Its Research Wizardry Serve the Bottom Line," *Wall Street Journal* (March 27, 1992), pp. A1, A4.
3. P. Carroll, "The Day Bill Gates Overthrew Big Blue," *Wall Street Journal* (August 16, 1993), p. B3. Taken from Carroll's 1993 book, *Big Blues: The Unmaking of IBM.*
4. C. A. Ferland, book review of *Third Generation R&D—Managing the Link to Corporate Strategy* by Roussel, Saad, and Erickson, in *Long Range Planning* (April 1993), p. 128.
5. J. H. Dobrzynski, "These Board Members Aren't IBM-Compatible," *Business Week* (August 2, 1993), p. 23.
6. C. Power, K. Kerwin, R. Grover, K. Alexander, and R. D. Hof, "Flops," *Business Week* (August 16, 1993), pp. 76–82.
7. B. R. Schlender, "How Sony Keeps the Magic Going," *Fortune* (February 24, 1992), p. 77.
8. N. Snyder, "Environmental Volatility, Scanning Intensity and Organizational Performance," *Journal of Contemporary Business* (September 1981), p. 16.
9. G. C. Hill and K. Yamada, "Motorola Illustrates How an Aged Giant Can Remain Vibrant," *Wall Street Journal* (December 9, 1992), p. A1, A14.
10. W. I. Zangwill, "When Customer Research Is a Lousy Idea," *Wall Street Journal* (March 8, 1993), p. A10.
11. D. F. Kuratko, J. S. Hornsby, D. W. Naffziger, R. V. Montagno, "Implement Entrepreneurial Thinking in Established Organizations," *SAM Advanced Management Journal* (Winter 1993), p. 29.
12. L. G. Franko, "Global Corporate Competition: Who's Winning, Who's Losing, and the R&D Factor as One Reason Why," *Strategic Management Journal* (September–October 1989), pp. 449–474. See also P. S. Chan, E. J. Flynn, and R. Chinta, "The Strategies of Growing and Turnaround Firms: A Multiple Discriminant Analysis," *International Journal of Management* (September 1991), pp. 669–675.
13. M. J. Chussil, "How Much to Spend on R&D?" *The PIMSletter of Business Strategy,* No. 13 (Cambridge, Mass.: The Strategic Planning Institute, 1978), p. 5.
14. J. S. Harrison, E. H. Hall, Jr., and R. Nargundkar, "Resource Allocation as an Outcropping of Strategic Consistency: Performance Implications," *Academy of Management Journal* (October 1993), pp. 1026–1051.
15. M. A. Hitt, R. E. Hoskisson, and J. S. Harrison, "Strategic Competitiveness in the 1990s: Challenges and Opportunities for U.S. Executives," *Academy of Management Executive* (May 1991), p. 13.

16. T. F. O'Boyle, "Steel's Management Has Itself to Blame," *Wall Street Journal* (May 17, 1983), p. 32.
17. E. F. Finkin, "Developing and Managing New Products," *Journal of Business Strategy* (Spring 1983), p. 45.
18. M. Silva and B. Sjogren, *Europe 1992 and the New World Power Game* (New York: John Wiley & Sons, 1990), p. 231.
19. E. Mansfield, M. Schwartz, and S. Wagner, "Imitation Costs and Patents: An Empirical Study," *Economic Journal* (December 1981), pp. 907–918.
20. G. Stalk, Jr., and A. M. Webber, "Japan's Dark Side of Time," *Harvard Business Review* (July–August 1993), p. 99.
21. R. D. Hof, "Inside Intel," *Business Week* (June 1, 1992), pp. 86–94; A. Deutschman, "If They're Gaining on You, Innovate," *Fortune* (November 2, 1992), p. 86.
22. P. Pascarella, "Are You Investing in the Wrong Technology?" *Industry Week* (July 25, 1983), p. 37.
23. Ibid., p. 38.
24. A. C. Cooper and C. G. Smith, "How Established Firms Respond to Threatening Technologies," *Academy of Management Executive* (May 1992), pp. 55–70.
25. H. I. Ansoff, "Strategic Management of Technology," *Journal of Business Strategy* (Winter 1987), p. 35. For further information on managing technological discontinuity, see R. G. McGrath, I. C. McMillan, and M. L. Tushman, "The Role of Executive Team Actions in Shaping Dominant Designs: Towards the Strategic Shaping of Technological Progress," *Strategic Management Journal* (Winter 1992), pp. 137–161.
26. R. D. Hof, "This Chip Battle Royal Ain't Over Till It's Over," *Business Week* (June 1, 1992), p. 94. Technological discontinuities can occur in both product and process innovations. See P. Anderson and M. L. Tushman, "Technological Discontinuities and Dominant Designs: A Cyclical Model of Technological Change," *Administrative Science Quarterly* (December 1990), pp. 604–633.
27. M. Robert, "Market Fragmentation Versus Market Segmentation," *Journal of Business Strategy* (September/October 1992), p. 52.
28. W. Shan and W. Hamilton, "Profiting from International Cooperative Relationships," *Handbook of Business Strategy, 1992/93 Yearbook,* edited by H. E. Glass and M. A. Hovde (Boston: Warren, Gorham and Lamont, 1992), pp. 6.1–6.14.
29. K. Kelly and M. Ivey, "Turning Cummins into the Engine Maker That Could," *Business Week* (July 30, 1990), pp. 20–21.
30. M. Silva and B. Sjogren, *Europe 1992 and the New World Power Game* (New York: John Wiley & Sons, 1990), pp. 239–241. See also P. Nueno and J. Oosterveld, "Managing Technology Alliances," *Long Range Planning* (June 1988), pp. 11–17.
31. P. R. Nayak, "Should You Outsource Product Development?" *Journal of Business Strategy* (May/June 1993), pp. 44–45.
32. W. M. Cohen and D. A. Levinthal, "Absorptive Capacity: A New Perspective on Learning and Innovation," *Administrative Science Quarterly* (March 1990), pp. 128–152.
33. "The Impact of Industrial Robotics on the World of Work," *International Labour Review*, Vol. 125, No. 1 (1986). Summarized in "The Risks of Robotization," *The Futurist* (May–June 1987), p. 56.
34. Hitt, Hoskisson, and Harrison, p. 9.
35. C. A. Lengnick-Hall, "Innovation and Competitive Advantage: What We Know and What We Need to Know," *Journal of Management* (June 1992), pp. 399–429.
36. P. R. Nayak, "Product Innovation Practices in Europe, Japan, and the U.S.," *Journal of Business Strategy* (May/June 1992), pp. 62–63.
37. D. Rowe, "Up and Running," *Journal of Business Strategy* (May/June 1993), pp. 48–50.
38. N. Freundlich and M. Schroeder, "Getting Everybody into the Act," *Business Week* (Quality 1991 edition), p. 152.
39. W. D. Guth and A. Ginsberg, "Corporate Entrepreneurship," *Strategic Management Journal* (Summer 1990), p. 5.
40. R. A. Burgelman, "Designs for Corporate Entrepreneurship," *California Management Review* (Spring 1984), pp. 154–166; R. A. Burgelman and L. R. Sayles, *Inside Corporate Innovation* (New York: Free Press, 1986).
41. C. Y. Woo, G. E. Willard, and S. M. Beckstead, "Spin-Offs: What Are the Gains?" *Journal of Business Strategy* (March–April 1989), pp. 29–32.
42. J. B. Levin and R. D. Hof, "Has Philips

Found Its Wizard?" *Business Week* (September 6, 1993), pp. 82–84.

43. Freundlich and Schroeder, pp. 149–152; "Patent Scorecard," *Business Week* (August 9, 1993), pp. 59–62.
44. O. Port, "Rating R&D: How Companies Get the Biggest Bang for the Buck," *Business Week* (July 5, 1993), p. 98.
45. I. Krause and J. Liu, "Benchmarking R&D Productivity," *Planning Review* (January/February 1993), pp. 16–21, 52–53.
46. McMurray, pp. A1, A4.

Strategic Issues in Entrepreneurial Ventures and Small Businesses

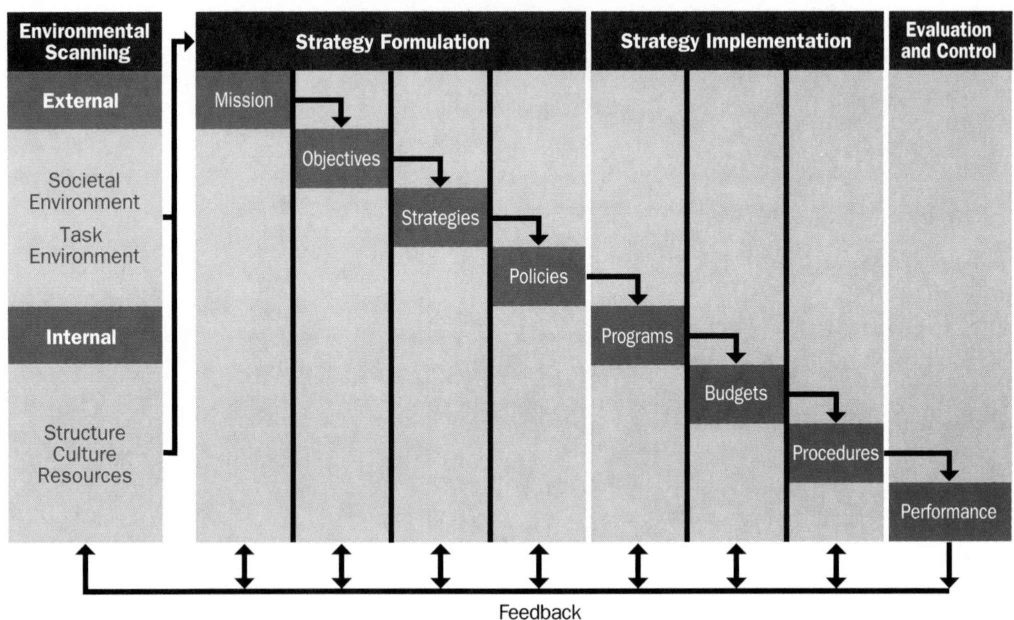

Wherever there's angst, there's an opportunity.[1]
[Cherrill Farnsworth, CEO, TME, Inc.]

Have you ever opened the refrigerator looking for a cold beer or a cola only to find the beverage shelf empty? You probably mumbled some curse and reached for one of those warm cans you had left in the pantry. You still want a cold drink but have only a few poor choices. If it's a soft drink, you can pour the contents of the can over ice cubes (if you had remembered to refill the ice trays), or you could put the can in the freezer and wait 20 minutes or so until it cools (or more likely forget and leave it there until it freezes and ruptures, spilling the still-liquid contents onto your left-over pizza). Or you might drive to the local convenience store to buy a cold drink, wasting time and gasoline.

F. X. Cretzmeyer III had a better idea. For $24.95 he will sell you a Chill Wizard, a patented device that will cool any 12-ounce canned beverage in only two minutes. According to Cretzmeyer, "With this product, you eliminate any potential of that hassle ever arising again." A Chill Wizard is a rectangular plastic box that holds crushed or cubed ice and a small battery-powered motor, which spins a 12-ounce can on top of the ice but doesn't cause the drink to foam when opened. "When people see it, they are so disbelieving," says Cretzmeyer. "It's almost like a magic trick in a way."

Cretzmeyer patented his invention in 1986 but couldn't find a company willing to manufacture and distribute it. So, to start Chill Wizard himself, he sold his successful equipment rental and video rental stores in Coralville, Iowa, and took out a second mortgage on his home. The first shipment of 10,000 Chill Wizards arrived from a Hong Kong factory in July 1990. Cretzmeyer hoped to sell them within a month, but stores were reluctant to stock the unusual product, most shoppers had no idea what the product could do, and sales were few and far between. As a result, cardboard boxes of Chill Wizard filled the Cretzmeyers' garage over the winter. Needless to say, the Cretzmeyer family ate a lot of French toast that year instead of the usual meat and potatoes.

In desperation, Cretzmeyer sent letters to catalog companies urging them to carry his product. Bankruptcy was closing in on Chill Wizard until upscale companies such as The Sharper Image, Hammacher Schlemmer, and Sporty's decided to feature the product in their summer 1991 catalogs. The beverage chillers began to sell spectacularly well. Cretzmeyer even received calls from NBC's "Today" program asking him to appear on television.

Why did this man risk everything on an idea—an idea that almost no one else was willing to support? Cretzmeyer explained it this way:

> I had enough faith in the product and was absolutely convinced. . . . One of the common complaints among older persons is that they didn't take enough risks [when they were younger]. If I hadn't, I'd never know and I could be sitting on an old folks' porch 40 years from now still kicking myself wondering. I never would have known, and I guess that was important to me.[2]

13.1 The Importance of Small-Business and Entrepreneurial Ventures

Strategic management as a field of study typically deals with large, established business corporations. However, small businesses cannot be ignored. Approximately 99% of the 17 million businesses in the United States employ fewer than 100 people. Small businesses account for approximately half of all U.S. employment and created over 80% of all new jobs in the United States between 1960 and 1985. Well over 60% of the total were created by new ventures. During the 1980s, Fortune 500 companies eliminated 3.5 million jobs, whereas small businesses created more than 20 million jobs.[3] Research reveals that small firms spend almost twice as much of their R&D dollars on fundamental research as large firms. As a result, small companies are responsible for a high proportion of innovative products and services.[4] For example, new small firms produce 24 times more innovation per research dollar than do the much larger Fortune 500 firms.[5] The National Science Foundation estimates that 98% of "radical" product developments result from the research done in labs of small companies.[6]

Despite the overall success of small businesses, however, every year tens of thousands of small companies fail. According to the U.S. Small Business Administration, 24% of all new businesses fail within two years and 63% fail within six years.[7] Similar failure rates occur in the United Kingdom, the Netherlands, Japan, Taiwan, and Hong Kong.[8] Although some studies indicate that the survival rate of new entrepreneurial ventures is higher,[9] new businesses definitely are risky. The causes of small-business failure (depending on the study cited) range from inadequate accounting systems to inability to cope with growth. The underlying problem appears to be an overall lack of strategic management—beginning with an inability to plan a strategy to reach the customer and ending with a failure to develop a system of performance measurement and controls. According to a review of new-business failures, "In nearly all cases, the practice of strategic planning by small firm owners and managers was found to be scanty and perfunctory."[10]

Definition of Small-Business Firms and Entrepreneurial Ventures

The most commonly accepted definition of a small business firm is one that employs fewer than 500 people and that generates sales of less than $20 million annually. According to the U.S. Small Business Administration, "A small business is one which is independently owned and operated, and which is not dominant in its field of operation."[11]

Although there is considerable overlap between what is meant by the terms small business and entrepreneurship, the concepts are different. The **small-business firm** is independently owned and operated, not dominant in its field, and doesn't engage in innovative practices. The **entrepreneurial venture,** in contrast, is any business whose primary goals are profitability and growth and that can be characterized by innovative strategic practices.[12] The basic difference between the small-business firm and the entrepreneurial venture, therefore, lies not in the type of goods or services provided, but in their fundamental views on growth and innovation. Thus, according to Donald Sexton, an authority on entrepreneurship, strategic planning is more likely to be an integral part of an entrepreneurial venture than of the typical small-business firm:

> Most firms start with just a single product. Those oriented toward growth immediately start looking for another one. It's that planning approach that separates the entrepreneur from the small-business owner.[13]

The Entrepreneur as a Strategic Manager

Often defined as a person who organizes and manages a business undertaking and who assumes risk for the sake of a profit, the entrepreneur is the ultimate strategic manager. He or she makes all the strategic and operational decisions. All three levels of strategy—corporate, business, and functional—are the concerns of the founder and owner–manager of the company. As one entrepreneur puts it, "Entrepreneurs are strategic planners without realizing it."[14]

The founding of Chill Wizard described at the beginning of this chapter contained the key elements of the entrepreneurial venture: a basic business idea that hadn't yet been tried successfully and a gutsy entrepreneur who, while working on a shoestring, creates a new business through a lot of trial and error, persistence, and hard work. Similar stories can be told of countless other people, including Will Parish, who founded National Energy Associates, and Debbie Fields, who created Mrs. Fields Cookies. Both were ridiculed at one time or another for their desire to start a business. Friends and family told Debbie Fields that starting a business to sell chocolate chip cookies "was a stupid idea." Will Parish, who built a power plant in California's Imperial Valley that burns "pasture patties," is called an "entre-manure." Every day the plant burns 900 tons of manure collected from nearby feedlots to generate 15 megawatts of electricity—enough to light 20,000 homes. Parish sells the power to Southern California Edison. He got the idea during a trip to India where the fuel used to heat meals often is cow dung. Now that the plant is earning a profit, Parish is building a larger plant nearby that will burn wheat straw and other crop wastes. The plants provide an environmentally sound, as well as profitable, way to dispose of waste. Says Parish, who is very interested in conservation, "I wanted to combine doing well with doing good."[15]

13.2 Use of Strategic Management

Research shows that strategic planning is strongly related to small-business financial performance.[16] Nevertheless, many small companies still do not utilize the process. Four reasons usually are cited for the apparent lack of strategic planning by many small-business firms.

- **Not enough time.** Day-to-day operating problems take up the time necessary for long-term planning. It's relatively easy to justify avoiding strategic planning on the basis of day-to-day crisis management. Some will ask, "How can I be expected to do strategic planning when I don't know if I'm going to be in business next week?"
- **Unfamiliarity with strategic planning.** The small-business CEO may be unaware of strategic planning or view it as irrelevant. Planning may be viewed as a straitjacket that limits flexibility.
- **Lack of skills.** Small-business managers often lack the skills necessary to begin strategic planning and don't have or want to spend the money necessary to bring in consultants. Future uncertainty may be used to justify a lack of planning. One entrepreneur admits, "Deep down, I know I should plan. But I don't know what to do. I'm the leader but I don't know how to lead the planning process."
- **Lack of trust and openness.** Many small-business owner–managers are very sensitive about the business's key information and unwilling to share strategic planning with employees or outsiders. For this reason also, boards of directors often are composed only of close friends and relatives of the owner–manager—people unlikely to provide an objective viewpoint or professional advice.[17]

Value of Strategic Management

There is some evidence, however, that an increasing number of small businesses are introducing strategic management very early in their existence. A 1990 survey by the national accounting and consulting firm of BDO Seidman found that 81% of firms 1–10 years old had strategic plans, whereas only 67% of companies 11–20 years old had such plans. Herb Goldstein, a partner with BDO Seidman, commented that older entrepreneurs were more likely to "manage by the seat of their pants." Of those firms with a strategic plan, 89% indicated that the plan had been effective. Reasons given for its effectiveness were that it had specific goals (64%), gave staff a unified vision (25%), and set up a time frame for achievements (11%). Reasons given for an ineffective strategic plan were that it was too vague (43%), lacked a time frame for goals (29%), did not identify goals (17%), and lacked staff input (11%).[18]

Degree of Formality

Researchers generally conclude that the strategic planning process should be far less formal in small companies than it is in large corporations.[19] Some studies have even found that too formal a process may actually hurt performance.[20] A heavy emphasis on structured, written plans may be dysfunctional to small entrepreneurial firms because it reduces the flexibility that is crucial to their success. *The process of strategic planning, not the plan itself, is probably the key to improving business performance.*

These observations suggest that an entrepreneurial venture begins in Henry Mintzberg's entrepreneurial mode of strategy formulation (see Chapter 2) and moves toward the planning mode as the company becomes established and the entrepreneur wants its growth to continue. However, if the entrepreneur chooses stability over growth, the venture moves toward the adaptive mode common to many small businesses.

Usefulness of Strategic Management Model

The descriptive model of strategic management presented in Fig. 1.2—and which prefaces each chapter in the book—also is relevant to entrepreneurial ventures and small businesses. This basic model holds for both an established small company and a new entrepreneurial venture. As the research mentioned earlier concluded, small and developing companies increase their chances of success if they make a serious attempt to work through the strategic issues embedded in the strategic management model. The key is to focus on what's important: the set of managerial decisions and actions that determine the long-run performance of the company. The list of informal questions presented in Table 13.1 may be more useful to a small company than the more formal approach used by large corporations.

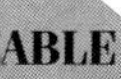

TABLE 13.1

Informal Questions to Begin the Strategic Management Process in a Small Company or Entrepreneurial Venture

Formal	Informal
Define mission	What do we stand for?
Set objectives	What are we trying to achieve?
Formulate strategy	How are we going to get there? How can we beat the competition?
Determine policies	What sort of ground rules should we all be following to get the job done right?
Establish programs	How should we organize this operation to get what we want done as cheaply as possible with the highest quality possible?
Prepare pro forma *budgets*	How much is it going to cost us and where can we get the cash?
Specify procedures	In how much detail do we have to lay things out, so that everybody knows what to do?
Determine performance measures	What are those few key things that will determine whether we make it? How can we keep track of them?

Usefulness of Strategic Decision-Making Process

One way to make the strategic management model action-oriented is to follow the strategic decision-making process presented in Fig. 2.3. Those eight steps are just as appropriate for small companies as they are for large corporations. Unfortunately, the process doesn't fit new entrepreneurial ventures. These companies must develop new missions, objectives, strategies, and policies by comparing their external opportunities and threats to their potential strengths and weaknesses. Consequently, as shown in Fig. 13.1, we propose a modified version of the strategic decision-making process that better suits the new entrepreneurial business.

The proposed **strategic decision-making process for new ventures** comprises the following eight interrelated steps.

1. **Develop a basic business idea** involving a product and/or service having target customers and/or markets. The idea can be based on a person's experience or generated in a moment of creative insight. For example, F. X. Cretzmeyer conceived the idea of the beverage cooler long before it became feasible as a product.
2. **Scan the external environment to locate strategic factors** in the societal and task environments that pose opportunities and threats. Scanning should focus particularly on market potential and resource accessibility.
3. **Scan the internal strategic factors** relevant to the new business. The entrepreneur should consider objectively personal assets, areas of expertise, abilities, and experience—all in terms of the organizational needs of the new venture.
4. **Analyze the strategic factors** in light of the current situation. The entrepreneur must evaluate the venture's potential strengths and weaknesses in light of opportunities and threats.

FIGURE 13.1 **Strategic Decision-Making Process for New Ventures**

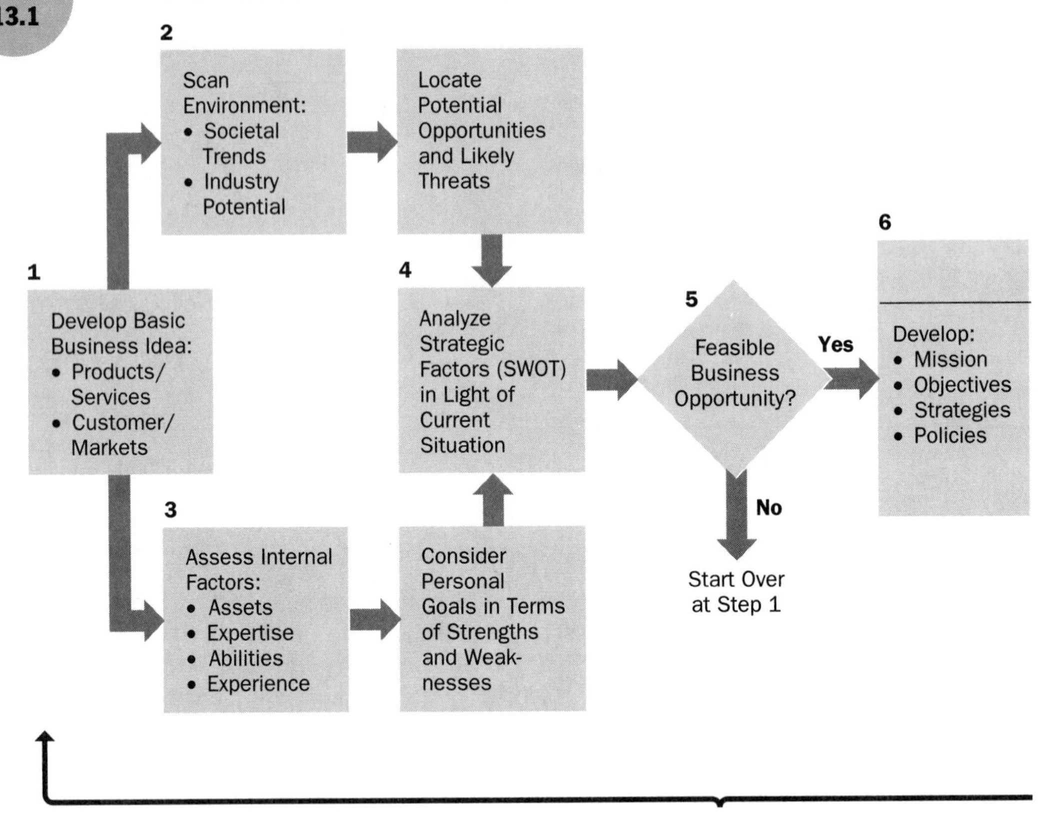

Source: T. L. Wheelen and C. E. Michaels, Jr., "Model for Strategic Decision-Making Process for New Ventures." Copyright © 1987 by T. L. Wheelen. Reprinted by permission.

5. **Decide to proceed or stop** by determining whether the basic business idea still appears to be a feasible business opportunity. If it is, continue the process. Otherwise, don't develop the idea further unless the strategic factors change.
6. **Generate a business plan** specifying how to transform the idea into reality. Table 13.2 lists the suggested contents of a strategic business plan. The proposed venture's mission, objectives, strategies, policies, likely board of directors (if a corporation), and key managers should be developed. Crucial internal factors should be specified and performance projections generated. (The *strategic audit* [in Chapter 2, pages 48–55] can be used to develop a strategic business plan. The audit's sections and subsections along with the questions within them provide a useful framework for developing a plan.) The

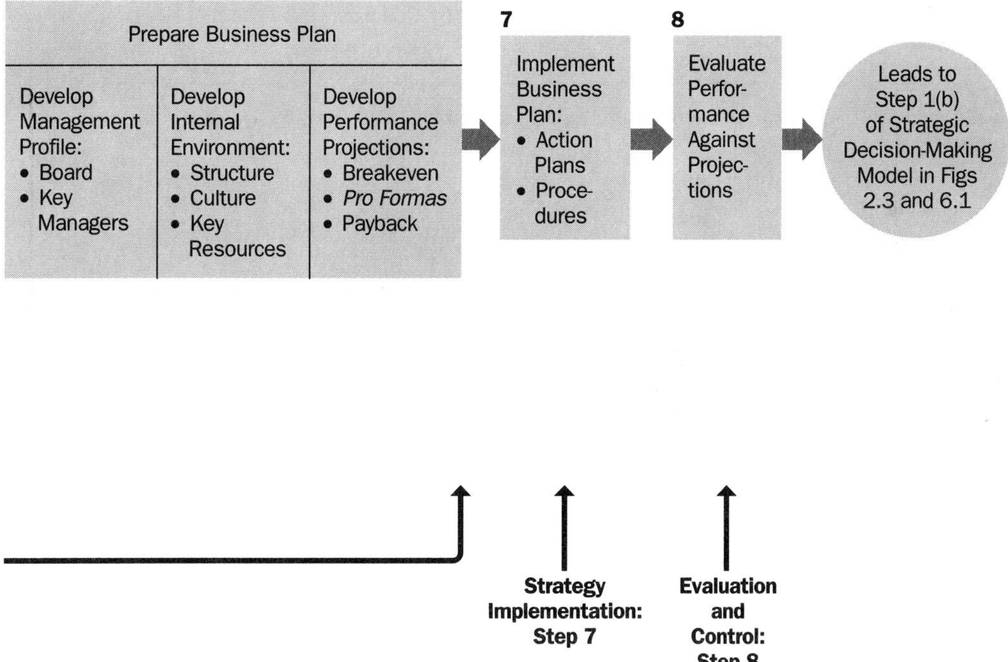

business plan serves as a vehicle through which financial support is obtained from potential investors and creditors. Starting a business without a business plan is the quickest way to kill a new venture. For example, one study of clothing retailers showed that 80% of the successful stores had written a business plan, whereas 65% of the failed businesses had not.[21]

7. **Implement the business plan** with action plans and procedures.
8. **Evaluate the implemented business plan** by comparing actual performance to projected performance. This step leads to Step 1(b) of the strategic decision-making process shown in Fig. 2.3. If actual results are much less or much greater than the anticipated results, the entrepreneur may need to reconsider the company's current mission, objectives, strategies, policies, and programs and make changes to the original business plan.[22]

TABLE 13.2 **Contents of a Strategic Business Plan for an Entrepreneurial Venture**

I. Table of Contents	X. Human Resources Plan
II. Executive Summary	XI. Ownership
III. Nature of the Business	XII. Risk Analysis
IV. Strategy Formulation	XIII. Timetables and Milestones
V. Market Analysis	XIV. Strategy Implementation—Action Plans
VI. Marketing Plan	XV. Evaluation and Control
VII. Operational Plans—Service/Product	XVI. Summary
VIII. Financial Plans	XVII. Appendixes
IX. Organization and Management	

Note: The strategic audit can be used to develop a business plan. It provides detailed questions to serve as a checklist.

Source: Thomas L. Wheelen, "Contents of a Strategic Business Plan for an Entrepreneurial Venture." Copyright © 1988 by Thomas L. Wheelen. Reprinted by permission.

13.3 Issues in Environmental Scanning and Strategy Formulation

Environmental scanning in small businesses is much less complicated than in large corporations. The business is usually too small to justify hiring someone to do only environmental scanning or strategic planning. Top managers, especially if they are the founders, tend to believe that they know the business and can follow it better than anyone else. A study of 220 small, rapidly growing companies revealed that the majority of CEOs were actively and personally involved in all phases of the planning process but especially in setting objectives. Only 15% of the companies used a planning officer or formed a planning group to assist in the planning process. In the rest of the firms, operating managers who participated in strategic planning provided input only to the CEO, who then formulated the plan.[23] Unfortunately, research suggests that few small businesses do much competitor analysis.

A fundamental reason for differences in strategy formulation between large and small companies lies in the relationship between owners and managers. The CEO of a large corporation has to consider and balance the varied needs of the corporation's many stakeholders. The CEO of a small business also is very likely to be the owner—the company's primary stakeholder. Personal and family needs may strongly affect the small company's mission and objectives and override other considerations.[24] For example, large corporations often choose growth strategies for their many side benefits for management as well as for shareholders. However, a small company may choose a stability strategy because (a) the owner is interested mainly in generating employment for family members, (b) providing the family a decent living, and (c) being the boss of a firm small enough to manage alone comfortably. "Thus in order to understand the goals of a small organization, it is first necessary to understand the motivation of the owner since the two are indistinguishable, certainly in the early days of the firm's start-up," according to S. Birley and D. Norburn.[25]

The basic SWOT analysis is as relevant to small businesses as it is to large ones. Both the greatest strength and the greatest weakness of the small firm, at least in the beginning, rest with the entrepreneur—the owner–manager of the business. The entrepreneur is *the* manager, the source of product/market strategy, and the dynamo who energizes the company. That is why the internal assessment of a new venture's strengths and weaknesses focuses in Fig. 13.1 on the personal characteristics of the founder—his or her assets, expertise, abilities, and experience. Just as an entrepreneur's strengths can be the key to a company's success, so too can personal weaknesses be a primary cause of failure. For example, a study of 270 clothing retailers showed that the managers of 85% of failed stores had had no prior retailing experience.[26]

Sources of Innovation

In his book *Innovation and Entrepreneurship,* Peter Drucker proposed that those interested in starting an entrepreneurial venture—either within an established company or as an independent small business—should monitor seven sources of innovative opportunity.[27] The first four exist within the industry itself, and the last three in the societal environment.

1. **The unexpected:** An unexpected success, an unexpected failure, or an unexpected outside event can be a symptom of a unique opportunity. When Don Cullen of Transmet Corporation spilled a box of very fine aluminum flakes onto his company's parking lot, he discovered that their presence in the asphalt prevented it from turning sticky in high temperatures. His company now produces aluminum chips for use in roofing. Sales have doubled every year since introduction of the product and will soon dominate the business.[28]
2. **Incongruity:** A discrepancy between reality and what everyone assumes it to be, or between what is and what ought to be, may create an opportunity for innovation. Realizing that the real costs of ocean freighter haulage were not crew wages but the time spent loading and unloading at port, Sea-Land changed the entire industry by introducing efficient containerized shipping to reduce handling time and costs.
3. **Innovation based on process need:** When a weak link is evident in a particular process, but people work around it instead of doing something about it, an opportunity is present for the person or company willing to forge a stronger link. For example, Alcon Laboratories came into being because of the discovery that a specific enzyme could enable doctors to avoid cutting a particular ligament when performing eye surgery.
4. **Changes in industry or market structure:** An innovative product, service, or approach to a business may emerge from a shift in the underlying foundation of an industry or a market. Black Entertainment Television, Inc., was born when Robert Johnson noticed that no television programmer was targeting the

increasing number of black viewers. Johnson then successfully expanded from television into print with *Young Sisters & Brothers,* a monthly magazine aimed at black teenagers.[29]

5. **Demographics:** Changes in the population's size, age structure, composition, employment, level of education, and income can create opportunities for innovation. For example, Pam Henderson started a company called Kids Kab to shuttle children and teenagers to private schools, doctor and dental appointments, lessons, and extracurricular activities. With the trend to dual careers, parents were no longer always available to provide personal transportation for their own children and needed such a service.[30]
6. **Changes in perception, mood, and meaning:** Opportunities for innovation can develop when a society's general assumptions, attitudes, and beliefs change. For example, the increasing dominance of a few national brewers has caused beer drinkers to look for alternatives to the same old national brands. By positioning Yuengling, a local Pennsylvania beer, as a full-flavored beer and providing it with an artsy, nostalgic-looking label, the small company was able to catch the fancy of young, trendy consumers who viewed it as Pennsylvania's version of Anchor Steam, the successful San Francisco beer.[31]
7. **New knowledge:** Advances in scientific and nonscientific knowledge can create new products and new markets. Advances in two different areas sometimes can be integrated to form the basis of a new product. For example, new software firms emerge weekly as new programs are needed to take advantage of technological advances in computers and telecommunications.

Factors Affecting a New Venture's Success

According to C. W. Hofer and W. R. Sandberg, three factors have a substantial impact on a new venture's performance. In order of importance, they are (1) the structure of the industry entered, (2) the new venture's business strategy, and (3) the behavioral characteristics of the entrepreneur.[32]

Industry Structure

Research shows that the chances for success are greater for entrepreneurial ventures that enter rapidly changing industries than for those that enter stable industries. In addition, prospects are better in industries that are in the early, high-growth stages of development because the competition often is less intense. Fast market growth also allows new ventures to make some mistakes without serious penalty. New ventures also increase their chances of success when they enter markets in which they can erect entry barriers to keep out competitors.

PIMS data reveal that a new venture is more likely to be successful when entering an industry in which one dominant competitor has a 50% or more market share than when entering an industry in which the largest competitor has less than a 25% market share. To explain this phenomenon, Hofer and Sandberg point out that, when an industry has one dominant firm, the remaining competitors are relatively weak and are easy prey for an aggressive entrepreneur. To avoid direct competition with a major rival, the new venture can focus on a market segment that others are ignoring (such as Yuengling beer did by avoiding Anheuser-Busch to compete in a Pennsylvania niche).

Industry product characteristics also have a significant impact on a new venture's success. First, a new venture is more likely to be successful when it enters an industry with heterogeneous (different) products than when it enters one with homogeneous (similar) products. In a heterogeneous product industry, a new venture can differentiate itself from competitors with a unique product; or, by focusing on the unique needs of a market segment, it can find a market niche. Second, according to research data, a new venture is more likely to be successful if the product is relatively unimportant to the customer's total purchasing needs than if it is important. Customers are more likely to experiment with a new product if its cost is low and product failure won't create a problem.

Business Strategy

The key to success for most new ventures is (1) to differentiate the product from other competitors in terms of quality and service and (2) to focus the product on customer needs in a segment of the market to achieve a dominant share of that segment (Porter's focused differentiation competitive strategy). Adopting guerrilla warfare tactics, these companies go after opportunities in market niches too small to justify retaliation from market leaders.[33]

To continue its growth after it has found a niche, the entrepreneurial firm can emphasize continued innovation and pursue natural growth in its current markets. It also can expand into related markets in which the company's core skills, resources, and facilities offer the keys to further success.[34]

Entrepreneurial Characteristics

Four behavioral factors are key to a new venture's success.[35]

1. Successful entrepreneurs are better than most people at *identifying potential venture opportunities*. They focus on opportunities—not on problems—and try to learn from failure. Entrepreneurs are goal-oriented and have a strong impact on the emerging culture of an organization. They are able to envision where the company is going and thus are able to provide a strong sense of strategic direction.
2. Successful entrepreneurs have a *sense of urgency* that makes them action-oriented. They have a high need for achievement, which motivates them to put their ideas into action. They tend to have an internal locus of control that leads them to believe that they can determine their own fate through their own behavior. They have a significantly greater capacity to tolerate ambiguity than do many in established organizations.[36] They also have a high need for control and may even be viewed as "misfits who need to create their own environment." They tend to distrust others and often have a need "to show others that they amount to something, that they cannot be ignored."[37]
3. Successful entrepreneurs have a *detailed knowledge of the key factors* needed for success in the industry and the physical stamina needed to make their work their lives. More than half of all entrepreneurs work at least 60 hours a week

TABLE 13.3

Some Guidelines for New-Venture Success

- Focus on industries facing substantial technological or regulatory changes, especially those with recent exits by established competitors.
- Seek industries whose smaller firms have relatively weak competitive positions.
- Seek industries that are in early, high-growth stages of evolution.
- Seek industries in which it is possible to create high barriers to subsequent entry.
- Seek industries with heterogeneous products that are relatively unimportant to the customer's overall success.
- Seek to differentiate your products from those of your competitors in ways that are meaningful to your customers.
- Focus such differentiation efforts on product quality, marketing approaches, and customer service—and charge enough to cover the costs of doing so.
- Seek to dominate the market segments in which you compete. If necessary, either segment the market differently or change the nature and focus of your differentiation efforts to increase your domination of the segments you serve.
- Stress innovation, especially new product innovation, that is built on existing organizational capabilities.
- Seek natural, organic growth through flexibility and opportunism that builds on existing organizational strengths.

Source: C. W. Hofer and W. R. Sandberg, "Improving New Venture Performance: Some Guidelines for Success," *American Journal of Small Business* (Summer 1987), pp. 17, 19. Copyright © 1987 by C. W. Hofer and W. R. Sandberg. Reprinted by permission.

in the start-up year, according to a study by the National Federation of Independent Business.[38]

4. Successful entrepreneurs *seek outside help* to supplement their skills, knowledge, and abilities. Over time, they develop a network of people having key skills and knowledge whom the entrepreneurs can call on for support. Through their enthusiasm, these entrepreneurs are able to attract needed investors, partners, creditors, and employees. For example, Mitch Kapor, founder of Lotus Development Corporation, didn't hesitate to bring in Jim Manzi as President because Manzi had the managerial skills that Kapor lacked.

In summarizing their conclusions regarding factors affecting the success of entrepreneurial ventures, Hofer and Sandberg propose the guidelines presented in Table 13.3.

13.4 Issues in Strategy Implementation

The implementation of strategy in a small business involves many of the same issues that concern a large corporation. The major difference between the large and small company is who must implement the strategy. In a large corporation, the implementors often are a very different group of people from those who formulated the strategy. In a small business, the formulators of the strategy are usually the ones who implement it. Hence the imaginary line between strategy formulation and implementation often becomes blurred in most small businesses. Two key implementation issues in small companies are organizing and staffing the growing company and transferring ownership of the company to the next generation.

Stages of Small Business Development

The implementation problems of a small business change as the company grows and develops over time. Just as the decision-making process for entrepreneurial ventures is different from that of established businesses, so do the managerial systems in small companies often vary from those of large corporations. Those variations are based on the stages of corporate growth and development discussed in Chapter 8 on pages 229–231. All small businesses are either in Stage I or trying to move into Stage II, implying that all successful new ventures eventually become Stage II, functionally organized companies. This outcome isn't always true, however. In attempting to show clearly how small businesses develop, N. C. Churchill and V. L. Lewis propose five *substages* of small business development: (A) Existence, (B) Survival, (C) Success, (D) Take-off, and (E) Resource Maturity.[39] By moving through these substages, a company can progress from the entrepreneurial Stage I to the functionally oriented, professionally managed Stage II.

Stage A: Existence

At first, the entrepreneurial venture faces the problems of obtaining customers and delivering the promised product or service. The organizational structure is a simple one. The entrepreneur does everything and supervises subordinates directly. Systems are minimal. The owner *is* the business.

Stage B: Survival

Those ventures able to satisfy a sufficient number of customers enter the survival stage. The rest of the ventures close when the owners run out of start-up capital. Those reaching the survival stage are concerned about generating the cash flow needed to repair and replace capital assets as they wear out and to finance the growth to continue satisfying the market segment it has entered.

The organizational structure is still simple, but it probably has a sales manager or general supervisor to carry out the well-defined instructions of the owner. A major problem of many small businesses at this stage is finding a person who is qualified to supervise the business when the owner can't be present but who is still willing to work for a very modest salary.[40] Entrepreneurs usually try to use family members rather than hire an outsider who lacks the entrepreneur's dedication to the business and (in the words of one owner–manager) "steals them blind." A company that remains in this stage long will earn marginal returns on invested time and capital (with lots of psychic income!) and eventually go out of business when "mom and pop" give up or retire.

Stage C: Success

By this point the company's sales have reached a level where the firm not only is profitable, but has sufficient cash flow to reinvest in itself. The key issue at the success stage is whether the company should be used primarily to support the owners

COMPANY SPOTLIGHT

MAYTAG Corporation

The Impact of F. L. Maytag as Entrepreneur

Much of Maytag Corporation's corporate culture derives from founder F. L. Maytag's personal philosophy and from lessons he learned when starting the business at the beginning of the twentieth century. This entrepreneur made a direct impact on the Maytag Company's development and indirectly on the Maytag Corporation's philosophy of management in the following areas.

- **Commitment to quality.** In the company's first year of operation (selling attachments to threshing machines), almost half the products sold were defective in some way. F. L. Maytag's insistence on fixing or buying back the faulty products resulted in losses for the new company but set a strong example in emphasizing the importance of quality. He commented that "*nothing was actually 'sold' until it was in the hands of a satisfied user.*"
- **Concern for employees.** Wages at Maytag have traditionally been some of the highest in the industry. F. L. Maytag's philosophy was that an "*uncommonly good company wants to pay its employees uncommonly well.*"
- **Concern for the community.** F. L. Maytag played a significant role in the development of the Newton (Iowa) YMCA. He also built a water treatment plant and sold it to the city at cost. Continuing his example, Maytag management has been active in community affairs and concerned about pollution.
- **View of innovation.** In the company's early years when the factory itself sent service people out

as they completely or partially disengage from the company or as a platform for growth. The company is transforming into a functionally structured organization but still relies on the entrepreneur for all key decisions. The two options are:

C(1) Disengagement The company can now successfully follow a stability strategy and remain at this stage almost indefinitely—provided that environmental change doesn't destroy its niche or poor management reduce its competitive abilities. By now functional managers have taken over some duties from the entrepreneur. By this time the company may be incorporated, but it is still primarily owned by the founder or founder's family. Consequently, the board of directors is either a rubber stamp for the entrepreneur or a forum for family squabbles. Growth strategies are not pursued, either because the market niche will not allow growth or because the owner is content with the company at a size he or she can still manage comfortably.

C(2) Growth The entrepreneur risks all available cash and the established borrowing power of the company to finance further growth. Strategic as well as operato far-flung dealers to repair defective products, F. L. Maytag noted that few calls ever came from a Minnesota dealer that employed a mechanic named Howard Snyder. Consequently, he hired Snyder to improve the company's products. Snyder wasn't interested in cosmetic changes for the sake of sales but in internal improvements related to quality, durability, and safety. This emphasis became the company's dominant view of product development.

- **Promotion from within.** F. L. Maytag strove to build company loyalty and trust. He was committed to hiring and training people to do the best work possible. He constantly told people: "*I'd rather make men than money . . . and I would because I can give money away. I can't give men away; I need them.*"
- **Dedication to hard work.** Imbued with the strong work ethic of the Midwest, F. L. Maytag spent huge amounts of time to establish and maintain the company. His trip West while Chairman of the Board to sell a train carload of washers personally set an example to his sales force and became a permanent part of company lore.
- **Emphasis on performance.** F. L. Maytag didn't like to boast about himself or his company. Preferring to be judged by his work rather than by his words, he was quoted in a company newsletter as saying: "*It's a good idea for a fellow to have a fair opinion of himself. . . . But it doesn't sound well to hear him broadcast it. It's a better idea to let his associates discover it by his deeds.*"

tional planning is extensive and deeply involves the owner. Managers with an eye to the company's future rather than its current situation are hired. The emphasis now is on teamwork rather than the entrepreneur's personal actions and energy. As noted in the Company Spotlight: Maytag Corporation feature on pages 374–375, a corporate culture based on the personal values and philosophy of the founder begins to form as the founder hires and trains a dedicated team of successors.

Stage D: Take-Off

The key problems in this stage are how to grow rapidly and how to finance that growth. The entrepreneur must learn to delegate to specialized professional managers or to a team of managers who now comprise the top management of the company.[41] A functional structure of the organization should now be solidly in place. Operational and strategic planning heavily involve the hired managers, but the entrepreneur's presence and stock control still dominate the company. Vertical and horizontal growth strategies are being seriously considered as the firm's management debates when and how to grow. This is the point at which the entrepreneur either is able to manage the transition from a small to a large company or recognizes personal limitations, sells his or her stock for a profit, and leaves the firm. The composition of the board of directors changes from dominance by the owner's friends and relatives to a large percentage of outsiders with managerial experience, who can help the owner during the transition to a professionally managed company. The biggest danger facing the firm in this stage is the owner's desire to remain in total control, as if the company were still a small entrepreneurial venture, even though the owner lacks the managerial skills necessary to run an established corporation.[42]

Stage E: Resource Maturity

Upon reaching resource maturity, the small company has taken on most of the characteristics of an established, large company. It may still be a small-to-medium-sized company, but it is recognized as an important force in the industry and a possible future candidate for the Fortune 500 list. The greatest concerns of a company at this stage are (1) controlling the financial gains brought on by rapid growth and (2) retaining its flexibility and entrepreneurial spirit. In terms of the stages of organizational growth and development discussed in Chapter 8 on pages 229–231, the company has become a full-fledged Stage II functional corporation.[43]

Transfer of Power and Wealth in Family Businesses

Small businesses often are family businesses. Even though the company founders are the primary forces in starting entrepreneurial ventures, their needs for business support and financial assistance will cause them to turn to trusted family members rather than unknown outsiders of unknown integrity with high salary demands. Sooner or later the founder draws spouse and children into the business, either because (1) the family standard of living is directly tied to the business or (2) the entrepreneur is in desperate need of help just to staff the operation. The children are guaranteed summer jobs and the business changes from dad's or mom's company to "our" company. The family members are extremely valuable assets to the entrepreneur because they often are willing to help the business succeed by putting in long hours for low pay. Even though spouse and children might have no official stock in the company, they know that they will somehow share in its future and perhaps even inherit the business. The problem is that only 30% of family firms in the United States make it to the second generation, and just 13% survive to the third generation.[44]

Churchill and Hatten suggest that family businesses go through four sequential phases, from the time at which the venture is strictly managed by the founder to the time at which the next generation takes charge.[45] Table 13.4 describes these phases, each of which must be particularly well managed if the company is to survive past the third generation. Some of the reasons that family businesses fail to transfer ownership successfully to the next generation are: (1) inherited wealth destroys entrepreneurial drive, (2) the entrepreneur doesn't allow for a chang-

TABLE 13.4 **Transfer of Power in a Family Business**

Phase 1. **Owner-managed business.** Phase 1 begins at start-up and continues until the entrance of another family member into the business on a full-time basis. Family considerations influence but are not yet a directing part of the firm. At this point, the founder (entrepreneur) and the business are one.

Phase 2. **Training and development of new generation.** The children begin to learn the business at the dining room table during early childhood and then through part-time and vacation employment. The family and the business become one. Just as the entrepreneur identified with the business earlier, the family now begins to identify itself with the business.

Phase 3. **Partnership between generations.** At this point, a son or daughter of the founder has acquired sufficient business and managerial competence so that he or she can be involved in key decisions for at least a part of the company. The entrepreneur's offspring, however, has to first gain respect from the firm's employees and other managers and show that he or she can do the job right. Another issue is the lack of willingness of the founder to share authority with the son or daughter. Consequently, a common tactic taken by sons and daughters in family businesses is to take a job in a large, established corporation where they can gain valuable experience and respect for their skills.

Phase 4. **Transfer of power.** Instead of being forced to sell the company when he or she can no longer manage the business, the founder has the option in a family business of turning it over to the next generation as part of their inheritance. Often the founder moves to the position of Chairman of the Board and promotes one of the children to the position of CEO. Unfortunately, some founders cannot resist meddling in operating affairs and unintentionally undermine the leadership position of the son or daughter. To avoid this problem, the founder should sell his or her stock (probably through a leveraged buy out to the children) and physically leave the company to allow the next generation the freedom it needs to adapt to changing conditions.

Source: N. C. Churchill and K. J. Hatten, "Non-Market-Based Transfer of Wealth and Power: A Research Framework for Family Businesses," *American Journal of Small Business* (Winter 1987), pp. 51–64.

ing firm, (3) emphasis on business means that the family is neglected, (4) the business's financial growth can't keep up with rising family lifestyles, (5) family members are not prepared to run a business, and (6) the business becomes an arena for family conflicts.[46] In addition, succession planning may be ignored because of the founder's or family's refusal to think about the founder's death, the founder's unwillingness to let go of the firm, the fear of sibling rivalry, or intergenerational envy.[47]

13.5 Issues in Evaluation and Control

The means of evaluating a large corporation's implementation of strategy and its control systems have evolved over a long period of time in response to pressures from the environment (particularly the government). Conversely, the entrepreneur creates what is needed as the business grows. Because of a personal involvement in decision making, the entrepreneur managing a small business has little need for a formal, detailed reporting system.[48] Thus the founder who has little understanding of accounting and a lack of cash might employ a bookkeeper instead of an accountant. A formal personnel function might never appear because the entrepreneur lumps it in with simple bookkeeping and uses a secretary to handle personnel files. As an entrepreneurial venture becomes more established, it will develop more complex evaluation and control systems, but they often are not the kind used in large corporations and probably are used for different purposes.

Financial statements, in particular, tell only half the story in small, privately owned companies. The formality of the financial reporting system in such a company usually is a result of pressures from government tax agencies, not from management's desire for an objective evaluation and control system. For example, the absence of taxes in Bermuda has been given as the reason that business owners there keep little documentation. Thus keeping track of inventory, monitoring sales, or calculating how much they are owed is nearly impossible.[49] Because balance sheets and income statements do not always give an accurate picture of small, privately owned companies, standard ratios such as return on assets and debt–equity are unreliable. R. I. Levin and V. R. Travis provide five reasons why owners, operators, and outside observers should be wary of using standard financial methods to indicate the health of a small, privately owned company.[50]

- **The line between debt and equity is blurred.** In some instances, what appears as a loan is really an easy-to-retrieve equity investment. The entrepreneur in this instance doesn't want to lose his or her investment if the company fails. Another condition is that retained earnings seldom reflect the amount of internal financing needed for the company's growth. This account may merely be a place in which cash is left so that the owner can avoid double taxation. To avoid other taxes, owner–managers may own fixed assets that they lease to the corporation. The equity used to buy those assets is really the company's, but it doesn't appear on the books.
- **Lifestyle is a part of financial statements.** The lifestyle of the owner and the owner's family often is reflected in the balance sheet. The assets of some firms include beach cottages, mountain chalets, and automobiles. In others, plants and warehouses that are used for company operations are not shown because they are held separately by the family. Income statements may not reflect how well the company is operating. Profitability is not so important in decision making in small, privately owned companies as it is in large, publicly held corporations. For example, spending for recreation or transportation and paying rents or salaries above market rates to relatives put artificially high costs on the books of small firms. The business might appear to be poorly managed to an outsider, but the owner is acting rationally. The owner–manager wants dependable income or its equivalent with the least painful tax consequences. Because standard profitability measures such as ROI are not useful in the evaluation of such a firm, Levin and Travis recommend return on current assets as a better measure of productivity.[51]
- **Standard financial formulas don't always apply.** Following practices that run counter to standard financial recommendations, small companies often use short-term debt to finance fixed assets. The absence of well-organized capital

markets for small businesses, along with the typical banker's resistance to making loans without personal guarantees, leaves the private owner little choice.

- **Personal preference determines financial policies.** Because the owner often is the manager of the small firm, dividend policy is largely irrelevant. Dividend decisions are based not on stock price (which usually is unknown because the stock isn't traded), but on the owner's lifestyle and the trade-off between taking wealth from the corporation and double taxation.
- **Banks combine personal and business wealth.** Because of the large percentage of small businesses that go bankrupt every year, bank loan officers are reluctant to lend money to a small business unless the owner also provides some personal guarantees for the loan. In some instances, part of the loan may involve a second mortgage on the owner's house. If the owner doesn't want to put up personal assets as collateral, he or she must be willing to pay high interest rates for a loan that doesn't place the family's assets at risk.

In Conclusion . . .

This chapter described the differences between large corporations' and small businesses' use of strategic management. Entrepreneurs and top managers of other small businesses inhabit a very different world from that of their counterparts in large corporations. They have few resources to draw on and operate with the knowledge that the difference between success and bankruptcy can be their willingness to risk all their personal possessions on a dream and to work extremely hard.

Cherrill Farnsworth typifies the classic entrepreneur. She is currently the CEO of TME, Inc., the fifth company she has founded. She founded her first company, a bus line, in 1974. After her husband was transferred to Houston in 1970, she noticed that people had no way to get downtown from her northwestern suburb. "Wherever there's angst, there's an opportunity," comments Farnsworth. Despite heavy opposition from major bus operators, she won a franchise to run a bus line. Soon, however, running the bus line became boring. After two years, she sold it at a profit. Remembers Farnsworth, "I realized at that point what value you could get by working hard and creating something new—especially if there's no competition." In her next three new ventures, she leased luxury vehicles, office equipment, and then oil field equipment.

In the early 1980s, Farnsworth was attracted to MRI machines—expensive machines used by hospitals to look inside a person's body without using X rays. At the time, hospitals couldn't buy the machines because Medicare hadn't yet approved reimbursements from health insurers for the service. According to Farnsworth, when she first proposed to hospital administrators that she provide the service, "they found the idea shocking. They giggled and rolled their eyes." Once they reviewed her financial analysis, however, they agreed. Financial backers soon followed.

In assessing her skills as an entrepreneur, Farnsworth sees herself not so much as a manager but as someone who builds something and then moves on to another challenge. She comments on the future of TME, Inc.:

> I'm not a 20-year player. I've got to develop an exit strategy, probably by going public. I'm very transaction oriented. I love to put something together, build stockholder value, and then raise money again for another venture. Nothing makes me happier.[52]

Points to Remember

- Entrepreneurial ventures and small businesses are managed far less formally than are large, established business corporations. Small, rapidly growing companies tend to follow the entrepreneurial mode of strategy formulation—characterized by bold moves and intuitive decisions.
- Small firms that engage in strategic management usually outperform those that don't. However, this doesn't mean that formal procedures are necessary. The process of strategic planning, not the plan itself, appears to be a key component of business performance.
- The strategic decision-making process discussed in Chapter 2 is a valuable tool for small businesses with a few adjustments made for entrepreneurial ventures.
- SWOT analysis is very useful, but environmental scanning can be much less formal than that performed in large corporations. A prospective entrepreneur should carefully monitor seven sources of innovation: the unexpected, incongruity, innovation, structural change, demographics, perceptual change, and new knowledge.
- A new venture's success is largely determined by (1) the industry's structure, (2) the venture's business strategy, and (3) the entrepreneur's behavioral characteristics.
- Small-business managers tend to make little distinction between formulation and implementation. The stages of growth and development for a small business also are quite different from those presented earlier in Chapter 8. Between Stages I and II are five distinct substages that characterize many small companies.
- The implementation of strategy is different for the many small companies (and for a few large companies, as well) that are privately held family businesses. The next generation must always be considered in decisions to fill key positions and organize for future growth.
- In a small company, evaluation and control procedures usually are rather informal and reflect the owner–manager's preferences and government taxation policies rather than strategic considerations. Small businesses often are run on a cash basis and have minimum reporting procedures. For these and other reasons, owners, operators, and outside observers should be wary of using standard evaluation methods to measure the health of a small, privately owned company.

Discussion Questions

1. What are some arguments for and against the use of strategic management concepts and techniques in a small or entrepreneurial business?
2. If the owner–manager of a small company asked you for some advice concerning the introduction of strategic planning, what would you tell her?
3. In terms of strategic management, how does a new venture's situation differ from that of an ongoing small company?
4. The strategic decision-making process for new ventures comprises interrelated steps. List and describe each step in sequence.
5. How should a small company engage in environmental scanning? To what aspects of the environment should management pay most attention?
6. What are the characteristics of an attractive industry from an entrepreneur's point of view?
7. What considerations should small-business entrepreneurs keep in mind when they are deciding whether a company should follow a growth or a stability strategy?
8. What are the substages of small business development? List and explain each stage.
9. How does being family-owned compared to publicly-owned affect a firm's strategic management?
10. What are the pros and cons of using a standard financial reporting system in a small business?

Notes

1. C. Burck, "The Real World of the Entrepreneur: The Rewards of Angst," *Fortune* (April 5, 1993), p. 64.
2. C. Bullard, "Coralville Man Bets on Chilling Invention," *Des Moines Register* (June 16, 1991), pp. 1G, 2G.
3. D. Hale, "For New Jobs, Help Small Business," *Wall Street Journal* (August 10, 1992), p. A10; C. W. Hofer and W. R. Sandberg, "Improving New Venture Performance: Some Guidelines for Success," *American Journal of Small Business* (Summer 1987), pp. 11–12.
4. *The State of Small Business: A Report to the President,* (Washington, D.C.: U.S. Government Printing Office, 1987), p. 117.
5. B. Keats and J. Bracker, "Toward a Theory of Small Firm Performance: A Conceptual Model," *American Journal of Small Business* (Spring 1988), pp. 41–58; D. Dougherty, "A Practice-Centered Model of Organizational Renewal Through Product Innovation," *Strategic Management Journal* (Summer 1992), pp. 77–92.
6. J. Castro, J. McDowell, and W. McWhirter, "Big vs. Small," *Time* (September 5, 1988), p. 49.
7. B. Bowers, "This Store Is a Hit But Somehow Cash Flow Is Missing," *Wall Street Journal* (April 13, 1993), p. B2.
8. M. J. Foster, "Scenario Planning for Small Businesses," *Long Range Planning* (February 1993), p. 123; M. S. S. El-Namacki, "Small Business—The Myth and the Reality," *Long Range Planning* (August 1990), p. 79.
9. Further analysis by Kirchhoff of the 814,000 firms in the Dun and Bradstreet small business database used in a 1992 Small Business Administration report disclosed that instead of 62% of new businesses dying within six years, the number

was only 18%. Changes of ownership or a switch from a partnership to a corporation accounted for 28% of the supposed failures. Including "voluntary terminations," such as retirement of the proprietor, the survival rate over the six-year period actually was 54%. See J. Aley, "Debunking the Failure Fallacy," *Fortune* (September 6, 1993), p. 21.
10. El-Namacki, p. 84.
11. G. d'Amboise and M. Muldowney, "Management Theory for Small Business: Attempts and Requirements," *Academy of Management Review* (April 1988), p. 226.
12. J. W. Carland, F. Hoy, W. R. Boulton, and J. A. C. Carland, "Differentiating Entrepreneurs from Small Business Owners: A Conceptualization," *Academy of Management Review* (April 1984), p. 358; J. W. Carland, J. C. Carland, F. Hoy, and W. R. Boulton, "Distinctions Between Entrepreneurial and Small Business Ventures," *International Journal of Management* (March 1988), pp. 98–103.
13. S. P. Galante, "Counting on a Narrow Market Can Cloud Company's Future," *Wall Street Journal* (January 20, 1986), p. 17.
14. S. Shirley, "Corporate Strategy and Entrepreneurial Vision," *Long Range Planning* (December 1989), p. 107.
15. D. Fields, "Mrs. Fields' Weekends," *USA Weekend* (February 3–5, 1989), p. 16; M. Alpert, "In the Chips," *Fortune* (July 17, 1989), pp. 115–116.
16. J. S. Bracker, B. W. Keats, and J. N. Pearson, "Planning and Financial Performance Among Small Firms in a Growth Industry," *Strategic Management Journal* (November–December 1988), pp. 591–603.
17. C. B. Shrader, C. L. Mulford, and V. L. Blackburn, "Strategic and Operational Planning, Uncertainty, and Performance in Small Firms," *Journal of Small Business Management* (October 1989), pp. 45–60; C. E. Aronoff and J. L. Ward, "Why Owners Don't Plan," *Nation's Business* (June 1990), pp. 59–60; J. D. Aram and S. S. Cowen, "Strategy Planning for Increased Profit in the Small Business," *Long Range Planning* (December 1990), pp. 63–70.
18. J. Walsh, *1990 Pulse of the Middle Market,* as reported in "A Solid Strategy Helps Companies' Growth," *Nation's Business* (October 1990), p. 10.
19. A. Thomas, "Less Is More: How Less Formal Planning Can Be Best," in *The Strategic Planning Management Reader,* edited by L. Fahey (Englewood Cliffs, N.J.: Prentice-Hall, 1989), pp. 331–336; Shrader, et al., pp. 45–60.
20. R. B. Robinson, Jr., and J. A. Pearce II, "The Impact of Formalized Strategic Planning on Financial Performance in Small Organizations," *Strategic Management Journal* (July–September 1983), pp. 197–207; R. Ackelsberg and P. Arlow, "Small Businesses Do Plan and It Pays Off," *Long Range Planning* (October 1985), pp. 61–67.
21. V. Fowler, "Business Study Focuses on Failures," *Des Moines Register* (August 9, 1992), p. G1; For information on preparing a business plan, see J. T. Broome, Jr., "How to Write a Business Plan," *Nation's Business* (February 1993), pp. 29–30 and P. D. O'Hara, *The Total Business Plan* (New York: John Wiley & Sons, 1990).
22. T. L. Wheelen and J. D. Hunger, "The Usefulness of Strategic Management Concepts to Small Businesses and Entrepreneurial Ventures," *International Journal of Management* (December 1992), pp. 399–405.
23. J. C. Shuman and J. A. Seeger, "The Theory and Practice of Strategic Management in Smaller Rapid Growth Firms," *American Journal of Small Business* (Summer 1986), p. 14.
24. S. Birley and P. Westhead, "Growth and Performance Contrasts Between 'Types' of Small Firms," *Strategic Management Journal* (November–December 1990), pp. 535–557.
25. S. Birley and D. Norburn, "Small vs. Large Companies: The Entrepreneurial Conundrum," *Journal of Business Strategy* (Summer 1985), p. 82.
26. V. Fowler, "Business Study Focuses on Failures," *Des Moines Register* (August 9, 1992), p. G1.
27. P. F. Drucker, *Innovation and Entrepreneurship* (New York: HarperCollins, 1985), pp. 30–129.
28. C. A. Jaffe, "Success by Surprise," *Nation's Business* (September 1989), pp. 30–33.
29. M. Lewyn, "The Very Picture of Success," *Business Week* (May 24, 1993), p. 67.
30. J. Chandler, "Filling the Transit Gap," *Nation's Business* (January 1993), pp. 39–42.
31. M. Charlier, "Yuengling's Success Defies

Convention," *Wall Street Journal* (August 26, 1993), pp. B1, B6.

32. C. W. Hofer and W. R. Sandberg, "Improving New Venture Performance: Some Guidelines for Success," *American Journal of Small Business* (Summer 1987), pp. 12–23. See also J. J. Chrisman and A. Bauerschmidt, "New Venture Performance: Some Critical Extensions to the Model," Paper presented to *State-of-the-Art Symposium on Entrepreneurship,* Iowa State University (April 12–14, 1992).
33. J. L. Ward and S. F. Stasch, "How Small-Share Firms Can Uncover Winning Strategies," *Journal of Business Strategy* (September/October 1988), pp. 26–31; K. R. Harrigan, "Guerrilla Strategies for Underdog Competitors," *Planning Review* (November 1986), pp. 4–11, 44–45.
34. Some studies do indicate that new ventures also can be successful following strategies other than going after an undefended niche. See P. McDougall and R. B. Robinson, Jr., "New Venture Strategies: An Empirical Identification of Eight 'Archetypes' of Competitive Strategies for Entry," *Strategic Management Journal* (October 1990), pp. 447–467; A. C. Cooper, G. E. Willard, and C. Y. Woo, "A Reexamination of the Niche Concept," in *The Strategy Process: Concepts, Contexts, and Cases,* 2nd ed., edited by H. Mintzberg and J. B. Quinn (Englewood Cliffs, N.J.: Prentice-Hall, 1991), pp. 619–628.
35. Hofer and Sandberg, p. 22.
36. H. P. Welsch, "Entrepreneurs' Personal Characteristics: Causal Models," Paper presented to *State-of-the-Art Symposium on Entrepreneurship,* Iowa State University (April 12–14, 1992).
37. M. F. R. Kets de Vries, "The Dark Side of Entrepreneurship," *Harvard Business Review* (November–December 1985), pp. 160–167.
38. R. Ricklefs and U. Gupta, "Traumas of a New Entrepreneur," *Wall Street Journal* (May 10, 1989), p. B1.
39. N. C. Churchill and V. L. Lewis, "The Five Stages of Small Business Growth," *Harvard Business Review* (May–June 1983), pp. 30–50; R. K. Kazanjian, in "Relation of Dominant Problems to Stages of Growth in Technology-Based New Ventures," *Academy of Management Journal* (June 1988), pp. 257–279, proposes the four stages of (1) conception and development, (2) commercialization, (3) growth, and (4) stability. Kazanjian's first two stages are similar to Churchill and Lewis's Stage A. Growth and stability are similar to Churchill and Lewis's Survival (Stage B) and Success (Stage C). The Churchill and Lewis model is used in this text because it is more comprehensive and generalizable to more types of entrepreneurial ventures than is the Kazanjian model.
40. R. Johnson, "Trying Harder to Find a No. 2 Executive," *Wall Street Journal* (June 19, 1989), p. B1.
41. K. G. Smith, "Managing Organizational Growth," *Handbook of Business Strategy, 1991/92 Yearbook* (Boston: Warren, Gorham and Lamont, 1991), pp. 22.1–22.13.
42. G. D. Meyer, R. M. Lenoir, and T. J. Dean, "The Executive Limit Scenario in High Technology Firms," in *Proceedings, Managing the High Technology Firm Conference,* edited by L. R. Gomez-Mejia and M. W. Lawless (Boulder: University of Colorado, January 13–15, 1988), pp. 342–349.
43. Even though much anecdotal evidence supports Churchill and Lewis's concept of substages of development, unfortunately little empirical evidence supports this model. See also Birley and Westhead, pp. 535–557.
44. J. Ward, *Keeping the Family Business Healthy* (San Francisco: Jossey-Bass, 1987), as reported by U. Gupta and M. Robichaux, "Reins Tangle Easily at Family Firms," *Wall Street Journal* (August 9, 1989), p. B1.
45. N. C. Churchill and K. J. Hatten, "Non-Market-Based Transfers of Wealth and Power: A Research Framework for Family Businesses," *American Journal of Small Business* (Winter 1987), pp. 51–64.
46. J. L. Ward and C. E. Aronoff, "Shirt Sleeves to Shirt Sleeves," *Nation's Business* (September 1992), pp. 62–63.
47. M. F. R. Kets de Vries, "The Dynamics of Family Controlled Firms: The Good and the Bad News," *Organizational Dynamics* (Winter 1993), pp. 59–71.
48. Birley and Norburn, p. 85; S. S. Cowen and J. K. Middaugh II, "Designing an Effective Financial Planning and Control System,"

Long Range Planning (December 1988), pp. 83–92.
49. J. Applegate, "Business People in Bermuda Get Sloppy Without Taxes," *Des Moines Register* (July 6, 1992), p. 8B.
50. R. I. Levin and V. R. Travis, "Small Company Finance: What the Books Don't Say," *Harvard Business Review* (November–December 1987), pp. 30–32.
51. Ibid., p. 31.
52. C. Burck, "The Real World of the Entrepreneur: The Rewards of Angst," *Fortune* (April 5, 1993), pp. 64–65.

Strategic Issues in Not-for-Profit Organizations

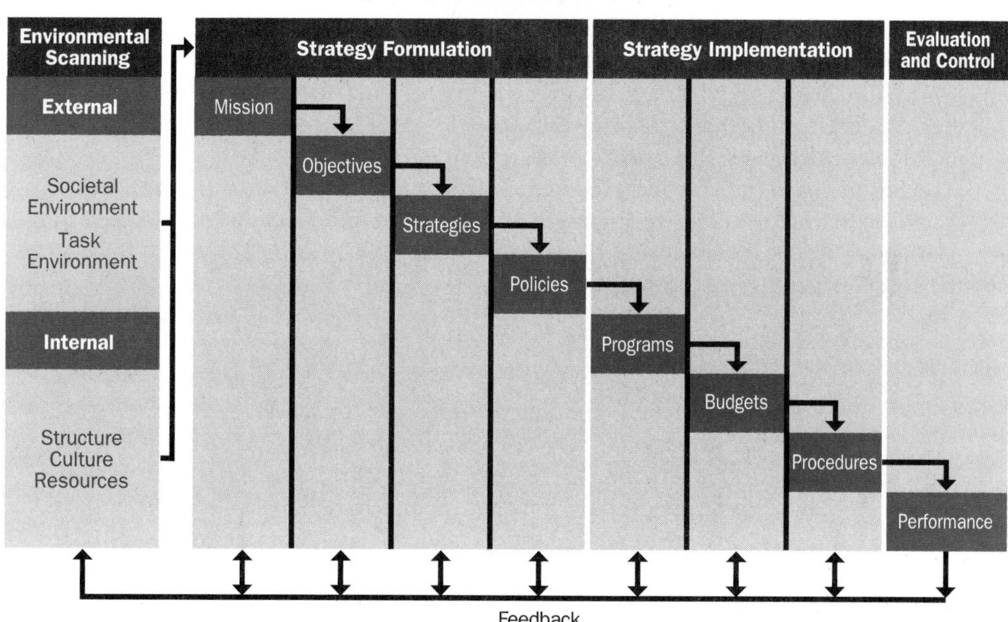

Twenty years ago, management was a dirty word for those involved in nonprofit organizations. It meant business, and nonprofits prided themselves on being free of the taint of commercialism and above such sordid considerations as the bottom line. Now most of them have learned that nonprofits need management even more than business does, precisely because they lack the discipline of the bottom line.[1]

[Peter Drucker]

New York City's Guggenheim Museum desperately needed to develop a strategy to cope with declining revenues. The tax breaks that allowed the rich to donate to museums (roughly 80% of all the objects in U.S. museums are gifts) were being eliminated. Public funding for the arts was declining rapidly. As many as 29 states were considering reductions of 50% or more in arts funding, so the Guggenheim wasn't alone in this situation. By the mid 1990s, most not-for-profit organizations were turning to strategic management to ensure their survival.[2]

A knowledge of not-for-profit organizations is important if only because they employ some 25% of the U.S. work force and own approximately 15% of the nation's private wealth.[3] In the United States alone—in addition to various federal, state, and local government agencies—there are about 10,000 not-for-profit hospitals and nursing homes (84% of all hospitals), 4,600 colleges and universities, more than 100,000 private and public elementary and secondary schools, almost 350,000 churches and synagogues, and thousands of charities and service organizations.[4]

Typically, the term not-for-profit includes **private nonprofit corporations** (such as hospitals, institutes, private colleges, and organized charities) and **public government units or agencies** (such as welfare departments, prisons, and state universities). Traditionally, studies in strategic management have dealt with profit-making firms to the exclusion of nonprofit or government organizations. The little, but growing, empirical research suggests that not-for-profit organizations are still in the early stages of using strategic management.[5]

Many scholars and practitioners now believe that various strategic management concepts and techniques can be adapted successfully for not-for-profit organizations.[6] Although the evidence isn't yet conclusive, there appears to be an association between strategic planning efforts and performance measures such as growth.[7] In this chapter we highlight briefly the major differences between the profit-making organization and the not-for-profit organization and their effects on the strategic management process.

14.1 Why Not-for-Profit?

The not-for-profit sector of an economy is important for several reasons. *First,* society desires certain goods and services (primarily services) that profit-making firms cannot or will not provide. These are referred to as *public* or *collective* goods because people who might not have paid for them also receive benefits from them. Paved roads, police protection, museums, and schools are examples of public goods. People cannot use private goods unless they pay for them. Generally, however, when a public good is provided, anyone can use it, benefit from it, or enjoy it.

Second, a private nonprofit organization tends to receive benefits from society that a private profit-making firm cannot obtain. Preferred tax status is one major benefit. Section 501(c)(3) of the U.S. Internal Revenue code exempts nonstock corporations from corporate income taxes. Private nonprofit organizations also enjoy exemptions from various other state, local, and federal taxes. Under certain conditions these organizations benefit from the tax deductibility of donors' contributions and membership dues. In addition, they qualify for special third-class mailing privileges.[8] These benefits are provided because private nonprofit organizations typically are service organizations, which are expected to use any excess of revenue over costs and expenses either to improve services or to reduce the price of their services. This service orientation is reflected in the fact that not-for-profit organizations do not use the term customer to refer to the recipients of services. They typically refer to the recipient as a patient, student, client, case, or simply "the public."

14.2 Importance of Revenue Source

The feature that best differentiates not-for-profit organizations from each other as well as from profit-making corporations is source of income.[9] The **profit-making firm** depends on revenues obtained from the sale of its goods and services to cus-

- To the extent that a not-for-profit organization depends more on its sponsors than on its clients for revenue, the less useful will be the standard concepts, techniques, and prescriptions of strategic management.
- Five characteristics of the not-for-profit organization constrain its behavior and affect its management: service often is intangible, client influence may be weak, employees often are more committed to their profession than to the organization, resource contributors may pressure management, and the use of rewards and punishments often are restrained. These characteristics affect strategy formulation, implementation, and evaluation and control.
- To cope with funding declines, not-for-profit organizations increasingly are turning to the strategies of strategic piggybacking and mergers and interorganizational linking.

Discussion Questions

1. Are not-for-profit organizations less efficient than profit-making organizations? Why or why not?
2. Do you agree that the source of revenue is the best way to differentiate between not-for-profit and profit-making organizations, as well as among the many kinds of not-for-profit organizations? Explain.
3. Is client influence always weak in an NFP organization? Why or why not?
4. Why does the employment of a large number of professionals complicate the strategic management process? How can it also occur in profit-making firms?
5. How does the lack of a clear-cut performance measure, such as profits, affect the strategic management of an NFP organization?
6. What are the pros and cons of strategic piggybacking? In what way is it "unfair competition" for NFPs to engage in revenue generating activity?
7. What are the pros and cons of mergers/interorganizational linking?
8. Recently, many NFP organizations in the United States have been converting to profit-making operations. Why would an NFP organization want to change its status to profit making?

Notes

1. Reprinted by permission of the *Harvard Business Review*. Excerpted from P. F. Drucker, "What Business Can Learn from Nonprofits," *Harvard Business Review* (July–August 1989). Copyright © 1989 by The President and Fellows of Harvard College. All rights reserved.
2. A. Prud'Homme, "The CEO of Culture Inc., *Time* (January 20, 1992), pp. 36–37.
3. G. Rudney, "The Scope and Dimensions of Nonprofit Activity," in *The Nonprofit Sector: A Research Handbook*, edited by W. W. Powell (New Haven: Yale University Press, 1987), p. 56; C. P. McLaughlin, *The Management of Nonprofit Organizations* (New York: John Wiley & Sons, 1986), p. 4.
4. M. O'Neill, *The Third America* (San Francisco: Jossey-Bass, 1989).
5. K. Ascher and B. Nare, "Strategic Planning in the Public Sector," *International Review of Strategic Management*, Vol. 1, edited by D. E. Hussey (New York: John

Wiley & Sons, 1990), pp. 297–315; M. S. Wortman, Jr., "Strategic Management in Nonprofit Organizations: A Research Typology and Research Prospectus," in *Strategic Management Frontiers,* edited by J. H. Grant (Greenwich, Conn.: JAI Press, 1988), pp. 415–442; J. W. Harvey and K. F. McCrohan, "Strategic Issues for Charities and Philanthropies," *Long Range Planning* (December 1988), pp. 44–55.

6. Ascher and Nare, pp. 297–315; I. Unterman and R. H. Davis, *Strategic Management of Not-For-Profit Organizations* (New York: Praeger, 1984), p. 2.
7. P. V. Jenster and G. A. Overstreet, "Planning for a Non-Profit Service: A Study of U.S. Credit Unions," *Long Range Planning* (April 1990), pp. 103–111; G. J. Medley, "Strategic Planning for the World Wildlife Fund," *Long Range Planning* (February 1988), pp. 46–54.
8. J. G. Simon, "The Tax Treatment of Nonprofit Organizations: A Review of Federal and State Policies," in *The Nonprofit Sector: A Research Handbook,* edited by W. W. Powell (New Haven: Yale University Press, 1987), pp. 67–98.
9. B. P. Keating and M. O. Keating, *Not-For-Profit* (Glen Ridge, N.J.: Thomas Horton & Daughters, 1980), p. 21.
10. "Revenues and Expenditures of Colleges and Universities, 1981–82," *Chronicle of Higher Education* (April 4, 1984), p. 14.
11. Ascher and Nare, pp. 297–315; R. McGill, "Planning for Strategic Performance in Local Government," *Long Range Planning* (October 1988), pp. 77–84.
12. E. Ferlie, "The Creation and Evolution of Quasi Markets in the Public Sector: A Problem for Strategic Management," *Strategic Management Journal* (Winter 1992), pp 79–97. Research has found that for profit hospitals have more mission statement components dealing with principal services, target customers, and geographic domain than do not-for-profit hospitals. See R. Subramanian, K. Kumar, and C. C. Yauger, "Mission Statements of Hospitals: An Empirical Analysis of Their Contents and Their Relationship to Organizational Factors," *Journal of Business Strategies* (Spring 1993), pp. 63–78.
13. J. D. Hunger and T. L. Wheelen, "Is Strategic Management Appropriate for Not-for-Profit Organizations?" in *Handbook of Business Strategy, 1989/90 Yearbook,* edited by H. E. Glass (Boston: Warren, Gorham and Lamont, 1989), pp. 3.1–3.8. The contention that the pattern of environmental influence on the organization's strategic decision making derives from the organization's source(s) of income agrees with the work of Emerson, Thompson, and Pfeffer and Salancik. See R. E. Emerson, "Power-Dependence Relations," *American Sociological Review* (February 1962), pp. 31–41; J. D. Thompson, *Organizations In Action* (New York: McGraw-Hill, 1967), pp. 30–31; J. Pfeffer and G. R. Salancik, *The External Control of Organizations: A Resource Dependence Perspective* (New York: HarperCollins, 1978), p. 44.
14. W. H. Newman and H. W. Wallender III, "Managing Not-For-Profit Enterprises," *Academy of Management Review* (January 1978), p. 26.
15. Ibid., p. 27. The following discussion of the effects of these constraining characteristics is taken from pp. 27–31.
16. P. C. Nutt, "A Strategic Planning Network for Non-Profit Organizations," *Strategic Management Journal* (January–March 1984), p. 57; F. Heffron, *Organization Theory and Public Administration* (Englewood Cliffs, N.J.: Prentice-Hall, 1989), pp. 100–103.
17. J. Denis, A. Langley, and D. Lozeau, "Formal Strategy in Public Hospitals," *Long Range Planning* (February 1991), pp. 71–82.
18. Heffron, p. 132.
19. Ibid., pp. 103–115.
20. Unterman and Davis, p. 174; J. A. Alexander, M. L. Fennell, and M. T. Halpern, "Leadership Instability in Hospitals: The Influence of Board–CEO Relations and Organizational Growth and Decline," *Administrative Science Quarterly* (March 1993), pp. 74–99.
21. R. M. Kanter and D. V. Summers, "Doing Well While Doing Good: Dilemmas of Performance Measurement in Nonprofit Organizations and the Need for a Multiple-Constituency Approach," in *The Nonprofit Sector: A Research Handbook,* edited by W. W. Powell (New Haven: Yale University Press, 1987), p. 163.
22. R. P. Nielsen, "SMR Forum: Strategic Piggybacking—A Self-Subsidizing Strategy for Nonprofit Institutions," *Sloan Management Review* (Summer 1982), pp. 65–69; R. P. Nielsen, "Piggybacking for Business and

Nonprofits: A Strategy for Hard Times," *Long Range Planning* (April 1984), pp. 96–102.

23. C. Crossen, " 'Sesame Street,' at 23, Still Teaches Children While Amusing Them," *Wall Street Journal* (February 21, 1992), pp. A1, A9.
24. D. C. Bacon, "Nonprofit Groups: An Unfair Edge?" *Nation's Business* (April 1989), pp. 33–34.
25. E. Skloot, "Should Not-For-Profits Go Into Business?" *Harvard Business Review* (January–February 1983), p. 21.
26. R. P. Nielsen, "Piggybacking Strategies for Nonprofits: A Shared Costs Approach," *Strategic Management Journal* (May–June 1986), pp. 209–211.
27. Skloot, pp. 20–24.
28. S. Collins, "A Bitter Financial Pill," *U.S. News & World Report* (November 29, 1993), pp. 83–86.
29. K. G. Provan, "Interorganizational Cooperation and Decision Making Autonomy in a Consortium Multihospital System," *Academy of Management Review* (July 1984), pp. 494–504; R. D. Luke, J. W. Begun, and D. D. Pointer, "Quasi-Firms: Strategic Interorganizational Forms in the Health Care Industry," *Academy of Management Review* (January 1989), pp. 9–19.
30. G. Fuchsberg, "Business Schools Team Up With Rivals to Enrich Offerings but Keep Costs Down," *Wall Street Journal* (August 18, 1992), pp. B1, B6.

Suggestions for Case Analysis

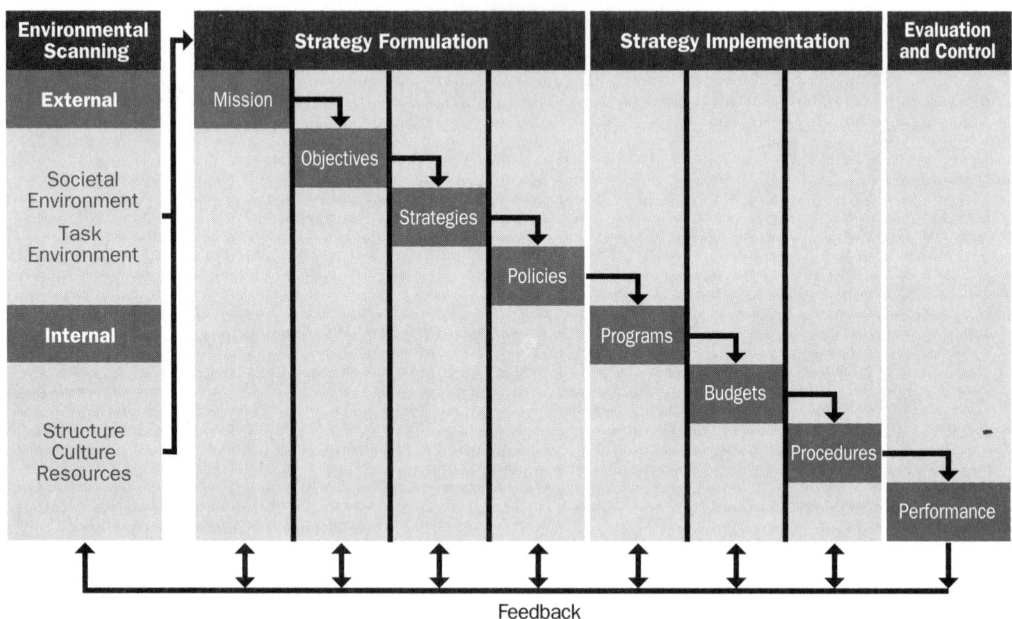

> *During the last 25 years the Case Method has enjoyed a steady and continuing increase in popularity and use.*[1]
> [Hans E. Klein]

An analysis of a corporation's strategic management calls for a comprehensive view of the organization. The case method of analysis provides the opportunity to move from a narrow, specialized view emphasizing technical skills to a broader, less precise analysis of the overall corporation emphasizing conceptual skills. Concentrating on strategic management processes forces you to develop a better understanding of the political, social, and economic environment of business, and to appreciate the interactions of the functional specialties required for corporate success.

15.1 The Case Method

The analysis and discussion of cases has been the most popular method of teaching strategy and policy for many years.[2] Surveys indicate that approximately 70%–90% of business schools use cases in the strategic management course.[3]

Studies also show that the case method emphasizes the manager's world, improves communication skills, offers the rewards of solving a mystery, possesses the quality of illustration, and establishes concrete reference points for connecting theory and practice.[4]

Cases present actual business situations and enable you to examine both successful and unsuccessful corporations. In case analysis, you might be asked to analyze critically a situation in which a manager had to make a decision of long-term corporate importance. This approach helps you understand what it is like to be faced with making and implementing strategic decisions.

15.2 Framework for Case Analysis

There is no one best way to analyze or present a case report. Each instructor has personal preferences for format and approach. Nevertheless, we suggest an approach for both written and oral reports in Appendix 15A, which provides a systematic method for successfully attacking a case.

The presentation of a case analysis may be organized on the basis of several frameworks. One obvious framework to follow is the **strategic audit** as detailed earlier in Chapter 2 on pages 48–55. Another is the McKinsey **7-S Framework,** composed of the seven organizational variables of *structure, strategy, staff, management style, systems and procedures, skills,* and *shared values.*[5] Regardless of the framework chosen, be especially careful to include a complete analysis of key environmental variables, especially trends in the industry and the competition and international developments.[6]

The focus in case discussion is on critical analysis and logical development of thought. A solution is satisfactory if it resolves important problems and is likely to be implemented successfully. How the corporation actually dealt with the problems has no real bearing on the analysis because management might have analyzed its problems incorrectly or implemented a series of flawed solutions.

15.3 Library Research

You should undertake outside research into the environmental setting of the case. Check each case to find out the date when the case situation occurred and then screen the business periodicals for that time period. Use the computerized company and industry information services such as COMPUSTAT, Compact Disclosure, and CD/International, which are available on CD-Rom or on-line at the library.

This background will give you an appreciation for the case situation as it was experienced by the participants in the case. A company's annual report and 10-K form from that year can be very useful. An understanding of the economy during that period will help you avoid making a serious error in your analysis—for example, suggesting a sale of stock when the stock market is at an all-time low or taking on more debt when the prime interest rate is above 15%. Information on the industry will provide insights on its competitive activities. Some resources available for research into the economy and a corporation's industry are suggested in Appendix 15B.

If you are unfamiliar with these business resources, we urge you to read *How to Use the Business Library: With Sources of Business Information* by H. W. Johnson, A. J. Faria, and E. L. Maier (South-Western Publishing).

15.4 Financial Analysis: A Place to Begin

A review of key financial ratios can help you assess the company's overall situation and pinpoint some problem areas. Ratios control for firm size and enable you to compare a company's ratios with industry averages (and quartile norms).[7] Table 15.1 lists some of the most important financial ratios: (1) **liquidity ratios,** (2) **profitability ratios,** (3) **activity ratios,** and (4) **leverage ratios.**

Analyzing Financial Statements

In your analysis do not simply make an exhibit including all the ratios but select and discuss only those ratios that have an impact on the company's problems. For instance, accounts receivable and inventory may provide a source of funds. If receivables and inventories are double the industry average, reducing them may provide needed cash. In this situation, the case report should include not only sources of funds, but also the number of dollars freed for use. Compare these ratios with industry averages to discover what quartile the company's ratios fit and whether the company diverges from others in the industry.

A typical financial analysis of a firm would contain a study of its operating statements for five or so years, including a trend analysis of sales, profits, earnings per share, debt-to-equity ratio, return on investment, and so on, plus a ratio study comparing the firm under study with industry standards. To begin, scrutinize historical *income statements* and *balance sheets.* These two basic statements provide most of the data needed for analysis. Statements of cash flow also may be useful. Compare the statements over time if a series of statements is available. Calculate changes that occur in individual categories from year to year, along with the cumulative total change. Determine the amount of change as a percentage and in absolute terms. You may also need to adjust for inflation if that was a significant factor. If examination of this information reveals developing trends, compare trends in one category with trends in related categories. For example, an increase in sales of 15% over three years may appear to be satisfactory until you note an increase of 20% in the cost of goods sold during the same period. The outcome of this comparison might suggest that further investigation of the manufacturing process is necessary.

Companies that want to show better financial results than are justified tend to get "creative" in preparing financial statements. Although many of these maneuvers may be legal, they are cause for concern. During the late 1980s, for example, IBM propped up its profits by recording immediately all the revenue from long-term computer leases and pushing the cost of investments into the future.[8] Watch for certain *red flags* when analyzing financial statements in an annual report or prospectus. These are often found in the notes section of the financial reports.

TABLE 15.1 **Financial Ratio Analysis**

	Formula	How Expressed	Meaning
1. Liquidity Ratios			
Current ratio	$\frac{\text{Current assets}}{\text{Current liabilities}}$	Decimal	A short-term indicator of the company's ability to pay its short-term liabilities from short-term assets; how much of current assets are available to cover each dollar of current liabilities.
Quick (acid test) ratio	$\frac{\text{Current assets} - \text{Inventory}}{\text{Current liabilities}}$	Decimal	Measures the company's ability to pay off its short-term obligations from current assets, excluding inventories.
Inventory to net working capital	$\frac{\text{Inventory}}{\text{Current assets} - \text{Current liabilities}}$	Decimal	A measure of inventory balance; measures the extent to which the cushion of excess current assets over current liabilities may be threatened by unfavorable changes in inventory.
Cash ratio	$\frac{\text{Cash} + \text{Cash equivalents}}{\text{Current liabilities}}$	Decimal	Measures the extent to which the company's capital is in cash or cash equivalents; shows how much of the current obligations can be paid from cash or near-cash assets.
2. Profitability Ratios			
Net profit margin	$\frac{\text{Net profit after taxes}}{\text{Net sales}}$	Percentage	Shows how much after-tax profits are generated by each dollar of sales.
Gross profit margin	$\frac{\text{Sales} - \text{Cost of goods sold}}{\text{Net sales}}$	Percentage	Indicates the total margin available to cover other expenses beyond cost of goods sold, and still yield a profit.
Return on investment (ROI)	$\frac{\text{Net profit after taxes}}{\text{Total assets}}$	Percentage	Measures the rate of return on the total assets utilized in the company; a measure of management's efficiency, it shows the return on all the assets under its control regardless of source of financing.
Return on equity (ROE)	$\frac{\text{Net profit after taxes}}{\text{Shareholders' equity}}$	Percentage	Measures the rate of return on the book value of shareholders' total investment in the company.

(continued)

TABLE 15.1 **Financial Ratio Analysis** *(continued)*

	Formula	How Expressed	Meaning
Earnings per share (EPS)	$\frac{\text{Net profit after taxes} - \text{Preferred stock dividends}}{\text{Average number of common shares}}$	Dollars per share	Shows the after-tax earnings generated for each share of common stock.
3. Activity Ratios			
Inventory turnover	$\frac{\text{Net sales}}{\text{Inventory}}$	Decimal	Measures the number of times that average inventory of finished goods was turned over or sold during a period of time, usually a year.
Days of inventory	$\frac{\text{Inventory}}{\text{Cost of goods sold} \div 365}$	Days	Measures the number of one day's worth of inventory that a company has on hand at any given time.
Net working capital turnover	$\frac{\text{Net sales}}{\text{Net working capital}}$	Decimal	Measures how effectively the net working capital is used to generate sales.
Asset turnover	$\frac{\text{Sales}}{\text{Total assets}}$	Decimal	Measures the utilization of all the company's assets; measures how many sales are generated by each dollar of assets.
Fixed asset turnover	$\frac{\text{Sales}}{\text{Fixed assets}}$	Decimal	Measures the utilization of the company's fixed assets (i.e., plant and equipment); measures how many sales are generated by each dollar of fixed assets.
Average collection period	$\frac{\text{Accounts receivable}}{\text{Sales for year} \div 365}$	Days	Indicates the average length of time in days that a company must wait to collect a sale after making it; may be compared to the credit terms offered by the company to its customers.
Accounts receivable turnover	$\frac{\text{Annual credit sales}}{\text{Accounts receivable}}$	Decimal	Indicates the number of times that accounts receivable are cycled during the period (usually a year).
Accounts payable period	$\frac{\text{Accounts payable}}{\text{Purchases for year} \div 365}$	Days	Indicates the average length of time in days that the company takes to pay its credit purchases.
Days of cash	$\frac{\text{Cash}}{\text{Net sales for year} \div 365}$	Days	Indicates the number of days of cash on hand, at present sales levels.

(continued)

TABLE 15.1 Financial Ratio Analysis *(continued)*

	Formula	How Expressed	Meaning
4. Leverage Ratios			
Debt to asset ratio	Total debt / Total assets	Percentage	Measures the extent to which borrowed funds have been used to finance the company's assets.
Debt to equity ratio	Total debt / Shareholders' equity	Percentage	Measures the funds provided by creditors versus the funds provided by owners.
Long-term debt to capital structure	Long-term debt / Shareholders' equity	Percentage	Measures the long-term component of capital structure.
Times interest earned	(Profit before taxes + Interest charges) / Interest charges	Decimal	Indicates the ability of the company to meet its annual interest costs.
Coverage of fixed charges	(Profit before taxes + Interest charges + Lease charges) / (Interest charges + Lease obligations)	Decimal	A measure of the company's ability to meet all of its fixed-charge obligations.
Current liabilities to equity	Current liabilities / Shareholders' equity	Percentage	Measures the short-term financing portion versus that provided by owners.
5. Other Ratios			
Price/earnings ratio	Market price per share / Earnings per share	Decimal	Shows the current market's evaluation of a stock, based on its earnings; shows how much the investor is willing to pay for each dollar of earnings.
Divided payout ratio	Annual dividends per share / Annual earnings per share	Percentage	Indicates the percentage of profit that is paid out as dividends.
Dividend yield on common stock	Annual dividends per share / Current market price per share	Percentage	Indicates the dividend rate of return to common shareholders at the current market price.

Note: In using ratios for analysis, calculate ratios for the corporation and compare them to the average and quartile ratios for the particular industry. Refer to Standard and Poor's and Robert Morris Associates for average industry data. For an in-depth discussion of ratios and their use, refer to a financial management text such as E. F. Brigham, *Fundamentals of Financial Management*, 5th ed. (Chicago: Dryden, 1987), pp. 265–286. Special thanks to Dr. Moustafa H. Abdelsamad, Dean, Business School, Texas A&M University, Corpus Christi, Texas, for his definitions of these ratios.

- **Special risks.** Potential problems often are grouped in a section called "special considerations," "investment considerations," or "special risks." For example, the preliminary prospectus of ZZZZ Best Company disclosed that a single customer was responsible for 86% of the company's recent revenue. The company went bankrupt a year later.
- **Earnings problems.** Earnings trending downward certainly indicate caution. Knowing where the money comes from also helps. Does the company depend on a single product for its profits or are there special, one-time items that artificially boost earnings? Look closely at *operating income* to learn whether the company is earning any profit in its primary business activity. The corporation may be showing a net profit only because management is selling the company's assets.
- **Too much debt.** Although the optimal ratio varies from industry to industry, most financial professionals believe that the amount of equity (common stock) should significantly exceed the amount of long-term debt.
- **Top management.** Some experts believe that officers and directors should own a significant amount of stock in the corporation—otherwise, their interests may not align with those of the shareholders. Watch, however, for insider trading of company stocks.
- **Questionable transactions.** Watch out for strange items buried in the notes to the financial statements. A stock prospectus for Crazy Eddie, Inc., disclosed that before the company went public it funded a medical school in the Caribbean, invested in oil and gas limited partnerships, and made interest-free loans to the chairman and other members of his family "to meet family needs." Not surprisingly, the company soon went bankrupt.
- **Lawsuits.** Legal actions against a company may be significant if they suggest that something may be seriously wrong with either the company's products or the way it conducts business.[9]

Common-Size Statements

Another approach to the analysis of financial statements is to convert both the income statement and balance sheet into *common-size statements.* Convert every category from dollar terms to percentages. For the *income statement,* net sales represent 100%: calculate the percentage of each category so that the categories sum to the net sales percentage (100%). The Company Spotlight: Maytag Corporation feature on page 405 shows the company's income statements for 1991 and 1992 done in *common-size* format. For the *balance sheet,* give the total assets a value of 100%, and calculate other asset and liability categories as percentages of the total assets. (Individual asset and liability items, such as accounts receivable and accounts payable, can also be calculated as a percentage of net sales.) To more easily note category changes, plot the annual percentages over a five-year period for each of the categories, such as cost of goods sold and accounts receivable. Connect the dots to view trends in each category. A poor trend indicates an underlying problem needing attention.

When you convert statements to this form, it is relatively easy to note the percentage that each category represents of the total. Comparisons of these percent-

COMPANY SPOTLIGHT

MAYTAG Corporation

Common-Size Income Statements (Dollar amounts in thousands)

	1992	%	1991	%
Net sales	$3,041,223	100.00	$2,970,626	100.00
Cost of sales	2,339,406	76.92	2,254,221	75.88
Gross profits	701,817	23.08	716,405	24.12
Selling, general, and administrative expenses	528,250	17.36	524,898	17.67
Reorganization expenses	95,000	3.12	—	—
Operating income	78,567	2.58	191,507	6.45
Interest expense	(75,004)	(2.46)	(75,159)	(2.53)
Other—net	3,983	0.13	7,069	.23
Income before taxes and accounting changes	7,546	0.25	123,417	4.15
Income taxes	(15,900)	(0.52)	(44,400)	(1.49)
Income before accounting changes	(8,354)	(0.27)	79,017	2.66
Effects of accounting changes for postretirement benefits	(307,000)	(10.09)	—	—
Net income (loss)	$ (315,354)	(10.36)	$ 79,017	2.66

ages over the years can point out areas for additional analysis. To get a valid perspective, however, compare these data to industry data, if available, to determine whether fluctuations merely reflect industrywide trends. If a firm's trends are generally in line with those of the rest of the industry, the likelihood of problems is less than if the firm's trends fall below industry averages. These statements are especially helpful in developing scenarios and pro forma statements (see Chapters 4 and 7) because they provide a series of historical relationships (for example, cost of goods sold to sales, interest to sales, and inventories as a percentage of assets).

Other Useful Calculations

If the corporation being studied appears to be in poor financial condition, use **Altman's Bankruptcy Formula** to calculate its *Z*-value. This formula combines five ratios by weighting them according to their importance to a corporation's financial strength. The formula is

$$Z = 1.2x_1 + 1.4x_2 + 3.3x_3 + 0.6x_4 + 1.0x_5,$$

where

x_1 = Working capital/Total assets (%),
x_2 = Retained earnings/Total assets (%),
x_3 = Earnings before interest and taxes/Total assets (%),
x_4 = Market value of equity/Total liabilities (%), and
x_5 = Sales/Total assets (number of times).

Scores below 1.81 indicate significant credit problems, whereas scores above 3.0 indicate a healthy firm. Scores between 1.81 and 3.0 indicate a questionable situation.[10]

If the corporation being studied is about to embark on a growth strategy, use the **Index of Sustainable Growth** (g^*) to learn how much of the growth rate of sales can be sustained by internally generated funds. The formula is

$$g^* = \frac{P(1 - D)(1 + L)}{T - P(1 - D)(1 + L)},$$

where

P = (Net profit before tax/Net sales) $\times$ 100,
D = Target dividends/Profit after tax,
L = Total liabilities/Net worth, and
T = (Total assets/Net sales) $\times$ 100.

If planned growth calls for a rate higher than g^*, external capital will be needed to fund the growth unless management can improve efficiency, decrease dividends, increase the debt-to-equity ratio, or reduce assets through renting or leasing arrangements.[11]

Takeover artists and leveraged buyout (LBO) specialists look at a corporation's financial statements for **operating cash flow,** which is the amount of revenue generated by a company before the cost of financing and taxes. It is the company's net income plus depreciation, depletion, amortization, interest expense, and income tax expense. When acquiring a company, LBO specialists will take on as much debt as the company's operating cash flow can support. Although operating cash flow is a broad measure of a company's funds, some takeover artists look at a much narrower **free cash flow,** which is the amount of money a new owner can take out of the firm without harming the business. It is net income plus depreciation, depletion, and amortization less capital expenditures and dividends.[12]

Economic Considerations

If you are analyzing a company over many years, you may need to adjust sales and net income for inflation to measure financial performance in **constant dollars.** One way to adjust for inflation is to use the **Consumer Price Index (CPI),** as shown in Table 15.2. Dividing sales and net income by the CPI factor for that year will change the figures to 1982–1984 constant dollars.

Another helpful analytical aid is the **prime interest rate (PIR),** also shown in Table 15.2. Better assessments of strategic decisions can be obtained by noting the prime interest rate at the time of the case. A decision to borrow money to build a new plant would have been a good one in 1987 but not such a good one in 1989.

When preparing a scenario for your pro forma financial statements, you also may want to use the **Gross Domestic Product (GDP)** from Table 15.2. Used worldwide, GDP measures the total output of goods and services within a country's

TABLE 15.2 **U.S. Economic Indicators: Gross Domestic Product (GDP), in Billions of Dollars; Consumer Price Index for All Items (CPI), 1982–1984 = 1.0; Prime Interest Rate (PIR), percent**

Year	GDP	CPI	PIR
1979	$2,488.6	.726	11.22%
1980	2,708.0	.824	15.27
1981	3,030.6	.909	18.87
1982	3,149.6	.965	14.86
1983	3,405.0	.996	10.79
1984	3,777.2	1.039	12.04
1985	4,038.7	1.076	9.93
1986	4,268.6	1.096	8.33
1987	4,539.9	1.136	8.21
1988	4,900.4	1.183	9.32
1989	5,250.8	1.240	10.87
1990	5,546.1	1.307	10.01
1991	5,722.9	1.362	8.46
1992	6,038.5	1.403	6.25
Mid 1993	6,327.6	1.444	6.00

Sources:

1. Gross Domestic Product from *Survey of Current Business* (September, 1993), Vol. 73, No. 9, Table 1, p. 47.

2. Consumer Price Index from U.S. Department of Commerce, *1992 Statistical Abstract of the United States,* 112th edition, Chart no. 738, p. 469; U.S. Bureau of Labor Statistics, *Monthly Labor Review* (September, 1993), Chart no. 31, p. 86.

3. Prime Interest Rates from D. S. Benton, "Banking and Financial Information," Table 1.1, p. 2, in *Thorndike Encyclopedia of Banking and Financial Tables,* 3rd ed., 1994 Yearbook (Boston: Warren, Gorham and Lamont, 1994).

borders. The previously used U.S. measure was Gross National Product (GNP), which covered production by a country's workers wherever they were in the world.[13]

15.5 Using the Strategic Audit in Case Analysis

The Appendix at the end of Chapter 2 on page 48 presents an example of a strategic audit proposed for use not only in strategic decision making, but also as a framework for the analysis of complex business policy cases.[14] The questions in the audit parallel the eight steps depicted in Fig. 2.3 on page 42, the strategic decision-making process. The audit provides a checklist of questions, by area or issue, that enables you to make a systematic analysis of various corporate activities. As a diagnostic tool, it is extremely useful in pinpointing problem areas and highlighting strengths and weaknesses. It isn't an all-inclusive list, but it presents many of the crucial questions that need to be addressed in the strategic analysis of any corporation. In a particular case, some of the questions or even some areas might be inappropriate; in other cases, the questions may be insufficient for a complete analysis. However, each question in a particular area of the strategic audit can be broken into a series of subquestions. It is up to you to develop these subquestions when you need to. Use the **Strategic Audit Worksheet,** shown in Fig. 15.1, to summarize your case analysis and recommendations. *It serves as a way to organize and structure your case notes for daily class discussions of a specific case.*

A strategic audit fulfills three major functions in a case-oriented strategy and policy course.

1. It serves to highlight and review important concepts from previously studied subject areas.
2. It provides a systematic framework for the analysis of complex cases and is especially useful if you are unfamiliar with the case method.
3. It generally improves the quality of case analysis and reduces the amount of time you might spend in learning how to analyze a case.

You also will find the audit helpful in organizing a case for written or oral presentation and in seeing that all areas have been considered. The strategic audit thus enables both you and the instructor to be efficient, both in analyzing why a certain area is creating problems for a corporation and in considering solutions to the problems.

The Strategic Audit found in the Appendix to Chapter 2 activates the Strategic Decision-Making Process shown in Fig. 2.3. Steps 3 and 4 of the Strategic Decision-Making Process are parts III and IV of the Strategic Audit and are carried out in the EFAS (Table 4.3) and IFAS (Table 5.2) Tables. Factors from the EFAS and IFAS Tables go in the Strategic Factor Analysis Summary (SFAS) in Fig. 6.2 and in the SWOT Matrix in Fig. 6.8. Following this procedure should help you do a complete analysis of a complex strategic management case.

In Conclusion . . .

Case study is one of the best ways to understand and remember the strategic management process. By applying the concepts and techniques you have learned to cases, you will be able to remember them long past the time when you have forgotten other memorized bits of information. The use of cases to examine actual situations brings alive the field of strategic management and helps build your analytic and decision-making skills. These are just some of the reasons why the use of cases in various disciplines from agribusiness to health care is increasing throughout the world.

FIGURE 15.1 **Strategic Audit Worksheet**

Strategic Audit Heading	Analysis		Comments
	(+) Factors	(−) Factors	
I. Current Situation			
A. Past Corporate Performance Indexes			
B. Strategic Posture: Current Mission Current Objectives Current Strategies Current Policies			
SWOT Analysis Begins			
II. Strategic Managers			
A. Board of Directors			
B. Top Management			
III. External Environment (EFAS): Opportunities and Threats (SWOT)			
A. Societal Environment			
B. Task Environment (Industry Analysis)			
IV. Internal Environment (IFAS): Strength and Weaknesses (SWOT)			
A. Corporate Structure			
B. Corporate Culture			
C. Corporate Resources			

(continued)

FIGURE 15.1 **Strategic Audit Worksheet** *(continued)*

Strategic Audit Heading	Analysis		Comments
	(+) Factors	(−) Factors	
1. Marketing			
2. Finance			
3. Research and Development			
4. Operations (Manufacturing/Service)			
5. Human Resources			
6. Information Systems			
V. Analysis of Strategic Factors (SFAS):			
A. Key Internal and External Strategic Factors (SWOT)			
B. Review of Mission and Objectives			
SWOT Analysis Ends			
VI. Alternatives and Recommendations			
A. Strategic Alternatives			
B. Recommended Strategy			
VII. Implementation			
VIII. Evaluation and Control			

Source: T. L. Wheelen and J. D. Hunger, "Strategic Audit Worksheet." Copyright © 1989 by Wheelen and Hunger Associates. Revised 1991 and 1994. Reprinted by permission. **Additional copies available for classroom use in Part D of Case Instructors Manual.**

Points to Remember

- A case can be analyzed within any of several organizing frameworks. Two suggested frameworks are the strategic audit and the 7-S framework. Keep in mind that there is no one right way to analyze a case. Your recommendations are less important than your processes of analysis and decision making.
- We recommend that, after you've read the case to get a sense of the situation, you calculate ratios and generate common-size statements over a five-year period. The figures will likely point to some symptoms of underlying problems that you will need to examine.
- You may want to do some library research to find out what was happening in the environment at the time the situation occurred. If you calculate ratios for the company, compare its ratios to average ratios for the industry and key competitors during that time period. See Appendix 15B for sources of information.
- Appendix 15A describes some ways for you to do case analysis and present the results in written reports and oral presentations.
- Consider following the analytic process illustrated in the Strategic Audit Worksheet shown in Fig. 15.1 to consider and weigh the essentials of the case for preparing your case analysis.

Discussion Questions

1. Why should you begin a case analysis with a financial analysis? When are other approaches appropriate?
2. What are common-size financial statements? What is their value to case analysis? How are they calculated?
3. When is adjusting financial statements for the effect of inflation useful?
4. When should you gather information outside the case by going to the library?

Notes

1. H. E. Klein, "Preface," *Forging New Partnerships with Cases, Simulations, Games and Other Interactive Methods,* edited by H. E. Klein (Needham, Mass.: World Association for Case Method Research & Application, 1992), p. xv.
2. T. A. Festervand and C. J. Hill, "The Case Method: A Managerial Assessment of Present Status and Future Directions," *Business Case Journal* (Fall 1993), pp. 141–151.
3. C. R. Decker and J. F. Bibb, "The Business Policy Course: Case and Other Course Components," (Millikin University Working Paper, 1990); C. H. Davis and G. T. Mills, "Offering Variety in Policy Case Courses," *Proceedings, Midwest Society for Case Research* (1990), pp. 89–95.
4. B. Keys and J. Wolfe, "Management Education and Development: Current Issues and Emerging Trends," *Journal of Management*

(June 1988), p. 214; R. G. Blunden and N. W. McGuinness, "The Real Case Method: A Response to Critics of Business Education," *Case Research Journal* (Winter 1993), pp. 106–119.

5. R. W. Waterman, Jr., T. J. Peters, and J. R. Phillips, "The 7-S Framework," in *The Strategy Process: Concepts, Contents, Cases,* 2nd ed., edited by H. Mintzberg and J. B. Quinn (Englewood Cliffs, N.J.: Prentice-Hall, 1991), pp. 309–314.
6. Software is available to add in strategic planning or to help in financial analysis. See R. J. Mockler, "A Catalogue of Commercially Available Software for Strategic Planning," *Planning Review* (May/June 1991), pp. 28–35.
7. S. Chan, H. Koh, and G. Sng, "The Demand for Accounting Ratios: An Empirical Study," *International Journal of Management* (March 1993), pp. 54–65.
8. M. W. Miller and L. Barton, "As IBM's Woes Grew, Its Accounting Tactics Got Less Conservative," *Wall Street Journal* (April 7, 1993), pp. A1, A6. One of the more recent tactics used is structuring borrowing as leases instead of listing them as debt. The companies can still list them as assets for tax purposes. This enables them to claim interest deductions and annual depreciation. The leasing arrangement means that analysts won't know how much the company actually owes. These transactions often are called "synthetic leases" or "off-balance-sheet loans" and reported in small print as a footnote in the annual report. See J. Egan, "A New Balance-Sheet Act," *U.S. News & World Report* (May 31, 1993), p. 79.
9. G. Jasen, "Red Flags: Putting a Company in Its Proper Prospectus," *Wall Street Journal* (September 7, 1989), p. C1.
10. M. S. Fridson, *Financial Statement Analysis* (New York: John Wiley & Sons, 1991), pp. 192–194.
11. D. H. Bangs, Jr., *Managing by the Numbers* (Dover, N.H.: Upstart Publications, 1992, pp. 106–107). (Thanks to Stan Mendenhall of Eastern Montana College for bringing the index and this reference to our attention.)
12. J. M. Laderman, "Earnings, Schmernings Look at the Cash," *Business Week* (July 24, 1989), pp. 56–57.
13. "Economics: Grossed Out," *Time* (December 16, 1991), p. 60.
14. J. D. Hunger and T. L. Wheelen, "The Strategic Audit: An Integrative Approach to Teaching Business Policy" (Paper presented at the Forty-third Annual Meeting of the *Academy of Management,* Dallas, Texas, August 1983).

Appendix 15A: Suggested Techniques for Case Analysis and Presentation

A. Case Analysis

1. Read the case to get an overview of the nature of the corporation and its environment. Note the date on which the case was written so that you can put it into proper context.
2. Read the case a second time, and give it a detailed examination according to the strategic audit (see the Appendix to Chapter 2 on pages 48–55) or some other framework of analysis. The audit, for example, will provide a conceptual framework for the examination of the corporation's objectives, mission, policies, strategies, problems, symptoms, and issues. Regardless of the framework used, you should end up with a list of the salient issues and problems in the case. Then perform a financial analysis.
3. Undertake outside research, when appropriate, to uncover economic and industrial information. Appendix 15B suggests possible sources for outside research into the corporation's environmental setting. Conduct an in-depth analysis of the industry. Analyze the important *competitors*. Consider the bargaining power of both *suppliers* and *buyers* that might affect the firm's situation. Consider also the possible threats of *future competitors* in the industry and the likelihood of new or different products or services that might *substitute* for the company's present ones. Consider *other stakeholders* who might affect strategic decision making in the industry.
4. Compile facts and evidence concerning selected issues and problems. Develop a framework or outline to organize your analysis. The following methods of organization are suggested for your consideration.
   a) Organize the analysis around the strategic audit or Strategic Audit Worksheet.
   b) Organize the analysis around the key individual(s) in the case.
   c) Organize the analysis around the corporation's functional areas: production, management, finance, marketing, and R&D.
   d) Organize the analysis around the decision-making process.
   e) Organize the analysis around the seven variables (the McKinsey 7-S Framework) of structure, strategy, staff, management style, systems and procedures, skills, and shared values.
5. Clearly identify and state the central problem(s) as supported by the information in the case. Use the SWOT format to sum up the key *strategic factors* facing the corporation: *S*trengths and *W*eaknesses of the company; *O*pportunities and *T*hreats in the environment. Use the external (EFAS) and internal (IFAS) strategic factor analysis summary tables shown in Tables 4.4, 5.2, and 6.2.

6. Develop a logical series of mutually exclusive alternatives that evolve from the analysis to resolve the problem(s) or issue(s) in the case. One of the alternatives should be to continue the company's current strategy. Develop at least two other strategic alternatives. However, don't present three alternatives and then recommend that all three be adopted. That's one alternative presented in three parts!
7. Evaluate each of the alternatives in light of the company's environment (both external and internal), mission, objectives, strategies, and policies. Discuss pros and cons. For each alternative, consider both the possible obstacles to its implementation and its financial implications.
8. Make recommendations assuming that action must be taken regardless of whether or not needed information is available. The individuals in the case may have had the same or even less information than given in the case.
   a) Base your recommendations on a total analysis of the case.
   b) Provide the evidence gathered above in **Step A4** to justify suggested changes.
   c) List the recommendations in order of priority.
   d) Show clearly how your recommendations deal with each of the *strategic factors* mentioned above in **Step A5**. How do they build on corporate *Strengths* to take advantage of environmental *Opportunities*? How do they deal with environmental *Threats* and corporate *Weaknesses*?
   e) Explain how each recommendation will be implemented. How do you intend to deal with anticipated resistance to the plan(s)?
   f) Suggest feedback and control systems to ensure that the recommendations are carried out as planned and to give advance warning of needed adjustments.

B. Written Report

1. Use the outline from **Step A4** to write the first draft of the case analysis. Follow **Steps A5–A8** as detailed above.
   a) Don't rehash the case material; rather, supply the salient evidence and data to support your analysis and recommendations.
   b) Develop exhibits on financial ratios and other data, such as strategic factors summary (SFAS table), for inclusion in your report. The exhibits should provide meaningful information. Refer to key elements of exhibits in the text of your written analysis. If you include a ratio analysis as an exhibit, explain the implications of the ratios and cite the critical ones in the text.
2. Review your written case analysis for content and grammar. Compare the outline (generated earlier in **Step A4**) with the final product. Be sure that you've presented sufficient data or evidence to support your analysis and recommendations. If the final product requires rewriting, do so. Keep in mind that the written report is going to be judged not only on what you say, but also on the manner in which you say it. *Style, grammar, and spelling are just as important as content in a written case analysis!*
3. If your written report requires pro forma statements, you may want to develop a *scenario* for each quarter and/or year in your forecast. A well-constructed scenario will help improve the accuracy of your forecast. (See Chapters 4 and 7 for information on constructing scenarios.)

C. Oral Presentation by Teams

1. A team should first decide on a framework or outline for analysis (**Step A4**). Although teams often divide the analysis work, each team member should follow **Steps A5–A8** to develop a preliminary analysis of the entire case and share it with team members.
2. The team should combine member input into one consolidated team analysis, including SWOT analysis, alternatives, and recommendation(s). Obtain agreement on the strategic factors and the best alternative(s) to support.
3. Divide further development and presentation of the case analysis and recommendation(s). Agree on responsibilities for the preparation of visual aids and handouts. As in written reports, scenarios and pro forma financial statements should support any recommendation.
4. Modify the team outline, if necessary, and have one or two rehearsals of the presentation. If exhibits are to be used, be sure to allow sufficient time to explain them. Check to ensure that any visual aids can be easily seen from the back of the room. Critique each others' presentations and modify the analysis as necessary. Again, *style, grammar, and delivery are just as important as content in an oral presentation!*
5. Dress appropriately and introduce yourselves to the audience. Begin your presentation by handing out a copy of the agenda, specifying the topics to be covered and who will present each topic. If a presenter misses a key fact, deal with it in summarizing the presentation.
6. Encourage questions from both the instructor and classmates. Begin the questioning period by calling on someone you consider a friend and who can be expected to ask a question you can easily field to get you off to a good start. You may wish to have one person act as a moderator for referring questions to the appropriate team member.

Appendix 15B: Resources for Case Library Research

A. Company Information

1. Annual Reports
2. *Moody's Manuals on Investment* (a list of companies in certain industries that contains a brief history and a five-year financial statement for each company).
3. Securities and Exchange Commission *Report Form 10-K* (annually) and *Report Form 10-Q* (quarterly).
4. Standard and Poor's *Register of Corporations, Directors, and Executives.*
5. Value Line *Investment Survey.*
6. *Findex: The Directory of Market Research Reports, Studies and Surveys* (a list by Find/SVP of more than 11,000 studies conducted by leading research firms).
7. *COMPUSTAT, Compact Disclosure,* and *CD/International* (computerized operating and financial information on thousands of publicly held corporations).

B. Economic Information

1. Regional statistics and local forecasts from large banks.
2. *Business Cycle Development* (Department of Commerce).
3. Chase Econometric Associates' publications.
4. U.S. Census Bureau publications on population, transportation, and housing.
5. *Current Business Reports* (U.S. Department of Commerce).
6. *Economic Indicators* (U.S. Joint Economic Committee).
7. *Economic Report of the President to Congress.*
8. *Long-Term Economic Growth* (U.S. Department of Commerce).
9. *Monthly Labor Review* (U.S. Department of Labor).
10. *Monthly Bulletin of Statistics* (United Nations).
11. *Statistical Abstract of the United States* (U.S. Department of Commerce).
12. *Statistical Yearbook* (United Nations).
13. *Survey of Current Business* (U.S. Department of Commerce).
14. *U.S. Industrial Outlook* (U.S. Department of Defense).
15. *World Trade Annual* (United Nations).
16. *Overseas Business Reports* (by country, published by the U.S. Department of Commerce).

Note: For further information, see M. A. Young, "Sources of Competitive Data for the Management Strategist," *Strategic Management Journal* (May–June 1989), pp. 285–293.

C. Industry Information

1. Analyses of companies and industries by investment brokerage firms.
2. *Business Week* (provides weekly economic and business information, and quarterly profit and sales rankings of corporations).
3. *Fortune* (each April publishes financial information on corporations in certain industries).
4. *Industry Survey* (published quarterly by Standard and Poor's Corporation).
5. *Industry Week* (late March/early April issue provides information on 14 industry groups).
6. *Forbes* (mid-January issue provides performance data on firms in various industries).
7. *Inc.* (May and December issues give information on small companies).

D. Directory and Index Information on Companies and Industries

1. *Business Periodical Index* (on computer in many libraries).
2. *Directory of National Trade Associations.*
3. *Encyclopedia of Associations.*
4. Funk and Scott *Index of Corporations and Industries.*
5. Thomas's *Register of American Manufacturers.*
6. *Wall Street Journal Index.*

E. Ratio Analysis Information

1. *Almanac of Business and Industrial Financial Ratios* (Prentice-Hall).
2. *Annual Statement Studies* (Robert Morris Associates).
3. *Dun's Review* (Dun and Bradstreet; published annually in September–December issues).
4. *Industry Norms and Key Business Ratios* (Dun and Bradstreet).

Contents

Cases in Strategic Management

Section A Strategic Managers: Questions of Executive Leadership

The Wallace Group

Laurence J. Stybel

Frances Rampar, President of Rampar Associates, drummed her fingers on the desk. Scattered before her were her notes. She had to put the pieces together in order to make an effective sales presentation to Harold Wallace.

Hal Wallace was the President of The Wallace Group. He had asked Rampar to conduct a series of interviews with some key Wallace Group employees, in preparation for a possible consulting assignment for Rampar Associates.

During the past three days, Rampar had been talking with some of these key people and had received background material about the company. The problem was not in finding the problem. The problem was that there were too many problems!

Background of the Wallace Group

The Wallace Group, Inc., is a diversified company dealing in the manufacture and development of technical products and systems (see Exhibit 1.1). The company currently consists of three operational groups and a corporate staff. The three groups include Electronics, Plastics, and Chemicals, each operating under the direction of a Group Vice-President (see Exhibits 1.2, 1.3, and 1.4). The company generates $70 million in sales as a manufacturer of plastics, chemical products, and electronic components and systems. Principal sales are to large contractors in governmental and automotive markets. With respect to sales volume, Plastics and Chemicals are approximately equal in size, and both of them together equal the size of the Electronics Group.

Electronics offers competence in the areas of microelectronics, electromagnetic sensors, antennas, microwave, and minicomputers. Presently, these skills are devoted primarily to the engineering and manufacture of countermeasure equipment for aircraft. This includes radar detection systems that allow an aircraft crew to know that they are being tracked by radar units on the ground, on ships, or on other aircraft. Further, the company manufactures displays that provide the crew with a visual "fix" on where they are relative to the radar units that are tracking them.

In addition to manufacturing tested and proven systems developed in the past, The Wallace Group is currently involved in two major and two minor programs, all involving display systems. The Navy-A Program calls for the development of a display system for a tactical fighter plane; Air Force-B is another such system for an observation plane. Ongoing production orders are anticipated following flight

This case was prepared by Dr. Laurence J. Stybel. It was prepared for class discussion rather than to illustrate either effective or ineffective handling of an administrative situation. This case is available from and distributed in looseleaf exclusively from Lord Publishing, Inc., One Apple Hill, Suite 320, Natick, Mass. 01760, (508) 651-9955. This case was edited by T. L. Wheelen and J. D. Hunger for this book. Reprinted by permission.

EXHIBIT 1.1

An Excerpt from the Annual Report

To the Shareholders:

This past year was one of definite accomplishment for The Wallace Group, although with some admitted soft spots. This is a period of consolidation, of strengthening our internal capacity for future growth and development. Presently, we are in the process of creating a strong management team to meet the challenges we will set for the future.

Despite our failure to achieve some objectives, we turned a profit of $3,521,000 before taxes, which was a growth over the previous year's earnings. And we have declared a dividend for the fifth consecutive year, albeit one that is less than the year before. However, the retention of earnings is imperative if we are to lay a firm foundation for future accomplishment.

Currently, The Wallace Group has achieved a level of stability. We have a firm foothold in our current markets, and we could elect to simply enact strong internal controls and maximize our profits. However, this would not be a growth strategy. Instead, we have chosen to adopt a more aggressive posture for the future, to reach out into new markets wherever possible and to institute the controls necessary to move forward in a planned and orderly fashion.

The Electronics Group performed well this past year and is engaged in two major programs under Defense Department contracts. These are developmental programs that provide us with the opportunity for ongoing sales upon testing of the final product. Both involve the creation of tactical display systems for aircraft being built by Lombard Aircraft for the Navy and the Air Force. Future potential sales from these efforts could amount to approximately $56 million over the next five years. Additionally, we are developing technical refinements to older, already installed systems under Army Department contracts.

In the future, we will continue to offer our technological competence in such tactical display systems and anticipate additional breakthroughs and success in meeting the demands of this market. However, we also believe that we have unique contributions to make to other markets, and to that end we are making the investments necessary to expand our opportunities.

Plastics also turned in a solid performance this past year and has continued to be a major supplier to Chrysler, Martin Tool, Foster Electric, and, of course, to our Electronics Group. The market for this group continues to expand, and we believe that additional investments in this group will allow us to seize a larger share of the future.

Chemicals' performance, admittedly, has not been as satisfactory as anticipated during the past year. However, we have been able to realize a small amount of profit from this operation and to halt what was a potentially dangerous decline in profits. We believe that this situation is only temporary and that infusions of capital for developing new technology, plus the streamlining of operations, has stabilized the situation. The next step will be to begin more aggressive marketing to capitalize on the group's basic strengths.

Overall, the outlook seems to be one of modest but profitable growth. The near term will be one of creating the technology and controls necessary for developing our market offerings and growing in a planned and purposeful manner. Our improvement efforts in the various company groups can be expected to take hold over the years with positive effects on results.

We wish to express our appreciation to all those who participated in our efforts this past year.

Harold Wallace
Chairman and President

Organizational Chart: The Wallace Group

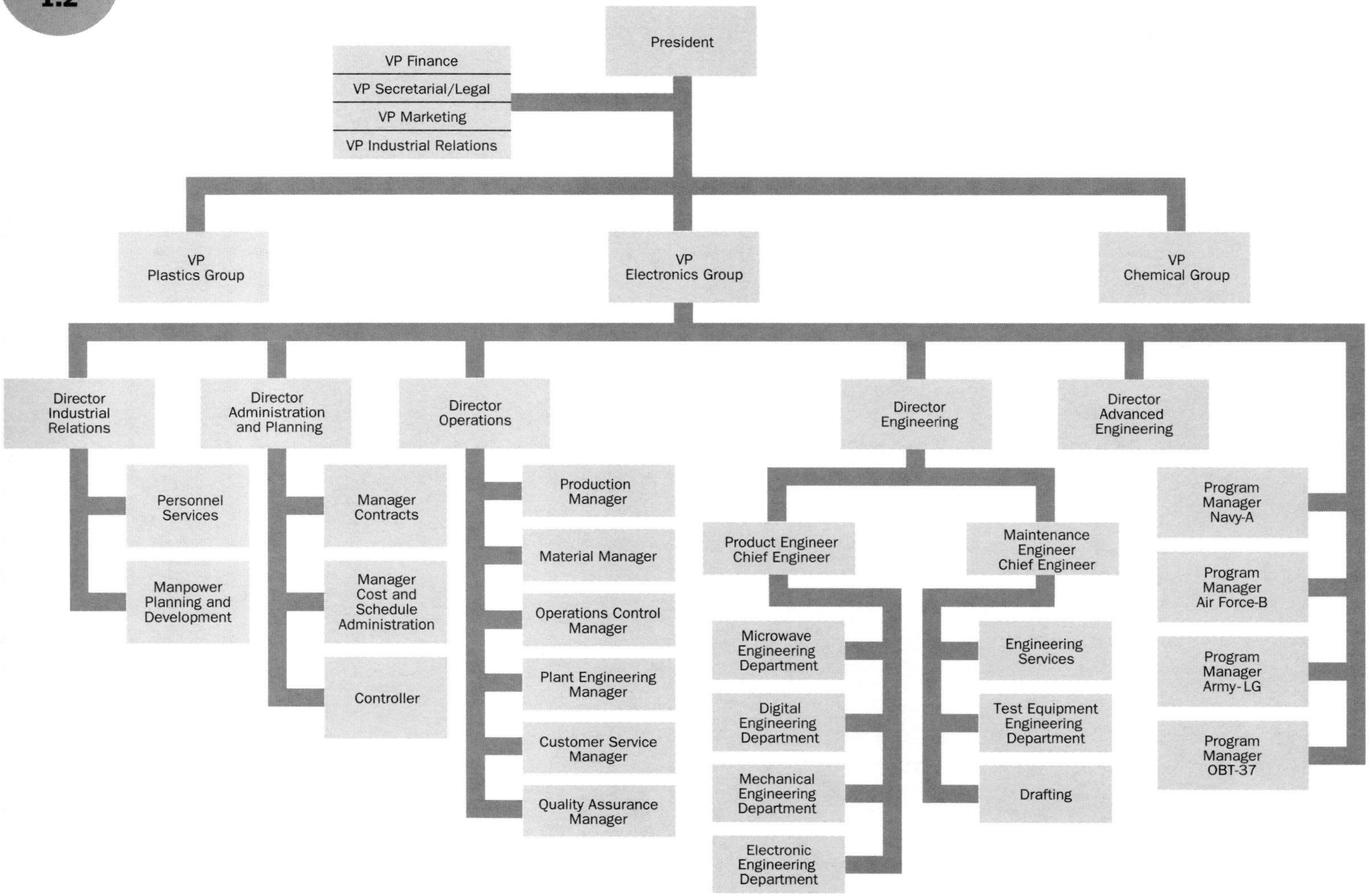

President

VP Finance
VP Secretarial/Legal
VP Marketing
VP Industrial Relations

VP Plastics Group

VP Electronics Group

VP Chemical Group

Director Industrial Relations
- Personnel Services
- Manpower Planning and Development

Director Administration and Planning
- Manager Contracts
- Manager Cost and Schedule Administration
- Controller

Director Operations
- Production Manager
- Material Manager
- Operations Control Manager
- Plant Engineering Manager
- Customer Service Manager
- Quality Assurance Manager

Director Engineering
- Product Engineer Chief Engineer
  - Microwave Engineering Department
  - Digital Engineering Department
  - Mechanical Engineering Department
  - Electronic Engineering Department
- Maintenance Engineer Chief Engineer
  - Engineering Services
  - Test Equipment Engineering Department
  - Drafting

Director Advanced Engineering

Program Manager Navy-A

Program Manager Air Force-B

Program Manager Army-LG

Program Manager OBT-37

EXHIBIT 1.3 The Wallace Group

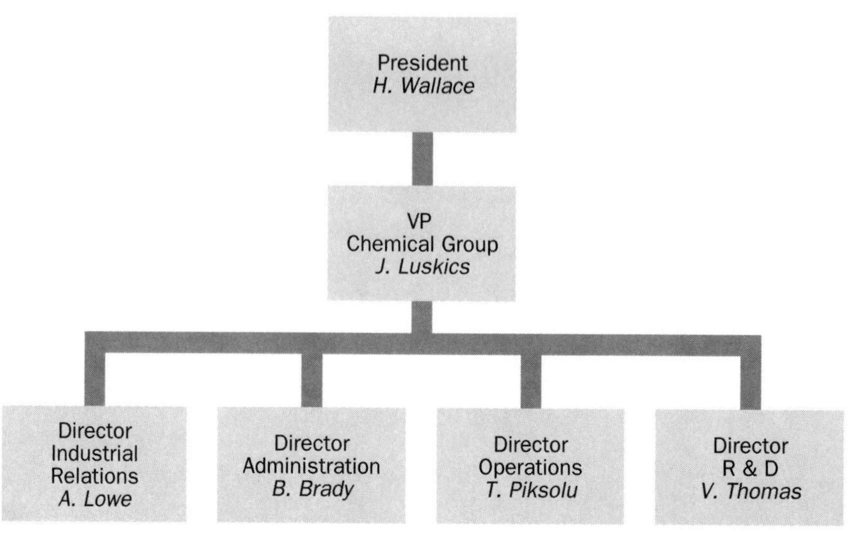

EXHIBIT 1.4 The Wallace Group

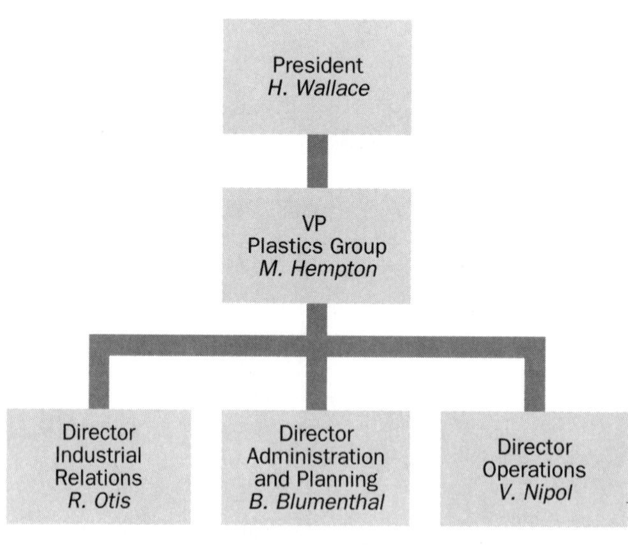

testing. The other two programs, Army-LG and OBT-37, involve the incorporation of new technology into existing aircraft systems.

The Plastics Group manufactures plastic components utilized by the electronics, automotive, and other industries requiring plastic products. These include switches, knobs, keys, insulation materials, and so on, used in the manufacture of electronic equipment and other small made-to-order components installed in automobiles, planes, and other products.

The Chemicals Group produces chemicals used in the development of plastics. It supplies bulk chemicals to the Plastics Group and other companies. These chemicals are then injected into molds or extruded to form a variety of finished products.

History of the Wallace Group

Each of the three groups began as a sole proprietorship under the direct operating control of an owner/manager. Several years ago, Harold Wallace, owner of the original electronics company, determined to undertake a program of diversification. Initially, he attempted to expand his market by product development and line extensions entirely within the electronics industry. However, because of initial problems, he drew back and sought other opportunities. Wallace's primary concern was his almost total dependence on defense-related contracts. He had felt for some time that he should take some strong action to gain a foothold in the private markets. The first major opportunity that seemed to satisfy his various requirements was the acquisition of a former supplier, a plastics company whose primary market was not defense-related. The company's owner desired to sell his operation and retire. At the time, Wallace's debt structure was such that he could not manage the acquisition and so he had to attract equity capital. He was able to gather a relatively small group of investors and form a closed corporation. The group established a Board of Directors with Wallace as Chairman and President of the new corporate entity.

With respect to operations, little changed. Wallace continued direct operational control over the Electronics Group. As holder of 60% of the stock, he maintained effective control over policy and operations. However, because of his personal interests, the Plastics Group, now under the direction of a newly hired Vice-President, Martin Hempton, was left mainly to its own devices except for yearly progress reviews by the President. All Wallace asked at the time was that the Plastics Group continue its profitable operation, which it did.

Several years ago, Wallace and the Board decided to diversify further because two-thirds of their business was still defense-dependent. They learned that one of the major suppliers of the Plastics Group, a chemical company, was on the verge of bankruptcy. The company's owner, Jerome Luskics, agreed to sell. However, this acquisition required a public stock offering, with most of the funds going to pay off debts incurred by the three groups, especially the Chemicals Group. The net result was that Wallace now holds 45% of The Wallace Group and Jerome Luskics 5%, with the remainder distributed among the public.

Organization and Personnel

Presently, Harold Wallace serves as Chairman and President of The Wallace Group. The Electronics Group had been run by LeRoy Tuscher, who just resigned as Vice-President. Hempton continued as Vice-President of Plastics and Luskics served as Vice-President of the Chemicals Group.

Reflecting the requirements of a corporate perspective and approach, a corporate staff has grown up, consisting of Vice-Presidents for Finance, Secretarial/Legal, Marketing, and Industrial Relations. This staff has assumed many functions formerly associated with the group offices.

Because these positions are recent additions, many of the job accountabilities are still being defined. Problems have arisen over the responsibilities and relationships between corporate and group positions. President Wallace has settled most of the disputes himself because of the inability of the various parties to resolve differences among themselves.

Current Trends

Presently, there is a mood of lethargy and drift within The Wallace Group (see Exhibits 1.5–1.11). Most managers feel that each of the three groups functions as an independent company. And, with respect to group performance, not much change or progress has been made in recent years. Electronics and Plastics are still stable and profitable, but both lack growth in markets and profits. The infusion of capital breathed new life and hope into the Chemicals operation but did not solve most of the old problems and failings that had caused its initial decline. For all these reasons Wallace decided that strong action was necessary. His greatest disappointment was with the Electronics Group, in which he had placed high hopes for future development. Thus he acted by requesting and getting the Electronics Group Vice-President's resignation. Hired from a computer company to replace LeRoy Tuscher, Jason Matthews joined The Wallace Group a week ago.

Last week, Wallace's net sales were $70 million. By group they were:

Electronics	$35,000,000
Plastics	$20,000,000
Chemicals	$15,000,000

On a consolidated basis, the financial highlights of the last two years are as follows:

	Last Year	Two Years Ago
Net sales	$70,434,000	$69,950,000
Income (pre-tax)	3,521,000	3,497,500
Income (after-tax)	1,760,500	1,748,750
Working capital	16,200,000	16,088,500
Shareholders' equity	39,000,000	38,647,000

Total assets	59,869,000	59,457,000
Long-term debt	4,350,000	3,500,000
Per Share of Common Stock		
Net income	$.37	$.36
Cash dividends paid	.15	.25

Of the net income, approximately 70% came from Electronics, 25% from Plastics, and 5% from Chemicals.

EXHIBIT 1.5 Selected Portions of a Transcribed Interview with H. Wallace

RAMPAR: What is your greatest problem right now?

WALLACE: That's why I called you in! Engineers are a high-strung, temperamental lot. Always complaining. It's hard to take them seriously.

Last month we had an annual stockholder's meeting. We have an Employee Stock Option Plan, and many of our long-term employees attended the meeting. One of my managers—and I won't mention any names—introduced a resolution calling for the resignation of the President—me!

The vote was defeated. But, of course, I own 45% of the stock!

Now I realize that there could be no serious attempt to get rid of me. Those who voted for the resolution were making a dramatic effort to show me how upset they are with the way things are going.

I could fire those employees who voted against me. I was surprised by how many did. Some of my key people were in that group. Perhaps I ought to stop and listen to what they are saying.

Businesswise, I think we're O.K. Not great, but O.K. Last year we turned in a profit of $3.5 million before taxes, which was a growth over previous years' earnings. We declared a dividend for the fifth consecutive year.

We're currently working on the creation of a tactical display system for aircraft being built by Lombard Aircraft for the Navy and the Air Force. If Lombard gets the contract to produce the prototype, future sales could amount to $56 million over the next five years.

Why are they complaining?

RAMPAR: You must have some thoughts on the matter.

WALLACE: I think the issue revolves around how we manage people. It's a personnel problem. You were highly recommended as someone with expertise in high-technology human-resource management.

I have some ideas on what is the problem. But I'd like you to do an independent investigation and give me your findings. Give me a plan of action.

Don't give me a laundry list of problems, Fran. Anyone can do that. I want a set of priorities I should focus on during the next year. I want a clear action plan from you. And I want to know how much this plan is going to cost me!

Other than that, I'll leave you alone and let you talk to anyone in the company you want.

EXHIBIT 1.6

Selected Portions of a Transcribed Interview with Frank Campbell, Vice-President of Industrial Relations

RAMPAR: What is your greatest problem right now?

CAMPBELL: Trying to contain my enthusiasm over the fact that Wallace brought you in!

Morale is really poor here. Hal runs this place like a one-man operation, when it's grown too big for that. It took a palace revolt to finally get him to see the depths of the resentment. Whether he'll do anything about it, that's another matter.

RAMPAR: What would you like to see changed?

CAMPBELL: Other than a new President?

RAMPAR: Uh-huh.

CAMPBELL: We badly need a management development program for our group. Because of our growth, we have been forced to promote technical people to management positions who have had no prior managerial experience. Mr. Tuscher agreed on the need for a program, but Hal Wallace vetoed the idea because developing such a program would be too expensive. I think it is too expensive *not* to move ahead on this.

RAMPAR: Anything else?

CAMPBELL: The IEWU negotiations have been extremely tough this time around, due to excessive demands they have been making. Union pay scales are already pushing up against our foreman salary levels, and foremen are being paid high in their salary ranges. This problem, coupled with union insistence on a no-layoff clause, is causing us fits. How can we keep all our workers when we have production equipment on order that will eliminate 20% of our assembly positions?

RAMPAR: Wow.

CAMPBELL: We have been sued by a rejected candidate for a position on the basis of discrimination. She claimed our entrance qualifications are excessive because we require shorthand. There is some basis for this statement since most reports are given to secretaries in handwritten form or on audio cassettes. In fact, we have always required it and our executives want their secretaries to have skill in taking dictation. Not only is this case taking time, but I need to reconsider if any of our position entrance requirements, in fact, are excessive. I am sure we do not want another case like this one.

RAMPAR: That puts The Wallace Group in a vulnerable position, considering the amount of government work you do.

CAMPBELL: We have a tremendous recruiting backlog, especially for engineering positions. Either our pay scales are too low, our job specs are too high, or we are using the wrong recruiting channels. Kane and Smith [Director of Engineering and Director of Advanced Systems] keep rejecting everyone we send down there as being unqualified.

RAMPAR: Gee.

CAMPBELL: Being head of Human Resources around here is a tough job. We don't act. We react.

EXHIBIT 1.7

Selected Portions of a Transcribed Interview with Matthew Smith, Director of Advanced Systems

RAMPAR: What is your greatest problem right now?

SMITH: Corporate brass keeps making demands on me and others that don't relate to the job we are trying to get done. They say that the information they need is to satisfy corporate planning and operations review requirements, but they don't seem to recognize how much time and effort is required to provide this information. Sometimes it seems like they are generating analyses, reports, and requests for data just to keep themselves busy. Someone should be evaluating how critical these corporate staff activities really are. To me and the Electronics Group, these activities are unnecessary.

An example is the Vice-President, Marketing (L. Holt), who keeps asking us for supporting data so he can prepare a corporate marketing strategy. As you know, we prepare our own group marketing strategic plans annually, but using data and formats that are oriented to our needs, rather than Corporate's. This planning activity, which occurs at the same time as Corporate's, coupled with heavy work loads on current projects, makes us appear to Holt as though we are being unresponsive.

Somehow we need to integrate our marketing planning efforts between our group and Corporate. This is especially true if our group is to successfully grow in nondefense-oriented markets and products. We do need corporate help, but not arbitrary demands for information that divert us from putting together effective marketing strategies for our group.

I am getting too old to keep fighting these battles.

RAMPAR: This is a long-standing problem?

SMITH: You bet! Our problems are fairly classic in the high-tech field. I've been at other companies and they're not much better. We spend so much time firefighting, we never really get organized. Everything is done on an ad hoc basis.
I'm still waiting for tomorrow.

EXHIBIT 1.8

Selected Portions of a Transcribed Interview with Ralph Kane, Director of Engineering

RAMPAR: What is your greatest problem right now?

KANE: Knowing you were coming, I wrote them down. They fall into four areas:

1. Our salary schedules are too low to attract good, experienced EEs. We have been told by our Vice-President (Frank Campbell) that corporate policy is to hire new people below the salary grade midpoint. All qualified candidates are making more than that now and in some cases are making more than our grade maximums. I think our Project Engineer job is rated too low.
2. Chemicals Group asked for and the former Electronics Vice-President (Tuscher) agreed to "lend" six of our best EEs to help solve problems it is having developing a new battery. That is great for the Chemicals Group, but meanwhile how do we solve the engineering problems that have cropped up in our Navy-A and OBT-37 programs?
3. As you know, Matt Smith (Director of Advanced Systems) is retiring in six months. I depend heavily on his group for technical expertise, and in some areas he depends heavily on some of my key engineers. I have lost some people to the Chemicals Group, and Matt has been trying to lend me some of his

(continued)

EXHIBIT 1.8

Selected Portions of a Transcribed Interview with Ralph Kane, Director of Engineering *(continued)*

people to fill in. But he and his staff have been heavily involved in marketing planning and trying to identify or recruit a qualified successor long enough before his retirement to be able to train him. The result is that his people are up to their eyeballs in doing their own stuff and cannot continue to help me meet my needs.

4. IR has been preoccupied with union negotiations in the plant and has not had time to help me deal with this issue of management planning. Campbell is working on some kind of system that will help deal with this kind of problem and prevent them in the future. That is great, but I need help now—not when his "system" is ready.

EXHIBIT 1.9

Selected Portions of a Transcribed Interview with Brad Lowell, Program Manager, Navy-A

RAMPAR: What is your . . .?

LOWELL: . . . great problem? I'll tell you what it is.
I still cannot get the support I need from Kane in Engineering. He commits and then doesn't deliver, and it has me quite concerned. The excuse now is that in "his judgment," Sid Wright needs the help for the Air Force program more than I do. Wright's program is one week ahead of schedule, so I disagree with "his judgment." Kane keeps complaining about not having enough people.

RAMPAR: Why do you think Kane says he doesn't have enough people?

LOWELL: Because Hal Wallace is a tight-fisted S.O.B. who won't let us hire the people we need!

EXHIBIT 1.10

Selected Portions of a Transcribed Interview with Phil Jones, Director, Administration and Planning

JONES: Wheel spinning—that's our problem! We talk about expansion, but we don't do anything about it. Are we serious or not?

For example, a bid request came in from a prime contractor seeking help in developing a countermeasure system for a medium-range aircraft. They needed an immediate response and a concept proposal in one week. Tuscher just sat on my urgent memo to him asking for a go/no go decision on bidding. I could not give the contractor an answer (because no decision came from Tuscher), so they gave up on us.

I am frustrated because (1) we lost an opportunity we were "naturals" to win, and (2) my personal reputation was damaged because I was unable to answer the bid request. Okay, Tuscher's gone now, but we need to develop some mechanism so an answer to such a request can be made quickly.

Another thing, our MIS is being developed by the Corporate Finance Group. More wheel spinning! They are telling us what information we need rather than asking us what we want! E. Kay (our Group Controller) is going crazy trying to sort out the input requirements they need for the system and understanding the complicated reports that come out. Maybe this new system is great as a technical achievement, but what good is it to us if we can't use it?

EXHIBIT 1.11 **Selected Portions of a Transcribed Interview with Burt Williams, Director of Operations**

RAMPAR: What is your biggest problem right now?

WILLIAMS: One of the biggest problems we face right now stems from corporate policy regarding transfer pricing. I realize we are "encouraged" to purchase our plastics and chemicals from our sister Wallace groups, but we are also committed to making a profit! Because manufacturing problems in those groups have forced them to raise their prices, should *we* suffer the consequences? We can get some materials cheaper from other suppliers. How can we meet our volume and profit targets when we are saddled with noncompetitive material costs?

RAMPAR: And if that issue was settled to your satisfaction, then would things be O.K.?

WILLIAMS: Although out of my direct function, it occurs to me that we are not planning effectively our efforts to expand into nondefense areas. With minimal alteration to existing production methods, we can develop both end-use products (e.g., small motors, traffic control devices, and microwave transceivers for highway emergency communications) and components (e.g., LED and LCD displays, police radar tracking devices, and word processing system memory and control devices) with large potential markets.

The problems in this regard are:

1. Matt Smith (Director, Advanced Systems) is retiring and has had only defense-related experience. Therefore he is not leading any product development efforts along these lines.
2. We have no marketing function at the group level to develop a strategy, define markets, and research and develop product opportunities.
3. Even if we had a marketing plan and products for industrial/commercial application, we have no sales force or rep network to sell the stuff.

   Maybe I am way off base, but it seems to me we need a Groups/Marketing/Sales function to lead us in this business expansion effort. It should be headed by an experienced technical marketing manager with a proven track record in developing such products and markets.

RAMPAR: Have you discussed your concerns with others?

WILLIAMS: I have brought these ideas up with Mr. Matthews and others at the Group Management Committee. No one else seems interested in pursuing this concept, but they won't say this outright and don't say why it should not be addressed. I guess that in raising the idea with you I am trying to relieve some of my frustrations.

The Problem Confronting Frances Rampar

As Rampar finished reviewing her notes, she kept reflecting on what Hal Wallace had told her:

> Don't give me a laundry list of problems, Fran. Anyone can do that. I want a set of priorities I should focus on during the next year. I want a clear action plan from you. And I want to know how much this plan is going to cost me!

Fran Rampar again drummed her fingers on the desk.

CASE 2

The Recalcitrant Director at Byte Products, Inc.: Corporate Legality versus Corporate Responsibility

Dan R. Dalton, Richard A. Cosier, and Cathy A. Enz

Byte Products, Inc., is primarily involved in the production of electronic components that are used in personal computers. Although such components might be found in a few computers in home use, Byte products are found most frequently in computers used for sophisticated business and engineering applications. Annual sales of these products have been steadily increasing over the past several years; Byte Products, Inc., currently has total sales of approximately $265 million.

Over the past six years increases in yearly revenues have consistently reached 12%. Byte Products, Inc., headquartered in the midwestern United States, is regarded as one of the largest volume suppliers of specialized components and is easily the industry leader with some 32% market share. Unfortunately for Byte, many new firms—domestic and foreign—have entered the industry. A dramatic surge in demand, high profitability, and the relative ease of a new firm's entry into the industry explain in part the increased number of competing firms.

Although Byte management—and presumably shareholders as well—is pleased about the growth of its markets, it faces a major problem: Byte simply cannot meet the demand for these components. The company currently operates three manufacturing facilities in various locations throughout the United States. Each of these plants operates three production shifts (24 hours per day), seven days a week. This activity constitutes virtually all of the company's production capacity. Without an additional manufacturing plant, Byte simply cannot increase its output of components.

James M. Elliott, Chief Executive Officer and Chairman of the Board, recognizes the gravity of the problem. If Byte Products cannot continue to manufacture components in sufficient numbers to meet the demand, buyers will go elsewhere. Worse yet is the possibility that any continued lack of supply will encourage others to enter the market. As a long-term solution to this problem, the Board of Directors unanimously authorized the construction of a new, state-of-the-art manufacturing facility in the southwestern United States. When the planned capacity of this plant is added to that of the three current plants, Byte should be able to meet demand for many years to come. Unfortunately, an estimated three years will be required to complete the plant and bring it on line.

Jim Elliott believes very strongly that this three-year period is far too long and has insisted that there also be a shorter range, stopgap solution while the plant is under construction. The instability of the market and the pressure to maintain leader status are two factors contributing to Elliott's insistence on a more immediate solution. Without such a move, Byte management believes that it will lose market share and, again, attract competitors into the market.

This case was prepared by Professors Dan R. Dalton, Richard A. Cosier, and Cathy A. Enz of the Graduate School of Business at Indiana University. This case was edited by T. L. Wheelen and J. D. Hunger for this book. Reprinted by permission of the authors.

Several Solutions?

A number of suggestions for such a temporary measure were offered by various staff specialists, but rejected by Elliott. For example, licensing Byte's product and process technology to other manufacturers in the short run to meet immediate demand was possible. This licensing authorization would be short-term, or just until the new plant could come on line. Top management, as well as the board, was uncomfortable with this solution for several reasons. They thought it unlikely that any manufacturer would shoulder the fixed costs of producing appropriate components for such a short term. Any manufacturer that would do so would charge a premium to recover its costs. This suggestion, obviously, would make Byte's own products available to its customers at an unacceptable price. Nor did passing any price increase to its customers seem sensible, for this too would almost certainly reduce Byte's market share as well as encourage further competition.

Overseas facilities and licensing also were considered but rejected. Before it became a publicly traded company, Byte's founders decided that its manufacturing facilities would be domestic. Top management strongly felt that this strategy had served Byte well; moreover, Byte's majority stockholders (initial owners of the then privately held Byte) were not likely to endorse such a move. Beyond that, however, top management was reluctant to foreign license—or make available by any means the technologies for others to produce Byte products—as they could not then properly control patents. Top management feared that foreign licensing would essentially give away costly proprietary information regarding the company's highly efficient means of product development. There also was the potential for initial low product quality—whether produced domestically or otherwise—especially for such a short-run operation. Any reduction in quality, however brief, would threaten Byte's share of this sensitive market.

The Solution!

One recommendation that has come to the attention of the Chief Executive Officer could help solve Byte's problem in the short run. Certain members of his staff have notified him that an abandoned plant currently is available in Plainville, a small town in the northeastern United States. Before its closing eight years before, this plant was used primarily for the manufacture of electronic components. As is, it could not possibly be used to produce Byte products, but it could be inexpensively refitted to do so in as few as three months. Moreover, this plant is available at a very attractive price. In fact, discreet inquiries by Elliott's staff indicate that this plant could probably be leased immediately from its present owners, because the building has been vacant for some eight years.

All the news about this temporary plant proposal, however, is not nearly so positive. Elliott's staff concedes that this plant will never be efficient and its profitability will be low. In addition, the Plainville location is a poor one in terms of high labor costs (the area is highly unionized), warehousing expenses, and inadequate transportation links to Byte's major markets and suppliers. Plainville is simply not a candidate for a long-term solution. Still, in the short run a temporary plant could help meet the demand and might forestall additional competition.

The staff is persuasive and notes that this option has several advantages: (1) there is no need for any licensing, foreign or domestic, (2) quality control remains firmly in the company's hands, and (3) an increase in the product price will be unnecessary. The temporary plant, then, would be used for three years or so until the new plant could be built. Then the temporary plant would be immediately closed.

CEO Elliott is convinced.

Taking the Plan to the Board

The quarterly meeting of the Board of Directors is set to commence at 2:00 P.M. Jim Elliott has been reviewing his notes and agenda for the meeting most of the morning. The issue of the temporary plant is clearly the most important agenda item. Reviewing his detailed presentation of this matter, including the associated financial analyses, has occupied much of his time for several days. All the available information underscores his contention that the temporary plant in Plainville is the only responsible solution to the demand problems. No other option offers the same low level of risk and ensures Byte's status as industry leader.

At the meeting, after the board has dispensed with a number of routine matters, Jim Elliott turns his attention to the temporary plant. In short order, he advises the 11-member board (himself, three additional inside members, and seven outside members) of his proposal to obtain and refit the existing plant to meet demand problems in the short run, authorize the construction of the new plant (the completion of which is estimated to take some three years), and plan to switch capacity from the temporary plant to the new one when it is operational. He also briefly reviews additional details concerning the costs involved, advantages of this proposal versus domestic or foreign licensing, and so on.

All the board members except one are in favor of the proposal. In fact, they are most enthusiastic; the overwhelming majority agree that the temporary plant is an excellent—even inspired—stopgap measure. Ten of the 11 board members seem relieved because the board was most reluctant to endorse any of the other alternatives that had been mentioned.

The single dissenter—T. Kevin Williams, an outside director—is, however, steadfast in his objections. He will not, under any circumstances, endorse the notion of the temporary plant and states rather strongly that "I will not be party to this nonsense, not now, not ever."

T. Kevin Williams, the senior executive of a major nonprofit organization, is normally a reserved and really quite agreeable person. This sudden, uncharacteristic burst of emotion clearly startles the remaining board members into silence. The following excerpt captures the ensuing, essentially one-on-one conversation between Williams and Elliott.

WILLIAMS: How many workers do your people estimate will be employed in the temporary plant?

ELLIOTT: Roughly 1,200, possibly a few more.

WILLIAMS: I presume it would be fair, then, to say that, including spouses and children, something on the order of 4,000 people will be attracted to the community.

ELLIOTT: I certainly would not be surprised.

WILLIAMS: If I understand the situation correctly, this plant closed just over eight years ago and that closing had a catastrophic effect on Plainville. Isn't it true that a large portion of the community was employed by this plant?

ELLIOTT: Yes, it was far and away the majority employer.

WILLIAMS: And most of these people have left the community presumably to find employment elsewhere.

ELLIOTT: Definitely, there was a drastic decrease in the area's population.

WILLIAMS: Are you concerned, then, that our company can attract the 1,200 employees to Plainville from other parts of New England?

ELLIOTT: Not in the least. We are absolutely confident that we will attract 1,200—even more, for that matter virtually any number we need. That, in fact, is one of the chief advantages of this proposal. I would think that the community would be very pleased to have us there.

WILLIAMS: On the contrary, I would suspect that the community will rue the day we arrived. Beyond that, though, this plan is totally unworkable if we are candid. On the other hand, if we are less than candid, the proposal will work for us, but only at great cost to Plainville. In fact, quite frankly the implications are appalling. Once again, I must enter my serious objections.

ELLIOTT: I don't follow you.

WILLIAMS: The temporary plant would employ some 1,200 people. Again, this means the infusion of over 4,000 to the community and surrounding areas. Byte Products, however, intends to close this plant in three years or less. If Byte informs the community or the employees that the jobs are temporary, the proposal simply won't work. When the new people arrive in the community, there will be a need for more schools, instructors, utilities, housing, restaurants, and so forth. Obviously, if the banks and local government know that the plant is temporary, no funding will be made available for these projects and certainly no credit for the new employees to buy homes, appliances, automobiles, and so forth.

If on the other hand, Byte Products does not tell the community of its "temporary" plans, the project can go on. But, in several years when the plant closes (and we here have agreed today that it will close), we will have created a ghost town. The tax base of the community will have been destroyed; property values will decrease precipitously; practically the whole town will be unemployed. This proposal will place Byte Products in an untenable position and in extreme jeopardy.

ELLIOTT: Are you suggesting that this proposal jeopardizes us legally? If so, it should be noted that the legal department has reviewed this proposal in its entirety and has indicated no problem.

WILLIAMS: No! I don't think we are dealing with an issue of legality here. In fact, I don't doubt for a minute that this proposal is altogether legal. I do, however, resolutely believe that this proposal constitutes gross irresponsibility.

I think this decision has captured most of my major concerns. These along with a host of collateral problems associated with this project lead me to strongly suggest that you and the balance of the board reconsider and not endorse this proposal. Byte Products must find another way.

The Dilemma

After a short recess, the board meeting reconvened. Presumably because of some discussion during the recess, several other board members indicated that they were no longer inclined to support the proposal. After a short period of rather heated discussion, the following exchange took place.

ELLIOTT: It appears to me that any vote on this matter is likely to be very close. Given the gravity of our demand capacity problem, I must insist that the stockholders' equity be protected. We cannot wait three years; that is clearly out of the question. I still feel that licensing—domestic or foreign—is not in our long-term interests for any number of reasons, some of which have been discussed here. On the other hand, I do not want to take this project forward on the strength of a mixed vote. A vote of 6–5 or 7–4, for example, does not indicate the board is of anything remotely of one mind. Mr. Williams, is there a compromise to be reached?

WILLIAMS: Respectfully, I have to say no. If we tell the truth, namely, the temporary nature of our operations, the proposal is simply not viable. If we are less than candid in this respect, we do grave damage to the community as well as to our image. It seems to me that we can only go one way or the other. I don't see a middle ground.

CASE 3

Section B Environmental Issues: Questions of Social Responsibility and Ethics

Burroughs Wellcome and AZT

Ram Subramanian

As the bell sounded to signify the opening of the New York Stock Exchange, it was soon drowned out by another noise. Five men, chained to a balcony inside the Exchange, were blowing a horn to draw attention to a banner that they held. The banner read: "Sell Wellcome."[1]

One April morning, four young men, nattily attired in business suits, audaciously walked into Burroughs Wellcome's headquarters in North Carolina. They ejected the occupant of an executive office, sealed the doors tight, and chained themselves to a radiator. Meanwhile one of their cohorts called the press to describe the break-in.[2]

Were these international terrorists attacking harmless establishments to seek release of their prisoner brothers? No, they were Acquired Immune Deficiency Syndrome (AIDS) activists protesting what they described as unfair pricing tactics employed by Burroughs Wellcome for the AIDS drug, azidothymidine, or AZT.

The Pharmaceutical Industry[3]

The major domestic players in the pharmaceutical industry (Standard Industrial Classification two-digit code 28) include: Merck, Abbott Labs, American Home Products, Eli Lilly, Johnson & Johnson, Bristol-Myers Squibb, Schering-Plough, and Burroughs Wellcome. The primary competition from outside the United States includes Glaxo Holdings, Hoechst, and Ciba-Geigy. The industry is very competitive, with no single company holding a dominant market share position. In 1989, the top four firms accounted for nearly 25% of industry sales.

After an unsuccessful attempt at unrelated diversification during the 1970s and early 1980s, pharmaceutical companies embarked on a strategy to build market share (within the industry) by investing heavily in research and development. Currently in 1991, the industry spends around 15% of sales on R&D, one of the highest among major U.S. industries. Industry experts believed that R&D spending was essential for effective product differentiation and consequently for improved economic performance. Past history also indicated that being the first to introduce new drugs resulted in increased profits.

The industry's marketing expenses are about 20% of sales. The expenses are mainly for recruiting and training salespeople who visit physicians and hospitals

---

This case was prepared by Professor Ram Subramanian of the F. E. Seidman School of Business at Grand Valley State University. The author wishes to thank Kathy Bartlett of Burroughs Wellcome Company for her helpful comments. Research assistance was provided by Cindy Hietala and Ron Villenueva. Every effort has been made to present the facts of the case objectively from available public data as well as company documents furnished to the author. This case was presented at the 1991 North American Case Research Association Meeting. This case was edited by T. L. Wheelen and J. D. Hunger for this book. Reprinted by permission.

to provide information about their company's products. Other marketing expenses include advertising in scientific journals and direct mailing costs.

The industry exhibited annual revenue growth of about 8% during 1975–1985. Its Return on Equity (ROE) has consistently been higher than other industries during the 1980s.

Several threats, however, have emerged for the U.S. pharmaceutical industry in recent times. A number of foreign companies, apart from marketing their products with increased vigor in the United States, have formed a large number of joint ventures with U.S. companies to strengthen their competitive position. The government has undertaken several steps to reduce the time span of patent protection, presumably to open up the competition. Finally, the increasing popularity of generic drugs also poses a significant threat for the industry.

Historical Background to the Development of AZT

AIDS is caused by a virus called human immunodeficiency virus (HIV). Actually a retrovirus, HIV has a unique capability that makes it very insidious. A retrovirus is a ribonucleic acid (RNA) virus that has a special enzyme. Ordinarily RNA viruses cannot replicate because they do not have deoxyribonucleic acid (DNA). But with the help of its special enzyme, a retrovirus is able to build DNA from its RNA. Sometimes these DNA copies become integrated into the host cells. Because they are similar, the host cell has no way of knowing that these are, in fact, "infected" DNAs manufactured by the retrovirus. Therefore these foreign DNAs also become part of the host cells and cause the disease when they multiply.

In 1964, a Michigan Cancer Foundation researcher first synthesized a compound called azidothymidine (AZT) as a possible cure for cancer. When tests showed that the compound was not effective as a cancer cure, the research was abandoned and the compound forgotten.

Burroughs Wellcome, a subsidiary of U.K.-based Wellcome PLC, has always encouraged its scientists to find cures for obscure diseases. In 1981, the company resynthesized AZT in its quest for a compound that would be effective against bacterial infection.[4] Meanwhile, one of its chemists, Janet Rideout, was studying the chemical structure of the HIV virus. The intention was to find a cure for the disease by studying the chemical structure of the disease-causing agent. She found that AZT was similar in structure to the enzyme that the retrovirus needed to replicate inside the host cell. Because AZT was toxic, she felt that it would effectively neutralize the retrovirus and prevent it from multiplying inside the host cell. When Burroughs Wellcome was actively looking for a cure for AIDS, Rideout suggested AZT.

By late 1984, Burroughs had determined that AZT was effective against some cat and mouse retroviruses. Because the company then did not have the facilities for testing AZT on live HIV, it sought the help of the National Cancer Institute (NCI). Sam Broder, a senior researcher at the institute, took an active part in the testing process.

The tests conducted by the NCI and others proved that AZT was effective against the HIV. Nineteen AIDS-affected patients were given the drug, and while two dropped out of the program, 15 showed improvement in their immune system and also noticeably gained weight.[5] The media and the medical community enthusiastically received public reports of these early results. In some ways, this enthusiasm sowed the seeds for Burroughs Wellcome's subsequent troubles with the drug.

Drug companies have to go through a lengthy period of field testing a drug before seeking approval from the Federal Drug Administration (FDA). After the initial tests by the NCI indicated the potency of the drug, the company established a program of wide-scale field testing. As the news of the drug's efficacy spread across the country, multitudes of AIDS patients begged the company to use them for the testing. The company then faced an ethical dilemma.

Drug companies test drugs in one of two ways. One, called the placebo trial, tests a drug by using two groups of people. The first group is given the drug while the second group is given a placebo (a harmless pill). In the second method of *historical trials,* the drug is given to every patient and the health changes of these patients are compared with untreated patients.

Because of problems associated with intervening variables in historical trials, the scientific community generally prefers placebo trials. This preference and the fact that the compound tested may turn out to be harmful prompted Burroughs Wellcome to use placebo trials.[6] A lot of negative publicity resulted from this decision. AIDS activists saw this decision as stemming from greed—greed, because the company wanted to use the faster placebo trials instead of historical trials. Also, the company had to give placebos to half the group tested, knowing full well that these patients were likely to die, while those given AZT were likely to live.

The company elected to proceed with large-scale testing using the placebo method. After the drug was tested almost the whole of 1986, the FDA approved it in March 1987. Before putting it on the market, the company thought long and hard about the drug's price. Finally, in mid 1987 the company marketed AZT under the brand name "Retrovir" with a price that effectively cost an AIDS patient $10,000 for a year's supply of the drug.

The company had not bargained for the backlash on its pricing policy. Through various media, AIDS activists voiced their protests and sought the help of the federal government. The principal AIDS activist group was Act-Up (Aids Coalition to Unleash Power), largely comprising homosexual middle-class professionals.[7]

Using sophisticated confrontational techniques and a grassroots approach to activism, Act-Up has considerable influence. In response to the strident protests of AIDS patients, led by Act-Up, Burroughs Wellcome lowered the price of AZT in December 1987 by 20% so that the annual cost to a patient was now $8,000. The company claimed that the price reduction was due to production efficiencies. The price was cut an additional 20% (to $6,400 per patient per year) in September 1989 because the drug was shown to benefit a substantially larger group of patients, thereby increasing its market.

Activists' Reasons for the Protests

AZT does not cure AIDS. However, it prolongs the victim's life by slowing the effect of the HIV virus.[8] Scientists calculated that with the help of AZT, an AIDS victim's life could be prolonged by as much as five years. When AZT was introduced commercially by Burroughs Wellcome in early 1987, it was one of the most expensive drugs ever. Typically, consumers of pharmaceuticals are not price sensitive because the cost of medication is covered by health insurance. However, in 1987, with Medicaid not yet authorized to cover the treatment of the disease, most AIDS patients did not have insurance that would cover treatment for AIDS.

The company's pricing policy outraged AIDS activists who soon banded together to voice their protests publicly. There was an underlying sense of urgency in the protesters' action. The federal government had funded a $20 million program to provide AIDS patients with AZT. The program was due to expire in October 1989, leaving the 7,000 patients in the program to deal with the problem of raising funds in addition to dealing with their illness. Even the subsequent cuts in prices that reduced the price of the drug from $10,000 to $6,400 for a year's supply did not mollify AIDS activists. The activists based their protest on two factors that surrounded the introduction of AZT.

One factor fueling the indignation of AIDS activists was that Burroughs Wellcome was reaping the profits of a drug that it did not develop. A chemical that was originally developed as a cancer cure by a Michigan Cancer Foundation researcher was resurrected by the company based on published reports in 1974 by a West German scientist, W. Ostertag, who demonstrated that AZT was effective in blocking the reproduction of certain kinds of retroviruses.[9] Subsequent research by Burroughs Wellcome researchers confirmed Ostertag's findings, and they developed AZT as a drug that was effective against AIDS. Protesters claimed that the company saved millions of dollars because much of the basic research had already been done for them by others. AIDS activists argued that since the drug did not cost nearly as much to develop as drugs normally do, the company's prices for the drug indicated its greed and its propensity to exploit ill people. Burroughs Wellcome did not reveal details about AZT costs and profit margins. However, analysts familiar with the drug industry believe that the company makes 70% to 80% gross profit on AZT, which, although high, is in line with average industry profit margins.[10] These high margins, argue those in the drug industry, are necessary to offset losses from hundreds of drugs that never see the light of day.

The second reason for the protests was that agencies such as the National Cancer Institute did much of the testing—a significant part of product development costs in the drug industry. Normally, a drug company pays for the testing of its products and adds these costs to the drug's development cost. Protesters argued that the company saved millions of dollars because NCI did much of the expensive hospital testing. The drug's prices did not reflect these savings.

Company's Point of View

Burroughs Wellcome is owned by the London-based Wellcome PLC. Ironically, the company that received a lot of negative publicity over its pricing policy for AZT is the largest charity in the United Kingdom, in 1989 distributing $55 million to fund medical libraries and research.[11]

Long known for concentrating its resources on finding cures for obscure diseases and providing an excellent atmosphere for scientific research, the company was totally unprepared for the wave of negative publicity that surrounded AZT. In recent interviews the company explained its rationale behind the pricing of AZT, which was meant to pacify the protesters and diffuse the situation.

According to company officials, even though Burroughs Wellcome did not create the chemical AZT, it spent more than six years and a lot of money (the company did not reveal actual figures) taking an abandoned compound and making it a potent drug to treat AIDS. The company performed years of expensive animal testing and also gave away the drug free to 5,000 people at a cost of $10 million as part of an Investigational New Drug (IND) program prior to obtaining FDA approval to market the drug.[12] To put the company involvement with the drug in perspective, a top executive of Burroughs Wellcome noted that, whereas a project of this size would have taken up only 20% of Merck's (the industry leader) time, it took 100% of Burroughs Wellcome's time.

Once the drug was approved by the FDA, the company had to spend more than $80 million in designing the production process for the compound.[13] A drug normally takes a decade from conception to commercial development, so a company usually has a lot of time to design the production process to make the drug at the lowest possible cost. But, in the case of AZT, because things began moving very quickly after the initial tests, the company had less than six months to perfect the production process. A key ingredient, thymidine, was hard to come by because worldwide demand for the compound, obtained as a side product from the DNA in salmon and herring sperms, was very low. Burroughs Wellcome had to locate companies with the appropriate technology to manufacture large quantities of both natural and synthetic thymidine. These sources, consequently, proved to be very expensive. The high price of AZT was justified, in part, by the expensive manufacturing costs incurred by the seven-month process of converting the raw material into the finished compound.[14] The company claimed that when the production process was streamlined in late 1987, the savings were passed on to the users.

The second reason for the high price of AZT, from the company's point of view, was the uncertainty about the market for the drug. When the drug was initially approved in 1987, the FDA permitted the use of the drug only for terminally ill patients—an estimated 50,000 people. This small market, coupled with the fear that a better drug to combat AIDS could come along at any time (as several companies were working on AIDS drugs), prompted the company to price AZT at $10,000 for a year's supply. The company has pointed out that when the FDA subsequently approved the sale of the drug to all people who showed AIDS symptoms, the company cut prices in response to the expanded market. Also, recent medical evidence indicates that AZT is effective even at half the normal dosage—reducing the per patient annual cost to around $3,000.

Did Burroughs Wellcome profit significantly from AZT? Estimated sales of AZT were $200 million in 1989 and $290 million in 1990—between 8% and 12% of Wellcome PLC's worldwide sales.[15] Its return on equity (ROE), at 23.9% in 1990, was among the lowest in the drug industry (primarily because it generally pursues the research and development of arcane, rather than useful, drugs), with industry leader in sales Merck showing a 44% ROE and American Home Products (the maker of Anacin) 56%.[16] To provide a financial incentive to spur drug manu-

EXHIBIT 3.1 **Selected 1989–1990 Financial Data for Firms in Drug Industry**

Company	Sales in Billions of Dollars	Profits in Millions of Dollars	ROE as a Percentage
Burroughs Wellcome	$2.40	$332.8	23.9%
Bristol-Myers Squibb	9.19	747.0	14.7
Johnson & Johnson	9.76	1,082.0	27.5
Merck	6.55	1,495.4	44.8
Eli Lilly	4.18	939.5	25.0
American Home Products	6.75	1,102.2	55.9

Source: *Business Week* (April 13, 1990).

facture, the U.S. federal government invoked the Orphan Drug Act in 1985 permitting Burroughs Wellcome to manufacture AZT on an exclusive basis for a period of seven years commencing from 1987. Exhibit 3.1 shows selected financial data for an illustrative list of companies.

Government's Role

As the protests against the pricing of AZT continued unabated, Congress, at first highly supportive of the company, called company executives to Washington to respond to charges of price gouging. A House Subcommittee on Health and the Environment conducted a hearing on the drug's pricing policy. Senator Edward Kennedy's office even researched the possibility of nationalizing the drug in an effort to control its prices. Partly in response to these investigations, the company slashed the drug's prices on two occasions. But company officials have always maintained that changing market conditions, not governmental interference, led to a reduction in AZT's price.

Notes

1. Marilyn Chase, "Burroughs Wellcome Reaps Profits, Outrage from Its AIDS Drug," *Wall Street Journal* (September 15, 1989), pp. A1, 5.
2. Cynthia Crossen, "AIDS Activist Group Harasses and Provokes to Make Its Point," *Wall Street Journal* (December 7, 1989), pp. A1, 9.
3. Adapted from Zahra, et al., "Merck: Strategy Making in America's Most Admired Corporation," in John A. Pearce II and Richard B. Robinson, *Strategic Management* (Homewood, Ill.: Richard D. Irwin, 1991).
4. "Retrovir Milestones," Burroughs Wellcome Company Press Release (April 1991).
5. Brian O'Reilly, "The Inside Story of the AIDS Drug," *Fortune* (November 5, 1990), pp. 112–129.
6. "Retrovir Milestones."
7. Crossen, "AIDS Activist Group Harasses and Provokes to Make Its Point."
8. John Mills and Henry Masur, "AIDS-Related Infections," *Scientific American* (August 1990), pp. 50–57.
9. Chase, "Burroughs Wellcome Reaps Profits, Outrage from Its AIDS Drug."

10. Ibid.
11. "Retrovir Milestones."
12. "The Development of Retrovir," Burroughs Wellcome Company Press Release (June 1990).
13. T. E. Haigler, "Testimony Before the House Committee on Energy and Commerce" (March 10, 1987).
14. Ibid.
15. Christine Gorman, "How Much a Reprieve from AIDS?" *Time* (October 2, 1989), pp. 81–82; and "Retrovir Milestones."
16. Brian O'Reilly, "The Inside Story of the AIDS Drug."

The Gift

John Kilpatrick, Gamewell Gantt, and George Johnson

You have recently been hired as a group leader in the purchasing department at CDI Electronics. You are getting settled in your new position and becoming acquainted with your people and the vendors with whom you do business.

It is nearly Christmas. Among your mail for the day is a small package containing an expensive watch from one of the large vendors. Your first reaction is to send the watch back because accepting expensive gifts from vendors clearly is contrary to company policy as stated in the policy manual, which all new employees receive and are required to read. (An excerpt from the company policy manual appears on the next page.) It is a very fine watch with your name engraved on the back along with the vendor's logo.

Before you get the chance to return the watch, however, Jim Fitzpatrick, an old hand in your department, approaches you about the situation. Apparently, everyone in the purchasing department received similar watches. According to Jim, the vendor sends some type of gift each Christmas, and members of the department look forward each year to see the gift. He goes on to say that everyone enjoys the presents and is most appreciative but, he hastened to add, no preferential treatment is given to the vendor nor is any expected.

Jim is concerned. He and others in your group have noticed that your watch has been sitting on your desk for the past two days. The group is wondering why and what you may be thinking. They are concerned that if you make an issue of the gift there will be trouble over gifts accepted in past years. In fact, the policy manual specifically states that anyone accepting such a gift could be subject to termination of employment.

According to Jim, the senior management in the purchasing department is aware of the practice and, in fact, also received gifts from this vendor. However, corporate executives apparently are not aware of the practice and nobody really knew how they might react.

After Jim leaves your office, you sit and think about your options. The easiest solution would be to accept the gift as others have done in the past, and as, apparently, your boss has done. Or, you could ask your boss for guidance and cover yourself in that way. There is the risk, of course, that bringing it to the attention of your boss will force him to crack down on the practice. You think that, in all likelihood, the boss will go along with past practice.

This case was prepared by Professors John Kilpatrick, Gamewell Gantt, and George Johnson of Idaho State University. This case was presented at the Midwest Society for Case Research Workshop Meeting, 1990. This case was edited by T. L. Wheelen and J. D. Hunger for this book. Reprinted by permission. This case also appears in *Annual Advances 1990,* pp. 300–301, edited by Roy A. Cook.

Excerpt from the Company Policy Manual

Gifts from vendors: Purchasing agents and other employees involved in contracts with vendors shall not accept gifts, whether in the form of merchandise, lunches, or other forms of gratuities. It is the intent of this policy that employees avoid even the appearance of compromising their fiduciary responsibility to advance the interests of the company to the best of their ability. Failure to comply may result in disciplinary action up to and including dismissal.

CASE 5

Dow Corning and Silicone Gel Breast Implants

Ram Subramanian and Marie McKendall

Flip through any popular magazine, watch television commercials, glance at the billboards that dot the landscape, or examine the pictures on package labels. Like any casual observer you can find ample evidence that our society emphasizes the pursuit and attainment of a rather narrow definition of physical beauty. Health clubs, cosmeticians, hair stylists, plastic surgeons, and others comprise a wide array of professionals who are eager to help people attain perfect hair, perfect skin, perfect clothes, perfect smiles, and perfect bodies.

Since the early 1960s, hundreds of thousands of women have chosen to reshape their bodies through breast implant surgery in an effort to adhere to societal standards of female beauty. Unfortunately, what began for many as an attempt to attain the physical ideal has deteriorated into a nightmare of doubt and fear. Following is a description of the role played by Dow Corning, the leading breast implant manufacturer, in a drama that made front page news in early 1992.

History of Breast Implants

During the past several decades, two million American women have chosen to have breast implant surgery. A woman typically decides to have a breast implant for one of two reasons. About 20% of 150,000 annual implant recipients are women who have undergone mastectomies as a treatment for breast cancer and subsequently decide to have reconstructive surgery. The remaining 80% of implant operations are performed for cosmetic reasons on women who want to augment their breasts.[1] By 1992, breast implants were the third most popular form of cosmetic surgery, topped only by rhinoplasty and liposuction.[2]

A woman electing to have breast implants had two types from which to choose. Implants consist of a plastic pouch filled with either a saline solution (sterile salt water) or silicone gel. Of the two million women who had received breast implants by 1992, approximately one million had selected the silicone gel type.[3] Women and physicians preferred the silicone gel implants because their appearance and feel best mimicked a real breast. Saline implants are more likely to shift, settle, and stretch the skin and are therefore inappropriate for thin women or those who had undergone a mastectomy.[4] Because of its apparent superiority, silicone was becoming the implant of choice; in 1991, 60% of operations being performed involved the silicone implant and the remaining 40% involved the saline implant.[5]

This case was prepared by Professors Ram Subramanian and Marie McKendall of the F. E. Seidman School of Business at Grand Valley State University. This case was presented at the Midwest Society for Case Research Workshop, 1992. This case also appears in *Annual Advances in Case Research, 1993*. This case was edited by T. L. Wheelen and J. D. Hunger for this book. Reprinted by permission of the authors.

Inbreeding largely created the silicone breast implant market. Dow Corning pioneered the development of silicone implants in the early 1960s. In 1972, five employees of Dow Corning left and accepted positions with Heyer-Schulte; they brought with them knowledge of how to manufacture and sell silicone breast implants. Two years later, the same five people opened their own company, McGhan Medical. Heyer-Schulte and McGhan Medical essentially duplicated the Dow Corning implant and began to sell it under their own names. At this point, breast implants were unregulated; consequently, the two companies did very little product testing, relying on the testing performed by Dow Corning. Minnesota Mining and Manufacturing (3M) bought McGhan Medical in 1977 and owned it for seven years, at which point 3M sold it back to its original owners. American Hospital Supply owned Heyer-Schulte from 1974 until 1984, when it sold the company to Mentor Corporation. Bristol Myers-Squibb also was an industry leader, but withdrew from the market in 1991 when it could not prove to the Food and Drug Administration (FDA) that its product was safe.[6]

Data on this industry are not readily available. Industry analysts estimate that at the end of 1991, Dow Corning was the leading manufacturer of silicone gel breast implants, controlling 35% of the approximately $49 million market. The company's 1991 silicone implant sales of $17 million represented less than 1% of Dow Corning's total sales. Mentor controlled about a third of the market, and McGhan came in third.[7]

Role of the FDA

The FDA is a U.S. federal agency charged with regulating all foods, drugs, cosmetics, and medical devices sold in interstate commerce. Its general responsibility is to protect the American public from all potential health hazards associated with the use of any of these products. Among its many duties, the FDA

1. regulates the safety, efficacy, and labeling of medical devices;
2. requires premarket testing of any potentially hazardous medical device;
3. establishes standards and enforces regulations governing the manufacture of medical devices; and
4. inspects the manufacturing facilities of companies that produce medical devices.

The FDA has the power to require that a manufacturer prove the safety of a new product before the company can market that product. The agency generally does not conduct its own research on new products; rather, it sets research standards for manufacturers to follow, reviews scientific literature and test results, and consults advisory boards composed of experts about any product in question. The FDA also monitors products after release through an "adverse reaction reporting system" and by recording and tracking consumer complaints. It relies on the manufacturer's legal obligation to report any excessive side effects.[8]

History of Dow Corning

Dow Corning is a joint venture of the Dow Chemical Company and Corning, Inc. Each parent company owns 50% of Dow Corning. Both Dow Chemical and Corning participate in a number of joint ventures. At the end of 1990, Dow Chemical had 53 such joint ventures in more than a dozen countries, and Corning was involved in 17 joint ventures (with investments ranging from 20%–50% in each of these companies) at the end of 1990. For Dow Chemical, joint ventures "offer benefits ranging from faster entry into new geographic markets to achieving the critical mass necessary to compete successfully in a particular business."[9] For Corning, the rationale for joint ventures is that they help "speed Corning technology into the marketplace."[10]

Dow Corning came into existence in 1943. Its principal business was to develop, manufacture, and market silicones, related specialty chemical materials, polycrystalline silicon, and certain specialty health care products. At the end of 1991, this high-technology company had approximately 5,000 products, 45,000 customers, 8,300 employees, and 4,900 worldwide patents and was spending $150 million annually on research and development.[11] Dow Corning's two parent companies each held five seats on the 14-member Board of Directors, although they claimed they were not involved in day-to-day management activities.[12]

Dow Corning traditionally placed a great deal of emphasis on maintaining ethical standards in its business practices. The company has one of the most comprehensive and highly respected ethics programs in corporate America.[13] Dow Corning's "values statement" (see Exhibit 5.1) includes the themes of integrity, quality, and safety. The company also has an ethical audit program. The firm started using these audits in the 1980s and holds about 20 meetings every year. At these meetings, managers and employees candidly discuss ethical issues such as conflicts of interest and better business conduct. A Business Conduct Committee oversees the audits and reports to the Board of Directors.[14]

The Implant Controversy

When Dow Corning created the first silicone gel breast implant in the early 1960s, these devices were not covered by FDA regulations. Dow Corning conducted a series of in-house tests to determine the safety of the product. These test findings, which were released years later as a result of a court order, indicated that the company's in-house testing revealed tumors in laboratory animals exposed to silicone gels. A review panel convened by the company confirmed the presence of malignant tumors in up to 80% of the test animals. However, the panel felt that this high occurrence probably was the result of faulty testing procedure and hence deemed the study inconclusive. A subsequent Dow Corning study found that tumors could be induced in rats when foreign agents, such as silicone implants, were introduced into their systems. However, company officials, relying on scientific studies, decided that the type of cancer caused by implants in rats was rare in humans.[15]

EXHIBIT 5.1

Dow Corning's Value Statement

Integrity: Our integrity is demonstrated in our ethical conduct and in our respect for the values cherished by the society of which we are a part.

Employees: Our employees are the source from which our ideas, actions and performance flow. The full potential of our people is best realized in an environment that breeds fairness, self-fulfillment, teamwork and dedication to excellence.

Customers: Our relationship with each customer is entered in the spirit of a long-term partnership and is predicated on making the customer's interests our interests.

Quality: Our never-ending quest for quality performance is based on our understanding of our customers' needs and our willingness and capacity to fulfill those needs.

Technology: Our advancement of chemistry and related sciences in our chosen fields is the value that most differentiates Dow Corning.

Environment: Our commitment to the safekeeping of the physical environment is founded on our appreciation of it as the basis for the existence of life.

Safety: Our attention to safety is based on our full-time commitment to injury-free work, individual self-worth and a consideration for the well-being of others.

Profit: Our long-term profit growth is essential to our long-term existence. How our profits are derived, and the purposes for which they are used, are influenced by our values and our shareholders.

Source: Dow Corning Corporation, 1991–1992.

Congress granted the FDA power to regulate medical devices in 1976. A 1978 FDA advisory panel, heavily staffed with plastic surgeons, recommended that implants be placed in a classification that would not require manufacturers to prove their safety. Staff members of the FDA disagreed, and in 1982 the FDA proposed a stiffer classification for breast implants. No action was taken for nine years as manufacturers and plastic surgeons fought the recommendation. Acting under the lenient classification, manufacturers continued to market and sell their product.[16]

In the meantime, news questioning the safety of the implants came to light. FDA documents, dating back to 1988, indicated that the agency's scientists had reviewed the results of hundreds of animal tests performed by Dow Corning and had serious concerns about the safety of implants. An agency representative acknowledged that the FDA knew of the concern, but felt that it had "higher priority devices to deal with."[17]

In 1984, a San Francisco federal court jury concluded that Dow Corning had committed fraud in marketing its implants as safe. The court awarded Maria Stern $1.5 million in punitive damages against Dow Corning. Following this judgment, in 1985 Dow Corning began to accompany its breast implants with safety literature. Although the company stated that it disagreed with the verdict, the new warnings cautioned product users about possible immune system deficiency and silicone migration following rupture. After an appeal by Dow Corning, the Stern case was eventually settled out of court. The judge who heard the case maintained that the company's own studies "cast considerable doubts about the safety of the product," which were not disclosed to patients.[18]

In April, 1991, the stricter classification was enacted, and the FDA ordered implant manufacturers to prove that their products were safe. By this time, the FDA had received about 2,500 reports of injuries and illnesses associated with breast implants.[19]

Momentum had grown, however, and the controversy over silicone breast implants could no longer be contained. Women from among those who pay doctors $450 million a year for the implants began to file suit alleging that, upon the deterioration or rupture of the implants, silicone bled or leaked into the body and caused numerous health problems. Two lawsuits were filed against the government. Bristol Myers-Squibb withdrew its implant from the market when the fact that the coating on the implant contained a known carcinogen became public knowledge.[20]

Finally, in December 1991, a California court ruled in favor of Mariann Hopkins in her suit against Dow Corning and awarded her $7.34 million in damages. A key witness for the prosecution was Thomas D. Talcott, an engineer who quit Dow Corning after 24 years because he believed the product to be unsafe. He told the court that he believed that Dow Corning had been conducting "experimental surgery on humans."[21] An internal Dow Corning memo revealed in open court documented the concern of a company scientist who wrote: "To my knowledge, we have no valid long-term implant data to substantiate the safety of gel for a long-term implant use."[22]

In response to the Hopkins judgment, on January 6, 1992, the FDA requested that plastic surgeons stop using silicone breast implants for 45 days. The FDA also demanded that Dow Corning release hundreds of internal documents detailing the timing and extent of the company's knowledge about problems with the implants.[23] On February 18, the FDA revealed its concern that the implants ruptured and released silicone into the body more often than previously thought. The FDA stated that the rupture rate might be up to 14% but was difficult to determine because of the lack of a uniform reporting system. Furthermore, the agency stated that 4%–6% of women with ruptured implants might exhibit no symptoms that a rupture had occurred.[24] The FDA also released information suggesting that silicone could "bleed" into the body even in the absence of a rupture.[25] Although the FDA maintained that it was not unduly alarmed, the agency did acknowledge that there were health questions that needed to be answered.[26]

The FDA announced that it had decided to form an advisory panel to investigate the safety of silicone implants and promised a decision about the future use of implants within 60 days of the panel's recommendation. On February 13, before the panel had begun to meet, one of its members was stripped of his vote for telling a reporter from *Time* magazine that he thought the implants should be removed from the market.[27] McGhan Medical also tried to stop the panel's scheduled hearing on the grounds that several of the panel members were biased against the implants; a district judge, however, denied the motion on February 14.[28] Functioning under an FDA-imposed gag order, the advisory panel met on February 18 and heard testimony for three days.

Testimony before the panel was mixed. The major controversy was not whether silicone bled through the implants or spilled in the event of a rupture, but whether such an occurrence posed a danger to the woman. Dr. Charles Balch of Anderson Hospital in Houston cited three studies involving 3,047 women that showed no increased incidence of autoimmune disease in women with the implants. Dow Corning maintained that, although silicone did leak from the implants, the process was benign and state-of-the-art studies showed no connection between the implants and diseases of the immune system. In contrast to this testimony was that of doctors who attributed a variety of conditions (including cancer, lupus, arthritis, rheumatism, arterial lateral sclerosis, and diseases of the muscles and connective tissue) to the leakage of silicone from the gel implants.[29] These physicians contended that the gel migrates to the lungs, liver, and lymph nodes, and triggers several autoimmune disorders as the immune system tries to defend itself against the foreign material.[30]

Meanwhile, the parent companies of Dow Corning (Dow Chemical and Corning) decided to act to attempt to repair the joint venture's tarnished image. The unfavorable Hopkins verdict, extensive news coverage of the implant controversy and the court-ordered release of the incriminating internal documents had propelled Dow Corning into a public relations nightmare. Keith R. McKennon replaced John S. Ludington as Chair of Dow Corning's Board of Directors. McKennon had the reputation of being a shrewd diplomat and peacemaker. As a Dow Chemical employee, he had successfully diffused the Agent Orange controversy in which the company was involved during the Vietnam War. In contrast to Dow Corning's previous confrontational style in the implant controversy, McKennon's first move was to reassure implant users. He suggested that the company might begin new research to answer safety concerns about the product and also offered to provide financial help to women who wanted to have their implants removed. He released more than 800 pages of company documents and adopted a more conciliatory tone when dealing with the press and the public.[31]

On February 20, the FDA's advisory panel concluded that it could not conclusively link the silicone breast implants to health problems. The panel did state, however, that it was "disturbed" by the possibilities and recommended that further use of the product be limited to women undergoing reconstructive surgery following mastectomies. The panel concluded its findings with an unanimous vote that implants be made available, but that all women receiving them be required to enroll in clinical studies that would monitor their health for years after the surgery.[32]

The Role of Plastic Surgeons

Breast augmentation represents a $450 million annual business to many of the nation's plastic surgeons. They contend that breast implants are often a medical necessity. In the early 1980s, the American Society of Plastic and Reconstructive Surgeons (ASPRS) issued a memo to the FDA that contained the statement: "There is a substantial and enlarging body of medical information and opinion to the effect that these deformities [small breasts]are really a disease," that, left uncorrected, results in a "total lack of well being."[33]

Many plastic surgeons are extremely angry with the FDA's ruling severely limiting the availability of silicone gel implants. They point to the fact that no plastic surgeon served as a member of the advisory panel and that some of the people who did serve had a clear bias against implants. In response to the FDA ruling, the ASPRS has launched a $3.5 million campaign to persuade both the public and the FDA that breast implants do more good than harm. Dr. Norman Anderson, an FDA panel member, contended that such an attitude is "more befitting a trade association than a professional organization." Other plastic surgeons, however, are as confused as their patients and welcome the studies that will now be undertaken and which will hopefully provide definitive answers to the safety questions.[34]

The Scientific Community's Position

Although the scientific community generally was divided in its view of implant safety, a number of studies provided support for the manufacturers' point of view. Two studies, conducted on samples of 11,676 and 1,700 women, show no increased risk of breast cancer associated with breast implants.[35] Critics have charged, however, that cancers can develop 20 to 30 years after exposure to a toxin and that neither of these studies tracked women long enough to produce valid results.[36]

In response to the charge that implants impede the interpretation of mammograms, an editorial in *The New England Journal of Medicine* noted that "the American College of Radiology believes that an adequate examination can be achieved with commonly available techniques and it does not support restricting the use of implants."[37]

In response to the FDA ruling, medical experts have argued that there is no scientific evidence linking implants with autoimmune disease and that the controversy has been exaggerated.[38] The American College of Rheumatology issued a statement in 1988 saying that, although it encouraged further research, there was no convincing evidence linking implants with any generalized disease.[39] The Mayo Clinic argued that there is no scientific proof that implants cause greater incidence of autoimmune disease and stated that removing implants from the market on the basis of the small number of women who experience problems (1 out of 2,000) is not justified. Its doctors also stated that the adverse publicity may erroneously "have led women to believe that every symptom that they experience, from fatigue to tiredness to joint pain and occasional fevers, are associated with their implants." The Clinic further contended that, even in the event of a rupture, in the great majority of women, the silicone does not travel and can be easily removed.[40]

In an editorial in *The New England Journal of Medicine,* Dr. Marcia Angell echoed the position of many members of the scientific community when she stated:

Demonstrating the safety and effectiveness of a drug or a device does not, of course, mean showing that there are no side effects or risks. If that were the standard, we would have no drugs or devices, since nearly all of them have possible adverse effects. The issue is the balance between risks and benefits. Greater risks are permitted for greater benefits. . . . Given the difficulties of assessing the benefits (of breast implants), the FDA has acted as though there were none. . . . In the case of breast implants, the benefit has to do with personal judgments about the quality of life, which are subjective and unique to each woman. . . . The FDA's decision has given rise to great fears among the 1 million women now living with implants—fears that in many women are all out of proportion to what is known about the risks.[41]

Reaction to the FDA Decision

On March 19, 1992, Dow Corning announced that it would permanently shut down its implant production facilities and get out of the business. Board Chair McKennon summarized the company's decision in the following statement:

> In making this announcement, let me make very clear that Dow Corning remains satisfied that Dow Corning implants produced over the years have filled an important medical need for thousands of women, and did not and do not represent an unreasonable risk. Our reasons for not resuming production and sales, therefore, are not related to issues of science or safety but to the existing condition of the marketplace . . . for us, this is a small business. The products represent less than 1% of our revenues and have not been profitable over their history. Given the continued controversial environment surrounding this product, I see no prospect for business improving. Instead, I believe the future use of this product will be curtailed to a considerable extent.[42]

Dow Corning said it would pay up to $1,200 for each patient desiring to have her implants removed. In addition, the company stated that it would set up a $10 million fund to conduct research on the safety of the device.[43]

Many in the medical community criticized the FDA's decision and said they hoped the implants would again become widely available. These doctors contend that implants serve a valuable purpose, particularly to those women who have undergone a mastectomy. Mayo Clinic's doctors stated that "it is ironic that women continue to smoke, drink, and undergo abortion, all of which have very real and proven consequences to their health; while there are those seeking to prevent the use of devices which have, to the present, not been shown to be associated with health hazards. . . ."[44] Other physicians, however, remain "appalled" that the product was allowed to remain on the market for 30 years without rigorous testing.[45]

The general public remains divided on the breast implant question. Some groups steadfastly maintain that what a woman does with her body is her business. These critics contend that once informed of risks, women have a right to make an informed choice about breast implants.[46] Others claim that "to choose a procedure that may harden the breasts, result in loss of sensation and introduce a range of serious health problems isn't a choice; it is a scripted response made in order to conform to the values of a society which prizes women most highly for their packaging."[47]

Dr. David Kessler, head of the FDA, while acknowledging that the decision was one of the most controversial ever made by the agency, defended the ruling by stating that there were too many unanswered questions about the safety of the implants. He further argued that continuing to make the implants available to those who had undergone a mastectomy was justifiable because "it makes little sense for the FDA to consider breast augmentation of equivalent importance with an accepted component of cancer therapy." Kessler also claimed that many experts continue to believe that breast implants impede full visualization of the breast during mammography. Finally, Kessler rebutted the "informed choice" position, stating:

> If members of our society were empowered to make their own decisions about the entire range of products for which the FDA has responsibility, then the whole rationale for the agency would cease to exist. . . . The FDA was established as a result of a social mandate. . . . Manufacturers have vested interests. Between those interests and the interests of patients, the FDA must be the arbiter. . . . Had the FDA failed to intervene, the uncontrolled and widespread availability of breast implants would probably have continued for another 30 years–without producing any meaningful clinical data about their safety and effectiveness.[48]

The Future

As long-term studies finally begin, no one knows what the testing and investigation will reveal about the safety of the silicone gel breast implants. Although the Hopkins and Stern trials resulted in the only two current verdicts against the company, Dow Corning faces potential liability on a variety of fronts. As of March 1992, 200 suits have been filed, and more were expected. Possible damages could run into hundreds of millions of dollars, and the company has quietly begun to settle some of the suits. Industry analysts speculate that bankruptcy may become an option. The company might also become the target of civil and criminal investigations by the Justice Department and the FDA. Possible charges include shipping adulterated products and filing false reports with a government agency.[49]

In the meantime, lawyers are investigating the potential liability of the parent companies. The stocks of both Dow Chemical and Corning have dropped in light of the negative publicity. Shareholders of the two companies have begun to file suit, alleging that the parent companies failed to disclose the implant risks. The two companies continue to claim that they were not involved in Dow Corning's decision process and therefore are not liable.[50]

Many recipients of the implants are worried and unsure about what they should do. Some women, many of whom have already undergone cancer treatment and reconstructive surgery, feel they cannot face another round of surgery. Others are not particularly worried and think the entire controversy has obscured reality.

Dow Corning steadfastly maintains that its product is safe and that the company acted in accordance with all laws and business standards. Doctors seem divided on the issue, as does the general public. The role and actions of the FDA also are being questioned, as consumers wonder which widely used product will next become controversial. Currently unregulated devices include respirators;

chin, cartilage, and testicular implants; kidney-dialyzing components; and artery catheters.[51] In the meantime, more than one million women are living with a product in their bodies about which many questions remain unanswered.

Notes

1. J. C. Fisher, "The Silicone Controversy—When Will Science Prevail?" *New England Journal of Medicine,* 1992, 326(25), pp. 1696–1698.
2. T. Smart, "This Man Sounded the Silicone Alarm—in 1976," *Business Week* (January 27, 1992), p. 34.
3. J. Ambrose, "Physicians Attempt to Relieve Public Scare on Breast Implants," *Grand Rapids Press* (February 2, 1992).
4. A. Purvis, "A Strike Against Silicone," *Time* (January 20, 1992), p. 40.
5. Ambrose.
6. T. Burton, "Several Firms Face Breast-Implant Woes," *Wall Street Journal* (January 23, 1992).
7. T. Burton, "Liability Problems Seen for Corning, Dow Chemical in Implant Controversy," *Wall Street Journal* (January 14, 1992). T. Burton, "Dow Corning Closes Production Lines for Breast Implants, Plans a Write-off," *Wall Street Journal* (January 23, 1992).
8. *Federal Regulatory Directory* (Washington, D.C.: Congressional Quarterly, Inc., 1986), pp. 318–351; J. Regush, "Toxic Breasts," *Mother Jones* (January–February 1992), pp. 25–31.
9. Dow Chemical Company, *1990 Annual Report.*
10. Corning, Inc., *1990 Annual Report.*
11. Dow Corning Corporation: *1992–93 Profile.*
12. Burton (January 14, 1992).
13. J. Bryne, "The Best Laid Ethics Programs . . . ," *Business Week* (March 9, 1992), pp. 67–69.
14. G. Laczniak and P. Murphy, "Fostering Ethical Marketing Decisions," *Journal of Business Ethics* (1991) 10, pp. 259–271.
15. T. Smart, "Breast Implants: What Did the Industry Know and When?" *Business Week* (June 10, 1991), pp. 94–98.
16. Ibid.
17. Ibid.
18. Ibid.
19. A. Stern, "Dow Hit by Media Firestorm on Implant Issue," *Grand Rapids Press* (February 9, 1992).
20. Smart (1991).
21. Smart (1992).
22. J. Seligman, G. Cowley, and K. Springen, "Another Blow to Implants," *Newsweek* (January 6, 1992), p. 45.
23. "Firm Aware of Implant Leads 20 Years Ago, Data Show," *Grand Rapids Press* (February 10, 1992).
24. "Implants, Diseases not Linked, Dow Corning Says," *Grand Rapids Press* (February 19, 1992); Fisher, p. 1697.
25. "Firm Aware of Implant Leads. . . ."
26. Ambrose.
27. "Doctor Loses His Vote on Implant Panel," *Grand Rapids Press* (February 13, 1992).
28. "Judge Won't Block Panel on Breast Implants," *Grand Rapids Press* (February 15, 1992).
29. Purvis.
30. "FDA May Require Registration of Future Implant Patients," *Grand Rapids Press* (February 20, 1992).
31. T. Burton and J. Rigdon, "Handling of Crisis Caused Shake-Up at Dow Corning," *Wall Street Journal* (February 12, 1992); L. Reibstein, "Fighting the Implant 'Fire': Dow Corning Scrambles to Rescue Image," *Newsweek* (February 24, 1992), p. 38.
32. "Panel's Findings Called a Plus for Implant Makers," *Grand Rapids Press* (February 21, 1992).
33. Regush.
34. J. Seligman, M. Hager, and K. Springen, "Another Tempest in a C Cup," *Newsweek* (March 23, 1992), p. 67.
35. H. Berkel, D. Birdsell, and H. Jenkins, "Breast Augmentation: A Risk Factor for Breast Cancer?" *New England Journal of Medicine* (1992) 326(25), pp. 1629–1633.
36. D. Haney, "Breast Implants Linked with Lower Risk of Cancer," *Grand Rapids Press* (June 17, 1992).
37. Fisher.

38. M. Angell, "Breast Implants—Protection or Paternalism?" *New England Journal of Medicine* (1992) 326(25), pp. 1695–1696.
39. Fisher.
40. Mayo Clinic (1992), p. 3.
41. Angell, p. 1695.
42. Dow Corning Press Release (1992).
43. Ibid.
44. Mayo Clinic (1992), p. 5.
45. G. Cowley and D. Glick, "A Boon or a Bust for Women?" *Newsweek* (November 25, 1992), p. 65.
46. P. Huber, "A Woman's Right to Choose," *Forbes* (February 17, 1992), p. 138.
47. L. Shapiro, K. Springen, and J. Gordon, "What Is It with Women and Breasts?" *Newsweek* (January 20, 1992), p. 57.
48. D. Kessler, "The Basis of the FDA's Decision on Breast Implants," *New England Journal of Medicine* (1992) 326(25), pp. 1713–1715.
49. M. Galen, J. Byrne, T. Smart, and D. Woodruff, "Debacle at Dow Corning: How Bad Will It Get?" *Business Week* (March 2, 1992), pp. 36–38.
50. Galen et al.
51. Regush.

CASE 6

Section C Issues in Strategic Management

Industry One Grocery/Merchandising

The Great Atlantic and Pacific Tea Company, Inc., and the Retail Grocery Industry

Jim Kendall, Dan Kopp, and Lois Shufeldt

Introduction

James Wood, Chairman of the Board, President, and Chief Executive Officer of the Great Atlantic and Pacific Tea Company, Inc. (A&P or Tea Company) was reflecting on some troubling trends in the retail grocery store industry. Among them were the following.

- From 1970 to 1990, industry sales quadrupled from $80.2 billion to $338.9 billion—an increase of $258.7 billion. However, 91.5% of this increase is inflation related and only 8.5% is growth in real sales. Real sales, therefore, increased only 27.5% during this period.
- From 1970 to 1990, grocery store sales as a percentage of disposable personal income decreased from 11.2% to 8.3%.
- During the 1980s, restaurants were getting a larger share of the consumer's food and beverage dollar. From 1983 to 1990, restaurants' market share increased from 31.0% to 33.2% while the market share for food stores dropped from 69.0% to 66.8%.

Even though the industry faces an avalanche of new products, the number of stores dropped 7.5% from 1985 to 1990. As a result, the retail grocery store industry is extremely competitive, with a profit margin averaging less than 1.5% and many firms operating at a loss.

Through an expansion and acquisition program involving an investment exceeding $2 billion from 1981 through 1990,[1] A&P grew to be the fourth largest retail grocery firm in the United States. With 1,275 stores[2] located primarily in the eastern United States and Ontario, Canada, A&P reported record sales and profits in the fiscal year ending February 23, 1991.

In the Company's *1990 Annual Report to Shareholders,* Wood remarked:

> A&P again achieved record sales and earnings in fiscal 1990, although results were affected by adverse economic conditions in most of the Company's major trading areas in the U.S. and particularly Canada. . . .
>
> After a positive first half, results from midyear onward reflected the recessionary conditions that gripped Ontario, Canada, as well as the northeastern, middle Atlantic and midwestern areas of the U.S.—the areas of A&P's greatest concentration. Cautious

This case was prepared by Mr. Jim Kendall of City Utilities, Springfield, Missouri, and Professors Dan Kopp and Lois Shufeldt of Southwest Missouri State University. This case was edited by T. L. Wheelen and J. D. Hunger for this book.

> consumer spending, and the promotional investment required on our part to protect market share, impacted both sales and earnings during the latter part of the year, and those conditions continue into 1991.[3]

Chairman Wood's comments were an accurate harbinger of things to come. The first three quarters of fiscal 1991 witnessed a dramatic decline in profits. They are down 54.3% compared to profits during the first three quarters of fiscal 1990, with successively lower profits in each quarter.

Chairman Wood foresaw major strategic challenges, including (1) how to reverse declining profit margins, (2) how to improve resource utilization, (3) how to position the company to lessen the impact of future economic recessions, and (4) how to structure the company's expansion and acquisition program, given industry trends.

Grocery Store Industry

Great A&P is included in the retail sales portion of the economy. Retail sales are shown in Exhibit 6.1 with 1990 sales of $1.8 trillion representing a 5.2%[4] increase over 1989 sales.

Grocery stores and *specialty food stores* (which include meat, seafood, fruit, and vegetable markets, as well as food stores such as confectioneries and bakeries) comprise the *food store industry.* The food store industry recorded sales of $362.3 billion in 1990 with 93.5% from grocery stores and 6.5% from specialty stores.

The grocery store segment, which is summarized in Exhibit 6.2, is further divided into *supermarkets, superettes,* and *other grocery stores.* Grocery stores also are divided into chains, those with 11 or more stores, and independents, which includes chains with less than 11 stores. Exhibit 6.3 shows a breakdown of grocery store sales by commodity.

According to *Industry Surveys,* "Changes in the composition, character, and shopping habits of American consumers have resulted in the emergence of the one-stop shopping phenomenon. The time-pressed working woman has been identified as the supermarkets' prime target customer."[5]

In response to these challenges, supermarkets are supplementing their traditional product mix with more nonfood and general merchandise items, including health and beauty aids, and prescriptions. Additionally, they are adding more specialty departments featuring gourmet and prepared foods. "Food retailers have also invested time and space to capitalize on the decade-long trend toward increased health-consciousness. According to a recent study by Towne-Oller & Associates, a New York–based market research firm, combination store outlets average three times more dollar volume of health and beauty products than do traditional supermarkets."[6]

Demand

As Exhibit 6.4 depicts, during the 1970s and the 1980s, the grocery store industry enjoyed a significant sales growth in nominal dollars. However, when stated in constant dollars (with 1970 as the base), the growth has been minimal. During the period depicted in Exhibit 6.4, actual sales quadrupled from $80.2 billion to $338.9

EXHIBIT 6.1

Retail Sales by Trade

(Dollar amounts in millions)

	1990 Sales	Percent of Total
Motor vehicle dealers	$ 382,069	21.1%
Grocery stores	338,857	18.7
General merchandise group	212,170	11.7
Eating and drinking establishments	180,077	10.0
All other retail stores	170,586	9.4
Gasoline service stations	131,839	7.3
Apparel group	94,839	5.2
Furnishings, appliances	93,155	5.1
Building supply, hardware stores	92,480	5.1
Drug and proprietary stores	68,588	4.0
Specialty food stores	23,477	1.3
Liquor stores	20,784	1.1
Total retail sales	$1,808,348	100.0%

Source: "1991 Consumer Expenditure Study," *Supermarket Business,* September 1991, p. 56.

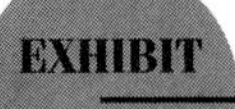

EXHIBIT 6.2

Grocery Store Industry—1990 Information

(Dollar amounts in thousands)

	Sales		Number of Stores	
Supermarkets	$264,935,354	78.2%	30,750	21.2%
Superettes	21,753,816	6.4	11,600	8.0
Other grocery stores				
Sales $500,000—$1,000,000	18,342,149	5.4	19,500	13.5
Sales less than $500,000	33,825,681	10.0	83,150	57.3
Total grocery stores	$338,857,000	100.0%	145,000	100.0%
Chains (11 or more stores)	$288,367,307	85.1%	22,600	15.6%
All other grocery stores	50,489,693	14.9	122,400	84.4
Total grocery stores	$338,857,000	100.0%	145,000	100.0%

Source: "Consumer Expenditure Study," *Supermarket Business,* September 1991, p. 53.

EXHIBIT 6.3

1990 Grocery Store Sales

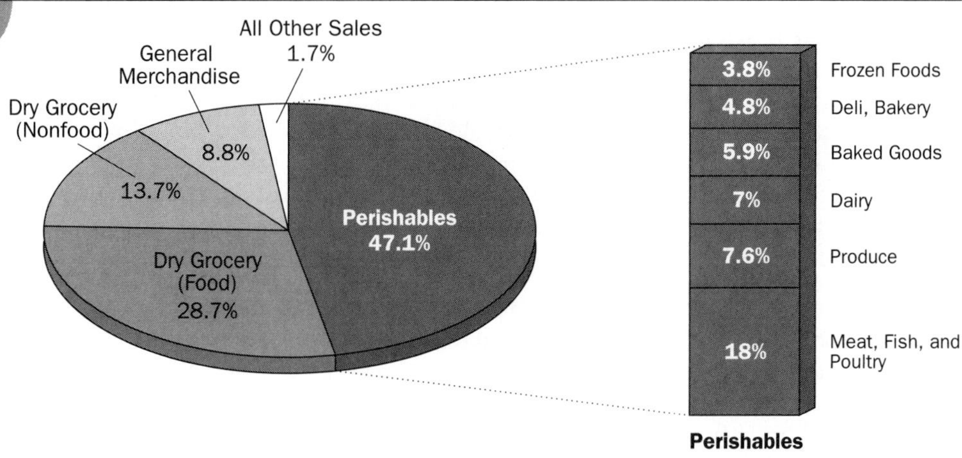

Source: *Supermarket Business,* September 1991, p. 61.

EXHIBIT 6.4

Grocery Store Sales

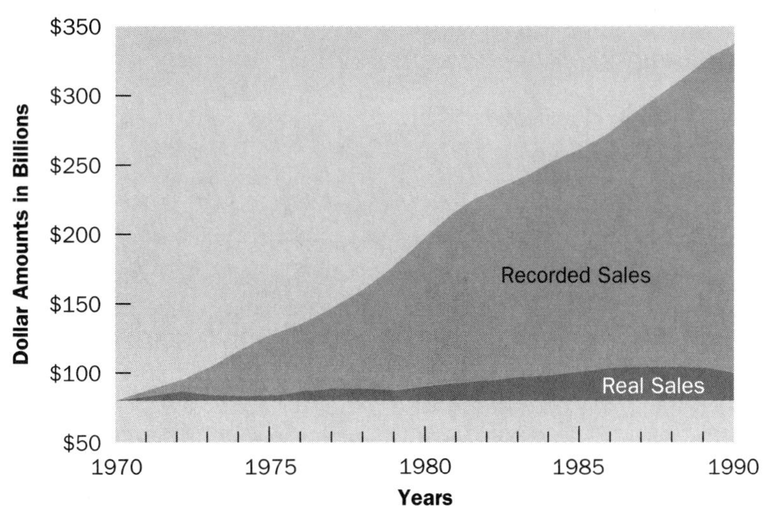

Source: Calculated from "CPI—Food at Home" Index and *Supermarket Business*' "Annual Consumer Expenditures Study."

billion. However, on a constant dollar basis, the increase is only 27.5%. Furthermore, during the past two years real sales have declined: down 0.4% in 1989, and down an additional 3.5% in 1990. *Supermarket Business* summarizes the situation by stating, "We're selling less product, but getting a little more money for it."[7]

The number of stores decreased 7.5% from 156,703 in 1985 to 145,000 in 1990. Even though spending per capita increased 22.3% during this same period, industry sales as a portion of total disposable personal income has been diminishing (see Exhibit 6.5). However, as shown in Exhibit 6.6, growth has not been even throughout the industry. Supermarkets have enjoyed the most consistent growth, with superettes and other grocery stores experiencing wide fluctuations.

Supermarket Business[8] categorizes stores as follows:

> *Supermarkets*: Supermarkets, which are complete, full-line, self-service and partial service food markets, with annual sales of at least $2 million, are gradually increasing their piece of industry sales. In 1985, they accounted for 76.0% of grocery store sales; by 1990, this had increased to 78.2%. Sales per store increased 30.3% from $6.6 million in 1985 to $8.6 million in 1990.
>
> *Superettes*: Superettes are self-service or partial service food stores handling groceries, meats, and produce, with annual sales of $1 million to $2 million. Superettes have also watched their market share edge upward, increasing from 6.0% in 1985 to 6.4% in 1990. This increase, however, has come in spurts with sales increases of 13.9% and 12.1% in 1986 and 1989, respectively, sandwiched around increases of 1.2% in 1987 and 1.7% in 1988. Sales per store increased 11.8% from $1.7 million in 1985 to $1.9 million in 1990.
>
> *Chains*: A chain is an operation of 11 or more retail food stores, regardless of individual dollar volume. The market share for chain stores has increased from 54.6% in 1985 to 79.6% in 1990. This increase is the result of two factors: (1) the number of stores increased from 18,178 to 22,600, and (2) sales per store jumped from $8.5 million to $12.6 million.

Because of the recession and rising food prices, consumers are buying generics and store brands, which tend to be priced lower than national brands. Therefore the U.S. Department of Commerce forecasts industry sales, adjusted for inflation, to rise about 1% annually during the next five years.[9] This rate is consistent with the growth experienced during the late 1980s, during which sales increased approximately 5% annually. It also is at the lower end of *Value Line*'s forecast, which foresees industry sales, not adjusted for inflation, growing in a range of 6.5% to 13.3% over the next two to four years.* Thus, assuming inflation of 4% to 5% for the next few years, the industry can expect sales to grow about 5% to 6% per year.

Stage in Life Cycle

According to Standard & Poor's *Industry Surveys*, "the supermarket industry is mature, with chains accounting for nearly 70% of volume. [Note: *Supermarket Business* gives chains a much higher market share.] Beyond this degree of consoli-

*Calculations based on information contained in "Grocery Store Industry," *Value Line Survey, Part 3, Ratings and Reports*, August 23, 1991, Edition 10, p. 1498.

EXHIBIT 6.5

Grocery Store Sales as a Percentage of Disposable Personal Income

Year	Percent
1970	11.2%
1975	11.3
1980	10.5
1981	10.4
1982	10.2
1983	9.9
1984	9.5
1985	9.4
1986	9.3
1987	9.2
1988	8.9
1989	8.7
1990	8.3

Source: Calculated by author.

dation, the slow rate of population growth in the U.S. and the overabundance of stores in many markets has placed a cap on the number of new stores the industry can accommodate."[10] This position is further supported by the dismal growth in real sales the industry has experienced during the past 20-plus years and the industry's profit margin, which is approximately 1.2%.[11]

Competitive Conditions

This industry is highly competitive, and no firm clearly dominates. *Forbes* lists 29 firms in the supermarket and convenience store industry. Based on sales, the largest firms are American Stores ($21.3 billion), Kroger ($21.2 billion), Safeway ($15.1 billion), Great A&P ($11.6 billion), and Winn-Dixie Stores ($10.1 billion). Four of the companies reported a net loss during the last 12 months. Furthermore, the median profit margin was 1.2%.[12]

EXHIBIT 6.6

Grocery Stores—Change in Sales

	1985	1986	1987	1988	1989	1990	Six-Year Total
Supermarkets	4.5%	5.7%	2.0%	9.8%	7.2%	3.4%	37.2%
Superettes	6.4	13.9	1.2	1.7	12.1	3.9	45.3
Others	4.8	0.6	23.2	(10.2)	(1.3)	(0.7)	14.3

Source: Calculations based on information in annual "Consumer Expenditures Study," *Supermarket Business.*

Labor

Labor costs are a supermarket's single largest operating expense, "typically two-thirds of non-inventory operating costs."[13] Plagued with a high turnover rate and a shrinking employee base, it is little wonder that Mark C. Hollis, President of Publix Supermarkets, feels that, "The single biggest challenge of the 1990s will be attracting and retaining an adequate staff of qualified employees."[14]

An astronomical turnover rate is the norm for this industry. According to *Progressive Grocer,* in 1990 chain supermarkets experienced a turnover rate of 45% for full-time employees and nearly 70% for part-time employees; part-time employees comprise approximately 41% of workers in chain stores.[15] Turnover extracts a heavy toll on stores—not only in direct costs, such as training, recruitment, and employee benefits, but also indirectly in areas such as efficiency, checkout speed and accuracy, cleanliness, and customer satisfaction. Furthermore, this situation is exacerbated by the fact that it is often these intangible areas that separate one store from another, attract and retain customers, and build customer loyalty.

The turnover problem is compounded by a shrinking employee base. Traditionally, teenagers have been a source of inexpensive, part-time labor. However, "the number of 14- to 17-year-olds dropped almost 20% from 1980 to 1990, and should remain about level until 1995."[16]

As Exhibit 6.7 indicates, from 1985 to 1990 average hourly wages increased 24.2%, from $5.94 to $7.38. Although this increase may have been partially in response to the shrinking employee base, real sales increased only 0.6% during this period. Furthermore, the ratio of households to employees has steadily declined. Presumably, this decline indicates that each employee serves increasingly fewer customers. Thus employee wages greatly exceeded productivity gains during this period.

The industry is attacking its labor problems with a three-pronged initiative. First, to attract and retain qualified employees, supermarket chains are reviewing career opportunities. This effort, coupled with the recession, has yielded positive results. In 1990, employee turnover declined 6% for full-time employees and 9% for part-timers.[17]

Second, the industry is looking outside the traditional teenage labor pool for new employees. According to the Food Marketing Institute,

> 86.2% of all food retailing companies actively recruit senior citizens, another 43.5% recruit developmentally disabled persons and 40.6% recruit the physically handicapped. In addition, companies are finding that women with young children will work either full-time or part-time if some kind of day-care assistance is provided.[18]

Third, the industry is taking a firmer stance against unions. Stores are withdrawing from markets where labor costs make them uncompetitive,[19] and there is a definite trend against unionization. According to a USDA report on labor costs in the food industry, the percentage of unionized employees in chain grocery stores dropped from 52% in 1989 to 45% in 1990. Additionally, the report said the reduction in union representation "largely reflects an industry practice of operating non-union stores in new locations."[20]

Predictably, independent stores are significantly less unionized than chain stores. However, as indicated in Exhibit 6.8, the degree of unionization is falling

EXHIBIT 6.7

Food Retailing

Employment (in thousands)	1991	1990	1989	1988	1987	1986	1985
Nonsupervisory	3,098	3,022	2,934	2,841	2,742	2,657	2,567
Supervisory	302	293	272	248	229	216	208
Total employment	3,400	3,315	3,206	3,089	2,971	2,873	2,775
Households per employee	NRA	27.7	29.0	29.5	30.6	30.8	31.3
Average hourly earnings	NRA	$7.38	$7.16	$7.01	$6.95	$7.06	$5.94

Note: NRA—not readily available.

fast at both types of stores. At independent stores, 17% of clerks and 22% of meat cutters were unionized in 1983. By 1990, however, these percentages had dwindled to 12% and 13%, respectively. At chain stores, the statistics are much the same. Unionized clerks declined from 52% to 43%, and unionized meat cutters dropped from 54% to 44% during this same seven-year period.

Five Competitive Forces

Rivalry

As a result of acquisitions and restructurings, many supermarket chains have huge debt burdens, which are affecting the competitive conditions within the industry. Because of this debt and its associated interest expense, these firms incur higher operating expenses and thus charge higher prices than competitors. Recognizing this opportunity, low-price firms are expanding into these markets, attempting to take market share away from vulnerable firms. The success of this strategy is dependent on customer sensitivity to lower prices.

EXHIBIT 6.8

Supermarket Unionization

	Clerks		Meat Cutters	
	Independents	Chains	Independents	Chains
1990	12%	43%	13%	44%
1989	12	50	15	51
1988	13	50	15	51
1987	13	52	16	53
1986	13	52	16	53
1985	14	51	17	52
1984	16	55	19	58
1983	17	52	22	54

Source: *Industry Surveys,* Standard & Poor's, May 2, 1991, p. R90.

When a new store enters a market or a discount store tries to expand its market share, a price war often results. Additionally, discount warehouses and supercenters are adding a new dimension to the competitive environment. Because of their minimal service levels and bare-bones premises, these firms generate enormous volume by offering rock-bottom prices. Because of these stores and with firms such as Kmart and Wal-Mart entering the food retailing business, competitiveness and rivalry are expected to intensify.

Potential Competitors

The industry faces competition from several directions. In January 1991, a McDonald's restaurant in Bloomington, Minnesota, began selling the following items through its drive-up window: milk, orange juice, eggs, margarine, bread products, and yogurt. Steve Whiteis, regional marketing consultant at McDonald's Minneapolis office, says, "This is simply a volume-building program being tested at a local store."[21] Local supermarket operators seem to agree that this is not a serious effort by McDonald's to bite into supermarket share. Nevertheless, if the experiment is successful, other fast food outlets may consider this possibility.

In July 1991, with the opening of the first Super Kmart Center in Medina, Ohio, Kmart Corporation is aggressively moving into the food retailing business. The Super Kmart Center covers 148,000 square feet and contains a 53,000 square foot supermarket inside. According to Kmart Chairman, Joseph Antonini, "We've been looking at this market for a long time. Food is a great draw. We know it's a tough market. But we want to create a mix and a balance that will make the whole store attractive."[22] Since Kmart is one of the largest retailers in the country, if this experiment is successful, Kmart could become a serious competitor.

Kmart is not the only retailer to enter the supermarket business. Wal-Mart operates six Supercenters from its Bentonville, Arkansas, headquarters, and seven more are scheduled to open in 1992. "By that time, Wal-Mart will be competing for food business in Arkansas, Missouri, Oklahoma, and Mississippi. This will vault it onto the list of the top 100 supermarket operators nationally."[23]

Competition is also coming from overseas. According to a new government analysis, foreign corporations are gobbling up the U.S. food industry at a rapid clip. For example, in April 1991, Ahold of the Netherlands, which owns the largest supermarket chain in the Netherlands with over 25% of the market, acquired Tops Markets of Buffalo, New York. Ahold also owns and operates Giant Food Store (Carlisle, Pennsylvania), Bi-Lo (Mauldin, South Carolina), and First National Supermarkets, Inc. (Cleveland, Ohio). With the Tops acquisition, Ahold became the seventh largest supermarket chain in the United States and the third largest East Coast chain.[24]

Substitute Products

Even though there are no apparent substitutes for the industry's products, customers certainly have the option of preparing their food at home or buying it out. Furthermore, customers have not been hesitant to exercise this option.

EXHIBIT 6.9 **Share of Food Dollar**

Year	Restaurants	Food Stores
1990	33.2%	66.8%
1989	33.2	66.8
1988	32.2	67.8
1987	32.0	68.0
1986	32.4	67.6
1985	31.7	68.3
1984	31.5	68.5
1983	31.0	69.0

Source: Annual "Consumer Expenditures Study," *Supermarket Business.*

"Demographic shifts and changing lifestyles have contributed to a pronounced change in the way consumers allocate their spending for food and beverages."[25] During the 1980s, more and more of the consumer's total expenditures for food and beverage was devoted to food consumed away from home (see Exhibit 6.9). The recession that began in 1990, however, altered this trend. As consumers felt the effects of the recession, they stabilized this expenditure pattern, and, as a result, grocery stores' market share was unchanged in 1990.

Bargaining Power of Buyers

Although there isn't a consumer's organization with sufficient clout to influence the industry, consumers are not without power. Most stores sell the same products, so price and convenience are significant to customers. According to *Value Line*, "Currently, of shoppers who switch to other stores, location appears to be a slightly more telling factor than price."[26]

Bargaining Power of Suppliers

The bargaining power of suppliers is questionable, but during the 1980s an adversarial relationship developed between manufacturers and retailers. This relationship led to several practices that manufacturers found questionable.

- From 1979 through 1989, the number of grocery stores dropped by 27,430 stores, or 15.7%. However, during this same time period the "number of items stocked by the typical grocery store doubled to 26,000."[27] Simultaneously, manufacturers raced to develop new products (more than 10,000 new products were introduced in 1990[28]) and invested heavily in advertising and promotion. With 80%[29] of the new products failing to gain a significant foothold in the market, retailers demanded and received high fees, called slotting allowances, for new products.

- Market development funds, or street money, is a lump sum payment designed to compensate the retailer for participating in special promotions, new product introductions, and the like.
- Diverting is a technique used by supermarket chains to reduce costs. A chain contracts for the purchase of a nationally advertised brand item in a low-price area, then diverts delivery of the product to a market where prices are higher.

Heading into the 1990s, relations among retailers, wholesalers, and manufacturers warmed. However, as long as manufacturers' profit margins are 3%[30] versus approximately 1%[31] for food distributors and wholesalers, the possibility for renewed tensions is present.

Government Regulation

The industry faces increased government regulation. According to *Supermarket Business,* following a report recently prepared by the General Accounting Office that lists "grocery stores among the top violators of the nation's child labor laws, U.S. Labor Department enforcers may set their sights on food retailers."[32] The report found that 23% of all violations detected last year occurred in grocery stores. Additionally, the report claimed that from 1983 through 1990, 14.9% of injuries involving illegally employed children occurred in grocery stores. *Supermarket Business* continued:

> Earlier this year [1991], new legislation took effect that sharply increased the maximum penalties in this area. And more recently, Labor Department officials indicated that they will be imposing stiffer sanctions for virtually all violations—even minor record keeping or paperwork infractions.
>
> Last year, child labor law penalties assessed by federal enforcers averaged $212 per violation. This year, Labor Department officials have announced plans to boost those penalties anywhere from 28 percent to 900 percent.[33]

Also, according to *Supermarket Business,*

> Controversial new workplace safety legislation under consideration in Congress would subject supermarketers and other employers to strict new criminal penalties for allowing potentially hazardous employment conditions. . . . Even small independent grocers with no more than a dozen employees would be required to set up labor-management advisory committees on workplace safety.[34]

In late 1990, Congress approved legislation setting a single, uniform national labeling standard for food products. The law, which is to be effective after the U.S. Food and Drug Administration (FDA) writes implementation regulations, requires grocers to label packaged food, fresh produce, and seafood with information about nutritional content, serving sizes, daily intakes, and reference values. The National Grocers Association feels that the regulations will be "counterproductive and excessively expensive to the food industry."[35]

Technology

Trends and Implications

According to *Progressive Grocer*, 80% of the chains and 60% of independent stores currently use electronic scanning technology.[36] Scanning has improved productivity and accuracy, and many new information-system applications are being developed to enhance the benefits associated with this technology. These new applications will allow managers to gather more information at the store level, to gather this information more quickly and accurately, and allow the manager to make better merchandising decisions. *Value Line* expects information systems to bolster operational efficiency by cutting labor needs and reducing human errors.[37]

The *1991 U.S. Industrial Outlook*[38] and *Value Line*[39] highlight the following developments, which may affect the industry in the future.

- ***Computer-assisted inventory reordering*** utilizes product code information to trigger reorder requirements for each store and automatically send orders to the store's distribution center. This method could reduce lost sales from stock-outs and eliminate labor intensive manual efforts currently being used by some stores.
- ***Direct store delivery*** is a store-based system that boosts order accuracy by automatically checking shipments against inventory order records. At the same time, slotting allowances and other fees due from suppliers aren't overlooked, as is often the case when checking is done by hand.
- ***Electronic shelf labels*** are capable of displaying a wide range of product information (product price, unit price, nutritional content, etc.) on command from an in-store computer. Although currently not cost effective, they help reduce labor costs and provide more accurate shelf-price marking. They also allow managers to make immediate price changes on items, thereby permitting special sales.
- ***New scanning technology*** is allowing some stores to test frequent-shopper programs. It allows instant discounts, electronically generated credits for coupons, and point-of-sale payment. It also gathers demographic and purchase information that could eventually help supermarkets improve marketing and merchandising decisions.

Economic Conditions

National

The year 1991 has been a tough one for the U.S. economy. After showing signs of life in the first half of the year, performance in the second half has been dismal (see Exhibit 6.10). In January 1992, *Value Line* summarized the economy by saying:

> The economy is hurting and, in our opinion, the task of turning this diverse and cumbersome giant around will prove both difficult and time consuming. This and similar

EXHIBIT 6.10

Selected Economic Data

	1991									
	Jan	Apr	May	Jun	Jul	Aug	Sep	Oct	Nov	Dec
Leading indicators[1]	138.8	141.9	143.0	143.9	145.5	145.5	145.3	145.5	145.1	144.8
Coincident indicators[1]	127.0	125.9	126.5	127.0	127.1	126.9	126.9	126.6	125.2	125.5
Unemployment rate	6.2%	6.6%	6.9%	7.0%	6.8%	6.8%	6.7%	6.8%	6.9%	7.1%
CPI-urban consumers[2]	134.6	135.2	135.6	136.0	136.2	136.6	137.2	137.4	NA	NA
Consumer confidence[3]	55.1	79.4	76.4	78.0	77.7	76.1	72.9	60.1	52.7	52.4
Capacity utilization	80.0%	78.6%	79.1%	79.6%	80.0%	79.8%	79.8%	79.6%	79.1%	NA
Personal income[4] (in trillions)	$4.724	$4.756	$4.787	$4.811	$4.802	$4.826	$4.847	$4.857	$4.886	$4.923

Notes: 1. 1982 = 100. 2. 1982–84 = 100. 3. 1985 = 100. 4. Stated in 1982 dollars. NA—Not available when case was written.

Source: Jan–Oct—"Business Cycle Indicators," *Survey of Current Business,* U.S. Department of Commerce, Economics and Statistics Administration, Bureau of Economic Analysis (November 1991), 71(11). Nov–Dec—*Wall Street Journal* articles on the economy citing data released by U.S. Department of Commerce.

downbeat assessments are being heard with increasing frequency among not only economic and stock market forecasters, but also the Congressional Budget Office, the Federal Reserve, and even the White House.[40]

According to the *Wall Street Journal,* "The newest figures [November's indices of leading economic and coincident indicators] offer further evidence that the economy has been dead in the water for some time and will remain sluggish in the near future. Between January and July, the index rose steadily, but it has since been lackluster."[41]

After trending upward during the first half of 1991, the Commerce Department's index of leading indicators leveled off at 145.5 during late summer and fall. During November, however, the index fell 0.3% with seven of the 11 indicators contributing to the decline, and it declined another 0.2% in December. The index rose only once during the last six months of 1991.

The Commerce Department's index of coincident indicators, which is designed to track the current health of the economy, after peaking at 127.1 in July, has since retreated to 125.2 by November—a decline of 1.5%. December reversed the trend as the index rose 0.2% to 125.5.

The unemployment rate has been on a roller coaster ride. After starting 1991 at 6.2%, it rose to 7.0% in June, dropped back to 6.7% by September, and rose again, reaching 7.1% in December.

Consumer confidence may be the key to the current economic situation. According to Dr. Irwin L. Kellner, chief economist for Manufacturers Hanover Trust:

> Consumer confidence is the lowest it has been since 1974, when Nixon resigned and equal to the level of 1980, when the government put tight controls on bank lending to bring down our double-digit inflation rate.
>
> [As a result] consumers aren't spending, depressing corporate profits, which in turn is spurring layoffs. This is the opposite of what normally happens at the end of a recession.[42]

The consumer confidence index (see Exhibit 6.11) jumped 47.2% from January (55.1) to its peak of 81.1 in March. The March peak coincided with the end of the war in the Persian Gulf. Since then, however, it declined steadily and finished the year at 52.4—down 35.4% from March's peak.

Many economists expect the economy to rebound in 1992. According to a *Wall Street Journal* survey of 42 economists, "Get ready for a bleak winter, followed by a mild economic recovery starting this spring or early summer."[43] This position is echoed by Donald Straszhelm, chief economist at Merrill Lynch & Co., "The year is going to start badly, but keep the faith. The economy will improve as the year progresses."[44] (Exhibit 6.12 contains *Value Line*'s forecast for the U. S. economy for the next 18 months.) *Fortune* magazine echoes the same prediction:

> The U.S. as a whole will grow a sluggish 1.5% in 1992, after declining nearly 1% in 1991. . . . [However] states outside the Northeast should expand nearly 2.5% after inflation in 1992. By contrast, the Northeast, which contracted 2.6% last year, is expected to shrink another half a percent this year.[45]

EXHIBIT 6.11 **Consumer Confidence**

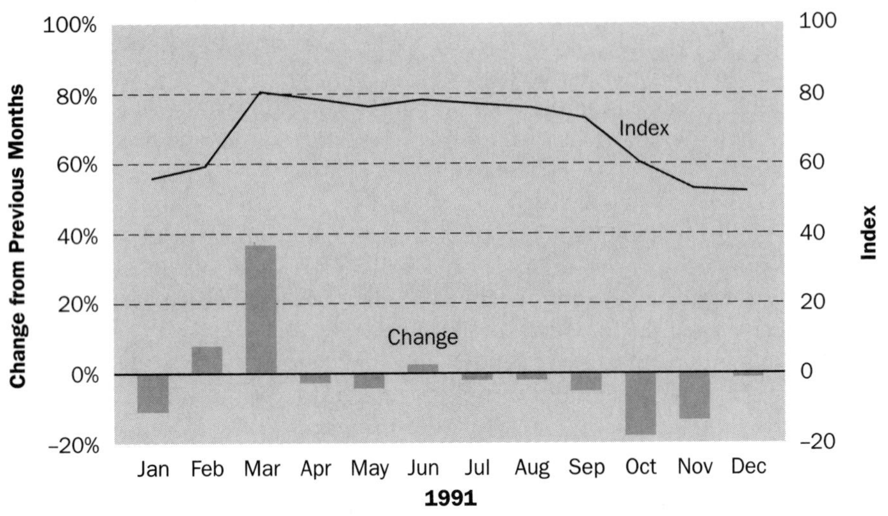

Source: *Survey of Current Business*, U.S. Commerce Department.

U.S. Regions

The economic situation has affected various regions of the country differently. During the late 1970s and 1980s, A&P's market area grew at approximately the same rate as the country. However, the current recession has hit particularly hard the New England, Mideast, and Great Lakes regions, which are A&P's primary market areas. David Wyss, research director of DRI/McGraw Hill, Inc., a Lexington, MA economic forecasting concern, says:

EXHIBIT 6.12 **Selected Quarterly Economic Data**

	Actual	Estimated						
	91:3	91:4	92:1	92:2	92:3	92:4	93:1	93:2
Real GNP (1982 dollars)[1]	$4,139	$4,146	$4,154	$4,178	$4,210	$4,240	$4,266	$4,296
Personal income (billions)	$4,824	$4,850	$4,896	$4,926	$4,973	$5,032	$5,122	$5,194
National unemployment	6.8%	7.0%	7.2%	7.0%	6.9%	7.0%	7.0%	6.9%
CPI—urban consumers								
Annualized rate of change	3.0	1.4	2.4	2.7	2.8	3.3	3.4	3.5

Note: 1. Real GNP stated in billions of dollars—seasonally adjusted.

Source: "Quarterly Economic Review," *Value Line Investment Survey* (January 3, 1992), pp. 471–486.

EXHIBIT 13 Regional Projections of GRP Growth

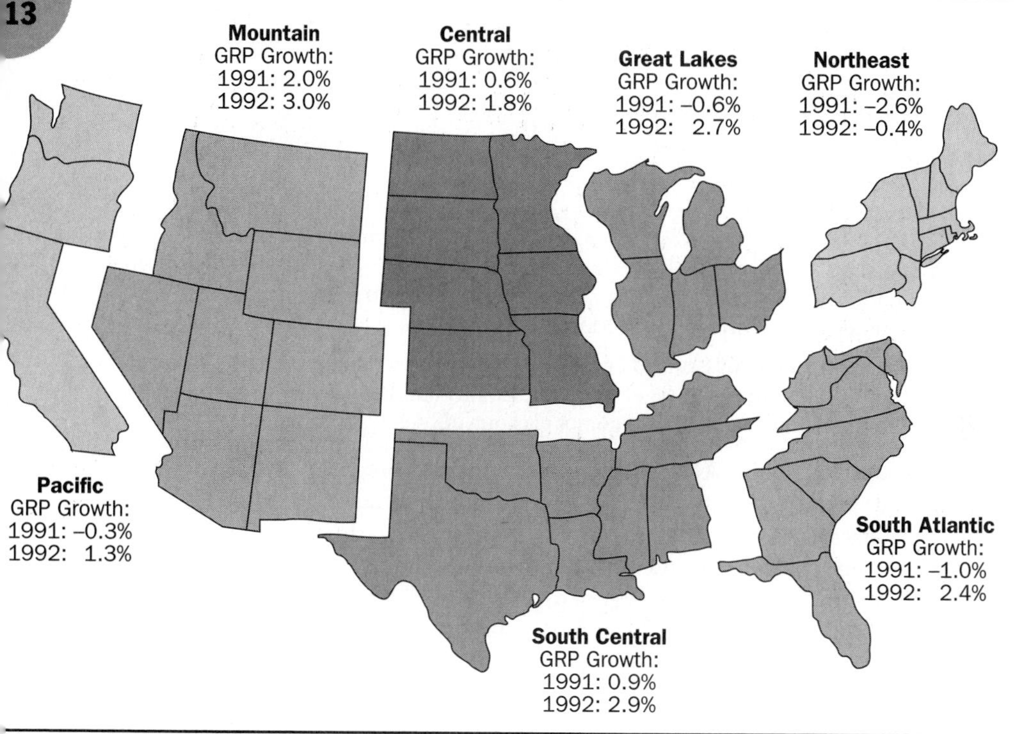

Note: GRP—Gross regional product.

Source: *Forbes,* January 27, 1992.

> New England is by far the sickest of any region. From Connecticut to the Canadian border, he says, the six New England states are mired in a recession that has cut deeper and probably will linger longer than anywhere else.
>
> The region's unemployment rate, at 7.8%, is a full point above the national average. Layoffs continue to shrink the computer, banking and defense industries. . . . Perhaps the biggest problem facing New England is that few jobs are being created to replace the ones lost.[46]

Exhibit 6.13 shows the regional projections from Regional Financial Associates, a consulting firm in West Chester, PA.[47]

Canada

The Canadian economy faces many of the same problems as the U.S. economy. According to the *Wall Street Journal:*

> The Canadian economy emerged from a yearlong recession this spring with a strong burst of growth in the April–June period. But growth has slowed since the summer, partly because of weak consumer and business confidence. . . . The Business Council

on National Issues, which represents the chief executive officers of 150 of Canada's largest companies, said, "Canada seems destined to experience one of the most anemic economic recoveries on record." But it said, "We do see some positive signs on the economic horizon."[48]

The Great A&P Tea Company

According to its *Form 10-K* (1990) and *1990 Annual Report to Shareholders:*

> The Great Atlantic & Pacific Tea Company, Inc., based in Montvale, New Jersey, is engaged in the retail food business.[49] The Company operates conventional supermarkets and larger superstores in 23 U.S. states, the District of Columbia, and Ontario, Canada, under the A&P, Waldbaum's, Food Emporium, Super Fresh, Farmer Jack, Kohl's, Dominion, and Miracle Food Mart trade names.
>
> Through its Compass Foods subsidiary, the Company also manufactures and distributes a line of coffees under the Eight O'Clock, Bokar, and Royale labels, both for sale through its own stores, and by other companies outside A&P's trading areas.[50]

On February 24, 1990, A&P operated two coffee roasting plants, three bakeries, and an ice cream plant in the United States and Canada. In addition, it maintained warehouses to service its stores. On February 23, 1991, A&P operated 1,275 stores[51] and believed that it enjoyed a prominent position in the industry.

> On the basis of reported sales for fiscal 1989, the Company believes that it had the fourth largest sales volume of any retail food company in the United States and the largest sales volume in metropolitan New York and Detroit and in the Province of Ontario, the Company's largest single markets in the United States and Canada.[52]
>
> Having shed the role as a mere distributor of commodities, A&P and its subsidiary companies are fully in the food service business. A high percentage of our stores feature extensive delicatessens with broad selections of hot and cold prepared foods plus catering service, and bakery departments combining the best elements of both counter and self-service configurations.[53]

Mission and Objectives

Reflecting on where the company has been and where it is going, Chairman of the Board, President, and Chief Executive Officer, James Wood remarked:

> Looking back, I believe we can take great pride in A&P's achievements in the decade of the 1980s. Against considerable odds, we restored and sustained the Company's profitability; became innovators in regional marketing and store format development; set the pace in growth by acquisition, and built one of the strongest balance sheets in the industry.
>
> Heading into the new decade, we will continue to increase our sales and customer base. . . . Our Company has the people, financial strength, store facilities and technology we need to assume industry leadership in this decade. Given our past accomplishments, I am confident we will be successful.[54]

Chairman Wood, however, tempered this vision for the future with a realistic look at the present. In the Company's *1990 Annual Report to Shareholders,* he explained:

> A&P again achieved record sales and earnings in fiscal 1990, although results were affected by adverse economic conditions in most of the Company's major trading areas in the United States and particularly Canada.
>
> After a positive first half, results from midyear onward reflected the recessionary conditions that gripped Ontario, Canada, as well as the northeastern, middle Atlantic, and midwestern areas of the U.S.—the areas of A&P's greatest concentration. Cautious consumer spending, and the promotional investment required on our part to protect market share, impacted both sales and earnings during the latter part of the year, and those conditions continue into 1991.[55]

Organization

Great A&P is organized into six regional operating groups. Each group has its own chief executive and is described in one of A&P's annual reports as a "company within a company in many ways." The Company's *1989 Annual Report to Shareholders* introduces the operating groups.

> **Canada:** A&P's Canadian Subsidiary operates 194 supermarkets in the Province of Ontario, including 156 A&P stores, 36 upscale Dominion stores in and around Metropolitan Toronto, and two Super Fresh stores. Our combined operations hold the leading market share in Ontario.
>
> **Midwest:** The Midwest Group operates 77 Farmer Jack stores and 58 A&P stores in Michigan, mostly in the Metro Detroit market, and 63 Kohl's Food Stores in Wisconsin. A&P acquired Kohl's in 1983 and Farmer Jack in 1989.
>
> **South:** The Southern Group operates 85 A&P stores in the Atlanta, GA and Charlotte, NC markets; 42 A&P stores in New Orleans, LA and along the Gulf Coast of Mississippi, and 16 Super Fresh stores in Baton Rouge, LA.[56]
>
> **Mid-Atlantic:** The Mid-Atlantic Group stores operate under the Super Fresh banner in the Philadelphia/southern New Jersey/Delaware Valley area (73 stores), Baltimore/Washington, D.C. (84 stores), Richmond, VA (60 stores) and Raleigh, NC (23 stores).
>
> **Metro New York:** A&P is the New York market leader with 190 A&P stores, 100 Waldbaum's stores and 30 Food Emporiums, with the combined operations encompassing all boroughs of New York City and its New York, New Jersey and nearby Connecticut suburbs.
>
> **Northeast:** The Northeast Group consists of 78 A&P stores and 42 Waldbaum's Food Marts in southern Massachusetts including Cape Cod, northern and central Connecticut, upstate New York, Maine, New Hampshire, Rhode Island, and Vermont.[57]

Marketing Strategies

According to its *Form 10-K* (1990):

> The Company has broadened its original focus on the "traditional" family and now strategically operates its stores with merchandise, pricing and identities tailored to appeal to different segments of the market. Discount shoppers, gourmet chefs, and single

professionals all now fit within the Company's family of supermarkets and superstores. Marketing strategies are targeted for reaching these distinct buying groups.[58]

Expanding on this strategy in its *1990 Annual Report to Shareholders,* A&P explained:

> The art and science of merchandising today is geared to our need to serve large cross-sections of consumers, yet not lose sight of the nature of the individual shopper; to respond to national and even global trends, without forgetting that regardless of our overall size, we remain essentially a local business.[59]
>
> . . . Satisfying the customer is a far more complex undertaking than ever before. To be sure, it still begins with the tried and true premise of offering customers the basics at the right prices. However, the dramatic increase in the value of the shopper's time in recent years has presented the supermarket operator with the challenge—and therefore the opportunity—to provide far more in the way of service.[60]
>
> Over the past nine years, the activities of A&P's retail design and development department have focused on converting the Company's store facilities from a chain of relatively small grocery outlets to a network of contemporary supermarkets and superstores.
>
> With the population having become increasingly regional and consumer demographics more segmented, management realized at the outset that chains such as A&P could no longer compete effectively in all territories with the same stores selling the same products, or even trading under the same name for that matter.
>
> Consequently, our marketing and merchandising was re-focused to cater to the customer preferences within the regional operating groups we organized, each a company within a company in many ways. As a result, we began that decade of the 1980s with one significant trading identity, and we began the 90s with eight.
>
> Finally, true "niche marketing" across geographic regions requires a portfolio of store formats that differ in size, product variety, service levels, pricing and shopping atmosphere.[61]

Geographic Areas

As indicated earlier, A&P operates in the United States and Canada. Exhibit 6.14 presents selected information for each area. In 1984, Canadian operations represented 15.9% of assets, 17.1% of sales, and 28.0% of income before income taxes. By February 1991, these percentages were: assets, 23.9%; sales, 19.3%; and income before income taxes, 23.4% (see Exhibit 6.15).

In general, A&P's Canadian operations have outperformed those in the United States. During the eight years ending in February 1991, return on assets and return on sales for the Canadian operations were 10.5% and 2.8%, respectively, compared to 7.1% and 1.8%, respectively, for U.S. operations.

This spread, however, which was considerable in the mid 1980s, has virtually been eliminated by 1991 (see Exhibit 6.15). In 1984, the return on sales in Canada was 2.8%, compared to 1.5% for sales in the United States. By 1991, the return for domestic sales had increased to 2.2%, whereas that in Canada remained constant at 2.8%. Similarly, in 1984, return on Canadian assets was 12.9%, or more than double the 6.3% return on U.S. assets. In 1991, A&P showed a greater return on domestic assets, 8.0%, than on Canadian assets, 7.8%.

EXHIBIT 6.14

Domestic and Foreign Operations[1]

(Dollar amounts in thousands)

Year	Assets		Sales		Income Before Taxes		Return on Assets		Return on Sales	
	U.S.	Canada	U.S.	Canada	U.S.	Canada	U.S.	Canada	U.S.	Canada
1990	$2,518,618	$788,878	$9,195,995	$2,194,948	$200,935	$61,416	8.0%	7.8%	2.2%	2.8%
1989	2,238,333	593,239	9,197,353	1,950,644	194,556	56,242	8.7%	9.5%	2.1%	2.9%
1988	2,210,213	430,157	8,204,675	1,863,101	176,587	47,195	8.0%	11.0%	2.2%	2.5%
1987	1,842,802	418,372	7,859,119	1,672,661	141,933	46,010	7.7%	11.0%	1.8%	2.8%
1986	1,700,010	380,216	6,178,519	1,656,340	80,559	48,851	4.7%	12.8%	1.3%	2.9%
1985	1,306,014	357,746	5,163,857	1,451,565	74,178	34,912	5.7%	9.8%	1.4%	2.4%
1984	1,184,199	178,902	4,955,686	922,600	57,296	30,079	4.8%	16.8%	1.2%	3.3%
1983	1,008,604	191,324	4,328,056	893,954	63,536	24,763	6.3%	12.9%	1.5%	2.8%

Note:
1. Fiscal years ending in February.

Source: A&P annual reports to shareholders.

EXHIBIT 6.15 **Canadian Operations**

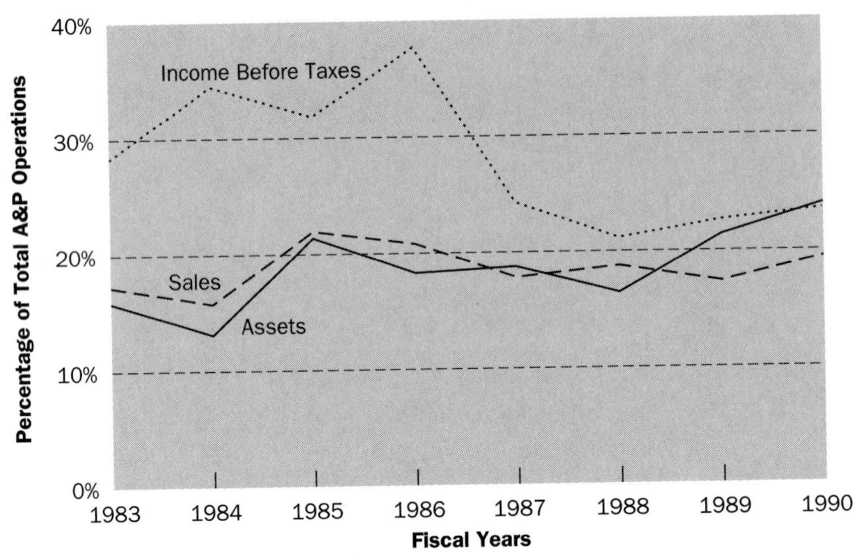

In the *1989 Annual Report to Shareholders,* Chairman Wood mentioned the "*intensified price competition from chains and aggressive independents in Ontario.*"[62] A year later Chairman Wood expanded on the competitive environment facing the Canadian operations and offered hope for the future:

> At present, the trading environment in Ontario remains adverse, with many consumers cross-border shopping to take advantage of lower prices in U.S. stores, and government opposition to Sunday openings continuing in the majority of our areas. . . . As the Canadian economy improves, the combined A&P, Dominion and Miracle Food Mart operations will resume a solid, long-term growth trend.[63]

Operations

In the nine years since fiscal 1981, the Company invested over $2 billion in acquiring, constructing, remodeling, and expanding stores.[64] As a result of this investment, from February 1984 to February 1990: (1) the number of stores increased 24.8% (from 1,022 to 1,275); (2) total store area increased 68.3% (from 23,376,000 square feet to 39,353,000 square feet); and (3) average store size increased 35.5% (from 22,775 square feet to 30,865 square feet). (See Exhibit 6.16.)

The Company's *1990 Annual Report to Shareholders* presents a three-pronged strategy to meet its objectives:

- New store development will proceed at a somewhat slower pace in the coming year, reflecting the recent inability of developers to obtain financing for the shopping center locations we seek to acquire. Nevertheless we continue the

EXHIBIT 6.16 **A&P—Stores Information**

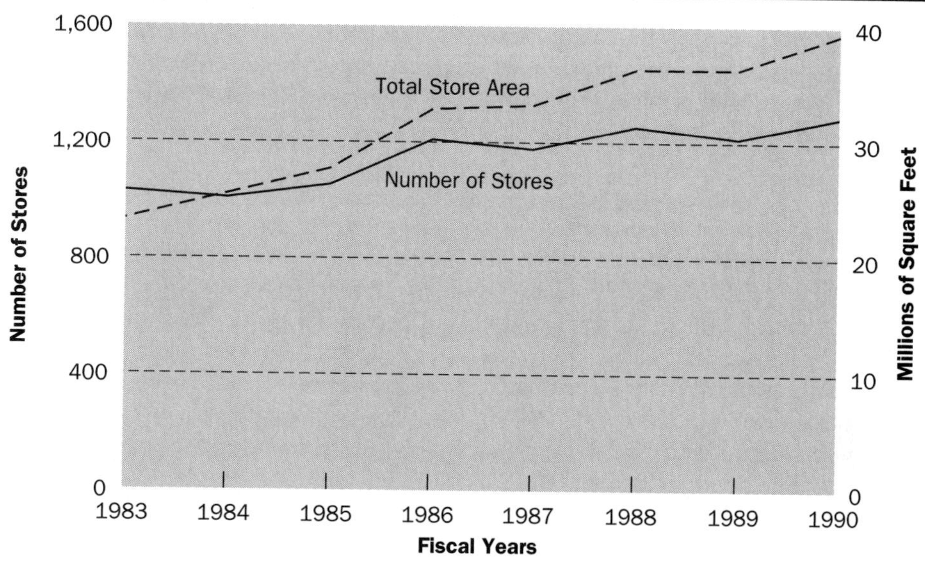

Source: A&P annual reports.

pursuit of high potential locations, and expect to resume our previous development pace in the years ahead as the building industry regains its momentum.

- Another key strategic element is our new marketing direction. . . . The corporate merchandising department is guiding the operating groups toward a more aggressive profile in their marketing regions, complementing their reputation for outstanding perishables, service departments and overall store facilities. This strategy is being communicated to consumers through greater emphasis on high-impact television and radio advertising.
- A major factor in our drive for sales progress will be the full deployment of our new central purchasing operation, which purchases national brand grocery products for the entire Company at Montvale headquarters. The leveraging of A&P's buying power will lower our total cost of goods appreciably—providing the flexibility to emphasize market share growth while maintaining strong margins and profitability.[65]

In 1989 and 1990, A&P consolidated its purchasing, merchandising, and advertising functions under a single corporate umbrella. The Company anticipates several benefits from this consolidation.

- Better inventory control and lower cost for goods can be achieved through "centralized, high-volume purchasing"[66] for the entire company. A&P feels this will be more efficient, eliminate duplicate efforts, and will qualify the

Company for the maximum promotional support offered by vendors. Previously, each geographic region negotiated separately for its purchases.

- A&P anticipates interfacing its "computer-assisted" buying and merchandising operations with its "computerized space management system."[67] Utilizing scanner-generated information for each product generated at the store level, the system will produce planograms or departmental shelf sets to improve sales volume and gross profit.

Financial

Great A&P's fiscal year ends on the last Saturday in February. Fiscal years 1985, 1987, 1988, 1989, and 1990 each contained 52 weeks, whereas the 1986 fiscal year contained 53 weeks. The first quarter of each fiscal year ends in mid June and consists of 16 weeks. Quarter two ends in early September, and quarter three ends in late November or early December. Quarters two, three, and four each contain 12 weeks.

As of February 23, 1991, Tengelmann Warenhandelsgesellschaft owned 53.0% of the Company's stock.[68]

Following a deficit in fiscal 1981, A&P earned profits in each of the nine succeeding years. In addition to the $757.3 million in profits shown for fiscal years 1982 through 1990, in the mid 1980s the company recorded $249.2 million of extraordinary items, bringing total profits during this nine-year period to $1,006.5 million.

However, the first three quarters of fiscal 1991 saw this trend reverse as profits plunged (see Exhibits 6.17 and 6.18). Except for the first quarter of fiscal 1991, ending in June 1991, quarterly profits have steadily declined. The first quarter of each fiscal year contains 16 weeks and is traditionally A&P's best quarter. Even then, however, profits for the first quarter of fiscal 1991 were $14.8 million, or 29.0% below those of the first quarter of fiscal 1990. Even so, quarterly revenues remain comparable to historical levels.

Profits for the second quarter of fiscal 1991 dropped $21.7 million, or 60.0%, and for the third quarter they decreased another $10.6 million, or 73.0%. Profits for the third quarter of fiscal 1991 were $28.1 million, or 87.8% below those for the same quarter a year earlier (see Exhibit 6.19). Refer to Exhibits 6.20–6.23 for financial statements.

Human Resources

According to *A&P's Form 10-K* (1990):

> The control of labor costs has been a major component of the Company's improved operating efficiency in recent fiscal years. The Super Fresh Food Markets and Kohl's Food Stores operate under a precedent-setting labor/management agreement under which employees have both a direct input to management and personal incentives to improve sales and productivity. This participatory concept has been adopted in the Company's operations in Baton Rouge, LA and in two Super Fresh stores in the Province of Ontario, Canada.[69]

EXHIBIT 6.17

Revenue and Net Income Before Extraordinary Items: A&P

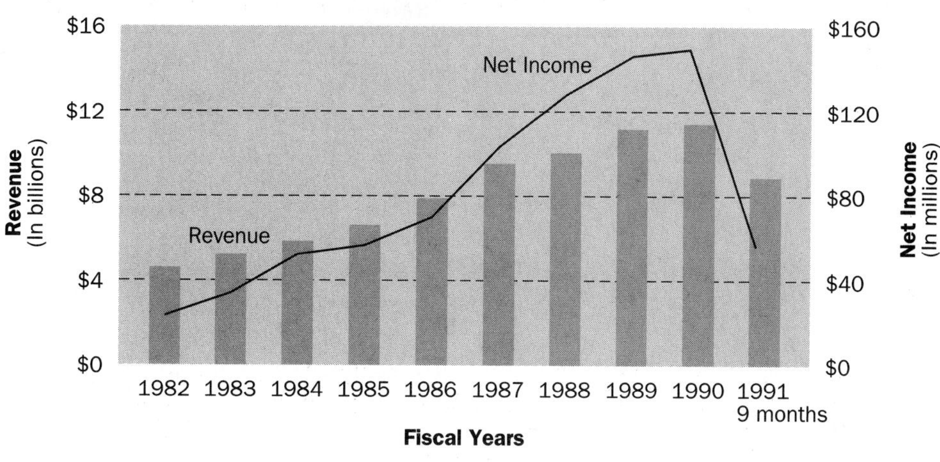

Source: Standard & Poor's and A&P annual reports.

EXHIBIT 6.18

Quarterly Revenue and Net Income: A&P

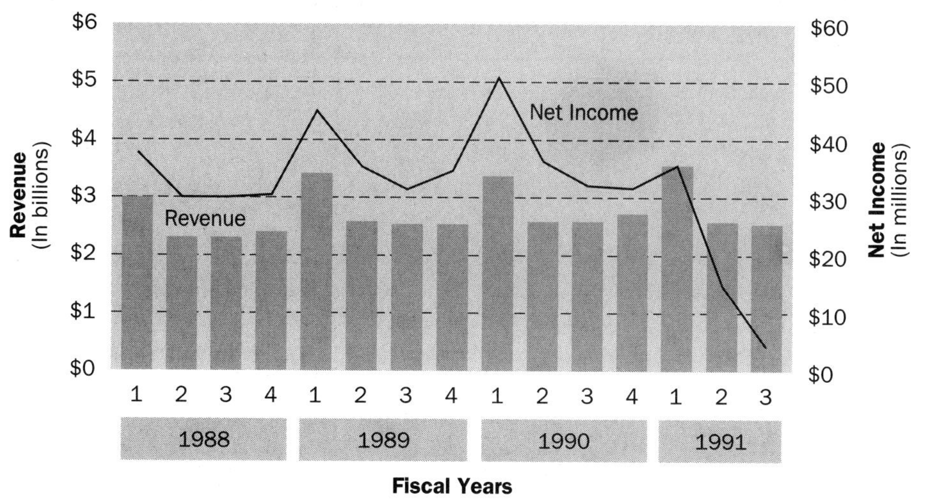

Source: Standard & Poor's and A&P annual reports.

EXHIBIT 6.19

Quarterly Financial Results
(Dollar amounts in thousands)

Fiscal Year	Quarter Ending	Revenues	Net Income
1991			
Q-I	June 1991	$3,590,694	$36,201
Q-II	September 1991	2,652,686	14,480
Q-III	November 1991	2,607,667	3,916
1990			
Q-I	June 1990	$3,402,690	$51,007
Q-II	September 1990	2,604,294	36,316
Q-III	December 1990	2,550,533	32,050
Q-IV	February 1991	2,833,426	31,581
		$11,390,943	$150,954
1989			
Q-I	June 1989	$3,439,591	$45,390
Q-II	September 1989	2,590,149	35,630
Q-III	December 1989	2,550,533	31,169
Q-IV	February 1990	2,567,724	34,509
		$11,147,997	$146,698
1988			
Q-I	June 1988	$3,004,014	$38,047
Q-II	September 1988	2,327,957	29,450
Q-III	December 1988	2,302,389	29,495
Q-IV	February 1989	2,433,417	30,590
		$10,067,777	$127,582

Source: A&P annual reports to shareholders and forms 10-K.

In February 1990, the Company had approximately 91,000 employees, of which 61% were part-time and 39% were full-time. As shown in Exhibit 6.24, from 1984 through 1991 the number of employees increased faster than either the number of stores or total store area. The number of employees grew 87.4% during this period, while the number of stores grew 24.8% (from 1,022 in 1984 to 1,275 in 1991). Total store area increased 69.1% (from 23,276,000 square feet in 1984 to 39,353,000 square feet in 1991).

With sales increasing 118.1% (from $5,222 million to $11,391 million) during this period, sales per employee increased from $98,528 to $114,713 (16.4%) for the fiscal years ending in 1984 and 1991, respectively. However, the "Food at Home" component of the consumer price index increased approximately 33.5%

EXHIBIT 6.20

Summary of Selected Information: The Great Atlantic & Pacific Tea Company, Inc.
(Dollar amounts in millions, except per share data and ratios)

	Fiscal 1990 (52 weeks)	Fiscal 1989 (52 weeks)	Fiscal 1988 (52 weeks)	Fiscal 1987 (52 weeks)	Fiscal 1986 (53 weeks)	Fiscal 1985 (52 weeks)
Operating Results						
Sales	$11,390.9	$11,148.0	$10,067.8	$9,531.8	$7,834.9	$6,615.4
Income before extraordinary credits	151.0	146.7	127.6	103.4	69.0	56.1
Net income	151.0	146.7	127.6	103.4	95.0	88.3
Per Share Data						
Income before extraordinary credits	3.95	3.84	3.34	2.71	1.82	1.48
Net income	3.95	3.84	3.34	2.71	2.50	2.33
Cash dividends	.775	.675	.575	.475	.40	.10
Financial Position						
Current assets	1,212.3	1,075.9	1,068.7	945.7	898.9	756.6
Current liabilities	1,096.1	995.7	978.1	883.0	805.4	582.5
Working capital	116.2	80.2	90.6	62.7	93.4	174.1
Current ratio	1.11	1.08	1.09	1.07	1.12	1.30
Total assets	3,307.5	2,831.6	2,640.4	2,243.2	2,080.2	1,663.8
Long-term debt	532.5	329.3	254.3	168.3	196.2	151.3
Capital lease obligations	220.9	233.6	252.6	225.7	223.9	196.4
Equity						
Shareholders' equity	1,221.3	1,092.2	970.8	851.3	755.7	668.7
Book value per share	31.96	28.59	25.42	22.32	19.85	17.63
Weighted average shares outstanding	38,206,000	38,198,000	38,164,000	38,106,000	38,017,000	37,839,000
Other						
Number of employees	99,300	91,000	92,000	83,000	81,500	60,000
Number of stores at year end	1,275	1,215	1,241	1,183	1,200	1,045
Total store area (square feet)	39,353,000	36,369,000	36,407,000	33,111,000	32,609,000	27,648,000

Source: A&P annual reports to shareholders.

EXHIBIT 6.21

Statements of Consolidated Operations: The Great Atlantic & Pacific Tea Company, Inc.

(Dollar amounts in millions, except per share data)

Fiscal Years	1990	1989	1988	1987
Sales	$11,390.9	$11,148.0	$10,067.8	$9,531.8
Cost of merchandise sold	(8,237.3)	(8,211.3)	(7,481.4)	(7,112.9)
Gross margin	3,153.6	2,936.7	2,586.4	2,418.9
Stores operating, general and administrative expense	(2,818.7)	(2,628.6)	(2,319.0)	(2,183.5)
Income from operations	334.9	308.1	267.4	235.4
Interest expense	(79.7)	(73.5)	(48.5)	(51.9)
Interest income	7.2	16.2	4.9	4.4
Income from operations	262.4	250.8	223.8	187.9
Provision for income taxes	(111.4)	(104.1)	(96.2)	(84.5)
Net income	$ 151.0	$ 146.7	$ 127.6	$ 103.4
Net income per share	$3.95	$3.84	$3.34	$2.71
Dividends per share	$ .775	$ .675	$ .575	$ .475

Source: A&P annual reports.

EXHIBIT 6.22

Quarterly Consolidated Statements of Operations: The Great Atlantic & Pacific Tea Company, Inc.

(Dollar amounts in millions, except per share data)

Quarters Ending	Nov. 30, 1991	Sept. 7, 1991	June 15, 1991	Feb. 23, 1991	Dec. 1, 1990	Sept. 8, 1990	June 19, 1990
Sales	$2,607.7	$2,652.7	$3,590.7	$2,773.0	$2,611.0	$2,604.3	$3,402.6
Cost of merchandise sold	(1,894.3)	(1,926.7)	(2,586.2)	(2,000.0)	(1,884.6)	(1,888.0)	(2,464.7)
Gross margin	713.4	726.0	1,004.5	773.0	726.4	716.3	937.9
Store operating, general and administrative expense	(688.6)	(683.1)	(914.7)	(697.0)	(652.1)	(638.4)	(831.2)
Income from operations	24.8	42.9	89.8	76.0	74.3	77.9	106.7
Interest expense	(18.3)	(17.6)	(26.7)	(21.0)	(19.7)	(16.5)	(22.5)
Interest income	.3	.2	.4	.4	1.6	2.2	3.0
Income before taxes	6.8	25.5	63.5	55.4	56.2	63.6	87.2
Income taxes	(2.9)	(11.0)	(27.3)	(23.8)	(24.1)	(27.3)	(36.2)
Net income	$3.9	$14.5	$36.2	$31.6	$32.1	$36.3	$51.0
Net income per share	$.10	$.38	$.95	$.83	$.84	$.95	$1.33
Dividends per share	$.20	$.20	$.20	$.20	$.20	$.20	$ .175

Source: A&P forms 10-Q.

EXHIBIT 6.23

Consolidated Balance Sheets: The Great Atlantic & Pacific Tea Company, Inc.
(Dollar amounts in millions)

Years Ending	Nov. 30, 1991	Feb. 23, 1991	Feb. 24, 1990	Feb.25, 1989
	(Unaudited)			
Assets				
Current assets				
Cash and short-term investments	$ 5.4	$ 28.5	$ 35.1	$ 44.5
Accounts receivable	196.8	201.8	164.0	152.0
Inventories	965.5	936.2	836.2	829.2
Prepaid expenses and other assets	40.5	45.8	40.6	43.0
Total current assets	1,208.2	1,212.3	1,075.9	1,068.7
Property				
Land	NRA	89.3	88.1	83.6
Buildings	NRA	220.1	212.8	197.4
Equipment and leasehold improvements	NRA	1,928.1	1,544.6	1,408.8
Total—at cost	NRA	2,237.5	1,845.5	1,689.8
Less accumulated depreciation and amortization	NRA	(612.9)	(507.5)	(396.9)
	1,581.1	1,624.6	1,338.0	1,292.9
Property leased under capital leases	159.8	173.7	188.2	209.0
Property—net	1,740.9	1,798.3	1,526.2	1,501.9
Other assets	300.4	296.9	229.5	69.8
Total assets	$3,249.5	$3,307.5	$2,831.6	$2,640.4
Liabilities and Shareholders' Equity				
Current liabilities				
Current portion of long-term debt	$ 6.0	$ 41.2	$ 54.9	$ 60.6
Current portion of capital lease obligations	19.2	20.4	20.7	21.1
Accounts payable	619.2	655.9	522.6	531.7
Accrued salaries, wages, and benefits	146.7	166.3	156.2	149.0
Accrued taxes	36.5	56.3	77.1	73.7
Other accruals	163.2	156.0	164.2	142.0
Total current liabilities	990.8	1,096.1	995.7	978.1
Long-term debt	533.3	532.5	329.3	254.3
Capital lease obligations	208.1	220.9	233.6	252.6
Deferred income taxes	161.0	152.2	8.8	57.2
Other non-current liabilities	97.3	84.5	92.1	127.3

(continued)

EXHIBIT 6.23

Consolidated Balance Sheets: The Great Atlantic & Pacific Tea Company, Inc. *(cont.)*
(Dollar amounts in millions)

Years Ending	Nov. 30, 1991	Feb. 23, 1991	Feb. 24, 1990	Feb.25, 1989
		(Unaudited)		
Shareholders' equity				
Preferred stock—none				
Common stock	38.2	38.2	38.2	38.2
Capital surplus	437.9	437.9	437.9	436.8
Cumulative translation adjustment	15.7	9.7	1.9	2.7
Retained earnings	767.4	735.8	614.4	493.5
Treasury stock, at cost	(0.3)	(0.3)	(0.3)	(0.3)
Total shareholders' equity	1,259.0	1,221.3	1,092.1	970.9
Total liabilities and shareholders' equity	$3,249.5	$3,307.5	$2,831.6	$2,640.4

Source: A&P annual reports to shareholders and forms 10-K.

Notes to A&P consolidated balance sheets:

1. NRA—not readily available.
2. In July 1986, the Company acquired all the outstanding shares of Shopwell, Inc. ("Shopwell") for approximately $70 million in cash. Shopwell, located in the Metropolitan New York area operated 53 retail supermarkets.
3. On April 25, 1985, the Company purchased Dominion Stores Limited, 92 stores, 2 warehouses, and an office complex ("Dominion") located in the Province of Ontario for approximately $116 million.
4. On October 1, 1983, the Company acquired the net assets of Kohl's Food Stores for approximately $31 million in cash.
5. During fiscal 1989 the Company loaned approximately $436 million to Newgateway Holdings Limited ("Newgateway"), a United Kingdom Company, which was formed to purchase the outstanding common shares of the Gateway Corporation PLC ("Gateway"), the third largest food retailer in the United Kingdom. Subsequently, Newgateway sold its Gateway shares to Isosceles PLC ("Isosceles"), the owner of a controlling interest in Gateway with cash and 19.9% off the common and cumulative preference shares of Isosceles. During fiscal 1990, Isosceles completed a recapitalization which resulted in the contribution of additional equity to Isosceles (in the form of cash and debt conversion) in the amount of at least 222 million Pounds Sterling. . . . After giving effect to the recapitalization (in which the Company did not participate), the Company owns approximately 7.2% of the equity of Isosceles. The Company uses the cost method to account for its Isosceles investment, which was $164 million at year-end exchange rates and is included in the balance sheet caption "Other Assets."

(from 99.1 to 132.3) during this time. Therefore "real" sales increased approximately 63.4% and "real" sales per employee slipped about 12.8%.

Acquisitions and Investments

According to its *1990 Annual Report to Shareholders,* "Since 1982, A&P has acquired 530 supermarkets and superstores"[70] involving six "major strategic" acquisitions: Waldbaum's and Shopwell/Food Emporium in the New York area; Farmer Jack in Detroit; Miracle Food Mart and Dominion Stores in Ontario, Canada; and

EXHIBIT 6.24 **Employees at Fiscal Year End**

Year	Employees: Number	Employees: Per Store	Employees: Sales Per Employee	Store: Area Per Employee
1990	99,300	77.9	$114,712	396.3
1989	91,000	74.9	$122,505	399.7
1988	92,000	74.1	$109,432	395.7
1987	83,000	70.2	$114,841	398.9
1986	81,500	67.9	$ 96,133	400.1
1985	60,000	57.4	$110,257	460.8
1984	53,000	52.9	$110,911	477.6
1983	53,000	51.9	$ 98,529	439.2

Source: A&P annual reports or calculated from information therein.

Kohl's Food Stores in Wisconsin. The following is discussed in the company's forms 10-K and its annual reports to shareholders.

- In October 1990, A&P acquired certain assets, including inventory, of the Miracle Food Mart Division of Steinberg, Inc. ("Miracle Food Mart") for approximately $270 million. Miracle Food Mart operates 70 retail supermarkets in the province of Ontario under the tradenames "Miracle Food Mart" and "Ultra Mart."
- In January 1989, the Company acquired all of the outstanding shares of Borman's, Inc. ("Borman's") for approximately $78 million in cash. Borman's operated 81 retail supermarkets principally in the Metropolitan Detroit area under the tradename of Farmer Jack.
- During the fourth quarter of 1986, the Company acquired a 95% interest in Waldbaum's for $277 million in cash. Waldbaum's operated 139 retail supermarkets in New York, Connecticut, and Massachusetts.

Notes

1. The Great Atlantic & Pacific Tea Company, Inc., *1990 Annual Report to Shareholders, for the Fiscal Year Ending February 23, 1991,* p. 2.
2. The Great Atlantic & Pacific Tea Company, Inc., *Form 10-K,* for the Fiscal Year Ending February 23, 1991.
3. A&P, Inc., *1990 Annual Report to Shareholders,* p. 1.
4. "Consumer Expenditures Study," *Supermarket Business* (September 1991), p. 56.
5. K. J. Sack, *Industry Surveys,* Standard & Poor's (May 2, 1991), 159(17, 1), p. R88.
6. Ibid.
7. "Consumer Expenditures Study," p. 48.
8. Annual "Consumer Expenditures Study," *Supermarket Business* (printed in September of each year).
9. *1992 U.S. Industrial Outlook—Retailing,* U.S. Department of Commerce (January 1992).
10. Sack, pp. R87–R88.

11. T. Gutner, "Food Distributors," *Forbes* (January 6, 1991), p. 150.
12. Ibid.
13. Sack, p. R90.
14. Ibid.
15. Ibid.
16. Ibid.
17. Ibid.
18. Ibid.
19. Ibid., pp. R90–R91.
20. "Industry's Union Membership Drops; Wage Rise Highest Since '83," *Supermarket Business* (October 1991), p. 9.
21. "McDonald's Tests Grocery Sales, But Supermarkets Aren't Worried," *Supermarket Business* (April 1991), p. 11.
22. M. Duff, "Kmart Plunges Feet First into Food," *Supermarket Business* (October 1991), p. 32.
23. Ibid., p. 31.
24. K. Partch, "The Dutch Are Coming (Again)," *Supermarket Business* (June 1991), p. 21.
25. *1991 U.S. Industrial Outlook—Retailing,* U.S. Department of Commerce (January 1991), pp. 40–44.
26. "Grocery Store Industry," *Value Line Investment Survey, Part 3, Ratings and Reports* (August 23, 1991), Edition 10, p. 1498.
27. *1990 U.S. Industrial Outlook—Retailing,* U.S. Department of Commerce (January 1990), pp. 41–45.
28. Sack, p. R90.
29. *1990 U.S. Industrial Outlook—Retailing,* pp. 41–45.
30. "The Largest U.S. Industrial Corporations," *Fortune* (April 22, 1991), p. 286.
31. Gutner, p. 148.
32. "Grocers Among Top Violators of Child Labor Laws," *Supermarket Business* (August 1991), p. 7.
33. Ibid.
34. "Criminal Penalties Proposed for Unsafe Working Conditions," *Supermarket Business* (October 1991), p. 9.
35. "NGA Protests Labeling Proposal," *Supermarket Business* (January 1991), p. 7.
36. Sack, p. R89.
37. "Grocery Store Industry."
38. *1991 Industrial Outlook—Retailing.*
39. "Grocery Store Industry."
40. "The Quarterly Economic Review," *The Value Line Investment Survey* (January 3, 1992), p. 471.
41. L. Harper, "Index Shows Sluggishness Is Widespread," *Wall Street Journal* (January 2, 1992), p. 2.
42. I. L. Kellner, "One Step Ahead," *Boardroom Reports* (January 15, 1992), 21(2), p. 2.
43. Harper, p. 2.
44. T. Herman, "Economists Predict Bleak Winter, Then Mild Recovery," *Wall Street Journal,* (January 2, 1992), p. 2.
45. J. Spiers, "Fortune Forecast: Areas Where Prospects Are Best," *Fortune* (January 27, 1992), p. 21.
46. J. R. Wilke, "New England's Economy Heads South," *Wall Street Journal* (December 10, 1991), p. A2.
47. Spiers, pp. 21–22.
48. J. Urquhart, "Canada's Gross Domestic Product Rose Just 0.1% in October from Month Earlier," *Wall Street Journal* (December 26, 1991), p. 2.
49. The Great Atlantic & Pacific Tea Company, Inc., *Form 10-K,* for the Fiscal Year Ending February 24, 1990, p. 1.
50. A&P, Inc., *1990 Annual Report to Shareholders,* inside front cover.
51. A&P, Inc., *Form 10-K* (1991).
52. A&P, Inc., *Form 10-K* (1990), p. 1.
53. A&P, Inc., *1990 Annual Report to Shareholders,* p. 9.
54. The Great Atlantic & Pacific Tea Company, Inc., *1989 Annual Report to Shareholders, for the Fiscal Year Ending February 24, 1990,* p. 30.
55. A&P, Inc., *1990 Annual Report to Shareholders,* p. 1.
56. A&P, Inc., *1989 Annual Report to Shareholders,* p. 4.
57. Ibid., p. 5.
58. A&P, Inc., *Form 10-K* (1990).
59. A&P, Inc., *1990 Annual Report to Shareholders,* p. 5.
60. Ibid., p. 9.
61. Ibid., p. 10.
62. A&P, Inc., *1989 Annual Report to Shareholders,* p. 1.
63. A&P, Inc., *1990 Annual Report to Shareholders,* pp. 1–2.
64. Ibid., p. 2.
65. Ibid., pp. 2–3.
66. A&P, Inc., *1989 Annual Report to Shareholders,* p. 3.
67. A&P, Inc., *1990 Annual Report to Shareholders,* p. 6.
68. A&P, Inc., *1990 Annual Report to Shareholders.*
69. A&P, Inc., *Form 10-K* (1990).
70. A&P, Inc., 1990 Annual Report to Shareholders, p. 2.

Casey's General Stores, Inc.

J. David Hunger and Phanos L. Pitiris

Donald Lamberti, founder and Chairman of the Board of Casey's General Stores, looked over the audience, smiled, and stepped to the microphone to address the Iowa Society of Financial Analysts on February 10, 1993. The six-month financial results were encouraging, and Lamberti knew that he had a good story to tell. The audience seemed to be receptive, but wasn't sure how long Casey's success would last. After all, the convenience store industry seemed to have reached maturity. Larger companies, such as 7-Eleven, Circle K, and National Convenience Stores, were either in bankruptcy or just emerging from it and were closing or selling stores by the hundreds. Petroleum companies were increasingly converting their well-located service stations to self-service convenience stores offering low-priced gasoline to attract customers. How could a midsized regional convenience store chain without a petroleum partner survive in a price war?

Lamberti wasn't worried in the slightest by these developments in the industry. Some argued that the 7-Elevens and Circle Ks of the industry were mismanaged, overextended, and suffering the consequences. Lamberti personally believed that his company was positioned in a niche that few could successfully attack. He told the analysts: "Eighty percent of our stores are in towns of 5,000 people or less." (Only 6% percent of the stores were located in communities with populations over 20,000.) He liked it that way because it made for better gasoline business. "There are a lot of cars in rural families. Mom, dad, son, daughter, they travel in all directions—greater distances—and they like to buy gas where they live if the price is right." The major oil companies had been closing or selling their gas stations in small towns so they could expand in metropolitan areas. In some towns, Casey's was now the only gas station.

Lamberti announced to the analysts that Casey's currently had 819 stores in eight Midwestern states and that the number should reach 1,000 by the end of 1996. In a companywide renovation program, stores were being expanded to allow more space for remodeled restrooms and a wider array of products, ranging from dog food to shotgun shells. With the renovation program nearing completion, new store construction would soon increase. The company was in the process of building 50 new stores in 1993 and planned to add at least one new store a week in 1994. He added that the company's territory could accommodate as many as 2,000 stores. "We are positioned for growth in the short- and long-term," asserted Lamberti.

This case was written by Professor J. David Hunger of Iowa State University and Phanos L. Pitiris of Elli Computers, with the research assistance of Kendra Fulk. This case appears in the Spring 1994 issue of *Business Case Journal*.

Jim Lawless, financial analyst of the *Des Moines Register*, had some reservations. He commented in a subsequent newspaper article:

> The jury is still out on the impact that the boss of Casey's General Stores, Inc. made on financial analysts Wednesday. There was a glowing outlook projection in terms that analysts are used to hearing. . . . But how do you weigh the effect on the bottom line of a company whose chief boasts, "Our customers don't have to ask for a key to the restroom anymore."[1]

Background

In 1935, Dominic Lamberti, an immigrant from Piandelogatti, Italy, started a small business in Des Moines, Iowa, delivering ice and coal door to door. At that time, nobody could suspect the key role it would play in the establishment of Casey's, the sixteenth largest convenience chain in North America.

Eventually, Lamberti opened a store that offered fuel oil, gasoline, coal, ice, and groceries. Lamberti Ice & Fuel had become a reality. His son, Donald Lamberti, graduated from the American Institute of Business in Des Moines. However, he was forced to abandon his plans for an accounting degree at Drake University and to take over management of the store because of his father's ill health. In reflecting on this time in his life, Donald Lamberti said: "My father's small grocery store was the forerunner to today's modern convenience store. I learned the importance of having a store that is spotlessly clean and operated by friendly, helpful people."[2]

In 1967, Kurvin C. Fish, a salesman for Northwestern Refining Company, the company that sold gasoline to Lamberti, approached Don Lamberti with a plan to purchase four service stations, including one in Boone, Iowa, from the Square Deal Company of Ames, Iowa. The proposal required Fish to provide the management and Lamberti the capital: $40,000 down on a total cost of $200,000, plus a $40,000 loan from the bank to change the Boone service station into a convenience store.[3] They closed the deal and changed the company's name to Casey's—from the first two initials (KC) of Fish's name. Lamberti and Fish opened their first Casey's store in July 1968 in Boone, Iowa.

The store was so successful that it enabled the two men to open four additional stores in the following two years. Northwestern Refining's dealer assistance program played a significant role in this initial expansion. Nevertheless, in 1970 when Ashland Oil acquired Northwestern, the capital dried up. Lamberti tried to finance new stores one by one, funding each with a loan from a different local bank. That proved to be time-consuming, and the two men, impatient to expand faster, decided to franchise new stores. Although the company would earn less money from a franchised store than from a company-owned store (the typical franchisee pays to the franchisor a royalty that is a percentage of store sales, regardless of profits), franchising would enable the company to expand much faster.

During the 1970s, the company grew from four stores to almost three hundred stores, with the majority of them located in small towns of Iowa and neighboring states. In 1980, Kurvin Fish retired. In 1983, the company went public with an initial stock offering that raised $10 million. In 1985, another $21 million of public stock was offered, which enabled the company to close the doors to new franchisees. As of April 30, 1992, Casey's operated 799 stores in Iowa, Nebraska, Kansas, Illinois, Minnesota, Wisconsin, and South Dakota. The company owned or leased 597 of these stores and franchisees owned 202.

Casey's mission was stated clearly in the company's *1989 Annual Report* and reaffirmed by Donald Lamberti in a 1992 interview:

- To provide clean stores, courteous service, quality products and competitive prices, at conveniently located sites.
- To provide a work environment where employees are treated with respect, dignity and honesty, and where high performance is expected and rewarded.
- To provide shareholders with a fair return on investment.

The specifics of how the corporation achieved this mission were spelled out in the corporation's *1992 Form 10-K Report:*

> Casey's General Stores seek to meet the needs of residents of small towns by combining features of both general store and convenience store operations. Smaller communities often are not served by national-chain convenience stores. The company has been successful in operating Casey's General Stores in small towns by offering, at competitive prices, a broader selection of products than a typical convenience store.

The company started in a small town and planned to remain in small towns. Don Lamberti, CEO and Chairman of the Board, emphatically stated in May 1990: "I would like to see a Casey's in every town of 1,000 people. Small towns are where we started. They've been good to us, and small towns are where we will stay."[4] Furthermore, in 1992 Lamberti asserted that the company's objective was to have 1,000 stores by 1996, with total sales of $1 billion. To achieve this objective meant adding 50 new stores in 1993 and 50–60 each in 1994, 1995, and 1996.[5]

The Convenience Store Industry in North America

The convenience store was a typical American phenomenon. It offered customers conveniently located stores where people could quickly find and purchase a necessity, such as bread or milk. Operating contrary to the supermarket or mass merchandiser, the convenience store offered fewer goods at higher prices. As small "mom and pop" grocery/general merchandise stores in neighborhoods and small towns were replaced by shopping centers containing huge Wal-Marts and Safeways far from these towns or neighborhoods, a market vacuum was created. Convenience stores stepped into this vacuum and justified their higher prices and limited selection in terms of saving time and making shopping easy. In contrast to many grocery stores in the 1950s, which were open only from 9:00 A.M. to 6:00 P.M., convenience stores opened earlier and closed later.

By the early 1990s, the convenience store industry in the United States and Canada faced maturity. In 1991 (and for the first time in the industry's history) net convenience store unit growth was nonexistent.[6] At the beginning of 1992, the number of stores was the same (84,500 units) as in 1990. This plateau was a significant change from the earlier years of rapid growth. For example, from 1982 to 1986, the number of convenience stores had increased from 54,000 to 76,000. During the next five years, however, the number had increased from 80,000 in 1987 to only 84,500 in 1991. The explosive growth of convenience stores during the early 1980s had far outpaced population growth.[7] Half the 50 largest chains operated fewer stores in 1991 than they did in 1990. With the stagnant 1992–1993 economy, the number of stores was not expected to increase anytime soon.

From 1987 through 1990, total industry sales were $72.4, $82.5, $93.2, and $103.5 billion, respectively. Total sales grew slightly in 1991 to $104 billion, primarily because of strong gasoline sales and the aggressive beer and cigarette merchandising. According to the National Association of Convenience Stores, annual pretax profits in the industry had peaked in 1986 at $1.4 billion and had dropped thereafter.[8] Kyle Krause, Vice-President of Krause Gentle Corporation, which owned the Kum & Go convenience store chain, agreed: "As the market matures, it won't be easy to make the dollars. Just because you grow doesn't mean you grow profitably."[9]

Lower profits also reflected the rising costs of labor and capital and the expense of complying with new Environmental Protection Agency rules for petroleum storage tanks and underground lines. Mandated minimum wage increases contributed to the problem. According to President F. Higgins of Minit Mart Foods, "As far as labor goes, our problem will still be supply, not cost. But when you factor in the cost of rising health insurance, higher wages do present a problem. As a result, marginal stores will come under even more pressure."[10]

The convenience store industry was commonly broken into two categories for analysis: *traditional convenience stores,* such as the Southland Corporation with its 7-Eleven stores emphasizing general merchandise, and *petroleum marketers,* such as Mobil Corporation with its Mobil Mart stores emphasizing gasoline sales. Although the total number of convenience stores in the early 1990s generally remained stable from year to year, the mix of stores was definitely changing. For example, during 1991, traditional operators closed 1,000 stores, but petroleum marketers increased the number of their stores by the same number. Large traditional companies such as Southland Corporation, Circle K, and National Convenience Stores faced financial difficulties. All three of these corporations were in bankruptcy during the period 1990–1993 and were either selling or closing many stores in order to improve cash flow. Some midsized traditional chains such as Uni-Marts, Casey's General Stores, and QuikTrip, however, continued to grow steadily.

During the 1980s and early 1990s, most North American oil companies converted the service bays of their gas stations to merchandise areas when they made the stations "self-service" and stopped offering less profitable repair services. The oil companies often had a competitive advantage over the traditional convenience store in terms of location. "The gas stations simply have nicer stores at nicer locations," commented C. Vroom, a food retailing analyst. "The only traditional convenience stores that are going to do well are those with special products, or geographic niches."[11] Although a number of oil companies such as Coastal, Mapco, and Marathon had cut the number of their stores, others such as Texaco, Exxon, Atlantic Richfield, and Sun increased the number of their stores. At the beginning of 1992, the number of traditional stores was 51,000, and the number of petroleum marketer stores was 33,500. Of the 84,500 total stores, 16.6% were in the eastern United States, 43% in the southern United States, 22.1% in the midwestern United States, 15.1% in the western United States, and 3.2% in Canada.

Products

Superficially, convenience stores were an undifferentiated product. They tended to offer the same mix of products and services, regardless of name or location. "We are the worst thieves around," commented Ray Cox, Senior Vice-President at Circle K. "As soon as one of us finds something that works, the copycats go to work."[12] Nevertheless, many industry observers contended that the key to success in maintaining a profitable convenience store during the 1990s was tailoring offerings to specific markets. "You have to study your market and judge each convenience store individually. Area and location play a significant role for the product mix in the convenience store. You have to know your market and what your customers want," explained W. Englefield, President and CEO of Englefield Oil Company.[13]

Over the period 1987–1991, gasoline sales gradually increased as a percentage of total industry sales from 44.6% to 57.2%. In part, this increase reflected the changing proportion of petroleum retailers in the convenience store industry. Almost 100% of the petroleum marketers sold gasoline, whereas only 65.6% of the traditional stores had gas pumps on their premises. In addition, petroleum marketers usually devoted more space to the dispensing of fuel and less space to in-store merchandise. For example, the average annual sales of in-store merchandise of a petroleum marketer was only $430,000 in 1991, compared to $590,000 for a traditional convenience store. In contrast, the average petroleum marketer pumped 981,000 gallons of gasoline in 1991, compared to 661,000 gallons by the average traditional convenience store. During 1991, although petroleum retailers' gross margin on gasoline sales held steady at 9%, the margin for traditional stores dropped 1% to 8%. Both categories of stores had been pouring large amounts of money into upgrading their underground gasoline storage tanks to comply with environmental regulations. The typical company spent approximately $45,000–$48,000 per gas site during 1991—a significant increase over 1990 and a primary reason for the recent closure of a large number of convenience stores.

The percentage of total sales derived from in-store merchandise (everything except gasoline) dropped from 55.4% in 1987 to 46.2% in 1989 to 42.8% in 1991. In fact, total in-store merchandise sales declined from $45.6 billion in 1990 to $44.5 billion in 1991. Even though the sales of beer/wine/liquor, soft drinks, and tobacco increased, grocery sales fell from $3.4 billion in 1990 to $2.5 billion in 1991, and health and beauty aids sales shrank to $1.05 billion from $1.3 billion. Price-sensitive consumers now appeared to be relying more on discounters and supermarkets for groceries and health and beauty aids. Aggressive merchandising by traditional stores boosted the unit sales of cigarettes from 16.7% to 20.3% of merchandise sales. Although 84% of all convenience stores sold beer, the average beer transaction dropped from $5.19 to $4.07 at traditional stores and increased from $3.81 to $4.48 at petroleum marketers from 1990 to 1991. (See Exhibit 7.1 for a list of in-store merchandise items for both traditional and petroleum stores in terms of average sales, profits, and gross margins.)

With overall in-store merchandise sales shrinking, the average number of products offered in traditional stores dropped from 3,400 in 1989 to 3,100 in 1991. The number offered by petroleum marketers (with their smaller stores) remained steady at 2,300 items. The average merchandise transaction for a traditional store dropped from a high of $3.50 in 1990 to $3.00 in 1991. In contrast, the average transaction for a petroleum marketer only dropped five cents to $2.80 during the same period.

Although there had been a recent trend toward offering fast food and various services, such as copy machines and automatic teller machines, sales of these services declined somewhat in 1991 because of strong competition from other retail stores and the decline in the number of traditional stores (which had more in-store space than did petroleum marketers for offering these types of goods and services). Many convenience stores had added fast food to their merchandise mix in the mid 1980s. According to Kirby LeBof, President of the National Association of Convenience Stores, "The movement into fast foods is obvious. Many started with beverages like soft drinks and coffee, then got into microwave foods. Now many are trying to differentiate themselves with delis and on-premise cooking."[14] Generally, the industry was divided into two approaches to fast food: chains focusing on self-service and labor-saving equipment versus chains serving higher quality products by investing in the labor required to run a competitive food service program.[15]

Operations

The average traditional convenience store measured 2,500 square feet of inside space. The average petroleum marketer's store measured 1,900 square feet. Although 66% of petroleum marketers had 24-hour operations (no change since 1987), the number of traditional stores open all night dropped from 80% in 1987 to 50% in 1991.

The typical convenience store at the beginning of 1992 employed four full-time and three part-time people. Increasingly, convenience stores had difficulty attracting and retaining competent workers. Throughout North America, there was a shortage of labor willing to work at the lower end of the wage scale, which

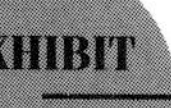

EXHIBIT 7.1

Merchandise Items for All Convenience Stores as a Percentage of Sales and Profits, and in Terms of Gross Margin

	Traditional			Petroleum		
	Percent of Merchandise			Percent of Merchandise		
	Sales	Profits	Gross Margin	Sales	Profits	Gross Margin
Food Items						
Beer/wine/liquor	13.2%	12.0%	25.0%	13.2%	11.3%	24.0%
Bottled/canned drinks	10.7	10.8	33.0	13.9	14.6	35.0
Prepared foods	8.6	9.5	46.0	6.4	8.4	46.0
Fountain/slush/coffee	7.8	10.3	60.0	7.5	10.1	59.0
Candy	6.2	7.0	41.0	7.2	8.1	38.0
Milk/dairy	6.7	5.4	22.0	3.6	2.8	22.0
Grocery	6.0	6.4	35.0	4.8	5.3	33.0
Packaged salted snacks	4.3	4.5	36.0	4.9	4.8	35.0
Packaged baked goods	3.4	3.3	29.0	2.0	2.1	33.0
Packaged ice cream	1.8	2.0	37.0	1.3	1.6	33.0
Packaged meats/deli	1.6	1.8	38.0	1.2	1.2	33.0
Ice	0.8	1.0	59.0	0.7	1.1	61.0
Other food Items	0.7	0.7	36.0	0.5	0.5	32.0
Nonfood Items						
Tobacco	20.3%	17.6%	25.0%	25.3%	21.1%	22.0%
Periodicals	3.4	2.7	21.0	1.5	1.1	22.0
Health and beauty care	2.6	2.8	38.0	1.9	1.8	37.0
Other nonfood items	1.0	1.0	38.0	2.1	2.1	36.0
Services	0.9%	1.2%	51.0%	2.0%	2.0%	32.0%
Total/Average	100.0%	100.0%	34.0%	100.0%	100.0%	32.0%

Note: Figures are based on 510 responses from representative firms.

Source: *Convenience Store News: 1992 Industry Report,* p. 24.

was what the convenience stores were able to pay. As a result, employee turnover always has been a significant problem. Firms in this industry usually considered any increase in the minimum wage a threat because of the impact of labor costs on profits. According to *Convenience Store News: 1992 Industry Report,* a combination of improved human resource programs and the recession's impact on employment slowed turnover in convenience stores during 1991.[16] At traditional stores, annual manager turnover declined from 25% a year earlier to

EXHIBIT 7.2

Average Companywide Expenses for All Convenience Stores

	Traditional		Petroleum	
Expense	1990	1991	1990	1991
Cost of goods sold	68%	72%	71%	77%
Payroll	12	11	12	8
Administrative	4	4	3	5
Rent/lease	4	4	3	2
Property operation	3	3	2	2
Depreciation	2	2	3	2
Property insurance	2	1	2	1
Advertising/promotion	1	1	2	1
Interest	2	1	1	1
Other expenses	2	1	1	1

Note: Figures are based on 510 responses from representative firms.

Source: *Convenience Store News: 1992 Industry Report*, p. 72.

15%, and clerk turnover declined from 101% to 81%. For petroleum marketers, turnover dropped from 19% to 12% for managers and from 93% to 89% for clerks. An improvement in the economy would likely increase turnover as better paying opportunities developed. The average salary for managers was $21,500 for traditional stores and $19,200 for petroleum marketers. The average clerk earned $4.70 and $4.50 per hour at traditional and petroleum stores, respectively.

As noted in Exhibit 7.2, the cost of goods sold category for the average convenience store increased as a percentage of total costs and expenses from 1990 to 1991. Stores were being increasingly pressured to improve the efficiency of their operations at a time when the market was becoming less interested in their higher margin in-store merchandise. Nevertheless, when *Convenience Store News* asked convenience store executives in early 1992 to indicate their companies' plans for the future, most anticipated growth. Over half the executives anticipated either building or acquiring new stores. Only 38% of traditional executives and 18% of petroleum marketers said "no" to expansion. Detailed responses are presented in Exhibit 7.3.

Customers

Many believed that convenience stores originally gained popularity as an increasing number of two-income and single-parent families tried to perform the most chores in the least time. According to John Rosco, a former convenience store operator,

EXHIBIT 7.3

Percentages of Convenience Store Executives Who Planned Expansion in 1992

Type of Expansion	Traditional	Petroleum
Build new stores	29%	46%
Acquire other stores	30	38
Expand food service departments	24	27
Expand current stores	15	41
Add food service departments	12	12
Add gasoline pumps	11	9
No planned expansion	38	18

Note: Figures include multiple responses and are based on 510 responses from representative firms.

Source: *Convenience Store News: 1992 Industry Report,* p. 76.

"the idea was that there were a lot of people who believed that their time was worth more than their money." These were key customers for convenience stores. Times had changed, however, felt Rosco. The vast majority of customers now "consider their money to be at least as important as their time, if not more so."[17]

Convenience stores' most loyal customers had always been working-class males. Unfortunately, the size of this group was declining.[18] Convenience stores thus had to broaden their appeal and invigorate their marketing to keep sales from falling. However, attracting women into the stores was difficult. The convenience store's reputation as a target of choice for armed robbery (because of its long hours and the usual presence of cash in the register) had not helped the typical store's image.

By the end of the 1980s, American convenience store operators were seriously considering worldwide growth opportunities. Both traditional chains and petroleum marketers agreed that abundant opportunities existed in other countries. They felt that Americans were not the only people on earth willing to pay a little extra to save time. The American convenience store format was extremely popular in many parts of the world, especially when compared to many types of native retail methods. Unfortunately, the chains that had taken the international route to growth, such as 7-Eleven and Circle K, found themselves having to sell their foreign holdings during the early 1990s to obtain needed cash.

Environmental Issues

The U.S. Environmental Protection Agency (EPA) identified one of the major problems with which the industry had to deal. The EPA (along with several state agencies, including Iowa's) required the operators and owners of underground petroleum storage tanks to notify state and local officials of the location, size, type, age, and contents of the tanks. More recently, regulations called on companies to upgrade certain tanks to meet specific technical standards, to undertake certain release prevention and detection efforts, and to abate known releases from underground storage tanks.[19] More specifically, some of these regulations dictated that any underground tank that was 25 or more years old (or of an unknown age) be replaced within a year. Iowa approved a revised law that classified underground storage tanks as high or low risk and set standards for licensing, monitoring, and cleaning them up.[20] Illinois required the use of fiberglass instead of steel for fuel-storage tanks. Partially as a result of the huge expense involved in digging up and replacing storage tanks (in many instances falling totally on the individual operator), at least 25% of the gas stations in Illinois and 15% of the gas stations in the Midwest closed during the period 1990–1992.[21]

Major Competitors

The original convenience stores always have faced strong competition, not only among themselves, but also from small stores selling "necessities," gas stations, 24-hour supermarkets, and (more recently) fast-food retailers. The targeting of the convenience store industry by oil companies during the 1980s had made the entire industry far more competitive. In 1987, three of the top 15 companies in the convenience store industry had been owned by petroleum firms. In 1989, that number had increased to six and by 1992, the oil companies occupied nine of the top 15 positions!

In 1992, Southland Corporation was the largest in the industry with 6,491 stores. The second largest was Circle K Corporation with 3,400 stores. The next four were Mobil Corporation with 2,900 stores, Amoco Corporation with 2,350 stores, Texaco with 1,533 stores, and Chevron with 1,180 stores. Next were Dairy Mart, Emro Marketing (owned by Marathon Oil), Cumberland Farms, and Silcorp Ltd. Surprisingly, of the five largest traditional convenience store companies, three operated in bankruptcy during the early part of the decade: Southland, Circle K, and Cumberland Farms. National Convenience Stores, previously one of the largest traditional convenience store companies, also was in bankruptcy and had dropped from tenth largest in 1991 to eighteenth in 1992. (See Exhibit 7.4 for a list of the top 20 convenience stores in 1992.) Industry analysts predicted in early 1993 that large traditional convenience store chains would continue to face considerable competitive pressure from gas station minimarkets and all-night grocery stores. According to Barbara Wedelstaedt, an analyst with Duff & Phelps of Chicago, "We're still seeing consolidation," adding that the industry "will have to operate on much lower margins than before."[22]

Southland Corporation

Founded in 1927, the Southland Corporation is believed to have originated the convenience store concept. By 1992, the company operated 6,269 7-Eleven stores throughout the United States and Canada and 222 units operating as High's Dairy

Stores, Quick Mart stores, and Super-7 gas outlets. (Licensees and other affiliates operated another 6,995 7-Eleven stores in more than 18 countries around the world.) About 47% of its stores were franchised. The company also operated five distribution centers and six food centers, which serviced more than 70% of its wide-spread stores. Even though the company had sold or closed over 600 stores since 1989, it was still considered to be the largest convenience store chain in the world.

In 1987, the company went private in a $4.9 billion leveraged buyout and actively sold assets to pay down debts. In February 1990, the company sold 50% of its interest in Citgo Petroleum Corporation, which had been the oil and gas branch of the company for many years. Southland used the net proceeds of the transaction to reduce senior bank debt related to the leveraged buyout. Citgo continued to supply Southland's convenience retailing operations with Citgo brand gasoline under a long-term product purchase agreement.[23] Southland filed for bankruptcy in October 1990. Ito-Yokado Company, a successful operator of 7-Eleven convenience stores in Japan, purchased 70% of Southland for $430 million. After bondholders exchanged some $1.8 billion in debt for new notes and stock, Southland emerged from Chapter 11 in March, 1991. According to Toshifumi Suzuki, Vice-Chairman of Southland's Board of Directors and Executive Vice-President of Ito-Yokado, "They forgot what a convenience store is supposed to be."[24]

Losses turned to profits in 1991, but profits reverted to losses in 1992. Still, an Austin, Texas, experiment with brighter lighting, wider aisles, and a new inventory system, increased sales by 10%. In addition, the experiment increased the percentage of women shoppers from 25% to about 50%. The company continued to be respected in the industry for its size, but analysts doubted that 7-Eleven would ever return to its past successes.

Circle K

In 1992, Circle K was the second largest operator of convenience stores in North America. Founded in 1951 in El Paso, Texas, the company was now headquartered in Phoenix, Arizona. In the 1980s, the company expanded greatly: from 1,200 stores in 1980, it grew to 4,689 by 1989. The company also had licensing agreements and joint ventures in Japan, Hong Kong, Indonesia, Canada, the United Kingdom, Finland, and Australia. Nevertheless, the corporation's aggressive acquisition program had led to financial trouble. The buying spree had left the company in chaos, with old operations left unconsolidated. In some cases, the company owned stores directly across the street from each other. Headquarters also increased prices and forced stores to take high-margin items that few people purchased. The company operated under a $1 billion debt load, and its stock plunged to $3. The company filed for bankruptcy protection under Chapter 11 in the spring of 1990.

By 1992, Circle K was down to 3,400 stores, located primarily in the southern United States. New management had dumped unprofitable stores and worked to refurbish the remaining units in order to climb out of bankruptcy. Nevertheless,

EXHIBIT 7.4 Largest Convenience Store Companies in North America, 1992

Company/Headquarters	Key Chain(s)	Total Stores	Company Operated	Franchise/ Dealer Operated	Number with Gas
1. SOUTHLAND, Dallas	7-Eleven, High's Dairy Stores, Quik Mart, Super 7	6,491	3,446	3,045	2,380
2. CIRCLE K, Phoenix	Circle K Food Stores	3,400	3,375	25	2,966
3. MOBIL, Fairfax, Va.	Mobil Mart	2,900	2,500	400	2,900
4. AMOCO, Chicago	Amoco Food Shops, Split Second	2,350	300	2,050	2,350
5. TEXACO, Houston	Food Mart, Star Mart	1,533	1,533	0	1,533
6. CHEVRON, San Francisco	Chevron Food Mart	1,180	527	653	1,180
7. DAIRY MART, Enfield, Conn.	Dairy Mart	1,134	685	449	432
8. EMRO, Springfield, Ohio	Speedway, Starvin' Marvin, Bonded, Cheker, Gastown, ECOL, Port	1,102	1,102	0	1,102
9. CUMBERLAND FARMS, Canton, Mass.	Cumberland Farms	973	973	0	650
10. SILCORP, Mississauga, Ontario	Mike's Mart, La Maissonee, Mac's, Hop-In Food Stores	970	866	104	207

11. DILLON, Hutchinson, Kan.	Kwik Shop, Quik Stop, Loaf n' Jug, Mini Mart, Turkey Mill Minit Markets, Tom Thumb Food Stores, Time Saver	938	842	96	776
12. SHELL, Houston	Food Mart	900	n/a	n/a	900
13. BP, Cleveland	BP Shop	872	872	0	872
14. COASTAL, Houston	Coastal Mart	860	520	340	860
15. ATLANTIC RICHFIELD, Los Angeles	am/pm	838	few	most	832
16. CASEY'S Ankeny, Iowa	Casey's General Stores	800	600	200	800
17: DIAMOND SHAMROCK, San Antonio	Corner Stores	764	764	0	764
18. NATIONAL CONVENIENCE STORES, Houston	Stop N Go	755	755	0	667
19. EXXON, Houston	Exxon Shop, Tiger Mart, Exxon Food Store	740	350	390	740
20. GETTY, Jericho, NY	GettyMart	735	166	569	735

Note: Petroleum marketers that also have stores run by jobbers: AMOCO (4,000), Texaco (4,476), Chevron (3,080), and Diamond Shamrock (1,155).

Source: *Convenience Store News: 1992 Industry Report,* p. 86.

according to Bart Brown, Chairman and Chief Executive Officer, the corporation planned eventually to shrink to fewer than 2,600 stores.[25] Unfortunately, even significant retrenching might not be enough to save the company. Four states were suing Circle K in 1993, charging that, at nearly 450 of the 900 abandoned locations, leaking underground gasoline storage tanks had contaminated groundwater. The cleanup could cost as much as $100 million and jeopardize the reorganization plan.

Mobil, Amoco, Texaco, and Chevron

The four largest petroleum company-owned convenience store chains, especially Texaco's and Chevron's, continued to grow through acquisitions and new-store construction. Mobil and Texaco operated throughout the United States, whereas Amoco was strongest in the Midwest and South and Chevron was strongest in the West and South. Texaco had introduced Dunkin' Donuts and Subway sandwich shops in selected stores. Chevron was in the midst of developing a new and larger convenience store prototype that would enable the chain to offer a wider product mix, such as Taco Bell fast food.

Regional and Local Competitors

Aside from 7-Eleven and several petroleum marketers, few convenience store chains operated throughout North America. Most focused on particular regions. For example, Circle K operated primarily in the southern United States. Dairy Mart (seventh largest chain) operated in an 11-state area from Massachusetts west to Indiana and south to Tennessee and North Carolina. Cumberland Farms (ninth largest) was located in 12 states in the East from Massachusetts to Florida. Silcorp, the tenth largest convenience store chain in North America in 1992, had 908 stores in Canada and 62 Hop-In stores in Michigan. However, analysts speculated that more than 200 of Silcorp's Canadian stores would soon be closed or sold, stemming from the company's filing for bankruptcy protection under Canada's Companies' Creditors Arrangement Act (CCAA).

In its eight-state marketing area, Casey's competed with numerous national and regional companies. 7-Eleven operated in cities and large towns. Petroleum marketers, such as Texaco, Amoco, Shell, Conoco, Phillips 66, Total, and Holiday operated throughout the area but were located primarily in the larger towns and along interstate highways. Dillon Companies, headquartered in Hutchinson, Kansas, operated 938 traditional convenience stores in 16 states under the Kwik Shop, Quik Shop, Loaf N' Jug, Mini Mart, Turkey Hill Minit Market, Tom Thumb Food Store, and Time Saver names. Other large traditional regional companies that competed in one or more states in Casey's marketing area were Convenient Food Mart of Schaumburg, Illinois, with 420 stores; QuikTrip Corporation of Tulsa, Oklahoma, with 300 stores; White Hen Pantry of Elmhurst, Illinois, with 387 stores in the Midwest and New England; E-Z Mart Stores of Texarkana, Texas, with 325 stores in Arkansas, Texas, Oklahoma, Louisiana, and Kansas;

Kwik Trip of La Crosse, Wisconsin, with 226 stores in Wisconsin, Minnesota, and Iowa; and Tom Thumb Food Markets of Hastings, Minnesota, with 173 stores in the upper Midwest. In addition, smaller regional chains such as Kum N Go, with under 200 stores, Four Sons with about 30 Handy Shops stores, and Pronto, with about 60 stores, competed with Casey's in its marketing area.[26]

In particular, Quik Trip Corporation of Tulsa, Oklahoma, was a strong and growing competitor of Casey's. Operating in the six-state area of Oklahoma, Kansas, Missouri, Iowa, Georgia, and Illinois, the company increased the number of its stores from 284 in 1990 to 300 in 1991. Future growth was expected in the St. Louis and Atlanta metropolitan areas. President Chester Cadieux wanted to redefine the chain to match "the mind set of a petroleum marketer" because petroleum marketers "are on the winning team, and I want to be on the winning team. . . . Our strategy is to focus on the core categories and be in the commodities business. That's where we've focused. . . . You have to decide if you are going to be in the convenience business and rely on convenience to drive sales or whether you are going to accept, as we have, that those core category items are basically commodities and price is very, very, important."[27]

Local "mom and pop" grocery/general merchandise stores and gas/service stations that sold "necessities" also competed with Casey's in small towns. In the past, small-town gas stations provided mainly fuel and repair services for cars. The shift in technology from primarily mechanically to electronically dependent cars had a negative impact, however, on their automobile service business. Less need for auto repair services forced the owners of small-town service stations to consider other options for better utilizing their locations. Unlike the major petroleum companies, which dropped repair services to convert to full-fledged convenience stores, small-town, independent dealers continued to offer repair services because they probably were the only local auto repair businesses. Their repair business also gave them a way to compete against the lower priced, but strictly fuel-only, self-service stations of the major petroleum firms. The profit squeeze in gasoline sales, however, did cause local independents to start selling products such as beer, milk, bread, and other high-margin sundries—thus becoming competitors of Casey's.

Competition in larger communities included local and national grocery and drug store chains, expanded gasoline stations, supermarkets, discount food stores, and traditional convenience stores. As Casey's (along with other convenience store chains) changed its in-store merchandise mix to include more prepared-food items, such as hot sandwiches and pizza, its stores were increasingly coming into competition with local restaurants and fast-food retailers, who aggressively defended their "turf."

Strategic Managers and Owners of Casey's

As with any entrepreneurial business, the founder, Donald Lamberti, has been (since the retirement of cofounder K. C. Fish) the primary strategic manager of Casey's General Stores. As the company grew and eventually sold stock to the general public, others became involved in strategic decision-making. Nevertheless, as of July 1992, Donald Lamberti was still the largest shareholder, with 1,777,728 shares of the company's common stock. The Board of Directors as a whole owned 21.81% of the stock. All except Donald Lamberti (16.05%), Ronald Lamb (3.27%), and Kenneth Haynie (1.92%) owned less than 1% of the corporation's common stock. Other shareholders owning more than 5% of the stock were Employees' Plan Trust (11.74%), College Retirement Equities Fund (5.97%), and Guardian Life Insurance Company of America (5.30%). The Employees' Plan Trust was an employee stock ownership plan (ESOP) funded by company contributions in money or stock, by which Casey's employees (including officers) who had completed one year of service received stock as part of their retirement plans.

Board of Directors

In 1993, the Board of Directors was composed of seven people, four of whom were members of the corporation's top management. The three outside directors were:

- **John R. Fitzgibbon,** age 70, a self-employed consultant who advised corporations regarding financial, personnel, and operational matters. A director of Casey's since 1983, Fitzgibbon had served as President, CEO, and Chairman of Iowa Des Moines National Bank (now Norwest) until 1985 and Vice-Chairman and CEO of First Group Companies of Des Moines from 1986 through 1988.
- **George A. Doerner,** age 74, an Iowa Agency Manager Emeritus for The Equitable Life Assurance Society of the United States, Des Moines. A director of Casey's since 1983, Doerner had served as Iowa Agency Manager from 1963 to 1981.
- **Kenneth H. Haynie,** age 59, a lawyer and shareholder in the Des Moines law firm of Ahlers, Cooney, Dorweiler, Haynie, Smith & Allbee, P.C. Haynie had been a director of Casey's since 1987.

The four management directors were Donald Lamberti, Ronald Lamb, Douglas Shull, and John Harmon. All directors were elected annually. The board had four standing committees: Executive Committee (Lamberti, Lamb, Fitzgibbon, and Doerner), Audit Committee (Shull, Fitzgibbon, Doerner, and Haynie), Compensation Committee (Fitzgibbon, Doerner, and Haynie), and Nominating Committee (Lamberti, Lamb, Shull, and Harmon).

At the annual Casey's shareholders meeting on September 18, 1992, shareholders voted to change the company's articles of incorporation to raise the maximum number of board members from seven to nine. Management indicated that raising the number of board members "would facilitate the orderly recruiting of director candidates and allow the Board to obtain the benefits of greater diversity of business backgrounds and experience to meet new challenges as they arise."[28]

Top Management

The top management group (corporate officers) of Casey's was composed of the following nine people.

Name	Age	Title	Years at Company
Donald Lamberti	55	Chairman and Chief Executive Officer	26
Ronald Lamb	57	President and Chief Operating Officer	17
Douglas Shull	50	Treasurer and Chief Financial Officer	6
Robert Bowersox	46	Vice-President—Transportation	17
Ronald Courson	50	Vice-President—Food Service	7
Robert Hood	49	Vice-President—Marketing	11
Cleo Kuhns	37	Vice-President—Store Operations	19
John Harmon	38	Secretary	17
Robert J. Myers	46	Vice-President—Property Management	4

The four managers (executive officers) who also served on the Board of Directors were Lamberti, Lamb, Shull, and Harmon.

- **Donald F. Lamberti** was a cofounder of the company. He served as President from 1975 until 1985, when he became Chief Executive Officer. Lamberti also served on the Board of Directors of Norwest Bank Iowa of Des Moines. During fiscal 1992, he received $452,444 in cash compensation, of which $200,000 was a bonus.
- **Ronald M. Lamb** started with the company in 1969 as a store manager. Before his election as Vice-President in 1976, he served as Operations Manager of the company. In September 1987, he assumed the title and responsibilities of Chief Operating Manager. In 1988, Lamb also became President. During fiscal 1992, he received $451,352 in cash compensation, of which $200,000 was a bonus.
- **Douglas K. Shull** was a certified public accountant and a principal in Shull & Co., Indianola, Iowa, from 1975 until joining Casey's as Treasurer in September 1987. He also served as Chief Financial Officer of the company. Shull & Co. had performed accounting and auditing services for Casey's and its officers since 1975. Shull had been associated with the accounting firm of Peat Marwick in Des Moines before forming his own accounting firm in 1975. During fiscal 1992, he received $201,588 in cash compensation, of which $80,000 was a bonus.
- **John G. Harmon** had been associated with the company since 1976. He served as Assistant Secretary from 1983 until his election as Secretary in September 1987. During fiscal 1992, he received $178,689 in cash compensation, of which $80,000 was a bonus.

Effective March 2, 1992, the corporation entered into new employment agreements with the executive officers (Lamberti, Lamb, Shull, and Harmon). For Lamberti, Lamb, and Shull, the terms were five years (with automatically renewed terms of three years for Lamberti and Lamb); for Harmon the term was three years. The terms of employment for Shull and Harmon would be extended for a three-year period in the event of a "change of control" of the corporation. Each agreement further provided for voluntary retirement at age 65 or upon reaching 59 years of age and having completed 25 years of employment with the company. However, the Board of Directors was empowered to extend an officer's employment on a year-to-year basis following age 65. In an interview April 24, 1992, Lamberti stated that he planned to retire in 1996. Ron Lamb is two years older than Lamberti, but Lamberti felt that he deserved the CEO spot. Thus Lamb will become CEO in 1996 "as things now stand," predicted Lamberti. Thinking about executive succession, Lamberti indicated that every top manager in the company had at least one backup to take over the job, if need be.

Operations and Facilities

The company supplied all company stores and over 90% of the franchised stores with groceries, fast food (including sandwiches prepared at the company's commissary in Creston, Iowa), health and beauty aids, and general merchandise from Casey's distribution center. The store managers ordered merchandise weekly from the distribution center in Ankeny by using a hand-held computer and transferring the information by telephone to the company's order entry computer. Company-owned trucks delivered weekly shipments from the distribution center. Headquarters polled every store every night to determine product sales and special needs. Management believed that the distribution center's efficient service area was 500 miles, which encompassed all the company's existing and proposed stores.[29]

Headquarters

In December 1989, the company had moved to its new consolidated headquarters on a 36-acre site in Ankeny, Iowa (15 miles north of Des Moines just off Interstate Highway 35). The facility included a two-story office building, distribution center, and vehicle maintenance center; it cost approximately $20 million.

The 140,000 square foot distribution center was three times the size of the previously leased facility in Des Moines. The new center featured state-of-the-art, automated product handling equipment and computerized control systems. Because the company owned a large fleet of cars and trucks, management believed that a vehicle maintenance service center would be an asset. This center occupied 20,000 square feet and combined operations that in the past had been conducted in separate locations. The new office building occupied 60,000 square feet and housed the corporate offices.[30]

The distribution center was built to serve a maximum of 1,200 stores. The facility was operating at 68% of its capacity in early 1993. Nevertheless, with a few modifications, the new facility could easily be upgraded to serve 2,000 stores.

In addition to the Ankeny facilities, the company owned a 10,000 square foot building on an eight-acre site in Creston, Iowa. It served as the commissary for preparation of the 12 different kinds of sandwiches sold in Casey's General Stores. After being frozen, the sandwiches were sent to the distribution center in Ankeny where they were stored and then shipped weekly to the stores. The facility produced 2.5 million sandwiches per year.[31]

Stores

Casey's General Stores units were free-standing, and, with a few exceptions to accommodate local conditions, conformed to standard construction specifications. The standard merchandising display layout had been designed to encourage customer traffic to flow throughout the stores. Store locations featured Casey's bright red and yellow pylon sign and building facade, both of which displayed the name and service mark of the company. Both company-owned and franchised stores offered substantially the same products and conformed to the same basic design. All of Casey's stores were open at least 16 hours a day, seven days a week. The majority of the stores were open from 7:00 A.M. to 11:00 P.M., although store hours could be adjusted to serve particular shopping patterns.[32]

During the fiscal year ending April 30, 1992, the aggregate investment in land, building, equipment, and initial inventory for a typical company store averaged $600,000. This amount represented an increase from $550,000 in 1991 and $280,000 in 1989 and reflected increases in store size (primarily in the kitchen and storage areas), the number of gasoline pumps (from one island in 1989), and the cost of materials. (For the industry as a whole, the cost for a typical new urban convenience store in 1988 was $773,300.)[33] According to Casey's management, a typical store generally was not profitable in its first year or two of operation owing to start-up costs, usually attaining representative levels of sales and profits during its third year of operation.[34] The standard building designed by the company was a preengineered steel-frame building mounted on a concrete slab. (The warehouse at company headquarters contained sufficient materials in one room to build or replace ten stores.[35]) The store design in 1992 measured 36 feet by 66 feet, with almost 1,300 square feet devoted to sales (no change in size since 1989), 500 square feet to the kitchen (up 100 square feet from 1989) and 575 square feet to storage and restrooms (up 115 square feet from 1989). Each store usually included two islands of gasoline pumps and storage tanks with a total capacity of 20,000 gallons of gasoline (compared to 16,000 gallons in 1989). The new stores were built with two restrooms because of customer demand. The company planned a 20-year life for a store before it would need to be remodeled or replaced.[36]

The kitchens were used for the preparation of items such as pizza, chicken, and sandwiches. Management had adopted the idea of "opening" the kitchen to the customers so they could see for themselves how the food was prepared and the quality of the kitchen equipment. According to Lamberti, "We are using this 'open kitchen' design concept in all new stores, and adding it to existing stores as they are remodeled."[37]

Management required that all stores maintain a bright and clean interior and provide a prompt checkout service. The company had committed $6 million to equip all stores with price scanners. After 250 of the stores had been converted to scanners, however, management placed the project on hold until it could learn whether employees could check out customers more quickly with scanners or manually. Casey's did not permit the installation of electronic games or sale of adult magazines in its store. Management believed that these policies created the positive, quality image required for success in the industry.

Franchisees

The corporation had franchised Casey's General Stores since 1970. In addition to generating income for the company, franchising had enabled Casey's to expand rapidly and to obtain desirable store locations from people who preferred to become franchisees to selling or leasing their locations to Casey's. As a result, the company had achieved operating efficiencies in its warehouse and distribution system and greater identification in its market area. As Casey's grew and became stronger financially, the advantages of franchising waned. Management, therefore, decided to grant a limited number of new franchises and only to existing franchisees. From 1983 to 1992, the percentage of company-owned stores had increased from 44% to 75% as the company gradually converted 124 franchised stores to company-owned stores by leasing or purchasing them.

Franchised stores generally followed the same operating policies as company-owned stores and were constantly subjected to supervision by the company to make sure that they followed the company's guidelines. Violation of any of the company's policies (e.g., clean-store requirements) was grounds for cancellation of a franchise agreement. When a franchisee wanted to sell a store, Casey's had first right of refusal. If the franchisee sold the store to someone else, Casey's reserved the right to decide whether to allow the new owner to use the Casey's name.

Although franchisees reserved the right to purchase products from any supplier, 95% of them bought their gasoline and 99% bought their groceries from Casey's. All franchisees paid the company a royalty fee of 3% of gross receipts from total store sales (subject to a minimum royalty fee of $300), excluding gasoline. Furthermore, Casey's assessed a royalty fee of $.018 per gallon on gasoline sales, although it had the right to increase this amount to 3% of retail gasoline sales. In addition, franchisees paid the company a sign and facade rental fee. According to the franchise agreement, Casey's had no authority over the prices charged by the franchisee. Finally, if the agreement between Casey's and the franchisee were terminated, the latter was not allowed to operate a convenience-type store in that area for the next two or three years.[38]

Casey's only wholesale sales were to franchised stores, to which the company sold groceries, prepared sandwiches, ingredients and supplies for donuts, sandwiches and pizza, health and beauty aids, general merchandise, and gasoline. The company made these sales (particularly gasoline sales) at narrow profit margins to increase franchised stores' competitiveness and increase Casey's sales to them.[39]

Products Offered by the Firm

Like any convenience store, Casey's divided its products into two categories: gasoline and grocery/general merchandise. Gross profit margins for prepared food items, which averaged approximately 50% during the three fiscal years 1990–1992, were significantly higher than the gross profit margin for retail sales of gasoline, which had averaged 8.2% in 1992 and 1991 (down from 9.2% in 1990, 9.0% in 1989, 12.0% in 1988, and 14.2% in 1987).[40]

Gasoline

All Casey's stores offered gasoline or gasohol for sale on a self-service basis. Stores located in Iowa, Nebraska, and Illinois sold primarily gasohol and, therefore, were able to take advantage of a tax break for such sales in those states. The gasoline and gasohol offered by the stores usually were sold under the Casey's name, although some franchised stores sold gasoline under a major oil company brand name.

Casey's purchased its gasoline from independent national and regional petroleum distributors. In response to a question, Mike Richardson, Advertising Manager of Casey's, stated that buying on the "spot" market was cheaper than having a long-term arrangement with a petroleum company. Although gasoline supplies might become scarce again someday, the company hadn't experienced any shortages in recent years.[41]

Gasoline sales were intensely competitive. Casey's competed with both independent and national brand gas stations, some of which had access to more favorable supply arrangements than did Casey's or the firms that supplied its stores. Management believed that the most direct competition for gasoline sales came from other self-service stores, some of which regularly offered noncash discounts, such as a "free" car wash or "miniservice." Casey's did not offer such discounts. In addition, management felt that Casey's competed for gasoline customers who regularly traveled outside their relatively small communities for shopping and employment purposes. Those customers generally were able to purchase gasoline while in nearby larger towns where retail gasoline prices often were lower. Hence Casey's attempted to offer gasoline at prices comparable to those in nearby larger towns and cities. One effect of this marketing strategy was the underpricing of local, independent gas stations. (See the section on Legal Considerations for more information.)

Approximately half of Casey's sales for the year ending April 30, 1992 came from retail sales of gasoline. Retail gasoline profit margins had a substantial impact on the company's net income. They could be adversely affected by factors beyond the control of the company, including oversupply in the retail gasoline market, uncertainty or volatility in the wholesale gasoline market (e.g., Persian Gulf crisis), and price competition from other gasoline marketers. Top management strongly believed that a significant amount of the company's nongasoline sales resulted from the patronage of customers primarily desiring to purchase gasoline. In an interview, Douglas Shull, Treasurer and Chief Financial Officer, emphasized the company's policy regarding gasoline sales and pricing: "We never want to be undersold in gasoline. We try to be at an equal level or less, but never undersold."

Grocery/General Merchandise

Each Casey's store usually carried over 2,500 food and nonfood items. This number was down from 1989 when each store reportedly carried more than 4,000 items.[42] The products offered were those normally found in a supermarket, except that the stores did not sell produce or fresh meats, and selection generally was limited to one or two well-known brands of each item stocked. Most staple foodstuffs were nationally advertised brands. Stores sold regional brands of dairy and bakery products, and approximately 94% of the stores offered beer. The nonfood items included tobacco products, health and beauty aids, school supplies, housewares, pet supplies, photo supplies, ammunition, and automotive products. In response to a question regarding the mix of merchandise in small towns versus larger cities, CEO Lamberti responded that the product mix was basically the same. He added that the product mix for small towns worked well at interstate highway locations.

During fiscal year 1992, Casey's purchased directly from manufacturers approximately 90% of the food and nonfood items sold from the company's distribution center. Casey's had no long-term contracts with any of its suppliers. According to management, "the absence of such contracts is customary in the industry for purchasers such as the company and enables Casey's to respond flexibly to changing market conditions."[43]

In December 1984, Casey's began marketing pizza "made from scratch" in its stores. By April 30, 1992, pizza was available in 750 (94%) of the stores. Top management believed that pizza was the company's most popular prepared-food product. The company continued to expand its prepared-food product line to include ham and cheese, beef, hot and mild sausage, and pork tenderloin sandwiches; pizza bread; garlic bread; and breakfast croissants. In addition, Casey's Crispy Fried Chicken, was available for take-out at 145 (18%) stores as of April 30, 1992. This number was down, however, from 226 (29%) of the stores in 1991. According to Donald Lamberti, in a typical day in 1991 Casey's sold 8,200 cinnamon rolls, 15,000 pizzas, 20,000 cookies, 123,300 cups of Folgers coffee, and 140,000 donuts![44]

Pizza and other prepared-food products were made on store premises with ingredients from Casey's distribution center. Pizza usually was available in three sizes with ten different toppings and was sold for take-out between 4:00 P.M. and 11:00 P.M. Furthermore, at selected store locations, the lunchtime menu consisted of pizza by the slice, sandwiches, pizza bread, and garlic bread.

The decision to add snack center items, freshly prepared donuts, and pizza to the company's product selection reflected management's strategy to promote high-profit-margin products that were compatible with convenience store operations. The company constantly experimented with new products at its stores. According to CEO Lamberti, Casey's wanted to "bring products to town that the town is deficient in." The company added pizza, for example, because towns with populations of less than 3,000 usually had no pizza restaurants. Videotape rental was another such offering. The company also considered installing ATM machines and post offices in the stores. Treasurer Douglas Shull explained top management's thinking: "The company's objective is to become the center of the small town. Casey's will be the Pizza Hut, the Kentucky Fried Chicken, the video store, the bank, and the gasoline station of small towns." By mid 1992, however, Casey's dropped videotapes because they had created clutter and had clogged the checkout lanes.[45]

In 1993, the company added its own private brand products. Stores were offering "Casey's" brand candy, motor oil, and charcoal briquettes. According to Donald Lamberti, "We were able to reduce the price on the charcoal by a dollar a bag" by going to the company label.[46]

The company decided whether to delete a product or add similar products by keeping track of warehouse shipments. Slow-moving goods with lower gross profits were dropped; fast-moving items were given more shelf space. When deciding whether to add a new product, top management first invited the 14 district managers to look at products that vendors were suggesting. If the district managers sensed that a particular item had profit potential, the company invited the supervisors to consider the product. If the supervisors agreed with the district managers, the company testmarketed the product in 25 stores. It then introduced successful products into the rest of the stores.

Marketing

An important part of the company's marketing strategy was to increase sales volume by competitive pricing on price-sensitive items. On items that were less price sensitive, the company's policy was to maintain—or in the case of franchised stores, to recommend—a companywide pricing structure in each store that was generally comparable to that of other convenience, gasoline, or grocery stores in the area. According to management, Casey's generally had been able to pass along cost increases by increasing the prices of products sold. Management attributed the company's ability to offer competitive prices to the centralized distribution system, purchasing practices that avoided dependence on jobbers and vendors by relying on a few large wholesale companies, and success in minimizing land, construction, and equipment costs.[47]

According to management, Casey's competitive advantage in the marketplace rests on several key factors:

> The company believes that the competitiveness of Casey's General Stores is based on price (particularly in the case of gasoline sales) as well as on a combination of store location, extended hours, a wide selection of name brand products, self-service gasoline facilities, and prompt checkout facilities.[48]

Store Location

Between 1988 and 1993, a period when the largest convenience store chains were retrenching, Casey's continued to expand.

Year	1988	1990	1992	1993
Stores	653	769	799	819

According to Donald Lamberti, the reason that new store growth had slowed recently was the EPA regulation that fuel storage tanks at the stores had to be upgraded to resist leakage. Casey's took advantage of this requirement by renovating each store when its fuel storage tank was replaced.[49]

Casey's convenience stores were located in the following states as of April 30, 1992.

State	Number of Stores	Number Franchised
Iowa	300	103
Missouri	209	35
Illinois	145	32
Kansas	70	5
Nebraska	32	10
Minnesota	27	15
South Dakota	15	1
Wisconsin	1	1
Total	799	202

The criteria set by the company for selection of the specific store site emphasized the population of the immediate area and the daily highway traffic volume. Management believed that, if there were no competing store, a Casey's General Store could operate profitably at a highway location in a community with a population of as few as 500.[50] Casey's was noted for placing its stores at the entrances (ends) of towns. Because three out of four of the company's stores were located in towns with less than 5,000 people and because many of these people worked in larger towns, high traffic volume was observed at the ends of the towns. According to Treasurer Douglas Shull:

> The policy of Casey's is that we want traffic by our stores and as a result of this, we try to place our stores at positions where there is traffic. . . . We want people to stop at our stores in the morning and buy their gas, their cigarettes and their coffee. We want them to stop again in the evening, after they return from work, and buy their dinner, their beer and their Coke.

Advertising and Promotion

Casey's primary approach to advertising was to locate its stores in extremely visible locations. An attractive Casey's—offering gasoline at a price competitive with that sold in larger cities plus coffee and donuts in the morning and milk, bread, and fresh pizza in the evening—was its own best advertisement. Television and newspaper ads had little value in the primarily rural areas that constituted the company's market.

Casey's did, however, rigorously promote its products. Besides specials, such as "three candy bars for $.99" printed on banners placed on store windows, the company's prepared-foods promotion included a free calendar for Casey's customers. This calendar featured artwork by a nationally syndicated newspaper cartoonist, and at the bottom of each page clip-out coupons offered discounts on various Casey's prepared-food items. In addition, in-store banners and displays—and a small amount of radio and television advertising—promoted the company and its prepared-food items.

Public Relations and Social Responsibility

Casey's formed a mutually beneficial partnership with the Des Moines Area Community College (DMACC) Foundation in Ankeny, and, as a result, in 1993 Casey's was constructing a complete Casey's store on the DMACC campus. The store was to serve 7,600 students and provide a training laboratory for DMACC students majoring in the college's retail and marketing programs. Casey's would manage the store and be responsible for providing merchandise and maintaining store equipment. All profits after expenses were to go into a scholarship fund in Casey's name to help marketing and culinary arts students pay for their education.

Moreover, management hoped that this partnership would provide well-trained store personnel, including candidates for manager and assistant manager positions.

The company's personnel also were prominent in local activities. Casey's focused financial and volunteer resources on the communities, including school-related activities, it served. Project Mainstreet was a program in which Casey's teamed with KCCI-TV in Des Moines to provide $1,000 cash awards to neighborhoods and communities that completed worthwhile community betterment projects.

Management encouraged employees to become involved in community and school affairs. The company was a leading sponsor of activities in support of needy children. Each year hundreds of Casey's employees helped raise funds for such activities.

Human Resources

As of April 30, 1992, Casey's had 2,553 full-time and 3,639 part-time employees, compared to 2,384 full-time and 3,677 part-time employees in 1989. The employees were not unionized, and there were no collective bargaining agreements between the company and any of its employees. The company had not experienced a strike in its history.

Structure

The Chief Operating Officer, assisted by the Vice-President of Store Operations, ultimately were responsible for all store operations, including those of franchisees. Three regional operations managers reported directly to the Vice-President of Store Operations. Fourteen district managers, with responsibility for an approximately equal number of stores, reported to one of the three regional operations managers. Each of the district managers was responsible for eight supervisors. Each of the 113 supervisors was responsible for the operations of approximately seven stores. The majority of store managers lived in the communities in which their Casey's stores were located.

Training and Development

The Human Resources Department, headed by the Director of Human Resources, trained store managers and other personnel. A central training facility was located at company headquarters in Ankeny. The Human Resources Department provided guidance and training in advertising and promotion, merchandising, accounting, record keeping, inventory control, and other operating and management procedures. New store managers were brought to the headquarters campus for a two-week intensive training program.

Top management supported a promote-from-within policy, thus providing the company's employees with incentives to stay and work hard for the company. Most district managers and store supervisors had previously worked as store managers. In an interview, Donald Lamberti proudly pointed out that Chief Operating Officer Ronald Lamb had started with the company as a store manager. Lamberti wanted employees to view the company as a family that would take care of its own. He and the other executives also believed that one of the company's great strengths was its employees—people from small towns who understood, believed in, and lived by the ethic of hard work. Scarcity of labor had never been a problem.

Corporate headquarters had a large, attractive child-development (day-care) center on its ground floor. It contained classrooms and play and nursery areas that could accommodate as many as 90 employees' children. The center was so attractive that it became part of visitors' tours. Lamberti referred to it as one of the most interesting parts of the new headquarters building. (Lamberti reportedly wanted this center in part for visits by his grandchildren.)

Legal Considerations

On December 4, 1990, Casey's was named defendant in a lawsuit filed by five Iowa retail petroleum dealers on behalf of an alleged class of such dealers. The complaint, filed in the U.S. District Court for the Southern District of Iowa (*Gilbert Bathkeet et al.* v. *Casey's General Stores, Inc.*), alleged that by selling gasoline at "very low prices" the company violated Federal antitrust laws and state unfair price discrimination laws and thereby interfered with the plaintiffs' prospective business opportunities.

Even though top management denied that it was trying to drive local operators out of business, the lawsuit put Casey's in an unusual position, according to an article in the *Des Moines Register:* that of "the big, bad chain from out of town.

While Casey's has worked to cultivate its image as the friendly neighborhood store, some critics see the Ankeny-based store as the Iowa equivalent of Wal-Mart—the company that puts everyone else out of business."[51] According to Ed Kistenmacher, a lobbyist for the station operators, "I think there's some of that. [Casey's stores] have economic superiority in those smaller towns. It's a management decision on how they use that."

The controversy dated back to 1988 when Casey's changed the way it priced gasoline. The chain had been losing market share since 1983 even though its gas prices were the lowest in town, explained CEO Lamberti. What management finally realized was that customers would buy gas in the next large town. "If we didn't price gasoline competitively with the town next-door, the gallons per day, per month fall rather rapidly. Before we redefined our markets, we had four years of declining market share," stated Lamberti. With the loss of gas sales went the sales of donuts, pizza, and other high-profit merchandise.

Small town gas station operators did not sympathize, however, with Casey's. The operators perceived the new pricing policy as a plot to destroy them. Del Nelson of Spirit Lake Amoco (and head of a "Predatory Pricing Committee" of the Iowa Petroleum Marketers Association) contended that Casey's varied its gas prices from town to town and was unfairly squeezing dealers by pricing below cost. Their situations were exacerbated by the expense of replacing old fuel storage tanks.

Although the matter was still in the courts, it was brought up at the September 18, 1992, annual shareholders meeting. A shareholder asked Chairman Lamberti about some "community hostility" toward Casey's. "Do you mean like we come into town like a Wal-Mart and destroy all the other businesses?" asked Lamberti. The Chairman then took the time to portray Casey's as a good neighbor: "We build stores in towns where there is a need for our service. We are the local baker. Most of those towns don't have a bakery. We are the local prepared-food pizza operation. A lot of those towns don't have that. . . . We have more mayors and city councils calling to say, 'Can you put a store in our town?' than the opposite."[52]

Financial

During fiscal years 1991 and 1992, Casey's General Stores, Inc., derived over 91% of its gross profits from retail sales by company-owned stores. It also earned income from franchised stores in the forms of royalties, wholesale sales of merchandise, sign and facade rental fees, and the provision of certain maintenance, transportation, and construction services. Sales at Casey's have historically been strongest during the company's first and second quarters (May through October) and relatively weak during its fourth quarter (February through April). In the warmer months of the year, customers tended to purchase greater quantities of gasoline and certain convenience items such as beer, soft drinks, and ice. Owing to the continuing emphasis on higher margin, freshly prepared food items, however, net sales and net income had recently become somewhat less seasonal.

Statements of Income: Casey's General Stores, Inc.
(Dollar amounts in thousands)

Fiscal Years Ending April 30	1992	1991	1990	1989	1988
Net sales	$606,585	$580,305	$500,657	$419,237	$336,381
Franchise revenue	4,991	4,806	4,797	4,677	4,585
	611,576	585,111	505,454	423,914	340,966
Cost of goods sold	480,357	463,090	394,201	335,193	263,607
Operating expenses	94,209	90,711	83,394	65,900	51,152
Depreciation and amortization	13,704	12,238	10,580	8,779	6,758
Interest, net	4,808	4,678	3,967	2,843	1,776
	593,078	570,717	492,142	412,715	323,293
Income before income taxes	18,498	14,394	13,312	11,199	17,673
Provision for income taxes	6,984	5,362	4,959	4,166	7,122
Net income	$ 11,514	$ 9,032	$ 8,353	$ 7,033	$ 10,551
Earnings per common and common equivalent share					
Primary	$1.04	$.81	$.73	$.61	$.90
Fully diluted	$1.00	$.80	$.73	$.61	$.88

Source: Casey's General Stores, Inc., *1989 Annual Report*, p. 10; *1992 Annual Report*, p. 9.

The 1992 fiscal year was a big success for Casey's General Stores. Sales topped $600 million for the first time. Perhaps because the retail price of gasoline was lower than in previous years (averaged $1.04/gallon in 1992 compared to $1.14 a year earlier), the company sold a record 289.5 million gallons. Earnings of $11.5 million were the highest in the company's history. Average earnings for the company-owned stores in 1992 reached $54,211, a 2.6% gain over the previous year. Over the five years 1988–1992, capital expenditures totaled more than $150 million. Most of the $35.4 million spent in 1992 was used to renovate existing stores, with particular emphasis on replacing fuel storage tanks. According to CEO Lamberti, "Through prudent cost-control measures, operating expenses as a percentage of sales declined to 15.5% in fiscal 1992. The savings came from improved efficiencies rather than from staff reductions or salary restrictions on store personnel."[53] Treasurer Douglas Shull reported that labor-related expenses accounted for 65% of the company's operating expenses.[54]

The company commenced paying cash dividends during fiscal 1991. The Board declared a $.03 per share dividend payable August 3, 1992, and stated that

EXHIBIT 7.6

Balance Sheets: Casey's General Stores, Inc.

(Dollar amounts in thousands)

Fiscal Years Ending April 30	1992	1991	1990	1989	1988
Assets					
Current assets					
Cash and cash equivalents	$ 1,527	$ 2,789	$ 1,332	$ 923	$ 176
Short-term investments	7,231	6,086	6,369	6,031	15,061
Receivables	1,926	1,932	2,080	2,427	2,096
Inventories	21,898	20,265	20,033	19,130	18,741
Prepaid expenses	429	574	554	575	554
Recoverable income taxes	—	—	137	1,974	2,073
Total current assets	33,011	31,646	30,505	31,060	38,701
Other assets, net of amortization	2,907	3,397	3,902	4,295	4,638
Property and equipment, at cost					
Land	21,539	17,890	15,358	13,831	11,153
Buildings and leasehold improvements	87,525	76,480	72,197	55,056	37,520
Machinery and equipment	124,949	107,051	91,651	79,450	60,034
Leasehold interest in property and equipment	12,363	13,615	14,409	11,536	10,917
	246,376	215,036	193,615	159,873	119,624
Less accumulated depreciation and amortization	62,818	52,338	42,575	33,681	26,027
Net property and equipment	183,558	162,698	151,040	126,192	93,597
Total assets	$219,476	$197,741	$185,447	$161,547	$136,936

(continued)

it intended to pay comparable dividends quarterly in the future. The stock price had risen from a 1990 high of $11.25 per share to $17.00 a share in February 1993. The corporation had established a type of "poison-pill" takeover defense: if anyone accumulated as much as 20% of the common stock, the corporation could issue more stock at a 50% discount to the rest of its shareholders. Of the six analysts following Casey's stock who were present at a company meeting on February 10, 1993, two rated the stock a "buy" and four had no opinion.[55] See Exhibits 7.5–7.8 for Casey's financial statements and other pertinent information on the company.

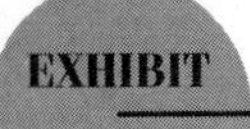

Balance Sheets: Casey's General Stores, Inc. *(continued)*
(Dollar amounts in thousands)

Fiscal Years Ending April 30	1992	1991	1990	1989	1988
Liabilities and Shareholders' Equity					
Current liabilities					
Notes payable to banks	$ 7,000	$ 3,250	$ 4,999	$ 7,750	$ 5,000
Current liabilities					
Current maturities of long-term debt	1,990	1,780	1,687	891	548
Accounts payable	29,326	24,096	19,471	17,222	16,112
Accrued expenses:					
Salaries and wages	2,263	1,517	1,205	743	363
Other	5,097	3,724	2,551	2,449	1,943
Income taxes payable	917	1,477	—	—	—
Total current liabilities	46,593	35,844	29,913	29,055	23,966
Long-term debt, net of current maturities	61,433	63,770	64,470	52,368	42,899
Deferred income taxes	14,916	12,716	11,071	8,558	7,285
Deferred compensation	680	597	524	450	378
Commitments and contingencies	—	—	—	—	—
Shareholders' equity	—	—	—	—	—
Capital stock	25,308	24,513	27,362	32,387	30,712
Retained earnings	70,546	60,301	52,107	43,754	36,721
Common stock held in treasury at cost, 352,158 shares	—	—	—	(5,025)	(5,025)
Total shareholders' equity	95,854	84,814	79,469	71,116	62,408
Total liabilities and shareholders' equity	$219,476	$197,741	$185,447	$161,547	$136,936

Source: Casey's General Stores, Inc., *1989 Annual Report,* p. 9; *1990 Annual Report,* p. 8; *1992 Annual Report,* p. 8.

The Future

In early 1993, analysts of the convenience store industry were somewhat pessimistic about its future prospects. The industry as a whole seemed to have reached maturity, with the traditional convenience store chains, in particular, apparently facing a rather bleak future. Large traditional chains were in financial difficulty and selling off or closing stores. Smaller traditional chains had to battle the large oil companies, which had begun to take over the industry. Even petroleum marketers were working with a very low profit margin on gasoline—not really enough to fund expansion. The EPA rules on fuel storage tanks were compound-

EXHIBIT 7.7

Net Sales and Gross Profits: Casey's General Stores, Inc.
(Dollar amounts in thousands)

Fiscal Years Ending April 30	1992	1991	1990	1989	1988
Net sales					
Retail sales					
Grocery/merchandise	$233,527	$213,667	$201,739	$174,628	$139,430
Gasoline	302,202	297,401	225,596	169,726	129,519
Total	$535,729	$511,068	$427,335	$344,354	$268,949
Wholesale sales					
Grocery/merchandise	$ 34,980	$ 33,345	$ 35,916	$ 34,176	$ 30,572
Gasoline	24,565	25,519	26,900	30,246	30,115
Total	$ 59,545	$ 58,864	$ 62,816	$ 64,422	$ 60,687
Gross Profits					
Retail sales					
Grocery/merchandise	$ 90,811	$ 82,833	$ 75,223	$ 59,154	$ 48,006
Gasoline	24,903	24,352	20,708	15,320	15,671
Total	$115,714	$107,185	$ 95,931	$ 74,474	$ 63,677
Wholesale sales					
Grocery/merchandise	$ 1,312	$ 1,486	$ 1,708	$ 1,825	$ 1,734
Gasoline	705	756	975	1,022	219
Total	$ 2,017	$ 2,242	$ 2,683	$ 2,847	$ 1,953

Note: These figures do *not* include either franchise revenue or charges to franchisees for certain maintenance, transportation, and construction services provided by the company.

Source: Casey's General Stores, Inc., *1992 Annual Report,* p. 18; *1989 Annual Report,* p. 19.

ing the situation and driving many companies to bankruptcy. How could a midsize traditional chain like Casey's, operating in sparsely populated areas continue to be successful in the future?

Donald Lamberti, CEO and Chairman of Casey's, viewed the situation quite differently:

> In my view, conditions for growth are more favorable now than they were in 1978 when we were adding new stores at a rate of 10 a month. As the high cost of meeting environmental rules continues to exert economic pressure on smaller, independent operations, voids are appearing throughout our market territory. This creates an opportunity for Casey's.[56]

EXHIBIT 7.8 **The Average Store: Casey's General Stores, Inc.**[1]

Fiscal Years Ending April 30	1992	1991	1990	1989	1988
Company Stores					
Average retail sales	$913,522	$895,042	$791,854	$726,058	$681,936
Average retail sales of grocery and general merchandise	399,731	375,326	375,358	368,983	355,467
Average gross profit on grocery and general merchandise	147,970	138,733	133,292	125,352	122,136
Average retail sales of gasoline	513,791	519,716	416,496	357,075	326,469
Average number of gallons sold	492,115	455,415	419,809	405,550	366,398
Average gross profit on gasoline	41,556	43,545	38,518	33,384	39,929
Average operating income[2]	54,211	52,852	46,846	41,533	58,955
Franchised Stores					
Average franchise revenue[3]	24,420	23,721	22,842	22,379	22,629

Notes:

1. Includes only those stores that had been in operation for at least one full year prior to April 30 of the fiscal year indicated.

2. Represents retail sales less cost of goods sold, including cost of merchandise, financing costs, and operating expenses attributable to a particular store, but excluding federal and state income taxes, operating expenses of the company not attributable to a particular store, and payments by the company to its benefit plans.

3. Includes a royalty fee equal to 3% of gross receipts derived from store sales of nongasoline items, a royalty fee of $0.18 per gallon on gasoline sales, and sign- and facade-rental fees.

Source: Casey's General Stores, Inc., *1989 Annual Report,* p. 20; *1992 Annual Report,* p. 19.

Notes

1. Jim Lawless, "Casey's Finishes Renovation, Plans to Add Stores," *Des Moines Register* (February 11, 1993), p. 1S.
2. "The First Casey's Store Was Located in Boone," *Des Moines Register* (May 20, 1990), advertising supplement.
3. *Forbes* (November 17, 1987).
4. "The First Casey's Store Was Located in Boone."
5. Interview with Donald Lamberti (April 24, 1992).
6. Much of the data presented on the industry was taken from *Convenience Store News: 1992 Industry Report.*
7. Chris Ebel, "Unit Growth Outpaces Population," *Convenience Store News* (November 13–December 5, 1989), p. 58.
8. Claudia Deutsch, "Rethinking the Convenience Store," *New York Times* (October 8, 1989), p. 15.
9. Frank Victoria and Peggy Smedley, "Why Oil Marketers Have C-Store Chains Circling Their Wagons," *National Petroleum News* (September, 1989), p. 36.
10. "Retailers Debate Impact of Minimum Wage Hike," *Convenience Store News* (January 15–February 11, 1990), p. 55.
11. Deutsch, p. 15.
12. Lisa Gubernick, "Stores for Our Times," *Forbes* (November 3, 1986), p. 41.
13. Victoria and Smedley, p. 43.
14. Joe Agnew, "Convenience Stores Testing Fast-Food Market," *Marketing News* (October 24, 1986), p. 10.

15. Andrew Glangola, "Foodservice vs. Labor Costs," *Convenience Store News* (October 16–November 12, 1989), p. 40.
16. *Convenience Store News: 1992 Industry Report,* p. 70.
17. Victoria and Smedley, p. 44.
18. Deutsch, p. 15.
19. Casey's General Stores, Inc., *Form 10-K,* (1991), p. 13.
20. Casey's General Stores, Inc., *1991 Annual Report,* p. 2.
21. Interview with Donald Lamberti.
22. B. Ortega, "Circle K Prepares to Emerge from Bankruptcy," *Wall Street Journal* (February 22, 1993), p. B6.
23. "Southland Completes Sale of Its Interest in Citgo," *Convenience Store News* (March 5, 1990), p. 62.
24. W. Zellner and K. L. Miller, "A New Roll of the Dice at 7-Eleven," *Business Week* (October 26, 1992).
25. B. Ortega, p. B6.
26. In an interview, Donald Lamberti mentioned Kum N Go, Pronto, and 4 Suns and their number of stores.
27. *Convenience Store News: 1992 Industry Report,* pp. 137–138.
28. Casey's General Stores, Inc., *Proxy Statement* (August 20, 1992), p. 15.
29. Casey's General Stores, Inc., *Form 10-K,* (1992), p. 9.
30. Casey's General Stores, Inc., *1989 Annual Report,* p. 5.
31. *Form 10-K* (1992), p. 5.
32. Ibid., pp. 6–7.
33. "C-Store Assessment 1988: Mixed Signals, Less Profit," *National Petroleum News* (July, 1989), p. 26.
34. Casey's General Stores, Inc., *1992 Annual Report,* p. 18.
35. Interview with Mike Richardson, Advertising Manager, Casey's General Stores, (February 16, 1993).
36. Interview with Donald Lamberti.
37. *1991 Annual Report,* p. 3.
38. *Form 10-K* (1992), p. 10.
39. Ibid., p. 9.
40. Ibid., p. 6; *Form 10-K* (1989), p. 8.
41. Interview with Mike Richardson.
42. *Form 10-K* (1989), p. 4; *Form 10-K* (1992), p. 4.
43. *Form 10-K* (1992), p. 10.
44. "A Lot of Dough(nuts)," *Des Moines Register* (February 24, 1991), p. F11.
45. Interview with Donald Lamberti.
46. Lawless, p. 1S.
47. *Form 10-K* (1992), p. 6.
48. Ibid., p. 12.
49. Interview with Donald Lamberti.
50. *Form 10-K* (1992), p. 7.
51. Dale Kasler, "'Mom and Pop' Stations Take on Mighty Casey's," *Des Moines Register* (December 23, 1990), p. 1G.
52. "Convenience Store Chain Plans 25 Percent Growth," *Ames Daily Tribune* (September 21, 1992), p. C8.
53. Donald F. Lamberti, "Letter to the Shareholders," Casey's General Stores, Inc., *1992 Annual Report,* p. 3.
54. Lawless, p. 1S.
55. Ibid.
56. Lamberti, "Letter to the Shareholders."

CASE 8

Food Lion Comes to Tulsa . . . "Hello, I'm Diane Sawyer"

Joseph Wolfe

On Thursday evening November 5, 1992, Diane Sawyer of the ABC network's top-rated investigative program "PrimeTime Live" leveled her gaze into the television camera and announced

> Tonight we have a story about what the consumer sees in the super market and what goes on behind the scenes . . . a "PrimeTime" investigation.
>
> Food Lion is the fastest growing grocery chain in the nation, a remarkable success story in an industry where profit margins tend to be perilously low. But six months ago we started talking to current and former employees. Seventy agreed to go on the record. People from different states, who didn't know each other, yet [all] told us similar stories about sanitation and food handling in some departments in their stores.
>
> Before we begin, a word about the Food Lion employees that were filmed with hidden cameras. They're hard working people who care about their jobs. But what this report will show is the kind of thing that *can* happen when the pressure for profit is great and you break the rules.

That introduction and the segments shown that evening and the following week threw Food Lion, Inc., into a maelstrom of negative publicity and harsh market reactions. The next day its two stocks plummeted 10.8% and 13.8%, respectively, and were NASDAQ's most active issues. Overnight the parent corporation's stock fell 6.2% in heavy trading on the Brussels stock exchange as many questioned the basis for the company's amazing success in the highly competitive and low-growth supermarket industry. By early March 1993, Standard & Poor's had designated up to $500 million of Food Lion's credit for review, and later that month Moody's Investors Service lowered the chain's senior long-term debt rating. In taking this action Moody's Vice-President Pam Stubing cited the investigation's negative publicity, the company's falling sales and growth rates, and the fact that the swift recovery Moody's felt would occur after the exposé "isn't happening and further pressures on earnings could occur."

Moreover, the televised exposé could not have come at a worse time for the company's struggling southwestern expansion. The company had opened 42 stores in the Dallas/Fort Worth area to disappointing sales in 1991. Its entry into the Tulsa, Oklahoma, market with seven new stores was scheduled for the following week, and even without the adverse publicity the chain faced strong competition from local and national firms in that city. Company officials in both Tulsa and its Salisbury, North Carolina, headquarters tried to minimize the television program's long-term consequences, but they admitted that short-term problems were causing concern. The company continued to press its September 1992 lawsuit against Capital Cities/ABC, Inc., over its investigative methods. Subsequently, in April 1993, the company amended the suit to a civil racketeering (RICO) action for damages amounting to at least $30 million.

Over that entire period, however, numerous forces from within Food Lion and the grocery industry generally had begun to exert themselves. The chain's same-store sales had been falling at an increasing rate over the past several years, and it had made some low-growth, "defensive expansions" to ward off new competition in its marketing territories. Food Lion's management believed that the company was both targeted and blameless regarding the food handling and employment practices detailed in the exposé. Moreover, various industry observers believed that the report merely highlighted the harsh realities of doing business in the supermarket industry.

Food Lion, Inc.

Today's food giant was started by Ralph Ketner, Brown Ketner, and Wilson Smith in 1957 as a one-store independent called Food Town. All former Winn-Dixie employees, they struggled for the next ten years to establish their company in its home state of North Carolina. They opened and closed various stores as the small chain strove to survive. Only after Ralph Ketner began a policy of everyday low prices did the 16-unit chain achieve stability and sales growth. Food Town went public in 1970, and four years later the Belgian grocery combine of Etablissements Delhaize Freres et Cie (Delhaize Le Lion) purchased a controlling interest in the company; it currently occupies half the company's Board seats. The entry of Delhaize Le Lion brought rapid expansion. In 1983, the chain changed its name to Food Lion, Inc., when it expanded into a territory already served by other stores carrying the Food Town name.

Delhaize Le Lion Group

Delhaize Le Lion is Belgium's second largest retailing conglomerate. It is also that country's most internationally oriented company, with over 60% of its sales coming from outside the country—principally the United States. The company adopted its overseas diversification strategy mainly in response to Belgium's 1975 "loi de cadenas," or padlock law. That legislation attempted to protect the country's small, independent retailers by controlling the expansion of its larger retail chains.

Before a group of entrepreneurs in June 1981, Delhaize Le Lion's Guy Beckers spoke of his company's thinking at the time of the law's passage. Because it was a Belgium-based supermarket chain, the company concluded that

> the number of domestic supermarkets could not increase indefinitely and that the rate of increase of the turnover of existing supermarkets would diminish some time or another. First, we took it for granted that manufacturing was not our job. We looked at the situation in a number of European countries. Everywhere the same constraints were evident—control by the State, pressure from the trade unions, and not many potential openings as far as sales points were concerned. This made us look toward the United States. We were looking for a region with a growing population and an expanding

economy. We chose the Sun Belt, which fulfilled these requirements: (1) lower energy consumption—with air-conditioning there is no problem about heat affecting the quality of work; (2) unemployment—the South is better situated from this point of view than other regions of the United States; (3) the South is the best region for lower wage scales; (4) increase of population—the South comes at the top of the list; (5) the South is at the top of the list for capital investments for equipment and next to the top for nonresidential investments.

In Belgium, Delhaize Le Lion operates more than 100 of its own supermarkets and has 144 franchisees and affiliates that include 64 AD Delhaize supermarkets and 41 neighborhood Delhaize food stores. In addition, it has long-term supply agreements with numerous traditional stores, including the Dial chain of 51 discount stores and a chain of some 60 DI drug stores. Exhibit 8.1 summarizes the holdings and operations of this conglomerate in both Western Europe and the United States.

Operational control of Food Lion rests with an American group headed by Tom E. Smith, the company's current CEO, who began working in the company's first store as a bagboy in 1958 when he was 17. After graduating from Catawba College in 1964 with an A.B. in Business Administration, he worked for Del Monte Foods for six years. He left Del Monte to become Food Lion's only buyer. Smith developed the company's strategy of mass buying at discount prices and simplifying store operations by stocking fewer brands and sizes than the chain's competitors. He became the company's Vice-President for Distribution in 1974 and its Executive Vice-President in 1977. At the age of 39, Smith became Food Lion's President in 1981 and its CEO in 1986. In 1992, his compensation consisted of the dividends on 1,534,089 shares of Food Lion stock, a base salary of $628,788 (a 20% raise from the previous year), and a $272,955 performance bonus. The Board of Directors voted him the bonus in December 1991, upon accomplishment of that year's record earnings. In late December 1991, the company's Class A and B stocks were trading at $25.125.

Food Lion Operating Characteristics

Food Lion has operated as a regional chain primarily in the southeastern United States, although it is now expanding north into Pennsylvania and southwest into Louisiana, Texas, and Oklahoma. Its typical store had approximately 25,515 square feet and served a trading area of fewer than 7,000 people. The simplicity and standardization of store operations has been a key factor in the company's success. Stores usually do not carry nonfood items but shelve approximately 16,000 stock keeping units (SKUs). Food Lion stores' selling space is roughly 20%–35% less than its competitors, such as Winn-Dixie or Kroger. Because of their size and simplicity, the stores are also cheaper to build—about $650,000 each versus $1.5 million for the average supermarket. Exhibit 8.2 presents the number of stores operated by Food Lion currently and in the recent past.

Originally, Food Lion leased its stores from developers who had them built by local construction companies, but in 1991 the company began to contract for construction of its new stores, which it then owned outright. Smith attributed the shift in its construction and ownership policy to "a credit crunch that has made it diffi-

EXHIBIT 8.1 Business Activities and Holdings: Delhaize Le Lion

- Belgian retail and wholesale operations:
  106 Delhaize Le Lion company-owned supermarkets
  64 AD Delhaize franchised supermarkets
  41 Delhaize neighborhood food stores
  39 independent stores supplied through food distribution arrangements
  51 Dial discount food stores
  62 DI drug stores
  4 warehouses operated by Delhaize Le Lion Coordination Center SA
- Full or partial operating control through ownership interests:

  Delimmo—A real estate company providing long-term leases to 14 of its supermarkets in Belgium. Owned by Delhaize Le Lion SA through a 99.9% stock interest.
  Delned—A holding corporation 100.0% owned by Delimmo. Through Delned (BV Delhaize The Lion Nederland) Delimmo has a 50.0% interest in Shipp's Corner Shopping Center, Virginia Beach, Virginia; and the Debarry Center, Jacksonville, Florida.
  Wambacq & Peeters—A transportation company delivering goods from Delhaize Le Lion's Belgium distribution centers; controlled by Delhaize through a 55.0% stock ownership.
  Pingo Doce—A 31-store supermarket chain operating in the Portuguese cities of Lisbon and Porto; Delimmo has a 38.8% stock interest.
  Artip SA—An airline ticket reseller 33.14% owned by Delhaize Le Lion.
  Deficom SA—An affiliate of the Defi holding company in the telecommunications industry; Delhaize Le Lion has a 10.0% ownership interest.
  Food Lion, Inc., USA—Controlled by Delhaize Le Lion's 50.3% ownership of Food Lion's Class A nonvoting shares and a 44.2% ownership of its Class B voting shares either directly or indirectly through its wholly owned U.S. subsidiary Delhaize The Lion America, Inc., USA.
  Delhaize the Lion America—A wholly owned company of Delhaize Le Lion SA (Detla).
  Super Discount Markets, Inc.—A seven-superstore food chain operating in Atlanta, Georgia, under the name Cub Foods of which Delhaize The Lion America, Inc., USA has 60.0% ownership.

Source: Summarized from "Retailer Profile No. 1: Delhaize Le Lion," *Marketing in Europe*. Brussels: Economist Intelligence Unit (July 1990), pp. 95–99.

EXHIBIT 8.2 Stores in Operation: Food Lion, Inc.

	Year				
Characteristic	1992	1991	1990	1989	1988
Number of stores	1,012	881	778	663	567
Total square footage (in thousands)	26,428	22,480	19,424	16,326	13,695
Scanning stores	1,012	801	508	315	130

Source: *1991 and 1992 Annual Reports*, pp. 4–5; press release, February 11, 1993, p. 3.

cult, if not impossible, for developers to build Food Lion stores and lease them to us as they have done in the past." Accordingly the chain used its own funds to build its Dallas/Fort Worth, Texas, stores and has indicated that it will continue to use debt to finance future growth. In 1992, the company spent approximately $200 million to build new stores and refurbish some of its older units.

Food Lion also utilizes other methods to increase operating efficiency. When building its distribution centers, the company looks for railroad access because it ships about 25% of its goods by rail, which is more than for most firms. In 1991 it opened three new combined 700,000 square foot dry/refrigerated facilities. Additional expansion in 1992 brought its total distribution center space to 8.7 million square feet at centers in

Salisbury, North Carolina
Dunn, North Carolina
Prince George County, Virginia
Elloree, South Carolina
Green Cove Springs, Florida
Plant City, Florida
Greencastle, Pennsylvania
Roanoke, Texas
Clinton, Tennessee

Food Lion also carefully nurtures its reputation for being a low-cost, efficient operation that translates into savings for its customers. Company lore is that the firm changed its name from Food Town to Food Lion because only two letters had to be changed on its store signs. All advertisements are prepared in-house, thereby keeping marketing costs to 0.5% of sales compared to the industry's average of about 1.1%. Smith appears in about half the company's advertisements, extolling, "At Food Lion, when we save, you save," thereby drawing customers with everyday low prices rather than costly weekly price-special advertisements. As one competitor acknowledges "They do a good job of promoting their everyday low-price image. They promise to deliver one thing—price—and they do, on groceries and frozens." He also added, however, that "their feature prices on produce are not that dramatic."

Other methods and procedures contribute further to lower store-level operating costs. When resetting or remodeling older stores, Food Lion places an adhesive covering over its old shelves, thus saving as much as $10,000 a store. This method also has reduced store reopening times by two to three weeks, thereby saving an additional $4,000 per unit. By 1992, Food Lion had converted all its stores to front-end scanning operations. In addition to using its scanners in the normal way, store visits by brokers and direct sales representatives are recorded on the store's computer, thereby ensuring that they visit each store every four weeks as requested.

To minimize "shrinkage" or theft the company is currently testing an electronic article surveillance (EAS) system in 25 of its stores. Food Lion's Director of Loss Prevention, Clayton Edwards, says, "We tagged health and beauty aids, cigarettes, meat, and, where applicable, wine." In an earlier test in six stores, Edwards found that "after six months, our gross profits were up nearly 10.0%. The biggest change was in the attitude of store management. With EAS, they feel as if they finally have a way of fighting theft." Edwards also observes that customers seem to like the system: "It makes for a safer shopping environment. We found that once word gets out—and it gets out very quickly—that a particular store is using EAS, the 'bad apples' or undesirables tend to go elsewhere. I think that supermarkets willing to invest in electronic tagging systems will definitely have a competitive advantage in years to come."

All buying is centralized and all stores in the chain are run in the same manner, resulting in a tightly disciplined, consistent, and centralized operation. Centralized buying has resulted in both lower procurement costs and food prices for the chain. As one of its vendors said, Food Lion has "the best buyers in the business. They will buy a year's worth of product if they can cut a deal and hold the price. Individual buyers have the authority to buy millions of dollars worth of a product with no second opinions needed. There is no buying committee. It's awesome." All stores are relatively small, layouts are almost identical, and store and district managers are told exactly what to do. As one competitor observes, Food Lion's "store managers have a checklist of what they should do, and they had better follow it. There's only one way to do things. Managers may have some leeway in supporting local charities, but that's about it. You can go into a Food Lion store in Florida and find the same end displays and planograms as in a store in North Carolina." Through both low corporate overhead costs (which ultimately must be supported at the store level) and efficient store operations, a typical Food Lion unit can make a profit on weekly volumes as low as $100,000.

To ensure conformity to its system, Food Lion offers one of the industry's most liberal employee benefits packages. Its stock purchase plan is open to all full-time employees over 18 years of age and all part-time employees who have been employed for at least one year. Other benefits include a profit-sharing plan and a comprehensive medical plan, including dental and vision care. Many laud the company's progressive benefits, but some believe that its overall management system encourages loyalty while discouraging initiative. Many managers reportedly have quit the company after a few years "because they felt the company was cold and impersonal, and they had no real feeling of security there." Others have claimed that Food Lion saves money by dismissing workers before they are fully vested in the company's profit-sharing plan or, as in the case of Rickey Bryant, who has filed a civil action suit against Food Lion with the help of the United Food and Commercial Workers Union (UFCW), that the company does not provide dismissed workers with an extension of their health insurance coverage as required by federal law.

Expansion Activities and Plans

Over the past five years, Food Lion has added more than 100 stores per year to its chain. The method used to enter new markets can be illustrated by the company's approach in Jacksonville, Florida. In August 1987 Smith blanketed the market with ads warning shoppers that "Food Lion is coming to town, and prices will be going down." After operating there for one year, Food Lion's five Jacksonville stores had 2.4% of the market. By 1991, the company had added 32 more stores and had obtained a 14.0% market share. The chain's entry into the market, however, did not go unchallenged. Months before, Winn-Dixie had lowered its prices 5% across the board, and by the time Food Lion opened its stores the entire market's prices were down almost 15%. Although Food Lion gained market share, Winn-Dixie still led with 36.0%. After Food Lion completed its Jacksonville expansion, Winn-Dixie's market share fell by 8.3%.

Based on Winn-Dixie's experience with Food Lion, others have learned how to withstand the company's entry into their markets. When Food Lion came to the already crowded Dallas/Fort Worth area in December 1990, many competitors had already reacted to earlier news announcements of the company's plans, pursuing areas in which they felt Food Lion was vulnerable. Because Food Lion does not emphasize service, many went to 24-hour operations, promoted home delivery, and added such services as FAX machines, Western Union money transfers, and money orders. Some emphasized the selection and variety of food offered, especially perishables and deli/bakery sections where, they felt, Food Lion was at a competitive disadvantage. Most, however, engaged in price competition in one form or another. They did so by promoting everyday low prices, advertising hot specials in weekly shopping guides, running one-cent sales, or offering triple coupons. All market participants increased their spending on advertising and promotions. Some used endcap displays, banners, and flags to compare their stores' prices to Food Lion's; others advertised that they would meet Food Lion's prices on comparable items; and many, such as Tom Thumb Food Stores and Kroger, ran advertisements twice a week rather than once a week. Kroger additionally guaranteed the lowest milk prices in town or triple the difference in cash.

Although customers may temporarily enjoy lower food prices, analysts have noted harmful, long-term aspects of Food Lion's market entry strategies. The Organization for Economic Cooperation and Development (OECD) has received formal complaints since 1985 against Delhaize/Food Lion, charging unfair marketing practices that threatened the host country's standard of living. The OECD asked its Trade Union Advisory Committee to investigate, and the committee concluded:

> Food Lion routinely opens a store in a town and launches a competitive war based on lower prices in order to take the market away from the already established supermarkets. The already established grocers are forced into closure or to lower their prices, which they can only do by lowering wages and benefits they pay in line with the level set by Food Lion.

After one year in the Dallas/Fort Worth market—and the attendant price war—Food Lion had garnered a 4% market share, or less than half its 10% objective. Although Food Lion's management expressed initial pleasure with its results, others believe that the company's success has been mixed. As Cleve Park, a local Russell-Moss real estate broker, observed, "In 75% of their stores they are extremely pleased, but in 25% they are extremely unhappy. They are in some terrible locations." Others have noted that many of the company's past successes have come in rural markets or less affluent communities with less sophisticated shoppers and weaker competition. To some extent this situation has been acknowledged by Vince Watkins, Food Lion's Vice-President of Operations. Referring to

EXHIBIT 8.3

Population and Income Statistics for Current and Projected Store Locations (States): Food Lion, Inc.

State	1990 Per Capita Income	1991 Population (in thousands)	1991 Population Rank	1980–1990 Percentage Growth	2000 Projected Population (in thousands)[1]
Current					
Delaware	$20,039	680	46	12.1%	802
Florida	18,586	13,277	4	32.7	16,315
Georgia	16,944	6,623	11	18.6	8,005
Kentucky	14,929	3,713	24	0.7	3,689
Maryland	21,864	4,860	19	13.4	5,608
North Carolina	16,203	6,737	10	12.7	7,717
Pennsylvania	18,672	11,961	5	0.1	12,069
South Carolina	15,099	3,560	25	11.7	3,962
Tennessee	15,978	4,953	18	6.2	5,424
Texas	16,769	17,349	3	19.4	17,828
Virginia	19,746	6,286	12	15.7	7,275
West Virginia	13,747	1,801	34	−8.0	1,651
Projected					
Alabama	$14,826	4,089	22	3.8%	4,358
Arkansas	14,218	2,372	33	2.8	2,509
Kansas	17,986	2,495	32	4.8	2,534
Louisiana	14,391	4,252	21	0.3	4,141
Mississippi	12,735	2,592	31	2.1	2,772
Missouri	17,497	5,158	15	4.1	5,473
Oklahoma	15,444	3,175	28	4.0	2,924

Note: 1. Series A migration assumptions used.

Source: *Statistical Abstract of the United States.* Washington, D.C.: U.S. Bureau of the Census (1992), pp. 22–23; *Current Population Reports: Population Estimates and Projections* (Series P-25). Washington, D.C.: U.S. Bureau of the Census (1989), p. 13; *Information Please Almanac 1992.* New York: Dan Golenpaul Associates (1993), p. 52.

the chain's relatively weak results in Texas, he admitted that "the competition out there was much better organized in preparing for our entry than perhaps they had been in other areas." Additionally, because of his chain's obsession with standardization, its stores failed to recognize local food preferences and stocked popular eastern brands unknown to those in the Southwest. After much delay, its Dallas/Fort Worth stores began to carry regional favorites such as ranch beans, various peppers, corn husks, plantain, and a select grade of beef popular with Texans.

Despite these results, Food Lion has designated its "primary expansion areas" for the 1990s as Kansas, Louisiana, Oklahoma, Missouri, Arkansas, Mississippi, and Alabama. The mobilizing cry of "2,000 by 2,000" can be heard throughout the chain. Exhibit 8.3 presents economic and population growth data for the company's current and projected operations, Exhibit 8.4 profiles the national competi-

EXHIBIT 8.4 **Selected Actual and Potential Food Lion Competitors**

- *Albertson's, Inc.,* operates more than 650 grocery stores in 19 western and southern states. Stores include about 250 combination food and drug stores having approximately 58,000 square feet of selling space per store, 250 superstores of about 42,000 square feet each, 118 conventional supermarkets of about 27,000 square feet each, and 32 warehouse stores. The company operates nine full-line distribution centers, which handle about 65% of the merchandise carried in its stores. In May 1992, Albertson's acquired 74 Jewel Osco stores. Future sales growth is expected to come from planned store space expansions of about 10% a year and population increases in its Florida and West Coast markets. The company competes through a strong private brand program, everyday low pricing, and superior service. Albertson's is 40% unionized.
- *Bruno's, Inc.,* is a southern chain that operates more than 250 supermarkets in Alabama, Florida, Georgia, Mississippi, and Tennessee under the names Food World, Consumer Warehouse, Bruno's, Food Max, and Piggly Wiggly. Its stores average about 35,000 square feet. In 1992, same-store sales fell 1%, and the company has been buffeted by high store opening costs and increased advertising expenditures to meet competition in some of its hotly contested markets. Bruno's plans to open 33 new units in 1993 and intends to install in-store computers to reduce inventory shrinkage and increase labor productivity.
- *Delchamps, Inc.,* is affiliated with the Topco cooperative grocery purchasing organization. The chain operates 115 supermarkets along the Gulf Coast (Alabama, Florida, Louisiana, and Mississippi) and ten liquor stores in Florida. All stores are leased under long-term agreements. Each contains about 35,345 square feet. Sales fell in 1992 because of food price deflation and competitive pressures. Delchamps responded to heavy local competition by doubling the value of coupons (up to $.60) and by making cash donations to schools equaling 1% of the cash register receipts collected by the schools. The chain has begun to reduce its selling costs by cutting its nighttime store hours and obtaining greater labor productivity.
- *Giant Food* is a highly integrated chain of 154 supermarkets concentrated in Washington, D.C., Baltimore, and adjoining areas in Virginia and Maryland. It has its own

(continued)

tion that Food Lion currently and potentially faces when it moves into its projected markets, and Exhibit 8.5 presents operating data for those competitors.

To maintain its expansion program, Food Lion needs a constant pool of new employees. The company's goal has been to obtain 80% of its new store management from existing operations, but it is actually getting only about 50% at this time. For 1993, Food Lion plans on opening about 110 new stores, primarily in Virginia, Maryland, West Virginia, and Texas. Exhibit 8.6 shows the estimated capital expenditures for those proposed stores.

Company Corporate Responsibility and Community Relations Efforts

Because of the chain's destabilizing effects on local markets, it is no stranger to controversy. However, Food Lion is proud of its recognition as a good corporate

EXHIBIT 8.4 **Selected Actual and Potential Food Lion Competitors** *(continued)*

warehouses and distribution network and a construction and maintenance company. Giant Food also produces its own private-label ice cream, baked goods, dairy products, soft drinks, and ice cubes. Same store sales, which have averaged about $22.7 million per store, fell in 1992, but the chain's high degree of vertical integration adds about 1% to its overall margins.

- *Kroger Company* is America's largest grocery chain, maintaining major market shares in the Midwest, South, and West. Kroger operates some 1,265 stores, of which 657 are combination food and drug units and 520 are superstores. The chain also operates more than 940 convenience stores. Kroger acquired the Mini-Mart Convenience store chain in 1987 and sold its free-standing drug stores in the same year. In October 1988, it underwent a major restructuring. To foil a takeover bid at that time, Kroger declared a special dividend that left the company with a heavy debt burden. Much of its current cash flow is now being used to retire that debt. Kroger processes food at 37 plants and offers over 4,000 private-label goods. The company is heavily unionized and has faced stiff competition in Houston, Cincinnati, Dayton, and Tennessee.
- *Weis Markets* has most of its 127 food outlets in southern Pennsylvania but also has a few in Maryland, Virginia, West Virginia, and New York. Other food retailers, including several low-price warehouse club chains, have moved into Weis's markets, forcing it to cut prices. Same-store sales and operating margins have fallen annually for the past few years. Weis owns about 55% of its sites, is debt free, and sells national brand merchandise and 1,800 items under its trademarks Big Top, Carnival, and Weis Quality. The company also operates five Amity House Ice Cream Shoppes and the Weis Food Service institutional supply company.
- *Winn-Dixie Stores* is America's fifth largest grocery chain and the largest in the Sunbelt. It operates about 1,200 supermarkets under the names Winn-Dixie and Marketplace. Each unit contains 31,400 square feet. The chain is nonunionized and has its own distribution centers, processing and manufacturing plants, and fleet of trucks. In 1990, Winn-Dixie began emphasizing everyday low prices in addition to its usual high-service orientation.

citizen. In 1986, the company received the Martin Luther King Award for its humanitarian efforts. One of its actions that led to the award was the donation of its trucks to aid southeastern farmers during the 1985 drought. With these trucks farmers were able to transport hay from Indiana to save their cattle. The company has also been praised for providing equal opportunity employment and for establishing express lanes for handicapped customers.

When dealing with controversy the company has traditionally met it head on. During one attack by Winn-Dixie in Jacksonville, Food Lion produced a television advertisement featuring Tom Smith in his office assuring consumers that "Winn-Dixie would have you believe that Food Lion's low prices are going to crumble and blow away. Let me assure you that as long as you keep shopping at Food Lion, our lower prices are to stay right where they belong—in Jacksonville." In 1984, Smith reacted quickly when rumors in eastern Tennessee linked the Food

EXHIBIT 8.5

1992 National and Regional Chain Comparisons

(Dollar amounts in millions)

Category	Albertson's	Bruno's	Delchamps	Giant Food	Kroger	Weis Markets	Winn-Dixie
Sales	$10,095.0	$2,618.2	$ 949.8	$3,550.0	$22,085.0	$1,320.0	$10,074.0
Gross margin	26.0%	22.2%	26.5%	31.5%	22.5%	27.7%	22.8%
Net profit margin	2.67%	2.34%	0.60%	1.85%	0.37%	5.90%	2.09%
Inventory turnover	13.0	11.2	10.0	16.0	15.0	14.5	10.9
Long-term debt	$ 575.0	$ 172.2	$ 42.2	$ 255.0	$ 4,250.0	$ 0.0	$ 90.3
Net worth	$ 1,340.0	$ 422.4	$ 112.8	$ 650.0	– $ 2,749.0	$ 692.0	$ 952.2

Sources: *Value Line Company Surveys* (November 20, 1992), pp. 1498, 1501, 1503–1505, 1508, 1515–1516.

EXHIBIT 8.6

1993 Estimated New Store Expenditures
(Dollar amounts in millions)

Capital Item	Expenditure
Construction	$60.0
Store equipment	85.0
Land costs and distribution center expansion	10.0
Total	$155.0

Lion logotype to Satanic worship. The company hired Grand Ole Opry star Minnie Pearl to appear in local advertisements until the stories disappeared.

Recent Operating Results

Food Lion has asserted that its general plans are still in effect and that it plans to double revenues by 1997. However, Smith's recent near-term sales and profit projections have been less optimistic. As shown in Exhibits 8.7 and 8.8, the chain's long-term and near-term, same-store sales have been falling, and the U.S. economy isn't very robust despite the Clinton administration's efforts to stimulate economic

EXHIBIT 8.7

Same-Store Sales Volume Changes: Food Lion, Inc.

Year	Growth
1989	8.6%
1990	4.5
1991	2.7
1992	(0.4)

EXHIBIT 8.8

Monthly 1992–1993 Same-Store Sales: Food Lion, Inc.

Period	Decrease
November 1992	9.5%
December 1992	6.2
January 1993	7.6
February 1993	5.4
March 1993	5.7

Source: Food Lion, Inc., *1992 Annual Report,* p. 15.

Balance Sheets: Food Lion, Inc.
(Dollar amounts in millions, except per share data)

	January 2, 1993	December 28, 1991 (restated)	December 29, 1990
Assets			
Current assets			
Cash and cash equivalents	$ 105.1	$ 4.3	$ 10.4
Receivables	96.0	97.1	77.0
Inventories	896.4	884.5	673.6
Prepaid expenses	50.3	36.5	6.7
Total current assets	1,147.9	982.5	767.7
Property at cost less depreciation and amortization	1,373.6	1,036.8	791.8
Total assets	$2,521.5	$2,019.3	$1,559.5
Liabilities and Shareholders' Equity			
Current liabilities			
Notes payable	$ 459.7	$ 122.5	$ 127.5
Accounts payable, trade	324.1	343.2	290.1
Accrued expenses	196.8	184.0	148.9
Long-term debt—current	0.6	1.1	3.4
Capital lease obligations—current	5.1	4.1	3.1
Income taxes payable	0.0	22.0	29.8
Total current liabilities	986.2	676.8	602.8
Long-term debt	248.1	247.2	97.9
Capital lease obligations	245.7	195.2	153.8
Deferred charges/income	84.0	67.4	36.3
Deferred compensation	1.7	1.7	0.0
Total liabilities	1,565.8	1,188.2	890.9
Shareholders' equity			
Common stock net common	241.9	161.2	161.1
Capital surplus	.2	2.0	1.2
Retained earnings	713.6	667.9	506.3
Total shareholders' equity	955.7	1,188.2	668.6
Total liabilities and shareholders' equity	$2,521.5	$2,019.3	$1,559.5
Dividends paid	$ 53.8	$ 48.0	$ 43.0

Source: Company *10-K Report;* February 11, 1993 press release; shareholder's reports for 1991 and 1992.

EXHIBIT 8.10

Statements of Income: Food Lion, Inc.
(Dollar amounts in millions)

Years Ending Nearest Saturday to December 31	1992	1991	1990	1989
Net sales	$7,196.4	$6,438.5	$5,584.4	$4,717.1
Cost of goods sold	5,760.0	5,103.0	4,447.2	3,772.5
Gross profit	1,436.4	1,335.5	1,137.2	944.6
Selling and administrative expenses	975.1	855.8	738.7	619.9
Interest expense	49.1	34.4	32.6	29.2
Depreciation and amortization	121.6	104.6	81.4	65.0
Income before taxes	290.6	340.7	294.5	230.5
Provision for income taxes	112.6	135.5	111.9	90.7
Net income	$ 178.0	$ 205.2	$ 172.6	$ 139.8

Source: Company *10-K Report;* February 11, 1993 press release.

growth. The chain's new real estate development strategy was a major factor in raising its long-term debt from 27% of capital to 35% last year. This debt load should increase, as Food Lion owned as many as 90 of the new stores built in 1992. However, Smith intends to start selling and leasing back the new stores in 1994 when he hopes the real estate market will have rebounded. Exhibits 8.9 and 8.10 present the company's balance sheets and income statements for 1989–1992. Exhibit 8.11 presents comparative quarterly sales and profit results for periods concurrent with the "PrimeTime Live" exposé.

EXHIBIT 8.11

Near-Term Sales and Income Results
(Dollar amounts in millions)

Quarter	Sales	Net Income
April 1991	$2,300.0	$60.8
April 1992	2,020.0	27.3
January 1992	$1,600.0	$49.6
January 1993	1,660.0	21.9

Source: "Food Lion's Payout Is Delayed Following Fallout of News Story," *Wall Street Journal* (February 3, 1993), p. B2; "Firm Posts 56% Decrease in 1st-Quarter Earnings," *Wall Street Journal* (April 8, 1993), p. C6.

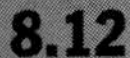

U.S. Food Expenditures

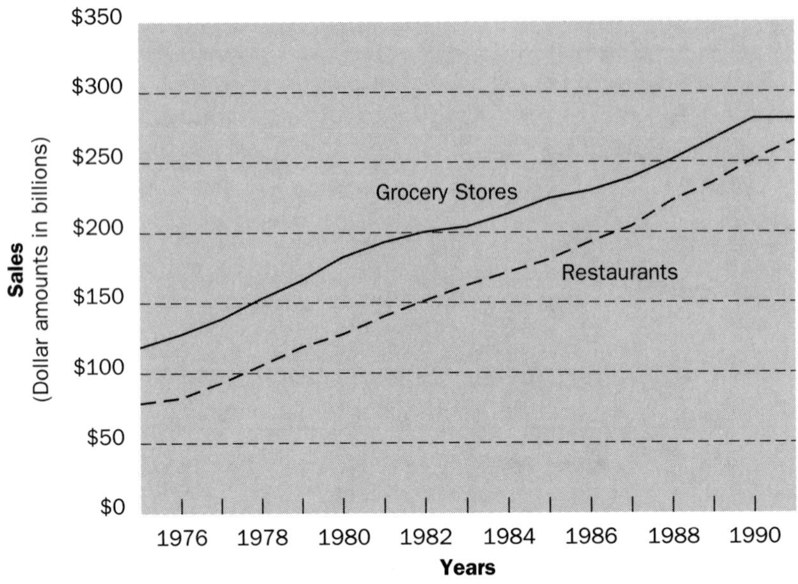

Source: From graphed data in Eben Shapiro, "A Page from Fast-Food's Menu," *New York Times* (October 14, 1991), p. D1.

The Grocery Industry

The grocery/supermarket industry has always been very competitive. Making it even more so have been recent trends of greater concentration, overlapping market and trading areas caused by both suburban sprawl and the quest for profits, falling real incomes for many families, and the effects of the two-career household on at-home food preparation. Although Americans consume more than 750 million meals a day, Exhibit 8.12 shows that the grocery store has been an ever-declining provisioner. In order to cater to changing tastes and shopping patterns, the industry's chains have responded by extending operating hours, increasing their assortments of prepared and ready-to-eat foods, and offering convenience services that help to build customer traffic while simultaneously providing greater markups than can be obtained from food retailing alone. Exhibit 8.13 displays the sales and food mix obtained by the nation's largest chains in 1991. Exhibit 8.14 shows the great variety of services offered by those responding to *Progressive Grocer*'s 1992 industry survey.

Because of the shrinking sales base caused by eating and dining out, America's declining population growth, and increasing interchain competition that has driven down prices and profit margins, most grocery chains are also attempting to reduce both store operating expenses and chainwide corporate expenses. Capital

EXHIBIT 8.13

1991 Food Chain Sales Proportions by Merchandise Type

Grocery	49.0%
Meat	15.0
Dairy	8.0
General merchandise/health and beauty aids	7.0
Produce	7.0
Frozen food	6.0
Service delicatessen	3.0
In-store bakery	2.0
Other	3.0

Source: "How Supermarkets Are Measuring Up," *Progressive Grocer 59th Annual Report* (April 1992), p. 37.

outlays have been made on in-store computer systems so that about 85% of all stores possess scanning systems. These systems track inventory levels, check out customers quickly, and schedule employees to respond efficiently to sales volumes and store traffic patterns. At the store level, also, much of the staffing is part-time labor, which is cheaper, more flexible, and not prone to unionization efforts.

At the area or district level many chains have begun to concentrate their stores within selected metropolitan areas to secure advertising economies of scale and minimize and consolidate shipping distances from centrally located food distribution centers. At the corporate level buying operations often are centralized to obtain dedicated, advanced buying volume discounts. Corporate-level real estate departments often have been successful in renegotiating store site leases, covenants, and/or payment terms and schedules. Exhibit 8.15 presents typical operating characteristics for chain stores. Over the past several years productivity per employee and square foot of selling space have been increasing slowly despite longer store operating hours, greater inventory levels, and larger store sizes.

In the face of the lingering 1991–1992 recession and falling real incomes, U.S. grocery chains have had to deal with the fact that shoppers have been trading down for the past few years. Through this process customers have been avoiding discretionary or impulse purchases and substituting lower priced, often generic or nonbrand, items for more expensive ones that yield more profit. Warehouse clubs, which offer lower prices for those who can buy in large quantities, have increased their market shares in many metropolitan areas. Club members typically pay an annual fee to shop for goods priced about 25% lower than in most supermarkets. Both the warehouse's operator and its patrons purchase products in bulk, providing savings for both. Items are stocked on pallets and placed on industrial-type shelves by forklift trucks rather than being stocked individually by hand. Many buying clubs also carry general merchandise items, resulting in more sales per customer and spreading operating expenses over a larger revenue base. Warehouse

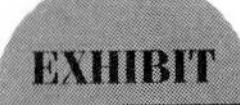

8.14

Grocery Store Services Offered

(Percentage of stores surveyed)

Service	Percentage
Plastic grocery bags[1]	90.0%
Carryout service[1]	82.0
Scanning checkouts[1]	77.0
Full-service delicatessen[1]	76.0
Reusable grocery bags	69.0
Film processing service	62.0
Trim-cut meat[1]	60.0
Full-service bakery[1]	56.0
Hot takeout food[1]	55.0
Recycling facilities	51.0
Nutritional information	48.0
Chilled prepared foods	47.0
Full-service meat department	45.0
Self-service delicatessen[1]	42.0
Hot food bars	37.0
Full-service fish department	36.0
Separate cheese department	34.0
Videocassette rentals	33.0
Accept credit cards	28.0
Automatic teller machines[1]	25.0
Salad bar	24.0
Combination in-house and bake-off bakery[1]	24.0
Bake-off bakery only	22.0
Coupon scanning	20.0
Catering	20.0
Sit-down eating	18.0
FAX ordering	18.0
Pharmacy	16.0
Accept debit cards	12.0
Frequent shopper programs	12.0
Scratch/mix bakery	10.0
Fruit/juice bar	8.0
Ethnic prepared foods	8.0

Note: 1. Services offered by Tulsa Food Lion stores.

Source: "How Supermarkets Are Measuring Up," *Progressive Grocer 59th Annual Report* (April 1992), p. 36.

EXHIBIT 8.15 **1991 Grocery Chain Operating Results and Characteristics**

Sales Volume	
Weekly sales per checkout	$26,375
Weekly sales per employee	$ 3,768
Sales per employee hour	$ 94.42
Weekly sales per square foot	$ 8.65
Average transaction size	$ 17.71
Annual inventory turns	13.9
Front-End Measures	
Percent of scanning stores	85.0%
Number of weekly transactions	13,082
Number of checkouts	8.8
Physical Measures	
Average square feet of selling area	26,656
Average total area in square feet	34,012
Items stocked	20,372
Store inventory value (in thousands)	$ 702.0
Store Hours	
Average hours open per week	127
Percentage open 24 hours per day all week	31.0%

Source: "How Supermarkets Are Measuring Up," *Progressive Grocer 59th Annual Report* (April 1992), p. 37.

club sales amounted to $34 billion in 1992. In 1983 there were 15 warehouse club stores in operation in the United States; by 1992, their number had grown to 577. Sam's Wholesale Clubs, Price Company, and Costco Wholesale currently are the largest buying club chains in the United States.

Supermarketers have engaged in various tactics to either combat or join this trend. Some now stock bulk-sized, "big box" items; others have increased their services to include home or office delivery, FAXed orders, and food clubs. A relatively few have opened their own warehouse-type markets. As tough as supermarket competition has been in the past, it probably will become even more competitive in the future. The new competition will be waged less and less against small, undercapitalized independents and more often by big, well-capitalized chains against each other. And despite the relatively low profits obtained by the nation's major chains, as shown in Exhibit 8.16, new cash infusions and new entrants are appearing. Wal-Mart, a super retailer in the general merchandise field, recently entered the supermarket industry and companies from the United Kingdom, Germany, and Belgium have acquired controlling interests in various U.S. food chains.

EXHIBIT 8.16 **Grocery Store Industry Financial Results**

	1993	1992	1991	1990	1989	1988
Revenues	$130,800.0	$120,400.0	$115,940.0	$113,019.0	$107,325.0	$97,401.0
Cost of goods sold	96,792.0	89,336.8	86,259.4	84,199.2	80,279.1	73,148.2
Operating profit	34,008.0	31,063.2	29,680.6	28,819.8	27,045.9	24,252.8
Overhead expense	30,222.9	27,996.5	26,998.1	26,261.0	25,164.5	22,517.6
Pretax income[1]	3,785.1	3,066.7	2,682.6	2,558.9	1,881.4	1,735.3
Income taxes	1,495.1	1,226.7	1,081.1	1,041.5	777.0	682.0
Net profit	$ 2,290.0	$ 1,840.0	$ 1,601.5	$ 1,517.4	$ 1,104.4	$ 1,053.3

Note: 1. Rounding errors.

Source: Philip S. Mulqueen, "Grocery Store Industry," *Value Line* (November 20, 1992), p. 1497. Includes results of only those companies studied by *Value Line.*

ABC "Primetime Live"'s Exposé

The Government Accountability Project, a group that provides support to company whistle-blowers, first brought the food-handling and sanitation practices at Food Lion to "PrimeTime Live"'s attention. Subsequently, ABC producer Lynn Neufer Litt began gathering material for the exposé by talking to 70 current and past Food Lion employees who had worked at 200 of the company's stores. To obtain independent confirmation of the various employee claims, several investigators (one of whom was Lynn Neufer Litt) applied for jobs in some 20 different Food Lion stores. Two were hired and worked in three stores, in two meat departments and a deli. Neufer Litt's hidden-camera footage and Diane Sawyer's employee interviews provided viewers a behind-the-scenes look at Food Lion's food-handling methods, deceptive labeling practices, pressures to protect profit margins, and unsanitary shortcuts that employees pursued to survive under the company's time-management system.

Food Freshness and Food-Handling Practices

With slim profit margins, supermarkets have to squeeze profits from every dollar spent. Food Lion's merchandise costs are about 79% of total expenses, so any savings achieved in this area are significant. Accordingly, top management went to great lengths to demonstrate frugality and the conservation of profit margins. Area managers and even vice-presidents would get into trash barrels and dumpsters and retrieve discarded food, stating that "you're throwing away profits." Bryan Rogers, an ex-produce manager told Diane Sawyer: "I've seen them *in* the dumpster, not just leaning over into it, climb *in* it, I mean be up in it" to get merchandise and have it recycled. "Just take a head of cauliflower, for instance, I mean to where it's just got tiny little black spots all over the top of it, and they'd bring it back in and want you to take a, like a Brillo pad type of thing, and scrub it to get the little black stuff off and stick it in a tray and reduce it and try to get something for it."

A meat manager stated: "We try to sell everything we can to keep from throwing anything away." Another worker, shown trimming off discolored portions of out-dated pork announced: "OK, these are conversions, they look just as good as fresh." Jean Bull, a meat wrapper who had worked in 12 different Food Lion stores over a 13-year period said:

> I have seen my supervisor take chicken back out of the bone can, make us wash it, and put it back out, and it was rotten. It's just unreal what they'll do to save a dime. They take *that* pork that's already starting to get a slime to it, it gets what they call a halo to it, a kind of a green tinge to it, and they take and put that into a grinder with sausage mixture, and they put it back out for anywhere from 7–10 days as fresh, home-made sausage. And it's *rotten.*

Larry Worley, an ex-market manager, told another tale of trimming away spoilage and the pressures placed on employees to perform: "We'd have this pack of cheese, sliced American cheese, and rats would get up on top of that and just eat, eat like the whole corner off of it. You'd have to trim it up and put it back out. You *had* to because if we didn't make our gross profit we were out the door."

Others told how Food Lion extended the shelf life of outdated products through repackaging or reformulation. Whole ham that was two weeks past the meat packer's "sell-by" date was sliced, placed in new number ten trays, and put on sale as fresh meat. A worker was observed unwrapping old ground beef and mixing it with fresh ground beef to be sold as new. Bleach was used creatively, according to Bonnie Simpson, a five-year Food Lion veteran meat wrapper: employees soaked outdated ham in Clorox to remove its foul odor, cut it up and cubed it, and sold it as cubed pork. Fish received a different treatment:

> Fish has a three-day shelf life. OK? After three days you're supposed to reduce it and sell it or throw it away. But we didn't do that. We soaked the fish in baking soda and then we'd squirt lemon juice on it. Then put it back in the case and sell them for three more days on it. The fish would be *so* rotten it would crumble in your hand.

The most elaborate method for dealing with outdated product was one manager's handling of "Country Pride" chicken parts. An on-camera segment showed him working with some cellophane wrapped packages, saying "Open them up and put a soaking pad, a couple of them in the tray. This way we can put three days' date on them." He then proceeded to spread barbecue sauce on the chicken parts and sent them to the gourmet section to be sold at full price.

Despite these practices, Diane Sawyer noted that no cases of food poisoning had been connected to Food Lion or any other grocery chain in North Carolina. Johanna Reese, of the state's Division of Environmental Health, stated that Food Lion has an "average to above-average record" regarding health inspections.

Time Management and Unsanitary Work Practices

In addition to squeezing as much profit as possible from its merchandise, Food Lion has attempted to be as labor efficient as possible. The company called in a consulting firm to time all work and establish standards. The firm then developed a time-management system called "Effective Scheduling." For example, a meat cutter must cut one box of meat every 32 minutes, and meat wrappers have one hour to unload and stock 50 boxes of product. Based on the standards established, headquarters sent each store a schedule mandating the work that departments should accomplish in 40 hours. Through this system, Tom Smith believes that "we don't work our employees hard. We work them smart."

Unfortunately, many employees have found it impossible to complete their work in the allotted time and have resorted to skipping work breaks and working illegally "off-the-clock." For three workers interviewed by Diane Sawyer, their weekly unpaid work amounted to 10–25 hours each, and they said the pace was grueling. Mark Riggs, a former manager of two Food Lion stores, felt pressured by higher management to get performance from his employees. He knew that he was asking too much from them: "I felt guilty, incredible guilt for the things I made people do. It was the biggest reason for me leaving [Food Lion]. I couldn't look at myself in the mirror at the end of the day. You had to push people, push people."

Employees also took many shortcuts to save time, which led to unsanitary workplace conditions. In one case, a beef grinder wasn't cleaned in the evening or the next morning, and the department's bandsaw blades and wheels weren't disassembled to eliminate spending time to reassemble them the next morning. As a result, meat residues rotted overnight and were deposited on newly ground or cut meat the next day. One deli clerk, casting a baleful eye around her workstation, commented after the hidden camera showed infrequently cleaned trays and tins and a meat cutter "ice skating" on a grease-covered floor:

> Well the floor and the meat slicer . . . God, comin' into a place and the glunk on the slicer is thick. The floor's got all kinds of crap all over it. I don't think it's real appealing for a deli.

Another exposé segment pointed out shipping problems associated with Food Lion's vaunted advance purchasing system. Although centralized advance purchases and volume buying resulted in lower product costs, shipping delays or problems with getting merchandise from distribution centers in a timely manner caused many meat products to arrive in stores near their "sell-by" dates. In one on-camera sequence the following dialogue transpired.

Meat manager: You *know* that the lamb that you cut on Monday is not gonna run, is not gonna go through Wednesday. Because the damn stuff is old when it comes in.

"PrimeTime": What do you mean it's old when it comes in?

Meat manager: It's ——— lamb. I been on their ass for three years to get some decent lamb, if they want to sell lamb.

Food Lion Responds

Prior to its broadcast, "PrimeTime Live" gave Food Lion a report on its investigation and invited the company to provide a spokesperson to be interviewed. Rather than appear under "PrimeTime"'s conditions, Food Lion immediately began running television advertisements. One showed Tom Smith strolling through a Food Lion store, mentioning the company's "A" sanitation rating and the chain's pride in its cleanliness standards. On the morning of the telecast, employees in Salisbury held a rally to prepare procompany petitions and letters. They were subsequently sent to members of Congress and Capital Cities/ABC, Inc. A Tulsa paper carried a story the morning of the telecast, anticipating the program's effect on the company's new stores and quoting Vince Watkins: "It is our understanding that this program will make some very serious and potentially devastating allegations about our company. These allegations will make excellent television but they will not be the truth."

The next day Food Lion distributed a media "Fact Sheet" outlining its position regarding food-handling and employee scheduling practices. Company executives visited each store shown in the segment and interviewed the employees involved. A company announcement promised quick action to accomplish the following.

1. Establish more stringent periodic testing of employees to ensure complete and clear understanding of all of Food Lion's policies and procedures.
2. Increase internal and external audits and internal inspections by management to ensure that these policies and procedures are rigorously implemented.
3. Continue to ensure that if there is ever any problem in any of our stores, anywhere, at any time, we fix it.

Other operating procedures were changed immediately. The company's previous meat-handling policy had been to open the packages on their "sell-by" date to check for freshness. Any spoiled meat was to be discarded, and still-fresh meat would be repackaged and sold at a discount. Now "so as not to create any further suspicions" about repackaging, Michael Mozingo said that prices would be reduced while the meat remained in the case after which it could be sold for only one more day.

Although the chain's executives believed that the furor would quickly subside, it didn't. Mozingo admitted that "our stock is down, but we expected that to occur and we expect it to go back up to its previous level. The reason Food Lion has been so successful is because our customers are happy with the job we're doing." In an effort to stem the company's sliding stock value Tom Smith made a 50-minute conference call to stock analysts, charging that most of the program's sources lacked credibility and were union sympathizers. He also made a television commercial in which he said, in part, "You've heard some shocking stories about Food Lion. We do have sound policies and procedures. However, occasionally a problem can exist." And within the chain itself another public relations strategy was tried: 60,000 video tapes of Food Lion's responses to the broadcast were sent to employees, and they were urged to show them to their families, friends, and local groups. Vincent Watkins also suggested that, along with showing the tapes, "they might want to have a party with their friends and serve them food from Food Lion's delis."

During the ensuing weeks Food Lion launched a counteroffensive in the press and on television against what it considered to be unfair, careless, and dishonest reporting. Vince Watkins asserted that "when unwarranted attacks are made on a company, you don't say, 'We'll take our hit and move on.' You come back with the truth." Food Lion questioned whether the outdated meat loaf actually was nine days old, as it would have become visibly black to the television cameras after only four days. The company pointed out that Food Lion never carried various products displayed in one televised sequence, such as Colombo yogurt and Healthy Choice lunch meats. Beef America products were shown, but actually 6–7-week-old Montford Beef was shipped in vacuum sealed packages, well within the prescribed 12–14 week freshness period. And in the damaging barbecue sauce segment, the chicken products changed from scene to scene.

Additionally, the company questioned the union's integrity and the motives of three people interviewed. Some 65 of the 70 people interviewed by "PrimeTime Live" were supplied by the UFCW and six of the seven people identified in the story were involved in UFCW-initiated lawsuits against Food Lion. The company reprimanded Joe Sultan, the former perishables manager, for poor conditions in his department and then fired him for requiring off-the-clock work from employees. Bryan Rogers, while denigrating the company's produce in the telecast, had shopped at a Food Lion the night of the "PrimeTime" program. Jean Bull, who talked about selling slime-covered pork, shops with her family at Food Lion each week. She was reprimanded for passing bad checks and has a lawsuit against Food Lion.

Food Lion also initiated numerous legal actions. The company filed its first suit in connection with the program by charging the network with fraud because ABC's producers lied to Food Lion to get jobs at its stores. Through this lawsuit Food Lion gained access to the program's unedited footage and the right to question Lynn Neufer Litt, the segment's producer. According to Mike Mozingo, "Some of the things we are finding out from our depositions makes it plain to us they engaged in extensive illegal acts and violated state and federal laws in doing so." The chain amended its original suit in April 1993, adding allegations that the network violated federal racketeering laws. Food Lion's suit now includes accusations of racketeering, trespassing, illicit eavesdropping, and wire fraud, allowing it to collect triple damages. The network's response to this emendation noted that "Food Lion does not challenge the truth of the ABC report. It challenges only the undercover methods used by ABC. We believe Food Lion's charges of racketeering are outrageous. We believe this is a legally baseless complaint."

In another lawsuit filed February 12, 1993, against the UFCW, Food Lion alleged that the union has waged a smear campaign in an attempt to increase union membership. In seeking actual and punitive damages, Food Lion has charged the union with the (1) "abuse of process," (2) use of "economic guerrilla tactics" to tarnish its image, and (3) filing of frivolous lawsuits to obtain proprietary information about company operations and finances.

In the face of all these legal actions, some have questioned the wisdom of Food Lion's public relations strategy. Said John Small of Fort Worth's Strategic Retail Consulting firm: "From a public relations standpoint, they were their own worst enemy. I would have advised a massive *mea culpa* as opposed to the defensive posture that they're taking." Food Lion, however, believes that it is pursuing the right strategy and takes comfort in General Motors' vindication after it had been severely damaged in an NBC "Dateline" exposé of safety hazards associated with its pickup trucks. Referring to GM's defense—and to television sensationalism in general—Vince Watkins said that the "Dateline" debacle only "illustrates that TV tabloid-type programs will go to extraordinary lengths to concoct or stage events."

Although Food Lion often has employed court actions to remedy challenges to its survival, numerous court actions have in turn been begun against it. The company began meeting with the U.S. Labor Department in January 1993 to head off federal charges of child-labor law and overtime violations. These charges were contained in a 183-person class action suit filed on September 11, 1991, with the help of the UFCW. The suit seeks $388 million in back pay and damages, although none in the action are members of the UFCW. Francis D. Carpenter claims to have regularly worked 60- and 70-hour weeks during his seven years at Food Lion's Southern Pines, North Carolina, grocery store. He said, "It got to the point where I just couldn't take it anymore. My supervisor would always say 'Do what you have to do to get the job done, but don't let me catch you working off the clock.' I took that to mean 'Work off the clock, but don't get caught.'" In its suit the union asserted that employees often worked up to 13 hours a week off the clock. Food Lion has already lost one such case when a U.S. District Court Judge ordered Food Lion to pay two former employees a total of $53,000 in overtime wages and damages.

The Labor Department is also investigating some 1,400 alleged violations of child-labor laws, including 1,200 involving teenagers working with or near potentially dangerous equipment. If the chain is ultimately charged with all these violations, it would be the largest case of its kind involving a single employer. Food Lion Vice-President Vince Watkins did not know the investigation's details, but he understood that about 90% were related to teenagers putting cardboard boxes into package balers that were turned off. He noted that the ban on teenagers doing that type of work had gone into effect less than a year ago and that the entire grocery industry is fighting the ban's scope. Food Lion's policy states that teenagers must sign statements acknowledging the ban. They must also wear a blue dot on their name tags so they will not be asked to perform forbidden work. Watkins said, "I don't think anybody violated it intentionally and I don't think anyone in management asked them to do it."

Food Lion's Tulsa Operations

Over a short period of time, Food Lion built and opened seven stores in the fastest-growing parts of the Tulsa metropolitan area. Exhibit 8.17 shows the

EXHIBIT 8.17 **Food Lion's Store Locations in the Tulsa Metropolitan Area**

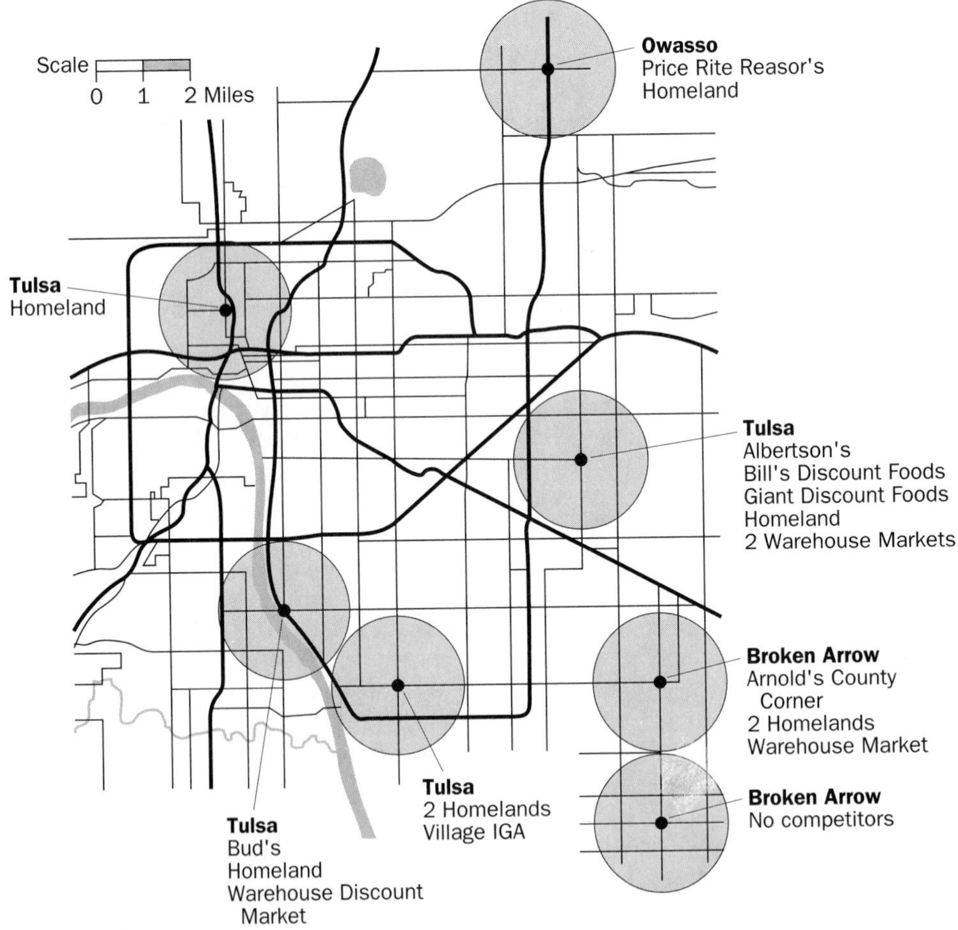

XHIBIT 8.18

Food Lion's Tulsa Supermarket Competition

Company	Stores
Albertson's	4
Bud's Food Stores	4
Consumer's IGA	2
Homeland	25
Payless Food Store	2
Price Mart	3
Price Rite Reasor's (Reasor's Foods)	2
Super H Discount Foods	5
Warehouse Market	12

store locations and their competitors within a two-mile radius. Exhibit 8.18 lists the major supermarkets operating in the Tulsa market. In addition to the large number of Warehouse Markets and Homelands stores blanketing the area, competition comes from at least three warehouse clubs and 135 convenience stores.

Food Lion's stores were open from 7:00 A.M. to 11:00 P.M. They were clean, well-lit, easily accessible, and utilitarian in appearance. The stores contained 28,000 to 32,000 square feet and cost $1–$2 million each, depending on the land cost. All were similarly configured, as shown in Exhibit 8.19, with the only difference being the use of 13 aisles in the smaller Broken Arrow and Owasso stores. The company pursued its usual low-price strategy, which it announced through comparative advertising of the type depicted in Exhibit 8.20. Well in advance of Food Lion's store openings, however, its competitors had begun cutting prices and featuring cents-off end displays and shelf specials. Other competitors renewed double redemptions on coupons, a practice that had been previously discontinued in the Tulsa market, and still others guaranteed lower prices on a product-by-product basis.

In addition to the actions taken by other supermarkets, the UFCW's Local 76 immediately challenged Food Lion. John Stone, the local's president, felt that the "PrimeTime Live" exposé would be effective for only about three weeks. To keep its message before the public, Stone's union mailed "informational literature" to households in each store's ZIP-code area and passed out leaflets at each store's parking lot entrance for several weeks. Exhibit 8.21 shows a copy of the postcard mailed to households during the week of December 3, 1992. Exhibit 8.22 is an example of the leaflets handed out. One side contained the words "Shop *American* DON'T SHOP FOOD LION," superimposed on an American flag.

EXHIBIT 8.19 **Typical Tulsa Food Lion Store Layout**

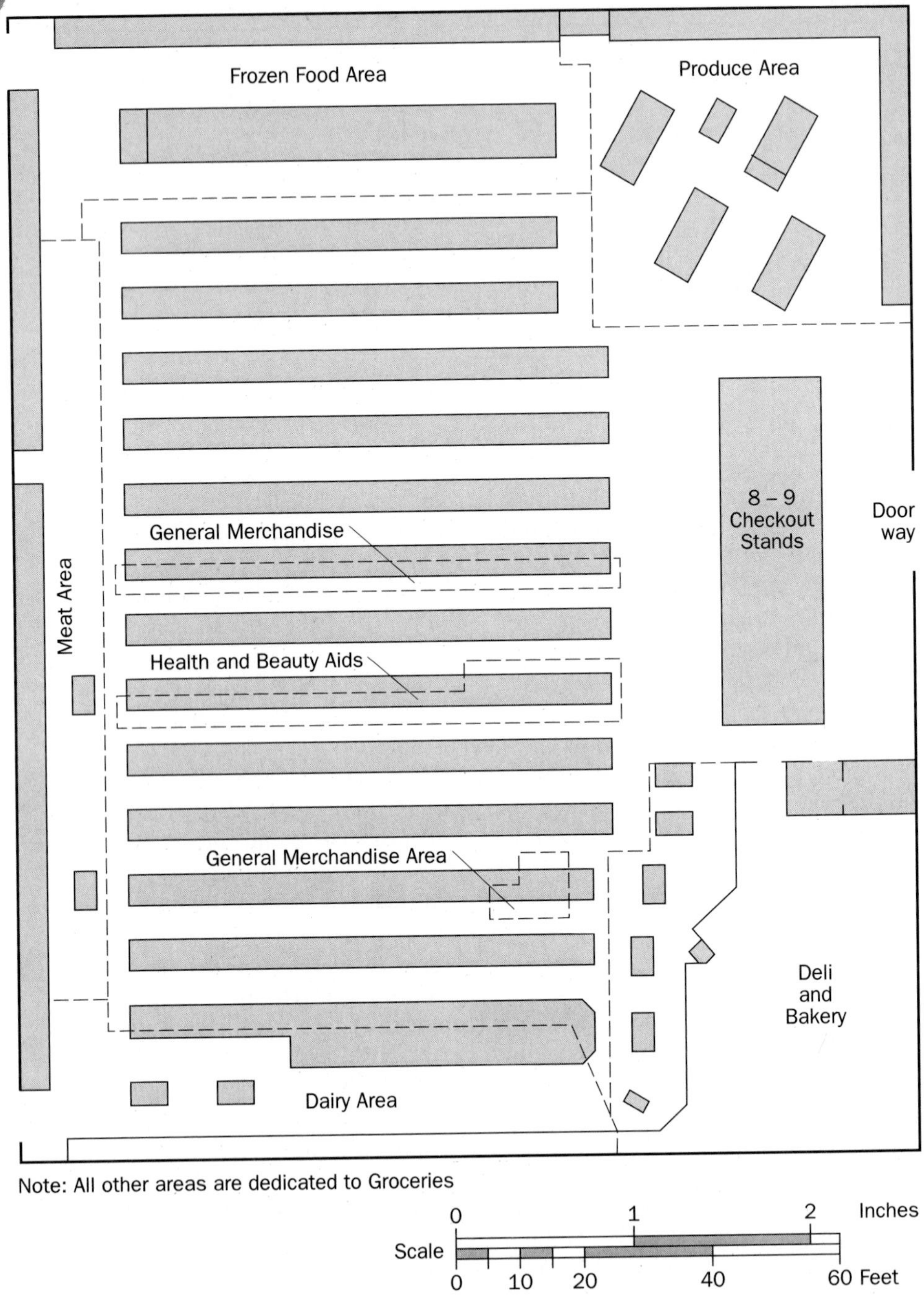

Frozen Food Area
Produce Area
8 – 9
Checkout
Stands
Door
way
General Merchandise
Meat Area
Health and Beauty Aids
General Merchandise Area
Deli
and
Bakery
Dairy Area
Note: All other areas are dedicated to Groceries
Scale
0
1
2
Inches
0
10
20
40
60 Feet

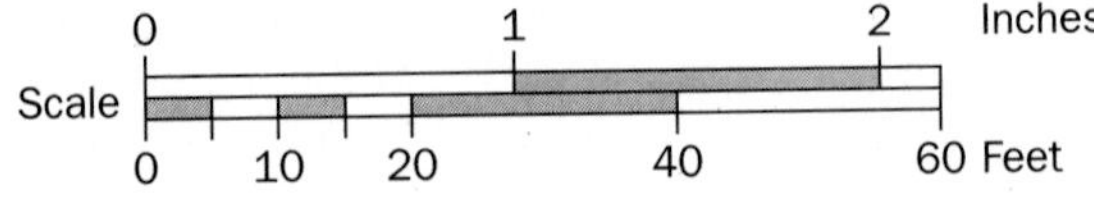

EXHIBIT 8.20 **Price Comparison Advertisement**

Comparison reveals

FOOD LION PRICES LOWER IN TULSA

Food Lion's Extra Low Prices are lower everyday on the items families buy most. Below are just a few examples. These represent thousands of items you can buy for less at Food Lion every day of the week. Visit Food Lion today and discover how much you can save each week on your total food bill.

	Price Mart	Homeland	Food Lion
Libby's Lite Sliced Peaches (16 Oz.)	$ .89	$ 1.19	$ .79
Del Monte Cut Green Beans (8 Oz.)	.43	.53	.34
Del Monte Creamed Corn (8.75 Oz.)	.43	.53	.34
Veg All (16 Oz.)	.59	.59	.48
Del Monte Green Peas (8.5 Oz.)	.43	.53	.30
Bush's Baked Beans (16 Oz.)	.69	.69	.50
Van Camp's Beanee Weenees (7.75 Oz.)	.74	.85	.55
Hunt's Whole Peeled Tomatoes (14.5 Oz.)	.73	.79	.48
Mahatma Yello Rice (5 Oz.)	.41	.39	.33
Campbell's Vegetable Soup (10.5 Oz.)	.64	.65	.55
Campbell's Cream of Chicken Soup (10.75 Oz.)	.69	.75	.64
Spam Deviled Spread (3 Oz.)	.59	.65	.56
Underwood's Deviled Ham (4.5 Oz.)	1.29	1.39	1.09
Libby's Vienna Sausages (5 Oz.)	.63	.75	.43
Bush's Hot Chili Beans (16 Oz.)	.49	.55	.38
Franco American Spaghetti (14.75 Oz.)	.65	.69	.50
Franco American Spaghetti O's W/Meatballs (14.75 Oz.)	1.13	1.16	.89
Chef Boyardee Beef-O-Getti (15 Oz.)	1.13	1.16	.89
Chef Boyardee Beef Ravioli (15 Oz.)	1.13	1.16	.79
Chef Boyardee Microwave Spaghetti W/Meatballs (7.5 Oz)	.99	1.09	.79
Prego Spaghetti Sauce W/Mushrooms (30 Oz.)	1.89	2.27	1.69
Old El Paso Taco Dinner (12/9.75 Oz.)	2.39	2.59	1.99
Kraft Deluxe Macaroni (14 Oz.)	1.69	1.77	1.39
Crisco Shortening (16 Oz.)	1.28	1.39	1.23
Totals	$21.95	$24.11	$17.92

America's Fastest Growing Supermarket Chain

This price comparison was made December 17, 1992. Some prices may have changed since that time.

EXHIBIT 8.21 **Union Local 76 Postcard Copy**

FOOD LION IS FOREIGN OWNED!
Every Dollar in Profit Goes Overseas to Belgium!

The U.S. Dept. of Labor has charged Food Lion with "substantial violations of overtime and child labor laws." Food Lion cheats its employees to gain an illegal advantage over American businessmen who obey the law! Investigative news reports indicate Food Lion engages in grossly unsanitary food handling practices including the repackaging of rancid meat and other food products. Don't let a foreign company dump its garbage on American consumers!

SHOP AMERICAN!
DON'T SHOP AT FOOD LION!

EXHIBIT 8.22 **United Food and Commercial Workers Union Local 76 Leaflet**

Help Stop Off the Clock Work at Food Lion!

In Congressional Hearings, Food Lion Employees testified that Food Lion pressured them to work off the clock without pay. Hundreds of other Employees have filed complaints with the U.S. Department of Labor or in Federal Courts challenging Food Lion's off the clock practices.

PLEASE DON'T SHOP FOOD LION

Food Lion Is Foreign Owned
Don't Send American Dollars Overseas

Please Shop American!

What Now?

In addressing the company's shareholders, Tom Smith acknowledged that problems have arisen during its southwestern market expansion, of which Tulsa is only an example:

> Operating results in this market have been less than originally expected and are significantly below the average for the Company's stores in other markets. We will closely monitor and evaluate performance in this market in light of the Company's performance objectives and will continue to do all things reasonably necessary to increase performance. However, at the present time, the Company does not plan any significant additional growth in the Southwest and is studying alternative strategies for this market.

Asked what Smith's remarks meant, Vince Watkins scoffed at any idea of the company's selling its southwestern stores and 1.1 million square foot Roanoke, Texas, distribution center. He went on to say that "we intend to battle hard for market share out there."

Meanwhile the company disclosed in late April 1993 the filing of three shareholder suits against it. One suit alleges that Food Lion's top executives conspired to inflate the market price of the company's securities. The second lawsuit maintains that executives misstated or omitted important information in its company reports dating back to September 1991. The third suit claims that the company's 1992 proxy statement was false and misleading when it failed to disclose the improper food-handling procedures documented by "PrimeTime Live."

APPENDIX A: How to Handle the Media

Progressive Grocer has provided general guidelines for handling inquiries from the media. Those guidelines and their rationales are as follows.

1. **Be prompt**
   If you cannot give an immediate and informed answer to the media, do not attempt to stall by replying "No comment," which raises a red flag to most reporters. State that you will have to look into the matter and that you will get back to them as soon as possible with a complete and conversant response.
   Have someone return all media calls as soon as possible. Do not assume that, by not responding, the problem will go away. The media will run the story with or without your company's response.
2. **Be informative**
   Do not consider the media a collective enemy but instead consider the situation an opportunity to explain your side of the story or event.
   Be sure that the media understands the conditions under which your industry operates as well as the various pressures to which your firm must respond.
3. **Be prepared**
   Have a formal program that details how the media will be handled by all store personnel regardless of their position. This formal program is administered best through a public affairs or communications department, with individuals assigned to specific media liaison duties.
   Be sure that your employees know what they can and cannot say to the media.
4. **Don't lie**
   Try to determine why the media is interested in your company. The question may be about food retailing in general, and your company may be a convenient source of information—or it may be about your particular firm, requiring a company-specific response.
   If the query is about something negative try to present a positive action that has already been taken, if such is the case, or state that corrective action will be taken if further investigation indicates that such action is required.
   Never lie to reporters; they invariably have more information about the particular issue than you do at the time of the query.

Source: Summarized from Steve Weinstein, "How to Handle the Media," *Progressive Grocer* (September 1991), pp. 90–93.

McDonald's Corporation

Patricia Feltes, Dan Kopp, and Lois Shufeldt

In the early Spring of 1992, McDonald's was confronting a dilemma that many corporations would have liked to face. How does the number one company in its industry increase market share? How can it maintain a ten-year compound annual growth rate in sales and net income of 11% and 12%, respectively?[1] And finally, if it can accomplish all of that, how can the company still retain some sense of what it traditionally had been?

Ray Kroc, who bought the franchise rights to McDonald's Corporation and turned it into a fast-food giant, was a firm believer in growth. One of his favorite sayings was: "If you're green, you're growing. If you're ripe, you rot."[2] He was also a firm believer in the strategy he chose for the organization: that McDonald's should set itself apart from the competition by offering simple, inexpensive food with fast, friendly, clean, convenient, and consistent service.[3]

Things had changed for McDonald's Corporation and the industry it created since Ray Kroc stated his philosophy. Enticed by McDonald's growth, other firms entered the market. These companies built on the lessons learned from McDonald's pioneering efforts to become competitors not only for customers but also for suppliers and restaurant sites. Demand for McDonald's traditional menu items had slowed and customers were increasingly turning to other choices. The industry that McDonald's Corporation created had matured.

In 1992, McDonald's was running out of good sites and room to grow in the United States without cannibalizing its present outlets, whether company or franchisee owned. Although international expansion was rapid, the 2,300 domestic franchisees would not benefit from that growth. They relied exclusively on sales and profits in their own markets and expected the parent company to support their efforts.[4] The chain also was becoming increasingly aware that the consumer base was outgrowing the McDonald's menu. The traditional response of massive marketing spending might not be enough to boost U.S. sales in the face of industry saturation, slowing demand, and tougher competition.[5]

As the market became more competitive, McDonald's became more responsive to market trends and customer demands. But adding too many new items to the menu and providing additional services could overtax kitchens, slow service, and cause the loss of its competitive advantage. In addition, a new policy of changing menus, varying options, and offering multiple services could undercut its popular image as *the* fast-food hamburger chain.

This case was prepared by Professors Patricia Feltes, Dan Kopp, and Lois Shufeldt of Southwest Missouri State University. This case was presented at the 1992 North American Case Research Meeting. This case was edited by T. L. Wheelen and J.D. Hunger for this book. Reprinted by permission.

Background

The giant McDonald's Corporation began as a tiny drive-in just east of Pasadena, California, in 1937. Dick and Maurice (Mac) McDonald owned and operated it. The brothers cooked hot dogs, mixed milk shakes, and waited on customers seated on a dozen canopy covered stools. Three carhops served patrons in the parking lot. The success of this unit led the brothers to open a larger outlet in San Bernardino with an expanded, 25-item menu that included time- and labor-intensive pit barbecue selections. By the mid 1940s, it was the town's most popular teenage hangout. That popularity, however, drove off the broader family trade while drawing additional carhop drive-ins into the competition.

The McDonald brothers reconsidered their operation. They studied their sales receipts for the previous three years and discovered that hamburgers generated 80% of their business. This discovery led to a revolution in the food service industry. Speed, lower prices, and volume became the McDonald brothers' strategy. They cut the menu from 25 to 9 choices, fired the carhops, and replaced the china and cutlery with paper wrappings. They introduced custom-built, six-foot long grills and reduced the price of a hamburger from $.30 to $.15. Within six months, the restaurant began to attract the working-class families who would be their market.[6]

The McDonalds continued to customize equipment and refine processes. They adopted rigid operational procedures, which they carefully taught to all employees. To fill orders in 30 seconds or less, the crew began cooking and packaging food products in anticipation of orders rather than in response to them.[7]

When they began to franchise their concept in 1952, they also saw that they needed a new, standard building design. They sketched a rough idea of what they wanted, including a large arch at each end of the building to give it height. The first architect they approached agreed to design the building but refused to include the gaudy arches. The McDonalds took his drawing and went to a local maker of neon signs, where they got their bright yellow arches.

In 1954, Ray A. Kroc, a food service equipment salesman, was impressed with the number of Multimixers the brothers bought for their operations. He quickly recognized that the best way to profit from their fast-food concept was to franchise them and allow others to invest their capital. The McDonalds had sold only 21 franchises since 1952, with nine of them becoming operating units. At first they sold their system of doing business for a flat fee of $1,000. They had already turned down an offer from Carnation Corporation to build a chain of their restaurants in partnership because they preferred things the way they were.

The brothers hired Kroc as their franchise agent. His contract gave Kroc 1.9% of the gross sales from franchisees; of that, the McDonalds took a 0.5% royalty. Kroc sold franchises under the name Franchise Realty Corporation. The brothers retained the rights to their name and insisted on adherence to their procedures. Ray Kroc's role was to sell the system developed by the McDonald brothers worldwide.[8]

In spite of a widely believed Harvard Business School study done in the mid 1950s, which proved beyond any doubt that the fast-food franchise concept could never succeed as a chain in the United States,[9] Ray Kroc continued to expand the operation. In 1960, Kroc's organization changed its name to McDonald's Corporation. A year later, the McDonald brothers sold out to Kroc and his associates for $2.7 million. At that time, there were 200 McDonald's units.[10] By 1989 McDonald's Corporation operated 12,400 outlets in 59 countries. Its 500,000 employees served 22 million customers a day and grossed almost $20 billion in revenue annually.[11]

Industry

Demand

The food service industry had revenues of $262 billion in 1991. The National Restaurant Association projected an inflation-adjusted restaurant sales growth of 1.8% in 1992, compared to 0.5% in 1991 and 0.9% in 1990. The total number of U.S. outlets was 269,000 in 1991, compared to 379,000 in 1989. Net profits in 1992 for the 74 largest public companies were expected to be flat at 7% to 8% of sales.[12]

Although the restaurant industry had outpaced the overall economy in recent years, indications of outlet saturation now appeared. This situation was attributed in part to the slowdown of population growth. A restaurant shakeout triggered by debt-laden balance sheets, an excess of outlets, and stiff competition from food stores was expected to continue. The fastest growing segment of the industry was expected to be in the sandwich area.[13]

Competitive Conditions

The biggest chains controlled a growing share of the market. The top 100 companies—led by McDonald's, PepsiCo (Taco Bell, Kentucky Fried Chicken, and Pizza Hut), and Grand Metropolitan (Burger King)—operated nearly 50% of the nation's stand-alone eating places, an increase from 30% in 1972. Independents owned 34% of the nation's upscale restaurants.[14]

Growth and increasing size did not necessarily result in profits for all entrants. Many formerly highly regarded investment opportunities fell on financial hard times. Debt-laden chains included Al Copeland Enterprises (Popeye's Famous Fried Chicken and Church's Fried Chicken) and Long John Silver's Holding, Inc.[15]

Fast-food chains constantly revised their menus to adjust to competitors' attacks and consumer tastes. At McDonald's, prepackaged salads (introduced in 1987) accounted for 7% of total sales. Mexican food, such as burritos and fajitas, have been introduced to combat Taco Bell's competitive pressures.[16]

In the past, prime suburban sites were the target of fast-food restaurants, but most of the choice locations were now gone. The competition for good locations had been extended to alternative sites such as hospitals, airports, railroad stations, tollways, military bases, tiny towns near highways, urban areas, and shopping malls.[17] Some relief in the cost of new locations was expected in 1992 as a result of declines in real estate values and lower interest rates.[18]

The consumer's perception of value, that is, a combination of product, price, service, and convenience, was considered a key factor of success in the restaurant business. Delivering "value," generally interpreted in practice as lower prices, was the industry's theme in 1991. Less expensive menus or selected "value" offerings were becoming commonplace at such giants as McDonald's, Taco Bell, and Wendy's.[19] Price cutting can hurt profit margins, so the large chains were reluctant to add items to the bargain lists. Instead, they were introducing "value combinations" (typically offering a deluxe sandwich, fries, and drink at a lower combo price).

On average in 1991, about 34% of each dollar spent by a restaurant went for the food itself. Payroll expenses, including fringe benefits, represented approximately 30%. Fixed costs in the industry were high and included much of a restaurant's labor costs, utility bills, and interest expense related to the acquisition of land, buildings, and equipment. A survey by the National Restaurant Association reported an average of 6% pretax profit but profitability varied, with the amount of sales being the key determinant.[20] Cost cutters were expected to get help in 1992, as forecasts of the industry's main expenses—labor and raw materials (food)—indicated rises no faster than inflation in 1992.[21]

Government Regulation

According to restaurateurs, rising taxes and government-mandated employee benefits took their toll on growth. The industry was concerned about Clinton administration and congressional efforts to develop a national health insurance plan. It was also lobbying for repeal of a 1987 law requiring restaurants to pay Social Security taxes on a share of their workers' tips. Restaurant owners contended that this requirement was unfair because they couldn't count the same tips toward minimum wage obligations.[22] The Americans with Disabilities Act of 1991 was also expected to have an impact on both hiring and customer access. The act required access to jobs and public facilities for individuals with certain disabilities.

McDonald's competitors had long resented the industry leader's refusal to join fights against minimum wage hikes and other potentially damaging legislation. The company rarely participated in industry associations and joined the National Restaurant Association only in 1985. A McDonald's senior Vice-President stated that the organization preferred to remain apolitical and avoid getting embroiled in legislative issues.[23]

Consumer Behavior

Fast-food industry research showed that there were three primary reasons for a consumer's choice of a fast-food restaurant: (1) time of day, (2) time required to eat, and (3) price. The type of food and its taste were not that important to the decision.[24]

Customers viewed fried chicken as too messy for a sit-down restaurant meal and too expensive for lunch. Pizza was suitable for dinner because it was relatively high priced and time-consuming. Hamburgers were primarily a lunchtime choice because they were fast, inexpensive, and could be eaten anywhere.[25]

Forecasts indicated that Americans aged 45 and above would comprise more than 25% of the population during the 1990s. An expected result was an increased emphasis on home delivery and healthier eating choices.[26]

American consumers overall had become more nutrition conscious. Phil Sokoloff, a multimillionaire nutrition activist, had been a particularly effective crusader. He took on McDonald's menu and U.S. eating habits with ads specifically critical of fast food. After spending more than $3 million of his own money, he began to see the fast-food giants change, including McDonald's introduction of a low-fat burger, the McLean Deluxe, in 1991.[27]

Labor Shortages

Labor shortages were expected to be a continuing challenge for the industry, particularly for the lower paying fast-food chains. Because of the declining birth rates in the 1970s, there were about 3 million fewer youths aged 16–20 in 1990 than there were in 1980; their ranks would continue to thin over the next five years.[28]

However, potential new labor sources were emerging. The two age groups having the greatest population growth—ages 45–54 (47%) and ages 35–44 (18%)—will also show an increase in labor participation as "baby boomer" mothers return to work. More than 84% of women aged 35–44 are expected to be working by the year 2000, compared to only 77% in 1990. For women in the 45–54 age group, the participation rate is expected to rise from 69% in 1990 to 75% in 2000.[29]

Competition

Although McDonald's characterized the competition as "anyone who sells food," according to a Paine Webber restaurant analyst,[30] its immediate competition can be categorized as fast-food establishments, midprice family restaurants, and supermarkets. Potential competition included regional chains with national appeal and new entrants such as Walt Disney Company's Mickey's Kitchen.[31] Many contract food service companies had also expanded from their school, worksite, and hospital cafeteria businesses to buy and operate restaurants. For example, Morrison, Inc., ran the 151-unit Ruby Tuesday chain.[32]

Fast-Food Competitors

Burger King Corporation

Owned by Grand Metropolitan PLC, Burger King was number two in the restaurant industry. In 1991, it had U.S. sales of about $5.4 billion from approximately 5,400 outlets. Internationally, the organization had nearly $1 billion in revenues.[33] A new advertising campaign and the introduction of product hits such as the BK broiler chicken sandwich and the double cheeseburger were credited with helping the company successfully turn around.[34]

Besides testing another 70 new items, including popcorn, frozen yogurt, and fresh fruit, Burger King was considering a joint offering with Weight Watchers Corporation as a response to nutrition concerns. Burger King management conceded that Weight Watchers' low-calorie offerings would not be big sellers in its restaurants. However, they would help to eliminate the "veto factor" by offering an alternative to a dieting family member.[35] Other brand names being tested as joint offerings at Burger King included Domino's pizza and Newman's Own salad dressings.[36]

Wendy's International, Inc.

In 1991, Wendy's had some $1.1 billion in sales from 3,776 units worldwide. The organization had successfully completed a five-year turnaround and planned to open 25 new units worldwide in 1992.

Although many fast-food chains became nutritionally aware and began to offer a variety of low-fat, low-calorie selections, Wendy's took a different approach. It had been an early entrant in the nutrition campaign, offering salad bars at some restaurants. It now began to offer the type of product most associated with fast-food menus. The company introduced and heavily promoted Dave's Deluxe, a burger smothered with bacon, sauteed onion, and cheese and named for founder Dave Thomas.[37]

PepsiCo, Inc.

Three of the largest restaurant chains in the industry were part of PepsiCo, Inc.: Kentucky Fried Chicken (KFC), Pizza Hut, and Taco Bell. In 1990, the total PepsiCo restaurant system had U.S. revenues of about $9.4 billion and operated some 14,921 U.S. outlets. The Kentucky Fried Chicken and Pizza Hut chains produced foreign sales of approximately $1.1 billion from about 4,579 outlets.[38] PepsiCo also purchased a small new walk-up/drive-up chain called Hot'n Now, which served a limited menu with no inside seating.

Kentucky Fried Chicken In 1990, Kentucky Fried Chicken produced $3.2 billion in U.S. sales for its parent company. Foreign sales added another $2.6 billion.

Broiled chicken, honey barbecue chicken wings, skinless fried chicken, and oriental wings were a few of the menu tests and changes being tried by Kentucky Fried Chicken.[39] In fact, the informal name change from Kentucky Fried Chicken to KFC was the result of the organization's concern over the image of "fried" food.

The systemwide introduction of skinless fried chicken was delayed in 1991, resulting in a $9 million write-off in the third quarter and an additional $50 million pretax charge in the fourth quarter.[40]

Pizza Hut In 1990, Pizza Hut had $3.8 billion in U.S. sales and $1.1 foreign sales.[41] Pizza Hut had introduced innovations during the past several years to counter the image of pizza as a food choice only for dinner. Personal pan pizzas became the mainstay of its lunch trade, and it instituted delivery service in most markets.[42]

In addition, Pizza Hut was planning to introduce "video juke boxes" to entertain customers while they waited for their pizzas. A quarter would buy the customer five minutes of rock video, vintage newsreels, or highlights of classic TV programs.[43]

Taco Bell PepsiCo's Taco Bell chain had successfully concentrated on the business philosophy popularized by McDonald's Ray Kroc. It served a limited menu at a low price and gave fast service. Estimated systemwide sales for 1991 were $2.6 billion.[44]

In the mid 1980s, Taco Bell cut costs by shifting as much food preparation as possible to outside suppliers, thereby cutting labor costs. It reduced kitchen space from 70% to 30% in each building, converting workspace to additional customer seating. To cut costs further, the company was testing taco-making robots.[45]

Subway Sandwiches and Salads

Subway was the fastest growing restaurant chain in 1989, jumping its sales by 58% to $782 million.[46] Sales generated by 5,595 units in 1990 rose an additional 40.1% to $1.4 billion. Privately held Subway specialized in sandwiches made with bread baked daily at each outlet. It attracted potential franchisees with a start-up cost of $75,000, compared to $1.6 million for a McDonald's. This low cost resulted in over 7,000 franchises worldwide, four times the number in 1987.[47]

Sonic Drive-Ins

Sonic Corporation parlayed 1950s style ambience with prices set 10% less than the competition to grow to 1,150 units. Giving the chain a unique image were 1950s features such as carhops, a menu of chili dogs, cherry limeades, onion rings, and hamburgers, as well as commercials featuring Frankie Avalon. Sonic's same-store sales growth averaged 11.3% for 16 quarters. In fiscal 1991, sales for franchised and company-owned units were expected to rise 13%, to $515 million.[48]

Rally's

Systemwide 1991 sales for Rally's burger chain were estimated to be $216 million from 327 outlets. First half of 1991 net income was $2.3 million, down slightly from 1990. The menu was a basic hamburger served fast from double drive-through windows at lower prices than the competition.[49] A typical Rally's unit was only 600 to 700 square feet in size, or about one-fifth the size of a McDonald's. It cost $350,000 to build and annual sales averaged about $1,300 a square foot, compared to a $1 million investment and $400 a square foot in sales for an average McDonald's.[50]

Most customers, even at lunchtime, were on their way within 30 seconds. They could buy a quarter-pound cheeseburger, French fries, and large Coke for $3, or $.85 less than at McDonald's. A customer commented that "the food isn't very good here, but it's cheap, quick and easy."[51]

Midprice Family Restaurants

Midprice chains such as Chili's, Baker's Square, Cracker Barrel Old Country Store, General Mills (Olive Garden and Red Lobster), Sizzler Buffet Court and Grill, and Shoney's were providing growing competition for fast-food chains. Meals ranged from $5 to $7, compared to an average $3 to $4 at most fast-food outlets. Additionally, they offered generous portions in comfortable, attractive surroundings with table service. Their success was likely to continue, as demographics were in their favor. In the early 1990s, baby boomers with children and the increasingly older population were expected to patronize such restaurants.[52]

Other Prepared Food Sources

The growth of at-home eating slowed a trend of away-from-home food consumption. Restaurants accounted for much of the total market for prepared takeout foods, capturing 78.1% of the $63.5 billion market in 1989. However, that share had declined from a high of 80.4% in 1986. Figures for 1991 were projected to be down again, to 77.6% of the market.[53]

Supermarkets and convenience stores accounted for more than 20% of the takeout market. In 1989, convenience stores captured 9.2% and supermarkets 12.7% of takeout revenues, respectively. By 1994, when the market is expected to have grown to $88.7 billion, supermarkets' share could increase to 16.5% at the expense of restaurants.[54]

The projected continuation of a rising birthrate should contribute to the number of families who would find going out for a meal more troublesome. Home prepared, microwaved "fast food" would meet many families' needs. Restaurant or store-prepared food that was easily obtained for at-home consumption should also be popular.[55] Competitors such as Domino's Pizza, Pizza Hut, and others were responding to the at-home trend by providing more and faster delivery services. Some upscale restaurants, such as Levy Restaurants, also were starting home delivery for their customers in densely populated and affluent city locations.[56]

McDonald's Corporation

Master Strategy

McDonald's corporate strategy for growth focused on three key elements: adding restaurants, maximizing sales and profits at existing restaurants, and improving international profitability. This emphasis on profitable marketing reflected the business philosophy of its top manager. Chief Executive Officer and Chairman of the Board Michael R. Quinlan stated that the number one objective of the firm was to "cement" the company's preeminent position in the eyes and taste buds of its customers. He further stated that "being the customer's first choice is what we're all about."[57]

In order to accomplish that objective, Thomas W. Glasgow, Jr., Executive Vice-President and Chief Operations Officer, stated that there are only four basic retailing messages for establishing a clear business identity. An organization can focus on being: (1) the cheapest by offering the lowest prices; (2) the easiest by providing top service in the most convenient place to shop; (3) the hottest by focusing on the trendiest new gimmicks; (4) the biggest by offering the widest variety of products. Referring to McDonald's, Glasgow said: "We're the easiest . . . the place that satisfies customers best, and gives them the best value."[58]

Marketing

According to Paul D. Schrage, Senior Executive Vice-President and Chief Marketing Officer:

> Value and customer satisfaction are our mission, and that will be our message. . . . The object of our messages must always be long-term brand building, and those messages should evoke a tinge of nostalgia for those magic moments when we have felt happy and satisfied. A more than $1 billion marketing budget is used to send those messages.[59]

Some impressive facts best describe the effectiveness of the organization's advertising budget and operations. McDonald's was the second-best-known brand in the world. An estimated 96% of the U.S. population between the ages of 16 and 65 have eaten at McDonald's at least once, and two-thirds of that age group did so at least once a month. Character recognition for Ronald McDonald was second only to Santa Claus among children aged 4 to 7.[60]

Other organizations recognized this effectiveness and approached the firm regarding joint marketing efforts. For example, McDonald's and NBC teamed up to sponsor a nationwide gamelike promotion of the network's primetime lineup in the fall of 1990. The effort reached almost 60 million people a day through network spots and traffic at the 8,400 McDonald's restaurants.[61]

Product Innovations

McSubs, McFish Fry, and Other Menu Developments

As eating-out became more popular and affordable, the fast-food-consuming public developed a taste for more than hamburgers and French fries. Hamburger consumption dropped from 19% of all restaurant orders in 1982 to 17% in 1990.[62] McDonald's faced competitors who provided the same service but used other products to meet customers' needs. To counter that challenge McDonald's tested and introduced a variety of alternative menu items.

To meet the growing competition of Subway Sandwiches and Salads, McDonald's introduced McSubs, a cold submarine sandwich, in Wisconsin test markets. To combat Pizza Hut's pizza for lunch features, McDonald's tested a six-inch personal-size pizza in Indiana. In addition, it offered full-size pizzas at other locations to test the dinner market. The company also introduced Mexican food, such as the breakfast burrito, to meet the challenge of Taco Bell, and tested fried chicken against the Kentucky Fried Chicken chain.[63]

Some of the products tested emphasized a healthier alternative: grilled chicken breast sandwich, grilled steak sandwich, and the McLean hamburger. The McLean Deluxe was a lean beef patty containing beef, water, encapsulated salt, carrageenan, and natural beef flavor. This entry offered a response to the Center for Science in the Public Interest, a Washington, D.C.–based consumer group that had described McDonald's Big Mac as containing eight teaspoons of fat.[64] Vegetable oil was now used systemwide for cooking French fries, and salads with reduced calorie dressings were available.[65]

As would be expected, some menu tryouts didn't make the grade. Choices such as Chicken McSwiss sandwich, Maple McKrisps, Calzone, Hulaburger, chopped beefsteak, country-style McChicken sandwich, and a donut-shaped hot dog on a hamburger bun never received enough customer support to be accepted by the chain.[66]

A Paine Webber analyst also wondered whether the company could meet all competition without losing its own distinct image along the way: "It can serve pizza, but it can't offer the variety Pizza Hut can. It can serve taco salad but not the varieties of Mexican food Taco Bell can."[67]

McExtras

Supermarkets in Bloomington, Minnesota, nervously watched as the local McDonald's began to sell McExtras (i.e., half-gallons of milk and orange juice, cartons of eggs, bread, and yogurt) through their drive-up window. This new product expansion was designed to meet the competition posed by convenience stores and supermarkets, which were increasing their sales of ready-to-eat prepared food.[68]

Thus far this strategy had been implemented at only one store, which had room for extra refrigeration units. "This is simply a volume-building program being tested at a local store," said Steve Whiteis, Regional Marketing Consultant for McDonald's.[69] But the store chosen for the test was flanked by a PDQ convenience store and a Country Club Market grocery store. The advertising slogan for the new concept was "Groceries on the go."[70]

McDonald's Express

The McDonald's Express was a new version of the original McDonald's concept of a limited-menu, speedy drive-up service. The units themselves were prefabricated and provided double lanes for faster service. Although walk-up business was possible, the units were designed to meet the competition of faster drive-through service.[71] Each unit contained 1,212 square feet, or less than one-third that of the average 4,500 square foot outlet, and required a staff of only 35 (rather than 65) to operate.[72]

Menus were limited to basic hamburger fare, ignoring breakfast entrees and salads. The menus did include two new items, hot dogs, a staple of convenience stores, and curly French fries, a big seller at competitor Hardee's. Advertising stressed both the convenience and the take-home market with the theme of "Driving it home."[73]

McDonald's Cafe

McDonald's also introduced another limited menu concept in test markets. Originally tested as the Golden Arch Cafe, three units now bore the McDonald's name. As the larger urban markets became saturated with fast-food outlets and good restaurant sites became scarce, small-town locations become more attractive.

McDonald's Corporation continues to be committed to its traditional growth rate of 500-plus new units a year worldwide, but good locations in the United

States are scarce and expensive. Moreover, in 1989 the building cost for a regular outlet rose by 10.2%, but average per outlet sales rose only 1.6%.[74] Thus the lower costs of more rural areas was appealing. Offsetting lower costs, however, was the lower volume of sales possible in small communities.

The McDonald's Cafe has about 60% of the square footage of a regular McDonald's restaurant. To produce the needed sales volume, the cafes served a broader menu, including roast chicken, hot dogs and beans, and a fish platter.[75]

New Service Innovations

Although McDonald's was famed for its commitment to standardized service and fare, the corporation also was well known for its interest in promoting innovations by successful franchisees. In addition, McDonald's also tests changes of its own. One of these changes has been the acceptance of credit cards for consumer purchases at some test-site restaurants.[76]

Franchise owners in Chicago turned their McDonald's units into theme restaurants. One of the units was dubbed the "rock'n'roll" restaurant and was decorated with a $1 million collection of memorabilia from, among others, James Dean, Elvis Presley, and the Beatles. This outlet alone regularly attracted 10,000 visitors during its 24-hour business day. It grossed $5 million annually, with a probable profit of 9%, or $450,000, making it possibly the highest volume McDonald's restaurant.[77]

McDonald's introduced pizza delivery at the Chicago franchise that had been the first McDonald's to deliver other products five years ago. The delivery area contained high office and population densities. At the same time, this unit also opened a retail souvenir shop featuring McDonald's T-shirts, jackets, sunglasses, buttons, mugs, and other novelties. The owners expected to sell $300,000 worth of souvenirs the first year.[78]

Management

Corporate Structure

McDonald's divided the country into 35 regions, each governed by a Regional Operators Advisory Board. The boards were composed of elected franchisees and managers from company-owned stores. They decided which menu items to promote and which regional products to offer and dealt with various topical problems, including employee recruitment. In addition, each region had an advertising cooperative that worked with regional advertising agencies to create local promotions and television ads. These regional agencies supplemented the advertising efforts of McDonald's national agencies.[79]

Management Training

Training began at the store level with videotapes and one-on-one instruction. Assistant managers progressed through a development program of self-study, operations and management classes, and regional seminars on equipment use. Upon completion, they were eligible to attend the two-week advanced course at Hamburger University.[80]

Only 10% of management training took place at Hamburger University. Founded in 1961, by 1991 the school had campuses in Oak Brook, Illinois; Munich, Germany; Tokyo, Japan; and London, United Kingdom.[81] Students in the program included franchisees in training, newly promoted store managers, and occasionally, an executive of a McDonald's supplier. They studied human relations skills, equipment training, and operations management.[82]

Human Resources

Corporate Employment

Longevity of service was a commonly held value at McDonald's Corporation. The average length of service for the 1,500 corporate employees was 15 years. Sixty percent of the corporate employees started out as crew members, and 40% were mostly financial executives who arrived with experience from other firms.

One of the primary reasons for low turnover was the corporate compensation package. It consisted of a pension plan, company stock, and a variety of unusual extras. For example, after ten years of service, an employee could take an eight-week paid sabbatical.[83]

Women's groups have expressed concern that the company has few female officers. In 1989, only seven of the company's 94 officers were women. A spokeswoman from Chicago Network, a respected association of female executives, said that no woman at McDonald's has even been nominated for the organization. McDonald's stated that 40% of corporate employees exclusive of secretaries were women, and that the company places promising female employees on a management fast track.[84]

Store Employment

Recruiting employees at the restaurant level often was difficult. To combat this problem in places such as Chicago's affluent northern suburbs, a "Bring a Friend" program was started. This program offered $50 to any employee who convinced a friend to work at McDonald's.[85]

McJobs was the company's National Special Employment program. From 1981 to 1989, more than 8,000 people with disabilities were put to work in McDonald's restaurants after receiving job training. In 1990, 1,000 new trainees were expected to complete the McJob training program in 29 states. Workers and company both benefited. Graduates from the program were good workers, were motivated, and had high retention levels, approaching 80%.[86]

Through the McMasters program, McDonald's recruits and trains people aged 55 and over. Participants were introduced to the McDonald's work environment through a four-week training program under the guidance of a coach. They were then recognized at a graduation ceremony and brought into the regular work force.[87]

International

Paul D. Schrage, Senior Executive Vice-President and Chief Marketing Officer, focused on the similarities of the world's five billion inhabitants: "Everyone needs to eat, and we see our market as everyone with an appetite."[88] During the past five years, 50% of systemwide additions have been outside the United States. Of the 427 restaurants added in 1991, 63% were in the six largest foreign markets (France, Japan, Germany, Australia, Canada, and England).

McDonald's operated in 59 countries in 1991. Seventy-one percent of McDonald's restaurants were located in the United States with 29% operating outside the country's borders. The U.S. operations provided 63% of the sales and 60% of the operating income, and international sales were 37% with operating income of 40%.[89]

In 1986, McDonald's was the number one fast-food business in Japan. Sales had grown from zero in 1971 to $770 million annually, making McDonald's (Japan) the U.S. company's largest overseas venture and accounting for 36% of foreign sales. McDonald's (Japan) imports 27% of the frozen potatoes (all Idahos), and 8% of Japanese beef imports.[90]

Corporate Citizen

Charities

Ronald McDonald Children's Charities was dedicated to helping children. It funded grants that developed and supported health care and medical research programs. The Ronald McDonald House program provided a place for families of seriously ill children to stay near hospitals where they were being treated. By the end of 1991, there were 151 such houses worldwide.

Environment

In 1990 after extensive campaigning by environmental and children's groups, McDonald's announced that it would phase out foam packaging. This change reduced the volume of its waste by 90%. Ironically, in 1976 McDonald's had switched from paper packaging to the polystyrene foam clamshells in response to a study on the relationship of paper consumption and rain-forest destruction. McDonald's had participated in a recycling effort involving foam packaging left on the restaurant's premises. The new layered sandwich packaging was not recyclable, would remain in landfills, but would require less space.[91]

McDonald's also turned to alternative sources of building materials as part of its environmental efforts. Two Chicago McDonald's restaurants participated in a joint venture with General Electric and Digital Equipment Corporation to boost plastic recycling. General Electric acquired reclaimed computer housings from Digital Equipment. They then melted and mixed the housings with 48% virgin plastic to create roof panels that resembled cedar shake shingles for use in McDonald's construction. McDonald's promised to spend $100 million annually to purchase recycled plastic for use in building and remodeling its U.S. restaurants.[92]

Financial

Assets and Liabilities

Financial statements for McDonald's are provided in Exhibits 9.1 and 9.2. McDonald's Corporation was a cash business without significant inventory. There-

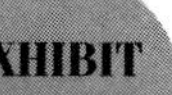

XHIBIT 9.1

Consolidated Statement of Income: McDonald's Corporation
(Dollar amounts in millions, except per share data)

Years Ending December 31	1991	1990	1989
Revenues			
Sales by company-operated restaurants	$4,908.5	$5,018.9	$4,600.9
Revenues from franchised restaurants	1,786.5	1,620.7	1,464.7
Total revenues	6,695.0	6,639.6	6,065.6
Operating costs and expenses			
Company-operated restaurants			
Food and packaging	1,627.5	1,683.4	1,560.3
Payroll and other employee benefits	1,259.2	1,291.0	1,174.4
Occupancy and other operating expenses	1,142.4	1,161.2	1,043.1
	4,029.1	4,135.6	3,777.8
Franchised restaurants—occupancy expenses	306.5	279.2	240.6
General, administrative and selling expenses	794.7	724.2	656.0
Other operating (income) expense—net	(113.8)	(95.3)	(46.5)
Total operating costs and expenses	5,016.5	5,043.7	4,627.9
Operating income	1,678.5	1,595.9	1,437.7
Interest expense—net of capitalized interest of $26.2, $36.0, and $29.8	391.4	381.2	301.9
Nonoperating income (expense)—net	12.3	31.6	21.4
Income before provision for income taxes	1,299.4	1,246.3	1,157.2
Provision for income taxes	439.8	444.0	430.5
Net income	$ 859.6	$ 802.3	$ 726.7
Net income per common share	$ 2.35	$ 2.20	$ 1.95
Dividends per common share	$ .36	$ .33	$ .30

fore inflation was not a substantial problem. In fact, owing to the organization's heavy investment in real estate, it could operate during highly inflationary periods by relying on the increasing value of its property.

Total Revenues

Total revenues consisted of sales by company-operated restaurants and fees from restaurants operated by franchisees and affiliates that were based on a percentage of sales with specified minimum payments. The minimum franchise fee has been 12% of sales for new U.S. franchise arrangements since 1987. Higher fees were charged when the company made a higher investment in a particular restaurant. Foreign fee arrangements varied according to local business conditions.

Revenues grew as restaurants were added and as sales increased at existing restaurants. Menu price adjustments affected revenues, as well as sales. However, different pricing throughout the McDonald's system, new products, promotions, and product mix variations made it impractical to quantify their impact.

Consolidated Balance Sheets: McDonald's Corporation
(Dollar amounts in millions)

Years Ending December 31	1991	1990	1989
Assets			
Current assets			
Cash and equivalents	$ 220.2	$ 142.8	$ 136.9
Accounts receivable	238.4	222.1	207.2
Notes receivable	36.0	32.9	27.2
Inventories, at cost, not in excess of market	42.6	42.9	46.1
Prepaid expenses and other current assets	108.8	108.3	77.3
Total current assets	646.0	549.0	494.7
Other assets and deferred charges			
Notes receivable due after one year	123.1	102.2	76.0
Investments in and advances to affiliates	374.2	335.2	291.0
Miscellaneous	278.2	250.0	229.0
Total other assets and deferred charges	775.5	687.4	596.0
Property and equipment			
Property and equipment, at cost	12,368.0	11,535.5	9,873.9
Accumulated depreciation and amortization	(2,809.5)	(2,488.4)	(2,115.6)
Net property and equipment	9,558.5	9,047.1	7,758.3
Intangible assets–net	369.1	384.0	326.0
Total assets	$11,349.1	$10,667.5	$9,175.0
Liabilities and Shareholders' Equity			
Current liabilities			
Notes payable	$ 278.3	$ 299.0	$ 75.8
Accounts payable	313.9	355.7	386.1

(continued)

Growth rates for sales by company-operated restaurants and revenues from franchised restaurants varied because of expansion and changes in ownership. Sales by company-operated restaurants were affected more by changing foreign currencies than were revenues from franchised restaurants, as 51% of sales by company-operated restaurants were outside the United States, compared to 27% of revenues from franchised restaurants.[93] The annual growth rate of sales revenues had been decreasing from its peak of 15.27% in 1987 to its ten-year low of 6.23% in 1991, a decline of 59%.

Profit Margins

Company-operated restaurant margins were 17.9% of sales in 1991, compared to 17.6% in 1990 and 17.9% in 1989. The annual growth rate for net income also

EXHIBIT 9.2

Consolidated Balance Sheets: McDonald's Corporation *(continued)*
(Dollar amounts in millions)

Years Ending December 31	1991	1990	1989
Liabilities and Shareholders' Equity			
Income taxes	$ 157.2	$ 82.6	$ 70.7
Other taxes	82.3	68.6	64.9
Accrued interest	185.7	133.2	126.0
Other accrued liabilities	201.4	194.9	184.1
Current maturities of long-term debt	69.1	64.7	58.6
Total current liabilities	1,287.9	1,198.7	966.2
Long-term debt	4,267.4	4,428.7	3,902.0
Security deposits by franchisees and other long-term liabilities	224.5	162.7	143.3
Deferred income taxes	734.2	695.1	613.1
Shareholders' equity			
Preferred stock, no par value, authorized—165.0 million shares; issued—9.9 and 6.9 million	298.2	199.7	200.0
Guarantee of ESOP Notes	(286.7)	(196.5)	(228.2)
Common stock, no par value; authorized—1.25 billion shares; issued—415.2 million	46.2	46.2	46.2
Additional paid-in capital	201.9	173.7	158.9
Retained earnings	5,925.2	5,214.5	4,545.5
Equity adjustment from foreign currency translation	32.3	46.7	
	6,217.1	5,484.3	4,722.4
Common stock in treasury, at cost; 56.5 and 56.1 million shares	(1,382.0)	(1,302.0)	(1,172.0)
Total shareholders' equity	4,835.1	4,182.3	3,550.4
Total liabilities and shareholders' equity	$11,349.1	$10,667.5	$9,175.0

had been declining, from its peak of 17.67% in 1987 to its ten-year low of 7.23% in 1991, a drop of 59%.

Declining food and packaging costs, payroll and employee benefit costs, and other operating costs (as a percentage of sales) offset increases in occupancy costs in 1991.[94]

Franchised restaurant margins were 82.8% of applicable revenues for 1991 and 1990 and 83.6% in 1989. Franchised margins include revenues and expenses associated with restaurants operating under business facilities lease arrangements. Under these arrangements, the company leases the businesses, including equipment, to franchisees who have options to purchase the businesses. The company charges higher fees under these arrangements, but margins generally are lower because of equipment depreciation. When franchisees exercise purchase options, the resulting gains compensate the company for the previous lower margins and are included in other operating (income) expense—net. At the end of 1991, 584 restaurants were operating under such arrangements, compared to 553 at the end of 1990.[95]

General, Administrative, and Selling Expenses

The increase for 1991 in general, administrative, and selling expenses reflected higher advertising costs worldwide. Higher employee costs outside the United States resulted from expansion.[96]

Store Ownership

At the end of fiscal 1991, McDonald's Corporation had 12,418 restaurants systemwide: franchisees operated 8,151, the Company operated 2,547, and other arrangements covered the remaining 1,720.[97] Unlike many competitors, McDonald's did not sign multiunit franchise agreements. Franchise ownership was limited to seven or eight restaurants at most, with the majority of franchisees operating only two or three units.[98]

According to Gerald Newman, Vice-President and Chief Accounting Officer:

> At McDonald's, total revenues include fees from franchised restaurants plus 100 percent of sales from restaurants we manage. We converted more than 400 Company-operated restaurants to franchises in 1990 and 1991. This resulted in lower total revenues but improved operating income and increased cash flow. We've lowered overhead and reduced invested capital. Most importantly, the licensees of those restaurants will put in the sweat equity that builds sales and improves profits. Don't misunderstand. We sell only the franchise. McDonald's still owns the land, the building or lease.[99]

The following information shows McDonald's changing restaurant business ownership.

	1991	1990	1989	1988
Operated by franchisees	8,151	7,578	7,135	6,732
Operated under business facilities lease arrangements[1]	584	553	438	378
Operated by the company	2,547	2,643	2,691	2,600
Operated by 50% or less owned affiliates	1,136	1,029	898	803
Systemwide restaurants	12,418	11,803	11,162	10,513

Note: 1. Franchisees operating under "business facilities lease arrangements" had options to purchase the business.

Franchisee Selection

McDonald's was highly selective in choosing its franchisees. It did not advertise to attract franchisees, but it did send approximately 20,000 brochures each year to interested parties. In return, it received some 5,000 applications for approximately 100–150 new placements.

Potential franchisees must show they have sufficient financial resources and business experience before the company will grant them a two-hour interview. In 1988, the initial standard cost of establishing a McDonald's outlet exceeded $500,000 for the franchisee and an additional $900,000 for the corporation. Thus the commitment and ability of the potential operator needed to be strong.

If the interview was successful, the applicant had to work 50 hours at a McDonald's in a job-experience program and then survive another interview and evaluation. A six-to-nine-month Basic Operations course and the initial part of the Registered Applicant Training Program then followed. After this training, applicants faced reevaluation by a licensing manager and field consultants. If they succeeded and McDonald's placed them on the registered applicants' list, they had to pay a substantial deposit ($4,000 in 1988) and begin 12–18 months of formal training. Most of the training was done at an established McDonald's, with four additional formal classroom sessions lasting one or two weeks required. The last of these sessions was held at Hamburger University. This training was done at the applicant's expense with no compensation for approximately 2,000 hours of effort. If all went well, the successful franchisee would then have to wait one to three years for a restaurant.[100]

Franchise Operations

Franchise arrangements generally provide for initial fees, continuing payments to the company, based on a percentage of gross sales (generally 12%), and minimal rent payments. Among other things, the company provides the use of restaurant facilities to franchisees, generally for a period of 20 years. Franchisees pay all related occupancy costs, including property taxes, insurance, maintenance and a refundable, non-interest-bearing security deposit.

At December 31, 1991, the net value of property and equipment under franchise arrangements was $5.2 billion. This net amount excluded accumulated depreciation and amortization of $1.4 billion but included land of $1.6 billion.[101]

Corporate Revenues from Franchised Restaurants
(Dollar amounts in millions)

	1991	1990	1989
Rent from franchisees	$ 798.2	$ 690.7	$ 597.6
Percentage fees	970.4	914.0	854.8
Initial fees	17.9	16.0	12.3
Total revenues	$1,786.5	$1,620.7	$1,464.7

Leasing Arrangements

At December 31, 1991, McDonald's held ground leases at 2,003 restaurant locations (the company leases land and constructs and owns buildings) and improved leases at 2,028 locations (lessor owns land and buildings). Land and building lease terms generally were for 20–25 years, and in many cases provided for rent increases and renewal options. In addition, some leases provided purchase options. The company was generally obligated for related occupancy costs, which included property taxes, insurance, and maintenance.[102]

Suppliers

Economies of scale were obvious in the operations of the supply network. Franchisees must buy food and paper products from approved suppliers and benefit especially when they form co-ops with other local franchisees.[103] "A meat plant, for example, can supply 300 restaurants more profitably than it can 150," says James R. Cantalupo, President and CEO of McDonald's International.[104]

A major consideration for systemwide rollout of any new menu item was the enormous demand placed on supplying thousands of units. McDonald's could "make or break" a supplier with its menu decisions because the tremendous volume used of an ingredient. For example, McDonald's used 3,500 tons of sesame seeds annually for Big Mac buns and prepared at least two million pounds of French fries daily.[105]

Corporate Controls

Corporate officers frequently visited the restaurants. They were interested in learning about the operations of the units they visited and the operators' views of corporate activities.

Three-day store exams known as "full fields" took place twice a year. Examiners looked at everything from the roof to the ketchup dispensers and graded the unit on quality, service, and cleanliness. Franchisees were not graded on "value" because, as independent business people, they were free to set prices. In addition, the examiners made suggestions to improve the operations.[106]

Shareholders

Gerald Newman said he realized that shareholders "won't get rich on a one-percent dividend. We reinvest profits into new and existing capital assets. But as we grow and increase profitability, we hope the '90s will bring shareholders the same returns that the '80s did." McDonald's return on equity has averaged 20% over the past ten years.[107]

Rumors continued to circulate that PepsiCo would be interested in acquiring McDonald's Corporation. With just 6.5% of the company's publicly held stock owned by Ray Kroc's widow, Joan Kroc, and 13.5% by McDonald's executives, franchisees, owner-partners, and suppliers,[108] such an acquisition is only an outside possibility.[109]

Conclusion

In the days of Ray Kroc and McDonald's super growth, running a franchise meant following the system's rules to the letter. Sandwiches were hamburgers with ketchup, mustard, and a pickle. A McDonald's deluxe sandwich was the Big Mac with two patties, special sauce, lettuce, pickles, onions, and cheese on a sesame seed bun. If customers didn't care for pickles, they could remove the offending ingredient themselves. The soft drink was company-mandated Coca-Cola and woe be to the franchisee who switched to another brand. Ray Kroc refused to renew licenses for uncooperative franchisees who made their own menu decisions.[110] That emphasis on standardization, quality control, and efficient operations led to McDonald's high market share and profits.

In 1992, Michael Quinlan, McDonald's Corporation CEO and Chairman, faced an almost mature industry that contained powerful competitors and sophisticated consumers. Quality and customer satisfaction were widely praised objectives throughout the U.S. business community. Quinlan responded to these forces by rephrasing McDonald's continuing commitment to the consumer. The new message was simply: "Do whatever it takes to make a customer happy."[111] Pickles were to be removed upon request.

Did this approach enhance or detract from McDonald's traditional competitive advantage? Some proponents viewed the changes as merely natural extensions of McDonald's desire to meet the market's needs. Changing menus, increasing discretion for franchisees, and redesigning decor were required to maintain company growth. The market, the industry, and the company were maturing—and that demanded flexible adaptation. Others worried that the changes would dilute the company's image, resulting in loss of brand identity. They suggested that the strategy of offering consistent, simple, and fast meals would be lost to the pressures of attempting to balance variety and efficiency.[112]

Notes

1. McDonald's Corporation, *1991 Annual Report.*
2. Lois Therrien, "McRisky: Lasagna? Tablecloths and Candles? What Would Ray Kroc Say?" *Business Week* October 21, 1991), pp. 114–122.
3. William C. Johnson, "Products 'Mature' Gracefully with Value-Added Features," *Marketing News* (December 5, 1988), 22, p. 4.
4. Therrien, "McRisky: Lasagna? . . ."
5. Scott Hume, "McD's Faces U.S. Slowdown," *Advertising Age* (May 14, 1990), 61, pp. 1, 64.
6. Ellen Graham, "McDonald's Pickle: He Began Fast Food but Gets No Credit," *Wall Street Journal* (August 15, 1991), pp. 1, A10.
7. Ibid.
8. John F. Love, "McDonald's Behind the Arches," *Restaurant Business Magazine* (February 10, 1987), 86, pp. 122–127.
9. Charles Bernstein, "McDonald's at 35: Unparalleled Success; Clouds on the Horizon," *Nation's Restaurant News* (August 27, 1990), 24, pp. 60–63.
10. Graham.
11. Lisa Bertagnoli, "McDonald's: Company of the Quarter Century," *Restaurants and Institutions* (July 10, 1989), 99, pp. 32–59.
12. Lois Therrien, "What's for Dinner? Humble Pie," *Business Week* (January 13, 1992), p. 88.
13. *1991 U.S. Industry Surveys—Leisure Time, Restaurants*, pp. L25–L28.
14. Lois Therrien, "Restaurants: Doing Well by Being Big," *Business Week* (January 14, 1991), p. 92.
15. Ibid.
16. Therrien, "McRisky: Lasagna? . . ."
17. Bruce Hager, "Podunk Is Beckoning," *Business Week* (December 23, 1991), p. 76.

18. *1992 U.S. Industry Surveys—Leisure Time, Restaurants,* pp. L44–L47.
19. Therrien, "What's for Dinner? . . ."
20. *1991 U.S. Industry Surveys.*
21. Therrien, "What's for Dinner? . . ."
22. Ibid.
23. Lisa Bertagnoli, "Inside McDonald's," *Restaurants and Institutions* (August 21, 1989), 99, p. 44.
24. John Harris, "I Don't Want Good, I Want Fast," *Forbes* (October 1, 1990), p. 186.
25. Ibid.
26. *1992 U.S. Industry Surveys.*
27. Leon Jaroff, "A Crusader from the Heartland," *Time* (March 25, 1991), 137, pp. 56–58.
28. *1990 U.S. Industry Surveys—Leisure Time, Restaurants,* pp. L39–L43.
29. Ibid.
30. Scott Hume and Leslie Bayer, "McD's Sizzles with New Ideas," *Advertising Age* (September 3, 1990), 61, pp. 1–2.
31. *1992 U.S. Industry Surveys.*
32. Ibid.
33. Ibid.
34. Scarpa (1991).
35. Kevin Maney, "A Taste of Fast Food's Future," *USA Today* (August 16, 1991), p. 1.
36. Scott Hume and Ray Serafin, "Burger King Attacks Big Mac with Brands," *Advertising Age* (July 16, 1990), 61, pp. 3–4.
37. Maney.
38. *1992 U.S. Industry Surveys.*
39. Maney.
40. Therrien, "What's for Dinner? . . ."
41. *1992 U.S. Industry Surveys.*
42. Scott Hume, "McD's Latest: Cold McSubs," *Advertising Age* (December 17, 1990), 61, pp. 3–4.
43. Ibid.
44. Therrien, "What's for Dinner? . . ."
45. Ibid.
46. Hume, "McD's Latest: Cold McSubs."
47. Barbara Marsh, "Franchise Realities," *Wall Street Journal* (September 16, 1992), pp. 1, A5.
48. Therrien, "What's for Dinner? . . ."
49. Ibid.
50. Harris.
51. Ibid.
52. Therrien, "Restaurants: Doing Well by Being Big."
53. Scott Hume, "McDonald's Takes Nip at Supermarkets," *Advertising Age* (March 11, 1991), 62, pp. 1–2.
54. Ibid.
55. *1991 U.S. Industry Surveys.*
56. Therrien, "Restaurants: Doing Well by Being Big."
57. McDonald's Corporation, *1991 Annual Report,* p. Q1.
58. Ibid., p. S1.
59. Ibid., p. Q3.
60. Bernstein.
61. Wayne Walley, "Networks Prime Joint Operations," *Advertising Age* (April 16, 1990), 61, p. 45.
62. Therrien, "McRisky: Lasagna? . . ."
63. Hume, "McD's Latest: Cold McSubs."
64. Bertagnoli, "Inside McDonald's."
65. Lois Therrien, "McDonald's Isn't Looking Quite So Juicy Anymore," *Business Week* (August 6, 1990), p. 30.
66. Maney.
67. Hume and Bayer, p. 53.
68. Hume, "McDonald's Takes Nip at Supermarkets."
69. "McDonald's Tests Grocery Sales, but Supermarkets Aren't Worried," *Supermarket Business* (April 1991), 46, p. 11.
70. Hume, "McDonald's Takes Nip at Supermarkets," p. 1.
71. "McDonald's Tests New Design," *Wall Street Journal* (May 9, 1991), p. B4.
72. Hume, "McDonald's Takes Nip at Supermarkets," p. 2.
73. Ibid.
74. Hume and Bayer.
75. Hager.
76. Johnson.
77. Jane Alexander, "A McDonald's Coins Big McMoney. The Secret Formula: Guts, Glitz and Rock'n'roll," *Money* (December 1987), 16, pp. 37–40.
78. Carolyn Walkup, "McD Licensee Rolls Pizza Delivery Test," *Nation's Restaurant News* (June 1990), 24, p. 3.
79. Bertagnoli, "Inside McDonald's."
80. McDonald's Corporation, *1991 Annual Report.*
81. Ibid.
82. Bertagnoli, "Inside McDonald's."
83. Ibid.
84. Ibid.
85. Ibid.
86. Michael DeLuca, "Independence Day: McDonald's Gives People with Disabilities a Shot at Self-Sufficiency," *Restaurant Hospitality* (August 1990), 74, p. 135.
87. McDonald's Corporation, *1991 Annual Report.*
88. Ibid., p. Q3.

89. Ibid.
90. Frederick Hiroshi Katayama, "Japan's Big Mac," *Fortune* (September 15, 1986), pp. 114–120.
91. Brian Quinton, "The Greening of McDonald's," *Restaurants and Institutions* (December 26, 1990), 100, pp. 28–42.
92. "GE, Firms Form Venture to Boost Plastic Recycling," *Wall Street Journal* (June 18, 1991), p. A9.
93. McDonald's Corporation, *1991 Annual Report.*
94. Ibid.
95. Ibid.
96. Ibid.
97. Ibid.
98. Bertagnoli, "Inside McDonald's."
99. McDonald's Corporation, *1991 Annual Report,* p. C1.
100. D. L. Noren, "The Economics of the Golden Arches: A Case Study of the McDonald System," *American Economist* (1988), 34(2), pp. 60–64.
101. McDonald's Corporation, *1991 Annual Report.*
102. Ibid.
103. Noren.
104. McDonald's Corporation, *1991 Annual Report,* p. Q2.
105. Bernstein.
106. Bertagnoli, "Inside McDonald's."
107. McDonald's Corporation, *1991 Annual Report,* p. C1.
108. Ibid.
109. Bernstein.
110. Therrien, "McRisky: Lasagna? . . ."
111. Ibid., p. 117.
112. Ibid.

CASE 10

Checkers Drive-In Restaurants, Inc.

Thomas L. Wheelen, Thomas Ladd, and Bryan McDonald

Introduction

On April 30, 1992, during the slow time of the day, the manager of McDonald's on Chandler Road in Atlanta, Georgia, stared idly out of the drive-thru window. He spotted an ominous-looking convoy of vehicles moving down the road single file: a black and white checkered building sat on the back of a flatbed tractor trailer. The convoy appeared to be heading toward a vacant lot a short distance away. As the last vehicle passed, the manager caught a glimpse of a large red sign reading "Checkers" in bold white letters. Suddenly, the manager realized that business on Chandler Road would be different from now on.

Meanwhile, back in his Clearwater, Florida, office, Herb Brown, Chairman of the Board of Checkers, picked up the morning edition of the *Tampa Tribune* and began leafing through its pages in search of the business section. Brown was used to seeing his company in the news. Since its initial public offering in November 1991, Checkers Drive-In Restaurants, Inc., had been one of Wall Street's hottest growth stocks. The April 30, 1992 headline read, "Checkers Drive-In Insiders To Sell Stock Valued At Nearly $83 Million."[1] The article detailed how Brown and other directors planned to sell 1.5 million shares of their personal holdings in the company, accounting for one-half of a new issue. This news would almost certainly spark much speculation, with Checkers stock currently trading at about 70 times its per share earnings, or several times that of most restaurant stocks. In fact, if an investor had bought 10,000 shares of Checkers stock on the date of the initial public offering in November 1991, the purchase price would have been $160,000. After adjusting for stock splits, that same block of stock currently would be worth about $405,000 (a 153% increase). Under Brown's leadership, Checkers more than doubled the number of its restaurants from 56 in 1990 to 117 in 1991 and expected 163 to be in operation by August 1, 1992. Of this total, 65 will be company owned (in five states), and the remaining 98 will be operated by franchisees (in 12 states) (see Exhibit 10.1). By the end of 1992, the total number of Checkers restaurants is expected to be approximately 218.[2] Brown leaned back in his chair and swivelled it to face the office window. He had seen Checkers' earnings climb from $71,121 in 1989 to $3.3 million in 1991, and many analysts saw 1992 as another record year with projected earnings reaching $10 million.[3] Staring off into the clear blue Florida sky, Brown stopped to reflect on the company's short history and uncertain future. Would this sale of insider stock be a signal to stockholders

This case was prepared by Thomas Ladd and Bryan McDonald, both Master of Accountancy students and graduate assistants, under the direction of Professor Thomas L. Wheelen of the University of South Florida.

EXHIBIT 10.1

Restaurant Locations: Checkers Drive-In Restaurants, Inc.
(Projected by August 1992)

State	Company	Franchise	Total
Alabama	12	4	16
Florida	43	48	91
Georgia	7	12	19
Illinois	0	17	17
Indiana	0	1	1
Louisiana	2	3	5
Michigan	0	2	2
Missouri	0	2	2
North Carolina	1	2	3
South Carolina	0	3	3
Tennessee	0	4	4
Total	65	98	163

Source: "Announcement," *Checkers Drive-In Restaurants, Inc.*, back cover.

that the company's founders lacked confidence? Could the company continue its rapid expansion in the future?

Background and History

Even in the 1940s, long before Ray Kroc revolutionized the fast-food industry with his golden arches, double drive-thru burger operations (McDonald's) were carving out a niche in the restaurant industry.[4] The basic concept behind these "burger boxes" is simplicity: high volume, low price, and fast service. Checkers' founder Jim Mattei concedes that Checkers is just a 1990s revision of the 1950s idea. The striking white-tiled McDonald's restaurants of the 1950s provided a limited menu, little or no seating, easy car access, and low prices. Today, McDonald's and other large burger chains seem to have abandoned this niche and are in Mattei's words "looking at all kinds of pastas, pizzas, and other foods" and "becoming more of a dinner-house concept."[5] The four largest chains—McDonald's, Burger King, Wendy's, and Hardee's—all have expanded their menus to include pizza, pasta, and breakfast items; they hardly seem like quick order burger chains anymore.[6]

Jim Mattei developed his business sense as a real estate developer in Mobile, Alabama. During the 1980s, he was involved in more than $60 million worth of construction and renovation projects, such as marinas, condominiums, office complexes, and shopping centers in and around downtown Mobile. Mattei also built some restaurants for a franchisee of Wendy's International, and when these restaurants failed, Mattei became their new owner. After carefully going over their books, Mattei noticed a startling trend: over half the sales came from the drive-thru and were characterized by some variation on the basic burger, fries, and cola combination. Mattei said, "I couldn't understand why you would have a big parking lot and dining room tables, and why you would have a big menu." Mattei added that he became increasingly disillusioned with the continual menu expansion at Wendy's and resolved to beat the giant chains at their own game by getting back to burger basics.[7]

Mattei opened his first Checkers in April 1986. This first store in Mobile was similar to the Checkers of today, with a limited menu, a drive-thru window on each side of the small building, and no dining room. Just months earlier, a competitor, Rollo's Through-Thru Inc., opened a low-overhead, high-speed burger box in Mobile, using a prefabricated trailer as its building. Taking advantage of the low start-up costs, other competitors soon jumped into the fray. The competition took its toll, but Mattei managed to open three more Checkers facilities by the end of the year. By early 1987, however, losses were approaching $20,000 a month. Realizing that he needed help to keep his dream alive, Mattei began to seek a partner.[8]

The pivotal point in Checkers' development came in the summer of 1987 when Jared Brown began looking for a way to enter the fast-food restaurant business without being forced to work for one of the large established chains. In the course of his research, Brown came across a little known but potentially profitable operation based in Alabama. After meeting with Jim Mattei in Mobile, Brown returned to his father's Clearwater, Florida, office anxious to get him involved, saying, "Dad this [Checkers] is your kind of place and Jim is your kind of person." Soon Herb Brown and Jim Mattei met in Mobile, and based on a handshake they formed the partnership that would help make Checkers what it is today.[9]

Herb Brown, the patriarch of the Brown family, is a deeply religious man who grew up during the Great Depression. He believes strongly in the simple traditional values of trust in God, dedication to family, loyalty to country, and hard work. Brown is a devoted family man and has always tried to include his family in his work. At the age of 18, Brown found himself running the family appliance store in Opelousas, Louisiana, following his father's death. After making a success of the appliance store, he began a chain of furniture stores known as Brown Furniture Stores, with locations in Florida and Louisiana. Next Brown started a chain of some 40 drug stores he later sold to the Jack Eckerd Corporation of Clearwater, Florida, in the late 1960s. While operating Brown's Thrift City Pharmacies, he developed his basic pricing strategy: buy in bulk and package small; keep the overhead down so that you can charge prices much lower than your competitors; and run clean stores in high traffic areas.[10]

Under CEO and President Jim Mattei and Board Chairman Herb Brown, Checkers has become a company that not only develops, owns, operates, and franchises restaurants but that also produces modular restaurant packages (see Exhibit 10.2). The company's success to date has been attributed to several key operating strategies developed by Mattei and Brown. By offering a limited menu (17 items), Checkers has been able to focus both on the quality of the food and the speed of its preparation while providing enough variety to satisfy most fast-food customers. The double drive-thru design and a computerized point-of-sale system has enhanced the speed of order delivery. Additionally, by utilizing modular restaurant

HIBIT 0.2 **Champion Modular Restaurant Company, Inc. and Checkers Drive-In Restaurants, Inc.**

Source: "Prospectus for Checkers Drive-In Restaurants, Inc.," *Dean Witter Reynolds, Inc., and Raymond James and Associates, Inc.* (November 15, 1991), back cover.

packages featuring an unusual design, the company and several franchise groups have been able to develop key markets rapidly.[11] "The same thing that Wal-Mart has done to Sears and Kmart, is about the same thing that we're doing to the big fast food restaurants," Jim Mattei once remarked.[12] A long-term objective at Checkers is to expand nationally through controlled growth—as Wal-Mart has done.

Industry

As a whole, hamburger restaurants face escalating competition in their mature, saturated markets. Traditionally, fast-food sales have held up during downturns in the economy, but experience during the current recession may prove to be different[13] (see Exhibit 10.3). A recent innovation in the industry has been the double drive-thru concept. A double drive-thru has no public restrooms, no indoor seating, and no other indoor space apart from the work space. "Double drive-thru" means that these restaurants have spaces on both sides of the small building for serving cars. Thus either a driver or a passenger can take the food from the hands of the server and pedestrians are encouraged to walk up to the serving windows.[14] This seemingly nostalgic return to the origins of the fast-food industry may reflect economic reality more than anything else. Apparently, more and more fast-food customers are feeling the effects of time and money constraints. Consumers are eating out more than ever, but the sluggish economy has made them more discriminating in terms of what they get for their dollar. Steven Rockwell, an analyst with Alex Brown & Sons, Inc., said that "eating away from home is a lifestyle today, not a luxury." He went on to say, "Therefore instead of staying away from restaurants, belt-tightening consumers worried about their jobs and the economy are flooding into those places that offer the most bang for their buck."[15] A dominant factor in the industry's outlook for 1992 and beyond will be the pace of the economic recovery.

Industry analysts also are finding that customers of traditional chains aren't staying on the premises to eat. Still other analysts believe that consumers are flocking to these new restaurants simply for a change of pace, an alternative to McDonald's. As Arthur Bonnel, portfolio manager of the MIM stock appreciation fund in Reno, said, "The restaurant industry is tricky, consumers are finicky and tastes in restaurants can be highly faddish."[16] There are now about 25 different double drive-thru chains, ranging from a few mom and pop businesses to regional franchises, all operating under the concept of limited, inexpensive menus and quick drive- and walk-up service.[17] These restaurants are capitalizing on industry research showing that the three most important factors in a consumer's decision on where to eat are: time of day, time devoted to eating, and price.[18]

Other double drive-thru chains include Central Park, Beefy's, Fast Track, Zipp's, and Rally's. Almost all these chains offer $.99 hamburgers, fries, and soft drinks, and some offer a slightly larger menu with such items as chicken breast and fish fillet sandwiches.[19] Central Park USA, Inc., is a Chattanooga-based chain that offers the fewest menu selections and the lowest prices—only three items: $.89

burgers, $.49 fries, and colas. Central Park now has 70 units but plans to open four units per month. A Nashville-based chain, Beefy's, Inc., currently operates 33 units, nine of which are company owned, but plans to add 30 more units by the end of 1992. A Beefy's modular unit can be erected in four days and lists for $63,660.[20]

The runaway leader in this category and one of the industry's fastest growing chains is Rally's, based in Louisville, Kentucky. Rally's had more than 250 units and $159 million in systemwide sales in 1990. Additionally, late in 1990, Rally's announced that it had reached an agreement with Snapps Drive-Thru, Inc., for Snapps to become a franchisee. Snapps will convert its 43 outlets into Rally's over a 42-month period.[21]

According to some analysts, Rally's has already confronted the problems of rapid growth, cannibalization of same-store sales, and a few weak franchisees. Checkers, which has about 30% of its units in or around Tampa, Florida (see Exhibit 10.1), has probably yet to encounter the problems that arise when a company tries to increase market penetration by clustering stores. To date, Checkers has only four markets with two or more stores in each, and same-store sales are likely to decline as markets become more developed. Additionally, Rally's multimedia marketing strategy emphasizing radio and television for promotion purposes has been characterized as being more aggressive and successful than that of Checkers.[22]

In 1990, there were 34,269 hamburger restaurants, which represented 9.1% of all restaurants. Of course, number one in the hamburger industry is McDonald's, with 12,468 restaurants (8,772 in the United States and 3,696 in other countries). In 1992, sales were $1.9 billion. Systemwide domestic volume grew by 6% in 1992 with a 2% increase in the number of restaurants. The company projects 700–900 new units a year for the next several years, about two-thirds outside the United States. Burger King is number two with 5,469 units in the United States and sales of more than $5 billion. Hardee's is number three with 4,022 units in the United States and had sales of $3.4 billion. Wendy's is number four with 3,962 units, of which 355 were international, and 1992 sales of $1.1 billion.[23] Pressure from lower priced rivals such as Checkers and Rally's has inspired some rather unusual changes by these larger chains. For example, in a break from its fast-food past, Burger King has introduced table service at some of its restaurants, offering higher priced items, tablecloths, napkin rings, dinner music, soft lighting, and no tipping.[24] This move is an apparent attempt to capitalize on the success of moderately priced sit-down chains such as Chili's and Applebee's, which currently represent the fastest growing sector of the restaurant industry.[25] "Since Burger King can't compete at the low end, because its buildings are a lot bigger and its rents a lot higher, they're trying to go in the other direction and see if they can entice people to spend more money," according to Michael Mueller, a restaurant analyst with Montgomery Securities in San Francisco.[26]

Niche hamburger outlets, such as Checkers, can serve a hamburger faster than a traditional burger restaurant because customers have fewer menu choices. Checkers and rival Rally's keep their selections down to 15 items or less, whereas McDonald's offers some 65 choices.[27] In fact, Checkers promises customers that

EXHIBIT 10.3

Fast-Food Industry Information

A. Basic Information

1. Americans eat about 750 million meals a day.
2. The sources of prepared food are (a) 51.0% fast-food restaurants, (b) 23.0% table-service restaurants, (c) 14.0% supermarkets, and (d) 12.0% other sources.
3. In 1993, total restaurant spending will be more than $268.0 billion.
4. From 1985 to 1990, the sandwich segment of the industry grew from 4.9% to 5.7% of total sales.
5. From 1985 to 1990, the sales of hamburger chains fell from 53.4% to 50.5% of total sales.
6. In 1992, the sandwich segment of the fast-food industry had sales of $5.3 billion, or a 0.8% increase over 1991.

B. Restaurant Revenue and Cost Structure

Restaurant Industry Economics—1990
(By type of restaurant)

Type of Restaurant	Full-Menu Table Service	Limited-Menu Table Service	Limited Menu, No Table Service	Cafeteria
Revenues				
Foods sales	76.3%	73.3%	97.6%	90.7%
Beverage sales	20.2	15.8	2.0	3.2
Other	3.5	10.9	0.4	6.1
Total	100.0%	100.0%	100.0%	100.0%
Costs				
(Percentage of total revenue)				
Food	27.3%	27.6%	33.1%	31.1%
Beverages	5.4	3.9	0.5	0.9
Payroll	28.8	26.6	23.9	29.7
Employee benefits	4.3	3.6	2.5	2.6
Rent	4.2	6.6	5.6	4.4
Advertising and promotion	2.4	3.5	5.7	2.0
Utilities	2.8	2.8	3.6	2.8
Depreciation	2.3	2.1	3.0	3.7
Repairs and maintenance	2.1	1.9	2.1	1.5

(continued)

they will have their food within 30 seconds of ordering. In comparison, a traditional fast-food restaurant may take as long as several minutes.[28] David Geraty, an analyst with Equitable Securities, has said that "the big four have expanded their menus to target a broader and broader market to the point that their speed and efficiency have been neglected."[29]

EXHIBIT 10.3 Fast-Food Industry Information *(continued)*

Type of Restaurant	Full-Menu Table Service	Limited-Menu Table Service	Limited Menu, No Table Service	Cafeteria
Administration and general	4.1	3.0	2.4	3.2
Interest	1.2	0.6	0.6	0.5
Other	11.2	11.7	8.5	12.2
Total	96.1%	93.9%	91.5%	94.6%
Pretax profit	3.9%	5.0%	9.8%	13.8%

C. Food Service Industry Sales by Category

Projected U.S. Food Service Industry Sales
(Dollar amounts in billions)

	Estimated[1] 1990	Projected[5] 1991	Projected[5] 1992
Fuller service restaurants	$ 75.9	$ 79.2	$ 83.2
Limited-menu restaurants[4]	69.8	73.6	78.3
Commercial cafeterias	4.4	4.6	4.8
Social caterers	2.2	2.4	2.6
Ice cream, frozen custard stands	2.0	2.1	2.1
Bars/taverns	8.8	8.6	8.9
Commercial eating and drinking places[1]	163.1	170.5	179.9
Food contractors	NA	15.0	16.1
Lodging places	NA	14.3	15.0
Other commercial sales	NA	19.9	21.2
Total commercial food service	211.0	219.5	232.2
Institutional food service[2]	26.6	27.5	28.8
Military food service[3]	1.1	1.0	1.0
Total U.S. food service	$238.7	$248.0	$262.0

Notes: All figures are weighted averages and are based on 1990 data from 1,270 restaurant operators. 1. Only for establishment with payroll. 2. Sales by institutional organizations operating their own food service. 3. Continental United States only. 4. Largely fast-food restaurants; includes refreshment places. 5. Projections based on data available in late September and early October 1991.

Source: National Restaurant Association, "Restaurant Industry Operations Report—1991," *Restaurants USA: Industry Surveys—Restaurants* (March 12, 1992), p. L-44, L-45.

Lower operating costs are another advantage of double drive-thru restaurants. Such units can operate with less labor than traditional fast-food chains such as McDonald's.[30] However, some industry observers are predicting a shakeout in the industry over the next five years, leaving two to four companies to emerge as the leaders in the drive-thru business.[31] One early casualty of this predicted shakeout was the Grand Junction double drive-thru chain that went bankrupt in 1990. "The real battle isn't going to be David versus Goliath, but David versus David," one owner has remarked.[32] Since price is a key selling point for the double drive-thru chains, each operator must minimize overhead. The low inflation rate over the past several years has benefited these chains. High unemployment has helped hold down wages, but as the economy improves restaurant workers probably will seek jobs in other, higher paying industries. The long-term picture for labor in the industry has been negative for the past several years, with the recession providing only a temporary hiatus in this trend.[33]

The double drive-thru segment of the business is expected to be the only fast-food industry sector to increase market share, according to most industry observers. "The decade of the 1990s will be the decade of the double drive-thru," Ron Paul, President of Technomic, Inc., a Chicago-based consulting group, has said.[34] From 1989 to 1990, the number of double drive-thrus increased from 300 to 500 units nationwide.[35] "The double drive-thru is giving the burger segment a migraine headache these days wherever they are in competition," said Jack B. Hayes of *Nation's Restaurant News*.[36] For example, Checkers are often intentionally built near Burger Kings or McDonald's to take advantage of their already completed marketing studies indicating a market for burgers at that location.[37] According to Herb Brown, several of the Checkers restaurants located in the Chicago area are "doing more volume than some McDonald's locations."[38]

The double drive-thrus are concentrated most heavily in the Southeast; however, both Rally's and Checkers aspire to become nationwide chains. Checkers has already gone head-to-head against Rally's in several markets. When Checkers announced plans to open 20 stores in Charlotte, North Carolina, Rally's reopened two stores previously closed in the area and developed plans to open six more units during the next two years.[39]

Atlanta may be the next battleground. A franchisee of Rally's plans to open ten new Rally's restaurants there by the end of 1992.[40] Rally's has been in the city since 1990 and currently has four operations. Jim Kochran, Area Director for Rally's, has said that the chain expects to have 50 franchise and company-owned restaurants in the Atlanta area within the next three years.[41] "We want to capture what we see as a growing market for quick meals at a really good cost, before they do," Kochran has said about Checkers.[42] Checkers has already teamed up with industry veteran La-Van Hawkins with plans to establish 40 franchised Checkers drive-ins in the Atlanta and Decatur area over the next five years.[43] In addition, Checkers has opened 21 restaurants in the two years it has been in metropolitan Atlanta.[44] The south is not the only region up for grabs: both chains are attempting to establish footholds in northern cities, including St. Louis, Chicago, and Philadelphia.

One possible problem looming on the horizon for the double drive-thru industry is the declining burger demand that pushed the major chains into offering chicken sandwiches and salads. Obviously, any decline in burger demand would be a threat to drive-thru only operators who stay with a burger menu. The major shifts in eating habits that have emerged over the past decade could signal a decline in burger demand. For example, chicken is much more popular now than it has been in the past, and the rapid growth of yogurt shops is an example of the population's attempt to reduce fat intake, at least at dessert time. However, according to U.S. Department of Agriculture data compiled over a 30-year period, Americans still eat more red meat than poultry or fish. One fast-food insider has been quoted as saying that "people talk thin, but eat fat."[45]

Major fast-food chains have begun to utilize their immense financial resources to gain a piece of the double drive-thru restaurant market. Taco Bell's purchase of California-based Hot'n Now hamburger chain was the first such purchase. The 3,000-unit Mexican food, quick-service leader wants to accelerate growth to reach 10,000 units by the year 2001 through the use of nontraditional outlets such as double drive-thrus.[46] Charleston, South Carolina; Fresno, California; and Birmingham, Alabama, will serve as test-market locations for 95 of these units.[47] Kentucky Fried Chicken has operated a double drive-thru in Miami for seven years and is expected to open more. McDonald's has opened the first "express" store, offering only walk-up and drive-in service in Atlanta.[48] Recently, McDonald's opened its first double drive-thru restaurant in Raleigh, North Carolina. It has no counters or seating and is about one-third the size of the typical McDonald's 4,500 square foot unit. This restaurant offers a limited menu and has about 35 employees compared to the 60 in typical units. Burger King and Hardee's also are testing double drive-thrus in various parts of the country.[49] Arby's has introduced a new franchising option called Daddy-O's Drive-Thru Express Hamburgers, which needs a site of only 1,500 to 2,000 square feet and costs one-third to one-half less than a standard Arby's.[50] Although only five are currently in existence, Arby's plans to build additional Daddy-O's units in Atlanta and Miami. George Nadvit, Arby's Executive Vice-President of Operations, has said that "the potential for double drive-thrus is especially good now."[51]

Strategic Management and Board of Directors

The Board at Checkers is made up of six directors, of which two are outsiders. One of the outsiders is 85-year-old James M. Roche, who served as Chairman and CEO of General Motors Corporation during the 1970s. The second outsider is Harry S. Cline, a Clearwater, Florida, attorney who has performed legal work for Checkers in the past (see Exhibit 10.4). Neither of these two directors has had significant experience in the fast-food industry.[52]

Herbert G. Brown has been a Director since July 1987 and has served as Chairman of the Board since February 1989. Throughout his business career, Brown has been committed to community service. For example, for the past 50 years, he has held numerous posts with Rotary International. Additionally, in 1991 The Institute of American Entrepreneurs selected Brown as Florida's retail entrepreneur of the year. Checkers' founder, James E. Mattei, has served Checkers as a Director since its organization, as Chief Executive Officer since February 1989, and as President since April 1990. Since 1981, Mattei has also been Director, Chief Executive Officer, and President of Mattei Companies of Mobile, Alabama, a company involved in commercial development and construction. Before

EXHIBIT 10.4 Directors and Top Managers: Checkers Drive-In Restaurants, Inc.

Name	Age	Position	Percentage of Stock Held
Herbert G. Brown	68	Chairman and Director	6.9%
James E. Mattei	43	Chief Executive Officer, President and Director	17.4
George W. Cook	59	Executive Vice-President and Director	5.1
Paul C. Campbell	37	Chief Financial Officer	NA
Jared D. Brown	32	Vice-President and Director	10.6
Robert G. Brown	31	Vice-President	10.6
Harry S. Cline	51	Director	NA

Source: Compact Disclosure, Checkers Drive-In Restaurants, Inc.

joining forces to develop Checkers, both Brown and Mattei had only limited experience in the fast-food industry.[53]

George W. Cook has been a Director and Executive Vice-President of Purchasing, Human Resources, Security, and Training for Checkers since February 1990. Mr. Cook has also served as President of Champion, a wholly owned subsidiary of Checkers, which manufactures its restaurants. Before joining Checkers, Cook served as Director and President of Brown Furniture stores in Florida. Paul C. Campbell, an 11-year veteran of the fast-food industry, has served as Chief Financial Officer since April 1990. Before joining Checkers, Campbell worked for six years in various finance-related positions for Taco Bell Corporation. Campbell's last job at Taco Bell was Manager of Business Planning, and in that capacity was responsible for more than 650 company-owned and 500 franchised units.[54]

Both of Herb Brown's sons have key roles at Checkers. Jared Brown has served the company as a Director, Vice-President—Franchising, Vice-President—Marketing and Advertising, and as Secretary and Treasurer. Robert Brown has served as a Director and is currently Vice-President—Development. The brothers gained their early business experience working as partners in the management and operation of Herbert G. Brown and Associates—a shopping center, mobile home park and office development partnership based in Florida.[55]

Restaurant Operations

As of April 1992, Checkers was operating 62 company-owned restaurants, and franchisees were operating another 96. The majority of the Checkers restaurants are located in Florida, with smaller numbers of outlets located in Alabama, Pennsylvania, Georgia, Louisiana, Illinois, Tennessee, Missouri, Michigan, North Carolina, and South Carolina.[56] Checkers' management believes that the location of every unit is essential to the company's success. Therefore Checkers' management inspects and approves each potential site prior to its final selection. Various factors, such as traffic volume and speed, convenient access, size and configuration, demographics, population density, visibility, and costs, are considered when making a site selection. Checkers' management also examines potential competition and the sales and traffic counts of national and regional chains operating in the same general area. Leased land is utilized whenever possible.[57] However, when purchasing property becomes necessary, real estate costs are approximately one-half of those faced by the traditional chains such as McDonald's and Burger King. For example, a Checkers restaurant can be placed on a 15,000 square foot lot, whereas most fast-food restaurants require 30,000 square feet to an acre.[58] Small site requirements allow Checkers to do well on long, narrow strips of land that larger chains wouldn't even consider.

All Checkers restaurants are built to company-approved specifications regarding size (approximately 14 feet by 48 feet), interior and exterior decor, equipment, fixtures, and other features (see Exhibit 10.2). All the modular buildings are distinctive because they are designed around a 1950s diner and art deco theme with the use of black and white tiles in a checkerboard pattern and neon lights. As noted earlier, the restaurants utilize the double drive-thru concept with serving windows located on opposite sides of the building, but service also is available at walk-up windows. Although none of the units have an interior dining area, most have a patio for outdoor eating.[59]

Each Checkers has a computerized point-of-sale system, which displays customer orders on a monitor in front of the food and drink preparers who are able to begin filling the order as it is being placed. The computerized point-of-sale system also is used to monitor sales, labor and food costs, customer counts, and other important information for each hour that a restaurant is open. Generally, each system at company-owned restaurants is polled daily by a computer at the company's head office. On a daily basis, management monitors the sales, food and labor costs, product mix, inventories, and customer counts for each company-owned store. Moreover, profit and loss statements and balance sheets are produced monthly.[60]

A typical menu at a Checkers' restaurant is shown in Exhibit 10.5. The typical cost of a meal consisting of a deluxe hamburger, French fries, and soft drink is usually less than $3.00—about $1 cheaper than the average check at McDonald's. Every restaurant, whether company owned or franchised, must purchase all food, beverages, and supplies from company-approved suppliers. These products must meet standards and specifications set by the company, and management constantly monitors the quality of the items being supplied. Checkers has been successful in negotiating price concessions from suppliers for bulk purchases of food and paper supplies. Additionally, all essential food and beverage products are available or could be procured from alternative qualified suppliers on short notice.[61] Each company-operated restaurant employs an average of 31 hourly employees, many of whom work part-time. Each Checkers restaurant usually has a manager and three assistant managers. The company has an incentive compensation program for each store manager that provides a monthly bonus for meeting certain defined goals.[62] However, there has been some management turnover because of the monotony and tedium of a manager's job. "The concept can lull people to sleep. You work in the same 12-foot-by-40-foot box every day, and you can slip a bit. There's not enough money in the world to keep some people in a job like that," according to Mike Ballard, President of Double Drive-Thru, Inc.

EXHIBIT 10.5

A Typical Checkers Menu

All burgers 100% U.S.D.A. beef

BURGER

Cajun Champ Burger[1]	1.29
1/4 lb Champ Burger	.99
Cheese Burger	1.29
1/2 lb Dbl Meat Hamburger	1.89
1/2 lb Dbl Meat Cheese Burger	2.09
Bacon Cheese Burger	1.89

SANDWICHES

Chicken Sandwich	1.96
Fish Sandwich	1.96
B.L.T.	1.24
Hot Dog	.96
Deluxe Chili Dog	1.24

FRIES

Large .99 Small .79

DRINKS/SHAKES

Ice Tea
Sweetened/Unsweetened
Large .99 Small .86
Coffee, Regular .55
Milk Shakes[2]
Lg. 1.99 Reg. 1.49 Sm. 1.19

COLAS

Coke Diet Coke
Cherry Coke
Sprite Dr Pepper
Lg. .99 Reg. .89 Sm. .79

DESSERTS

Apple Nuggets .99

Notes: 1. Deleted part of menu. 2. Deleted the four flavors.

Every restaurant manager is required to have had prior restaurant experience, preferably in the fast-food industry, and reports directly to a District Manager who has responsibility for five to seven restaurants. Each District Manager reports to a Director of Operations, one of whom is responsible for Florida operations and the other for Alabama, Georgia, and Louisiana.[63]

Since its inception, Checkers has maintained a limited advertising program at the restaurant level, consisting mainly of fliers, handouts, coupons, and small newspaper ads focused on each restaurant's immediate market area. Some analysts warn that being identified with couponing and discounting will cause consumers to view Checkers' products as inferior.[64] However, Checkers' management believes that the visual appeal of its restaurants and satisfied customers provide the most effective advertising. One goal at Checkers is to develop a sufficient number of restaurants in each of its markets to make radio and television advertising effective. As a cost-cutting measure, the company requires franchisees to spend 2% of their annual gross receipts for local advertising and promotion.[65]

By fast-food industry standards, Checkers restaurants are extremely profitable. Excluding real estate costs, the $408,000 initial investment in a Checkers unit generates an average of $916,000 in sales—for a return on investment ratio of about 2.2 to 1.[66] In comparison, a McDonald's restaurant costs about $1.3 million to build and produces an average of $1.5 million in annual sales—a ratio of about 1.15 to 1.

U.S. Food Expenditures

Food expenditures in the United States have risen almost every year since the end of the Great Depression. Even though the amount of money spent on food has been steadily rising, as a percentage of income spending on food has declined. The reason is that income generally has risen faster than food expenditures. Spending on food has risen over the years partly because more people eat at higher priced restaurants as their incomes rise. Home-produced food, once a major food source, has declined since 1929 from 19% to less than 2% of total food expenditures.

Rising incomes are chiefly responsible for the increased spending on food away from home (Exhibit 10.6). Items most affected by income are foods prepared away from home, frozen and refrigerated bakery products, and all alcohol except beer, ale, and whiskey. American households, on average, spend 53% of their food and beverage budgets on food prepared at home, another 40% on food prepared away from home, and about 7% on alcohol. But households with incomes of $50,000 or more spend more than half their food dollars at restaurants or on carry-out meals. Exhibit 10.6 lists the percentage of total average annual expenditures spent on food away from home by consumer unit.

Spending on food varies dramatically by age, and the biggest spenders are aged 35 to 54. Away-from-home spending peaks among 45- to 54-year-olds, at 37% above the average. Those under 25 years of age have the highest percentage of carry-outs, and those 75 years old and older have the lowest percentage of restaurant, carry-out, and other types of away-from-home meals (6.57% and 3.46% respectively). Expenditures on food at home and away from home by urban consumer unit were $4,320 and $2,445 in 1990, respectively. Total average urban consumer unit spending was $29,161. The rural consumer unit spent $4,147 on food at home and $2,727 on food away from home in 1990. Total average annual rural consumer unit spending was $24,327.

Single, employed persons living alone spend substantially more on eating out than any other group, but they also spend more per person on food at home than any other group. Larger households generally spend less on eating out than do smaller households, partly because they have more children. Married couples with no children at home devote 44% of their food dollars to restaurants, take-outs, and other food prepared away from home. Married couples with children spend 41% of their food budgets at restaurants and for carry-outs.

Contributing to the greater food spending away from home is the fact that more working mothers result in more lunches being eaten away from home. People under 25 years of age lead in eating lunch away from home and dining out, with percentages of 2.55% and 2.69%, respectively, of their total average annual expenditures going to these types of meals out.

EXHIBIT 10.6 Consumer Spending on Food

	All Consumer Units	Under $10,000	$10,000–$19,999	$20,000–$29,999	$30,000–$39,999	$40,000–$49,999	$50,000 and Over
Meals away from home	6.17%	5.75%	6.06%	6.39%	6.41%	6.32%	6.09%
Meals at restaurants, carry-outs	4.83	4.61	5.04	5.20	5.03	4.98	4.49
Lunch	1.89	1.82	1.87	2.07	1.96	1.89	1.83
Dinner	2.08	1.88	2.14	2.21	2.09	2.19	2.02
Snacks and alcohol	0.54	0.60	0.63	0.59	0.60	0.60	0.40
Breakfast and brunch	0.32	0.31	0.41	0.34	0.38	0.30	0.25
Board (including at school)	0.17	0.22	0.04	0.11	0.12	0.10	0.29
Catered affairs	0.16	0.04	0.04	0.14	0.16	0.13	0.27
Food on out-of-town trips	0.74	0.57	0.57	0.67	0.80	0.80	0.86
School lunches	0.16	0.10	0.13	0.17	0.21	0.23	0.13
Meals as pay	0.11	0.21	0.24	0.11	0.10	0.09	0.03

Consumer Eating Habits

Consumer eating habits varied greatly during the 1980s. As medical research continues to confirm the importance of healthy eating habits in order to avoid the number one killer disease—cardiovascular disease—Americans are trying to improve their eating habits. Trends in food consumption are affected by three factors: (1) the constant battle to maintain a low cholesterol level, (2) the benefits of eating fiber-rich food, and (3) the continuous struggle for thin and fat-free bodies. Medical research focused attention on all three factors, but they were exaggerated by the media and became more fads than medical concerns. The following are the effects that each factor had on food consumption.

Cholesterol

Because of increased concern with diseases related to high cholesterol, Americans began to consume less poultry and fish. Vegetable oils began to replace animal oils. In 1991, per capita poultry consumption in the United States was 94.8 pounds (on average, ¼ lb per day); beef and veal consumption was 97.0 pounds (on average, ¼ lb per day); and pork consumption was 65.5 pounds (on average, ⅙ lb per day).

Fibers

Fiber-rich diets are responsible for the decreased consumption in processed vegetables and bakery items made of bleached flour. In contrast, consumption of cereals, whole-grain breads/bakery items, and fresh fruit and vegetables increased dramatically in the 1980s.

Weight

The weight issue increased consumption of fresh fruits and vegetables; poultry is consumed instead of other meats. Foods traditionally rich in fat are now available in low-fat or fat-free versions; consumption of the latter increased greatly. Overall, consumption of all sweets and sugar-laden foods declined.

Another trend in consumer eating habits is that of eating already prepared meals, at home or away from home. The reason is that both parents in many families work full-time, thus having more disposable income and less time for food preparation. In just a few years, the time allotted for food preparation has shrunk from 30 to 20 minutes. This shift in eating habits has enabled the food service industry to grow considerably, especially the fast-food segment. Expenditures for fast food as a percentage of total food expenditures increased from 1.5% in 1950 to 15.7% in 1990. Current trends in fast-food restaurants include increases in

- menu-item selections,
- low-fat and fat-free items,
- fiber-rich items,
- cost-saving combination menus, and
- ethnic cuisines (Mexican, Chinese, Italian, Cajun, etc.).

Foods affected most negatively by health concerns are

- shortening,
- whole milk,
- potato chips,
- French fries, and
- sausage.

Attitudes versus Behaviors

A substantial portion of the preceding figures were obtained through surveys, so a word of caution about interpreting them is necessary. The trends toward healthier eating habits are certainly true; however, they are not as significant as the media and marketing/advertising agencies would like the public to believe. Inconsistencies in results occur when surveyed consumers truthfully express a concern about such or such an item and declare that they have changed their behavior regarding this item. However, this answer might not represent reality, as most surveyed consumers say what they wish they were doing instead of what they *really* do.

In the 1988 National Eating Trends Survey, for example, 39% of the people surveyed expressed concerns about French fries (1985–1988). However, analysis of consumption figures revealed that the number of people who consumed French fries at least once in two weeks declined only 7%. The same observation applied to consumption of fried chicken: a substantial change in attitude was reported, but only a moderate change in behavior was observed. Although other decreases in food consumption might indeed be real, the causes may be wrongly attributed. A good example is the declining consumption of eggs, which is attributed to concern about cholesterol-laden products. However, it also could be the result of less time spent on food preparation, and cooking eggs in the morning is time-consuming.

Overall, the consumption of "unhealthy" foods has been declining over the past decade; however, it still outweighs the consumption of "healthy" foods by more than 30%. A restaurant analyst said, "People may have changed their eating habits at home, but when they eat out—they still want red meat, fried foods, potatoes with sour cream and butter—so they revert to their old eating habits."

Manufacturing Operations

"People eat with their eyes," Jared Brown once said, and the design of a Checkers restaurant certainly whets a customer's appetite. To attract the attention of busy motorists, the prefabricated buildings have been fitted with black and white checkered tile and, as one business writer noted, "enough chrome and glass to restore a small fleet of '55 Buicks."[67] The result is a building that serves as perhaps the company's best form of advertising.

Champion, a wholly owned Checkers subsidiary, currently leases a 48,615 square foot building in Largo, Florida, for its manufacturing operations. Under the terms of the lease, Champion has an option to purchase the building and an adjacent 7,853 square foot fully furnished office facility for a total purchase price of $625,000 (see Exhibit 10.2). At the Largo facility, Champion produces a complete modular restaurant package ready for delivery and installation. This capability, when compared to the conventional on-site construction methods used by the major fast-food chains, provides several competitive advantages to Checkers: less construction time and cost, direct quality control, and consistent and uniform image.[68] In 1991, revenue from the sale of modular restaurant packages accounted for 24% of total revenues and 42% of earnings.

Gregory T. deCelle has been General Manager of Champion since it was organized in May 1990. Before joining Champion, deCelle was a representative of Grier's Office Machines, Inc., where he was involved in the creation, development, and maintenance of restaurant-related computerized point-of-sale computer systems, computerized accounting systems, and customer-polling software. He gained knowledge of the construction industry by serving for eight years as Vice-President of deCelle Builders, a company involved in the construction of residential and commercial properties.[69]

Each modular restaurant package consists of a modular building complete with all mechanical, electrical, and plumbing systems; a computerized point-of-sale system; all restaurant and cooking equipment, such as walk-in coolers and freezers, grills, desks, filing cabinets, sinks, preparation tables, fryers, milkshake machines, drink stations, dispensing equipment, and small wares and utensils; delayed-time safes; and security and smoke detection systems. Even though the modular building is designed to be permanent when placed on its site, it can later be lifted intact and moved to another location at a cost estimated by management to be approximately $6000 plus $12 per mile; the cost includes site improvement, moving, and installation. This ability to relocate provides great flexibility in the selection and control of prospective sites and enables the owner, whether the company or a franchisee, to adapt rapidly to changing traffic patterns.[70]

The Champion production facility presently operates one shift per day, five days a week, and can produce 12–15 modular restaurant packages per month. Independent contractors hired and supervised by Champion personnel handle most of the construction and assembly operations. Manufacturing time from the date the order is received to the date the package is ready for delivery is generally five to six weeks. Normally, Champion does not maintain an inventory of completed packages. Rather, it produces packages only in anticipation of new company-operated restaurants or against firm orders received from franchisees. To date, Checkers' management does not require franchisees to buy a modular restaurant package; however, it expects that most franchisees will elect to do so because of the relatively low cost.[71]

During 1991, the cost of producing a modular restaurant package ranged from $221,000 to $223,000, which included an average building price of $128,000 and equipment package prices ranging from $93,000 to $95,000.[72] These packages are sold to franchisees for $408,000, whereas a Rally's unit conventionally constructed costs $360,000 or 11.8% less.[73] Building and operating these restaurants costs about a third to a half of what it costs major competitors.

Champion maintains quality control at each stage of production and installation. It includes inspection in the plant by independent third parties to test compliance with government construction and performance standard regulations. In addition, Champion personnel supervise all phases of installation, approve all site improvements, and inspect all mechanical, plumbing, and electrical systems. After a modular restaurant package has been delivered to a site by an independent trucking contractor, in only 14–21 days the restaurant is fully operational.[74]

Franchise Operations

One of Checkers' growth strategies is to focus primarily on the controlled development of franchised restaurants in existing markets and certain contiguous states, including South Carolina, Texas, Virginia, and Wisconsin. "Checkers cannot successfully penetrate a market on our own—we create a big network of franchisees as well as company-owned stores; we use the franchise system to help solidify a given market."[75] The two primary criteria considered by Checkers in the approval of potential franchisees are (1) the availability of sufficient capital (net worth of about $2 million) to open and operate the number of restaurants franchised and (2) prior experience in the operation of fast-food restaurants. During the next several years, Checkers expects a ratio of approximately 30% company-operated restaurants to 70% franchised restaurants. Under existing franchise agreements, franchisees are required to open 286 restaurants by 1995.[76]

Checkers maintains a staff of well-trained and experienced restaurant operations personnel. They help train franchisees, assist them in opening new restaurants, and monitor the operations of existing restaurants. These services constitute an integral part of Checkers' franchise program. In addition, when a new franchised restaurant opens, Checkers sends a four-member restaurant management team to assist the franchisee during the critical first four days of operation. This team works in the new restaurant to ensure that Checkers' standards of quality and speed will be maintained. The team also provides on-site training for all restaurant personnel.[77] Before a new restaurant opens, Checkers requires each franchisee and restaurant manager to attend a comprehensive five-week training program consisting of both classroom and in-store training. Hands-on experience is incorporated into this training program by requiring each attendee, prior to completion of the course, to work in and eventually manage an existing company-operated restaurant.[78] A McDonald's insider has criticized this short training program saying that "you can't just pop these places open . . . and have instant training." A comparable training program at McDonald's lasts approximately 18 months.[79]

Construction of a new franchised restaurant cannot begin until Checkers has approved the site plans. These plans include details of building location, internal traffic patterns, utility locations, walkways, driveways, signs, parking lots, and landscaping. When a modular restaurant package is not used by a franchisee, the company still must approve the plans and specifications for the restaurant to ensure uniformity of the design of the building and accompanying site improvements.[80] All franchise agreements require that the franchisee select various proposed sites within the franchised area and submit these potential sites to Checkers' management for approval. Each Checkers' franchisee is required to purchase all fixtures, equipment, inventory, products, ingredients, and other supplies used in the operation of its restaurants from company-approved suppliers, all in accordance with company specifications.[81]

The three franchise service representatives at Checkers each supervise approximately 18 franchised restaurants in defined geographic areas. These representatives have been fully trained to assist franchisees in implementing operating procedures and policies of the company. They also rate each restaurant's hospitality, food quality, service speed, cleanliness, and facility maintenance. The franchisees receive written findings of these inspections and, if any deficiencies are noted, recommendations for correcting the deficiencies.[82]

Unless a franchisee operates a single restaurant under a unit franchise agreement, each franchisee ordinarily signs an area development agreement. It grants the franchisee the right to develop and open a specified number of restaurants in a defined geographic area within a limited period of time and thereafter to operate each restaurant in accordance with the terms and conditions of a unit franchise agreement. Each area development agreement establishes the number of restaurants (normally five to ten) the franchisee is to construct and open in the franchised area during the term of the agreement. The number of restaurants required is based on factors such as the residential, commercial, and industrial characteristics of the area; geography and population of the area; and previous experience of the franchisee. Generally, the area development agreement contains the development schedule. Checkers may terminate an agreement if a franchisee fails to meet the development schedule.

A unit franchise agreement (for a single restaurant), generally requires a franchisee to pay a $25,000 fee. Under an area franchise agreement, the franchisee must pay a fee for each restaurant opened. The amount of the fee varies and is based on the number of restaurants that company management estimates the franchisee can develop within the franchised area. Each franchisee also is generally required to pay Checkers a semimonthly royalty fee of 4% of each restaurant's gross sales and to expend monthly 2% of gross sales for local advertising and promotion.[83]

Finance: Going Public

By the end of 1989, Checkers' total revenues were some 200% greater than they had been in 1988. In 1990, total revenues surpassed the $20 million mark—growing by another 150% (Exhibits 10.7 and 10.8). Between 1988 and 1991, the average annual sales volume per restaurant climbed from $460,000 to $916,000.[84] In midsummer of 1991, Jim Mattei and Herb Brown decided to take Checkers public.

The initial offering completed November 15, 1991, consisted of 2,100,000 shares of common stock, of which 300,000 shares were offered by insiders. The offering price range originally discussed was between $10 and $12 per share, but when demand proved to be much greater than anticipated the price was boosted to $16 per share.[85] Total proceeds from the offering were $33,600,000, of which $2,352,000 went to underwriting discounts and commissions and $4,464,000 went to the selling shareholders. Of the net proceeds, $9,200,000 was earmarked for development of additional company-operated restaurants ($1,900,000 for use

EXHIBIT 10.7

Statement of Operations: Checkers Drive-In Restaurants, Inc.
(Dollar amounts in thousands)

	First Quarter	Fiscal Years Ending December 31			
	March 1992	1991	1990	1989	1988
Revenues					
Restaurant sales	$12,047	$29,019	$18,357	$8,765	$2,834
Royalties	795	1,764	682	112	11
Franchise fees	345	1,280	563	275	37
Modular restaurant packages	2,982	10,088	3,323	—	—
Total revenues	16,529	42,151	22,925	9,152	2,882
Costs and expenses					
Costs of revenues—					
Restaurant sales	9,165	21,902	14,099	7,021	2,430
Modular packages	2,422	8,594	2,847	—	—
Depreciation/amortization	422	1,015	534	285	200
Selling, general, and administration	1,548	4,549	2,884	1,263	786
Total costs and expenses	13,557	36,060	20,364	8,569	3,416
Operating income	2,972	6,091	2,561	583	(534)
Interest expense (income)	(209)	418	483	491	203
Earnings (loss)	3,181	5,673	2,078	92	(737)
Minority interest in income	104	294	206	21	—
Earnings (loss)	3,077	5,379	1,872	71	(737)
Income tax expense	1,094	1,699	659	16	—
Earnings (loss)	1,983	3,680	1,213	55	(737)
Extraordinary item/loss carry	—	—	320	16	—
Net earnings (loss)	$ 1,983	$ 3,680	$ 1,533	$ 71	$ (737)

Source: *Checkers Investor Information Packet,* p. 11.

during 1991 and $7,300,000 for use during 1992 and 1993), and $5,743,000 was set aside to repay long-term debt.[86]

Since this first offering, Checkers' stock hit a high of $36 but then eased off to $27. Lately, Checkers' stock has caught the attention of short sellers who believe that the lofty price–earnings ratio of 46 is too high and hence expect a collapse.[87] Veteran restaurant analyst Roger Lipton of Laden Thalmann disagrees with the short sellers, stating that "the stock could double in price in another 12 months."[88]

Citing a doubling of revenues and lower operating costs, Checkers reported a 214% increase in operating income—to $3 million—for the first quarter of 1992. Among other things, company officials indicated that the jump in revenues was linked to a 9.5% increase in same-store sales for the quarter and greater royalties resulting from a large base of franchised units.[89] Checkers' Chief Financial Officer Paul Campbell noted that the company also managed to trim food costs because

EXHIBIT 10.8

Consolidated Balance Sheets: Checkers Drive-In Restaurants, Inc. and Subsidiaries

Years Ending December 31	1991	1990
Assets		
Current assets		
Cash and cash equivalents	$13,120,036	$ 562,886
Investments, at cost	2,839,671	—
Royalties receivable	127,679	94,461
Other franchisee receivables	131,387	119,854
Other receivables	947,276	202,183
Inventory	182,316	136,081
Costs and earnings in excess of billings on uncompleted contracts	377,087	—
Prepaid expenses and other	7,973	156,148
Pre-opening costs, net of accumulated amortization of $59,515 in 1991 and $34,746 in 1990	155,848	78,991
Total current assets	17,889,273	1,350,604
Property and equipment, at cost, net of accumulated depreciation and amortization	18,905,654	9,741,309
Long-term investments, at cost	6,235,348	—
Goodwill, deposits and other	462,856	423,093
Total assets	$43,493,131	$11,515,006
Liabilities and Shareholders' Equity		
Current liabilities		
Notes payable to bank	$ —	$ 718,980
Current installments of long-term debt	738,887	830,934
Current installments of notes payable to shareholders	—	347,289
Accounts payable	4,951,373	1,586,752
Accrued wages	556,435	292,831
Other accrued expenses	656,516	448,211

(continued)

"Checkers is becoming a fairly large chain, and we have been able to negotiate some pretty good prices." Campbell also attributed the same-store sales hike to combination meal promotions, such as a quarter-pound Champ burger, a small order of fries, and a medium soft drink for $2.29.[90]

On April 29, 1992, Checkers announced a secondary offering of 3 million shares (half by the company and half by insiders) to be sold for $25.25 per share, or approximately $83 million for the total offering. The net proceeds from this offering, along with the remaining proceeds of its initial offering, have been earmarked for development of additional company-operated restaurants and working capital.[91]

EXHIBIT 10.8

Consolidated Balance Sheets: Checkers Drive-In Restaurants, Inc. and Subsidiaries *(continued)*

Years Ending December 31	1991	1990
Billings in excess of costs and earnings on uncompleted contracts	—	148,422
Income taxes payable	838,765	146,835
Deferred franchise fee income, net of deferred costs	278,195	558,134
Total current liabilities	8,020,171	5,078,388
Long-term debt, less current installments	1,768,408	3,808,395
Notes payable to shareholders, less current installments	—	539,867
Deferred area development franchise fee income	352,500	360,000
Deferred income taxes	987,000	190,000
Minority interests in joint ventures	419,826	394,858
Total liabilities	11,547,905	10,371,508
Shareholders' equity		
Preferred stock, $.001 par value. Authorized 2,000,000 shares, no shares outstanding	—	—
Common stock, $.001 par value. Authorized 15,000,000 shares, issued and outstanding 13,582,500 shares in 1991 and 10,887,482 shares in 1990	13,776	10,888
Additional paid-in capital	29,129,475	703,204
Retained earnings	3,201,975	429,406
	32,345,226	1,143,498
Less treasury share, at cost	400,000	—
Net shareholders' equity	31,945,226	1,143,498
Commitments and related party transactions		
Total liabilities and shareholders' equity	$43,493,131	$11,515,006

Source: Checkers Drive-In Restaurants, Inc., *1992 Annual Report,* p. 17.

Conclusion

Herb Brown turned back toward his desk and set the newspaper down. In one fluid motion, he sprang from his chair and moved down the hall to Jim Mattei's office. Already in Mattei's office were Brown's sons, Jared and Robert. Herb Brown smiled and began talking excitedly about ways to beat the company's current growth projections for 1992 and to have 403 restaurants by the end of 1993. Mattei said, "We are going back to the traditional roots of fast food by offering a burger and fries and colas."[92] This approach will allow Checkers to become the leading double drive-thru burger chain in this country. By returning to traditional roots, Mattei added, "More and more people [will] . . . eat at Checkers every day."[93]

Meanwhile, back on Chandler Road in Atlanta, the McDonald's manager held each side of an aluminum ladder firmly so that an employee could descend safely. As the young man climbed down, the manager could begin to make out the new wording on the marquee. The fluorescent orange lettering read: "Big Macs for just 99 cents." The manager wondered just how long this change would have to remain in effect.

Notes

1. Dave Szymanski, "Checkers Drive-In, Insiders to Sell Stock Valued at Nearly $83 Million," *Tampa Tribune* (April 30, 1992).
2. Gene G. Marshall, "A Burger Joint That Could Sizzle," *Business Week* (August 24, 1992), p. 3280.
3. James R. Hagy, "After Fast Growth What's The Next Move," *Florida Trend* (November 1992), p. 30.
4. R. D. R. Hoffman, "Curb Appeal at Checkers," *Florida Business,* Tampa Bay edition (December 1, 1989), p. 4.
5. Dave Szymanski, "Checkers Jumps the Competition," *Tampa Tribune* (March 26, 1992), p. 30.
6. Cathleen Ferraro, "Drive-Ins: Newest Old Idea in Burger Wars," *Investor's Business Daily* (March 26, 1992), p. 30.
7. Hagy, p. 42.
8. Ibid.
9. Szymanski.
10. Ibid.
11. Checkers Drive-In Restaurants, Inc., *Prospectus* (November 15, 1991), p. 5.
12. Kenneth Bohannon, "Checkers Earns Triple Earnings in First Quarter," *West Palm Beach Post* (April 9, 1992).
13. James Scarpa, "Hamburger," *Restaurant Business* (January 1, 1991), p. 95.
14. Beth Wolfensburger, "Double Drive-Thrus Challenge the Burger Big Boys," *Boston Business Journal* (December 11, 1989), p. 12.
15. Lisa Lee Freeman, "Steak, Burger Chains Are Street's Darlings," *Investor's Business Daily* (September 28, 1992), p. 1.
16. Ibid.
17. Nancy Ryan, "It's Back to the Future in the Fast-Food Business," *Chicago Tribune* (October 10, 1990), p. B1.
18. John Harris, "I Don't Want Good, I Want Fast," *Forbes* (October 1, 1990), p. 186.
19. Carolyn Walkup, "Drive-Thru-Only Shift to Compete in the Fast Lane," *Nation's Restaurant News* (August 29, 1988), p. 4.
20. Scarpa, pp. 104–110.
21. Ibid.
22. S. D. Weinress, "Rally's Company Report," *Thompson Financial Network* (November 29, 1991).
23. J. J. Rohs et al., "Fast-Food Restaurants," *Wertheim Schroder & Co.* (April 16, 1992).
24. Edwin McDowell, "Whoppers by Candlelight: Fast Food Slows Down a Bit," *New York Times* (September 19, 1992), p. D-1.
25. Ibid.
26. Ibid.
27. Ferraro, p. 30.
28. Szymanski.
29. Ferraro, p. 30.
30. Walkup, p. 4.
31. Ibid.
32. Jack Hayes, "Drive-Thrus Get into the Fast Lane," *Nation's Restaurant News* (November 20, 1989), p. 1.
33. Rohs et al. (April 16, 1992).
34. Peter O. Keegan, "Fast Feeders Seeing Double from Drive-Thru Mania," *Nation's Restaurant News* (April 8, 1991), p. 27.
35. Ibid.
36. Hoffman, "Curb Appeal at Checkers."
37. Teresa Burney, "Checkers Serves Up Burger Battle," *St. Petersburg Times* (July 1, 1990).
38. Herb Brown, "Checkers," *Beta Alpha Psi Fall Accounting Conference*, University of South Florida, Tampa (November 13, 1992).
39. Katherine Snow, "Burgers by the Bushel," *The Business Journal—Charlotte* (May 25, 1992), p. 1:1.
40. Ernest Holsendolph, "Checkers, Rally's Openings Put Fast Food on Fast Track," *Atlanta Journal and Constitution* (June 7, 1992), p. H-3.

41. "Rally's Puts Bigger Bite on Atlanta," *Atlanta Journal and Constitution* (September 12, 1992), p. C-2.
42. Ibid.
43. Ernest Holsendolph, "Franchisee Not Moving Checkers at a Leisurely Pace," *Atlanta Journal and Constitution* (March 18, 1992), D-1.
44. "Rally's Puts Bigger Bite on Atlanta."
45. Ferraro, p. 30.
46. Keegan, p. 27.
47. Hagy, p. 45.
48. Ernest Holsendolph, "Restauranteur Takes a Gamble on Ponce Shop," *Atlanta Journal and Constitution* (July 5, 1991), p. D-1.
49. Ben Eubanks, "Burger Battle Rally's Falters," *St. Louis Business Journal* (February 27, 1989), p. 1:1.
50. "What Ever Happened to Off the Rack?" *Restaurant Business* (March 20, 1992), p. 67.
51. Scarpa, p. 104.
52. Hagy, p. 44.
53. Checkers *Prospectus* (November 15, 1991), p. 29.
54. Ibid., p. 30.
55. Ibid.
56. Hagy, p. 42.
57. Checkers *Prospectus* (November 15, 1990), p. 20.
58. Hoffman.
59. Checkers *Prospectus* (November 15, 1991), p. 20.
60. Ibid., p. 22.
61. Ibid., pp. 20–21.
62. Ibid., p. 21.
63. Checkers *Prospectus* (November 15, 1991), p. 21.
64. Weinress.
65. Checkers *Prospectus* (November 15, 1991), p. 27.
66. Adam S. Levy, "Checkers Drive-Ins to Jump into Stock Market," *Tampa Tribune* (September 28, 1991).
67. Hoffman.
68. Checkers *Prospectus* (November 15, 1991), p. 25.
69. Ibid., p. 31.
70. Paul Campbell, "Checkers," *Beta Alpha Psi Summer Meeting* (June 22, 1992).
71. Checkers *Prospectus* (November 15, 1991), p. 25.
72. Ibid.
73. Weinress.
74. Checkers *Prospectus* (November 15, 1991), p. 25.
75. Jared Brown, "Checkers," *Beta Alpha Psi Fall Accounting Conference,* University of South Florida, Tampa (November 13, 1992).
76. Checkers Drive-In Restaurants, Inc. *1991 Annual Report.*
77. Checkers *Prospectus* (November 15, 1991), p. 22.
78. Ibid.
79. Hagy, p. 44.
80. Checkers *Prospectus* (November 15, 1991), p. 23.
81. Ibid., pp. 23–24.
82. Ibid., p. 23.
83. Ibid., p. 24.
84. Szymanski.
85. Ibid.
86. Checkers *Prospectus* (November 15, 1992), p. 10.
87. Marcial, p. 68.
88. Ibid.
89. Alan Liddle, "Checkers Sees 1st Q Jump in Operating Income," *Nation's Restaurant News Newspaper* (April 27, 1992), p. 14.
90. Ibid.
91. "Checkers Drive-In Restaurants Announces a Secondary Offering of Common Stock," *Business Wire* (May 22, 1992).
92. Lisa Blackman, "Checkers Step Up Expansion Plans as IC Seeks to Be Number 1," *Tampa Tribune* (May 11, 1993), p. F-1.
93. Ibid.

PepsiCo and the Fast-Food Industry

Joseph Wolfe

As PepsiCo, Inc., entered the early 1990s, Wayne Calloway, the company's Board Chairman and Chief Executive Officer, had every right to be optimistic. From 1991 to 1992 sales had increased 14.0%, earnings were up 21.0%, and per share dividends had increased 20.0%. Moreover, the firm's primary industry segments of soft drinks, snack foods, and restaurants had hiked sales 10.0%, 17.0%, and 16.0%, respectively. Since 1987, PepsiCo's compounded annual sales had increased 16.8%, and its income from continuing operations had grown at an 18.4% rate. Based on these results, Calloway set a new goal for the corporation's 338,000 employees by asking the question, "How does a $20.0 billion company add another $20.0 billion in just five years?"

The CEO answered that question by identifying two main growth opportunities: (1) global expansion, and (2) redefinition of the company's basic businesses. Calloway stated:

> Not too long ago we would have described ourselves as a company in the business of soft drinks, snack chips and quick service restaurants. Today, we're in the business of beverages, snack foods and quick service food distribution. A soft drink company sells only carbonated colas and the like; a beverage company might sell things like water and tea or fruit-based drinks. Also, a restaurant company is constricted to certain physical locations. A food distribution company can take its products wherever there's a customer, without necessarily making an investment in a large restaurant. We also reconsidered our geographic limitations. Up until a few years ago, we were basically a strong U.S. company with a solid but limited international presence. Not so today. In 1991, nearly one out of every four sales dollars came from our international operations. When you consider that 95.0% of the world's population is outside the U.S., you can see what that means in terms of opportunity. And this is doubly true for our kinds of products, which are in great demand everywhere on earth, with almost no economic or cultural barriers.

Although numerous opportunities appear to exist for PepsiCo, many industry observers have noted that overall domestic soft drink industry sales increases have been marginal and that the cola segment has plateaued. The cola market amounted to $34.0 billion in 1992, but its growth was only 1.5%, far lower than the 5.0% to 7.0% annual growth rates experienced in the 1980s despite changes in packaging, logotypes, and advertising campaigns by both Coke and Pepsi. In 1992, the market share for diet soft drinks, for years a growth segment, showed its first annual drop—from 29.8% in 1991 to 29.4%—and overall consumption rose only marginally—from 47.8 gallons to 48.0 gallons per capita. In the United States Coca-Cola maintained its 40.7% share of the soft-drink market, but PepsiCo slipped from 31.5% to 31.3% in 1992. Additionally, the first-move advantages

---

This case was prepared by Professor Joseph Wolfe. This case was submitted to the 1993 North American Case Research Meeting. This case was edited by T. L. Wheelen and J. D. Hunger for this book.

claimed by Pepsi in the former Warsaw Pact nations quickly evaporated after Coca-Cola began an 18-month, $400 million assault in Central Europe's post-Socialist countries in "Operation Jumpstart." Health concerns have affected the sales of both snack foods and fast foods, with strong implications for PepsiCo's other two divisions. Although snack chip and cracker manufacturers have introduced new products and all the fast-food chains have launched new, leaner burgers and menu assortments, these innovations have met with mixed success.

In charting his company's future, Wayne Calloway knows that he must correctly interpret the sources of PepsiCo's potential growth while carefully balancing the resource needs of the company's various divisions, businesses, and products. Known worldwide for its soft drinks, PepsiCo actually obtains more sales (about 36.0% of its revenues) from its restaurant operations than its soft drinks. Although the restaurant operations increased their sales, the division's costs and profit performances have been spotty. What can be done to correct this situation? Again Calloway is optimistic for at least the company's Pizza Hut and Taco Bell systems:

> A steadily growing interest in eating away from home and the continued gravitation to convenience foods are creating an atmosphere of excitement for our restaurants. Our strategy is to take advantage of these trends by accelerating our growth in existing markets and introducing our products to new markets. At Pizza Hut, we'll continue to expand delivery aggressively. We're testing alternatives to our traditional dine-in concept and we're adding innovative distribution channels. Taco Bell is also continuing its break with tradition. Alternative distribution points and the increasing use of technology to drive costs down make Taco Bell the market innovator. The situation at KFC in the U.S. is challenging. We're in the process of restructuring our business to greatly improve productivity and customer service. We're reorganizing our kitchens, upgrading our units and adding nontraditional distribution points.

PepsiCo, Inc.

PepsiCo, Inc., is an international company currently operating in three industries: soft drinks, snack foods, and restaurants. As Exhibit 11.1 shows, it evolved to its current status as an annual $20 billion revenue giant. It all began in 1893 in New Bern, North Carolina. A soda fountain drink known as "Brad's drink" became the trademark drink Pepsi-Cola in 1902 when the Pepsi-Cola Company was formed as a North Carolina corporation. Profitable operations ensued until heavy losses on sugar inventories caused its bankruptcy in 1922. A new Pepsi-Cola Corporation was formed the following year and all operations were moved to Richmond, Virginia. This corporation lost money for the next five years and then was only marginally profitable until it too went bankrupt in June 1931.

Using the assets and borrowing power of the New York–based Loft, Inc., candy company, Charles Guth subsequently purchased Pepsi-Cola's proprietary rights for $10,500. Guth reformulated the drink to his tastes and sold Pepsi's syrup mainly to Loft's candy stores, but the operation continued to lose money. Mired in the depths of the Great Depression the company began to bottle its soft

EXHIBIT 11.1 **Significant Company Events: PepsiCo, Inc.**

1893 "Brad's Drink" concocted in Caleb B. Bradham's pharmacy in New Bern, North Carolina.

1902 Pepsi-Cola Company incorporated in North Carolina.

1908 First bottling franchise created.

1920 Sugar prices rise dramatically from $.055 to $.265 per pound. Bradham invests heavily in sugar inventories. Prices drop to $.35 per pound in December and the company reports a $150,000 loss on operations.

1922 Company files for bankruptcy. Bradham forced to resign and R.C. Megargel & Company forms "The Pepsi-Cola Company" as a wholly owned Delaware corporation. Company lapses on March 18, 1925 for nonpayment of taxes.

1923 Craven Holding Corporation of North Carolina purchases all of Pepsi-Cola's assets and trademark. Roy C. Megargel forms the "Pepsi-Cola Corporation" in Richmond, Virginia, after purchasing Pepsi's trademark, business, and good will from the Craven Holding Corporation for $35,000. Operations in New Bern closed and moved to Richmond.

1928 Company is merged with the "National Pespi-Cola Corporation," of which Megargel owned 90%.

1931 Company goes bankrupt. Charles Guth uses $10,500 from the Loft, Inc., candy store company to buy Pepsi's proprietary rights. A new Pepsi-Cola Company is founded in Long Island City and loses money for the next three years.

1933 Company begins to bottle its soft drinks in used 12-oz. beer bottles. Within five months more than 1,000 cases a day are being sold.

1935 Loft, with support from Phoenix Securities Corporation, sues Guth for control of Pepsi-Cola. Guth loses suit but appeals the decision. Company managed by a court-appointed team during the appeal process.

1938 Coca-Cola files a trademark violation suit against Pepsi over its use of the word Cola. Coke loses the lawsuit.

1939 Charles Guth loses his appeal. All legal and financial control of the company reverts to Phoenix Securities, which has a dominant stock interest in Loft. "Pepsi-Cola hits the spot" jingle created.

1941 Pepsi jingle played on over 469 radio stations and later voted America's best-known tune in 1942.

1946 Sales level off at about $45 million for the next few years and earnings drop by 70%.

1950 Pepsi nears bankruptcy. Alfred N. Steele leaves Coca-Cola to become Pepsi's President and vows to "Beat Coke." Pepsi's Cuban sugar plantation sold for $6.0 million. Over the next five years $38.0 million is invested in new plants and equipment.

1955 Steele marries film star Joan Crawford. Pepsi's advertising budget is $14.0 million, or 18% of the industry's total. Advertising theme is "Be Sociable with Light Refreshment." Sales have risen 112% since 1950. Company owns 120 plants in more than 50 countries.

1958 Steele attempts to merge company with Pabst Brewing Company.

(continued)

EXHIBIT 11.1 **Significant Company Events: PepsiCo, Inc.** *(continued)*

1959 Steele dies of a heart attack after completing "Adorama," a $200,000 national sales promotion tour. Donald Kendall, head of Pepsi's overseas operations, photographs Nikita Khrushchev drinking six cupfuls of Pepsi at a Moscow trade fair. Drink becomes an instant hit with the Russians and in Eastern Europe.

1962 Advertising theme is "Now, it's Pepsi, for those who think young."

1963 Coke introduces diet Tab and Pepsi-Cola introduces Patio Diet Cola and later Diet Pepsi to fill low-calorie segment pioneered by Royal Crown's Diet Rite Cola.

1964 Advertising theme is "Come Alive, You're in the Pepsi Generation." Company establishes the Pepsi-Cola Equipment Corporation to lease trucks and equipment to bottlers. Company later acquires and adds to this unit Lease Plan International, a trucking concern, National Trailer Convoy, North American Van Lines, Lee Way Motor Freight, and Chandler Leasing. Pepsi-Cola United Bottlers buys Rheingold Breweries for $26 million; PepsiCo later acquires a 51% interest in the United Bottlers operation. Company acquires Tip Corporation, the Virginia manufacturer of Mountain Dew.

1965 Company develops Devil Shake to compete with the Yoo-Hoo chocolate drink. Attempts to buy controlling interest in Miller Brewing Company. Purchases Wilson Sporting Goods from LTV. Company merges with Frito-Lay of Dallas to become PepsiCo, Inc. Herman W. Lay becomes PepsiCo's largest stockholder and Chairman of its Board.

1966 Advertising theme is "Taste That Beats the Others Cold . . . Pepsi Pours It On." Company closes its up-state New York sugar refinery after losing $12 million on operations.

1969 Pepsi's late-year advertising theme becomes "You've Got a Lot to Live, and Pepsi's Got a Lot to Give." Soft drink sales are $940 million, compared to Coke's $1.3 billion.

1970 Corporation moves from its Manhattan headquarters to suburban Purchase, New York.

1974 Company fined $50,000 for conspiring to fix sugar cane prices in 1972 and 1973.

1977 Company acquires Pizza Hut for about $300 million. Coca-Cola outbids PepsiCo for Taylor Wines of New York for $96 million. Pepsi's management admits that its overseas executives have made $1.7 million in questionable payments to local officials; Coke's questionable payments had been $1.3 million.

1978 Company acquires Taco Bell, Inc., the nation's largest Mexican fast-food chain, for $148 million in stock.

1982 Lee Way Motor Freight loses $12.8 million.

1984 Taco Bell unit experiments with La Petite Boulangerie, a franchised chain of bakeries. Introduces Slice to compete in the "natural fruit" drink segment. Sells Lee Way Motor Freight for a $15 million after tax loss.

1985 Company sells North American Van Lines for an after-tax gain of $139 million. Sells Wilson Sporting Goods for an $18 million after-tax loss.

1986 Acquires Kentucky Fried Chicken, the world's largest chicken chain. Acquired Mug Root Beer, and 7UP for distribution in all non-U.S. markets.

(continued)

EXHIBIT 11.1 **Significant Company Events: PepsiCo, Inc.** *(continued)*

1989 Acquires the United Kingdom's Smiths Crisps Limited and Walkers Crisps Holdings Limited for $1.34 billion. Acquires General Cinema's domestic bottling operations for $1.77 billion.

1991 Taco Bell acquires Hot 'n Now hamburger franchiser.

1992 Company acquires Evercrisp Snack Productos de Chile SA and Mexico's Kas SA and Knorr Elorza SA. Buys out joint venture partners Hostell Frito-Lay in Canada and Gamesa Cookies in Mexico. Acquires a 50% interest in California Pizza Kitchen, Inc., and an equity position in Carts of Colorado, Inc.

1993 Pepsi-Cola International begins to distribute Cadbury Schweppes products in Central Europe through a franchise partnership. Increased distribution of H2Oh! sparkling water and Avalon still water in the United States. PepsiCo creates a $600 million European snack food joint venture with General Mills after failing in its bid to purchase the company's European operations. PepsiCo's snack companies in Spain, Portugal, and Greece are joined with General Mills' French, Belgium, and Dutch operations into Snack Ventures Europe.

drink in used 12-oz. beer bottles and promoted the slogan "Two large glasses in each bottle." Thus Pepsi offered almost twice as much for the same $.05 price charged by Coca-Cola in its 6.5-oz. container. Sales and profits rose dramatically, but this revival in profits generated court battles on two fronts. Loft's management, with the help of the company's major stockholder, Phoenix Securities, sued Guth for company control, and Coca-Cola simultaneously filed a trademark infringement suit over Pepsi's use of the word "Cola." After four years of court-appointed management, Charles Guth lost all claims to the company. In the intervening period, Coca-Cola also lost its lawsuit against Pepsi after successfully suing many other soft drink manufacturers for the same violation and having watched more than 1,100 other cola manufacturers go out of business.

For the next 20 years the company operated as a soft drink firm, battling the firmly entrenched Coca-Cola Company. Pepsi-Cola narrowly averted another bankruptcy in 1950 and attempted or consummated various conglomerate diversifications from the late 1950s to the mid 1960s. Upon its merger with Frito-Lay in 1965, the company became PepsiCo, Inc., and subsequently grew through concentric acquisitions, new product introductions, and product line extensions.

Soft Drinks Division

Today, PepsiCo's soft drinks division markets Pepsi-Cola, Mountain Dew, and Slice in regular and diet versions in both the U.S. and international markets, and 7UP in non-U.S. markets. This division also operates various soft drink joint bottling and distribution ventures, such as those with Ocean Spray and Lipton Tea in the United States; Canada's Avalon spring water on the U.S. East Coast; A&W's

root beer and cream soda, Squirt, and Vernors brands in Asia; and Kas brands with Knorr Elorza SA in Spain. The company introduced Crystal Pepsi and Diet Crystal Pepsi (the firm's clear, uncolored "New Age" soft drink) during Super Bowl XXVII with 90 seconds of advertising at $28,000 a second. It also slowly rolled out All Sport, as it tried to crack America's $800 million-a-year sports drink market.

Snack Foods Division

The company's snack foods division makes and distributes its products throughout the world. Its major offerings are Lay's Potato Chips, Cheetos, Doritos, Crunch Tators, Tostitos, Ruffles, Rold Gold Pretzels, Fritos, and Santitas Tortilla Chips. New snack and chip products include Sunchips multigrain snacks, Suprimos wheat-based snack chips, McCracken's cracker crisps, and the Sonric sweet snack in Mexico. In a related move, Frito-Lay introduced a line of salsa and picante sauces, which garnered an 11% share of 1992's $496.8 million market. In the spring of 1993, the division rolled out a premium brand of salsa and picante named after its popular Tostitos restaurant-style chips. Major manufacturing and processing operations are located in the United Kingdom, Spain, Mexico, Portugal, and Brazil. Joint ventures are underway in various countries, such as in Mexico with the Gamesa Company in the cookie business, in Poland with Wedel in the sweet snack segment, and in Australia with complete ownership of the Arnotts snacks and cracker company, after initial operation as a joint venture.

Restaurant Division

PepsiCo also operates the world's largest system of restaurants through its Pizza Hut, Taco Bell, and KFC (Kentucky Fried Chicken) chains. Included in this division are the sales of PepsiCo Food Systems Worldwide (PFS), which supplies all company-owned and franchised units with food, paper goods, equipment, and promotional materials. The division's revenues come from company-owned store sales, initial franchising fees, royalty and rental payments from franchisees, and net wholesale sales to franchisees by PFS. Although already a worldwide presence, the company continues to penetrate new markets: Pizza Hut has opened in Aruba, Cyprus, and Gibraltar; KFC has opened in France and Chile; and Taco Bell has opened in Aruba, Korea, and Saudi Arabia. Pizza Hut and KFC each operate in more than 60 countries, and Taco Bell operates in eleven countries, with 20 more countries being considered. In the United States, Taco Bell is experimenting in Charleston, South Carolina, and Fresno, California, with its Hot 'n Now acquisition, an express drive-thru burger concept, as well as additions to the fare served in its three main restaurant systems. Exhibits 11.2 and 11.3 present PepsiCo's income statements and balance sheets for fiscal years 1988–1992. Exhibit 11.4 summarizes PepsiCo's international sales. Exhibits 11.5 and 11.6 present each segment's overall performance, its assigned assets, and its geographic area of concentration. Exhibit 11.7 shows recent one-time and unusual expenditures associated with PepsiCo's restaurant division.

EXHIBIT 11.2

Income Statements: PepsiCo, Inc.
(Dollar amounts in millions)

Years Ending	December 26, 1992	December 28, 1991	December 29, 1990	December 31, 1989
Net sales	$21,970.0	$19,607.9	$17,802.7	$15,242.4
Cost of goods sold	10,492.6	9,395.5	8,549.4	7,421.7
Gross profit	11,477.4	10,212.4	9,253.3	7,820.7
Selling and general administration	8,840.3	7,880.8	7,008.6	5,887.4
Pretax operating income	2,637.1	2,331.6	2,244.7	1,933.3
Nonoperating income	113.7	(45.4)	111.2	26.8
Interest expense	586.1	615.9	688.5	609.6
Pretax income	2,164.7	1,670.3	1,667.4	1,350.5
Provision for taxes	597.1	590.1	576.8	449.1
Less exceptional items and discontinued operations[1,2]	1,567.6	—	13.7	—
Net income	$ 374.3	$ 1,080.2	$ 1,076.9	$ 901.4

Notes:
1. 1990 net charges for discontinued operations.
2. 1992 net charges for required accounting changes for retiree health benefits and income taxes.

Source: Adapted from PepsiCo, Inc., *Form 10-K Report;* and *News from PepsiCo, Inc.* (February 2, 1993), p. 2.

The Fast-Food Restaurant Industry

Americans eat about 750 million meals a day, but over the years the proportion of food consumed in the home has declined. Exhibit 11.8 shows that, in the battle for "stomach share," by 1991 Americans spent almost as much, or about $262 billion, on restaurant meals as they spent for prepared and nonprepared grocery store food. Prepared food is a growth industry because of the two-person working family and the provision of an escape from cooking chores. Exhibit 11.9 demonstrates that fast-food restaurants have increased their market share but that the table service or "white linen" restaurant share has declined. In 1993, restaurant spending will total more than $268 billion for meals served both on and off the restaurant's premises, as depicted in Exhibit 11.10.

The 1980s were a decade of high industry growth, with average sales increases amounting to 8.7% a year. Lately, however, real growth and the industry's returns on net worth have declined. Exhibit 11.11 shows the combined actual and estimated operating profits for selected restaurant chains. After adjusting for inflation, analysts noted that total industry sales increased only 1.8% from 1991 to 1992. Price wars have periodically broken out in response to outlet proliferation

EXHIBIT 11.3

Balance Sheets: PepsiCo, Inc.

(Dollar amounts in millions)

Years Ending	December 26, 1992	December 28, 1991	December 29, 1990	December 31, 1989
Assets				
Cash	$ 169.6	$ 186.7	$ 170.8	$ 76.2
Marketable securities	1,888.5	1,849.3	1,644.9	1,457.7
Receivables	1,588.5	1,481.7	1,414.7	1,239.7
Inventories	768.8	661.5	585.8	546.1
Other current assets	426.8	386.9	265.2	231.1
Total current assets	4,842.2	4,566.1	4,081.4	3,550.8
Property, plant and equipment	7,442.0	6,594.7	5,710.9	5,130.2
Advances to subsidiaries	1,707.0	1,681.9	1,505.9	970.8
Intangibles	6,959.0	5,932.4	5,845.2	5,474.9
Total assets	$20,951.2	$18,775.1	$17,143.4	$15,126.7
Liabilities and Shareholders' Equity				
Notes payable	$ 706.8	$ 228.2	$ 1,626.5	$ 866.3
Accounts payable	1,164.8	1,196.6	1,116.3	1,054.5
Income taxes	387.9	492.4	443.7	313.7
Other current liabilities	2,064.9	1,804.9	1,584.0	1,457.3
Total current liabilities	4,324.4	3,722.1	4,770.5	3,691.8
Deferred charges	1,682.3	1,070.1	942.8	856.9
Long-term debt	7,964.8	7,806.2	5,600.1	5,777.1
Other long-term liabilities	1,624.0	631.3	925.8	909.8
Total liabilities	15,595.5	13,229.7	12,239.2	11,235.6
Common stock	14.4	14.4	14.4	14.4
Capital surplus	667.6	476.6	365.0	323.9
Retained earnings	5,439.7	5,470.0	4,753.0	3,978.4
Less treasury stock	667.0	745.9	611.4	491.8
Currency adjustment	(99.0)	330.3	383.2	66.2
Shareholder equity	5,355.7	5,545.4	4,904.2	3,891.1
Total liabilities and shareholders' equity	$20,951.2	$18,775.1	$17,143.4	$15,126.7

Source: Adapted from PepsiCo, Inc., *Form 10-K Report; 1992 Stockholders' Report,* p. 32.

EXHIBIT 11.4

Sales and Profits by Geographic Area: PepsiCo, Inc.
(Dollar amounts in millions)

	Net Sales				Operating Profit			
Area	1992	1991	1990	1989	1992	1991	1990	1989
United States	$16,551.0	$15,167.8	$14,046.9	$12,519.4	$2,059.6	$1,842.2	$1,853.3	$1,601.9
Europe	1,349.0	1,486.0	1,344.7	771.7	52.6	61.8	108.5	53.8
Canada and Mexico	2,214.2	1,434.7	1,089.2	899.0	251.0	198.7	164.2	117.1
Other	1,855.8	1,519.4	1,321.9	1,052.3	138.6	123.8	98.4	122.9
Total	$21,970.0	$19,607.9	$17,802.7	$15,242.4	$2,501.8	$2,226.5	$2,224.4	$1,895.7

Source: PepsiCo Inc., *1990 Stockholders' Report,* p. 35; *1991 Stockholders' Report,* p. 35; *1992 Stockholders' Report,* p. 29.

EXHIBIT 11.5

Domestic and International Segment Sales and Profits: PepsiCo, Inc.
(Dollar amounts in millions)

Segment		Net Sales 1992	Net Sales 1991	Net Sales 1990	Net Sales 1989	Operating Profit 1992	Operating Profit 1991	Operating Profit 1990	Operating Profit 1989
Beverages	Domestic	$5,485.2	$5,171.5	$5,034.5	$4,623.3	$686.3	$746.2	$673.8	$577.6
	International	2,120.4	1,743.7	1,488.5	1,153.4	112.3	117.1	93.8	98.6
Total		7,605.6	6,915.2	6,523.0	5,776.7	798.6	863.3	767.6	676.2
Snack Foods	Domestic	3,950.4	3,737.9	3,471.5	3,211.3	775.5	616.6	723.3	667.8
	International	2,181.7	1,827.9	1,582.5	1,003.7	209.2	171.0	202.1	137.4
Total		6,132.1	5,565.8	5,054.0	4,215.0	984.7	787.6	934.4	805.2
Restaurants	Domestic	7,115.4	6,258.4	5,504.0	4,684.8	597.8	479.4	447.2	365.5
	International	1,116.9	868.5	684.8	545.9	120.7	96.2	75.2	57.8
Total		8,232.3	7,126.9	6,188.8	5,230.7	718.5	575.6	522.4	414.3
Total	Domestic	16,551.0	15,167.8	14,010.0	12,519.4	2,059.6	1,842.2	1,853.3	1,601.9
	International	5,419.0	4,440.1	3,755.8	2,703.0	442.2	384.3	371.1	293.8
Grand Total		$21,970.0	$19,607.9	$17,765.8	$15,222.4	$2,501.8	$2,226.5	$2,224.4	$1,895.7

Source: PepsiCo, Inc., *1990 Stockholders' Report,* p. 35; *1991 Stockholders' Report,* p. 35; *News from PepsiCo, Inc.* (February 2, 1993), p. 5.

EXHIBIT 11.6

Identifiable Assets by Division and Geographic Area: PepsiCo, Inc.

(Dollar amounts in millions)

	1992	1991	1990	1989
Division				
Soft Drinks	$ 7,857.5	$ 6,832.6	$ 6,465.2	$ 6,198.1
Snack Foods	4,628.0	4,114.3	3,892.4	3,310.0
Restaurants	5,097.1	4,254.2	3,448.9	3,070.6
Total	$17,582.6	$15,201.1	$13,806.5	$12,578.7
Area				
United States	$11,957.0	$10,777.8	$ 9,980.7	$ 9,593.4
Europe	1,948.4	2,367.3	2,255.2	1,767.2
Canada and Mexico	2,395.2	917.3	689.5	409.5
Other	1,282.0	1,138.1	881.1	808.6
Total	$17,582.6	$15,201.1	$13,806.5	$12,578.7

Source: PepsiCo, Inc., *1990 Stockholders' Report*, p. 35; *1991 Stockholders' Report*, p. 35; *1992 Stockholders' Report*, p. 29.

EXHIBIT 11.7

Assorted Restaurant Division Charges: Pepsi Co, Inc.

(Dollar amounts in millions)

Pizza Hut	1990—$9.0 for closing underperforming domestic units; $8.0 to consolidate domestic field operations; $2.4 to relocate headquarters
Taco Bell	1989—$5.5 to consolidate domestic field operations
	1990—$4.4 for closing underperforming domestic units
Kentucky Fried Chicken	1989—$8.0 reorganization
	1990—$4.0 for closing underperforming domestic units
	$0.6 for closing underperforming international units
	1991—$32.8 to restructure domestic operations; $1.2 to restructure international operations; $9.0 for delay of Skinfree Crispy introduction

Source: PepsiCo, Inc., *1990 Stockholders' Report*, p. 35; *1991 Stockholders' Report*, p. 35.

EXHIBIT 11.8

U.S. Consumer Food Expenditures

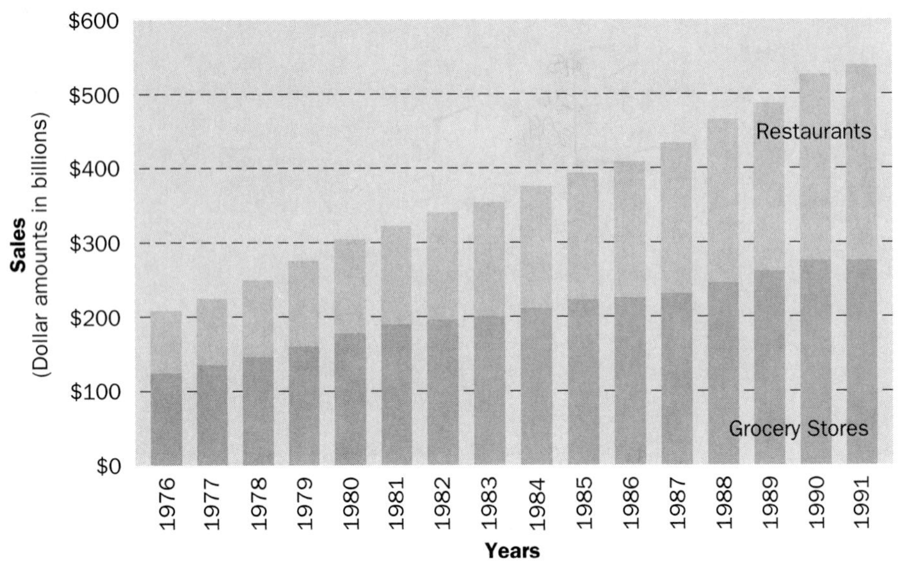

Source: Derived from graphic data presented in Eben Shapiro, "A Page from Fast-Food's Menu," *New York Times* (October 14, 1991), p. D1.

EXHIBIT 11.9

Sources of Prepared Foods in the United States

	Food Source			
Year	Fast-Food Restaurant	Table-Service Restaurants	Supermarkets	Other
1991	51.0%	23.0%	14.0%	12.0%
1990	46.0	27.0	14.0	13.0
1989	41.0	33.0	12.0	14.0

Source: Adapted from Charles S. Clark, "Fast-Food Shake-Up," *CQ Researcher* (November 8, 1991), 1(25), p. 837.

EXHIBIT 1.10

Where America Ate Its Restaurant Food in 1991

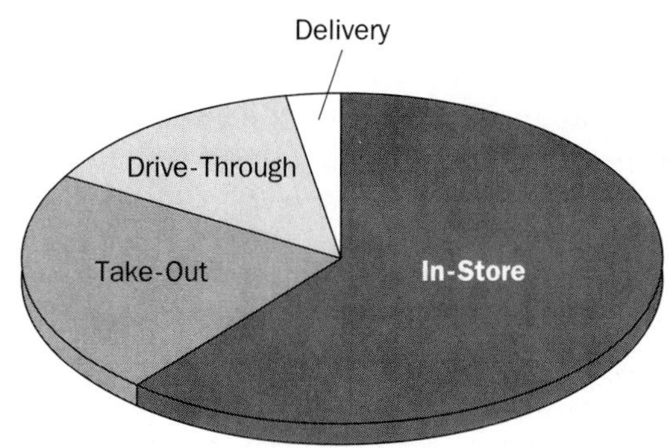

Source: From data and graphs in "Forget Candlelight, Flowers, and Tips: More Restaurants Tout Takeout Service," *Wall Street Journal* (June 18, 1992), p. B1.

EXHIBIT 1.11

Restaurant Industry Income and Expenses

(Dollar amounts in millions)

	1995–1997 (Estimated)	1993 (Estimated)	1992 (Estimated)	1991	1990	1989
Sales	$21,275.0	$15,315.0	$14,085.0	$13,330.0	$12,943.0	$12,048.0
Cost of sales	16,062.6	11,716.0	10,845.5	10,277.4	10,017.9	9,445.6
Gross profit	5,212.4	3,599.0	3,239.5	3,052.6	2,925.1	2,602.4
Administrative overhead	640.7	401.0	325.8	473.0	459.1	426.0
Depreciation	1,155.0	895.0	845.0	800.9	758.9	604.9
Pretax profit	3,416.7	2,303.0	2,068.7	1,778.7	1,707.1	1,571.5
Less taxes	1,161.7	783.0	713.7	601.2	602.6	573.6
Net profit	$2,255.0	$1,520.0	$1,355.0	$1,177.5	$1,104.5	$997.9
Net worth	$13,075.0	$8,860.0	$7,640.0	$6,624.8	$5,762.3	$4,937.7

Note: Summary results for Bob Evans Farms, Carl Karcher Enterprises, Frisch's Restaurants, International Dairy Queen, JB's Restaurant, Luby's Cafeterias, McDonald's, Morrison Restaurant, National Pizza, Perkins Family Restaurant, Piccadilly Cafeterias, Ryan's Family Steak Houses, Shoney's, Sizzler International, TCBY Enterprises, Vicorp Restaurants, and Wendy's International.

Source: William G. Barr, "Restaurant Industry," *Value Line* (September 25, 1992), p. 295.

and the lingering 1991 recession. The use of discounting to generate traffic has been widespread, but the major chains are now redefining the nature of a "bargain." This new definition regards "value" as the use of combination meals to guide customers to higher markup food items while simultaneously emphasizing the food's quality and the restaurant's service and atmosphere.

Overall growth has declined, but some segments and food delivery services have had healthy growth. From 1985 to 1990, the fast-food industry's sandwich segment rose from 4.9% to 5.7% of total sales while hamburger chain sales fell from 53.4% to 50.5% of all sales. Sandwich segment sales amounted to about $5.3 billion in 1992, or 0.8% more than in 1991. In 1991, America's 100 largest restaurant chains added only 413 hamburger outlets, but pizza makers opened 1,095 additional restaurants. By the beginning of 1992 the nation had about 18,600 pizza and 26,600 burger restaurants. Ice cream and yogurt outlets ranked third in number but had a net loss of 142 outlets in 1991. Reflecting on the pizza category's growth, Technomic President Ronald Paul says that "pizza's a very friendly product." He observes that crusts can vary in thickness and can be crunchy or chewy, the pizza's cheese base is rich in protein, and a great variety of toppings can be offered. Moreover, home delivery pizza holds up better over longer distances than do either burgers or fries. Exhibit 11.12 lists the current high-growth food segments, and Exhibit 11.13 lists America's fastest growing fast-food chains.

Although the upscale, casual dining segment has lost market share in recent years, each unit generates relatively high profits. Rather than relying on the fast-food restaurant's "table turn" for profits, white linen restaurants profit by changing higher markups, generating bar and table liquor sales, and serving multicourse meals rather than finger food and limited combos. General Mills has been especially successful in the casual dining, ethnic food restaurant segment. To supplement its aging Red Lobster seafood restaurant chain, in 1982 General Mills simultaneously created the Olive Garden (based on an Italian theme) and purchased Darryl's (a North Carolina fern-bar restaurant chain), The Good Earth (a California health-food restaurant), and Casa Gallardo (a Mexican-food chain). Of the four concepts, the Olive Garden appeared to have the greatest potential; market research revealed that Italian cuisine was America's most identifiable ethnic food. In 1985, the company opened seven more restaurants, and by 1992 the chain had grown to 320 restaurants with sales of $808 million. Success didn't come easily, however, as management spent five years and about $28 million before settling on the chain's optimal recipes, flavorings, and decor. The Olive Garden learned that it had to recognize regional taste differences if it was to cater to the white-collar, evening dinner crowd. It discovered through taste tests and trial menus that chunky tomato sauce did poorly in St. Louis but that patrons in California loved it; customers in Rhode Island uniquely favored veal saltimbocca.

Based on General Mills' success with Olive Garden, it is now in its third year of testing Chinese cuisine at its China Coast restaurant in Orlando, Florida. The company first tried oriental cuisine with its Minneapolis-based Leeann Chin buffet and take-out chain seven years ago after extensive testing. When this approach failed, the company hired Terry Cheng, a Chinese-American chef and food biolo-

EXHIBIT 11.12

Growth of Food Segments in 1991

Food Segment	Growth
Pizza	5.4%
Chicken	6.8
Fish	11.6
Mexican	12.6
Oriental	28.4

Source: Adapted from PepsiCo, Inc., *1991 Stockholders' Report*, p. 31.

EXHIBIT 11.13

Fastest Growing Fast-Food Chains
(Dollar amounts in millions)

Chain	Menu/Theme	1990 Sales
Taco Bell	Inexpensive Mexican food	$2,600.0
Subway	Deli-style submarine sandwiches	1,400.0
Sonic	1950s-style drive-ins	515.0
Sbarro	Fast Italian food	277.0
Rally's	Double drive-through burgers	215.0

Source: Louis Therrien, "The Upstarts Teaching McDonald's a Thing or Two," *Business Week* (October 21, 1991), p. 122.

gist, to produce a more satisfying menu for American tastes. The result has been the creation of six main dishes revolving around moo goo gai pan, fried rice, egg rolls, and sweet-and-sour chicken and definitely not authentic Chinese dishes (such as chicken feet, jellyfish, and bird's nest soup). Exhibit 11.14 presents the ratings from a *1992 Consumers Reports* reader survey for various national chains that offer diverse fare and upscale dining accommodations.

Trends in the Fast-Food Industry

Prepared foods represented a $63.5 billion business in 1989. The market research firm Find/SVP's projection of this market is $88.7 billion by 1994, with the supermarkets' share increasing to 16.5% at the expense of fast-food restaurant sales. In addition to price wars and niche hunting as strategies for dealing with the fast-food industry's declining growth, other methods are being tried to continue the industry's development. These strategies entail the creation of more convenient outlets, development of alternative food delivery methods, greater attempts to capture the after-six eating crowd, and an increasing reliance on foreign or internationally derived sales.

EXHIBIT 11.14

Selected National Restaurant Chains by Type

Family Restaurants	
Big Boy	963 units. Originally known for its hamburgers but now offers a variety of meals and a soup, salad, and fruit bar. Lowest rated restaurant in this category. Value and prices were average.
Denny's	1,391 units. 24-hour service, well-known for breakfast menu and grilled sandwiches. Menus for senior citizens and children. Alcohol served at many locations. Food taste and selection rated less than average for average prices.
International House of Pancakes	500 units. Traditional breakfast stop with a wide variety of all-day meals of average value and price. Menus for seniors and children. Most patrons were seated immediately.
Po Folks	137 units. Large portions of "home style cookin'." Special menus for seniors and children. Take-out service and catering facilities. Considered a good value with lower than average prices. Highest rated restaurant in this category.
Village Inn	229 units. Focuses mainly on breakfast with a limited selection of lunch and dinner meals. Senior citizen discount and low-fat, low-calorie breakfasts. Most diners were seated immediately.
Steak and Buffet Restaurants	
Golden Corral	458 units. Mostly steak but limited grilled chicken and seafood. Food, salad, and dessert bar with more than 100 items. Menus for seniors and children. Bar. Prices and food value rated better than average.
Mr. Steak	60 units. Steak, chicken, and seafood. Take-out service and children's menu. Highest rated restaurant in this category.
Sizzler	634 units. Features chicken, steak, and seafood with a large salad, soup, taco, and pasta bar. Senior citizen and children's menus. Entertainment lounge and wine. Take-out service. Taste, food selection, price and value rated average.
Casual Dinner Houses	
Bennigan's	223 units. Menu varies throughout the United States but emphasizes southwestern dishes and finger foods. Children's menu, takeout, and bar. Lowest rated restaurant in this category. Value and prices lower than average but atmosphere much better than average.

(continued)

Off-Premises Dining

Restaurant take-out, drive-through, and delivery services comprise the off-premises dining segment of the fast-food industry. It grew 5.9% in 1991, whereas the fast-food industry's on-premises sales were flat. Over the years, certain chains have been more successful than others in obtaining off-premises sales. These sales accounted for 65% of Wendy's volume in 1992, a 30% increase since 1988, and they accounted for 70% of Burger King's sales. Despite the growth of this food delivery method, off-premises sales may conflict with on-premises dining. One way to eliminate the problems of offering both types of sales from the same location is

EXHIBIT 1.14 **Selected National Restaurant Chains by Type** *(continued)*

Chili's	267 units. Southwest grill, Tex–Mex, burgers, and salads. Senior's and children's menus. Bar. Fare above average in tastiness. Rates about average for this group.
El Torito	169 units. Clearly Mexican, featuring fajitas, quesadillas, and chimichangas and daily specials. Sunday brunch. Bar. Dinner portions larger than average.
Houlihan's	54 units. Steaks, burgers, and fajitas. Kids menu. Bar and lounge. Value and prices rated lower than average for this group.
Olive Garden	Homemade pasta, regional Italian meat, and seafood specialties. Large Italian wine list. Children's menu, take-out service and catering. Highest rated restaurant in this category with much better than average taste and better than average menu selection. Dinner portions larger and food quality more consistent than average. At least 25 percent of the raters had to wait more than ten minutes to be seated for dinner.
Red Lobster	550 units. Seafood, chicken, and steak with catch-of-the-day specials. Children's menu, take-out service, and bar. Prices much higher than average although fare above average in taste and selection. 25 percent of the raters had to wait more than ten minutes to be seated.
Ruby Tuesday	151 units. Menu varies throughout the United States with international appetizers and main courses. Salad bar and weekend brunch. Senior citizen discounts and children's menus. Bar. Below average price and value.
Steak and Ale	158 units. Well-appointed atmosphere, featuring steak, seafood, pasta, and chicken. Salad bar. Bar. Food much tastier than average and above average in selection. Prices were higher than average. Second-highest rated restaurant in this group.
T.G.I. Friday's	202 units. Very eclectic menu. Also has "lite" and children's menus. Take-out service and bar. Prices much higher than average. Tastiness and selection better than average.
Tony Roma's	222 units. Barbecued ribs and chicken entrées. Take-out, bar, and children's menu. Food higher than average in tastiness but below average in value and cost.

Source: Adapted from "Best Meals Best Deals," *Consumer Reports* (June 1992), 57(6), pp. 361–362.

to operate restaurants that prepare meals exclusively for off-premises consumption. Pizza Hut has opened Fastino's, a chain that sells pasta and pizza on a take-out and drive-through basis only. Pizza Hut's Vice-President of Development, Pat Williamson, predicts that Fastino's will eventually become as big as the 8,000-unit Pizza Hut chain. A variant of this concept is the use of double drive-throughs. McDonald's is experimenting with this concept in Raleigh, North Carolina, which uses tandem drive-through windows on both sides of a small food preparation and cashiering building. The store has no counter or seating, has one-third the space of a typical McDonald's 4,500 square foot outlet, and has only 35 employees instead of 60. To accelerate food preparation and simplify order-taking, its limited menu excludes salads and breakfast entrees (such as pancakes). Other companies experimenting with this concept are Taco Bell and Arby's, which bought the Hot 'n Now and Daddy-O's Express Drive-Thru chains, respectively, in 1991.

Other attempts to capitalize on the desire for off-premises dining—and to compensate for the scarcity of prime sites for full-scale restaurants—involve the creation of smaller outlets and greater access to fast-food from alternative locations. Two forms of the smaller outlet are kiosks and portable food carts. Taco Bell has operated one-person kiosks in supermarkets in Phoenix, and its first Mexico City outlet was a two-person food cart, started in June 1992, with two more locations planned for Mexico City and one in Tijuana. Pizza Hut, which already has 500 carts in operation, has plans to set up more than 10,000 carts in the United States and 100,000 in overseas locations. Kentucky Fried Chicken opened a cart unit in a General Motors plant in January 1992 and has plans for carts in train stations, office buildings, sports stadiums, and amusement parks. PepsiCo is negotiating with Wal-Mart to put its units in the mass merchandiser's chain throughout the United States. As an indication of the company's commitment to this concept, PepsiCo purchased a strong minority interest in Carts of Colorado, Inc., in February 1992.

Additional Outlets

Chains also are planning for additional outlets. McDonald's is attempting to develop "niche" outlets in airports and hospitals and in small, rural towns by opening smaller units called Golden Arch Cafes. These cafes are about half the size of a standard McDonald's, seat about 50 people, and offer counter service. Other examples of niche locations are Wendy's in the downtown Atlanta Day's Inn lobby and Marriott Hotels' provision of Pizza Hut room service from its own kitchens despite the fact that most of its hotels have restaurants and that it once owned the Gino's and Roy Rogers restaurant chains. Hotels and motels find that they can charge more for the franchised products they offer than their own because of instant brand name recognition. As of early 1992 Pizza Hut's offerings were available in about 40 Marriott Hotels, with 25 more scheduled for July 1992. Economy hotels and motels, which usually do not have dining facilities or are losing money on them, are now the fast-food industry's target. They account for about 38% of the nation's 44,500 hotels and motels and are the lodging industry's fastest growing segment.

Dinner Service

Another attempt to increase sales in the fast-food industry is its renewed efforts to attract the evening dinner customers and to profit from the rise of the "casual dining out experience." Many customers want to relax and spend more time over dinner than they do at breakfast or lunch. Norman K. Stevens, former marketing chief for Hardee's, explains that "people's expectations at dinner are totally different than at lunch" and that dinner is a more leisurely event—not something to be gotten through as quickly as possible. As an example of this trend, 1991 sales at sit-down ethnic restaurants totaled $8.0 billion, a 10.0% increase over 1990's sales.

However, changing the nation's fast-food eating habits or a chain's food delivery system or concept is difficult. After finally establishing its breakfast menu, McDonald's created a "Mac Tonight" promotion featuring a piano-playing Moonman character in 1987 to induce customers to have an evening meal at its restaurants. The campaign wasn't very successful, with only about 20% of McDonald's sales coming after 4:00 P.M.

Burger King has initiated a dinner menu and table service to revive its stagnant sales and attract a different, dinner customer. Although it serves about 2 million Whoppers a day, the company realized that its customers were switching to other menu items late in the day. Burger King's Cory Zywotow also found that customers said "they'd like to relax and spend more time" over dinner. At certain outlets, tablecloths and napkin rings are provided to heighten the ambiance. Starting at 4:00 P.M. each Burger King offers four main courses priced between $3.00 and $5.00: a hamburger, steak sandwich, fried shrimp, or fried chicken filet in a dinner basket, with either a baked potato or French fries, and a salad or cole slaw. Customers receive trays, beverage cups, and numbered plastic markers, along with free popcorn. When their orders are ready, servers bring them to the tables. Management believes that its sit-down dinner service was a major factor in increasing the company's operating profit by more than 9% from 1991 to 1992. Table service is an innovation for a fast-food restaurant, but the value of a different evening menu should not be overestimated. About 65% of Kentucky Fried Chicken's sales and 73% of Pizza Hut's sales are at the dinner hour despite the lack of both table service and special dinner items.

International Operations

Because of the decline in industry sales growth and saturation in various fast-food segments and geographic markets, many chains have turned to overseas operations. A 1992 Arthur Anderson & Co. survey of 366 franchisers found that only about one-third have foreign outlets but that nearly half of those without foreign operations intend to grow internationally in the next five years. Gary L. Copp, President of Spee-Dee Oil Change Systems, Inc., speaks for many when he reasons, "'Why take on Chicago when I can go to Brazil and find a virgin market?"

In the fast-food industry, international sales have become very important and very profitable. McDonald's first-quarter 1992 international sales rose 14% to $1.9 billion, or 39% of its total revenue and 42% of its total operating profits. Steven A. Rockwell of Alex. Brown & Sons estimates that the company's overseas profits will surpass domestic profits by 1995 owing to both the number of units operated and the high unit volumes they produce. In early 1992, McDonald's added 50 restaurants to its system; most were in foreign countries, and as many as 450 new overseas units were planned for the year. By April 1992, McDonald's had 8,772 American and 3,696 foreign restaurants. In that month it also opened its largest outlet: a 700-seat facility in Beijing, China.

Other chains also have profited from foreign operations. Kentucky Fried Chicken posted a 26% third-quarter worldwide profit increase while its same-store U.S. sales declined 1%. The company opened its first Eastern European restaurant in Budapest, Hungary, in partnership with Hungarian franchisee Hemingway Holding AG in October 1992, after working nearly two years to develop local suppliers. Pizza Hut opened two restaurants in Moscow in September 1990, with one selling pizzas for hard currency and the other selling them for rubles. About 20,000 customers a week are served, or about the number served by ten Pizza Huts in the United States.

As profitable as foreign operations are for fast-food franchisers, numerous problems accompany the application of their standardized operating systems in foreign cultures. McDonald's U.S. success has come from its manufacturing and operating routines. Its operations manual contains 600 pages, and the company demands mass production and absolute uniformity. A crew person must get a manager's approval before replacing a malted drink order or a spilled soft drink. Dressing a hamburger is always done in the same order—mustard first, then ketchup, then onions, and then two pickles. The result is a Big Mac that looks and tastes the same in Toledo as in Tacoma. In coming to Hungary, however, McDonald's found that the country's native potatoes were dark and did not fry "golden brown" and that the requisite iceberg lettuce was not home-grown. To replicate the chain's eye appeal and taste standard, the company initially flew entire Boeing 747 planeloads of potatoes and shredded lettuce to Budapest when it opened its first restaurant there.

Meeting Nutritional Concerns

A continuing concern is fast-food's nutritional value, and this concern has grown with America's greater awareness of health and diet issues. To many consumers, fast food has always meant "bad food." PepsiCo has attempted to avoid this stereotype of fast not being good by calling its chains "quick service" restaurants. Others, such as McDonald's, emphasize the enjoyment of eating fast, tasty meals with friends, family, and co-workers. Americans' health concerns are real, however, and the national chains have begun to introduce low-fat, low-calorie items while emphasizing the nutritional value of fast-food dining. In early 1990, McDonald's introduced its McLean Deluxe, a 91% fat-free hamburger containing carrageenan, a seaweed-based additive, to wide acclaim. Unfortunately, its sales weren't sizzling. Two years later, as part of a nutritional public information effort, the company aired a dozen animated 55-second televised spot announcements called "What's on Your Plate." These announcements attempted to explain the basics of well-balanced eating and how it could be accomplished. In each restaurant, McDonald's posts nutritional information about all its fare, and leaflets about its food are available for the asking. Burger King displays posters with the calorie, fat, cholesterol, and sodium content of all its food. The company is also test marketing (in 350 of its restaurants) menus based exclusively on Weight Watchers foods and is experimenting with foods containing less than 300 calories, including chicken on angel-hair pasta and chocolate mocha pie. About 60% of Taco Bell's company-owned outlets offer complete nutritional product information, and Wendy's has taken the position that it will match its competition regarding the amount of information supplied.

Many critics, however, are dissatisfied with the industry's efforts to provide a healthy diet. Michael Jacobson, Executive Director of the Center for Science in the Public Interest, believes that the fast-food industry could do more: "The charts and posters don't convey much to the average person. The information is presented as a matrix with 10 or 15 numbers for every food. Most people aren't going to lose their places in line to read about nutritional values."

Both nutritionists and industry participants emphasize the role of self-choice in making food purchases mixed with a bit of cynicism regarding America's eating intentions versus its actions. Sandwich shops have capitalized on the desire for greater nutrition. Many customers believe that deli meats sandwiched between two slices of fresh bread is healthier than a quarter-pound burger on a bun. Subway's "fattiest" sandwich is a six-inch meatball sub. "[I]t's not particularly healthy," observes Bonnie Liebman, Director of Nutrition at the Center for Science in the Public Interest, "but it has only half as much fat as a McDonald's Big Mac." Michael Evans of Burger King notes that by eating a Whopper without mayonnaise the customer saves 140 calories. With mayonnaise, which is the way most people like it, a Whopper contains 619 calories. Understandably, many chain operators are frustrated regarding the health issue. According to Maurice Bridges, Hardee's Director of Public Affairs, "After spending millions on research, we found, just by listening to the consumer, that people are talking nutrition, but they buy on taste." And industry observer Rajan Chaudhry of *Restaurants and Institutions* magazine believes that "people talk healthy but what they're really looking for is something to let them off the hook and let them believe they're eating healthier than they were otherwise."

Exhibit 11.15 displays the results of eating typical fast foods for an entire day. The average adult needs between 1,200 and 3,000 calories daily for weight maintenance. Approximately 50%–60% of those calories should come from carbohydrates, 15%–20% from protein, and 25%–30% from fat. Nutritionists also recommend that healthy adults limit their sodium intake to 3,000 milligrams and cholesterol to 300 milligrams per day.

Franchise–Franchisee Relations

Another serious concern relates to franchisee–franchisor relations. Although these relations often have been contentious, many franchisees have been hit hard by franchiser actions that were taken to maintain sales growth at the unit level. Accordingly, in the early 1990s franchisees have developed a new militancy that often frustrates the designs of the national chains.

Since the early 1960s McDonald's has exemplified the virtues of franchising as a key to rapid business development. Frandata Corporation of Washington, D.C., estimates that more than 3,000 franchisers operate some 540,000 franchised outlets in the United States. And, according to the International Franchise Association, a new outlet of some type opens about every 16 minutes. As a result, franchised business sales have risen dramatically, by 6.1% in 1991 alone, to $757.8 billion and now represent more than 35% of all retail sales. Although

EXHIBIT 11.15

A Day of Fast-Food Dining

Meal	Nutrition				
	Carbohydrates	Protein	Fat	Cholesterol	Calories
Breakfast at McDonald's					
Orange Juice	19	1	0	0	80
McMuffin Sausage/Egg	28	23	27	263	440
Hashbrown Potatoes	15	1	7	9	130
Total	62	25	34	272	650
Lunch at Pizza Hut					
3 Slices Medium size					
Peperoni Pizza	75	42	6	75	750
1 Regular Pepsi	40	0	0	0	159
Total	115	42	6	75	909
Supper at Kentucky Fried Chicken					
3 Drumsticks	12	39	27	201	438
Cole Slaw	13	2	7	5	119
2 Buttermilk Biscuits	56	10	24	2	470
1 Regular Pepsi	40	0	0	0	159
Total	121	51	58	208	1,186
Grand Total	298	118	128	555	2,745

Note: Amounts of carbohydrates, protein, fat, and cholesterol are in grams.

Source: *Eating Out Made Simple.* Tulsa: St. Francis Hospital (1991), pp. 16–17, 22, 25–26.

some franchisees work long, hard hours and often make little profit, franchising in general makes good business sense. In four of five industries surveyed by Francorp, an Olympia Fields, Illinois, consulting firm, franchisees' 1991 per unit sales grew faster or declined less than their industries' national averages. For restaurants, which constitute the franchising industry's largest single group, 1991 per unit sales increased 6.2% versus an overall restaurant industry growth rate of 3.0%.

Despite these generally favorable results, many restaurant franchisees have become increasingly dissatisfied with their franchisers. When Great Britain's Grand Metropolitan PLC purchased Burger King from Pillsbury in 1989, it ordered changes in floor tile designs and background music and cut back field management help. It also created an advertising campaign that many franchisees felt was unsuccessful. Burger King's management group now faces a disgruntled, 1,300 member National Franchisee Association, Inc., which it met in 1991 for the first time in seven years. The association's grievances were so great that it even explored buying Burger King from Grand Met.

Other militant franchisee associations have entered the fray. Almost all of Taco Bell's franchisees joined an independent group in January 1992 to oppose PepsiCo's aggressive price-cutting strategy and to challenge a contract clause that allows PepsiCo to open company-owned stores within a franchisee's market. In protest against the advertised prices PepsiCo sets for its company-owned stores, some 30% of the franchised units priced their products higher than the nationally promoted prices in September 1992. Taco Bell officials said in March 1992, however, that it would maintain the $.59, low-price strategy that many believed started the industry's price war in late 1988. Although the chain rang up 50% sales increases to $2.4 billion in two years, its profit growth dropped rapidly. Earnings increases of 108% and 19% for 1991's first two quarters sank to 2% and 5% in the following two quarters. As a result of Taco Bell's discounting, McDonald's engaged in retaliatory price cutting in 1991. Joseph S. Capser, a Tampa, Florida, licensee with 29 McDonald's restaurants, reported that price cutting increased his customer count by 15% but that overall sales increased by only 4%–5% and profits fell 10%–15%.

Accordingly, many franchisees feel that they are bearing the brunt of the price wars being conducted by their chains. Taco Bell franchisees want higher priced items featured in its advertisements, but Tim Ryan, the system's Senior Vice-President of Marketing, maintains that "our customers' focus on price is unchanged. Value continues to be the primary driver." Accordingly, he is testing a Value Menu that is priced $.10 lower. Actions by Taco Bell's Hot 'n Now management group has engendered a similar response by some franchisees. Encouraged to feature $.39 prices for hamburgers, French fries, and soft drinks, many of the chain's independent franchisees are upset. They claim that they cannot make a profit at those prices and that the company's advertisements are confusing; 15 franchisees formed an independent association to confront PepsiCo in October 1992.

PepsiCo's Quick Service Restaurant Division

Under Wayne Calloway's leadership, PepsiCo's success has been attributed to the slogan "Love change. Learn to dance. And leave J. Edgar Hoover behind." He asserts that change is inevitable, so initiating change is better than reacting to a situation. He goes on to say that "the worst rule of management is 'If it ain't broke, don't fix it.' In today's economy, if it ain't broke, you might as well break it yourself, because it soon will be." By "learning to dance" the CEO wants PepsiCo to deal with customers in new ways, and "leaving J. Edgar Hoover behind" means practicing a "hands off" management style that the former FBI chief would have detested. Calloway's loose management style has allowed each chain a wide degree of latitude, although he is not averse to moving people around when necessary and setting high financial goals for each operation. He brought John Cranor from Frito-Lay in 1991 to fix the Kentucky Fried Chicken operation and sent Pepsi's Worldwide Beverages chief Roger Enrico to head the snack division after he suffered a mild heart attack in Turkey. To accomplish this latter move he created a new unit for Michael Jordan after Enrico replaced him. Within the past eight years three soft drink Senior Vice-Presidents of Sales and Marketing have left the company after falling off their career ladders.

Although much of the public's attention has been focused on the cola wars, Calloway has had a different priority: to double his company's quick service business within the decade. He explains, "For us the restaurant business is the most compelling action around. We're not going to prosper if we just wait for busy people to come to our restaurants. We want to move toward the day when pizzas, chicken, and tacos are as convenient and readily available as a bag of Doritos is now." To help accomplish his goals, Calloway named the following top executives.

- Kentucky Fried Chicken Corporation
  Louisville, Kentucky
  John M. Cranor III, President and Chief Executive Officer, 46, 15 years PepsiCo service
- Taco Bell Worldwide
  Irvine, California
  John E. Martin, President and Chief Executive Officer, 47, 9 years PepsiCo service
- Pizza Hut Worldwide
  Wichita, Kansas
  Steven S. Reinemund, President and Chief Executive Officer, 44, 8 years PepsiCo service

The restaurant division's financial results are shown in Exhibits 11.16–11.19. The company's overall sales and operating results are shown in Exhibit 11.20.

Kentucky Fried Chicken Corporation

As shown in Exhibit 11.16, Kentucky Fried Chicken's same-store sales have not risen for the past two years, and it has failed in various attempts to diversify its offerings. Certain factors, however, should help John Cranor turn this operation around. Michael Mueller, restaurant analyst with Montgomery Securities, observes that "regular hamburger customers, for health and variety, are switching to chicken." Within the restaurant industry itself, chicken entree and sandwich sales climbed from 10.9% in 1987 to 12.4% of all transactions in 1990, whereas hamburgers fell from 19% to 17% during the same period. Moreover the chain's nearest rivals, Church's and Popeye's, recently merged and ultimately were forced into bankruptcy.

Kentucky Fried Chicken dominates America's chicken segment with at least a 50% market share, as shown in Exhibit 11.17, but many fast-food chains have entered the marketplace with their own chicken-based meals. Wendy's has introduced a grilled chicken sandwich and Burger King has come out with its BK Broiler. McDonald's began offering chicken fajitas in mid 1991 and has been testing both grilled sandwiches and oven-baked chicken. Closer to home, additional

EXHIBIT 1.16

Same-Store Sales Growth by Chain: PepsiCo, Inc.

Chain	1992	1991	1990	1989
Pizza Hut	0.0%	0.5%	5.5%	9.2%
Taco Bell	6.0	4.1	11.5	15.3
Kentucky Fried Chicken	0.0	0.0	7.0	2.0

Source: Derived from E.S. Ely, "Some High Hurdles Loom for Pepsico's Fast-Food Hotshots," *New York Times* (February 16, 1992), Section 3, p. 5; *News from PepsiCo, Inc.* (February 2, 1993), pp. 7–9.

EXHIBIT 1.17

Restaurant Division's 1990 U.S. Market Shares by Food Category: PepsiCo, Inc.

(Dollar amounts in billions)

Chain	Food Category	Market Share	Total Market
Kentucky Fried Chicken	Chicken	48.6%	$ 7.0
Pizza Hut	Italian	26.2	16.4
Taco Bell	Mexican	69.6	4.6

Source: Based on data presented in PepsiCo, Inc., *1992 Stockholders' Report*, p. 23.

EXHIBIT 1.18

1992 Unit Ownership by Area and Chain

Area	Pizza Hut	Taco Bell	Kentucky Fried Chicken
United States			
Company-owned	4,301	2,498	1,994
Licensed	402	134	21
Franchised	3,307	1,446	3,074
Total	7,608	4,078	5,089
Overseas			
Company-owned	539	51	726
Joint venture	370	—	474
Franchised	937	24	2,440
Total	1,846	75	3,640
Grand Total	9,454	4,153	8,729

Notes:

1. Unit totals include 477 primarily Pizza Hut kiosks and 293 other special concepts.
2. Taco Bell U.S. unit count includes 99 company-owned and 38 franchised Hot 'n Now restaurants. U.S. count does not include 29 California Pizza Kitchen, Inc., units.

Source: Abstracted from PepsiCo, Inc., *1992 Stockholders' Report,* p. 24.

EXHIBIT 11.19

Results by Restaurant Chain: PepsiCo, Inc.
(Dollar amounts in millions)

	Net Sales				Operating Profit			
Chain	**1992**	**1991**	**1990**	**1989**	**1992**	**1991**	**1990**	**1989**
Pizza Hut	$3,603.5	$3,258.3	$2,949.9	$2,453.5	$335.4	$314.5	$245.9	$205.5
Taco Bell	2,460.0	2,038.1	1,745.5	1,465.9	214.3	180.6	149.6	109.4
Kentucky Fried Chicken	2,168.8	1,830.5	1,530.3	1,331.3	168.8	80.5	126.9	99.4
Total	$8,232.3	$7,126.9	$6,225.7	$5,250.7	$718.5	$575.6	$522.4	$414.3

Source: PepsiCo, Inc., *1990 Stockholders' Report,* p. 35; *1991 Stockholders' Report,* p. 35; *News from PepsiCo, Inc.* (February 2, 1993), p. 6.

EXHIBIT 1.20

Current and Estimated Sales and Operating Results from Continuing Operations: PepsiCo, Inc.

(Dollar amounts in millions)

	1995-97 Estimated	1993 Estimated	1992 Estimated	1991	1990	1989	1988
Sales	$32,500.0	$24,500.0	$22,200.0	$19,608.0	$17,803.0	$15,242.0	$13,007.0
Cost of sales	26,650.0	20,212.5	18,426.0	16,274.6	14,847.7	12,681.3	11,016.9
Operating profit	5,850.0	4,287.5	3,774.0	3,333.4	2,995.3	2,560.7	1,990.1
General overhead	1,775.0	1,357.5	1,234.0	1,098.7	1,021.3	902.3	598.6
Depreciation	1,600.0	1,250.0	1,100.0	1,034.5	884.0	772.0	629.3
Pretax profit	2,475.0	1,680.0	1,440.0	1,200.2	1,050.0	886.4	762.2
Income taxes	866.3	588.0	504.0	417.7	346.5	295.2	251.5
Posttax profit	$ 1,608.7	$ 1,092.0	$ 936.0	$ 782.5	$ 703.5	$ 591.2	$ 510.7

Source: Stephen Sanborn, "PepsiCo, Inc.," *Value Line* (November 20, 1992), p. 1539.

competition is coming from within the PepsiCo family itself. Taco Bell introduced four chicken products in April 1991, and Pizza Hut began testing marinated, rotisserie-cooked chicken in mid 1992. Two of Taco Bell's items were $.79 chicken tacos and $.99 chicken-and-cheese filled tortillas called MexiMelts. Elliot Bloom of Taco Bell insisted that his chicken products would not steal business from Kentucky Fried Chicken: "You're talking about apples and oranges. What we're offering fills a void, a different niche."

Many see Kentucky Fried Chicken's reliance on fried chicken products as its main menu problem. Although chicken itself is lean and potentially healthy, the batters and frying processes used offset those advantages. The chain has informally renamed itself KFC to eliminate the "fried" from its logotype. It introduced a new skinless, but still fried, product called Lite 'N Crispy in the spring of 1991. The product was an embarrassment: it was too expensive and tasteless, and the division's franchisees protested its low margin. Initially announced as a phased national introduction, the product had to be renamed Skinfree Crispy and withdrawn until 1992 because of production and taste problems. The delay ultimately resulted in charges of $9 million against domestic operations in 1991. For some industry observers, Lite 'N Crispy's flop is indicative of the entire Kentucky Fried Chicken operation. "There doesn't seem to be a strategic direction. There is a disjointedness, and the skin-free chicken is a microcosm of that," states Emanuel Goldman of Paine Webber, Inc. Moreover Lite 'N Crispy's failure is particularly significant, as John Cranor intended it to be the bridge from flavored chicken, such as lemon, barbecue, and teriyaki, to other nonfried fare.

This experience also caused the division to back away from other new product introductions, although it did introduce Popcorn Chicken in July 1992. Popcorn Chicken consists of small pieces of marinated, breaded, and fried chicken. The

Center for Science in the Public Interest, however, in its *Nutrition Action Healthletter* described it as "nuggets of grease-drenched breading that are oozing with fat and salt." A standard 5.3-oz. serving contains 45 grams of fat, or almost twice as much as in two Big Macs, and 1,775 mg of sodium. Other new products have been stalled in Kentucky Fried Chicken's test kitchens, and a line of eight new sandwiches failed in test markets. The sandwiches, including barbecue, spicy, and chicken salad designed for the lunch trade, increased sales only when heavily promoted. Moreover, they cannibalized the company's higher margin fried chicken sales.

William McDonald, Kentucky Fried Chicken's Senior Marketing Vice-President, says that reformulating the chicken isn't easy: "It's not a no-brainer. We've learned a product has got to be unbelievably indulgent, special and unique and not eminently substitutable at home." The chain has been trying hard to come up with a nonfried chicken offering, first trying baking and then trying open-hearth grilling. When those two methods were unsatisfactory, it tried char-grilling and then broiling. It has recently scrapped its most recent effort, Monterey Broil, and is starting over to make it stand out from home-prepared chicken by adding spice to its flavor. Doctoring this product's recipe could take another year and a half.

The chain also has been working on its image. By early 1992, 85% of its U.S. outlets had invested an average of $7,500 for new landscaping, new atriums, coats of fresh red roof paint, and brighter wallpaper. John McDonald says that "KFC has a '60s image and it's the '90s. We've got to turbo-charge." Beginning in the spring of 1992, the chain's advertising focused on the make-believe town of Lake Edna and its single KFC restaurant. The campaign's purpose was to capture the positive, feel-good aspects associated with good food and the traditional values and security of small towns. Colin Moore, the company's Senior Marketing Vice-President, said in defense of the campaign's strategy: "Clearly we were looking for a 'campaign-able' idea. And we think we've found it. Lake Edna is obviously a fictitious place that is simultaneously nowhere and everywhere. This notion of a small town is as much a state of mind as a physical location." The chain spent almost $120 million on advertising in 1991, compared to McDonald's $387.3 million, Pizza Hut's $118.4 million, and Taco Bell's $92.7 million.

Management has undertaken various economy and efficiency actions and John Cranor has recruited Pizza Hut executives to teach him the fast-food business. As a first step, Kentucky Fried Chicken has begun to use more frozen products to reduce in-house chicken preparation labor costs. A restructuring of the chain's administrative level cost $43 million in 1991, but it could save the division as much as $25 million a year. The move eliminated about 750, or one-half, of the company's managers and support staff at both the 800-employee Louisville, Kentucky, headquarters and the 700-employee field management offices. After the restructuring, the remaining middle managers supervised more stores, and headquarters became more involved in field operations. The company stressed that the restructuring was necessary because the division had become bloated. However, as Ron Paul, President of Technomic, Inc., observes, "All this does is improve their margins in the short run. It does not fundamentally change the menu and the way consumers view the store."

In attempting to turn Kentucky Fried Chicken around, John Cranor has been faced by another source of problems. Franchisees, who own about two-thirds of the chain's U.S. outlets, are an independently minded group. Many of their outlets are in middle- or low-income neighborhoods, and their customers, less concerned about nutrition, are partial to fried food. Besides, many franchisees remain loyal to Colonel Sanders' original Kentucky Fried Chicken concept, which is why they initially purchased their franchises, and are antagonistic towards some of the new products headquarters has created for them. They have expressed this antagonism in many ways and even have had PepsiCo in court for three years over various contract disputes. PepsiCo has begun to buy out some of its franchisees to at least partially deal with these frustrations.

When asked how Kentucky Fried Chicken's turnaround has progressed under his leadership, Cranor responded, "I didn't expect turning KFC around was going to be an easy proposition. We're all impatient with everything. We need direction, we need a unified focus. We just want to make sure we don't screw up a $6.0 billion business while we decide how to get from there to $10.0 billion." Gary Stibel, of the New England Consulting Group, agrees that the division's President has the right idea: "The marketing challenge is a matter of attracting new users without losing their current loyal following."

Pizza Hut Worldwide

Steven S. Reinemund, division President and former Marriott Corporation executive, believes that he heads a pizza distribution company. Accordingly, Pizza Hut has been creative in finding alternative methods for obtaining off- and on-premises pizza sales. It began delivering pizza in 1987 and has built the most units dedicated to delivery and carryout. Says George Rice, Chairman of a food service consulting firm, "Since 1984 the entire growth in restaurant sales has been in take-out, delivery, and other consumption outside the stores. That makes Pizza Hut one of the industry's best-positioned companies." Although Pizza Hut has captured about 26.2% of the pizza delivery market, as shown in Exhibit 11.17, it still lags well behind Domino's and is just even with Little Caesars in the number of outlets devoted to take-out and delivery service. Moreover, Little Caesars is adding this type of units in the United States faster than Pizza Hut.

In 1992, Steven Reinemund implemented a strategic shift in reaction to a long-term trend in operating results. By the third quarter of 1991, Pizza Hut's delivery sales increases were not compensating for its declining sit-down sales. It began to refocus on its in-store business, and part of this effort involved installation of all-you-can-eat buffets.

The buffets were tested for four months at Pizza Huts in Dallas, Indianapolis, Savannah, and Tulsa, and were later installed in 2,000 restaurants in 1992 at a cost of tens of millions of dollars. "We're into it hot and heavy," said Reinemund, adding that "it is phase one of our effort to revitalize our dine-in business." For

$3.99, patrons can load their plates at a 14-foot-long table spread with pastas, salads, and pizza. Although its buffets were initially open only for lunch, dinner buffets may be added. However, certain risks accompany buffet service. As observed by Michael Mueller, a restaurant analyst with Montgomery Securities, "It's not an easy business to operate well. The risk is the quality of the food you offer." To maintain product quality, Pizza Hut designed a screen that sits inside a pan and allows air to circulate around the pizza, keeping it hot and fresh at the buffet table for as long as 20 minutes.

Steven Reinemund is also exploring the upscale pizza market with a concept called Pizza Hut Cafes. The chain believes that a market exists for this concept, although the field is already crowded with others offering pastas, desserts, and gourmet pizzas in casual dining atmospheres. Its cafe, which has been tested in Wichita, featured tablecloths, desserts, sauteed chicken, and a wider variety of pizzas than regular Pizza Huts offer.

Taco Bell Worldwide

Under John Martin's leadership, Taco Bell has become the fast-food industry's value leader. In late 1988, the chain introduced its $.59 Value Menu. Sales climbed 50% in two years to $2.4 billion, causing McDonald's and Burger King to retaliate in late 1990 but to their disadvantage, as their operations were not as efficient as Taco Bell's. Continuing the trend of offering everyday bargains in the fall of 1990, Martin reorganized most of his menu into three price tiers: $.59, $.79, and $.99. Although he later had to back away from rigid enforcement of these tiers because of franchisee pressures for higher margins, he believes that offering value menus is his chain's key to success; he also believes that Taco Bell alone can become as big as the entire PepsiCo corporation is today. In responding to questions about his low-price strategy, Martin says, "Radical thought, huh? Low prices are what got our business started. The other guy has gotten away from it."

To be a low-cost producer, Taco Bell began to shift as much food preparation to outside suppliers as possible and to rationalize its production methods in the mid 1980s. Its ground beef is precooked outside the store and then reheated, its tortillas are already fried, precooked dishes are placed in boil bags, and all its onions are prediced in a factory. These actions have sliced 15 work hours daily from every outlet and reduced kitchen space from 70% to 30% of a typical building. "Our entire Taco Bell restaurant can fit into a McDonald's kitchen," says Elliot Bloom.

Other operating efficiencies have come from greater automation and simplified food production, enabling Taco Bell permanently to slash prices to a $.69, 29-item core menu. Martin refigured the menu to emphasize plain tacos and burritos, which take only eight seconds to make, compared to the 20 seconds needed to make a Mexican pizza or a taco salad. Through various efficiencies, a new Taco Bell restaurant can handle twice the volume of five years ago with half the labor, and it is currently testing taco-making robots in its quest for even lower operating costs.

Although it is the industry's low-price leader, various industry analysts question Taco Bell's strategy. They point out that low pricing hurts profit margins, cannibalizes the sales of full meals, can leave customers unfilled, and creates an image of low quality. Hugh Zurkuhlen of Weiss, Peck & Greer says that the chain is "a potential victim of their own success" and would have a difficult time abandoning that image when facing the ultimate pressures of rising ingredient and labor costs.

1993 and Beyond

As 1993 began, Wayne Calloway's overall goal for PepsiCo "is simply to be the best consumer products company in the world." He went on to explain:

> In 1992 we took dramatic steps to keep us on a strong growth path. Our domestic beverage division is being completely restructured to serve our customers better. And our aggressive acquisition activity, over 50 in all, is doing a lot to expand and strengthen our core businesses. We're entering 1993 with solid momentum and well positioned to address changing consumer needs. Low cost Mexican food is still a novelty to most Americans, there are more ways to sell pizza, and new products and value combinations at KFC will bring customers back more often.

Jay Nelson, an analyst with Brown Brothers Harriman, observes that "PepsiCo doesn't participate in rapid-growth industries with favorable demographic trends [see Exhibit 11.21]. But managers there think it's their destiny to win."

EXHIBIT 11.21

Annual Per Capita Consumption of Various Consumer Goods and Wealth for Selected Countries

Country	Soft Drinks[1]	Income[2]	TVs[3]	Newspapers[4]	Literacy[5]
United States	770	$19,678	769	255	99.0%
Mexico	512	2,222	123	142	88.0
Australia	403	14,994	500	308	99.0
Germany[6]	255	19,637	385	417	99.0
Japan	75	21,845	244	569	99.0
Confederation of Independent States[7]	46	3,606	313	345	99.0
India	3	339	16	16	36.0

Notes:

1. 1991 per capita 8 oz. servings per year.
2. 1988 GDP per capita in U.S. dollars.
3. Television sets per 1,000 population.
4. Newspaper circulation per 1,000 population.
5. Percent literacy rate.
6. Former Federal Republic of Germany.
7. Former Union of Soviet Republics.

Source: Adapted from PepsiCo, Inc., *1992 Stockholders' Report,* pp. 9, 15; *World Almanac and Book of Facts,* New York: Pharos Books (1992), pp. 687, 712, 718, 723, 733, 760, 765; "Indicators of Market Size for 117 Countries," *Business International* (July 30, 1990), pp. 248, 250.

The U.S. Major Home Appliance Industry in 1993: From Domestic to Global

J. David Hunger

In 1993 the major home appliance industry in the United States was a very successful domestic industry in the process of becoming global. In contrast with the U.S. automobile and consumer electronics industries, U.S. major appliance manufacturers had been able to ward off Japanese competition and were actually on the offensive internationally. Imports to the United States were holding steady at 17% of the total domestic major appliance market. Over 90% of these imports were microwave ovens, small refrigerators, and room air-conditioners.[1] About 85% of the "white goods" sold in the United States were made domestically.[2] ("White goods" is the traditional term used for major home appliances—refrigerators, freezers, washing machines, dryers, ranges, microwave ovens, and dishwashers. The term "brown goods" refers to home electronics products such as radios and televisions.)

The industry had been very successful in keeping prices low and improving the value of its products. During the last decade, the increase in appliance prices had been less than the increase in U.S. earnings. Thus the average American consumer in 1993 could earn a new appliance in fewer hours on the job than in years past. For example, consumers in 1993 could actually buy a high-quality vacuum cleaner at the same price as in 1927 (when automobiles cost about $700).[3] In addition, the energy efficiency of the most common major appliances had increased every year since 1972.[4] After a prolonged recession, there were some indications that the economy was improving. The year 1993 was expected to be the second consecutive year of increasing unit sales after four years of decreasing sales (Exhibit 12.1).

The major home appliance industry was, nevertheless, facing some significant threats as well as opportunities as it moved through the last decade of the twentieth century. After 40 years of rising sales, both in units and in dollars, the North American market had reached maturity in the 1980s. Aside from some normal short-term fluctuations, future unit sales were expected to grow only 1%–2% annually on average for the foreseeable future. Operating margins had been dropping as appliance manufacturers were forced to maintain competitively low prices despite rising costs.

In Western Europe, however, a market already 25% larger than the mature North American appliance market, unit sales were expected to grow 5% annually on average. This percentage was expected to increase significantly as Eastern European countries opened their economies to world trade. In addition, the continuing economic integration of the 12 member countries of the European Community

This industry note was prepared by Professor J. David Hunger, with the research assistance of Kendra Fulk of Iowa State University. This case appears in the Fall 1993 issue of *Case Research Journal*.

(EC)—the Netherlands, Belgium, Luxembourg, Germany, France, Italy, Denmark, the United Kingdom, the Irish Republic, Greece, Spain, and Portugal—was providing the impetus for a series of mergers, acquisitions, and joint ventures among major household appliance manufacturers. Economies in Asia and South America were becoming more important to world trade as numerous countries moved more toward a free-market economy. The industry was under pressure from governments around the world to make environmentally safe products and to significantly improve appliance energy efficiency.

Development of the U.S. Major Home Appliance Industry

In 1945, there were approximately 300 major appliance manufacturers in the United States. By 1993, however, the "big five" of Whirlpool, General Electric, A.B. Electrolux (not to be confused with Electrolux Corporation, a U.S. company selling Electrolux brand vacuum cleaners), Maytag, and Raytheon controlled almost 98% of the U.S. market. The consolidation of the industry during that period was a result of fierce domestic competition. Emphasis on quality and durability coupled with strong price competition drove the surviving firms to increased efficiencies and a strong concern for customer satisfaction.

Industry History

All of the major U.S. automobile firms except Chrysler had participated at one time in the major home appliance industry. Giants in the consumer electronics industry had also been involved heavily in appliances. Some of the major auto, electronics, and diversified companies active at one time in the appliance industry were General Motors (Frigidaire), Ford (Philco), American Motors (Kelvinator), Studebacker (Franklin), Bendix, International Harvester, General Electric, RCA, Emerson Electric, Westinghouse, McGraw Edison, Rockwell, United Technologies, Raytheon, Litton, Borg-Warner, and Dart & Kraft. By 1990, only General Electric, Raytheon, and Litton remained in appliances. Emerson Electric continued only through its In-Sink-Erator line of disposers and as a supplier of electronic parts to the remaining appliance makers. Most of the other firms had divested their appliance business units, many of which were acquired by White Consolidated Industries, which itself was acquired by A.B. Electrolux in 1986 and subsequently renamed Frigidaire.

Prior to World War II, most appliance manufacturers produced a limited line of appliances deriving from one successful product. General Electric made refrigerators, Maytag focused on washing machines, and Hotpoint produced electric ranges. Each offered variations of its basic product, but not until 1945 did firms begin to offer full lines of various appliances. By 1955, the major appliance industry had begun to experience overcapacity, leading to mergers and acquisitions and a proliferation of national and private brands.

The industry as a whole almost doubled in size during the 1960s as sales of several products grew rapidly. Unit sales of dishwashers almost quadrupled, and unit sales of clothes dryers more than tripled. Product reliability improved even though real prices (adjusted for inflation) declined some 10%.

EXHIBIT 12.1

U.S. Manufacturers' Unit Shipments of Major Home Appliances (Including Imports)

(Unit amounts in thousands)

Product	1992	1991	1990	1989	1988	1987	1986	1985	1980
Compactors	126	129	185	213	243	226	194	177	235
Dishwashers									
Built-in	3,619	3,360	3,419	3,456	3,647	3,763	3,663	3,327	2,354
Portable	210	211	217	213	260	269	255	248	384
Disposers	4,195	4,002	4,137	4,363	4,233	4,439	4,269	4,105	2,962
Dryers									
Compact	275	268	275	267	250	218	200	189	207
Electric	3,563	3,295	3,318	3,522	3,554	3,381	3,108	2,891	2,287
Gas	1,154	1,018	1,002	1,052	1,047	1,037	936	834	682
Freezers									
Chest	1,005	794	723	677	727	692	661	634	963
Compact	360	355	351	336	295	260	250	237	310
Upright	686	620	573	541	622	567	561	602	78
Microwave Ovens									
Combination ranges	110	128	146	158	177	185	285	314	265
Countertop	6,990	7,233	8,193	9,290	9,500	11,000	11,064	9,727	3,320
Microwave/Convection	280	300	303	306	310	320	280	256	—
Over-the-range	625	694	780	844	1,000	1,100	1,100	900	—
Range/Oven Hoods	2,522	2,342	2,450	2,602	2,600	2,595	2,600	2,588	2,400

Ranges, Electric									
Built-in	624	568	631	648	635	655	596	574	555
Free-standing	2,508	2,332	2,358	2,400	2,566	2,691	2,717	2,567	1,975
Glass/Ceramic	72	69	68	69	70	65	94	86	155
Surface units	442	409	455	480	506	495	423	409	NA
Ranges, Gas									
Built-in	91	92	106	112	126	120	86	84	102
Free-standing	2,221	2,041	2,061	2,055	2,100	2,046	1,854	1,729	1,437
Surface units	301	268	262	247	230	176	150	—	NA
Refrigerators									
Compact	950	925	932	925	1,000	830	810	783	543
Standard	7,761	7,273	7,101	7,099	7,227	6,972	6,510	6,080	5,124
Washers									
Automatic	6,515	6,197	6,192	6,251	6,190	5,998	5,765	5,278	4,426
Compact	365	358	344	334	329	320	315	303	266
Wringer	12	14	18	22	26	30	33	37	124
Water Heaters									
Electric	3,399	3,170	3,226	3,369	3,333	3,396	3,389	3,452	2,451
Gas	4,241	3,936	3,906	4,130	3,956	3,951	3,329	3,529	2,818
Total Appliances[1]	54,671	51,828	53,170	55,419	56,219	57,289	55,269	51,305	37,134

Note: 1. Numbers may not add because of rounding and minor changes in categories.

Source: *Appliance* (April 1990), p. 33; (April 1993), p. 53.

Although the 1970s was a time of high inflation and high interest rates, unit sales in the major home appliance industry continued to increase. Profit margins were squeezed even more as the industry continued to consolidate around fewer firms. Antitrust considerations prevented GE and Whirlpool from acquiring other appliance units, so White was able to buy the troubled appliance divisions of all the automobile manufacturers and Westinghouse's as they were put up for sale.[5]

The market continued to expand in the early 1980s, thanks partially to the acceptance by the U.S. consumer of the microwave oven. Nevertheless, total sales actually began to fall in the late 1980s. By the early 1990s, U.S. appliance manufacturers offered a full range of products even if they did not make the items themselves. A company would fill the gaps in its line by putting its own brand name on products it purchased from another manufacturer. For example, Whirlpool made trash compactors for Frigidaire (A.B. Electrolux), In-Sink-Erator (Emerson Electric), Jenn-Air and Magic Chef (Maytag), and Sears. Caloric (Raytheon) made gas ranges not only for its in-house Amana brand, but also for Whirlpool. General Electric made some microwave ovens for Caloric (Raytheon), and for Jenn-Air and Magic Chef (Maytag), as well as for its own Hotpoint and RCA brands.[6]

Product and Process Design

Innovations in the industry tended to be of three types: (1) new products that expanded the appliance market, (2) new customer-oriented features, and (3) process improvements to reduce manufacturing costs.

New Products

New products that had strongly increased industry unit sales were dishwashers in the 1960s and microwave ovens in the 1980s. The combination washer–dryer and compact versions of other appliances, such as refrigerators and washers, were not popular in the United States but had been successful in Europe and Asia where household space was at a premium and cultural norms favored daily over weekly food shopping.

Customer-Oriented Features

Customer-oriented features included the self-cleaning oven, pilotless gas range, automatic ice-cube-making refrigerator, and others. In most cases, features were introduced on top-of-the-line models and made available on lower priced models later. Manufacturers' own brands usually had the newest and most elaborate features, followed by national retailers such as Sears Roebuck and Montgomery Ward, whose offerings usually copied the most successful features from the previous year. In this competitive industry, aside from patented features, no one producer could successfully keep a new innovation to itself for more than one year.

In the early 1990s, two trends were evident. First, European visual product design was having a strong impact on appliance design worldwide. Frigidaire, for example, introduced a "Euroflair" line of appliances. Second, manufacturers were introducing "smart" appliances with increasingly sophisticated electronic controls and self-diagnostic features. The Japanese firms of Matsushita, Hitachi, Toshiba, and Mitsubishi were using "fuzzy logic" computer software to replace the many selector switches on an appliance with one start button. In February 1990, for example, Matsushita Electric Industrial Company introduced a washing machine containing sensors that judged size and dirtiness to determine optimal cycle time and water level for each laundry load.[7] At first, U.S. manufacturers showed little interest in fuzzy logic technology, saying that the consumer did not want electronics to completely take away the individual's opportunity to make choices. Nevertheless, by 1993 Whirlpool added fuzzy logic to its successful VIP series microwave ovens. The firm's new Sixth Sense oven could determine the necessary settings for reheating or defrosting food with no guesswork from the cook. The user simply pressed a single button for defrost—the oven then calculated on its own the correct time and power output.[8]

Process Improvements

Process improvements for more efficient manufacturing of current products (rather than new product development) had dominated research and development efforts in the U.S. major home appliance industry. Although modern appliances were much more effective and efficient, a refrigerator or a washing machine in the 1990s still looked and acted very much the same as it did in the 1950s. It was built in a far different manner, however. In 1990, Richard Topping, Director of the Center for Product Development of the consulting firm Arthur D. Little, indicated that the appliance industry had historically been characterized by low-intensity in research and development because of intense cost competition and demand for higher reliability. Topping went on to stress that the basis for effective competition in the future would be in producing the fewest basic components necessary in the most efficient plants. Although individual designs might vary, the components inside the appliances would become more universal and would be produced in highly automated plants using computer integrated manufacturing processes.[9] Examples of this emphasis on product simplification were Maytag's Dependable Drive and Whirlpool's frame fabrication for its Eye Level ranges. Maytag's new washer transmission was designed to have 40.6% fewer parts than the transmission it replaced. Fewer parts meant simplified manufacturing and less chance of a breakdown. The results were lower manufacturing costs and higher product quality.

Most industry analysts agreed that steady process improvements had kept U.S. major home appliance manufacturers dominant in their industry. The emphasis on quality and durability, coupled with a reluctance to make major design changes simply for the sake of change, resulted in products with long average life expectancy (Exhibit 12.2). The average useful life of a refrigerator or range approaching 20 years and that of washers and dryers approaching 15 years was one reason why the Japanese manufacturers had been less successful in entering the U.S. appliance market than the automobile market.[10] Another reason was a constant unrelenting pressure to reduce costs or be driven from the marketplace.

EXHIBIT 12.2 **Average Life Expectancy of Major Home Appliances**

Appliance Type	Years
Compactors	10
Dishwashers	10
Disposers	11
Dryers—electric	13
Dryers—gas	13
Freezers	15
Microwave ovens	11
Ranges—electric	17
Ranges—gas	19
Refrigerators	16
Washers	13
Vacuum cleaners	10
Floor polishers	12
Water heaters—electric	14
Water heaters—gas	11

Source: *Appliance* (September 1992), pp. 46–47.

Manufacturing and Purchasing

Although many manufacturing operations took place in an appliance factory, much of the process focused on proper preparation of the metal frame within which the washing, drying, or cooking components and elements would be attached. Consequently, appliance manufacturers could be characterized as "metal benders" who fabricated different shapes of metal boxes out of long coils of metal. Sophisticated machines would form and even weld the frames, and automated assembly lines and robots would add porcelain to protect the metal and add color to the finish. Human workers usually were still needed to install the internal components in the frame and to wire sophisticated electronic controls. Quality control often was a combination of electronic diagnostics and worker inspection.

Manufacturing costs were generally in the range of 65%–75% of total operating costs (Exhibit 12.3). Although direct labor costs were still an important part of the cost of completed goods (about 10%), most companies were carefully examining material, general administration, and overhead costs for potential cuts. The optimal size of an assembly plant traditionally had an annual capacity of 500,000 units for refrigerators, ranges, washers, dryers, or dishwashers. Even though production costs were believed to be 10%–40% higher in plants with smaller capacity, current analysis suggested that with the use of robotics, smaller plants would not operate at a cost disadvantage.[11] A 1988 survey of 44 U.S. appliance-related companies revealed that 24 were using robots to reduce costs, improve product consistency and quality, and gain flexibility.[12]

EXHIBIT 12.3

The Major Home Appliance Value Chain

Sales			100%
Manufacturing costs		65–75%	
Fully integrated			
• raw materials	30–40%		
• labor	6–10		
• plant and equipment	12–20		
• general administration	12–20		
Not integrated			
• components	35–45		
• labor and overhead	30–40		
Transportation and warehousing		5–7	
Advertising		1–2	
Sales and marketing		4–8	
Service		2–5	
Product research and development		2–5	
Overhead		2–10	

Source: C. R. Christensen, K. R. Andrews, J. L. Bower, R. G. Hamermesh, and M. E. Porter, "Note on the Major Home Appliance Industry in 1984 (condensed)," in *Business Policy,* 6th ed. (Homewood, Ill.: Irwin, 1987), p. 339.

The 1990s continued the trend toward dedicated manufacturing facilities, combining product line production in fewer larger plants to gain economies of scale. Although a dedicated production line for washing machines could be adjusted to make many different models, it could still only be used to make washing machines. Each product category required its own specialized equipment.

All the major home appliance manufacturers were engaged in renovating and building their production facilities to gain economies of scale, improve quality, and reduce labor and materials costs. From 1986 to 1989, for example, Frigidaire (A.B. Electrolux) invested $500 million in state-of-the-art production and design facilities.[13] Whirlpool completely renovated the manufacturing processes and labor management system in its aging tooling and plating factory in Benton Harbor, increasing productivity by more than 19% from 1988 to 1992.[14]

The purchasing function and relationship with suppliers changed considerably in the 1980s as more companies used fewer suppliers and more long-term contracts to improve quality and assure just-in-time (JIT) delivery. David Simpson, Senior Editor of *Appliance* magazine, explained why this trend was likely to continue through the 1990s:

> Today, many OEMs [original equipment manufacturers] are demanding—and receiving—computer links with their suppliers, nearly just-in-time delivery, supplier input from the early stages of appliance design, statistical process control, global availability, and more. As OEMs broaden their demands, they are establishing close relationships

EXHIBIT 12.4

Major Home Appliance Saturation in the United States, Western Europe, and Japan

(Households with at least one of a particular appliance)

Appliance	United States	Western Europe[1]	Japan
Dishwashers	48%	25%	NA%
Freezers	33	42	NA
Microwave Ovens	85	27	79
Ranges/Ovens	99	92	57
Refrigerators	99	97	99
Dryers	67	17	17
Washers	73	88	99
Vacuums	97	82	98
Water Heaters	99	NA	30

Note: 1. Composite of Austria, Belgium/Luxembourg, Switzerland, Germany, Denmark, Spain, France, Great Britain (U.K.), Greece, Italy, Ireland, Norway, the Netherlands, Portugal, Sweden, and Finland.

Source: *Appliance* (September 1992), p. 42; (July 1992), p. 43; (March 1993), p. 55.

with those suppliers that fit their ever-more-varied needs. While price is still a critical consideration, it is far from being the only one.[15]

Some of the key materials purchased by the U.S. appliance industry were steel (primarily in sheets and coils from domestic suppliers), plastics, coatings (paint and porcelain), motors, glass, insulation, wiring, and fasteners.

Marketing and Distribution Channels

Due to relatively high levels of saturation in the United States, the market for major home appliances was driven primarily by the demand for replacements. As shown in Exhibit 12.4, more than 70% of U.S. households had washers, ranges, refrigerators, and even microwave ovens. Generally speaking, replacements accounted for 75% of sales, new housing for 20% of sales, and new household formation for about 5% of sales of major home appliances. Replacement demand usually was driven by existing housing turnover, remodeling, changing trends in living arrangement, introduction of new features, and price levels in the economy.[16] The National Kitchen and Bath Association estimated that about $4 billion of the total $25 billion spent annually on kitchen remodeling was for home appliances. The National Association of Home Builders predicted some 1.3 million housing starts in 1993, compared to 1.2 million in 1992 and 1.0 million in 1991 (a 46-year low).[17] Each new house had the potential to add four to six new appliances. Both the new-housing and remodeling markets in the late 1980s and early 1990s tended to emphasize more upscale appliances as contrasted to the previous tendency for builders to economize by buying the cheapest national brand appliances.[18] A study by Simmons Market Research Bureau for *New Home* magazine revealed that more than $13 billion was spent annually by new-home owners on household goods, especially appliances. In order of priority, the appliances typically bought within the first three months by the owner of a new home were refrigerator, washer, dryer, microwave oven, vacuum cleaner, dishwasher, coffeemaker, and range.[19]

A study of the appliance industry by Jerome Fischer of *Value Line* concluded that changes in demographics in the 1990s favored the highly profitable high-end, high-profile segment of the business.[20] This trend worked to the detriment of the mass market business, which emphasized cost over features. The coming of age of the baby boomers and the increase of two-income families had increased the upscale market, which demanded more style and costly features. General Electric, Whirlpool, and Maytag were responding by expanding product lines that emphasized quality and features.

As recently as 1981, U.S. appliance exports exceeded imports. Microwave oven popularity altered this situation significantly. Exports declined through the mid 1980s but began to improve toward the end of the decade. In 1987, total U.S. appliance exports of all kinds were $1.2 billion, compared to imports of $3.2 billion. Export growth was especially strong for refrigerators, vacuum cleaners, and laundry appliances. The largest export markets for U.S. appliances in 1987 were Canada ($347 million), Taiwan ($95 million), and the United Kingdom, West Germany, Japan, and Saudi Arabia, each of which imported some $40–$50 million worth of U.S. appliances. Recent export growth partially reflected a decline in the value of the dollar. According to a report by the Office of Consumer Goods of the U.S. Department of Commerce, several developing countries, among them Mexico, Chile, and South Korea, offered great export potential because of recent government actions to reduce tariffs and importing restrictions.[21] Nevertheless, much of Asia, Africa, and significant parts of South America were not yet sufficiently developed in economic terms to be significant markets for U.S. major home appliances. For one thing, electricity and natural gas service were not yet widely available in most developing countries. Even in those locations where electricity was available, it was not always reliable—power outages were a common occurrence in some countries.

The two major distribution channels for major home appliances in the United States were contract and retail. A third, but less important, distribution channel was the commercial market, comprising laundromats and institutions.

Contract Sales

Manufacturers made contract sales to large home builders and to other appliance manufacturers, with direct sales accounting for about 80% of contract sales. Firms sold appliances on contract both directly to large builders and indirectly through local builder suppliers. Because builders were very cost conscious, they liked to buy at the middle to the low end of a well-known appliance brand. Consequently, appliance manufacturers with strong offerings in this range, such as Whirlpool and General Electric, tended to do well in this market. However, Maytag and other companies traditionally emphasizing high-end products, sold little (except for the lower priced Magic Chef brand) to home builders. Whirlpool and GE designed whole kitchen "concepts" and sold the entire design package—and their appliances—to builders.

Retail Sales

Retail sales in the United States were made to three major kinds of retail outlets: (1) national chain stores/mass merchandisers; (2) department, furniture, and discount stores; and (3) appliance dealers. Sales to *national chain stores/mass merchandisers* usually consisted of private brands promoted by the retailers. For example, Whirlpool has traditionally been a heavy supplier of Sears and Kenmore brand appliances to Sears Roebuck. Magic Chef sold similar private brand appliances to Montgomery Ward. Some 30%–40% of white goods were traditionally sold through this channel. Sears Roebuck alone sold one of four major appliances sold in the United States.

Department stores, furniture stores, and discount stores were another important channel for major appliances—selling about 20% of white goods sold in the United States. These stores usually purchased well-known brands to offer their customers. During the 1980s, as department stores tended to alter their product offerings in favor of more soft goods (clothing items) over hard goods (furniture and appliances), discount stores became more important in major home appliance sales. Their concern with price, however, put even more pressure on manufacturers to sell in large quantity at low price.

Appliance dealers traditionally had been an important retail outlet for white goods. Some 30%–40% of major home appliances were sold through this channel. In the late 1980s and early 1990s, many locally owned stores were being replaced by national chains. In 1989, Richard Haines, Executive Vice-President of Maytag Corporation, explained the impact of changes in distribution channels on his firm:

> When we [Maytag Company] decided to expand our offerings beyond laundry and dishwashers, one of the reasons we did so was the changing marketplace. What we saw happening was a significant decrease in the number of independent Mom and Pop dealerships that used to be the mainstay of the retail appliance business. The field was becoming increasingly dominated by national power retailers and by regional super stores.
>
> These new age marketers make their livings on high volume sales with relatively low unit margins. To maintain profitability, they must seek out the lowest wholesale prices possible from manufacturers on large volume buys. By purchasing only a few full lines of major appliances, today's retailers develop the clout they need with individual appliance producers to get the best pricing at wholesale and, therefore, the best margins at retail.
>
> Manufacturers who wish to compete in this new arena need a full line of products plus the capacity and manufacturing efficiency to make the volume sales mass merchants require.[22]

By the 1990s, the so-called "power retailers"—Sears, Montgomery Ward, and regional appliance chains such as Circuit City—were selling over 60% of all retail appliances in the United States.

The Commercial Market

Although never as important to manufacturers as the contract and retail channels, the commercial market was nevertheless an important set of customers for sales of washing machines and dryers. Laundromats and institutions, such as college dormitories, typically bought the most durable appliances made for the home market. Manufacturers simply added coin meters to the top of the washers and dryers destined for use in these commercial or public establishments. Although home laundry appliances adapted for the commercial market comprised over 50% of the sales to this channel, there were some indications that this market might be moving to commercial washers built to last 2–3 times longer than the adapted home variety.[23] Freezers, refrigerators, and ranges for use in business establishments such as restaurants generally were made by a different group of companies (e.g., Traulsen, Hobart, and Glenco) from those manufacturing home appliances.

Appliance manufacturing in 1993 seemed to be shifting from an emphasis on quality and reliability to speed and agility. This meant that manufacturers were working to improve their use of logistics in order to provide better service to their distributors. The just-in-time (JIT) concept had been introduced during the 1980s to improve manufacturing efficiency. Similar concepts were now being applied in the 1990s in terms of distribution and marketing. For example, Whirlpool introduced Quality Express in 1992 as part of its revamped distribution system. Quality Express used dedicated trucks, personnel, and warehousing to deliver Whirlpool, KichenAid, Roper, and Estate brand appliances to 90% of all dealer and builder customers within 24 hours, and 100% within 48 hours. As part of the service, drivers delivering the products unloaded units from the truck and put them where the customer wanted them. This service even included uncrating, customizing, and installation if desired. According to Tom Ellspermann, Manager of Special Projects for the Whirlpool Appliance Group, "The system lets dealers increase inventory turns and reduce interest charges and other related costs, all of which can increase profitability substantially."[24]

Environmental Issues and Government Regulation

The major home appliance industry had rarely been a target of criticism regarding safety or pollution as had the U.S. steel and automobile industries (among others). By the 1980s, however, this situation had changed. Chlorofluorocarbons (CFCs) used in refrigerator and freezer insulation and in refrigerant had been identified as a causative agent in the depletion of the earth's ozone layer—thus contributing to an increased exposure to ultraviolet light and the incidence of skin cancer. A 1987 meeting of the developed nations in Montreal resulted in a document called the Montreal Protocol, signed by 46 countries, which signaled the intent of the participating countries to eliminate the ozone-depleting gases. In November 1992 the members of the Montreal Protocol and others met to enter into agreements for eliminating the use of chlorine-containing, ozone-depleting CFCs and to adopt a schedule for eliminating the use of hydrochlorofluorocarbons (HCFCs), which had substantially lower ozone-depleting potential. The schedule for the phaseout of CFCs required a cap of 100% of 1986 levels as of January 1, 1993; a cap of 25% on January 1, 1994; and elimination, insofar as the refrigeration industry was concerned, on January 1, 1996. The schedule for the phaseout of HCFCs called for a similar series of steps leading to complete elimination by January 1, 2030.[25]

Thus U.S. refrigerator and freezer manufacturers faced a serious dilemma. On the one hand, governments were requiring less use of chemicals crucial to cooling. On the other hand, the U.S. Department of Energy (DOE) was requiring energy conservation improvements for refrigerators and freezers. These appliances had traditionally been notorious energy hogs—consuming about 20% of the electricity used in the American home.[26] The appliance industry had worked to make their products more energy efficient over the decades. For example, from 1972 to 1990, the amount of energy consumed by a typical top-mount, automatic defrost refrigerator (the most popular U.S. refrigerator) declined from 1,986 kilowatt-hours per year to 950 kilowatt-hours per year. Chest freezer energy consumption dropped during the same period from 1,268 kilowatt-hours per year to 575 kilowatt-hours per year. Nevertheless, the DOE mandated further energy reductions for all refrigerators and freezers. Its standards required that the average residential refrigerator/freezer manufactured after January 1, 1993, use no more energy than that used by a 75-watt lightbulb.[27] Units imported into the United States also were required to meet the regulations. The dilemma being faced by the industry in the 1990s was that a reduction in the use of CFCs for cooling tended to reduce the efficiency of the appliance, thus increasing energy consumption.

Another issue facing appliance manufacturers was the presence of widely different quality and safety standards for major appliances in countries around the world. These standards were promulgated by bodies such as the British Standards Institute (BSI) in the United Kingdom, Japanese Industrial Standards Committee (JISC), AFNOR in France, DIN in Germany, Canadian Standards Association (CSA) in Canada, and Underwriters Laboratories (UL) in the United States. These standards had traditionally created entry barriers that served to fragment the major home appliance industry by country. In 1986, CSA signed a memorandum with UL to harmonize Canadian and U.S. standards. The European Community also agreed that all member countries would have common product standards for most industries. By 1993, common world standards, without which there could not be a true global market in major home appliances, were beginning to emerge.[28]

Products

White goods were generally classified as *laundry* (washers and dryers), *refrigeration* (refrigerators and freezers), *cooking* (ranges and ovens), and *other* (dishwashers, disposers, and trash compactors) appliances. In addition to making white goods, some appliance manufacturers also made and sold floor care appliances, such as vacuum cleaners and floor polishers.

Laundry Appliances

Except for a slight drop in 1990, sales of washers and dryers in the United States had shown consistent growth in recent years (see Exhibit 12.1). However, U.S. saturation levels had remained fairly steady at 73% for washers and 67% for dryers. Market share had remained reasonably stable over the ten-year period 1983–1992 for laundry appliances (Exhibit 12.5). Over 50% of the market was controlled by Whirlpool. General Electric, Maytag, and A.B. Electrolux (Frigidaire) had market shares in the teens with Raytheon in the single digits. Exhibit 12.6 lists the results of 1990, 1991, and 1992 surveys conducted by *Consumer Reports* that rated the reliability of washing machine and other major home appliance brands from most to least reliable (in terms of repairs required).

Refrigeration Appliances

Except for microwave ovens in the 1980s, refrigerators had historically been the largest selling major home appliance. Refrigerators were one of the few major appliances with saturation levels approaching 100%. Compact refrigerators had increased in importance in the U.S. refrigeration market, from 9.4% in 1983 to almost 11% in 1992. The demand for compacts was much greater in Europe and Asia where space limitations and a culture emphasizing daily over weekly food shopping tended to reduce the demand for the large refrigerators so much in demand in the United States. Except for a slight drop in 1989, sales of both standard and compact refrigerators in the United States increased steadily from 1980 to 1992. General Electric, Whirlpool, and A.B. Electrolux (Frigidaire) together controlled almost 80% of the U.S. market. Maytag through Admiral and Raytheon through Amana controlled most of the rest.

Cooking Appliances

The acceptance by the American public of the microwave oven in the 1980s radically changed the situation for home cooking appliances. As sales of microwave ovens jumped from 3.6 million in 1980 to 10.6 million in 1989, sales of electric and gas ranges slowed. As the microwave oven market approached saturation in the 1990s (the percentage of U.S. homes with a microwave oven had increased dramatically, from under 2% in 1980 to 85% in 1992), sales of microwaves slowed and electric and gas range sales began to increase once again. Since the 1960s, electric ranges have had a slight sales edge over gas ranges. The combined saturation level of electric and gas ranges slightly exceeded 100% (more than one range per home). General Electric and Whirlpool controlled about 60% of the electric range market; whereas Maytag (through Magic Chef), A.B. Electrolux (Frigidaire), and Raytheon controlled over 70% of the gas range market. Matsushita, Sharp, Samsung, Goldstar, A.B. Electrolux (Frigidaire), and Sanyo Fisher controlled over 80% of the U.S. microwave market. Maytag, Raytheon, Whirlpool, Toshiba, and others each had 6% or less of the market.

EXHIBIT 12.5

U.S. Market Shares in Percentage by Category

Category	1992	1988	1983
White Goods			
Compactors			
Whirlpool	70[1]	67	48
GE	14	14	26
Broan	14	6	NA
Emerson Contract	—	8	NA
Thermador/Waste King	1	3	4
Others	1	2	22[2]

1. Includes Emerson Contract, a Whirlpool unit.
2. Includes 12 for Hobart's KitchenAid, 6 for Tappan, 4 for Amana.

Category	1992	1988	1983
Disposers			
In-Sink-Erator	65	60	61
Electrolux (Anaheim)	17	30	NA
Thermador/Waste King	10	5	8
KitchenAid	2	NA	NA
Watertown Metal Products	2	2	NA
Maytag	2	1	NA
Others	2	2	31[1]

1. Includes 12 for Tappan, 11 for GE, 7 for Hobart's KitchenAid.

Category	1992	1988	1983
Dishwashers			
GE	40	40	22
Whirlpool	31[1]	19	13
Electrolux (Frigidaire)	20[2]	7	7
Maytag	8	7	7
Thermador/Waste King	1	1	2
Design & Manufacturing	—	20	36
Emerson Contract	—	5	13
Others	—	1	—

1. Includes Emerson Contract, a Whirlpool unit.
2. Includes Design & Manufacturing, an Electrolux unit.

Category	1992	1988	1983
Dryers, Electric			
Whirlpool	52	52	47
GE	18	16	17
Maytag	15[1]	12	15
Electrolux (Frigidaire)	12	11	15
Raytheon (Speed Queen)	3	3	5
Norge	—	2	NA
Others	—	4	1

1. Includes Norge, a Maytag unit.

Category	1992	1988	1983
Dryers, Gas			
Whirlpool	53	52	47
Maytag	17[1]	12	12
GE	14	16	16
Electrolux (Frigidaire)	10	11	15
Raytheon (Speed Queen)	4	3	5
Norge	—	2	4
Others	2	4	1

1. Includes Norge, a Maytag unit.

(continued)

EXHIBIT 12.5

U.S. Market Shares in Percentage by Category *(continued)*

Category	1992	1988	1983
Freezers			
Electrolux (Frigidaire)	76	32	30
W.C. Wood	14	NA	NA
Whirlpool	5	36	34
Raytheon (Amana)	5	6	6
Maytag (Admiral)	—[2]	22	22
Others	—	4	8[1]

1. Includes 5 for GE.

2. No longer makes freezers.

Category	1992	1988	1983
Microwave Ovens			
Sharp	20	17	11
Samsung	18	18	7
Matsushita (Panasonic, Quasar)	17	13	5
Electrolux (Frigidaire)	10	5	9
Goldstar	10	19	1
Sanyo Fisher	7	5	13
Maytag (Magic Chef)	6	2	4
Raytheon (Amana)	4	6	11
Whirlpool	3	2	4
Toshiba	1	2	3
Others	4	11[2]	20[1]

1. Includes 16 for GE.

2. Includes 6 for Litton.

Category	1992	1988	1983
Range Hoods			
Broan	51[1]	35	30
Nutone	14	19	20
Rangaire	12	13	18
Watertown Metal Products	12	14	NA
Fasco	4	NA	NA
Aubrey	—	15	12
Others	7	4	20[2]

1. Includes Aubrey, now part of Broan.

2. Includes 10 for GE.

Category	1992	1988	1983
Ranges, Electric			
GE	30	30	32
Whirlpool	30[1]	13	12
Maytag	17[2]	10	—
Electrolux (Frigidaire)	15[3]	15	16
Raytheon (Caloric)	7	7	8
Thermador/Waste King	1	NA	—
Roper	—	14	10
Tappan	—	7	6
Others	—	4	1

1. Includes Roper, Whirlpool unit.

2. Includes Magic Chef, Hardwick, Jenn-Air as Maytag units.

3. Includes Tappan, an Electrolux unit.

(continued)

EXHIBIT 12.5

U.S. Market Shares in Percentage by Category *(continued)*

Category	1992	1988	1983
Ranges, Gas			
Maytag	27[1]	24	—
Electrolux (Frigidaire)	25[2]	7	6
Raytheon (Caloric)	22	15	18
GE	19[3]	—	—
Brown	3	4	7
Peerless-Premier	3	3	—
Tappan	—	25	NA
Roper	—	15	14
Others	1	7	7

1. Includes Jenn-Air, Hardwick, Magic Chef as Maytag units.
2. Includes Tappan, an Electrolux unit.
3. GE purchased Roper's manufacturing facilities.

Category	1992	1988	1983
Refrigerators			
GE	35	35	31
Whirlpool	25	28	30
Electrolux (Frigidaire)	17	21	23
Maytag (Admiral)	13	10	12
Raytheon (Amana)	8	5	7
Others	2	1	—
Washers			
Whirlpool	52	50	48
GE	16	17	18
Maytag	17	16	15
Electrolux (Frigidaire)	11	10	15
Raytheon (Speed Queen)	4	4	4
Others	—	3	—
Floor Care			
Vacuum Cleaners			
Hoover	34	34	40
Eureka	16	21	21
Royal	13	NA	—
Regina	9	7	—
Whirlpool (Kenmore)	9	8	4
Electrolux	6	5	10
Ryobi (Singer)	5	7	16
Kirby	4	6	8
Matsushita (Panasonic)	2	3	—
Rexaire (Rainbow)	2	2	1
Others	—	7	—
Floor Polishers			
Hoover	58	55	30
Regina	33	38	25
Electrolux	9	2	15
Others	—	5	30

Source: *Appliance Manufacturer* (February 1993), pp. 18–21; (February 1989), pp. 32–34.

EXHIBIT 12.6

Ratings of Major Home Appliance Reliability

(Listed in order from most to least reliable in terms of repairs required)

Washers	Dryers (Electric)	Dryers (Gas)
Hotpoint	Maytag	Whirlpool
Maytag	Whirlpool	Hotpoint
GE	Hotpoint	Amana (tied for 1st: Whirlpool, Hotpoint, Amana, GE, Sears)
Whirlpool	Amana	GE
Sears	GE	Sears
Speed Queen	Sears	
Montgomery Ward	Speed Queen	
White-Westinghouse	White-Westinghouse	Maytag
Frigidaire	Montgomery Ward	Speed Queen
	Frigidaire	White-Westinghouse

Refrigerators (No Icemakers)	Refrigerators (with Icemakers)	Microwave Ovens
Sears	Sears	Sanyo
Whirlpool	Whirlpool	Panasonic
Amana (tied for 2nd: Whirlpool, Amana, Magic Chef)	Amana	Quasar
Magic Chef	Hotpoint	GE
Montgomery Ward	Frigidaire	Sharp
Gibson	GE	Sears
Hotpoint (tied for 6th: Gibson, Hotpoint, White-Westinghouse)		Samsung
White-Westinghouse		J. C. Penney
Admiral		Magic Chef
Frigidaire		Tappan
GE		Amana
		Whirlpool

Ranges (Electric)	Ranges (Gas)	Dishwashers
Hotpoint	Magic Chef (tied for 1st: Magic Chef, Tappan)	Magic Chef
Whirlpool	Tappan	General Electric
GE		Hotpoint
Tappan		Whirlpool
Frigidaire	Sears	Tappan
Sears	Caloric	KitchenAid
Caloric		Sears
White-Westinghouse		White-Westinghouse
Magic Chef		Caloric
		Maytag
		Frigidaire

Source: From various issues of *Consumer Reports*. "Washing Machines" (February 1991), p. 115; (August 1992), p. 538. "Clothes Dryers" (January 1992), p. 48. "Refrigerators" (July 1992), p. 461. "Electric Ranges: Coil or Disk" (March 1990), p. 149. "Cooking With Gas" (August 1990), p. 526. "Microwave Ovens" (November 1991), p. 738. "Dishwashers Plain and Fancy" (May 1990), p. 342.

Other Major Home Appliances

Dishwashers, disposers, and trash compactors comprised the remaining category of white goods appliances.

Dishwashers

Sales of dishwashers peaked in the 1970s, dropped in the early 1980s, and settled into a pattern of 3.4 to 3.8 million units in sales annually from 1984 through 1992. The percentage of built-in units when compared to portables increased from 86% of all dishwasher sales in 1980 to 95% in 1992. Even though the U.S. saturation level of dishwashers had increased from 34.3% in 1973 to 47.7% in 1991, this appliance appeared to offer some real growth potential in contrast to some other major home appliances. Dishwashers were one of the most complicated appliances to make because they involved a combination of electrical, mechanical, and hydraulic technology. In 1992, three firms controlled 90% of the U.S. dishwasher market. General Electric led with a 40% market share. Whirlpool increased to 31% with its purchase of Emerson Contract. A.B. Electrolux (Frigidaire) moved to third place with a 20% market share after its purchase of Design and Manufacturing (a firm specializing in dishwashers). Maytag was a distant fourth with an 8% market share.

Garbage Disposers

In contrast to all other major home appliances, garbage disposers were sold primarily through plumbing contractors and could not be considered a white good. In-Sink-Erator was the leader with a greater than 60% market share. A.B. Electrolux (Anaheim) was in second place with 17% of the market. The remainder of the market was divided among a number of other brands. The saturation level increased from 35.3% in 1973 to 47% in 1991.

Compactors

Whirlpool dominated the trash compactor market with a 70% market share, followed by General Electric and Broan, each with 14% of the market. Although saturation was less than 5% of U.S. homes, potential growth appeared limited. With annual sales of less than 150,000 units in 1992, manufacturers did not attach much importance to this product.

Floor Care Appliances

Consisting of vacuum cleaners and floor polishers, the U.S. floor care market had realized greater recent growth than had many other home appliances. Nearly 18 million vacuum cleaners were sold in 1992 (Exhibit 12.7). Continued growth was predicted even though 97.2% of U.S. households had at least one vacuum cleaner. Like white goods, the life expectancies of floor care appliances were more than ten years. Hoover, now a part of Maytag Corporation, controlled the U.S. floor care

EXHIBIT 12.7

U.S. Manufacturers' Unit Shipments of Floor Care Appliances
(Dollar amounts in thousands)

Product	1992	1991	1990	1989	1988	1987	1986	1985	1984
Vacuum cleaners									
Cannisters	2,100	2,385	2,741	3,010	3,177	2,983	2,860	2,998	3,066
Handheld electric	3,610	2,900	2,500	1,900	1,050	935	670	564	470
Handheld rechargeable	2,740	3,500	5,000	5,125	5,300	5,750	5,000	5,440	4,730
Stick	1,500	1,500	1,644	1,893	1,725	1,700	1,093	1,077	943
Upright	7,870	6,960	6,578	6,470	5,750	5,527	4,870	4,438	4,377
Floor polishers	NA	NA	NA	191	185	200	200	190	NA

Source: *Appliance* (April 1990), p. 35; (April 1993), p. 55.

market with a 34% share of vacuum cleaner sales and a 58% share of floor polisher sales (see Exhibit 12.5). Eureka, part of A.B. Electrolux of Sweden, was second in vacuum cleaner sales with a market share of 16%. Electrolux Corporation of Marietta, Georgia, held second place in the sales of floor polishers and third place in vacuum cleaner sales as a result of its 1989 purchase of the Regina Company. Royal had been advertising heavily its "Dirt Devil" recently to boost its sales of vacuum cleaners. The Japanese companies of Ryobi (Singer brand) and Matsushita (Panasonic) were working to build U.S. vacuum cleaner sales. As a result of increasingly aggressive foreign competition, U.S. floor care appliance manufacturers were busily engaged in defending their market shares by renewing their manufacturing facilities and/or acquiring other floor care companies or were considering exiting the manufacturing part of the business.

Competitors

In 1993, five appliance manufacturers controlled almost 98% of the U.S. major home appliance market, led by Whirlpool with 33.8% and General Electric with 28.2% (Exhibit 12.8). Of these five, only A.B. Electrolux and Whirlpool appeared to be in good position to similarly dominate the European market. General Electric's joint venture with GEC (General Electric Corporation) of the United Kingdom and Maytag's acquisition of Hoover's international business improved their international positions in 1989. General Electric's and Maytag's European market shares, however, needed to be improved significantly if either was to be an important factor in Europe.

EXHIBIT 12.8

Approximate Shares of U.S. and European Markets in White Goods[1]
(Refrigerators, washing machines, dryers, ranges, and dishwashers)

United States

Company	Market Share	Brands
Whirlpool	33.8%	Whirlpool, KitchenAid, Roper
General Electric	28.2	GE, Hotpoint, RCA, Monogram
A.B. Electrolux (Frigidaire)	15.9	Frigidaire, Gibson, Kelvinator, Tappan, White, Westinghouse
Maytag	14.2	Maytag, Hardwick, Jenn-Air, Magic Chef, Admiral, Norge
Raytheon	5.6	Amana, Speed Queen, Caloric
Others	2.3	

Western Europe

Company	Market Share	Brands
A.B. Electrolux (Sweden)	19%	Electrolux, Buderus, Zanker, Zanussi, Thorn-EMI, Cobero
Bosch-Siemens (Germany)	13	Bosch, Siemens, Neff, Constructa, Balay, Pitsos
Whirlpool (United States)	10	Philips, Whirlpool, Bauknecht, Ignis
Miele (Germany)	7	Miele, Imperial
Temfa (France/Spain)	6	Thomson, Fagor, DeDetriech
AEG (Germany)	5	AEG
Merloni (Italy)	4	Merloni, Ariston, Indesit, Scholtes
General Domestic Appliances (United States/United Kingdom)	4	Hotpoint, Creda, General Electric
Candy (Italy)	4	Candy, Rosieres, Kelvinator, Gasfire
Others	28	

Note: 1. U.S. share data for 1991; Western Europe share data for 1990.

Source: *Appliance* (September 1992), p. 44; (July 1992), p. 41.

Whirlpool

Whirlpool and GE traditionally have dominated the U.S. major home appliance industry. Whirlpool owed its leadership position to its 50-plus years' relationship with Sears, which historically accounted for about 40% of the company's North American sales. Sears stocked Whirlpool's own brand and Whirlpool's Kenmore and Sears brands. Sears' movement away from a heavy reliance on its private Sears and Kenmore brands toward its new Brand Central concept in the late 1980s meant that Sears no longer dominated Whirlpool's sales. Nevertheless, Sears continued to be Whirlpool's largest single customer in 1992.

In 1989, Whirlpool paid Philips Electronics N.V. $470 million for a 53% stake in the Dutch firm's appliance operations. Two years later in July 1991 Whirlpool paid Philips some $610 million to complete the acquisition. By 1993, Whirlpool had become a serious global competitor in the emerging worldwide major home appliance industry. Sales and profits had increased in 1992 in every geographical area served. Whirlpool was first in North America and third in Western Europe in terms of market share. It had developed a series of joint ventures and equity arrangements with appliance manufacturers throughout Asia and South America. Although its share of the Asian market was still fairly small, Whirlpool together with its affiliates in Argentina and Brazil had the largest manufacturing base and market share in South America. The emphasis in the company was clearly on making the Whirlpool name a global brand.

General Electric

General Electric, with a U.S. major home appliance market share of 28.2%, was a strong competitor in many industries. It had a powerful name and brand image and was the most vertically integrated of the major home appliance manufacturers. Like others, it manufactured some of its components, but it was the only appliance producer to own its entire distribution and service facilities. The operating income of General Electric's major appliance division declined in both 1991 and 1992 but the division was still profitable. Realizing that GE's manufacturing facilities at its 40-year-old Appliance Park near Louisville, Kentucky, were slowly losing their competitiveness, management announced in March 1993 that the company would modernize the washing machine plant at a cost of $70 million. According to Richard Stonesifer, chief of GE Appliances, more modernizing would soon be needed at Appliance Park because washing machines were not the only product line losing money at that location.[29]

Given the relatively slow growth in the North American market, GE Appliances planned to continue its movement into faster-growing international locations. In 1989, GE paid $580 million for a joint appliance venture and other ventures with the U.K.'s General Electric Corporation (GEC). In Europe, GEC was known for its mass market appliances, whereas GE was known for its high-end appliances. Named General Domestic Appliances (GDA), the joint venture was a leading (and profitable) competitor in the U.K. market with its GE, Hotpoint, and Creda brands; GDA shipped only small quantities of appliances to the European continent. General Electric was also involved with international partners in Mexico (MABE), Venezuela (Madosa), India (Godrej & Boyce Mfg. Co.), the Philippines (Philacor), and Japan (Toshiba). Appliances manufactured by the joint ventures were primarily sold in the country of origin, with small amounts going to contiguous markets. By 1992, approximately 30% of the GE Appliance Division's sales came from outside the United States.[30]

A.B. Electrolux

A.B. Electrolux of Sweden, after its purchase of White Consolidated Industries (WCI) in 1986, sold nearly 17 million appliances under 41 brand names in countries around the world. After acquiring Zanussi in Italy, Tricity and Thorn EMI in the United Kingdom, and WCI in the United States, Electrolux considered itself the world's largest major home appliance manufacturer. By 1992, Electrolux was first in market share in Western Europe and third in North America. Europe accounted for about 65% of its major home appliance sales, and North America accounted for approximately 30%. Although overall household appliance sales increased from 1990 to 1991, operating income dropped for the second consecutive year. Electrolux needed to carefully plan to take full advantage of a proliferation of brands around the world without getting bogged down with competing internal demands for attention to each brand. In 1992, the company introduced its own pan-European brand under the Electrolux name. The company planned to spend about SEK600 million ($1US = approximately SEK8) over five years to market the Electrolux products throughout Europe.[31]

In 1991, the WCI Major Appliance Group was renamed Frigidaire Company in order to provide A.B. Electrolux's U.S. subsidiary the recognition earned by its pioneering namesake brand. Previously, the company's brands had competed against each other and had not been designed for automated manufacturing. Consequently, the quality of many of its well-known branded products had deteriorated over time. Frigidaire President Hans Backman stated that quality would be raised and costs reduced through investments in production facilities and new product innovation.[32]

Maytag

In 1993, Maytag Corporation, with a U.S. market share of 14.2%, but less than 4% in Western Europe through the Hoover brand, was working hard to keep from being outdistanced by the three powerhouses—Whirlpool, Electrolux, and GE. Knowing that the company could not successfully compete in the major home appliance industry as just a manufacturer of high-quality laundry products, the company embarked during the 1980s on the acquisition of Hardwick Stoves, Magic Chef, and Jenn-Air. These acquisitions provided Maytag the full line of appliances it needed to compete effectively in the U.S. market. Realizing that the industry was going global as well, Maytag purchased Hoover Company, a successful floor care company in the United States and a strong white goods producer in the United Kingdom and Australia with a solid distribution network in continental Europe. Maytag's recently completed state-of-the art dishwasher plant in Tennessee and its heavy investments in its Magic Chef and Admiral manufacturing facilities, and in Hoover's appliance plants in the United Kingdom, suggested that Maytag did not plan to be left behind by the big three in the future.

In acquiring Hoover, Maytag unfortunately also acquired a significant amount of debt. This debt and the heavy amount of investment needed to upgrade and integrate its newly-acquired facilities and operations strained Maytag's profitability. Although sales rebounded in 1992 from a relatively weak 1991, the year brought the company its first net loss since the 1920s. Even without the interest expense, operating profits had consistently dropped every year since 1989 (Exhibit 12.9). Part of the problem was that Hoover Europe had shown a loss every year

EXHIBIT 12.9

Major Home Appliance Operating Results for Primary U.S. Competitors
(Dollar amounts in millions)

Company	Category	1992	1991	1990
General Electric	Revenue	$5,330	$5,225	$5,592
	Operating income	386	400	435
	Assets	2,248	2,503	2,666
Whirlpool	Revenue	$7,301	$6,757	$6,605
	Operating income	479	393	349
	Assets	6,118	6,445	5,614
Electrolux[1]	Revenue	SEK46,540	SEK45,481	SEK44,890
	Operating income	SEK955	SEK1,081	SEK1,194
	Assets	NA	NA	NA
Maytag	Revenue	$3,041	$2,971	$3,057
	Operating income	79	192	231
	Assets	2,501	2,535	2,587
Raytheon	Revenue	$1,071	$998	$1,041
	Operating income	34	17	4
	Assets	754	674	670

Note: 1. Amounts given in Swedish kronor (SEK). One U.S. dollar equals approximately 8 Swedish krona.

Source: Annual reports of respective companies.

since it was acquired. Nevertheless, operating profits for the North American part of the corporation also had been dropping since 1989. With the company's stock price declining consistently since it had acquired Hoover, the financial community was wondering how long it would take to turn Maytag around.

Raytheon

Raytheon Company, an electronics as well as an appliances firm, was the fifth important player in the U.S. major home appliance industry. Raytheon's Appliances Group was composed of Amana Refrigeration, Caloric Corporation, and Speed Queen Company. Operating under the belief that its technological leadership in the electronics and defense industries could drive innovations in the appliance industry, Raytheon acquired enough appliance companies to assemble the full line of products necessary to compete effectively in the U.S. market. Charles Schmidt, Senior Vice-President and Group Executive of the Raytheon Appliances Group, stated that the company was interested in broadening its offerings in home and commercial appliances: "We are interested in either internally growing or cooperating in mutually agreed upon acquisitions."[33] Given the likely decrease in defense-related business in the 1990s, Raytheon would need a strong appliance business. To that end, the company invested $173 million in new appliance plants and equipment from 1989 through 1992.[34]

Unfortunately, Raytheon's appliance sales had consistently fallen from 1989 to 1991, but they rebounded slightly in 1992. Net income improved in 1991 and again in 1992 from a rather dismal showing in 1990 but was still dwarfed by the income from each of the company's other business units. Only Amana continued to show increasing sales and income, from strong refrigerator sales. The Appliances Group was working to consolidate functions within its three product lines to improve operating efficiencies and reduce costs.[35] The recent trend toward global acquisitions and consolidation in the appliance industry left analysts wondering whether Raytheon would be able to compete successfully in the world appliance market of the future.

The Future: A Global Appliance Market?

In the short run, the outlook for major home appliance sales was conservatively positive. In North America, sales for 1993 were expected to be not much greater than in 1992. Housing starts for 1993 were forecasted to be no more than 2% above those in 1992. Brian Beaulieu, Economics Editor for *Appliance Manufacturer,* predicted that robust housing starts and economic prosperity would be delayed until 1994. According to Beaulieu, "The years 1994 and 1995 are projected to be significantly positive in the U.S., the rest of North America, and abroad."[36]

Europe

The focus of everyone's attention in the major home appliance industry at the beginning of the 1990s had been Europe—the anticipated 1992 economic integration of the European Community and the rapidly opening markets of Eastern Europe. Because Western Europe was going through a demographic shift similar to that of the United States—toward a more middle-aged population—coupled with lower overall saturation levels (see Exhibit 12.4) of major home appliances, sales were predicted to grow annually in the 5%–6% range in contrast to the 1%–2% growth rate predicted for the United States. The barriers to free trade existing among the 12-nation European Community before 1992 were steadily being eliminated. The EC requirement of at least 60% local content to avoid tariffs made a European presence imperative for both U.S. and Japanese major home appliance manufacturers.

European appliance manufacturers were well aware of the need for consolidation in the European home appliance industry and the increasing pressure from non-EC appliance manufacturers. The Swedish firm A.B. Electrolux, with its acquisitions of the powerful Italian Zanussi company, the U.K.'s Thorn-EMI, the U.S.'s White Consolidated Industries (Frigidaire), and three Spanish companies, was in a good position to battle Whirlpool for the coming global market. It already had a strong presence in every European country from Finland to Portugal.

Other changes that would affect the industry in Europe were Whirlpool's acquisition of Philip's appliance business, the General Domestic Appliance joint venture, and Maytag's acquisition of Hoover. (General Domestic Appliances and Hoover dominated the U.K. appliance market but were only a minor presence on the continent.)

Other strong European competitors were Thomson-Brandt, which traditionally dominated France, Bosch-Siemens and AEG, which used their domination of the German market to export aggressively, and Merloni and Candy of Italy. In 1992, AEG Hausgerate AG, a subsidiary of Daimler Benz's AEG unit, agreed with A.B. Electrolux to merge some dishwasher and laundry production lines and product development. In that same year, Bosch-Siemens formed an alliance with Maytag Corporation to explore mutually beneficial business opportunities in Europe and elsewhere.

In early 1993, Italian appliance manufacturer Ocean Elettrodomestici joined TEMFA (renamed "Eurodom"), a group originally established in 1990 by Thomson Electromenager of France and Fagor Electrodomesticos of Spain. General Domestic Appliances of the United Kingdom also joined Eurodom later in the year. Eurodom was designed to offer member companies opportunities in R&D, coordinating purchasing agreements, cross-sourcing of finished products to improve product line, and exchange of practices in design and manufacturing.[37] Slovakia's Tatramat A.S., the country's largest maker of washing machines, formed a home appliance joint venture with Whirlpool International B.V. Both Whirlpool and A.B. Electrolux had relationships with appliance manufacturers in Hungary. As late as 1990, the European appliance industry had about 10% excess capacity and 250 manufacturers in 1990.[38] By 1993, although the number of firms had been significantly reduced, the industry was still fragmented, especially in Germany and Italy, where there were many national competitors. Electrolux, Whirlpool, and Bosch-Siemens controlled almost half the European market, but the remaining half was held by more than 55 manufacturers.[39]

Unlike the U.S. appliance market, the European market was heavily segmented into a series of national markets. In cooking appliances, for example, over 90% of the ranges purchased in Germany were electric, whereas gas prevailed through the rest of Europe. In Germany, 65% of ranges were built in, but the percentage of built-ins outside Germany was considerably less. Top-loading washers, long dominant in the United States, commanded 80% of the market in France, but front loaders dominated the rest of Europe, where washers and dryers must fit into a kitchen under a work surface or in a bathroom. Although built-in refrigerators formed only a small part of refrigerator sales in most of Europe, they comprised over 50% of the German market. The large, free-standing home appliances preferred by Americans were much less popular in Europe where smaller, energy efficient units were generally preferred.

The general feeling in the industry in 1993 was that the phase of European consolidation—dominated by acquisitions and joint ventures involving Europe-based firms—was winding down.[40] The largest appliance manufacturers were already engaged in developing opportunities elsewhere in the world—primarily in Mexico as well as in South America and Asia.

Mexico and NAFTA

In preparation for the North American Free Trade Agreement (NAFTA), Whirlpool had entered into a joint venture with Vitromatic S.A., which included three facilities in Mexico, and General Electric had formed a joint venture with MABE, a consortium of Mexican appliance producers. These arrangements were beginning to affect the competitiveness of U.S. firms without Mexican white goods operations: Maytag, Raytheon, and Frigidaire. For example, Maytag laid off workers at its Magic Chef plant in Cleveland, Tennessee, because of increasing imports of free-standing gas ranges from a MABE plant.[41]

South America

Regional trade agreements and the lowering of tariffs had made it easier to sell products such as home appliances in South America in the 1990s. General Electric had part ownership of Madosa, a leading appliance maker in Venezuela. Whirlpool, with its Brazilian and Argentine affiliates, had a strong presence in the area.

Asia

In 1993, Asia was already the world's second largest home appliance market and opportunities were still emerging. According to Roger Merriam, Vice-President of Sales and Marketing for Whirlpool Overseas Corporation, "In the U.S., we talk of households equipped with between seven and nine major appliance products. In Asia, which already accounts for 40% of the world market, it's more like four appliances per home." The saturation level of clothes washers in India, for example, was about 6%, compared to 54% in Mexico.[42] About 27% of the roughly 190 million units sold worldwide in 1992 were sold in Asia—more than in North America and fewer only than in Europe. The combined economies of the Asian region were expected to grow by about 6% annually through the 1990s, with industry shipments of appliances likely to grow more rapidly. Although Japanese and Korean manufacturers dominated the Asian home appliance market in the early 1990s, the industry was still fragmented and no single company dominated the market.[43] According to Jeff Immelt, Vice-President of Worldwide Marketing and Product Management at GE Appliances, the Asian market was still young enough to justify building a company's own brand instead of acquiring someone else's established brands, as was done in Europe.[44]

Already, Whirlpool had established a joint venture in India, and General Electric had part ownership of Philcor in the Philippines.

Emerging Global Industry

The largest players in the major home appliance industry were preparing for the emerging global market. Anders Sharp, CEO and President of A.B. Electrolux, announced that expansion in the 1990s would be based on a higher proportion of internationally generated growth in appliances—especially in the EC, North America, and the Far East.[45] Whirlpool, in cooperation with its affiliates in Brazil and joint venture partners in India and Mexico, had built facilities in those countries to produce what the company called the "world washer." This new compact washing machine had debuted in 1992 in Mexico and its production was intended to meet the increasing consumer demand in developing countries.

The technology and materials used in appliance manufacture were the same around the world. Products were becoming more alike as the European visual style of appliance design was being copied in Asia and the Americas. Consequently, developments in one part of the world were being quickly copied elsewhere. Appliance manufacturers could buy steel and other components internationally. For example, Whirlpool was already beginning to consolidate its purchases globally.

The Next 25 Years

Completing its first 25 years in 1992, the Association of Home Appliance Manufacturers (AHAM) through its President, Robert L. Holding, considered what might happen in the home appliance industry during the next 25 years. Holding pointed out that even though the U.S. industry had a strong base from which to operate, it would face continuing pressures on profits. Although U.S. appliance firms were successfully moving into Europe and Latin America, they lacked a real presence in Asia. He predicted that in 25 years the number of global appliance makers would shrink significantly, with five to ten firms becoming dominant.

Holding predicted that environmental issues and product quality would be crucial considerations. "Creating a basic design that can be manufactured into a 'family' of brands or models will be important."[46] Because retailers have been gaining increasing leverage over manufacturers, "speed to market" and flexible low-cost manufacturing would be essential to future success. In addition to energy-use and air-pollution laws, government would probably enact legislation requiring that the parts of worn-out appliances be recyclable, with disposal fees charged for any parts taken to the dump. Led by the trend to locate more appliances in main living areas of the house instead of in the basement, consumers would demand quieter appliances. According to Holding, the future of individual major home appliance manufacturers would depend on their ability to provide value to the consumer:

> There are a lot of brands competing for a limited market in terms of growth. These brands are competing for all segments, high, low, and in between. As features are introduced at the high end, they flow down quickly to the low end. The result will be great consumer value at all points in the market. In other words, we meet consumer needs "the old fashioned way" through hard competition.[47]

Notes

1. R. Holding, "1990 Shipment Outlook," *Appliance* (January 1990), p. 64; T. A. Stewart, "A Heartland Industry Takes on the World," *Fortune* (March 12, 1990), p. 110.
2. A. J. Takacs, "A New Order, a New Agenda," *Appliance* (April 1993), p. 58.
3. P. F. Dowling, Jr., "Continued Sales Records Expected," *Appliance* (January 1993), p. 56.
4. T. Somheil, "The Incredible Value Story—Part 3," *Appliance* (June 1992), pp. 25–32.
5. Summarized from C. R. Christensen, K. R. Andrews, J. L. Bower, R. G. Hamermesh,

and M. E. Porter, "Note on the Major Home Appliance Industry in 1984 (condensed)," in *Business Policy,* 6th ed. (Homewood, Ill.: Irwin, 1987), pp. 340–344.
6. "The 1989 Private Brand Picture," *Appliance* (September 1989), pp. 68–70.
7. N. C. Remich, Jr., "Is a Global, Look-Alike Design in Our Future?" *Appliance Manufacturer* (April 1988), pp. 38–45; L. Armstrong and N. Gross, "Why 'Fuzzy Logic' Beats Black-or-White Thinking," *Business Week* (May 21, 1990), pp. 92–93.
8. R. Dzierwa, "Converging on Cologne," *Appliance* (April 1993), p. 51.
9. S. Stevens, "Finessing the Future," *Appliance* (April 1990), pp. 42–43.
10. "The Life Expectancy/Replacement Picture," *Appliance* (September 1992), pp. 46–47.
11. Christensen et al., p. 340.
12. "Survey of Robots and Vision Systems in the Appliance Industry," *Appliance* (December 1988), pp. 36–37.
13. "WCI's $500-Million Investment to Payoff Soon," *Appliance Manufacturer* (March 1990), p. 66.
14. R. Wartzman, "A Whirlpool Factory Raises Productivity—And Pay of Workers," *Wall Street Journal* (May 4, 1992), pp. A1, A4.
15. D. E. Simpson, "Emphasis Purchasing: Making It in a New Decade," *Appliance* (January 1990), p. 43.
16. "Appliance Shipments Expected to Wane," *Industry Surveys,* Vol. 2, Standard & Poor's Corporation (January 1990), p. T98.
17. R. J. Buchert, "On the Rebound," *Appliance* (January 1993), p. 52.
18. Holding, p. 64.
19. "Buying Power—Home Purchase Triggers Sales of Appliances," *Appliance Manufacturer* (February 1989), p. 31.
20. J. D. Fischer, "Home Appliance Industry," *Value Line* (December 22, 1989), p. 132.
21. "Export Opportunities for Household Appliances," *Appliance* (August 1988), p. 21.
22. R. J. Haines, "Appliance Newsquotes," *Appliance* (June 1989), p. 21.
23. S. Stevens, "When Appliances Mean Business," *Appliance* (May 1989), p. 48.
24. "Whirlpool's Quality Express a JIT Distribution System for Retailers," *Appliance Manufacturer* (February 1992), p. 6.
25. T. Somheil, "Refrigeration's Revitalization," *Appliance* (February 1993), p. 54.
26. "You Can Win $30 Million," *Appliance Manufacturer* (August 1992), p. 8.
27. Somheil, "Refrigerations' Revitalization," p. 54.
28. D. W. Munson, "Lennox Gets a Jump on Europe 1992," *Appliance Manufacturer* (September 1989), pp. 36–40; J. Stevens, "Charting the Course," *Appliance* (August 1989), p. 7.
29. Z. Schiller, "GE's Appliance Park: Rewire, or Pull the Plug?" *Business Week* (February 8, 1993), p. 30; "GE to Spend $70 Million on Washing Machine Plant," *Appliance* (March 1993), p. 17.
30. "Global Growth Strategies," *Appliance Manufacturer* (January 1992), p. GEA-13.
31. A.B. Electrolux, *1991 Annual Report,* p. 16.
32. "All Systems 'Go,'" *Appliance Manufacturer* (October 1991), p. F-6.
33. S. Stevens, "Pursuing Innovation's Forefront," *Appliance* (October 1988), p. R-15.
34. G. Smith, "Raytheon's Strategy: Guns and Lots More Butter," *Business Week* (November 16, 1992), p. 96.
35. Raytheon, *1991 Annual Report,* p. 6.
36. B. Beaulieu, "Cooking-Appliance Output Flat but Rising for '94," *Appliance Manufacturer* (April 1993), p. 20.
37. "Ocean Joins Eurodom," *Appliance* (February 1993), p. 18.
38. Stewart, p. 110.
39. "European Cleaning Appliance Market Steadily Grows," *Appliance* (April 1993), p. 13; "Best Sellers in Europe," *Appliance Manufacturer* (April 1992), p. 66.
40. C. Birkner, "Final Sprint to the European Market," *Appliance* (August 1992), p. 18.
41. "NAFTA and Appliances," *Appliance* (April 1993), p. 16.
42. S. Stevens, "Taking on the World," *Appliance* (June 1991), p. W-55.
43. Whirlpool Corporation, *1992 Annual Report,* p. 19.
44. "Global Growth Strategies," p. GEA-13.
45. A. Sharp, "Appliance Newsquotes," *Appliance* (September 1989), p. 13.
46. N. C. Remich, Jr., "AHAM: The Next 25 Years," *Appliance Manufacturer* (March 1993), p. 71.
47. Ibid.

Maytag Corporation, 1993: Strategic Reassessment

J. David Hunger

Driving 30 miles east from Des Moines on Interstate 80 through a rainy mist punctuated with spurts of rain showers, a traveler nears the Newton exit. The winter has been long, and even in mid April it is hard to visualize the soaked black soil of the rolling Iowa countryside in its future summer abundance of ripening corn and soybean plants. Turning north for a few miles and then east on U.S. 6, the traveler enters the quiet town of Newton—population 15,000 and location of the headquarters of Maytag Corporation. After passing through the town square, the visitor turns right heading towards Newton Senior High School, the traditional site of Maytag's annual shareholders' meeting. It is a school day, so parking is limited and shareholders and others must park on one of the nearby streets, which are lined with well-kept houses and flower gardens. Executive jets fly low through the dark clouds in preparation for landing at Newton's small airport a few miles away. People exiting from cars and buses try to ignore the blowing rain as they enter the building. Another wet dreary day is predicted for April 27, 1993. It is 9:00 A.M. The meeting will begin in half an hour.

Notices at the door direct people to a large room with booths where the shareholders obtain their name tags and various meeting materials. Examples of the corporation's products (such as the redesigned Maytag dishwasher fresh from the brand-new Jackson plant and the new lines of Magic Chef and Maytag ranges) line the back walls. Nearby, visitors are welcomed with coffee, punch, and doughnuts. Maytag executives with their distinctive blue nametags mingle with the growing crowd. The mood is relatively friendly but charged with the expectation that management might face some difficult questions today.

Newspaper reporters are expecting trouble. "Management will be facing quite a round of questions because of recent events," stated David Lebowitz, an analyst who followed Maytag for American Securities in New York. "As a result, they're going to have to come very well prepared to explain what transpired in the past and more importantly how they envision the future."[1]

Anticipating an interesting meeting, people move toward the auditorium entrance hoping to get a good seat. A group of visiting high school students is ushered to the back of the room as a combination of young and old, known and unknown wander into the room in their coats and ties and heels and hose. From their comments and age, a significant number of the shareholders appear to be retired Maytag employees living in the area. Seated on the stage on both sides of a

This industry note was prepared by Professor J. David Hunger of Iowa State University with the research assistance of Kendra Fulk. This case appears in the Fall 1993 issue of *Case Research Journal*.

speaker's podium behind a long table are the members of Maytag Corporation's Board of Directors. The auditorium is filled to capacity, but hushes respectfully as Leonard Hadley, Chief Executive Officer and Chairman of the Board, steps forward to the podium and begins to speak.

Strategic Managers

One by one, the CEO introduces the 13 other members of the Board of Directors. Each nods briefly as his name is announced (see Exhibit 13.1 for a list of the board). Although the present board had shrunk in size from 17 members in 1989 and one-third of the board is elected every year for three-year terms, the same 14 current members have served on the board continuously since 1989. The audience notes the presence of Robert Ray, the highly respected ex-governor of Iowa, Daniel Krumm, the immediate past-Chairman and CEO of Maytag Corporation, and Lester Crown, Harvey Kapnick, and Neele Stearns, previous directors of the former Chicago Pacific Corporation who had joined Maytag's board when Maytag acquired Chicago Pacific in 1989. Dr. Ann Reynolds, the only woman on the board, is absent. Lester Crown personally owns 4.51% of Maytag's stock, but through holdings by associates and family members effectively controls 5.3% of the shares—far more than any other member of the board. Counting only personally owned shares (including Crown's), all officers and directors own only 5.44% of Maytag's outstanding shares. Although more than 60% of Maytag's stock is owned by individual shareowners, 8.2% of the stock is owned by INVESCO MIM PLC of London, England.

The CEO then introduces the executive officers seated in the center first two rows of the auditorium (see Exhibit 13.2 for a list of the officers). Each stands briefly as he or she is presented. Except for three people, the executives had worked their way up through Maytag Corporation and for the most part had spent their entire careers immersed in the Maytag Company culture. Prior to joining Maytag in 1991, Terry Carlson had been Vice-President of Purchasing for Estée Lauder, Inc. John Jansen came to the corporation in 1992 from Ridge Tool Company, a division of Emerson Electric, where he was Vice-President of Engineering. Steven Wood joined the corporation in 1989 from a position as Senior Manager with Ernst & Young, Chicago. With introductions over, Leonard Hadley looks over the packed auditorium and presents his report on the state of the corporation.

> This is my first report to you as Chairman and Chief Executive Officer, and I would like to express my sincere appreciation for your continuing interest in Maytag Corporation. I've been associated with Maytag for almost 34 years now, and I know many of you go back further than that. Together, we've seen ups and downs in appliance business cycles: we've seen favorable and unfavorable overall economic conditions; and more recently, we've seen a dividend cut and lackluster share prices. We've seen hot wars, the end of one cold one, and rapid, dramatic change in all aspects of our lives.
>
> Through it all, Maytag has prospered in the good times and weathered the storm in difficult periods. We will continue to do that in this our 100th year, and in the process we

EXHIBIT 13.1 Board of Directors: Maytag Corporation

Director	Joined Board	Position	Term Expires	Shares Owned
Edward Cazier, Jr.[1]	1987	Partner, law firm of Morgan, Lewis, & Bockius	1994	8,900
Howard L. Clark, Jr.	1986	Vice-Chairman of Shearson, Lehman, Hutton Holdings, Inc.	1996[4]	8,836
Frank W. Considine[1]	1974	Chairman of Executive Committee, American National Can Co.	1994	7,800
Lester Crown[1,3]	1989	Chairman, Material Service Corporation	1994	4,831,707
Leonard A. Hadley	1985	Chairman and Chief Executive Officer, Maytag Corporation	1996[4]	149,571
Harvey Kapnick	1989	Vice-Chairman, General Dynamics Corporation	1996[4]	32,000
Daniel J. Krumm	1970	Former Chair and Chief Executive Officer, Maytag Corporation	1995	266,215
Robert D. Ray[3]	1983	Chief Executive Officer, IASD Health Services Corporation	1996[4]	12,600
Dr. W. Ann Reynolds[2,3]	1988	Chancellor, City University of New York	1995	9,300
Jerry A. Schiller	1985	Exeuctive Vice-President and Chief Financial Officer, Maytag Corporation	1996[4]	107,411
John A. Sivright[2,3]	1976	Senior Relationship Executive, Harris Bankcorp, Inc.	1995	20,417
Neele Stearns, Jr.[1,2]	1989	Chief Executive Officer, CC Industries	1994	11,090
Fred G. Steingraber[2]	1989	Chair and Chief Executive Officer, A.T. Kearney, Inc.	1995	12,000
Peter S. Willmott	1985	Chair and Chief Executive Officer, Willmot Services	1996[4]	32,000

Notes:

1. Member of audit committee.
2. Member of compensation committee.
3. Member of nominating committee.
4. Reelected at April 27, 1993 annual meeting.

Source: Maytag Corporation, *1993 Notice of Annual Meeting & Proxy Statement,* pp. 2–6.

EXHIBIT 13.2 **Executive Officers: Maytag Corporation**

Officer	Office	Became an Officer	Age
Leonard A. Hadley	Chairman and Chief Executive Officer	1979	58
Jerry A. Schiller	Executive Vice-President and Chief Financial Officer	1984	60
Thomas H. Chapman	Senior Vice-President, Human Resources	1991	47
Carleton F. Zacheis	Senior Vice-President, Planning and Business Development	1988	59
Terry A. Carlson	Vice-President, Purchasing	1991	50
Robert L. Chaplin	Vice-President and Corporate Controller	1986	62
Janis C. Cooper	Vice-President, Public Affairs	1989	45
Randall J. Espeseth	Vice-President, Taxes	1992	46
Edward H. Graham	Vice-President, General Counsel, and Assistant Secretary	1990	57
Gregory P. Irwin	Vice-President, Labor Relations	1991	47
John H. Jansen	Vice-President, Technology	1992	53
Thomas C. Ringgenberg	Vice-President and Treasurer	1989	54
Steven H. Wood	Vice-President, Information Services	1992	35
E. James Bennett	Secretary and Assistant General Counsel	1985	51

Source: Maytag Corporation, *Form 10-K* (December 31, 1992), p. 6.

will become an even stronger, more competitive corporation in the days ahead. We're in this business for the long haul, and we fully intend to succeed.

As Hadley continues his speech, it becomes increasingly apparent that Maytag Corporation has come a long way from the days when F. L. Maytag sold agricultural machinery to local farmers. Has it really been 100 years?

History

Early Years: Achieving Industry Dominance

Fred L. Maytag (or F. L., as he was commonly called), who came to Newton, Iowa, as a farm boy in a covered wagon, joined three other men in 1893 to found the Parsons Band Cutter and Self Feeder Company. The firm produced attachments invented by one of the founders to improve the performance of threshing machines. The company built its first washing machine, the "Pastime," in 1907 as a sideline to its farm equipment, hoping that this product would fill the seasonal slumps in the farm equipment business and enable the company to have year-round production. Noting the presence of "too much manual labor in family washings," the company made and sold a washer primarily to farm wives as a replacement for the traditional washboard and tub. The *Pastime* had a wooden tub with a hand crank that turned an inside dolly with pegs, which was attached to the underside of the lid. As the user turned the dolly, it pulled the clothes through the water and against the corrugated tub sides.

In 1909, F. L. Maytag became sole owner of the firm and changed its name to the Maytag Company. With the aid of Howard Snyder, a former mechanic whose inventive genius had led him to head Maytag's development department, the company generated a series of product improvements. In 1910, Maytag offered a washer with a patented swinging reversible wringer. Like its competitors, Maytag attached an electric motor to its washer in 1911 to power both the turning of the dolly and the rubber rolls of the wringer. Unlike its competition, however, in 1915 the company also offered a gasoline engine-powered washer for rural customers without electricity. This washer became so popular that Maytag soon dominated the small-town and farm markets in the United States. (Maytag's success in rural America led the company to consciously direct its marketing strategy to the farm and small-town markets. For example, rather than focus on growing urban markets after World War II, Fred Maytag II, F. L.'s grandson, advocated a policy of establishing Maytag dealerships in all towns with populations greater than 1,000 that were not then being actively served by a franchise.)[2] In 1917, Maytag introduced the "divided wringer"—a wringer with an instant tension release providing ease of operation and a significant safety feature. In 1919, the company succeeded in casting the first aluminum washer tub. It achieved this result after many aluminum experts outside the company had said that such a tub could not be mass-produced.

Under the leadership of Lewis B. Maytag, a son of the founder, the company expanded from 1920 to 1926 into a national company. In looking for ways to simplify the aluminum dolly, Howard Snyder devised a way to invert the dolly, put it in the bottom of the tub, and replace the pegs with blades so that water would be forced through the clothes instead of pulling the clothes through the water. Using this newly invented Gyrafoam™ principle, Maytag introduced its Model 80 in 1922 with a Gyratator™ instead of a pegged dolly. F. L. Maytag, then serving as Chairman of the Board, was so impressed with the new product that he personally took one of the first four washers on a western sales trip. Sales of the Model 80 went from 16,000 units in 1922 to more than 258,000 units in 1926! The company went from a $280,000 loss in 1921 to profits exceeding $6.8 million in 1926.

In 1925, the company was organized as a Delaware corporation and went public with a listing on the New York Stock Exchange. From 1926 to 1940, Elmer H. Maytag, another of F. L. Maytag's sons, headed the company. Throughout the 1920s and 1930s, Maytag Company had an average U.S. market share of 40–45% in washing machines. During the Great Depression of the 1930s, Maytag never suffered a loss. With the death of E. H. Maytag in 1940, his son Fred Maytag II assumed the presidency at the age of 29. During World War II, the company discontinued the manufacture of washers and instead produced numerous components for military airplanes.[3]

The Middle Years: Becoming a Niche Producer

With the end of World War II in 1945, the Maytag Company returned to the manufacture of washing machines. Unfortunately, the innovative genius and entrepreneurial drive of the company's early years were no longer present. Bendix, a newcomer to the industry, introduced an automatic washing machine that used a spin cycle instead of a wringer to squeeze excess rinse water out of the clothes. Industry sales of wringer washers began to decline in 1948. Maytag, however, did not convert to the manufacture of automatics until 1949. This reluctance cost the company its industry leadership. Even with automatics, Maytag's share of the U.S. washer market was only 8% in 1954.[4]

According to Orville Butler, Maytag archivist, the company delayed its entry into automatic washers for several reasons. First, management believed that the automatic washer needed more research before it would meet Maytag quality standards. Second, management did not want to pay for the use of someone else's patent. Third, a large backlog of orders for Maytag's wringer machine caused management to emphasize satisfying current waiting customers instead of attracting potentially new customers. Fourth, management was reluctant to go into debt to finance new manufacturing facilities. Nevertheless, changing market demand soon forced Maytag's management to add automatics to the product line. After considering other locations, Maytag management bowed to strong pressure from local residents and built a large new factory, called Plant Two, in Newton to make its new automatic washing machine.

In 1962, after the death of Fred Maytag II, professional managers took charge of the company, and Maytag family members were no longer involved in company management. George M. Umbreit served as Chairman and CEO, and E. G. Higdon served as President. Both men had a conservative philosophy and were mainly concerned with continuing the practices that had served the company well in the past. They strongly emphasized product quality and cost control.

Throughout the 1950s and 1960s, Maytag continued to add to and improve its product line. Clothes dryers were added in 1953; dishwashers in 1966; and food waste disposers in 1968. An attempt begun in 1946 to market ranges and refrigerators made by other companies under the Maytag brand was discontinued by 1960 because of concerns over quality. The development of the Helical Drive Transmission in 1956 eliminated a possible source of washer failure—thus contributing to the high-reliability image of the company. By 1969, Maytag's market shares in washers and dryers were 10% and 9%, respectively. The company had become a profitable manufacturer of high-quality, high-priced home laundry appliances. Because of concerns of quality and cost control, the company had vertically integrated over time to the point that it did more of its own manufacturing than did other appliance manufacturers.

The Krumm Years: Growth Through Acquisitions

In 1972, Daniel J. Krumm succeeded E. G. Higdon as Maytag President and Treasurer. Two years later he was named Chief Executive Officer. Joining Maytag in 1952 in the Sales Analysis Department, Krumm had served in Belgium and Germany as Manager of European Operations from 1962–1967. At that time, Maytag's foreign operations were a minor part of the company's sales. Krumm returned to Newton in 1967 as Administrative Assistant to the President. He was subsequently named Vice-President and elected to the Board of Directors in 1970.

During the 1970s, Maytag reaped the benefits of its heavy orientation on quality products and cost control. *Consumer Reports* annually ranked Maytag washers and dryers as the most dependable on the market. Research had indicated that Maytag washers lasted longer, needed fewer repairs, and had lower service costs when they did require service.[5] Beginning in 1967, the Leo Burnett advertising agency dramatized Maytag brand dependability in its "Old Lonely" ad campaign, featuring a Maytag repairman who, because Maytag products were so good, had nothing to do and was thus "lonely." The company's "Old Lonely" ads consistently ranked among the most effective on television. Profit margins were the highest in the industry. The company increased capacity, improved its dishwasher line, and changed the design of its clothes dryers. Industry analysts soon viewed Maytag's plants as being the most efficient in the industry.[6] By 1977, Maytag's share of the market had risen to approximately 15% in both washers and dryers.

However, Daniel Krumm was not satisfied with Maytag's situation in 1978. Although the company had added products to its original line of washers, it was still relatively small, regarded in the industry as a specialty manufacturer operating only in the higher priced end of the laundry market. Whirlpool, through its long-term relationship with Sears, and General Electric, with its strong distribution network and huge resources, dominated the major home appliance industry in the United States. Unlike the competition, Maytag was not a full-line major appliance manufacturer, lacking cooking appliances and refrigeration products. Krumm wanted Maytag to move beyond its position as a successful niche manufacturer in a maturing U.S. market, and Maytag's management adopted a strategy to become a full-line manufacturer and develop a stronger position in the U.S. appliance industry. The decision was made to grow by acquisition within the industry.

In 1981, Maytag purchased Hardwick Stove Company, a manufacturer of low-priced gas and electric ranges with an estimated 5% share of the range market. In 1982, the company acquired Jenn-Air, a niche manufacturer of high-quality, built-in electric grill ranges. In 1986, Maytag acquired Magic Chef, Inc., a successful manufacturer of mass-marketed appliances in the mid- to low-price segment of the market. The acquisition included not only Magic Chef's best-selling ranges and other products, but also appliances sold under the Admiral, Norge, and Warwick labels, plus Dixie-Narco, a leading manufacturer of soft-drink vending equipment. Most important, this acquisition provided Maytag with what it needed most to become a full-line, major home appliance manufacturer—Admiral's refrigeration facilities. On May 30, 1986, Maytag Company and the Magic Chef family of companies were merged under a parent Maytag Corporation headed by Chairman and CEO Daniel Krumm.

In 1988, realizing that the U.S. home appliance market had reached maturity, top management of the new Maytag Corporation decided to extend the corporation's growth strategy to the international arena. Maytag offered nearly $1 billion in cash and Maytag stock for Chicago Pacific Corporation (CP), the owner of Hoover Company. Consequently, by June 30, 1989, Maytag's debt had soared to

$923 million from $134 million just nine months earlier. Its total outstanding shares increased to 105 million from 75 million during the same period. Although Maytag soon reduced its debt by $200 million with the sale of CP's furniture companies, interest payments leaped to $70 million in 1989 from $20 million in 1988 and its stock price dropped from $26.50 in October 1988 to $20.00 in January 1989.[7] This was a significant change for a company that until eight years earlier had no long-term debt!

In this one step Maytag Corporation moved into the international home appliance marketplace with nine manufacturing operations in the United Kingdom, France, Australia, Mexico, Colombia, and Portugal. Hoover was known worldwide for its floor care products and throughout Europe and Australia for its washers, dryers, dishwashers, microwave ovens, and refrigerators. Before this acquisition, Maytag's international revenues were too small to report. Maytag's management anticipated some valuable future synergies in design and manufacturing technology. However, they believed it unlikely that Hoover's overseas appliances would be marketed in the United States or that Maytag products would be introduced in Europe through Hoover because of differences in American and European consumer preferences. Krumm pointed out the importance to Maytag Corporation of the purchase:

> American appliances are virtually unsalable in Europe, or most places in the world, and vice-versa. Our homes are different, the sizes of our kitchens, even the standard dimensions of things are so different. . . . The addition of Hoover makes Maytag about a $3 billion-a-year corporation consisting of twelve companies. We now have 28 manufacturing operations in eight countries, and approximately 28,000 employees.[8]

Major Home Appliance Industry: White Goods

In 1993, the major home appliance industry faced some significant threats as well as opportunities. After 40 years of rising sales both in terms of units and dollars, the North American market had reached maturity. Aside from some normal short-term fluctuations, future unit sales were expected to grow only 1%–2% annually on average for the foreseeable future. Operating margins had been dropping as appliance manufacturers held down prices to be competitive, even though costs kept increasing. In Western Europe, however, a market already 25% larger than the mature North American appliance market, unit sales were expected to grow 5% annually on average. This figure was expected to increase significantly as Eastern European countries opened their economies to world trade. In addition, the continuing economic integration of the 12 member countries of the European Community (EC) was providing the impetus for a series of mergers, acquisitions, and joint ventures among major household appliance manufacturers. Economies in Asia and South America were becoming more important to world trade as numerous countries moved more toward a free-market economy. The industry was under pressure from governments around the world to make environmentally safe products and to significantly improve appliance energy efficiency. (For additional information, see Case 12, "The U.S. Major Home Appliance Industry in 1993: From Domestic to Global.")

Business Segments and Products

In 1993, Maytag Corporation operated in two business segments, home appliances and vending equipment. The vending equipment segment consisted of Dixie-Narco, a manufacturer of soft drink vending machines. Although home appliances were reported as a single segment, they were managed geographically in terms of North American Major Appliances, Hoover North America, Hoover Europe, and Hoover Australia. The home appliance business was not seasonal and the corporation did not depend on a few customers. In contrast, the vending equipment segment depended on a few primary soft-drink customers, and sales were typically stronger in the first six months of the year than in the last six months of the year.

North American Major Appliances

North American Major Appliances contained the original Maytag Company, the Admiral Company, Magic Chef Company, Jenn-Air Company, Jackson Appliance Company, Maycor Appliance Parts and Service Company, Maytag International, Inc., and Maytag Financial Services Corporation. Within the industry, Maytag's North American Major Appliance group generally ranked third or fourth in U.S. market share in each major home appliance category—usually far behind either Whirlpool or General Electric—except in gas ranges and clothes dryers (see Exhibit 13.3 for details). Washers and dryers were Maytag's traditional strength. Market surveys consistently showed Maytag brand laundry appliances to be not only the brand consumers desired most (when price was not considered) but also the most reliable. Refrigeration was a traditional strength of Admiral. Although Admiral's quality had dropped under previous management, it was reemphasized after the Maytag acquisition. Gas ranges had always been a particular strength of Magic Chef and were perceived as very reliable in *Consumer Reports* surveys.

In terms of marketing, the Maytag brand has always been sold through Maytag-affiliated dealers and heavily advertised to consumers. Magic Chef also had been sold through its own affiliated dealers, but its advertising was primarily directed toward the dealers in terms of cooperative advertising and promotions. Jenn-Air was marketed through distributors who then sold the products to dealers. Like Magic Chef, Jenn-Air's advertising was aimed only at distributors and dealers. Because Maytag Corporation had primarily used Admiral as a manufacturing facility to make refrigerators for other brands and for private labels (e.g., Montgomery Ward's Signature line), it did little advertising of its own brand. A 1992 decision to reorganize the corporation's marketing included positioning the Admiral brand as a mid-price product to be sold through Maytag dealers.

Maytag Company

Headquartered in Newton, Iowa, the company was the flagship of the corporation and manufactured Maytag brand washing machines and dryers in its Newton plant. It also marketed Maytag brand cooking products made by the Magic Chef and Jenn-Air Companies, a refrigerator line manufactured by Admiral Company, and dishwashers manufactured by the Jackson manufacturing facility. Market emphasis was on the premium price segment and the upscale home builders' market.

EXHIBIT 13.3

Share of U.S. Market Compared to Market Leaders' Share by Major Home Appliance Category in 1992: Maytag Corporation

Appliance Category	Market Leader	Leader Share	Maytag Share	Maytag Rank
Disposers	In-Sink-Erator	65%	2%	4
Dishwashers	General Electric	40	8	4
Dryers, electric	Whirlpool	52	15	3
Dryers, gas	Whirlpool	53	17	2
Freezers	Frigidaire	76	—	—
Microwave Ovens	Sharp	20	6	7
Ranges, electric	General Electric	30	17	3
Ranges, gas	Maytag	27	27	1
Refrigerators	General Electric	35	13	4
Washers	Whirlpool	52	17	3

Source: *Appliance Manufacturer* (February 1993), pp. 18–21.

A survey of Americans found the Maytag brand to be fifteenth in a list of the strongest brand names based on consumer recognition and perception of quality.[9]

Named President in June 1989 after then-President Leonard Hadley had been promoted to Corporate Executive Vice-President, Richard Haines developed a mission statement for the Maytag Company: *To provide our customers with products of unsurpassed performance that last longer, need fewer repairs, and are produced at the lowest possible cost.* Now the core unit of a larger corporation, Maytag Company was striving not only to produce the industry's most dependable appliances, but also to develop products that were uniquely Maytag. According to Haines:

> It is very important that our products retain their Maytag identities. Our goal is to generate additional business, not to take business away from our sister companies, so we avoid taking products made at these plants and simply putting our label on them. A Maytag refrigerator, for example, is a high featured unit, unlike any others produced by Admiral. . . . Quality has gotten us to where we are today, and we have to make sure it continues to carry us into the future.[10]

The company sold Maytag and Admiral brand appliances through more than 9,000 retail dealers in the United States and Canada. A relatively small number of appliances were sold overseas through Maytag Corporation's international sales arm, Maytag International. Maytag appliances were also sold through Montgomery Ward, but not through Sears. According to Leonard Hadley, Maytag Company refused to join the Sears Brand Central concept because it did not want to antagonize its carefully nurtured dealers. Maytag dealers accepted distribution through Montgomery Ward because Ward had not traditionally been as dominant a force in appliance retailing as had Sears with its strong Kenmore brand. Maytag dealers, in turn, were very loyal and appreciated the company's emphasis on qual-

Maycor Appliance Parts and Service Company

Headquartered in Cleveland, Tennessee, Maycor handled all parts and service for Maytag Corporation appliance brands. The recently consolidated and automated warehouse facility in Milan, Tennessee, replaced the four separate parts distribution operations of Maytag, Admiral, Jenn-Air, and Magic Chef.

Hoover North America

Founded in 1875 in what is now North Canton, Ohio, Hoover Company originally manufactured sweepers as a sideline to its leather business. In 1908, Murray Spangler, a cousin of the founder's wife, invented the first vacuum cleaner. Like Maytag, Hoover established dealerships throughout the United States with salesmen who would demonstrate the product in a potential customer's home. By 1912, the vacuum cleaner sideline was producing 3,926 units and had become the primary business of the company.

In contrast to Maytag, however, Hoover successfully went international early in its existence. Demand for vacuum cleaners in Ontario, Canada, led Hoover to establish a manufacturing plant in Hamilton in 1920. The British Empire at that time had the slogan "Buy Empire" and correspondingly low import tariffs for members of the Empire. Cleaners with a "Made in Canada" label were welcomed in Great Britain. From Britain, it was a simple matter to ship to other parts of the British Empire and to Holland, France, and Germany. By 1937, however, Great Britain changed its slogan to "Buy British." Frank Hoover, a son of the founder, built a plant west of London to support expanding European demand. To market the sweepers, Hoover introduced the "hire-purchase" plan, the British equivalent to America's buying on installments.[17]

Headquartered in North Canton, Ohio, Hoover North America manufactured and marketed (to all price segments) upright and canister vacuum cleaners, stick and hand-held vacuum cleaners, disposable vacuum cleaner bags, floor polishers and shampooers, central cleaning systems, and commercial vacuum cleaners. Hoover also sold washing machines in Mexico. It heavily advertised to the consumer. In addition to the North Canton headquarters and three Stark County, Ohio, manufacturing plants, Hoover North America controlled four other facilities—in El Paso, Texas, Ciudad Juarez, Mexico (a maquiladora assembly plant), Burlington, Ontario (Hoover Canada), and Industrial Vallejo, Mexico (Hoover Mexicana).

In the United States, Hoover held a 34% market share of the residential vacuum cleaner market and a 58% share of the floor polisher market. It was the market leader in both categories in 1992 with almost twice the sales of its nearest competitor. Eureka (now part of A.B. Electrolux of Sweden) was second in 1992 cleaner sales, with a U.S. market share of 16%. Regina (now part of Electrolux Corporation of Marietta, Georgia, not to be confused with A.B. Electrolux of Sweden) was second in floor polisher sales in 1992 with a U.S. market share of 33%. Growth in the U.S. floor care market exceeded that of many other appliance segments. Almost 18 million vacuum cleaners were sold in 1992, and continued growth was predicted. Over 97% of U.S. households had at least one vacuum cleaner, and many had two or three full size vacuums plus hand-held vacuums. Like those of major appliances, the average life expectancies of floor polishers and vacuum cleaners exceeded 10 years. Surprisingly, 70 dealers accounted for approximately 80% of Hoover's floor care sales. In light of this fact, Hoover restructured its sales organization in 1992 to better serve these "power retailers." It continued to maintain service to its small dealers through a telemarketing division.[18]

Facing an upsurge in competition—especially from Japanese manufacturers—in the mid 1980s, Hoover's management developed a five-year plan to maintain its market dominance. In effect, the company planned to replace all of Hoover's floor care lines and drastically upgrade its manufacturing facilities. The company already was almost totally vertically integrated. Hoover built maquiladora twin plants in Juarez and El Paso to make the Quick Broom II, a stick vacuum, and the Sprint and Tempo compact canister cleaners. The North Canton plant was redesigned at a cost of $38 million to manufacture the new Elite line of upright vacuum cleaners to replace the low- to mid-priced segments of Hoover's 30-year old Convertible line. Praised by industry experts as one of the best manufacturing facilities in the United States, the new North Canton "factory within a factory" had been designed by an interdisciplinary team to reduce costs and improve quality. According to Keith Minton, Hoover's Vice-President of Manufacturing, quality was higher than at any time in the company's history—in large part because of facility automation.

Meanwhile, competition was not standing still in floor care products. Electrolux Corporation of Marietta, Georgia, automated its plants and in 1989 purchased The Regina Company. A.B. Electrolux of Sweden acquired Eureka brand floor care products when it purchased White Consolidated Industries (WCI) in 1986. Whirlpool Corporation arranged a joint venture in 1990 with Matsushita Electric Industrial Company Ltd. The venture was to own and operate Whirlpool's manufacturing plant in Danville, Kentucky, to provide vacuums for Sears. Matsushita was expected to use the Kentucky facilities to expand its manufacturing and marketing base in North America.[19]

Hoover Europe

Overseas, where nearly 70% of its total revenues had been generated prior to joining Maytag, Hoover had become successful, in manufacturing and marketing not only upright and canister vacuum cleaners, but also (especially in Great Britain and Australia) washing machines, dryers, refrigerators, dishwashers, and microwave ovens. Headquartered in Merthyr Tydfil, South Wales, Hoover Europe manufactured washers, dryers, and dishwashers in a nearby factory. It also produced upright vacuum cleaners, motors for washers and dryers, and disposable vacuum cleaner bags in a facility at Cambuslang (near Glasgow), Scotland. Although Americans were split almost equally in their preference for canister and upright vacuums, the British preferred uprights and the rest of Europeans preferred canisters. Hoover Europe marketed its products in the mid-priced segment of European markets.

British consumers accounted for 75% of Hoover's $600 million European sales.[20] Although Hoover vacuum cleaners were big sellers in continental Europe, its major appliances were not. This concentration in Great Britain became a serious problem for Hoover in the late 1980s and early 1990s when a combination of a recession and high interest rates sharply reduced Hoover's European sales. In terms of market share, Hoover's position in the key major appliances during 1991 in the United Kingdom is shown below:

Washers		Dryers		Dishwashers	
G.D.A.	66%	Crosslee	48%	G.D.A.	68%
Hoover	34	G.D.A.	47	Hoover	19
		Hoover	5	Candy	13

When the market share figures from the United Kingdom, France, Italy, Spain, Scandinavia, and Germany were consolidated, however, Hoover's position dropped considerably—to 2.8% in washers, 1.6% in dryers, and 0.9% in dishwashers.[21] According to Leonard Hadley in a 1992 interview, "Our white goods position in Europe is what needs work." With only $600 million in revenues, Hoover Europe was at a significant disadvantage against established European competitors such as A.B. Electrolux ($3.9 billion in revenues), Whirlpool ($2.25 billion), and GE/GEC ($1 billion).[22]

Although Hoover's North American operations always have been very profitable, Hoover Europe has not shown a profit since being acquired by Maytag. Unknown to Maytag Corporation's top management before the acquisition, Hoover's U.K. facilities were in desperate need of renovation and the product line needed to be upgraded. Some weaknesses at the South Wales plant were apparent before the purchase, but the corporation was too preoccupied with learning about the vacuum cleaner business to investigate further. South Wales "concerned me the least," explained then-CEO Daniel Krumm.[23] After recognizing the need to modernize the U.K. facilities, Maytag Corporation committed $25 million to renovate the laundry and dishwasher plant in South Wales. This investment was in addition to Hoover's in its Scotland floor care plant. To oversee the renovation and to improve efficiency, Maytag Corporation sent a task force to the South Wales plant in October 1990. By 1993, Hoover Europe had cut 700 jobs, combined marketing offices, and put operations in the United Kingdom, France, and Portugal under a single head office in Wales. Although some former executives talked of a culture clash between the collegial Hoover and the more rigid Maytag executives, CEO Leonard Hadley blamed Hoover's woes purely on the poor business environment.[24]

Hoover Australia

Hoover Australia was divided into two parts. Hoover Pty, Ltd, was located near Sydney and manufactured vacuum cleaners, washers, and dryers. Hoover Appliances Ltd produced refrigerators and freezers near Melbourne. The Melbourne plant had earlier been purchased from Philips and was producing Admiral and Norge refrigerators in addition to the Hoover brand. Maytag Corporation was considering the possibility of manufacturing Admiral and/or Norge laundry equipment at the Sydney plant. Hoover Australia marketed its products in the mid-priced segment of the Australian and New Zealand markets.

Dixie-Narco

Dixie-Narco, Inc., was a subsidiary of Maytag Corporation that made canned and bottled soft drink and juice vending machines that it sold to soft drink syrup bottlers and distributors, canteen owners, and others. Headquartered in Williston, South Carolina, the group manufactured vending machines in its factory there. It also had an Electronics Division (previously called Ardac, Inc.) outside Cleveland in Eastlake, Ohio. The Eastlake facility made dollar bill acceptors, changers, and foreign currency acceptors for soft drink vending machines. In 1990, a year after Maytag Corporation had decided to stop manufacturing home freezers and compact refrigerators, Dixie-Narco had spent $31 million to convert the Admiral freezer and refrigerator factory in Williston into its new headquarters. Dixie-Narco's president, Gerald Kamman, referred to the Williston facility as "the largest and most highly automated vending machine producing facility of its type in the country—and probably in the world."[25] The Maytag Corporation had decided to stop manufacturing home freezers and compact refrigerators in 1989 because of declining profit margins and low sales and to buy what they needed from others.

According to Douglas C. Huffer, Sales and Marketing Director of Domestic Operations, Dixie-Narco's management believed that the company provided the best value in vending in the industry, not only in terms of high quality and reliability, but also through manufacturing expertise and a good support network. The company sold vending equipment directly to independent bottlers and full-service operators who installed banks of vending machines in offices and factories. It also marketed through bottlers directly to company-owned syrup bottlers.

According to Maytag Corporation management, although sales of vending machines continued to be relatively flat during 1992, the company had been able to increase its share of the U.S. market owing to strong demand for Dixie-Narco products. International vending growth was slower than anticipated—especially in Europe where customers were not accustomed to purchasing soft drinks from a machine. Sales of the Dixie-Narco bill validator set a new high in 1992, generating increased production levels at the Eastlake factory.

Corporate Culture

Impact of F. L. Maytag

Much of Maytag Corporation's corporate culture derived from F. L. Maytag's personal philosophy and lessons the founder learned when starting the Maytag Company at the turn of the century. Orville Butler, Maytag archivist, and Ronald Krajnovich, Maytag Company's Public Relations Director, identified several areas in which F. L. Maytag had made a direct impact on the Maytag Company's development and on the corporation's philosophy of management. These were (1) commitment to quality, (2) concern for employees, (3) concern for the community, (4) concern for innovation, (5) promotion from within, (6) dedication to hard work, and (7) emphasis on performance.

- *Commitment to Quality.* In the company's first year of operation as the Parsons Band Cutter and Self Feeder Company, almost half the products sold were defective in some way. In F. L. Maytag's words, "It was then that we learned that *nothing was actually 'sold' until it was in the hands of a satisfied user,* no matter if it had been paid for." His insistence on fixing or purchasing back the faulty products resulted in losses for the new company. Maytag's employees over the years have taken great pride in the company's reputation for high-quality products.
- *Concern for Employees.* Long before they were required by law, Maytag Company established safety standards in the workplace and offered its employees accident and life insurance policies. Wages have traditionally been some of the highest in the industry. F. L. Maytag's philosophy was that an "uncommonly good company wants to pay its employees uncommonly well."
- *Concern for the Community.* F. L. Maytag played a significant role in the development of the Newton YMCA. He also built a water plant and sold it back to the city at cost. He served on the City Council and as Mayor in addition to serving as an Iowa State Senator. Following his example, Maytag management has been active in community affairs and concerned about pollution. Maytag's decision to build its new automatic washer plant in Newton after World War II indicated the company's loyalty to the town.
- *Concern for Innovation.* From its earliest years, the company had not been interested in cosmetic changes for the sake of sales, but in internal improvements related to quality, durability, and safety. This orientation dominated the company's view of product development. One example was the careful way the company chose to replace the venerable helical drive transmission with a new Dependable Drive™ transmission for its automatic washers in 1989. The new drive was delivered in 1975, patented in 1983, and put into test market in 1985 after testing showed that the drive would contribute to a 20-year product life. The Dependable Drive contained only 40 parts, compared to the previous drive's 65, and allowed the agitator to move 153 strokes a minute, compared to only 64 previously.
- *Promotion from Within.* F. L. Maytag was concerned about building company loyalty and trust and committed to hiring and training people to do the best work possible. He constantly told people, "I'd rather make men than money . . . and I would because I can give money away; I can't give men away; I need them." This orientation was evidenced by the fact that a majority of the corporation's top management had begun their careers with Maytag Company.
- *Dedication to Hard Work.* In tune with the strong work ethic permeating the Midwest, F. L. Maytag worked huge amounts of time to establish and maintain the company. His fabled trip West, while Chairman of the Board, to personally sell a train-car load of washers set an example to his sales force and became a permanent part of company lore.
- *Emphasis on Performance.* F. L. Maytag did not like to boast about himself or his company, preferring to be judged by his work rather than by his words.

The Maytag "Family" of Companies

In 1993, the Maytag Corporation still reflected its strong roots in the Maytag Company culture molded by founder F. L. Maytag. The corporate headquarters were housed on the second floor of a relatively small building (compared to Maytag Company's Plant 1 and the Research and Development building surrounding it). Built in 1961, the Newton, Iowa, building still housed Maytag Company administrative offices on the first floor. Responding to a question in 1990 regarding a comment from outside observers that the corporation had "spartan" offices, Leonard Hadley, then-Chief Operating Officer, looked around at his rather small, windowless office and said, "See for yourself. We want to keep corporate staff to a minimum." Hadley believed that the headquarters location and the fact that most of the corporate officers had come from Maytag Company resulted in an overall top management concern for quality and financially conservative management. This belief supported then-CEO Daniel Krumm's position that the corporation's competitive edge was its *dedication to quality*. According to Krumm, "We believe quality and reliability are, ultimately, what the consumer wants."[26] This devotion to quality was exemplified by a corporate policy that no cost reduction proposal would be approved if it reduced product quality in any way.[27]

A corporate publication referred to the designing and manufacturing of the Maytag refrigerator as "a perfect example of how Maytag Corporation's family of companies can work together toward a common goal."[28] Under the direction of Leonard Hadley, while he was serving as Maytag Company President, the project combined Admiral's engineering expertise in refrigeration with Maytag Company's manufacturing and quality skills. When Hadley first visited Admiral's facilities in Galesburg, Illinois, to discuss the design of a Maytag line of refrigerators, there was some concern in Newton that the Admiral plant might not be able to produce the level of quality needed for Maytag products. When Admiral personnel asked Hadley when the name on the plant water tower would be changed from Admiral to Maytag, Hadley responded, "When you earn it."

The refrigerator resulting from the Maytag-Admiral collaboration was a huge success. The project crystallized corporate management's philosophy for forging synergies among the Maytag companies, while simultaneously allowing the expertise among those units to flourish.

Human Resources and Labor Relations

At the beginning of 1993, the total number of Maytag Corporation employees was 20,140 in home appliances and 1,137 in vending equipment. This total of 21,277 employees was significantly less than the 26,019 employees in 1989 after the Hoover acquisition, but considerably more than the 12,913 employees in 1988 before the Hoover purchase. Throughout the corporation, employees were organized into various labor unions. The bargaining unit representing Maytag Company unionized employees in Newton was the United Auto Workers (UAW). The unions representing employees at other U.S. Maytag Corporation companies were the Sheet Metal Workers International Association (Jenn-Air), the International Brotherhood of Electrical Workers (Hoover North America), and the International

Association of Machinists and Aerospace Workers (Magic Chef). All the presidents of union locals belonged to a Maytag Council, which met once a year to discuss union issues.

Traditionally, the Maytag Company had maintained cordial relations with its local union, but the change to a large corporation seemed to alter that relationship. When asked about the often-heard remark that there were two kinds of people in Newton—those who worked at Maytag and those who wished they did—Lonnie White, President of UAW Local 997 in Newton, commented, "It has been a very good place to work. My son also works at Maytag." Regarding wages and benefits, White said Maytag Company was comparable to none. White felt, however, that there had been a change in tone of the relationship between labor and management since 1989. Management now seemed more formal and less flexible. Somewhat ruefully, White summed up the situation: "We're no longer dealing with Mother Maytag. Now we're dealing with a corporation."

Nevertheless, the corporation has not had any strikes with any of its unions since a one-day affair at Maytag Company in 1974. This record is worthy of note considering that during the three-year period 1990–1992 the corporation had reduced employment by 4,500 people. There was, however, significant employee unhappiness in Newton when top management decided in 1990 to move the manufacturing of dishwashers to a new location in Jackson, Tennessee. The three-year contract signed in 1992 with Newton's UAW Local 997 encouraged increased involvement of employees in matters affecting their work.[29]

Financial Situation

By the time of the shareholders meeting on April 27, 1993, most of the corporation's shareholders knew how much the company had changed since the days when Maytag sold washing machines only as a sideline. Most appreciated management's attempts to build the company. A significant number were concerned, however, that the corporation no longer had the best profit margin in the industry. Most knowledgeable investors knew that return on equity has been a weakness of the corporation since it first embarked on the strategy of growth through acquisitions. According to a recent article in *Financial World,* "Return on equity was more than 25% before the Magic Chef merger in 1986, peaked at over 30% in 1988, and was nearly halved to 18.3% in 1989 after the Chicago Pacific acquisition. . . . and by 1991 Maytag was earning just 8% on equity."[30] 1993 marked the first time since the 1920s that the annual report showed a net loss.

The Shareholders' Meeting

Now, sitting in the Newton High School auditorium, the shareholders await the chairman's explanation of Maytag's relatively poor financial performance. They especially want to know what is wrong with Hoover Europe, the unit that, according to some analysts, seems to be sucking Maytag dry. Chairman Hadley pauses after his introductory remarks and looks out over the audience before he moves to probably what would be the most controversial topic of the meeting.

The Hoover Fiasco

From August 1992 through January 1993, Hoover Europe had run promotions to increase sales of its appliances. Under the plan, customers in Great Britain and the Irish Republic who bought Hoover appliances for as little as $150 to $375 were eligible for a pair of round-trip tickets to destinations in either Europe or the United States. The programs had been arranged in cooperation with two travel agencies. The agencies were to obtain low-cost "space available" tickets and would help Hoover support the expense by earning commissions on "land packages," such as car rental and hotels at the destination. However, a bigger than expected response, coupled with a much smaller than anticipated "fall-out" rate of purchasers who for one reason or another failed to meet the requirements of the promotions, overwhelmed the promotions. Realizing that the tickets were worth more than the appliances, some 200,000 people bought appliances and filled out forms seeking tickets—thus creating a monstrous paperwork "bottleneck." In addition, the travel agencies' sale of land packages was "far below expectations" and had the result of "greatly reducing support money" for the seriously underfunded promotions. The costs ran $49 million over budget! Customers were outraged at Hoover's slowness to honor its obligations. London's *Daily Mail* reported that some British Labour Party politicians were calling for the government's Minister of Consumer Affairs to resign for failing to investigate the promotion sooner. The corporation fired two top executives of Hoover Europe: William Foust, President (Maytag Corporation's Senior-Vice President of Human Resources until 1991) and Brian Webb, Vice-President of Marketing.[31]

Hadley spends little time summarizing what happened. It is obviously a painful memory for him.

> I'm sure you've all read and heard more than you care to about this subject, so I'll be brief. Essentially, Hoover Europe got involved in two very poorly designed free-flight programs, and the travel agencies Hoover contracted with couldn't hold up their end of the agreements. This was a risk to Hoover that should have been covered, and it wasn't.
>
> We publicly acknowledged the Hoover Europe problem; we replaced the top management people who were accountable; we put a task force in place to solve the problem, and we committed $30 million (after tax) to help ensure that Hoover customers who were qualified for a free flight would get just that. We have announced in the British press today the block purchase of seats on 11 airlines—on over 1,100 flights over the next six months.

Results for 1992

As the Chairman moves on to the 1992 results, shareholders who brought the *1992 Annual Report* to the meeting are turning to the section containing Maytag's financial statements (see Exhibits 13.4–13.7). Sales were up slightly from 1991. According to Hadley, earnings were down because of continued losses in Europe, costs associated with new production facilities, intense price competition, and sluggish economic conditions. Raw materials costs had not increased significantly during the year. He then points to the corporation's achievements. Unit shipments of the five core products—washers, dryers, dishwashers, refrigerators, and cooking appliances—were strong in North America, and the corporation gained market share overall in core appliances. During 1992, Jenn-Air reduced product development time and Magic Chef introduced new products. The year was a challenging one for Hoover North America because competitors introduced more new products in a six-month period than they had in the previous two years combined. Dixie-Narco improved its performance in 1992, primarily because of stronger demand for its products in the United States.

Strategic Planning

Continuing his speech to the Maytag shareholders, Hadley moves from financial results to the corporation's strategy—a topic that in recent years has dominated top management's attention. Hadley states that the corporation's successful brands are a result of its collective competencies in floor care, laundry, cooking, refrigeration, vending, and commercial appliances. Referring to the various companies that are now a part of Maytag Corporation, Hadley states:

> It's not Maytag *Company,* or Jenn-Air *Company,* or Magic Chef *Company,* or Hoover or Admiral anymore. Those independent companies, as many of us knew them just over a decade ago, undoubtedly would not have survived on their own in this day of the mega-retailer with the buying clout they now have. Dealer base consolidation in the last five years has been amazingly rapid, and none of these short-line manufacturers could meet their needs.
>
> We all exist as a family today because Maytag Corporation pulled these historically great companies together under one shield. We are alive and well; we have preserved our strong brands; improved our products and invested in our people—and we are appliance people. We are not owned by an irrelevant conglomerate, and we are marching steadily forward. Although we now have substantial debt and have incurred a number of special financial charges over the past couple of years, we remain a financially sound corporation.
>
> As we've changed, I know you shareholders have suffered. Additionally, a number of employees have been displaced. In fact, in the last three years, we've reduced employment by 4,500; we've closed plants, delayed salary increases twice and reduced bonuses. . . . Also, I would add that despite disruptions brought about by change, I firmly believe that our underlying strategy is right, our management team is strong and there will be brighter days for us ahead.

Hadley was referring to the strategic plan that management had developed to take Maytag Corporation through the 1990s. Such a plan was quite a change from just 16 years earlier when "strategic planning" meant preparing the next year's budget!

Beginning of Strategic Planning

In 1978, when Leonard Hadley was working as Maytag Company's Assistant Controller (he had joined the company in 1959 as a cost accountant), CEO Daniel Krumm asked him and two others from manufacturing and marketing to serve as

EXHIBIT 13.4

Statement of Consolidated Income: Maytag Corporation

(Dollar amounts in thousands, except per share data)

Years Ending December 31	1992	1991	1990	1989[1]	1988	1987
Net sales	$3,041,223	$2,970,626	$3,056,833	$3,088,753	$1,885,641	$1,822,106
Cost of sales	2,339,406	2,254,221	2,309,138	2,312,645	1,413,627	1,318,122
Gross profit	701,817	716,405	747,695	776,108	472,014	503,984
Selling, general/ administrative expenses	528,250	524,898	517,088	496,165	—	—
Reorganization expenses	95,000	—	—	—	—	—
Operating income	78,567	191,507	230,607	279,943	226,207	255,373
Interest expense	(75,004)	(75,159)	(81,966)	(83,398)	(19,738)	(10,788)
Other—net	3,983	7,069	10,764	10,427	8,753	8,393
Income before income taxes and accounting changes	7,546	123,417	159,405	206,972	215,222	252,978
Income taxes	15,900	44,400	60,500	75,500	79,700	105,300
Income before accounting changes	(8,354)	79,017	98,905	131,472	135,522	147,678
Effect of accounting changes for postretirement benefits	(307,000)	—	—	—	—	—
Income from discontinued operations	—	—	—	—	23,040	5,025
Net income (loss)	$(315,354)	$79,017	98,905	$131,472	$158,562	$152,703
Average number of shares of common stock	106,077,000	105,761,000	105,617,000	103,694,000	76,563,000	80,151,000
Per share data						
Income (loss) before accounting changes	$(.08)	$.75	$.94	$1.27	$1.77	$1.84
Effect of accounting changes	(2.89)	—	—	—	—	—
Net income (loss) per share	$(2.97)	$.75	$.94	$1.27	$2.07	$1.91

Note: 1. 1989 numbers reflect the acquisition of Hoover on January 25, 1989.

Source: Maytag Corporation, *1992 Annual Report,* p. 23; Maytag Corporation, *1989 Annual Report,* p. 25.

EXHIBIT 13.5

Statements of Consolidated Financial Condition: Maytag Corporation

(Dollar amounts in thousands)

Years Ending December 31	**1992**	**1991**	**1990**	**1989[1]**	**1988**
Assets					
Current assets					
Cash and cash equivalents	$ 57,032	$ 48,752	$ 69,587	$ 39,261	$ 10,503
Accounts receivable, less allowance—(1992, $16,380; 1991, $14,119; 1990,$17,600; 1989, $8,730; 1988, $3,820)	476,850	457,773	487,726	502,992	250,299
Inventories—finished goods	249,289	314,493	335,417	336,721	135,581
Inventories—raw materials, in process, supplies	151,794	174,589	200,370	210,196	127,124
Deferred income taxes	52,261	24,858	22,937	34,594	33,876
Other current assets	28,309	56,168	52,484	15,938	6,251
Total current assets	1,015,535	1,076,633	1,168,521	1,139,702	563,634
Noncurrent assets					
Marketable securities	—	—	—	9,488	11,045
Deferred income taxes	71,442	—	—	—	—
Pension investments	215,433	232,231	235,264	185,693	26,020
Investment in Chicago Pacific Corporation	—	—	—	—	384,561
Intangibles less allowance for amortization (1992, $37,614; 1991, $28,295; 1990, $18,980; 1989, $9,737)	328,980	338,275	347,090	356,309	—
Miscellaneous	35,989	52,436	45,209	38,794	29,640
Total noncurrent assets	651,844	622,942	627,563	590,284	451,266

(continued)

EXHIBIT 13.5

Statements of Consolidated Financial Condition: Maytag Corporation *(continued)*
(Dollar amounts in thousands)

Years Ending December 31	**1992**	**1991**	**1990**	**1989**[1]	**1988**
Property, plant and equipment					
Land	47,370	51,147	50,613	51,941	7,737
Buildings and improvements	286,368	296,684	282,828	256,727	143,576
Machinery and equipment	962,006	895,025	828,464	713,688	399,050
Construction in progress	90,847	92,954	61,775	47,921	71,803
	1,386,591	1,335,810	1,223,680	1,070,277	622,166
Less allowances for depreciation	552,480	500,317	433,223	363,944	306,997
Total property, plant and equipment	834,111	835,493	790,457	706,333	315,169
Total assets	$2,501,490	$2,535,068	$2,586,541	$2,436,319	$1,330,069
Liabilities and Shareowners' Equity					
Current liabilities					
Notes payable	$ 19,886	$ 23,504	$ 56,601	$ 68,713	$ 7,700
Accounts payable	218,142	273,731	266,190	179,496	101,379
Compensation to employees	89,245	63,845	53,753	60,312	31,649
Accrued liabilities	180,894	165,384	154,369	158,198	77,621
Income taxes payable	11,323	17,574	13,736	5,486	21,491
Current maturities of long-term debt	43,419	23,570	11,070	16,592	6,649
Total current liabilities	562,909	567,608	555,719	488,797	246,489
Noncurrent liabilities					
Deferred income taxes	89,011	75,210	71,548	60,434	52,260
Long-term debt	789,232	809,480	857,941	876,836	518,165
Postretirement benefits other than pensions	380,376	—	—	—	—
Other noncurrent liabilities	80,737	72,185	86,602	72,055	11,677
Total noncurrent liabilities	1,339,356	956,875	1,016,091	1,009,325	582,102

Shareowners' equity					
Common stock					
Authorized—200,000,000 shares (par value $1.25)					
Issued—117,150,593 shares in treasury; 89,674,506 shares (1988)	146,438	146,438	146,438	146,438	112,093
Additional paid-in capital	478,463	479,833	487,034	488,137	41,022
Retained earnings	328,122	696,745	670,878	672,359	640,819
Cost of common stock in treasury					
(1992—10,545,915 shares; 1991—10,808,116 shares; 1990—11,424,154 shares; 1989—11,586,073 shares; 1988—13,094,035 shares)	(234,993)	(240,848)	(254,576)	(258,356)	(291,115)
Employee stock plans	(65,638)	(66,711)	(63,590)	(67,117)	(1,341)
Foreign currency translation	(53,167)	(4,872)	(28,547)	(43,264)	—
Total shareowners' equity	599,225	1,010,585	1,014,731	938,197	501,478
Total liabilities and shareowners' equity	$2,501,490	$2,535,068	$2,586,541	$2,436,319	$1,330,069
Number of employees	21,407	22,533	24,273	26,019	12,913
Stock price/share (high-low)	$21–$13	$17–$10	$21–$10	$27–$19	$27–$19

Note: 1. 1989 numbers reflect the acquisition of Hoover on January 26, 1989.

Source: Maytag Corporation, *1992 Annual Report,* pp. 24–25; *1991 Annual Report,* pp. 26–27; *1989 Annual Report,* pp. 26–27.

Geographic Information: Maytag Corporation
(Dollar amounts in thousands)

Years Ending December 31	1992	1991	1990	1989
Net sales[1]				
North America	$2,407,591	$2,332,365	$2,403,779	$2,545,230
Europe	501,857	495,517	496,672	396,859
Other	131,775	142,744	156,382	146,664
Total	$3,041,223	$2,970,626	$3,056,833	$3,088,753
Income (loss) before taxes and effect of accounting changes				
North America	$ 145,991	$ 190,820	$ 246,182	$ 299,777
Europe	(67,061)	(865)	(22,863)	(8,612)
Other	(51)	1,561	8,548	9,607
Corporate (excluding interest expense)	(71,333)	(68,099)	(72,462)	(93,800)
Total	$ 7,546	$ 123,417	$ 159,405	$ 206,972
Identifiable assets				
North America	$1,677,131	$1,681,304	$1,679,599	$1,685,843
Europe	452,995	507,746	562,690	450,835
Other	109,954	130,929	130,480	133,275
Corporate	261,410	215,089	213,772	166,366
Total	$2,501,490	$2,535,068	$2,586,541	$2,436,319

Note:
1. Sales between affiliates of different geographic regions are not significant. The amount of exchange gain or loss included in operations in any one of the years presented was not material. The corporation incurred $95 million of reorganization expenses for marketing and distribution changes in North America and plant closings and other organizational changes in Europe in 1992. Of the $95 million allocated to Home Appliances, $40 million was allocated to North America and $55 million to Europe.

Source: Maytag Corporation, *1992 Annual Report,* p. 38; *1991 Annual Report,* p. 38.

a strategic planning task force. Krumm posed a question: "*If we keep doing what we're now doing, what will the Maytag Company look like in five years?*" The question was a challenge to answer—the company had never done financial modeling, and none of the three assigned the task knew much about strategic planning. Hadley worked with a programmer in his MIS section to develop "what if" scenarios. The task force presented its conclusion to the board of directors: A large part of Maytag's profits (the company had the best profit margin in the industry) were coming from products and services with no future. These were repair parts, portable washers and dryers, and wringer washing machines.

Looking back, Hadley felt that 1978 had been a crucial time for the company. The Board of Directors was becoming less conservative as more outside directors

EXHIBIT 13.7

Principal Business Groups: Maytag Corporation
(Dollar amounts in thousands)

Performance	North American Appliances	Vending Equipment	European Appliances
1992			
Sales	$2,242,270	$165,321	$501,857
Operating income	129,680	16,311	(67,061)
1991			
Sales	2,182,567	149,798	495,517
Operating income	186,322	4,498	(865)
1990			
Sales	2,212,335	191,444	496,672
Operating income	221,164	25,018	(22,863)

Source: Maytag Corporation, *1992 Annual Report,* p. 1; *1991 Annual Report,* p. 1.

came from companies that were growing through acquisitions. With the support of the board, Krumm promoted Hadley to the new position of Vice-President of Corporate Planning. Hadley was given the task of analyzing the industry to search for acquisition candidates. Until then, most planning had been internal, with little external analysis.

The Planning Process

After helping Maytag acquire Hardwick, Jenn-Air, and Magic Chef, Hadley was promoted in 1986 to Maytag Company President. His replacement as Vice-President of Planning and Business Development was Carleton F. Zacheis (pronounced ZIGH-HIGH), who had joined the company in 1958 as a trainee and served as planning associate since 1984. According to Zacheis, his was the "most creative, free-form job there is." He served with four other corporate top managers on a Strategic Issues Committee. Under Dan Krumm's leadership and with Zacheis's input, the committee did a lot of "brainstorming" throughout the year to develop a strategic proposal for the corporation. The proposal usually revolved around a strategic issue facing the firm, such as the recent topic of "synergy." At an annual summer meeting, the committee unveiled the latest strategic proposal to business unit heads and top-level corporate staff. The committee encouraged participation to question and flesh out the proposed plan. The resulting strategic plan dealt with implementation in addition to providing general direction for the corporation as a whole. The corporation's strategic plan usually had a three-year time horizon and was updated annually.

Current Strategic Plan

As the audience listened to Leonard Hadley discussing the corporation's strategic position, many of them thought back to the 1990 shareholders' meeting in which then-Chairman Daniel Krumm presented Maytag Corporation's strategic plan. In addition to stressing quality, synergy, and globalization as keys, Krumm had said:

> Increasing *profitability* is essential. . . . Our objective is to be the profitability leader in the industry for each product line we manufacture. We intend to out-perform the competition in the next five years striving for a 6.5 percent return on sales, a 10% return on assets, and a 20% return on equity. . . . However, . . . we must not emphasize market share at the expense of profitability. . . .

The basic elements of Krumm's 1990 strategic plan were still in place in 1993. As part of the corporation's emphasis on globalization, for example, Maytag had formed an alliance in September 1992 with Bosch-Siemens Hausgerate GmBH of Munich, Germany. According to Maytag, the two companies were forming a joint committee to study "opportunities for marketing each other's products. The possibilities of consolidating product distribution and service in certain geographic areas was also being considered. . . . The alliance also will develop common purchasing strategies for components and materials."[32] Herbert Worner, Bosch-Siemens' Chief Managing Director, had stated that his company would supply dishwashers to Hoover for sale in Britain and that he expected the companies to move jointly into markets where neither had much presence, such as South America, China, and Southeast Asia.[33]

In his speech, Chairman Hadley updates the strategic plan by stating, "Our collective mission is to develop world-class quality. This principle expands Maytag's long-standing belief in product quality to all aspects of our operations." He continues by presenting the corporation's three current goals:

1. Increased profitability.
2. Be number one in total customer satisfaction.
3. Grow the North American appliance business and become the 3rd largest appliance manufacturer (in unit sales) in North America.

According to Hadley, "our top goal has to be increased profitability." The principal way to achieve it would be through profitable market share growth in the core North American appliance and floor care business. "Last year, this segment accounted for about 75% of our corporatewide sales, and 98% of our operating income, before reorganization charges." A primary vehicle to boost profitability is the revised marketing structure put into place the first of this year. "We've consolidated our U.S. major appliance marketing efforts from three sales organizations to two. One direct-to-dealer sales force is handling the Maytag and Admiral brands, while the other one sells our Jenn-Air and Magic Chef lines to builders and retailers. Having sales organizations go directly to retail dealers with both a high-end and a middle price brand makes a lot of sense." Jenn-Air products thus would be sold through Magic Chef dealers instead of through independent distributors. Hoover North America's field sales force is also being reorganized and reduced to give more attention to the large retailers. The corporation took a $40 million charge during 1992 to cover these marketing and distribution changes as well as a $55 million charge for the European reorganization. To boost Hoover Europe's profitability, the corporation is phasing out the Dijon, France, plant and taking a large charge against earnings. Pointing to the large amount of investment by the corporation over the past five years in new plants, renovations, and new product development, Hadley asserts that "we not only have the best sales and marketing organization we've ever had, we have the strongest product lines the corporation has ever had." Regarding customer satisfaction, Hadley points out that "Maytag Corporation wants all its brands to beat the competition in satisfying the customer, be that customer a dealer, builder, or end-user of the product."

Regarding growth, Hadley points out that Whirlpool currently is first in unit sales, followed by GE, Frigidaire (the former White Consolidated Group owned by Electrolux), Maytag, and Raytheon. "I know our profits exceed the current third place player, but in total unit shipments in a year, we aren't quite in third place."

Questions from the Shareholders

Reaching the end of his prepared remarks, Chairman Hadley looks up from the podium and states, "The meeting is now open for questions." As people slowly raise their hands, ushers with microphones move rapidly throughout the auditorium to get into position. A shareholder asks what steps the corporation is taking to ensure that the Hoover fiasco doesn't happen again. Are more controls needed or should the divisions still have autonomy? The Chairman responds that he is confident that dismissing executives was appropriate but that the question of controls versus autonomy is under review.

Raised hands are now appearing throughout the auditorium, indicating shareholder concern about the management of their company. An angry shareholder from Des Moines poses two questions that would be reported in the *Des Moines Register* the next day: "How long will it be before earnings get back to the 1988 level of $1.77 per share from continuing operations?" and "why should we have any confidence in your answer, given the performance of the past five years?" Murmurs and sporadic clapping sweep through the audience. Obviously uncomfortable with such antagonistic questions, the Chairman responds by pointing out that Maytag is a very different corporation from the one in 1988. The business environment and customer base have changed dramatically. A return to those levels would take a shift in market conditions. That type of change is unlikely for the balance of the decade, predicts Hadley. "During the years 1983–1988 we were able to charge more money than the year before for the Maytag brand. 1989 was the last year of a Maytag brand price increase. Actually, the average selling price is going down. We are unlikely for the balance of this decade to have price increases." Hadley does not attempt to answer the second question.

A question is raised regarding Whirlpool's "Quality Express" by which the company is using sophisticated logistics and information systems to improve service to its dealers. The shareholder points out that Whirlpool is using dedicated trucks, personnel, and warehousing to deliver appliances to 90% of all dealer and builder customers within 24 hours, and 100% within 48 hours. Hadley responds that "all of our competitors are embracing this kind of approach." (General Electric had introduced a similar service during 1992.) He adds that this approach is included in Maytag Corporation's ongoing North American reorganization projects to improve logistics, MIS, and customer service. "It's in process. We are responding to it. Whirlpool will still have to deal with us," concludes Hadley.

A shareholder from the back of the room stands to address the chairman. "I'm not a happy camper," she begins. "For five years, earnings have been constantly down. What can we do to boost profits? Also, why are there no Maytags at home shows? Why are Maytag appliances so expensive? Is the price justified? Is a Maytag really that much better?" Choosing to respond first to the home-show part of the question, Hadley explains that in the building industry, relationships are built over time. He further reports from memory that the percentages of new homes that include major appliances are: cooking appliances, 90%; dishwashers, 80%; refrigerators, 30%; and laundry appliances in the teens. "Since the Maytag brand has been traditionally weak in cooking, we have not had a strong relationship with builders. We have used other brands to do that." He further explains that "the premium for that Maytag name is a key part of our income stream. A Maytag dishwasher sells today for less (price) than 2 or 5 or even 7 years ago."

Another question focuses on marketing: "How has the corporation changed in terms of marketing and appealing to consumers? Are you aware of what consumers want? Are you too smug about your marketing approach?" The chairman responds that there is a lot of change going on in the corporation. "We have a lot of people who are very close to the customer. Elimination of Jenn-Air's distributors allows us to get closer to the retailer. This will help."

As there are no more questions, Hadley announces that the meeting will now move on to (1) the election of Ernst & Young as the auditing firm for 1993 and (2) the election of six directors (Clark, Hadley, Kapnick, Ray, Schiller, and Willmot) for three-year terms. Each is currently serving on the board. All except Kapnick, who began serving in 1989, have served continuously since 1986 or before.

Presentation on the Jenn-Air/Magic Chef Marketing Partnership

While waiting for the votes to be collected and assembled with the proxies already received, Hadley calls on Carl Moe, President of Jenn-Air, a long-time Maytag employee and the son of a Maytag employee, to describe the consolidation of Magic Chef's sales and marketing force with the Indianapolis headquarters of Jenn-Air. Moe describes how, in November 1992, Leonard Hadley came to Indianapolis to talk about the idea of merging Jenn-Air's sales into those of Magic Chef. Moe describes how the partnership approach would enable both Jenn-Air and Magic Chef to pick the best sales and marketing people from both companies, resulting in one direct sales force for both brands. This merger would be a boost to Jenn-Air, as only 25% of Magic Chef dealers were also Jenn-Air dealers. Jenn-Air's historically strong relationship with small quality builders means that these builders would now be available to Magic Chef. Moe gave the example of a California builder who agreed to put Magic Chef in his low-end homes, Jenn-Air in his high-end homes, and both in his moderately priced homes. The sales organization now has four brands to market and can cover all quality and price levels: Norge and Hardwick as the low-end brands for special opportunities; Jenn-Air as the mid-range to high-end brand with unique styling and innovative features; and Magic Chef as the mid-range to low-end brand with less innovative, but more value-oriented features.

Both Jenn-Air and Magic Chef have moved their advertising to Leo Burnett, the same agency responsible for Maytag's "lonely repairman" ads. No longer will the two brands focus only on dealer ads and promotions to market their products. Magic Chef will use some of the money it has been spending on dealer ads to run consumer-type ads to build market awareness.

Moe continues, "In 1991, we looked at ourselves and we had become a bureaucracy. It was taking too long to get products to market." A three-person task force was established with the goals of reducing the bureaucracy, developing new products with a shorter design process, and lowering costs. Jenn-Air set up what it called a "discovery center" with people from various functional areas combined in a new product team. Moe adds, "The cooking product market is expanding rapidly. Referring to the recent renovation of its Indianapolis facility, Moe asserts that "our factory is brand new." "We now have a division dedicated to selling to the builders," concludes Moe. To close, he shows a ten-minute videotape entitled, "Magic Chef and Jenn-Air: A Winning Combination."

Conclusion of the Meeting

"Thank you, Carl," remarks Leonard Hadley as he returns to the podium to present the results of the voting.

> Each of the six directors was elected. The current auditor continues. There will be a board meeting at Maytag headquarters in one-half hour [to reelect the current corporate officers]. Plant tours are available for those who would like to see how Maytag washers and dryers are made. Unless there is any further business, I hereby declare this year's meeting of shareholders adjourned.

As Hadley turns from the podium to speak with a director, people begin to head for the exits, stepping into a gray overcast day as they leave the building. The rain has stopped for the moment, but people have to sidestep puddles as they climb into the buses that will transport them to their parked cars.

A group of financial analysts compare notes as they plan for lunch at the nearby Village Inn. In 1991, one takeover investor had concluded that based on assets Maytag was worth $20 per share.[34] Maytag's common stock is currently trading at $13¼ per share. Some analysts were wondering if the corporation might soon be forced to sell Hoover or have no choice but to sell out to a competitor by the end of the decade.[35] Others are wondering whether this will be the year that Maytag finally turns things around.

Notes

1. "Maytag Has Some Explaining to Do," *Ames Daily Tribune* (April 26, 1993), p. A3.
2. Correspondence from O. R. Butler, Maytag archivist (September 24, 1990), p. 2.

3. Material on the Maytag Company's early years came from: A. B. Funk, *Fred L. Maytag: A Biography* (Cedar Rapids: Torch Press, 1936); *Maytag Company* (Newton, Iowa: Maytag Company, 1945); *Brief History of Maytag* (Newton, Iowa: Maytag Company, 1990); "3 Years and Counting," *Maytag Monthly Bulletin* (April 1990), pp. 1–6; Interview with O. R. Butler, Maytag Archivist for the Center for the Historical Studies of Technology and Science, Iowa State University (June 1, 1990).
4. C. R. Christensen, K. R. Andrews, J. L. Bower, R. G. Hamermesh, and M. E. Porter, "Note on the Major Home Appliance Industry in 1984 (Condensed)," *Business Policy,* 6th ed. (Homewood, Ill.: Irwin, 1987), p. 353.
5. "Dependability Ads Endure," Maytag Company advertising supplement to *Des Moines Register* (May 16, 1993), p. 6.
6. G. Erb, "Maytag Flexes Magic Chef Muscle; Industry Gets Brawny New Contender," *Des Moines Register* (July 26, 1986), p. 4F.
7. H. S. Byrne, "Remaking Maytag," *Barron's* (August 21, 1989), p. 12.
8. Remarks by D. J. Krumm to the East Coast Financial Community in Boston, Hartford, and Philadelphia on August 15–17, 1989, p. 3 and P. Lewine, "Maytag to Acquire Chicago Pacific," *The Weekly Home Furnishings Newspaper* (October 31, 1988), p. 112.
9. M. Ho, "Maytag Scores in Brand-Name Ranking," *Des Moines Register* (July 17, 1991), p. 5S.
10. R. Dzierwa, "Dependably Maytag," *Appliance* (June 1990), pp. M-13, M-17.
11. R. L. Rose, "Maytag's Acquisitions Don't Wear as Well as Washers and Dryers," *Wall Street Journal* (January 31, 1991), p. A6.
12. Ibid.
13. R. Dzierwa, "Cool Diligence," *Appliance* (June 1990), pp. M-49, M-51.
14. "Nelms of Magic Chef," *Appliance* (July 1992), p. 24.
15. S. Barlas, "NAFTA and Appliances," *Appliance* (April 1993), p. 16.
16. J. A. Tannenbaum, "Distributors' Links to Producers Grow More Fragile," *Wall Street Journal* (October 28, 1992), p. B2.
17. Much of the early history of The Hoover Company was taken from: Frank G. Hoover, *Fabulous Dustpan: The Story of the Hoover* (Cleveland, Ohio: World, 1955).
18. Maytag Corporation, *1992 Annual Report,* p. 10.
19. "Whirlpool, Matsushita Sign Joint Venture," *Des Moines Register* (June 6, 1990), p. 5S.
20. C. Hillinger, "Maytag and Hoover: Heaven for Housekeeping and Appliance Makers," *Los Angeles Times* (May 30, 1989), p. 3, Part IV; B. Bremner and M. Maremont, "Maytag's Foreign Fling Isn't Much Fun After All," *Business Week* (September 4, 1989), pp. 32–33.
21. "Portrait of the European Appliance Industry," *Appliance* (July 1992), pp. 41–42.
22. J. Dubashi, "Taken to the Cleaners," *Financial World* (August 4, 1992), p. 30.
23. D. Kasler, "Maytag Hunkering Down to Ride Out War, Recession," *Des Moines Register* (February 24, 1991), p. 2G.
24. K. Kelly, F. Guterl, and R. Lewald, "Can Maytag's Repairman Get Out of This Fix?" *Business Week* (October 26, 1992), p. 55.
25. J. R. Stevens, "The Dixie-Narco Story," *Appliance* (June 1990), p. M-31.
26. S. Stevens, "Maytag's Corporate Mission," *Appliance* (June 1990), p. M-7.
27. D. J. Krumm, "Satisfying the Customer Is Serious Business," *Directors and Boards* (Fall 1988), p. 16.
28. "A Refrigerator Is Born," *Maytag Corporation Corporate News* (May 1989), p. 7.
29. W. Ryberg, "Maytag UAW OKs New Contract," *Des Moines Register* (June 5, 1992), p. 8S.
30. Dubashi, p. 30.
31. J. P. Miller, "Maytag U.K. Unit Finds a Promotion Is Too Successful," *Wall Street Journal* (March 31, 1993), p. A9; further information supplied by Janis Cooper, Vice-President, Public Affairs, Maytag Corporation.
32. D. Kasler, "Maytag Forms Alliance," *Des Moines Register* (September 15, 1992), p. 8S.
33. Kelly, Guterl, and Lewald, p. 55.
34. "Maytag: Will a Suitor Clean Up?" *Business Week* (April 1, 1991), p. 73.
35. W. Ryberg, "Has Maytag Swept to Glory?" *Des Moines Register* (September 6, 1992), p. G1; Dubashi, p. 30.

Whirlpool Corporation, 1993: A Metamorphosis

Arieh A. Ullmann

The mood was upbeat as David Whitwam, President, Chief Executive Officer, and Chairman of the Board of Whirlpool Corporation, emerged from the meeting with Whirlpool's senior management in January 1993. He and his associates had briefed the board on the results of the 1992 fiscal year. "Outstanding" and "The best year in the company's 81-year history," were words used by the attendees to describe the accomplishments of the past year. Evidently, the strategy that had been formulated almost a decade ago was finally coming to fruition. Whirlpool's performance, measured in terms of shareholder value, the company's foremost objective, was clearly above average (see Exhibit 14.1).

The U.S. Appliance Industry

Products, Manufacturing and Distribution[1]

Home appliances were generally classified as laundry (washers and dryers), refrigeration (refrigerators and freezers), cooking (ranges and ovens), and other (dishwashers, disposals, and trash compactors) appliances. Many appliance manufacturers also made floor care goods such as floor polishers and vacuum cleaners.

Manufacturing operations consisted mainly of preparation of a metal frame to which the appropriate components were attached in automated assembly lines and by manual assembly. Manufacturing costs comprised about 65%–75% of total operating costs, with labor representing less than 10% of total operating costs.[2] Optimally sized assembly plants had an annual capacity of about 500,000 units for most appliances except microwave ovens. Unlike other industries, such as textiles, variable costs played an important role in the cost structure; changes in raw material and component costs also were significant. Component production was fairly scale sensitive. Doubling compressor output for refrigerators, for instance, reduced unit costs by 10%–15%.[3] There were also some scale economies in assembly, but the introduction of robotics tended to reduce them, in addition to improving quality, raising performance consistency, and enhancing flexibility.[4]

Distribution of major appliances occurred either directly through contract sales to home builders and other appliance manufacturers or indirectly through local builder suppliers. Traditionally, these customers were very cost conscious and thus preferred less expensive appliance brands. Retail sales represented the second

---

This case was prepared by Professor Arieh A. Ullmann of the State University of New York at Binghamton. Special thanks to Carol L. Sizler, Manager of Media and Community Relations, Whirlpool Corporation, for her helpful comments. This case was edited by T.L. Wheelan and J.D. Hunger for this book.

Five-Year Cumulative Return: Whirlpool, S&P Index, and S&P Household Furniture & Appliance Group[1,2]

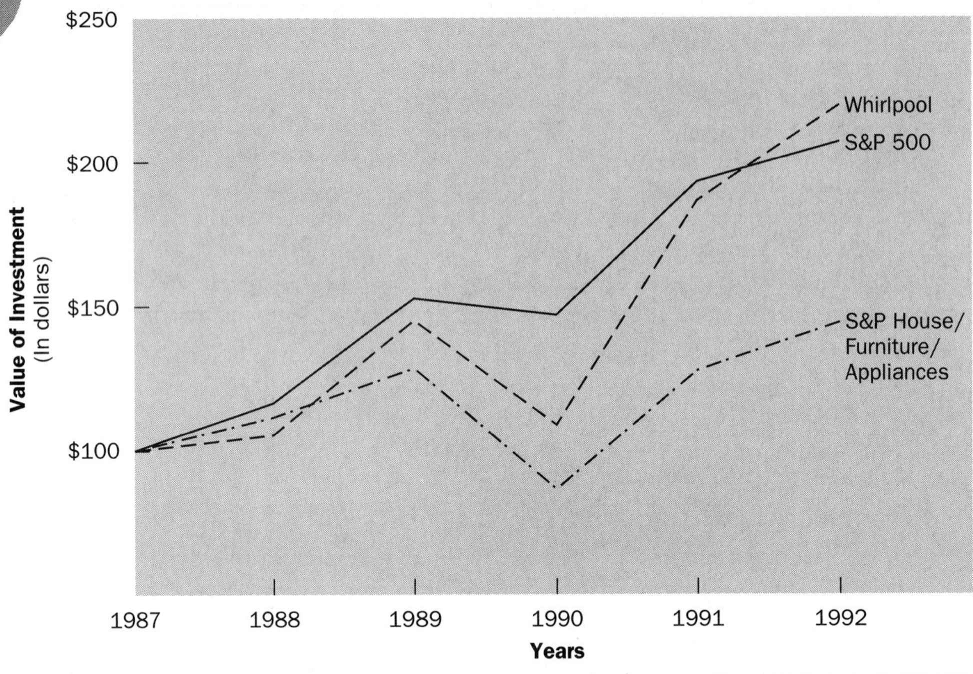

Notes:

1. Assumes $100 invested on December 31, 1987 in Whirlpool Common Stock, S&P 500, and S&P Household Furniture and Appliance Group.
2. Cumulative total return is measured by dividing (i) the sum of (A) the cumulative amount of the dividends for the measurement period, assuming dividend reinvestment, and (B) the difference between share price at the end and the beginning of the measurement period by (ii) the share price at the beginning of the measurement period.

Source: Whirlpool Corporation, *1992 Proxy Statement.*

distribution channel, with national chain stores and mass merchandisers such as department, furniture, discount, and appliance stores acting as intermediaries. In recent years, independent appliance stores, which in the past sold about a third of all white goods, were being replaced by national chains such as Sears' Brand Central and mega-appliance dealers such as Circuit City. The consolidation of the appliance distributors led to the current situation where about 45% of the total appliance volume was being sold through ten powerful mega-retailers, with Sears leading with a market share of about 29%.[5] A third, less visible channel was the commercial market, encompassing laundromats, hospitals, hotels, and other institutions.[6]

Consolidation

Before World War II, each company produced many varieties of one product. In the mid 1940s, over 250 firms manufactured appliances in the United States, including all the major U.S. automobile firms except Chrysler. The industry experienced a period of mergers in the 1950s and 1960s while sales grew approximately 50% owing to increased reliability, advances in technology, and a decline in prices. With the 1970s came high inflation and interest rates, but unit sales still continued to climb.

The last merger wave occurred in 1986 when, within less than one year, A.B. Electrolux purchased White Consolidated, Whirlpool acquired KitchenAid, and Maytag bought Magic Chef. Maytag's acquisition of Jenn-Air and Magic Chef increased its overall revenues by giving Maytag brand name appliances at various price points. Likewise, Whirlpool's acquisition of KitchenAid and Roper, respectively, broadened Whirlpool's presence at the high end and low end of the market.[7] In 1992, the number of domestic manufacturers varied by type of product—seven for home laundry appliances, 15 for home refrigeration and room air-conditioning equipment, and five for dishwashers.[8]

Broad Product Scope

In the 1980s, the U.S. market continued to grow primarily because of consumer acceptance of the microwave oven. Microwave oven unit sales tripled from 1980 to 1989 while washer and dryer sales increased only 34% and 52%, respectively. Appliance manufacturers realized that they must offer a complete line of appliances even if they did not manufacture all of them themselves, which was one reason for merger activities and the practice of interfirm sourcing. For example, Whirlpool made trash compactors for Frigidaire (A.B. Electrolux/White Consolidated), In-Sink-Erator (Emerson Electric), and Sears. General Electric manufactured microwave ovens for Caloric (Raytheon) and Jenn-Air and Magic Chef (Maytag).[9]

In 1992, five major competitors controlled 98% of the core appliance market (cooking equipment, dishwashers, dryers, refrigerators, and washers), each of which offered a broad range of product categories and brands targeted to different customer segments. With a 33.8% domestic market share, Whirlpool was ahead of GE (28.2%), reversing the leadership position of two years earlier. A.B. Electrolux (15.9%), Maytag (14.2%), and Raytheon (5.6%) followed. Whirlpool held market share leadership positions in several appliance categories (see Exhibit 14.2).

Market Saturation

Throughout the 1980s and into the 1990s, competition in the United States was fierce. Industry demand depended on the state of the economy, disposable income levels, interest rates, housing starts, and consumers' ability to defer purchases. Saturation levels remained high and steady; over 70% of households had washers and over 65% had dryers (see Exhibit 14.2). Refrigerators had become fully efficient at

EXHIBIT 14.2

Domestic Market Shares of Major Appliance Manufacturers, 1991

(Shipments are in thousands of units)

Major Producers	Market Share	Saturation	Shipments
Refrigerators		99.9%	7,273
GE	35%		
Whirlpool	25		
Electrolux	17		
Maytag	12		
Freezers		33.0	1,414
Electrolux	70		
W.C. Wood	16		
Whirlpool	6		
Raytheon	3		
Washers		73.0	6,197
Whirlpool	51		
Maytag	18		
GE	16		
Electrolux	12		
Dishwashers		47.7	3,571
GE	40		
Whirlpool	33		
Electrolux	19		
Maytag	7		
Disposers		47.0	4,002
In-Sink-Erator	59		
Electrolux	29		
Waste King	7		
Electric ranges		56.7	2,900
GE	43		

(continued)

preserving food, and that segment was saturated. Sales of electric ranges slowed as those of microwave ovens zoomed. Microwave sales, which had jumped from 3.5 million units in 1980 to more than 10 million by 1989, started leveling out.[10] Sales of ranges had dropped off drastically, owing to market maturation (more than one gas or electric range in a home was not uncommon).

Factors of Competition

In this environment all rivals worked hard to keep costs down. Over four years, A.B. Electrolux spent more than $500 million to upgrade old plants and build new ones for its acquisition, White Consolidated Industries (renamed Frigidaire). General Electric automated its Louisville, Kentucky, plant which, over ten years,

EXHIBIT 14.2

Domestic Market Shares of Major Appliance Manufacturers, 1991 *(continued)*
(Shipments are in thousands of units)

Major Producers	Market Share	Saturation	Shipments
Electric ranges		56.7	2,900
GE	43		
Whirlpool	18		
Electrolux	17		
Maytag	12		
Gas ranges		45.7	2,132
Maytag	25		
GE	24		
Electrolux	22		
Raytheon	21		
Electric dryers		50.6	3,295
Whirlpool	52		
GE	17		
Maytag	15		
Electrolux	14		
Gas dryers		16.1	1,018
Whirlpool	52		
GE	14		
Maytag	14		
Electrolux	12		
Microwave ovens		85.2	8,207[1]
Sharp	23		
Samsung	19		
Matsushita	16		
Goldstar	11		

Note: 1. Domestic and imported units except for combination microwave ovens/ranges.

Source: *Appliance* (September 1992).

halved the work force and raised output by 30%. Had the appliance manufacturers been making automobiles, the price of a Chevrolet Caprice would have risen from $7,209 in 1980 to $9,500 in 1990, not to $17,370.[11]

Toward the end of the 1980s, lowering costs, monitoring margins, and achieving economies of scale became even more important. The Big Four were renovating and enlarging existing facilities. Maytag built new facilities in the South to take advantage of lower cost, nonunion labor. Others built twin plants on the Mexican border to profit from cheap labor. Still others built focus factories, where each plant produced only one type of product, covering all price points.[12]

Also, all competitors started to push into the high-end segment of the market, which was more stable and profitable. Once the domain of Maytag, it became increasingly crowded with the appearance of GE's Monogram line, Whirlpool's acquisition of KitchenAid, and White's Euroflair models. This trend had its roots in the 1980s, reflecting increased new-home construction and home expansions and remodelings. Each new home was expected to contain four to six new appliances. Purchases emphasized upscale models, compared to the previous tendency for builders to economize by buying the cheapest national brand appliances.[13]

Quality, too, became an important feature in the competitive game, as symbolized by Maytag's lonely repairman. The number of service calls dropped across the board in the wake of rising consumer expectations. Defect rates dropped from 20 per 100 appliances made in 1980 to 10 per 100 twelve years later.[14] Relationships with suppliers changed as companies used fewer of them than in years past. Contracts contained longer terms to improve quality and provisions to keep costs low with just-in-time deliveries.[15]

A recent development was the demand by the powerful distributors for faster delivery to curtail inventory costs, their biggest expense. At a recent meeting of the Association of Home Appliance Manufacturers, Bernard Brennan, CEO of Montgomery Ward, declared:

> We would like to carry even more brands, but we have to find a way to move products more quickly. Sharing information with manufacturers is critical. Logistics are more than distribution; they cover disposal of major appliances, next-day delivery guaranteed in a three-hour period, and emergency repairs. But we have to work with manufacturers to get the costs down.[16]

As a consequence, manufacturers started to improve delivery systems. For instance, General Electric created its Premier Plus Program, which guaranteed three-day delivery. Also, sales departments were reorganized so that one sales representative would cover all manufacturer's brands of a given product category. Customer information services via 800-number telephone lines also were strengthened.

Innovation

Two developments, government regulation and advances in computer software, combined with intense competition accelerated product innovation. New energy standards to be enforced under the 1987 National Appliance Energy Conservation Act limited energy consumption of new appliances, with the objective of reducing energy use in appliances by 25% every five years. At the same time, the possible ban on ozone-depleting chlorofluorocarbons (CFCs) in refrigerators by 1995 was forcing the industry to redesign its refrigerators. Pressures also were exerted to change washer and dishwasher designs to reduce water consumption.

In 1989, the Natural Resources Defense Council, several utilities, and the Environmental Protection Agency organized the Super Efficient Refrigerator Program, Inc. (SERP).[17] Refrigerator makers had to revamp their product lines for EPA-mandated improvements in energy efficiency and an impending ban on CFCs, so SERP organizers created a $30 million contest financed by 24 utilities to develop a refrigerator prototype free from CFCs and at least 25% more energy efficient than the 1993 federal standards. The outcome of the competition was to be announced in July 1993. The winner, who would receive the entire $30 million, had to manufacture and sell more than 250,000 refrigerators between January 1994 and July 1997.

Advances in computer technology was the second development accelerating innovation. New programs called fuzzy logic or neural networks that mimicked the human brain's ability to detect patterns were being introduced in many industries, including white goods.[18] In Asia, elevators, washers, and refrigerators using fuzzy logic to recognize use patterns were already widespread.[19] In late 1992, AEG Hausgeräte AG, a subsidiary of Daimler Benz's AEG unit, introduced a washer using fuzzy logic to automatically control water consumption depending on the size of the load and to sense how much dirt remained in clothes.[20] United Technology was working on a line of air conditioners that automatically adjusted room temperature as a function of the number of people in a room and their preference for comfort, humidity, and air flow.[21]

Outlook

For the future, demand in the United States continued to appear weak, with growth rates of 1%–2% forecasted from a level that was 15% below 1988 industry shipments. At the prevailing saturation levels demand was restricted mostly to replacement purchases (79%), with the remainder going to new housing and new household formation.[22]

The one positive element in this otherwise bleak outlook was a demographic trend in that the aging baby boomers were demanding more stylish appliances with new features.[23] During the late 1980s, new technologies in cooking surfaces emerged: ceramic–glass units, solid elements, and modular grill configurations. Other new customer-oriented features included the self-cleaning oven, automatic ice cube makers, self-defrosting refrigerators, pilotless gas ranges, and appliances that could be preset. Manufacturers normally accessorized their own brands first and then those of the national retailers they outfitted. Sears and Montgomery Ward usually copied the previous year's most successful products. However, the industry was so competitive that no one manufacturer could keep an innovation to itself for more than a year without a patent. Finally, consumers became more concerned with the way appliances looked. Sleek European styling—smooth lines, rounded corners, and a built-in look with electronic controls—became fashionable.[24] Another trend was the white-on-white look that suggested superior cleanability and made the kitchen look larger.[25]

The Globalization of the Appliance Industry

Foreign Competition

The white goods industry was as American as baseball and apple pie. In 1992, 98% of the dishwashers, washing machines, dryers, refrigerators, freezers, and ranges sold in the United States were made there. Exports represented about 5% of shipments. The manufacturing plants of industry leaders were located in places such as Newton, Iowa (Maytag), Benton Harbor, Michigan (Whirlpool), and Columbus, Ohio (White Consolidated Industries/Frigidaire). Each of the Big Four was headquartered closer to a corn stalk than a parking meter. Combined, these companies practically owned the market for each major appliance, with one exception—microwave ovens, which represented the lion's share of imports and about 17% of total appliance sales.[26]

The acquisition of White Consolidated Industries by A.B. Electrolux of Sweden in 1986 marked a major change in the industry. Until then, foreign competition was largely restricted to imports of microwave ovens, a segment controlled by Far Eastern competitors from Korea (Goldstar and Samsung) and Japan (Sharp and Matsushita). Aware of the fate of other industries, many observers expected that it was only a matter of time before these companies would expand from their beachhead in microwave ovens and compact appliances into other segments. Indeed, the general manager of the overseas office of Matsushita, the market leader in Japan's white goods industry, stated:

> Foreign makers are right to expect that Matsushita and other Japanese companies will enter the U.S. and European markets soon enough. The traditional makers won't be number 1 and number 2 forever.[27]

Europe's Promise

Of prime attractiveness to U.S. manufacturers was Western Europe, which represented 27% of the global market. Eastern Europe, the Middle East, and Africa comprised 16%, Asia's share was 27%, North America followed with 24%, and Latin America had 6%.[28] Since 1985, Western Europe had rapidly moved toward a unified market of some 320 million consumers, which was not nearly as saturated as Canada and the United States. Appliance demand was expected to grow at 5% annually. Political changes in Eastern Europe integrated these countries into the world trade system and thus added to Europe's long-term attractiveness.

During the 1970s and 1980s the European white goods industry had experienced a consolidation similar to that in the United States. In the late 1980s, six companies—Electrolux Zanussi, Philips Bauknecht, Bosch-Siemens, Merloni-Indesit, Thompson, and AEG—controlled 70% of the market (excluding microwave ovens and room air conditioners). Until the mid 1980s most companies were either producing and selling in only one national market or exporting to a limited extent to many European markets from one country. Observed Whirlpool CEO Whitwam, "What strikes me most is how similar the U.S. and European industries are."[29] Research by Whirlpool also indicated that the working components of washers were basically alike around the world.[30]

However, the European market was segmented, and consumer preferences differed greatly from country to country with regard to almost every type of appliance. For example, the French preferred to cook food at high temperatures, splattering grease on oven walls. Thus oven ranges manufactured for France should have self-cleaning capability. However, this feature was not a requirement in Germany where lower cooking temperatures were the norm.[31] In contrast to Americans who preferred to stuff as many clothes into the washer as possible, Europeans overwhelmingly preferred smaller built-in models. The continental European "engineering" mentality disliked the U.S. and British one-touch button models. They preferred the built-in concept developed in the United States, where it had failed to attract buyers.[32] In France, 80% of washing machines were top-loaders, whereas elsewhere in Western Europe, 90% were front-loaders. Also, European washers frequently contained heating elements, and the typical European homemaker preferred to wash towels at 95° Celsius. Gas ranges were common throughout Europe, except for Germany where 90% were electric.

Given this situation, some observers were skeptical about the possibility of establishing pan-European models that would yield a sustainable competitive advantage through manufacturing, procurement, and marketing efficiencies. They claimed that the European market was actually many smaller individual markets—the respective countries. Furthermore, many of these national markets featured strong competitors.

A.B. Electrolux was a major force in Europe with an overall 25% market share.[33] Over 20 years the $14 billion multinational from Sweden had undertaken more than 200 acquisitions in 40 countries that spanned five businesses: household appliances, forestry and garden products, industrial products, metal and mining, and commercial services. Its expertise in managing acquisitions and integrating the newly acquired units into the organization was unequalled. For instance, in 1983, A.B. Electrolux took over the money-losing Italian white goods manufacturer with 30,000 employees, 50 factories and a dozen foreign sales companies. Within four years the Swedes turned a company that in 1983 lost L120 billion into an efficient organization netting L60 billion.[34] The acquisitions of Zanussi of Italy, Tricity of Britain, and three Spanish companies in anticipation of the changes in Western Europe marked the beginning of a new era in this mature industry. Industrial Design Centers and Research Centers were being established in Stockholm, Sweden, Venice, Italy, and Columbus, Ohio, to share product and operation ideas and to accelerate product development among the many brands. Instead of combining production, marketing, and sales market by market, a search for synergies began, first to establish pan-European brands for a unified Europe and then to explore cross-Atlantic opportunities. The newly formed Electrolux Components Group was charged with taking advantage of the available integration opportunities, primarily by coordinating and developing strategic components worldwide. The company created a parallel organizational layer on the marketing side to combine sales and marketing in several countries on a regional basis.

In Germany, Bauknecht (Philips), Siemens-Bosch, and AEG-Telefunken were dominant; in Britain GEC's Hotpoint, and in France Thomson-Brandt were forces to be reckoned with. Italy's Merloni pursued a different approach by flooding Europe with machines produced in Italy with lower cost labor. In 1987, Merloni gobbled up Indesit, an Italian producer in financial trouble, to enlarge its manufacturing base and take advantage of Indesit's marketing position in many Euro-

EXHIBIT 14.3

Core Appliance Market Share of Major Competitors in the United States and Europe, 1991 versus 1989

U.S. Market	1991	1989	European Market	1991	1989
Whirlpool	33.9%	32.7%	Electrolux	19%	20.5%
General Electric	28.2	25.5	Bosch-Siemens	13	11.0
Electrolux	15.9	18.4	Whirlpool	10	11.5
Maytag	14.2	14.8	Miele	7	NA
Raytheon	5.6	NA	Thompson	6	NA
Other	2.2	8.6	AEG	5	NA
			Merloni	—	10.0
			Maytag	—	2.0
			Other	40	40.0

Source: Hiawatha Bray, "Plugging into the World," *Detroit Free Press* (May 17, 1993); *Appliance* (September 1992).

pean countries. However, in the late 1980s no brand had more than 5% of the overall market, even though the top ten producers generated 80% of the volume.

General Electric was another important rival. In 1989, GE entered into an appliance joint venture with Britain's General Electric Corporation (GEC), which had a strong presence in the low-priced segment of the European market, especially the United Kingdom, and thus complemented GE's high-end European products.

In the same year, Maytag also entered the European market. It had acquired the Hoover Division through the purchase of Chicago Pacific. Best known for its vacuum cleaners, Hoover also produced washers, dryers, and dishwashers in the United Kingdom using a highly integrated process in aging facilities. Hoover also was present in Australia and, through a trading company, served other parts of the world. By acquiring Hoover, Maytag assumed a significant debt load and experienced a negative reaction from the stock market. However, the company's official strategy entailed continued globalization through expansion in Europe and the Pacific Rim.

Thus, in spite of these concerns about differing consumer preferences in Europe, the largest U.S. appliance manufacturers decided to enter the European market before the 1992 EC Program became a reality. Within two years, GE, Maytag, and Whirlpool entered Western Europe and thus began closing the gap relative to the geographical scope of A.B. Electrolux (see Exhibit 14.3). European Community rules required a 60% local content to avoid tariffs, which, combined with the fear of EC-wide tariffs after 1992, excluded exports as a viable strategy.

Within a short time further agreements followed, greatly reducing the number of independent competitors in Europe. AEG-Telefunken started cooperating with

A.B. Electrolux in washer and dishwasher production and development, Bosch-Siemens formed an alliance with Maytag, and the European Economic Interest Group combined several manufacturers with France's Thompson-Brandt as the leader. Despite this trend toward consolidation, Whirlpool estimated that in 1992 European manufacturers of home appliances numbered some 100.[35]

Asia

Asia, the world's second largest home appliance market, was expected to experience rapid economic growth in the near future, primarily because of the booming economies of the Pacific Rim countries. Home appliance shipments were expected to grow by at least 6% annually through the 1990s—more than in Europe or North America. The market was dominated by some 50 widely diversified Asian manufacturers, primarily from Japan, Korea, and Taiwan, with no clear leader emerging yet. The biggest promise, of course, lay in the huge markets of the world's most populous countries—China and India.

Latin America

Another market promising attractive growth in appliances was Latin America, once these countries began to follow Chile's example and emerge from decades of political instability, economic mismanagement, and hyperinflation. Indeed, many such changes in the 1990s were accompanied by efforts to lower tariffs to stimulate trade. Whirlpool expected appliance sales in Latin America to expand faster than in North America and Europe.[36]

Whirlpool Corporation

Company Background

Whirlpool Corporation, headquartered in Benton Harbor, Michigan, was one of the world's leading manufacturers and marketers of major home appliances. The company's plants were located in 12 countries, and it distributed its products in more than 120 countries under major brand names (see Exhibit 14.4).

Whirlpool was founded in St. Joseph, Michigan, in 1911. At the time, it was producing motor driven wringer washers under the name Upton Machine, with the hope of selling them in large quantities to large distributors. In 1916, the first order was sold to Sears, Roebuck and Company. In 1992, this enduring relationship with its oldest and largest customer continued, with Sears representing 19% of Whirlpool's sales. In 1929, Upton merged with Nineteen Hundred Corporation of Binghamton, New York, and plants operated in both locations until the Binghamton facility was closed in 1939. In 1948, the company introduced the Whirlpool brand automatic washer. This action established the dual distribution system: one product line for Sears, the other for Nineteen Hundred. The Nineteen Hundred Corporation was renamed Whirlpool in 1950 with the addition of auto-

EXHIBIT 14.4 **Milestones of Globalization: Whirlpool Corporation**

1957	Whirlpool invests in Brazilian appliance market through purchase of equity interest in Multibras S.A., renamed Brastemp S.A. in 1972.
1969	Entry into the Canadian appliance market through a 52% equity interest in Inglis Ltd. Sole ownership established in 1990.
1976	Increased investment in Brazil through purchase of equity interests in Consul S.A., an appliance manufacturer, and Embraco S.A., a maker of compressors.
1986	Purchase of majority interest in Aspera S.r.l. of Fiat S.p.A., a manufacturer of compressors, located in Turin and Riva, Italy.
1987	Entry into the Indian appliance market through TVS Whirlpool Ltd, a 33% each joint venture company formed with Sundaram–Clayton Ltd of Madras.
	Ownership in Inglis Ltd increased to 72%.
1988	Vitromatic, S.A. de C.V. is formed with Vitro, S.A., of Monterrey, Nuevo Leon, to manufacture and market major home appliances for Mexican and export markets. Whirlpool has a 49% interest.
	Whirlpool operates a maquiladora, Componentes de Reynosa, in Reynosa, Tamaulipas, to manufacture components for final assembly in the United States.
1989	Whirlpool and N.V. Philips of the Netherlands consummate an agreement under which Whirlpool acquires a 53% interest in a joint venture company made up of Philips former major domestic appliance division. The new company, Whirlpool International B.V. (WIBV), will manufacture and market appliances in Western Europe. The joint venture brand names are Bauknecht, Philips, Ignis, and Laden.
	North American Appliance Group formed from streamlined U.S., Canadian, and Mexican operations.
	Affiliates in Brazil, India, and Mexico complete construction of facilities and start producing the "world washer."

(continued)

matic dryers to the company's product line. In 1955, Whirlpool merged with Seeger Refrigerator Company of St. Paul, Minnesota, and the Estate range and air-conditioning divisions of R.C.A. The company, now named Whirlpool-Seeger Corporation, established the RCA Whirlpool brand name, which was used until 1967. In 1957, the company's name was changed back to Whirlpool Corporation. In the same year, the company established the Appliance Credit Corporation as a wholly owned finance subsidiary, whose name later was changed to Whirlpool Financial Corporation. Also in 1957, Whirlpool for the first time entered the foreign market through the purchase of equity interest in Multibras S.A. of Sao Paulo, Brazil, later renamed Brastemp S.A. In 1967, Whirlpool was the first competitor in the industry to take advantage of AT&T's new 800-number service. Whirlpool

EXHIBIT 14.4 **Milestones of Globalization: Whirlpool Corporation** *(continued)*

1990	A program is launched to market appliances in Europe under the dual brands Philips and Whirlpool.
	Formation of a joint venture company with Matsushita Electric Industrial Company of Japan to produce vacuum cleaners for the North American market.
	Creation of Whirlpool Overseas Corporation as a wholly owned subsidiary to conduct industrial and marketing activities outside North America and Western Europe.
	Inglis Ltd becomes a wholly owned subsidiary.
1991	Whirlpool acquires remaining interest in WIBV from Philips Electronics N.V.
	Creation of two new global business units: Whirlpool Compressor Operations and Whirlpool Microwave Cooking Business.
1992	Creation of Whirlpool Tatramat in the Slovak Republic. Whirlpool Tatramat a.s. will manufacture clothes washers for Slovakia and neighboring countries and import other WIBV major appliances for sale.
	Begins gradual phaseout of dual-branded advertising to sole Whirlpool brand by removing the Philips name in Europe.
	Whirlpool assumes control of SAGAD S.A. of Argentina from Philips.
	Reorganization of Whirlpool Europe. Name is changed from WIBV to WEBV.
	Didier Pineau-Valencienne, Chairman and CEO of Groupe Schneider S.A., France, becomes a Whirlpool director, the first non-American on the board.
1993	Reorganization of NAAG. Start of the implementation of a new Asian strategy.
	Sales subsidiaries are opened in Poland and the Czech Republic.
	In May, Whirlpool announces joint venture with Teco Electric & Machinery Company, Ltd of Taiwan to market and distribute home appliances in Taiwan.

created the Cool-Line Telephone Service which provided customers a toll-free number to call for answers to questions and help with service. Over the years, Whirlpool consistently upgraded its manufacturing capacity by constructing new plants and closing old ones. In 1968, it completed the Elisha Gray II Research and Engineering Center in Benton Harbor, thereby establishing a solid R&D basis. In 1986, Whirlpool's purchase of the KitchenAid division of Hobart Corporation from Dart & Kraft marked the company's entry into the upscale segment of the appliance market. In the same year, Whirlpool sold its central heating and cooling business to Inter-City Gas Corporation of Canada.

The company's sole effort to diversify came in 1985. It purchased the assets of Mastercraft Industries Corporation, a Denver-based manufacturer of kitchen cabinets. A year later the newly formed Whirlpool Kitchens, Inc., acquired a second cabinet maker, St. Charles Manufacturing Company. Whirlpool Kitchens lost money, so it discontinued operations in 1988 and then was sold due to lack of fit in March 1989.

North American Appliance Group

In 1988, Whirlpool reorganized its North American operations into four brand-oriented business units: Whirlpool Appliance Group (1988 sales: $1,678 million), KitchenAid Appliance Group (1988 sales: $308 million), Kenmore Appliance Group (1988 sales: $1,440 million), and Inglis Ltd (1988 sales: $351 million). This structure was supposed to allow the company to capitalize on the success of its brands and at the same time reap scale effects through an integrated manufacturing network. KitchenAid served the upscale market based on its reputation for quality blenders and dishwashers, the Whirlpool brand served the midprice segment, and the Roper brand name, which Whirlpool acquired in 1988 and was part of the Whirlpool Group, focused on the lower segment and provided Whirlpool with gas range production capability. Thus, within the North American Appliance Group (NAAG), a clear market segmentation existed, ensuring complete coverage and minimal overlap. The NAAG's scope had been further extended in 1988 with the acquisition of Emerson Electric's dishwasher and trash compactor business.

In 1990, Whirlpool sold its vacuum cleaner business to a joint venture with Matsushita Electric Industrial Company, which would operate Whirlpool's Danville, Kentucky, vacuum cleaner plant. In the early 1990s, the company streamlined its refrigerator business by concentrating production of certain models in one plant and closing older facilities. Similar decisions also affected the production of dishwashers and trash compactors. In 1992, as a result of a year-long strategic reassessment of the entire company, a new organizational structure was designed for NAAG. Effective January 1, 1993, the new organizational units focused on process, brand, and customer management; product and service creation; manufacturing; and logistics. The new structure was intended to provide better support for a customer-oriented strategy. The sales and distribution organization was responsible for brand and customer management for the retail and contract sales business. Marketing focused on product and service creation and on enhancing brand awareness and loyalty. Logistics was responsible for managing availability and inventory by means of warehouses, plants, and vendors. A separate unit, the Kenmore organization, was charged with supporting Sears, Whirlpool's largest single customer.

In June 1993, Whirlpool was named the winner in the $30 million Super Efficient Refrigerator Program. CEO Whitwam attributed this success to the multidisciplinary team that had been assembled from all over the world. "Each member of the Whirlpool team is an expert in his or her field," Whitwam said. "Their combined efforts and unrelenting focus on bringing a SERP refrigerator to market has resulted in the development of a superior product in a remarkably short time."[37]

The first SERP model would be a 22 cubic foot side-by-side refrigerator/freezer, which would be introduced in early 1994. The SERP model eliminated CFCs completely by using a different refrigerant and a blowing agent to expand foam insulation between the walls of the refrigerator liner and cabinet. The product achieved energy efficiency gains through better insulation, a high-efficiency compressor, and an improved condenser fan motor in conjunction with a microchip controlled adaptive defrost control that incorporated fuzzy logic.[38] Jeff Fettig, Vice-President, Group Marketing and Sales for NAAG declined to discuss details of the new technology but added, "I can say that these changes allowed us to surpass SERP's very tough requirement that the refrigerators be at least 25% more efficient than 1993 federal energy standards." Whirlpool had entered the SERP contest because it was consistent with the company's strategy to exceed customer expectations. Fettig went on to say that "the SERP program allowed us to accelerate the development process and bring these products to the market sooner. Future products will be designed with these consumer expectations [regarding environmental concerns] in mind, giving people even more reason to ask for a Whirlpool-built product next time they are in the market for a major home appliance."[39]

In its *1993 Annual Report* Whirlpool announced that, since 1988, NAAG had increased its regional market share by nearly a third. The North American business remained Whirlpool's core group: "NAAG has been the source of much of the cash flow required to fund the company's expansion into new markets, and in 1992 accounted for nearly 60 percent of corporate revenues."[40]

Whirlpool's Globalization

In 1992, Whirlpool's ongoing efforts to establish a global presence were more than ten years old. In its *1984 Annual Report* Whirlpool announced that it had concluded a two-year study and adopted a plan for the next five years. Among the steps mentioned were developing new international strategies and adding sound new businesses that would complement existing strengths. The company formed Whirlpool Trading Corporation to consolidate existing international activities and explore new ventures. In January 1985, the company increased its equity interest in Inglis, which dated back to 1969, from 48% to more than 50%. In the following year, Whirlpool purchased Aspera S.r.l. in Torino, Italy, a large compressor maker, from Fiat. Also, the company held talks with Philips about global opportunities. The *1986 Annual Report* discussed the reasons for the emphasis on internationalization and explained the company's ambition to become an international leader:

> Against the backdrop of recent mergers and acquisitions that are both consolidating and globalizing our industry, we're determined to emerge as one of the few key players expected to prevail on the appliance scene, worldwide, by the year 2000.[41]

Indeed, Whirlpool itself was actively involved in the market for companies acquiring KitchenAid on January 31, 1986, for cash.

In the late 1950s, Whirlpool had undertaken its first foreign expansion when it entered Brazil and then Canada in 1969 (see Exhibit 14.5). In 1976, Whirlpool strengthened its position in Brazil. However, globalization exploded in the 1980s when Whirlpool added Mexico, India, and Europe to its markets through a series of joint ventures. The moves in South America and Asia were motivated by the expectation that the rising disposable incomes in these continents combined with better education and a broadening middle class would result in a growing demand for appliances that would "at least partially mirror the American consumer boom of the 1950s and 1960s."[42]

Among Whirlpool's top management, David R. Whitwam was known as a champion of Whirlpool's globalization (see Exhibit 14.6). Whitwam had succeeded Jack Sparks who had retired in 1987 after 47 years of service, including five as CEO. Sparks had given Whirlpool the focus it had lacked. His legacy to the company was aptly summarized by a colleague: "He is a risk taker who challenges the status quo and a visionary who is value driven. He believes in people and recognizes and embraces a changing world."[43]

It was not an easy task to follow in the footsteps of such a distinguished leader. Born in Madison, Wisconsin, Whitwam graduated from the University of Wisconsin with a B.S. in economics with honors. After eight years in the U.S. Army and the Wisconsin National Guard he joined Whirlpool as a marketing management trainee in July 1968. One year later he was named territory sales manager of the Southern California sales division, and from there job descriptions did not change, only the locations. Whitwam spent time in New York and then in Southern California.[44] A soft-spoken man with midwestern charm, Whitwam was never one to gloat, but his success in California was immense. His forward thinking and innovative spirit sparked Ed Herrelko, Vice-President of Marketing and Sales for Caloric to exalt, "He's a legend out there."[45]

Whitwam moved to corporate headquarters in Benton Harbor in 1977 when he was named Merchandising Manager for Range Products. Then came promotions to Director of Builder Marketing and to Vice-President, Whirlpool Sales, in 1983. In 1985, he was elected to the company's Board of Directors. On December 1, 1987, he assumed his current position as President, CEO, and Chairman of the Board of Whirlpool Corporation. Since then, he has transformed a domestically oriented $4 billion company into a $7 billion global force.

Whirlpool Europe B.V.

Among those most strongly convinced of the promise of the European market was David Whitwam: "The only people who say you can't have a pan-European brand are the people who don't have one themselves."[46] In the *1987 Annual Report* Whitwam elaborated on the company's rationale for globalization:

> The U.S. appliance market has limited growth opportunities, a high concentration of domestic competitors and increasing foreign competition. Further, the U.S. represents only about 25% of the worldwide potential for major appliance sales.

HIBIT 14.5 Global Presence: Whirlpool Corporation

Principal Products	Major Brand Names	Principal Locations
North America		**Corporate**
Automatic dryers	Acros[1]	Benton Harbor, Michigan
Automatic washers	Admiral (Canada)	
Dehumidifiers	Crolls[1]	**Subsidiaries**
Dishwashers	Estate	Inglis Ltd
Freezers	Inglis	Mississauga, Ontario
Microwave ovens	KitchenAid	Whirlpool Financial Corporation
Ranges	Roper	Benton Harbor, Michigan
Refrigerators	SpeedQueen (Canada)	
Room air conditioners	Supermatic[1]	**Affiliates**
Trash compactors	Whirlpool	Matsushita Floor Care Company
		Danville, Kentucky
		Vitromatic S.A. de C.V.
		Monterrey, Mexico
		Manufacturing Facilities
		Benton Harbor, Michigan
		Cambridge, Ontario
		Clyde, Ohio
		Columbia, South Carolina
		Evansville, Indiana
		Findlay, Ohio
		Fort Smith, Arkansas
		Greenville, Ohio
		La Vergne, Tennessee
		Marion, Ohio
		Montmagny, Quebec
		Oxford, Mississippi
		Reynosa, Mexico
		Parts Distribution Centers
		LaPorte, Indiana
		Mississauga, Ontario
		Sales Divisions
		Atlanta
		Boston
		Charlotte, North Carolina
		Chicago
		Dallas
		Dayton, Ohio
		Denver
		Kansas City, Kansas
		Knoxville, Tennessee
		Little Rock, Arkansas
		Los Angeles
		Miami
		New York City
		Orlando
		Philadelphia
		Pittsburgh
		Santurce, Puerto Rico
		San Francisco
		Seattle

(continued)

EXHIBIT 14.5 **Global Presence: Whirlpool Corporation** *(continued)*

Principal Products	Major Brand Names	Principal Locations
Europe Automatic dryers Automatic washers Dishwashers Freezers Microwave ovens Ranges Refrigerators	Bauknecht Ignis Laden Whirlpool	**Strategic and Group Center** Comerio, Italy **Subsidiary** Whirlpool Europe B.V. Eindhoven, Netherlands **Affiliate** Whirlpool Tatramat a.s. Poprad, Slovakia **Manufacturing Facilities** Amiens, France Barcelona, Spain Calw, Germany Cassinetta, Italy Naples, Italy Neunkirchen, Germany Norrköping, Sweden Poprad, Slovakia Riva di Chieri, Italy Schorndorf, Germany Siena, Italy Trento, Italy **Parts Distribution Centers** Comerio, Italy Schorndorf, Germany **Sales Subsidiaries** Barcelona Brussels Budapest, Hungary Comerio, Italy Dublin, Ireland Eindhoven, Netherlands Espoo, Finland Herlev, Denmark Lenzburg, Switzerland Lisbon, Portugal London Nürnberg, Germany Oosterhout, Netherlands Oslo, Norway Paris Stuttgart, Germany Vienna, Austria

(continued)

EXHIBIT 14.5 **Global Presence: Whirlpool Corporation** *(continued)*

Principal Products	Major Brand Names	Principal Locations
Latin America		**Subsidiaries**
Automatic dryers	Bauknecht	Whirlpool Argentina
Automatic washers	Brastemp[1]	Buenos Aires, Argentina
Freezers	Consul[1]	Whirlpool Overseas Corporation
Ranges	Ignis	Benton Harbor, Michigan
Refrigerators	KitchenAid	
Room air conditioners	Roper	
	Semer[1]	
	Whirlpool	**Affiliates**
		Brasmotor S.A.
		Sao Paulo, Brazil
		Brastemp S.A.
		Sao Paulo, Brazil
		Consul S.A.
		Joinville, Brazil
		Embraco S.A.
		Joinville, Brazil
		South American Sales Company
		Sao Paulo, Brazil
		Manufacturing Facilities
		Joinville, Brazil
		Sao Paulo, Brazil
		San Luis, Argentina
Asia		**Subsidiary**
Automatic dryers	Bauknecht	Whirlpool Overseas Corporation
Automatic washers	Ignis	Benton Harbor, Michigan
Cooking products	KitchenAid	
Dishwashers	Roper	
Microwave ovens	Whirlpool	**Affiliate**
Refrigerators		TVS Whirlpool Limited
Room air conditioners		Madras, India
		Manufacturing Facility
		Pondicherry, India
		Sales Subsidiaries
		Bangkok
		Hong Kong
		Kuala Lumpur
		Melbourne
		Singapore

Note: 1. Affiliate owned.

EXHIBIT 14.6

Directors and Senior Management: Whirlpool Corporation

(As of February 8, 1993)

Directors

Victor A. Bonomo
Former Executive Vice-President
PepsiCo, Inc.
Committees: Audit, Organization, Strategic Planning

Robert A. Burnett
Former Chairman of the Board,
Meredith Corporation
Finance, Human Resources, Organization, Strategic Planning

Herman Cain
President and Chief Executive Officer,
Godfather's Pizza, Incorporated
Organization

Douglas D. Danforth
Former Chairman of the Board
and Chief Executive Officer,
Westinghouse Electric Corporation
Finance, Human Resources, Organization, Strategic Planning

Allan D. Gilmour
Vice-Chairman and Director,
Ford Motor Company,
and President, Ford Automotive Group
Finance, Organization, Strategic Planning

William D. Marohn
President and Chief Operating Officer
of the corporation

Miles L. Marsh
Chairman of the Board
and Chief Executive Officer,
Pet, Incorporated
Audit, Organization, Strategic Planning

Didier Pineau-Valencienne
Chairman and Chief Executive
Officer, Groupe Schneider S.A.
and Societe Parisienne d'Entreprises
et de Participation
Organization

Philip L. Smith
Former Chairman of the Board,
President and Chief Executive
Officer, Pillsbury Company
Finance, Organization, Strategic Planning

Jack D. Sparks
Former Chairman of the Board
of the corporation
Finance, Organization, Strategic Planning, Pension Fund

Paul G. Stern
Chairman, Northern Telecom Limited
Human Resources, Organization, Strategic Planning, Technology

Janice D. Stoney
Former Executive Vice-President,
US WEST Communications Group,
Incorporated
Audit, Organization, Strategic Planning, Technology

Kenneth J. Whalen
Former Executive Vice-President,
American Telephone & Telegraph
Company
Finance, Organization, Strategic Planning, Technology

David R. Whitwam
Chairman of the Board and
Chief Executive Officer of the corporation

(*continued*)

XHIBIT 14.6

Directors and Senior Management: Whirlpool Corporation *(continued)*
(As of February 8, 1993)

Corporate Officers

David R. Whitwam
Chairman of the Board
and Chief Executive Officer

William D. Marohn
President and Chief Operating Officer

Jeff M. Fettig
Group Sales and Marketing, NAAG

Robert D. Hall
Global Procurement Operations

Stephen F. Holmes
Group Manufacturing and Technology, NAAG

Executive Vice-Presidents

Harry W. Bowman
Whirlpool Europe B.V.

Michael J. Callahan
Chief Financial Officer

Robert Frey
Whirlpool Overseas Corporation

Ralph F. Hake
North American Appliance Group

Ronald J. Kerber
Chief Technology Officer

James R. Samartini
Chief Administrative Officer

Edward J.F. Herrelko
Sales and Distribution, NAAG

Daniel F. Hopp
General Counsel and Secretary

Halvar Johansson
Group Manufacturing and Technology, WEBV

Kenneth W. Kaminski
Kenmore Appliance Group

Jan Karel
Group Sales, WEBV

James E. LeBlanc
Chairman of the Board
and Chief Executive Officer,
Whirlpool Financial Corporation

Vice-Presidents

Bradley J. Bell
Treasurer

Bruce K. Berger
Corporate Affairs

E.R. (Ed) Dunn
Human Resources
and Assistant Secretary

Ivan Menezes
Group Marketing, WEBV

Charles D. (Chuck) Miller
Marketing, NAAG

P. Daniel Miller
President, Whirlpool do Brasil

Robert G. Thompson
Controller

Source: Whirlpool Corporation, *1992 Annual Report.*

> Most importantly, our vision can no longer be limited to our domestic borders because national borders no longer define market boundaries. The marketplace for products and services is more global than ever before and growing more so every day.
>
> Consumers in major industrialized countries are living increasingly similar lifestyles and have increasingly similar expectations of what consumer products must do for them. As purchasing patterns become more alike, we think that companies that operate on a broad global scale can leverage their strengths better than those which only serve an individual national market. Very likely, appliance manufacturing will always have to be done regionally. Yet the ability to leverage many of the strengths of a company on an international basis is possible only if that company operates globally.[47]

On August 18, 1988, Whitwam and Whirlpool made their boldest move so far toward global dominance in the white goods industry: they announced a joint venture with N.V. Philips, the second largest appliance manufacturer in Europe behind A.B. Electrolux. The deal for a 53% interest in Philips's worldwide Major Domestic Appliance Division was consummated on January 2, 1989, for $361 million in cash; the new company was called Whirlpool International B.V. Two years later, on July 31, 1991, Whirlpool exercised its option to purchase from Philips the remaining interest in WIBV. With this move, Whirlpool became the world's largest appliance manufacturer, overtaking archrival A.B. Electrolux.

Whirlpool phased out Philips's decentralized organization and split WIBV into two customer-focused business units—one for the Bauknecht brand and the other for the dual-branded Philips/Whirlpool products and Ignis and Laden products. Brands thus were positioned to fit the niches and conditions in Europe, an approach employed earlier in the United States where each brand was given a particular segment. Bauknecht—Philips's most profitable brand—was aimed at the high end of the market, Philips/Whirlpool at the middle, and Ignis at the lower end. Sales and marketing were kept completely separate for the Bauknecht and Whirlpool appliance groups, yet nonmarketing support from each of the 14 countries was combined. The manufacturing organization also was completely revamped. However, several strategically located plants were maintained, in contrast to Maytag. This approach turned out to be a significant advantage in a Europe with fragmented consumer tastes. Explained Lisa Mendheim of Maytag, referring to the company's Hoover operations, "We're very limited in adapting washers and dryers made in Wales to European standards."[48] Logistics, distribution after-sales service, and information were tied together with assembly under one person. Distribution was reconfigured toward a pan-European approach and ten of 28 finished goods warehouses were closed.

The management team acquired a global outlook. Instead of having primarily Dutch managers, the top seven-member team comprised five nationalities. Managers rotated between Europe and the United States to foster global thinking. This move paid off in late 1991 when the VIP Crisp microwave oven, developed by a new "advanced global technology unit" in Norrköping, Sweden, was introduced and quickly became Europe's best-selling model. The VIP Crisp has a heated base plate that allows Italians to bake crisp pizza crusts and the British to fry eggs. Now the company is starting to import the VIP Crisp to the United States.[49]

WIBV also made a series of moves to establish itself in the emerging markets of Central and Eastern Europe, which in 1991 represented about 11% of the world appliance market and promised attractive growth opportunities over the long term.[50] Bauknecht was first in setting up a distribution system in East Germany after the opening of the border. In early 1992, WIBV developed distribution networks in the entire region and established a wholly owned sales subsidiary in Hungary, Whirlpool Hungarian Trading, Ltd. In May 1992, Whirlpool acquired a 43.8% minority investment in Whirlpool/Tatramat a.s., a joint venture in Slovakia; in October it started manufacturing and selling automatic washers and marketing products assembled at other WIBV locations. In 1993, the company opened sales subsidiaries in Poland and the Czech Republic adding to WEBV's position in Eastern Europe. By the end of 1992, WIBV with headquarters in Eindhoven, Holland, employed 14,000 people and maintained manufacturing facilities in six countries (see Exhibit 14.4).

In 1992, WIBV started redesigning its products in order to increase manufacturing efficiency and to improve product quality and customer satisfaction. In September, WIBV, now called Whirlpool Europe B.V. (WEBV), was restructured. WEBV replaced the Bauknecht and Philips/Whirlpool Appliance Groups with centralized sales and marketing functions that supported all of Whirlpool's European brands. The company consolidated national sales subsidiaries into three sales regions, which recognized the growing European cross-border trade. The marketing function included separate, brand-oriented components to strengthen brand identity while at the same time ensuring coordination internally. Manufacturing and technological activities were reorganized around product groups and development centers, with Germany focusing on laundry and dishwashing products and Italy on refrigeration and cooking. Key support functions (consumer services, information technology, logistics, and planning) remained separate, centrally managed entities.[51] Explained WEBV president Hank Bowman, "The idea is to put systems support in place so we can deliver products more accurately and in a more timely manner."[52] A central account-management function was established to serve transnational buying groups. WEBV also assumed responsibility for the Middle East and Africa, formerly housed in Whirlpool Overseas Corporation (WOC), which accounted for $100 million in sales, mainly in the form of kits in an attempt to boost local content and thus preempt the emergence of domestic-content rules. WEBV supported WOC by supplying products, components, and technology sold by WOC in its geographic domain. In June 1993, WEBV sold its refrigerator plant in Barcelona (Spain) to an Italian appliance maker in order to make better use of its remaining facilities. By mid 1993, WEBV had established itself as the third largest appliance manufacturer in Europe behind A.B. Electrolux and Bosch-Siemens and anticipated that, by achieving increased efficiencies coupled with volume growth, it would raise operating margins to the North American level.[53]

The World Washer[54]

Another initiative, which encountered widespread skepticism in the industry, was the development of a compact washer, dubbed the "world washer." It went into production in new manufacturing facilities in Brazil in late 1990 and in Mexico and India in early 1991. Lightweight, with substantially fewer parts than its U.S. counterpart, it had good test scores and received favorable evaluations based on such features as stainless steel and porcelain baskets. According to Samuel J. Pearson, Director, International Engineering, its performance was equal to or better than anything on the world market while being competitive in price with the most popular models in these markets.

Although many of the circumstances surrounding the decision to start world washer production in India, Brazil, and Mexico differed, all three countries presented a clear opportunity. In 1986, market penetration for washers in the targeted areas stood at only 6%, 22%, and 54%, respectively. Whirlpool estimated that about 10%–15% of India's 840 million people could afford clothes washers but that only about 250,000 low-quality machines were sold annually.[55] Further, a weakened U.S. dollar provided the right "window" that Whirlpool and its partners needed to get the new design into production before competitors could capitalize on the same opportunities. The goal of the world washer effort was to develop a complete product, process, and facility design package versatile enough to satisfy conditions and market requirements in various countries but with low initial investment requirements. At the same time, the world washer established a beachhead, especially against the company's Far Eastern rivals.

Extensive market research and intensive analysis of almost every washer model marketed in Japan, Korea, Europe, New Zealand, and the United States preceded development. Originally, the plan was to replicate the project design in each of the three countries, but, eventually, three, slightly different variations had to be developed. "Each of the affiliates presented different expertise both in the washer business and in working with various materials," said Lawrence J. Kremer, Senior Vice-President, Global Technology and Operations. "Our Mexican affiliate, Vitromatic, has porcelain and glassmaking capabilities. Porcelain baskets made sense for them. Stainless steel became the preferred material for the others."

Costs also varied widely, further affecting both product and process decisions. "In India, for example, material costs may run as much as 200 to 800 percent higher than elsewhere, while labor and overhead costs are comparatively minimal," added Kremer. Another consideration were the garments to be washed in each country. "Saris—those beautiful, 18-foot lengths of cotton or silk with which Indian women drape themselves—posed a special challenge," recalled Pearson.

The plants also varied subtly from each other, although the goals were identical: to minimize facility investment and to avoid big finish systems and welding stations requiring extensive machinery for material cleanup and environmental safety. Brastemp, Whirlpool's Brazilian partner, put its new plant in Rio Claro, 100 kilometers northwest of Sao Paulo. Made of precast concrete, it was designed as a creative convection cooling system to address the problem of high humidity. In India, the new facility was built in Pondicherry, just 12° north of the equator. Although the plant looked similar to the one in Brazil—except for the overhead fans—the method of construction was different. Concrete was hand mixed on location, then carried in wicker baskets to forms constructed next to the building site. The Indian construction crew cast the concrete, allowed it to cure, and then five or six men, using chain, block, and tackle, raised each three-ton slab into place. In Mexico, two plants comprised the facility in Monterrey. Internacional de Lavadores housed the flexible assembly lines, stamping operations, and some machine operations. Viplasticos, the adjacent facility, housed injection moulding and extrusion processes.

Pearson underscored the fact that the project resulted not only in new plants and a new product, but also in team members from different cultural backgrounds. They gained experience in how to manage a project differently, employing a small team with the authority to do many things. "Our foreign colleagues have become partners in every sense of the word," Pearson said, adding that "when we make the final handoff to Gopal Srinivasan in India, to Francisco Fiorotto in Brazil, and to Luis Hernandez in Mexico, we will be placing the ventures in the hands of good people, good colleagues, good friends."

Whirlpool Overseas Corporation

Whirlpool Overseas Corporation (WOC) was formed in the spring of 1990 as a wholly owned subsidiary to conduct marketing and industrial activities outside North America and Europe. It included U.S. Export Sales, the Overseas Business Group acquired from Philips in the WIBV transaction, and three wholly owned sales companies in Hong Kong, Thailand, and Australia. Industrial activities encompassed technology sale and transfer, kit and component sales, joint venture manufacturing, and project management for affiliates. WOC also oversaw the activities in Brazil and the joint venture in India.

One of WOC's key responsibilities was to feed the new technologies from Whirlpool's bases in North America and Europe to its other units. A second responsibility was to ensure optimal brand positioning in each country and to analyze specific appliance designs for their suitability to various markets because conditions could vary greatly from country to country. For instance, the company sold so-called giant ovens in Africa and the Middle East. These ovens were 39 inches and 42 inches wide, compared to the standard 30 inches in the United States and were large enough to roast a sheep or goat.[56]

In January 1992, WOC strengthened its position in South America by taking over control of SAGAD, Philips's white goods operation in Argentina. In July, Whirlpool created a joint venture with its affiliates to distribute both their products to independent distributors. As a result of these moves, Whirlpool and its affiliates were the leading marketers and manufacturers of major home appliances in the region.

WOC's activities reflected the belief that global leadership implied a strong presence in all major markets. With the company's major presence in North America and Europe and its 30-year history in South America, Asia represented the last, and what many believed, biggest challenge and opportunity. "In the U.S. we talk of households equipped with between seven and nine major appliance products. In Asia, which already accounts for 40 percent of the world market, it's more like four appliances per home," remarked Roger E. Merriam, Vice-President, Sales and Marketing, WOC. With growing income levels, significant market growth could be expected.[57]

In October 1992, WOC reorganized, adopting a regional structure concentrating on Latin America and Asia that would go into effect in 1994. WOC Asia with headquarters in Tokyo was further subdivided into three subregions: Asia Pacific (Southeast Asia, India, Australia), Greater China (Hong Kong, Peoples Republic of China, Taiwan), and Japan. By adopting this regional structure, the company believed that it was in a better position to expand from its regional market share of 1% against the strong local manufacturers. This optimism was based on the fact that some of Whirlpool's products were being met with good customer acceptance. For instance, a top-load automatic washer sold in Hong Kong had about one third of the market.[58] Whirlpool moved very quickly in Asia, creating a headquarters in Tokyo and establishing sales subsidiaries and regional offices. Whirlpool realized that a viable position implied more than selling imports from NAAG and WEBV and having kits assembled by licensees. This belief also was reinforced by the fact that consumer preferences in Asia were different from those in the United States and Europe. For instance, Japanese usually wash with cold water, but to get clothes clean Japanese machines have soak cycles that may range from 30 minutes to several hours. In May 1993, Whirlpool announced a joint venture with Teco Electric & Machinery Company, Ltd to market and distribute home appliances in Taiwan as an insider. Teco was Whirlpool's largest international distributor of Whirlpool products.

Fine-tuning the Strategy

With the new global structure established, Whirlpool fine-tuned its strategy aimed at creating sustainable shareholder value. Comparisons with leading global firms established four areas essential for value creation: customer satisfaction, total quality, people commitment, and growth and innovation. Excellence in these four areas combined would lead to the targeted return on equity of 18% (see Exhibit 14.7). For each of the four areas, measures to track progress and drive decision making and accountability were developed and reported in the company's *1991 Annual Report.*[59]

In pursuing the customer satisfaction objective, the company conducted extensive studies of dealer and customer satisfaction in North America and Europe. Based on the results, the company developed a new "Quality Express" physical distribution system, initiated product improvements, and created two consumer assistance centers that greatly expanded the Cool Line service and were designed to handle nine million consumer calls by 1995.

The total quality objective led to the introduction of the Worldwide Excellence System as a single framework to incorporate total quality standards, the Malcolm Baldrige National Quality Criteria, and the ISO 9000 system. First successes were already being reported: The New Generation dishwasher models, produced in Findlay, Ohio, reported a first-year service rate already lower than those they replaced. Quality improvements also were recorded in the automatic washer manufacturing plant in Amiens, France, the cooking products facility at Cassinetta, Italy, and the Hong Kong subsidiary.

To show its commitment to people, in 1991 Whirlpool introduced PartnerShare, a stock option plan for its 22,000 U.S. employees to encourage employee ownership and dedication to building shareholder value. A gain-sharing program at the Benton Harbor components division slashed rework by 31%, total scrap cost by 62%, and its parts-per-million rejection rate by 99% over the previous three years. The program also paid each of the plant's 265 employees an extra $2,700 in 1991.[60]

The growth objective resulted in many acquisitions, joint ventures, and aggressive expansion of Whirlpool brands into new territories in recent years. The world washer and the SERP win underscored the company's growth and innovative orientation.

Besides optimizing the structure of its businesses, Whirlpool also adjusted the overall organization and board composition to support its strategy. In 1991, management created the position of Chief Technology Officer, which subsequently led to the creation of Whirlpool Compressor Operations and Whirlpool Microwave Cooking Business, two new business units with global responsibility. The company added a fourth new entity with global responsibility in 1992 with the formation of the Water and Portable Appliance business unit, charged with managing the company's small appliance business. Also, a centrally managed Global Technology Organization with systemwide responsibility was formed for advanced technology development, advanced product and manufacturing process creation, nontraditional new product opportunities, and procurement. The objective was to anticipate changes in technology better and to enhance new product creation and the technology management process. Furthermore, Didier Pineau-Valencienne, Chairman and CEO of the Groupe Schneider S.A., headquartered in Paris (France), joined the board to provide a broader perspective (see Exhibit 14.6).

At the beginning of 1993, Whirlpool's global direction and geographic position were largely complete. However, by its own admission Whirlpool was not yet a truly global home appliance company. It claimed only to have made significant progress toward becoming the leader in the developing global home appliance industry by being the only player active in all four major regions:

> But being a real global home-appliance company means more than just trading in countries around the world. It means identifying and respecting genuine national or regional differences in what customers demand from products and services—and simultaneously recognizing and responding to similarities across markets.[61]

The financial results for the first six months of 1993 showed continued improvement despite unfavorable economic conditions worldwide (see Exhibits 14.8–14.14).

Strategy for the 1990s: Whirlpool Corporation

Overall objective	Create shareholder value by achieving a return on equity of about 18%.
Rationale	"In order to attract investors in a rapidly changing world, it is not enough for Whirlpool to lead the developing global home-appliance industry. The company's financial performance must be competitive with the best of all large, publicly traded companies." (*1991 Annual Report,* p. 7.)

Whirlpool believes that it must excel in four areas in order to create sustainable value for its shareholders and, in turn, other stakeholders. For each area, the company has specific objectives that drive measurement, decisions, and accountability:

Customer satisfaction	Through the intense customer focus of all Whirlpool people, we will measure and deliver the highest levels of customer satisfaction in all of our markets and with all of our products and services, assuring that we are the company of preference with our customers.
Total quality	Our Worldwide Excellence System (WES) will deliver products and services that by measurement exceed customer expectations and outperform all of our competitors. We will achieve at least a 30% annual improvement in WES implementation through 1994. This will also improve our corporate total-cost productivity to a sustainable 5% per-year improvement level as we assure that we are always doing the right things, the right way, the first time.
People commitment	A high performance partnership with all of our people will encourage and enable contribution and commitment from each individual and team, and will provide a dynamic and diverse workplace environment which is valued by all.
Growth and innovation	Our accomplishments and management systems will assure innovation in all areas of global business conduct, and create consistent internal growth in our revenues of at least 6% per year.

Source: Whirlpool Corporation, *1992 Annual Report; 1991 Annual Report.*

EXHIBIT 14.8

Consolidated Income Statement: Whirlpool Corporation

(Dollar amounts in millions, except per share data)

Years Ending December 31	1992	1991	1990	1989	1988
Revenues					
Net sales	$7,097	$6,650	$6,424	$6,138	$4,314
Financial services	204	207	181	136	107
Total revenues	7,301	6,757	6,605	6,274	4,421
Expenses					
Cost of products sold	5,365	4,967	4,955	4,846	3,506
Selling and administrative	1,323	1,257	1,180	932	607
Financial services interest	82	91	85	65	47
Intangible amortization	27	27	14	11	—
Restructuring costs	25	22	22	9	—
Total expenses	6,822	6,364	6,256	5,863	4,160
Operating profit	479	393	349	411	261
Other income (expense)					
Interest and sundry	38	49	19	19	25
Interest expense	(145)	(138)	(148)	(122)	(53)
Earnings before taxes and other items	372	304	220	308	233
Income tax	154	130	110	132	87
Earnings before equity earnings and other items	218	174	110	176	146
Equity in net earnings of WFC	—	—	—	—	—
Equity in net earnings (losses) of affiliated companies and other	(13)	(4)	(38)	11	15
Loss from discontinued operations	—	—	—	—	(67)
Net earnings	$ 205	$ 170	$ 72	$ 187	$ 94
Per share of common stock	$ 2.90	$ 2.45	$ 1.04	$ 2.70	$ 1.36
Cash dividends	1.10	1.10	1.10	1.10	1.10
Average number of common stock outstanding (millions)	70.6	69.5	69.4	69.3	69.3

Source: Whirlpool Corporation, annual reports.

EXHIBIT 14.9

Consolidated Balance Sheet: Whirlpool Corporation

(Dollar amounts in millions)

Years Ending December 31	1992	1991	1990	1989	1988
Assets					
Current assets					
Cash and equivalents	$ 66	$ 42	$ 78	$ 78	$ 98
Trade receivables less allowances	851	846	943	930	420
Financing receivables less allowances	980	1,190	943	828	685
Inventories	650	698	801	947	537
Prepaid expenses and other	119	111	110	71	62
Deferred income taxes	74	33	25	35	25
Total current assets	2,740	2,920	2,900	2,889	1,827
Other assets					
Investment in affiliated companies	282	296	281	299	248
Investment in WFC	—	—	—	—	—
Financing receivables less allowances	912	828	628	497	387
Intangibles, net	795	909	437	350	111
Other	64	92	19	31	17
Total other assets	2,053	2,125	1,365	1,177	763
Property, plant, and equipment					
Land	73	78	74	69	20
Buildings	588	586	559	474	317
Machinery and equipment	2,052	2,026	1,823	1,289	888
Accumulated depreciation	(1,388)	(1,290)	(1,107)	(544)	(405)
Total property, plant, and equipment	1,325	1,400	1,349	1,288	820
Total assets	$ 6,118	$ 6,445	$ 5,614	$ 5,354	$ 3,410

(continued)

XHIBIT 14.9

Consolidated Balance Sheet: Whirlpool Corporation *(continued)*
(Dollar amounts in millions)

Years Ending December 31	1992	1991	1990	1989	1988
Liabilities and Shareholders' Equity					
Current liabilities					
Notes payable	$ 1,425	$ 1,467	$ 1,268	$ 1,105	$ 695
Accounts payable	688	742	580	564	352
Employee compensation	164	177	133	120	90
Accrued expenses	495	478	506	399	198
Income taxes	87	38	42	27	5
Current maturities of long-term debt	28	29	122	36	36
Total current liabilities	2,887	2,931	2,651	2,251	1,374
Other liabilities					
Deferred income taxes	213	166	167	184	139
Accrued pensions and expenses	203	303	322	296	38
Long-term debt	1,215	1,528	874	982	474
	1,631	1,997	1,363	1,462	651
Minority interests	—	2	176	220	64
Shareholders' equity					
Capital stock	76	75	74	74	74
Paid-in capital	47	37	12	10	8
Retained earnings	1,721	1,593	1,499	1,503	1,392
Unearned restricted stock	(18)	(12)	—	—	—
Cumulative translation adjustments	(49)	(1)	16	11	24
Treasury stock—at cost	(177)	(177)	(177)	(177)	(177)
Total shareholders' equity	1,600	1,515	1,424	1,421	1,321
Total liabilities and shareholders' equity	$ 6,118	$ 6,445	$ 5,614	$ 5,354	$ 3,410

Source: Whirlpool Corporation, *1992 Annual Report.*

EXHIBIT 14.10

Consolidated Statements of Cash Flows: Whirlpool Corporation
(Dollar amounts in millions)

Years Ending December 31	1992	1991	1990	1989
Operating activities				
Net earnings	$ 205	$ 170	$ 72	$ 187
Depreciation	275	233	247	222
Deferred income taxes	9	3	(29)	16
Equity in net losses (earnings) of affiliated companies including dividends received	16	(1)	35	(31)
Gain on business disposition	—	—	(36)	—
Provision for doubtful accounts	55	55	20	16
Amortization of goodwill	27	27	14	11
Minority interest	—	5	5	27
Other	15	(19)	(9)	6
Changes in assets and liabilities, net of effects of business acquisitions and dispositions	(24)	344	209	(72)
Cash provided by operating activities	578	817	528	382
Investing activities				
Net additions to properties	(288)	(287)	(265)	(207)
Financing receivables originated and easing assets purchased	(2,497)	(3,129)	(2,749)	(2,268)
Principal payments received on financing receivables and leases	2,665	2,409	2,506	1,938
Business acquisitions less cash acquired	—	(595)	(134)	(345)
Business disposition	—	—	80	—
Other	(92)	(82)	1	(35)
Cash provided by (used for) investing activities	222	(1,684)	(561)	(917)
Financing activities				
Proceeds of short-term borrowings	12,066	9,268	10,611	10,084
Repayments of short-term borrowings	(12,299)	(9,142)	(10,728)	(9,477)
Proceeds of long-term debt	50	667	212	4
Repayment of long-term debt	(73)	(134)	(41)	(36)
Proceeds of non-recourse debt	—	269	—	45
Repayment of non-recourse debt	(17)	(17)	(20)	(14)
Dividends paid	(77)	(76)	(76)	(76)
Other	8	(4)	75	(15)
Cash provided (used for) financing activities	(342)	831	33	515
Increase (decrease) in cash and equivalents	24	(36)	—	(20)
Cash and equivalents at beginning of year	42	78	78	98
Cash and equivalents at end of year	$ 66	$ 42	$ 78	$ 78

Source: Whirlpool Corporation annual reports.

EXHIBIT 4.11

Revenues by Business Unit and Line of Product: Whirlpool Corporation

(Dollar amounts in millions)

A. REVENUES BY BUSINESS UNIT

Years Ending December 31	1992	1991	1990	1989	1988
Business Unit					
Whirlpool Appliance Group	$ NA	$ 1,819	$ 1,795	$ 1,691	$ 1,678
Kenmore Appliance Group	1,050	1,000	1,011	1,110	1,447
KitchenAid Appliance Group	NA	447	400	344	308
Inglis Ltd (Canada)	NA	315	327	337	357
Service and other, net of intercompany transactions	NA	335	357	368	—
Total North America	4,059	3,916	3,890	3,850	3,790
Whirlpool Europe	2,476	2,249	2,156	1,917	—
Whirlpool Overseas Corporation	336	223	178	—	—
Other, including export in 1989, net of intercompany transactions	226	162	200	371	495
Total appliance business	7,097	6,550	6,424	6,138	4,285
Whirlpool Financial Corporation, net of intercompany transactions	204	207	181	136	136
Total revenue	$ 7,301	$ 6,605	$ 6,757	$ 6,274	$ 4,421

B. REVENUES BY LINE OF PRODUCT

	1992	1991	1990	1989	1988
Line of Product					
Major home appliances					
Home laundry appliances	$ 2,489	$ 2,300	$ 2,220	$ 2,108	$ 1,485
Home refrigeration and room air-conditioning equipment	2,525	2,329	2,209	2,066	1,501
Other home appliances	2,083	1,921	1,995	1,964	1,328
Financial services	204	207	181	136	107
Total revenue	$ 7,301	$ 6,757	$ 6,605	$ 6,274	$ 4,421

Source: Whirlpool Corporation annual reports.

EXHIBIT 14.12

Geographic Segment Data: Whirlpool Corporation

(Dollar amounts in millions)

Years Ending December 31	1992	1991	1990	1989	1988
Revenues					
North America	$4,471	$4,224	$4,157	$4,116	$4,192
Europe	2,645	2,479	2,405	2,169	244
Corporate (and eliminations)	185	54	43	(11)	(15)
Consolidated revenues	$7,301	$6,757	$6,605	$6,274	$4,421
Operating profit					
North America	$ 359	$ 314	$ 269	$ 311	$ 271
Europe	101	82	86	101	(3)
Corporate (and eliminations)	19	(3)	(6)	(1)	(6)
Consolidated operating profits	$ 479	$ 393	$ 349	$ 411	$ 262
Identifiable assets					
North America	$3,511	$3,672	$3,216	$3,065	$2,710
Europe	1,917	2,284	1,905	1,678	210
Corporate (and eliminations)	690	489	493	611	490
Consolidated identifiable assets	$6,118	$6,445	$5,614	$5,354	$3,410
Depreciation expense					
North America	$ 142	$ 129	$ 140	$ 134	$ 126
Europe	132	104	107	88	17
Corporate (and eliminations)	1	—	—	—	—
Consolidated depreciation expenses	$ 275	$ 233	$ 247	$ 222	$ 143
Net capital expenditures					
North America	$ 174	$ 183	$ 158	$ 135	$ 171
Europe	111	104	106	94	9
Corporate (and eliminations)	3	—	1	—	—
Consolidated capital expenditures	$ 288	$ 287	$ 265	$ 229	$ 180

Source: Whirlpool Corporation annual reports.

EXHIBIT 4.13

Industry Segment Data: Whirlpool Corporation
(Dollar amounts in millions)

Years Ending December 31	1992	1991	1990	1989	1988
Revenues					
Major home appliances	$7,097	$6,550	$6,424	$6,138	$4,315
Financial services	235	233	210	163	135
Corporate (and eliminations)	(31)	(26)	(29)	(27)	(29)
Consolidated revenues	$7,301	$6,757	$6,605	$6,274	$4,421
Operating profit					
Major home appliances	$ 447	$ 353	$ 300	$ 377	$ 233
Financial services	18	30	35	23	22
Corporate (and eliminations)	14	10	14	11	7
Consolidated operating profits	$ 479	$ 393	$ 349	$ 411	$ 262
Identifiable assets					
Major home appliances	$3,612	$3,835	$3,513	$3,438	$1,865
Financial services	1,941	2,143	1,632	1,337	1,049
Corporate (and eliminations)	565	467	469	579	496
Consolidated assets	$6,118	$6,445	$5,614	$5,354	$3,410
Depreciation expense					
Major home appliances	$ 271	$ 228	$ 243	$ 218	$ 137
Financial services	3	3	3	2	4
Corporate (and eliminations)	1	2	1	2	2
Consolidated expenses	$ 275	$ 233	$ 247	$ 222	$ 143
Net capital expenditures					
Major home appliances	$ 284	$ 283	$ 260	$ 224	$ 175
Financial services	4	5	5	4	4
Corporate (and eliminations)	—	(1)	—	1	1
Consolidated net capital expenditures	$ 288	$ 287	$ 265	$ 229	$ 180
Percentage of sales to Sears, Roebuck and Company	19%	19%	20%	23%	38%

Source: Whirlpool Corporation annual reports.

EXHIBIT 14.14

Consolidated Statement of Earnings: Whirlpool Corporation
(Dollar amounts in millions, except per share data)

Six Months Ending June 30	1993	1992
Revenues		
Net sales	$ 3,633	$ 3,444
Financial services	87	109
Total revenues	3,720	3,553
Expenses		
Cost of products sold	2,750	2,615
Selling and administrative	708	645
Financial services interest	32	46
Intangible amortization	12	13
Restructuring costs	8	7
Total expenses	3,510	3,326
Operating profit (loss)	210	227
Other income (expense)		
Interest and sundry	(8)	15
Interest expense	(57)	(71)
Earnings before taxes, other items and accounting change	145	171
Income tax	58	71
Earnings before equity earnings, accounting change and other items	87	100
Equity in net earnings of WFC	—	—
Equity in net earnings (losses) of affiliated companies and other	5	(12)
Net earnings (loss) before cumulative effect of accounting change	92	88
Cumulative effect of accounting change for postretirement benefit	(180)	—
Net earnings (loss)	$ (88)	$ 88
Per share of common stock		
Primary earnings before accounting change	$ 1.29	$ 1.25
Primary earnings (loss)	(1.23)	1.25
Cash dividends	0.58	0.55

Source: Whirlpool Corporation annual reports.

Notes

1. J. D. Hunger, "The Major Home Appliance Industry in 1990: From U.S. to Global," (1990) mimeo.
2. J. L. Bower and N. Dossabhoy, "Note on the Major Home Appliance Industry in 1984" (Condensed), Case #385-211 (Cambridge, Mass.: Harvard Business School, 1984).
3. S. Ghoshal and P. Haspeslagh, "The Acquisition and Integration of Zanussi by Electrolux: A Case Study," *European Management Journal* (December 1990), 8(4), pp. 414–433.
4. Hunger.
5. "Poised for a Moderate Recovery," *Standard & Poor's Industry Surveys,* Vol. 2 (November 1992), pp. T96–T101.
6. "Waiting for the Next Replacement Cycle," *Standard & Poor's Industry Surveys,* Vol. 2 (November 1991) , pp. T102–T105.
7. *Standard & Poor's Industry Surveys* (November 1992).
8. Whirlpool Corporation, *Form 10-K Report* (1992).
9. S. Weiner, "Growing Pains," *Forbes* (October 29, 1990), pp. 40–41.
10. T. A. Stewart, "A Heartland Industry Takes on the World," *Fortune* (March 12, 1990), pp. 110–112.
11. Ibid.
12. *Standard & Poor's Industry Surveys* (November 1992).
13. *Appliance Manufacturer* (February 1990), pp. 36–37.
14. Hiawatha Bray, "Plugging into the World," *Detroit Free Press* (May 17, 1993), pp. 10F–11F.
15. T. DuPont, "Whirlpool's New Brand Name," *The Weekly Home Furnishings Newspaper* (April 11, 1988).
16. *Standard & Poor's Industry Surveys* (November 1992).
17. Ibid.; James B. Treece, "The Great Refrigerator Race," *Business Week* (July 15, 1993), pp. 78–81.
18. Ivan Botskor, Michel Chaouli, and Bernhard Müller, "Boom mit Grauwerten," *Wirtschaftswoche* (May 28, 1993), 22, pp. 64–75; Amal Kumar Naj, "Air Conditioners Learn to Sense if You're Cool,"*Wall Street Journal* (August 31, 1993), p. B1; Gene Bylinsky, "Computers That Learn By Doing," *Fortune* (September 6, 1993), pp. 96–102.
19. Botskor et al.
20. Ibid.
21. Naj.
22. Bray.
23. J. D. Fisher, "Home Appliance Industry," *Value Line* (December 22, 1989), p. 132.
24. *Standard & Poor's Industry Surveys* (November 1991).
25. *Standard & Poor's Industry Surveys* (November 1992).
26. *Standard & Poor's Industry Surveys* (November 1991).
27. Ghoshal and Haspeslagh.
28. Whirlpool Corporation, *1992 Annual Report.*
29. Stewart.
30. S. Kindel, "World Washer: Why Whirlpool Leads in Appliance: Not Some Japanese Outfit," *Financial World* (March 20, 1990), 159(6), pp. 42–46.
31. Weiner.
32. Robin Tierney, "Whirlpool Magic," *World Trade* (May 1993).
33. *Standard & Poor's Industry Surveys* (November 1991).
34. Ghoshal and Haspeslagh.
35. Whirlpool Corporation, *Form 10-K Report* (1992).
36. Whirlpool Corporation, *1992 Annual Report.*
37. Whirlpool Corporation, *News Release*, "Whirlpool Corporation Named Winner in $30 Million Super-Efficient Refrigerator Competition" (July 1993).
38. Treece.
39. Whirlpool Corporation, *News Release.*
40. Whirlpool Corporation, *1992 Annual Report*, p. 9.
41. Ibid., p. 39.
42. Whirlpool Corporation, *1989 Annual Report.*
43. Stewart.
44. T. DuPont, "The Appliance Giant Has a New President and a Global Vision," *The Weekly Home Furnishings Newspaper* (July 2, 1987), p. 1.
45. W. Zeller, "A Tough Market Has Whirlpool in a Spin," *Business Week* (May 2, 1988), pp. 121–122.
46. Stewart.

47. Whirlpool Corporation, *1987 Annual Report.*
48. Tierney.
49. Bray; Tierney.
50. Whirlpool Corporation, *1991 Annual Report.*
51. Whirlpool Corporation, *Form 10-K Report* (1992).
52. Tierney.
53. Whirlpool Corporation, *1992 Annual Report.*
54. Whirlpool Corporation, *News Release*, "Whirlpool 'World Washer' Being Marketed in Three Emerging Countries" (undated).
55. Whirlpool Corporation, *1990 Annual Report.*
56. *Appliance* (June 1991).
57. Ibid.
58. Whirlpool Corporation, *1992 Annual Report.*
59. Whirlpool Corporation, *1991 Annual Report.*
60. R. Wartzman, "A Whirlpool Factory Raises Productivity—And Pay of Workers," *Wall Street Journal* (May 4, 1992), p. A-1.
61. Whirlpool Corporation, *1992 Annual Report.*

Apple Computer, Inc., 1993: The New Competitive Environment

David B. Croll and Thomas L. Wheelen

Apple Computer's *1992 Annual Report* glowed with optimism. John Sculley, CEO, stated in his letter to the shareholders, "For many companies, 1992 will be remembered as a year of recession, price wars, and cutbacks. For Apple Computer, it was a year of growth, investment, and innovation. We maintained strong momentum in our personal computing business. We invested in new businesses. And we emerged as a company well positioned to be a leader in the digital information industry. It was, by virtually any measure, a tremendously successful year."[1]

By February 1, 1993, however, the tone had changed with the filing of Apple's *Form 10-K Report.* John Akers, the CEO of Apple Computer's chief rival, IBM, had been forced to resign. The tone of Apple's *Form 10-K Report* contrasted greatly with that of its annual report just four months earlier. *Form 10-K* contained the following statement:

> The market for the design, manufacture, and sale of personal computers and related software and peripheral products is highly competitive. . . . The Company believes that its products compete favorably in the personal computer marketplace based on their ease of use, integration of hardware and proprietary operating system software, networking capabilities, consistency across a multitude of applications, and price relative to performance; however, there can be no assurance that comparable or superior products incorporating more advanced technology or other features will not be introduced by the Company's competitors. Many U.S., Japanese, and other international companies, some of which have considerably greater financial resources than Apple, are very active in the personal computer market and related industries. While the personal computer market is highly competitive, Apple remains one of the most prominent manufacturers of products for this market. No assurance can be given, however, that Apple will have the financial resources; marketing, distribution, and service capability; depth of key personnel; or technological knowledge to continue to compete successfully in the numerous markets which comprise the personal computing marketplace.[2]

Industry analysts asked, "Why all the caution? Where did all the bravado go? What happened to Apple Computer in 1992? What must Apple Computer do in 1993?"

Apple achieved some substantial goals in 1992. It sold more personal computers in the first half of the calendar year (the latest period for which figures were published) than any other vendor.[3] In fiscal year 1992,* unit shipments of Macintosh personal computers were up 20% over 1991. Net sales grew to $7.1 billion, a 12% increase over FY 1991, and net income was $530.4 million, compared to $309.8 million in 1991 (see Exhibit 15.1). Apple spent $602 million, or 8.5% of net sales, on research and development for the company's future. Apple's alliance with IBM resulted in the introduction of new connectivity products, and Apple forged partnerships with Sharp and Toshiba to work on future products. It launched its own personal interactive electronics business by unveiling a revolutionary technology called "Newton." An industry source described Newton as a video cassette–sized device that combined a souped-up Rolodex, appointment book, Nintendo Game Boy, and fax machine. The user controlled it by writing on its screen instead of typing on a keyboard, and the user could store addresses and appointments and send and receive memos by fax.[4]

Historical Background

Founded in a California garage in 1976, Apple created the personal computer revolution with powerful yet easy-to-use machines for the desktop. Steve Jobs sold his Volkswagen van and Steve Wozniak hocked his programmable calculator to raise seed money to begin the business. Not long after, a mutual friend helped recruit A. D. "Mike" Markkula to help market the company and give it a $1 million image. By 1993, all three founders had left the company's management team, but Mike Markkula remained as a board member.

Apple's early success was largely attributable to marketing and technological innovation. In the high-growth industry of personal computers in the early 1980s, Apple grew rapidly. It stayed ahead of its competitors by contributing key products that stimulated the development of software specifically for its computers. Landmark programs such as Visicalc (a forerunner of Lotus 1–2-3 and other spreadsheet programs) was developed first for the Apple II. Apple also achieved early dominance in the education and consumer markets by awarding hundreds of thousands of dollars in grants to schools and individuals for the development of educational software.

Even with enormous competition, Apple's revenues continued to grow at an unprecedented rate, reaching $583.1 million in 1982. The introduction of the Macintosh graphics–user interface in 1984, which included icons, pull-down menus, and windows, became the catalyst for desktop publishing and instigated the second technological revolution attributable to the company. Apple kept the architecture of the Macintosh proprietary; that is, it could not be cloned like the "open system" IBM PC. This allowed the company to charge a premium for its distinctive "user-friendly" features.

A shakeout in the personal computer industry began in 1983, when IBM entered the PC market, first affecting companies selling low-priced machines to con-

*For the companies discussed, the reporting periods are the companies' fiscal years (e.g., years ending September 25 for Apple) unless otherwise stated.

EXHIBIT 15.1 Ten-Year Net Sales and Income: Apple Computer, Inc.

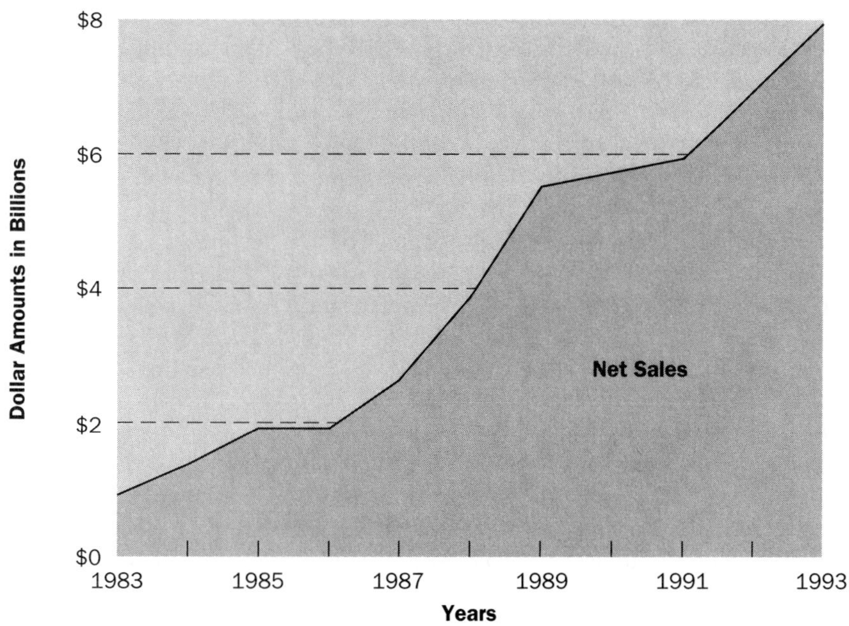

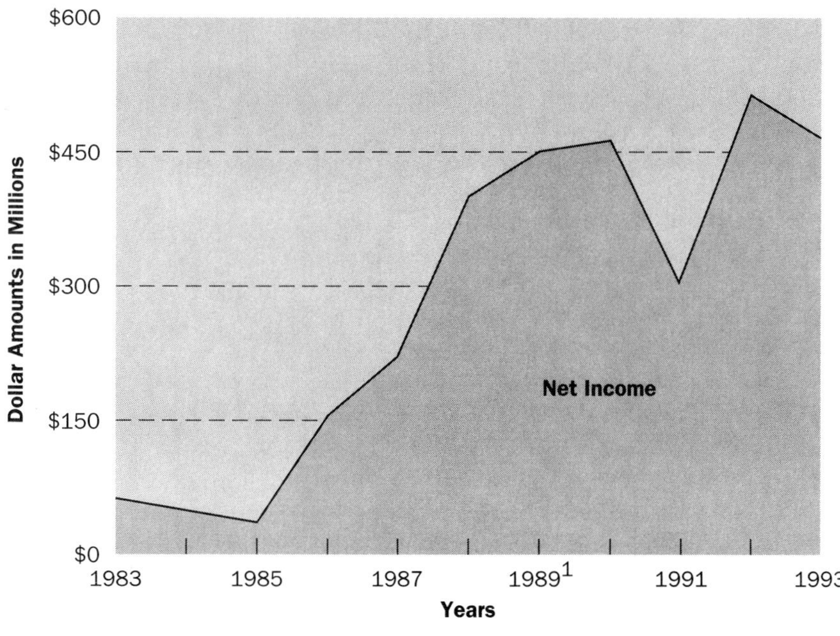

Note: 1. Includes a one-time gain of $48 million.

Source: Data from company reports; "Apple's Future," *Business Week* (July 5, 1993), p. 25.

sumers. Companies that made strategic blunders or that lacked sufficient distribution or brand awareness for their products disappeared. By 1985, only the largest computer and software companies seemed positioned to survive.

In 1985, amidst a slumping market, Apple's founders, Jobs and Wozniak, departed. The company instituted a massive reorganization to streamline operations and expenses, and, under the leadership of John Sculley, it engineered a remarkable turnaround. Macintosh sales gained momentum through 1986 and into 1987. Sales increased 40%, from $1.9 billion in 1986 to $2.7 billion in 1987, and earnings jumped 41% from $154 million to $217 million. Nearly half the company's sales and most of its profits came from the business sector. Apple introduced dozens of new software and peripheral products. The new technology carried over into 1988, with the introduction of products specifically designed to improve the networking and connectivity capabilities of Apple Computers.

In the early 1990s, Apple Computer sold more personal computers than any other computer company. In 1992, the shipment of Macintosh personal computers was up 20% over that of 1991, largely because of strong sales in Macintosh PowerBook computers.[5] Net sales grew to over $7 billion, net income to over $530 million, and earnings per share to $4.33. On October 2, 1991, Apple and IBM signed a series of agreements, including establishment of joint ventures in multimedia and object-based system software and other joint product development initiatives.[6] Development of PowerOpen, a key element of the alliance with IBM, was in process.[7] PowerOpen was a new standards-based operating system that combined Macintosh ease of use with AIX, IBM's popular version of the UNIX operating system. Fabrication of the first PowerPC chip, the RISC-based microprocessor that supports both PowerOpen and future versions of the Macintosh operating system, was completed in September of 1992.[8] In 1992, Apple reached new customers by significantly broadening its distribution channels. Nearly 1,800 retail stores in the United States, including Circuit City, Silo, and Sears, handled the new Macintosh Performa line. Net sales for Apple's European and Pacific operations increased by 13% in 1992 and represented 45% of total net sales. Sales in Japan alone totaled more than $500 million.

Current Situation

In 1992, the company's net sales grew 12% over that of the prior year, compared with net sales growth of 14% in 1991 over 1990. Net sales growth reflected strong sales of the new Macintosh models: Macintosh Classic II, Macintosh LCII, Macintosh PowerBook, and Macintosh Quadra computers, all introduced in 1992.[9] However, declines in the unit sales of certain older, more established products offset this growth. Although total Macintosh sales increased by 20% in 1992, the growth rate was substantially less than the sales increase of 60% in 1991. Average revenue per unit increased only slightly in 1992 owing to a shift in product mix toward the company's PowerBook and Macintosh Quadra computers and the pricing and promotion costs of introducing these models.[10]

International sales slowed from 22% growth in 1991 to 13% growth in 1992. Even so, this 13% growth in international sales was higher than the 11% growth in 1992 for domestic sales.

Operating expenses declined both as a percentage of total costs and in absolute terms in 1992, compared to 1991. This result reflected the elimination of restructuring costs and a decrease in selling, general, and administrative costs, highlighting Apple's continued progress in its ongoing efforts to control the growth of expenses. Its objective was to manage the selling, general, and administrative expenses to reduce the level of expenditures as a percentage of net sales in 1993, compared to 1992.[11] The company charged no restructuring costs to operating expenses in 1992, compared to more than $224 million in 1991. In the third quarter of 1991, the company had initiated a plan to restructure its operations worldwide, recording a $197.5 million charge to operating expenses. The restructuring charge included $114.5 million of estimated facilities, equipment, and other expenses, and $83 million of estimated employee-related expenses associated with consolidation, relocation, and termination of certain operations and employees.[12] Also in the third quarter of 1991, Apple recorded a reserve in the amount of $26.5 million in connection with certain trademark litigation filed against the company. In 1990, Apple recorded a $34 million charge for damage to facilities and equipment caused by the October 1989 earthquake in the San Francisco Bay Area.[13]

Apple anticipated that R&D expenditures in 1993 would approximate current spending levels of 8.5% of net sales.[14] Interest and other income declined slightly in 1992 because of lower interest rates and the increased cost of hedging certain foreign currency exposures. Income from interest fell 26% from the high of $67 million it had generated in 1990.

Management

The management style at Apple has been characterized as feel good and fun loving. However, recent hard times at Apple have resulted in layoffs and increased dependence on temporary help. When John Sculley was brought in as President and CEO in April 1983, Apple had been in trouble. Its management was strong on technology and innovation but didn't know how to manage the large worldwide corporation that Apple had become. Sculley had been president of PepsiCo and was acknowledged to be one of the best young corporate executives in the United States. He consolidated divisions, eliminated vice-presidents, and had more people report directly to him. When the personal computer market became saturated in 1985, Sculley weathered the downturn in the industry by letting go 20% of the company's work force and returning to a fairly traditional functional management structure. The reorganization cost the company $40.3 million. Although the reorganization was expensive, Sculley favored making the change over defending the status quo. Since then, management reorganization has occurred frequently at Apple.

In the changing environment of the early 1990s, Sculley again favored reorganization. Jean-Louis Gassee, Apple Products President, resigned under pressure in February 1990. Rather than seek a replacement, John Sculley assumed responsibility for directing Apple's research and development efforts.[15] He quickly consolidated development units, created a quarterly operations review, and instituted daily 7:30 A.M. meetings with his chief Macintosh engineer. "What I wanted to do was to dramatically improve the conversion rate of technologies into products," he explained. This most recent reorganization also resulted in the promotion of Michael H. Spindler, previously President of Apple Europe, to the position of Chief Operating Officer. As COO, Spindler was known as a hard-driving leader who could "breathe fire into people." Soren Olsson, head of Apple's highly successful Swedish subsidiary since 1984, and General Manager for Northern Europe since 1988, assumed Spindler's role as President of Apple Europe in February 1990. In July 1990, Robert Puette joined Apple as President of Apple USA, replacing Allan Loren, who had resigned under pressure in January. Puette was a 24-year veteran of Hewlett-Packard; he is responsible for Apple USA's sales, marketing support, and channel activities.

Ian Diery joined Apple as Senior Vice-President of Apple and President, Apple Pacific Division, in October 1989. Before joining Apple, Diery was employed by Wang Laboratories, where he had been Executive Vice-President of Worldwide Operations. Diery was promoted to Executive Vice-President, Worldwide Sales and Marketing in July of 1992. John Floisand replaced him as President, Apple Pacific.

G. Fred Forsyth joined Apple in June 1989 as Vice-President, Worldwide Manufacturing, Apple Products Division. After only a six-month stay as Senior Vice-President, Worldwide Manufacturing, he was promoted to Senior Vice-President and General Manager, Macintosh Systems Division. Prior to joining Apple, Forsyth was employed by Digital Equipment Corporation (DEC).

Two other senior vice-presidents joined Apple in the late 1980s. David C. Nagel came to Apple in June 1988 from the NASA Ames Research Center. Nagel was promoted to Senior Vice-President, Advanced Technology Group, in November 1991. Roger Heinen, Jr., joined Apple in January 1990 from DEC. In April 1992, Heinen was promoted to Senior Vice-President and General Manager, Macintosh Software Architecture Division.

Since the 1990–1991 reorganization, the Board of Directors and the officers of Apple Computer, Inc., have stayed fairly constant (see Exhibits 15.2 and 15.3). Their priorities are clearly defined in the *1992 Annual Report:*

> We believe Apple is at the forefront of the most dramatic business trend of our times. Diverse technologies—from telecommunications and television to computers and cameras—are converging. As they converge, they are creating what may become the largest industry in the world: the digital information industry. This industry offers incredible opportunities for growth opportunity to open up new markets—opportunity to extend the reach of current technologies—and opportunity to create new and better ways of working and learning. We are building a company to meet those opportunities—a new kind of systems company. It will integrate many different products and technologies to create total solutions, making it easy for people to organize, manage, and complete every aspect of their work.[16]

EXHIBIT 15.2

Board of Directors and Elected Executive Officers: Apple Computer, Inc.

Board Members

John Sculley, Chairman	Chief Executive Officer, Apple Computer, Inc.	**A. C. Markkula, Jr. Vice-Chairman**	Chairman, ACM Aviation, Inc.—Fixed-base operation at San Jose International Airport; Vice-Chairman, Echelon Corporation—Control and communications technology company
Peter O. Crisp	General Partner, Venrock Associates—Venture capital investments	**Arthur Rock**	Principal, Arthur Rock & Co.—Venture capital investments
Albert A. Eisenstat	Executive Vice-President and Secretary, Apple Computer, Inc.	**John A. Rollwagen**	Chairman and Chief Executive Officer, Cray Research, Inc.—Supercomputer manufacturer
Bernard Goldstein	Partner, Broadview Associates—Venture capital investments	**Michael H. Spindler**	President and Chief Operating Officer, Apple Computer, Inc.

Officers

John Sculley	Chairman of the Board, Chief Executive Officer, and Chief Technology Officer	**David C. Nagel**	Senior Vice-President, Advanced Technology Group
Michael H. Spindler	President and Chief Operating Officer	**Soren Olsson**	Senior Vice-President and President, Apple Europe
Albert A. Eisenstat	Executive Vice-President and Secretary	**Robert L. Puette**	Senior Vice-President and President, Apple USA
Joseph A. Graziano	Executive Vice-President and Chief Financial Officer	**Kevin J. Sullivan**	Senior Vice-President, Human Resources
Ian Diery	Executive Vice-President, Worldwide Sales and Marketing	**John Floisand**	Vice-President and President, Apple Pacific
G. Frederick Forsyth	Senior Vice-President and General Manager, Macintosh Systems Division	**Jeanne Seeley**	Vice-President, Finance, and Company Controller
Roger Heinen, Jr.	Senior Vice-President and General Manager, Macintosh Software Architecture Division	**Edward B. Stead**	Vice-President, General Counsel, and Assistant Secretary
		Morris Taradalsky	Vice-President and General Manager, Enterprise Systems Division

Source: Apple Computer, Inc., *1992 Annual Report,* p. 39.

EXHIBIT 15.3

Executive Officers of the Registrant: Apple Computer, Inc.

The following sets forth certain information regarding the executive officers of Apple as of December 9, 1992:

John Sculley, Chairman of the Board, Chief Executive Officer, and Chief Technology Officer (age 53). Mr. Sculley joined Apple as President and Chief Executive Officer, and as a director in May 1983, and was named Chairman of the Board of Directors in January 1986. Mr. Sculley continued to serve as Chief Executive Officer and Chairman of the Board of Directors after the appointment of Mr. Spindler as President in November 1990. In November 1991, Mr. Sculley was elected to the additional position of Chief Technology Officer.

Michael H. Spindler, President and Chief Operating Officer (age 50). Mr. Spindler joined Apple as European Marketing Manager in September 1980, was promoted to Vice-President and General Manager, Europe, in January 1984, was named Vice-President, International, in February 1985, and was promoted to Senior Vice-President, International Sales and Marketing, in November 1986. Mr. Spindler was appointed Senior Vice-President, International, in January 1988; Senior Vice-President, Apple Europe Division in April 1988, and was promoted to President, Apple Europe Division in August 1988. While remaining President Apple Europe Division, Mr. Spindler was also named Senior Vice-President of Apple in February 1989. In January 1990, Mr. Spindler was promoted to Chief Operating Officer and Executive Vice-President, and in November 1990, he was elected President. In January 1991, Mr. Spindler was elected a member of Apple's Board of Directors.

Albert A. Eisenstat, Executive Vice-President and Secretary (age 62). Mr. Eisenstat joined Apple in July 1980 as Vice-President, General Counsel and Secretary. In November 1985, Mr. Eisenstat was promoted to Senior Vice-President and was appointed a member of the Board of Directors. Mr. Eisenstat served as General Counsel until January 1987, and as Acting General Counsel from April 1989 to June 1989. He also served as Acting Chief Financial Officer from January 1989 to June 1989. In November 1990, Mr. Eisenstat was elected Executive Vice-President. Mr. Eisenstat is also a director of Commercial Metals Company and of Sungard Data Systems, Inc.

Joseph A. Graziano, Executive Vice-President and Chief Financial Officer (age 49). Mr. Graziano joined Apple in June 1989 as Senior Vice-President and Chief Financial Officer. In November 1990, Mr. Graziano was elected Executive Vice-President. Before joining Apple, Mr. Graziano was employed by Sun Microsystems, Inc., a manufacturer of high performance engineering workstations, as Chief Financial Officer from June 1987 to June 1989. Mr. Graziano is also a director of ShareData, IntelliCorp, and StrataCom, Inc.

Ian Diery, Executive Vice-President, Worldwide Sales and Marketing (age 43). Mr. Diery joined Apple as Senior Vice-President of Apple and President, Apple Pacific Division, in October 1989. In July 1992, Mr. Diery was promoted to Executive Vice-President, Worldwide Sales and Marketing. Prior to joining Apple, Mr. Diery was employed by Wang Labo-

(continued)

ratories, Inc., a manufacturer of computer systems and related products, from August 1978 to August 1989, where he served in various senior management positions, including Senior Vice-President of USA Operations from December 1986 to December 1987, and Executive Vice-President of Worldwide Operations from June 1988 to August 1989.

G. Frederick Forsyth, Senior Vice-President and General Manager, Macintosh Systems Division (age 48). Mr. Forsyth joined Apple in June 1989 as Vice-President, Worldwide Manufacturing, Apple Products Division. Mr. Forsyth was named Senior Vice-President, Worldwide Manufacturing in November 1990, and in April 1991 Mr. Forsyth was promoted to Senior Vice-President and General Manager, Macintosh Systems Division. Prior to joining Apple, Mr. Forsyth was employed by Digital Equipment Corporation (DEC), a manufacturer of networked computer systems and associated peripheral equipment, from November 1979 to June 1989, where he served in various managerial positions, most recently as Group Manager, Low End Systems Manufacturing from November 1986 to June 1989.

Roger Heinen, Jr., Senior Vice-President and General Manager, Macintosh Software Architecture Division (age 41). Mr. Heinen joined Apple in January 1990 and Vice-President, System Software Engineering. In April 1992, Mr. Heinen was promoted to Senior Vice-President and General Manager, Macintosh Software Architecture Division. Prior to joining Apple, Mr. Heinen was employed by DEC from June 1973 to January 1990, where he served most recently as Corporate Consulting Engineer, Software, from July 1985 to January 1990.

David C. Nagel, Senior Vice-President, Advanced Technology Group (age 47). Dr. Nagel joined Apple in June 1988 as Manager of the Applications Technology Group within the Advanced Technology Group. Between June 1988 and May 1990, Dr. Nagel was promoted to Manager of User Technologies, then Director of User Technologies, and finally Vice-President of the Advanced Technology Group in May 1990. In November 1991, Dr. Nagel was promoted to Senior Vice-President, Advanced Technology Group. Prior to joining Apple, Dr. Nagel was employed by NASA Ames Research Center, a field center within the National Aeronautics and Space Administration, which is a federal agency of the Executive Branch of the U.S. government responsible for aerospace research and technology development. Dr. Nagel joined NASA as Research Scientist in 1973, and served most recently as Chief of the Aerospace Human Factors Research Division from March 1985 until June 1988.

Soren Olsson, Senior Vice-President and President, Apple Europe Division (age 47). Mr. Olsson joined Apple in August 1984 as Managing Director, Sweden. He was named Managing Director, Sweden and Nordic Area, in January 1985, promoted to Director and Managing Director, Sweden and Nordic Area, in April 1988, and in November 1988 was promoted to Vice-President and Managing Director, Sweden and Europe North, Apple Europe. Mr. Olsson was promoted to Senior Vice-President and President, Apple Europe Division in February 1990.

(continued)

EXHIBIT 15.3 **Executive Officers of the Registrant: Apple Computer, Inc.** *(continued)*

Robert L. Puette, Senior Vice-President and President, Apple USA Division (age 50). Mr. Puette joined Apple in July 1990 as Senior Vice-President and President, Apple USA Division. Before joining Apple, Mr. Puette was employed from 1966 until July 1990 by Hewlett Packard Company, a manufacturer of measurement products and computation systems, in various senior management positions, most recently as General Manager of the Personal Computer Group from June 1981 to June 1990.

Kevin J. Sullivan, Senior Vice-President, Human Resources (age 51). Mr. Sullivan joined Apple in April 1987 as Vice-President, Human Resources. In October 1988, Mr. Sullivan was promoted to Senior Vice-President, Human Resources.

John Floisand, Vice-President and President, Apple Pacific (age 48). Mr. Floisand joined Apple in May 1986 as Director of Sales, Apple Computer, Ltd., United Kingdom. In October 1988, Mr. Floisand was named Director of Sales Development, Customer Services and Operations, Apple Pacific Division, and in February 1992 was promoted to Vice-President, Sales Development, Customer Services and Operations, Apple Pacific Division. Mr. Floisand was named Vice-President and President, Apple Pacific, in August 1992.

Jeanne Seeley, Vice-President, Finance and Company Controller (age 43). Ms. Seeley joined Apple in October 1981 as Controller with the Peripherals Division. In June 1985, Ms. Seeley was promoted to Senior Controller for the Operations Group, was named Director in July 1986, and was promoted to Senior Director in January 1989. In November 1990, Ms. Seeley was promoted to Vice-President, Finance. Ms. Seeley was appointed Vice-President, Finance, and Company Controller in May 1992.

Edward B. Stead, Vice-President, General Counsel, and Assistant Secretary (age 45). Mr. Stead joined Apple in September 1988 as Associate General Counsel, Apple USA Division. He was named Vice-President, General Counsel, and Assistant Secretary of Apple in June 1989. Prior to joining Apple, Mr. Stead was employed by Cullinet Software, Inc., a developer and distributor of mainframe computer software products, from December 1985 to January 1988 as Vice-President, General Counsel, and Secretary, and from January 1988 to May 1988 as Senior Vice-President, General Counsel, and Secretary.

Morris Taradalsky, Vice-President and General Manager, Enterprise Systems Division (age 46). Mr. Taradalsky joined Apple in December 1988 as Vice-President, Customer Support and Information Systems and Technology. In April 1990, Mr. Taradalsky was promoted to Vice-President, Customer Support Products and Services, and in April 1992 he was named Vice-President and General Manager, Enterprise Systems Division. Prior to joining Apple, Mr. Taradalsky was employed by IBM, a computer manufacturer, from 1983 until December 1988, in various senior management positions; most recently as IBM's Vice-President and General Manager of Programming, Santa Teresa Laboratory, from January 1987 to December 1988.

Source: Apple Computer, Inc., *Form 10-K Report* (1992), pp. 8–10.

The Alliance

On October 2, 1992, Apple and IBM signed a series of agreements, establishing joint ventures in multimedia and object-based system software and other joint product initiatives.[17] At that time, Apple and IBM were the largest computer companies, having a combined U.S. market share of 25%.[18] However, this combined market share (12% IBM and 13% Apple) was a considerable drop from their earlier market shares. The changing marketplace had forced both companies to make some painful adjustments, including the forced resignation of John Akers, IBM's CEO.

Another problem that drove IBM and Apple into each other's arms was their growing friction with some powerful partners, most notably Microsoft, the suburban Seattle software giant. Microsoft had created MS-DOS, the software that ran the IBM PC. In 1992, IBM and Microsoft had a disagreement over the next generation, called OS/2, that ran IBM's line of PS/2 computers. Microsoft developed OS/2, but IBM believed that the software company had undermined sales of its software by pushing the highly successful Window 3.0 program, which enabled old MS-DOS software to work much like a Macintosh. That had also alienated Apple, which contended that Microsoft stole elements of Windows from Macintosh programs. The new alliance between Apple and IBM, which will develop its own software, could spell the end of OS/2 and any remaining relationship IBM has with Microsoft.[19]

The new alliance scorned another powerful company, Intel, which had supplied the microprocessors for IBM's machines and had commanded an almost monopolistic position as a maker of IBM-compatible chips. Possibly to foster more competition, the new Apple–IBM partnership said that it would buy advanced processors from Motorola, whose chip business had been suffering because some of its largest customers, including Unisys, had declined. IBM also had been busy lining up other partnerships. Only a day after announcing its deal with Apple, IBM said that it would join forces with Germany's Siemens A.G. to produce a powerful new 16-megabit memory chip, which would hold four times as much data as current models. This alliance could create a competitive advantage against the Japanese companies in bringing the new chip to market. The Apple–IBM agreement contained the following main elements.

1. The two companies were to form a joint venture, Taligent, Inc., to develop an advanced operating system, the basic controlling software of the computers, which IBM and Apple would use in their machines and sell to other companies.
2. Apple's user-friendly Macintosh system would be integrated into IBM's product line, including the large computers that served as the heart of corporate systems.
3. Apple would gain access to IBM's advanced, high-speed microprocessors, which would be incorporated into future editions of the Macintosh and other machines.
4. The two computer makers would seek to develop a new generation of high-powered, multimedia hardware and software, which could be marketed under both brand names.[20]

In January 1993, Taligent, Inc., announced that the joint venture was ahead of schedule and already vying aggressively for the allegiance of leading applications makers. It expected to deliver its first operating system the next year.

The business aspects of the alliance made a great deal of sense, considering the growth of Microsoft and its capacity to hurt both IBM and Apple. Yet their corporate environments were drastically different. As Richard Shaffer, publisher of *ComputerLetter,* declared, "Who would have thought these two companies could possibly see eye to eye on anything? It's like a surfer girl marrying a banker."[21] Joseph M. Guglielmi, a veteran IBM executive who heads Taligent, said that the idea of a culture clash was overstated. "The notion of having an Apple culture or an IBM culture is really being left behind very rapidly," said Guglielmi. He said that Taligent, which was developing advanced software, was establishing its own culture, aided by the "dilution factor" of new employees who have never worked at either parent company.[22]

Taligent was attempting to change the rules in desktop computing by transforming operating software, which controlled the basic functions of a personal computer. Operating software determined the look and feel of various applications and could run on only one type of computer hardware. Microsoft's standard DOS operating software ran only on computers built around Intel Corporation microprocessors, and Apple's Macintosh software ran only on Motorola chips. Apple and IBM pledged that Taligent would run on a variety of computers, including their own. People familiar with the inner workings of Taligent said that the company had rather painlessly meshed the different IBM and Apple cultures, largely because of their common rivalry with Microsoft.[23]

Since the alliance with IBM, Apple has announced other alliances. In March 1992, Apple announced a licensing and development agreement with Sharp Corporation for the Newton technology. That June, Apple disclosed a development and manufacturing agreement with Toshiba Corporation for Apple's new CD-ROM–based personal digital assistants (PDA's). Apple announced plans in January 1992 to use technology developed by America Online, Inc. Analysts said that, in allying with America Online, Apple wanted to extend its information services beyond a base of primarily business users. The company stated that "these alliances will allow us to make use of the best technologies from other businesses, while focusing our resources on what we do best."[24]

The Industry

Investors in common stocks were nervous about first-quarter 1993 earnings from some of the largest computer makers. A weak recovery of the U.S. economy suggested that the earnings figures could fall short of earlier projections. Analysts expected DEC and IBM to show continued losses. Some even believed that other personal computer makers would come in below earlier estimates as capacity constraints, continued pressure on prices, and unfavorable currency trends reduced earnings. "Everyone's on the edge of his seat," said George Elling, a Merrill Lynch analyst.[25] John B. Jones of Solomon Brothers said that, despite some signs of a domestic recovery, "capital spending on computers is weak and overseas, virtually every non-English speaking country is showing slower growth this year than last."[26] IBM's mainframe sales were down as much as 50% from 1992 levels, as deep price cutting continued and customers evaluated less costly alternatives.

By 1993, the personal computer industry was no longer just a hardware and services industry. The vital component in the modern computer mainframe was the semiconductor chip. Even computer giants like Apple and IBM found that their success was tied to the availability and compatibility of computer software. The main competition to Apple and IBM was not other computer manufacturers but, rather, software developers such as Microsoft and semiconductor chip manufacturers such as Intel and Motorola. Therefore Apple was affected substantially by three interrelated industries, not just by the computer and peripherals industry.

At the close of trading on January 14, 1993, IBM held a slim lead over Microsoft in total stock market value: $27.83 billion to $27.28 billion. Coming up fast in the technology race was third-place Intel Corporation, valued at $24.47 billion. "This shows us that value in the technology business is added by software, not hardware," stated Hugh Johnson, chief investment officer at First Albany Corporation.[27] Many money managers suggested that, at least psychologically, Microsoft long ago supplanted IBM as the leader in the technology arena, regardless of the company's relative stock market value. "It's the nature of the computer industry that one company be the leader, and that company is Microsoft," stated Roger McName, a money manager at Integral Partners in Palo Alto, California.[28] Analysts knew that Microsoft would not hold the stock market value mantle forever; Intel was nipping at its heels. Intel's semiconductor chips had become the computer for all intents and purposes (see Exhibit 15.4).

Life in the computer and peripherals industry was becoming ever more difficult, with the move to lower cost, commoditylike computers. The major players were slicing prices and cutting costs to the maximum, leading to a shakeout in the industry, with only the largest, strongest, and most flexible likely to survive. The equity securities of many computer industry companies were battered during 1992.

The computer and peripherals industry was more vicious competitively than ever before, raising questions about the very survival of some of the companies.[29] Many of the problems the industry faced were simply a matter of bad timing. The mainframe makers—IBM, Amdahl, and DEC—had rolled out new generations of their large machines just as the United States entered a recession in 1990. Consequently, potential customers adopted a conservative attitude. In addition to the bad timing, the computer environment changed; users were developing an increasing number of applications that ran on cost-competitive networks of personal computers and workstations. Also arriving on the scene were more powerful computers built by lashing together inexpensive microprocessors. Finally, to maintain market share, companies were resorting to price cutting, which also eroded revenues and margins.

Makers of midsized computers faced the same problems as the mainframe builders. Personal computer makers faced competition from clone manufacturers. These manufacturers bought off-the-shelf components and built very competitive

EXHIBIT 15.4 **Computer Industry Leaders: Net Income**

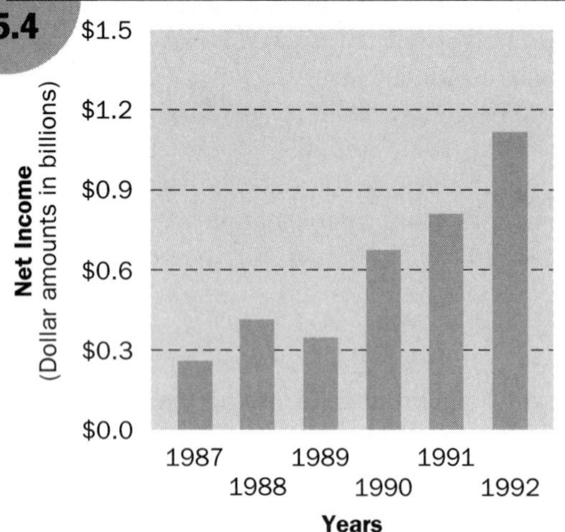

(a) Intel—Leading chip maker

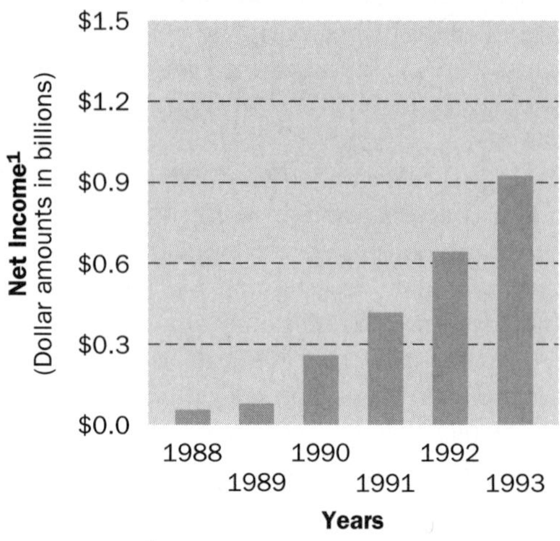

[1]Fiscal year ending June 30.

(b) Microsoft—Leading PC software developer

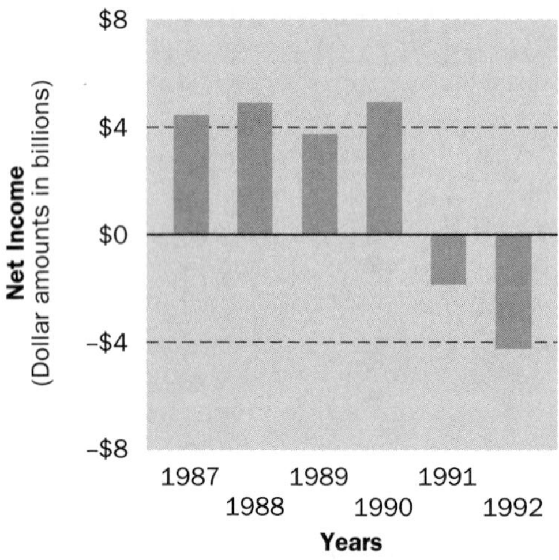

(c) IBM—Diversified computer maker

Source: G. Pascal Zachary and Stephen Yoder, *Wall Street Journal* (January 27, 1993), pp. A-1 and A-4.

products for less (based on their low administrative and R&D costs). To compete, Apple, Compaq, DEC, and IBM all have cut prices to meet, and often beat, the offerings of the clone makers. As margins shrank to the vanishing point, many of the weaker players were likely to fail. The price cuts have caused some difficulties to the computer manufacturers, and nowhere was the pain greater than at IBM.

Management announced that 25,000 IBM jobs would be lost in 1993—in addition to the 40,000 lost in 1992. Unisys earlier cut its work force drastically and trimmed the number of lines of computers it manufactured, focusing on a few niche markets where it had the expertise to help customers solve their problems.[30] Unisys was profitable in 1992.

Many computer manufacturers were recasting themselves as service and software providers—two areas that were growing much faster than the traditional hardware field. These businesses should have a reasonable chance for success, with many companies focusing on their main businesses, shedding many activities (such as data processing operations) that were peripheral to their core competencies.

The prospects for the computer hardware industry were looking good in 1993. The lower price for products should continue to increase unit sales even though price discounting was expected to return soon to more normal levels.[31] The cost-cutting efforts should also help widen margins. With an upturn in the economy, durable equipment orders should increase, leading to a rise in orders for computer gear, providing both revenue and earnings increase. Exhibits 15.5 and 15.6 illustrate the highly volatile nature of the computer hardware industry during the past several years.

The computer hardware and peripherals industry was not a Wall Street favorite in 1992, owing in large part to the plunge in IBM stock. Values of other computer company stocks fell as a reaction to poor quarterly earnings at Amdahl, Cray, DEC, and Storage Technology. Companies with rising stock values were Compaq, Dell, Unisys, and others. Nevertheless, the industry as a whole looked good as an investment.[32]

The computer software and services industry had attributes that allowed its companies to continue to grow regardless of economic conditions generally. The industry was changing rapidly, as IBM was being supplanted in mainframe production by hordes of increasingly powerful microprocessor-based machines. Software and services companies with marketing interests in this emerging market were obviously going to benefit.

The computer software and services industry survived the 1990–1992 recession with few problems. The reason was that many of the companies produced goods and provided services that were essential to their customers. Customers responded to tough times by concentrating on their core businesses and outsourcing peripheral operations, such as payroll processing. Some companies even outsourced the entire information services operation.

Potential customers were increasingly moving applications down from mainframes and minicomputers to networks of personal computers, which should be very good for developers of personal computer software such as Microsoft and Lotus. Computer Associates, System Software, and other companies that focused on data center mainframes and midrange computers had to expand their offerings to include a full range of applications for personal computers and workstations.

The semiconductor industry was well into a major business upswing. This revival became evident when the semiconductor industry coasted through its normal seasonal slump in the summer of 1992 with no loss in demand. Monthly orders for chips had turned around in late 1991 and had set new highs in mid 1992.[33] De-

EXHIBIT 15.5

Office and Computer Machine Orders

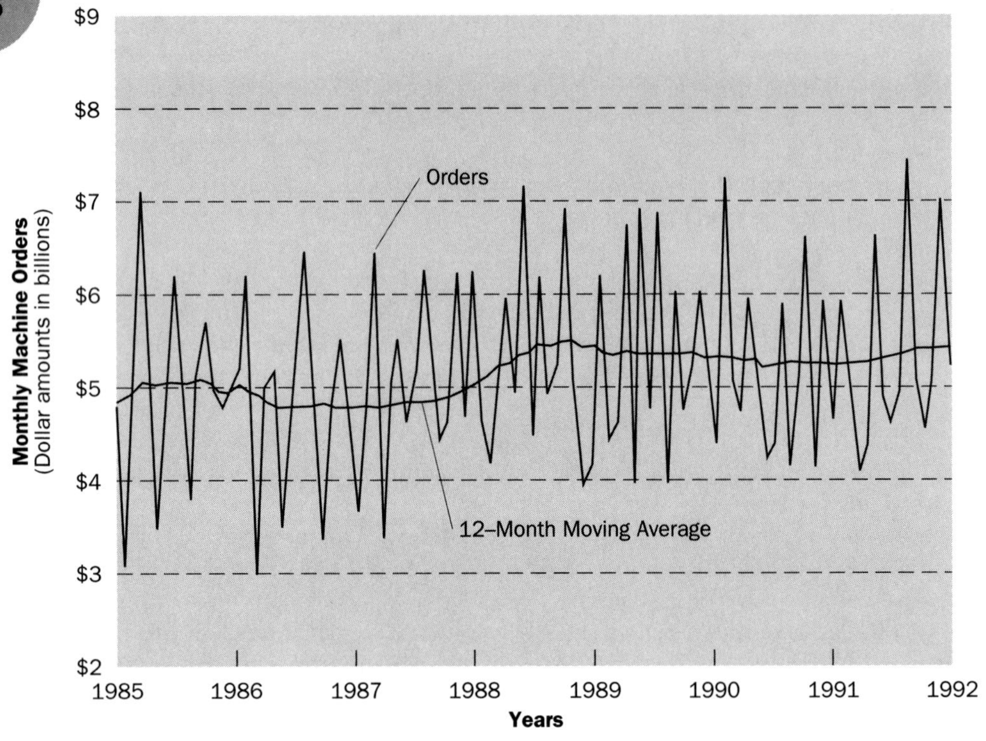

Source: "Computers and Peripherals Industry," U.S. Department of Commerce (January 29, 1993), p. 1076.

mand had continued to grow, with orders exceeding shipments, building substantial backlogs. The semiconductor industry association reported that, in the last three months of 1992, U.S. orders exceeded $1.9 billion, a 38% year-to-year advance. During the same period, the number of orders exceeded the number of chips shipped by 13%.[34]

Verification of the strong revival in the semiconductor business came in the fourth-quarter figures for 1992. Intel, with 17% of the industry's profits, disclosed a 54% jump in sales and a more than doubling of earnings for the last three months of 1992. The timing of this success coincided with a period of recession for much of the computer industry, the largest market for integrated circuits. The cause of this contradiction was the rapid advances in microprocessor performance in desktop computers. Many companies viewed desktop computers as convenient and economical substitutes for mainframe computers.

XHIBIT 15.6 **Office and Computer Machine Orders**

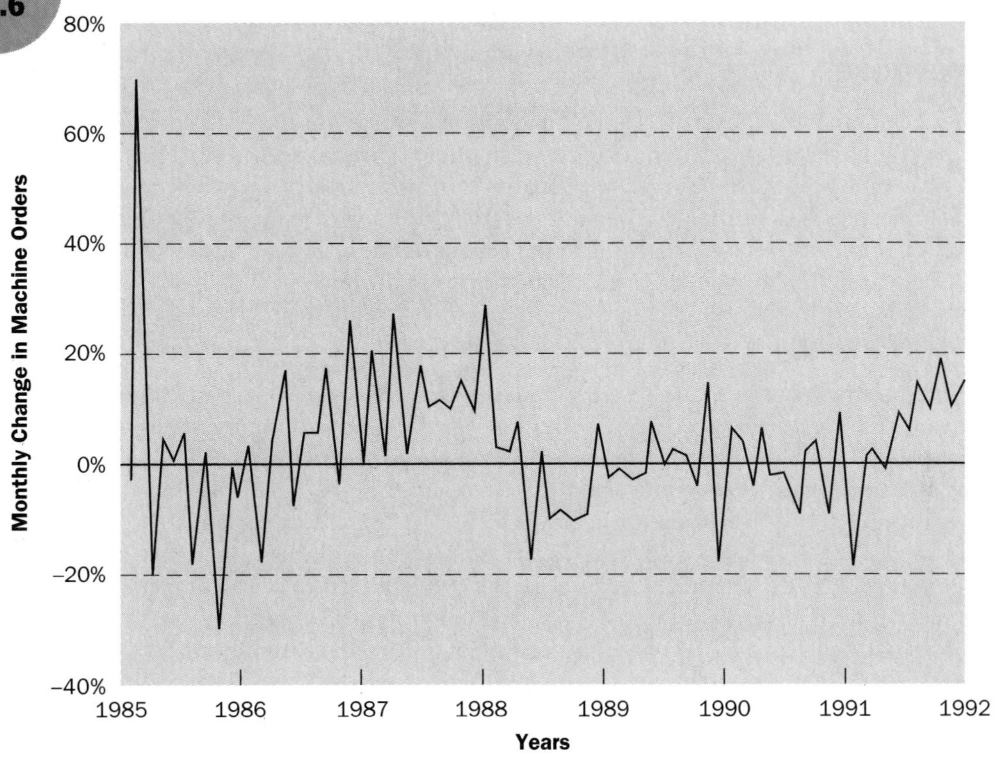

Source: "Computers and Peripherals Industry," U.S. Department of Commerce (January 29, 1993), p. 1076.

Volume increased to meet the increased demand, lowering unit costs and freeing up considerable amounts of cash for R&D programs. Aggressive research efforts in turn generated sharp advances in performance and manufacturing economy. Prices to computer makers were being lowered regularly, permitting reductions in computer selling prices. Reduced computer prices created more market demand. An additional result of research was miniaturization, which opened up a market based not on price but on convenience. Among the fastest growing markets for microprocessors in 1993 were applications in portable and notebook computers.[35] That market should evolve and expand to include both hand-held computers and multimedia communication devices.

The strong increase in price in semiconductor stocks during 1992 raised questions about how far it would go. Support for these high prices came from the unsatisfied demand for the product, reflected by the number of orders compared to the number shipped. Still, important user industries had yet to complete their recoveries from the recession. Edmund Swort of *Value Line* stated, "The semiconductor industry growth potential over the very long term is virtually unlimited."[36]

Competition

Just as the computer industry has gone through a major expansion and repositioning, the companies in direct competition with Apple have changed to include the main players in both the computer software and services industry and the semiconductor industry. The future of computer manufacturers was indisputably tied to the software that they could run and to the semiconductor chip advances needed for the new, small, and innovative products they were developing.

IBM

The International Business Machines Company was the world's largest supplier of advanced information processing technology and communication systems and services. The 1992 sales breakdown by products was 57% software, 16% maintenance, 11% services, 9% rentals, and 7% financing. Foreign business had accounted for 51% of 1991 revenues and over 99% of 1991 pretax earnings.[37]

However, 1992 was a bad year for IBM. Demand for large systems and the midrange AS/400 dropped because of the weak economy and competition from more powerful workstations and personal computers. The earnings per share of IBM stock fell from $10.51 in 1990 to $3.69 in 1991 and finally to $2.48 a share in 1992. IBM was planning to cut 25,000 more jobs in 1993. This force reduction and other cost reductions were expected to cut expenses by about $3 billion dollars.[38]

The lower priced line of personal computers had been selling so well that IBM hadn't been able to meet the demand for some models (see Exhibit 15.7). Workstations also were selling well, and the service business was growing. The move to split the company into independent business units (IBUs) was speeding up. According to analysts, splitting up the company should allow it to react faster to changes in the business environment. John F. Akers, IBM's departing chief recently told the company's top managers that he had hired Morgan Stanley & Co. and the Boston Consulting Group to help the computer giant further break itself up. He singled out the big PC and disk-drive units as the first candidates for change. A key issue for Morgan Stanley and Boston Consulting Group was the federal regulations requiring subsidiaries to have three years of audited results before any public offering. IBM didn't start keeping separate books for most units until 1993.[39]

Compaq

Compaq Computer Corporation produced portable and desktop personal computers that were IBM compatible. It was a leading player in the market for portable computers and had a large share of the IBM-compatible desktop market. Compaq sold its products exclusively through approximately 3,800 dealers. Foreign business amounted to 58% of total sales.[40] Sales had been going up consis-

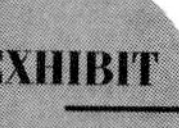

EXHIBIT 15.7

Top Ten Companies in World Sales of Personal Computers
(Dollar amounts in millions)

Company	Revenue 1992	Revenue 1991	% Change	Market Share[1] 1992	Market Share[1] 1991
1. IBM	$7,654.5	$8,505.0	−10.0%	17.2%	19.3%
2. Apple	5,412.0	4,900.0	10.4	12.1	19.3
3. Compaq	4,100.0	3,271.4	25.3	9.2	7.4
4. NEC	3,986.8	4,135.8	−3.6	8.9	9.4
5. Fujitsu	2,618.5	2,319.7	12.9	5.9	5.3
6. Toshiba	1,949.4	2,093.5	−6.9	4.4	4.7
7. Dell	1,812.5	667.4	171.6	4.1	1.5
8. Olivetti	1,348.7	1,586.1	−15.0	3.0	3.6
9. AST Research	1,140.5	800.7	42.4	2.6	1.8
10. Gateway 2000	1,107.1	627.0[2]	76.6	2.5	1.4

Notes:
1. Percentage share of DTM100 revenues.
2. Restated figure.

Source: "The DATAMATION 100," *DATAMATION* (June 15, 1993), p. 22.

tently, from $2,875,100,000 in 1989 to a projected $4,100,000,000 in 1992. Earnings also had improved (but not as fast), owing to the surge in sales of cheaper PCs. The PC price war appeared to be winding down, and, with increased demand by the larger PC manufacturers, there was less incentive to cut prices further. To stay competitive, Compaq was attempting to control rising costs by letting 1,000 employees go. The PC price war may have been about over, but the market share war was just heating up. Compaq's products were not the cheapest, so to maintain market share the company offered standard features rarely found in similarly configured competitors' models. For example, two of its desktop PC lines included a chip to record and play back sound. To expand its markets, Compaq greatly enlarged the number of its distribution channels. The company's early marketing focus had been on large businesses, but it shifted the focus to small businesses and retail stores that concentrated on the home user. Additionally, Compaq provided a free three-year warranty with every PC sold. Compaq hoped to improve its performance by changing its sales mix, introducing higher margin products, and marketing additional printers and high-end notebooks.[41]

Dell

Dell Computer Corporation made notebook and desktop computers, servers, and workstations that were compatible with standard IBM computers. Dell marketed to corporate, government, and educational customers through sales teams. To reach individuals and smaller institutional buyers, it used direct marketing, including mass merchandising arrangements with CompUSA, Staples, and Price Club. Indications were that, in 1992, Dell would have total sales of $2,015,000,000, compared to $889,900,000 in 1991 and $388,600,000 in 1989.[42] Expected 1992 total sales consisted of $1,813,000,000 in PCs and $202,000,000 in software and peripherals. Net sales grew nearly 130% during the first nine months of 1992. Domestic sales had grown by 126% over the same period in 1991, primarily because of Dell's success in obtaining large resellers to be approved vendors for major corporate, government, and education users. International sales more than doubled in the first nine months of 1992 and were approximately 38% of total sales. Plans were in place to enter the Japanese market. Dell's earnings per share had increased steadily from $.18 per share in 1989 to a projected $2.55 a share for 1992. However, Dell's gross margins dropped throughout 1992. By many accounts, Dell was now in a class with personal computer's Big Three: IBM, Apple, and Compaq. "We certainly see them as a first-tier vendor," said John Biglin, systems analyst/programmer at General Waterworks Management Services Company.[43] Although some Dell users stopped short of calling Dell a first-tier company, most said that they were drawn to Dell because it offered a lower priced, quality alternative to IBM and Compaq and offered effective service. In a reliability rating survey of the 500 largest PC sites in the country, Dell Computer outpaced all PC manufacturers in every category (see Exhibit 15.8)—only the second time a company had scored best in every category.[44]

A negative comment about Dell Computer's earnings surfaced on November 20, 1992, when Kidder, Peabody & Co. analyst David R. Korus suggested that Dell may have used foreign currency speculation to buttress its earnings. Dell's Chief Executive Officer, Michael S. Dell, responded quickly, denying any improprieties in the company's currency trading. Korus worried that, if Dell had to change its accounting, the restatement could wipe out its healthy gains.[45] Dell Computer had acknowledged a $38 million unrealized currency loss in 1992. Accounting rules required companies that incur losses as a result of currency speculation to take those losses immediately, whereas hedging losses could be deferred over future quarters.[46]

Dell replaced its old line of 486 desktops with new 486-based machines that offered higher performance and additional features at a lower price. Dell cut prices on its Dimension line and on its floor-standing and notebook systems as well. New machines based on Intel's Pentium (586) microprocessor were not likely to have the same sales growth as the low-priced 486-based machines, and Dell had already cut marketing and general expenses as much as possible. Thus any volume growth slowdown caused by price wars would affect Dell's profitability.

Microsoft

Although not a competitor in computer manufacturing, Microsoft Corporation was a leading player in the expanded computer industry as the largest independent maker of personal computer software. In 1980, IBM sought out the fledgling Microsoft to obtain its disk operating system (DOS) to run the first IBM personal

EXHIBIT 15.8

Customer Satisfaction Survey: Reliability Ratings, 1992 PC Vendor Survey[1]

Service		Technical Support		Price	
1. Dell	8.63	1. Dell	8.09	1. Dell	8.82
2. Apple	8.06	2. IBM	7.99	2. Compaq	6.62
3. IBM	8.01	3. Apple	7.72	3. Apple	6.58
4. Compaq	8.00	4. Compaq	7.71	4. IBM	6.01
Reliability		**Upgradeability**		**Functionality**	
1. Dell	8.96	1. Dell	8.52	1. Dell	8.73
2. Compaq	8.95	2. Apple	7.64	2. Compaq	8.45
3. Apple	8.58	3. Compaq	7.48	3. Apple	8.40
4. IBM	8.54	4. IBM	6.91	4. IBM	7.96
Monitor		**Overall Satisfaction**			
1. Dell	8.31	1. Dell	8.77		
2. Apple	8.08	2. Compaq	8.45		
3. Compaq	7.60	3. Apple	8.14		
4. IBM	7.38	4. IBM	7.89		

Note:
1. Based on customer ratings from a sample of the 500 largest PC sites in the United States.

Source: *Wall Street Journal* (October 12, 1992), p. C-3.

computer. Together, the two companies made the Term MS-DOS the world standard for PCs. However, in 1992, Microsoft joined with IBM's rival, DEC, to move into the minicomputer business. Microsoft and IBM then broke off their 12-year alliance, but Microsoft still had partnerships with every major computer maker except Apple. Its Windows software had a huge following, and MS-DOS was the most widely used operating system for IBM PCs and IBM compatibles. Systems software and languages, including MS-DOS, amounted to 40% of Microsoft's 1992 business. Microsoft also had developed XENIX and LAN Manager. Its applications software, including word processing, spreadsheet, and other business programs, comprised 49% of 1992 sales. Microsoft Mouse, other hardware, and books comprised the remaining 11% of 1992 sales.[47]

Both sales and earnings per share reached all-time highs in 1992. Sales for 1992 were more than $2.75 billion, compared to $803.5 million in 1989. Earnings per share were $2.41 in 1992, compared to $.67 in 1989. Both sales and earnings per share advanced by 40% in the first quarter of 1993, and the company wasn't planning to release any new products in 1993. Windows was still selling at the rate of one million units a month. Microsoft also offered a strong group of applications that were tuned to work with Windows.

Microsoft was planning to expand from software for individual computers to software applications for groups of workers. This market became important as corporations built on their investments in personal computers by tying them together so that users could share data and work together on projects. The first step in this direction was Windows for work groups, which integrated networking and work-group functions. Microsoft may repeat the strategy that was so successful with Windows—seeding as many computers as possible with the product and then reaping the benefits by selling applications that were tailored to take advantage of the system's features.

On February 5, 1993, a sharply split Federal Trade Commission declined to seek a preliminary injunction to force Microsoft Corporation to halt certain business practices. On a two-to-two vote, the commissioners rejected staff recommendations that the agency seek an injunction to prevent Microsoft from creating built-in incompatibility in its software. That incompatibility, for example, allowed Microsoft's popular Windows programs to work only with the company's disk operating system MS-DOS, and not with a competitor's.[48]

Intel

Both Intel Corporation and Motorola were major U.S. players in the semiconductor market. Intel was the leading supplier of semiconductors in the world, gaining a 7.7% share of the market and displacing Japan's NEC Corporation from the top spot in 1992. NEC fell to second, Toshiba Corp. dropped to third, and Motorola remained in fourth position, according to *Dataquest, Inc.*[49]

Intel served two markets: computers (75% of sales); and communications, industrial automation, and military and other electronic equipment (25% of sales).[50] Intel's major products were microprocessors, related peripherals, microcontrollers, and memory components. Intel's foreign business amounted to about 51% of sales. Intel's total annual sales increased from $3,127,000,000 in 1989 to $5,844,000,000 in 1992. During the same period, earnings per share doubled from $2.35 to $5.04. Fourth-quarter earnings per share for 1992 were $1.97, more than doubling the $.90 a share in the fourth quarter of 1991.[51] Surging demand by personal computer makers for high-performance Intel 486 microprocessors boosted sales for the last quarter of 1992 by 54%. With shipments at a quarterly rate close to $1.9 billion, high plant utilization and fixed overhead expense absorption improved profit margins. Drastic price cuts by manufacturers of personal computers created steep growth in demand for PCs by businesses. Intel's strategy was to roll out successive waves of devices at the high end, each generation protected by copyrights that gave the company time to develop the next generation. By the time competition in the i486 generation became substantial, Intel's Pentium chip was ready. The Pentium chip offered mainframe-like performance at a comparatively low price. The company's investment in plant and reduction in fabrication costs made each new model more profitable.

Motorola

Motorola, Inc., was a leading manufacturer of electronic equipment and components. It was one of the winners of the first Malcolm Baldrige National Quality Award in 1988, in recognition of its superior companywide quality management. Motorola's principal products were communications, semiconductors, and general systems. The semiconductors comprised a broad line of integrated circuits and products. Foreign business accounted for 42% of Motorola's sales. Annual sales figures went from $9,620,000,000 in 1989 to $13,711,000,000 in 1992. At the same time, the earnings per share increased only modestly, from $2.06 to $2.16, but a 22% increase in fourth-quarter sales in 1992 produced the largest quarterly per share figure in four years, $.67.

Year-to-year growth in orders exceeded sales increases for Motorola's three key business sectors in the last three months of 1992, creating appreciable product backlogs. A large demand for semiconductor chips produced strong demand well into 1993. The 22% revenue increase in 1992 for semiconductor products had a good chance of repeating, in view of the hefty 35% rise in fourth-quarter bookings. The semiconductor division was the company's leading profit contributor, with $464,000,000 of Motorola's total net profits of $576,000,000.[52]

In October 1992, IBM and Motorola announced the production of the PowerPC 601 microprocessor chip. The companies raced through design and first fabrication in 12 months to produce a reduced instruction set computing (RISC) chip that they claim equals the performance of leading RISC microprocessors, but was only half the size. The PowerPC chip has 2.8 million transistors packed into dimensions of approximately four-tenths of an inch per side.[53]

Marketing

Apple sold its products primarily to business and government customers through independent resellers—sellers that added value to the product prior to sale (VAR) and companies that integrated Apple components into their systems. In order to provide products and service to its independent resellers on a timely basis, Apple maintained numerous Apple distribution and support centers. The company also began to reach individual home sales by new distribution systems, such as general merchandise stores (Sears), consumer electronics outlets (Circuit City), and office product superstores (Silo).

Business customers contributed the largest portion of Apple's revenues. These customers reported that they were attracted to the Macintosh for various reasons, including the availability of a wide variety of software, low training costs, and the ability of the Macintosh to network and communicate with other computer systems.

Apple first introduced personal computers to education customers in the late 1970s. In the United States, Apple was one of the leading suppliers of personal computers to both elementary and secondary school customers and to college and university customers. Apple officials claimed that sales of its products to the education market accounted for more than half of Apple USA's 1991 revenues, or about $1.6 billion. Apple dominated the K–12 segment of the market during the 1991–1992 school year, with more than 65% of the market and a 35% slice of the higher education market.[54] The push into the educational arena had been mostly through low-end systems. Apple's closest competitor in the educational market was IBM, with a 17% market share.

In the United States, Apple's commitment to serve the federal government began in 1986 with the formation of the Apple Federal Systems Group. Although Apple had contracts with various U.S. government agencies, these contracts were not material to the company's overall financial condition.

In 1993, the United States represented Apple's largest geographic marketplace and was served by Apple USA's sales, marketing, and support efforts. Products sold domestically were manufactured primarily in Apple's facilities in Fremont, California; Fountain, Colorado; and Singapore.

Apple's personal computing business was strong in 1992. Shipments of Apple Macintosh personal computers grew by 20% during the year to more than 2.5 million units, outpacing the entire industry. Sales of Macintosh PowerBook computers accounted for much of the growth. Apple also sold more than 400,000 PowerBook computers in 1991, representing $1 billion in net sales. The most affordable color Macintosh computers, the Macintosh LC and Macintosh LC II, sold well in many markets. These products were especially popular in the education market, where the transition from Apple II systems to Macintosh systems continued. The Macintosh Quadra 950, the most powerful computer Apple ever developed, was popular with people who demanded high performance, such as publishers and engineers.

Apple continued to perform well in international markets. Net sales for Apple's European and Pacific operations increased by 13% in 1992 and represented 45% of total net sales. The personal computer business in Japan grew dramatically, generating more than $500 million in net sales. In Europe, Apple experienced strong growth in its largest markets. The major marketing improvement in 1992 was the expanded distribution channels. Not only did Apple expand hardware distribution by including consumer retail stores, but it also now marketed Macintosh system software and system extensions through software retail stores. Apple had made its personal computer products available to more people through more channels than ever before.

In general, Apple's resellers purchased products on an as-needed basis. Apple attempted to fill orders on the requested delivery dates and had not had a significant backlog of unfilled orders until November 1992, when they totaled approximately $950 million (compared to approximately $483 million in November 1991). This increase reflected strong demand for certain of the company's new products that had been introduced in September and October 1992.

Apple Computer allowed distributors to increase the number of Value Added Resellers (VARs) that they could support from 150 to 500 and loosened restrictions on recruitment by markets. "We had so many qualified VARs that had to be turned away that Apple was simply hurting itself and us by not allowing additional recruitment," said Dave Jaskulks, Director and General Manager of Ingram Micro's Macintosh division.[55] In the past, VARs that accessed Apple products through distributors had to obtain servicing for the products through a dealer holding Apple's standard authorization. In 1992, Apple developed a program to allow VARs to supply services to customers.

Market Segmentation

Apple Corporation concentrated on one principal industry segment: the design, manufacture, and sale of personal computing products. The company's net sales, transfers, operating income, and identifiable assets for 1990, 1991, and 1992 are shown in Exhibit 15.9. Although the largest amount of assets and sales were located in the United States, most of the operating income came from the European, Pacific, and Canadian markets.

In 1993, Apple had the largest share of the U.S. PC market, accounting for 13% of the total, with IBM slightly behind at 12%. The total PC market is shown in Exhibit 15.10. Although Apple had the largest single share of the market, the top 20 PC clone makers accounted for the largest portion of the total market. Small computer makers ("No-names") captured a phenomenal 16% of the total $50 billion PC market in 1992. Despite their small size, these companies have helped force prices down, with no-frills service and mail-order distribution. Suddenly, however, the market became more hostile for these companies (see Exhibit 15.11). IBM, Compaq, and the other large PC makers slashed the huge price differential that had allowed the no-names to flourish. By some counts, more than 300 no-name PC makers had sprung up in the United States since 1988, nibbling away at both IBM and larger second-tier brands such as Dell and AST Research. The no-names had once undercut Compaq and IBM by as much as $1,000 a unit, but the gap had closed to $400 to $500 in the summer of 1992 and had all but vanished in 1993.

Raytheon Company reported that it saved $1 million by buying no-name PCs, but it recently ordered some Apple computers after price cuts made them attractive again. Blair Kanbar, the purchasing agent for the city of Newton, Massachusetts, bought from Compaq. "They have become a lot more competitive lately," he said.[56]

The PC industry, normally producing a mind-numbing mix of technobabble and arcane product comparisons in order to sell its products, had turned to a new wave of direct, combative print advertising. Compaq, the PC maker that sparked the price war in June 1992, ran a two-page ad (that ran for weeks in major newspapers) that featured a gummy, oversized gluepot next to three tiny signs, ostensibly the nameplate for archrival Dell's new Dimension line. "Some companies must think you're willing to pay for a name," the headline says of the Dell machines. "On their computers, it's the only part they make."[57] In September 1992, IBM ran a two-page ad comparing Dell and Compaq machines to IBM's new PS/2. The ad featured a chart comparing the service features and warranty of its machines to Dell's and Compaq's. The ads became even more personal a few days after the *Wall Street Journal* ran an article detailing the behind the scenes power struggle at Compaq, which led to the ouster of Chairman Joseph R. Canion. Advanced Logic

EXHIBIT 15.9

Industry Segment and Geographic Information: Apple Computer, Inc.
(Dollar amounts in thousands)

The Company operates in one principal industry segment: the design, manufacture, and sale of personal computing products. The Company's products are sold primarily to the business, education, home, and government markets. Products are distributed principally through third-party computer resellers.

	1992	1991	1990
Net sales to unaffiliated customers			
United States	$3,885,042	$3,484,534	$3,241,061
Europe	1,950,039	1,824,641	1,545,091
Pacific and Canada	1,251,461	999,675	772,283
Total net sales	$7,086,542	$6,308,850	$5,558,435
Transfers between geographic areas (eliminated in consolidation)			
United States	$934,673	$774,059	$559,069
Europe	246,745	147,713	33,531
Pacific and Canada	979,566	1,099,448	373,118
Total transfers	$2,160,984	$2,021,220	$965,718
Operating income			
United States	$245,810	$9,036	$229,016
Europe	301,865	222,893	367,499
Pacific and Canada	246,181	227,690	103,770
Eliminations	11,952	(12,235)	11,727
Interest and other income, net	49,634	52,362	66,505
Income before income taxes	$855,442	$499,746	$778,517
Identifiable assets			
United States	$1,536,705	$1,440,332	$1,054,169
Europe	767,765	734,836	591,534
Pacific and Canada	456,472	461,555	350,966
Eliminations	(43,716)	(56,693)	(27,455)
Corporate assets	1,506,467	913,567	1,006,493
Total assets	$4,223,693	$3,493,597	$2,975,707

Net sales to unaffiliated customers is based on the location of the customers. Transfers between geographic areas are recorded at amounts generally above cost and in accordance with the rules and regulations of the respective governing tax authorities. Operating income consists of total net sales less operating expenses, and does not include either interest and other income, net, or income taxes. U.S. operating income is net of corporate expenses. Identifiable assets of geographic areas are those assets used in the Company's operations in each area. Corporate assets include cash and cash equivalents, joint-venture investments, and short-term investments.

Source: Apple Computer, Inc., *1992 Annual Report*, p. 37.

EXHIBIT 5.10

Fragmented PC Market

(Percentage of U.S. market by type of PC maker, June 1992)

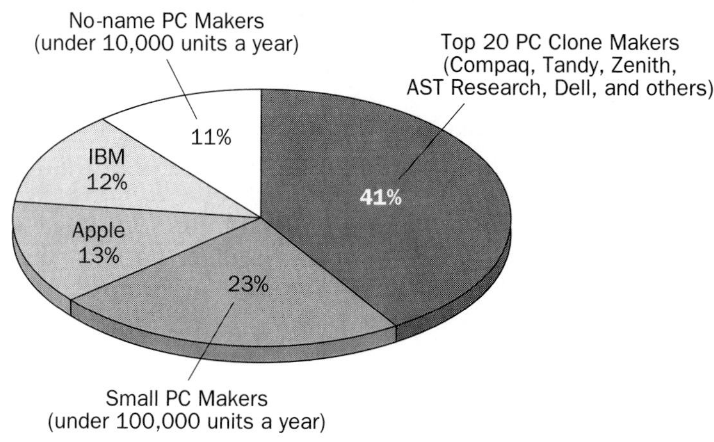

Source: *Wall Street Journal* (November 12, 1992), p. B-1.

EXHIBIT 5.11

No-Name PC Makers

(Number of units shipped by the smallest PC makers (below the top 100 vendors) and market share)

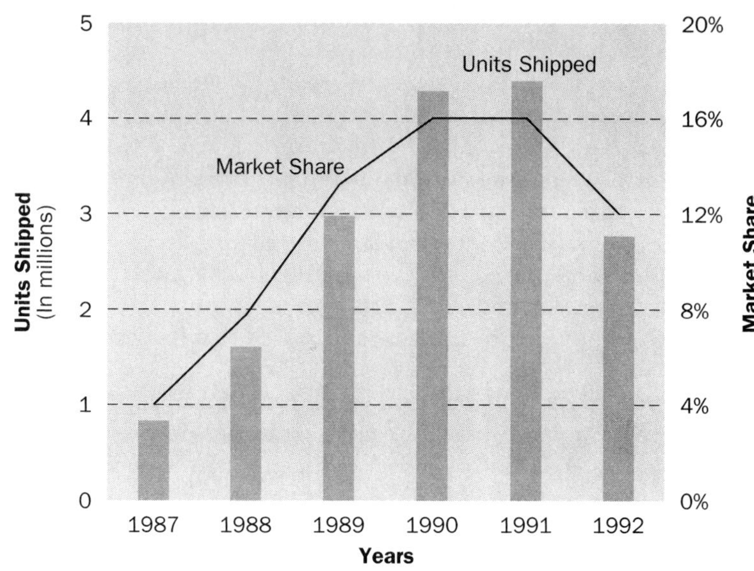

Source: *Wall Street Journal* (November 12, 1992), p. B-1.

Research focused on the turmoil in a biting ad in trade publications: "No betrayed friendship, no new CEO," the ad declared, "At ALR we're the same team."[58]

To make sure that they were getting their messages across, many computer companies boosted their ad budgets (see Exhibit 15.12). Compaq, which had announced three major new product families since June 1992, spent 76% more in the first eight months of 1993. The increase to $27.7 million from $15.7 million came despite an austerity program that claimed the jobs of 1,000 workers. AdScope, Inc., a company that tracked computer industry ad spending, said that, in all, the top ten PC advertisers spent $194.7 million during 1992's first eight months, up 43% from a year earlier.[59] Interestingly, that ad boom wasn't being led by the no-name clone computer makers that once dominated the pages of the industry trade magazines. Instead, the industry's leaders were the big spenders, using advertising to convince customers that, despite the popular perception, all personal computers were not the same.

For years, IBM did not sell directly to customers, unlike its upstart competitors. Instead, IBM opted for the traditional route: marketing its PCs exclusively through stores. IBM was expected to announce sometime in 1993 that it was stepping up its direct response sale of PCs. The cost of advertising for this step was expected to exceed $15 million and could ultimately be as much as $30 million.[60]

The top ten PC manufacturers accounted for 58% of international PC sales in 1992, up from 51% in 1991. "By the end of 1995, the five top computer companies will provide 75% of the world's computers," said Tim Bajarin, an analyst with Creative Strategies.[61] Things have gotten so competitive that Dataquest, Inc., a market research firm, has a "death watch" on some 60% of PC and peripherals companies. When these companies leave the business, said Dataquest analyst Robert Corpuz, "Most of them aren't likely to reappear."[62]

Apple has dramatically reversed its fortunes in Japan. Since 1989, Apple has increased its market share there nearly fivefold, to 5.4%, selling 120,000 units in 1991. That was still a small amount compared to sales by industry giant NEC, which controlled more than 50% of the personal computer market in Japan. Apple hoped to reach a 7% share and sell 50% more computers in Japan in 1992. In relatively short order, Apple Japan hired a Japanese management team, appointed a local board of directors, listed its shares on the Tokyo stock exchange, and dropped its prices to competitive levels. Apple also went after youthful consumers by backing a 1990 Janet Jackson concert and a Japanese Ladies Pro Golf tournament.[63]

At the vast Comdex/Fall trade show held in Las Vegas, Nevada (in November 1992), the action in mobile computing was all-American. From Motorola's range of hand-held wireless communicators to Apple Computer's new Duo notebook computers, the U.S. computer industry demonstrated that any fears that the Japanese would inevitably control personal computing—as they did the manufacture of television sets—were groundless. The Japanese share of the U.S. market was 6.4%, 13.2%, and 9.1% for 1991, 1990, and 1989, respectively.

Although the Japanese continued to dominate the supply of flat-panel display screens used in portable computers and had a leading position in producing computer memory chips, U.S. companies still dominated the production of many other

EXHIBIT 5.12

Computer Industry: Advertising Is Hot
(Number of pages, January 1–August 31)

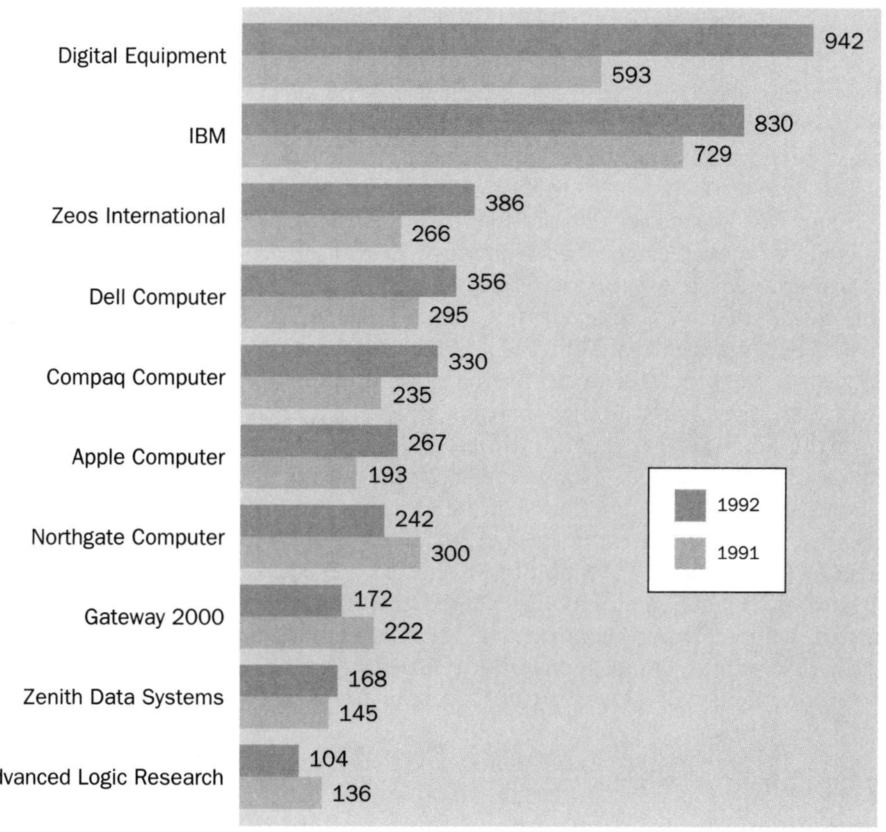

Source: "P.C. Marketers Punchup Combative Ads," *Wall Street Journal* (October 21, 1991), p. B-1.

components, such as microprocessors and hard disks. Charles H. Ferguson, an MIT researcher, stated, "American companies, primarily the Microsoft Corporation, . . . and Apple Computer, have been very successful in retaining leadership by setting standards adopted by large segments of the industry."[64] Computer makers have grown expert in thumping the Japanese in those areas where they are weakest: developing products in relatively short cycles and redesigning an entire product line in six to 12 months. "Suddenly the Japanese have become more conservative, and they're not taking risks," said Alain Rossman, a former Apple executive who was President of EO Computer. "Today, winning comes from speed-based competition," he continued. "The Japanese are quick when everything is specified, but in innovation and path-seeking, they're slower."[65]

Products

Apple Corporation offered a wide range of personal computing products, including personal computers, related software, peripherals, and networking and communication products. The Apple II and Apple Macintosh lines were Apple's two central product families. First introduced in 1977, the Apple II family is the company's oldest product family. The Macintosh product family, first introduced in 1984, featured an intuitive ease of use, an innovative applications base, and a built-in networking capability.

The Macintosh product family included a broad range of personal computer offerings. The Macintosh Classic II was affordable, did not take up much room, and could be moved easily. The Macintosh LCII offered a larger range of display options, both color and monochrome, at a reasonable price. The notebook-sized Macintosh PowerBook computers combined convenience, simplicity, and a wide range of performance availability. The Macintosh II and Quadra computers were designed for high performance, flexibility, and expansion—with a range of options for memory, mass storage, displays, graphics, and communication.

In the fall of 1992, Apple introduced several new personal computers: the Macintosh Performa 200, 400, and 600 computers; the PowerBook 145, 160, and 180; the Macintosh IIvi and IIvx; and the Macintosh Duo System. The Duo System combined the PowerBook Duo 210 or Duo 230 notebook computer with the Macintosh Duo Dock docking station to provide the versatility of a desktop computer and the convenience of a notebook computer. Apple also offered a full line of associated computer peripherals, including the LaserWriter, ImageWriter, and StyleWriter printer families; the Apple CD 150 memory drive, and the Apple OneScanner modem. In October 1992, Apple also introduced the 14-inch Macintosh Color Display.

On February 9, 1993, Apple announced that it was adding more power to the Macintosh. Apple planned to build its midrange Macintosh machines with a fast microprocessor "Brain" previously available only in its most expensive computers. Apple also planned to put color screens in some low-priced models that until then had offered only monochrome.[66] Apple's move to push power and color down into lower priced models came as its main competition, makers of PCs using Intel's chips and Microsoft's basic software, were driving down prices of powerful and feature-laden PCs. Apple said that it would unveil in 1993 a line of midpriced computers that used Motorola's 68040 microprocessor. This microprocessor had been available only in Apple's Quadra machines, which cost thousands of dollars more than Apple's new midpriced systems that have suggested retail prices ranging from $1,900 to $4,400. Apple also said that it would begin selling color screen versions of its most basic Macintosh, the Classic, and a version of its notebook-sized PowerBook computer. Apple's aggressiveness in selling upgraded Macintosh models has served to broaden its product line. The company said that it expected to announce in February 1993 that it had shipped its ten millionth Macintosh.[67]

Operating system software, such as Apple's Macintosh system software and A/UX, extend the power of Apple computers. Claris Corporation, a wholly owned Apple subsidiary, also developed and marketed innovative software applications and extensions to the Macintosh system software. Apple also provided networking and communications products that connected Apple systems to local area networks, providing access to other computers and computing environments. These computing environments included IBM's large and small systems and DEC's Vax system.

Apple developed every part of the Macintosh computer platform: the computer hardware, the system software, and the system extensions. With its third-party partners, it also developed peripherals, application software, and networking and communications products. Consequently, Apple could integrate hardware and software to create new personal computing systems that allowed users to do things with their computers that they were unable to do previously. It integrated high-resolution displays with scalable fonts and graphics capabilities, allowing users to create sophisticated publications on a personal computer. It also integrated a microphone and a CD-ROM drive with QuickTime software, so that users could work with sound, video, and animation. In addition, it integrated the all-in-one design of the PowerBook computer with a built-in modem and AppleTalk Remote Access software so that users could do their work anywhere.

A fundamental change was occurring in the way organizations manage and use information. Historically, organizations have used networks of "dumb terminals" connected to mainframes and minicomputers to share information, known as the host–terminal method of computing. Now businesses manage with a client–server model of computing networks of workstations and personal computers. The Macintosh systems were well suited to client–server environments because of their superior ease of use and broad networking capabilities.

Apple's Enterprise Systems Division pursued this opportunity by creating client–server systems to help people work together better. These systems work in different computing environments, from AppleTalk networks to IBM SNA networks. They can support many different types of work groups, from small businesses to classrooms to large multinational companies.

Raw Materials

The raw materials, processes, and components needed by Apple Corporation were generally available from multiple sources; however, certain key components were available only from single sources. For example, certain microprocessors used in some of the company's products were available only from Motorola, Inc. Additional key components and processes obtained from single sources included certain of the company's displays, microprocessors, mouse devices, keyboards, disk drives, printers, and printer components.[68] New products introduced by the company often initially utilized custom components obtained from only one source.

If the supply of a key single-source material, process, or component were delayed or stopped, Apple's ability to ship the related product would be adversely affected. Companies that could adversely affect Apple's production were Canon, Hitachi, Hosiden, Sharp, Motorola, Sony, TEC, and VLSI Technology. In 1993, Apple was attempting to reduce these risks by working closely with these and other key suppliers, all of whom were reliable multinational firms with multiple plans and long-standing business relationships with Apple. Apple had a supply agreement with TEC for an indefinite term and one with Motorola for five years from January 31, 1992.[69] The company single-sourced ImageWriter printers from TEC and microprocessors from Motorola.

Properties

Apple's headquarters were located in Cupertino, California, with manufacturing facilities in Fremont, California; Fountain, Colorado; Cork, Ireland; and Singapore. As of September 1992, Apple had leased 7.9 million square feet of space. The leases were generally for terms of five to ten years, with options to renew. Some of these leases had been initiated to facilitate the 1991 corporate restructuring. The amount of space leased may decline as the restructuring actions are completed.

The company owned its manufacturing facilities in Fountain, Colorado; Cork, Ireland; and Singapore. Apple also owned a new distribution facility in Apeldoorn, Netherlands. In the first quarter of 1992, Apple purchased a 30-acre parcel of land in Sacramento, California, to be used as a manufacturing, service, and support center. Apple owned a building in Napa, California, which it used as a centralized domestic data center.

In the fourth quarter of 1992, Apple announced a plan to realign its worldwide manufacturing and distribution activities. Consequently, the manufacturing functions currently performed in Fremont, California, were to be relocated to the Sacramento, Fountain, Cork, and Singapore sites. The lease on the Fremont plant ended in 1993.

Apple's management believed that its existing facilities and equipment were well maintained and in good operating condition and that it had ample manufacturing capacity. Management acknowledged in the *1992 Annual Report* that "the majority of the Company's research and development activities, its corporate headquarters, and other critical business operations are located near major earthquake faults. Operating results could be materially adversely affected in the event of a major earthquake."[70]

Litigation

In March 1988, Apple filed suit against Microsoft and Hewlett-Packard, alleging that the Microsoft Windows and HP NewWave computer programs infringed on Apple's registered copyrights that protected the Macintosh user interface. Microsoft and Hewlett-Packard countersued. On April 16, 1990, Apple asked the court for a summary judgment, holding that the company's copyrights for the Lisa and Macintosh computers were valid, and to strike the defendants' defenses challenging the validity and scope of the copyrights. Microsoft and Hewlett-Packard each filed a motion for summary judgment challenging the validity of Apple's copyrights and seeking to narrow the scope of the protection. On April 14, 1992, a court ruling unfavorable to Apple substantially narrowed the scope of the issues in the case. The court held that most of the Windows and NewWave interface elements were either licensed by Apple to Microsoft or made up of elements common to Apple that cannot be protected. Apple believed that "the final resolution of this matter will not have a material adverse effect on its financial condition and results of operations. . . ."[71]

In 1984, class action complaints were filed against Apple and 14 of its officers and directors, alleging violations of securities laws based on the company's alleged failure to make certain disclosures regarding the Lisa computer and the "Twiggy" disk drive. A fund of $16 million was created to settle the case under an agreement approved by the court in March 1992. In May 1991, class action complaints were filed against Apple and certain officers and directors alleging violations of securities laws, based on statements made about business prospects and the outlook for growth in earnings in 1991. Apple created a fund of $3.8 million to settle the case under an agreement approved by the court in May 1992. Apple's insurance coverage provided a substantial portion of the settlement in the two securities' class action cases.[72]

Finance

In 1992, competitive pressures forced price reductions in the personal computing industry, resulting in record increases in the number of units sold. However, Apple's gross margin dropped from 47.5% of net sales in 1991 to 43.7% of net sales in 1992. This decline in gross margin in 1992 did not translate into a drop in net income for two reasons: (1) Apple increased revenues greatly by selling more Apple products than ever before; and (2) the company reduced operating expenses by streamlining its operations and moving facilities to lower cost areas. Operating expenses decreased from 36.8% of net sales in 1991 to 32.3% of net sales in 1992. Unfortunately, this decline did not continue in the first quarter of 1993; even with record first-quarter revenues, pressures on profit margins depressed earnings by 2.8%. Competitive price cuts, coupled with the costs of introducing laptop products, reduced profits to $161.3 million, from $166 million a year earlier. With its margins caught in a vise, Apple enforced strict cost controls, forcing operating expenses down to a seven-year low of 29% of net sales[73] (see Exhibits 15.13–15.15).

The company hedged certain portions of its exposure to foreign currency and interest rate fluctuations with various strategies and financial instruments. Gains and losses associated with these financial instruments were recorded in income. All highly liquid investments with a maturity of three months or less at date of purchase were considered to be cash equivalents. Short-term investments were carried at cost plus accrued interest to approximate market value. A substantial portion of the company's cash and equivalents was held by foreign subsidiaries but listed in dollar amounts. No U.S. income taxes were accounted for on the earnings of the company's foreign subsidiaries. Apple intended that these earnings would be invested indefinitely in operations outside the United States.

In the third quarter of 1991, Apple initiated a plan to restructure its operations worldwide. In connection with this plan, it recorded a $197.5 million charge to operating expenses. The restructuring charge for 1991 included $114.5 million

EXHIBIT 15.13

Consolidated Balance Sheets: Apple Computer, Inc.

(Dollar amounts in thousands)

Years Ending September 25, 1992, and September 27, 1991	1992	1991
Assets		
Current assets		
Cash and cash equivalents	$ 498,557	$ 604,147
Short-term investments	936,943	288,572
Accounts receivable, net of allowance for doubtful accounts of $83,048 ($53,993 in 1991)	1,087,185	907,159
Inventories	580,097	671,655
Prepaid income taxes	199,139	222,980
Other current assets	256,473	169,097
Total current assets	3,558,394	2,863,610
Property, plant, and equipment		
Land and buildings	255,808	198,107
Machinery and equipment	516,335	485,872
Office furniture and equipment	155,317	146,433
Leasehold improvements	208,180	205,602
	1,135,640	1,036,014
Accumulated depreciation and amortization	(673,419)	(588,036)
Net property, plant, and equipment	462,221	447,978
Other assets	203,078	182,009
Total assets	$4,223,693	$3,493,597
Liabilities and Shareholders' Equity		
Current liabilities		
Notes payable	$ 184,461	$ 148,566
Accounts payable	426,936	357,084
Accrued compensation and employee benefits	142,382	119,468
Income taxes payable	78,382	14,857
Accrued marketing and distribution	187,767	136,712
Accrued restructuring costs	105,038	162,365
Other current liabilities	300,554	277,999
Total current liabilities	1,425,520	1,217,051
Deferred income taxes	610,803	509,870
Commitments and contingencies	—	—
Shareholders' equity		
Common stock, no par value; 320,000,000 shares authorized; 118,478,825 shares issued and outstanding in 1992 (118,385,899 shares in 1991)	282,310	278,865
Retained earnings	1,904,519	1,492,024
Accumulated translation adjustment	541	(2,377)
	2,187,370	1,768,512
Notes receivable from shareholders	—	(1,836)
Total shareholders' equity	2,187,370	1,766,676
Total liabilities and shareholders' equity	$4,223,693	$3,493,597

Source: Apple Computer, Inc., *1992 Annual Report,* p. 27.

EXHIBIT 15.14

Consolidated Statements of Income: Apple Computer, Inc.
(Dollar amounts in thousands, except per share data)

Fiscal Years Ending September 25	1992	1991	1990
Net sales	$7,086,542	$6,308,849	$5,558,435
Costs and expenses			
Cost of sales	3,991,337	3,314,118	2,606,223
Research and development	602,135	583,046	478,019
Selling, general and administrative	1,687,262	1,740,293	1,728,508
Restructuring costs and other	—	224,043	33,673
Total costs and expenses	6,280,734	5,861,500	4,846,423
Operating income	805,808	447,349	712,012
Interest and other income, net	49,634	52,395	66,505
Income before income taxes	855,442	499,744	778,517
Provision for income taxes	325,069	189,903	303,622
Net income	$ 530,373	$ 309,841	$ 474,895
Earnings per common and common equivalent share	$ 4.33	$ 2.58	$ 3.77
Common and common equivalent shares used in the calculations of earnings per share	$ 122,490	$ 120,283	$ 125,813

Source: Apple Computer, Inc., *1992 Annual Report,* p. 26.

of estimated facilities and $83 million of estimated employee-related expenses. Subsequently, Apple continued to phase in the restructuring plan.

The Future

Apple planned to introduce as many personal computing products in 1993 as it introduced in 1991 and 1992 combined. These products will expand its present offerings in desktop computing, notebook computing, system software, and peripherals. It planned to continue to expand its distribution channels, making the purchase of Apple products even easier. It also planned to expand its distribution system to sell certain Macintosh products by mailorder catalogs.

Apple planned to expand its enterprise systems—products to help groups of users share information and collaborate on projects. These systems will include new server, network management, and remote-access products. Apple expected to ship its first Personal Interactive Electronics Systems, called personal digital assistants (PDAs), in 1993. Alliances play a key role in Apple's personal interactive electronics business. In March 1992, Apple announced a licensing agreement with Sharp Corporation for the Newton technology. In June 1992, Apple announced a development and manufacturing agreement with Toshiba for its new CD-ROM–based PDAs.

Because of the nature of the personal computer industry, Apple's ability to compete depended heavily on its ability to produce a continuing and timely flow

EXHIBIT 15.15

Eleven-Year Financial History: Apple Computer, Inc.

(Dollar amounts in thousands, except per share data)

Fiscal Years Ending September 25	1992	1991	1990	1989
A. RESULTS OF OPERATIONS				
Net sales				
Domestic	$3,885,042	$3,484,533	$3,241,061	$3,401,462
International	3,201,500	2,824,316	2,317,374	1,882,551
Total net sales	7,086,542	6,308,849	5,558,435	5,284,013
Costs and expenses				
Cost of sales	3,991,337	3,314,118	2,606,223	2,694,823
Research and development (R&D)	602,135	583,046	478,019	420,083
Selling, general and administrative (SG&A)	1,687,262	1,740,293	1,728,508	1,534,794
Restructuring costs and other	—	224,043	33,673	—
Total costs and expenses	6,280,734	5,861,500	4,846,423	4,649,700
Operating income	805,808	447,349	712,012	634,313
Interest and other income, net	49,634	52,395	66,505	110,009
Income before income taxes	855,442	499,744	778,517	744,322
Provision for income taxes	325,069	189,903	303,622	290,289
Net income	$ 530,373	$ 309,841	$ 474,895	$ 454,033
Earnings per common and common equivalent share	$ 4.33	$ 2.58	$ 3.77	$ 3.53
Common and common equivalent shares used in the calculations of earnings per share	122,490	120,283	125,813	128,669
B. FINANCIAL POSITION				
Cash, cash equivalents, and short-term investments	$1,435,500	$ 892,719	$ 997,091	$ 808,950
Accounts receivable, net	1,087,185	907,159	761,868	792,824
Inventories	580,097	671,655	355,473	475,377
Net property, plant, and equipment	462,221	447,978	398,165	334,227
Total assets	4,223,693	$3,493,597	$2,975,707	$2,743,899
Current liabilities	1,425,520	$1,217,051	$1,027,055	$895,243
Deferred income taxes	610,803	509,870	501,832	362,910
Shareholders' equity	2,187,370	1,766,676	1,446,820	1,485,746
Cash dividends declared per common share	$ .48	$ .48	$ .44	$ .40

1988	1987	1986	1985	1984	1983	1982
$2,766,328	$1,940,369	$1,411,812	$1,490,396	$1,187,839	$764,416	$440,895
1,305,045	720,699	490,086	427,884	328,037	218,353	142,166
4,071,373	2,661,068	1,901,898	1,918,280	1,515,876	982,769	583,061
1,990,879	1,296,220	891,112	1,117,864	878,586	505,765	288,001
272,512	191,554	127,758	72,526	71,136	60,040	37,979
1,187,644	801,856	609,497	588,156	480,303	290,845	154,872
—	—	—	36,966	—	—	—
3,451,035	2,289,630	1,628,367	1,815,512	1,430,025	856,650	480,852
620,338	371,438	273,531	102,768	85,851	126,119	102,209
35,823	38,930	36,187	17,277	23,334	20,003	14,563
656,161	410,368	309,718	120,045	109,185	146,122	116,772
255,903	192,872	155,755	58,822	45,130	69,408	55,466
$ 400,258	$ 217,496	$ 153,963	$ 61,223	$ 64,055	$ 76,714	$ 61,306
$3.08	$1.65	$1.20	$.49	$.53	$.64	$.53
129,900	131,615	128,630	123,790	121,774	119,734	115,596
$545,717	$565,094	$576,215	$337,013	$114,888	$143,284	$153,056
638,816	405,637	263,126	220,157	258,238	136,420	71,478
461,470	225,753	108,680	166,951	264,619	142,457	75,368
207,357	130,434	107,315	90,446	75,868	67,050	34,483
2,082,086	1,477,931	1,160,128	936,177	788,786	556,579	357,787
827,093	478,678	328,535	295,425	255,184	130,094	87,808
251,568	162,765	137,506	90,265	69,037	48,584	12,887
1,003,425	836,488	694,087	550,487	464,565	377,901	257,092
.32	.12	—	—	—	—	—

(continued)

Eleven-Year Financial History: Apple Computer, Inc. *(continued)*
(Dollar amounts in thousands, except per share data)

Fiscal Years Ending September 25	1992	1991	1990	1989
C. OTHER DATA (UNAUDITED)				
Permanent employees	12,166	12,386	12,307	12,068
Temporary employees	2,632	2,046	2,221	2,449
International net sales as a percentage of total net sales	45%	45%	42%	36%
Gross margin as a percentage of net sales	44	47	53	49
R&D as a percentage of net sales	8	9	9	8
SG&A as a percentage of net sales	24	28	31	29
Operating margin as a percentage of net sales	11	7	13	12
Return on net sales	7	5	9	9
Return on average total assets	14	10	17	19
Return on average shareholders' equity	27	19	32	36
Price range per common share	\$69⅞–\$43¼	\$72¾–\$25	\$49½–\$28¼	\$49⅝–\$33¾

of competitive products to the marketplace. Apple's research and development expenditures totaled \$602 million in 1992, up from \$478 million in 1990.[74]

On February 8, 1993, American Telephone & Telegraph Company, Sony Corporation, Motorola, Inc., Phillips Electronics, and Matsushita Electric Industrial Company announced investments in General Magic, a secretive, three-year-old venture started by Apple Computer, Inc. Apple began the work, but Sculley decided that General Magic should operate as an independent alliance to secure the support of other giant concerns for communications software called Telescript. It would allow any computer or communicator to talk to other devices on any kind of network using Telescript. The lack of such a common language had stunted the growth of the desktop market for years, and overcoming it was considered vital to the spread of personal intelligent communicators (PICs). Every General Magic investor, as well as IBM, planned to use Telescript. Independent observers felt that General Magic was onto something big with Telescript, but they cautioned that it would mean little unless service providers flock to it. Apple will put Telescript inside both its best selling PowerBook portable computers and Newton. The General Magic partners were motivated by something even more powerful than the technology: the potential for billions of dollars of new revenue. For instance, AT&T expected an enormous volume of electronic messages over its Telescript-based network, linking millions of PICs and databases. Oddly enough, the more successful the General Magic alliance may become, the more second-guessing Sculley may have to endure. He has already been attacked within Apple for allowing the other companies to invest in General Magic.[75]

1988	1987	1986	1985	1984	1983	1982
9,536	6,236	4,950	4,326	5,382	4,645	3,391
1,300	992	636	325	—	—	—
32%	27%	26%	22%	22%	22%	24%
51	51	53	42	42	49	51
7	7	7	4	5	6	7
29	30	32	31	32	30	27
15	14	14	5	6	13	18
10	8	8	3	4	8	11
22	16	15	7	10	17	20
44	28	25	12	15	24	28
$59¼–$28	$57½–$16¼	$19 7/16–$7½	$15 5/16–$7¼	$16 9/16–$8⅞	$13 5/16–$9 1/16	$11 7/16–$5 9/16

Notes:

1. The number of shares and per share amounts for fiscal years 1982–1986 have been adjusted to reflect the 2-for-1 stock split effected on May 15, 1987.
2. Net income for fiscal year 1989 includes a pretax gain of approximately $79 million ($48 millon, or $.37 per share, after taxes) from the company's sale of its common stock.

Source: Apple Computer, Inc., *1992 Annual Report,* pp. 18, 19.

During the 1980s, Apple grew from a $100 million company to a $5 billion company by selling general-purpose personal computers. In the 1990s, Apple intended to expand beyond personal computing to develop products and solutions in many different businesses. It intended to become a new kind of systems company. Or, as management concluded in the *1992 Annual Report,* "We believe that our actions in 1992 have positioned Apple . . . to become a leader in the most dynamic, most exciting, and most promising industry in the world."[76]

Notes

1. Apple Computer, Inc., *1992 Annual Report,* p. 1.
2. Apple Computer, Inc., *Form 10-K Report* (1992), pp. 5–6.
3. Apple Computer, Inc., *1992 Annual Report,* p. 1.
4. Bart Ziegler, "A New Apple Looks for Rapid Growth," *Tampa Tribune* (May 24, 1992), pp. 1, 8.
5. Apple Computer, Inc., *1992 Annual Report,* p. 1.

6. Apple Computer, Inc., *Form 10-K Report* (1992), p. 6.
7. Apple Computer, Inc., *1992 Annual Report,* p. 9.
8. Ibid., p. 9.
9. Ibid., p. 21.
10. Ibid.
11. Ibid., p. 22.
12. Ibid., p. 23.
13. Ibid.
14. Ibid., p. 22.
15. Ziegler, "A New Apple Looks for Rapid Growth," pp. 1, 8.
16. Apple Computer, Inc., *1992 Annual Report,* p. 2.
17. Apple Computer, Inc., *Form 10-K Report* (1991), p. 6.
18. *The Wall Street Journal* (November 12, 1992), p. B-1.
19. Ibid.
20. Ibid.
21. Ibid.
22. Bart Ziegler, "Apple-IBM Pact Proving More Successful Than Some Envisioned," *Tampa Tribune* (September 27, 1992), p. 8.
23. G. Pascal Zachary, "IBM-Apple Operating System Taligent Is Ahead of Schedule," *Wall Street Journal* (January 12, 1992), p. B-12.
24. Apple Computer, Inc., *1992 Annual Report,* p. 11.
25. John R. Wilke, "Computer Firm Results Likely to Be Gloomy," *Wall Street Journal* (April 12, 1993), p. A-5.
26. Ibid.
27. Douglas Sease, "More Big Blues as Microsoft's Total Market Value Could Soon Pass Lead of Humbled Giant IBM," *Wall Street Journal* (January 15, 1993), pp. C-1, C-8.
28. Ibid.
29. "Computer and Peripherals Industry," *Value Line* (January 29, 1993), p. 1075.
30. Ibid.
31. Ibid.
32. Ibid.
33. "Semiconductor Industry," *Value Line* (January 29, 1993), p. 1057.
34. Ibid.
35. Ibid.
36. Ibid.
37. "International Business Machines," *Value Line* (July 29, 1993), p. 1097.
38. Ibid.
39. Lawrence Hooper, "Akers Moves to Speed Split of IBM Units," *Wall Street Journal* (February 8, 1993), p. B-1.
40. "Compaq Computer, Inc.," *Value Line* (January 29, 1993), p. 1086.
41. Ibid.
42. "Dell Computer," *Value Line* (January 29, 1993), p. 1090.
43. Michael Fitzgerald, "Dell Hits the Big Time," *Computer World* (December 7, 1992), p. 1.
44. James Daly, "User Survey Says Dell PC's Bested the Competition," *Computer World* (September 21, 1992).
45. Catherine Arnst and Stephanie Anderson, "Dell Tries to Put Out the Fire," *Business Week* (December 7, 1992), p. 42.
46. Kyle Pope, "Dell Computer at War with Analyst Critical of Its Currency Trades," *Wall Street Journal* (November 30, 1992), p. 1.
47. "Microsoft," *Value Line* (January 29, 1993), p. 2124.
48. Joe Davidson, "Microsoft Wins FTC Reprieve on Injunction," *Wall Street Journal* (February 8, 1993), p. A-3.
49. "Intel Leads Semiconductor Suppliers in 1992," *Dataquest* (January 5, 1993), p. 1.
50. "Intel," *Value Line* (January 29, 1993), p. 1064.
51. Ibid.
52. "Motorola," *Value Line* (January 29, 1993), p. 1068.
53. Maryfran Johnson, "IBM Motorola Bow RISC Chip," *Computer World* (October 5, 1992).
54. Lisa Picarille, "Students Give Apple High Marks," *Macweek* (August 24, 1992).
55. "Year in Review," *Computer Reseller News* (November 23, 1992).
56. John R. Wilke, "PC Giants' Price War Hurts Tiny Makers," *Wall Street Journal* (November 12, 1992). p. B-1.
57. Kyle Pope, "PC Marketers Punch Up Combative Ads," *Wall Street Journal* (October 21, 1992), p. B-1.
58. Ibid.
59. Ibid.
60. Kevin Goldman, "IBM to Expand Direct-Response PC Sales," *Wall Street Journal* (January 29, 1993), p. B-8.
61. "Who's Next? Victims of PC Shakeout Rise," *Dataquest* (January 19, 1993).
62. Ibid.
63. Robert Desmond, "Byting Japan," *Time Magazine* (October 5, 1992), p. 69.
64. John Markoff, "Yankee Ingenuity Wins Out in PC's," *New York Times* (November 23, 1992), p. D-1.
65. Ibid.

66. Ken Yamada, "Apple Boosts Level of Power in Some Models," *Wall Street Journal* (February 9, 1993), p. B-1.
67. Ibid., p. B-6.
68. Apple Computer, Inc., *Form 10-K Report* (1993), p. 3.
69. Ibid., p. 4.
70. Apple Computer, Inc., *1992 Annual Report,* p. 4.
71. Ibid., p. 36.
72. Ibid.
73. Marilyn Clare, "Apple Computer Profit Fell 28% Despite First-Period Sales Record," *Wall Street Journal* (January 15, 1993), p. B-6.
74. Ibid., p. 22.
75. G. Christian Hill and Ken Yamada, "Five Electronics Giants Hope General Magic Will Turn the Trick," *Wall Street Journal* (February 8, 1993), p. A-1.
76. Apple Computer, Inc., *1992 Annual Report,* p. 16.

CASE 16

AST Research, Inc., 1993: Signs Letter to Acquire a Major Competitor

Thomas L. Wheelen, Moustafa H. Abdelsamad, Kathryn E. Wheelen, Richard D. Wheelen, Thomas L. Wheelen II

Announcement

On May 26, 1993, AST Research issued the following news release:

> Today [the company] announced that it has executed a letter of intent with Tandy Corporation concerning AST's purchase of certain assets and assumption of certain liabilities relating to Tandy's personal computer manufacturing operations. The assets to be purchased will include GRiD, Tandy GRiD Europe, and computer manufacturing plants in Texas and Scotland. The specific assets to be purchased (which will exclude accounts receivable) and liabilities to be assumed will be detailed in a definitive purchase agreement to be entered into by the parties. The purchase price is estimated not to exceed \$175 million. The consideration will be paid in the form of either cash and three-year promissory notes, or all cash, at the election of AST. It is currently anticipated that, after review of the assets to be purchased and liabilities to be assumed, a significant portion of the purchase price will be paid in the form of three-year promissory notes.[1]
>
> We are pleased to announce the proposed acquisition of Tandy's personal computer operations," said Safi Qureshey, AST President and Chief Executive Officer. "Tandy's strength in multimedia and pen-based technology strongly complements AST's existing product line-up. Also, the additional manufacturing capacity and purchasing leverage this transaction brings is important as AST continues to execute its market share capture strategy.[2]

According to the IDC, for calendar 1992 Tandy/GRiD Systems ranked seventh in U.S. personal computer vendors market share with 3.4%, and AST ranked eighth with 2.8%.[3]

Completion of the transaction was subject to various conditions, including negotiation and approval (by each company's Board of Directors) of a definitive purchase agreement and obtaining regulatory approvals. If all conditions could be met, the transaction was expected to conclude in July 1993.[4]

This case was prepared by Dr. Thomas L. Wheelen of Thomas Wheelen Company (ca 1879) and the University of South Florida; Kathryn E. Wheelen, B.A. from the University of Tampa and administrative assistant; Richard D. Wheelen, student at the University of South Florida and case research assistant; Thomas L. Wheelen II, graduate of Boston College and a graduate student at the University of Colorado; and Dean Moustafa H. Abdelsamad of the College of Business, Texas A&M University at Corpus Christi.

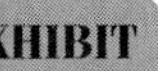
16.1

Consolidated Statement of Income: AST Research, Inc.
(Dollar amounts in thousands, except per share data.)

Years Ending June 27	1992	1991	1990
Net sales	$944,079	$688,477	$533,814
Cost of sales	650,819	440,130	360,439
Gross profit	293,260	248,347	173,375
Selling and marketing expenses	120,072	91,289	71,596
General and administrative expenses	45,201	36,328	28,911
Engineering and development expenses	30,461	26,647	18,441
Total operating expenses	195,734	154,264	118,948
Operating income	97,526	94,083	54,427
Interest income	7,009	8,199	4,804
Interest expense	(2,439)	(3,665)	(5,966)
Other expense, net	(1,812)	(241)	(1,694)
Income before provision for income taxes	100,284	98,376	51,571
Provision for income taxes	31,780	33,652	16,504
Net income	$ 68,504	$ 64,724	$ 35,067
Net income per share			
Primary	$ 2.16	$ 2.13	$ 1.43
Fully diluted	—[1]	—[1]	1.21
Weighted average common and common equivalent shares outstanding			
Primary	31,758	30,413	24,530
Fully diluted	—[1]	—[1]	30,960

Note:
1. Fully diluted earnings per share were antidilutive or not materially different from primary earnings per share.

Source: AST Research, Inc., *1992 Annual Report,* p. 31.

The Company

Ranked number 367 on the Fortune 500 list of America's largest industrial companies, AST Research, Inc., is a prominent market share holder in desktop, file server, and notebook computers. The company does business in 100 countries and operates 35 international subsidiaries and sales offices.[5]

General Business

AST Research, Inc. ("AST" or the "company") was incorporated in California on July 25, 1980 and reincorporated as a Delaware corporation effective July 1, 1987. The company designs, manufactures, markets, services, and supports a broad line of personal computers including desktop, notebook, and network server systems, which together accounted for 98% of total fiscal 1992 revenues [see Exhibit 16.1].[6]

Significant Business Developments in Fiscal 1992

In . . . 1992, the $26 million long-term mortgage note on the company's headquarters facility was prepared by AST Realty Partners, a California partnership of which the company and AST Realty, Inc. (a California corporation and wholly-owned subsidiary of the company) were the sole partners [see Exhibit 16.2].

In April 1992, the company entered into a new $100 million unsecured revolving credit facility agreement with five international banks. This facility replaced a previous $55 million unsecured revolving credit facility agreement. The new credit facility has a termination date of October 1, 1994.

During fiscal 1992, the company continued to strengthen its international presence by forming wholly-owned subsidiaries in Belgium, Mexico, Spain, and Sweden. The subsidiary locations provide sales and service assistance to distributors and dealers including local educational, technical, and marketing customer support.

On June 26, 1992, AST's co-founder, Thomas C. K. Yuen, resigned his position as Co-Chairman of the Board of Directors and Chief Operating Officer. Effective July 22, 1992, he also resigned his position as Director of the company. Also on June 26, Safi U. Qureshey resigned his position as Co-Chairman of the Board of Directors while retaining his positions as President and Chief Executive Officer. Mr. Qureshey continues to serve as a Director. Concurrent with Mr. Qureshey's resignations as Co-Chairman, Dr. Carmelo J. Santoro, a Director of the company since 1990, was elected Chairman of the Board [see Exhibit 16.3].[7]

Industry Segments and Geographic Information

AST operates in one industry segment: the manufacture, sale, and support of personal computers, including desktop, notebook and network server systems, and selected board-level enhancement products for personal computers. [Exhibit 16.4 provides]a summary of the company's operations by geographic area including net sales, operating income (loss), and identifiable assets. . . . [8]

Business Strategy and Market

The company's business strategy is to use its technological expertise, worldwide manufacturing capabilities, brand name recognition, and distribution channels to offer its customers a broad range of personal computers to meet a variety of user needs. In pursuing this strategy, the company offers multiple product lines from the entry level Bravo 3/25s to high performance i486-based systems and color notebook computers. The company's personal computers incorporate either Industry Standard Architecture (ISA) or Extended Industry Standard Architecture (EISA) and are compatible with major industry standard operating systems including MS-DOS, UNIX/XENIX, and OS/2. The company also intends to ensure that its products retain their compatibility with new major industry standards as they are developed. In addition to personal computer systems, the company offers board-level enhancement and connectivity products.

The company believes that its success depends upon the ability to identify products required by customers and to design high quality, innovative products compatible with industry standards. The company also believes that the price/performance features of its products are key factors in the purchase decisions of its customers and, as a result, has developed a series of product lines each specifically targeting a certain market seg-

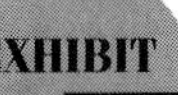
EXHIBIT 16.2

Consolidated Balance Sheet: AST Research, Inc.

(Dollar amounts in thousands, except per share data.)

Years Ending June 27	1992	1991
Assets		
Current assets		
Cash and cash equivalents	$ 87,874	$153,305
Short-term investments	52,831	—
Accounts receivable, net of allowance for doubtful accounts of $9,831 ($6,132 in 1991)	152,851	108,675
Inventories	182,498	128,131
Prepaid income taxes	24,897	24,472
Other current assets	14,026	9,874
Total current assets	514,977	424,457
Property and equipment	94,733	84,295
Accumulated depreciation and amortization	(30,946)	(25,013)
Net property and equipment	63,787	59,282
Other assets	1,849	1,692
Total assets	$580,613	$485,431
Liabilities and Shareholders' Equity		
Current liabilities		
Short-term borrowings	$ 1,374	$ 1,194
Accounts payable	95,351	58,511
Accrued salaries, wages and employee benefits	18,202	22,564
Other accrued liabilities	50,292	34,549
Income taxes payable	16,602	24,359
Current portion of long-term debt	363	602
Total current liabilities	182,184	141,779
Long-term debt	2,431	30,110
Deferred income taxes and other noncurrent liabilities	32,731	31,380
Commitments and contingencies		
Shareholders' equity		
Common stock, par value $.01;70,000,000 shares authorized, 30,786,790 shares issued and outstanding in 1992 (30,227,564 shares in 1991)	308	302
Additional paid-in capital	120,515	107,920
Retained earnings	242,444	173,940
Total shareholders' equity	363,267	282,162
Total liabilities and shareholders' equity	$580,613	$485,431

Source: AST Research, Inc., *1992 Annual Report,* p. 30.

EXHIBIT 16.3 **Directors and Corporate Officers: AST Research, Inc.**

Safi U. Quereshey
President, Chief Executive Officer, and Director

Bruce C. Edwards
Senior Vice-President, Finance and Chief Financial Officer, and Assistant Secretary

Richard P. Ottaviano
Senior Vice-President, Administration

Chetan M. Lekhani
Vice-President, Information Services

Dennis R. Leibel
Vice-President, Legal and Treasury Operations and Secretary

James T. Schraith
Vice-President, U.S. Sales and Service

Wai S. Szeto
Vice-President, Engineering

Richard J. Goeglein
Director, AST Research, Inc.
Chairman, ConServ International
A consulting and real estate development business
Principal, Market Value Partners Company
A remedial management/turnaround business

Carmelo J. Santoro
Chairman and Director, AST Research, Inc.
Chairman, Silicon Systems, Inc.
A semiconductor manufacturer

Delbert W. Yocam
Director, AST Research, Inc.
Private investor
Effective August 1, 1992

Source: AST Research, Inc., *1992 Annual Report,* p. 48.

ment. This multi-brand strategy provides for a variety of price points from the entry level *Advantage!* and Bravo product lines to the higher-end Premium and network server lines, all designed to meet the specific requirements of the end-user. Typically, new product entries are priced aggressively as AST highlights the price/performance advantages offered by its products. Price reductions which are periodically required in order to maintain favorable price/performance characteristics are determined with reference to then existing competitive factors, including the prevailing pricing strategy of other major computer manufacturers.

International market expansion has been a major factor in the company's growth during fiscal 1992. International sales revenue contributed 44% of total revenues in fiscal 1992, as compared to 42% and 36% in fiscal 1991 and 1990, respectively [see Exhibit 16.4]. The company's strategy of establishing a presence in areas with developing markets for computer products and providing products that meet local needs, such as customized systems and local language documentation, has contributed to acceptance of its products worldwide. In addition to expanding its European and Pacific Rim operations, the company is continuing to pursue opportunities in developing countries within the Middle East, Latin America, Africa, and Southeast Asia.[9]

Products

The company's products include desktop, notebook, and network server computer systems and enhancement products. The company also manufactures certain custom desktop system and board-level products for original equipment manufacturer

EXHIBIT 16.4

Segment and Geographic Information: AST Research, Inc.

(Dollar amounts in thousands)

The company operates in one industry segment: the manufacture and sale of personal computers, including desktop, notebook and network server systems, and selected board-level enhancement products for personal computers.

	North/Latin America	Europe	Pacific Rim	Eliminated	Consolidated
Year Ending June 27, 1992					
Sales to unaffiliated customers	$550,887	$215,396	$177,796	—	$944,079
Transfers between geographic areas	168,346	62,056	432,563	(662,965)	—
Net sales	$719,233	$277,452	$610,359	$(662,965)	$944,079
Operating income (loss)[1]	$ 40,090	$ (9,851)	$ 59,087	$ 8,200	$ 97,526
Identifiable assets[2]	$359,550	$129,683	$ 91,380	$ —	$580,613
Year Ending June 28, 1991					
Sales to unaffiliated customers	$415,373	$159,318	$113,786	$ —	$688,477
Transfers between geographic areas	176,724	52,732	480,878	(710,334)	—
Net sales	$592,097	$212,050	$594,664	$(710,334)	$688,477
Operating income (loss)[1]	$ 41,081	$ 42	$ 68,433	$ (15,473)	$ 94,083
Identifiable assets[2]	$325,936	$ 96,325	$ 63,170	$ —	$485,431
Year Ending June 30, 1990					
Sales to unaffiliated customers	$350,099	$ 96,804	$86,911	$ —	$533,814
Transfers between geographic areas	78,995	2,033	335,980	(417,008)	—
Net sales	$429,094	$ 98,837	$422,891	$(417,008)	$533,814
Operating income (loss)[1]	$ 11,498	$ (2,099)	$ 45,207	$ (179)	$ 54,427
Identifiable assets[2]	$224,936	$ 51,321	$ 47,918	$ —	$324,175

Notes:

1. In determining operating income (loss) for each geographic area, sales and purchases between geographic areas have been accounted for on the basis of internal transfer prices set by the company.
2. Identifiable assets are those tangible and intangible assets used in operations in each geographic area.
3. Certain previously reported amounts have been reclassified to conform to current period presentation.

Source: AST Research, Inc., *1992 Annual Report*, p. 43.

EXHIBIT 16.5

New Products and Product Recognition: AST Research, Inc.

A. SELECTED PRODUCT INTRODUCTIONS FISCAL YEAR 1992

Bravo
3/25S, 4/33

AST's lowest priced basic professional computer is designed for everyday business applications and a high-end 486DX computer which delivers power and speed for heavy duty applications.

Power Premium
3/25S, 3/33
3/25, 4/25S
4/33, 4/50D
(EISA)

The Power Premium product line provides high-performance Cupid-32 upgradeable solutions for all processor levels. The 486/33 is an ideal personal workstation, while the 486/50D has ultra-fast performance for processor-intensive applications.

Premium Servers
SE 4/33
SE 4/50

The 486/33 and 486/50 Cupid-32 upgradeable Premium Servers are designed for large multi-user and networking environments.

Premium Exec
386SX/25C

AST's vivid VGA color notebook computer is priced below many of our competitors' monochrome notebook computers.

(continued)

(OEM) customers. The company offers a complete family of personal computer systems products designed to meet various performance levels and price points [see Exhibit 16.5].[10]

Premium Exec Notebooks

The company offers lightweight, notebook-sized portable systems products under the AST Premium Exec name. The line includes the Premium Exec 386SX/20 and Premium Exec 386SX/25. . . . [11]

Bravo Desktops

Bravo systems are designed for the business user and feature high quality, reliability, and performance at an affordable price. The series includes the Bravo 3/25s and the Bravo 4/33 models. . . . [12]

New Products and Product Recognition: AST Research, Inc. *(continued)*

A. SELECTED PRODUCT INTRODUCTIONS FISCAL YEAR 1992 *(continued)*

Advantage!
386SX/25
486SX/20
486DX/33
NB-SX25
NB-SX25C

The *Advantage!* desktop and notebook computers, bundled with popular software, are sold through Mass Merchant and Consumer Electronics Retailers.

B. AST PRODUCTS HONORED

In 1992, AST Research products received favorable reviews and outstanding press mentions from numerous leading industry publications.

Premium Exec 386SX/20
"Analyst's Choice"
PC Week
—and—
"Best Buy"
PC Magazine
—and—
"Product of the Year"
PC Laptop

Premium II 386SX/20
"Editor's Choice"
PC Magazine

Source: AST Research, Inc., *1992 Annual Report,* p. 17.

Premium Family

1. Premium II and Power Premium lines feature advanced personal computer technology in AST's innovative Cupid-32 upgradeability and offer additional speed, expansion, and storage performance features. The Premium II desktop series optimizes power and performance into a small-footprint, ergonomically-designed enclosure and includes the following models: Premium II 386SX/20, Premium II 386SX/25, Premium 486SX/20 and Premium II 486/33. . . .

2. The Power Premium series includes the Power Premium 3/25s, 3/25, 3/33, 4/25s, 4/33 and 4/50d. In order to provide optimal performance under graphical user interfaces, Power Premium systems combine the most popular features of the Premium II line with the latest PC technology, including Premium VGA high-performance graphics support, EISA I/O bus architecture, upgradeable CUPID-32 processors, and AST Flash-BIOS, which allows downloading of the latest BIOS upgrades, thus eliminating the need for physical replacement of the BIOS chip. . . .

3. During fiscal 1992, the company introduced its new line of Premium Servers, engineered specifically for large multi-user and networking environments. . . .

4. The company announced its first fully symmetric multiprocessor system, AST Manhattan SMP, in early fiscal 1993. The AST Manhattan SMP features next-generation technology based on open system architecture ideal for LAN and multi-user UNIX environments. . . . [13]

Advantage!

In early fiscal 1992, the company introduced a complete line of *Advantage!* products available through consumer electronic mass merchants and superstores. Typically, the *Advantage!* system is combined with various factory installed software applications and custom configured with memory, hard drives, and other features to produce a complete hardware and software solution designed to meet both small business and home computer requirements. The *Advantage!* line includes desktop models 386SX/20, 286XS/25, 486SX/20, 486SX/25 and 486/33 and three notebook configurations, including the NB-SX/20, NB-SX25 and NC25C (color). . . . They are covered by AST's one-year ExeCare service program.[14]

Other Products

1. The company also has products designed especially for certain markets. During fiscal 1992, AST announced the PCvision 4/33 computer system which runs DOS/V 5.0, a version of Microsoft's DOS operating system that operates in both English and Japanese. . . . The system also features AST's own BIOS and a 106-key keyboard exclusively developed by AST within Open Architecture Developers Group standards.

2. Early in fiscal 1993, the company introduced the PCvision 3/25s, which replaces an earlier model, the PCvision 386SX/20, and 20 Mhz system introduced in October 1991. PCvision 3/25s is the third DOS/V-compatible system introduced by AST in less than a year. It also features AST's own BIOS and 106-key keyboard. . . . Optional . . . features provide faster processing power for Windows applications and higher resolution for better kanji character display.

3. AST's enhancement product line provides various combinations of increased memory, additional input/output ports and other features. . . .

4. AST offers monochrome (720 x 480 resolution) and Super VGA (1024 x 768 resolution) monitors. Super VGA monitors are also available in 14 and 17 inch low radiation versions which were introduced in fiscal 1992.[15]

Product Development

Due to the rapid pace of advances in personal computer technology, the company's continued success depends on the timely introduction of new products that are accepted in the marketplace. Accordingly, the company is actively engaged in the design and development of new products and the enhancement of existing products. Unlike many of its competitors, AST designs and develops its own products, utilizing the company's in-house engineering organization. As a result, AST is often able to quickly transform the latest technological advancements into commercially available products. During the fiscal years ending June 27, 1992, June 28, 1991, and June 30, 1990, the company's engineering and development expenses were $30,461,000, $26,647,000, and $18,441,000, respectively.

Strengthening the company's ability to bring new technology to the marketplace are its longstanding relationships with major software and hardware developers such as Banyan Systems, Inc., IBM Corp., Intel Corp., Microsoft Corp., Novell, Inc., and SCO, Inc. Working with these developers as partners in both compatibility testing and software support programs allows the company to introduce products incorporating the latest hardware technology and with the capability to operate the most current software available in the marketplace.

AST is firmly committed to the establishment of industry standards and actively participates in their development. The company was one of the nine original high technology companies which participated in the development of the Extended Industry Standard Architecture ("EISA"). As one of the original seven participants in the Open Architecture Development Group, organized to promote a standard personal computer operating system for Japan, AST was recently able to broaden its product offerings for this market with PCvision models 3/25s and 4/33.

The company believes that its technical expertise is key to its development of new innovative products. The company's engineering staff uses computer-aided design techniques which assist in the development of new products and enable faster adaption of printed circuit board layouts for the manufacturing process. An in-house Application Specific Integrated Circuits ("ASIC") group develops large scale integrated circuits and custom chips for use in the company's products resulting in both improved performance and reduced manufacturing costs.

Current major engineering and development efforts include final work on the company's multiprocessor system, expected to ship in fiscal 1993, which is designed to provide minicomputer-level performance using more cost-efficient microcomputer technologies. Efforts are also underway on development of new generations of portable and Premium systems and product enhancements of both the Bravo and *Advantage!* product lines.[16]

Manufacturing

AST's manufacturing operations include procurement and inspection of components, assembly and testing of printed circuit boards and assembly, testing, and packaging of finished products. The company's manufacturing locations in Fountain Valley, California, Hong Kong, and Taiwan represent over 400,000 square feet of state-of-the-art production facilities.

In its Fountain Valley facility the company manufactures desktop and notebook computer systems for sales to North America and Latin America, as well as printed circuit board ("PCB") assemblies for new product introductions. The Hong Kong facility produces PCB assemblies in support of worldwide systems manufacturing as well as desktop and notebook computers for its own Asia-Pacific marketplace. In order to accommodate high volume, both facilities use state-of-the-art PCB assembly equipment including single and double-sided surface mount machines. The company's Taiwan facility is dedicated to the production of desktop system products for sale principally in Europe.[17]

Outsourcing

The company currently procures all of its components from outside suppliers. AST factory sites located in Hong Kong and Taiwan provide close proximity to many key international vendors. Source inspections are conducted at the plants of selected strategic suppliers, while other parts are sampled for inspection upon receipt at the company's manufacturing facilities.

The company has generally been able to obtain parts without difficulty. However, as with others in the industry, the company has at times paid premium prices to obtain components that were in short supply. In the future, there can be no assurance that such shortages will not re-occur [sic] and significantly increase the costs or delay the shipment of AST's products, thereby adversely affecting both sales and gross profit margins.

Nearly all parts used in AST products are available from multiple sources. To achieve improvements in cost, AST has implemented a program that results in the development of multiple sources for existing sole-source components. Nevertheless, some key components are still only available through sole-source suppliers. AST purchases components pursuant to purchase orders placed in the ordinary course of business and has no guaranteed supply arrangements with sole-source suppliers. An extended supply interruption could have an adverse impact on the revenues and profitability of the company until an alternative source becomes available.[18]

Quality Control

Quality and reliability are emphasized both in the design and manufacture of the company's products. AST continues to focus on successful new product introductions through a process of concurrent product and process design efforts which attempt to simplify and streamline the manufacturing process in the earliest stages of product design. Products undergo quality inspection and testing throughout the manufacturing process. This is evidenced through programs which have been implemented for process measurement and improvement, reduction of the cost structure, maintenance of on-time delivery, increase of in-process yields, and improvement in product field reliability. Additional manufacturing verification and testing programs include failure analysis, out-of-box audit programs that consist of extended diagnostic and software testing, and extended early life reliability testing of products taken from finished goods. Extensive use is also made of automatic test equipment, some of which has been designed by the company's in-house personnel.

The company is currently seeking International Standards Organization ("ISO") 9000 certification at each manufacturing site in order to formalize and visibly demonstrate its continued commitment to ongoing process and quality improvements.[19]

Customized Products

During fiscal 1992, the company established a flexible manufacturing line which is committed to serving the customer base that orders non-standard product configurations. This flexible manufacturing center is staffed with dedicated manufacturing and technical support groups which provide real time solutions to the software/hardware configuration needs of our customers.[20]

Marketing and Sales

The company employs a worldwide multi-channel distribution strategy which allows it to reach a variety of customers. While each channel provides AST with access to a specific target market, the company has differentiated itself from the industry by continuing to realize significant revenues through its established network of authorized dealers and resellers. The company believes that its dealers and resellers continue to favor AST because of its product line breadth, the quality and reliability of its products, and the high level of service and support provided by the company. Despite AST's past success within these channels, the company continues to focus on broadening its product distribution channels.[21]

North American Distribution

The company's North American distribution channels include authorized independent resellers, dealers, national distributors, major chains, mass merchants, and government sales through GSA approved dealers. The company sells directly to large VADs and VARs who typically purchase personal computers from the manufacturer and add enhancement products and software to assemble a turn-key system which is sold in selected vertical markets. The company's VADs and VARs include customers such as JWP Businessland and CompuCom Systems. The company also sells its products to smaller dealers and resellers through major national distributors including Gates/FA Distributing, Ingram Micro, Merisel and Tech Data Corp. In addition, the company sells to corporate and computer store chains such as Computerland and Sears Business Systems Centers.

The company's *Advantage!* line designed for small office and home use is marketed primarily by mass merchants including BJ's Wholesale Club, Computer City Supercenter, Costco Wholesale Club Stores, Circuit City Stores, Inc.[owned by Tandy Corporation], and Sam's Wholesale Club, a division of Wal-Mart Stores.

The Federal Systems Division of AST focuses on the $2.5 billion federal government market and supports large government suppliers such as Electronic Data Systems and Digital Equipment Corporation. The Federal Systems Division also supports integrators on proposals requiring customized hardware and software platforms, as well as directly pursuing government procurement contracts on behalf of AST.

Fiscal 1992 North American revenues showed a 32% increase over the prior year, from $402.2 million to $532.8 million. The VAD/VAR channel and sales to distributors accounted for 64% and 20%, respectively, of total North American revenues in fiscal year 1992. Significant growth was also experienced in both the company's OEM and mass merchant channels, as 1992 revenues rose to 11% and 5% of North American revenues, respectively [see Exhibit 16.1].[22]

International Distribution

The company markets its products internationally through subsidiaries and sales offices in 34 locations worldwide. In countries where the company does not have subsidiary operations, product is sold to retail dealers and distributors. The company intends to continue to increase its investment in sales and marketing activities within Europe and the Pacific Rim and to pursue opportunities within other developing countries as they arise.

Fiscal 1992 international revenues rose 44% to $411.3 million. European revenues rose by approximately 35% to $218.5 million and represented 23% of total fiscal 1992 revenues. Sales in the company's Pacific Rim region were up 56% to $177.8 million, or approximately 19% of total worldwide revenues. A significant portion of the company's Pacific Rim revenues are derived from sales to the Hong Kong government and within the People's Republic of China ("PRC"). Current trade negotiations between the United States and China could result in sanctions on United States exports to China including such products as computers. Future sales and growth within the PRC are dependent upon continuing favorable trade relations.[23]

Customer Support and Training

AST believes that customer support, service, and training are crucial to maintaining strong relationships with its customers and that the high level of its service and support helps differentiate it from other manufacturers in the personal computer industry. The company provides technical support to resellers, dealers, and end-users through toll-free telephone lines, AST On-Line!, a 24-hour electronic bulletin board system, and through an AST Info-Fax system which can transmit technical information about the company's products via a facsimile machine 24-hours a day.

All AST computers include a one year parts and labor warranty. Service is provided by AST authorized dealers, third party maintenance organizations, and the company's in-house service and support organization. AST has trained service technicians in more than 1,500 Authorized Service Centers worldwide. On-site maintenance is available anywhere within a 50-mile radius of more than 250 authorized AST on-site service locations. ExeCare is AST's notebook service program which guarantees the expedited repair or replacement of any AST notebook product anywhere in the United States. The company also maintains a professional training staff that conducts ongoing sales and service training classes for dealers and distributors.[24]

Advertising

AST advertises its products domestically and internationally in selected computer and business publications and outdoor advertising including airport dioramas and cooperative billboards. Through the AST cooperative advertising program, the company encourages its dealers, resellers, and distributors to advertise AST products by funding a portion of joint advertising and promotion efforts. The company also participates in major computer and business trade shows.

During fiscal 1992, the company's advertising emphasized AST's industry-leading move to brand segmentation, encompassing a multi-brand strategy which addresses the price/performance needs of all business buyers, including small business and home office users.

In July 1992, the company announced a shift in advertising strategy by hiring an external advertising agency to handle the AST account. This shift towards outside advertising assistance is designed to enhance the company's brand name recognition.[25]

Backlog

The company manufactures products according to its forecast of near-term demand and maintains inventories of finished products in advance of receipt of firm orders from its customers. Orders from retail accounts are usually placed by the customer on an as-needed basis and are usually shipped by the company shortly after receipt. Customers generally may cancel or reschedule orders with little or no penalty. While certain EOMs normally place orders for scheduled deliveries, the amount and quantities are not significant at the present time. For these reasons, the company's backlog at any particular time is generally not indicative of the future level of sales.[26]

Patents and Licenses

The company relies on a combination of contract, copyright, trademark, and trade secret laws to protect its proprietary interests in its products. The company has been granted U.S. federal registration for its trademarks, including "AST," the AST logo, "AST PREMIUM," "AST RESEARCH," "SIX PAK PLUS," "RAMVANTAGE," "ADVANTAGE," "CUPID," and "PREMIUM EXEC." At June 27, 1992, the company had acquired patents through application and purchase and had additional patent applications pending with the United States Patent and Trademark Office relating to various aspects of its products.

AST has royalty license agreements for various products, including operating system software for its personal computer systems.[27]

Competition

The personal computer industry is characterized by rapidly changing technology and intense competition from both domestic and foreign manufacturers. Due to its broad range of product offerings, the company faces many different competitors in various marketplaces. Many of these competitors have better market positions and greater financial, marketing, and other resources than the company. The company competes primarily with manufacturers offering performance oriented personal computers, such as IBM and Compaq Computer Corporation and, to a lesser extent, with a number of other companies that offer lower-priced ISA and EISA compatible systems [see Exhibit 16.6].

The company competes principally on the basis of its distribution channels, brand name awareness, product line breadth, service, support, and the reliability, quality, and favorable price/performance characteristics of its products. AST believes that it is able to compete successfully with respect to all of these factors.

The personal computer market has continued to be highly price competitive. As a result, price reductions were made during fiscal 1992, and the company made additional price reductions of up to 47% in the first quarter of fiscal 1993. Gross profit margins declined from fiscal 1991 to fiscal 1992 primarily due to the impact of these price reductions. The company anticipates competitive pricing pressures to continue and, as a result, price adjustments are expected to continue to impact gross profit margins. The company will attempt to mitigate the effects of these pricing pressures by controlling operating expenses as a percentage of sales and through asset management programs.[28]

Employees

As of August 28, 1992, the company had 3,560 employees, 1,764 of whom were employed in manufacturing, 337 in engineering, and 1,459 in the areas of general management, sales, marketing, and administration. Of the total, 1,642 were employed in North America, 1,526 were employed in the Pacific Rim, and 392 were employed by the company's European subsidiaries. The company has been successful to date in attracting and retaining qualified personnel, but believes future success will depend in part on its continued ability to attract and retain highly qualified engineers, technicians, marketing, and management personnel. To assist in attracting qualified employees at all levels, the company has adopted stock option, profit sharing, and other benefit plans. The company considers its employee relations to be good. No employee of the company is represented by a union.[29]

EXHIBIT 16.6

Computer Industry: Top 15 Global Leaders in PC Sales, 1992 and 1991
(Dollar amounts in millions)

1992			1991		
Company	Rank	Sales	**Company**	Rank	Sales
IBM	1	$7,654.5	IBM	1	$8,505.0
Apple	2	5,412.0	Apple	2	4,900.0
Compaq	3	4,100.0	NEC	3	4,135.8
NEC	4	3,986.9	Compaq	4	3,271.4
Fujitsu	5	2,613.5	Fujitsu	5	2,319.7
Toshiba	6	1,949.4	Toshiba	6	2,093.5
Dell	7	1,812.5	Olivetti	7	1,586.1
Olivetti	8	1,348.7	Unisys	8	1,061.0
AST	9	1,140.5	Intel	9	1,050.0
Gateway 2000	10	1,107.1	Commodore	10	1,038.5
AT&T	11	998.9	AT&T	11	950.0
Hitachi	12	891.8	Group Bull	12	899.3
Acer	13	880.0	Hitachi	13	825.3
Packard Bell	14	878.8	AST	14	800.7
Seiko Epson	15	741.4	Tandy	15	790.0

Source: "The DATAMATION 100," *DATAMATION* (June 15, 1993), p. 23; *DATAMATION* (June 15, 1992), p. 26.

DATAMATION Assessment of AST's Performance

The 1993 "DATAMATION 100" survey stated that AST ". . . deftly executed a PC development and marketing strategy balanced midway between daring and timid, accompanied by rigorous cost control [in 1992]."[30] In 1991, Safi Qureshey, President of AST, described AST's approach as "value marketing—having the right product at the right time at the right price."[31] He explained that "this meant a multi-brand strategy that tackled every major market. He promised that this plan would carry AST past the billion-dollar revenue in 1992."[32] The company met and exceeded this objective.

Qureshey said, "We get paid for execution."[33] The company charged into the manufacture of 486s and notebooks when the 386 models lost profitability. *DATAMATION* noted that "comparing the second half of 1992 with that of 1991, revenue from machines using Intel Corp.'s 486 chips soared 203%, revenue from 386s sagged 17%, 286 chips plummeted 95% and notebooks rose 18%."[34] Execution also meant continuing on the strategy on some existing products. Larry Devlin, Vice-President of U.S. sales, "vows that AST will continue to market only through resellers, avoiding direct mail."[35] In 1993, the company developed a strategy to sell its products through high-end resellers.

DATAMATION stated, "The first half of 1993 saw SMP [fully symmetrical multiprocessing] servers shipped in volume, along with the new state-of-the-art

Premmia PC line, with local bus video and upgradeability to Intel's new Pentium chip."[36] In April 1993, AST introduced a new pen/keyboard convertible computer manufactured by GRiD Systems Corporation, a Tandy Corporation subsidiary. Devlin said that, "no other product line will be introduced in 1993, but existing lines will be enhanced with features like local bus video."[37] One way AST has accomplished this enhancement is by discontinuing use of its proprietary CUPID upgradeable processor board architecture in Premmias. The 486 Intel chip made this architecture unnecessary. Devlin "also promised that AST will stay price-competitive."[38] He went on to warn that "it would be hard to drive more cost out of these products."[39]

In 1992, AST ranked ninth in global sales of PCs. In 1991 it had ranked fourteenth (see Exhibit 16.6).

1993 AST Research Highlights

Safi Qureshey, President and CEO, said that "acceleration of AST's market share position remains our strategy."[40] He went on to say, "Third quarter revenues have increased to 53% [$241,550,000 to $370,352,000], from 45% in the first half of the current fiscal year. In addition, our market share continues to be well in excess of the industry."[41] Year-to-date revenues (nine months) in fiscal 1993 totaled $1.003 billion, a 48% increase over the same period a year ago. Net income for nine months was down by $16,590,000, or 33.3%.[42] Quershey added that

> while successful, the company's aggressive market share strategy has had a near-term impact on net margins and profitability. Issues, such as air freight shipping costs and selective component shortages, are in part responsible for the lower figures. To remedy the situation, AST is actively pursuing additional sources of component supply and has positioned key management staff to strengthen worldwide procurement activities.[43]

AST shipped a record number of PCs (211,000) during the third quarter of fiscal year 1993. This amount represented an 80% increase over the same period a year earlier but with a shift to higher performance Intel-based 486 systems. The quarter's total included 126,000 Intel 86–based desktop PCs.[44]

Qureshey said, "Our dramatic unit volume increases clearly position AST as a long-term, top-tier PC manufacturer."[45] According to StoreBoard, a service of InfoCorp/Computer Intelligence, for calendar year 1992, AST increased its market share by 45.3% over the preceding year. This growth strengthened the company's third-place ranking of 7.4% of Intel-based systems sold through the reseller channel.[46]

New products introduced during the third quarter of fiscal 1993 included the Premmia, a full-featured EISA-based line that replaces the Power Premium. This new line adds quick-response local bus graphics capabilities and an upgrade path to Pentium-based processing consistent with AST's price leadership strategy. It is priced 10%–20% lower than competitive offerings.[47]

AST introduced the PenExec, a pen-based system developed from the company's strategic alliance with TE Electronics. The product was aimed at bringing its pen-based computing to mainstream users.[48]

Value Line reported that "the company is achieving top-tier status. This may not seem to be of much importance, but it amounts to a great deal. Users are less willing to place large orders with vendors that may not deliver the service and support they promise."[49] It went on to say, "AST is having great success in the mass merchant channels, thanks to the introduction of several new *Advantage!* network and tower products aimed at small business and home-office users. Mass merchant sales account for approximately 25% of sales. . . ."[50]

Personal Computer Industry

According to *Value Line,* personal computer makers have never faced a "more vicious battlefield [competition] of late, bring[ing] the very survival, and certainly the prosperity, of some of the companies in this sector into question."[51] It went on to say, "Finally, to maintain market share, companies are resorting to price cutting, which also erodes revenue and margins."[52]

The personal computer manufacturers face competition from "so-called clone manufacturers, which take inexpensive off-the-shelf components and put them together. . . ."[53] at a much lower price. These newcomers don't have high overhead, expensive administration and R&D expenses. Many of the established companies (Apple, IBM, Compaq) decided to join the price war with a vengeance, meeting or bettering the prices of the clone companies. Consumers are benefiting from low prices and sales are increasing. This price war has clone companies retaliating with even lower prices, thereby shrinking margins "to the vanishing point [where] many of the weaker players will fall by the wayside."[54] The no-name clone companies have about 16% of the market, and their failure would increase market share for the big companies. Michael Miller, Editor-in-Chief of *PC Magazine,* estimates that there are more than 100 PC clone manufacturers. See Exhibits 16.7–16.10 for information about the PC industry.

Tandy Corporation

On January 11, 1993, John V. Roach, Chairman and CEO of Tandy Corporation, announced a proposed spin-off of Tandy's technology and manufacturing operations (27 plants) into a separate company, TE Electronics, Inc., with an estimated $1.5 billion in annual sales (see Exhibit 16.11). Tandy has an excellent history of spin-off companies, such as Pier One Imports, Color Tile, Inc., and Bombay Company.

Tandy will have sales of approximately $3.4 billion after the spin-off (see Exhibit 16.11). The spin-off announcement also stated Tandy's intent to close 100 of its 448 Tandy Name Brand retail stores. The 100 stores to be closed will be the smaller stores in the McDuff/Video Concepts (180 stores) and McDuff Supercenters (237 stores) chains.[55]

Within days of the announcement of the spin-off of TE Electronics by Tandy, both Standard & Poor Corporation and Moody's Investment Services, Inc., began 90-day studies of Tandy's credit to ascertain whether the company's credit rating

EXHIBIT 16.7

Computer Industry: World Revenues and Product Market Segments

(Dollar amounts in billions)

In 1992, North America's total revenues for information technology was up by 11.2% to $211.99 billion, while total world revenues were up by 9.7% to $317.99 billion. North American revenues account for 66.5% of total world revenues. Growth of all 10 product segments was not up equally in 1992.

Product Market Segment	Product Market Share				
	1992	1991	1990	1989	1988
Large-scale systems	9.0%	9.5%	9.6%	11.0%	11.5%
Mid-range systems	6.9	7.6	7.7	8.1	9.3
Personal computers	14.3	15.2	14.7	14.2	12.3
Workstations	4.5	4.7	3.8	2.8	1.4
Software	11.6	11.5	10.2	9.7	8.8
Peripherals	20.3	20.9	22.3	22.0	24.9
Data communications	5.5	5.3	6.3	7.7	7.3
Service	15.6	11.0	10.1	9.0	8.0
Maintenance	8.8	11.1	11.5	11.4	12.0
Other	3.5	3.2	3.8	4.1	5.4
Total revenue	$318.0	$290.0	$278.5	$255.8	$243.1

Source: "The Datamation 100," *DATAMATION* (June 15, 1993), p. 23.

EXHIBIT 16.8

Computer Industry: U.S. Consumption of PC Units

Customer Segment	Percentage of Total Units
Household[1]	36%
Small business (1–99 employees)	20
Medium business (100–999 employees)	15
Large business (1000+ employees)	12
Education	9
Government	8
Total	100%

Note:
1. Includes home office and home-based businesses in addition to hobbyists.

Source: "Computers," *Industry Survey* (December 21, 1992), p. C-81.

EXHIBIT 16.9

Computer Industry: PCs Gain Dominance in the United States
(Percentage of change in manufacturing revenue, 1991 to 1992)

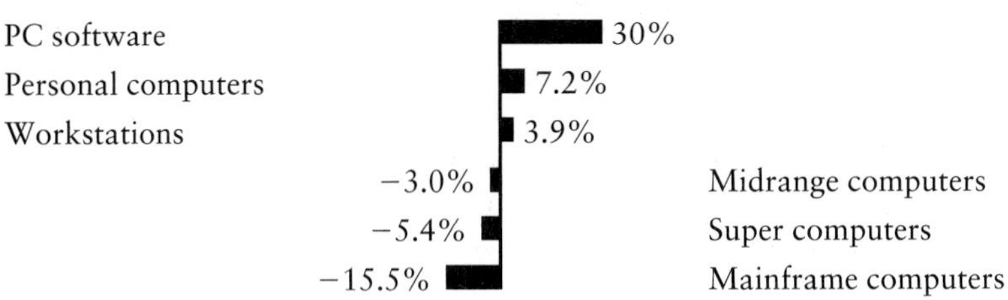

Source: G. Pascal Zachary, "Computer Industry Divides into Camps of Winners and Losers," *Wall Street Journal* (January 27, 1993), p. A-1.

on $2.3 billion of debt should be lowered. Standard & Poor's put the company on a "credit watch," based on Tandy's "loss of the manufacturing business . . . and . . . the company's lack of experience in running extremely low-margin stores."[56] A Tandy representative responded, "We have more than a little experience in the field."[57]

Tandy will receive $500 to $600 million from the sale of its manufacturing operations, including $175 million from AST sales. Exhibit 16.12 shows selected company financial information. The money, according to a Tandy executive, "would be used to pay down debt, buy back Tandy shares, and fund Tandy's existing retail business—now Tandy's key focus."[58] Tandy's retail outlets consist of the following store chains.

1. *Radio Shack* is the largest electronics retail chain store. It has 6,756 stores, of which 4,533 are company owned and 2,302 are dealer–franchiser owned. The average company-owned store contained 2,362 square feet of space. Tandy refers to this chain as the "ultimate electronic convenience store." The total number of stores has declined overall during the past three years, despite an increase in 1991. (See Exhibit 16.13.)

2. *Computer City* was established in 1991 as superstores that carry about 5,000 items. They are the only superstores authorized to carry IBM, Apple, AST, Compaq, Hewlett-Packard, Tandy, and other brand name competitor software, accessories, and office equipment. Tandy has formulated an aggressive expansion plan for this chain and expects to have more than 100 stores by the end of 1994. Chairman Roach forecasted that "over a five-year period, it would be a billion dollar business."[59] In March 1993, the company opened its first store in Europe.

3. *Incredible Universe* stores are approximately 160,000 square feet in size. They are devoted to a wide selection of consumer electronics, computer products, appliances, cameras, and music (Karaoke—Japanese singing style—studios), restaurants, and supervised children's play areas. The first store opened in Oregon in September 1992, and the second opened in Arlington, Texas. Many retail analysts question the viability of this size and concept of electronic store, but CEO Roach fully supports the concept and its future growth.[60]

EXHIBIT 16.10

Computer and Peripherals Industry: Composite Statistics

(Dollar amounts in millions)

Measure	Actual				Estimated		
	1988	1989	1990	1991	1992	1993	1995–1997
Sales	$118,743	$130,171	$142,365	$141,892	$155,000	$170,000	$230,000
Operating margin	20.0%	17.9%	17.9%	14.3%	15.5%	16.5%	18.0%
Depreciation	$7,775.3	$9,015.5	$9,489.6	$11,418	$12,300	$12,900	$16,000
Net profit	$10,417	$8,095	$8,934.7	$4,738.5	$6,300	$8,300	$14,100
Income tax rate	35.5%	40.4%	40.0%	38.0%	40.0%	40.0%	40.0%
Net profit margin	8.8%	6.2%	6.3%	3.3%	4.1%	4.9%	6.1%
Working capital	$34,843	$31,172	$30,816	$26,375	$28,800	$32,700	$52,300
Long-term debt	$14,936	$18,427	$18,114	$19,860	$20,400	$21,000	$22,800
Net worth	$68,371	$68,318	$75,470	$79,524	$74,900	$81,300	$109,100
% earned total capital	13.3%	10.1%	10.4%	6.3%	7.5%	9.0%	11.5%
% earned net worth	15.2%	11.8%	11.8%	6.7%	8.5%	10.5%	13.0%
% retained to common equity	11.1%	7.3%	7.8%	2.4%	4.5%	4.5%	8.0%
% all dividends to net profit	29%	40%	36%	63%	48%	38%	39%
Average annual P/E ratio	12.7	14.8	12.7	24.1			14.0
Relative P/E ratio	1.05	1.12	.94	1.54			1.10
Average annual dividend yield	2.2%	2.6%	2.7%	2.7%			2.5%

Source: "Computer and Peripheral Industry," *Value Line* (January 29, 1993), p. 1075.

EXHIBIT 16.11 **Tandy Corporation and the Spinoff Company, TE Electronics, Inc.**

A. NEW BUSINESS SNAPSHOT

1. Tandy Corporation (current retail operations): company would consist of Radio Shack, Computer City, The Incredible Universe, and Tandy Brand Group, which includes McDuff, Video Concepts, and The Edge in Electronics.
2. TE Electronics, Inc.: company would consist of two separate divisions. The computer direct sales division would be composed of GRiD System Corporation, Victor Technologies, and Tandy Electronics Manufacturing. The other marketing and manufacturing operations division would be composed of Memtek Products, O'Sullivan Industries, and Tandy Electronic Manufacturing (non-computer sales).

B. RECAST NET SALES AND GROSS PROFITS OF THE TWO COMPANIES

(Dollar amounts in thousands)

		Net Sales Year Ending June 30					Gross Profits, Year Ending June 30		
New Companies	**Present Divisions**	1992	% Change	1991	% Change	1990	1992	1991	1990
Tandy Corporation	Retail operations	$3,369,180	3.9%	$3,241,758	1.0%	$3,209,484	50.5%	52.3%	54.9%
	% of Total	72%		71.1%		71.3%			
TE Electronics, Inc.	Computer direct sales	620,952	(15.4%)	733,559	1.4%	732,656	23.9	31.0	34.9
	% of Total	13.3%		16.1%		16.1%			
	Other marketing and manufacturing	690,024	17.7%	586,465	3.5%	566,464	18.7	20.3	18.4
	% of Total	14.7%		12.8%		12.6%			
	Totals	$4,680,156	2.6%	$4,561,782	1.4%	$4,499,604	42.3%	44.8%	47.1%
		100%		100%		100%			

Source: Kyle Pope, "Tandy's Roach Decides to Try His Hand at Megastores," *Wall Street Journal* (January 13, 1993), p. 8; Tandy Corporation, *1992 Annual Report,* p. 10.

EXHIBIT 16.12

Selected Financial Information: Tandy Corporation

Year	Net Sales	Cost of Products Sold	Net Income
1992	$4,680,156,000	$2,701,969,000	$183,847,000
1991	4,561,782,000	2,519,309,000	195,444,000
1990	4,499,604,000	2,380,224,000	290,347,000
1989	4,180,703,000	2,140,464,000	323,504,000
1988	3,793,767,000	1,870,429,000	316,354,000
1987	3,452,178,000	1,700,109,000	242,329,000
1986	3,035,969,000	1,471,310,000	197,659,000
1985	2,595,695,000	1,218,353,000	186,060,000
1984	2,490,473,000	1,083,157,000	281,871,000
1983	2,241,443,000	923,346,000	278,521,000

Source: Tandy Corporation, *1990 Annual Report,* p. 22; *1987 Annual Report,* p. 14.

EXHIBIT 16.13

Radio Shack: Sales of Microcomputers, Peripherals, and Software

Year	Percentage of Total Sales
1992	NA%
1991	22.6%
1990	25.2%
1989	28.2%
1988	30.6%
1987	30.4%
1986	31.4%
1985	30.9%
1984	34.7%
1983	34.4%

Source: Tandy Corporation, *1990 Annual Report,* p. 22; *1987 Annual Report,* p. 14.

4. *McDuff Electronic and Appliance Supercenters* offers brand name audio, video, personal electronics, and major appliances. The approximately 257 stores have an average of 11,328 square feet of space. Thirty-nine new stores were opened during the past two years.

5. *The Edge Electronic* stores are designed for mall shoppers, who are attracted to fashionable, state-of-the-art personal and portable name brand elec-

tronic products. These boutique-style stores are situated in high-traffic mall locations. Seventy more stores were added in 1992.

6. *Tandy Name Brand* operates two types of stores: (a) the full-line McDuff Supercenters, which offer both consumer electronics and major appliances; and (b) McDuff and Video Concepts, which operate a total of 417 stores in smaller malls (a substantial increase from the 231 stores acquired in 1985). The average size store is 3,088 square feet.

John Roach said, "We had clearly decided to be primarily in the retail business."[61] He added that "at any moment, you just have to look at the hand of cards you hold and say this is what's best."[62] AST still will have access to all of Tandy's retail chain for selling its products.

In 1991, Victory Technologies Group Europe—Tandy's international PC distributor—was renamed Tandy GRiD Europe. It is headquartered in Stockholm. GRiD Systems, which AST Research will purchase, markets GRiD and Tandy desktop, laptop/portable and pen-based computers and networking systems to large business and government accounts in the United States and Canada through its direct sales force and value-added retailers. Gross profit percentages on computer direct sales were 23.9%, 31.0%, and 34.9% for 1992, 1991, and 1990, respectively.

Since the 1989 introduction of GRiDPAD, the first clipboard that recognized printed handwriting, GRiD has been the acknowledged industry leader in pen-based computers. In 1991, it introduced GRiDPAD RF, the first pen computer with integrated wireless communication capabilities that provided real-time data collection. In 1992, it introduced the first wearable pen computer, PalmPad.

DATAMATION reported that, "the PC price wars of 1992 were not kind to Tandy Corp. . . ."[63] It estimated that Tandy's 1992 revenues consisted of (1) $650 million in PC sales, (2) $15 million in software sales, (3) $90 million in peripheral sales, and (4) $15 million from services (see Exhibit 16.12). In 1992, computer sales were down by $300 million ($1.07 billion in 1991 to $770 million in 1992). *DATAMATION* went on to say that "PC price competition heated up following Compaq's . . . June 15, 1992 announcement of a new line of lower-priced PCs [and that] Tandy's PC lines suffered in Radio Shack channels."[64] A company executive said, "the bright side [is that] customers opted for more higher-end, fully loaded PCs than in the past. But to get customers into the stores, prices had to be slashed."[65] Tandy ranked fifteenth in global sales of PCs in 1991 but dropped out of the ranking in 1992 (see Exhibit 16.6).

Tandy also is trying to sell O'Sullivan Industries, which manufactures ready-to-assemble furniture for home and office, and Memtek Products, which includes Memorex tape products and stereo equipment, and most of the rest of its computer manufacturing not purchased by AST Research.[66]

Recently, investors have grown increasingly wary about the proposed spin-off of TE Electronics, which was scheduled for the summer 1993. The new company's sales would have had a loss of $9 million for the last half of 1992 and $16.2 million for the first quarter of 1993. Tandy was expected to record a $47.5 million charge against pretax earnings as of December 31, 1992, and TE Electronics was expected to record a similar charge of $20 million. Executives of Tandy responsible for setting up the new company estimated that TE would lose money for two more quarters because of the small margins in the manufacture of personal computers.[67]

Notes

1. AST Research, Inc., *News Release* (May 26, 1993), p. 1.
2. Ibid.
3. Ibid., p. 2.
4. Ibid.
5. Ibid.
6. AST Research, Inc., *Form 10-K* (June 27, 1992), p. 2.
7. Ibid.
8. Ibid.
9. Ibid., p. 3.
10. Ibid.
11. Ibid.
12. Ibid.
13. Ibid., p. 4.
14. Ibid., pp. 5–6.
15. Ibid., p. 6.
16. Ibid.
17. Ibid., p. 6.
18. Ibid.
19. Ibid.
20. Ibid.
21. Ibid., p. 7.
22. Ibid.
23. Ibid., p. 8.
24. Ibid.
25. Ibid.
26. Ibid.
27. Ibid., p. 9.
28. Ibid.
29. Ibid., p. 10.
30. "The DATAMATION 100," *DATAMATION* (June 15, 1993), p. 70.
31. Ibid.
32. Ibid.
33. Ibid.
34. Ibid.
35. Ibid.
36. Ibid.
37. Ibid.
38. Ibid.
39. Ibid.
40. AST Research, Inc., *News Release,* "Third Quarter Unit Shipments and Revenues Post Record Levels as AST Research Continues Market Share Push" (April 20, 1993).
41. Ibid.
42. Ibid., p. 4.
43. Ibid., p. 2.
44. Ibid.
45. Ibid.
46. Ibid., pp. 2–3.
47. Ibid., p. 3.
48. Ibid.
49. "AST Research," *Value Line* (January 29, 1993), p. 1077.
50. Ibid.
51. "Computer and Peripherals Industry," *Value Line* (January 29, 1993), p. 1075.
52. Ibid.
53. Ibid.
54. Kyle Pope, "Tandy's Roach Decides to Try His Hand at Megastores," *Wall Street Journal* (January 13, 1993), p. B-48.
55. Ibid.
56. *Wall Street Journal* (January 14, 1993).
57. Ibid.
58. Ken Yamada and Kyle Pope, "AST to Acquire PC Business of Tandy Corporation," *Wall Street Journal* (May 27, 1993), p. B-1.
59. Pope, p. B-48.
60. Ibid.
61. Ibid.
62. Yamada and Pope, p. B-1.
63. "The DATAMATION 100," p. 83.
64. Ibid.
65. Ibid.
66. Yamada and Pope, p. B-1.
67. Ibid.

CASE 17

Microsoft Corporation

Sexton Adams and Adelaide Griffin

Bill Gates sat in the waiting room of IBM's headquarters in Boca Raton, Florida, in October 1980, fidgeting with his new tie and weighing the probabilities that "Big Blue" would be interested in his young company's unproven operating system. He wondered if he would have to compromise his standards and whether his company would become another conquered land within the IBM empire.

As his mind wandered, Gates recalled the time five years earlier when he had decided to drop out of Harvard and pursue his dream of founding his own company. He and Paul Allen had concluded that the challenges offered through programming opportunities were financially and intellectually more rewarding than campus life. The pair headed West with the first opportunity to fulfill their ambitions of beginning a software company.

The gamble paid off. The team was fortunate enough to establish a reputation for creating quality programs for a number of smaller clients, which paid the bills. The opportunity of a joint venture with a company such as IBM was surely a chance of a lifetime, one that could provide success and financial independence.

Gates's nervousness was combined with sheer determination and confidence that his company, Microsoft, could compete with the best. He tried to imagine the effect that a positive outcome of today's meeting would have on Microsoft. The opportunities seemed unlimited.

The approaching men in blue suits snapped Gates out of his daydream and back to reality (seeing their attire, he was glad he had stopped to purchase a tie—even though he felt that it clashed with his Levis). The time had come for Gates to demonstrate that his young company had the right stuff and to convince IBM that Microsoft was able to deliver the desired product.

History

The Early Years

William Gates III, Chairman and co-founder of one of the world's largest computer software companies, may have found his destiny through an act of fate. Gates's mother, in conjunction with the Lakeside Mothers Club of Seattle, held a rummage sale and they purchased a computer from the proceeds. Bill's father claimed that his son "became hooked on it" from that time on.[1] Gates was only 14 years old.

This case was prepared by Jim Howard, Michelle Lee, Bob Mason, John Ray, and Sheryl Stein under the supervision of Professor Sexton Adams, University of North Texas, and Professor Adelaide Griffin of Texas Woman's University. This case was edited by T. L. Wheelen and J. D. Hunger for this book.

Gates and three friends (one of whom was Paul Allen, who eventually became Gates's partner and co-founder at Microsoft) formed an informal club called the Lakeside Programming Group and computer programming soon become an obsession for the young hackers. The group would frequently skip school to go to the computer center and stay until the wee hours of the night.[2] This obsession soon paid off for the entrepreneurs.

The group designed a computerized payroll system for the local school as well as a program that read punched cards used in monitoring highway traffic. The proceeds from these endeavors bought additional computer time for the club, and the computer was linked by phone to a local computer company.[3]

In 1973, Gates left Seattle for Harvard, where he and Paul Allen teamed up once again in search of new business opportunities. After two years of attending classes, Gates dropped out to pursue a business opportunity in Albuquerque with Allen. The two formed a partnership, Microsoft, and attempted to condense a popular computer language into a form that was compatible with a local engineering firm. However, the engineering firm folded and Microsoft moved to Seattle.[4]

The four years spent in Albuquerque were not fruitless for Microsoft. The fledgling company had developed a reputation with several clients that eventually led to the unthinkable. While some of Microsoft's clients were gained through referrals, most were obtained by the old-fashioned method of knocking on doors. In 1980, the giant of them all, IBM, came knocking on Gates's front door with the opportunity of a lifetime.[5]

Alliance with IBM

IBM was developing its line of personal computers and was interested in an operating system. Gates's first reaction was to refer IBM to another software manufacturer because Microsoft did not have the type of system IBM wanted. However, IBM again asked Microsoft if it could develop the system. This time Gates accepted. By this time Gates had learned of a system developed by Tim Patterson at Seattle Computer Products, Inc., and he thought the system could be adapted to IBM's needs. Microsoft bought the rights to the program, which became the highly successful MS-DOS. MS-DOS was exactly what IBM was looking for, and IBM and Microsoft negotiated a deal. Microsoft's staff grew from 80 in 1980 to 125 in 1981 and its revenues grew to $16 million, all due to the contract with IBM.[6] Microsoft had entered the big leagues.

The alliance with IBM allowed Microsoft to benefit from the larger company's marketing prowess, which led to MS-DOS becoming the standard operating system for IBM-compatible personal computers. In 1981, Gates persuaded IBM to let Microsoft sell DOS to anyone, thus allowing other manufacturers to make PC clones. The resulting sales amounted to over 50 million copies of MS-DOS sold through the 1980s.[7] During that decade, the company enhanced the original operating system many times, culminating in the most recent release, MS-DOS 5.0, which has received excellent critical acclaim.[8] This latest release demonstrated to its customers that Microsoft would provide continuing innovations for its baseline products while developing new software products.

Software Innovations

In addition to its commitment to MS-DOS, Microsoft developed a graphics computer environment in 1985 called Windows, which resembled the famous interface found on the Apple Macintosh.[9] With this innovation, the computer user worked with pictures (icons) instead of having to learn long, wordy commands. However, users who wanted a graphics interface were still a lot more comfortable with the Macintosh—at least until the release of Windows 3.0 in 1990.[10] This latest release became the first real competition for Apple, which responded by filing a lawsuit claiming that the graphics interface used in Windows infringed on their copyrights.[11]

While developing two of the most popular operating environments for personal computers, Microsoft also was active in producing a multitude of programs to work with these operating systems.[12] These programs include computer language compilers for programmers, word processors, spreadsheet applications, and other general business programs. The success of these products has led to increased sales of the operating system software, especially Windows, and vice versa. In the process, Microsoft has become an industry leader in both application software and operating systems.

Changes in the Relationship with IBM

Microsoft's strategic alliance with IBM led to another joint venture in which Gates agreed to develop a more sophisticated operating system called OS/2, which was released in 1987.[13] This innovation served as a shield against competitors' products such as UNIX, which were showing potential to decrease Microsoft's market share.[14] The OS/2 endeavor was not as profitable as expected, and the relationship between Microsoft and IBM became strained. Although Microsoft's success to this point had been very dependent on IBM, the company had become successful enough over the years with its own products that it was in a position to sever most ties with the industry giant. Microsoft had developed a strong foothold in the personal computer market that no longer relied on sales to IBM.

Problems with the FTC

In spite of Microsoft's differences with IBM, their long-standing relationship brought with it immense success, as well as an investigation by the Federal Trade Commission (FTC). The FTC's 1991 investigation focused on the 1989 agreement between Microsoft and IBM to cooperate on OS/2 and Windows, which it felt might indicate monopolization of the personal computer software market.[15]

Management

The personality of Microsoft as a corporation personified co-founder, Bill Gates, who was the Chairman of the Board and Chief Executive Officer. His influence extended from the secluded and forested corporate headquarters in a quiet Seattle suburb to the effect he had on his employees. Gates commanded such respect and adoration from those who worked for him that his mannerisms often could be observed in his employees.[16] Remarkably, Gates had kept the same level of intensity and drive from the inception of the corporation as a small, struggling software venture to a successful, publicly held entity that in 1991 had a firm grasp on the software market.

Business Units

Gates participated in every stage of product innovation from brainstorming sessions used to develop new ideas to marketing the final product. He managed to stay abreast of the various projects through the use of "business units." These units were designed to develop new software, and each was responsible for distinct projects. Gates met with each unit approximately every two weeks in order to stay informed on the progress of each project.[17]

Brenton Schlender of *Fortune* attributes much of Microsoft's success to the use of these business units through which Gates effectively delegated authority. Each unit was small enough (the average number was 30) that Gates could sit around the table and discuss the project with the members, allowing Gates to inject his thoughts and ideas personally. According to Gates, "It's very important to me and to the guys that work for us that Microsoft feel like a small company, even though it isn't one anymore. I remember how much fun it is to be small, and the business units help preserve that feeling."[18] Gates's hands-on approach to management demanded a premium on commitment from his employees. "I give people a hard time," he said. Using his own brand of computerspeak (referred to as "Gatespeak" within the company), he added, "When they come to meetings they'd better be ready to respond to my questions in real time and at high bandwidth."[19] (Real time refers to immediate responses and high bandwidth refers to an individual's intelligence.)

Organizational Culture

When the company was young, Gates and Allen managed the small enterprise efficiently and effectively. However, after the corporation began to grow, Allen contracted Hodgkin's disease and resigned from Microsoft in 1983. The disease later went into remission and Allen started his own software company, Asymetrix.[20] Asymetrix survived for a few years, but eventually folded and Allen has since rejoined Microsoft via a position on the Board.[21]

Many credit Gates's success with Microsoft to the fact that he realized the importance of hiring professional managers at an early stage. In 1983, after Allen resigned, Gates hired Jon A. Shirley and gave him the responsibility of managing the day-to-day activities.[22] Although this move enabled Gates to concentrate more on the long-term strategy of Microsoft, he was still very active in the various business units.

A workaholic, Gates set the standard for Microsoft employees. His typical day was 12 to 15 hours, which included Saturday and at least four hours on Sunday. In finding employees who fit into his organization, each prospective employee was subjected to several intense interview sessions in which he or she was grilled on technical issues and assessed for determination and dedication. A former employee said, "They'll make you write code right in front of them. And if they do hire you, you'll have flexible hours; you can work any 90 hours a week that you want."[23]

The expectations that Gates had of his employees often created moments of despair, as he was prone to cutting remarks and even threatening to fire team members. He was quick to reprimand employees who made mistakes but slow to praise them when they did well. According to Gates, "We don't try to make rock stars out of them."[24] James A. Towne, who served a brief stint as President in 1983, claimed: "Bill is a perfectionist who demands that his people move at his speed."[25]

Although the pressure on Microsoft's employees was great, the corporation experienced the lowest turnover in the industry. Shirley attributed this fact to the exciting atmosphere created by Gates and to being a part of a company that was trailblazing the path for the industry. Shirley summed it up by saying, "There must be some reason for all the people you see working around here at three or four in the morning."[26]

Shirley must have been right, as Gates did not set any standards for high salaries. However, Microsoft employees did have excellent fringe benefits, including attractive stock options. The options were based on achievement levels, ranging from 10 to 15, in which the options increase with the level. The level achievable by each employee was based on accomplishments rather than on position or seniority. When Microsoft went public in 1986, dozens of participating employees became paper millionaires.[27]

Despite the demanding workload placed on Microsoft's employees, they were privileged to have a casual dress code; corporate headquarters was often compared to a college campus. The majority of Microsoft employees, including Gates, avoided wearing the conventional suit and tie except when absolutely necessary. While the Microsoft staff regularly put on a tie and jacket when they attended functions at off-site locations, they dressed informally when they were the hosts. At one such meeting, an IBMer who could not recall a programmer's name referred to him as "the guy without shoes."[28]

Top Management and Board of Directors

Bill Gates held the positions of Chairman of the Board and Chief Executive Officer. Jon Shirley retired from Microsoft effective June 1, 1991, and was replaced as President and COO by Michael R. Hallman, a 20-year veteran of IBM. The organization chart in Exhibit 17.1 reflects this change. The Board of Directors was composed of Bill Gates as Chairman and CEO, Michael Hallman as President and COO, Paul Allen as co-founder and past-President of the company, Jon Shirley as immediate past-President of the company, and R. D. O'Brien, D. F. Marquardt, and W. G. Reed as outside directors having no other association with Microsoft Corporation.

Officers and directors owned approximately 54% of Microsoft's common stock. Of this amount Bill Gates owned 33% and Paul Allen owned 14%. In addition, institutions held some 31% of the common stock.[29]

EXHIBIT 17.1 Corporate Organizational Chart: Microsoft Corporation

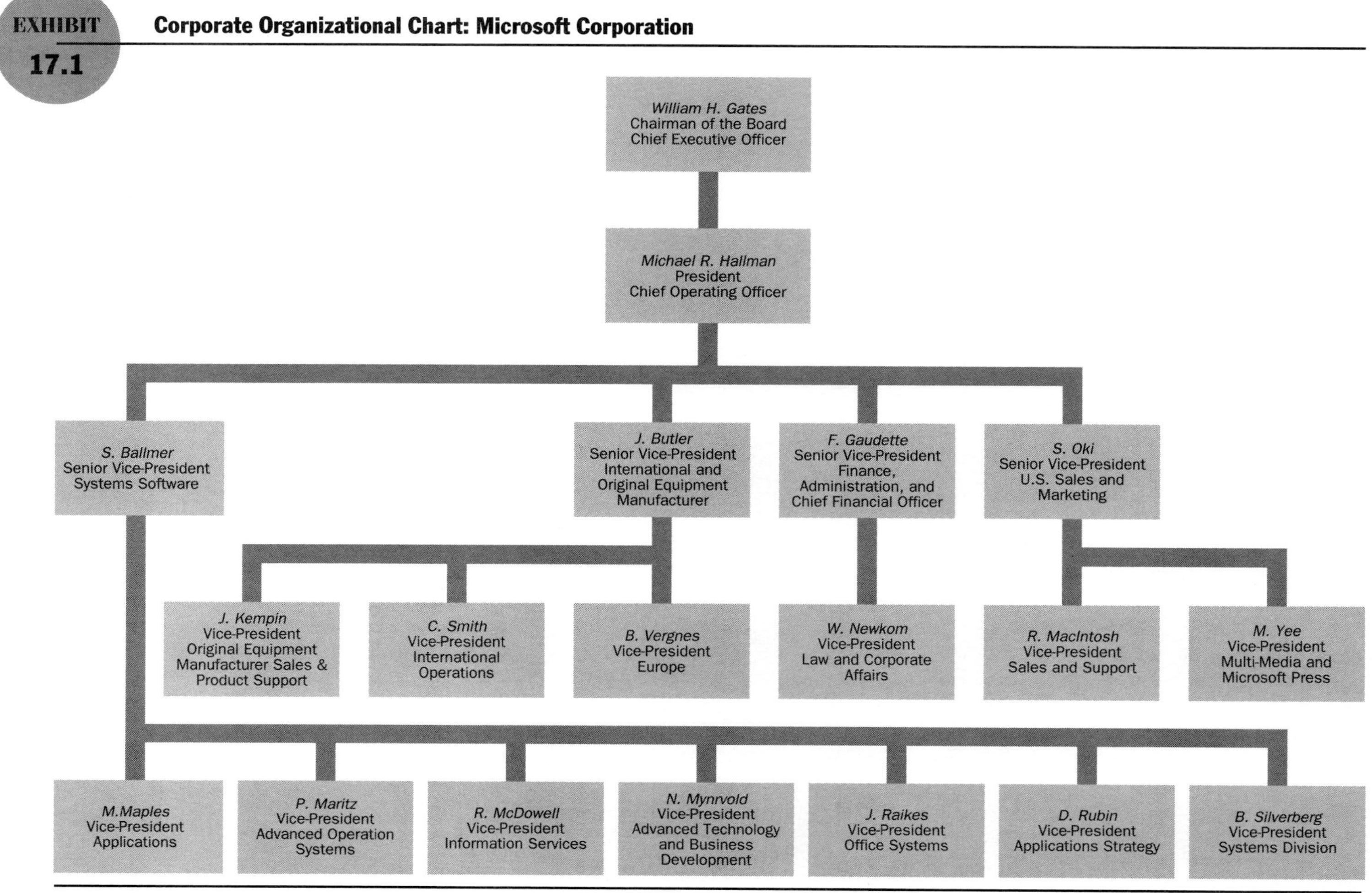

Source: Microsoft Corporation, *1990 Annual Report*, p. 36.

A Major Force in the Industry

Under Gates's direction, the software giant had earned the respect of its peers as an industry leader possessing a keen competitive edge and an insatiable hunger for developing new operating systems and software applications.

In 1991, Gates was the last of the young PC pioneers who developed their own companies and were still with the original operation (compared with Steven Jobs of Apple Computer and Mitchell Kapor, who started Lotus Development Corporation). Along the way he had continuously defined the edge of technology with innovative products. A prominent industry analyst with *P.C. Letter* felt that Gates had had an historical impact on the personal computer industry. He stated, "Gates sometimes reminds me of the nineteenth-century industrial barons who by force of will and business genius built the oil, steel, and banking monopolies. He's been that important to the computer industry."[30]

Although he had had an unequalled impact on the computer world, Gates was not without his critics. Mitch Kapor, founder of Lotus, stated that Microsoft products did not offer the ease of operation that most computer users wanted—though the technology was sound: "I give Bill Gates an A for vision, because as a business person and a strategist he's brilliant. His flaw is that his view is not informed by a humanistic or compassionate vision of how to make computers work for people."[31]

Michael Swavely, President of Compaq Computer's North American operations, had another view of Microsoft's shortcomings. "Microsoft is a very seat-of-the-pants operation in certain ways. In particular, their marketing tends not to be well thought out, and their understanding of market research is only rudimentary. But that is typical of a fast-growing company, and it's fixable."[32]

Product/Competition Overview

When Bill Gates founded Microsoft with Paul Allen, they had one mission: "a computer on every desk and in every home, all running Microsoft software."[33] Although this may sound like an impossible goal, Microsoft was well on its way to achieving it. Microsoft had earned the position of world leader in personal computer software through designing, developing, and manufacturing quality software products.

One of Microsoft's primary goals was to provide software products that made people more productive. This goal was supported by three guiding principles.[34]

1. Products are designed to work together, simply and intelligently.
2. Although products are designed to be used separately, they are more powerful when used together.
3. Microsoft products are designed to be at the leading edge of what people need and want.

Microsoft targeted a variety of market segments, both domestically and internationally, by offering (operating) system products, application products, hardware products, and Microsoft Press published materials. Microsoft also accommodated various types of personal computer users by selling software products that worked on the IBM PC and the Apple Macintosh computers.[35] By offering a broad range of integrated products, Microsoft was able to dominate the PC software market. Microsoft generated $1.18 billion in total sales in 1990, of which system products accounted for 39%, applications accounted for 48%, and hardware, books, etc., accounted for 13%.[36]

Although many PC hardware manufacturers and software developers have viewed Microsoft as some sort of impenetrable monolith, a recent internal memo from Bill Gates to his senior staff showed some real concern at the top:

> Our nightmare—IBM "attacking" us in systems software, Novell "defeating" us in networking and . . . competitors getting their Windows act together is not a scenario but a reality.[37]

System Products

DOS 5.0

In 1991, Microsoft released a DOS 5.0 that was both "Sexy and Bullet Proof."[38] DOS 5.0 was a brilliant marketing ploy because most DOS users were two or three versions behind at the time of the release, creating potential sales of 50 million copies.[39]

"DOS 5.0 has fixed the problems that users have been griping about for years," said Paul Somerson.[40] DOS 5.0 offered innovations such as online help and many other features unavailable in earlier releases. Thus Microsoft continued to improve on the operating system that gave rise to its empire.

Some competitors tried to compete with this product by developing an operating system that was similar, yet loaded with enhancements that many DOS users appreciated. One such firm was Digital Research, Inc., makers of DR DOS.[41] The efforts of such companies received high marks from reviewers in the PC press. However, Microsoft always seemed to nullify such efforts by including any worthwhile changes found in its competitors' products. In the process, Microsoft maintained its product as the standard in the industry, with firms such as Digital Research gaining an infinitesimal share of the market.

Windows 3.0

May 22, 1990, was the D-Day of personal computing as Microsoft introduced Windows 3.0. Windows offered features that DOS (even DOS 5.0) could never provide, such as GUI (Graphical User Interface). GUI, jokingly referred to as the W.I.M.P. interface,[42] gave a user a visual point-and-click interface using windows, icons, mice, and pulldown menus. Windows 3.0 also offered PC users a multitasking capability that was similar to "walking and chewing gum at the same time."[43] For example, a user could be editing a letter in Microsoft Word, while in the background a large spreadsheet in Microsoft Excel would be calculating complex algorithms.

Multitasking was possible because Windows 3.0 took advantage of the capabilities of the 286, 386, and 486 CPUs (central processing units) found on newer PCs. Less noticed, but useful, features of Windows were the extended memory management facility and cut/paste feature (e.g., cut/paste allows a user to copy a Lotus 1–2-3 graph into a graphic box in WordPerfect).

When Microsoft released Windows 3.0, it was able to offer four Windows business applications (MS Word, MS Power Point, MS Project, and MS Excel) that made the product more attractive to the public. By creating the popular Windows environment, as well as a number of first-rate compatible applications, the company strove to be a "one-stop, work-group provider to corporate accounts."[44] Not surprisingly, Windows 3.0 sold one million copies in the first four months after its release.[45]

OS/2

When the PC clones started cutting heavily into IBM's share of the PC market in the mid 1980s, IBM, with the help of Microsoft, sought to develop a new standard operating system called OS/2. Although DOS 5.0 had solved many of the old problems with the operating system, software developers had known for some time that DOS's inherent limitations would soon cripple its usefulness in a world moving toward increasingly powerful PCs and a desire for the GUI—a key feature of the Macintosh and Windows operating systems. A more powerful IBM operating system would allow IBM to take advantage of these trends and thus sell more hardware, preventing other manufacturers from benefiting from IBM's technological successes. Unfortunately, the marketplace was not impressed by OS/2. Despite IBM's large installed base, prestige, and immense marketing power, sales of the initial version of OS/2 were significantly below expectations and confined to a few well-defined niches.[46]

Although Microsoft had committed itself to IBM in the joint development of new OS/2 operating system, it was also committed to maintaining DOS and to the further development of Windows. The huge success of Windows 3.0 coupled with the disappointing sales performance of the initial version of OS/2 during 1990 prompted Microsoft's top management to rethink its plans for a next-generation operating system. Microsoft soon decided to build its own "New Technology" (NT) operating system for Windows and to deemphasize its development work on OS/2.

IBM responded to Microsoft's decision by seizing total control of OS/2 development. IBM initiated a development program not only to correct the problems users had found with OS/2, but also to provide an operating system superior to both Microsoft's DOS and Windows. Meanwhile, IBM continued to defend and support the initial version of OS/2 even though sales were marginal.[47,48] Nevertheless, some of the large software developers that had previously supported OS/2 were beginning to switch their orientation to Windows.[49] Realizing that an operating system could not succeed unless highly regarded application programs (such as WordPerfect and Lotus 1–2-3) were written to use with the system, IBM worked feverishly to stop the erosion of confidence in OS/2.[50] The company reduced the price of OS/2 and announced planned features for the second version that had never been contemplated by Microsoft, such as a graphic shell capable of simultaneously running both DOS and Windows applications.

Initial tests of IBM's OS/2 2.0 in 1991 by selected software analysts indicated that OS/2 might very well deliver on its promise to be a "better DOS than DOS, a better Windows than Windows." A senior technical editor for *Byte* magazine concluded that "version 2.0 promises to do what OS/2 should have done from the start: embrace the family of lesser PC operating systems and provide a smooth upgrade path. Ultimately, it's not just a better DOS or a better Windows that I want, but a better system. I think that's what OS/2 2.0 will be."[51] The marketplace appeared to agree. By mid 1992, IBM announced that it had delivered one million copies of OS/2 2.0. (The one-million mark traditionally denotes the level at which software developers can start making money with application programs made for that system.)[52]

UNIX

A less visible competitor to Microsoft in the operating system arena was UNIX. It was a product that had been around for over 20 years in many different forms; however, it was receiving more and more notice in 1991. "Many developers, frustrated with what they called the proprietary limitations of DOS and the muddy future of OS/2, were using UNIX to cover their bets."[53]

Although DOS had been quite suitable for many years and still met the needs of millions of users, there were demands for features that DOS could not provide. Such features included the ability to do two things at the same time or connect many users to the same programs. UNIX contained these and other features, whereas DOS required other networking or "environment" packages to be run on top of it, without nearly the same efficiency.[54] Moreover, some versions of UNIX had the capability to run DOS software as well as its own, giving those users the best of both worlds.[55]

In the mid 1980s, Microsoft ventured into the UNIX arena with its version for PCs, Xenix, which was popular in some circles around the country. However, with its early commitments to OS/2 and IBM, Xenix became less and less a prominent part of its product mix.

Several daunting factors kept UNIX from being a standard in the marketplace: the political maneuvering of different standards organizations, the proprietary nature of many companies' versions of the product, and the difficulty of use.[56] However, Egil Juliussen, President of the *Computer Industry Almanac,* felt that these problems would be overcome and UNIX's popularity would increase. He predicted that "shrink-wrapped UNIX software will be on computer store shelves by 1995."[57]

Nevertheless, the general feeling was that "UNIX will plod along in 1991 gaining favor with IS [Information Systems professionals] slowly but surely. . . . If UNIX had a superhero, he'd probably spend most of 1991 in a telephone booth trying to figure out how to put on his cape."[58] Although UNIX's progress in the standards and other areas had been slow and Microsoft probably would not face any real competition from it for another few years, UNIX's longevity and growing popularity, along with its many sophisticated features, made it a force to contend with over time.

Network Software

For many years Novell, Inc.'s Netware had been the leader in network software, which allows multiple DOS–based PCs to access the same programs and data. Microsoft made a strong attempt to cut into this market with its product, OS/2 LAN Manager, which had been called "functionally equivalent [to Netware] as a result of massive revisions that Microsoft included."[59] Novell did not sit idly by, as it released strong enhancements to its networking software for different levels of PCs.[60]

The April 1990 proposed merger of Lotus Development Corporation and Novell was seen as "both a response to the Microsoft Corporation juggernaut and as recognition by Lotus of the need to better align systems software with applications development."[61] Mitch Kapor, who founded Lotus, noted that the merger could "represent a significant challenge to Microsoft's complete dominance of systems software."[62] From these comments, the intentions of the parties were clear: stop Microsoft.

Over time, however, the merger collapsed, although Netware maintained strong support among purchasers of network software. Quite apart from these events, Microsoft itself cut back on funding for LAN Manager in 1991. Company officials' refusal to admit a lessening of commitment to LAN Manager may have been a response to the lackluster acceptance of OS/2 and LAN Manager relative to the increased attention paid to Windows and the strength of Netware. An electronic memo from Bill Gates to his managers read: "We knew it wasn't going to be easy, but it has been harder than we expected to build a position in networking."[63]

Recent developments concerning Novell, Inc., and Digital Research, Inc. (maker of DR DOS), indicated an increase in network competition for Microsoft. In a deal announced in the July 22, 1991, issue of *Computerworld,* Novell, Inc., was buying Digital Research, Inc., for $80 million. Analysts likened the agreement to an insurance policy for Novell, which ensured a stronger presence in the network applications market against competitors such as Microsoft.[64]

Computer Languages

Microsoft marketed a complete line of PC development languages. Microsoft C, Microsoft Macro Assembler, and Microsoft Quick C were considered state-of-the-art development languages and were the standard development packages for many large corporations (e.g., AMR [American Airlines]and JC Penney).[65] Microsoft BASIC and QuickBASIC had started slowly but had recently gained popularity as Microsoft improved the products. Microsoft also offered the software languages FORTRAN, COBOL, and PASCAL. The main selling features of these language products were their ease of use and extensive debugging capabilities.

Application Products

Microsoft offered a broad range of business application software (12 distinct, high-quality products) that provided PC users with the ability to do word processing, spreadsheet manipulation, database storage/retrieval, (graphics) presentation formatting, electronic mail, and project management. "Last year Microsoft surpassed competitor Lotus Development, maker of the popular 1–2-3, as the biggest seller of application software—word processors, spreadsheets, and the like."[66]

"Excel 3.0 [Microsoft's spreadsheet] is an example of what the new friendlier, smarter software is all about. . . . Smart software understands the user, and does as much of the work as possible."[67] Microsoft Excel was a main competitor of Lotus 1–2-3. Excel was doing very well because it worked with Windows 3.0, unlike the current version of 1–2-3, which ran exclusively with DOS.

Microsoft Word was another Microsoft product that was a key player in the word processing market. MS Word had a common interface, whether it was running under DOS, Windows, OS/2, or on a Macintosh. This feature made MS Word especially attractive to large corporations that had a hodgepodge of computing equipment, as it allowed them to select a standard word processing package for all their PCs.[68]

Microsoft Works was a multifunction, integrated business application. It allowed users to perform word processing, spreadsheet, and database functions with one software product. This capability was especially useful for small companies that wanted one product that served many purposes.[69]

Thus Microsoft's approach to high-quality, integrated business application software had resulted in Microsoft's ability to gain a sizable share of the applications market. By offering products that were suited to small and large corporations alike, Microsoft was able to accommodate the needs of most PC users. "While Microsoft is the leading developer of software for Apple Computers, it is not yet a leader in any of the three big IBM PC applications: word processors, spreadsheets, and databases. But no one doubts that it is only a matter of time before it gets there," said Kathleen K. Wiegner and Julie Pitta of *Forbes*.[70]

The heavyweights in the word processing and spreadsheet fields, WordPerfect Corporation and Lotus Development Corporation, respectively, were not about to take this threat lying down. With the popularity of Windows 3.0 being quite evident, Lotus quickly wrote a number of its programs to run with Windows, particularly its famous Lotus 1–2-3. Lotus President Jim Manzi clearly was combatting the one-stop-shopping image that Microsoft was trying to portray to its customers by keeping its old customers faithful even if they moved to the Windows environment.[71] Lotus worked hard to enhance its product to take full advantage of the graphic environment in order to counter any feelings that only Microsoft could truly optimize software on Windows.

Publications and Peripheral Products

In 1991, the publishing division of Microsoft marketed more than 123 titles on computers, software, science, and technology. These books were distributed through computer and software retail outlets and in many foreign languages.

Microsoft also marketed hardware accessories. For example, Microsoft had sold more than one million MS Mouse units since 1984 when the product was first introduced.[72] CD-ROM was another new market that Microsoft was pursuing. CD-ROM, which was the same storage media used by the record companies, was able to store millions of bytes of information on a single disk. This type of mass storage was especially attractive to companies that maintained many historical records or performed research on a regular basis.[73]

Other Competitive Issues

Apple

While the DOS-based IBM PC clones had taken over the business world, Apple had maintained a strong share of the personal computer market because of its easy-to-use graphics interface. However, Windows 3.0 had the potential to cut heavily into Apple's previously dedicated following.

> If the revamped Windows 3.0 lives up to expectations, some analysts said it will not only affect OS/2 migration but could also take the wind out of the sails of Apple's Macintosh by closely imitating the Mac's classic windows-and-icons graphical user interface. . . . This leveling of the playing field could be the deciding factor for many users, particularly those who hedge at the Mac's comparatively high price.[74]

Software executives whose companies made products used on the Macintosh, speaking at the Macworld Expo in April 1990, said that Apple's "party line, which holds that the Macintosh is unaffected by the recent challenge of Windows 3.0," was itself out of line.[75] These executives cited a number of factors that made Apple less competitive than its counterpart in the marketplace, including spending too much time and too many resources on copyright infringement litigation, focusing on niches that were too narrow (e.g., desktop publishing), replacing too many top managers in the organization, and, in particular, high cost. One software executive, referring to a recent TV advertising spot, said, "You need to introduce laptops that someone other than Bo Jackson can carry around."[76]

Apple had been trying to counter the "Windows onslaught" by releasing cheaper Macintoshes and a highly touted new release of its operating system, called System 7.0.[77] However, there were signs that Apple's efforts were too little too late. The new System 7.0 had received praise from many industry observers, but some problems had arisen that could affect users' dedication to the product. These problems included the need to add more memory to many existing machines and some incompatibilities with software written for previous versions of the operating system.[78]

However, these types of problems were not insurmountable. Although they could give more users reason to go to Windows instead of the Macintosh, other signs of the times for Apple could be more telling, such as die-hard Macintosh software developers rushing to write applications for Windows. International Data Corporation, a reputable market research firm for the computer industry, confirmed the following:

> Now that Microsoft Corporation's Windows 3.0 gives IBM Personal Computers and clones the simplified windows-and-icons appearance of the Macintosh, recession-wary developers are hungrily eyeing a DOS market that, at upwards of 40 million users, is nearly 10 times larger than Apple's steadily shrinking slice of the PC industry's pie.[79]

Another sign that Apple could have been suffering from the Windows competition was its recent layoff of 1,500 workers.[80] This move was a direct response to the newfound ability to put a sophisticated graphics interface on the masses of DOS-based PCs and the need to cut costs and lower prices in order to maintain market share.

The Rift with IBM

In May 1991, Bill Gates's memo to Microsoft executives predicted a "fairly cold" relationship with IBM during the next 24 months.[81] The reason for this "unhappy marriage" was that IBM was committed to moving all personal computer users to OS/2, whereas Microsoft's vision was decidedly different. Microsoft viewed Windows as the "target operating system" for the majority of users, supporting OS/2 primarily for what it perceived as a smaller, high-end market that needed some of the features that DOS-based Windows did not have.[82] Microsoft's perception of the market seemed to have been correct in 1991, as most DOS users interested in moving to a graphics interface for whatever reason had found Windows more than adequate for the task and a much less expensive transition as well.[83]

IBM had not been complacent after breaking with Microsoft. In fact, its actions seemed to be geared toward isolating Microsoft during the next several years. IBM was implementing this apparent strategy by aligning itself with other companies. One such alliance was with Lotus, producing an agreement that "is widely viewed as the latest in a series of alliances designed in part to put some distance between IBM and its estranged development partner, Microsoft Corporation."[84]

The Apple/IBM Partnership

The most important alliance that IBM had entered into recently had been with Apple, its longtime rival in the PC business. This proposed partnership led Bill Gates to tell top Microsoft executives with great trepidation that "IBM is proposing to take over the definition of PC desktop operating systems."[85] The alliance was aimed at developing a new operating system that would run on both IBM and Apple machines and allow users of the Macintosh, OS/2, and AIX, which was IBM's version of UNIX, to easily migrate to the new system.[86] The advantages to both companies were enormous. IBM could take advantage of Apple's superior graphics interface, and Apple could gain entrance into IBM's vast installed base in corporate America and benefit from IBM's enormous marketing clout.[87] The primary loser if the IBM/Apple deal went through and was successful would be Microsoft, who would be "served notice that it may no longer set the desktop agenda."[88] IBM said that OS/2 eventually would be replaced by the new proposed operating system with Apple, though it promised continued support for OS/2 and its users over the long haul.[89]

This proposed alliance presented the first major challenge to Microsoft in its role of being more independent of IBM, but there was no certainty that the alliance would meet expectations. The agreement between IBM and Apple had not been finalized in 1991, and many details still needed to be worked out.[90] Moreover, there was no guarantee that, if the deal was eventually finalized, IBM and Apple would be able to do what they set out to do. However, there was reason to expect that the enormous talents of Apple and the equally enormous resources of IBM would be up to the task, a fact that led Bill Gates to exclaim that "eventually, we need to have at least a neutral relationship with IBM."[91] Gates's remarks indicated second thoughts about Microsoft's decision to break with IBM, the company that helped make MS-DOS a household word.

Marketing and Distribution

Microsoft relied on four primary channels of distribution to market its software and hardware products. These channels included domestic Original Equipment Manufacturers (OEMs), domestic retail, international OEMs, and international finished goods.[92]

Microsoft's operating systems, as well as languages and application programs, were marketed mostly through OEMs. Major OEMs that had agreements with Microsoft included AT&T, Compaq, Digital Equipment Corporation, Hewlett-Packard, IBM, Olivetti, Tandy, Wang, and Zenith.[93]

Approximately 49% of domestic retail revenue for the year ending June 30, 1990, came through independent distributors, and dealers accounted for 36%. Microsoft had established a network of field sales representatives and field support to maintain relationships with customers. These representatives and support personnel received orders and provided product training seminars to integrate Microsoft software into the customers' existing operations.[94]

Microsoft's international market was virtually worldwide, but the largest markets were in Japan, South Korea, and Europe. Over the years, Microsoft had nurtured a relationship with various Japanese microcomputer manufacturers, which had resulted in a sharp increase in the use of Microsoft software.

Microsoft had also utilized various subsidiaries to assist in its foreign operations. For example, a Microsoft subsidiary in Japan handled the OEM marketing, a subsidiary in South Korea marketed Microsoft products to OEMs in that country, and a subsidiary serviced the European market by taking care of OEM marketing and business technical relations.[95]

In some foreign countries such as Belgium, Israel, Norway, and Switzerland, Microsoft marketed its finished goods through its marketing-only subsidiaries. In addition to marketing and distribution, the foreign subsidiaries also had helped localize Microsoft products.[96]

Marketing Highlights

The success of Windows had enabled Microsoft to reach $1.18 billion in sales for 1990, representing a market value of $12 billion—eight times larger than its nearest rival, Lotus Development.[97] Microsoft had gained market share by aggressively promoting Windows.

The company introduced Windows 3.0 in May 1990 with an all-out campaign intended to make the product a success. The plan consisted of a $10 million marketing budget, a ten-month advertising campaign, a shipment of 40,000 demonstration disks, a shipment of 120,000 copies to retailers for first-day display, and an agreement with 30 systems vendors to provide Windows 3.0 with their hardware sales.[98]

Microsoft's marketing effort was an obvious success. More than one million copies had been sold in the first three months, and the demand for Windows was still growing.[99] One analyst explained the reason for Windows' popularity: "The MIS guys are the only ones doing anything with OS/2. It's not on anyone's desk; why should it be. Windows [3.0] is a quick fix."[100]

As a promotion for its Windows software, Microsoft made a limited-time offer during February, March, and April 1991, cutting the prices on its Excel spreadsheet and Microsoft Word from $495 to $129. Windows 3.0 was such a success that it triggered a price war among software companies to sell their application software for Windows 3.0. The company's competitors, such as Borland International, Inc., and Lotus Development Corporation, followed Microsoft's price promotion by offering low prices and giveaways.[101]

Although Microsoft boosted the sales of Windows 3.0 through low pricing, management was skeptical about such an underpricing strategy. Scott Oki, Senior Vice-President of Sales, Marketing, and Services at Microsoft, said, "Long-term, it would be a pretty dead-end strategy. We couldn't afford to continue to invest heavily in research and development by giving away software."[102]

Microsoft's efforts to maintain its standards and openness was evident in its user-support programs. A variety of services were available from which Microsoft software users could obtain information ranging from technical support to application use. They were offered over the telephone through a system that could handle 6,500 calls per day, 24 hours a day.[103]

Financial Highlights

Microsoft's revenues reached a record high in fiscal 1990, topping $1 billion for the first time in the company's history. Microsoft's 1990 revenues of $1.18 billion represented a 47% increase over 1989 revenues of $803.5 million[104] (see Exhibits 17.2–17.4). This increase in revenues was a result of many factors, including the introduction of new products, enhancement and localization of existing products, worldwide growth of personal computer hardware shipments, and expansion of the company's international operations into new geographic areas.[105] Larger sales volumes rather than price increases were largely responsible for the company's revenue growth. New products, such as Microsoft Word for Windows and Microsoft Windows 3.0, comprised roughly 7% of the company's 1990 revenues.[106] International revenues increased significantly from 1988 to 1990, jumping 48% from 1989 to 1990 and 55% from 1988 to 1989.[107] This growth stemmed mainly from successful localization of products and expanding overseas markets, particularly in Europe.

EXHIBIT 17.2

Consolidated Statements of Income: Microsoft Corporation
(Dollar amounts in thousands, except net income per share)

Years Ending June 30	1990	1989	1988
Net revenues	$1,183,446	$803,530	$590,827
Cost of revenues	252,668	204,185	148,000
Gross profit	930,778	599,345	442,827
Operating expenses			
Research and development	180,615	110,220	69,776
Sales and marketing	317,593	218,997	161,614
General and administrative	39,332	27,898	23,990
Total operating expenses	537,540	357,115	255,380
Operating income	393,238	242,230	187,447
Non-operating income	23,326	16,566	10,750
Stock option program expense	(6,000)	(8,000)	(14,559)
Income before taxes	410,564	250,796	183,738
Provisions for income taxes	131,378	80,258	59,830
Net income	$ 279,186	$170,538	$123,908
Net income per share	$ 2.34	$ 1.52	$ 1.11

Source: Microsoft Corporation, Inc., *1990 Annual Report,* p. 23.

EXHIBIT 17.3

Net Revenues: Microsoft Corporation
(Dollar amounts in millions)

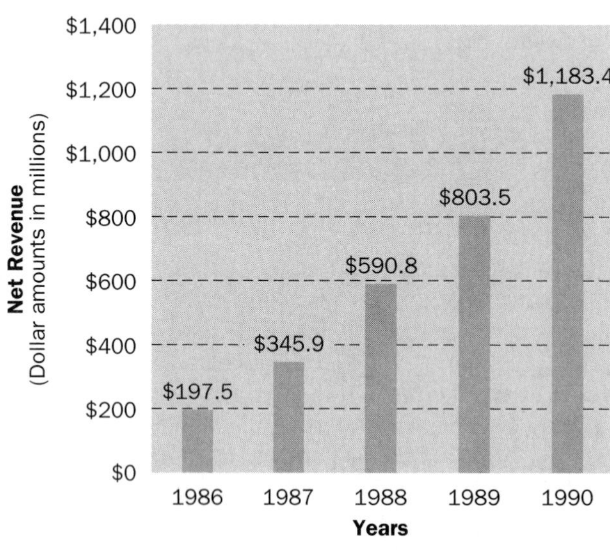

Source: Microsoft Corporation, Inc., *1990 Annual Report,* p. 34.

EXHIBIT 17.4

Consolidated Balance Sheets: Microsoft Corporation
(Dollar amounts in thousands)

Years Ending June 30	1990	1989
Assets		
Current assets		
Cash and short-term investments	$ 449,238	$300,791
Accounts receivable	180,998	111,180
Inventories	55,565	37,755
Other	34,089	19,223
Total current assets	719,890	468,949
Property, plant, and equipment	325,447	198,825
Other assets	60,012	52,824
Total assets	$1,105,349	$720,598
Liabilities and Shareholders' Equity		
Current liabilities		
Accounts payable	$ 51,012	$ 41,953
Customer deposits	17,172	10,043
Accrued compensation	28,770	25,718
Notes payable	6,500	25,619
Income taxes payable	42,582	30,069
Other	40,750	25,416
Total current liabilities	186,786	158,818
Commitments and contingencies	—	—
Stockholders' equity		
Common stock and paid in capital—shares authorized 160,000; issued and outstanding 113,699 and 109,172	219,520	110,480
Retained earnings	688,874	455,552
Translation adjustment	10,169	(4,252)
Total shareholders' equity	918,563	561,780
Total liabilities and shareholders' equity	$1,105,349	$720,598

Source: Microsoft Corporation, Inc., *1990 Annual Report,* p. 25.

Approximately 40% of Microsoft's revenues were collectible in foreign currencies in fiscal 1990. Accordingly, the company's net income was affected by fluctuations in foreign currency exchange rates.[108] The company's 47% increase in revenues in 1990 consisted of a 46% operational increase and a 1% exchange rate increase.[109] The latter was caused by the lower value of the U.S. dollar in 1990. The effect of these fluctuations on revenue collected in foreign currencies was offset to the extent that international operating expenses were incurred in the same currencies as its revenues.

EXHIBIT 17.5

Net Income: Microsoft Corporation
(Dollar amounts in millions)

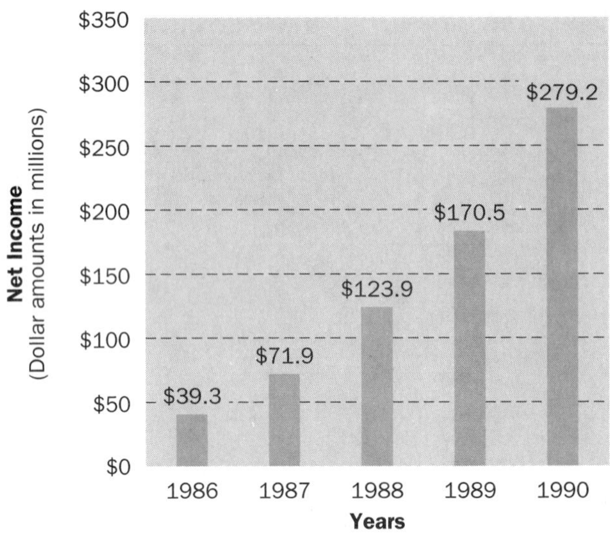

Source: Microsoft Corporation, Inc., *1990 Annual Report,* p. 34.

The 1990 costs of revenues as a percentage of net revenues decreased 24% from 1989 to 1990.[110] A multitude of factors contributed to this decline, including product cost reductions, economies of scale in manufacturing and distribution, and a shift in the revenue mix to a greater contribution from higher margin applications products.[111] Like Microsoft's revenues, 1990 net income and net income per share had also climbed to record levels. Net income increased 64% from $170.5 million in 1989 to $279.2 million in 1990[112] (see Exhibit 17.5). Similarly, net income per share rose from the $1.52 recorded in 1989 to $2.34 in 1990, a 54% increase[113] (see Exhibit 17.6). These financial results occurred because all aspects of the company's business had continued to prosper, including the international finished goods channel, the domestic retail channel, and Microsoft's worldwide OEM business.

Research and development expenses as a percentage of net revenues had increased in both 1989 and 1990 owing to planned additions to the company's software development staff. The product research and development staff had increased 54% from 1989 to 1990.[114] Management projected that sales and marketing expenses would increase in 1991 because of expansion and enhancement plans in the product support services area, and it planned to develop a reseller channel for networking products.[115] General and administrative expenses also had increased, reflecting the growth in administrative staff and systems necessary to run the company smoothly in the wake of its overall growth.

EXHIBIT 17.6 **Net Income Per Share: Microsoft Corporation**

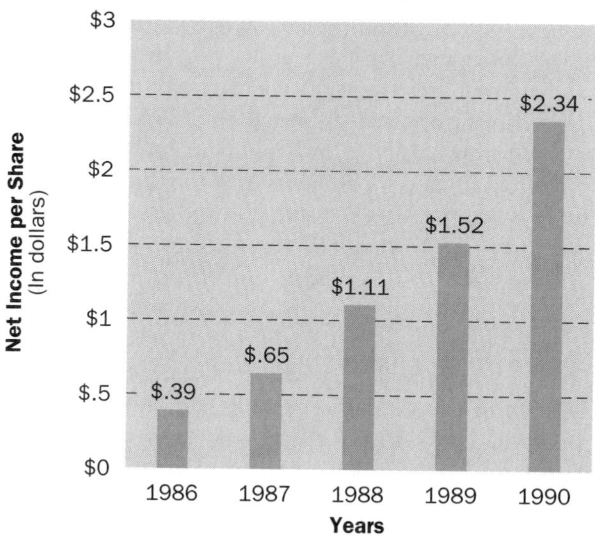

Source: Microsoft Corporation, Inc. *1990 Annual Report,* p. 34.

Legal Affairs

"If the judge rules against us without making it clear what we have to change or asks us to eliminate something fundamental to all windowing systems, it would be disastrous," Bill Gates lamented when recently asked to comment on Apple Computer, Inc.'s lawsuit.[116] Apple sued Microsoft in March 1988 for alleged copyright infringements, claiming that the visual displays of Microsoft Windows version 2.03 infringed Apple's copyrights and exceeded the scope of a 1985 Settlement Agreement between Microsoft and Apple.[117] Microsoft was licensed to simulate the look and feel of Apple's Macintosh screen appearance when Windows Version 1.0 was created. However, Apple contended that Microsoft had overstepped the boundaries of the 1985 agreement when the "audiovisual expression" of the Macintosh was copied too closely.[118] Apple won a key court round in this suit in March 1991, when the court upheld Apple's claim that the visual elements of the Macintosh screen display were not part of the 1985 licensing agreement.[119] If Apple were to prevail in this ongoing case, it could draw large royalty payments from Microsoft or even halt the sales of Windows. According to one market analyst, "Apple has been hurt in the marketplace, so they're becoming more combative in the courtroom."[120] From management's point of view, competitors were trying to punish Microsoft for its success, and Microsoft would not take these efforts lying down.

An investigation by the Federal Trade Commission into Microsoft's business practices, in response to complaints from third parties, created another legal concern for the company. The FTC would examine "third-party allegations that Microsoft has monopolized or attempted to monopolize the market for operating systems, operating environments, computer software and computer peripherals for personal computers."[121] The current investigation was substantially broader than its earlier investigation, which was originally limited to a 1989 agreement between Microsoft and IBM to cooperate on OS/2 and Windows. If the Commission concluded that Microsoft had conducted its business in a monopolistic manner, it could order remedies ranging from a cease-and-desist order to restitution.[122] "It's clear that Microsoft wants to be the IBM of the software industry," stated one journalist. "It's a super strategy; it's just that they don't implement it with sensitivity."[123]

The software development community was concerned that Microsoft unfairly used its position as purveyor of the standard PC operating system to seek dominance in applications also.[124] Microsoft was cooperating fully with authorities and vowed to continue to be competitive. "We will not back away from our commitment to the industry and the business, or from being a very aggressive company. We are not trying to win a popularity contest," stated company President Mike Hallman.[125] Instead, Hallman stressed the importance of "creating vision, innovation, and standard," which he said was the proper definition of leadership in the marketplace.[126] Microsoft did have a chance to escape this antitrust challenge via the new IBM/Apple alliance, which was formed to enter into UNIX-based, object-oriented platform design.[127] This IBM/Apple combination could provide enough of a competitive punch to erase any view of Microsoft as an unfair heavy hitter.

Epilogue

Flying the "red-eye" late-night plane back to Seattle on that very special day in 1980, Bill Gates couldn't stop grinning. They had pulled it off! Microsoft had contracted to supply IBM with its new operating system, which in turn would open a floodgate of opportunities. It truly seemed that the sky was the limit.

Even then, Gates was planning and scheming on how they would put a computer on every desk, each one running Microsoft software. And the rest, as they say, is history. . . .

Notes

1. Richard Brandt, "The Billion-Dollar Whiz Kid," *Business Week* (Industrial/Technology Edition) (April 13, 1987), p. 70.
2. Ibid.
3. Ibid.
4. Ibid., p. 71.
5. Ibid.
6. Ibid.
7. Paul Somerson, "The DOS You've Been Waiting For," *PC Computing* (July 1991), p. 97.
8. James Daly, "'All Systems Go' for Desktop Launches," *Computerworld* (May 6, 1991), pp. 1, 109.

9. Rachel Pred, "Looking Back, Looking Ahead," *PC Today* (December 1990), p. 16.
10. Ibid., p. 19.
11. James Daly, "Apple Looks to Include Windows 3.0 in Lawsuit," *Computerworld* (April 22, 1991), p. 4.
12. James Daly, "Excel Packs Windows Punch," *Computerworld* (January 14, 1991), p. 6.
13. Pred, p. 20.
14. Patricia Keefe, "UNIX Jumps Into the Breach," *Computerworld* (May 20, 1991), p. 100.
15. Patricia Keefe, "Microsoft Feels Heat of FTC Investigation," *Computerworld* (March 18, 1991), pp. 1, 101.
16. Brenton Schlender, "How Bill Gates Keeps the Magic Going," *Fortune* (June 18, 1990), p. 83.
17. Ibid., pp. 83, 84.
18. Ibid.
19. Bro Uttal, "A Computer Jock's $550-Million Jackpot," *Fortune* (January 5, 1987), pp. 84, 85.
20. Lindsay Van Gelder, "The Nerd Who Roars," *Business Month* (April 1988) p. 58.
21. Schlender, p. 89.
22. Thomas J. Murray, "Management by Obsession," *Business Month* (April 1988), p. 59.
23. Van Gelder, p. 60.
24. Ibid.
25. Murray, p. 59.
26. Ibid.
27. Schlender, p. 84.
28. Brandt, p. 72.
29. *Standard OTC Stock Reports,* Vol. 58, No. 86, Sec. 16 (New York: Standard and Poor's Corp., July 29, 1992), p. 4688M and *Standard and Poor's Register of Corporations, Directors, and Executives 1992,* Vol. 1 (New York: Standard and Poor's Corp., January 1992), p. 1763.
30. Schlender, p. 83.
31. Ibid., p. 88.
32. Ibid., p. 86.
33. Ibid., p. 82.
34. Microsoft Corporation, Inc., *1990 Annual Report,* p. 10.
35. Kathleen K. Wiegner and Julie Pitta, "Can Anyone Stop Bill Gates?" *Forbes* (April 1, 1991), p. 108.
36. Microsoft Corporation, Inc., *1990 Annual Report,* p. 4.
37. Jim Nash, "Gates's Words of Caution," *Computerworld* (June 24, 1991), p. 6.
38. Lynn Schwebach, "Microsoft's Latest: DOS 5.0," *PC Today* (July 1991), p. 6.
39. Ibid.
40. Somerson, p. 96.
41. Patricia Keefe, "Digital Research Hopes to Exploit MS-DOS Gaps," *Computerworld* (March 4, 1991), p. 8.
42. Pred, p. 16.
43. Ibid.
44. Patricia Keefe, "Lotus Faces Off With Microsoft," *Computerworld* (June 10, 1991), p. 14.
45. Ibid., p. 18.
46. Patricia Keefe and Charles Von Simson, "Overblown Promises Give Way to Reality," *Computerworld* (April 30, 1990), pp. 1, 118.
47. Patricia Keefe, "IBM Not Singing the OS/2 Blues," *Computerworld* (May 14, 1990), pp. 39, 50.
48. Patricia Keefe, "IBM Sticks to Its Guns on OS/2," *Computerworld* (April 1, 1991), pp. 37, 42.
49. Patricia Keefe, "Windows Blurs OS/2 Developers' Vision," *Computerworld* (April 23, 1990), pp. 1, 4.
50. Patricia Keefe, "Developer Shift to Windows Puts IBM OS/2 in Quandry," *Computerworld* (February 25, 1991), p. 8.
51. J. Udell, "OS/2 2.0: A Pilgrim's Journey," *Byte* (December 1991), p. 48.
52. L. Hooper, "IBM Trumpets Sales Milestone for OS/2 as Skeptical Microsoft Blows Own Horn," *Wall Street Journal* (August 13, 1992), p. B-3.
53. James Daly, "The UNIX PC Allure," *Computerworld* (November 26, 1990), pp. 1, 14.
54. Keefe, "UNIX Jumps Into the Breach," p. 100.
55. Deborah McAllister, "The Age of the Workstation," *D/FW Computer Currents* (January 1991), pp. 29–33.
56. J. A. Savage and Johanna Ambrosio, "UNIX Slow to Scrap Custom Wrappers," *Computerworld* (July 8, 1991), pp. 1, 105.
57. McAllister, p. 31.
58. Johanna Ambrosio, "Faster Than a Speeding . . . ," *Computerworld* (December 24, 1990), p. 36.
59. David Simpson, "Netware vs. LAN Manager: And the Winner Is?" *Systems Integration* (February 1991), pp. 25–31.

60. Jim Nash, "Network Update Has Users Cheering," *Computerworld* (March 25, 1991), p. 10.
61. Patricia Keefe and Jim Nash, "Lotus/Novell Merger Aims at Microsoft," *Computerworld* (April 9, 1990), pp. 1, 108.
62. Ibid., p. 1.
63. Jim Nash, "Memo Raises Doubt on LAN Manager," *Computerworld* (June 24, 1991), p. 6.
64. Jim Nash, "Novell Nets DRI in $80M Deal," *Computerworld* (July 22, 1991), p. 99.
65. Bob Mason, Senior Systems Analyst, AMRIS/TS (American Airlines), previously worked for JC Penney Corporate MIS Department.
66. Daly, "Excel Packs Windows Punch," p. 6.
67. Esther Dyson, "Microsoft's Spreadsheet, on Its Third Try, Excels," *Forbes* (April 1, 1991), p. 118.
68. James Daly, "Word Gets Better Definition," *Computerworld* (November 12, 1990), p. 47.
69. Jean S. Bozman, "Eyes on Microsoft Databases," *Computerworld* (May 20, 1991), p. 52.
70. Wiegner and Pitta, p. 108.
71. Patricia Keefe, "Lotus Shows Windows Suite, Users Say They Like the View," *Computerworld* (May 27, 1991), p. 106.
72. Geoff Lewis, "Microsoft Is Like an Elephant Rolling Around, Squashing Ants," *Business Week* (October 30, 1989).
73. Ibid.
74. James Daly, "Windows Could Be Apple Worm," *Computerworld* (April 9, 1990), pp. 35, 40.
75. Richard Pastore, "Software Vendors Rip Apple," *Computerworld* (August 13, 1990), pp. 1, 4.
76. Ibid., p. 4.
77. John Webster, "Apple's Future May Rest in Relying on Its Strengths," *Computerworld* (April 1, 1991), pp. 37, 44.
78. James Daly, "IS Confronts Chore in Move to System 7.0," *Computerworld* (May 20, 1991), pp. 1, 8.
79. James Daly, "More Macintosh Developers Writing for Windows Arena," *Computerworld* (January 1, 1991), p. 43.
80. James Daly, "Apple Cuts Back, Eliminates 1,500 Jobs," *Computerworld* (May 27, 1991), p. 109.
81. Nash, "Gates's Words of Caution," p. 6.
82. James Daly, "Microsoft, IBM Diverge on OS/2 Direction," *Computerworld* (February 4, 1991), pp. 1, 93.
83. David Coursey, "Not a Happy Marriage," *D/FW Computer Currents* (October 1990), p. 28.
84. Patricia Keefe, "User Gains Possible in IBM/Lotus Deal," *Computerworld* (July 8, 1991), p. 37.
85. Nash, "Gates's Words of Caution," p. 6.
86. Thomas McCarroll, "Love at First Byte," *Time* (July 15, 1991), pp. 46–47.
87. Patricia Keefe and J. A. Savage, "Who'll Win in Alliance Game," *Computerworld* (July 8, 1991), p. 102.
88. Ibid.
89. Patricia Keefe, "IBM, Apple in Pact to Control Desktop Standards," *Computerworld* (July 8, 1991), pp. 1, 103.
90. Patricia Keefe, "No Done Deal: Details Remain to Be Resolved," *Computerworld* (July 8, 1991), p. 102.
91. Nash, "Gates's Words of Caution," p. 6.
92. Microsoft Corporation, Inc., *Form 10-K Report,* (1990), p. 5.
93. Ibid.
94. Ibid., p. 6.
95. Ibid.
96. Ibid.
97. Thomas McCarroll, "The Next 800 Lb. Gorilla," *Time* (May 20, 1991), p. 44.
98. Charles Von Simson, "Microsoft Leads DOS Revival," *Computerworld* (May 28, 1991), pp. 1, 116.
99. Kate Bertrand, "Software Marketers Responding to Demand for 'Windows'," *Business Marketing* (December 1990), p. 14.
100. Von Simson, p. 116.
101. James Daly, "Competition = Bargains for Windows Software Buyers," *Computerworld* (February 18, 1991), p. 1.
102. Ibid., p. 101.
103. Microsoft Corporation, Inc., *Form 10-K Report,* (1990), p. 7.
104. Microsoft Corporation, Inc., *1990 Annual Report,* p. 2.
105. Ibid., p. 21.
106. Ibid.
107. Ibid.
108. Ibid.
109. Ibid.
110. Ibid.
111. Ibid.
112. Ibid., p. 2.
113. Ibid.

114. Ibid., p. 21.
115. Ibid.
116. Nash, "Gates's Words of Caution," p. 6.
117. Microsoft Corporation, Inc., *1990 Annual Report,* p. 32.
118. James Daly, "Apple Lawsuit Moves at Snail's Pace," *Computerworld* (August 27, 1990), p. 4.
119. James Daly, "Apple Wins Key Court Round," *Computerworld* (March 11, 1991), p. 4.
120. Daly, "Apple Looks to Include Windows 3.0 in Lawsuit," p. 4.
121. Clinton Wilder and James Daly, "Microsoft Probe Broadens," *Computerworld* (April 15, 1991), p. 1.
122. Patricia Keefe, "Microsoft Feels Heat of FTC Investigation," *Computerworld* (March 18, 1991), p. 1.
123. Wilder and Daly, p. 1.
124. Ibid., p. 8.
125. Patricia Keefe, "FTC Probe Won't Tame Microsoft," *Computerworld* (March 25, 1991), p. 1.
126. Ibid., p. 6.
127. Nell Margolis, "IBM/Apple Deal Could Take Heat Off Microsoft," *Computerworld* (July 15, 1991), p. 79.

CASE 18

Tandy Corporation, 1993: Proposed Spin-Off of TE Electronics, Inc.

Thomas L. Wheelen, Charles E. Michaels, Jr., Kimberly Jursa, and Penko K. Ivanor

The cover of Tandy Corporation's *1992 Annual Report* stated that "Tandy Corporation is committed to being the nation's leading retailer of consumer electronic and personal computers. . . . We believe this strategy will accelerate growth and enhance value for our shareholders."[1] Net income for fiscal 1992 was $183,847,000 on total sales and revenues of $4,680,156,000. It was the fourth consecutive year of decline in net income and the lowest level in the past decade. The decline in net income paralleled the slide in Radio Shack sales (except for a 3.0% rebound in 1992) and Tandy's PC market share. Matthew Upchurch, grandson of founder Charles Tandy and whose family is Tandy's largest noninstitutional shareholder, said, "There was so much focus put on computer manufacturing that Tandy lost sight of its roots: that it's a retailer."[2] Tandy has been a major disappointment in recent years to Wall Street because of its weak earnings and lackluster stock price performance.[3]

On January 11, 1993, John Roach, Chairman and CEO of Tandy, announced a proposed spin-off of Tandy's technology and manufacturing operations into a separate company—TE Electronics, Inc.—with an estimated $1.5 billion in annual sales (see Exhibit 18.1). Historically, the manufacturing unit had sold two-thirds of its products to other companies. Tandy's management has a record of successful spin-offs, including Pier One Imports, Color Tile, Inc., and Bombay Company, a specialty furniture retailer. Roach said, "Tandy has kind of had a history of re-inventing itself over the years," adding that "this allows the company to focus with a passion."[4] The spin-off of TE Electronics was scheduled for the summer of 1993, and Tandy was to provide the management team for the new Company. The spin-off announcement also signaled the closing of 100 of its 448 Tandy Name Brand retail stores. The 100 stores to be closed will be the smallest stores of the McDuff/Video Concept (180 stores) and McDuff SuperCenters (237 stores) chains. Tandy presently employs approximately 41,000 employees worldwide.

At Moody's Investment Service, Inc., and Standard & Poor's Corporation, the immediate reaction to the announcement was to consider reducing Tandy's credit rating on about $2.3 billion of debt; Standard & Poor's placed the company on a credit watch. The credit watch was based on Tandy's "loss of the manufacturing business . . . and . . . the company's lack of experience in running extremely low-priced stores."[5] A Tandy Company spokesperson's response was that "we have

---

EXHIBIT 18.1 Tandy Corporation: The Spinoff Company – TE Electronics, Inc.

A. NEW BUSINESS SNAPSHOT

1. *Tandy Corporation (current retail operations).* Company would consist of Radio Shack, Computer City, The Incredible Universe, and Tandy Brand Group, which includes McDuff, Video Concepts, and The Edge in Electronics.
2. *TE Electronics, Inc.* Company would consist of two separate divisions: the computer direct sales division will be composed of GRiD System Corporation, Victor Technologies, Tandy Electronics Manufacturing; the other marketing and manufacturing operations division will be composed of Memtek Products, O'Sullivan Industries, and Tandy Electronics Manufacturing (non-computer sales).

B. RECAST NET SALES AND GROSS PROFITS OF THE TWO COMPANIES
(Dollar amounts in thousands)

		Net Sales Years Ending June 30					Gross Profits Years Ending June 30		
New Companies	**Present Divisions**	1992	% Change	1991	% Change	1990	1992	1991	1990
Tandy Corporation	Retail operations	$3,369,180	3.9%	$3,241,758	1.0%	$3,209,484	50.5%	52.3%	54.9%
	% of total	72%		71.1%		71.3%			
TE Electronics, Inc.	Computer direct sales	620,952	(15.4%)	733,559	1.4%	723,656	23.9	31.0	34.9
	% of total	13.3%		16.1%		16.1%			
	Other marketing and manufacturing	690,024	17.7%	586,465	3.5%	566,464	18.7	20.3	18.4
	% of total	14.7%		12.8%		12.6%			
	Totals	$4,680,156	2.6%	$4,561,782	1.4%	$4,499,604	42.3%	44.8%	47.1%
		100%		100%		100%			

Source: Kyle Pope, "Tandy's Roach Decides to Try His Hand at Megastores," *Wall Street Journal* (January 13, 1993), p. 8; Tandy Corporation, *1992 Annual Report,* pp. 10–11.

had more than a little experience in the field."[6] Both companies are studying the proposed situation and were to make an announcement concerning Tandy's credit rating within 90 days.

History

When Radio Shack was founded in 1921 in Boston, the name originated from an invention that was to change our lives and the world—the radio. Early wireless equipment was installed on World War I ships in wooden structures built on the upper deck to serve as a radio room. This shelter became known as the "radio shack."

Charles Tandy, a Harvard Business School drop-out, converted common sense, salesmanship, and employee motivation into business success. During the 1950s, Tandy turned his family's small leathercraft business, Tandycrafts, Inc., into a national chain. He then sold Tandycrafts to a leather and sportswear company but shortly afterwards reacquired it, along with the leather and sportswear firm, in a proxy fight.

In 1960, Tandy bought an option on 51% of Radio Shack stock. He paid $5,000 cash and took out a $300,000 loan for the option, which allowed him to purchase the stock at book value. Book value, as the auditors later determined, was a negative $1.5 million. The loan was later converted to stock, and Charles Tandy was left with control of Radio Shack on a personal investment of only $5,000.

Some analysts would say that the purchase of a losing proposition at any price is not a bargain—and there was little doubt that Radio Shack was a losing proposition. In addition to its huge debts, the chain had posted a $4.0 million loss the year before Tandy took control. However, he believed that the firm, which at the time was selling electronic equipment to "ham" operators and other electronics buffs, would complement his recent acquisition of Electronic Crafts Company of Fort Worth. In addition, Tandy was attracted by the chain's $9.0 million annual sales and by the high quality of its personnel, a characteristic that he considered essential for growth in the electronics area.

Charles Tandy set out to prove his doubters wrong "with a vengeance." The first order of business was to reduce the firm's accounts receivable balance. Radio Shack had a policy of selling on a no-money down, two-years-to-pay basis, which had resulted in a large number of bad debts. Tandy quickly eliminated this problem by hiring a legal team to "go after Radio Shack's deadbeats."

Also of concern to Tandy were the high inventory levels and excessive number of products offered. Tandy reduced inventory by using aggressive direct mail advertising campaigns and sidewalk sales. He also whittled the number of products down from more than 25,000 to just 2,500. Products that had a low turnover were cut, as were those that generated anything less than a 50% gross profit margin. Radio Shack eventually focused on a relatively small group of diverse, highly profitable products.

Tandy also decided to eliminate brand name items, realizing that larger profits could be made by marketing private-label merchandise. He was particularly successful in negotiations with Japanese manufacturers, who at the time were actively seeking an opening into U.S. markets.

Tandy believed that the company's overhead costs should be spread over as many stores as possible. That belief led to the rapid expansion of Radio Shack's retail outlets. In less than ten years the company was opening new stores at the rate of one a day. By 1969, the firm was ready to begin producing its own goods, and built the first of its 26 manufacturing plants.

But the development of Radio Shack was not Tandy's only concern during the 1960s. The company acquired, developed, and eventually spun off Color Tile, Inc., Stafford Lowden, Inc. (a printing firm), and Pier One Imports and Bombay Company (specialty furniture retailers). It also spun off Tandycrafts and Tandy Brands. The Radio Shack Division, however, remained, and became one of the world's leading distributors of technology to the individual consumer.[7]

The firm was more than ready for the CB radio boom of the mid 1970s. "As consumers stampeded to get the chance to say 'breaker one nine,' Tandy saw its net income rise from $26.8 million in 1975 to $69 million in 1977, a 157% increase."[8] But CBs proved to be a short-lived fad and "Tandy had to scramble in 1977 to switch from its heavy CB manufacturing commitment."[9]

In 1977, the firm began developing its first home computer. Tandy was among the first companies to enter the market, and that move provided much of the firm's growth in the early 1980s. Tandy developed and marketed home and business computers and transportable cellular telephones. Emergence of the PC caused a major and permanent shift in the company's strategic direction and sales. In the late 1980s, John Roach sponsored the ambitious strategy change to make Tandy a major technology creator along the lines of Apple Computer. Matthew Upchurch said, "The computer was a great thing that happened to Tandy. But it's also the product that ate the company."[10]

The proposed TE Electronics will include O'Sullivan Industries, Memtek Products, and GRiD Systems Corporation. These companies make computers, audio equipment, office furniture, and other consumer products. After spinning off the computer and electronic manufacturing functions, Tandy, the retailer, will retain about $3.8 billion in sales (see Exhibit 18.1).

Management

In the past, Tandy had an extremely young management team that relied for the most part on Charles Tandy's successful management techniques (see Exhibit 18.2). The Tandy Board of Directors consists of 11 outside directors, a former company executive, and John Roach (see Exhibit 18.3).

Charles Tandy

Charles Tandy has been described as the "founder, architect, and driving force behind the corporation that bears his name."[11] Tandy's influence at the company remained strong for more than five years after his death. According to one source,

EXHIBIT 18.2 Officers: Tandy Corporation

John V. Roach
Chairman of the Board
and
Chief Executive Officer

William C. Bousquette
Executive Vice-President
and
Chief Financial Officer

Bernard S. Appel
Senior Vice-President
and
Chairman, Radio Shack

Herschel C. Winn
Senior Vice-President
and
Secretary

Dwain H. Hughes
Vice-President,
Treasurer

Ronald L. Parrish
Vice-President,
Corporate Development

Richard L. Ramsey
Vice-President,
Controller

John W. Burnam
Vice-President
Community Relations

Jana R. Freundlich
Assistant Secretary

James B. Sheets
Assistant Secretary

RETAIL OPERATIONS

David Christopher
Executive Vice-President
Radio Shack
Office of the President

James T. Nichols
Executive Vice-President
Radio Shack
Office of the President

Joseph V. Tanner
Executive Vice-President
Radio Shack
Office of the President

Alan C. Bush
President,
Computer SuperCenters
International, Inc.

Victor J. Sholis
President,
Tandy Name Brand Retail
Group

MARKETING AND MANUFACTURING

Robert M. McClure
President,
Tandy Electronics

Daniel F. O'Sullivan
President,
O'Sullivan Industries, Inc.
Lamar, Missouri

Lars-Olaf Svensson
President,
Tandy GRiD Europe
Stockholm, Sweden

D. Bruce Walter
President,
GRiD Systems Corporation
Fort Worth, Texas

Source: Tandy Corporation, *1992 Annual Report,* p. 34.

"even today, Radio Shack executives characterize their performance by saying, 'Charles Tandy would have been proud of what we've done.'"[12]

Tandy's rise to the top closely paralleled that of his company. "He had no hobbies, no children," said one Tandy executive, adding that "he ate, drank and slept that business, from dawn until as late as anyone was willing to talk about his

EXHIBIT 18.3 **Board of Directors: Tandy Corporation**

John V. Roach Chairman of the Board and Chief Executive Officer[2,3]	**Lewis F. Kornfeld, Jr.** Retired Vice Chairman Tandy Corporation Fort Worth, Texas[1,2]	**Alfred J. Stein** Chairman and CEO VLSI Technology, Inc. San Jose, California[3,4]
Norman E. Brinker Chairman and CEO Brinker International, Inc. Dallas, Texas[1,3]	**William G. Morton, Jr.** Chairman and CEO Boston Stock Exchange, Inc. Boston, Massachusetts[1,3]	**William E. Tucker** Chancellor Texas Christian University Fort Worth, Texas[2,4]
James I. Cash, Jr. Professor, Harvard University Graduate School of Business Administration Boston, Massachusetts[1,4]	**Thomas G. Plaskett** Business Consultant Irving, Texas[1,4]	**Jesse L. Upchurch** Chairman, CEO and President Upchurch Corporation Fort Worth, Texas[2,4]
Caroline Rose Hunt President Lady Primrose's Shopping English Countryside/ Public Relations, Rosewood Hotels and Investments Dallas, Texas[3,4]	**William T. Smith** Business Consultant Fort Worth, Texas[2,3]	**John A. Wilson** Retired Chairman, CEO and President Color Tile, Inc. Fort Worth, Texas[2,3]

Notes:
1. Member of Audit Committee.
2. Member of Executive Committee.
3. Member of Nominating Committee.
4. Member of Organization and Compensation Committee.

Source: Tandy Corporation, *1992 Annual Report,* p. 35.

business with him." Executives described him as "larger than life . . . throwing off boundless energy, laughing into his ever-busy phone, while waving a 30-cent cigar with his free hand. . . ."[13]

In his own unique style, Tandy "set the rules and pattern successors have carried on since he died. . . ." Among his favorite Tandyisms were: "You can't sell from an empty wagon" (a conviction that led the firm to stock high levels of inventory in its retail outlets); "Who wants dividends when they can have capital gains?" (thus the firm never paid dividends, using all earnings for growth); and "If you want to catch a mouse, you have to make a noise like a cheese" (the philosophy that justified an exceptionally large advertising budget). He also emphasized gross profit: "Tandy never entered a market or sold a product without a 50% gross margin."[14] The company's computer products have not achieved this Tandyism.

Vertical integration was another important part of Tandy's management philosophy. He kept everything from production to distribution to retailing to advertising in-house whenever possible. By 1982, one observer was moved to remark, "No retailer—not even Sears—has that kind of vertical integration."[15]

Charles Tandy's real genius was in motivation. He offered store managers large bonuses and profit-sharing plans based on their stores' performance. Former Chairman Phil North recounted, "Charles would call the employees into a room when it was time to hand out the bonus checks. He would not let them out until they bought Tandy stock."[16] He was so successful at convincing employees to invest in the company that today employees own an estimated 24% of Tandy's stock.

Journalist Harold Seneker described Tandy's death: "Charles D. Tandy, 60, lay down for a nap one Saturday afternoon in November [1978] and never got up. He couldn't have timed his passing much better if he had planned it." The firm's directors and top officers were in Fort Worth for a stockholders' meeting, and by the time the stock market opened on Monday they had decided on their course of action, business as usual, and on Charles Tandy's successor, Phil North.[17]

Phil North

Phil North was named President and Chairman of Tandy when his long-time friend and business associate, Charles Tandy, passed away. As a young man, North had been a reporter with his family's newspaper, the *Fort Worth Star-Telegram.* During World War II, he served as General Douglas MacArthur's personal press secretary. In 1964, Tandy convinced him to invest $100,000 in Tandy, and in 1966, North became a member of the firm's Board of Directors.

North was less than delighted by the prospect of taking control of the firm. "I'd rather be perfecting my duplicate bridge or seeing friends around the world," he said. He agreed to accept the position only "to provide a smooth transition of management for an interim period," saying that it was "one of the last things I can do for Charles, and by God, I'm going to do it."[18]

North described himself as "the company philosopher"; others described him as "Charles Tandy's alter ego." He was determined to carry on the Tandy philosophy, saying, "We will achieve the goals Charles set."[19]

As soon as practical, North relinquished the presidency to John Roach. In 1982, Roach also took over as Chairman of the Board. Phil North returned to his position as a director, and presumably, to his bridge.[20]

John Roach

John Roach, Chairman and CEO, took charge of Tandy Corporation at the age of 43. He was born and raised in Texas, as were the majority of Tandy's executives, and received his MBA from Fort Worth's Texas Christian University. Roach came to Tandy in 1967 as a data processing specialist and embarked on what was to become his pet project: development of the home computer. Ten years later, after rapidly rising within the firm, his project was complete. One day in early 1977 Charles Tandy came down to his office to see the home computer and was hooked. The computer was a success, and Roach's future with the company was assured.

In spite of his youth, *Financial World* awarded Roach the 1982 Chief Executive of the Year Award. Roach's management philosophy was:

> We are continuing to build Tandy's business on the strong fundamentals that have yielded extraordinary operating results for a retailer in one of the most competitive segments of the retail industry. Our basic philosophies of private label merchandising, strong promotion . . . convenient locations, vertical integration and the institutionalization of individual entrepreneurship truly make Tandy and Radio Shack unique.[21]

Executive Vice-Presidents

Bernard Appel (age 61), Senior Vice-President and Chairman of Radio Shack, has been with the company for some 34 years. He was President of Radio Shack until the 1992 reorganization when he was promoted to Senior Vice-President of Tandy Corporation and Chairman of Radio Shack. The reorganization also resulted in three Executive Vice-Presidents being named to the Office of the President for Radio Shack. They report directly to Tandy Chairman and CEO John Roach.

Appel was strongly committed to the Tandy philosophy, or as he put it, "Charles Tandy was a genius."[22] Appel's approach, like Tandy's, was that "our own product line, sold through our own distribution system via our own marketing plan . . . will enable us to remain the Number One retailer of electronics to the world."[23] On April 18, 1993, Appel announced his resignation—effective June 30, 1993. One analyst felt that the reorganization had reduced his authority and status. Bernard Appel said simply that "it was time for a change."[24] He will remain with the company as a consultant for three and a half years and may also consult with other companies if he wants to.[25]

William C. "Bill" Bousquette, 55, Executive Vice-President and Chief Financial Officer of Tandy Corporation, was appointed in November 1990. "Bill Bousquette has broad experience in corporate finance, accounting, and financial planning that I believe will complement and provide mature leadership to our financial staff. He has exhibited creativity in acquisitions, spin-offs, and credits that are highly desirable in his new position," says John Roach. Before joining Tandy, Bousquette was Executive Vice-President and Chief Financial Officer for Emerson Electric Company. From 1981–1984 he was Vice-President of Finance at Rockwell International.[26]

The Office of the President established at Radio Shack comprised three new Executive Vice-Presidents: Dave Christopher, James Nicholas, and Joe Tanner. Each has been with the company about 25 years. These positions focus the responsibilities of the three senior managers on actions to accelerate the growth of sales in the Radio Shack stores, particularly in advertising, merchandising, and sales. These changes will build on Radio Shack's strengths, which include product category dominance and technology. Radio Shack needs to strengthen the perception that it is still the shopper's ultimate convenience store for consumer electronics products and service.[27]

Dave Christopher, 49, will be responsible for merchandising and advertising and will retain his current duties as President of A & A International, Inc. James Nichols, 48, will be responsible for the operations of company-owned stores in the eastern United States, as well as training and store design. Joe Tanner, 49, will be responsible for retail store operations in the western United States and the Radio Shack distribution system.

Other members of top management include Dwain Hughes, who was elected Vice-President and Treasurer of Tandy in June 1991. From June 1989 until June 1991, Hughes was Assistant Treasurer of Tandy and from 1984 until June 1989, he was Audit Director of the Company's internal audit department.

Ronald Parrish was elected Vice-President of Corporate Development in April 1987. Prior to joining Tandy, he was responsible for 16 banks as the President of the Fort Worth Banking Division of InterFirst Corporation from July 1986 to April 1987.

Robert McClure was elected Vice-President of Tandy Electronics division in August 1987. He held the position of Senior Vice-President of Tandy Electronics division from 1985 to August 1987.[28]

On April 14, 1993, Bruce Walter, President of GRiD Systems Corporation since July 1991, resigned (see Exhibit 18.2). This division manufactured notebook and pen-based personal computers. The division was to become part of TE Electronics. He said, "We decided the ideal time [to leave]would be before we made the actual split."[29] He went on to say that "I just felt that now was the time to go and do something else."[30]

Corporate Structure

Tandy's strategic objective is simple: to be the major distributor of PCs in America. Tandy is implementing this growth strategy in various ways. Tandy's information and communication technology provides management with the operating tools for decentralized merchandising and marketing. Information developed at the point of sale is analyzed to track and project sales trends and automatically replenish store inventory.

The company will close 100 of its small McDuff's and VideoConcepts stores, which have failed to keep pace with changes in the way consumers buy electronics equipment. These chains have been hurt by the recent explosion of superstore consumer electronics outlets, such as Circuit City Stores, Inc., and Best Buy Company. These closures will allow Tandy to focus its attention on its Computer City and Incredible Universe chains. David Coursey, editor of *P.C. Letter,* stated, "People are looking for hyper-selection, hyper-convenience and hyper-low prices."

TE Electronics, Inc., will continue to supply Tandy outlets with computers and other consumer electronics. It also will handle all new product development efforts for Tandy and any other customers it can attract. In addition, it will enter some retailing areas that conflict with Tandy's core storefront business, including mail-order PC sales, a strategy long resisted by CEO Roach. Some analysts say that Roach is taking a risk by "shuttling" away his technology operations while applauding the company's return to its retailing roots.[31]

Roach obviously is abandoning the company's ambitious attempts to become a major technology creator like Apple Computer, Inc., and is betting the company's future in part on a megastore retailing concept that makes some analysts

EXHIBIT 18.4

Retail Highlights and Product Highlights, 1991–1992: Tandy Corporation and Subsidiaries

A. RETAIL HIGHLIGHTS

September '91—Radio Shack is first retailer to ship multimedia personal computers using industry-backed MPC standard.

November '91—Computer City chain launched with opening of the first eight stores.

April '92—Incredible Universe plans unveiled. Openings scheduled for Fall 1992.

May '92—First Computer City SuperCenter opens in Europe.

July '92—Tandy International Corporation and Grupo Gigante S.A. de C.V. form joint venture to open Radio Shack stores in Mexico.

September '92—First Incredible Universe opens near Portland, Oregon.

B. PRODUCT HIGHLIGHTS

October '91—GRiD introduced GRiDPAD RF, the first pen computer with integrated wireless communications capability providing real time data collection.

March '92—GRiD Systems Corp. introduces PalmPAD personal computer—The First Wearable Pen Computer.

May '92—Tandy announces an initiative to develop with Casio a new class of personal, portable information devices—Personal Information Processors.

June '92—Tandy subsidiary, A&A International Corporation and Nokia Mobile Phone, form joint venture in U.S. to produce cellular telephones in large volume.

August '92—Tandy Sensation Multimedia PC with WinMate software introduced. Tandy introduces new Video Interactive System (VIS) technology and presents the Optimus Digital Cassette (OCC) Recorder. *These are the first all-new computer electronics technologies manufactured in the U.S. in decades.*

Source: Tandy Corporation, *1992 Annual Report,* p. 1.

nervous. To meet emerging formats and changing market dynamics, Roach wants to vary Tandy's distribution channels while seeking the most cost effective method. Tandy's distribution channels fall into the following categories.

Consumer Electronic Specialty Stores

Radio Shack

The foundation of Tandy's retail growth is Radio Shack, America's largest consumer electronics retail chain. It is a market leader in calculators, radios, tape recorders, telephones, microcomputers, speakers, scanners, CB radios, batteries, test equipment, and electronic parts (see Exhibit 18.4).

New factory-direct programs offered by the stores are enhancing the competitiveness and breadth of Radio Shack's new product line. A new build-to-order computer program will permit customers to configure their own systems, and have them factory tested and shipped directly to their homes or businesses at significant savings.

In 1992, Radio Shack had 6,756 retail stores, of which 4,533 were company-owned and 2,223 were dealer–franchisee owned. The average size of company-owned stores is 2,362 square feet. The total number of stores has declined over the past three years, despite an increase in 1991. In 1991, Radio Shack closed about 200 Computer Centers. It then used some of the locations for sales offices.

Internationally, Mexico is leading the way in Latin America with rapid growth, which provides attractive opportunities for expansion. Radio Shack's Franchise International Division, in agreement with Gigante S.A., one of Mexico's largest retail chains, will open additional Radio Shack stores throughout Mexico.

Exhibit 18.5 shows the shift in classes of product sales over the period 1984–1992. In its *1992 Annual Report,* Tandy presented information on product sales to Radio Shack's customers differently than in previous years, as shown. Exhibit 18.6 shows sales by price range in Radio Shack's *Consumer Catalog.*

Aside from selling a broad range of high-quality private label electronics and Tandy personal computers, Radio Shack is the major distributor of electronic parts and accessories and certain specialty end-equipment, such as telephones, calculators, scanners, and CBs. The company's primary growth in 1992 came from the profitable traditional business of electronic accessories, components, and specialty items. Radio Shack had 55 million customers and sales of $2.8 billion in 1992.

Falling PC prices and corresponding lower gross margins have made the high-cost, high-price computer-dedicated retail store format obsolete. As a result, Tandy decided to close some and convert others of the Radio Shack Computer Centers from retail stores with relatively high-cost structures to sales offices with significantly lower support costs. The restructuring of the Radio Shack Computer Centers is only one aspect of a companywide program to reduce operating costs and enhance competitive position for PC distribution.

In 1991, 51 million individual customers purchased from Radio Shack retail stores. A 1991 consumer study conducted by one of the country's leading research firms reported that

- the "America's Technology Store" message is well received;
- shoppers have very favorable impressions of Radio Shack; and
- Radio Shack was rated highly for its well-organized stores and friendly, knowledgeable salespeople.

Radio Shack provides about 83% of Tandy's retail sales and is largely responsible for the decline in sales at the company's stores (open for at least one year) in both 1991 and 1992. On a comparable store basis, retail store sales declined by 1% in 1992 after a similar decline in 1991.

To maintain Radio Shack's leadership role, the company is implementing several growth-enhancing programs, including

- new brands,
- broader product assortment,

EXHIBIT 18.5 Sales to Customers, 1988–1992: Radio Shack

Class of Products	Years Ending June 30	
	1992	1991
Consumer electronics	48.6%	48.8%
Electronic parts, accessories, and specialty equipment	34.4	33.5
Personal computers, peripherals, software, and accessories	17.0	17.7
Total	100.0%	100.0%

Note: Excludes Radio Shack Computer Centers closed at fiscal year 1991 year end.

Class of Products	Years Ending June 30							
	1991	1990	1989	1988	1987	1986	1985	1984
Radios, tape recorders, tapes, and accessories	10.1%	10.7%	10.9%	15.9%	16.0%	17.0%	17.9%	19.8%
Audio equipment, phonos, and accessories	11.3	10.9	10.5	14.1	15.5	16.4	17.5	17.6
Video equipment and accessories	12.4	11.1	10.2	15.1	14.0	13.8	11.9	9.7
Citizen band radios, communication equipment scanners, and PA systems	7.2	6.7	6.7	8.9	8.8	8.6	8.8	8.3
Telephones, intercoms, and pagers	10.7	11.4	11.6	16.4	16.6	16.9	15.8	16.2
Electronics parts, test equipment, and related items	16.7	15.4	14.1	19.4	19.4	19.0	19.3	19.2
Personal electronics and toys	9.0	8.6	7.8	10.2	9.7	8.3	8.8	9.2
Microcomputers, peripherals, and software	22.6	25.2	28.2	—	—	—	—	—
Total	100.0%	100.0%	100.0%	100.0%	100.0%	100.0%	100.0%	100.0%

Notes:
1. Data prior to January 1990 are based on suggested retail prices.
2. Data for 1984–1988 are unaudited.

Sources: Tandy Corporation, *1992 Annual Report,* p. 11; *1991 Annual Report,* p. 14; *1988 Annual Report,* p. 14.

EXHIBIT 18.6 Analysis of Products in Consumer Catalog by Selling Price: Radio Shack

Price Range	Years Ending June 30 1991	1990	1989
Less than $10.00	2,024	2,020	1,962
$10.00–$49.99	657	650	606
$50.00–$199.99	247	235	217
$200.00–$599.00	42	41	44
$600.00–up	9	10	9
Total number of products	2,979	2,956	2,838

Note: Excludes microcomputer items.

Source: Tandy Corporation, *1991 Annual Report,* p. 15.

- training,
- focused marketing,
- inventory management, and
- larger stores.

Tandy recently updated and gave facelifts to the more than 3,000 Radio Shack Technology Store IIs. CEO Roach gets upset at analysts' suggestions that he missed a chance to remake Radio Shack. The strategy behind store upgrading was to transform the chain from a collection of technology stores to what the company terms the "ultimate electronics convenience store."[32] Roach said, "We feel like we're not making an offering to the customer that is in keeping with the times."[33]

Warehouse Stores

Computer City SuperCenter

To address the broader market shift in PC distribution, Tandy established the new Computer City SuperCenter chain in November 1991 with a warehouse format. These "category killer" warehouses are major forces in other sectors of retailing. Computer City has already become the nation's fastest-growing chain of computer supercenters and is considered the new "power retailing" format. Industry research indicates that computer superstores will be the fastest growing PC distribution channel. Computer City is positioned to take advantage of the turmoil in the traditional computer reseller channel by representing most of the major PC brands.

Operated as a Tandy subsidiary, Computer City SuperCenters average about 25,000 square feet in size, or roughly ten times the size of a typical Radio Shack, and stock approximately 5,000 items. The Computer City approach is simple: offer a leading-edge selection of the best brands and unsurpassed service at guaranteed great prices. Computer City is the only superstore authorized to carry IBM, Apple, AST Research, Compaq, Hewlett-Packard, and Tandy, as well as other name brand computers, software, accessories, and office equipment. Computer City offers customer services by a salaried sales staff and in-store repair facilities.

The company's *1991 Annual Report* stated that Tandy has formulated "an aggressive expansion plan which calls for a chain of over 100 stores by the end of 1994."[34] This growth strategy has been cut back by half, so there will be 50 stores in 1994. Roach's original strategic plan was to add 12 to 14 new stores per year. Roach forecasted that "over about a five-year period, it would be a billion dollar business."[35] In March 1992, the first Computer SuperCenter opened in Europe, and the second one opened a few months later.

Incredible Universe

Incredible Universe is large (approximately 160,000 square feet) and devoted to a selection of consumer electronics, computer products, appliances, cameras, and music. Incredible Universe's $9 million inventory of consumer electronics offers both breadth and depth of selection at low prices. As the likely next generation of retailing, it offers highly interactive displays and services that include repair, delivery and installation, training, a supervised children's play area, Japanese-style *Kareoke* studios with disc jockeys to broadcast customers' performances on huge screens, a restaurant, and a recycling center. The store will be more like a minimall than an industrial store and will display 300 TV and 90 VCR brands and models on the floor. The first opened near Portland, Oregon, in September 1992, and a second opened later in Arlington, Texas.

Also operated as a Tandy subsidiary, Incredible Universe will utilize highly efficient proprietary computerized sales and inventory management techniques to establish and maintain a competitive advantage through lower operating costs. Roach says that "low operating costs, buying clout and economics of scale will give Incredible Universe the 'flexibility to price very competitive' . . . [plus] the experience and financial muscle of . . . [the] nation's largest consumer electronics retailer will help."[36] Eugene Glazer of Dean Witter says, "If they're priced at a premium to their discount competitors, what you will find is that people will go to the Incredible Universe for the incredible experience, but they'll do their buying somewhere else."[37]

Roach stated that the two stores have "hit the middle part" of their projected forecasts for earnings," but few industry observers are convinced of these results. David Goldstein, retailer consultant, said, "I can't possibly fathom in my mind that they could make a profit."[38] He went on to say, "I am very skeptical about its success."[39] Seymour Merrin, computer industry consultant, said, "These stores do not appear to be hacking it."[40] Roach's responses to these negative statements were: "It's a very bad mischaracterization of the facts"[41]; "Incredible Universe is going to make history,"[42] says Roach from his penthouse office in a tower high above Fort Worth. "It may be because it didn't work or it may be because it did. It's a radically different . . . [retailing] shopping experience."[43]

McDuff Electronics and Appliance SuperCenters

McDuff Electronics and Appliance SuperCenters' 237 stores offer name brand audio, video, and personal electronics and major appliances. Thirty-nine new stores have been added in the past two years. The average store size is 11,328 square feet. An analyst said, "Superstores clearly are winning the day."

The Edge in Electronics

Tandy's strategic objective of addressing the complete array of the consumer electronics and personal computer markets created two new retail formats in 1991: The Edge in Electronics and Computer City.

The Edge in Electronics stores are designed for shoppers attracted to fashionable, state-of-the-art personal and portable name brand electronic products. Situated in high-traffic mall locations, these boutique-style stores create an image of uniqueness and product exclusivity and offer a high degree of service. Nine stores in Texas and the Washington, D.C., area opened in 1991. Seven more stores were added in 1992. The company will continue to expand this chain.

Tandy Name Brand

Tandy Name Brand (TNB) operates two types of stores: full line McDuff SuperCenters, offering both consumer electronics and major appliances; and smaller mall-located electronics stores that carry major name brand audio and video products. These smaller mall stores operate under either the McDuff or VideoConcepts name. The two distinct store formats provide TNB additional flexibility for covering its chosen markets.

The Tandy Name Brand Retail Group has been one of the industry's fastest growing electronics and appliance chains. Same-store sales growth at Tandy Name Brand has been among the industry's strongest over the past three years. The 5% achieved in 1991, in a difficult retail environment, follows the division's industry-leading increases of 19% and 11% in the two preceding years.

Since 1985, TNB has expanded its chain of McDuff and VideoConcepts stores from 231 to nearly 417 outlets, making it an emerging force in the highly competitive name brand electronics and appliance market. An aggressive store opening program was planned for 1992. TNB's strong showing stems from attention to operational details such as sales training, advertising, and (especially) customer service. The emphasis on customer service is driven by the philosophy that "the one who takes care of the customer will be the winner in the electronics–appliance business." TNB has thus made "Customer Satisfaction Guaranteed" its cornerstone.

In an industry that is experiencing a shakeout, TNB's strong growth, backed by Tandy's financial stability, provides assurance to top vendors concerned about the handling of their products.

McDuff/VideoConcepts

McDuff/VideoConcepts stores are located in nearly 180 major shopping malls and offer a broad selection of name brand audio and video products. The average store size is 3,088 square feet. In 1992, comparable-store sales were down by 10% from

1991 sales. Intense competition is the main pressure on store profitability. During 1992, 18 new stores opened, but this chain also planned to close stores in 1992.

Direct Marketing

GRiD Systems

GRiD Systems markets GRiD and Tandy desktop, laptop/portable and pen-based computers, and networking systems. Its primary customers are large businesses and governments in the United States and Canada, which it serves through a direct sales force and value-added resellers.

Since the 1989 introduction of GRiDPAD, the first clipboard-sized computer that recognizes printed handwriting, GRiD has been acknowledged as the industry leader in pen-based computers. The technology that recognizes printed words and numbers and transforms them into computer-usable input provides the pen-based computer market with explosive growth potential.

In October 1991, GRiD introduced GRiDPAD RF, the first pen computer with integrated wireless communications capabilities providing real-time data collection. In March 1992, GRiD Systems Corporation introduced the PalmPad personal computer, the first wearable pen computer (see Exhibit 18.4). In 1992, Tandy/GRiD ranked seventh in the U.S. PC market with a 3.4% market share.

Radio Shack Direct Sales

Radio Shack markets Tandy personal computers to school systems, educational institutions, and small businesses.

The Radio Shack Education Division is making Tandy Computers synonymous with quality education. Roach says that he encouraged and supported the development of a special awards program for outstanding mathematics and science students because he wanted Tandy to be out front in rewarding excellence in public schools. Initially, the company developed a program to reward excellence in math, science, and computer science for high schools in Fort Worth, Texas, where the $4.67 billion company is headquartered. The local program was so successful that Roach took steps to make it national in scope and launched the Tandy Technology Scholars program in 1990. Each year the program, which is administered by Texas Christian University, makes cash awards to outstanding math, science, and computer science teachers and students throughout the nation. One hundred teachers receive $2,500 each, and 100 students receive scholarships of $1,000 each.

Roach says that he is quite pleased with the program's results. "We know that the program is bringing attention to the right things in education," he says. "The program is one of the few in the country that places a large emphasis on recognition of teachers. We have found that teachers are highly appreciative of this. It is giving them opportunity to make a bigger difference in their schools and communities."[44]

International Distribution

Tandy Corporation's operations outside the United States include manufacturing and purchasing operations in the Orient and Scotland and product distribution channels in Canada, the United Kingdom, and Continental Europe. Although the

EXHIBIT 18.7

Operations by Geographic Area: Tandy Corporation and Subsidiaries
(Dollar amounts in thousands)

	United States	Europe, Asia and Other Operations Outside the United States	Eliminations	Consolidated
1992				
Sales and operating revenues—unaffiliated customers	$4,138,460	$354,807	$ —	$4,493,267
Sales to InterTAN	182,567	4,322	—	186,889
Transfers between geographic areas	26,788	581,020	(607,808)	—
Total sales and operating revenues	$4,347,815	$940,149	$(607,808)	$4,680,156
Operating profit (loss)	$ 326,952	$ (24,319)	$ 5,374	$ 308,007
General corporate expenses				(19,150)
Interest income, net				11,138
Income before income taxes				$ 299,995
Identifiable assets at June 30, 1992	$2,528,013	$485,335	$ 5,405	$3,018,753
Corporate assets				146,411
Total assets at June 30, 1992				$3,165,164
1991				
Sales and operating revenues—unaffiliated customers	$4,031,056	$358,033	$ —	$4,389,089
Sales to InterTAN	170,059	2,634	—	172,693
Transfers between geographic areas	21,405	539,970	(561,375)	—
Total sales and operating revenues	$4,222,520	$900,637	$(561,375)	$4,561,782
Operating profit (loss)	$ 361,026	$ 12,461	$ (10,356)	$ 363,131
General corporate expenses				(35,459)

(continued)

manufacturing and import/export operations in the Orient primarily supply products for the Company's retail outlets, those companies also sell to unaffiliated customers.[45] The amounts of transfers between the geographic areas shown in Exhibit 18.7 represent primarily intercompany transfers of goods from the Asian region. Sales to InterTAN are purchases of merchandise for its retail outlets. Operating profit represents all revenues of the geographic segment less all operating expenses

XHIBIT 18.7

Operations by Geographic Area: Tandy Corporation and Subsidiaries *(continued)*
(Dollar amounts in thousands)

	United States	Europe, Asia and Other Operations Outside the United States	Eliminations	Consolidated
1991				
Interest income, net				11,218
Income before income taxes				$ 338,890
Identifiable assets at June 30, 1991	$2,440,707	$430,346	$ 100	$2,871,153
Corporate assets				206,992
Total assets at June 30, 1991				$3,078,145
1990				
Sales and operating revenues—unaffiliated customers	$3,961,318	$303,518	$ —	$4,264,836
Sales to InterTAN	233,810	958	—	234,768
Transfers between geographic areas	7,110	653,372	(660,482)	—
Total sales and operating revenues	$4,202,238	$957,848	$(660,482)	$4,499,604
Operating profit (loss)	$ 499,570	$ (3,654)	$ 1,989	$ 497,905
General corporate expenses				(18,027)
Interest expense, net				(5,939)
Income before income taxes				473,939
Identifiable assets at June 30, 1990	$2,615,390	$482,080	$ 10,423	$3,107,893
Corporate assets				132,087
Total assets at June 30, 1990				$3,239,980

Source: Tandy Corporation, *1992 Annual Report*, p. 32.

attributable to that segment. The operating profit of a geographic area excludes corporate expenses, net interest income or expense, and income taxes. Transfers between geographic areas generally are recorded at market price.[46] In 1992, sales and revenues from foreign customers were some $940,149,000, or 20.6% of total company sales and revenues. The company suffered a $24,319,000 loss on these sales.

Victor Technologies

In 1989, Tandy Corporation acquired from Datatronic AB of Stockholm, Sweden, its Victor microcomputer and micronic hand-held computer subsidiaries in Europe. In addition, Tandy acquired the rights to the Victor, Micronic, and GRiD personal computers in 11 European countries through a network of dealers and distributors. The company's principal offices are located in Sweden, France, the United Kingdom, Germany, Switzerland, the Netherlands, Belgium, Norway, Denmark, and Austria; Victor also has distributors in other European countries. During 1988, sales of Victor and Micronic computer products exceeded $200 million, placing Victor among the top PC companies in Europe. John Roach said:

> With Victor, Tandy is acquiring an important name in the European microcomputer industry, which will further Tandy's commitment to this very significant market. Victor's past success in the European dealer and distributor market channels is complementary to Tandy's distribution through the InterTAN retail channel. Further, there are other synergies in this proposed transaction, such as the field automation solutions of Micronic hand-held computers and our GRiD Systems Division.[47]

Other Distribution and Marketing

Memtek Products

Memtek Products manufactures and markets Memorex audio and video tapes and accessories. Memorex products are sold in approximately 43,000 stores throughout the United States, Europe, Canada, Mexico, and the Caribbean.

Tandy's Memtek Products and O'Sullivan Industries reach a broad cross section of today's consumer electronics customers by distributing through several mass merchandising mediums, superstores, and electronics specialty stores. Sales of Memorex products increased slightly in 1992.

O'Sullivan Industries

O'Sullivan's high-quality products offer consumers a low-cost alternative to preassembled furniture. The company is a leading producer in the United States of ready-to-assemble racks for electronics products and, more recently, office desks and cabinets. O'Sullivan products are sold by major retailers across the country and by Tandy's retail divisions.

O'Sullivan Industries utilizes mass merchandising channels to market ready-to-assemble (RTA) furniture for the home and office under its own brand and as an original equipment manufacturer. The company is capitalizing on its reputation as the largest manufacturer of quality RTA electronics furniture in the United States by rapidly moving into home, office, and home-theater lines. Trends toward home-theater and entertainment centers are a major component of O'Sullivan's product development and distribution. As additional opportunities for the retail environment appear, the company is positioned to respond to the needs of the consumer.

Tandy Electronics Marketing

Tandy Electronics Marketing was formed to develop alternative channels of distribution for selected Tandy products. This unit became the OEM (Original Equip-

EXHIBIT 18.8

Sales of Personal Computers in the United States

Customer Segment	Percentage of Total Units
Household[1]	36%
Small business (1–99 employees)	20
Medium business (100–999 employees)	15
Large business (1000+ employees)	12
Education	9
Government	8
Total	100%

Note:
1. Includes home offices and home-based businesses in addition to hobbyists.

Source: "Computers," *Industry Survey* (December 21, 1992), p. C-81.

ment Manufacturer) for the company. In 1989, Digital Equipment Corporation (DEC) and Panasonic selected Tandy's computers for their product lines. In 1992, DEC announced a program to build its own computers, instead of selling Tandy's computers.

The Consumer Electronics Industry

The United States has a $265 billion a year consumer electronics industry, and the battle for tomorrow's mass-market telecommunications, information, and interactive services is being fought on too many fronts to begin to choose winners and losers. The prize for which these companies compete is not yet defined, owing to a slow economy and lack of hot technologies that resulted in weak spending in consumer electronics specialty stores in 1991 and 1992. In addition, the Persian Gulf crisis and ensuing recession heightened consumer caution in the early months of fiscal 1991. Generally weak consumer spending further troubled the already slow consumer electronics business.

However, an important trend in consumer electronics retailing is the growth in sales of PCs and home-office electronics.[48] Exhibit 18.8 shows the distribution of PC ownership by customer segment. Exhibit 18.9 illustrates the dramatic gains by PCs and PC software at the expense of larger and far more costly types of computers.

Performance of other companies in the computer and peripherals industry varied widely in 1992. Industry sales were just under $141.9 billion (see Exhibit 18.10), and personal computer manufacturers were locked in a price war. Personal computer companies that cut prices and trimmed expenses found that demand for their products soared and profits increased. However, for other computer manufacturers, the weak economic recovery made maintaining sales and profitability more difficult. Sixteen percent of the PC market belongs to no-name computers.

EXHIBIT 18.9 **Percentage Change in Manufacturing Revenue, 1991–1992: By Computer Type**

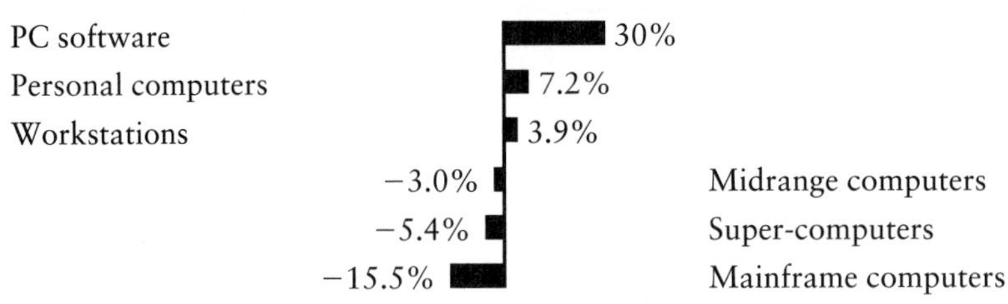

Source: G. Pascal Zachary, "Computer Industry Divides into Camps of Winners and Losers," *Wall Street Journal* (January 27, 1993), p. A-1.

Value Line predicted that GDP will advance only at a 2.1% rate in 1992. Of more interest to this industry was the forecasted increase in spending on durable goods of 4.0% in 1992. In 1993, the pace of economic recovery was expected to quicken, with a 3.1% gain in GDP, which should lead to increased spending for computers and peripherals, and a strong 7.5% advance in durable goods spending. The environment is likely to remain very competitive, and the PC price war is likely to continue as manufacturers attempt to maintain market share. Looking to 1995–1997, *Value Line* expected the economy to expand steadily with GDP growth in the 3%–4% range and spending for durable goods advancing from 3.5% to slightly more than 4%.[49]

Some analysts say that the computer industry, in striving to energize slowing sales growth, is staking its future on an outpouring of potentially confusing new products, including operating systems, multimedia computers, and pen-based computers. This confusion, the recession, and the inability of the personal computer to further penetrate the home market are cutting into industry sales. Although expanding applications into additional areas may confuse consumers, it appears to be a critical component in re-energizing the computer marketplace.[50]

The number of notebook personal computers was expected to increase from about 2.5 million in 1990 to 12.5 million or more by the end of 1991. As portable PCs grow in power and shrink in price, an increasing number of companies are looking at them not just for their field sales personnel, but also as the main computer for headquarters-based employees.[51]

Competition

The consumer electronics industry is highly competitive. Tandy competes in the sale of its products with department stores, mail-order houses, discount stores, general merchants, home appliance stores, and gift stores that sell the same types of products manufactured by others. Domestic competitors range in size from local drug and hardware stores to large chains and department stores. Computer store chains and franchise groups, independent computer stores, and several major retailers compete with Tandy in the microcomputer marketplace. Consumer elec-

EXHIBIT 18.10

Composite Statistic: Computer and Peripherals Industry

(Dollar amounts in millions)

	Actual				Estimated		
Category	1988	1989	1990	1991	1992	1993	1995–1997
Sales	$118,743	$130,171	$142,365	$141,892	$155,000	$170,000	$230,000
Operating margin	20.0%	17.9%	17.9%	14.3%	15.5%	16.5%	18.0%
Depreciation	$7,775.3	$9,015.5	$9,489.6	$11,418	$12,300	$12,900	$16,000
Net profit	$10,417	$8,095.0	$8,934.7	$4,738.5	$6,300	$8,300	$14,100
Income tax rate	35.5%	40.4%	40.0%	38.0%	40.0%	40.0%	40.0%
Net profit margin	8.8%	6.2%	6.3%	3.3%	4.1%	4.9%	6.1%
Working capital	$34,843	$31,172	$30,816	$26,375	$28,800	$32,700	$52,300
Long-term debt	$14,936	$18,427	$18,114	$19,860	$20,400	$21,000	$22,800
Net worth	$68,371	$68,318	$75,470	$79,524	$74,900	$81,300	$109,100
% earned total capital	13.3%	10.1%	10.4%	6.3%	7.5%	9.0%	11.5%
% earned net worth	15.2%	11.8%	11.8%	6.7%	8.5%	10.5%	13.0%
% retained to common equity	11.1%	7.3%	7.8%	2.4%	4.5%	4.5%	8.0%
% all dividends to net profit	29%	40%	36%	63%	48%	38%	39%
Average annual P/E ratio	12.7	14.8	12.7	24.1			14.0
Relative P/E ratio	1.05	1.12	.94	1.54			1.10
Average annual dividend yield	2.2%	2.6%	2.7%	2.7%			2.5%

Note: Data for 1992, 1993, and 1995–1997 are estimated.

Source: "Computer and Peripheral Industry," *Value Line* (January 29, 1993), p. 1075.

tronic and computer mail-order companies also compete with Tandy. Products that compete with Tandy's are manufactured by numerous domestic and foreign manufacturers, and many of them carry nationally recognized brand names or private labels. Some of its competitors have financial resources equal to or greater than Tandy's.

Management believes that price, quality, service, and a broad selection of electronic products and computers carried at conveniently located retail outlets are important to its competitive position. Tandy's utilization of trained personnel and its ability to use national and local advertising media are important to Tandy's ability to compete in the consumer electronics market.[52]

Both an opportunity and a threat, the discount superstore is changing computer retailing, as it changed the office supply and consumer electronics segments. By 1995, computer superstores such as CompUSA and CompuAdd are expected to sell 20% of all PCs to the corporate market, up from 2% in 1990, according to *Dataquest*. Mass merchandisers also will gain share from their current 6% to 15% of unit sales. The superstores' gains primarily will be made at the expense of traditional computer dealers, which still sell the most PCs. Their share of the market will drop from 47% to 33%, and mail-order and direct sales also will suffer share declines.[53] The following competitors operate in Tandy's environment.

Apple Computer

Apple Computer, Inc., is a major developer, manufacturer, and marketer of personal computer systems for use in business, education, government, and the home. The company's strategy of gaining market share by cutting prices has been successful, and cost controls have kept margins at reasonable levels, despite price cuts. Moreover, Apple has handled smoothly the transition from the Apple II to the more powerful Macintosh in the education market.[54] In 1992, Apple had sales of nearly $7.2 billion, of which $5.4 billion were in PCs, $1.5 billion in peripherals, and $276 million in software. The company ranks second in world sales of PCs according to *DATAMATION*[55] (see Exhibit 18.11).

AST Research

AST Research, Inc., designs, manufactures, markets, services, and supports a broad line of personal computers (including desktop, notebook, and network server systems), which accounted for 98% of its 1992 revenue on sales of $1.14 billion. The company ranked fourteenth in world PC sales in 1991, but in 1992 did not rank among the top 15 companies[56] (see Exhibit 18.11).

Compaq

Compaq Computer Corporation produces portable and desktop personal computers that are IBM compatible. The company is a leader in both the portable computer and the IBM-compatible desktop markets. Compaq sells its products exclusively through about 3,800 dealers. To help gain market share, the company recently cut prices on several selected desktop and laptop models. In its quest to be the "price leader," Compaq's already lower gross margins will feel further pres-

EXHIBIT 18.11

Top 15 Global Leaders in PC Sales, 1992 and 1991
(Dollar amounts in millions)

1992			1991		
Company	Rank	Sales	Company	Rank	Sales
IBM	1	$7,654.5	IBM	1	$8,505.0
Apple	2	5,412.0	Apple	2	4,900.0
Compaq	3	4,100.0	NEC	3	4,135.8
NEC	4	3,986.9	Compaq	4	3,271.4
Fujitsu	5	2,613.5	Fujitsu	5	2,319.7
Toshiba	6	1,949.4	Toshiba	6	2,093.5
Dell	7	1,812.5	Olivetti	7	1,586.1
Olivetti	8	1,348.7	Unisys	8	1,061.0
AST	9	1,140.5	Intel	9	1,050.0
Gateway 2000	10	1,107.1	Commodore	10	1,038.5
AT&T	11	998.9	AT&T	11	950.0
Hitachi	12	891.8	Group Bull	12	899.3
Acer	13	880.0	Hitachi	13	825.3
Packard Bell	14	878.8	AST	14	800.7
Seiko Epson	15	741.4	Tandy	15	790.0

Source: "The DATAMATION 100," *DATAMATION* (June 15, 1993), p. 23; *DATAMATION* (June 15, 1992), p. 26.

sure.[57] In 1992, Compaq had PC sales of $4.1 billion. Compaq ranked third in world sales of PCs according to *DATAMATION*[58] (see Exhibit 18.11).

Data General

Data General Corporation manufactures computers (chiefly midrange), communication systems, and peripheral equipment. The company markets both directly and through resellers.[59] In 1992, Data General had sales of $1.1 billion. The breakdown was $325 million in mid-range computers, $70 million in PCs, $75 million in workstations, $25 million in software, $165 million in peripherals, $100 million in service, and $340 million in maintenance sales.[60]

Dell Computer

Dell Computer Corporation makes notebook and desktop computers, servers, and workstations that are compatible with individual standards. The company markets to corporate, governmental, and educational customers through sales teams. It also markets to individuals and smaller institutional buyers through direct marketing and has mass-merchandising arrangements with CompUSA. The company's strategy is to increase its share of the personal computer market, while controlling costs, with the aim of achieving a net return on sales of 5%–6%. The main feature of this strategy is what the company refers to as "value pricing."[61] In 1992, Dell had sales of just over $2 billion, of which $1.8 billion were in PCs, $101 million in software, and $101 million in peripherals. The company ranked seventh in world sales of PCs according to *DATAMATION*[62] (see Exhibit 18.11).

Hewlett-Packard

Hewlett-Packard Company (HP) is a major designer and manufacturer of precision electronic products and systems for measurement and computation. Its major product categories are measurement, design, information, and manufacturing equipment, peripherals and network products, medical electronic equipment, and instrumentation.[63] In 1992, HP had sales of nearly $12.7 billion. The breakdown was $75 million in large-scale computers, $1.3 billion in mid-range computers, $725 million in PCs, $1.5 billion in workstations, $413 million in software, $4.6 billion in peripherals, $630 million in Datacom, $280 million in maintenance, and $600 million in service sales.[64]

International Business Machines

International Business Machines Corporation (IBM) is the world's largest supplier of advanced information processing technology, communication systems and services, and program products. IBM has felt pricing pressures, especially in personal computers, and has cut margins. In addition, economic and computer industry uncertainty has caused many European businesses to defer purchases.[65] In 1992, IBM had sales of $64.5 billion. The breakdown was $8.2 billion in large-scale computers, 5.8 billion in mid-range computers, $7.7 billion in PCs, $1.9 billion in workstations, $11.4 billion in software, $7.9 billion in peripherals, $2.2 billion in Datacom, $7.6 billion in maintenance, $6.4 billion in service, and $5.5 billion in other sales. The company ranked first in world sales of PCs according to *DATAMATION*[66] (see Exhibit 18.11).

Tandem

Tandem Computers, Inc., designs, assembles, and sells fault-tolerant computer systems under the trademark Non-Stop, for on-line transaction processing. It designs and sells enterprise networks, terminal, and communications controller products. At one time Tandem dominated the on-line transaction computing market, but that's no longer true. Previously rapid revenue growth has slowed while smaller computer companies were growing at rates that Tandem used to enjoy.[67] In 1992, Tandem had sales of nearly $2.1 billion. The breakdown was $845 million in mid-range computers, $118 million in workstations, $559 million in peripherals, $204 million in Datacom, $310 million in maintenance, and $30 million in service.[68]

Wang

Wang Laboratories, Inc., is a leading worldwide provider of computer-based information processing systems, including text, data, image, voice, telecommunications, and networking. The company produces mid-range and desktop systems and resells under the Wang logo some computers made by IBM.[69] In 1992, Wang had sales of some $1.5 billion. The breakdown was $240 million in mid-range computers, $220 million in PCs, $60 million in software, $200 million in peripherals, $40 million in Datacom, $630 million in maintenance, and $100 million in service.[70]

An International Note

According to a report from Evans Research Corporation, IBM and Apple each ended 1991 with 10.6% of the Canadian personal computer market. Atari Canada had 4%; Tandy, 3.2%; Epson Canada, 3.1%; and Compaq, 3%. In 1991, PC shipments to Canada grew by 9% to almost one million units. Shipments in 1992 were estimated to show a 14% increase over 1991.[71]

Unlike the growth foreseen in Canada, general economic growth throughout the European Community, which had averaged 3.2%, was expected to fall to 1.4% in 1991. The unemployment rate, which had been declining, was expected to rise by a full point to 9.4%. An analyst said, "These trends did not offer much encouragement for short-term PC market growth in EC countries."

Advertising

An in-house Tandy group, Radio Shack Advertising, is responsible for almost all the company's advertising.[72] One of Tandy's great strengths has been its ability to hold customers through heavy, targeted advertising, and direct-mail catalogs have been its core. Tandy recently developed a confidential customer database with demographics and psychographic information. The system is used to (1) segment the customer mailing list by product category preference in order to customize Radio Shack's monthly direct mailing; (2) personalize individual mailing of advertisements by emphasizing the customer's special interest based on a purchase profile; and (3) analyze customer preference by stores so as to tailor merchandise by store and region.[73] Exhibit 18.12 shows Tandy's advertising expenditures for 1990–1992.

Research and Development

To support the development of leading-edge technologies and manufacturing techniques, Tandy Electronics maintains five major research and development and electronic design centers. The newest Tandy Technology Center contains 270,000 square feet. Tandy Information Systems (TIS) is the home of Tandy's Research and Design group. In 1989, these design centers generated four new computer products: the Tandy 1100 FD, a lightweight, inexpensive PC-compatible notebook computer; FaxMate, an easy-to-use FAX system for PCs; Open Desktop, a graphical user interface for UNIX-based systems; and GRiDPad, a four-pound portable computer that uses handwritten input.

Notebook-sized, pen-based computers that can run common personal computer software represent the newest computing frontier. In 1991, GRiD Systems Corporation, a Tandy subsidiary, was the market leader with about 20,000 units

EXHIBIT 18.12

Breakdown of General Selling and Administrative Cost for 1992–1990: Tandy Corporation and Subsidiaries

(Dollar amounts in thousands)

Years Ending June 30	1992			1991			1990		
Category	Amount	% of Sales and Revenues	% Change	Amount	% of Sales and Revenues	% Change	Amount	% of Sales and Revenues	% Change
Payroll and commissions	$ 632,958	13.5%	3.4%	$ 611,982	13.4%	2.2%	$ 598,761	13.3%	3.0%
Advertising	274,322	5.9	(5.6)	290,558	6.4	(2.0)	296,526	6.6	5.1
Rent	218,297	4.7	5.0	207,986	4.6	10.1	188,963	4.2	7.9
Other taxes	87,097	1.9	7.7	80,880	1.8	12.3	72,048	1.6	10.2
Utilities and telephone	67,400	1.4	2.5	65,731	1.4	3.8	63,321	1.4	3.7
Insurance	49,628	1.0	(3.6)	51,464	1.1	4.3	49,322	1.1	11.1
Stock purchase and savings plans	21,591	0.4	(2.2)	22,078	0.5	(25.1)	29,456	0.7	5.2
Foreign currency transaction gains	(10,869)	(0.2)	(7.5)	(11,755)	(0.3)	261.7	(3,250)	(0.1)	54.5
Other	186,552	4.0	(23.7)	244,477	5.4	11.3	219,575	4.9	23.8
Subtotals	1,562,976	32.6%	(2.3%)	1,563,401	34.3%	3.2%	1,514,722	33.7%	7.0
Credit operations	59,073	1.3	14.3	51,702	1.1	58.3	32,655	0.7	12.7
Totals	$1,586,049	33.9%	(1.8)%	$1,615,103	35.4%	4.4%	$1,547,377	34.4%	7.3%

Note: Certain 1991 and 1990 amounts have been reclassified to conform to the 1992 presentation.

Source: Tandy Corporation, *1992 Annual Report*, p. 12.

sold. However, sales of pen-based computers were expected to jump to 125,000 units in 1992 and to one million units by 1995, according to a consulting group, which forecasts that sales generated by this segment will rise from $90 million in 1991 to $2.8 billion by 1995.[74]

All of Tandy's retail stores are linked and enhanced by Tandy's solid financial resources and extensive R&D, manufacturing, and administrative support. To increase the value of this support, Tandy is emphasizing the development and manufacturing of products for which it has a competitive advantage, such as electronics, digital compact cassettes, and personal computer products, including multimedia and pen-based computers.

Tandy also is continuing to reduce the technology and inventory-value risks of the personal computer business by shortening the response time of all activities, outsourcing as many services as possible to minimize investment and volume-dependent costs, and eliminating development, manufacturing, and selling activities that do not add value. Tandy R&D groups work closely with major semiconductor, component, hardware, and software manufacturers to identify emerging technologies that will maintain Tandy state-of-the-art product lines. Toshiba Corporation, a leading Japanese electronics manufacturer, and GRiD Systems Corporation, a wholly owned subsidiary of Tandy, have reached a patent cross-license agreement for the manufacture, use, and sale of laptop computers.

Suppliers

Tandy obtains merchandise from a large number of suppliers from various parts of the world. No supplier accounted for more than 10% of the cost of products sold in fiscal 1991. Alternative sources of supply exist for most merchandise and raw materials purchased by Tandy. Because Tandy's product line is diverse, management would not expect unavailability of a product to materially affect its operations.[75]

Manufacturing

Tandy Electronics is a world-class manufacturing organization that produces more than $1.3 billion worth of products. It develops and manufactures high-quality, innovative, and affordable products for Tandy's retail divisions, providing a substantial portion of the private-label products sold exclusively through Tandy's Radio Shack chain. Tandy Electronics also manufactures computers and other products for outside companies on an OEM basis.

Tandy Electronics has 27 manufacturing facilities, 22 in the United States and one each in the United Kingdom and Taiwan and three joint ventures—one each in the United States, China, and South Korea. The Chinese facility gives Tandy the opportunity to sell some of its products to Chinese consumers, a market that potentially is enormous.

Tandy's manufacturing capabilities are integral to the company's overall strategy of being the preeminent retailer of consumer electronics and personal computers by providing a "competitive edge" in product design and margin. Tandy is the most vertically integrated consumer electronics company in the United States, which provides consistent control over cost, availability, and quality. These controls in turn enable Tandy to deliver its products at competitive prices and maintain higher than average margins. The company's functional strategies include the implementation of total quality management (TQM) and just-in-time (JIT) product scheduling systems.

Human Resource Management

Following the example of its founder, Tandy values its employees highly. The company employs about 41,000 people worldwide and offers them stock purchase and savings plans. The purposes of these plans are twofold: (1) employees may invest to provide for retirement, and (2) employees may participate in the firm's growth. Charles Tandy was outspoken and persistent about employees owning stock in the corporation, and at one point its employees owned almost 25% of the corporation. Today, the company matches 40%, 60%, or 80% of employee contributions depending on the length of participation in the plan. Tandy usually funds the program with treasury stock that it acquires in the open market. For the period 1989–1991, Tandy contributed approximately $20 million per year to the stock purchase plan. Tandy also has a deferred salary and investment plan that allows employees to defer up to 5% of their annual compensation. No taxes are levied on this contribution as long as the money remains in the plan. In matching portions of employee contributions, Tandy contributed more than $9 million to this plan in 1990. As of June 28, 1990, the company also offered the Tandy Employee Stock Ownership Plan (TESOP). To fund this program, the company borrowed $100 million at 9.34% and guaranteed the repayment of the notes. The company provides comprehensive sales and product training over the Tandy Satellite Television Network. This training is conducted as an interactive, two-way communication effort.

Finance

Moody's lowered the ratings of Tandy Corporation and its credit subsidiary, Tandy Credit Corporation, on October 27, 1992. It lowered long-term debt ratings from A2 to A3 and short-term rating for commercial paper from Prime-1 to Prime-2. Standard & Poor's long-term debt and commercial paper ratings for the company remained unchanged at A and A-1, respectively. Management does not expect Moody's action to have an adverse impact on the company's ability to borrow funds, but it may increase slightly borrowing costs. Tandy's credit rating is under review by Moody's and Standard & Poor's because of the company's announcement to spin off TE Electronics and the proposed closing of 100 stores.

The company expected to record a $47.5 million charge to pretax earnings as of December 31, 1992, and TE Electronics expected to record a similar charge totaling $30 million. CEO Roach stated that the "separation has potential to improve profit ability of the companies."[76]

Exhibits 18.13–18.15 provide financial information for Tandy Corporation.

EXHIBIT 18.13

Consolidated Statement of Income: Tandy Corporation and Subsidiaries
(Dollar amounts in thousands, except per share data)

	1992		1991		1990	
Years Ending June 30	Amount	% of Revenues	Amount	% of Revenues	Amount	% of Revenues
Net sales and operating revenues	$4,680,156	100.0%	$4,561,782	100.0%	$4,499,604	100.0%
Cost of products sold	2,701,969	57.7	2,519,309	55.2	2,380,224	52.9
Gross profit	1,978,187	42.3	2,042,473	44.8	2,119,380	47.1
Expenses						
Selling, general and administrative	1,586,049	33.9	1,615,103	35.4	1,547,387	34.4
Depreciation and amortization	103,281	2.2	99,698	2.2	92,115	2.0
Net interest (income) expense	(11,138)	(0.2)	(11,218)	(0.2)	5,939	0.1
	1,678,192	35.9	1,703,583	37.4	1,645,441	36.5
Income before income taxes	299,995	6.4	338,890	7.4	473,939	10.6
Provision for income taxes	116,148	2.5	132,827	2.9	183,592	4.1
Income before cumulative effect of change in accounting principle	183,847	3.9	206,063	4.5	290,347	6.5
Cumulative effect on prior years of change in accounting principle, net of taxes	—	—	(10,619)	(0.2)	—	—
Net income	$ 183,847	3.9%	$ 195,444	4.3%	$ 290,347	6.5%
Net income per average common and common equivalent share						
Income before cumulative effect of change in accounting principle	$ 2.24		$ 2.58		$ 3.54	
Cumulative effect on prior years of change in accounting principle, net of taxes	—		(0.14)		—	
Net income per average common and common equivalent share	$ 2.24		$ 2.44		$ 3.54	
Average common and common equivalent shares outstanding	79,893		78,258		81,943	

Source: Tandy Corporation, *1992 Annual Report,* p. 16.

EXHIBIT 18.14

Consolidated Balance Sheets: Tandy Corporation and Subsidiaries

(Dollar amounts in thousands)

Years Ending June 30	1992	1991
Assets		
Current assets		
Cash and short-term investments	$ 106,454	$ 186,293
Accounts and notes receivable, less allowance for doubtful accounts	727,836	662,118
Inventories	1,391,295	1,301,854
Other current assets	114,664	111,833
Total current assets	2,340,249	2,262,098
Property, plant and equipment, at cost, less accumulated depreciation	531,100	504,906
Other assets, net of accumulated amortization	293,815	311,141
Total assets	$3,165,164	$3,078,145
Liabilities and Shareholders' Equity		
Current liabilities		
Notes payable	$ 220,497	$ 171,418
Current portion of guarantee of TESOP indebtedness	10,600	8,400
Accounts payable	243,893	202,206
Accrued expenses	293,136	297,405
Income taxes payable	15,688	31,821
Total current liabilities	783,814	711,250
Notes payable, due after one year	253,087	313,771
Guarantee of TESOP indebtedness	74,380	84,980
Subordinate debentures, net of unamortized bond discount	30,058	29,116
Deferred income taxes	60,272	62,010
Other non-current liabilities	32,813	30,256
Total other liabilities	450,610	520,133
Shareholders' equity		
Preferred stock, no par value, 1,000,000 shares authorized		
Series A junior participating, 100,000 shares authorized and none issued	—	—
Series B convertible, 100,000 shares authorized and issued	100,000	100,000
Series C PERCS, 150,000 shares authorized and issued	429,982	—
Common stock, $1 par value, 250,000,000 shares authorized with 85,645,000 shares issued	85,645	85,645
Additional paid-in capital	92,984	105,650
Retained earnings	2,039,782	1,917,851
Foreign currency translation effects	2,279	(1,198)
Common stock in treasury, at cost, 22,456,000 and 7,250,000 shares, respectively	(734,132)	(267,153)
Unearned deferred compensation related to TESOP	(85,800)	(94,033)
Total shareholders' liabilities and equity	1,930,740	1,846,762
	$3,165,164	$3,078,145

Source: Tandy Corporation, *1992 Annual Report,* p. 17.

EXHIBIT 18.15

Selected Supplemental Financial Data (Unaudited): Tandy Corporation and Subsidiaries

(Dollar amounts in thousands, except per share data)

Years Ending June 30	1992	1991	1990	1989	1988
A. OPERATIONS					
Net sales and operating revenues	$4,680,156	$4,561,782	$4,499,604	$4,180,703	$3,793,767
Income before income taxes and cumulative effect of accounting change	$ 299,995	$ 338,890	$ 473,939	$ 527,399	$ 514,680
Provision for income taxes	116,148	132,827	183,592	203,895	198,326
Income before cumulative effect of change in accounting principle	183,847	206,063	290,347	323,504	316,354
Cumulative effect on prior years of change in accounting principle, net of taxes	—	(10,619)	—	—	—
Net income	$ 183,847	$ 195,444	$ 290,347	$ 323,504	$ 316,354
Net income per average common and common equivalent share	$ 2.24	$ 2.44	$ 3.54	$ 3.64	$ 3.54
Average common and common equivalent shares outstanding	79,893	78,258	81,943	88,849	89,466
Dividends declared per common share	$ .60	$ .60	$ .60	$ .60	$ .575
Net interest (income) expense	$ (11,138)	$ (11,218)	$ 5,939	$ (12,217)	$ (588)
Ratio of earnings to fixed charges	3.26	3.11	4.34	5.94	6.10
B. YEAR-END FINANCIAL POSITION					
Inventories	$1,391,295	$1,301,854	$1,452,065	$1,285,373	$1,287,854
Total assets	$3,165,164	$3,078,145	$3,239,980	$2,574,310	$2,530,092
Working capital	$1,556,435	$1,550,848	$1,312,517	$1,373,311	$1,336,812
Current ratio	2.99 to 1	3.18 to 1	2.12 to 1	3.41 to 1	3.06 to 1
Capital structure					
Current debt	$ 231,097	$ 179,818	$ 695,871	$ 192,096	$ 306,475

(*continued*)

EXHIBIT 18.15

Selected Supplemental Financial Data (Unaudited): Tandy Corporation and Subsidiaries *(continued)*
(Dollar amounts in thousands, except per share data)

B. YEAR-END FINANCIAL POSITION *(continued)*					
Long-term debt	357,525	427,867	252,540	141,124	180,598
Total debt	$ 588,622	$ 607,685	$ 948,411	$ 333,220	$ 487,073
Total debt, net of cash and short-term investments	$ 482,168	$ 421,392	$ 813,214	$ 274,822	$ 298,849
Stockholders' equity	$1,930,740	$1,846,762	$1,723,496	$1,782,838	$1,603,112
Total capitalization	$2,519,362	$2,454,477	$2,671,907	$2,116,058	$2,090,185
Long-term debt as a percent of total capitalization	14.2%	17.4%	9.5%	6.7%	8.6%
Total debt as a percent of total capitalization	23.4%	24.8%	35.5%	15.7%	23.3%
Stockholders' equity per common share[1]	$ 24.53	$ 23.48	$ 21.78	$ 20.65	$ 18.10
Stock price ranges	31¼–23⅜	39½–23¼	48⅛–38⅛	56½–28	NA
C. FINANCIAL RATIOS					
Return on average stockholders' equity[2]	9.7%	11.5%	16.6%	19.1%	21.2%
Percent of sales					
Income before income taxes and cumulative effect of change in accounting principle	6.4%	7.4%	10.6%	12.6%	13.6%
Income before cumulative effect of change in accounting principle	3.9%	4.5%	6.5%	7.7%	8.3%

Notes:
1. Computed assuming the Series C PERCS will convert into 15,000,000 shares of common stock.
2. Computed using income before cumulative effect of accounting change.

Source: Tandy Corporation, *1992 Annual Report,* and *1990 Annual Report.*

Tandy commenced a "Dutch Auction" self-tender offer on February 28, 1992, for 12 million shares, or approximately 16% of its existing outstanding shares. Tandy intended to use proceeds from the recent issue of preferred equity redemption cumulative stock™ (PERCS™) to fund the share repurchase plan. Each shareholder could tender his or her shares at prices not greater than $32.00 or less than $27.50. The stock closed at $30.75 per share on February 26, 1992, the tender offer expired on March 26, 1992,[77] the company purchased 13,500,000 shares of stock at $32.00 a share.[78]

Notes

1. Tandy Corporation, *1992 Annual Report,* cover.
2. Ibid.
3. Stephen A. Forest, "Thinking Big—Very Big—at Tandy," *Business Week* (July 20, 1992), p. 85.
4. Kyle Pope, "Tandy's Roach Decides to Try His Hand at Megastores," *Wall Street Journal* (January 13, 1993), p. 48.
5. Ibid.
6. *Wall Street Journal* (January 14, 1993).
7. Ibid.
8. Sexton Adams and Adelaide Griffin, "Tandy Inc.," (case) in Thomas L. Wheelen and J. David Hunger, *Strategic Management and Business Policy,* 2nd ed. (Reading, Mass.: Addison-Wesley, 1986), pp. 752–754.
9. Paul Borenstein, "Can Tandy Stay on Top?" *Forbes* (April 11, 1983), p. 43.
10. Ibid.
11. Forest, p. 85.
12. "A Computer that Builds Radio Shack Image," *Business Week* (February 1, 1982), p. 23.
13. Harold Seneker, "What Do You Do After You Bury the Boss?" *Forbes* (March 3, 1979), p. 7.
14. Edmund Faltermayer, "U.S. Companies Come Back Home," *Fortune* (December 30, 1991), pp. 106–112.
15. Seneker, p. 7.
16. Harold Rudinsky and Roni Mach, "Sometimes We Are Innovators, Sometimes Not," *Forbes* (March 29, 1982), p. 66.
17. Ibid.
18. Seneker, p. 7.
19. Ibid.
20. "Tandy Man," *Forbes* (December 11, 1978), p. 118.
21. Ibid.
22. Adams and Griffin, pp. 752–780.
23. Tandy Corporation, *1983 Annual Report,* p. 3.
24. Bernard Appel, "Advantages of Being Self-Contained," *Marketing and Media Decisions* (Spring 1982, special issue), p. 71.
25. "Appel, Chairman of Radio Shack, to Leave Tandy," *Wall Street Journal* (April 19, 1992), p. B-5.
26. Ibid.
27. Tandy Corporation, *News Release* (November 8, 1990), p. 1.
28. Tandy Corporation, *Second Quarter Report* (December 31, 1991), p. 1.
29. Tandy Corporation, *Form 10-K Report* (1991), p. 5.
30. "President of Tandy's GRiD Systems Corp. Resigns Before Spinoff," *Wall Street Journal* (April 15, 1993), p. B-12.
31. Ibid.
32. Kyle, p. 48.
33. Ibid.
34. Tandy Corporation, *1991 Annual Report,* p. 13.
35. Kyle, p. 48.
36. Forest, p. 85.
37. Alexandra Biesada, "Incredible Gamble" (June 2, 1992), p. 49.
38. Ibid., p. 50.
39. Pope, p. 48.
40. Ibid.
41. Ibid.
42. Ibid.
43. Biesada, p. 49.
44. Ibid.
45. Joan Szabo, "Business Initiatives for Better Schools," *Nation's Business* (September 1992), pp. 44–48.

46. Tandy Corporation, *1992 Annual Report,* p. 32.
47. Tandy Corporation, *News Release* (September 13, 1989), p. 1.
48. Ken Hewes, "Weak Economy Makes Hard Times for Headlines," *Chain Storage Age Executive* (August 1992), pp. 29A–31A.
49. "Computers and Peripherals," *Value Line* (October 30, 1992), p. 1075.
50. Johnson Bailey, "Technology Marketing: Real Optimism Reigns—But Only If Segments Learn to Communicate," *Advertising Age* (November 11, 1991), pp. 53–54.
51. Jon Pepper, "Portable PC's Power Up," *Nation's Business* (September 1991), pp. 29–34.
52. Tandy Corporation, *Form 10-K Report,* p. 5.
53. Christy Fisher, "Technology Marketing: People Are Buying Computers Like Toasters," *Advertising Age* (November 11, 1991), pp. S9–S11.
54. "Apple Computer," *Value Line* (October 30, 1992), p. 1079.
55. "The DATAMATION 100," *DATAMATION* (June 15, 1993), pp. 30–31.
56. Ibid., p. 70.
57. "Compaq Computer," *Value Line* (October 30, 1992), p. 1085.
58. "The DATAMATION 100," p. 32.
59. "Data General," *Value Line* (October 30, 1992), p. 1088.
60. "The DATAMATION 100," p. 73.
61. "Dell Computer," *Value Line* (October 30, 1993), p. 1089.
62. "The DATAMATION 100," p. 51.
63. "Hewlett-Packard," *Value Line* (October 30, 1992), p. 1079.
64. "The DATAMATION 100," pp. 28–29.
65. "International Business Machines," *Value Line* (October 30, 1992), p. 1097.
66. "The DATAMATION 100," p. 28.
67. "Tandem Computers," *Value Line* (October 30, 1992), p. 1111.
68. "The DATAMATION 100," p. 51.
69. "Wang Laboratories," *Value Line* (October 30, 1992), p. 1115.
70. "The DATAMATION 100," p. 63.
71. Alison Eastwood, "Apple, IBM Level in PC Race," *Computing Canada* (February 3, 1992), p. 19.
72. Telephone conversation with Tandy Corporation marketing representative (May 12, 1993).
73. Tandy Corporation, *1991 Annual Report,* p. 10.
74. Alan Radding, "Technology Marketing: Pen Is Mightier Than. . .," *Advertising Age* (November 11, 1991), pp. S6–S7.
75. Tandy Corporation, *Form 10–K Report,* p. 2.
76. Robert Tomsho, "Tandy Unveils Major Overhaul of Operations," *Wall Street Journal* (January 13, 1993).
77. Tandy Corporation, *News Release* (February 27, 1992), pp. 1–2.
78. Tandy Corporation, *1992 Annual Report,* p. 30.

Clearly Canadian Beverage Corporation

Frank J. Fish III

Introduction

The employees at Vancouver, B.C.–based Clearly Canadian Beverage Corporation were brimming with excitement as shares of their company, which had been ignored by Canadian and U.S. analysts, hit a new high. The sudden attention came after Clearly Canadian's stock had been selected as the top choice among growth shares in the "Investment Dartboard" column of the *Wall Street Journal* in its March 5, 1991 issue. Analysts flooded the company with calls seeking information as the stock traded as high as $27 (U.S. dollars) on the Over the Counter market; its normal trading range was between $19 and $22 (U.S. dollars). New York analysts had long ignored the company and had only recently begun recommending the stock. Until a few years ago, Clearly Canadian was known as International Beverage Company—an unprofitable company with incredible sales potential.

Clearly Canadian Beverage Corporation is a small, 35-person Vancouver, B.C.–based bottler run by a 44-year-old former grocery store district manager named Douglas Mason. Since launching the brand three years ago, Mason has increased sales from $8 million to $85 million (Canadian dollars).

Actually, Clearly Canadian is Mason's second branded beverage. His first was a cola soda called Jolt, which had "twice the sugar and twice the caffeine" of competing colas. In 1986, Jolt was hot; the company's shares catapulted from 2½ to 17½ (U.S.) on the Vancouver exchange—only to collapse to 2 when Jolt's sales died. (These prices are adjusted for a 2-for-7 reverse stock split in 1990.) The costs associated with developing and producing Jolt made competing in the cola wars almost impossible. Unlike Jolt, Pepsi and Coca-Cola had extensive financial support to promote their marketing efforts. Mason renamed the company Clearly Canadian in 1990.

Clearly Canadian was originally incorporated under the name of Cambridge Development Corporation on March 19, 1981. It changed its name to Bridgewest Development Corporation on October 28, 1983, and to BDC Industries Corporation on November 15, 1984. On September 3, 1986, the Company again changed its name to The Jolt Beverage Company, Ltd. Jolt Beverage Company Ltd became The International Beverage Corporation on May 13, 1988. International Beverage Corporation then became the Clearly Canadian Beverage Corporation on May 14, 1990.

From its inception in 1981 until November of 1987, the company evolved through several unrelated business activities, including real estate development, oil and gas exploration, new-product distribution, mining, and restaurant operations.

This case was prepared by Frank J. Fish III as a basis for class discussion of the issues described in the case. This case was edited by T. L. Wheelen and J. D. Hunger for this book. Reprinted by permission of the author.

In April 1986, the Jolt Beverage Company agreed in principle to acquire exclusive rights to distribute a new product, Jolt Cola, in Canada.

Between June 1986 and March 1987, the Jolt Beverage Company successfully obtained distribution in 12 states of the United States and four western Canadian provinces for its product, Jolt Cola. In October 1987, the rather severe stock market correction adversely affected the success of Jolt Cola in the United States and Canada.

The Jolt Beverage Company was forced to surrender its U.S. distribution rights for Jolt Cola in Washington, Oregon, Alaska, Hawaii, Texas, Oklahoma, New Mexico, Montana, Idaho, California, Arizona, and Nevada for two major reasons.

1. Jolt Beverage Company, owing to the financial constraints resulting from the October 1987 stock market crash, was unable to keep current its commitments to Jolt Rochester, the inventor and sole supplier of Jolt Cola.
2. A diminishing sales performance, directly related to the company's inability to fund marketing expenditures, resulted in missing sales performance targets and therefore the subsequent cancellation of the U.S. distribution rights.

Jolt Beverage Company also had the exclusive marketing, bottling, and distribution rights for Jolt Cola beverages in Canada. However, as Jolt Cola sales diminished in the latter part of 1988 and early 1989, the company decided to abandon the project and liquidated all inventories by November 1989.

Overview of the Company

Clearly Canadian is a rapidly growing marketer and distributor of Clearly Canadian brand carbonated mineral water and sparkling water beverages with natural fruit flavors. First introduced in California markets in January 1988, Clearly Canadian has quickly become the category leader in the "New Age" beverage market, the fastest growing segment of the beverage industry. Clearly Canadian is a hybrid product designed to capitalize on the rapid growth of the $2 billion bottled water industry and the $29 billion soft-drink market. Consumer demand for products perceived as upscale, healthy, natural, and containing no alcohol led New Age beverage sales to grow from $246 million in 1986 to $757 million (U.S. dollars) in 1991. Clearly Canadian has grown faster than the category; in fiscal 1989, its first year, the company earned $8 million in revenues, which rose to $85 million (Canadian dollars) in fiscal 1992. Clearly Canadian's success had been achieved with virtually no major advertising campaign and without incurring any long-term debt. Management at Clearly Canadian has been focused on making the company profitable for the short term and has not devoted a lot of time to defining a mission statement or business goals and objectives.

Management

A management team with vision, operating depth, and financial acumen guided Clearly Canadian. The Company had eight executive officers:

Name	Position
Douglas L. Mason	Chief Executive Officer and President
D. Bruce Horton	Chief Financial Officer and Secretary
Glen D. Foreman	Chief Operating Officer
Stuart R. Ross	Senior Vice-President, Administration
Ron Kendrick	Vice-President, Operations
Elliot (Swede) Ewing	Vice-President, Marketing and Sales
Nigel G. Woodall	Vice-President, Accounting and Administration
Daniel Evans	Director, Investor Relations

The Company paid an aggregate of $506,708 (Canadian dollars) to the Company's executive officers for services rendered to the Company during the Company's financial year ending June 30, 1992.

Douglas L. Mason: Douglas Mason was appointed to his present position in June 1986. In 1984 and 1985, he was a partner with D. Bruce Horton in Continental Consulting Services. (The consulting service developed financing and marketing plans for a variety of businesses in Texas, Illinois, British Columbia, Japan, and Hong Kong.) From 1978 to 1983, he was engaged in two entrepreneurial businesses that entailed extensive market research and development and product distribution. From 1970 to 1978, he was district manager of a major retail grocery store operation with 18 retail outlets.

D. Bruce Horton: Bruce Horton was appointed to his present position in June 1986. In late 1984 and 1985, he was a partner with Douglas Mason in Continental Consulting. In 1984, Horton was consultant in connection with the reorganization, refinancing, and ultimate sale of California Cooperage U.S.A. to the Coleman Company of Wichita, Kansas. From 1972 to 1984, he was a partner of Horton, Butler and Schneider, Certified General Accountants of Kelowna, British Columbia.

Glen D. Foreman: Glen Foreman joined the company in October 1988 as Director of Marketing. In July 1989, he was appointed Vice-President of Sales and Marketing. Before joining the Company, Foreman had been with the Coca-Cola Company for 15 years as a marketing executive.

Stuart R. Ross: Stuart Ross joined the company in September 1986. From 1981 to 1986, he was controller for a medium-sized automobile dealership. Before that, he held positions as accountant and controller with various corporations in British Columbia.

The Product

Clearly Canadian had attained a "must carry" status in most major U.S. supermarkets and grocery outlets. Sold primarily in the United States and Canada and positioned as a premium brand, the company produces an unflavored, natural carbonated mineral water and a sparkling water beverage that comes in six natural flavors—wild cherry, orchard peach, western loganberry, mountain blackberry, country raspberry, and coastal cranberry. The unflavored water competes in the $2 billion (U.S. dollars) bottled water industry, which is predicted to grow 10%

annually over the next several years. The flavored products compete in the soft-drink market, which is estimated to grow 2.5%–3.0% annually in unit volumes.

The products consist of natural fruit flavors, Canadian water, fructose, malic acid, citric acid, sodium benzoate, and tartaric acid. They contain two-thirds of the calories of general carbonated soft drinks, or about 100–110 calories per 11-ounce bottle. Retail prices range from $.70 to $1.30 per 11-ounce bottle and from $2.50 to $4.00 for four-packs at retail. A 23-ounce family-size bottle also is available for $1.50 to $2.00.

Marketing

The Company initially introduced its product into new markets through convenience stores and "on-premises" accounts (stores that sell cold, single bottles such as delis, liquor stores, and restaurants) which created the perception that the product was everywhere. When the company felt that the product had sufficient brand recognition, it introduced four-packs and 23-ounce bottles to supermarkets. Consumer awareness of the product allowed the distributors to reduce the high cost of supermarket slotting allowances from the start. Only about 20% of the company's sales come from supermarkets, about 60% of sales were single-serve bottles or sold through convenience stores, and the remaining 20% of sales came from restaurants, hotels, and institutional accounts.

Beverage Marketing Corporation (New York) published an annual report on the category entitled *New Age and Isotonic Beverages in the U.S.* According to this report, 176.1 million gallons of New Age beverages were consumed in the United States in 1989, of which 34.7% were flavored waters (compared to 12.7 billion gallons of soft drinks and 2.7 billion gallons of fruit beverages). Clearly Canadian had been a strong beneficiary of the growth trends in New Age beverages, being deemed by Beverage Marketing as one of the hottest brands in the all natural soda category. According to A. C. Nielsen studies, Clearly Canadian had been able to secure a 5%–25% market share (averaging 10%) in markets where it has been established for one year. In fact, 60% of sales occurred in on-premises outlets and convenience stores. (A. C. Nielsen reflects sales data only for major supermarket chains.) In more mature markets, Clearly Canadian is still achieving 15%–20% growth, which is not surprising considering its award-winning packaging and the quality of the product, made with pure Canadian water and natural fruit flavors.

The award-winning blue-tinted bottles with attractive silk-screened graphics have contributed to the strong initial trial trends for the product; the product's quality and taste have led to repeat purchases and the success of the brand. Although this packaging was more expensive, it had distinguished Clearly Canadian from competitors' products, which often were in clear bottles with paper labels, and has even served as its own form of advertising. However, another New Age beverage called Mystic had pirated the unique design of Clearly Canadian's packaging to the extent that, at first glance, discerning the two brands was difficult.

Clearly Canadian was available in all 50 states in the United States and in Canada, Japan, the United Kingdom, and the Caribbean Islands. The company distributed and sold its products through a network of distributors. Master distributors are contractually responsible for bottling and distributing the product in a given area after purchasing the water and the concentrates from Clearly Canadian. In the United States, these partnerships handle most of the distribution. The spread between the end-user price and the production cost (in 1991, about $2 per case [U.S. dollars] for purchases primarily of concentrate and water) is divided. Master distributors are contractually required to pay for various marketplace costs, including local promotion. Many of these distributors have an equity investment in the company and were required to spend a minimum of $.50 per case (U.S. dollars) sold on advertising. Distributors often subcontract distribution of the product within their regions. Exhibit 19.1 shows the company's nine master distributors in the United States.

On March 3, 1992 Clearly Canadian announced that, through Nippack Company Ltd, the Company's Japanese master distributor, it had entered an exclusive distribution agreement with Asahi Breweries Limited. Asahi will distribute the Company's line of sparkling beverages to the Japanese market, which has a population of 150 million. Asahi's opening order was 500,000 cases, which translates into approximately $10 million (U.S. dollars) at wholesale. Asahi has committed to launching a multimillion dollar aggressive advertising campaign using television, radio, and print media. Headquartered in Tokyo, Asahi was one of the largest beer companies in Japan, with annual sales in excess of US$6 billion. Clearly Canadian will be sold by the nonalcoholic division of Asahi, which also handles the distribution of Schweppes and other premium juices and soft drinks.

Clearly Canadian also sought a European partner that could take up to a 20% stake in the company. To date, the largest single owner of stock was its Japanese master distributor, Nippack Company Ltd of Tokyo, which had about a 7% equity ownership. Currently, Japanese distribution and marketing methods are being reviewed and improved. One such improvement is the planned introduction of a smaller, lower priced 200-ml bottle solely for this market, a redesign expected to do much to revive sagging sales.

All the master distributors have experience in marketing premium brands and must meet minimum sales requirements in their territories to maintain distribution rights. Together these distributors constitute a sales force of about 14,000 people.

Clearly Canadian's flexible distribution system plays a pivotal role in its accomplishments. Strong partnerships with its suppliers, bottlers, and distributors, coupled with Clearly Canadian's experienced management team, are the driving forces behind its success.

Production

Clearly Canadian owns land and water rights at two well sites in Canada. One site, located about 300 miles north of Vancouver in Okanagan Valley, B.C., is situated on about 150 acres; it has five wells and the capacity to produce 18 million cases of product per year. Water drawn from this source is used to produce the company's natural mineral water. The excess is used to produce flavored water products for the western U.S., western Canada, and Japanese markets. The second

EXHIBIT 19.1 **Master Distributors by Territory: Clearly Canadian Beverage Corporation**

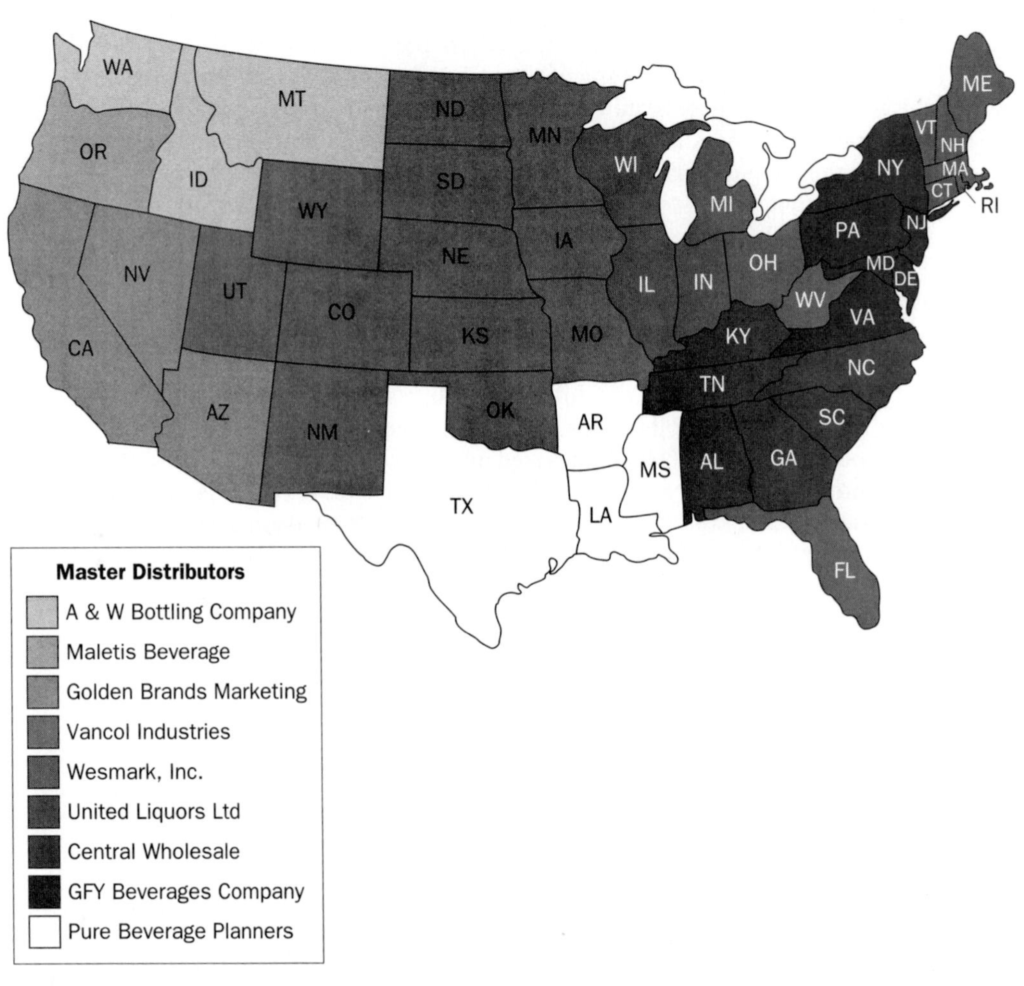

Source: Company data, 1992.

well site, located on five acres in Thornton, Ontario, can produce 23 million cases and is used to supply the eastern U.S., eastern Canada, and European markets with the company's flavored water products. Combined, these well sites can supply enough water to produce about 41 million cases. Water is shipped to the bottlers in stainless steel tankers specifically dedicated to Clearly Canadian. Clearly Canadian pays the cost of transporting the water from the well site to the bottler but

XHIBIT 19.2 **U.S. Bottlers' Production Facilities: Clearly Canadian Beverage Corporation**

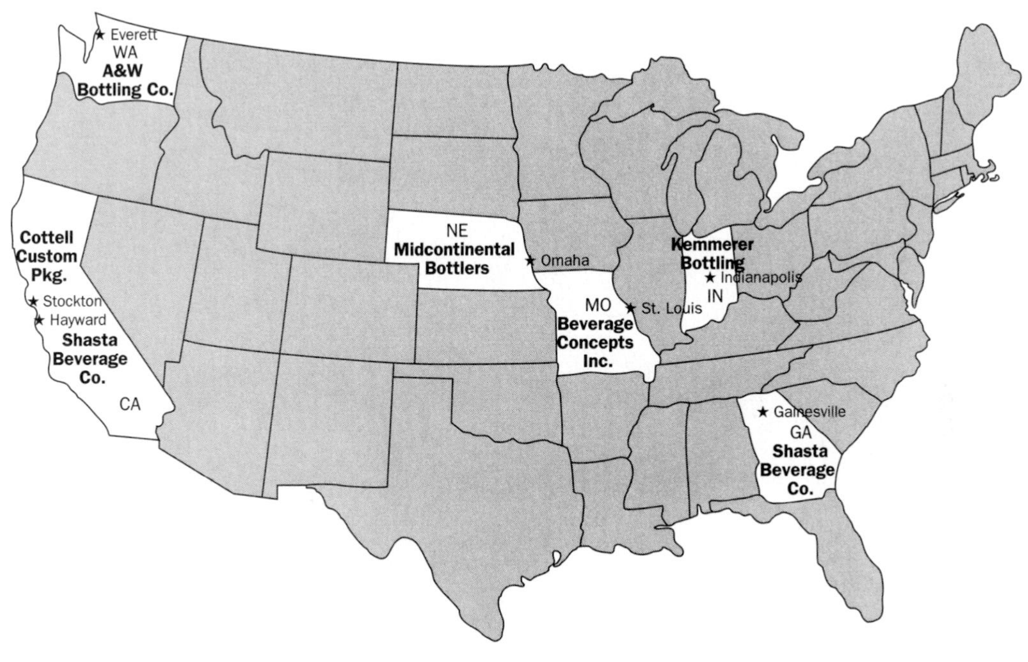

Note:
Annual U.S. Production Capacity = 30 million cases.

Source: Company data, 1992.

passes it on in the price paid by bottlers. The company is reviewing the acquisition of other Canadian land and water sources in strategic locations to serve international markets in the long term.

The company contracts bottling to nine carefully selected, strategically located bottling facilities in North America, seven in the United States and two in Canada. Exhibit 19.2 shows Clearly Canadian's U.S. bottlers' production facility locations. Exhibit 19.3 shows Canadian bottlers' production facility locations and well sites. Additional facilities that will begin operation in late 1992 will bring total bottling capacity to 50 million cases per year. Negotiations are continuing to increase production capacity.

Other raw materials included bottles and flavoring. The company contracted with four glass manufacturers: Vitro Packaging of Monterrey, Mexico; Owens-Brockway, Oakland, California; Consumer Glass Ltd of Lavington, B.C.; and Consumers Glass of Bramalea, Ontario. For flavorings, Clearly Canadian pro-

EXHIBIT 19.3

Canadian Bottlers' Production Facilities and Well Sites: Clearly Canadian Beverage Corporation

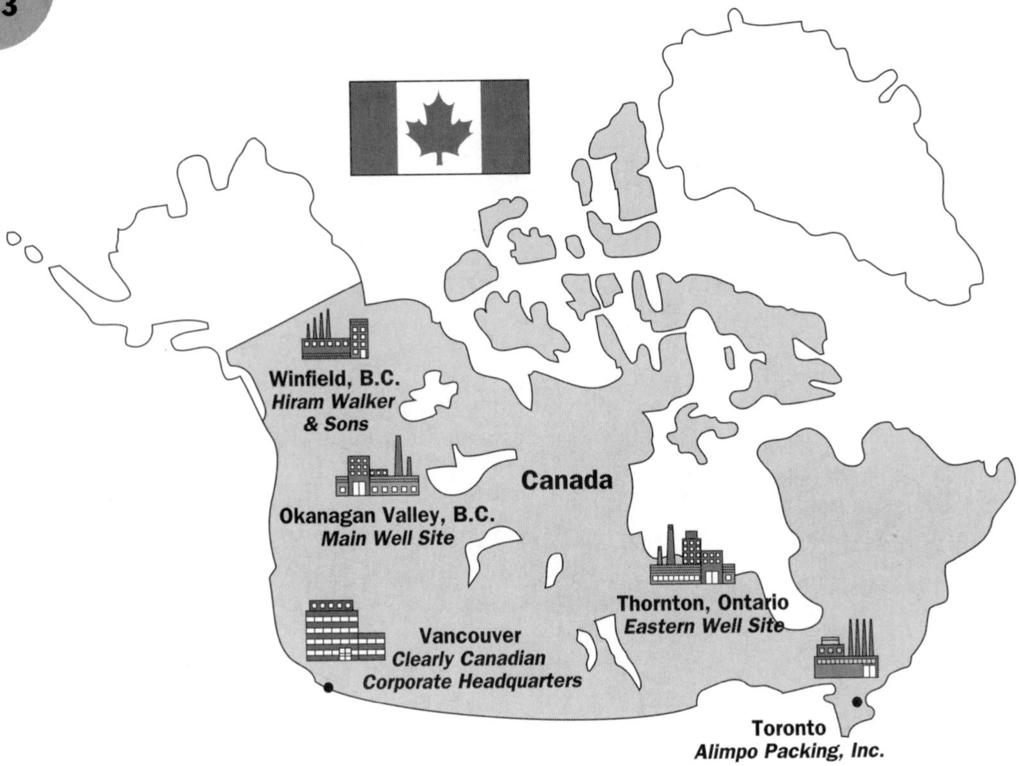

Winfield, B.C.
Hiram Walker & Sons

Okanagan Valley, B.C.
Main Well Site

Canada

Thornton, Ontario
Eastern Well Site

Vancouver
Clearly Canadian Corporate Headquarters

Toronto
Alimpo Packing, Inc.

Note:
1. Annual Canadian Well Site Capacity = 41 million cases.
2. Annual Canadian Bottler Production Capacity = 11 million cases.

Source: Company data, 1992.

vided the flavoring recipes to two suppliers. Each supplier had the technology to produce all the flavors. New flavors are under development and being tested.

Clearly Canadian's capital expenditure requirements are low because it doesn't own any manufacturing plants, bottling facilities, or trucks—nor does it need to pay a large sales force. Instead, it enters into long-term contracts with the industry's leading bottlers, distributors, and transportation companies.

Quality Control

The company's quality control system is state-of-the-art and the finest in the beverage industry. The quality of the company's products exceeds the most stringent requirements of any regulatory agency in the United States or Canada. Water is pumped through stainless steel pipes from several wells 250–300 feet below the surface, with quality continuously monitored. It is then stored in stainless steel storage tanks and shipped in dedicated stainless steel tankers to the bottlers' dedicated stainless steel tanks. The tankers are sealed and returned empty to the well sites. The water is tested a second time at the bottling facility and then again as a finished product. A quality control team randomly inspects the quality control systems at each bottling facility. The bottler tests every production run to ensure that product specifications are met and, in addition, sends water samples to two independent testing labs. Clearly Canadian's Quality Control process also measures torque on bottle caps and the sugar, PH level, and microbiological content of the product.

Management Information Systems

Clearly Canadian had not devoted much time or many people to development of an information system to report on its general operations. Douglas Mason for the most part had been reluctant to budget money for an MIS system because of the costs associated with hardware, software, development, and training.

Clearly Canadian needed a system to monitor operations and report on operational data. There was an urgency to report on domestic retail markets (including supermarkets) and international markets. Management had no formalized method of measuring the performance of distributors and bottlers, forecasting inventory levels, or tracking the performance of each beverage product.

Financial Situation

Exhibit 19.4 presents the company's balance sheets, Exhibit 19.5 presents the income statements, and Exhibit 19.6 presents the geographic sales segmentation for the years 1990–1992. The Company follows Canadian accounting principles, and all figures are reported in Canadian dollars. Monetary assets and liabilities are translated into Canadian dollars at the balance sheet date rate of exchange and non-monetary assets and liabilities at historical rates. Revenues and expenses are translated at appropriate transaction date rates except depreciation, which is translated at historical rates. Inventories are stated at the lower of cost or net realizable value. Cost is generally determined on a first-in, first-out basis. Investments represent marketable securities and are valued at the lower of cost or quoted market value. Property, plant, and equipment are recorded at cost. Depreciation is provided as follows: water storage facilities, 10% on a straight-line basis; equipment, 20%–30% on a diminishing balance basis; leasehold improvements, straight-line basis over the term of the lease. The company has a $3 million line of credit with a chartered bank. A mortgage charge against certain real property of Clearly Canadian and a security interest on all its present and future property is pledged as security for the line of credit. No borrowing against this line of credit was outstanding as of October 31, 1992.

Clearly Canadian recorded equivalent case sales of 14,451,954 for the first six months of 1992, compared to 6,164,496 for the same period the previous year.

EXHIBIT 19.4

Consolidated Balance Sheet: Clearly Canadian Beverage Corporation
(Amounts in Canadian dollars)

Years Ending June 30	1992	1991	1990
Assets			
Current assets			
Cash	$15,507,002	$479,001	$140,895
Accounts receivable	31,870,531	16,263,794	4,499,569
Inventories	14,913,178	11,785,532	1,821,083
Prepaid expenses and deposits	593,824	465,460	218,966
Investments	—	—	104,412
Total current assets	62,884,535	28,993,787	6,784,925
Property, plant and equipment	3,858,589	3,201,208	1,210,594
Total assets	$66,743,124	$32,194,995	$7,995,519
Liabilities and Shareholders' Equity			
Current liabilities			
Accounts payable and accrued liabilities	$14,288,100	$15,161,437	$3,515,025
Current portion of investments	17,738	23,335	—
Total current liabilities	14,305,838	15,184,772	3,515,025
Capital leases	41,390	84,058	—
Total liabilities	14,347,228	15,268,830	3,515,025
Shareholders' equity			
Share capital			
Issued and Outstanding, 14,852,035 common shares without par value (1991—12,400,889) (1990—10,895,884)	39,058,928	28,528,448	22,978,765
Retained earnings (deficit)	5,760,854	(11,602,283)	(18,498,271)
Total shareholders' equity	44,819,782	16,926,165	4,480,494
Total liabilities and shareholders' equity	$68,136,010	$32,194,995	$7,995,519

Clearly Canadian improved on gross profits per case for the six months ending June 30, 1992, to $1.57 per case compared to $1.19 for the same period in 1991.

On August 4, 1992, Clearly Canadian announced plans to raise US$35 million to US$45 million through a common share issue to investors outside North America, subject to regulatory approval. It retained investment dealer Deacon Barclays de Zoete Wedd Ltd to manage the offering in Europe. The shares will be offered at a price to be determined by the company and Deacon Barclays, an executive of Clearly Canadian, said. Proceeds of the issue, which were expected to close in Sep-

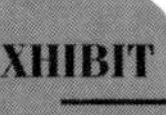

EXHIBIT 19.5

Consolidated Statements of Operations and Retained Earnings: Clearly Canadian Beverage Corporation
(Amounts in Canadian dollars)

Years Ending June 30	1992	1991	1990
Sales	$85,438,026	$ 71,408,918	$ 20,373,885
Cost of sales	66,193,226	57,566,490	16,449,786
Gross profit	19,244,800	13,842,428	3,924,099
Selling, administrative and general expenses	6,184,048	6,869,242	4,971,196
Depreciation	163,873	171,064	121,971
Other (income) expenses	(456,138)	(93,866)	247,894
Net income (loss) before income taxes	13,353,017	6,895,988	(1,416,962)
Income taxes			
Current	5,765,077	2,988,000	—
Utilization of prior year's income			
Tax losses	—	(2,988,000)	—
Net income (loss)	$ 7,587,940	$ 6,895,988	$ (1,416,962)
Rated earnings (deficit), beginning of year	$ (1,827,086)	$(18,498,271)	$(17,081,309)
Retained earnings (deficit), end of year	$ 5,760,854	$(11,602,283)	$(18,498,271)
Basic earnings (loss) per share	$ .49	$ .59	$ (.16)

tember 1992, were to be used to finance future capital spending and for working capital.

New Age Beverage Industry

Underscoring the importance of New Age beverages, New York–based Beverage Marketing Corporation this fall published its second annual report on the category *New Age & Isotonic Beverages in the U.S. 1991*. The report establishes three basic criteria for New Age beverages. They must be

1. relatively new to the marketplace (the report tracks sales back to 1985);
2. perceived by consumers as healthy, "riding a wave of goodwill" and allow consumers to feel good about the products and themselves for drinking them; and
3. natural products free of artificial ingredients, preservatives, or flavors.

According to Beverage Marketing, three types of beverages meet these standards: sparkling juices, flavored waters, and natural sodas. Club sodas, unflavored seltzers, and sparkling and noncarbonated bottled waters are not included in the New Age group. None are classified as New Age beverages because, like 100% juices, they are not new.

EXHIBIT 19.6

Geographic Sales Segmentation: Clearly Canadian Beverage Corporation
(Amounts in Canadian dollars)

	Years Ending June 30		
Geographic Segment	1992	1991	1990
United States	$73,464,741	$61,402,321	$13,654,107
Canada	10,440,526	8,733,097	6,279,626
Japan	695,467	572,600	347,731
Europe	837,292	700,900	92,421
Total	$85,438,026	$71,408,918	$20,373,885

New Age drinks are expected to have an increasingly important impact on beverage consumption in years to come. Consumers are increasingly aware of artificial ingredients and preservatives in beverages, and New Age beverages offer a healthy, yet satisfying alternative. The likely entry of new major producers capable of offering national distribution and advertising campaigns also will cultivate the growth of this evolving market.

Several trends will contribute to popularizing flavored and unflavored bottled water in the coming years. Growing concern about tap water purity will spur domestic demand for bottled water. So too will greater health consciousness. Particularly in the U.S. market, as consumers continue to cut alcohol and sugar from their diets, reduced calorie beverages and naturally flavored water will benefit. Noteworthy is the attempt of several alcoholic beverage companies to revive their moribund earnings by diversifying into bottled water.

Demand will also increase as domestic consumers become more accustomed to bottled water, perhaps viewing it one day as a staple, much as do the French, who drink 26 gallons a year compared to Americans' six. Exhibit 19.7 provides a demographic analysis of New Age beverage consumers.

Competition

The introduction of a similar beverage product by a larger international beverage company represents an unquantifiable risk to Clearly Canadian. Many companies have already introduced similar beverages without much success. Examples include Pepsi with $H_2OH!$, Coca-Cola with Clarte, McKesson with WallaRoo, and Seagrams with Soho. Many large companies spend $30–$40 million to roll out a product nationally; Clearly Canadian has been able to achieve its current success without any major television or ad campaigns.

Overall, approximately 15 beverage companies worldwide produce and distribute New Age beverages. These major producers include: New Era Beverage Company (Sundance); Perrier Groups (Perrier, Poland Spring, Calistoga); Cadbury Schweppes (Canada Dry, Schweppes), Snapple Natural Beverage (Snapple); and Clearly Canadian Beverage Corporation (Clearly Canadian).

Coca-Cola Company

The Coca-Cola Bottling Company of Philadelphia is adding Clearly Canadian to the line of beverages it distributes. Joe Casey, Vice-President of Marketing for Coca-Cola, indicated that the decision to add Clearly Canadian to its distribution system was based on Clearly Canadian's three-year sales performance in the United States. Unlike competitors Snapple, Mystic, and Best of Health, Casey said, "Clearly Canadian has the potential to be a category leader among light soft drinks," the main reason that Coca-Cola Bottling chose to distribute the product. Coca-Cola Corporation says that it has no current plans to come out with a similar product; but the company has repositioned FRESCA as a diet grapefruit soda in new green bottles.

Recently a marketing innovation gave the company a competitive edge: the introduction of talking vending machines. Each costs more than $3,000 and is equipped with computerized voice synthesizers to converse with consumers. Other new designs included energy-efficient machines and vendors equipped with electronic games for play after purchase.

Perrier Group

The Perrier Group was the first company to introduce a sparkling water with an essence of fruit flavor into the American market. In 1985, a flavored Perrier brand was introduced and was immediately successful. Since then, many of its other regional domestic water brands have added lines with natural essences of fruit or have extended selected lines to include sparkling or still-flavored water products.

The Perrier Group has been on the cutting edge of several movements in the beverage industry, starting with its pioneering work in promoting an imported sparkling water into a much-sought-after symbol of urban upscale living. The group also added flavored essence, first to its flagship brand and later to the Poland Spring and Calistoga lines. Arrowhead and Ozarka also marketed flavored essences as line extensions. In early 1992, Calistoga introduced Calistoga Country Orchard, a line of flavored noncarbonated juice-based products in Northern California.

Perrier is slowly regaining the national distribution that it had before the 1990 product recall. Perrier's flavored line did not recover its vibrancy in 1991 because distribution voids in the off-premises trade continued. The flavored products were the last to be reintroduced in late 1990 and early 1991. Wholesale volume dropped to $10.6 million from 1990's $14.4 million. The total Calistoga flavored line had relatively flat volume in 1991 at $34.8 million, down by 2.2% from 1990's $35.6 million (see Exhibit 19.8). In the case of Poland Spring, the flavored sparkling juice line was being phased out. Consumers had a mental picture of Poland Spring as a flat water, and the sparkling line had not proven to be a winner for the brand. The Arrowhead brand was strong in southern California and appeared to be gaining market share at the expense of Evian in that area. Ozarka was strong in Texas and had continued to build its flavored water market share in that state.

Each company's New Age flavored products has very different distribution patterns. Distribution of Poland Spring's flavored products is limited to New En-

EXHIBIT 19.7

Demographics of New Age Beverage[1] Consumers, 1992

Classification	Total U.S.[2] (Millions)	Number of Users[2] (Millions)	User Incidence[3]	User Profile[2]
Total Adults	182.5	14.2	7.8%	100.0%
Males	87.1	6.4	7.4	45.3
Females	95.4	7.8	8.1	54.7
Age				
18–24 years	25.5	2.5	9.9	17.8
25–34	44.1	4.7	10.7	33.3
35–44	37.5	3.3	8.9	23.5
45–54	25.3	1.6	6.4	11.4
55–64	21.0	1.2	5.6	8.3
65 or Older	28.9	0.8	2.8	5.8
Education				
Graduated college	35.3	3.5	9.8	24.4
Attended college	35.2	3.8	10.7	26.6
Graduated high school	70.9	4.8	6.8	34.0
Did not graduate high school	41.1	2.1	5.2	15.0
Employment				
Professional/manager	31.8	3.3	10.3	23.2
Technical/clerical/sales	39.6	3.6	9.1	25.5
Precision/craft	14.8	0.9	6.2	6.5
Other employed	39.0	2.7	7.0	19.4
Marital Status				
Single	40.2	4.1	10.3	29.1
Married	108.8	7.7	7.1	54.2
Divorced/separated/widowed	33.5	2.4	7.0	16.6
Parents	60.9	5.8	9.5	40.9

(continued)

gland and some parts of New York, New Jersey, and Pennsylvania and the District of Columbia and Baltimore. Calistoga and Arrowhead are strong in northern and southern California, respectively, and Ozarka's strength is in Texas.

The Perrier New Age beverages had the resources of The Perrier Group and its French parent strongly behind these new ventures. With the recent acquisition of Source Perrier by Switzerland's Nestlé, the new owners are expected to continue to support the New Age products that the American subsidiary so successfully introduced. The Perrier Group had an extremely able group at its Greenwich, Connecticut, U.S. headquarters. Ron Davis, President and CEO, and Kim Jeffrey, Executive

EXHIBIT 19.7

Demographics of New Age Beverage[1] Consumers, 1992 *(continued)*

Classification	Total U.S.[2] (Millions)	Number of Users[2] (Millions)	User Incidence[3]	User Profile[2]
Ethnic Groups				
White	156.5	11.4	7.3	80.6
Black	20.5	2.0	9.8	14.2
Other	5.5	0.7	13.5	5.2
Geographical Area				
Northeast	38.6	2.8	7.3	19.9
Midwest	44.3	3.0	6.8	21.3
South	62.6	3.4	5.4	24.0
West	37.0	4.9	13.3	34.8
Income				
$60,000 or more	36.8	3.8	10.5	27.3
$50,000 or more	53.2	4.8	9.0	33.7
$40,000 or more	75.3	6.7	9.0	47.6
$30,000 or more	102.4	8.9	8.6	62.5
$30,000–$39,999	27.1	2.1	7.8	14.9
$20,000–$29,999	30.3	2.5	8.3	17.8
$10,000–$19,999	29.9	1.5	5.1	10.7
Under $10,000	19.9	1.3	6.4	9.0

Notes:
1. Includes sparkling water flavored with both 100% juices and essences.
2. Some of the population categories do not add up to the totals shown because of rounding, and some of the percentage categories do not add up to 100% because of no responses or duplicate answers.
3. Used in the last seven days.

Source: Simmons Market Research Bureau, *1991 Media and Markets Study.*

Vice-President and COO, both have had wide experience in the soft drink industry and are seasoned executives of the bottled water industry.

EverFresh Beverages, Inc.

In February 1992, participants announced that EverFresh Beverages, Inc., had been formed, with James T. Pomroy as President and Chief Executive Officer. The new company combined the former EverFresh USA and EverFresh Canada, previously owned by John LaBatt Ltd of Canada, and the New Era Beverage Company,

EXHIBIT 19.8

Estimated Dollar Sales, 1986–1991: Top Ten New Age Brands

(Dollar amounts in millions)

			Estimated Wholesale Volume[1]					
Brand	**Rank**	**Parent Company**	**1991**	**1990**	**1989**	**1988**	**1987**	**1986**
Clearly Canadian	1	Clearly Canadian	$ 71.4	$ 20.3	$ 16.2	$ 7.1	—	—
Sundance	2	EverFresh Beverages, Inc.	55.0	66.5	80.0	75.0	$ 35.0	$ 14.0
Original NY Seltzer	3	Original NY Seltzer	44.0	55.0	85.0	95.0	100.0	60.0
Crystal Geyser	4	Crystal Geyser	39.0	34.0	18.7	12.2	5.0	3.0
Canada Dry	5	Cadbury Schweppes	36.7	35.6	34.5	29.5	24.0	10.0
Koala Springs	6	Koala Springs International	36.0	32.0	30.4	14.5	8.0	1.0
Snapple	7	Snapple Natural Beverages	35.0	20.8	16.0	9.5	6.0	3.5
Calistoga	8	Perrier Group	34.8	35.6	33.3	32.2	21.5	9.4
Tropicana Sparklers	9	Seagrams	30.0	15.0	—	—	—	—
Quibell	10	Quibell	19.0	12.4	—	—	—	—
Subtotal			$456.9	$344.4	$314.1	$275.0	$199.5	$100.9
All others			300.3	295.6	305.9	268.0	227.5	145.1
Total			$757.2	$640.0	$620.0	$543.0	$427.0	$246.0

Note:

1. Sales volume includes *only* New Age beverage sales. Excluded are each brand's sales for unflavored sparkling and nonsparkling waters, regular sodas, iced teas, juices, juice drinks, etc.

Source: Beverage Marketing, *Annual Industry Survey*.

whose previous owners were Guiness PLC and Stroh Brewery. The new company will feature flavored sparkling juices and fruit-based drinks in both the United States and Canada. The New Age products marketed by EverFresh Beverages are Sundance Sparkling Juice and the EverFresh sparkling juice line.

EverFresh Sparkling Juice, introduced into the U.S. market in 1990, is a combination of about 70% fruit juice and 30% sparkling mineral water. The brand contains no added sugar, fructose, artificial sweeteners, caffeine, preservatives, added color, or sodium. The flavors are summer peach, wild blackberry, pink grapefruit, orange passion fruit, red raspberry, cranberry raspberry, and strawberry kiwi.

Introduced in California in 1986, Sundance expanded into additional markets in 1987 before going national in 1988. In 1991, it had a wholesale volume of \$55.0 million, down from \$66.5 million in 1990, a 17.3% drop (see Exhibit 19.8). The product contains no added sugar or preservatives and is low in sodium. During the past two years, sales of this brand declined steadily. The main reason given for these declines was that the company elected to concentrate advertising, marketing, and promotional dollars in its most profitable markets and to phase out distribution in secondary markets and low-priced warehouse outlets.

Sundance was a target of all the New Age beverages that flooded the market in 1989. Whatever the New Age category, all natural sodas, sparkling juices or flavored waters, Sundance was the brand to beat. The 1990–1991 recession slowed the growth of New Age beverage sales. Additionally, there appeared to be some consumer resistance to the higher cost of the sparkling juice category. In March 1991, the company introduced two new flavors: passion fruit/pineapple and Concord twist.

The company distributes its New Age beverages nationally. For Sundance, distribution is concentrated in major markets, with special emphasis on the large metropolitan areas of New York, Los Angeles, and Dallas. Sundance's greatest concentration of sales is in retail trade. The EverFresh sparkling juice line has its greatest strength in the Midwest (Minnesota, Wisconsin, and Iowa) and the Washington, D.C./Baltimore areas. Sale of this product line relies heavily on cold-box distribution in quick-stop stores and in upscale supermarkets and gourmet food stores in urban and suburban stores and malls.

Cadbury Schweppes, Ltd.

Cadbury Schweppes has two entries in the flavored water segment of the New Age beverage market, which are line extensions under its Canada Dry and Schweppes lines. Canada Dry introduced its all-natural, flavored water on the West Coast in 1986. As a sparkling water, the brand has less carbonation than does the seltzer product. The same is true for the Schweppes product. Canada Dry's flavored sparkling water line had sales of \$36.7 million in 1991. (See Exhibit 19.8.) Canada Dry seltzer/sparkling water comes in nine flavors. It is distributed throughout the country, but not all flavors in all markets. The flavors include: original, lemon/lime, Mandarin orange, raspberry, black cherry, strawberry, peach, grapefruit, and cranberry/lime. Schweppes Sparkling Water also is marketed as a seltzer in certain markets, such as New York. The brand has eight flavors in various stages of distribution: original, lemon, lime, lemon/lime, orange, black cherry, wild raspberry, and peaches and creme.

Cadbury Schweppes established separate distribution networks for its flavored sparkling water brands. Each brand's existing soft-drink bottler network received each flavored line extension.

Cadbury Schweppes was strong financially. The Company has made several acquisitions in the U.S. market, solidifying its place as a niche marketer. Through its U.K. parent company, it has sufficient resources to back its American ventures. John Carson is President of Cadbury Schweppes North America. He has a knowledgeable staff, and the company has been making steady progress in its markets.

Snapple Natural Beverage Company

Snapple is based in the New York metropolitan area and until recently was privately owned. Two brothers-in-law and a mutual friend founded the company. In 1990, it moved its headquarters to Valley Stream, Long Island, from Ridgewood, New York, adding considerable space to the headquarters' operation. In its early years, the company had fairly slow growth, all of which was funded internally. However, in recent years, its growth has accelerated, and it has become a healthy business. It has strong consumer support in its base areas of the Northeast and mid-Atlantic states and growing support in new areas as it rapidly expands distribution.

In 1991, Snapple's line of New Age products reached an estimated sales volume of $35.0 million, excluding the iced tea line. The company has products in all the natural soda, sparkling flavored water, and juice added to nonsparkling water lines. In April 1992, a newly formed corporate entity, Snapple Beverage Corporation, acquired Snapple's owners, the Unadulterated Food Corporation, for an estimated $140.0 million. Thomas H. Lee Company, a successful investment firm, obtained 70% of the new entity, and Snapple's three founders control the remaining 30%.

In 1991, Snapple's New Age, all-natural soda line had seven flavors: lemon/lime, cherry/lime, orange, French cherry, passion supreme, raspberry, and peach melba. In 1992, the company brought back Cola, a flavor that had been deleted from the line in 1990, because the distributors (and presumably their customers) demanded it. Flavors added in 1992 were Jamaican ginger beer and strawberry. In addition, the orange flavor was reformulated.

Included in the all-natural soda category are the company's 100% natural seltzers, which have four regular and four diet flavors. These products are flavored with all natural essences and have no caffeine; the diet products contain Nutrasweet. The nonsparkling juice line has 10% pure fruit juice and 90% nonsparkling water. In 1991, Snapple added pink lemonade to a line that included fruit punch, grapeade, lemonade orangeade, and kiwi strawberry. The Company is planning to add more tropical flavors to this line.

Snapple's flavored seltzer line is distributed only in the Northeast, where seltzers are both recognized and appreciated. The brand continued to be strongest in the Boston–New York–Washington, D.C., corridor, with some sales spilling over into the suburbs of these cities. The rest of the product lines are now distributed in all 50 states.

Seagram Beverage Company, Inc.

Seagram had just introduced a New Age product, Quest, a two-calorie flavored mineral water that contains Nutrasweet. Seagram tested the brand for two years in four markets: Sacramento, California; Atlanta, Georgia; Columbus, Ohio; and Portland, Maine. Two-Calorie Quest is sold in four flavors: black cherry, raspberry, and two proprietary flavors (peach citrus and tangerine lime). It is packaged in a unique spiral-shaped bottle of clear glass and has an attractive pear-shaped label. It also has grooves near the base to make it easier to hold. It is priced competitively to Clearly Canadian, with a four-pack of 10-ounce bottles retailing for about $2.99 and a 23-ounce bottle for approximately $1.49. Advertising features Howie Mandel with the theme "Amazing Taste." Both radio and television ads were used in the four test markets.

In September 1990, Seagram's Tropicana Products, Inc., launched Tropicana Juice Sparklers nationally, after a successful test in Maine. The brand is a blend of juices with "just a touch of carbonation" and was Tropicana's first entry into the New Age category. Tropicana Juice Sparklers' introduction was backed by a reported $13.5 million advertising campaign. The product is marketed in four flavors: tropical orange, golden grapefruit, cranberry orchard, and wild berries.

The product is packaged in 10-ounce and 23-ounce glass containers and is priced at $2.59 per four-pack of 10-ounce bottles and $1.29 for the 23-ounce bottle. In January 1991, Seagram's recalled this brand after pressure build-up in some glass bottles caused them to explode on grocery and pantry shelves. The pressure apparently was caused by a contaminant from a chemical cleaning fluid. The company immediately removed all existing stock from the nation's grocery shelves and alerted consumers, asking them to bring back any bottles that they might have had in their homes. By February 1991, most distribution was reestablished and the product again was selling well. The brand is natural and follows the distribution of its sister brands. Tropicana moved all its brands into food service, convenience stores, and military food stores in 1991.

With Seagram's backing, Tropicana is part of a well-financed multinational corporation that gives its brands strong support. Seagram has invested heavily in R&D, and Tropicana sparklers have been backed by strong advertising budgets since they were introduced.

In September 1991, Tropicana announced the resignations of Robert Soran, President, and George Sulanas, Executive Vice-President, Finance and Procurement. In January 1992, William G. Pietersen, President of the Seagram Beverage Group based in Montreal, who had been filling the job temporarily, was formally named President.

PepsiCo, Inc.

PepsiCo, Inc., has introduced a clear, colorless cola called Crystal Pepsi in three test markets. The new cola is sold alongside traditional Pepsi in Dallas; Providence, Rhode Island; and throughout Colorado.

Crystal Pepsi is priced at regular cola prices, which often are less than two-thirds the price of current new age drinks ($.89 to more than $1). The new product will make its debut in both clear bottles and silver cans and has 130 calories in a 12-ounce serving, compared to 150 calories in the usual Pepsi. It touts low sodium, all-natural flavorings, and no preservatives, which is no different from the regular Pepsi. The new product's main appeal is image, according to beverage analysts. With the can and bottle label tinted blue, the product is designed to convey "good health, purity, and icy cold water," says Tom Pirko, president of Bevmark, Inc., a consulting firm.

Pepsi hopes that Crystal will boost sales among less frequent cola drinkers, or those who might now be trying New Age products besides drinking cola. Clear sodas tend to appeal to 21-to-25-year-olds, compared to regular colas, which are most popular among 14-to-21-year-olds, says Michael Bellar, president of Beverage Marketing Corporation.

Crystal and similar entries into the market by other big companies are expected to steamroll the current New Age category and may turn the niche into a mainline brand. Pepsi, in its new venture with Ocean Spray, also is working on a sparkling fruit juice called Splash, and the beverage maker is expected to introduce a line of fruit-flavored clear beverages patterned after Crystal.

Pepsi has been tenacious in its crusade to dominate the fast-food and vending machine markets. In 1990, Pepsi entered into a joint venture, nondisclosure agreement with American Business Computers, a NASDAQ-listed company, to develop a state-of-the-art beverage dispensing machine for its fast-food markets. The objective was to increase dispensing speed and machine quality. Pepsi also worked closely with Dixie Narco, a premier vending machine manufacturer in West Virginia, to develop a vending machine for its 12-ounce can beverage line.

References

Beverage Industry (1 East First Street, Duluth, MN 55802).

Beverage Marketing Corporation (850 Third Avenue, New York, NY 10022).

Beverage World (150 Great Neck Road, Great Neck, NY 11021).

Clearly Canadian Beverage Corporation (1700-355 Burrared Street, Vancouver, B.C., Canada V6C 268. *Phone:* [604] 683-0312).

Gretchen Morgensen, "Clearly Fuzzy," *Forbes* (November 11, 1991), p. 132.

Michael E. Porter, *Competitive Advantage* (New York: Free Press, 1985).

John F. Rockart and David W. DeLong, *Executive Support Systems* (Homewood, Ill.: Business One Irwin, 1988).

J. Fred Weston, Kwang S. Chung, and Susan E. Hoag, *Mergers, Restructuring and Corporate Control* (Englewood Cliffs, N.J.: Prentice-Hall, 1990).

Anheuser-Busch Companies, Inc., 1993: Globalization

Thomas L. Wheelen and David B. Croll

Introduction

On March 22, 1993, Anheuser-Busch management announced an agreement to acquire an 18% interest (for $477 million) in Grupo Modelo S.A. of Mexico. Eventually, Anheuser-Busch could acquire 50% of Modelo, which controls 51% of the Mexican beer market. This was Anheuser-Busch's first real international investment, not simply a joint venture.[1] Several weeks earlier, the company had announced a joint venture with Kirin Brewery Company, Ltd, of Japan. Kirin is the fifth largest brewer (2.9% world market share) in the world.[2] Anheuser-Busch is the world's largest brewer, with an 8.9% market share, which is almost double that of the next two largest world brewers, Heineken NV and Miller Brewing, both of which have a 4.5% world market share (see Exhibit 20.12).

Beer sales in the United States declined by 2.4% in 1991, and the beer market seemed to be saturated. On March 28, 1990, Patrick K. Stokes had been appointed President of Anheuser-Busch, Inc., the company's beer subsidiary (see Exhibit 20.1). He succeeded August A. Busch III, who had served as President of the subsidiary for the three previous years. Busch stated that he would continue to participate in the management of the subsidiary, but would devote more time to corporate duties and working with other subsidiaries.[3] Busch charged Stokes with the company objective to achieve a 50% market share in the domestic market. An analyst said, "Stokes will be under extra pressure since the achievement of this objective is a top priority of Mr. Busch." Anheuser-Busch's market shares were 44.3%, 44.2%, 43.5%, 37.1%, and 28.2% in 1992, 1991, 1990, 1985, and 1980, respectively.

Company History (1852–1992)

An Entrepreneurial Tradition

In 1852, George Schneider founded the Bavarian Brewery in St. Louis, Missouri. On the brink of bankruptcy in 1857, a competitor bought the brewery and renamed it Hammer and Urban. By 1860, the new company had defaulted on a loan

A special note of appreciation and thanks goes to Marvin R. Shanken, Chairman of M. Shanken Communications, Inc., for his kindness in providing the authors with a copy of *The U.S. BEER MARKET IMPACT DATABANK Review and Forecast—1992 Edition.* Without this extensive survey of the beer industry, this case could not have been developed. So, we want to say thank you for ourselves and the students. This case was prepared by Professor Thomas L. Wheelen of the University of South Florida and Professor David B. Croll of the McIntire School of Commerce at the University of Virginia.

EXHIBIT 20.1

Historical Evolution: Anheuser-Busch Companies, Inc.

1. STEPS IN OWNERSHIP DEVELOPMENT

Year	Firm	Type
1852–1857	Bavarian Brewery	Proprietorship
1857–1858	P. and C. Hammer & Company	Partnership
1858–1860	Hammer & Urban	Partnership
1860–1875	E. Anheuser & Company	Partnership
1875–1879	E. Anheuser Company's Brewing Association	Corporation
1879–1919	Anheuser-Busch Brewing Association	Corporation
1919–1979	Anheuser-Busch, Inc.	Corporation
1979–present	Anheuser-Busch Companies, Inc.	Corporation

2. PRESIDENTS OF ANHEUSER-BUSCH

Name	Tenure
Eberhard Anheuser	President E. Anheuser & Company from 1860 to July 7, 1875. President of E. Anheuser Company's Brewing Association from April 29, 1879, to May 2, 1880 (death).
Adolphus Busch	President of Anheuser-Busch Brewing Association from May 10, 1880, to October 13, 1913 (death).
August A. Busch, Sr.	President of Anheuser-Busch Brewing Association from December 8, 1913, to November 22, 1919. President of Anheuser-Busch, Inc., from November 22, 1919, to February 13, 1934 (death).
Adolphus Busch III	President of Anheuser-Busch, Inc., from February 22, 1934, to August 29, 1946 (death).
August A. Busch, Jr.	President of Anheuser-Busch, Inc., from September 5, 1946, to April 27, 1971.
Richard A. Meyer	President of Anheuser-Busch, Inc., from April 27, 1971, to February 27, 1974.
August A. Busch III	President of Anheuser-Busch, Inc., from February 27, 1974, to October 1, 1979. President of Anheuser-Busch Companies, Inc., from October 1, 1979, to March 28, 1990.
Patrick K. Stokes	President of Anheuser-Busch Companies, Inc., from March 28, 1990 to present.

to Eberhard Anheuser. A successful soap manufacturer, Anheuser assumed control of Hammer and Urban. Four years later, he asked his son-in-law, Adolphus Busch, to join the brewery in the position of salesman. Busch became the driving force behind the new venture, rising to partner (1873), and eventually to President (1880–1913). In 1879, the name of the brewery was changed to Anheuser-Busch Brewing Company (see Exhibit 20.1).

Adolphus Busch was a pioneer in the development of a new pasteurization process for beer, and he became the first American brewer to pasteurize beer. In 1894, he and Carl Conrad developed a new beer that was lighter in color and body than the company's previous beer. The new beer, Budweiser, gave Busch a national beer, for which he developed many marketing techniques (such as give-aways, tokens, and pocketknives) to increase sales. By 1901, annual sales of Anheuser-Busch had surpassed the million-barrel mark.

In 1913, August A. Busch succeeded his father as President of the company and served as President through the Prohibition era (1920–1933) to 1934. He led the company into diversification, entering businesses such as truck bodies, baker's yeast, ice cream, corn products, commercial refrigeration units, and nonalcoholic beverages. With the passage of the Twenty-first Amendment, Anheuser-Busch returned to the manufacture and national distribution of beer, and in 1934 the company went public.

August A. (Gussie) Busch, Jr., succeeded Adolphus Busch III as President and Chief Executive Officer in 1946. In 1949, Eberhard Anheuser was elected the first Chairman of the Board. August A. Busch, Jr., was elected Chairman in 1956. During his tenure, the company constructed eight new breweries, and sales increased elevenfold, from three million barrels in 1946 to 34 million barrels in 1974. He also guided the company's pursuit of diversification strategies into real estate, family entertainment parks, transportation, the St. Louis Cardinals baseball team, and can manufacturing. Busch was serving as Honorary Chairman of the Board of Anheuser-Busch Companies, Inc., and Chairman and President of the St. Louis National Baseball Club, Inc., upon his death on September 29, 1989 at age 90. Busch had said of his life, "I've had a wonderful, competitive life filled with challenge and reward." He had continued, "And I'm thankful for it all. Most of all, I'm thankful for my heritage, for my family, and for my children. I'm thankful for my life with my company, Anheuser-Busch."[4] His death marked the last of the legendary "beer barons" and the end of an era.[5]

August A. Busch III, born June 16, 1937, was the fifth generation of the Busch brewing dynasty. He started his career hauling beechwood chips out of 31,000-gallon aging tanks. In his youth, "Little Augie" was a hell raiser, but he is now a conservative workaholic. He attended the University of Arizona and the Siebel Institute of Technology (a Chicago school for brewers), where he received a brewmaster's diploma.

August A. Busch III was elected President of the company in 1974 and Chief Executive Officer in 1975 (see Exhibit 20.1). By 1986, he was serving as both Chairman and President. During his tenure, sales increased by more than two and one-half times, or 255%, from 34 million barrels in 1974 to 86.8 million barrels in 1992. The company had 12 breweries, with a total annual capacity of 91.7 million barrels, and under his direction, Anheuser-Busch has continued its successful diversification efforts. The company's thirteenth plant opened in 1993, increasing capacity to 98.4 million barrels.

On March 28, 1990, Patrick K. Stokes was appointed President of Anheuser-Busch Companies, Inc., succeeding August A. Busch III (see Exhibit 20.2). In 1993, Stokes remains as President, and August A. Busch III is the Chairman and CEO.[6]

During Busch's 18 years of managing the company, he transformed it from a large, loosely run company into a tightly run organization with an emphasis on the bottom line. Busch is known for his tough mindedness and intensity, his highly competitive nature, and his attention to detail. As Dennis Long, former President of the company's brewing subsidiary, said, "There is little that goes on that he doesn't know something about." Busch, a brewmaster, is known for making unscheduled visits to the breweries at all hours of the day and night.

Busch starts his day at 5:30 A.M., then pilots his helicopter from his 1,000-acre farm in Saint Peters, Missouri, to the company's headquarters on the south side of St. Louis, a 30-mile flight. He holds his first meeting over breakfast before 7:00 A.M. and rarely leaves the office before 6:00 P.M. One of his final rituals before retiring at 8:30 P.M. is to taste-test daily samples of beer that are flown in from the company's 13 breweries. Few batches of Budweiser—or any other Anheuser-Busch beer—are shipped without his personal approval.[7] Busch is described "as a man who never, absolutely never, wastes his time."[8] "When you have a meeting with him, it is boom, boom, boom," states Jerry Steinman, publisher of *Beer Marketer's Insights,* an industry newsletter.[9] Professor Armand C. Stalnaker, who is on the company's Board of Directors, puts it another way: "He's not a guy who sits back, puts his feet up on the desk, and says, 'Let's chat about this for an hour or two.' But I would call it intensity rather than abruptness."[10] Long added, "Let there be no doubt. He's at the helm and he sets the tone."[11] "For him, planning and management are one and the same; once a plan is drawn up, he tracks the follow-through to make sure that it is carried out."[12]

Encouraging openness and participation from his executives, Busch provides them with plenty of responsibility and freedom and promotes group decision making. Henry King, former President of the United States Brewing Association, says that "the reason Anheuser-Busch leads the field is because it's got dynamic leadership. August Busch picks very talented people; he gives them enormous responsibilities; but he gives them the authority to exercise those responsibilities and he holds people accountable."[13]

Busch's Policy Committee is a 15-member forum in which each member must present an opinion on the current topic or issue and substantiate his position. Busch believes that "executives do not learn from success, they learn from their failures." What is his philosophy of success? As he states, "The more successful we become . . . the more humble that we must be . . . because that breeds future success."[14]

According to Robert S. Weinberg, a brewing industry analyst and former consultant to the company, "The thing that is extraordinary about A-B is their depth of management talent. . . . This is a very extraordinary team. They're not compet-

XHIBIT 20.2 **Executive Officers, 1993: Anheuser-Busch Companies, Inc.**

August A. Busch III (age 55) is presently Chairman of the Board and President, and Director of the Company and has served in such capacities since 1977 and 1963, respectively. Since 1979 he has also served as Chairman of the Board and Chief Executive Officer of the Company's subsidiary, Anheuser-Busch, Inc. During the past five years he also served as President of that subsidiary from 1987–1990. He is a member of the *Corporate Office* and the Policy Committee.

Jerry E. Ritter (age 58) is presently Executive Vice-President—Chief Financial and Administrative Officer of the Company and was appointed to serve in such capacity in 1990. He is also Vice-President—Finance of the Company's subsidiary, Anheuser-Busch, Inc., and has served in such capacity since 1982. During the past five years he also served as Vice-President and Group Executive of the Company (1984–1990). He is a member of the *Corporate Office* and the Policy Committee.

Michael J. Roarty (age 64) is presently Executive Vice-President—Corporate Marketing and Communications of the Company and was appointed to serve in such capacity in 1990. He is also presently Chairman of the Board of the Company's subsidiary, Busch Media Group, Inc., and Chairman of the Board and Chief Executive Officer of the Company's subsidiary, Busch Creative Services Corporation, and was appointed to serve in each such capacity in 1990. During the past five years, he also served as Vice-President of the Company (1988–1990) and Executive Vice-President—Marketing of the Company's subsidiary, Anheuser-Busch, Inc. (1983–1990). He is a member of the *Corporate Office* and the Policy Committee.

Patrick T. Stokes (age 50) is presently Vice-President and Group Executive of the Company and has served in such capacity since 1981. He is also presently President of the Company's subsidiary, Anheuser-Busch, Inc., and was appointed to serve in such capacity in 1990. During the past five years he also served as Chairman of the Board and Chief Executive Officer of the Company's subsidiary, Campbell-Taggart, Inc. (1985–1990) and Chairman of the Board and President of the Company's subsidiary, Eagle Snacks, Inc. (1987–1990). He is a member of the *Corporate Office* and the Policy Committee.

John H. Purnell (age 51) is presently Vice-President and Group Executive of the Company and has served in such capacity since January 1991. He is also Chairman of the Board and Chief Executive Officer of the Company's subsidiary, Anheuser-Busch International, Inc., and has served as Chairman since 1980 and as Chief Executive Officer since January 1991. During the past five years he also served as Senior Vice-President—Corporate Planning and Development (1987–1991).

Barry H. Beracha (age 51) is presently Vice-President and Group Executive of the Company and has served in such capacity since 1976. He is also presently Chairman of the Board and Chief Executive Officer of the Company's subsidiary, Metal Container Corporation, and has served in such capacity since 1976. During the past five years he also served as Chairman of the Board and Chief Executive Officer of the Company's subsidiary, Anheuser-Busch Recycling Corporation (1978–January 1993).

W. Randolph Baker (age 46) is presently Vice-President and Group Executive of the Company and has served in such capacity since 1982. During the past five years he also served as Chairman of the Board and President of the Company's subsidiaries, Busch Properties, Inc., and Busch Entertainment Corporation (1978–1991).

(*continued*)

EXHIBIT 20.2

Executive Officers, 1993: Anheuser-Busch Companies, Inc. *(continued)*

Stephen K. Lambright (age 50) is presently Vice-President and Group Executive of the Company, and has served in such capacity since 1984.

Stuart F. Meyer (age 59) is presently Vice-President and Group Executive of the Company and has served in such capacity since April 1991. He has also served as Vice-President—Corporate Human Resources of the Company (1984–March 1991). He was appointed President and Chief Executive Officer of the Company's subsidiary, St. Louis National Baseball Club, Inc., in January 1992, and prior to that served as Executive Vice-President and Chief Operating Officer (April 1991–December 1991). He is also President and Chief Executive Officer of the Company's subsidiary, Civic Center Corporation, and has served in such capacity since April 1991.

Raymond E. Goff (age 47) is presently Vice-President and Group Executive of the Company and has served in such capacity since 1986. He is also presently Chairman of the Board and Chief Executive Officer of the Company's subsidiary, Busch Agricultural Resources, Inc., and has served in such capacity since 1986.

Jaime Iglesias (age 62) is presently Chairman of the Board and Senior Vice-President—Europe of the Company's subsidiary, Anheuser-Busch Europe, Inc. (ABEI), and was appointed to these positions in January 1993. Prior to that he served as Chief Executive Officer (1989–January 1993) and as President (1988–January 1993) of ABEI. He was appointed President—International Operations of the Company's subsidiary, Campbell-Taggart, Inc. (CTI), in 1991 and prior to that served as Vice-President—International (1983–1991). He is also Chairman of CTI's subsidiary, Bimbo S.A., and President and Senior Vice-President—Europe of the Company's subsidiary, Anheuser-Busch International, Inc. (ABII), and served in such capacities since 1978 and January 1993, respectively. He also served as President and Managing Director—Europe of ABII (1988–January 1993).

Aloys H. Litteken (age 52) is presently Vice-President—Corporate Engineering of the Company and has served in such capacity since 1981.

David S. Leavenworth(age 55) is presently Chairman of the Board and Chief Executive Officer of the Company's subsidiaries, Campbell-Taggart, Inc., and Eagle Snacks, Inc., and has served in such capacities since 1990. During the past five years he also served as President of Campbell-Taggart, Inc. (1989–1990), and Executive Vice-President, Administration and Bakery Division (1984–1989).

William L. Rammes (age 51) is presently Vice-President—Corporate Human Resources of the Company and has served in such capacity since June 1992. During the past five years he also served as Vice-President—Operations of the Company's subsidiary, Anheuser-Busch Inc. (1990–June 1992) and Vice-President—Administration (1986–1989).

John B. Roberts (age 48) is presently Chairman of the Board and President of the Company's subsidiary, Busch Entertainment Corporation, and has served in such capacities since June 1992 and May 1991, respectively. During the past five years he also served as Executive Vice-President and General Manager of Busch Entertainment Corporation (1990–May 1991) and Vice-President and General Manager (1987–1990) and Vice-President—Operations (1979–1987).

Source: Anheuser-Busch Companies, Inc., *Form 10-K Report* (1993) pp. 6–8.

ing with each other; they're all working together for the common goal."[15] A former employee warns, "The biggest mistake as an Anheuser executive is to wake up one morning and think you're a Busch," even though Mr. Busch speaks in endearing, almost emotional terms about the A-B family (employees).[16]

Busch's 29-year-old son, August A. Busch IV, has been learning the business for the past eight years. He is a graduate of St. Louis University and is presently Brand Manager for Bud Dry. Commenting on the success of his four children, Busch says, "If they have the competency to do so, they'll be given the opportunity. You learn from the ground up. Those of us who are in the company started out scrubbing the tanks."[17] "The fact that he [August IV] is August III's son does not mean a free lunch," states a friend of the immediate family.[18]

In July 1991, August IV was appointed Brand Manager for the Budweiser family of beers. He began to try to reach out to women, partly by downplaying the role of jiggly females in Budweiser commercials.[19] According to Beverage Marketing Corporation, women now comprise 35% of the overall domestic beer market and 45% of the light beer market. Michelob management estimates that 30% of its market are women.[20] A brewery source said, "August is not afraid to listen."[21] He went on to say that "He also knows the industry and has brought in a lot of his own marketing ideas." A co-worker said, "He's not out there alone. He's getting a lot of help. You have to assume his father is keeping a close eye on the marketing. He always has in the past."[22] In 1991, Budweiser sales volume increased by 5.8%. August IV has been a forceful advocate in devising a strategic plan to boost Budweiser sales.

Corporate Structure: Business Segments and Reorganization

On October 1, 1979, Anheuser-Busch Companies, Inc., was formed as a new holding company. It is composed of 18 subsidiaries, of which 16 comprise the company's major operations (see Exhibit 20.3).

The new company's name and organizational structure clearly reflect Anheuser-Busch's mission and diversification endeavors of the past decades. Because each subsidiary of Anheuser-Busch Companies, Inc., has its own Board of Directors and officers, management has gained operational and organizational flexibility. The Policy Committee for Anheuser-Busch Companies, Inc., establishes policies for all the subsidiaries, one of which is Anheuser-Busch, Inc. Fifteen members comprise the Policy Committee.

During 1989—and as a result of the acquisition of Sea World in September 1989—Anheuser-Busch reorganized and redefined its principal three business segments from prior years. For 1992, the company's principal three business segments for strategic planning purposes were (1) *beer and beer-related operations,* which produces and sells the company's beer products; (2) *food products,* which consists of the company's food and food-related operations (Campbell-Taggart, Inc., and Eagle Snacks, Inc.); and (3) *entertainment,* which consists of the company's theme parks (Sea World, Cypress Gardens, Busch Gardens, Adventure Island, and Sesame Place), baseball team (St. Louis Cardinals), stadium (Busch

EXHIBIT 20.3

Subsidiaries: Anheuser-Busch Companies, Inc.

Anheuser-Busch, Inc.[1]	Campbell-Taggart, Inc.[1]
Anheuser-Busch International, Inc.[1]	Civic Center Corporation[1]
Anheuser-Busch Investment Capital Corporation	Eagle Snacks, Inc.[1]
Anheuser-Busch Recycling Corporation[1]	International Label Company[2]
Busch Agricultural Resources, Inc.[1]	Manufacturers Railroad Company[1]
Busch Creative Service Corporation[1]	Metal Container Corporation[1]
Busch Entertainment Corporation	Promotional Product Group
Busch Media Group, Inc.[1]	St. Louis National Baseball Club, Inc.[1]
Busch Properties, Inc.[1]	St. Louis Refrigerator Car Company[1]

Notes:
1. Major operations.
2. Joint-venture company.

Source: Anheuser-Busch Companies, Inc., *Fact Book, 1992/1993*, pp. 2–14.

Stadium and Civic Center), and real estate development operations (see Exhibit 20.4 for more details on each segment).

Prior to the reorganization, the three principal business segments were (1) beer and beer-related, (2) food products, and (3) diversified operations. The diversified operations segment consisted of the company's entertainment, real estate, transportation, and communications operations. Since 1989, the transportation and communication operations have been included in the beer and beer-related segment. Each of the subsidiary companies of the business segments has its own management organization, which is headed by a Chairman of the Board.[23]

The Board of Directors of Anheuser-Busch Companies, Inc., consists of 14 members and one advisory member, with August A. Busch III being the only internal member (see Exhibit 20.5). The members of the Corporate Office are August A. Busch III, Jerry E. Ritter, Patrick K. Stokes, and Michael J. Roarty. Exhibit 20.2 lists the company's executive officers.

In 1992, the beer and beer-related business segment contributed 75.5% of the corporation's net sales and 92.7% of its operating revenue (see Exhibit 20.6). Exhibit 20.4 briefly describes the 18 companies that comprise the three business segments, and Exhibit 20.6 presents the financial information for each segment. Beer will remain the top priority, according to Busch.

The company's vertical integration strategy increased the knowledge of the economics of those businesses, ensured the quantity and quality of supply, and allowed the strict control of both packaging and raw materials. In cultivating internally developed businesses such as Eagle Snacks, Anheuser-Busch continues its philosophy of maintaining premium quantity and quality of supply and control of

EXHIBIT 20.4 **Business Segments: Anheuser-Busch Companies, Inc.**

Company	Year Founded	Activities
1. BUSINESS SEGMENT: BEER AND BEER-RELATED		
Anheuser-Busch, Inc.	1852	It ranked as the world's largest brewer, selling 86.8 million barrels of beer in 1991, and has been the industry leader since 1957. Market share was 44.63% (up 0.4 since last year). The company distributes 14 naturally brewed beers, a nonalcoholic brew, and 3 imports through 11 company-owned wholesalers and approximately 900 independent wholesalers. Barrels sold have increased by 72.9% (86.8–50.2 million barrels) since 1980.
Anheuser-Busch International, Inc.	1981	It is the company's international and national licensing and marketing subsidiary. The world beer market is 3.5 times as large as the domestic market. The Company exports to 50 countries and license-brews in 5 countries. The company posted record volume (up 10%) and profits in 1992.
Anheuser-Busch Investment Capital Corporation	1984	It shares equity positions with qualified partners in A-B distributorships. It is currently invested in 22 wholesale dealerships.
Anheuser-Busch Recycling Corporation	1978	It recycled more than 550 million pounds of aluminum (or more than 16 billion cans) and 81 million pounds of glass (153 million bottles) and 35 million pounds of paper goods. It recycled more than 93% of the Anheuser-Busch beer cans that were sold.
Busch Agricultural Resources, Inc.	1962	It processes barley into malt. In 1992, it supplied 33% of the company's malt requirements. It grows and processes rice and has the capacity to meet 50% of the company's rice needs.
Busch Creative Service Corporation	1980	It is a full-service business and marketing communications company, selling its services to Anheuser-Busch and other Fortune 500 companies. In 1986, it acquired Innervision Productions, Inc., which produces video programming and industrial films. In 1986, it acquired Optimus, Inc., which is a post-production facility.

(continued)

both packaging and raw materials through self-manufacture. Anheuser-Busch's stated philosophy is:

> Anheuser-Busch's vision of greatness is today a reality. But the company isn't about to rest on its history of achievement. There are many new challenges to be met. And, as always, Anheuser-Busch will lead the way, because we believe that excellence is not just the act of achievement, but the process of constantly striving to achieve even more. We also believe that while a single achievement may signify luck, a history of many

EXHIBIT 20.4

Business Segments: Anheuser-Busch Companies, Inc. *(continued)*

Company	Year Founded	Activities
Busch Media Group, Inc.	1985	It serves as the company's in-house agency to purchase all national broadcast media time and to develop and place local advertising schedules. This allows Anheuser-Busch to better control its substantial television and radio advertising expenditures.
International Label Company	1979	Joint venture with Illochroma International, S.A. of Brussels, Belgium, and Metal Label Company. It produces more than 10 million labels annually, for it sells both to Anheuser-Busch and other customers.
Manufacturers Railway Company	1878	It operates 42 miles of track in the St. Louis area, 247 insulated railroad cars used to ship beer, and hopper cars and boxcars. It has three trucking subsidiaries with a fleet of 240 specially designed trailers. It also runs the warehousing for 12 brewery locations.
Metal Container Corporation	1974	It operates 10 can and lid manufacturing plants. In 1991, it produced nearly 10 billion cans and 14 billion lids. This represents 40% of the company's container requirements. This subsidiary is rapidly expanding into the soft-drink container market. MCC is the third-largest U.S. aluminum beverage container manufacturer, and it increased its market share to 16% in 1992.
Promotional Products Group	NA	It is responsible for licensing, developing, selling, and warehousing the company's promotional merchandise. Each year, more than 1,500 new promotional items are created, and approximately 5,000 different items are available at any one time.
St. Louis Refrigerator Car Company	1878	It is one of the company's transportation subsidiaries, with three facilities. It provides commercial repair, rebuilding, maintenance, and inspection of railroad cars.
2. BUSINESS SEGMENT: FOOD PRODUCTS		
Campbell-Taggart, Inc.	1982	It has 66 plants and approximately 18,000 employees in the U.S., Spain, and France. It is a highly diversified food products company with operations in about 35% of the U.S. It consists of the following divisions: Bakery Operations, Refrigerated Products, Frozen

(continued)

achievements signifies great endeavor and the promise of more to come. Anheuser-Busch has lived that philosophy. And the result speaks for itself.[24]

The company acquired Sea World for $1.1 billion from Harcourt Brace Jovanovich, Inc., in November 1989. The acquisition consisted of three parks in central Florida—Boardwalk and Baseball (near Haines City), Cypress Gardens

EXHIBIT 20.4 **Business Segments: Anheuser-Busch Companies, Inc.** *(continued)*

Company	Year Founded	Activities
		Food Products (Eagle, Crest Foods, Inc.), International—Spain and France. Other interest—makes folding cartons. It just began to adopt TQM concepts. In its 10 years, it has a 10.1% compound growth rate in profit contribution.
Eagle Snacks, Inc.	1978	It produces and distributes a premium line of snack foods and nuts. In 1984 it began self-manufacturing virtually all of its snack products, and in 1985 it purchased Cape Cod Potato Chip Company. In continues to move toward its goal of gaining significant market share in the snack food industry (estimated sales in excess of $12 billion). It is an intensely competitive industry, where the leader has aggressively responded to Eagle's growth with pricing strategy. Eagle Snacks' net sales in 1992 were up only by 6%, while sales volume was up 15%, and it still remains unprofitable.
3. BUSINESS SEGMENT: ENTERTAINMENT		
Busch Entertainment Corporation	1959	It operates 10 U.S. theme parks. More than 18 million people visited the parks in 1992 (up over 1991). The company is always developing new attractions and rides. Conservation and education continue to be priorities for the parks. The profits for the parks increased by 20% despite a slow economy.
Busch Properties, Inc.	1970	It is the company's real estate development subsidiary, with commercial properties in Virginia, Ohio, and California. It continues to develop a planned community, Kingsmill, in Williamsburg, Virginia. Busch Corporate Centers is engaged in leasing and selling property at the Company's three commercial property sites (565 acres). Busch Properties of Florida is selling 300 acres adjacent to Sea World.
Civic Center Corporation	1981	It owns Busch Stadium, Civic Center, and two and three-fourths downtown city blocks currently used for parking.
St. Louis National Baseball Club, Inc.	1953	St. Louis Cardinals. In 1992, the team celebrated its 100th anniversary in the National League.

Source: Anheuser-Busch Companies, Inc., *1992 Annual Report,* pp. 3–5, 10–16; *Fact Book, 1992/1993,* pp. 2–14

(Winter Haven), and Sea World (Orlando)—and the Sea World marine parks in San Antonio, Texas; Aurora, Ohio; and San Diego, California. Harcourt Brace Jovanovich sold the parks because it had accumulated $2.9 billion of debt while fighting a 1987 hostile takeover bid by British publisher Robert Maxwell.[25]

In January 1990, the company closed the Boardwalk and Baseball amusement park operations because neither had ever been profitable. Harcourt Brace Jo-

EXHIBIT 20.5 **Board of Directors: Anheuser-Busch Companies, Inc.**

Name	Organizational Affiliation
August Busch III	Chairman of the Board and President
Richard T. Baker	Former Chairman and presently Consultant for Ernst & Young, certified public accountants
Andrew B. Craig III	Chairman, President, and Chief Executive Officer—Boatmen's Bancshares, Inc., a multibank holding company
Bernard A. Edison	Director Emeritus—Edison Brothers Stores, Inc., retail specialty stores
Peter M. Flanigan	Director—Dillon, Read & Company, Inc., an investment banking firm
John E. Jacob	President and Chief Executive Officer—National Urban League, Inc., a community-based social and advocacy agency
Charles F. Knight	Chairman of the Board and Chief Executive Officer—Emerson Electric Company, a manufacturer of electrical and electronic equipment
Vernon R. Loucks, Jr.	Chairman and Chief Executive Officer—Baxter International Inc., an international manufacturer and marketer of health care products, systems, and services
Sybil C. Mobley	Dean of the School of Business and Industry, Florida A&M University
Vilma S. Martinez	Partner—Munger, Tolles & Olson, attorneys
James B. Orthwein	Partner—Huntleigh Asset Partners, a private investment firm
Douglas A. Warner III	President—J.P. Morgan & Company, Inc., and Morgan Guaranty Trust Company of New York, an international commercial and investment banking firm
William H. Webster	Partner—Milbank, Tweed, Hadley & McCloy, attorneys
Edward E. Whitacre, Jr.	Chairman and Chief Executive Officer—Southwestern Bell Corporation, a national communications corporation
Advisory Member	
Fred L. Kuhlmann	Vice-Chairman—St. Louis National Baseball Club, Inc.

Source: Anheuser-Busch Companies, Inc., *1992 Annual Report,* p. 70.

vanovich had bought the money-losing Circus World in 1986 for $18 million and spent an additional $50 million to renovate the Coney Island–style amusement park, add a baseball stadium, and rename it Boardwalk and Baseball. According to Vicki Pearlman, Busch spokeswoman, "It's been a concept with problems since its inception."[26] She went on to say, "It was historically unprofitable." Attendance

EXHIBIT 20.6

Financial Information for Business Segments: Anheuser-Busch Companies, Inc., 1990–1992
(Dollar amounts in millions)

	Beer and Beer-Related	%	Food Products	%	Entertainment	%	Eliminations	%	Consolidated
1992									
Net sales	$8,609.6	75.7	$2,131.1	18.7	$604.3	6.0	($31.3)	(0.2)	$11,393.7
Operating income	1,645.4	92.7	75.4	4.2	54.9	3.1		0.0	1,775.7
Depreciation and amortization expense	395.1	69.7	100.9	17.8	71.8	12.5		0.0	567.0
Capital expenditures	490.4	66.5	109.5	14.9	137.3	18.6		0.0	737.2
Identifiable assets	6,864.8	68.4	1,584.1	15.8	1,508.2	15.8		0.0	10,037.1
Corporate assets									500.8
Total assets									10,537.9
1991									
Net sales	$8,338.5	75.7	$2,068.7	18.8	$617.9	5.6	($13.8)	0.1	$10,996.3
Operating income	1,581.5	91.8	95.0	5.5	45.0	2.6		0.0	1,599.0
Depreciation and amortization expense	381.4	71.4	89.5	16.8	63.2	11.8		0.0	534.1
Capital expenditures	511.5	69.4	82.5	11.2	108.5	14.8		0.0	737.2
Identifiable assets	6,660.5	69.5	1,359.7	14.2	1,565.7	16.3		0.0	9,586.0
Corporate assets									400.5
Total assets									9,986.5
1990									
Net sales	$8,151.2	75.9	$1,982.4	18.4	$625.3	5.8	(15.3)	(0.1)	$10,743.6
Operating income	1,455.1	91.0	85.6	5.4	58.3	3.6		0.0	1,599.0
Depreciation and amortization expense	351.5	70.9	84.7	17.1	59.5	12.0		0.0	495.7
Capital expenditures	722.4	80.3	95.8	10.7	80.7	9.0		0.0	898.9
Identifiable assets	6,348.5	68.8	1,337.2	14.5	1,540.0	16.7		0.0	9,225.7
Corporate assets									408.6
Total assets									9,634.3

Source: Anheuser-Busch Companies, Inc., *1992 Annual Report*, p. 59.

peaked in 1988 at 1.35 million visitors, dropping 24% in 1989 to 1.04 million visitors. The company owns 250 undeveloped acres next to the 135-acre theme park. Pearlman said, "The company could sell the property or put it to some other use."[27] In 1993, the company was trying to negotiate with the Kansas City Royals, who use the baseball park for its spring training headquarters, to move to another baseball complex. The move would allow the company to sell the entire facility.

In 1989, the company announced a joint venture to build a $300 million resort and theme park near Barcelona, Spain. The resort was scheduled to open in 1993, but at present the project is in jeopardy unless Anheuser-Busch can find a new partner for the project. The project's majority shareholder (80.1%), Grand Tibidabo S.A. has been plagued by problems: (1) a financial scandal involving the majority partner; (2) a frozen bank loan guarantee; and (3) the changing government of Catalonia province (site of the project). However, Jerry E. Ritter, Executive Vice-President, said, "I don't think we have to write off the project."[28]

In 1989, the company sold its wholly owned subsidiary, Busch Industrial Products Corporation, to Gist-Brocades N.V. of the Netherlands. This subsidiary produced yeast products.[29] In 1988, the company sold its majority interest in Exploration Cruise Lines, Inc., which it had acquired in 1985.[30]

The company sold its sparkling water brands, Saratoga and àSanté, and its Zeltzer Seltzer natural soda line to Evian Waters of France, Inc. These sales included production facilities. The company also disposed of its Master Cellar's line of premium-quality California table wines, which it had introduced in 1982.

In 1985, the company became an investor in its first venture capital fund, Innoven, an established fund that has been very successful over the years. With this company, Anheuser-Busch gained exposure to new business ventures being developed by the small start-up companies in which Innoven invests capital.

The company extended its research and development program with the acquisition of Interferon Sciences, which develops and clinically tests both material and recombinant forms of interferon, an antiviral agent found in the human body. Anheuser-Busch expects to continue its long-term diversification efforts, which are to be maintained as long as they are consistent with the company's objectives.

In 1990, Anheuser-Busch International, Inc., formed Anheuser-Busch Europe, Inc., to develop sales, distribution, and marketing of its beer brands in Europe. Anheuser-Busch Europe will also continue to oversee Anheuser-Busch's licensed-brewing partners. In 1992, the volume for the unit was up by more than 25%.

Anheuser-Busch has encountered tough times in its nonbeverage businesses. In 1992, Campbell-Taggart, Inc. (in the food products segment) had what the company called "a slight profit decline" on a 3% sales volume increase. Campbell-Taggart, Inc. (acquired in 1982) was unable to raise prices because recession-minded consumers were opting for low-priced, nonbranded bakery goods.[31] The company had invested millions of dollars in plant modernization and a distribution system. David Goldman, an investment analyst, said, "We think there is reason to believe that Anheuser-Busch may consider restructuring of the company, to include the sale of the food [products business segment, which includes] both Campbell-Taggart, Inc., and Eagle Snacks. We believe these businesses might be worth approximately $1.5 billion to $2 billion." He went on to suggest that "the after-tax portion of the proceeds might be used to acquire a threshold in the international brewing market."[32] In 1992, the beer and beer-related segment had sales of $8.6 billion and operating income of $1.6 billion, whereas the food products segment had sales of $2.1 billion and operating income of $75 million (see Exhibit 20.6).

Similarly, Anheuser's Eagle Snacks (formed in 1978) came under competitive pressure from PepsiCo's Frito-Lay division in the chips market. This competition has seriously depressed Eagle Snacks' profit margins. Dollar sales were up 6%, but tonnage (volume output) was up 15%, so Eagle remains unprofitable. Jerry Ritter, Executive Vice-President, said, "We plan that it will lose considerably less in 1993 as it gains market share. Eagle Snacks did reduce its losses in 1992 as compared with 1991 losses."[33] In 1991, Kevin Bowler, Eagle Snacks' President, had announced that Eagle Snacks was not projected to earn a profit until at least 1993. Eagle Snacks is in third place in this industry, behind Frito-Lay and Borden.[34] One of Eagle's strategies was to "rely primarily on price discounts and secondary shelf space to move our products."[35] The Eagle executive went on to say that "we do little in the way of creative marketing because historically this is the way it's been done. Since snacks are impulse purchases, conspicuous presentations and good value are most effective. We feel the customers are cynical about sweepstakes, so we don't use them."[36] A vice-president of a regional snack-food company said, "It's a price war between Frito-Lay and Eagle; and they're bringing everyone into it. Eagle is putting all the money into buying shelf space (a few retailers are charging snack companies up to $1,000 a year for a foot of shelf space) and promotions, and the regional companies are forced to come back with comparable deals. But without the deep pockets behind us, it's hurting us all."[37]

The U.S. retail snack chips industry includes potato, corn, and tortilla chips, pretzels, and ready-to-eat popcorn, and has sales of approximately $10 billion. Frito-Lay has about half the market share.

During the first half of 1993, the theme parks in Florida were recording extremely strong attendance gains, reflecting more foreign visitors.[38] During the same period, several foreign visitors have been shot and killed in Florida. Canadian organizations warned Canadians about the dangers of visiting Florida. The German government was considering issuing a similar warning to its citizens who were considering traveling to Florida. The California and Virginia theme parks have not yet seen a big upswing in attendance. Overall, the Busch Entertainment segment reported a 2% attendance increase.[39]

David Goldman summed up Anheuser-Busch's diversification strategy. "Even the casual observer realizes that the company's investment in diversified business has not 'paid off.'"[40]

Alcohol Abuse and Corporate Citizenship

Anheuser-Busch "is deeply concerned about the abuse of alcohol and the problem of driving while intoxicated. It supports the proposition that anything less than responsible consumption of alcoholic beverages is detrimental to the individual, to

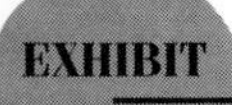

EXHIBIT 20.7

Programs to Promote Responsible Drinking: Anheuser-Busch Companies, Inc.

I. INTRODUCTION

Alcohol Awareness—Anheuser-Busch is deeply concerned about alcohol abuse, drunk driving, and underage drinking. It supports the position that anything less than responsible consumption of alcoholic beverages can be detrimental to the individual, to society, and to the brewing industry.

The company continues to factually address alcohol-related issues, emphasizing that beer is a legal, socially acceptable beverage enjoyed responsibly by the vast majority of 80 million adult Americans.

The Department of Consumer Awareness and Education is responsible for coordinating the advertising and grass-roots program contained under the company's "Know When to Say When" umbrella campaign. Anheuser-Busch believes these programs promote responsible drinking without imposing costs on responsible drinkers or infringing on the rights of individuals.

II. SPECIFIC PROGRAMS

"Know When to Say When" is an advertising campaign that makes millions of impressions annually with messages about responsible drinking. The campaign includes national and local television, radio, magazine, newspaper, and billboard advertising.

"The Family Talk about Drinking" program offers a set of parental guides, developed with authorities in the fields of alcohol research, child development, and family therapy. The guides encourage effective communication between parents and children to help prevent underage drinking and are sent free to those who call 1-800-359-TALK. To date, more than 1 million copies of "Family Talk" materials have been sent to parents and educators across the country.

"I'm Driving"is an Anheuser-Busch sponsored program promoting the use of designated drivers. Through this program, a consumer typically receives free soft drinks or discounts on food from an establishment in exchange for being named the designated driver in a group and refraining from drinking alcoholic beverages on that occasion. In 1991, Anheuser-Busch and its wholesalers worked with almost 5,000 community organizations to establish local designated driver programs. In addition, O'Doul's, the company's non-alcoholic brew, introduced a designated driver program in collaboration with the National Commission Against Drunk Driving.

(continued)

society, and to the brewing industry."[41] Anheuser-Busch has been a leader in developing programs that support this position and has designed programs to meet the needs of its employees, wholesalers, retailers, and customers (see Exhibit 20.7 for the specific programs).

The company's Department of Consumer Awareness and Education is responsible for coordinating the advertising and grass-roots programs under the company's "Know When to Say When" umbrella campaign. In 1992, the company

EXHIBIT 20.7 **Programs to Promote Responsible Drinking: Anheuser-Busch Companies, Inc.** *(continued)*

"The Alert Cab" program brings Anheuser-Busch wholesalers, cab companies, restaurants and taverns together to provide free cab rides home to those who may have had too much to drink. Last year, more than 30,000 such rides were given through this or similar cab programs sponsored by Anheuser-Busch wholesalers.

"Your Alcohol IQ" is a video production that uses well-known entertainers and alcohol authorities to discuss the consumption and abuse of alcoholic beverages. Through a question-and-answer format, viewers are challenged to learn more about alcohol and responsible drinking. The videotape is available on a free-loan basis through many video stores nationwide and through Anheuser-Busch wholesalers.

Good Sport" is a program of communication, training, and management activities designed to help stadium operators, team owners, and concessionaires promote positive fan behavior by encouraging personal responsibility. In addition to sporting events, the program can be adapted to street festivals, music concerts, and other special events that might attract large crowds.

"Pit Stop" is a program designed to give motorists a place to take a break from driving, have a free snack, and receive information about Anheuser-Busch programs that promote responsible consumption among adults who choose to drink. The program is often set up at public rest stops during holidays or other high-traffic times, such as football game weekends and hunting season.

"TIPS" (Training for Intervention Procedures by Servers of Alcohol) teaches techniques to help servers of alcohol recognize the signs of intoxication in customers and respond effectively to prevent alcohol abuse and drunk driving situations. TIPS was developed by Dr. Morris Chafetz, the founding director of the National Institute of Alcohol Abuse and Alcoholism.

"The Buddy System" is an Anheuser-Busch awareness campaign designed specifically for *college students* and other young adults of legal drinking age. Aimed at reducing alcohol abuse through education, the program reminds college students to take care of each other. The program promotes responsible drinking among students 21 and older who choose to drink. For those under 21, it promotes respect for the law.

"BACCHUS" (Boost Alcohol Consciousness Concerning the Health of University Students), a national student organization that works with fraternity and sorority houses, residence units, higher education associations, government officials, and others to promote student-to-student alcohol awareness education, positive peer pressure, and action

(continued)

made two of its most popular programs, "Family Talk About Drinking" and "Make the Right Call," available on videotape. It aired "Know When to Say When" ads on programs such as the World Series, NCAA basketball tournament, "Good Morning America," "Today," and the Super Bowl.[42]

According to the U.S. Department of Transportation, between 1991 and 1992, the decline in alcohol-related auto fatalities was the largest ever recorded for a year. In the past ten years, teenage drunk-driving fatalities have decreased by

EXHIBIT 20.7

Programs to Promote Responsible Drinking: Anheuser-Busch Companies, Inc. *(continued)*

programs supporting a safe campus environment. Anheuser-Busch is a major sponsor of BACCHUS.

"NCAAW" (National Collegiate Alcohol Awareness Week) is an annual week of on-campus activities to promote safety, education, and alcohol awareness. Each year, activities are held on approximately 3,500 campuses. Anheuser-Busch is a major sponsor of NCAAW. The Company also awards 26 scholarships to the winners of its annual NCAAW "Know When to Say When" poster contest.

"Project ARK" (At Risk Kids)—Anheuser-Busch wholesaler network offers a 39-minute video, "How to Be A Positive 'I Can' Person," to schools on a free-loan basis. Designed by Lt. Jerry Agnew of the Pulaski County, Arkansas, Police Department for fourth, fifth, and sixth graders, the video uses visual aids, audience participation, magic tricks, and a high-tech police car robot to tell children that they can achieve their dreams without using or experimenting with illegal drugs.

Alcohol I.D. is an Anheuser-Busch print advertisement titled "Susie Collins" that graphically demonstrates how difficult it can be to detect the correct age of some individuals. It encourages retailers to be diligent in identifying legal-age patrons. To help retail establishments better identify those customers they are legally able to serve, Anheuser-Busch makes available through its wholesalers plastic bands that are snapped on wrists of those who show a valid identification. Anheuser-Busch wholesalers also make available booklets that contain photographs of valid drivers' licenses from all 50 states and Canadian provinces.

Educational Lecture Series is a factual and impactful presentation to high school students to discourage teen drinking as well as drinking and driving. Barbara Babb, a former flight nurse from St. Louis, delivers the presentation. Anheuser-Busch sponsorship has helped Barbara take her live presentation to high schools across the country. In addition, Anheuser-Busch has developed a video and teacher's guide to further broaden the reach of Barbara's important message.

Other Support: Internally, the company's Employee Assistance program continues to offer employees and their families counseling on personal problems, including alcohol abuse. It has been used as a model for the development of other similar programs by many Anheuser-Busch wholesalers and other U.S. corporations.

Source: Anheuser-Busch Companies, Inc., *Fact Book, 1992/1993,* pp. 17–18.

nearly 50%. A University of Michigan study stated that high school seniors who reported drinking in the past month declined by 25% from 1978 to 1991.[43]

U.S. Beer Industry

In 1991, the beer market declined by 5.3 billion gallons (or 2.4%). Total U.S. sales were 188.5 million barrels. The top seven U.S. brewers accounted for 99.5% of all domestic sales (see Exhibit 20.8). Over the decades, the beer industry had

EXHIBIT 20.8

Top 10 Beers in the United States, 1991
(Shipments in millions of barrels)

Rank	Brand	Brewer/Importer	Segment	Shipments	Market Share
1	Budweiser	Anheuser-Busch, Inc.	Premium	45.0	23.9%
2	Miller Lite	Miller Brewing Company (Philip Morris)	Light	19.1	10.1
3	Bud Light	Anheuser-Busch, Inc.	Light	12.4	6.6
4	Coors Light	Adolph Coors Company	Light	12.2	6.5
5	Busch	Anheuser-Busch, Inc.	Popular	9.8	5.2
	Total top 5			98.5	52.3
6	Milwaukee's Best	Miller Brewing Company (Philip Morris)	Popular	6.6	3.5
7	Miller Genuine Draft	Miller Brewing Company (Philip Morris)	Premium	6.4	3.4
8	Old Milwaukee	Stroh Brewing Company	Popular	5.6	3.0
9	Miller High Life	Miller Brewing Company (Philip Morris)	Premium	5.1	2.7
10	Natural Light	Anheuser-Busch, Inc.	Light	4.3	2.3
	Total Top 10			126.5	67.2
	Total Top 15			140.9	74.7
	Total Top 20			150.5	79.8
	Total Top 25			158.0	83.8
	Other brands			30.5	16.2
	Total beer market			188.5	100.0%

Source: *IMPACT DATABANK—1992 Edition,* Table 4-A, p. 141.

first splintered and then had concentrated. In 1850, 430 brewers produced 750,000 barrels per year. By the end of the 1890s, the number of brewers had grown to 1,169, and they produced more than 1,000,000 barrels each year. However, by midcentury, the industry had begun to consolidate. In 1954, there were only 310 plants and 263 brewers, and, by 1963, these numbers had shrunk to 211 plants and 171 brewers. This concentration of the industry continued through the next decade, so that by 1980 there were 88 plants and 41 brewers.

In 1991, the big three brewers—Anheuser-Busch (44.2% market share), Miller Brewing (22.4% market share), and Coors (10.3% market share)—controlled 76.9% of the market, and in 1990 their combined market share was 75.4%. Anheuser-Busch suffered an unaccustomed downturn in shipments, from 84.1 million barrels in 1990 to 83.3 million barrels in 1991 (see Exhibit 20.9). Sales of the Budweiser family of beers were down despite heavy increases in adver-

EXHIBIT 20.9

Sales of Leading U.S. Brewers
(Volume in thousands of barrels)

Company	1970 Volume	1970 Market Share	1980 Volume	1980 Market Share	1985 Volume	1985 Market Share	1990 Volume	1990 Market Share	1991 Volume	1991 Market Share
Anheuser-Busch	22,202	18.1%	50,160	28.2%	68,000	37.1%	84,100	43.5%	83,300	44.2%
Miller Brewing	5,150	4.2	37,300	21.0	37,100	20.3	42,500	22.0	42,200	22.4
The Stroh Brewery	3,276	2.7	6,161	3.5	23,400	12.8	15,400	8.0	14,000	7.4
G. Heileman Brewing	3,000	2.4	13,270	7.4	16,200	8.8	10,700	5.5	9,800	5.2
Adolph Coors	7,277	5.9	13,779	7.7	14,738	8.1	19,200	9.9	19,400	10.3
Total top 5	40,905	33.3	120,670	67.8	159,438	87.1	171,900	88.9	168,700	89.5
Other domestic	80,995	66.0	52,830	29.6	15,662	8.6	12,500	6.5	11,900	6.3
Total domestic	121,900	99.3	173,500	97.4	175,100	95.7	184,400	95.4	180,600	95.8
Imports	900	0.7	4,600	2.6	7,900	4.3	8,800	4.6	7,900	4.2
Total	122,800	100.0%	177,900	100.0%	183,000	100.0%	193,200	100.0%	188,500	100.0%

Note: 1. Excludes tax-free, malt-based, coolers and non-alcoholic.

Source: IMPACT, Vol. 19, No. 16 and 17 (August 15 and September 1, 1990) and *IMPACT DATABASE—1992 Edition,* Table 3-D, p. 98.

tising expenditures. The premium beer segment, where Budweiser is sold, decreased from 72.1 million barrels in 1990 to 67.4 million barrels in 1991, a 6.5% drop in sales (see Exhibit 20.10).

The beer market is projected to remain stagnant until the year 2000 and probably beyond. The consumption of all alcoholic beverages (wines, coolers, distilled spirits, and beer) is declining, from 39.10 gallons per adult in 1990 to a projected 33.48 gallons in 2000. Consumption patterns of beer have shifted from one of the nine beer segments to another and are likely to continue. Over the past several years, there have been extensive price wars in the nine beer segments. Jerry Steinman, publisher of *Beer Market's Insights,* said, "There's certainly more promotion [in other words, price cutting] in 1991 than in previous years." He went on to say that the price cutting episodes "lasted longer, they were deeper, [and] the competition was fierce."[44] Price cutting, sweepstakes, refunds, and coupon offers have reached the point that, in some markets, as much as 90% of the beer on retailers' shelves is being sold at less than regular price.[45]

During the past decade, the second-tier brewers (Stroh, Heileman, etc.) have faced new competition from the big three brewers as they introduced new low-priced brands. The second-tier brewers had maintained a niching strategy of lower priced beer brands.

The industry is intensely competitive—campaigns against underage drinking and against drinking and driving, price wars, new product introductions, expensive advertising budgets, and possible market saturation. This situation has hindered Anheuser-Busch management's attempts to attain its objective of a 50% market share. It has made each market share point harder, but not impossible, to achieve.

Anheuser-Busch Domestic Beer Products

According to those in the industry, the five hallmarks of beer as a consumer beverage are convenience, moderation, health, value, and thirst-quenching properties. Each member of the Anheuser-Busch family of 16 beers is positioned to take advantage of contemporary lifestyles and their hallmarks. The company also distributes three imported beers—Carlsburg, Carlsburg Lite, and Elephant Malt Liquor.

In 1991, the company introduced three new beers—Natural Pilsner, Michelob Golden Draft, and Michelob Golden Draft Lite (see Exhibit 20.11). All are still being tested, with good results.

Sales of the flagship beer, Budweiser, declined in 1990 and 1991. Although 1991 sales declined by 6.3%, Budweiser remains the number one beer, both in total beer shipments (45 million gallons), and in its popular beer segment (45%). During 1991, the company spent $77.1 million to advertise Michelob Dry, introduced in 1988, and Bud Dry, introduced in 1989. The results of the campaign were that Bud Dry eclipsed Michelob Dry sales (3.2 million barrels to 2.3 million barrels). Sales of both brands declined in 1991. Bud Dry sales were down by 9.4%, and Michelob Dry's sales decreased by 4.3%. Management cut Michelob Dry's advertising budget from $36.7 million in 1991 to $4.8

EXHIBIT 20.10

Beer Consumption Information

(Barrels in millions)

1. BEER CONSUMPTION BY SEGMENTS—VOLUME AND SHARE—1970–2000

	1970		1975		1980		1985	
Segment	Barrels	Share	Barrels	Share	Barrels	Share	Barrels	Share
Popular	71.6	58.3%	65.4	43.5%	30.0	16.9%	33.3	18.2%
Premium	46.1	37.5	71.6	47.6	102.3	57.5	86.1	47.1
Super-premium	1.1	0.9	5.0	3.3	11.5	6.5	8.8	4.8
Light	—	—	2.8	1.9	22.1	12.4	39.4	21.6
Low alcohol	—	—	—	—	—	—	—	—
Imported	0.9	0.7	1.7	1.1	4.6	2.6	7.9	4.3
Malt liquor	3.1	2.5	3.8	2.5	5.5	3.1	5.5	3.0
Ale	NA	NA	NA	NA	1.9	1.1	1.3	0.7
Dry	—	—	—	—	—	—	—	—
Total[2]	122.8	100.0%	150.3	100.0%	177.9	100.0%	182.7	100.0%

Notes:

1. Less than 50,000 barrels.
2. Addition of columns may not agree because of rounding.

Source: *IMPACT DATABANK—1988 Edition,* Table 4-E, p. 30; Table 4-6, p. 31, and Table 8-A, p. 75; *1992 Edition,* Table 4-E, p. 143; Table 4-F, p. 144; and Table 9-A, p. 286.

2. BEER GROWTH RATES BY SEGMENTS: 1970–2000

Segment	**1970–1975**	**1975–1980**	**1980–1985**	**1985–1990**
(Average annual compound growth rate)				
Popular	−1.8%	−14.4%	2.1%	−1.7%
Premium	9.2	7.4	−3.4	−1.1
Super-premium	35.4	18.1	−5.2	−4.5
Light	—	51.2	12.3	4.5
Low alcohol	—	—	—	−24.2
Imported	13.5	22.2	11.6	6.8
Malt liquor	4.2	7.7	—	−1.1
Ale	NA	NA	−7.3	−5.1
Dry	—	—	—	—
Total	4.1%	3.4%	0.5%	0.3%

Source: *IMPACT DATABANK—1988 Edition,* Table 8-B, p. 76; *1992 Edition,* Table 9-B, p. 287.

1990		1991		1995 (Estimated)		2000 (Estimated)	
Barrels	Share	Barrels	Share	Barrels	Share	Barrels	Share
35.7	18.5%	33.8	17.9%	31.6	16.6%	28.0	14.9%
72.1	37.3	67.4	35.8	62.1	32.6	58.1	30.9
5.6	2.6	4.4	2.3	3.5	1.8	3.0	1.6
59.6	30.9	63.2	33.5	70.0	36.7	74.5	39.6
—[1]	—[1]	—[1]	—[1]	2.3	1.2	2.5	1.3
8.8	4.5	7.9	4.2	8.0	4.2	8.0	4.3
6.5	3.4	6.6	3.5	6.6	3.5	5.5	3.0
0.9	0.5	0.9	0.5	0.8	0.4	0.7	0.4
4.6	2.4	4.3	2.3	5.6	2.9	6.6	3.5
193.2	100.0%	188.5	100.0%	190.5	100.0%	188.0	100.0%

1990–1995	Estimated Projections 1995–2000
−2.4%	−2.4%
−2.9	−0.9
−6.9	−3.0
3.3	1.3
8.9	1.7
−1.9	—
0.3	—
−2.3	−2.6
4.0	3.3
−0.4%	−0.3%

3. PER CAPITA CONSUMPTION

Category	Year 1990	Year 2000[2]
(Gallons per adult)		
Wine	2.54	2.12
Distilled spirits	2.15	1.63
Beers	33.79	19.37
Coolers	0.59	0.35
Total alcoholic beverages	39.10[1]	33.48

Notes:
1. Rounding error.
2. Estimated.

Source: *Market Watch,* Table 9-B, p. 267.

EXHIBIT 20.11 **Selected Information, Beer Products: Anheuser-Busch, Inc.**

A. ESTABLISHED ANHEUSER-BUSCH BEER PRODUCTS

Brand	Impact Databank Segment	Shipments in Millions of Barrels 1990	1991	Percentage Change 1990–1991	Market Share of Total Beer Shipments 1990	1991
1. Budweiser	Premium	66.6	66.8	6.3%	24.6%	24.9%
2. Bud Light	Light	11.8	12.4	5.1	6.1	6.6
3. Bud Dry	Dry	3.2	2.9	–9.4	1.7	1.5
4. Busch	Popular	9.3	9.8	5.4	4.8	5.2
5. Busch Light	Light	1.9	2.7	42.1	1.0	1.4
6. King Cobra	Malt	0.6	0.7	16.7	NA	NA
7. Michelob	Super-premium	3.1	2.7	–12.9	1.6	1.4
8. Michelob	Super-premium Classic dry	0.1	0.1	0.0	NA	NA
9. Michelob Dry	Dry	1.1	0.8	–27.3	NA	NA
10. Michelob Light	Light	2.3	2.2	–4.3	1.2	1.2
11. Natural Light	Light	3.0	4.3	43.3	1.6	2.3

Brand	Impact Databank Segment	Shipments in Thousands of 2.25 Gallon Cases 1990	1991	Percentage Change 1990–1991
12. O'Douls	Non-Alcoholic	3,650	6,850	87.7%

million in 1992. Exhibit 20.11 provides an overview of Anheuser-Busch's beer products.

World Beer Market

In 1991, the top 20 world brewers combined had a 49.1% market share, selling 485.1 million barrels of beer (see Exhibit 20.12). These sales increased by 0.4% from 1990's 483.3 million barrels and a 48.5% market share. Exhibit 20.12 shows that four of the top 15 beer companies were U.S. brewers. Anheuser-Busch, with a world market share of 8.9%, has almost double the sales of the next two companies, Heineken N.V. (Netherlands), and Miller Brewing, which have a 4.5% market share each. Extrapolating the sales in Exhibit 20.12 gives a total estimated world beer sales of 987.9 million barrels in 1991 and 996.5 million barrels in

Market Share in Its Segment		Ranking Position in Beer Segment		Rank in Top 10 Beers		Advertising Budget (in millions)		
1990	1991	1990	1991	1990	1991	1990	1991	Year Introduced
48.0%	45.0%	1	1	1	1	$85.5	$93.0	1876
19.8	19.6	2	2	3	3	56.1	64.9	1982
69.6	67.4	1	1			41.4	54.4	1955
26.1	29.0	1	1	5	5	18.6	7.4	1989
3.2	4.3	5	5			NA	NA	1984
9.2	10.6	4	4			NA	NA	1896
62.0	61.4	1	1			NA	NA	1981
2.0	2.3	5	5			NA	NA	1988
23.9	18.6	2	2			35.7	4.8	1978
3.9	3.5	6	6	10	10	0.8	0.5	1977
5.0	6.8	4	4			NA	NA	1991

Market Share in Its Segment		Ranking Position in Segment		Advertising Budget (in millions)		
1990	1991	1990	1991	1990	1991	Year Introduced
19.9%	28.4%	2	2	$7.2	$11.2	1990

(continued)

1990. Overall, world beer sales were down by approximately 0.2%. Total world beer sales are almost four times U.S. domestic sales. In recent years, Guinness (United Kingdom) acquired Cruz delCampo (Spain), Heineken (Netherlands) purchased Komaromi Sorgyar (Hungary), and Grolsch purchased Wickuler.[46]

Anheuser-Busch International, Inc., was formed in 1981. The company's mission is to develop and explore beer markets outside the United States. Budweiser is now brewed in five overseas markets and is exported to more than 50 countries.[47] Exhibit 20.13 shows the top ten imported beers; in 1991, total U.S. beer *imports* were 113.5 million, 12.25 gallon cases (down 7.6% from 1990). Exhibit 20.14 shows that total U.S. beer *exports* in 1991 were 73.3 million barrels (up 19.3% from 1990).

In Canada, Budweiser and Bud Light are brewed and distributed by Labatt Brewing Company. In 1989, Modelo S.A. introduced Budweiser into Mexico under an export agreement. Anheuser-Busch exports Budweiser to Central America

EXHIBIT 20.11 **Selected Information, Beer Products: Anheuser-Busch, Inc.** *(continued)*

B. NEW BEER PRODUCTS IN 1991

Brand
13. Michelob Golden Draft
14. Michelob Golden Draft Light
15. Natural Pilsner

C. IMPORTS DISTRIBUTED BY ANHEUSER-BUSCH

Brand	Information
Carlsburg	None Available
Carlsburg Light	None Available
Elephant Malt Liquor	None Available

D. MARKET SHARE BY BEER SEGMENTS—EACH SEGMENT IS 100%

Company	Year	Popular	Premium	Super-Premium	Light
Anheuser-Busch	1985	17%	53%	67%	24%
	1990	26	67	64	32
	1991	29	67	61	34

E. SHARE OF TOTAL COMPANY VOLUME BY SEGMENT

Brewer	Year	Popular	Premium	Super-Premium	Light
Anheuser-Busch	1985	9%	68%	9%	14%
	1990	11	57	4	22
	1991	12	54	3	26

and recently began exporting it to Brazil, the seventh largest beer market in the world.[48]

In Japan, Suntory Ltd has distributed Budweiser since 1981, and the brand is firmly established as the leading imported beer in Japan. In 1986, Anheuser-Busch signed a similar agreement with Oriental Brewing Company Ltd of Seoul, Korea. Budweiser produces and markets more than 60% of the international beer brands. In 1992, Anheuser-Busch Asta, Inc., was formed to develop the sales, distribute, and market Anheuser-Busch beer brands in Asia.[49]

Anheuser-Busch European Trade Ltd (ABET) was formed in 1990. Its mission is similar to Asta's but for Europe. Sales were up by 25% in 1992. ABET trades in 17 countries including 10 of the 12 EC countries. Budweiser has been brewed, marketed, and distributed in Europe since 1986 by Guinness-Ireland.

In March 1993, Anheuser-Busch announced a joint venture with Japan's largest brewer, Kirin Brewery, the fifth largest brewer in the world. Kirin sold 29.0 million and 27.5 million barrels of beer in 1991 and 1992, respectively. The com-

Malt Liquor	Dry	Non-Alcoholic	Ales and Other Low Alcohol
2%	—%	—%	17%
9	93	—	—
11	86	29	—

Malt Liquor	Dry	Non-Alcoholic	Other	Last Year
—%[1]	—%	—%	—%[1]	0%
1	5	—[1]	—	0
1	4	1	—	0

Note:
1. Less than 0.5%

Source: *IMPACT DATABANK—1992 Edition,* Table 4-A, p. 141; Table 4-C, p. 151; Table 3-G, p. 101; Table 3-F, p. 100.

pany had 2.9% and 2.8% shares of the world beer market in 1991 and 1990, respectively (see Exhibit 20.12).

The joint venture company, Budweiser Japan Company, will be 90% owned by Anheuser-Busch and 10% owned by Kirin. The company will start selling Budweiser in September 1993. Anheuser-Busch management envisions eventually selling other beer brands in Japan.[50]

On March 22, 1993, Anheuser-Busch announced an agreement (A-B invested $477 million) to acquire an 18% interest in Grupo-Modelo S.A. Modelo is Mexico's largest brewer, with a 51% market share and is the brewer of Corona beer. Eventually, Anheuser-Busch could acquire about 50% of Modelo, which is a closely held company, but no change of control is contemplated. Modelo represents Anheuser-Busch's first investment in a foreign brewer, though it had participated in a joint venture earlier. A senior Anheuser-Busch executive said, "We're looking at acquiring other brewers and other brands outside of Mexico."[51] The agreement requires each company to have board representatives on the other's

EXHIBIT 20.12

Top 20 Beer Marketers Worldwide

(Shipments in millions of barrels)

Rank	Company	Headquarters	Shipments[1] 1990	Shipments[1] 1991	Change	Share of World Beer Market 1990	Share of World Beer Market 1991
1	Anheuser-Busch, Inc.	United States	88.1	88.0	−0.1%	8.8%	8.9%
2	Heineken NV	Netherlands	45.6	44.7	−1.9	4.6	4.5
3	Miller Brewing Company (Philip Morris)	United States	44.3	44.4	0.2	4.4	4.5
4	Foster's Brewing Group	Australia	30.7	29.8	−2.8	3.1	3.0
5	Kirin Brewery Company, Ltd	Japan	27.5	29.0	5.3	2.8	2.9
	Total top 5		236.2	236.0	−0.1	23.7	23.9
6	Companhia Cervejaria Brahma	Brazil	24.7	26.1	5.5	2.5	2.6
7	Coors Brewing Company (Adolph Coors)	United States	20.0	20.2	0.9	2.0	2.0
8	Groupe BSN	France	21.3	20.0	−6.0	2.1	2.0
9	South Africa Breweries, Ltd	South Africa	19.1	19.1	—	1.9	1.9
10	Carlsberg Ltd	Denmark	16.4	18.2	10.4	1.6	1.8
	Total top 10		337.8	339.5	0.5	33.9	34.3
11	Companhia Antarctica Paulista	Brazil	17.0	18.1	6.0	1.7	1.8
12	Cerveceria Modelo SA	Mexico	16.7	18.0	7.7	1.7	1.8
13	Guinness PLC	United Kingdom	17.0	17.1	1.0	1.7	1.7
14	FEMSA	Mexico	16.6	16.8	1.0	1.7	1.7
15	The Stroh Brewery Company	United States	16.1	14.8	−7.9	1.6	1.5
	Total top 15		421.2	424.3	0.7	42.2	42.9
16	Asahi Breweries, Ltd	Japan	13.8	14.1	2.5	1.4	1.4
17	Santo Domingo Group	Colombia	12.8	13.0	1.3	1.3	1.3
18	Bass PLC	United Kingdom	12.4	12.0	−3.4	1.2	1.2
19	San Miguel Corporation	Philippines	12.7	10.8	−14.8	1.3	1.1
20	Sapporo Breweries, Ltd	Japan	10.3	10.8	5.2	1.0	1.1
	Total top 20		483.3	485.1	0.4	48.5%	49.1%
	Total world market[2]		996.5	987.9	−0.2%	100.0%	100.0%

Notes:

1. The authors projected the world total for beer shipments based on the information for the Top 20.
2. Additions of columns may not agree because of rounding.
3. The notes to original Table 3-U were deleted.

Source: *IMPACT DATABANK—1992 Edition,* Table 3-U, p. 120.

EXHIBIT 20.13

Top 10 Imported Beer Marketers

(Millions of 2.25 gallon cases)

		Depletions			Change		Market Share		
Rank	Importer	1989	1990	1991	1989–1990	1990–1991	1989	1990	1991
1	Van Munching & Company, Inc. (Heineken N.V.)	34.6	35.6	31.2	2.9%	−12.4%	28.5%	29.0%	27.5%
2	Molson Breweries USA, Inc.	20.1	20.5	21.0	2.0	2.4	16.6	16.7	18.5
3	Guinness Import Company	14.0	14.0	13.3	—	−5.0	11.5	11.4	11.7
4	Barton Beers, Ltd	12.5	11.0	9.6	−12.0	−12.7	10.3	9.0	8.5
5	Dribeck Importers, Inc.	10.1	10.7	9.3	5.9	−13.1	8.3	8.7	8.2
	Total top 5[1]	91.3	91.8	84.4	0.5	−8.1	75.3	74.7	74.4
6	Labatt's USA, Inc.	8.6	9.0	8.6	4.7	−4.4	7.1	7.3	7.6
7	Gambrinus Importing Company, Inc.	6.4	5.5	5.8	−14.1	5.5	5.3	4.5	5.1
8	Wisdom Import Sales Company, Inc.	4.6	5.3	4.8	15.2	−9.4	3.8	4.3	4.2
9	Associated Beverage Importers, Inc. (Allied-Lyons)	3.1	3.0	2.6	−3.2	−13.3	2.6	2.4	2.3
10	Sapporo USA, Inc.	1.3	1.3	1.3	—	—	1.1	1.1	1.1
	Total top 10[1]	115.3	115.9	107.5	0.5	−7.2	95.1	94.3	94.7
	Other Importers	6.0	7.0	6.0	16.7	−14.3	4.9	5.7	5.3
	Total imported beer[1]	121.3	122.9	113.5	1.3%	−7.6%	100.0%	100.0%	100.0%

Note:
1. Additions of columns may not agree because of rounding.

Source: *IMPACT DATABANK—1992 Edition,* Table 3-T, p. 119.

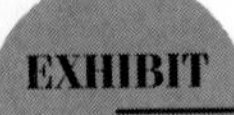

EXHIBIT 20.14

Commercial Exports of U.S. Beer by Country of Destination
(In millions of gallons)

		Shipments				Average Annual Compound Growth Rate		Change
Rank	Country	1980	1985	1990	1991	1980–1985	1985–1990	1990–1991
1	Japan	1.8	1.0	17.8	17.3	−11.8%	78.8%	−3.2%
2	Canada	17.4	13.7	15.0	13.5	−4.7	1.9	−10.3
3	Hong Kong	4.9	1.5	5.4	9.2	−21.1	29.1	69.0
4	Mexico	0.4	—[1]	4.4	5.0	−34.1	—[2]	12.9
5	Commonwealth of Independent States	NA	NA	—[1]	3.0	NA	NA	—[2]
	Total top 5	24.5	16.2	42.6	48.0	−8.0	21.4	12.3
6	Taiwan	3.8	0.1	3.2	3.0	−57.3	—[2]	−4.6
7	United Kingdom	0.3	0.3	1.2	2.5	−1.3	32.0	—[2]
8	Brazil	NA	NA	0.9	2.0	NA	NA	—[2]
9	Argentina	NA	NA	0.2	1.7	NA	NA	—
10	Trust Territories of Pacific	0.9	1.1	1.4	1.3	5.7	3.7	−3.2
	Total top 10	29.5	17.7	49.5	58.5	−9.7	22.9	18.3
	Other Countries	5.7	4.1	12.0	14.8	−6.3	23.9	23.5
	Total U.S. beer exports	35.2	21.8	61.5	73.3	−9.1%	23.1%	19.3%

Notes:
1. Less than 50,000 gallons.
2. Excludes shipments to Puerto Rico and U.S. possessions and armed forces overseas.

Source: *IMPACT DATABANK—1992 Edition,* Table 2-HH, p. 71.

board and to swap six executives for two-year tours of duty. John H. Purnell, Chairman and CEO of Anheuser-Busch International, Inc., said, "We are seeking equity positions in other brewers that will make a significant impact on the growth of our company." He further stated that "Modelo holds a 51% share of the Mexican beer market, which is growing faster than the U.S. market."[52] The negotiations lasted almost two years.

Marketing and Advertising

Anheuser-Busch, probably the largest sponsor of sporting events, racing vehicles, and broadcasting, has affiliated its beers with sports for years (see Exhibit 20.15). In 1993, Anheuser-Busch is expected to announce that the company will become the fifth company to become a national sponsor of the 1996 Summer Olympic Games in Atlanta. The other four are Home Depot, IBM, Sara Lee, and NationsBank. The sponsor fee will be approximately $40 million.

EXHIBIT 20.15 **Sports Affiliation and Sponsorships: Anheuser-Busch Companies, Inc.**

Sport	Event	Sport	Event
Budweiser		**Bud Light**	
Horse Racing	Irish Derby Breeders' Cup Budweiser International	Powerboat Racing	Powerboat Racing Team
		Bowling	ABC Masters; Bud Light Hall of Fame PBA Events
Hydroplane Racing	Miss Budweiser	Triathlons	Bud Light Triathlons Series
CART/Indy Car	Truesports Indy Car	IMSA	Bud Light Jugar
Drag Racing	Budweiser King Top Fuel Dragster	Pool/Darts	Bud Light Pool and Dart Leagues
		Busch	
NASCAR	Junior Johnson Ford	NASCAR	Official Beer of NASCAR Busch Pole Award Busch Clash
PGA Golf	Anheuser-Busch Golf Classic		
Olympics	Corporate Sponsor Olympic Job Opportunities Program	**Michelob**	
Boxing	Golden Globes Top-Rated Pad Bouts	Golf	Golf Advisory Staff
Soccer	U.S. National Team		
Shooting	Series of State Trap Skeet Shoots across the Country		
Waterskiing	Bud Water Ski Tour		
Beach Sports	Budweiser Pro Surfing Tour Bud Pro Beach Volleyball Team Bud Pro Jetski Team		
Skiing	Bud Mogul Tour Bud Ski Challenge		

Source: Anheuser-Busch Companies, Inc., *Fact Book, 1992/1993*, p. 24.

The beer industry spent more than $751 million in 1992 and $659 million in 1991 on advertising (see Exhibit 20.16). The 1992 increase of some $92 million was preceded by two years of cutbacks. Anheuser-Busch increased its budget by $18,883,000, or 7.1%, but "deep pockets" Miller Brewing increased its budget by $54,184,500, or 29.2%. Combined, the two companies increased their total advertising budgets by $73,067,500, or 16.2%. The combined advertising budgets of Anheuser-Busch and Miller were $524,955,500, or 69% of the industry total of $751,221,500. Coors' budget increased by $7,468,600, or 6.1%. Stroh Brewery increased its budget by $10,949,800, or 70.4%. The largest advertising budget increase by an imported beer company was for Van Munching & Company, Inc., a Dutch corporation, which increased its budget by $5,546,900, or 40.8%. But overall, the imported beer companies continued to cut their advertising budgets: in 1991, their combined budgets were $42 million, which represented an 8.7% reduction from 1990.

EXHIBIT 20.16

Beer Media Advertising
(Dollar amounts in thousands)

A. TOP 10 BEER MEDIA ADVERTISERS

Rank	Brewer/Importer	1990	1991
1	Anheuser-Busch, Inc.	$266,329.6	$285,212.6
2	Miller Brewing Company (Philip Morris)	185,557.9	239,742.4
3	Coors Brewing Company	121,825.7	129,294.3
4	The Stroh Brewery Company	15,563.7	26,513.5
5	Van Munching & Company, Inc.	13,592.3	19,139.2
6	G. Heileman Brewing Company[1]	11,309.5	14,331.8
7	Molson Breweries USA, Inc.	10,907.5	8,202.6
8	S & P Company	5,534.7	7,459.0
9	Dribeck Importers, Inc.	8,137.1	5,946.6
10	Labatt's USA, Inc.	5,075.4	5,246.4
	Total top 10	643,833.1	741,088.4
	Other brewers/importers	15,511.8	10,133.1
	Total beer advertising[2]	$659,344.9	$751,221.5

B. SHARE OF BEER ADVERTISING EXPENDITURES BY MEDIUM

Medium	1975	1990	1991
Network television	39.3%	39.5%	40.6%
Spot television	33.0	29.6	25.9
Syndicated television	NA	5.4	7.2
Cable television	—	5.3	5.2
Spot radio	17.3	9.9	9.5
Network radio	1.1	0.5	0.1
Total broadcast	90.7	90.2	88.4
Magazines	3.2	4.6	4.4
Newspapers	4.3	2.1	2.5
Newspaper supplements	0.4	0.1	0.5
Outdoor	1.4	3.0	4.2
Total print and outdoor	9.3	9.8	11.6
Total[1]	100.0%	100.0%	100.0%

Note: 1. Addition of columns may not agree because of rounding.

Source: *IMPACT DATABANK—1992 Edition,* Table 6-F, p. 220.

Change		Share of Total	
Dollars	Percentage	1990	1991
$18,883.0	7.1%	40.4%	38.0%
54,184.5	29.2	28.1	31.9
7,468.6	6.1	18.5	17.2
10,949.8	70.4	2.4	3.5
5,546.9	40.8	2.1	2.5
3,022.3	26.7	1.7	1.9
−2,704.6	−24.8	1.7	1.1
1,924.3	34.8	0.8	1.0
−2,190.5	−26.9	1.2	0.8
171.0	3.4	0.8	0.7
97,255.3	15.1	97.6	98.7
−5,378.7	34.7	2.4	1.3
$91,876.6	13.9%	100.0%	100.0%

Notes: 1. Excludes Pittsburgh Brewing Company. 2. Addition of columns may not agree because of rounding.

Sources: *IMPACT DATABANK—1992 Edition,* Table 6-L, p. 223.

Beer companies prefer broadcast media to all other forms of advertising (see Exhibit 20.15). They spent 88.4% of their advertising dollars on broadcast media; television alone—both network and spot—represents 66.5% of their entire advertising expenditures. A corporate executive at Anheuser-Busch said, "Our competitors continue to focus the majority of their television advertising in sports sponsorships, and I would think that would continue to be a competitive area."[53]

The alcoholic beverage industry spent the following amounts (in millions of dollars) on advertising.

Category	1991	1990	1985
Beer	$751.2	$659.3	$770.0
Coolers	31.2	30.9	75.2
Distilled spirits	277.7	290.6	303.0
Wine	72.8	74.2	145.5
Total	$1,133.0	$1,055.0	$1,293.7

Note: Addition of columns may not agree because of rounding.

The industry's expenditures on advertising have declined over the period 1985–1991. In 1991, beer companies spent $.11 to advertise each gallon of beer; cooler producers spent $.35 a gallon; distilled spirits makers spent $.71 a gallon; and the wine producers spent $.18 a gallon.

The following table shows advertising expenditures by the top five selling beer manufacturers' on a *per barrel* basis. Some of the wide differences in a given year reflect the introduction of new beer products.

Rank	Brand	1991	1990	1985
1	Budweiser	$2.11	$1.80	$2.07
2	Miller	4.05	3.56	4.95
3	Bud Light	10.17	4.76	5.23
4	Coors Light	3.92	5.98	5.46
5	Busch	4.17	2.00	.75

Anheuser-Busch, Inc.'s Promotional Products Group markets approximately 5,000 different items at any one time. They include items such as caps, glassware, mugs, clothing, and key chains, all bearing the A-B Eagle, Clydesdale, or beer brand logos. Each year, more than 1,500 new promotion items are created and authorized.

Overall, Anheuser-Busch Companies, Inc., spent $747,600,000, $632,600,000, and $613,600,000 on advertising in 1992, 1991, and 1990, respectively.

Distribution Channels

The company distributes its beer in the United States and the Caribbean through a network of ten company-owned wholesale operations that employ approximately 1,600 people and about 900 independently owned wholesale companies that employ approximately 30,000 people. The Anheuser-Busch Wholesaler Advisory Panel, a representative group of wholesalers, meets regularly with the company's top management. Canadian and European distribution is handled through special arrangements with foreign brewing companies, including joint venture and ownership.

The Anheuser-Busch Investment Capital Corporation, a subsidiary company, was formed in 1984 to share equity positions with qualified partners in Anheuser-Busch, Inc., distributorships. This subsidiary allows operating general partners to function as independent wholesalers while increasing their equity and building toward total ownership. Anheuser-Busch Investment Capital Corporation plays a key role in strengthening the brewer–wholesaler team. Currently, the company has invested in 22 wholesaler operations.[54]

When Busch was "asked if strong brewers and beer products make strong wholesalers or strong wholesalers make strong brewers, Busch lays the 'chicken-or-egg theory' to rest, noting succinctly, 'It takes both.'"[55] Henry King, former President of the United States Brewing Association, recalls, "I've been with August when we've been driving along and he's spotted an A-B distributor's truck. He pulled up behind it and spoke into his little cassette to dictate a memo to his secretary to send a letter of compliment to the wholesaler because his truck was beautifully cleaned and everything. Had the truck been dirty, there would have been a letter reprimanding him as well."[56] Busch counts on wholesalers as "one of our most important assets, who provide critical service to retailers. Personal service is a key . . . they are the front-line merchandisers for the entire system and . . . indispensable to the system."[57]

Wholesalers are responsible for the marketing, sales, and distribution of the company's beers within their assigned exclusive territories. Wholesalers implement programs to develop brand awareness for all Anheuser-Busch products and provide the retailer with the finest service in the industry in order to ensure that the customer receives only the freshest beer.[58] These exclusive wholesale-distribution rights have been questioned by congressional committees. Only the state of Indiana forbids the exclusive distribution contracts, and 27 states require the contract. Anheuser-Busch always lobbies for no change in the exclusive contract. The U.S. Brewers Association and the National Beer Wholesale Association also lobby for this contract, and any other legislation impacting on the industry and the membership interest.

"Together with our wholesalers," Busch stated, "we share a commitment to provide the consumer with the highest quality, best tasting, and freshest beer products through the three-tier system, in which the brewer, wholesaler, and retailer each play an important role." He went on to say, "Strong products, suppliers, wholesalers, and service equal retailer profitability. Quality to the consumer and product presentation equal sales 'success.'"[59]

Production Facilities

Anheuser-Busch operates 12 breweries in ten states, with an annual capacity of 85.1 million barrels of beer (see Exhibit 20.17). A thirteenth brewery at Cartersville, Georgia, is scheduled to open in 1993. This six-million-barrel-capacity plant will cost approximately $300 million. The expansion by Anheuser-Busch is in contrast to the other brewers, who are and have been consolidating capacity. Busch eyes the company's "expansion as necessary for 'market penetration and growth,' never blinking from Anheuser-Busch's projected 50% share by the mid-1990's."[60] Anheuser-Busch has developed an extensive modernization and expansion program for all its operations and plants.

The company completed a 3.6-million-barrel expansion at the Newark brewery in 1990, and expanded capacity at the Tampa brewery by 800,000 barrels, to 2.7 million. Mini-expansions were completed at six other plants, adding approximately 2.5 million barrels of capacity.[61]

Capital expenditures for the company's three segments were $737,200,000 in 1992, an increase of $34,700,000 over 1991. Capital expenditures were down from 1989's high of $1,076,700,000. The maintenance costs were $403,000,000, in 1992 and $405,500,000 in 1991.

Talking about the cost of ingredients to make beer (barley, rice, corn, hops, and others), Busch said, "We pay premium to the market because we demand the highest quality ingredients that money can buy. We have the highest cost of

EXHIBIT 20.17

Production Facilities: Anheuser-Busch Companies, Inc.
(Annual shipping capacity in millions of barrels)

Brewery	Year Opened	Site Size (Acres)	Annual Shipping Capacity
St. Louis, Missouri	1880	100	13.3
Newark, New Jersey	1951	87	10.2
Los Angeles, California	1954	95	11.7
Tampa, Florida	1959	317	2.7
Houston, Texas	1966	136	9.3
Columbus, Ohio	1968	252	6.7
Jacksonville, Florida	1969	867	7.2
Merrimack, New Hampshire	1970	300	3.2
Williamsburg, Virginia	1972	144	9.2
Fairfield, California	1976	200	4.0
Baldwinsville, New York	1982	211	8.2
Fort Collins, Colorado	1988	1,130	6.0
Total capacity in 1992			91.7
Cartersville, Georgia[1]	1993	1,700	6.7
Total capacity in 1993			98.4

Note:
1. Scheduled to be on line in 1993.

Source: Anheuser-Busch Companies, Inc., *Fact Book 1992/1993*, p. 1.

ingredients of anybody in the brewing industry. I can prove it to you. We [also] must make sure we are the lowest cost producer."[62] Busch went on to say, "We're trying to provide a balance of the highest liquidity costs in the industry with the most efficient production possible." He continued, "Quality comes first."[63] Busch's statements tie directly into the two primary reasons the company gives for Anheuser-Busch's outstanding record:

> Quality—first, and most importantly, Anheuser-Busch believes in quality. Quality is never sacrificed for economic reasons—or for any other reason. The company is firmly convinced that its belief in and strict adherence to quality is the fundamental, irreplaceable ingredient in its successful performance for more than 100 years. That quality is there for everyone to see, to taste, to experience, and to enjoy. "Somebody still cares about quality" is more than a corporate slogan at Anheuser-Busch. It is a way of life.
>
> Along with quality, Anheuser-Busch is committed to growth and innovation. That commitment has seen the company through some rough times—two World Wars, Prohibition, the Great Depression. While hundreds of breweries succumbed to difficult times like these and closed their doors, Anheuser-Busch survived and grew. During these trying periods, the company devised innovative ways to use its resources, its people, and its expertise. But in good times as well as bad, the company has always realized that while you have to do the best you can in the present, you must always keep your eyes turned toward the future. That is the way to greatness.[64]

Productivity continues to be an integral part of Anheuser-Busch's growth strategy, and the company has received many productivity awards over the years. In 1985, Anheuser-Busch, Inc., received the Excellence in Productivity Award from the Institute of Industrial Engineers because of the company's continued commitment to reducing waste and increasing efficiency. Also, the Williamsburg Brewery received the U.S. Senate Productivity Award. Since 1980, the company has generated more than $720 million in expense reductions. Anheuser-Busch also is deeply involved in the environmental issue of recycling waste materials. In 1979 it formed Anheuser-Busch Recycling Corporation. In 1992, this subsidiary recycled more than 550 million pounds of aluminum, 16 billion cans, 35 million pounds of paper goods, and 81 million pounds of glass.

The beer industry has suffered from excess plant capacity over the past decade. For example, in 1984, Miller mothballed its Trenton, New Jersey, plant because of excess capacity in its system. Anheuser-Busch's plant capacity utilization factor is normally above 94%—tops in the industry. Industrywide average plant utilization has varied from approximately 75% to 86% over the past decade. During that time, many plants were closed. In 1991, the seven leading U.S. breweries (not including Miller's mothballed Trenton, New Jersey, plant) in terms of capacity utilization were:

Brewery	**Capacity Utilization**
Miller Brewing	96.7%
Anheuser-Busch	94.0
Coors Brewing Company	83.0
The Stroh Brewing Company	82.7
G. Heileman Brewing Company	77.3
S&P Company	59.3
The Genessee Brewing Company	55.0
Average utilization	88.4%

Legislation, Litigation, and Special Issues

In recent years, Anheuser-Busch has become more active in monitoring and taking positions on issues that could have a major impact on the company. Management expanded the Industry and Government Affairs Division in order to identify such issues and to respond to them with specific programs.

The National Minimum Drinking Age Act of 1984 granted the federal government the authority to withhold federal highway funds from states that failed to raise the legal drinking age to 21 by 1986. Although several states contested the act, all the states currently have a 21-year-old minimum drinking age.

Specific Legislative Issues

1. Excise Tax. In 1992, Anheuser-Busch paid $1.67 billion in state and federal excise taxes. The company "believes that excise taxes discriminate against both the industries involved and consumers.[65]

2. **Warning Labels.** In 1988, Congress passed legislation requiring a warning statement to appear on all alcoholic beverage containers by November 1989. The two-part statement read: "Government Warning: (1) According to the Surgeon General, women should not drink alcoholic beverages during pregnancy because of the risks of birth defects. (2) Consumption of alcoholic beverages impairs your ability to drive a car or operate machinery and may cause health problems." The legislation requires only this two-part statement and restricts state governments from requiring any additional statements.[66]
3. **Deposit Laws.** The company "remains firmly opposed to forced deposit legislation.[67]
4. **Advertising and Marketing Restrictions.** There are proposals to ban beer and wine advertising from radio and television. Also, some groups are calling for the restriction on the brewing industry's ability to advertise or promote beer and wine at sporting events. Anheuser-Busch "strongly opposes such restrictions."[68]

Concentration and the Possibilities of Antitrust Review

Leonard Weiss of the University of Wisconsin at Madison developed a way to delineate the impact of mergers on an industry's structure. Using his methodology, Kenneth Elzinga of the University of Virginia found that mergers accounted for a negligible amount of the concentration occurring in the brewing industry. In fact, concentration trends in the brewing industry are rather unique in that most of the increased concentration was brought about by internal expansion rather than by merger or acquisition. Strict enforcement of the antitrust laws by the Department of Justice is one reason that mergers have accounted for such a small share of the increase in concentration. The Department of Justice, nevertheless, through its enforcement may have promoted the result it was trying to prevent—increased national concentration. With the elimination of the merger route, national brewers were forced to expand internally. They built large new breweries, which were more efficient than the older, smaller ones. If mergers had been permitted, the national firms might have acquired old small breweries and might have grown more slowly than they actually did.

In analyzing the effect of a proposed horizontal merger on competition in the brewing industry, Antitrust Chief William F. Baxter was said to rely on the Herfindahl Index. Named for Orris Herfindahl, an economist, the index is based on the premise that market leaders have even greater economic power in an industry than can be assumed by simply looking at their market shares. The index is thus a measure of industry concentration, obtained by summing the square of all participating firms' market shares. An industry in which one firm had 100% of the market would have an index of $(1)(100^2)$, or 10,000. An industry with ten firms, each having 10% of the market, would have an index of $(10)(10^2)$, or 1,000. In April 1982, the beer industry's Herfindahl Index was 1,600. Any merger that increased the index by 75 points was a likely candidate for rejection. Other measures also have been used. For example, the level of concentration in a local market would be a serious consideration.[69]

A knowledgeable beer market analyst has wondered whether the Department of Justice will take or propose antitrust action as Anheuser-Busch's market share approaches 50%. Growth over the past decade, from 28.2% in 1980 to 44.2% in 1991, has come in a maturing industry. If Anheuser-Busch had tried to grow by mergers to achieve its 50% market share, the Department of Justice probably would have rejected the mergers (under the Herfindahl Index). A possibility exists that one of the remaining small brewers could ask the Department of Justice for protection or relief under the antitrust laws.

Human Resources Management

In 1983, management established Anheuser-Busch's Office of Corporate Human Resources to focus on human resource activities and issues. Human resource planning has become an integral component of the business planning process at all levels of the organization.

The company's philosophy concerning its approximately 44,871 employees (declining employment) is that all employees are to be treated with courtesy and respect. The company tries to foster open, two-way communication. Labor–management committees function on a national level to involve employees in issues and decisions that directly affect them and their working conditions. Additionally, in 1985, Anheuser-Busch, Inc., introduced "The New A-BI," a communication program designed to encourage employee participation in productivity improvement and cost reduction.

The International Brotherhood of Teamsters represents some 13,838 employees in Anheuser-Busch Companies, Inc., and 23 other unions represent another 10,277 employees. The current labor agreement expires February 28, 1994. The company initiated an employee stock ownership plan (ESOP) in 1989 and considers its employee relations to be good.

Total quality management (TQM) is a major focus of the company's training and development programs. The emphasis is on creating experience(s) with TQM principles that focus on service quality and improved profitability by satisfying all customer product and service needs, thereby maximizing the value added by all employees and continually improving Anheuser-Busch's system.[70]

The company initiated TQM in 1992 to build on its industry leadership and quality reputation. Anheuser-Busch management believes that TQM will result in higher customer satisfaction, which will translate to larger market share and profits, higher productivity, and greater employee empowerment. Busch said that "empowering our employees to meet or exceed customers' needs most effectively can be best achieved through a total quality management (TQM) approach" and that the company is in a "position to take advantage of this new 'value decade' . . . because of our established strengths. . . ."[71]

On September 21, 1992, Miller Brewing Company announced that John N. MacDonough had become the new President and Chief Operating Officer of the company, replacing Warren Dunn. Dunn had become President and CEO a year earlier, was appointed Chairman when MacDonough was hired, and remains CEO. MacDonough had been Executive Vice-President for Marketing in Anheuser-Busch's

International Division. The appointment caught Anheuser-Busch executives and the rest of the industry by surprise.

The Anheuser-Busch Ethics Manual contains the company's policy statement concerning standards of business conduct. It provides guidelines for employees to follow in conducting their day-to-day business activities in order to avoid any situation involving potentially illegal or improper acts. Areas covered by the policy statement include political contributions, trade practices, conflicts of interest, antitrust practices, and compliance with securities laws.[72]

Finance

In 1992, Anheuser-Busch Companies, Inc., completed its most successful year in its 150-year history (see Exhibits 20.18, 20.19, and 20.20). During the 1980s, the company's net sales increased by 187.7% ($3,295,400,000 to $9,481,300,000). Net income rose by 346.6% ($171,800,000 to $767,200,00), gross profits increased by 332.3% ($741,500,800 to $3,205,500,000), and total assets increased by 268.4% ($2,449,700,000 to $9,025,700,000).

In 1992, Anheuser-Busch's sales increased by 3.4% to $13,062,300,000, and net income declined by $22,300,000, or 2.4%. The decline in net income was the result of implementing FAS 106, which changed the accounting rules for post-retirement benefits. This one-time charge was $76,700,000. The company increased its line of credit to $800 million, allowing it to select from various loan arrangements with different maturity dates.

The cost of products and services as a percentage of net sales has changed from 63.8% in 1992 to 65.0% in 1991 to 66.0% in 1990. For 1992, 1991, and 1990, the company's federal and state excise taxes were $1.67 billion, $1.64 billion, and $868.1 million, respectively. On January 31, 1991, the federal excise tax on beer was increased by 100%.

Fortune magazine recognized the company's outstanding financial performance by naming Anheuser-Busch one of the 20 most profitable companies over the past decade. Anheuser-Busch also was rated the single best stock overall for the individual investor for the past ten years in a book published by Longman Press.

The company has paid a dividend for 59 consecutive years. During this period, the stock split seven times, and three stock dividends were paid. On November 26, 1989, Anheuser-Busch Companies, Inc., registered with the Securities and Exchange Commission more than 8 million shares of common stock that may be sold periodically by the heirs of August Busch, Jr., who died in September 1989. The secondary share offer represents about 8.4% of the company's outstanding common stock. Before Busch's death, about 23% of the company was closely controlled—12% by Busch, 11% by Centerre Trust Company of St. Louis, and 1% by other directors.

During 1989, the company established an employee stock ownership plan (ESOP) for its salaried and hourly employees (see Exhibit 20.19). Under the ESOP and other stock ownership plans, employees eventually will own approximately 10% of the company's shares.

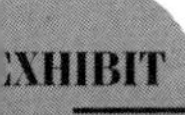

EXHIBIT 20.18

Consolidated Statement of Income: Anheuser-Busch Companies, Inc., and Subsidiaries

(Dollar amounts in millions, except per share data)

Years Ending December 31	1992	1991	1990
Sales	$13,062.3	$12,634.2	$11,611.7
Less federal and state excise taxes	1,668.6	1,637.9	868.1
Net sales	11,393.7	10,996.3	10,743.6
Cost of products and services	7,309.1	7,148.7	7,093.5
Gross profit	4,084.6	3,847.6	3,650.1
Marketing, distribution and administrative expenses	2,308.9	2,126.1	2,051.1
Operating income	1,775.7	1,721.5	1,599.0
Other income and expenses			
Interest expense	(199.6)	(238.5)	(283.0)
Interest capitalized	47.7	46.5	54.6
Interest income	7.1	9.2	7.0
Other income (expense), net	(15.7)	(18.1)	(25.5)
Income before income taxes	1,615.2	1,520.6	1,352.1
Provision for income taxes			
Current	561.9	479.1	429.9
Deferred	59.1	101.7	79.8
	621.0	580.8	509.7
Net income, before cumulative effect of accounting changes	994.2	939.8	842.4
Cumulative effect of changes in the method of accounting for post-retirement benefits (FAS 106) and income taxes (FAS 109), net of tax benefit of $186.4 million	(76.7)	—	—
Net income	$ 917.5	$ 939.8	$ 842.4
Primary earnings per share			
Net income, before cumulative effect	$ 3.48	$ 3.26	$ 2.96
Cumulative effect of accounting changes	(.26)	—	—
Net income	$ 3.22	$ 3.26	$ 2.96
Fully diluted earnings per share	(.26)	—	—
Net income, before cumulative effect	$ 3.46	$ 3.25	$ 2.95
Cumulative effect of accounting changes	(.26)	—	—
Net income	$ 3.20	$ 3.25	$ 2.95

Source: Anheuser-Busch Companies, Inc., *1992 Annual Report,* p. 46.

EXHIBIT 20.19

Consolidated Balance Sheet: Anheuser-Busch Companies, Inc., and Subsidiaries

(Dollar amounts in millions)

Years Ending December 31	1992	1991
Assets		
Current assets		
Cash and marketable securities	$ 215.0	$ 97.3
Accounts and notes receivable, less allowance for doubtful accounts of $4.9 in 1992 and $5.5 in 1991	649.8	654.8
Inventories		
Raw materials and supplies	417.7	397.2
Work in process	88.7	92.5
Finished goods	154.3	145.9
Total	660.7	635.6
Other current assets	290.3	240.0
Total current assets	1,815.8	1,627.7
Investments and other assets		
Investments in and advances to affiliated companies	171.6	116.9
Investment properties	164.8	159.9
Deferred charges and other non-current assets	356.3	365.6
Excess of cost over net assets of acquired businesses, net	505.7	519.9
Total	1,198.4	1,162.3
Plant and equipment		
Land	273.3	308.9
Buildings	3,295.2	3,027.8
Machinery and equipment	7,086.9	6,583.9
Construction in progress	729.7	669.0
	11,385.1	10,589.6
Accumulated depreciation	(3,861.4)	(3,393.1)
Total	7,523.7	7,196.5
Total assets	$10,537.9	$ 9,986.5

(continued)

During the next five years (1993–1997), capital expenditures are expected to exceed $4.0 billion. At the end of 1992, the company had spent $2.3 billion. The company is not opposed to long-term financing for some of its capital programs, but cash flow from operations will remain the principal source of funds to support these programs. For short-term capital requirements, the company had access to an $800 million bank line of credit. The company currently has an AA bond rating.

In 1992, the beer and beer-related segment had sales of $8,609,600,000 (75.5%) and operating income of $1,645,400,000 (92.7%); the food products segment had sales of $2,131,100,000 (18.7%) and operating income of $75,400,000 (4.2%); and the entertainment segment had sales of $684,300,000

EXHIBIT 20.19

Consolidated Balance Sheet: Anheuser-Busch Companies, Inc., and Subsidiaries *(continued)*

(Dollar amounts in millions)

Years Ending December 31	1992	1991
Liabilities and Shareholders' Equity		
Current liabilities		
Accounts payable	$ 737.4	$ 709.8
Accrued salaries, wages and benefits	257.3	223.3
Accrued interest payable	52.4	58.5
Due to customers for returnable containers	48.2	44.5
Accrued taxes, other than income taxes	117.0	110.9
Estimated income taxes	38.8	45.2
Other current liabilities	208.7	210.6
Total current liabilities	1,459.8	1,402.8
Postretirement benefits	538.3	—
Long-term debt	2,642.5	2,644.9
Deferred income taxes	1,276.9	1,500.7
Common stock and other shareholders' equity		
Common stock, $1.00 par value, authorized 400,000 shares	341.3	338.5
Capital in excess of par value	762.9	654.5
Retained earnings	5,794.9	5,209.8
Foreign currency translation adjustment	(1.4)	20.7
Total	6,897.7	6,223.5
Treasury stock, at cost	(1,842.9)	(1,324.2)
ESOP debt guarantee offset	(434.4)	(461.2)
Total	4,620.4	4,438.1
Commitments and contingencies	—	—
Total liabilities and shareholders' equity	$10,537.9	$ 9,986.5

(6.0%) and operating income of $54,900,000 (see Exhibit 20.6). A former Anheuser-Busch executive attributes the poor performance of the non-beer segments to the fact that they were managed by beer-oriented people. "They continue to use 'beer guys' on the diversifications. It's a big mistake."[73] The company fully hedges its foreign currency exposure for interest and principal payments on its foreign currency denominated debt.[74]

A beverage analyst wondered about the impact of the failure of management in not meeting the company's stated objective of 50% market share in the early 1990s. He said, "This is the first time that Augie has not met a stated 'company objective.'" Another analyst said, "The international growth strategy will be more

EXHIBIT 20.20

Ten-Year Financial Summary—Consolidated Summary of Operations: Anheuser-Busch Companies, Inc

(Dollar amounts in millions, except per share and statistical data)

Years Ending December 31	1992	1991	1990	1989
Barrels sold	86.8	86.0	86.5	80.7
Sales	$13,062.3	$12,634.2	$11,611.7	$10,283.6
Federal and state excise taxes	1,668.6	1,637.9	868.1	802.3
Net sales	11,393.7	10,996.3	10,743.6	9,481.3
Cost of products and services	7,309.1	7,148.7	7,093.5	6,275.8
Gross profit	4,084.6	3,847.6	3,650.1	3,205.5
Marketing, distribution and administrative expenses	2,308.9	2,126.1	2,051.1	1,876.8
Operating income	1,775.7[1]	1,721.5	1,599.0	1,328.7
Interest expense	(199.6)	(238.5)	(283.0)	(177.9)
Interest capitalized	47.7	46.5	54.6	51.5
Interest income	7.1	9.2	7.0	12.6
Other income (expense), net	(15.7)	(18.1)	(25.5)	11.8
Gain on sale of Lafayette plant	—	—	—	—
Income before income taxes	1,615.2[1]	1,520.6	1,352.1	1,226.7
Income taxes	621.0	580.8	509.7	459.5
Net income, before cumulative effect of accounting changes	994.2[1]	939.8	842.4	767.2
Cumulative effect of changes in the method of accounting for postretirement benefits (FAS 106) and income taxes (FAS 109), net of tax benefit of $186.4 million	(76.7)	—	—	—
Net income	$ 917.5	$ 939.8	$ 842.4	$ 767.2
Primary earnings per share				
Net income before cumulative effect	$ 3.48[1]	$ 3.26	$ 2.96	$ 2.68
Cumulative effect of accounting changes	(.26)	—	—	—
Net income	$ 3.22	$ 3.26	$ 2.96	$ 2.68
Fully diluted earnings per share				
Net income before cumulative effect	$ 3.46[1]	$ 3.25	$ 2.95	$ 2.68
Cumulative effect of accounting changes	(.26)	—	—	—
Net income	$ 3.20	$ 3.25	$ 2.95	$ 2.68
Cash dividend paid				
Common stock	338.3	301.1	265.0	226.2
Per share	1.20	1.06	.94	.80
Preferred stock	—	—	—	—
Per share	—	—	—	—
Average number of common shares				
Primary	285.8	287.9	284.6	286.2
Fully diluted	290.8	292.9	289.7	286.2

Notes:

1. All per share information and average number of common shares data reflect the September 12, 1986 two-for-one stock split and the June 14, 1985 three-for-one stock split. All amounts reflect the acquisition of Campbell-Taggart, Inc., as of November 2, 1982, and acquisition of Sea World as of December 1, 1989. Financial information prior to 1988 has been restated to reflect the adoption in 1988 of Financial Accounting Standards No. 94, Consolidation of Majority-Owned Subsidiaries.
2. 1992 operating income, income before income taxes, net income and earnings per share reflect the 1992 adoption of the new Financial Accounting Standards pertaining to Postretirement Benefits (FAS 106) and

1988	1987	1986	1985	1984	1983	1982
78.5	76.1	72.3	68.0	64.0	60.5	59.1
$9,705.1	$9,110.4	$8,478.8	$7,756.7	$7,218.8	$6,714.7	$5,251.2
781.0	760.7	724.5	683.0	657.0	624.3	609.1
8,924.1	8,349.7	7,754.3	7,073.7	6,561.8	6,090.4	4,642.1
5,825.5	5,374.3	5,026.5	4,729.8	4,464.6	4,161.0	3,384.3
3,098.6	2,975.4	2,727.8	2,343.9	2,097.2	1,929.4	1,257.8
1,834.5	1,826.8	1,709.8	1,498.2	1,338.5	1,226.4	758.8
1,264.1	1,148.6	1,018.0	845.7	758.7	703.0	499.0
(141.6)	(127.5)	(99.9)	(96.5)	(106.0)	(115.4)	(93.2)
44.2	40.3	33.2	37.2	46.8	32.9	41.2
9.8	12.8	9.6	21.3	22.8	12.5	17.0
(16.4)	(9.9)	(13.6)	(23.3)	(29.6)	(14.8)	(5.8)
—	—	—	—	—	—	20.4
1,160.1	1,064.3	947.3[2]	784.4	692.7	618.2	478.6
444.2	449.6	429.3	340.7	301.2	270.2	191.3
715.9	614.7	518.0[2]	443.7	391.5	348.0	287.3[3]
—	—	—	—	—	—	—
$ 715.9	$ 614.7	$ 518.0[2]	$ 443.7	$ 391.5	$ 348.0	$ 287.3[3]
$ 2.45	$ 2.04	$ 1.69[2]	$ 1.42	$ 1.23	$ 1.08	$ 1.00[3]
—	—	—	—	—	—	—
$ 2.45	$ 2.04	$ 1.69[2]	$ 1.42	$ 1.23	$ 1.08	$ 1.00[3]
$ 2.45	$ 2.04	$ 1.69[2]	$ 1.42	$ 1.23	$ 1.08	$ 0.98[3]
—	—	—	—	—	—	—
$ 2.45	$ 2.04	$ 1.69[2]	$ 1.42	$ 1.23	$ 1.08	$ 0.98[3]
188.6	148.4	120.2	102.7	89.7	78.3	65.8
1.20	1.06	.94	.36[2,3]	.31[1,3]	.27	.23
—	20.1	26.9	27.0	27.0	29.7	—
—	3.23	3.60	3.60	3.60	3.60	—
292.2	301.5	306.6	312.6	317.4	321.0	288.6
292.2	301.5	306.6	312.6	317.4	321.0	294.5

Income Taxes (FAS 109). Excluding the financial impact of these Standards, 1992 operating income, income before income taxes, net income, and fully diluted earnings per share would have been $1,830.8, $1,676.0, $1,029.2, and $3.58, respectively.

3. Effective January 1, 1986, the company adopted the provisions of Financial Accounting Standards No. 87 (FAS 87), Employers' Accounting for Pensions. The financial effect of FAS 87 adoption was to increase 1986 income before taxes $45 million, net income $23 million, and earnings per share $.08.

profitable to the company over the next twenty years than 50% U.S. market objective. The market may have forced Augie's hand to go with the international growth strategy."

Notes

1. Richard Gibson, "Anheuser-Busch to Buy 18% Stake in Mexican Brewer," *Wall Street Journal* (March 23, 1993), p. B-4.
2. Ibid.
3. "August Busch III Names Beer Successor," *Beverage World* (May 1990), p. 10.
4. Anheuser-Busch Companies, Inc., *1989 Annual Report,* p. 1.
5. Ibid.
6. "August Busch III Names Beer Successor," p. 10.
7. Christy Marshall, "The Czar of Beers," *Business Month* (June 1988), p. 26.
8. Ibid.
9. Ibid.
10. Ibid.
11. "How Anheuser Brews Its Winners," *New York Times* (August 4, 1985), p. 28.
12. Ibid.
13. Larry Jabbonsky, "What Keeps Anheuser-Busch Hot?" *Beverage World* (September 1988), p. 22.
14. "How Anheuser Brews Its Winners," p. 28.
15. Jabbonsky, p. 22.
16. Ibid., p. 26.
17. "How Anheuser Brews Its Winners," p. 28.
18. Jabbonsky, p. 22.
19. Rick Desloge, "August IV Puts His Stamp on Budweiser," *St. Louis Business Journal* (August 24, 1992), pp. B7-B8.
20. Cyndee Miller, "Michelob Ads Feature Women—and They're Not Wearing Bikinis," *Marketing News* (March 2, 1992), p. 2.
21. Desloge, p. B-8.
22. Ibid.
23. Anheuser-Busch Companies, Inc., *1989 Annual Report,* pp. 58, 66–67.
24. Anheuser-Busch Companies, Inc., *Fact Book, 1989/1990,* p. 3.
25. David Szymansi, "HBJ Writes Final Chapter on Theme Parks," *Tampa Tribune* (September 24, 1989), pp. 1–3.
26. Brian O'Donnell, "What's Next?" *Tampa Tribune* (January 1, 1990), pp. 1D–2D.
27. Ibid.
28. Gibson, p. B-4.
29. Anheuser-Busch Companies, Inc., *Form 10-K Report* (1988), p . 4.
30. Anheuser-Busch Companies, Inc., *Form 10-K Report* (1989), p . 4; Anheuser-Busch Companies, Inc., *Fact Book, 1986/1987,* p. 16.
31. Gibson, p. B-4.
32. Rick Desloge, "Analyst: A-B May Be Near to Exiting Bakery Business," *St. Louis Business Journal* (June 8, 1992), p. F-14.
33. Gibson, p. B-4.
34. Kevin Doyle, "Snack Makers Feel the Crunch," *Incentive* (November 1991), p. 51.
35. Ibid.
36. Ibid.
37. Ibid., p. 52.
38. Gibson, p. B-4.
39. Ibid.
40. Desloge, p. F-14.
41. Anheuser-Busch Companies, Inc., *Fact Book, 1992/1993,* p. 16.
42. Anheuser-Busch Companies, Inc., *1992 Annual Report,* p. 8.
43. Ibid.
44. Erik Gunn, "Prices Get Drafted in Latest Beer Wars," *Milwaukee Journal* (January 12, 1992), Suppl. p. 16.
45. James P. Miller, "Anheuser Plans Pretax Charge of $565 Million," *Wall Street Journal* (September 23, 1993), p. 4.
46. *IMPACT DATABANK—1992 Edition,* p. 95.
47. Anheuser-Busch Companies, Inc., *1992 Annual Report,* p. 13.
48. Anheuser-Busch Companies, Inc., *Fact Book, 1992/1993,* p. 4.
49. Ibid.
50. Gibson, p. B-4.
51. Ibid.
52. Ibid.
53. *IMPACT DATABANK—1992 Edition,* Table 6-B, p. 217.
54. Anheuser-Busch Companies, Inc., *1992 Annual Report,* p. 13.
55. Jabbonsky, p. 28.

56. Ibid.
57. Ibid.
58. Anheuser-Busch Companies, Inc., *Fact Book, 1992/1993,* p. 2.
59. Jabbonsky, p. 28.
60. Ibid.
61. Anheuser-Busch Companies, Inc., *Fact Book, 1990/1991,* p. 3.
62. Jabbonsky, p. 28.
63. Ibid.
64. Anheuser-Busch Companies, Inc., *Fact Book, 1990/1991,* p. 3.
65. Ibid.
66. Anheuser-Busch Companies, Inc., *Fact Book, 1992/1993,* p. 2.
67. Ibid.
68. Ibid.
69. Anheuser-Busch Companies, Inc., *1989 Annual Report,* p. 19.
70. Jabbonsky, p. 28.
71. Ibid.
72. Anheuser-Busch Companies, Inc., *Fact Book, 1990/1991,* p. 3.
73. Marshall, p. 30.
74. Anheuser-Busch Companies, Inc., *1992 Annual Report,* p. 3.

CASE 21

Celestial Seasonings, Inc.

Ram Subramanian and Pradeep Gopalakrishna

As Morris J. (Mo) Siegel looked up from the sheaf of papers he was reading, his eyes caught the portrait of Abraham Lincoln juxtaposed between paintings depicting the covers of the company's herb tea products, and he thought of the task at hand. He had returned to Celestial Seasonings as its Chairman and CEO nine months ago, and it was now 1992. The company that he had created had undergone many changes in the interim. After being owned by Kraft for four years, its management team brought back the company with the help of a venture capital firm. The buyout had been funded largely by debt, which left little money for expansion and new product development. Also, the industry had undergone changes, principally the increased market power of competitors such as Lipton.

Next week was the annual management retreat that Siegel had started when he founded the company. The retreat was an informal, free-for-all brainstorming session where important decisions concerning the company's future were made. The current session was the first since Siegel's return to the company. As Siegel leaned back and thought about the decisions to be made, he reflected on the company and the long and winding path it had taken from its early days.

Company History[1]

The birth of Celestial Seasonings was almost simultaneous with the birth of the herb tea industry in the United States. In 1968, Mo Siegel, along with his then wife, Peggy, friend Wyck Hay, and Wyck's girlfriend Lucinda Ziesing, roamed the mountains around Colorado picking herbs to make tea. Soon they picked enough herbs to fill 10,000 muslin bags with what was called Mo's 36 Herb Tea, which they sold to the Grainery, a health food store in Boulder, Colorado. They called their enterprise "Celestial Seasonings," after Lucinda Ziesing's nickname. The initial capital came from the sale of Wyck Hay's Volkswagen for $800. At this time, Wyck's brother John Hay joined the company. In 1970, they established the company's first production facilities in a barn in Boulder. Shortly thereafter, John Hay and Mo Siegel incorporated the company and served as co-presidents. The demand for their products led to Mo Siegel's having to travel worldwide to purchase herbs because the local supply was inadequate. John Hay eventually opted out of the company's management in 1978, though he retained his investment in the company.

This case was prepared by Professor Ram Subramanian of the F.E. Seidman School of Business at Grand Valley State University and Professor Pradeep Gopalakrishna, of the Department of Marketing and International Business at Hofstra University. This case was presented at the 1992 North American Case Research Meeting. This case was edited by T.L. Wheelen and J.D. Hunger for this book. Reprinted by permission of the authors.

Initially, the company sold its products in health food stores. But the health craze of the 1970s swept the company along, and soon the company's products began appearing on supermarket shelves. Revenues grew from $3 million in 1976 to $27 million in 1984. Meanwhile, the heady growth brought with it an increasing need for capital. When General Mills offered to buy the company for $8.3 million in 1979, the then Vice-President of Finance, Barney Feinblum, suggested that the company sell stock to its employees instead. When even this approach was inadequate to fund its needs, the company decided to make a public offering of its stock in 1983. However, just four days after the offering, disaster struck. A woman who consumed the equivalent of 16 cups of one of Celestial Seasonings' teas in one sitting suffered an adverse reaction. Medical investigation indicated that the tea contained toxins. Apparently, the pickers of a particular batch of herbs (from Eastern Europe) had mistakenly included herbs from a toxic plant that were not detected by the company's quality control process. This adverse publicity led to a withdrawal of the public offering, and the company's search for capital continued.

In 1984, Kraft, Inc., bought Celestial Seasonings for $40 million and put it, along with other niche players such as Lender's Bagels and Tombstone Pizza, into a separate division. Kraft invested money in advertising and product development, and Celestial's sales increased to $45 million by 1988. However, it soon became clear to Feinblum (who stayed on as Celestial's CEO after Mo Siegel departed) that Kraft was not happy with Celestial. Although Celestial was profitable under Kraft, it was simply too small to make an impression. When Kraft bought Budget Gourmet frozen dinners, it got the critical mass that it needed in the niche-driven frozen food industry, and put Celestial on the selling block. Kraft sold Celestial to tea industry leader Lipton, but R.C. Bigelow, a specialty tea maker, challenged the sale. Bigelow successfully argued that acquiring Celestial would give Lipton more than 80% of the herb tea market. While the case was dragging on for several months, Kraft offered to sell Celestial to a management group led by Feinblum (with the help of a venture capital firm). So, in 1988, just a short while before Kraft itself was acquired by the tobacco giant Philip Morris, Celestial got its independence. The story goes that Feinblum sent two dozen red roses to Eunice Bigelow, the Vice-President of R.C. Bigelow, with a note that said "thank you for standing up to the giants."

Today, in 1992, Celestial Seasonings is a privately held company with more than 40 products in the two subgroups in the tea industry: specialty teas (herb tea, caffeine-free tea, and flavored tea) and traditional teas (also called "black" or "orange pekoe"). It had 1991 revenues of approximately $51 million and a market share of about 50% in the herb tea industry, which it helped to create. Exhibit 21.1 gives a timeline of significant events for Celestial Seasonings, and Exhibit 21.2 presents the company's statement of beliefs.

The Tea Industry

The tea industry traces its origins to the Chinese Emperor Shen Nung in 2737 B.C. The Emperor, who had a fetish for boiled water, once accidentally boiled leaves that fell from a nearby tree. Legend has it that he was immediately struck by the

EXHIBIT 21.1

Timeline of Significant Events in Celestial Seasonings' History

1968	Mo and Peggy Siegel, Wyck Hay, and Lucinda Ziesing began picking herbs in the mountains around Boulder, Colorado.
1969	10,000 muslin bags of Mo's 36 Herb Tea were sewn, filled, and sold to the Grainery, a health food store in Boulder.
1970	Company's first production facility established in a barn in Boulder.
1971	Began purchasing herbs worldwide.
1973	Company began serving free family-style hot lunches to employees.
1974	Sales topped $1 million.
	Implemented strategic planning.
1977	Began selling teas internationally.
1983	First public stock offering (later canceled before completed).
1984	Company purchased by Kraft, Inc.
1986	Mo Siegel resigned as President after appointing Vice-President of Finance Barney Feinblum as successor.
1987	Kraft announced plans to sell Celestial Seasonings to Thomas J. Lipton, Inc.
1988	Sale of company to Lipton blocked by R.C. Bigelow, Inc.
	Celestial Seasonings management and Vestar Capital Partners bought company from Kraft through leveraged buyout. The day of buyout is referred to by company employees as "independence day."
1991	Mo Siegel rejoined the company as Chairman and CEO.

Source: Adapted from "Celestial Seasonings: Corporate Timeline," company publication.

delightful aroma and invigorating taste. Soon, tea entered China's trading arena. Europeans learned about tea when the Dutch brought it back from Far Eastern ports. It became the beverage of choice in Europe's royal households. When English colonists arrived in America, they brought with them an ample supply of tea. As students of American history recall, tea played a dramatic part in the establishment of the United States of America. In 1767, the British government levied a tax on the tea used by American colonists. Infuriated by what they called "taxation without representation," the colonists decided to stop buying tea and refused to allow tea ships to be unloaded. One December night in 1773, a group of men dressed as Indians boarded British ships in Boston harbor and threw more than 300 chests of tea into the sea; this "Boston Tea Party" sparked the American War of Independence.[2]

From these beginnings, tea sales in the United States have grown to more than $1 billion per year. Led by women 30 years of age and older, Americans consumed 128 million pounds of tea in 1991—an increase of 2% over 1990. This increase in demand is greater than that for canned and frozen juices and drinks and coffee. The declining sales of soft drinks coupled with Americans' increasing tendency toward healthier dietary and lifestyle habits signal a positive trend for the tea industry.[3]

The United States is the second largest consumer of tea in the world, next only to the United Kingdom. Whereas at one time China supplied nearly all the tea used in the world, today about 70% of the tea Americans drink comes from India, Sri Lanka, Indonesia, Kenya, and Tanzania. When the tea chests arrive in U.S. ports aboard freighters and ocean liners, samples are tested to guarantee high quality. The U.S. Board of Tea Experts, made up of members of government and industry, annually sets the minimum standards for tea that can be imported. The U.S. Tea Examiner tests all tea that comes into the country during the year against these standards. After it has passed inspection, the tea, which is sold through auctions, goes to various tea companies for blending and packaging. Expert tea tasters choose which teas to combine (sometimes as many as 20 to 30) to produce the special flavor, color, and aroma for their particular brands.

Americans buy tea in several forms: tea bags, iced tea mix, herbal bags, instant tea, loose tea, and liquid tea. Exhibit 21.3 indicates tea sales trend by type. The 2% increase in sales for total tea was driven by the growth of tea bags and iced tea mixes. The liquid tea category showed double-digit increases in each of the three years, albeit from a relatively small base.

The herb tea segment is a subset of the larger tea industry and part of the specialty tea segment, which includes loose tea, herb tea, black tea flavored with lemon, orange, or spices, and decaffeinated tea—in other words, everything except the plain black tea that traditional tea lovers consumed.[4] As overall tea consumption has stagnated or even declined over the past several years, the specialty tea category has shown an average growth rate of over 20% since 1983.[5] Like many others in the food and beverage industries, tea manufacturers have had to respond to consumers' increasingly health-conscious demands and to their changing tastes. These concerns are largely responsible for the boom in the sales of specialty teas.

Herb teas make up about 60% of the specialty tea market.[6] In 1991, the herb tea market was estimated to be some $100 million.[7] In the United States, tea is a name used for any infusion, be it fruit, flower, root, or herb. Herb teas, which are tea only in name, as they are infusions not of tea but of other plants, are now being packaged in the same manner as tea bags. Advocates of herb tea claim that it stimulates, puts an "out of gear" system back to complete health, lifts melancholy and depression, soothes and induces sleep, acts as a daytime tranquilizer, alleviates pain, and functions as a mild digestive aid. Currently, more than 100 varieties of herb teas are sold in health food stores and supermarkets. These include jasmine, rose, geranium, lime, orange, aniseseed, caraway, and dill. Herb tea is made by boiling fresh green herbs or seeds that have been sun dried or hung in a dry, warm atmosphere. This infusion of dried herbs is used both as a beverage and for medicinal purposes.[8]

Herb teas have become an important segment of the tea industry. As Exhibit 21.4 shows, they accounted for 4.6% of total tea sales (in metric tons) in 1990—a significant increase from a share of 0.9% in 1980. Also, because herb teas are more expensive than traditional teas, their share of total tea dollars is 10%.

EXHIBIT 21.2 **Celestial Seasonings Beliefs**

OUR QUEST FOR EXCELLENCE
We believe that in order to make this world a better place in which to live, we must be totally dedicated to the endless quest for excellence in the important tasks which we endeavor to accomplish.

OUR PRODUCTS
We believe in marketing and selling healthful and naturally oriented products that nurture people's bodies and uplift their souls. Our products must be superior in quality, of good value, beautifully artistic, and philosophically inspiring.

OUR CONSUMERS AND CUSTOMERS
We believe that our past, current and future successes come from a total dedication to excellent service to those who buy our products. Satisfying our customer and consumer needs in a superior way is the only reason we are in business, and we shall proceed with an obsession to give wholeheartedly to those who buy our products. Our customers and consumers are king, and we are here to serve them.

OUR GROWTH
We believe in aggressive, steady, predictable and well planned growth in sales and earnings. We are intent on building a large company that will flourish into the next century and thereafter.

DIGNITY OF THE INDIVIDUAL
We believe in the dignity of the individual, and we are totally committed to the fair, honest, kind, and professional treatment of all individuals and organizations with whom we work.

(continued)

The major players in the herb tea industry are Celestial Seasonings, Lipton, and R.C. Bigelow. Current details of market share are not available, but in 1988, Celestial Seasonings had a 50% share, Lipton 31%, and R.C. Bigelow 15%, with regional brands accounting for the remaining 4%.[9] Celestial Seasonings is credited with creating the herb tea industry in 1970 and giving it legitimacy by moving it out of health food and specialty food stores to supermarkets. In 1979, Lipton, part of the worldwide Unilever Group and the leading company in the tea industry, launched its herb teas and quickly captured a respectable market share. Also, in the same year, privately owned R.C. Bigelow, which had created the specialty tea segment in 1945 when it launched its Constant Comment brand by blending black tea leaves with orange peel and spices, entered the herb tea market.

In 1991, Celestial Seasonings had sales of approximately $51 million, R.C. Bigelow reported sales of approximately $40 million, and Lipton recorded sales of $1.374 billion.[10] Each company has strong brand names in the niche market, making it difficult for new entrants in this industry. Also, limited shelf space in supermarkets and economies of scale make competing with these existing companies difficult for new entrants.

EXHIBIT 21.2 **Celestial Seasonings Beliefs** *(continued)*

OUR EMPLOYEES
We believe that our employees develop a commitment to excellence when they are directly involved in the management of their areas of responsibility. This team effort maximizes quality results, minimizes costs, and allows our employees the opportunity to have authorship and personal satisfaction in their accomplishments, as well as sharing in the financial rewards of their individual and team efforts.

We believe in hiring above average people who have a "hands on" approach to work and quest for excellent results. In exchange, we are committed to the development of our good people by identifying, cultivating, training rewarding, retaining and promoting those individuals who are committed to moving our organization forward.

OUR ENVIRONMENT
We believe in fostering a working environment which promotes creativity and encourages possibility thinking throughout the organization. We plan our work to be satisfying, productive, and challenging. As such, we support an atmosphere which encourages intelligent risk taking without the fear of failure.

OUR DREAM
Our role at Celestial Seasonings is to play an active part in making this world a better place by unselfishly serving the public. We believe we can have a significant impact on making people's lives happier and healthier through their use of our products. By dedicating our total resources to this dream, everyone profits: our customers, consumers, employees, and shareholders. Our actions are building blocks in making this world a better place now and for future generations.

Source: Celestial Seasonings Corporation, company publication.

Herb tea competes not only with other tea segments but also with other types of beverages. Exhibit 21.5 shows market shares in the beverage industry for 1990. Note that tea has maintained a market share of about 4%, with its largest competitors being soft drinks and bottled water.

Tea is monitored by the Food and Drug Administration (FDA) as are other beverages, food, and drugs. In the near future tea, along with all other consumer foodstuffs, will have to meet FDA regulations for package labeling. The FDA is cracking down on the use of language such as fresh, diet, fat-free, and caffeine-free.

Company Profile

Manufacturing[11]

Celestial Seasonings acquires the more than 100 items used in its teas from 45 different countries and more than 200 suppliers. Although many suppliers come to the company with their products, Kay Wright (Botanicals Purchasing Manager)

EXHIBIT 21.3

Tea Sales Trend by Type

(Stated as a percentage of change)

Type	1991	1990	1989
Tea bags	+1%	(1%)	(3%)
Iced tea mix	+8	+3	+3
Herbal bags	−2	+ 3	+4
Instant tea	−4	−10	−7
Loose tea	−9	−10	−11
Liquid tea	+28	+24	+24

Source: Nielsen Marketing Research Report provided by the Tea Council of the U.S.A., Inc.

EXHIBIT 21.4

Herbal Tea Sales and Percentage of Total Tea Sales

(Sales in metric tons)

Year	Sales	Percentage of Total Tea Sales
1980	645	0.90%
1981	1010	1.41
1982	1875	2.60
1983	2096	2.81
1984	2109	2.99
1985	2151	3.10
1986	2350	3.50
1987	2141	4.00
1988	2191	4.20
1989	2235	4.40
1990	2337	4.60

Source: Nielsen Marketing Research Report provided by the Tea Council of the U.S.A., Inc.

travels a month each year looking for new sources of herbs. This quest for alternative sources is necessary because herb prices depend on many changing factors, such as droughts and volatile political conditions. Various countries supply herbs to the company: China supplies hibiscus; Mongolia, ginseng; Guatemala, lemon grass; France, lavender; and the hills of Missouri, passionflower and blackberries. As part of its health consciousness, the company insists that its cultivated herbs be organic. Purchases from some Third World countries where such a certification is not possible are rejected if they show residues of spraying. The company annually buys some 2,300 tons of items. In 1990, the total cost of purchases was $6.5 million.

Shipments that arrive at the manufacturing facility in Boulder are first inspected and then cleaned. After cleaning, the items are rolled into the milling machine. In the milling process the items are cut, shredded, and sifted until the particles are of the proper size. Care is taken to utilize as much as possible of the material. For example, products that are cut too fine and become dust are pelletized and cut again.

Blending is the next step in the production process. A 15-year veteran, Charlie Baden, oversees this crucial process. Each week Baden gets a schedule from production control telling him what to make. His first task is to create a prototype of the actual recipe to be used in the run. The object is to match the reference sample provided by the Product Development Department. Sometimes, different herb shipments produce subtle variations in flavor, making Baden's job difficult. Flavors vary constantly, depending on soil conditions and the amount of water a crop receives. Baden works closely with Kay Wright to find sources that yield similar flavors of the same herb. After Baden produces the prototype, he makes up the recipe and sends it to the mixers. The recipe formula is dialed in on a computer, which monitors how the mix comes out on the conveyor belt. Large barrels hold each batch before it is fed into the packaging system. Either Baden or the quality control taster taste every batch in a production run.

The production line operates 24 hours a day, producing 250,000 pounds of tea per week during the winter months when the demand for hot tea is at its peak. The blended product is fed through a tube by gravity onto the fully automated packaging line where it is measured into tea-bag-sized quantities. Paper is wrapped around each package and then heat-sealed. Each lined box contains 24 tea bags.

Celestial Seasonings is the only herb tea manufacturer that has a highly integrated production process, from milling to blending. Its only manufacturing facility is located in Boulder, Colorado. Exhibit 21.6 gives a manufacturing timeline for the company.

Marketing

Since its inception in 1969, Celestial Seasonings has marketed more than 40 different types of teas. The company's overwhelming success is due in part to the customer focus as well as the integrated, goal-oriented philosophy of the firm—in short, its marketing concept. The company's marketing strategies reflect the philosophy of cofounders John Hay and Mo Siegel. Celestial Seasonings strives to give consumers products that embody goodness, truth, and beauty: goodness comes from the 100% natural and healthy herb teas; beauty from the original artwork that adorns each package; and truth from the quotes, essays, and aphorisms that are part of every Celestial Seasonings communication. Consumers responded positively to this unique approach to packaged goods marketing. Despite the company's lofty goals, Celestial Seasonings personnel try not to take themselves too seriously.

Celestial Seasonings' marketing strengths are focused growth via health consciousness, brand awareness, strong consumer loyalty, and distinctive packaging

EXHIBIT 21.5

Beverage Industry Market Shares, 1979–1990

(Stated as a percent)

	1990	1989	1988	1987	1986	1985	1984	1983	1982	1981	1980	1979
Soft drinks	26.0%	25.5%	25.2%	24.2%	23.1%	22.4%	21.3%	20.3%	19.5%	19.1%	18.7%	18.2%
Coffee[2]	13.8	13.9	13.9	14.1	14.1	14.1	14.5	14.6	14.6	14.9	15.0	15.2
Beer	12.8	12.9	13.0	13.1	13.2	13.0	13.1	13.3	13.4	13.5	13.3	13.0
Milk	10.4	10.5	10.6	10.8	10.9	10.8	10.8	10.7	10.8	11.1	11.3	11.5
Tea[2]	3.9	4.0	4.1	4.0	4.0	4.0	3.9	3.9	4.1	4.1	4.0	4.2
Bottled water	4.8	4.4	3.9	3.5	3.1	2.8	2.2	1.9	1.8	1.8	1.5	1.4
Juices	3.8	3.7	3.9	3.7	3.8	3.8	3.6	4.3	3.7	3.7	3.8	3.7
Powdered drinks	2.9	3.0	2.8	3.0	3.3	3.4	3.5	3.6	3.3	3.3	3.3	3.3
Wine[3]	1.1	1.2	1.2	1.3	1.3	1.3	1.3	1.2	1.2	1.2	1.2	1.1
Distilled spirits	0.8	0.8	0.9	0.9	0.9	1.0	1.0	1.0	1.0	1.1	1.1	1.1
Subtotal	80.4[1]	79.8[1]	79.5	78.5	77.8[1]	76.8[1]	75.2	74.8	73.4	73.7[1]	73.2	72.7
Imputed water consumption[4]	19.6	20.2	20.5	21.5	22.2	23.2	24.8	25.2	26.6	26.3	26.8	27.3
Total	100.0%	100.0%	100.0%	100.0%	100.0%	100.0%	100.0%	100.0%	100.0%	100.0%	100.0%	100.0%

Notes:

1. Rounding errors are present in the subtotals.
2. Coffee and tea data are based on a three-year moving average to counterbalance inventory swings, thereby portraying consumption more realistically.
3. Includes wine coolers beginning in 1984.
4. Includes all others.

Source: John C. Maxwell, Jr., Wheat First Securities.

EXHIBIT 21.6

Manufacturing Timeline: Celestial Seasonings, Inc.

1970	First production facility established in a barn in Boulder, Colorado.
1971	Growth necessitated moving into larger manufacturing facility.
1976	Installed first tea-bag packaging equipment.
1977	Instituted use of purchase orders. Time-shared first computer for production with University of Colorado.
1979	Changed herb tea packaging from vertical to horizontal boxes.
1982	Invented and installed current raw herb processing equipment.
1988	Introduced tamper-resistant cellophane overwrap to packaging process.

Source: Adapted from "Celestial Seasonings: Corporate Timeline," company publication.

(considered a significant advantage over the competition). During the 1990s, increased consumer interest in health and natural foods continues to predominate.[12] Celestial Seasonings has capitalized on this trend by positioning several of its products according to particular consumer groups. To cater to the maturing baby-boomer market's needs, Celestial produces specialty teas and traditional teas. The herb tea segment has brand names such as "Red Zinger," "Mandarin Orange Spice," "Sleepytime," and "Peppermint." The traditional tea segment comprises "Classic English Breakfast" and "Extraordinary Earl Grey Distinctive." "Orange Spice Distinctive" makes up the flavored tea segment.

Celestial Seasonings' primary target market consists of women between the ages of 18 and 49. Within this age category, however, Celestial believes that its loyal customers are women aged 30 and over. Demographic trends continue to favor Celestial Seasonings. By the year 2000, the number of people in the 35–54 age category are expected to have increased dramatically—up 18 million over 1990. As Exhibit 21.7 indicates, the number of 45–54-year-olds will have increased by almost 50%.

Despite steadily declining consumer brand loyalty since the late 1970s, Celestial Seasonings has been able to capture and sustain loyalty by selling quality teas coupled with offers of consumer involvement, as evidenced by the copy on its package: "Please write, we like to respond. We are interested in your suggestions, ideas, queries, quotations and short essays for use on the package."[13]

In its pre-Kraft years, Celestial Seasonings' advertising budget was about $2 million a year. Print advertisements appeared in magazines such as McCall's and Redbook. The print advertisements tended to be (and still are today) simple, dignified, and information oriented. In addition, the company used special cause-related marketing in the form of sponsorship of a bicycle race called the Red Zinger Classic. During its Kraft years (1984–1988) the advertising budget was boosted to some $6 million per year. National television commercials featuring actress Mariette Hartley as spokesperson were aimed at the upscale working women's market.

EXHIBIT 21.7

Demographic Trends
(Numbers of people and changes in millions)

Age Group	Number of People in 1990	Number of People in 2000	Change 1990–2000
Under 18	64	66	+2
18–24	26	25	−1
25–34	44	37	−7
35–44	38	44	+6
45–54	25	37	+12
55–64	21	24	+3
65 plus	32	35	+3

Source: William L. Wilkie, *Consumer Behavior,* 2nd. ed. (New York: John Wiley and Sons, 1990).

During its early days Celestial Seasonings concentrated its distribution on health food stores. Over time, it expanded its distribution to supermarket chains, gourmet stores, and foreign markets such as Canada.

The company has adopted a penetration pricing strategy to position several of its products at a price of $.055 a bag, a price lower than its competitors Lipton and Bigelow. Exhibit 21.8 shows a price comparison of herb teas. Also, Celestial packs 24 bags to a box, compared to Lipton's 16 bags.

Human Resources

In 1985, Celestial Seasonings was rated as one of the 100 best companies to work for in America.[14] One survey by the book's authors gave high marks to the company in the areas of benefits, job security, advancement opportunities, and ambience. In an interview, Chairman Mo Siegel succinctly summarized his management philosophy by saying, "What is important is creating a condition in which the work force feels better about their lives, because what is good for labor should be good for management and vice versa."[15] The company, with its 216 employees (as of 1990), does not have time clocks and is not unionized. The company has a number of plans aimed at motivating its employees. There is an employee stock ownership plan (ESOP) and a gain-sharing program that pays cash dividends to employees if corporate goals are exceeded. Although these two programs were suspended during the Kraft years, Celestial Seasonings has reintroduced them. Employees receive a $25 check on birthdays, $50 at Thanksgiving, and $100 at Christmas. The company also provides opportunities for self-advancement. For example, an office secretary was put in charge of automating the office with word processing stations, and a janitor who suggested saving money by having an in-house fleet of trucks to transport teas to market was given the job of organizing such a fleet.[16] Turnover is low and, because of its reputation as a good place to work, the company receives 100 applications for each job opening.[17]

EXHIBIT 21.8

Price Comparison of Selected Specialty Tea Brands

Brand	Cost per Quart
Lipton's Cinnamon Apple	$.48
Celestial's Red Zinger	.32
Celestial's Wild Forest Blackberry	.32
Lipton's Gentle Orange	.48
Bigelow's Constant Comment	.36
Celestial's Caffeine-Free	.20
Lipton's Decaffeinated	.43
Bigelow's Constant Comment Decaff.	.48

Source: 1991 survey provided by Celestial Seasonings.

Finances

Celestial Seasonings does not disclose its financial statements because it is privately held. A top management group led by Barney Feinblum acquired the company in a leveraged buyout from Kraft for an estimated $60 million in 1988. A venture capital firm, Vestar Capital Partners, financed the buyout by putting in $15 million of equity and the rest in debt. The $45 million in debt requires annual interest payments of about $6 million, taking up almost all the profits. Exhibit 21.9 summarizes the company's financial details.

Management

Soon after the sale of Celestial Seasonings to Kraft (in 1984), the company's founder, Morris J. (Mo) Siegel, resigned as President after appointing the then Vice-President of Finance, Barney Feinblum, as his successor. After engineering the leveraged buyout from Kraft (in 1988), Feinblum continued as President of the company. After Siegel left Celestial Seasonings, he embarked on a personal odyssey that led him to found the Jesusonian Foundation, which furthers the teachings of Jesus. Siegel wasn't comfortable with being a philanthropist, and in an effort to get back into the business world he founded Earth Wise, Inc. Earth Wise sells environmentally friendly household cleaning products and trash bags that are made from 100% recycled plastic.[18] In 1991, Mo Siegel returned to Celestial Seasonings as Chairman and CEO, making an equity investment in the company after it offered to buy Earth Wise. Earth Wise became a brand of Celestial Seasonings, finding a comfortable niche in Celestial's existing natural foods market, although because of its LBO status Celestial Seasonings could not invest in the infant brand. In a newspaper interview, Vestar Capital Partners' managing partner, James Kelley, gave the rationale for bringing Mo Siegel back as CEO: "Mo is a marketing genius who created a category and a company. It takes a marketing expert to grow the [herb tea] category. We think Mo will help expand it."[19]

EXHIBIT 21.9

Summary of Financial Details: Celestial Seasonings, Inc.[1]
(Dollar amounts in millions)

Year	Sales	Percentage Change in Sales	Operating Profits
1980	11.56	—%	$—
1981	16.66	+44.0	1.00
1982	23.33	+40.0	1.70
1983	26.50	+13.6	2.20
1984	26.00	−1.89	4.00
1985	29.75	+14.4	4.46
1986	35.00	+17.6	5.25
1987	40.00	+14.2	6.00
1988	45.00	+12.5	6.00
1989	47.00	+4.4	7.00
1990	49.00	+4.3	7.35
1991	51.00	+4.1	7.65

Note:
1. Since Celestial Seasonings is a privately held company, these are estimates and not actual figures.

Sources: Henry Dubroff, "Celestial Seasonings Grows Up," *CFO* (October 1989), pp. 36–50; Sandra D. Atchison, "Why Celestial Seasonings Wasn't Kraft's Cup of Tea," *Business Week* (May 8, 1989), p. 76; Sandra D. Atchison, "Putting the Red Zinger Back in Celestial," *Business Week* (November 4, 1991), pp. 74–78.

In an effort to give the company a new marketing focus and to build a hand-picked team of his own, Siegel replaced Celestial's Chief Executive in the functions of marketing, finance, operations, and human resources. Siegel also created the positions of strategic planning and corporate development to give the company a growth orientation.

Culture

Celestial Seasonings was a product of the 1970s: a free-spirited enterprise created by flower children to provide a healthy alternative to coffee and traditional black tea. In keeping with such a background, the company took its name from that of the girlfriend of one of the founders, sold its products through natural-food stores, had executives who kept their hair long and rode bicycles to work, and practiced what a business reporter called "cosmic capitalism."[20] But, as herb tea grew to a $100 million business with powerful competitors such as Lipton, Celestial Seasonings found that it had to go mainstream. Mo Siegel always believed in a button-down approach to management and in fact resented the hippie label attached to his company.[21] He constantly took pains to point out that Celestial Seasonings, although a relaxed company to work for, was also a hard-nosed competitor in the herb tea industry. An intensely religious person, Mo Siegel nevertheless wanted the company to become one of America's leading corporations that could compete effectively in the marketplace.[22]

During the early years, the company thrived on its informal ambience. There were volleyball games every lunch hour, employees' toddling children walked in and out of Mo Siegel's office, and eight-hour all-company meetings to discuss policy issues were common.[23] Employees were treated well and there was no clear demarcation between management and workers.

When Kraft acquired Celestial Seasonings, understandably things changed. Executives now wore suits, even though CEO Barney Feinblum still rode a bicycle to work, and a clear dividing line emerged between management and workers. More important, many Celestial Seasonings executives felt that their company, an erstwhile nimble, entrepreneurial outfit, was becoming stodgy and cautious like Kraft.[24] Opportunities were missed because Kraft wanted to move slowly, and paperwork increased tremendously. Also, Kraft severed Celestial's ties to bicycle racing, which Celestial had sponsored for several years. Relations between Kraft's more conservative managers and Feinblum deteriorated further when, in response to anonymous letters, Kraft put an undercover agent in Celestial's plant to check for drug use among employees.[25]

Currently, after gaining its independence from Kraft, Celestial Seasonings is a blend of 1970s-style informality and 1990s-style professional management. Employees are treated well, as evidenced by low turnover rates. Decisions are made quickly to take advantage of opportunities. Also, the company is heavily involved in preserving the environment. It has changed its packaging, is active in recycling, and maintains a toll-free telephone service offering environmental information to consumers across the country. For these reasons, the company was a nominee in the Fifth Annual America's Corporate Conscience Award in the environment category.[26]

The Future

As Mo Siegel looked back on the company's past, he realized that the annual management retreat was crucial for the company. The huge debt incurred as part of the buyout meant that the company had to generate large sales and profits to service the debt. However, interest and principal payments took a large part of the cash flow, leaving less money for expansion or new product development. The herb tea industry is currently a $100 million business but it is highly seasonal (sales occur largely in the winter months) putting additional strain on managing cash flow. Also, other segments of the tea industry are showing higher growth rates than the herb tea segment. The iced tea segment has sales of $700 million a year and is growing at an annual rate of 8%. Celestial Seasonings has only just launched its entry in this segment. The nascent liquid tea segment, where ready-to-drink tea is sold in plastic containers, shows the largest growth rate (28% in 1991) in the industry, but the company does not have a presence in this segment. Should the company enter the liquid tea segment? Should it diversify into other related health food areas? What should the company do to expand and pay off its debt? Mo Siegel realized that these crucial questions had to be answered at the next management retreat.

Notes

1. This section was based on the following sources: "Teas . . . More Tastefully Done," Celestial Seasonings Company Brochure; Henry Dubroff, "Celestial Seasonings Grows Up," *CFO Magazine* (October 1989), pp. 36–50; Mary Rowland, "Change Is Brewing in Tea," *Working Woman* (April 1989), pp. 85–86.
2. The historical details are from the following sources: "The Story of Tea," "Two Leaves and a Bud," and "A Short History of One of the World's Oldest Beverages," booklets provided by the Tea Council of the U.S.A., Inc.
3. *Tea World,* 1991.
4. Celestial Seasonings, company brochure.
5. Rowland, pp. 85–86.
6. Ibid.
7. Sandra D. Atchison, "Putting the Red Zinger Back into Celestial," *Business Week* (November 4, 1991), pp. 74–78.
8. Celestial Seasonings, company brochure.
9. John Birmingham, "Strange Brew," *Adweek's Marketing Week* (November 21, 1988), pp. 18–22.
10. Celestial Seasonings, company documents.
11. This section is based mainly on Wendy Worrall, "Tea Tales," *Daily Camera* (December 1991).
12. Henry Assall, *Consumer Behavior and Marketing Action,* 4th ed. (Boston: PWS-Kent, 1992).
13. Celestial Seasonings, company brochure.
14. Robert Levering, Milton Moscovitz, and Michael Katz, *100 Best Companies to Work for in America* (New York: New American Library, 1985).
15. Ibid.
16. Ibid.
17. Company documents.
18. Atchison, "Putting the Red Zinger Back into Celestial," pp. 74–78.
19. Jeffrey Leib, "Herb Tea Guru Comes Full Circle," *The Denver Post* (August 6, 1991).
20. Eric Morganthaler, "Herb Tea's Pioneer: From Hippie Origins to $16 Million a Year," *Wall Street Journal* (May 6, 1981), pp. 1, 22.
21. Rowland, pp. 85–86.
22. Nora Gallagher, "We're More Aggressive Than Our Tea," *Across the Board* (July–August 1983), pp. 46–50.
23. Ibid.
24. Sandra D. Atchison, "Why Celestial Seasonings Wasn't Kraft's Cup of Tea," *Business Week* (May 8, 1989), p. 76.
25. Ibid.
26. Celestial Seasonings, company press release.

CASE 22

Church & Dwight Company, Inc., 1993: Preparing to Enter the Twenty-first Century

Roy A. Cook

Background

For almost 150 years, Church & Dwight Company, Inc., has been building market share on a brand name that is rarely associated with the company. This brand name has become so pervasive that it can now be found on many consumer products in 95% of all U.S. households. As the world's largest producer and marketer of sodium bicarbonate–based products, Church & Dwight has achieved consistent growth in sales and earnings. Sodium bicarbonate is used in many products because it can perform a variety of functions, including cleaning, deodorizing, leavening, and buffering. Although Church & Dwight may not be a household name, the company's ubiquitous yellow box of ARM & HAMMER[1] brand baking soda is.

Shortly after its introduction in 1878, ARM & HAMMER Baking Soda became a fundamental item on the pantry shelf as homemakers found many uses for it other than baking, such as cleaning and deodorizing. It can also be used as a dentifrice, a chemical agent to absorb or neutralize odors and acidity, a kidney dialysis element, a blast media, and a potentially effective pollution control agent.

Over the past decade, company sales, on average, increased almost 15% annually, reaching a total of $516.4 million in 1992 (see Exhibits 22.1 and 22.2). Church & Dwight has also achieved consistent growth in earnings and return on equity by "selling related products in different markets all linked by common carbonate and bicarbonate technology."[2]

Management

The slow but steady course that Church & Dwight has traveled reflects top management's efforts to focus the company's activities. The ability to remain focused may be attributable to the fact that more than 50% of the outstanding shares of common stock are owned by descendants of the company's co-founders. Dwight C. Minton (age 58) has directed the company since becoming C.E.O. in 1969. Minton, a direct descendant of the company founder, succeeded his father as Chairman of the Board in 1981 after serving on the Board since 1965.

Many companies in the consumer products field with strong brand names have been susceptible to leveraged buy-outs and hostile takeover attempts. However, a series of calculated actions spared Church & Dwight's management from having to make last-minute decisions to ward off unwelcome suitors. Besides maintaining majority control of the outstanding common stock, management pro-

EXHIBIT 22.1

Consolidated Statements of Income: Church & Dwight Company, Inc.
(Dollar amounts in thousands, except per share data)

Years Ending December 31	1992	1991	1990	1989	1988
Net sales	$516,438	$485,487	$428,546	$387,641	$346,779
Cost of goods	278,534	283,664	263,761	261,779	238,077
Gross profit	237,904	201,823	164,785	125,862	108,702
Selling, general, and administrative expenses	193,130	161,490	130,943	95,685	81,739
Income from operations	44,774	40,333	33,842	30,177	26,963
Nonoperating income	2,636	3,339	8,753	(8,781)[1]	2,428
Interest expense	260	1,672	3,623	4,340	4,463
Income before taxes	47,150	42,000	38,973	17,056	24,928
Income taxes	17,647	15,525	15,767	8,408	8,454
Net income	$ 29,503	$ 26,475	$ 22,482[2]	$ 8,648	$ 16,474
Weighted average—outstanding shares	20,338	19,831	20,455	20,728	21,985

Notes:

1. Reflects a $15,360,000 loss on the disposal of product lines.
   (a) Includes a $6.4 million loss on the sale of the milk products lines of the National Vitamin Products Company and the Quantock Corporation.
   (b) Includes a $9.0 million write-down of assets of the DeWitt product line in anticipation of sale.
2. Reflects a $724,000 charge for the early retirement of $20,000,000 in debt.

Source: Church & Dwight Company, Inc., *1992 Annual Report.*

posed and the Board amended the company's charter in 1986. This amendment gave current shareholders four votes per share but required future shareholders to buy and hold shares for four years before receiving the same privilege. The Board of Directors also was restructured into three classes so that the directors in each class serve staggered three-year terms.

As a further deterrent to would-be suitors and unwelcome advances, the company entered into an employee severance agreement in 1989 with its key officials. This agreement provides severance pay of up to three times the individual's highest annual salary and bonus plus benefits for the preceding three years if the individual is terminated within one year after a change in control of the company. Change of control is defined as "the acquisition by a person or group of 25% or more of Company Common Stock; a change in the majority of the board of directors not approved by the pre-change board of directors; or the approval by the stockholders of the Company or a merger, consolidation, liquidation, dissolution, or sale of all the assets of the Company."[3]

As Church & Dwight pushed into the consumer products field, the company added several individuals with extensive consumer product marketing experience to the management team. William C. Egan III joined the company in 1990 as Vice-

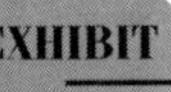

EXHIBIT 22.2

Consolidated Balance Sheets: Church & Dwight Company, Inc.
(Dollar amounts in thousands)

Years Ending December 31	1992	1991	1990	1989	1988
Assets					
Cash	$ 17,536	$ 4,706	$ 26,987	$ 24,610	$ 15,095
Marketable securities	8,060	3,999	18,717	18,711	10,893
Receivables	45,597	48,439	39,226	38,348	38,965
Inventories	45,603	54,710	40,289	34,864	43,161
Other current assets	6,762	4,733	4,999	13,277	4,609
Total current assets	123,558	116,587	130,218	129,810	112,723
Property, plant, and equipment	120,537	113,728	103,055	102,203	111,449
Intangibles	4,152	4,341	4,111	4,282	7,821
Other long-term assets	14,100	10,341	12,995	8,563	12,004
Total assets	$262,347	$244,997	$250,379	$244,858	$243,997
Liabilities and Shareholders' Equity					
Accounts payable	$ 69,740	$ 71,632	$ 71,394	$ 57,362	$ 46,414
Income taxes	6,841	7,049	8,127	1,057	3,264
Current long-term debt	—	—	1,401	1,422	1,439
Total current liabilities	76,581	78,681	80,922	59,841	51,117
Long-term debt	7,744	7,811	29,635	52,193	55,586
Deferred charges	18,971	19,351	21,120	21,269	25,262
Shareholders' equity	159,051	139,154	118,702	111,555	112,032
Total liabilities and shareholders' equity	$262,347	$244,997	$250,379	$244,858	$243,997

Source: Church & Dwight Company, Inc., *1992 Annual Report*

President and President of the ARM & HAMMER Division. He had served for more than 15 years with Johnson & Johnson, Inc., reaching the position of President of that organization's Baby Products Company before leaving. Anthony P. Deasey, Vice-President—Finance and Chief Financial Officer, served as Controller of the Prince Matchabelli Division of Chesebrough-Pond's, Inc., before joining the company in 1988.

The most recent additions to the senior management team were Kenneth J. Gaicin and James E. Barch. Gaicin, Vice-President—New Business Development, ARM & HAMMER Division, joined the company in 1991 after holding various senior-level management positions with Johnson & Johnson over a 17-year period. Just prior to joining Church & Dwight, he held the positions of Vice-President—Business Development and Director—Business Development. Barch, Vice-President—Marketing Household Products, joined the organization in 1992 after a seven-year stint at Procter & Gamble where he served as Associate Advertising Manager.[4]

Consumer Products

Baking soda has become synonymous with environmental safety in consumers' minds. Church & Dwight has long been known for environmental education, conservation, and products that are environmentally sound. According to William Egan, "As a result, environmentally conscious consumers instinctively turn to the yellow box."[5]

Church & Dwight has selected an overall family brand strategy to further penetrate the consumer products market in the United States and Canada by introducing additional products displaying the ARM & HAMMER logo. The ARM & HAMMER brand controls a commanding 85% of the baking soda market. By capitalizing on its easily recognizable brand name, logo, and established marketing channels, Church & Dwight has moved into such product lines as laundry detergent (approximately 5% of the market), carpet deodorizers (approximately 35% of the market), air deodorizers (approximately 13% of the market), and toothpaste (10% of the market). This strategy has allowed the company to promote multiple products using only one brand name.

The strategy to move more aggressively into consumer products can be traced to Dwight Minton. From the company's founding until 1970, it produced and sold only two consumer products: ARM & HAMMER Baking Soda and a laundry product marketed under the name Super Washing Soda. In 1970, under Minton, Church & Dwight began testing the consumer products market by introducing a phosphate-free, powdered laundry detergent, which since has been reformulated. Several other products, including a liquid laundry detergent, fabric softener sheets, an all-fabric bleach, tooth powder and toothpaste, and deodorizers (carpet, room, and pet) have been added to the expanding list of ARM & HAMMER brands.

The company's largest selling consumer product line is laundry detergent, which has approximately 5% of the market. "Despite a virtual absence of advertising, the detergent is positioned to offer quality cleaning at a substantial discount [15%–20%] to Procter & Gamble Co.'s 'Tide'".[6] The mature $10 billion domestic detergent market is growing at a sluggish 0.5% annually, but it is far from tranquil. Environmental concerns continue to increase, and competition from the introduction of innovative products has intensified.

New products must muscle their way into markets by taking market share from current offerings, and heavy-duty liquid detergents appear to have been the most successful in doing so. Faced with the problems of a mature domestic market, marketers are utilizing a segmentation approach to gain market share. They also are beginning to focus their attention outside the United States and Canada. The key difference in the U.S. and Canadian markets is that they are both marketing driven, whereas the markets in the rest of the world are still product driven.[7]

Household products traditionally have been heavily promoted (but not advertised) and sold at prices below market leaders. At times, these price differentials are as much as 25%. Church & Dwight had to modify this generic strategy some-

EXHIBIT 22.3

Market Share of Toothpaste Brands

Brand	Market Share
Crest	31.2%
Colgate	22.1
ARM & HAMMER	10.1
AquaFresh	9.2
Close-Up	5.1
Sensodyne	3.5
Ultra Brite	2.5

Source: Kathleen Deveny, "Toothpaste Makers Tout New Packaging," *Wall Street Journal* (November 10, 1992), p. B-1.

what as it rolled out ARM & HAMMER DENTAL CARE from regional test markets into nationwide distribution during the summer of 1989. The offerings in the toothpaste line expanded in 1990, 1991, and 1992.

The task of successfully implementing a nationwide marketing campaign is not new to the company. In 1972, Church & Dwight made marketing history when it introduced ARM & HAMMER Baking Soda as a refrigerator deodorizer. A national television advertising campaign and point-of-sale promotions in grocery stores were used. The outcome was accelerated growth and a 74% increase in volume over a three-year period.[8]

The company's consumer products strategy has focused on niche markets to avoid a head-on attack from competitors with more financial and marketing clout. In exploring new and existing markets the common thread was to seek new uses of the basic baking soda ingredient for loyal users. To further this objective, Church & Dwight has developed its own consumer research studies on trends in baking soda use for health care and household applications, identifying users by age, gender, income level, and education level.[9]

The company's most aggressive entrants into the consumer products market have been its dental care products. Although it is entering a crowded field of specialty products, Church & Dwight is planning to ride the crest of increasing interest by both dentists and hygienists in baking soda as an important element in a regimen for maintaining dental health.[10] Church & Dwight has been able to move rapidly from the position of a niche player in the toothpaste market (along with products such as Topol, Viadent, Check-Up, Zact, and Tom's of Maine) to that of a major competitor. In only five years, the company has captured a significant market share and the attention of major competitors. There appears to be room for growth in this $1.5 billion plus domestic market; the market leaders—Crest and Colgate—have 31.2% and 22.1% of the toothpaste market, respectively. However, a better perspective of the relative standing of the company's dental care products can be gained from the relative standings in the toothpaste market. The market is attractive because the typical manufacturer realizes a $.34 profit on a $1.99 retail sale of a tube of toothpaste[11] (see Exhibit 22.3).

Church & Dwight's dramatic success in penetrating the toothpaste market has not gone unnoticed or unchallenged. Both Procter & Gamble and Colgate have introduced similar products. In addition, Procter & Gamble has indicated that it will compete on a price basis (possibly lowering prices on baking soda toothpaste by as much as 30%) supported by heavy advertising.

New and expanded consumer product offerings continue to drive sales growth. The newest entrants into these markets are a cat litter deodorizer and ARM & HAMMER Concentrated Automatic Dishwashing Detergent.

For the most part, Church & Dwight's entries into the consumer products market have been successful. However, some products have failed to meet expectations or can even be termed failures. Most notable among the company's marketing missteps were an oven cleaner and an underarm deodorant. The company eventually sold off the oven cleaner line and pulled the underarm deodorant from test markets during the mid 1970s. Another potential marketing problem may be looming on the horizon. ARM & HAMMER could be falling into the precarious line-extension snare. Placing a well-known brand name on a wide variety of products could cloud its position and cause it to lose marketing pull.[12]

Specialty Products

The Specialty Products Division of Church & Dwight basically consists of the manufacture and sale of sodium bicarbonate for two market segments: industrial and animal feed products. Manufacturers utilize sodium bicarbonate as a leavening agent for commercial baked goods; an antacid in pharmaceuticals; a chemical in kidney dialysis; a carbon dioxide release agent in fire extinguishers; and an alkaline in swimming pool chemicals, detergents, and various textile and tanning applications. Animal feed producers use sodium bicarbonate predominantly as a buffer, or antacid, for dairy cattle feeds and make a nutritional supplement that enhances milk production in dairy cattle. Church & Dwight maintains a dominant position in the production of the required raw materials for both its consumer and industrial products. It manufactures almost two-thirds of the sodium bicarbonate sold in the United States and is the only U.S. producer of ammonium bicarbonate and potassium carbonate.

Although management has focused attention increasingly on consumer products, the following table shows the relevant contributions of consumer products and specialty products to total sales over the past six years.

	1987	1988	1989	1990	1991	1992
Consumer products	73%	72%	76%	77%	80%	79%
Specialty products	27	28	24	23	20	21
Total	100%	100%	100%	100%	100%	100%

Fluctuations in the significance of specialty products sales can be traced to a series of acquisitions, partnership agreements, and divestitures completed from 1985 through

1989. These included the acquisition of a 40% interest in Brotherton Chemicals Ltd, a producer of ammonium-based chemicals; a 49% interest in Sales y Oxidos S.A., a Mexican producer of strontium carbonate; a partnership agreement entered into with Occidental Petroleum Corporation to form Armand Products Company, which produces and markets potassium chemicals; and control of National Vitamin Products Company, which specializes in animal nutrition products.

The company currently has the largest share (approximately 60%) of the sodium bicarbonate capacity in the United States, with 350,000 tons of annual production. Its closest competitor, FMC, has an estimated annual capacity of only 60,000 tons.[13] As reported in a 1988 letter to shareholders, "The strategies for the Chemicals Division [later renamed Specialty Products Division] involve the expansion of the sodium bicarbonate business through the development of new applications and markets, and broadening the business base by diversifying into related products with similar technology and markets."[14]

A third competitor, NaTec, increased its ability to supply sodium bicarbonate from 20,000 to 125,000 tons in 1993, although it has not put this new capacity into production. NaTec also has not yet invested in the technology to match the varying quality levels of Church & Dwight's products. In addition, 10,000 tons per year are imported from Mexico.[15] Church & Dwight produces sodium bicarbonate from two basic raw materials: soda ash and carbon dioxide. "The primary source of soda ash used by the company is the mineral trona which is found in abundance in southwestern Wyoming near the company's Green River plant."[16]

Although the flurry of chemical-related acquisitions appeared to have the potential for accelerating growth, management soon decided to divest some of the recently acquired companies. Both the milk products line of specialty feeds marketed through National Vitamin Products Company and the 49% interest in Sales y Oxidos S.A. were divested. According to Anthony P. Deasey, Vice-President and Chief Financial Officer, "The reason for these sales was a realization that while sales increased in 1986 through 1988, profits lagged, pulling down return on investment."[17] The remaining assets of National Vitamin were disposed of during 1991 and 1992.

Pollution control processes at coal-fired electrical plants where sodium compounds are used to clean flue gases may open up an entirely new market for Church & Dwight's specialty products in the environmental area. The company has tested a process whereby dry injection rather than the typical wet scrubbers can be used to remove sulfur oxide and nitrogen oxides from smokestack emissions. The company is hoping that it may help to provide solutions to the country's acid-rain problems. The process of dumping baking soda into incinerators of all types to neutralize various pollutants causing acid rain has been successfully tested,[18] and municipalities are adding it to their water supplies in order to cut lead and neutralize excess acidity.

Although pollution control applications are presently providing minimal revenues, the potential for future sales is enormous. Public Service Company of Colorado (PSC) was the first utility to test the viability of this process commercially. The test was successful, but PSC also is testing other pollution control processes and therefore have not yet committed to using sodium bicarbonate. Reducing sulfur dioxide from smokestack emissions also is being explored in waste incinerator applications.

Additional opportunities are being examined for ARMEX Blast Media and potable water treatment. ARMEX Blast Media is a sodium bicarbonate-based product used as a paint stripping compound. It was utilized successfully for the delicate task of stripping the accumulation of years of paint and tar from the interior of the Statue of Liberty without damaging the fragile copper skin. It is now being considered for other specialized applications in the transportation and electronics industries and in industrial cleaning because of its apparent environmental safety. ARMEX also has been introduced into international markets.

The company launched another specialty chemical product, ARMAKLEEN, in 1992. It is an aqueous cleaner used for cleaning printed circuit boards. This potentially promising product may have an enormous market because it may be able to replace chlorofluorocarbon-based cleaning systems. "ARMAKLEEN, a carbonate and bicarbonate technology, is the first nonsolvent-based system for this market," says John Berschied, Vice-President—Research and Development. "It is also the company's first venture into the electronics market."[19]

Sodium bicarbonate also has been used to remove lead from drinking water and, when added to water supplies, coats the inside of pipes and prevents lead from leaching into the water. This market could grow in significance with additions to the Clean Water Bill.

International Operations

Church & Dwight has enjoyed a great deal of success in North American markets. It has achieved full distribution in the United States and Canada and limited distribution in Mexico.[20] "Moving into overseas markets will put Church & Dwight into heightened competition with major oral-care and household product marketers such as Procter & Gamble Company, Unilever, and Colgate-Palmolive Company."[21]

Church & Dwight expanded its presence in the international consumer products markets with the 1986 acquisition of DeWitt International Corporation, which manufactures and markets personal care products, including toothpaste. The DeWitt acquisition not only provided the company with increased international exposure but also with much needed toothpaste production facilities and technology. Even with this acquisition, the company still derives over 95% of its revenues from the United States and Canada. Owing to the perceived limited market potential of the DeWitt product line, Church & Dwight divested the subsidiary's brands and its overseas operations in 1990 but retained its U.S. toothpaste manufacturing facilities in Greenville, South Carolina.

Attempts to enter international markets have met with limited success, probably for two reasons: (1) lack of name recognition, and (2) transportation costs. Although ARM & HAMMER is one of the most recognized brand names in the United States (in the top ten), it does not enjoy the same name recognition elsewhere. "International transportation represents 40 to 45% of Church & Dwight's sales expense, versus 5 to 10% domestically."[22]

Church & Dwight's Future

The company's stated mission for the 1990s is:

> We will supply customers quality ARM & HAMMER Sodium Bicarbonate and related products, while performing in the top quarter of American businesses.[23]

The core business and foundation on which the company has been built remain the same after 144 years. However, as the management team at Church & Dwight looks to the future, new ventures and products and extensions of existing product lines are being planned to enhance the shareholder wealth of this publicly traded but family controlled company.

Notes

1. ARM & HAMMER is a registered trademark of Church & Dwight Company, Inc.
2. "C&D Sees Growth Despite Competition," *Chemical Marketing Reporter* (December 11, 1989), 236, p. 9.
3. Church & Dwight Company, Inc., *Notice of Annual Meeting of Stockholders* (1989), p. 17.
4. Church & Dwight Company, Inc., *Notice of Annual Meeting of Stockholders* (1993).
5. William C. Egan III, "Brand Equity: The Value of a Trademark," *Editor & Publisher* (December 5, 1992), p. 6T.
6. "C&D Sees Growth Despite Competition," p. 19.
7. Gregory D. L. Morris, "Soap and Detergents," *Chemicalweek* (January 18, 1989), pp. 24ff.
8. Church & Dwight Company, Inc., *1988 Annual Report.*
9. Carrie M. Wainwright, "Church & Dwight: Slow But Steady into Personal Care," *Drug & Cosmetic Industry* (February 1987), p. 28.
10. David Kiley, "Arm & Hammer Mixes Its Own," *Adweek's Marketing Week* (July 4, 1988), p. 3.
11. Based on the information from Towne-Oller & Associates, New York.
12. Ronald Alsop, "Arm & Hammer Baking Soda Going in Toothpaste as Well as Refrigerator," *Wall Street Journal* (June 24, 1988), p. 2-24.
13. "C&D Sees Growth Despite Competition," pp. 9, 19.
14. Church & Dwight Company, Inc., *1987 Annual Report,* p. 2.
15. Gretchen Busch, "New Bicarb Pact Could Have Impact on Supply Picture," *Chemical Marketing Reporter* (November 30, 1992) 242(22).
16. Church & Dwight Company, Inc., *Form 10-K Report* (1992), p. 5.
17. "C&D Sees Growth Despite Competition," p. 19.
18. Kathleen Deveny, "Marketing," *Wall Street Journal* (April 27, 1990), p. B-1.
19. Rick Mullin, "Soaps and Detergents: New Generation of Compacts," *Chemicalweek* (January 27, 1993), p. 29.
20. Riccardo A. Davis, "Arm & Hammer Seeks Growth Abroad," *Advertising Age* (August 17, 1992), pp. 3, 42.
21. Ibid., p . 42.
22. Robert J. Bowman, "Quality Management Comes to Global Transportation," *World Trade* (February 1993), p. 38.
23. Church & Dwight Company, Inc., *1989 Annual Report.*

References

Church & Dwight Company, Inc., *1989 Annual Report.*

Church & Dwight Company, Inc., *1990 Annual Report.*

Church & Dwight Company, Inc., *1991 Annual Report.*

Church & Dwight Company, Inc., *1992 Annual Report.*

Nordstrom, Inc., 1993

Stephen E. Barndt

Nordstrom, Inc., a Seattle-based fashion specialty retail chain, operates 52 apparel, accessory, and shoe department stores; 16 clearance clothing stores; and four youth-oriented clothing stores in Alaska, Arizona, California, Illinois, Maryland, Minnesota, New Jersey, Oregon, Utah, Virginia, and Washington.

The company attained a position of leadership and an outstanding reputation for service: salesperson attention to the customer, selection of goods, product return policy, and amenities to make shopping an enjoyable experience are acknowledged to be extraordinary in the industry. Capitalizing on this trend-setting customer service to differentiate itself from its competition, Nordstrom has grown aggressively while major competing chains have not.

After many years as a regional retail chain serving the Northwest, in the late 1970s Nordstrom started a major expansion into California and Utah. Growth in the northern and southern California areas was steady through the 1980s, and in 1988 the company started a move from western regional focus to that of a national retailer with the opening of a store in Virginia. As a result of growth in both number of stores and sales per store, net sales grew 750% from fiscal year (FY) 1980 through FY 1992. Sales in FY 1992 approximated \$3.42 billion.

Company History[1]

John W. Nordstrom emigrated from Sweden to the United States in 1887 at the age of 16 and worked for years as a logger, miner, and laborer. After earning \$13,000 gold mining in the Klondike, he settled in Seattle where, in 1901, he opened a shoe store in partnership with shoemaker Carl Wallin. In 1923, Wallin and Nordstrom opened a second store in Seattle. John Nordstrom's three sons bought his interest in the store in 1928 and Carl Wallin's in 1929, establishing the "family" ownership and management that has continued to the present.

In the early years, John Nordstrom developed two basic philosophies that have guided business practice since. The first is a customer orientation in which the company emphasizes outstanding service, selection, quality, and value. The second is a policy of selecting managers from among employees who have experience on the sales floor. All of the Nordstrom family members who attained management positions started their careers as salesmen.

Rapid growth did not begin until after World War II. Starting an expansion in 1950 with the opening of two new stores, the company continued to grow so that

This case was prepared by Professor Stephen E. Barndt of Pacific Lutheran University. This case was edited by T. L. Wheelen and J. D. Hunger for this book.

EXHIBIT 23.1

Growth, 1977–1993: Nordstrom, Inc.

Years Ending January 31	Company-Operated Stores	Total Square Footage
1978	24	1,446,000
1979	26	1,625,000
1980	29	1,964,000
1981	31	2,166,000
1982	34	2,640,000
1983	36	2,977,000
1984	39	3,213,000
1985	44	3,924,000
1986	52	4,727,000
1987	53	5,098,000
1988	56	5,527,000
1989	58	6,374,000
1990	59	6,898,000
1991	63	7,655,000
1992	68	8,590,000
1993	72	9,224,000

Source: Nordstrom, Inc., 1985, 1986, 1987, 1989, and 1992 annual reports.

by 1961 there were eight shoe stores and 13 leased shoe departments in Washington, Oregon, and California.

In 1963, Nordstrom diversified into women's fashion apparel with the acquisition of Best's Apparel and its stores in Seattle and Portland. Before the 1960s ended, five new Nordstrom Best stores offering clothes, shoes, and accessories had opened.

During the 1970s, Nordstrom continued to change and grew rapidly and steadily. Management passed to the third generation of Nordstroms in 1970, and the company went public in 1971, accompanied by a change in name to Nordstrom, Inc. Continued growth in the Northwest provided the company with 24 stores by 1978. Geographic expansion to California began in 1978 and has continued. By 1987, Nordstrom's southern California presence was reflected in its position of first or second in market share for women's suits, women's blazers, men's tailored pants, women's dresses, women's coats, women's shoes, and men's shoes in the Los Angeles market.[2] In early 1993, Nordstrom operated 31 stores in California, including six Nordstrom Rack discount stores. Started in 1983, the Rack line of stores had grown to 15 in the western states by 1992. Exhibit 23.1 shows the growth in Nordstrom, Nordstrom Rack, Place Two (youth fashion), and Last Chance (clearance) stores during the 15 years ending January 31, 1993.

The Fashion Specialty Retail Industry

Fashion specialty goods include apparel, shoes, and accessories. The market for such goods is relatively mature, with a 1981 to 1991 ten-year growth rate approximating 6%. Through most of the 1980s, sales growth averaged 7% per year, but the recession starting in 1990 resulted in an overall growth in apparel sales of only 0.9% between 1990 and 1991. In 1991, total U.S. sales of apparel were $95.3 billion. Women's apparel and accessory stores accounted for 35% of the total, and shoe stores accounted for 18%. Men's and boy's wear sales only amounted to 9%.[3]

The fashion goods market is segmented into several imprecise levels of perceived quality and price. The custom-made goods market is at the high end followed by designer/style-setting goods; then popular, mid-priced goods; and finally the low-priced utility goods market.

Through the 1980s, the aging of the population into higher income categories, economic prosperity in general, and increased representation of women in the work force and in higher salaried positions resulted in greater appeal of high-quality, style-setting fashions. Retailers that catered to market segments, such as fashion conscious women that desire upscale goods, did well.

Entering the 1990s, three conditions combined to reduce the nature and growth of the fashion apparel market. First, the economic boom of the 1980s ended. With home values declining or not appreciating, weakened inflation and income growth, and a soft job market, a significant portion of the population felt less secure financially. Second, an aging population, although it had more to spend, tended to spend a lower proportion of its income on clothing. Third, fewer women were entering the work force, reducing the boost they provided the apparel industry as they outfitted themselves.[4] As a result of these conditions, retailers faced a less favorable market.

Analysts expect specialty niche merchants to flourish only if they are able to adapt their lines to changing tastes such as those appropriate to the maturing population of shoppers.

Competition

Fashion retailing traditionally has been very competitive, with stores relying heavily on product differentiation through an emphasis on quality, service, or other means of adding value. Competitors include traditional department stores (e.g., Bullock's, Macy's, and Lazarus), general merchandise chain stores (e.g., Sears and K mart), specialty retailer chains (e.g., The Limited, Brooks Brothers, I. Magnin, and Nordstrom), and independent boutiques.

Most retailers position themselves to serve a single segment of the market. Many department stores are exceptions, offering stylish fashions "upstairs" and discounted standard or clearance goods in their bargain basement departments. Exhibit 23.2 provides a general view of the kinds of retailers that tend to serve the various market segments and what they offer.

Competition often is intense, with rivals in close proximity to one another, especially for firms located in shopping malls. Nordstrom, which caters to the

EXHIBIT 23.2 **Competitor Specialization by Segment**

Market Segment	Types of Stores Serving the Segment	Emphasis in Marketing
Custom	Independent specialty shops	One of a kind, quality
Style-setting/fashion conscious	Upscale department fashion specialty chains, boutiques	Name, quality, service
Popular, mid-priced	Department stores, independent and chain specialty stores	Availability, variety, price, service
Low-priced	Discount department stores, general merchandisers	Price, accessibility, convenience

upscale, fashion conscious market, is located in malls and downtown shopping districts. Consequently, Nordstrom is typically in face-to-face competition with strong, major competitors. For example, in its California markets a Nordstrom store is likely to face several of the following competitors: Macy's, Broadway, Robinson's, Neiman Marcus, I. Magnin, and Saks Fifth Avenue. The Tysons Corner, Virginia, store competes directly with Macy's, Bloomingdale's, and Saks Fifth Avenue. A planned new store in the mall at Short Hills, New Jersey, will compete with Neiman Marcus, Saks Fifth Avenue, Bloomingdale's, and Abraham & Straus. All these competitors are major chain department stores or chain specialty stores. Nordstrom also faces competing independent boutiques and specialty stores in all of its locations.

When the economy is strong, discount clothing retailers do not present a direct competitive threat, as they serve a distinctly different market segment. During an economic recession, however, customers who suffer a loss or are uncertain of income tend to become much more price sensitive. When this happens, fashion clothing customers may become more cautious in their spending and more price-value (rather than quality-value) conscious. As a result, fashion retailers may lose sales because of both nonspending and switching to cut-price retailers, which is what happened during the recession starting in 1990. Nordstrom was particularly hard hit because 48.3% of its square footage was in California, a state with severe economic woes.

Common Industry Practices

Although fashion retailers do not all follow the same strategies, several popular strategic moves have been widely followed to varying degrees. They include market segmentation, selective location, growth through acquisition, cost containment, and price discounting.

Most fashion retailers focus on a single market segment. In recent prerecession years, the higher priced, higher quality stylish market was particularly attractive because of the greater growth in this segment and the higher margins available on such goods. This attractiveness led some firms to establish new lines of focused stores and others to refocus current stores. Each of these alternatives presented disadvantages. Developing new retail lines can require considerable capital to start new businesses or acquire existing businesses. Refocusing has been difficult for many because an identity, once established, is difficult to change. For example, Sears, long a retailer of low-priced and popular fashions, clouded its image and confused potential customers when it tried to upgrade its product offerings.

In contrast to focusing on single market segments, many department stores have sought further market diversification in order to serve higher income customers without losing others. This diversification involves creating stores within a store, with departments divided into mini-boutiques each aimed at a specific fashion niche.

Another market diversification move has aimed at competing for the value-conscious customer. Outlet malls have been taking business away from traditional shopping malls. Now large mid-priced to high-end retailers are opening clearance stores to compete. Macy's, Saks Fifth Avenue, Bloomingdale's, and Nordstrom are among those setting up cut-price outlets.[5]

A shift in shopping from neighborhood and downtown locations to suburban and urban shopping malls has made locating stores in malls or close proximity thereto essential. Picking the malls and other locations that are attractive with respect to customer demographics and then gaining access to needed square footage are key factors for success. Firms that gain the new prime locations in growing areas tend to have significant advantages over competitors with older stores in declining shopping areas.

In the mature fashion market with its low (6%) rate of growth, companies that desire growth must capture the business of competitors. To do so can involve enticing competitors' customers through superior marketing. Alternatively, it can involve acquiring going-concern competitors to gain market share or broader segment coverage. The latter, a growth through acquisition strategy, has been widely followed in the industry. Federated Department Stores, Macy's, The Limited, the May Company, and Carter Hawley Hale Stores, among others, have used acquisition to grow.

Rapid expansion through acquisition has left many chains in debt and strapped for cash. For example, Campeau Corporation, which owned Allied Stores and Federated Department Stores, entered bankruptcy in late 1989 and subsequently sold its Bullocks and I. Magnin chains to Macy's and its Filene's chain to the May Company. Later, as the recession reduced cash flow, the Carter Hawley Hale and Macy's department store chains also were forced into Chapter 11 bankruptcy. The Campeau Corporation's former department store chains emerged from bankruptcy in 1992, as an independent Federated Department Stores, Inc. Aside from such drastic measures as divestiture, debt-laden firms commonly are searching perpetually for ways to reduce operating costs. They also tend to be conservative, not investing in innovation or taking major risks. Many such firms are followers, attempting to duplicate the moves of a competitor only after those moves have proved successful.

Price competition is common, especially among department stores. This competition includes constant rounds of sale prices, in place of stocking top-of-the-line goods, to lure customers. Such heavy reliance on price discounting to increase sales rather than on enhanced merchandising and marketing is reflected in advertising that is typically price-oriented.

Lower prices (with lower margins), in general, and heavy debt burdens, in particular, have driven many of the larger corporations toward cost reduction. Because labor and inventory are major costs, they have been the target of cutbacks. Among many stores, inventories are maintained at low to moderate levels and emphasize a limited breadth of fast turnover styles. Labor cost reduction has affected direct selling and support. Sales cost reductions have been achieved by replacing commission pay with straight hourly wages, increased use of relatively inexperienced lower paid people for sales, and a reduction of work hours and therefore the size of the on-duty sales force. At the same time, centralization of the buying and warehousing functions have reduced support manpower and labor costs.

Nordstrom's Strategic Posture

The Nordstrom strategy emphasizes merchandise and service tailored to appeal to the affluent and fashion-conscious shopper without losing its middle-class customers. The large Nordstrom specialty department stores cater to their target market with an unparalleled attention to customers, guaranteed service, and a wide and deep line of merchandise. The success of this strategy has made the company one that competitors fear and attempt to follow. Its competitive strength is implied in the statement: "Nordstrom is sometimes known as the 'Black Hole,' into which shoppers disappear, never to enter nearby stores."[6]

In addition to its mainline stores, Nordstrom also operates four smaller Place Two stores specializing in youth fashions, one Last Chance cut-price clearance store, and 15 Nordstrom Rack stores. The Racks serve as discount outlets offering clearance merchandise from the main stores and some merchandise purchased directly from manufacturers. They cater to bargain shoppers who value Nordstrom quality.

Store architecture and merchandise differ from store to store. Each is designed to fit lifestyles prevailing in the local geographic and economic environment. For example, the downtown San Francisco and Seattle stores provide their mainstay clientele, upscale professionals, with large men's clothing and accessories selections. In every location, merchandise selection, local tastes, and customer preferences help shape what the store looks on the inside. Approximately 70% of the merchandise featured is available at all Nordstrom stores, and the other 30% is unique to each store or region.[7]

Product Lines

Nordstrom's specialty department stores carry focused lines of classically styled, relatively conservative merchandise. A *New York Times* writer described the mer-

EXHIBIT 23.3

Merchandise Sales by Category: Nordstrom, Inc.

Merchandise Category	Share of 1991 Sales
Women's apparel	39%
Women's accessories	20
Shoes	19
Men's apparel and furnishings	16
Children's apparel and accessories	4
Other	2

Source: Nordstrom, Inc., *1992 Annual Report.*

chandise as "primarily classic and not trendy, the selection limited to styles with broad appeal. . . ."[8]

Women's fashions account for the largest share of the Nordstrom product line. However, men's wear appears to be gaining in emphasis in some locations. For example, men's wear comprised 18% of the inventory and 21–22% percent of total sales in the downtown San Francisco store.[9] Company-wide, sales from men's wear constitute 16% of total sales. Exhibit 23.3 shows the company-wide sales breakdown by merchandise category.

Nordstrom carries both designer and private-label merchandise. In the past, it has carried private labels on 15% of the merchandise. Men's apparel and men's and women's shoes were the largest private-label lines, with approximately 50% of men's clothes and 25% of shoes carrying the Nordstrom name. Designer lines have made up the bulk of the merchandise. Nordstrom has featured apparel lines by Claude Montana, Gianfranco Ferre, Christian Lacroix, Carolina Herrera, Carolyne Roehm, Calvin Klein, Anne Klein, Donna Karan, and Gianni Versace, among others, in its various stores. The Facconnable line of men's wear is sold throughout the chain. Selection of lines and styles is based largely on wants indicated in direct customer feedback.

The company stays alert to changes in both taste for and profitability of its product offerings and has a history of change. If a new line of merchandise appears to serve customers better than an existing one, Nordstrom doesn't hesitate to make the switch. For example, recently the company closed out its fur salons and converted the space into departments carrying more profitable merchandise, such as large-size women's apparel.

The volume of its orders has allowed Nordstrom to develop a broad supplier base. No one supplier has significant bargaining power.

Merchandising

Nordstrom's merchandising is noted for its extensive inventories and dedicated, helpful sales force. However, Nordstrom also differs from rivals in several other ways.

The typical store has 50% more salespeople on the floor than similar sized competitors. The sales force uses its product knowledge to show appropriate merchandise to customers, assist them in their selections, and suggest accessories. Salespeople keep track of their regular customers' fashion tastes and sizes and then call or send them notes about new merchandise in which they may have an interest.

The company carries a large inventory, providing an unusually wide selection of colors and sizes. With an inventory almost twice as large per square foot as its department store competitors, Nordstrom has a depth of inventory almost comparable to smaller specialty stores but offers a more complete line. As an indication of the inventory intensity, the San Francisco Center (downtown) store had $100 million invested in opening-day inventory, including 100,000 pairs of shoes, 10,000 men's suits, and 20,000 neckties.

Nordstrom is one of the industry leaders in dividing its stores into small boutiques featuring targeted merchandise mixes. Rather than feature a single type of merchandise, departments offer a variety of items (e.g., coats, suits, dresses, etc.), all of which are keyed to a particular lifestyle. Nordstrom adds or changes departments to serve evolving customer needs. For instance, in response to growth in the number of women in higher level management positions, it added women's tailored clothing departments. Although designer fashions generally are not given special treatment in display, the company has introduced special departments to display some of its higher priced designer apparel.

Luxurious settings that use polished wood and marble contrast with the chrome and bright colors common in competing stores. Merchandise is arranged in departments according to lifestyles. Stores feature clusters of antiques and open displays of merchandise, usually arranged at right angles to each other. Mannequins are used sparingly. A piece of antique furniture is a more commonly used display prop. Merchandise is displayed without bulky anti-theft tags. In addition, there is no closed-circuit television, presenting a less intimidating atmosphere to customers. Instead, Nordstrom relies on the presence of its large sales force to discourage theft.

Nordstrom spends less than 2% of sales on advertising, or half as much as is commonly spent in the industry. The company relies heavily on word-of-mouth to attract customers. The advertising that is used emphasizes styles and breadth of merchandise selection rather than price.

Pricing

Prices are competitive with comparable merchandise. Nordstrom follows the same mark-up practices common to retail fashion stores, but prices tend to be high, reflecting the company's selectivity in providing high-quality merchandise. However, the company is committed to providing value and will not be undersold. If a customer finds an item carried by Nordstrom for sale cheaper at another store, Nordstrom will match that lower price.

Consumer caution in spending during the recession that started at the end of the 1980s placed downward pressure on prices in the industry. Nordstrom responded with a shift to a greater share of value-priced merchandise. The primary means of providing lower priced, quality merchandise has been the substitution of Nordstrom-label goods for brand-label goods.

Customer Service

High inflation in the 1970s and significant increases in the cost of goods and labor caused most department stores and specialty retailers to cut services. They did so to prevent prices from skyrocketing and to remain competitive with the discount retailers that had become popular. This period of rising costs forced consumers to accept less service in exchange for affordable prices.

Under recent conditions of lower inflation and higher incomes, consumers have raised their expectations of service. Many Americans have become tired of self-service or inattentive sales help. Two-income households and busy professionals have become hooked on convenience and are willing to pay for it. At the same time, retailers who shifted to lower levels of customer service are having difficulty in upgrading service. Understaffing in sales positions and overwork, coupled with low pay and lack of a career path, do not provide the conditions necessary to motivate employees to improve service.

Nordstrom has never cut service and therefore does not have to overcome structural, motivational, or cultural barriers to provide satisfying service. The company is already there—it is the undisputed leader in customer service. Nordstrom's excellent service is anchored on the sales force and supported by company policy and investment in facilities and personnel.

At Nordstrom, a customer can expect to be in a department no longer than two minutes before a salesperson is in attendance to answer questions, explain merchandise, and make suggestions. This salesperson might lead the customer to merchandise in other departments to help find what he or she wants. As an example of this kind of service, a sales representative showed up at a Nordstrom store as it opened at 9:30 A.M. The sales representative, who was dressed in jeans and complementary casual attire, explained that she needed to be completely outfitted so that she could make a sales presentation at a college over an hour away in two hours. She had arrived in town with only her briefcase because an airline had misdirected her luggage. A sales clerk helped her select a suit and then brought merchandise to fill out the outfit from other departments, including such items as shoes, hose, a slip, blouse, and scarf. The sales clerk also facilitated opening a charge account to make the purchase possible. The sales representative left Nordstrom 45 minutes later, suitably attired for her presentation.

Sales clerks routinely attend customers in dressing rooms, bringing them alternative items of apparel or sizes to try on. They also routinely send thank you notes and announcements of sales and arrival of merchandise that should be of interest to the customer. Other examples of the extraordinary out-of-the-way types of service that have been noted of Nordstrom sales personnel include warming up customers' cars on cold days, paying parking tickets for customers who couldn't find legal parking, personally delivering items to the customer's home, and ironing a newly bought item of apparel so the customer could wear it back to work.

Extraordinary service stems from several mutually supportive factors. First, the number of salespeople on the floor is high—50% higher than is common in the industry. Thus the sales clerks are not badly rushed and have the time to wait on customers. Second, the sales force is carefully recruited. Third, pay is higher than in comparable positions elsewhere and, in addition, is partly based on performance (volume of sales). That means that the sales clerk who satisfies customers earns more. In addition, there is peer pressure to sell more (satisfy more customers) because those who earn more are viewed as role models. Last, Nordstrom has a powerful corporate culture that stresses attentiveness to the customer. This culture is well established, having been instituted under John W. Nordstrom and reinforced ever since. The company has successfully transferred this culture to its new stores at their start-up. A key practice in establishing the Nordstrom culture in new stores is to open them under the leadership of a cadre of experienced Nordstrom managers and sales people who provide guidance and training to locally hired personnel. For example, when Nordstrom opens its new store in Indianapolis, about 50 of 500 employees will be moved there from other Nordstrom stores.[10]

In keeping with the feeling that the customer is "king" and is always right, Nordstrom has a no-questions-asked merchandise return policy. The company willingly replaces or refunds the price of any item of merchandise whether new or used, with or without a sales receipt. Probably the best known of many refund folklore tales is that of an individual who had bought a pair of tires from the same store when it was under other ownership and returned them to Nordstrom for a refund. Nordstrom refunded the purchase price of the pair of tires even though it does not and never has sold tires.

Luxurious settings and furnishings make the shopper feel special. Standard extras in many of the stores include a musician playing enjoyable music on a baby-grand piano, free coat and package checking, play areas for children, extra large dressing rooms, free gift wrap at the cash register, and tea for weary customers as they try on apparel in the dressing rooms. Newer, larger stores feature even more extras. For example, the San Francisco Center store has a beauty treatment spa, four restaurants, a pub in the men's department, and valet parking to help it differentiate itself from competition.

Location

Nordstrom targets growing affluent communities for its stores. Although the majority of its stores are located in suburban shopping centers, others are located in large and small city central business districts. In either type of location, Nordstrom chooses to locate close to other retailers because of the drawing power of a concentration of shopping facilities. Exhibit 23.4 shows the locations and sizes of Nordstrom and Nordstrom Rack stores in 1993.

As a late entrant in many regions (e.g., the East, Midwest and southern and northern California), Nordstrom has had an advantage in its selection of store sites in growing high-income areas. Early entrant chains often find themselves doing business in outdated stores in older, less economically attractive areas. However, the industry is mature, with most attractive shopping districts saturated with retailers. Finding locations attractive for growth with adequate available square footage requires buying out competitors or a geographically extended search. Fol-

EXHIBIT 23.4

Stores: Nordstrom, Inc.

Store Location	State	Square Feet	Year Started
Portland Lloyd Center	Oregon	150,000	1963
Seattle downtown	Washington	245,000	1963
Seattle Northgate	Washington	122,000	1965
Portland downtown	Oregon	174,000	1966
Tacoma Mall	Washington	132,000	1966
Bellevue Square	Washington	184,000	1967
Seattle Southcenter	Washington	170,000	1968
Yakima	Washington	44,000	1972
Spokane	Washington	121,000	1974
Portland Washington Square	Oregon	108,000	1974
Anchorage	Alaska	97,000	1975
Vancouver	Washington	71,000	1977
South Coast Plaza	California	235,000	1978
Alderwood Mall	Washington	125,000	1979
Brea Mall	California	195,000	1979
Crossroads Plaza	Utah	140,000	1980
Salem	Oregon	71,000	1980
Clackamas Town Center	Oregon	121,000	1981
Fashion Place Mall	Utah	110,000	1981
Fashion Valley	California	156,000	1981
Los Cerritos Shopping Center	California	122,000	1981
Hillsdale Mall	California	149,000	1982
Ogden City Mall	Utah	76,000	1982
Clackamas Rack	Oregon	28,000	1983
Glendale Galleria	California	147,000	1983
Santa Ana Rack	California	21,000	1983
Broadway Plaza	California	193,000	1984
Stanford Shopping Center	California	187,000	1984
Topanga Plaza	California	154,000	1984
University Towne Center	California	130,000	1984
Woodland Hills Rack	California	48,000	1984
Alderwood Rack	Washington	25,000	1985
Galleria at South Bay	California	161,000	1985
Horton Plaza	California	151,000	1985

(continued)

lowing its coverage of virtually all major Pacific Northwest markets in the 1970s and early 1980s, Nordstrom channeled its growth into California. By the late 1980s, Nordstrom had covered most of the attractive California markets, limiting its further growth there. This saturation forced the company to search for expansion opportunities in several other, more slowly growing geographic regions.

EXHIBIT 23.4 **Stores: Nordstrom, Inc.** *(continued)*

Store Location	State	Square Feet	Year Started
Mission Valley Rack	California	27,000	1985
Oakridge Mall	California	150,000	1985
Pavilion Rack	Washington	39,000	1985
Village at Corte Madera	California	115,000	1985
Westside Pavilion	California	150,000	1985
Montclair Plaza	California	133,000	1986
North Country Fair Center	California	156,000	1986
Portland Rack	Oregon	19,000	1986
Chino Rack	California	30,000	1987
Main Place Mall	California	169,000	1987
280 Metro Center Rack	California	31,000	1987
Seattle Rack	Washington	42,000	1987
Valley Fair Shopping Center	California	165,000	1987
San Francisco Center	California	350,000	1988
Stonestown Galleria	California	174,000	1988
Tysons Corner Center	Virginia	238,000	1988
Arden Fair	California	190,000	1989
Fashion Centre at Pentagon City	Virginia	241,000	1989
Garden State Plaza	New Jersey	272,000	1990
Marina Square Rack	California	44,000	1990
Paseo Nuevo	California	186,000	1990
Potomac Mills Rack	Virginia	46,000	1990
Stoneridge Mall	California	173,000	1990
The Galleria at Tyler	California	164,000	1991
Menlo Park Mall	New Jersey	266,000	1991
Montgomery Mall	Maryland	225,000	1991
Oakbrook Center	Illinois	249,000	1991
Sugarhouse Center Rack	Utah	31,000	1991
City Place Rack	Maryland	37,000	1992
Freehold Raceway Mall	New Jersey	174,000	1992
Mall of America	Minnesota	240,000	1992
Towson Rack	Maryland	31,000	1992
Towson Town Center	Maryland	205,000	1992

Source: Nordstrom, Inc., *1992 Annual Report.*

Nordstrom currently plans to open stores in various selected locations in the East, Northeast, Southcentral, and Midwest regions and is considering opening stores in the Southeast and Intermountain West. Such growth is opportunistic, involving new shopping mall space in growth areas or occupancy of vacated space in older shopping centers. An example of the latter is Nordstrom's entry into the Paramus,

New Jersey, market in a store vacated when May Department Stores closed its Hahne's chain.

Seven regional distribution centers are located to serve stores quickly and efficiently. These include recently opened distribution centers in Maryland and Iowa to serve the growing number of stores in the surrounding states.

Management and Organization

Nordstrom practices selective centralized and decentralized decision making. Strategic and significant financial decisions are made at the top level in the organization, whereas operational decisions are made at the regional and store levels. The managers in each region, store, and department are responsible and accountable for profit. They have the autonomy and authority to make decisions regarding their areas. This decentralized management allows managers to be entrepreneurially creative in tailoring each store's merchandise and layout to its customers. Freed from decision making for regional and store operations, top management has been able to concentrate on future expansion.

The company structure can be described in terms of three levels of management responsibility: top or executive level, mid level, and store level. The top level consists of four Co-Chairmen of the Board: brothers James F. Nordstrom, 53, and John N. Nordstrom, 55, and cousin Bruce A. Nordstrom, 59, often collectively referred to as the "family"; and John A. McMillan, 61, who is married to a Nordstrom. The Co-Chairmen retain strategic management responsibility, concentrating on setting the strategic direction and making expansion location decisions. The "family" is deeply involved in providing the overall guidance to the company and exercises effective control with about 40% ownership. When a new store opens, at least one Nordstrom will be there—on the floor. During a downturn in 1987, family members returned to the floor for stints of selling and visible leadership to help motivate the meeting of goals. They are visible leaders and approachable to employees and customers but are close-lipped about themselves and the company.

While the Co-Chairmen share strategic management, operational management is delegated to an Office of the President. In 1991, the Co-Chairmen appointed four Co-Presidents to manage the day-to-day operations. These four share the office by focusing on different aspects of the business. Raymond Johnson, 51, handles accessories, lingerie, children's clothes, personnel, and legal matters; Darrel Hume, 45, is in charge of store planning, finance, and men's apparel; Galen Jefferson, 43, handles women's wear and merchandise systems; and John Whitacre, 40, concentrates on shoes, restaurants, and budgeting. Each has authority to make decisions that clearly fall in his or her area. They meet formally once a week and informally communicate with one another throughout the week as necessary. Disagreements that arise among the Co-Presidents usually are resolved by choosing the view or course of action that best serves the customer.[11]

The mid-management level consists of the corporate Treasurer; geographic group general managers for the northern California, southern California, Oregon, Washington and Alaska, Utah, Northeast, Midwest, and capital groups of stores;

EXHIBIT 23.5 **Management Structure: Nordstrom, Inc.**

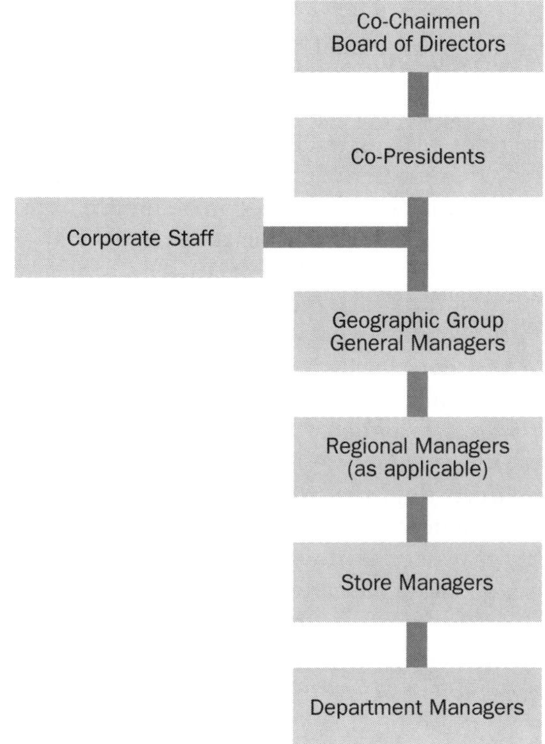

regional managers responsible for smaller groups of stores in several of the geographic store groups; and various managers in charge of merchandise categories and staff support areas such as public relations, legal affairs, and sales promotion.

Operational management of the stores is the responsibility of store managers with the assistance of their staffs and department managers. Stores and departments have their own buyers. Exhibit 23.5 shows the general chain of command at Nordstrom.

Throughout the company, idea generation and operational decision making are encouraged, expected, and supported at the lowest levels where the individual has the appropriate information. For example, managers in the sales departments routinely make decisions on what inventory to carry and whether to accept checks, lower prices to stay competitive, and accept returned merchandise, without consulting higher level managers or staff specialists.

Units and the individuals in them are goal-driven. As stated by Richard Stevenson in a *New York Times Magazine* article, "the life of a Nordstrom salesperson is defined by goals. Departmental, storewide, and company goals. Qualitative and quantitative goals."[12] Store goals are set for the year and both reflect and influence departmental goals. Departmental goals influence salesperson goals. Yearly goals are translated into monthly goals. Daily goals are more changeable and reflect pro rata accomplishment of monthly goals as well as historical performance. On a daily basis, departments aim to surpass sales of the same day last year by a set level, and individual goals are adjusted accordingly. If a department is behind in reaching its monthly goal, daily goals of the department and each sales clerk are likely to be pegged higher to get it back on track.

Salespeople and departments are kept aware of the level of their goal accomplishment and are rewarded for goal achievement. Salespeople are reminded of the day's goal and may be asked during the day how they are doing. Reaching goals is praised and when longer term goals (e.g., annual personal goals), are achieved, recognition is public, often in the form of an announcement or letter from a Nordstrom. Top-performing salespeople are admitted to the Pacesetters' Club. Pacesetters receive a certificate, a new "Pacesetter" business card, a 33% discount on Nordstrom merchandise (rather than the standard 20%), and a night on the town.

The company also promotes performance and conformity to its standards of customer service through the widespread use of heroics. The exploits of employees who make unusual or extraordinary efforts to please customers or who have specially noteworthy levels of sales are communicated throughout the organization, formally and informally, so that they may serve as role models. This technique, along with the use of goals, serves as a powerful indicator of the kinds of behavior the company wants and rewards.

Human Resources

Nordstrom has about 33,000 year-round employees plus seasonal hires. The company likes to hire young people who have not learned behaviors inconsistent with the Nordstrom customer service values and start them in sales positions. The actual decision of who to hire is left to the sales department managers rather than to a staff personnel department. The company's hiring practice, in conjunction with its major expansion in recent years, has left the company with a work force that is relatively young and often college educated. Even its mid- and top-level managers are young. Top managers are in their early 40s to mid 50s. Mid-level vice-presidents range in age from the low 30s to mid 50s, with most less than 45 years of age.

The company follows a promote-from-within policy. Because the company is growing fast, this policy serves as a motivator to those who aspire to rapid advancement. Promotions to line management positions are made from among employees with sales and customer contact experience. Those who are promoted to higher level positions are encouraged and expected to keep in contact with customers. For example, the company's buyers, who all started in sales positions, spend a large amount of their time on the sales floor to learn what customers want.

Initial training is brief, taking about one and a half days, and stresses product knowledge and how to work cash registers and attend the customer. Formal indoctrination takes the form of reading a handbook and either viewing a videotape or listening to a lecture on the company's history.

Acceptable behavior is not narrowly specified. For the most part, the culture takes care of that. Employees are given basic guidance in a short, one page 5″ × 8″ employee handbook on card stock that says:

Our number one goal is to provide
outstanding customer service.
Set both your personal and
professional goals high.
We have great confidence in your
Ability to achieve them.
Nordstrom Rules:
Rule #1: **Use your good**
judgment in all situations.
There will be no additional rules.[13]

Other expectations are transmitted in various ways and will bring on corrective actions if violated. One of these is dress. Employees are expected to wear neat business attire. Further, it is understood that the attire *should* be acquired from Nordstrom. Personal business, including telephone calls, is not to be conducted in a customer area. Abuse of employee discount privileges, violation of criminal law, rudeness to a customer, and unacceptable personal conduct are grounds for immediate dismissal. Underperforming employees usually leave on their own, as do those who are uncomfortable with constant pressure to meet goals and be nice to the customer no matter what the customer does or how he or she behaves. Those who remain are loyal to the company and accepting of its cultural values.

To motivate its sales force, Nordstrom uses goals, heroics, recognition, and promotion from within as already discussed. Additional major motivational forces are monetary compensation and morale boosting and attitude shaping programs.

High pay is an important factor in attracting, retaining, and motivating employees. Pay ranges from about \$6 to \$9 per hour plus commissions of 6.5%–10%. With combined hourly and commission pay, first-year salespeople average \$20,000 to \$22,000 and after three years about \$50,000 per year.[14] Top salespeople can earn \$80,000 to \$100,000. These levels of earnings make Nordstrom's sales employees' compensation high relative to that of the rest of the industry.

Commission pay ties rewards directly to sales and customer service performance. The higher the sales to satisfied customers, the greater is the reward. Subtracting the price of returned merchandise from sales clerks' sales decreases commission income and discourages selling for the sake of a sale alone.

Motivational speeches, skits, and pep-talk meetings supplement monetary rewards and public recognition. The objectives of these techniques are to build employees' confidence in their ability to perform better, in general, and to get them worked up to capitalize on the selling opportunities associated with one of the four major annual sales, in particular.

With its high level of compensation and culture that emphasizes the employee and her or his contributions, Nordstrom is ranked among the better employers.

The company attempts to make union representation unnecessary and unattractive. The only locations where employees had been represented by a union was the western part of Washington state. From mid 1989, Nordstrom was engaged in an open dispute with locals 1001 and 367 of the United Food & Commercial Workers Union. The union, through these locals, represented approximately 2,000 Nordstrom employees. After a long and bitter contest, Nordstrom employees elected to decertify local 1001 in 1991. A year later, in 1992, local 367 withdrew its representation on the eve of a decertification election when it was clear the union would lose.

Image and Public Relations

Nordstrom's reputation for service and selection of merchandise provide the company with a mystique. As a result, Nordstrom receives a great deal of favorable free publicity. New store openings are preceded with numerous articles in the local press that help create perceptions that Nordstrom offers a superior shopping experience. Continuing favorable reports in the media reinforce that perception. For example, the press recently reported the results of a nationwide survey that ranked Nordstrom first among the top 70 U.S. retail department and discount store chains in overall customer satisfaction.[15]

Although much of the publicity has been favorable, some unfavorable charges and accusations have surfaced in recent years. These include labor union allegations of wrongdoing and black-interest charges of discrimination.

In late 1989, the United Food & Commercial Workers Union charged that Nordstrom encouraged its salespeople to work off-the-clock taking inventory, writing thank you notes, making home deliveries, or tracking down hard-to-find garments over the phone. Thus the union was claiming that salespeople spent time working for the company for which they were not compensated. The Washington State Department of Labor and Industries subsequently found Nordstrom in violation of state wage laws and directed the company to reimburse workers for work performed without pay. The union followed up with a class-action lawsuit on behalf of 50,000 past and present Nordstrom employees in Washington, Oregon, California, Utah, Alaska, and Virginia seeking compensatory damages and penalties. Without admitting guilt, the company has agreed to pay back wages and legal fees to qualifying present and former employees. Total cost to the company has been estimated at $15–$30 million.[16] Earlier the company established a $15 million contingency liability reserve for retroactive wage claims.[17]

The union also engaged in an attempt to discredit Nordstrom's image with customers. The union alleged that the company requires its employees to wear garments it is promoting during work hours, then allows them to put the merchandise back on the rack, sometimes without cleaning. Subsequently, Oregon sued Nordstrom for selling used lipstick, shoes, and other merchandise at its Oregon stores. Without admitting any wrongdoing, Nordstrom settled the suit with Oregon, paying the state $25,000.[18] The company claims that its employees are encouraged but not required to wear Nordstrom clothing. The Nordstrom clothing they wear must be purchased and employees can buy at a discount.

In an unrelated incident a sales clerk in a California Nordstrom store filed a lawsuit alleging that Nordstrom invaded her privacy through the use of a hidden video camera placed in a small room used by some employees to change clothes and relieve themselves. Nordstrom contended that the room was not an employee lounge and that the camera was there to monitor a safe containing high-value merchandise.[19]

In 1992, black interests targeted the company. First, seven blacks filed a class-action lawsuit claiming discrimination against blacks in recruitment, hiring, and promotion. Subsequently, a group calling itself People Against Racism at Nordstrom (PARAN) targeted Nordstrom for a national boycott based on the allegations of discrimination.[20] Later, another six plaintiffs entered the lawsuit. However, by late 1992, 12 had withdrawn.

In spite of union and black interest charges, Nordstrom generally is considered to be a good community citizen. It has a record of supporting benefits for social program fund-raising in its communities. For example, in its hometown it recently provided the Seattle Housing Group with $4.7 million, more than half the cost to build a 100 unit low-income housing project.

Nordstrom started a "Healthy Beginnings" free program to help expectant mothers avoid risks during their pregnancies. Under the program, they receive educational materials, pregnancy risk screenings, a toll-free hot line, and a Nordstrom gift certificate.[21] Within the company, Nordstrom introduced a family leave program in 1991, allowing up to 12 weeks of unpaid leave to care for newborn or newly adopted children or seriously ill family members.

Nordstrom has been a leader in catering to people with disabilities. In 1992, the company was awarded an "Excellence in Access Award" for making its stores accessible to disabled customers and providing special services to them. Also in 1992, Nordstrom received an Equality/Dignity/Independence (EDI) award from the National Easter Seal Society for featuring models with disabilities in its catalogs.[22]

Support for minorities includes a minority vendor program started in 1989 that, by 1992, had awarded $20 million in contracts to minority-owned businesses. The company committed $220,000 for advertising in West Coast African-American newspapers over ten months and contributed $10,000 to the United Negro College Fund. Within the company, 27% of the work force are members of minorities, as are 16% of its managers. Further, Nordstrom claims that it employs a greater percentage of African-Americans in every region where it does business than that minority's share of the population.[23] Many special and minority interest groups support and praise Nordstrom for its efforts.

Financial Position

Over the ten-year period from February 1983 through January 1993, Nordstrom enjoyed continuous growth in sales. Net earnings grew each year except fiscal years 1989 and 1990 (see Exhibit 23.6). Fiscal year 1988, ending January 31, 1989, was the best year of the ten in terms of return on sales, assets, and equity. Exhibit 23.7 shows the company's consolidated balance sheet, and Exhibit 23.8 provides a ten-year summary of financial information.

EXHIBIT 23.6

Statement of Profit and Earnings: Nordstrom, Inc., and Subsidiaries

(Dollar amounts in thousands, except per share amounts)

Years Ending January 31	1993	1992	1991	1990	1989	1988	1987	1986	1985	1984
Net sales	$3,421,979	$3,179,820	$2,893,904	$2,671,114	$2,327,946	$1,920,231	$1,629,918	$1,301,857	$958,678	$768,677
Costs and expenses										
Cost of sales and related buying and occupancy	2,339,107	2,169,437	2,000,250	1,829,383	1,564,056	1,300,883	1,095,584	893,874	648,270	509,133
Selling, general and administrative	902,083	831,505	747,770	669,159	582,973	477,488	408,664	326,758	243,845	192,813
Net interest	44,810	49,106	52,228	49,121	39,977	32,952	34,910	30,482	20,682	12,109
Service charge income	(86,140)	(87,443)	(84,660)	(55,958)	(57,492)	(53,825)	(49,479)	(36,636)	(26,630)	(19,217)
Total costs and expenses	3,199,860	2,962,605	2,715,588	2,491,705	2,129,514	1,757,498	1,489,679	1,214,478	886,167	694,838
Earnings before taxes	222,119	217,215	178,316	179,409	198,432	162,733	140,239	87,379	72,511	73,839
Income taxes	85,500	81,400	62,500	64,500	75,100	70,000	67,300	37,300	31,800	33,600
Net earnings	$ 136,619	$ 135,815	$ 115,816	$ 114,909	$ 123,332	$ 92,733	$ 72,939	$ 50,079	$ 40,711	$ 40,239
Earnings per share	$ 1.67	$ 1.66	$ 1.42	$ 1.41	$ 1.51	$ 1.13	$ .91	$ .65	$ .54	$ .54
Dividends per share	$ .32	$ .31	$ .30	$ .28	$ .22	$ .18	$ .13	$ .11	$ .10	$ .07
After-tax return on sales	$ .040	$ .043	$ .040	$ .043	$ .053	$ .048	$ .045	$ .038	$ .042	$ .052
Asset turnover	1.67	1.56	1.52	1.56	1.54	1.56	1.52	1.37	1.34	1.49
Return on assets	$ .067	$ .067	$ .061	$ .067	$ .082	$ .075	$ .068	$ .053	$ .057	$ .078
Return on equity	$ .13	$ .14	$ .14	$ .16	$ .19	$ .17	$ .16	$ .16	$ .15	$ .17

Source: Nordstrom, Inc., 1991 and 1992 annual reports.

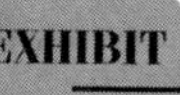
EXHIBIT 23.7

Consolidated Balance Sheets: Nordstrom, Inc. and Subsidiaries
(Dollar amounts in thousands)

Years Ending January 31	1993	1992
Assets		
Current assets		
Cash and cash equivalents	$ 29,136	$ 14,651
Accounts receivable, net	603,198	608,227
Merchandise inventories	536,739	506,632
Prepaid expenses	50,771	48,128
Total current assets	1,219,844	1,177,638
Property, buildings and equipment, net	824,142	856,404
Other assets	9,184	7,833
Total assets	$2,053,170	$2,041,875
Liabilities and Shareholders' Equity		
Current liabilities		
Notes payable	$ 38,319	$ 134,735
Accounts payable	220,176	216,432
Accrued salaries, wages, and taxes	158,028	145,792
Accrued expenses	31,141	31,741
Accrued income taxes	22,216	16,402
Current portion of long-term debt	41,316	8,801
Total current liabilities	511,196	553,903
Long-term debt	440,629	502,199
Deferred income taxes	49,314	46,542
Contingent liabilities		
Shareholders' equity	1,052,031	939,231
Total liabilities and shareholders' equity	$2,053,170	$2,041,875

Source: Nordstrom, Inc., *1993 Annual Report.*

While the company has been profitable every year, it suffered reduced profitability in relative and absolute terms starting in its fiscal year 1989. A continuing recession, particularly in California, where Nordstrom has nearly 50% of its square footage, is a major factor explaining the reduced profitability. Profits suffered in two ways: (1) growth in demand and sales was less than in the years prior to the recession, and (2) competition for customers forced price markdowns. As a consequence, overall sales per store continued to climb but at a reduced rate while net earnings per store declined relative to FY 1988, the best year of the past ten. As Exhibit 23.9 shows, earnings per store in FY 1989–1992 failed to continue the upward climb started in 1986. The company does not disclose profitability by geographic region, but indications are that the East Coast, Midwest, Pacific Northwest, and Utah regions have done relatively well during the recession.

EXHIBIT 23.8

Ten-Year Statistical Summary: Nordstrom, Inc., and Subsidiaries

(Dollar amounts in thousands, except square footage and per share amounts)

Years Ending January 31	1993	1992	1991	1990
Financial Position				
Customer accounts receivable, net	$ 584,379	$ 585,490	$ 558,573	$ 519,656
Merchandise inventories	536,739	506,632	448,344	419,976
Current assets	1,219,844	1,177,638	1,090,379	1,011,148
Current liabilities	511,196	553,903	551,835	489,888
Working capital	708,648	623,735	538,544	521,260
Operating working capital	724,577	749,780	668,150	595,083
Working capital ratio	2.39	2.13	1.98	2.06
Property, buildings and equipment, net	824,142	856,404	806,191	691,937
Long-term debt	481,945	511,000	489,172	468,412
Debt/capital ratio	33.09	40.74	43.59	43.78
Shareholders' equity	1,052,031	939,231	826,410	733,250
Shares outstanding	81,974,797	81,844,227	81,737,910	81,584,710
Book value per share	12.83	11.48	10.11	8.99
Total assets	2,053,170	2,041,875	1,902,589	1,707,420
Operations				
Net sales	$ 3,421,979	$ 3,179,820	$ 2,893,904	$ 2,671,114
Costs and expenses				
Cost of sales and related buying and occupancy	2,339,107	2,169,437	2,000,250	1,829,383
Selling, general and administrative	902,083	831,505	747,770	669,159
Interest, net	44,810	49,106	52,228	49,121
Service charge income and other, net	(86,140)	(87,443)	(84,660)	(55,958)
Total costs and expenses	3,199,860	2,962,605	2,715,588	2,491,705
Earnings before income taxes	222,119	217,215	178,316	179,409
Income taxes	85,500	81,400	62,500	64,500
Net earnings	$ 136,619	$ 135,815	$ 115,816	$ 114,909
Earnings per share	$ 1.67	$ 1.66	$ 1.42	$ 1.41
Dividends per share	.32	.31	.30	.28
Net earnings as a percent of net sales	3.99%	4.27%	4.00%	4.30%
Return on average shareholders' equity	13.72%	15.38%	14.85%	16.74%
Sales per square foot for company-operated stores	381	388	391	398
Stores and Facilities				
Company-operated stores	72	68	63	59
Total square footage	9,224,000	8,590,000	7,655,000	6,898,000

Source: Nordstrom, Inc., *1993 Annual Report.*

1989	1988	1987	1986	1985	1984
$ 465,929	$ 391,387	$ 344,045	$ 296,030	$ 214,831	$ 162,610
403,795	312,696	257,334	226,017	162,361	129,588
913,986	730,182	645,326	546,756	402,898	309,039
448,165	394,699	324,697	339,503	239,331	164,628
465,821	335,483	320,629	207,253	163,567	144,411
549,588	423,378	355,950	337,308	237,221	187,290
2.04	1.85	1.99	1.61	1.68	1.88
594,038	502,661	424,228	397,380	313,818	205,597
389,216	260,343	271,054	276,419	199,387	109,534
43.12	39.57	41.57	56.41	50.12	39.07
639,941	533,209	451,196	314,119	271,709	237,734
81,465,027	81,371,106	80,981,722	74,504,392	74,382,408	74,141,420
7.86	6.55	5.57	4.22	3.65	3.21
1,511,703	1,234,267	1,071,124	945,880	717,557	514,679
$ 2,327,946	$ 1,920,231	$ 1,629,918	$ 1,301,857	$ 958,678	$ 768,677
1,563,832	1,300,720	1,095,584	893,874	648,270	509,133
582,973	477,488	408,664	326,758	243,845	192,813
39,977	32,952	34,910	30,482	20,682	12,109
(57,268)	(53,662)	(49,479)	(36,636)	(26,630)	(19,217)
2,129,514	1,757,498	1,489,679	1,214,478	886,167	694,838
198,432	162,733	140,239	87,379	72,511	73,839
75,100	70,000	67,300	37,300	31,800	33,600
$ 123,332	$ 92,733	$ 72,939	$ 50,079	$ 40,711	$ 40,239
$ 1.51	$ 1.13	$ .91	$ .65	$ .54	$ .54
.22	.18	.13	.11	.10	.07
5.30%	4.83%	4.48%	3.85%	4.25%	5.23%
21.03%	18.84%	19.06%	17.10%	15.98%	18.32%
380	349	322	293	267	243
58	56	53	52	44	39
6,374,000	5,527,000	5,098,000	4,727,000	3,924,000	3,213,000

EXHIBIT 23.9

Average per Store Performance: Nordstrom, Inc.
(Dollar amounts in thousands)

Fiscal Year	Number of Stores	Net Sales per Store	Net Earnings per Store
1983	39	$19,710	$1,032
1984	44	21,788	925
1985	52	25,036	963
1986	53	30,753	1,376
1987	56	34,290	1,656
1988	58	40,137	2,126
1989	59	45,273	1,948
1990	63	45,935	1,838
1991	68	46,762	1,997
1992	72	47,527	1,897

Source: Nordstrom, Inc., 1987–1992 annual reports.

The company is a leader in sales per square foot, a key measure of efficiency in the industry. In 1989, the department store industry averaged $173 in sales per square foot. Although Nordstrom is not directly comparable to general department stores because it sells only apparel, shoes, and accessories that can be stocked densely, it can be compared to specialty stores. In 1988 and 1989, specialty stores averaged $248 and $243 in sales per square foot, respectively.[24] As Exhibit 23.10 shows, Nordstrom stores averaged $398 in FY 1989 and $381 in FY 1992. Many of the company's new stores exceed $400 per square foot in their first year. The company's best sales of $600 per square foot occurred at the South Coast Plaza store in 1987. Nordstrom stores also get off to a quicker start than is common. "On the average, it takes a Nordstrom store between one and two years before it reaches chainwide sales per square foot performance. This compares to an industry average of about three years."[25] Nordstrom's per foot sales increased in both real and constant dollar terms through January 31, 1990, but the three following years showed a decline.

Efforts to improve profitability have included both cost cutting and revenue enhancement. Management began a continuing pressure to reduce costs in September 1990, when it directed all stores to cut expenses by 3%–12%, depending on store performance. The exact nature of cost reductions, whether in personnel, inventories, or advertising, was at the discretion of each store manager. The company has undertaken a systematic attack on inventory costs through information transfer. Nordstrom has instituted an improved management information system to improve its inventory ordering and vendor service. Its vendor information partnership lets suppliers and Nordstrom buyers communicate and obtain updated information about inventories, status of orders, and payments. Buyers can initiate reorders through the system. The company also is evaluating a PC-based system for tracking sales demand by item by store, identifying the level and location of inventories, and initiating transfer of inventory between locations.

EXHIBIT 23.10 Sales per Square Foot: Nordstrom, Inc.

Fiscal Year	Sales per Square Foot	Customer Price Index of Retail Apparel and Upkeep[1] (1982–1984=100)		Sales per Square Foot Corrected for Price Rises
		Year	Index	
1981	$184	1980	90.9	$202
1982	200	1981	95.3	210
1983	205	1982	97.8	210
1984	243	1983	100.2	243
1985	267	1984	102.1	262
1986	293	1985	105.0	279
1987	322	1986	105.9	304
1988	349	1987	110.6	316
1989	380	1988	115.4	329
1990	398	1989	118.6	336
1991	391	1990	124.1	315
1992	388	1991	128.7	301
1993	381	1992	131.9	289

Note:

1. Retail apparel price index is a composite that includes men's and boy's apparel, women's and girl's apparel, infant's and toddler's apparel, footwear, other apparel, and apparel services.

Source: Nordstrom, Inc., 1988 and 1991 annual reports: U.S. Department of Commerce, *Statistical Abstract of the United States 1992;* U.S. Labor Department, *Monthly Labor Review* (March 1993), p. 87.

Nordstrom spends considerably less on advertising than its competitors. Compared to an industry average of 4% of sales, Nordstrom spends less than 2% on advertising. Total company advertising expenditures amounted to only $58,424,000, $55,320,000, $50,412,000, $47,150,000, and $41,556,000 in FYs 1992, 1991, 1990, 1989, and 1988, respectively. The low level of advertising expenditures allows the company to pay more in salesperson compensation without eroding profit margins. One reason that Nordstrom can get by with less advertising is that it is able to capitalize on the mystique created by the many feature articles that continue to be written about the company and its services.

To increase sales in an otherwise depressed market, the company has recently shifted to more lower priced merchandise. This shift largely has been carried out by replacing national-brand merchandise with goods produced for the company to its specifications and bearing the Nordstrom label. This approach has allowed selling at lower prices without major reductions in margins. Another move to boost revenues involved establishing the Nordstrom National Credit Bank in Colorado to issue and service its credit card operations. With a federally chartered national bank, Nordstrom can charge its cardholders in any state the maximum interest

EXHIBIT 23.11 **Liquidity and Debt Ratios: Nordstrom, Inc.**

Ratio	Years Ending January 31				
	1993	1992	1991	1990	1989
Current ratio	2.28	2.13	1.98	2.06	2.04
Quick ratio	1.34	1.21	1.16	1.21	1.14
Long-term debt/Equity	0.42	0.54	0.59	0.64	0.61
Long-term debt/Total assets	0.21	0.25	0.26	0.27	0.26
Total debt[1]/Total assets	0.49	0.53	0.57	0.57	0.58

Note:
1. Total debt is calculated as total liabilities and equity less equity.

Source: Nordstrom, Inc., 1991 and 1992 annual reports.

allowed in the state where chartered. The bank does not engage in any checking or saving and loan operations–it only handles credit card operations.

The company has used internally generated operating earnings, debt, and proceeds from the sale of common stock to finance its growth. Currently, debt is preferred over equity as a source of capital. However, Nordstrom has avoided the high level of debt that plagues many of its competitors. Incremental, store-by-store growth has been managed so that only relatively modest increases in debt have been needed to supplement operating earnings in financing growth. In fact, Exhibit 23.11 shows a decline in relative use of debt over the past five years. Capital expenditures in the near future will not require any major increase in debt. Opening new stores and modernizing present stores is expected to require the expenditure of approximately $550 million through 1995.

Nordstrom's current ratio has hovered near 2.0 during the preceding five fiscal years. Over the past ten fiscal years the current ratio ranged from a low of 1.61 to a high of 2.38. The quick ratio exceeds 1.0. In addition, Nordstrom has a $150-million line of credit to use as liquidity support for short-term debt.

At the end of FY 1992, 250 million shares of common stock had been authorized and 81,974,797 shares had been issued. Book value per share increased steadily from $3.21 in FY 1984 to $12.83 in FY 1992. Exhibit 23.12 shows total shareholders' equity and other elements of the company's financial structure for the past ten years.

Current Industry Trends

The general trend followed by chain specialty and department stores is to become more like Nordstrom. Its success has awakened many of its competitors. They now perceive customer satisfaction with sales-force efficiency, competence, and attitudes as a key success factor in market segments other than the low-price end.

EXHIBIT 23.12

Selected Financial Indicators: Nordstrom, Inc.

(Dollar amounts in thousands)

Years Ending January 31	1993	1992	1991	1990	1989	1988	1987	1986	1985	1984
Cash, prepaid expenses, and miscellaneous current assets	$ 98,726	$ 85,516	$ 83,462	$ 71,516	$ 44,262	$ 26,099	$ 43,947	$ 24,709	$ 25,706	$ 16,841
Accounts receivable, net[1,2]	584,379[2]	585,490[2]	558,573	519,656	465,929	391,387	344,045	296,030	214,831	162,610
Merchandise inventories	536,739	506,632	448,344	419,976	403,795	312,696	257,334	226,017	162,361	129,588
Total current assets	1,219,844	1,177,638	1,090,379	1,011,148	913,986	730,182	645,326	546,756	402,898	309,039
Property, plant, and equipment, net	824,141	856,404	806,191	691,937	594,038	502,661	424,228	397,980	313,818	205,597
Other assets	9,184	7,833	6,019	4,335	3,679	1,424	1,570	1,744	841	43
Total assets	2,053,170	2,041,875	1,902,589	1,707,420	1,511,703	1,234,267	1,071,124	945,880	717,557	514,679
Current liabilities	511,196	553,903	551,835	489,888	448,165	394,699	324,697	339,503	239,331	164,628
Long-term debt and capitalized leases less current portion	481,945	502,199	478,742	440,613	369,520	260,343	271,054	276,419	199,387	109,534
Other liabilities	49,314	46,542	45,602	43,669	54,077	46,016	24,177	15,839	7,130	2,783
Shareholders' equity	$1,052,170	$939,231	$826,410	$733,250	$639,941	$533,209	$451,196	$314,119	$271,709	$237,734

Notes:

1. Accounts receivable equals customer accounts receivable minus allowance for doubtful accounts.
2. Accounts receivable for 1993–1992 include noncustomer receivables such as licensors and others.

Sources: Nordstrom, Inc., 1985–1992 annual reports.

This realization has prompted competing chains to start switching from an emphasis on rock-bottom costs to one of serving the customer.

Actually improving services is easier said than done. Years of understaffing and lack of attention to the customer have resulted in sales forces that are not accustomed to providing excellent service. Efforts to upgrade customer service can clash with the corporate culture that has developed in chain stores under these conditions. Changing customer service values is slow and requires consistent communication and reinforcement of desired attitudes and behaviors.

The first and most pronounced change being introduced in major chains to boost sales and upgrade customer service is the conversion of salespeople's compensation from hourly pay to commissions. The general intent of this change to commissions is to foster greater concern for satisfying the customer and therefore making both the immediate and future sales. The following examples illustrate the scale of the trend toward commission pay. Macy's converted stores located in competition with Nordstrom's to commission sales compensation. Carter Hawley Hale Stores has its chains and their stores' sales forces on 100% commission. Prior to entering bankruptcy, Campeau Corporation had made plans to have 90% of the salespeople in its Jordan Marsh, Maas Brothers–Jordon Marsh, Stern's, Bon Marche, Abraham & Straus, Bloomingdale's, Burdines, Lazarus, and Rich-Goldsmith's chains on commission by the end of 1990. Bloomingdale's already had 13 of its 17 stores' sales forces on 100% commission by mid 1989.

Conversion to commission pay is costly initially and payoffs come slowly. However, the payoffs can be significant. For example, one chain reduced its selling costs as a percentage of sales by 1 percentage point, while at the same time, increasing sales staff hours by 10%.[26]

Several other trends are less pronounced than the movement to commission pay but have a potential impact on service competitiveness. One is the addition of sales staff. Macy's increased both its sales force and the amount of training. Macy's also eliminated departments such as home furnishings, linens, housewares, and electronics and replaced them with expanded apparel, shoes, and accessories departments. This movement indicates a focus on higher margin and higher priced merchandise, including designer labels. In addition, consolidation of operations and centralization of selected functions has continued, and building medium-sized stores is favored.

As mentioned earlier, in the current economic uncertainty, fashion retailers are losing sales to outlet stores that offer brand name clothing at low prices. Many large department stores and fashion specialty chains are opening cut-price outlets to capture the growing price–value segment.

Company Plans

Growth can be expected to continue at the approximate rate of three to four new large specialty department stores per year. These stores will range in size from about 150,000 to 250,000 square feet. In addition, the Nordstrom Racks will continue their steady expansion. Distribution centers will be established to serve the stores in new geographic areas.

EXHIBIT 23.13

Planned Additions to Large Specialty Store Chain: Nordstrom, Inc.

Location	Year
Annapolis Mall, Maryland	1994
Circle Centre Mall, Indianapolis, Indiana	1994
Old Orchard Mall, Skokie, Illinois	1994
Santa Anita Mall, Arcadia, California	1994
Washington Square, Portland, Oregon[1]	1994
White Plains (Westchester County), New York	1994
Dallas Galleria, Texas	1995
Mall at Short Hills, New Jersey	1995
Woodfield Mall, Schaumberg, Illinois	1995
King of Prussia Plaza, Pennsylvania	1996

Note:
1. To replace old, small store.

Nordstrom has no plans to expand its operations to foreign nations. At least initially, national expansion will be targeted at the Washington to Boston corridor and the Southeast, Southcentral, and Midwest regions.

When the company enters a new area it will open several stores within a few years to make more efficient use of the required supporting distribution center and regional staff. The company will open its new stores under the leadership of experienced employees relocated or promoted from other Nordstrom stores. As in the past, this cadre will be relied on to anchor and communicate the Nordstrom culture.

Nordstrom's pace of expansion was slowed for 1993 when two large stores originally scheduled for opening were postponed until 1994 because of construction and environmental impact slowdowns. In 1993, only one Rack and one outlet store will open. However, plans call for opening ten new large specialty stores between 1994 and 1996 (see Exhibit 23.13). The schedule reflects an emphasis on gaining a critical mass of stores between Washington and New York City and in the upper Midwest. The Dallas store is the first in the Southcentral region. Additional stores will follow, with Houston, Austin, and San Antonio being considered. The company also is actively considering or seeking store sites in Connecticut and the Atlanta, Boston, Phoenix, Detroit, Las Vegas, and Denver areas. Nordstrom particularly likes to enter areas where competitors are not very profitable and where it can woo previously neglected customers with its outstanding service.

Within the mainline Nordstrom stores, service, quality, and selection are expected to remain the major bases of differentiation. Merchandising will remain the same, except that the company is placing greater emphasis on value merchandise.

The growth of off-price clothing sales at 15% from 1986 to 1990, opposed to 6% for general merchandise, has prompted Nordstrom to enter that market on an experimental basis.[27] Nordstrom planned to try two different cut-price discount store concepts to specifically cater to the low-priced brand-goods market. One of these trial stores was to be similar to the Rack discount stores but would carry non-Nordstrom goods and a different name. This Last Chance outlet store was in operation in Arizona as the company entered 1993. The second discount-type store was to bear the Nordstrom name and open in Philadelphia in 1993. This Nordstrom Factory Direct outlet store was to offer quality Nordstrom-label merchandise.

Notes

1. This brief history of Nordstrom, Inc., draws heavily on the Nordstrom, Inc., *1987 Annual Report,* pp. 5–12.
2. "Nordstrom's Expansion Blitz," *Chain Store Age Executive* (December 1988), pp. 49–50, 53.
3. Standard & Poor's, *Industry Surveys* (October 1989 and January 1993), p. R63.
4. Standard & Poor's, *Industry Surveys* (January 1993), p. R-75.
5. Adrienne Ward, "Department Stores Play the Outlet Game," *Advertising Age* (January 27, 1992), 63(4), p. 56.
6. Jan Shaw, "Executives Catch Nordstrom Fever in Opening Week," *San Francisco Business Times* (October 10, 1988), p. 10.
7. Nordstrom, Inc., *1987 Annual Report,* p. 12.
8. Richard W. Stevenson, "Watch Out Macy's, Here Comes Nordstrom," *New York Times Magazine* (August 27, 1989), p. 35.
9. Robert Sharoff, "Chicago Seen as Good Move for Nordstrom," *Daily News Record* (January 6, 1989), pp. 2, 11.
10. Nordstrom, Inc., IN, Proposal," *Sales Prospector–Illinois and Indiana* (Westgate Publishing Company, Inc., March 3, 1992).
11. "Nordstrom's Gang of Four," *Business Week* (June 15, 1992), pp. 122–123.
12. Stevenson, p. 39.
13. Nordstrom, Inc., *Employee Handbook* (undated).
14. Melinda Wilson, "Upscale Nordstrom's May Land in Detroit," *Crain's Detroit Business* (May 23, 1989).
15. Pat Baldwin, "You Can Get Satisfaction: Nationwide Survey Ranks Nordstrom's No. 1," *The Dallas Morning News* (January 9, 1993), p. 2F.
16. "Nordstrom Labor Suit Is Settled," *Los Angeles Times* (January 12, 1993), pp. D-1, D-2.
17. Nordstrom, Inc., *1989 Annual Report.*
18. "Nordstrom Settles Merchandise Resale Complaint in Oregon," *Seattle Post Intelligencer* (March 27, 1991), p. B-6.
19. "Nordstrom Clerk Sues, Says Store Invaded Her Privacy," *Seattle Times* (July 8, 1990), p. A-7.
20. Debra Prinzing, "Nordstrom and Minorities," *Puget Sound Business Journal* (May 29, 1992), p. 12.
21. "Healthy Beginnings," *Seattle Times* (December 2, 1991), p. D-9.
22. "Nordstrom Receives Easter Seal Award for Innovative Catalogs," *PR Newswire* (September 23, 1992).
23. Prinzing, p. 12.
24. Standard & Poor's, *Industry Surveys* (January 1993), p. R-81.
25. "Nordstrom's Expansion Blitz," p. 50.
26. "Now Salespeople Really Must Sell for Their Supper," *Business Week* (July 31, 1989), pp. 50, 52.
27. Stephanie Strom, "Nordstrom in No-Frills Arena," *New York Times* (June 24, 1992), p. D-1.

K mart Corporation, 1991: Corporate Strategy at the Crossroads

James W. Camerius

In early 1991, K mart Corporation comprised various retail formats, including discount department stores, membership warehouse clubs, sporting goods stores, home improvement centers, super drugstores, and specialty shops in the United States and several foreign countries, including Canada, Australia, and Puerto Rico. Measured in sales volume it was the second largest retailer and the second largest discount department store chain in the United States.

By the late 1980s, the discount department store industry was perceived to have reached maturity. As part of that industry, K mart had a retail management strategy that was developed in the late 1950s. The firm was at the crossroads, in terms of corporate strategy. The problem was what to do over the next 20 years.

The Early Years

K mart was the outgrowth of an organization founded in 1899 in Detroit by Sebastian S. Kresge. The first S.S. Kresge store represented a new type of retailing that featured low-priced merchandise for cash in low-budget, relatively small (4,000–6,000 square foot) buildings with sparse furnishings. The adoption of the "5-cent and 10-cent" or "variety store" concept, pioneered by F. W. Woolworth Company in 1879, led to rapid and profitable development of what was then the S.S. Kresge Company.

Kresge Company believed that it could substantially increase its retail business by centralizing buying and control, developing standardized store operating procedures, and expanding with new stores in heavy traffic areas. In 1917, the firm was incorporated. It had 150 stores and, next to Woolworth's, was the largest variety chain in the world. Over the next 40 years, the firm experimented with mail-order catalogs, full-line department stores, self-service, a variety of price lines, and the opening of stores in planned shopping centers.

By 1957, corporate management had become aware that the development of supermarkets and the expansion of drugstore chains into general merchandise lines had made inroads into market categories previously dominated by variety stores. Moreover, management recognized that a new form of store with a discount merchandising strategy was emerging.

This case was prepared by James W. Camerius of Northern Michigan University. This case was edited by T. L. Wheelen and J. D. Hunger for this book. Reprinted by permission of the author.

The Cunningham Connection

In 1957, in an effort to regain its competitiveness and possibly save the company, Frank Williams, then President of the S.S. Kresge Company, nominated Harry B. Cunningham as General Vice-President. This maneuver freed Mr. Cunningham, who had worked his way up the organization, from operating responsibility. He was being groomed for the presidency and was given the assignment of studying existing retailing business and recommending marketing changes.

In his visits to Kresge stores, and those of the competition, Cunningham became interested in discounting—particularly in a new operation in Garden City, Long Island. Eugene Ferkauf had recently opened large discount department stores called E.J. Korvette. Their discount mass-merchandising emphasis featured low prices and margins, high turnover, large free-standing departmentalized units, ample parking space, and a location typically in the suburbs.

Cunningham was impressed with the discount concept, but he knew that he had to first convince the Board of Directors, whose support would be necessary for any new strategy to succeed. He studied the company for two years and presented the following recommendation:

> We can't beat the discounters operating under the physical constraints and the self-imposed merchandise limitations of variety stores. We can join them—and not only join them, but with our people, procedures, and organization, we can become a leader in the discount industry.

In a speech delivered at the University of Michigan, Cunningham made his management approach clear by concluding with an admonition from the British author, Sir Hugh Walpole: "Don't play for safety; it's the most dangerous game in the world."

The Board of Directors had a difficult job. Change is never easy, especially when the company has a proud heritage. Before Cunningham could make his first presentation to the Board, rumors were circulating that one shocked senior executive had said:

> We have been in the variety business for 60 years—we know everything there is to know about it, and we're not doing very well in that, and you want to get us into a business we don't know anything about.

The Board of Directors accepted Cunningham's recommendations. When President Frank Williams retired, Cunningham became the new President and Chief Executive Officer and was directed to implement his recommendations.

The Birth of K mart

Management conceived the original K mart as a conveniently located one-stop shopping unit where customers could buy a wide variety of quality merchandise at discount prices. The typical K mart had 75,000 square feet, all on one floor. It generally stood by itself in a high-traffic, suburban area, with plenty of parking space. All stores had the same floor plan.

The firm made an $80 million commitment in leases and merchandise for 33 stores before the first K mart opened in 1962 in Garden City, Michigan. As part of this strategy, management decided to rely on the strengths and abilities of its own people to make decisions rather than employing outside experts for advice.

The original Kresge five-and-ten variety store operation, upon which the company was founded, was characterized by low gross margins, high turnover, and concentration on return on investment. The main difference in the K mart strategy would be the offering of a much wider merchandise mix.

The company had the knowledge and ability to merchandise 50% of the departments in the planned K mart merchandise mix, and contracted for operation of the remaining departments. In the following years, K mart took over most of those departments originally contracted to licensees. Eventually, K mart operated all but the shoe departments.

The Nature of the Competitive Environment

For retailers, the 1980s was considered a very unstable period. Campeau Corporation with its Federated and Allied Department Store Divisions was in bankruptcy. The Bloomingdale specialty store division of Federated Stores was offered for sale and then withdrawn. To avert a takeover attempt, the British B.A.T. Industries sold Marshall Field department stores to Dayton Hudson Corporation and offered for sale the Saks Fifth Avenue specialty store division. L.J. Hooker Corporation tried to raise cash by selling its Bonwit Teller and Sakowitz stores; it liquidated the B. Altman chain and parts of Bonwit after fruitless sale efforts. May Department Stores sold its Caldor and Venture discount divisions, each with annual sales of more than $1 billion. After decades of development work, Dayton Hudson Corporation sold Lechmere, its appliance and electronics retail unit.

By the late 1980s, the discount department store industry had gone through a series of fundamental changes. Nearly a dozen firms, such as E. J. Korvette, W. T. Grant, Arlans, Atlantic Mills, and Ames, passed into bankruptcy or reorganization. Many historically regional firms such as Wal-Mart Stores, Target Stores, and ShopKo Stores began carrying more fashionable merchandise in more attractive facilities and shifted their emphasis to more national markets. Wal-Mart, based in Bentonville, Arkansas, was especially growth-oriented and emerged in 1991 as the nation's largest retailer and largest discount chain in sales volume. Specialty discounters such as Toys 'R' Us were making big inroads in toys, sporting goods, paint, and other lines. The so-called "superstores" of drug and food chains were rapidly discounting increasing amounts of general merchandise. Some firms, such as Woolworth (Woolco Division), had withdrawn from the field entirely after years of disappointment. Sears, Roebuck & Company, in a state of stagnated growth for several years, fell from first to third place in sales in the ranking of retail organizations in 1991. Exhibit 24.1 shows a competitive analysis of K mart versus selected competitors at the end of fiscal years 1980 and 1990.

Many retailers, such as Target, that adopted the discount concept attempted generally to go after an upscale customer. The upscale customer tended to have a

EXHIBIT 24.1

A Competitive Analysis, 1980 and 1990

(Dollar amounts in millions, except sales per square foot)

	K mart	Sears	Wal-Mart	Target	Caldor
A. FISCAL YEAR 1980 COMPARISON INFORMATION					
Sales	$14,204	$ 25,194	$ 1,643	$1,531	$ 666
Number of stores	1,968	856	368	148	75
Sales per square foot	$ 104	$ 145	$ 120	$ 154	$ 129
Sales growth	11.6%	2.6%	31.6%	36.7%	18.4%
Gross margin	26.7%	32.1%	21.6%	26.7%	22.2%
Overhead	23.4%	29.9%	15.3%	20.5%	15.6%
B. FISCAL YEAR 1990 COMPARISON INFORMATION					
Sales	$32,070	$25,093.2	$32,601	$8,175	$1,700
Number of stores	2,350	1,765	1,721	420	122
Sales per square foot	$ 189	$ 341	$ 263	$ 198	$ 213
Sales growth	1.1%	0.4%	26.0%	10.0%	5.1%
Gross margin	24.5%	30.8%	21.8%	27.7%	29.8%
Overhead	21.9%	30.3%	15.8%	21.2%	24.5%

Source: Company records.

household income of $25,000–$44,000 annually. Other pockets of population were being served by firms such as Zayre, which served consumers in the inner city, and Wal-Mart, which served the needs of the more rural consumer in secondary markets. Senior management at K mart believed that many firms in the industry faced the same situation. First, they were very successful five or ten years ago, but were not changing and therefore were becoming somewhat dated. Management that had a historically successful formula, particularly in retailing, was perceived as having difficulty adapting to change, especially at the peak of success. Management would wait too long and then would have to scramble to regain competitiveness.

K mart executives found that discount department stores were being challenged by several new retail formats. Some retailers were assortment-oriented, with a much greater depth of assortment within a given product category. To illustrate, Toys 'R' Us was an example of a firm that operated 20,000 square foot toy supermarkets. Toys 'R' Us prices were very competitive within a competitive industry. When consumers entered a Toys 'R' Us facility, they were confident that, if a product wasn't there, no one else had it.

Other retailers were experimenting with the "off-price" apparel concept, where name brands and designer goods were sold at 20%–70% discounts; home improvement centers, which were warehouse-style stores with a wide range of hardline merchandise for both do-it-yourselfers and professionals; and drug supermarkets, which offered a wide variety of high-turnover merchandise in a convenient location. In these cases, competition was becoming more risk-oriented by putting $3 or $4 million in merchandise (retail value) in an 80,000 square foot facility and offering genuinely low prices. The F & M stores in the Detroit market, Drug Emporium in the Midwest, and a series of independents were examples of organizations employing the entirely new concept of the drug supermarket.

Competition was offering something new and different in terms of depth of assortment, competitive price image, and format. K mart management recognized the threat of these viable businesses that were keeping the firm from improving and maintaining market share in specific merchandise categories.

The Maturation of K mart

Corporate research revealed that, on the basis of convenience, K mart served 80% of the population. One study concluded that one of every two adults in the United States shopped at a K mart at least once a month. Despite this popular appeal, strategies that had allowed the firm to have something for everybody no longer seemed appropriate for the 1990s. K mart found that it had a broad customer base because it operated nationally. It had assumed that the firm was serving everyone in the markets where it was established.

K mart was often perceived as aiming at the low-income consumer. The financial community believed that the K mart customer was blue-collar, low-income, and upper-lower-class. The market served, however, was more professional and middle-class because K mart stores initially were located in suburban communities where the growth was occurring.

K mart has made a major commitment in more recent years to secondary or rural markets that it previously had not cultivated. In its initial strategies, the firm perceived the rural consumer as different from the urban or suburban customer. In re-addressing the situation, it discovered that its product assortments in rural areas were too limited and that the company had too many preconceived notions regarding what the "Nebraska farmer" really wanted. The firm discovered that the rural consumer didn't always shop for bib overalls and shovels, but shopped for microwave ovens and all the things everyone else did.

The goal was not to attract more customers, but to get the customer coming in the door to spend more. Management believed that, once in the store, the customer would demonstrate more divergent tastes. The upper-income consumer would buy health and beauty aids, cameras, and sporting goods. The lower-income consumer would buy toys and clothing.

In the process of trying to capture a larger share of the market and get people to spend more, the firm began to recognize a market that was more upscale. Consumer research showed that the profile of the trade area and the profile of the person who shopped at K mart in the past month were identical. That is, K mart was serving predominantly the suburban consumer in suburban locations.

In "lifestyle" research in markets served by the firm, K mart determined that there were more two-income families, that families were having fewer children, that there were more working wives, and that more customers tended to be homeowners than it had originally thought. Customers were careful about how they spent their money and wanted quality. This customer profile was a distinct contrast to that of the 1960s and early 1970s, which tended to have a "throw away" orientation. The customer now said, "What we want is products that will last longer. We'll have to pay more for them, but we'll still want them and at the lowest price possible." Customers wanted better quality products but still demanded competitive prices. According to a K mart annual report, "Consumers today are well-educated and informed. They want good value and they know it when they see it. Price remains a key consideration, but the consumers' new definition of value includes quality as well as price."

Corporate management at K mart considered the discount department store to be a mature idea. Although maturity was sometimes looked on with disfavor, K mart executives believed that it did not mean a lack of profitability or lack of opportunity to increase sales. They perceived the industry as being "reborn." In this context they developed a series of new retailing strategies designed to upgrade the K mart image.

Retailing Strategies

Several new marketing strategies emerged as the result of an overall reexamination of existing corporate strategies. They included accelerating store expansion and refurbishment; capitalization on dominant lifestyle departments; centralizing merchandising; investing more capital in retail automation; undertaking an aggressive and focused advertising program; and fostering continued growth through new specialty retail formats.

In February 1990, K mart announced a five-year, $2.3 billion new store opening, enlargement, relocation, and refurbishment program. This program involved virtually all 2,300 K mart discount stores. There would be approximately 250 new full-size K mart stores, 620 enlargements, 280 relocations, and 30 closings. In addition, 1,260 stores would be refurbished to bring their layout and fixtures up to new store standards.

One area receiving initial attention and improvement was the way products were displayed. The traditional K mart layout was by product category. Often these locations for departments were holdovers from the old variety store days. Many departments would not give up prime locations. As part of the new marketing strategy, the shop concept was introduced. Management recognized that it had a sizable do-it-yourself store. As planning management discussed the issue, "nobody was aware of the opportunity. The hardware department was right smack in the center of the store, because it was always there. The paint department was over here and the electrical department was over there." "All we had to do," management contended, "was put them all in one spot and everyone could see that we had a very respectable do-it-yourself department." The concept resulted in a variety of new departments such as Soft Goods for the Home, Kitchen Korners, and Home Electronic Centers. The goal behind each department was to sell an entire lifestyle-oriented concept to consumers, making goods complementary so that shoppers would want to buy several interrelated products rather than just one item.

The program also involved utilizing and revitalizing the space K mart already controlled. It took the form of remodeling and updating existing stores. The program would involve virtually all U.S. K mart discount stores. The new look featured a broad poppy red and gold band around interior walls as a "horizon"; new round, square, and honeycombed racks that displayed the full garment; relocation of jewelry and women's apparel to areas closer to the entrance; and redesigned counters to look more upscale and hold more merchandise.

Name brands were added in soft and hard goods as management recognized that the customer transferred the product quality of branded goods to perceptions of private-label merchandise. In the eyes of K mart management, "if you sell Wrangler, there is good quality. Then the private label must be [of the same quality as the name brand]."

Additional programs emphasized the quality image. In a joint venture with *McCall's,* the company launched a new magazine called *Betsy McCall,* aimed at girls aged 6 to 12. It engaged pro golfer Fuzzy Zoeller to promote golf equipment and associated products. Mario Andretti, who races in the Championship Auto Racing Teams' Indy car series, agreed to co-sponsorship of his car with associated promotion. Dusty Lenscap, an animated marketing character, promoted photo developing equipment.

K mart hired Martha Stewart, an upscale Connecticut author of lavish best-selling books on cooking and home entertaining, as its lifestyle spokesperson and consultant. She was to be a corporate symbol for housewares and associated products in advertising and in-store displays. Management visualized her as the next Betty Crocker, a fictional character created some years ago by General Mills, Inc., and a representative of its interest in lifestyle trends. Management created a separate division to develop strategy for all Martha Stewart–label goods and programs. In addition, the company featured merchandise in a redesigned once-a-week K mart newspaper circular that now carried the advertising theme: "The quality you need, the price you want."

K mart reduced several thousand prices in 1989 to maintain price leadership across America. As management noted, "It is absolutely essential that we provide our customers with good value, quality products at low prices." Although lower prices hurt margins and contributed significantly to an earnings decline, management was convinced that unit turnover of items with lowered prices increased significantly to "enable K mart to maintain its pricing leadership, which will have a most positive impact on our business in the years ahead."

Management introduced a centralized merchandising system to improve communication. A computerized, highly automated replenishment system tracked how rapidly merchandise sold and quickly put fast-moving items back on the shelves. Satellite capability and a point-of-sale (POS) scanning system were part of the program. Regular, live satellite communication from K mart headquarters to the stores enabled senior management to communicate with store managers and allowed for questions and answers. The POS scanning system recorded every sale and transmitted data to headquarters. This capability enabled K mart to respond quickly to what was new and in demand and what would keep customers coming back.

In the mid 1970s and throughout the 1980s, K mart became involved in the acquisition or development of several smaller new operations. K mart Insurance Services, Inc., acquired as Planned Marketing Associates in 1974, offered a full line of life, health, and accident insurance in 27 K mart stores primarily in the South and Southwest.

In 1982, K mart initiated its own off-price specialty apparel concept called Designer Depot. Twenty-eight Designer Depot stores opened in 1982 to appeal to customers who wanted quality, upscale clothing at a budget price. A variation of this concept, called Garment Rack, opened to sell apparel that normally would not be sold in Designer Depots. A distribution center was added in 1983 to supplement both of the above ventures. K mart attempted an unsuccessful joint venture with the Hechinger Company of Washington, D.C., a warehouse home center retailer. However, after much deliberation, K mart instead chose to acquire Home Centers of America of San Antonio, Texas. The division would be building 80,000-square-foot warehouse home centers, each named Builders Square. Builders Square would capitalize on K mart's real estate, construction, and management expertise and Home Centers of America's merchandising expertise.

K mart acquired Waldenbooks, a chain of 877 bookstores, from Carter, Hawley, Hale, Inc., in 1984. It was part of a strategy to capture a greater share of the market for a product category that K mart already had in its stores and had been interested in building on for some time.

The Bruno's, Inc., joint venture in 1987 formed a partnership to develop large combination grocery and general merchandise stores or "hypermarkets." The giant, one-stop-shopping facilities of 225,000 square feet would capitalize on the grocery expertise of Bruno's and the general merchandise knowledge of K mart to offer a wide selection of products and services at discount prices.

In 1988, the company acquired a controlling interest in Makro, Inc., a Cincinnati-based operator of warehouse "club" stores. Makro, with annual sales of about $300 million, operated "member only" stores that were stocked with low-priced fresh and frozen groceries, apparel, and durable goods in suburbs of Atlanta, Cincinnati, Washington, and Philadelphia. In 1989, K mart acquired PACE Membership Warehouse, Inc., a similar operation.

The company's specialty retail group included Builders Square, warehouse home improvement stores; Pay Less Stores Northwest, Inc., super drugstores; the Waldenbooks Company, specialty bookstores; and Bargain Harold's Discount Limited, Canadian mini variety stores. K mart Canada also included K mart discount stores and Kresge and Jupiter variety stores.

On April 6, 1987, K mart Corporation announced that it had agreed to sell most of its 55 Kresge and Jupiter variety stores in the United States to McCory Corporation, a unit of the closely held Rapid American Corporation of New York. The move left the firm with approximately 4,000 retail units in the various divisions.

A new corporate logo symbolized the new program. The logo featured a big red "K" with the word "mart" written in smaller white script inside the "K." It was designed to "signify the changes taking place inside the store," indicated chairman Joseph Antonini. "This is what we have to do," he maintained.

The Planning Function

Corporate planning at K mart was the result of executives, primarily the senior executive, recognizing change. The role played by the senior executive was to get others to acknowledge that nothing is good forever. Good planning required that they get involved in determining the company's future. Poor planning was done by those who didn't recognize the need to grasp the future until it was too late to survive. Good planning, if done on a regular and timely basis, resulted in improved performance. K mart's Director of Planning and Research contended:

> Planning, as we like to stress, is making decisions now to improve performance tomorrow. Everyone looks at what may happen tomorrow, but the planners are the ones who make decisions today. That's where I think too many firms go wrong. They think they are planning because they are writing reports and are aware of changes. They don't say, "Because of this, we must decide today to spend this money to do this to accomplish this goal in the future."

The Director of Planning and Research of K mart believed that it had been very successful in the area of strategic planning. "When it became necessary to make significant changes in the way we were doing business," he stated, "that was accomplished on a fairly timely basis." When the organization made the change in the 1960s, it recognized a powerful investment opportunity and capitalized on it—far beyond what anyone else would have done. "We just opened stores," he continued, "at a great, great pace. Management, when confronted with a crisis, would state, 'It's the economy, or it's this, or that, but it's not the essential way we are doing business.'" He continued, "Suddenly management would recognize that the economy may stay like this forever. We need to improve the situation and then do it." Strategic planning probably arose from some difficult times for the organization.

K mart had a reasonably formal planning organization that involved a constant evaluation of what was happening in the marketplace, what competition was doing, and what kinds of opportunities were available. Management felt a need to diversify because it would not be a viable company unless it was growing physically. Management believed that the company was not going to grow physically by staying with the same K mart format forever. It needed physical growth and opportunity, particularly if the company was to open 200 new stores on a regular basis. The Director of Planning and Research felt that, "Given a corporate culture that was accustomed to challenges, management would have to find ways to expend that energy. A corporation that is successful," he argued, "has to continue to be successful. It has to have a basic understanding of corporate needs and be augmented by a much more rigorous effort to be aware of what's going on in the external environment."

A planning group at K mart reported directly to the Chairman of the Board through its Director of Planning and Research. The group represented several

Consolidated Statements of Income: K mart Corporation
(Dollar amounts in millions, except per share data)

Years Ending	January 30, 1991	January 31, 1990	January 25, 1989	January 27, 1988
Sales	$32,070	$29,533	$27,301	$25,627
Licensee fees and rental income	269	260	249	237
Equity in income of affiliated retail companies	113	105	105	92
Interest income	10	24	33	22
Total	32,462	29,922	27,688	25,978
Cost of merchandise sold (including buying and occupancy costs)	23,895	21,745	19,914	18,564
Selling, general, and administrative expenses	6,435	6,071	5,603	5,296
Advertising	577	571	581	617
Restructuring of K mart stores and other charges	—	640	—	—
Interest expense				
Debt	232	205	172	156
Capital lease obligations	177	175	174	174
Total expenses	31,316	29,407	26,444	24,807
Income before income taxes	1,146	515	1,244	1,171
Income taxes	390	192	441	479
Net income	$ 756	$ 323	$ 803	$ 692
Earnings per common and common equivalent share	$ 3.78	$ 1.61	$ 4.00	$ 3.40
Weighted average shares	200.1	200.7	200.6	203.5

Source: K mart Corporation, *1991 Annual Report; 1989 Annual Report.*

functional areas of the organization. Management described it as an "in-house consulting group" with some independence. It comprised (1) financial planning, (2) economic and consumer analysis, and (3) operations research. The Chief Executive Officer (CEO) was the organization's main planner.

Finance

The company's financial position is shown in Exhibits 24.2–24.5. An 11-year (1980–1990) record of financial performance by K mart and Wal-Mart is shown in Exhibit 24.6. The company's 1990 fiscal year (FY) was from January 31, 1990 through January 30, 1991. K mart's FY 1990 sales were $32.1 billion.

EXHIBIT 24.3

Consolidated Balance Sheets: K mart Corporation

(Dollar amounts in millions)

Years Ending	January 30, 1991	January 31, 1990
Assets		
Current assets		
Cash (includes temporary investments of $26 and $35, respectively)	$ 278	$ 353
Merchandise inventories	6,891	6,933
Accounts receivable and other current assets	727	698
Total current assets	7,896	7,984
Investments in affiliated retail companies	609	512
Property and equipment	4,361	3,850
Other assets and deferred charges (includes goodwill, net of accumulated amortization, of $692 and $441, respectively)	1,033	799
Total assets	$13,899	$13,145
Liabilities and Shareholders' Equity		
Current liabilities		
Long-term debt due within one year	$ 51	$ 11
Notes payable	658	601
Accounts payable—trade	2,307	2,319
Accrued payrolls and other liabilities	906	830
Taxes other than income taxes	316	322
Income taxes	139	216
Total current liabilities	4,377	4,299
Capital lease obligations	1,598	1,549
Long-term debt	1,701	1,549
Other long-term liabilities including K mart restructuring obligations	682	745
Deferred income taxes	157	100
Total liabilities	8,515	8,242
Shareholders' equity		
Common stock, 500,000,000 shares authorized; shares issued 204,710,587 and 204,918,993, respectively	205	205
Capital in excess per value	593	671
Restricted stock deferred compensation	(2)	(1)
Retained earnings	4,753	4,341
Treasury shares	(131)	(146)
Foreign currency translation adjustment	(34)	(29)
Total shareholders' equity	5,384	4,972
Total liabilities and shareholders' equity	$13,899	$13,145

Source: K mart Corporation, *1991 Annual Report.*

EXHIBIT 24.4

Business Group Information: K mart Corporation
(Dollar amounts in millions)

Years Ending	January 30, 1991	January 31, 1990	January 25, 1989	January 27, 1988
Sales[1]				
General merchandise	$24,891	$24,959	$23,187	$22,140
Specialty retail	7,179	4,574	4,114	3,487
Total	32,070	29,533	27,301	25,627
Licensee fees and other income				
General merchandise	257	274	273	252
Specialty retail	12	10	9	7
Total	269	284	282	259
Equity in income of affiliated retail companies	113	105	105	92
Total revenues from operations	$32,452	$29,922	$27,688	$25,978
Operating income[2]				
General merchandise	$ 1,299	$ 720	$ 1,436	$ 1,384
Specialty retail	165	87	72	75
Total	1,464	807	1,508	1,459
Equity in income of affiliated retail companies	113	105	105	92
Interest expense—Debt—net	(222)	(205)	(172)	(156)
Capital lease obligations	(177)	(175)	(174)	(174)
Corporate expense	(32)	(17)	(23)	(50)
Income before income taxes	1,146	515	1,244	1,171
Income taxes	390	192	441	479
Net income	$ 756	$ 323	$ 803	$ 692
Identifiable assets[3]				
General merchandise	$ 9,640	$10,139	$ 9,108	$ 8,254
Specialty retail	3,581	2,427	2,426	2,364
Total	$13,221	$12,566	$11,534	$10,618

(*continued*)

The Challenge

At the beginning of 1991, K mart Corporation announced its intention to continue as "America's most dominant retail nameplate by remaining the leader in everyday low prices and by implementing strategies designed for real gains in sales, earnings, and cash flow." These strategies included: accelerated store expansion and refurbishment, capitalization on dominant lifestyle departments, centralized merchandising, more capital investment in retail automation, an aggressive and focused advertising program, and continued growth through specialty retail formats.

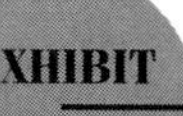

EXHIBIT 24.4

Business Group Information: K mart Corporation *(continued)*
(Dollar amounts in millions)

Years Ending	January 30, 1991	January 31, 1990	January 25, 1989	January 27, 1988
Investments in affiliated retail companies	609	512	506	379
Assets of discontinued operations	69	67	86	109
Total assets	$13,899	$13,145	$12,126	$11,106
Capital expenditures—owned and leased				
General merchandise	$ 790	$ 587	$ 583	$ 421
Specialty retail	184	102	111	163
Total capital expenditures	$ 974	$ 689	$ 694	$ 584
Depreciation and amortization expense				
General merchandise	$ 405	$389	$374	$349
Specialty retail	126	98	63	52
Total depreciation and amortization expense	$ 531	$ 487	$ 437	$ 401

Notes:

1. The dominant portion of the company's business is general merchandise retailing through the operation of a chain of K mart discount department stores, PACE warehouse clubs, Makro warehouses, and an American Fare store. Operations identified as specialty retailing include Pay Less Drug Stores, Waldenbooks, Builders Square, Bargain Harold's Canada, Office Square, and Sports Giant.
2. Operating income in 1989 (Fiscal Year ending January 31, 1990) for the general merchandise and specialty retail groups was reduced by $598 million and $42 million, respectively, due to the K mart restructuring provision and other charges.
3. Identifiable assets are those assets of the company associated with a specific business group or discontinued operations. Corporate and foreign assets are insignificant. Investments in affiliated retail companies include the company's investments in Coles Myer and Meldisco.

Source: K mart Corporation, *1991 Annual Report.*

EXHIBIT 24.5

Financial Performance, 1970–1989: K mart Corporation
(Dollar amounts in millions)

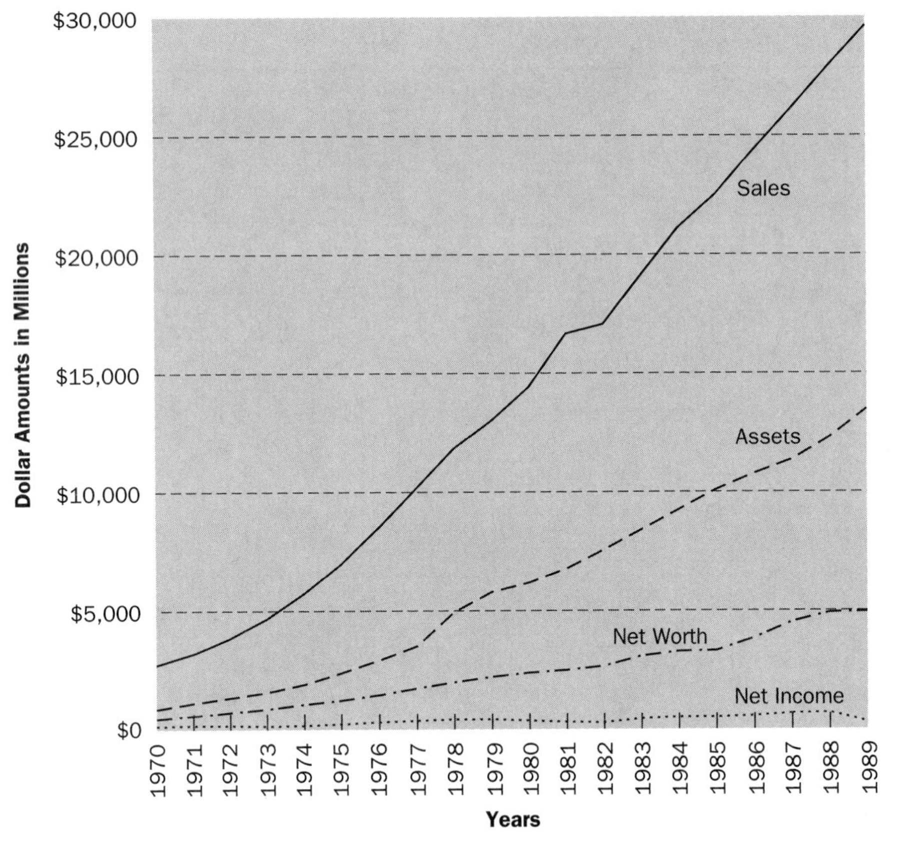

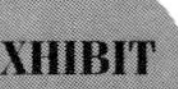

EXHIBIT 24.6

Comparison of Financial Performance of K mart and Wal-Mart, 1980–1990
(Dollar amounts in thousands)

A. K MART: 1980–1990 FINANCIAL PERFORMANCE

Fiscal Year[1]	Sales	Assets	Net Income	Shareholders' Equity	K mart Stores
1980	$14,204,381	$ 6,102,462	$260,527	$2,343,172	1,722
1981	16,527,012	6,673,004	220,251	2,455,594	2,055
1982	16,772,166	7,343,665	261,821	2,601,272	2,117
1983	18,597,900	8,183,100	492,300	2,940,100	2,160
1984	20,762,000	9,262,000	503,000	3,234,000	2,173
1985	22,035,000	9,991,000	472,000	3,273,000	2,332
1986	23,035,000	10,578,000	570,000	3,939,000	2,342
1987	25,627,000	11,106,000	692,000	4,409,000	2,273
1988	27,301,000	12,126,000	803,000	5,009,000	2,307
1989	29,533,000	13,145,000	323,000	4,972,000	2,361
1990	32,070,000	13,899,000	756,000	5,384,000	2,350

B. WAL-MART: 1980–1990 FINANCIAL PERFORMANCE

Fiscal Year[1]	Sales	Assets	Net Income	Shareholders' Equity	K mart Stores
1980	$ 1,643,199	$ 592,345	$ 55,682	$ 248,309	330
1981	2,444,997	937,513	82,794	323,942	491
1982	3,376,252	1,187,448	124,140	488,109	551
1983	4,666,909	1,652,254	196,244	737,503	642
1984	6,400,861	2,205,229	270,767	984,672	745
1985	8,451,489	3,103,645	327,473	1,277,659	849
1986	11,909,076	4,049,092	450,086	1,690,493	980
1987	15,959,255	5,131,809	627,643	2,257,267	1,114
1988	20,649,001	6,359,668	837,221	3,007,909	1,259
1989	25,810,656	8,198,484	1,075,900	3,965,561	1,573
1990	32,601,594	11,389,915	1,291,024	5,365,524	1,721

Note:
1. Fiscal year is January through December, and the accounting year is February through January.

Source: *Fortune* Financial Analysis; K mart Corporation, annual reports; Wal-Mart Stores, Inc., annual reports.

References

John Bussey, "K mart Is Set to Sell Many of Its Roots to Rapid–American Corp's McCory," *Wall Street Journal* (April 6, 1987), p. 24.

Eleanore Carruth, "K mart Has to Open Some New Doors on the Future," *Fortune* (July 1977), pp. 143–150, 153–154.

Subtrata N. Chakravarty, "A Tale of Two Companies," *Forbes* (May 27, 1991), pp. 86–96.

Robert E. Dewar, "The Kresge Company and the Retail Revolution," *University of Michigan Business Review* (July 2, 1975), p. 2.

Melinda G. Guiles, "Attention, Shoppers: Stop that Browsing and Get Aggressive," *Wall Street Journal* (June 16, 1987), pp. 1, 21.

Melinda G. Guiles, "K mart, Bruno's Join to Develop 'Hypermarkets,'" *Wall Street Journal* (September 8, 1987), p. 17.

Paul Ingrassia, "Attention Non–K mart Shoppers: A Blue-Light Special Just for You," *Wall Street Journal* (October 6, 1987), p. 42.

"It's Kresge . . . Again," *Chain Store Executive* (November 1975), p. 16.

"K mart Looks to New Logo to Signify Changes," *Wall Street Journal* (September 13, 1990), p. 10.

"K mart Will Expand Line with Purchase of Warehouse Club," *Wall Street Journal* (December 14, 1990), p. 4.

Janet Key, "K mart Plan: Diversity, Conquer: Second Largest Retailer Out to Woo Big Spenders," *Chicago Tribune* (November 11, 1984), pp. 1–2.

Jerry Main, "K mart's Plan to Be Born Again," *Fortune* (September 21, 1981), pp. 74–77, 84–85.

Russell Mitchell, "How They're Knocking the Rust Off Two Old Chains," *Business Week* (September 8, 1986), pp. 44–48.

Faye Rice, "Why K mart Has Stalled," *Fortune* (October 9, 1989), p. 79.

Bill Saporito, "Is Wal-Mart Unstoppable?" *Fortune* (May 6, 1991), pp. 50–59.

Francine Schwadel, "Attention K mart Shoppers: Style Coming to this Aisle," *Wall Street Journal* (August 9, 1988), p. 6.

Francine Schwadel, "K mart to Speed Store Openings, Renovations," *Wall Street Journal* (February 27, 1990), p. 3.

Patricia Sellers, "Attention, K mart Shoppers," *Fortune* (January 2, 1989), p. 41.

Barry Stavro, "Mass Appeal," *Forbes* (May 5, 1986), pp. 128, 130.

Patricia Sternad, "K mart's Antonini Moves Far Beyond Retail 'Junk' Image," *Advertising Age* (July 25, 1988), pp. 1, 67.

Michael Wellman, Interview with Director of Planning and Research, K mart Corporation (August 6, 1984).

"Where K mart Goes Next Now That It's No. 2," *Business Week* (June 2, 1980), pp. 109–110, 114.

"Why Chains Enter New Areas," *Chain Store Executive* (December 1976), pp. 22, 24.

Woodruff, David, "Will K mart Ever Be a Silk Purse?" *Business Week* (January 22, 1990), p. 46.

CASE 25

Wal-Mart Stores, Inc., 1992: Strategies After Sam Walton's Death

James W. Camerius

It was dusk in the foothills of the Ozark Mountains in north central Arkansas. One of the most successful retailing entrepreneurs in modern history was driving a battered red 1980 Ford pickup minus two hubcaps down a rural road. A hunting dog named Buck was seated next to him, inside the cab. Some coffee and conversation with friends awaited at Fred's Hickory Inn in Bentonville.

Sam Walton was "down-to-earth and old-fashioned in his views of the past, the present and the future," noted the *Arkansas Gazette*. It then quoted Walton further:

> I didn't sit down one day and decide that I was going to put a bunch of discount stores in small towns and set a goal to have a billion-dollar company some day. I started out with one store and it did well, so it was a challenge to see if I could do well with a few more. We're still going and we'll keep going as long as we're successful.

From this beginning, Wal-Mart Stores, Inc., has emerged as a modern retail success story.

An Emerging Organization

Wal-Mart Stores, Inc., in 1993, had completed its twenty-ninth consecutive year of growth in both sales and earnings. The firm, with corporate offices in Bentonville, Arkansas, operated stores under a variety of names and retail formats, including Wal-Mart stores, which were discount department stores; Sam's Wholesale Clubs, which were wholesale/retail membership warehouses; and Hypermarket*USA stores, which were combination grocery and general merchandise stores, each having in excess of 200,000 square feet. It also operated Wal-Mart Supercenters, scaled down versions of hypermarkets; Dot Discount Drugstores, a super discount drug chain; and Bud's stores, off-price outlets. It was not only the nation's largest discount department store chain, but had recently surpassed the retail division of Sears, Roebuck, & Company in sales volume as the largest retail company in the United States.

The Sam Walton Spirit

Much of the success of Wal-Mart derived from the entrepreneurial spirit of its founder and Chairman of the Board, Samuel Moore Walton. One of the most influential retailers of the century, Walton died on April 5, 1992, at the age of 74.

This case was prepared by James W. Camerius of Northern Michigan University. This case was edited by T. L. Wheelen and J. D. Hunger for this book. Reprinted by permission of the author.

Sam Walton or "Mr. Sam," as some referred to him, had traced his down-to-earth, old-fashioned, home-spun, and evangelical ways to growing up in rural Oklahoma, Missouri, and Arkansas. Although he was remarkably blasé about his roots, some suggested that it was a simple belief in hard work and ambition that had "unlocked countless doors and showered upon him, his customers, and his employees . . . , the fruits of . . . years of labor in building [this] highly successful company." "Our goal has always been in our business to be the very best," Sam Walton once said in an interview, "and, along with that, we believe that in order to do that, you've got to make a good situation and put the interests of your associates first. If we really do that consistently, they in turn will cause . . . our business to be successful, which is what we've talked about and espoused and practiced." "The reason for our success," he noted, "is our people and the way that they're treated and the way they feel about their company." Many have suggested that it is this "people first" philosophy, which guided the company through the challenges and setbacks of its early years, and allowed the company to maintain its consistent record of growth and expansion in later years.

Little about Walton's background would suggest his amazing success. He was born in Kingfisher, Oklahoma, on March 29, 1918, to Thomas and Nancy Walton. Thomas Walton was a banker at the time and later entered the farm mortgage business and moved to Missouri. Sam Walton, growing up in rural Missouri in the depths of the Great Depression, discovered early that he "had a fair amount of ambition and enjoyed working," he suggested in a company interview. He completed high school in Columbia, Missouri, and received a Bachelor of Arts Degree in Economics from the University of Missouri in 1940. "I really had no idea what I would be," he said, adding as an afterthought, "at one point in time, I thought I wanted to become President of the United States."

A unique, enthusiastic, and positive individual, Sam Walton was called "just your basic home-spun billionaire" by *Business Week* magazine. One source suggested that "Mr. Sam is a life-long small-town resident who didn't change much as he got richer than his neighbors." He had tremendous energy, enjoyed bird hunting with his dogs, and flew a corporate plane. When the company was much smaller he could boast that he personally visited every Wal-Mart store at least once a year. A store visit usually included Walton leading Wal-Mart cheers that began "Give me a W, give me an A, . . ." To many employees, he had the air of a fiery Baptist preacher. Paul R. Carter, a Wal-Mart Executive Vice-President, said that "Mr. Walton has a calling." He became the richest man in America, by 1991 creating a personal fortune for his family in excess of $21 billion.

For all the chronicling of Walton's success, its magnitude was hard to comprehend. Sam Walton was selected by the investment publication *Financial World* in 1989 as the "CEO of the Decade." He received honorary degrees from the University of the Ozarks, the University of Arkansas, and the University of Missouri. He also received many of the most distinguished professional awards of the industry, including "Man of the Year," "Discounter of the Year," and "Chief Executive Officer of the Year," and was the second retailer to be inducted into the Discounting Hall of Fame. He was recipient of the Horatio Alger Award in 1984 and acknowledged by *Discount Stores News* as "Retailer of the Decade" in December 1989.

EXHIBIT 25.1 **The Penney Idea, 1913**

1. To serve the public, as nearly as we can, to its complete satisfaction.
2. To expect for the service we render a fair remuneration and not all the profit the traffic will bear.
3. To do all in our power to pack the customer's dollar full of value, quality, and satisfaction.
4. To continue to train ourselves and our associates so that the service we give will be more and more intelligently performed.
5. To improve constantly the human factor in our business.
6. To reward men and women in our organization through participation in what the business produces.
7. To test our every policy, method, and act in this wise: "Does it square with what is right and just?"

Source: Vance H. Trimble, *Sam Walton: The Inside Story of America's Richest Man* (New York: Dutton, 1990).

"Walton does a remarkable job of instilling near-religious fervor in his people," says analyst Robert Buchanan of A. G. Edwards. "I think that speaks to the heart of his success." In late 1989, Sam Walton was diagnosed as having multiple myeloma, or cancer of the bone marrow. He planned to remain active in the firm as Chairman of the Board of Directors for as long as he was able.

The Marketing Concept

Genesis of an Idea

Sam Walton started his retail career in 1940 as a management trainee with the J. C. Penney Company in Des Moines, Iowa. He was impressed with the Penney method of doing business and later modeled the Wal-Mart chain on many Penney principles, including "The Penney Idea" (see Exhibit 25.1). In a manner similar to Penney's, Wal-Mart employees were called "associates" rather than "clerks." As a "main street merchant" in Kemmerer, Wyoming, Penney had found strength in cultivating rural markets.

Following service in the U.S. Army during World War II, Walton acquired a Ben Franklin variety store franchise in Newport, Arkansas, which he operated successfully until losing the lease in 1950. He opened a store under the name of Walton's 5 & 10 in Bentonville, Arkansas, the following year. By 1962, he was operating a chain of 15 stores.

The early retail stores owned by Sam Walton in Newport and Bentonville, Arkansas, and later in other small towns in adjoining southern states, were variety store operations. They were relatively small operations (6,000 square feet of floor space), were located on "main street," and displayed merchandise on plain wooden tables and counters. Operated under the Ben Franklin name and supplied by Butler Brothers of Chicago and St. Louis, they were characterized by a limited price line, low gross margins, high merchandise turnover, and concentration on return on investment. The firm, operating under the Walton 5 & 10 name, was the largest Ben Franklin franchisee in the country in 1962. The company phased out the variety stores by 1976 to concentrate on the growth of Wal-Mart Stores.

Foundations of Growth

The original Wal-Mart discount concept was not a unique idea. Sam Walton became convinced in the late 1950s that discounting would transform retailing. He traveled extensively in New England, the cradle of "off-pricing." "He visited just about every discounter in the United States," suggested William F. Kenney, the retired president of the now-defunct Kings Department Stores. He tried to interest Butler Brothers executives in Chicago in the discount store concept. The first K mart, a "conveniently located one-stop shopping unit where customers could buy a wide variety of quality merchandise at discount prices," had opened in 1962 in Garden City, Michigan. His theory was to operate a discount store in a small community and in that setting, he would offer name brand merchandise at low prices and would add friendly service. Butler Brothers executives rejected the idea. The first "Wal-Mart Discount City" opened in late 1962 in Rogers, Arkansas.

Wal-Mart stores would sell nationally advertised, well-known brand merchandise at low prices in austere surroundings. As corporate policy, it would cheerfully give refunds, credits, and rain checks. Management conceived the firm as a "discount department store chain offering a wide variety of general merchandise to the customer." Initially, management emphasized opportunistic purchases of merchandise from whatever sources were available. It pushed the health and beauty aids (H&BA) product line and presented merchandise by "stacking it high." By the end of 1979, 276 Wal-Mart stores were operating in 11 states.

The firm developed an aggressive expansion strategy as it grew from its first, 16,000 square foot discount store in Rogers. It located new stores primarily in towns of 5,000 to 25,000 population. Store size ranged from 30,000 to 60,000 square feet, with 45,000 being the average. The firm also expanded by locating stores in contiguous areas, town by town, state by state. When its discount operations came to dominate a market area, it moved to an adjoining area. Whereas other retailers built warehouses to serve existing outlets, Wal-Mart built distribution centers first and then located stores all around it, pooling advertising and distribution overhead. Most stores were less than a six-hour drive from one of the company's warehouses. The first major distribution center, a 390,000 square foot facility, opened in Searcy, Arkansas, outside Bentonville in 1978.

National Perspectives

At the beginning of 1993, the firm had 1,880 Wal-Mart and 256 Sam's Club stores in 35 states, with expansion planned for adjacent states. The stores were designed to offer one-stop shopping in 36 departments, including family apparel, health and beauty aids, household needs, electronics, toys, fabric and crafts, automotive supplies, lawn and patio, jewelry, and shoes. In addition, certain stores provided a pharmacy, an automotive supply and service center, a garden center, or a snack bar. Wal-Mart stressed "everyday low prices" rather than special price promotions. Each store was expected to "provide the customer with a clean, pleasant, and friendly shopping experience."

Although Wal-Mart carried much the same merchandise, offered similar prices, and operated stores that looked much like its competition, there were many differences. The typical Wal-Mart store featured employees who wore blue vests to identify themselves, wide aisles, apparel departments carpeted in warm colors, store employees who followed customers to their cars to pick up their shopping carts, and a "people greeter" who welcomed the customer at the door, gave directions, and struck up conversations. Associates bagged merchandise in brown paper sacks rather than plastic bags when customers wanted them to. A simple Wal-Mart logo in white letters on a brown background on the front of the store identified it. Consumer studies determined that the chain was particularly adept at striking the delicate balance of convincing customers that its prices were low without making them feel that its merchandise was cheaply made. In many ways, competitors such as K mart sought to emulate Wal-Mart by introducing people greeters, upgrading interiors, developing new logos and signs, and introducing new inventory response systems. In 1992, sales per square foot of retail space at Wal-Mart were $297. In contrast, K mart sold only $181 per square foot that year.

Wal-Mart introduced a "satisfaction guaranteed" refund and exchange policy to give customers confidence in its merchandise quality. Technological advancements such as scanner cash registers, hand-held computers for ordering merchandise, and computer linkages of stores to the general office and distribution centers improved communications and merchandise replenishment. Management encouraged each store to initiate programs that would make it an integral part of the community in which it operated. The company encouraged associates to "maintain the highest standards of honesty, morality, and business ethics in dealing with the public."

The External Environment

Industry analysts had labeled the 1980s as a time of economic uncertainty for retailers, and some firms faced difficulty upon merger or acquisition. After acquiring U.S.-based Allied Department Stores in 1986 and Federated Department Stores in 1988, Canadian developer Robert Campeau declared bankruptcy, with more than $6 billion in debts. Upon reevaluation, several divisions and units of the organization were either sold or closed. The flagship downtown Atlanta store, Rich's, a division of Federated, closed after completing a multimillion dollar remodeling program. Reevaluation of specific merchandise programs in divisions such as Bloomingdale's lowered inventory and raised cash. The ability to service existing debt became a significant factor in the success or failure of a retailing organization

EXHIBIT 25.2 **Selected Acquisitions of U.S. Retailers by Foreign Firms, 1980–1990**

U.S. Retailer	Foreign Acquirer	Country of Acquirer
Allied Stores (general merchandise)	Campeau	Canada
Alterman Foods (supermarkets)	Delhaie-Le Leon	Belgium
Bonwit Teller (general merchandise)	Hooker Corporation	Australia
Brooks Brothers (apparel)	Marks & Spencer	Great Britain
Federated Department Stores (diversified)	Campeau	Canada
Great Atlantic & Pacific (supermarkets)	Tengelmann	Germany
Herman's (sporting goods)	Dee Corporation	Great Britain
International House of Pancakes (restaurants)	Wienerwald	Switzerland
Talbots (apparel)	Jusco Ltd	Japan
Zale (jewelry)	PS Associates	Netherlands

Source: Barry Berman and Joel R. Evans, *Retail Management: A Strategic Approach,* 4th Ed. (New York: Macmillan, 1989).

in the latter half of the decade. Exhibit 25.2 summarizes selected acquisitions of U.S. retailers by foreign firms over the past decade.

Other retailers experienced changes in ownership. The British B.A.T. Industries PLC sold the Chicago-based Marshall Field department store division to the Dayton Hudson Corporation. L. J. Hooker Corporation, the U. S. arm of Australia's Hooker Corporation, sold its Bonwit Teller and Sakowitz stores; it liquidated its B. Altman chain after fruitless sale efforts. The R. H. Macy Company saddled itself with $4.5 billion in debt as a result of acquiring Bullock's and I. Magnin specialty department stores. Chicago-based Carson, Pirie, Scott & Company was sold to P. A. Bergner & Company, operator of the Milwaukee Boston Store and Bergner Department Stores. Bergner declared a Chapter 11 bankruptcy in 1991.

Many retail enterprises confronted heavy competitive pressure by lowering prices or changing merchandise strategies. Sears, Roebuck & Company, in an effort to reverse sagging sales and less than defensible earnings, unsuccessfully introduced a new policy of "everyday low pricing" (ELP) in 1989. It later introduced name brand items such as Whirlpool alongside its traditional private-label merchandise (e.g., Kenmore) and introduced the "store within a store" concept to feature the name brand goods. Montgomery Ward—and to a lesser extent K mart and Ames Department Stores—followed similar strategies. The J. C. Penney Company, despite repositioning itself as a more upscale retailer, believed that the recession and concerns about the Persian Gulf War had combined to erode consumer confidence. "As a result," the company noted in its *1990 Annual Report,* "sales and profits within the industry were more negatively impacted than at any time since the last major recession of 1980–82."

The discount department store industry by the early 1990s had changed in important ways and many analysts thought that it had reached maturity. Several formerly successful firms, including E. J. Korvette, W. T. Grant, Atlantic Mills, Arlans, Federals, Zayre, Heck's, and Ames, had declared bankruptcy and as a result either liquidated or reorganized. Regional firms such as Target Stores and Shopko Stores began carrying more fashionable merchandise in more attractive facilities and shifted their emphasis to national markets. Specialty retailers such as Toys 'R' Us, Pier 1 Imports, and Oshmans began making big inroads in toys, home furnishings, and sporting goods. The "superstores" of drug and food chains were rapidly discounting increasing amounts of general merchandise. The company's specialty stores—Caldor and Venture—and the F. W. Woolworth Company's discount store (Woolco) have withdrawn from the field by either selling their discount divisions or closing them down entirely.

Several new retail formats had emerged in the marketplace to challenge the traditional discount department store format. The superstore, a 100,000–300,000 square foot operation, combined a large supermarket with a discount general merchandise store. Originally a European retailing concept, these outlets were known as "malls without walls." K mart's Super K mart and American Fare and Wal-Mart's Super Center Store and Hypermarket were examples of this trend toward large operations. Warehouse retailing, which involved some combination of warehouse and showroom facilities, used warehouse principles to reduce operating expenses and thereby offer discount prices as a primary customer appeal. Home Depot combined the traditional hardware store and lumber yard with a self-service home improvement center to become the largest home center operator in the nation.

Some retailers responded to changes in the marketplace by selling goods at price levels (20%–60%) below regular retail prices. These off-price operations appeared as two general types: (1) factory outlet stores such as Burlington Coat Factory Warehouse, Bass Shoes, and Manhattan's Brand Name Fashion Outlet; and (2) independents such as Loehmann's, T. J. Maxx, Marshall's, and Clothestime, which bought seconds, overages, closeouts, or leftover goods from manufacturers and other retailers. Some retailers chose to dominate a product classification as super specialists: Sock Appeal, Little Piggie Ltd, and Sock Market, for example, offered a single narrowly defined classification of merchandise with an extensive assortment of brands, colors, and sizes. Others, as niche specialists (e.g., Kids Mart, a division of F. W. Woolworth, and McKids, a division of Sears) targeted an identified market with carefully selected merchandise and appropriately designed stores. Some retailers, including Silk Greenhouse (silk plants and flowers), Office Club (office supplies and equipment), and Toys 'R' Us (toys) were called "category killers" because they had achieved merchandise dominance in their respective product categories. The Limited, Victoria's Secret, and Banana Republic became minidepartment specialists by showcasing new lines and accessories alongside traditional merchandise lines.

Wal-Mart became the nation's largest retailer and discount department store chain in sales volume in 1991. Many industry analysts and consumers in several

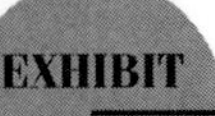
EXHIBIT 25.3

Competitive Sales and Store Comparison, 1980–1992
(Dollar amounts in thousands)

	K mart		Wal-Mart[1]	
Year	Sales	Stores[2]	Sales	Stores[2]
1992	$37,724,000	2,435	$55,483,771	1,880
1991	34,580,000	2,391	43,886,902	1,720
1990	32,070,000	2,350	32,601,594	1,573
1989	29,533,000	2,361	25,810,656	1,402
1988	27,301,000	2,307	20,649,001	1,259
1987	25,627,000	2,273	15,959,255	1,114
1986	23,035,000	2,342	11,909,076	980
1985	22,035,000	2,332	8,451,489	859
1984	20,762,000	2,173	6,400,861	745
1983	18,597,000	2,160	4,666,909	642
1982	16,772,166	2,117	3,376,252	551
1981	16,527,012	2,055	2,444,997	491
1980	14,204,381	1,772	1,643,199	330

Notes:
1. Wal-Mart Fiscal Year ends January 31. Figures are assigned to previous year.
2. General Merchandise Stores. Sales figures are net sales for the firm.

independent studies perceived K mart—now the industry's second largest retailer and discount department store chain, with 2,435 stores and $37.7 billion in sales in FY 1992—as a laggard, even though it had been the industry sales leader for many years. The same respondents perceived Wal-Mart as the industry leader, even though, according to the *Wall Street Journal,* "they carry much the same merchandise, offer prices that are pennies apart and operate stores that look almost exactly alike." "Even their names are similar," noted the newspaper. The original K mart concept of a "conveniently located, one-stop shopping unit where customers could buy a wide variety of quality merchandise at discount prices," had lost its competitive edge in a changing market. As one analyst noted in an industry newsletter: "They had done so well for the past 20 years without paying attention to market changes. Now they have to." Exhibit 25.3 shows Wal-Mart and K mart sales growth over 13 fiscal years. Exhibit 25.4 shows a competitive analysis for four major retail firms.

Some retailers (e.g., K mart) initially had focused on professional, middle-class consumers who lived in suburban areas and who were likely to be price sensitive. Other firms (e.g., Target), which had adopted the discount concept early, generally attempted to go after upscale consumers having annual household incomes of $25,000 to $44,000. Fleet Farm and Menard's served rural consumers, and firms

EXHIBIT 25.4

An Industry Competitive Analysis, 1992
(Dollar amounts in thousands, except per share data)

	Wal-Mart	Sears	K mart	J.C. Penney
Sales	$55,483,771	$ 31,961,000	$37,724,000	$18,009,000
Net income	$ 1,994,794	$ (2,977,000)	$ 941,000	$ 777,000
Net income per share	$ .87	$ —	$ 2.06	$ 2.95
Dividends per share	$ .11	$ —	$ 1.72	$ 1.32
Number of stores	2,136[1]	1,701[2]	4,792[3]	3,862[4]
Percent of sales change	26.0%	1.7%	9.1%	11.2%

Notes:

1. **Wal-Mart and Subsidiaries** (number of outlets)
   Wal-Mart Stores—1,880
   Sam's Wholesale Club—256
2. **Sears Roebuck & Company** (all divisions)
   Sears Merchandise Group (number of outlets)
   Multi-line stores—813
   Small hard-line stores—46
   Western Auto—595
   Paint and hardware stores—103
   Homelife Furniture Stores—34
   Appliance stores—37
   Free-standing tire and auto centers—20
   Retail outlet and other—53
3. **K mart Corporation** (number of outlets)
   General Merchandise—2,435
   Specialty retail stores—2,357
   PACE Membership Warehouse—114
   Builders Square—165
   Payless Drug Stores—552
   Waldenbooks—179
   The Sports Authority—56
   Borders—31
4. **JC Penney Company, Inc.** (number of outlets)
   Stores—1,312
   Metropolitan market stores—697
   Geographic market stores—615
   Catalog units—2,090
   JC Penney Stores—1,312
   Free standing sales centers—626
   Drug stores—136
   Other, principally outlet stores—16
   Drug stores (Thrift Drug or Treasury Drug—487

Source: Company records.

such as Chicago's Goldblatt's Department Stores returned to their immigrant heritage to serve blacks and Hispanics in the inner city.

In rural communities, Wal-Mart's success often came at the expense of established local merchants and units of regional discount store chains. Hardware stores, family department stores, building supply outlets, and stores featuring fabrics, sporting goods, and shoes were among the first either to close or to relocate elsewhere. Regional discount retailers in the Sunbelt states (e.g., Roses, Howard's, T. G. & Y., and Duckwall-ALCO), who once enjoyed solid sales and earnings, had to reposition themselves by renovating stores, opening larger and more modern units, remerchandising, and offering lower prices. In many cases, Coast-to-Coast, Pamida, Ben Franklin, and other chains closed stores when Wal-Mart announced plans to build in a specific community. "Just the word that Wal-Mart was coming made some stores close up," indicated a local newspaper editor.

Corporate Strategies

The corporate and marketing strategies that emerged at Wal-Mart to challenge a turbulent and volatile external environment reflected two main objectives that had guided the firm through its growth years in the 1980s. The first objective featured the customer: "customers would be provided what they want, when they want it, all at a value." The second objective emphasized team spirit: "treating each other as we would hope to be treated, acknowledging our total dependency on our Associate-partners to sustain our success." The approach included aggressive plans for new store openings; expansion to additional states; upgrading, relocation, refurbishing, and remodeling of existing stores; and opening of new distribution centers. The plan was to not have a single operating unit that had not been updated in the past seven years. In its *1991 Annual Report,* the company considered the 1990s to be "a new era for Wal-Mart; an era in which we plan to grow to a truly nationwide retailer, and should we continue to perform, our sales and earnings will also grow beyond where most could have envisioned at the dawn of the 80's."

Wal-Mart introduced several new retail formats in the 1980s. The first Sam's Wholesale Club opened in Oklahoma City, Oklahoma, in 1983. Other firms had developed the wholesale club idea earlier, but it found its greatest acceptance and success at Wal-Mart. Sam's Wholesale Clubs featured a vast array of product categories, with limited selection of brand and model; cash-and-carry business, with limited hours; large (100,000 square foot), bare-bones facilities; rock-bottom wholesale prices; and minimal promotion. The limited membership plan permitted consumers who bought memberships and others who usually paid a percentage above the ticket price of the merchandise to shop at Sam's Clubs. At the beginning of 1993, there were 256 Sam's Wholesale Clubs in 28 states. Effective February 2, 1991, Sam's Clubs merged the 28 units of The Wholesale Club, Inc., of Indianapolis, Indiana, into the organization.

The first Hypermarket*USA, a 222,000 square foot superstore, which combined a discount store with a large grocery store, a food court of restaurants, and other service businesses (such as banks or video tape rental stores) opened in 1988 in the Dallas suburb of Garland. A scaled-down version of Hypermarket*USA was the Wal-Mart Super Center, which offered similar merchandise but was about half the size of hypermarts. These expanded outlets also included convenience stores and gasoline service to "enhance shopping convenience." The company proceeded slowly with these plans and later suspended its plans for building any more hypermarkets in favor of the super-center concept.

In 1991, Wal-Mart acquired McLane Company, Inc., a provider of retail and grocery distribution services for retail stores. In October 1991, management announced that it was starting a chain of stores called Bud's, which would sell damaged, outdated, and overstocked goods at discounts even deeper than those of regular Wal-Mart stores.

Several programs were launched to highlight popular social causes. Wal-Mart initiated the "Buy American" retail program in 1985. The theme was "Bring It Home To The USA," and its purpose was to communicate Wal-Mart's support for

American manufacturing. The company encouraged manufacturers to produce goods in the United States rather than import them from other countries. It attracted vendors to the program by contacting manufacturers directly with proposals to sell goods made in the United States. Buyers also targeted specific import items in their assortments on a state-by-state basis to encourage domestic manufacturing. According to Haim Dabah, president of Gitano Group, Inc., a maker of fashion discount clothing that imported 95% of its clothing and now makes about 20% of its products here: "Wal-Mart let it be known loud and clear that if you're going to grow with them, you sure better have some products made in the U.S.A." Farris Fashion, Inc. (flannel shirts), RoadmasterCorporation (exercise bicycles), Flanders Industries, Inc. (lawn chairs), and Magic Chef (microwave ovens) were examples of vendors that chose to participate in the program.

From the Wal-Mart standpoint the "Buy American" program centered on producing and selling quality merchandise at competitive prices. The promotion included television advertisements featuring factory workers, a soaring American eagle, and the slogan: "We buy American whenever we can, so you can too." Also used were prominent in-store signs and store circulars. One store poster read: "Success Stories—These items formerly imported, are now being purchased by Wal-Mart in the U.S.A."

Wal-Mart was one of the first retailers to embrace the concept of "green" marketing. The program offered shoppers the opportunity to purchase products that were better for the environment in terms of manufacturing, use, and disposal. The company introduced it with full page advertisements in the *Wall Street Journal* and *USA Today*. In-store signs identified those products which were environmentally safe. As Wal-Mart executives saw it, "Customers are concerned about the quality of land, air, and water, and would like the opportunity to do something positive." To initiate the program, Wal-Mart notified 7,000 vendors of its corporate concern for the environment and asked for their support in a variety of ways. Wal-Mart television advertising showed children on swings, fields of grain blowing in the wind, and roses. Green and white store signs, printed on recycled paper, marked products or packaging that had been developed or redesigned to be more environmentally sound.

Wal-Mart had become the channel commander in the distribution of many brand name items. As the nation's largest retailer—in many geographic areas the dominant distributor—it exerted considerable influence in negotiations for the best price, delivery terms, promotion allowances, and continuity of supply. It passed on many of these benefits to consumers in the form of quality name brand items at lower than competitive prices. As a matter of corporate policy, management often insisted on doing business only with a producer's top sales executive rather than going through a manufacturer's representative. Wal-Mart had been accused of threatening to buy from other producers if firms refused to sell directly to it. In the ensuing power struggle, Wal-Mart executives refused to talk about the controversial policy or even admit that it existed. As a representative of an industry association representing a group of sales agencies representatives suggested, "In the Southwest, Wal-Mart's the only show in town." An industry analyst added, "They're extremely aggressive. Their approach has always been to give the customer the benefit of a corporate saving. That builds up customer loyalty and market share."

Another key factor in the mix was an inventory control system recognized as the most sophisticated in retailing. A high-speed computer system, linked virtually all the stores to headquarters and the company's distributions centers. It electronically logged every item sold at the checkout counter, automatically kept the warehouses informed of merchandise to be ordered, and directed the flow of goods to the stores and even to the proper shelves. Most important for management, it helped detect sales trends quickly and speeded up market reaction time substantially.

Decision Making in a Market-Oriented Firm

One principle that distinguished Wal-Mart was the unusual depth of employee involvement in company affairs. Corporate strategies emphasized human resource management. Employees of Wal-Mart became "associates," a name borrowed from Sam Walton's early association with the J. C. Penney Company. Management encouraged input at meetings at the store and corporate level. The firm hired employees locally, provided training programs, and through a "Letter to the President" program, management encouraged employees to ask questions. Words such as "we," "us," and "our" quickly became part of the corporate language. Various special award programs recognized individual, department, and division achievement. The company introduced stock ownership and profit-sharing programs as part of a "partnership concept."

The editors of the trade publication *Mass Market Retailers* saluted Wal-Mart's corporate culture when it recognized all 275,000 associates collectively as the 1989 "Mass Market Retailers of the Year." The editors noted that "in this decade that term [the Wal-Mart associate] has come to symbolize all that is right with the American worker, particularly in the retailing environment and most particularly at Wal-Mart. . . ." The "store within a store" concept, as a Wal-Mart corporate policy, trained individuals to be merchants by being responsible for the performance of their own departments as if they were running their own businesses. Seminars and training programs afforded them opportunities to grow within the company. "People development, not just a good 'program' for any growing company but a must to secure our future," is how Suzanne Allford, Vice-President of the Wal-Mart People Division explained the firm's decentralized approach to retail management development.

Management used the phrase "The Wal-Mart Way" to summarize the firm's unconventional approach to business and development of the corporate culture. As management noted in Wal-Mart's *1991 Annual Report* in reference to a recent development program, "We stepped outside our retailing world to examine the best managed companies in the United States in an effort to determine the fundamentals of their success and to 'benchmark' our own performances." Management used the term *Total Quality Management* (TQM) to identify this "vehicle for proliferating the very best things we do while incorporating the new ideas our people have that will assure our future."

The Growth Challenge

David Glass, 54, had assumed the role of President and Chief Executive Officer at Wal-Mart, the position previously held by Sam Walton. Known for his hard-driving managerial style, Glass gained his experience in retailing at a small supermarket chain in Springfield, Missouri. He joined Wal-Mart as Executive Vice-President for Finance in 1976 and became President and Chief Operating Officer in 1984.

And what of Wal-Mart without Mr. Sam? "There's no transition to make," said Glass, "because the principles and the basic values he used in founding this company were so sound and so universally accepted." "As for the future," he suggested, spinning around in his chair at his desk in his relatively spartan office at corporate headquarters in Bentonville, "there's more opportunity ahead of us than behind us. We're good students of retailing and we've studied the mistakes that others have made. We'll make our own mistakes, but we won't repeat theirs. The only thing constant at Wal-Mart is change. We'll be fine as long as we never lose our responsiveness to the customer."

For more than 25 years Wal-Mart Stores, Inc., had experienced tremendous growth and, as one analyst suggested, had "been consistently on the cutting edge of low-markup mass merchandising." Much of the forward momentum had come from the entrepreneurial spirit of Samuel Moore Walton. Following Walton's death, the company announced on Monday, April 6, 1992, that his son, S. Robson Walton, Vice-Chairman of Wal-Mart, would succeed his father as Chairman of the Board. David Glass would remain President and CEO. A new management team was in place. Management felt that it had positioned the firm as an industry leader to meet the challenges of the next decade.

Finance

The financial position of the company is presented in Exhibits 25.5–25.8. The company's 1992 fiscal year was from February 1, 1992 through January 31, 1993. Hence Wal-Mart's FY 1992 sales were just under $55.5 billion.

Epilogue

The post–Sam Walton era in the company's history brought new challenges. In early 1993, Wal-Mart management confirmed that sales growth for stores open more than a year would likely slip into the 7%–8% range for FY 1993. Analysts also were concerned about the increased competition in the warehouse club business and the company's move from its roots in southern and midwestern small towns to the more competitive and costly markets of the Northeast. Wal-Mart Supercenters faced more resilient rivals in the grocery field. Unions representing supermarket workers delayed and in some cases killed expansion opportunities. Some analysts said that "the company is simply suffering from the high expectations its stellar performance over the years has created."

Consolidated Statements of Income: Wal-Mart Stores, Inc., and Subsidiaries

(Dollar amounts in thousands, except per share data)

Years Ending January 31[1]	1993	1992	1991
Revenues			
Net sales	$55,483,771	$43,886,902	$32,601,594
Rentals from licensed departments	36,035	28,659	22,362
Other income—net	464,758	373,862	239,452
Total	55,984,564	44,289,423	32,863,408
Costs and expenses			
Cost of sales	44,174,685	34,786,119	25,499,834
Operating, selling, and general and administrative expenses	8,320,842	6,684,304	5,152,178
Interest costs			
Debt	142,649	113,305	42,716
Capital leases	180,049	152,558	125,920
Total	52,818,225	41,736,286	30,820,648
Income before income taxes	3,166,339	2,553,137	2,042,760
Provision for federal and state income taxes			
Current	1,136,918	906,183	737,020
Deferred	34,627	38,478	14,716
Total	1,171,545	944,661	751,736
Net income	$ 1,994,794	$ 1,608,476	$ 1,291,024
Net income per share	$ .87	$ .70	$ .57

Notes:

1. Financial information is for the previous (1993–1992, 1992–1991, and 1991–1990) calendar year.
2. Adjusted to reflect the two-for-one stock split on July 6, 1990.

Source: Wal-Mart Stores, Inc., *1993 Annual Report,* p. 10.

EXHIBIT 25.6 **Net Income for Ten Years: Wal-Mart Stores, Inc., and Subsidiaries**

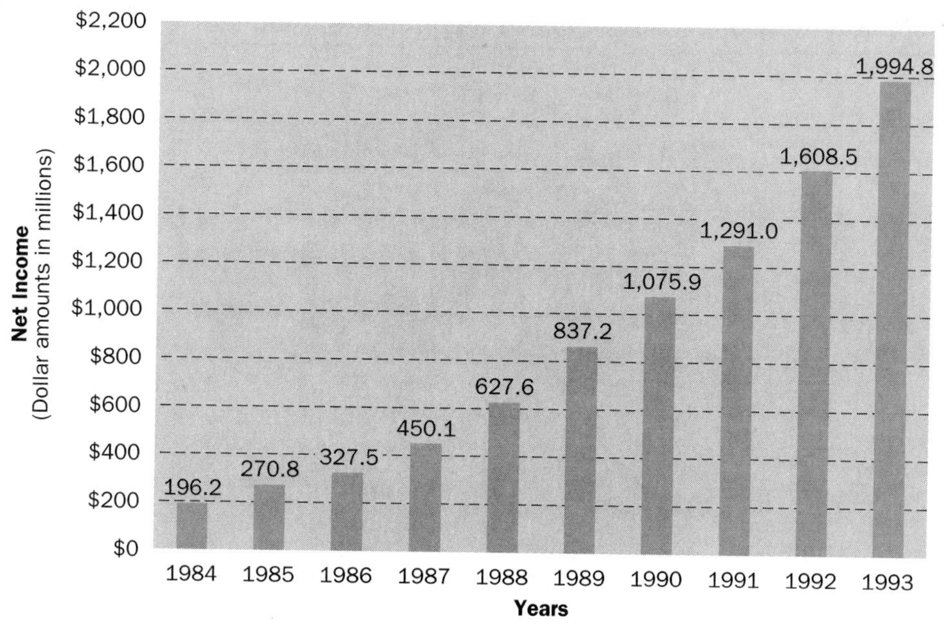

Source: Wal-Mart Stores, Inc., *1993 Annual Report*, p. 10.

EXHIBIT 25.7

Consolidated Balance Sheets: Wal-Mart Stores, Inc., and Subsidiaries

(Dollar amounts in thousands)

Years Ending January 31	1993	1992
Assets		
Current assets		
Cash and cash equivalents	$ 12,363	$ 30,649
Receivables	524,555	418,867
Recoverable costs from sale/leaseback	312,016	681,387
Inventories		
At replacement cost	9,779,981	7,856,871
Less LIFO reserve	511,672	472,572
LIFO	9,268,309	7,384,299
Prepaid expenses	80,347	60,221
Total current assets	10,197,590	8,575,423
Property, plant, and equipment, at cost		
Land	1,692,510	1,077,658
Buildings and improvements	4,641,009	2,569,095
Fixtures and equipment	3,417,230	2,683,481
Transportation equipment	111,151	86,491
Total	9,861,900	6,416,725
Less accumulated depreciation	1,607,623	1,338,151
Net property, plant, and equipment	8,254,277	5,078,574
Property under capital leases	1,986,104	1,724,123
Less accumulated amortization	447,500	368,896
Net property under capital leases	1,538,604	1,355,227
Other assets and deferred charges	574,616	434,165
Total assets	$20,565,087	$15,443,389

(continued)

25.7

Consolidated Balance Sheets: Wal-Mart Stores, Inc., and Subsidiaries *(continued)*
(Dollar amounts in thousands)

Years Ending January 31	1993	1992
Liabilities and Shareholders' Equity		
Current liabilities		
Commercial paper	$ 1,588,825	$ 453,964
Accounts payable	3,873,331	3,453,529
Accrued liabilities	1,042,108	829,381
Accrued federal and state income taxes	190,620	226,828
Long-term debt due within one year	13,849	5,156
Obligations under capital leases due within one year	45,553	34,917
Total current liabilities	6,754,286	5,003,775
Long-term debt	3,072,835	1,722,022
Long-term obligations under capital leases	1,772,152	1,555,875
Deferred income taxes	206,634	172,007
Shareholders' equity		
Preferred stock ($.10 par value; 100,000 shares authorized, none issued)		
Common stock ($.10 par value; 5,500,000 shares authorized, 2,299,638 and 1,149,028 issued and outstanding in 1993 and 1992 respectively)	229,964	114,903
Capital in excess of par value	526,647	625,669
Retained earnings	8,002,569	6,249,138
Total shareholders' equity	8,759,180	6,989,710
Total liabilities and shareholders' equity	$20,565,087	$15,443,389

Source: Wal-Mart Stores, Inc., *1993 Annual Report,* p. 11.

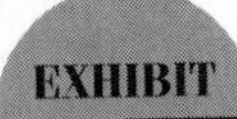

Ten-Year Financial Summary: Wal-Mart Stores, Inc. and Subsidiaries

(Dollar amounts in thousands, except per share data)

Years Ending January 31[1]	1993	1992	1991	1990
Operating results				
Net sales	$55,483,771	$43,886,902	$32,601,594	$25,810,656
Net sales increase	26%	35%	26%	25%
Comparative store sales increase	11%	10%	10%	11%
Rentals from licensed departments and other income-net	500,793	402,521	261,814	174,644
Cost of sales	44,174,685	34,786,119	25,499,834	20,070,034
Operating, selling, and general and administrative expenses	8,320,842	6,684,304	5,152,178	4,069,695
Interest costs				
Debt	142,649	113,305	42,716	20,346
Capital leases	180,049	152,558	125,920	117,725
Provision for federal and state income taxes	1,171,545	944,661	751,736	631,600
Net income	$ 1,994,794	$ 1,608,476	$ 1,291,024	$ 1,075,900
Per share of common stock[2]				
Net income	$ .87	$ .70	$ .57	$ .48
Dividends	$ .11	$ .09	.07	.06
Financial position				
Current assets	$10,197,590	$ 8,575,423	$ 6,414,775	$ 4,712,616
Inventories at replacement cost	9,779,981	7,856,871	6,207,852	4,750,619
Less LIFO reserve	511,672	472,572	399,436	322,546
Inventories at LIFO cost	9,268,309	7,384,299	5,808,416	4,428,073
Net property, plant, equipment and capital leases	9,792,881	6,433,801	4,712,039	3,430,059
Total assets	20,565,087	15,443,389	11,388,915	8,198,484
Current liabilities	6,754,286	5,003,775	3,990,414	2,845,315
Long-term debt	3,072,835	1,722,022	740,254	185,152
Long-term obligations under capital leases	1,772,152	1,555,875	1,158,621	1,087,403
Preferred stock with mandatory redemption provisions	—	—	—	—
Shareholders' equity	8,759,180	6,989,710	5,365,524	3,965,561
Financial ratios				
Current ratio	1.5	1.7	1.6	1.7
Inventories/working capital	2.7	2.1	2.4	2.4
Return on assets[3]	12.9%	14.1%	15.7%	16.9%
Return on shareholders' equity[3]	28.5%	30.0%	32.6%	35.8%
Other year-end data				
Number of Wal-Mart Stores	1,880	1,720	1,573	1,402
Number of Sam's Clubs	256	208	148	123
Average Wal-Mart Store size	81,200	75,000	70,700	66,400
Number of Associates	434,000	371,000	328,000	271,000
Number of Shareholders	180,584	150,242	122,414	79,929

Notes: 1. Financial information is for the previous (1993-1992, 1992-1991, 1991-1990, etc.) calendar year. 2. Restated to reflect the two-for-one stock split announced January 22, 1993. 3. On beginning of year balances.

1989	1988	1987	1986	1985	1984
$20,649,001	$15,959,255	$11,909,076	$8,451,489	$6,400,861	$4,666,909
29%	34%	41%	32%	37%	38%
12%	11%	13%	9%	15%	15%
136,867	104,783	84,623	55,127	52,167	36,031
16,056,856	12,281,744	9,053,219	6,361,271	4,722,440	3,418,025
3,267,864	2,599,367	2,007,645	1,485,210	1,181,455	892,887
36,286	25,262	10,442	1,903	5,207	4,935
99,395	88,995	76,367	54,640	42,506	29,946
488,246	441,027	395,940	276,119	230,653	160,903
$ 837,221	$ 627,643	$ 450,086	$ 327,473	$ 270,767	$ 196,244
$ .37	$ .28	$ .20	$ .15	$ .12	$ .09
.04	.03	.02	.02	.01	.01
$ 3,630,987	$ 2,905,145	$ 2,353,271	$1,784,275	$1,303,254	$1,005,567
3,642,696	2,854,556	2,184,847	1,528,349	1,227,264	857,155
291,329	202,796	153,875	140,181	123,339	121,760
3,351,367	2,651,760	2,030,972	1,388,168	1,103,925	735,395
2,661,954	2,144,852	1,676,282	1,303,450	870,309	628,151
6,359,668	5,131,809	4,049,092	3,103,645	2,205,229	1,652,254
2,065,909	1,743,763	1,340,291	992,683	688,968	502,763
184,439	185,672	179,234	180,682	41,237	40,866
1,009,046	866,972	764,128	595,205	449,886	339,930
—	—	—	4,902	5,874	6,411
3,007,909	2,257,267	1,690,493	1,277,659	984,672	737,503
1.8	1.7	1.8	1.8	1.9	2.0
2.1	2.3	2.0	1.8	1.8	1.5
16.3%	15.5%	14.5%	14.8%	16.4%	16.5%
37.1%	37.1%	35.2%	33.3%	36.7%	40.2%
1,259	1,114	980	859	745	642
105	84	49	23	11	3
63,500	61,500	59,000	57,000	55,000	53,000
223,000	183,000	141,000	104,000	81,000	62,000
80,270	79,777	32,896	21,828	14,799	14,172

Source: Wal-Mart Stores, Inc., *1993 Annual Report,* pp. 6–7.

References

"A Supercenter Comes To Town," *Chain Store Age Executive* (December 1989), pp. 23–30ff.

Jules Abend, "Wal-Mart's Hypermart: Impetus for U.S.Chains?" *Stores* (March 1988), pp. 59–61.

"Another Record Year at Wal-Mart," *Chain Store Age, General Merchandise Edition* (June 1984), p. 70.

Ray Bard and Susan K. Elliott, *The National Directory of Corporate Training Programs* (New York: Doubleday, 1988), pp. 351–352.

Michael Barrier, "Walton's Mountain," *Nation's Business* (April 1988), pp. 18–20ff.

Wayne Beamer, "Discount King Invades Marketer Territory," *National Petroleum* (April 1988), pp. 15–16.

Joan Bergman, "Saga of Sam Walton," *Stores* (January 1988), pp. 129–130ff.

Karen Blumenthal, "Marketing With Emotion: Wal-Mart Shows the Way," *Wall Street Journal* (November 20, 1989), p. B-3.

Michael Bradford, "Receiver Sued to Recoup Comp Payments," *Business Insurance* (September 11, 1989), p. 68.

Arthur Bragg, "Wal-Mart's War on Reps," *Sales & Marketing Management* (March 1987), pp. 41–43.

Molly Brauer, "Sam's: Setting a Fast Pace," *Chain Store Age Executive* (August 1983), pp. 20–21.

Faye Brookman, "Will Patriotic Purchasing Pay Off?" *Chain Store Age, General Merchandise Trends* (June 1985), p. 95.

Susan Caminiti, "What Ails Retailing," *Fortune* (January 30, 1989), pp. 63–64.

Thomas N. Cochran, "Chain Reaction," *Barron's* (October 16, 1989), p. 46.

Pat Corwin, Jay L. Johnson, and Renee M. Rouland, "Made in U.S.A.," *Discount Merchandiser* (November 1989), pp. 48–52.

"David Glass's Biggest Job Is Filling Sam's Shoes," *Business Month* (December 1988), p. 42.

"Discounters Commit to Bar-Code Scanning," *Chain Store Age Executive* (September 1985), pp. 49–50.

Jerry Edgerton and Jordon E. Goodman, "Wal-Mart for Hypergrowth," *Money* (March 1988), p. 12.

R. Craig Endicott, "'86 Ad Spending Soars," *Advertising Age* (November 23, 1987), pp. S-2ff.

R. Craig Endicott, "Leading National Advertisers (Companies Ranked 101–200)," *Advertising Age* (November 21, 1988), pp. S-1ff.

"Explosive Decade," *Financial World* (April 4–17, 1984), p. 92.

"Facts About Wal-Mart Stores, Inc.," *Press Release,* Corporate and Public Affairs, Wal-Mart Stores, Inc.

Christy Fisher and Patricia Strand, "Wal-Mart Pulls Back On Hypermart Plans," *Advertising Age,* (February 19, 1990), p. 49.

Christy Fisher and Judith Graham, "Wal-Mart Throws 'Green' Gauntlet," *Advertising Age* (August 21, 1989), pp. 1ff.

Margaret A. Gilliam, "Wal-Mart and the Investment Community," *Discount Merchandiser* (November 1989), pp. 64ff.

"Glass Is CEO at Wal-Mart," *Discount Merchandiser* (March 1988), pp. 6ff.

"Great News: A Recession," *Forbes* (January 8, 1990), p. 194.

Christina Gruber, "Will Competition Wilt Rose's?" *Chain Store Age, General Merchandise Edition* (May 1984), p. 40.

Michael Hartnett, "Resurgence in the Sunbelt," *Chain Store Age, General Merchandise Trends* (October 1985), pp. 13–15.

Kevin Helliker, "Wal-Mart's Store of the Future Blends Discount Prices, Department-Store Feel," *Wall Street Journal* (May 17, 1991), pp. B-1, B-8.

Kevin T. Higgins, "Wal-Mart: A Pillar in a Thousand Communities," *Building Supply Home Centers* (February 1988), pp. 100–102.

John Huey, "America's Most Successful Merchant," *Fortune* (September 23, 1991), pp. 46–48ff.

John Huey, "Wal-Mart, Will It Take Over the World?" *Fortune* (January 30, 1989), pp. 52–56ff.

"Hypermart USA Makes a Few Adjustments," *Chain Store Age Executive* (May 1988), p. 278.

"In Retail, Bigger Can Be Better," *Business Week* (March 27, 1989), p. 90.

"Jack Shewmaker, Vice Chairman, Wal-Mart Stores, Inc.," *Discount Merchandiser* (November 1987), pp. 26ff.

Steve Jacober, "Wal-Mart: A Boon to U.S. Vendors," *Discount Merchandiser* (November 1989), pp. 41–46.

Steve Jacober, "Wal-Mart: A Retailing Catalyst," *Discount Merchandiser* (November 1989), pp. 54–58.

Jay L. Johnson, "Are We Ready for Big Changes?" *Discount Merchandiser* (August 1989), pp. 48, 53–54.

Jay L. Johnson, "Hypermarts and Supercenters—Where Are They Heading?" *Discount Merchandiser* (November 1989), pp. 60ff.

Jay L. Johnson, "Hypermarket USA Does a Repeat Performance," *Discount Merchandiser* (March 1988), pp. 52ff.

Jay L. Johnson, "Internal Communication: A Key to Wal-Mart's Success," *Discount Merchandiser* (November 1989), pp. 68ff.

Jay L. Johnson, "Supercenters: Wal-Mart's Future?" *Discount Merchandiser* (May 1988), pp. 26ff.

Jay L. Johnson, "The Future of Retailing," *Discount Merchandiser* (January 1990), pp. 70ff.

Jay L. Johnson, "The Supercenter Challenge," *Discount Merchandiser* (August 1989), pp. 70ff.

Jay L. Johnson, "Walton Honored by Harvard Business School Club," *Discount Merchandiser* (June 1990), pp. 30, 34.

Bill Keith, "Wal-Mart Places Special Emphasis on Pharmacy," *Drug Topics* (July 17, 1989), pp. 16–17.

Kevin Kelly, "Sam Walton Chooses a Chip off the Old CEO," *Business Week* (February 15, 1988), p. 29.

Kevin Kelly, "Wal-Mart Gets Lost in the Vegetable Isle," *Business Week* (May 28, 1990), p. 48.

Dick Kerr, "Wal-Mart Steps Up 'Buy American,'" *Housewares* (March 7–13, 1986), pp. 1ff.

Marvin Klapper, "Wal-Mart Chairman Says His Buy American Program Working," *Women's Wear Daily* (December 3, 1985), p. 8.

"Leader in New Construction," *Chain Store Age Executive* (November 1985), p. 46.

Robert Levering, *The 100 Best Companies to Work For in America* (1984), pp. 351–354.

Bruce A. Lloyd, "Wal-Mart to Build Major Distribution Center in Loveland, Colo.," *Site Selection* (June 1989), pp. 634–635.

"Management Style: Sam Moore Walton," *Business Month* (May 1989), p. 38.

Barbara Marsch, "The Challenge: Merchants Mobilize to Battle Wal-Mart in a Small Community," *Wall Street Journal* (June 5, 1991), pp. A-1, A-4.

Todd Mason, "Sam Walton of Wal-Mart: Just Your Basic Homespun Billionaire," *Business Week* (October 14, 1985), pp. 142–143ff.

Douglas McLeod, "Miro Exceeded Authority on Wal-Mart Cover: Judge," *Business Insurance* (July 20, 1987), p. 28.

Douglas McLeod, "Transit Liquidator Can't Collect from Wal-Mart, Court Rules," *Business Insurance* (October 3, 1988).

"$90 Million Expansion Bill at Wal-Mart," *Chain Store Age Executive* (November 1982), p. 73.

"Number of Units Set to Climb by 62%," *Chain Store Age Executive* (November 1983), p. 34.

"Our People Make the Difference: The History of Wal-Mart," Videocassette, (Bentonville, Arkansas: Wal-Mart Video Productions, 1991).

Tim Padgett, "Just Saying No to Wal-Mart," *Newsweek* (November 13, 1989), p. 65.

"Perspectives on Discount Retailing," *Discount Merchandiser* (April 1987), pp. 44ff.

Tom J. Peters and Nancy Austin, *A Passion for Excellence* (New York: Random House, 1985), pp. 266–267.

Cynthia Dunn Rawn, "Wal-Mart vs. Main Street," *American Demographics* (June 1990), pp. 58–59.

Susan Reed, "Talk About a Local Boy Making Good! Sam Walton, the King of Wal-Mart, Is America's Second-Richest Man," *People* (December 19, 1983), pp. 133ff.

Sharon Reier, "CEO of the Decade: Sam M. Walton," *Financial World* (April 4, 1989), pp. 56–57ff.

"Rex Chase—Pure Wal-Mart Lore," *Chain Store Age, General Merchandise Edition* (March 1983), p. 35.

Howard Rudnitsky, "How Sam Walton Does It," *Forbes* (August 16, 1982), pp. 42–44.

Howard Rudnitsky, "Play It Again, Sam," *Forbes* (August 10, 1987), p. 48.

"Sam's Wholesale Club Racks Up $1.6 Billion Sales in 1986," *Discount Merchandiser* (February 1987), p. 26.

"Sam Walton, the Retail Giant: Where Does He Go from Here?" *Drug Topics* (July 17, 1989), p. 6.

"Sam Moore Walton," *Business Month* (May 1989), p. 38.

Bill Saporito, "The Mad Rush to Join the Warehouse Club," *Fortune* (January 6, 1986), pp. 59ff.

Michael Schachner, "Wal-Mart Chief Fined $11.5 Million for Court Absence," *Business Insurance* (January 9, 1989), pp. 1ff.

Francine Schwadel, "Little Touches Spur Wal-Mart's Rise," *Wall Street Journal* (September 22, 1989), p. B-1.

Kenneth R. Sheets, "How Wal-Mart Hits Main St.," *U.S. News & World Report* (March 13, 1989), pp. 53–55.

"Small Stores Showcase Big Ideas," *Chain Store Age, General Merchandise Trends* (September 1985), pp. 19–20.

"Small Town Hit," *Time* (May 23, 1983), p. 43.

Sarah Smith, "America's Most Admired Corporations," *Fortune* (January 29, 1990), pp. 56ff.

Alison L. Sprout, "America's Most Admired Corporations," *Fortune* (February 11, 1991), pp. 52ff.

Stephen Taub, "Gold Winner: Sam M. Walton of Wal-Mart Stores Takes the Top Prize," *Financial World* (April 15, 1986), pp. 28ff.

Marianne Taylor, "Wal-Mart Prices Itself in the Market," *Chicago Tribune* (April 28, 1991), Section 7, pp. 1ff.

"Tending Wal-Mart's Green Policy," *Advertising Age* (January 29, 1991), pp. 20ff.

The Almanac of American Employers (Chicago: Contemporary Books, 1985), p. 280.

"The Early Days: Walton Kept Adding 'a Few More' Stores," *Discount Store News* (December 9, 1985), p. 61.

"The Five Best-Managed Companies," *Dun's Business Month* (December 1982), p. 47.

Shannon Thurmond, "Sam Speaks Volumes About New Formats," *Advertising Age* (May 9, 1988), p. S-26.

Vance H. Trimble, *Sam Walton: The Inside Story of America's Richest Man* (New York: Dutton, 1990).

"Wal-Mart's 1990 Look," *Discount Merchandiser* (July 1989), p. 12.

"Wal-Mart Associates Generate Over $5.5 Million for United Way," *Press Release* (January 2, 1990), Corporate and Public Affairs, Wal-Mart Stores, Inc.

"Wal-Mart Beats the Devil," *Chain Store Age* (August 1986), p. 9.

"Wal-Mart Expands; Tests New 'Wholesale' Concept," *Chain Store Age, General Merchandise Trends* (June 1983), p. 98.

"Wal-Mart's Glass to Reps: 'That's a Bunch of Baloney!'" *Discount Merchandiser* (September 1987), p. 12.

"Wal-Mart's Goals," *Discount Merchandiser* (January 1988), pp. 48–50.

"Wal-Mart Goes on Its Own," *Progressive Grocer* (June 1987), p. 9.

"Wal-Mart's 'Green' Campaign to Emphasize Recycling Next," *Adweek's Marketing Week* (February 12, 1990), pp. 60–61.

"Wal-Mart Has No Quarrel with 1984," *Chain Store Age, General Merchandise Trends* (June 1985), p. 36.

"Wal-Mart on the Move," *Progressive Grocer* (August 1987), p. 9.

"Wal-Mart Policy Asks for Supplier Commitment," *Textile World* (May 1985), pp. 27–28.

"Wal-Mart Raises Over $3 Million for Children's Hospital," *Press Release* (June 1989), Corporate and Public Affairs, Wal-Mart Stores, Inc.

"Wal-Mart Rolls Out Its Supercenters," *Chain Store Age Executive* (December 1988), pp. 18–19.

"Wal-Mart Stores Penny Wise," *Business Month* (December 1988), p. 42.

"Wal-Mart: The Model Discounter," *Dun's Business Month* (December 1982), pp. 60–61.

"Wal-Mart to Acquire McLane, Distributor to Retail Industry," *Wall Street Journal,* (October 2, 1990), p. A-8.

Steve Weiner, "Golf Balls, Motor Oil and Tomatoes," *Forbes* (October 30, 1989), pp. 130–131ff.

Steve Weiner, "Pssst! Wanna Buy a Watch? A Suit? How About a Whole Department Store?" *Forbes* (January 8, 1990), pp. 192ff.

"Wholesale Clubs," *Discount Merchandiser* (November 1987), pp. 26ff.

"Why Wal-Mart Is Recession Proof," *Business Week* (February 22, 1988), p. 146.

"Work, Ambition—Sam Walton," *Press Release,* Corporate and Public Affairs, Wal-Mart Stores, Inc.

Jason Zweig, "Expand It Again, Sam," *Forbes* (July 9, 1990), p. 106.

The Blockbuster Video Challenge

John Dunkelberg and Tom Goho

When Mike Gibbons, the owner of Video Station, picked up the morning newspaper, the headline got his immediate attention: "Blockbuster Video Opens in September [1991]." As he read the article under the headline, he learned that Blockbuster Video was planning to open a 6,500 square foot video tape rental store within 50 yards of his own 5,000 square foot video rental store. Although he had heard that Blockbuster had done a market survey in the early spring and that it had inquired about leasing two different pieces of commercial property, Mike had not expected them to come to a town as small as Lumberton, North Carolina.

As he finished the article, he started making notes on the possible consequences of the arrival of Blockbuster on his business and to map a strategy for the four-month period before the proposed opening. Mike had visited Blockbuster stores to learn about their operations, and he felt that he knew the volume of sales they needed to be profitable. He believed that it would be very hard for both him and Blockbuster to be profitable in the limited (population was 26,000) Lumberton market.

Background

Mike Gibbons was born and raised in Lumberton, North Carolina, and had graduated as a business administration major from a nearby private university. While in college, he was active in his fraternity and had always been interested in assuming leadership positions. His goals had been to be self-employed and start a business that offered a better product and/or service than its competitors. He also wanted to establish a business that was interesting and that had the potential for rapid growth. Mike's business experience involved working at his father's retail clothing store, where he had worked since he was twelve. While in college, he and a friend had started Video Station. After Mike graduated, his friend dropped out of the business and went to law school.

Lumberton's Video Market

Lumberton, a small city located in the eastern part of North Carolina, has a population of about 26,000. According to the Chamber of Commerce, the per capita income in Lumberton is approximately $10,000, and the average total household income is $28,000. Currently there are ten video rental stores in Lumberton. (Exhibit 26.1 presents additional demographic information.)

This case was prepared by Professor John Dunkelberg and Tom Goho of Wake Forest University. This case appears in *International Journal of Case Studies and Research*, Vol. 1, No. 1 (November 1, 1992). This case was edited by T. L. Wheelan and J. D. Hunger for this book. Reprinted by permission of the authors.

EXHIBIT 26.1 **Demographic Profile: Lumberton, North Carolina**

Principal Industries		Number of Wage Earners		Average Weekly Wage
Textiles		3,984		$243
Chemical and allied products		2,413		421
Apparel		1,269		186
Transportation, communication, and utilities		1,132		389
Population	24,150			
Households	8,968			
Per capita income	$10,000			
Percent high school graduates			55.7%	
Percent college graduates			20.1	
Percent population: Age 0–19 years old			24.3	
Age 20–49 years old			35.1	
Over 50 years old			40.6	

First Year

Mike Gibbons and a partner started Video Station in 1988, when Mike was 21 years old, with $22,000 in start-up capital. The basic concept was to deliver rental videos to customers' homes just like pizza was delivered. Customers could order from a video library of just over 500 tapes, and, for $2.99, Video Station would deliver the requested tapes to their homes. The next day the tapes could be dropped in one of four drop boxes located throughout Lumberton. Since opening the store, Mike had lowered the price to $1.99 for one night. The business quickly outgrew the original 143 square foot room, and Video Station expanded into an adjacent room, remodeled to handle walk-in business. During the first year of business, Mike's partner ran the day-to-day business while Mike finished his last year of college and worked at Video Station on the weekends. Revenues that first year were $64,000, with all surplus cash being used to purchase additional tapes.

Second Year

During the second year, the partner, who had finished college the previous year, decided to enter law school, so Mike bought him out. Video Station expanded to a second store located in a small shopping mall. The 1,200 square foot store contained about 1,500 video tapes. This expansion required additional capital, which Mike obtained by a $100,000 bank loan based on his personal assets. He used the money to remodel space for the second store, purchase the initial inventory for the second store, increase the inventory in the first store, and to purchase a general-purpose vehicle for use in deliveries. Revenues during the second year were

EXHIBIT 26.2

Income Statement: Video Station, Inc.
(Six months ending June 30, Year Four)

Revenues		$167,842
Expenses		
Salaries	$ 41,743	
Payroll taxes	3,848	
Depreciation	46,102	
Utilities	7,301	
Rent	11,514	
Office expenses	12,661	
Maintenance	838	
Interest expense	14,558	
Total expenses		$138,565
Income before taxes		$ 29,277

$173,000. Mike received an annual salary of $12,000 and used all other profits to purchase additional tapes.

Third Year

During the third year, Video Station opened a third store that had 5,000 square feet of retail floor space and additional space for offices. This store stocked 12,000 tapes and required an additional $200,000 loan for the remodeling and the purchase of tapes. Revenues grew each month, and total revenue for the year was $278,000. Video Station was just beginning its fourth year when Mike read the announcement of the planned arrival of Blockbuster Video.

Present Position (Year Four)

The growth of Video Station had come partly at the expense of some of the smaller video rental stores, and, over the past two years, ten had gone out of business, leaving only nine smaller competitors. Mike estimated that his remaining competitors had an average of less than 1,000 video tapes each and, combined, had less than half the total video rental business in Lumberton. He also estimated that the present annual revenues from video rentals in Lumberton was about $600,000. This total did not seem to be enough business for both big stores (Video Station and Blockbuster) to be profitable.

Although the growth of Video Station had been phenomenal, it had not been very profitable. The sales mix had been 90% in-store rentals and 10% home deliveries. To furnish the last two stores and purchase a large inventory of tapes, Mike had borrowed almost $300,000. The growth of revenues, however, had met his expectations, and he believed that Video Station would become profitable this year. The income statement for the first six months indicates that his estimates are on target (see Exhibit 26.2).

EXHIBIT 26.3

Cash Flow: Video Station, Inc.
(Three months, April–June, Year Four)

Cash received		$85,774
Cash expenditures		
Purchases	$26,308	
Salaries	22,768	
Payroll taxes	2,391	
Utilities	3,614	
Rent	5,754	
Maintenance	395	
Office expenses	7,876	
Interest expense	7,279	
Total cash expenditures		$76,385
Net cash inflows		$ 9,389

Although the income statement indicated a healthy firm, Mike knew that cash flows would be more important in the next few months; cash would be needed to keep the business afloat after Blockbuster opened, when sales could drop significantly because of the promotional campaign that Blockbuster normally used to open new stores. His cash flows for the past three months were positive (see Exhibit 26.3), although he had purchased slightly more video tapes than usual. Finally, he examined his most recent balance sheet (see Exhibit 26.4). Two items looked ominous: notes payable and retained earnings.

The notes payable (money borrowed to purchase the tape inventory, make leasehold improvements, and purchase fixtures and office furniture for the last two stores) required only interest payments for the next three years. The other item, retained earnings, was negative because during the first three years of operation, Video Station had large depreciation expenses. Before Blockbuster announced its opening, Mike had felt that Video Station had gone through its growth period and was finally poised to be a profitable operation. Profitability now seemed far away.

Blockbuster Video

Blockbuster Entertainment Corporation operates and licenses Blockbuster Video stores, which rent video tapes. The firm has grown from 19 stores in 1986 to 1,079 stores by the end of 1990 (561 company-owned and 518 franchises) in 43 states, Canada, the United Kingdom, and Guam. The typical Blockbuster store carries 7,000 to 13,000 tapes and the stores range in size from 4,000 to 10,000 square feet. In 1990 the 301 company-owned stores that had been in operation for more than one year were averaging monthly revenues of $65,984.

Although the growth in the United States in consumer spending on video rentals seems to have slowed, Blockbuster Video believes that it has the opportu-

EXHIBIT 26.4

Balance Sheet: Video Station, Inc.
(June 30, Year Four)

Cash	$ 5,264	Accounts payable	$ 15,429
Inventory	3,700	Withholding/FICA payable	2,270
Prepaid expenses	1,390	Sales tax payable	1,240
Total current assets	10,354	Notes payable	256,378
		Total current liabilities	275,317
Office equipment	48,499	Common stock	10,400
Furniture and fixtures	53,400	Retained earnings	(25,409)
Video tapes	223,068		
Leasehold improvements	39,800		
Accumulated depreciation	(114,913)		
Total assets	$260,208	**Total liabilities and equity**	$260,208

nity to take market share away from smaller competitors through its strategy of building large stores with a greater selection of tapes than most of its competitors. As the largest video chain in the United States, Blockbuster Video also has advantages in marketing and purchasing inventory. Blockbuster Video's pricing is $3.50 per tape for two nights. However, there apparently has been some discussion within the organization about giving local stores some pricing discretion.

According to a prospectus, Blockbuster plans for the Lumberton store include the purchase of a vacant lot for about $310,000 and then to lease a 6,400 square foot building that will be built to their specifications, under a long-term lease agreement for $8.50 per square foot per year. The cost of completely furnishing the building, including the video tapes, will be approximately $375,000, and Blockbuster plans to spend more than $150,000 on the grand opening promotion. Blockbuster's operating costs are similar to Video Station's because the computer checkout equipment is similar and both firms have approximately the same personnel costs. Both firms depreciate their tapes over 12 months.

Efforts to Negotiate

After analyzing Blockbuster's plans, Gibbons called George Atkins, President of SEC Video, who had the Blockbuster Video licensee agreement for Virginia, South Carolina, and North Carolina. Mike thought that a meeting with Atkins could be beneficial to learn more about Blockbuster's plans and to find out whether Blockbuster was interested in purchasing Video Station. Video Station had about the same size store that Blockbuster was planning to build, used the same type of computer checkout system, many of the same fixtures, and had the same open store layout. Mike's thinking was simple: there was not enough business for both stores to be profitable. Blockbuster would save a lot of money by moving into his store and needed to make only minor changes to have a store that looked just like all other Blockbuster stores. Mike had not thought about owning a video store all his life and had been thinking of returning to graduate school even before the Blockbuster announcement.

Atkins seemed happy to meet with Mike and invited him to his office in Sumter, South Carolina. During the meeting Atkins made a tentative offer to purchase Video Station for 40% of current sales plus the value of the existing tapes, and he seemed willing to purchase the leases on Mike's two stores. Each of these leases had two more years to run. He did state that he would not consider a move into Mike's store because there was not enough parking area. In addition, all Blockbuster stores were to be new and the company had a policy against moving into existing stores. Interestingly, during the meeting in which Atkins tried hard to learn what Video Station's revenues were, he stated that he thought the potential video rental market in Lumberton was about $1,000,000 per year. Mike thanked Atkins for his time and agreed to think about his offer.

After calculating what he thought was a reasonable point to start negotiating, Mike called Atkins and they agreed to meet in Lumberton. About one month after the first meeting, Atkins flew into the Lumberton airport in his private plane. Mike met him in a private office at the airport. Mike opened the meeting with a brief statement of what had transpired during the last meeting and again asked whether Blockbuster would consider using Video Station's existing building, as the saving to Blockbuster would be enormous. Atkins again stated that Blockbuster had a policy about new stores because of the image the company wanted to maintain. He then reminded Mike that Video Station was worth more right now than it ever would be again, about how large Blockbuster was compared to Video Station, and how it would soon be able to take Mike's customers through promotions such as giving away a Bronco or other popular cars each month until they had the market share they wanted.

He then offered to purchase Video Station for 40% of the last 12 months' sales. This figure included all of Video Station's assets but none of its liabilities, such as the store leases. This offer was so far from the previous offer that Mike did not attempt to negotiate but did leave the possibility of future talks open. Atkins stated that this was his final offer and he told Mike that "I will not call you again." He then hurried off to his waiting plane to fly to a similar sized town about 40 miles away to discuss the purchase of that town's largest video store. As the plane taxied from the control tower, Mike began mentally analyzing his options and wondering about the future of Video Station when Blockbuster Video opened its store in less than three months.

L.A. Gear, Inc.

A. J. Almaney

Overview

In February 1989, Robert Y. Greenberg stood on the floor of the New York Stock Exchange and watched as the letters "LA" flashed across the ticker tape for the first time. "It was my proudest moment. It was my dream," Greenberg said. "You see, I always wanted to be the president of a company on the New York Stock Exchange,"[1] he added.

For more than 14 years, L.A. Gear promoted the southern California lifestyle with attractively styled shoes designed primarily for women. Later, however, the company altered its focus to include products that appealed to the men's performance athletic market. The company continued to produce fashion shoes for women, but its core business became the performance athletic market where sales were not as dependent on swings in consumer tastes. The company achieved its position as the number three brand maker of footwear products when it surpassed Converse, Inc., in 1989. Greenberg set his sights on the number one position in the industry by challenging Nike and Reebok.

However, L.A. Gear began to experience financial difficulties in 1991. Its market share dropped from a high of 12% in 1990 to 8% in 1991 to 5% in 1992. And its net sales declined from $820 million in 1990 to $619 million in 1991 to $430 million in 1992. The company incurred losses of $45 million in 1991 and $72 million in 1992. As a result, L.A. Gear was unable to obtain credit from its traditional lenders. To enhance its credit rating, L.A. Gear managed to lure a new investor, Trefoil Capital Investors L.P., who, in September 1991, paid $100 million for a 34% stake in the company.

After the Trefoil deal, L.A. Gear's internal operations underwent major restructuring. As part of the restructuring, the Trefoil team replaced L.A. Gear's top management, including the company's founder, Robert Y. Greenberg. Stanley P. Gold, Managing Director of Trefoil Capital Investors L.P., and Mark R. Goldston, former Reebok executive, took over. Gold succeeded Greenberg as the company's new Chairman and Chief Executive Officer, and Goldston was appointed President and Chief Operating Officer.

Gold and Goldston developed a survival strategy to nurse the ailing L.A. Gear back to health. At the core of the turnaround strategy was a new advertising campaign built around the theme, "Get in Gear." In an effort to create a clear identity

---

This case was prepared by Professor A. J. Almaney and the following MBA students under Professor Almaney's direction: S. Green, S. Slotkin, and H. Speer of DePaul University. This case was accepted by the refereed *Midwest Society for Case Research Meeting, 1993*. This case was edited by T. L. Wheelen and J. D. Hunger for this book. Reprinted by permission.

for L.A. Gear, Goldston reorganized product lines into three groups: athletic, lifestyle, and children. The new management also launched a restructuring program aimed at paring the company's costs.

In their letter to the shareholders, Gold and Goldston stated, "We believe that the accomplishments of the past year have laid the groundwork upon which we can build to achieve our ultimate objective—to make L.A. Gear a leader in the footwear industry and one of the most admired companies in America." But, will they be able to accomplish their objective in this highly competitive industry?

History

Robert Y. Greenberg, L.A. Gear's founder, had a knack for selling. First, it was wigs. Later it was roller skates and jeans for the trendy residents of Venice Beach, California. Then it was sneakers. As one analyst described him, "Greenberg is the quintessential salesman."[2]

Greenberg's story is a 1980s financial fairy tale with a 1990s climax: a street-smart shoemaker who always feared being poor would create a pair of sneakers that brought him fortune. As a kid working in his Brooklyn family's produce business and reading his father's copies of *Forbes* magazine, Greenberg set his sights on starting his own company. He took his first step toward that goal by enrolling in a beauticians' school. After graduation, he opened a chain of hair salons in Brooklyn in the mid 1960s. Later, he started a wig-importing business. As that venture petered out, Greenberg spotted another trend—fashion jeans—and began importing them from South Korea. By 1979, the jeans business had started to fade, and Greenberg decided to pack up for southern California.

His next inspiration came soon after his arrival in Los Angeles, as he waited three hours at Venice Beach to rent roller skates for his wife and kids. "I figured the guy must be taking in $4,000 to $5,000 a day," he said. So, Greenberg walked out of that skate shop and immediately plunked $40,000 into his own, which he soon expanded to nine locations. Not only did he sell skates through the stores, but he established a skate-manufacturing business. The market for skates quickly soured, though. Greenberg then opened a clothing store on Melrose Avenue, which he named L.A. Gear. By 1985, the L.A. Gear store was losing money.

Greenberg started looking for the next trend to ride. Having watched Reebok storm the market a year earlier with its fashionable aerobics shoes, Greenberg went after Reebok with his own candy-colored sneakers, all aimed at a market he knew: trend-conscious teenage girls. In what proved to be a brilliant marketing strategy, he opted to sell his shoes not just to sporting goods stores but also to big department stores such as Nordstrom, the May Company, and Bullock's. L.A. Gear's big break came the following year, 1987, when Reebok underestimated the demand for its wildly popular black-and-white athletic shoes. Greenberg stepped in to meet the demand by marketing "The Workout," a simple canvas shoe that became the flagship of the company.

During Greenberg's Venice Beach tenure, he had become friends with Sandy Saemann, who was making skating safety equipment while Greenberg was hawking skates. After Saemann launched his own advertising agency, Greenberg brought him into the company to help craft L.A. Gear's frothy image of sun and sex.

The Greenberg–Saemann combination worked. L.A. Gear soon became a highly profitable operation. Sales mushroomed from $200,000 per month at the beginning of 1985 to $1.8 million per month by mid year. As the company grew to an operation of 51 employees, it needed outside funds for more development and opted for an initial public offering, which was completed on July 1, 1986.

The company used the $16.5 million in proceeds from the offering to fund its growing working-capital requirements and to fund a hefty advertising and promotion budget. The initial single style of footwear exploded into 150 styles, and L.A. Gear's preeminence in the youth market expanded to include footwear for customers of all ages. In 1986, L.A. Gear launched lines for men, children, and infants and expanded its women's line to include athletic shoes for basketball, aerobics, and cross-training.

In 1989, sales rocketed to $617 million from $71 million in 1987, and the company surpassed Converse, Inc., to become the nation's third-largest seller of athletic shoes. In 1989, L.A. Gear's stock switched from trading in the over-the-counter market to the New York Stock Exchange (NYSE). L.A. Gear's stock price in 1988 was $10.94 based on $224 million in sales. By early December 1989, L.A. Gear's stock had climbed more than 178%, more than any NYSE stock.[3] The *Wall Street Journal, Business Week,* and *Fortune* named L.A. Gear the best performing stock on the NYSE in 1989. Greenberg boasted that he would push L.A. Gear past Reebok and Nike by 1991. Mark R. Goldston, L.A. Gear's current President, described the company's early success as a phenomenon achieved by innovative styling and unique abilities to have its ear to the market and to respond quickly.

In 1990, however, the company's stock price started to decline, and investors became concerned that L.A. Gear was losing its appeal to fashion-conscious young women. Some analysts marked the beginning of L.A. Gear's troubles with the failure of its Michael Jackson shoes.[4] In 1989, Sandy Saemann, Executive Vice-President, signed a $20 million contract with Michael Jackson for endorsement of a line of black, silver-buckled shoes. But the shoes were a failure. Other signs of trouble included reports of stock selling by insiders and a Justice Department investigation of alleged underpayment of customs duties.[5]

In April 1991, L.A. Gear posted a fiscal first-quarter loss of $12.5 million. Sales fell 8.8% to $171 million from 187 million. L.A. Gear posted a tangible net worth of $193 million as of February 28, 1991.[6]

In May 1991, L.A. Gear agreed to sell a 30% stake to Roy E. Disney's Trefoil Capital Investors L.P. for $100 million. Under the agreement, Trefoil would also receive three seats on L.A. Gear's Board of Directors and the first option to buy Greenberg's 3.5 million in common shares should he decide to sell. L.A. Gear also agreed to hire Disney's Shamrock Capital Advisors, Inc., as consultants for three years, paying fees of $500,000 the first year, $600,000 the second year, and $700,000 the third year.

Shortly after initiation of the Trefoil agreement, Sandy Saemann—the flamboyant, gold-chain–decked Executive Vice-President—resigned. Saemann was the architect of L.A. Gear's sexy marketing campaign that often featured scantily

EXHIBIT 27.1 **Board of Directors: L.A. Gear, Inc.**

Stanley P. Gold
Chairman of the Board and Chief Executive Officer
L.A. Gear, Inc.
President and Managing Director
Trefoil Investors, Inc., and
Shamrock Capital Advisors, Inc.

Mark R. Goldston
President and Chief Operating Officer
L.A. Gear, Inc.

Richard W. Schubert
General Counsel and Secretary
L.A. Gear, Inc.

Alan E. Dashling
Chairman of the Board and Chief Executive Officer
Sterling West Bancorp

Willie D. Davis
President and Chief Executive Officer
All-Pro Broadcasting

Stephen A. Koffler
Executive Vice-President and
Director of Investment Banking
Sutro & Co., Inc.

Ann E. Meyers
Sports Commentator
KMPC Radio, Prime Ticket, ESPN,
Sportschannel, and ABC

Clifford A. Miller
Chairman
The Clifford Group, Inc.

Robert G. Moskowitz
Managing Director
Trefoil Investors, Inc., and
Shamrock Capital Advisors, Inc.

R. Rudolph Reinfrank
Executive Vice-President
Shamrock Holdings, Inc.

Vappalak A. Ravindran
Chief Executive Officer
Paracor Company
President
Elders Finance, Inc.

Source: L.A. Gear, *1992 Annual Report,* p. 29.

clad models. He also was credited with gathering celebrity endorsers for L.A. Gear. Saemann agreed to provide consulting services to L.A. Gear for two and a half years. Analysts said that Saemann resigned because his flamboyant personality conflicted with those of the Trefoil team.[7] Kevin Ventrudo, 32, Senior Vice-President of Administration and a Board member, also resigned. Mark R. Goldston succeeded Robert Greenberg as President. Greenberg remained as Chairman and Chief Executive.

On January 27, 1992, Robert Greenberg, L.A. Gear's founder, was eased out as Chairman and Chief Executive and a director, along with Gil N. Schwartzberg, Vice-Chairman. Stanley P. Gold, 50, Managing Director of Trefoil, was appointed Chairman and Chief Executive Officer of L.A. Gear.

Board of Directors

As shown in Exhibit 27.1, the Board of Directors contained 11 members. Three were insiders, and the others were outsiders. One of the outside directors was sports commentator Ann E. Meyers. The Chairman of the Board was Stanley P.

Gold who also served as Chief Executive Officer. The Board carried out its duties through the Executive and Nominating Committees. The Executive Committee consisted of Stanley Gold, R. Rudolph Reinfrank, and Mark Goldston. Reinfrank served as Chairman of the Executive Committee. The Nominating Committee consisted of Stephen A. Koffler, Robert G. Moskowitz, and Mark Goldston. Koffler served as Chairman of the Nominating Committee.

Top Management

L.A. Gear's top management underwent major changes after Trefoil invested $100 million in the company. A profile of each key executive follows.

Stanley P. Gold: Stanley Gold, 50, succeeded Greenberg as Chairman and Chief Executive Officer of L.A. Gear, Inc. He had been President and Chief Executive Officer of Shamrock Holdings, Inc., a Burbank, California–based company wholly owned by the Roy Disney family. Gold was considered to be a turnaround expert. He proved himself by helping revive Walt Disney Company, oil driller Enterra, and soybean processor Central Soyal. Prior to assuming his positions at Shamrock, Gold was a Managing Partner of Gange, Tyre, Ramer & Brown, Inc., a prominent Los Angeles law firm he joined in 1968. For a number of years, he specialized in corporate acquisitions, sales, and financing. Earlier in his legal career, he served as a trial lawyer in major corporate and civil litigation.[8]

A native of Los Angeles, Gold first studied at the University of California at Berkeley and subsequently graduated from the University of California at Los Angeles with an A.B. degree in political science. After receiving his J.D. degree from the University of Southern California Law School in 1967, he did postgraduate work at Cambridge University in England.[9] Gold's professional and civic affiliations included the American Bar Association and the Copyright Society. He served as a guest lecturer at the Wharton School at the University of Pennsylvania. He was Chairman of the Board of Governors of Hebrew Union College, a Trustee of the Center Theater Group in Los Angeles, member of The George C. Marshall Foundation, and a member of the USC Law Center Board of Councilors.

Mark R. Goldston: Mark Goldston, 38, succeeded Robert Y. Greenberg, the company's founder, as President and Chief Operating Officer. Greenberg also was eased out as Chairman, Chief Executive Officer, and a director at a Board meeting in an apparent effort by the company's largest investor, Trefoil Capital Investors L.P., to bury the "old" L.A. Gear.[10] Despite Greenberg's assertions that "the company is left in great hands," the ouster capped a four-month battle between the laid-back Greenberg and the buttoned-down Trefoil team for the soul of L.A. Gear.[11]

Goldston was a principal of Odyssey partners, a leverage buyout and investment firm. At Odyssey, Goldston was part of an internal operating unit that supervised the management of certain portfolio companies. His responsibilities included the development, execution, and management of operating plans and the evaluation of strategic alternatives for those portfolio companies. Prior to joining

Odyssey, Goldston had been Senior and Chief Marketing Officer of Reebok International Ltd where he spearheaded the marketing effort for "The Pump," a $500 million line of athletic footwear products. As one of the inventors of the Reebok "Visible Energy Return System Technology," Goldston was on the U.S. patent for that technology. Additionally, Goldston was involved in the development of the Hexalite and Energaire product lines for Reebok. Prior to joining Reebok, Goldston had been President of Fabergé USA, Inc., a cosmetics and personal care products company. During his tenure there, the company's U.S. sales increased by about 50%.

Goldston was on the J. L. Kellogg Graduate School of Management Dean's Advisory Board at Northwestern University. In addition, he sat on the Board of Directors of Revel/Monogram, Inc., ABCO Markets, and Collection Clothing Corporation. Goldston's book, entitled *The Turnaround Prescription,* detailing a step-by-step blueprint for effecting a corporate marketing turnaround, was published in 1992.[12]

In his new position as President and Chief Operating Officer, Goldston brought in fresh talent by hiring former Reebok employees Gordie Nye, Robert Apatoff, and Christopher Walsh. Gordie Nye, Vice-President of Marketing Athletic Footwear, joined the company in December 1991. Previously, he had been at Reebok where he was Senior Director of Fitness Marketing, with responsibility for marketing men's and women's fitness products.

Christopher Walsh: Christopher Walsh, 43, joined L.A. Gear as Senior Vice-President of Operations in December 1991. Previously, he was Vice-President of Production at Reebok for three years, where he was in charge of worldwide supply sources. Prior to joining Reebok, he spent two years at Toddler University, a children's shoe manufacturer as Vice-President of Operations. Before that, he worked as a senior consultant for Kurt Satmon Associates for two years, focusing on strategic planning. Earlier in his career, he worked at Nike for 10 years in production and sourcing.[13]

William L. Benford: William Benford, 50, was appointed Chief Financial Officer in September 1991.[14] Prior to that, he had been Senior Vice-President and Chief Financial Officer of Central Soya company. Before that he had been Vice-President and Treasurer of Dekalb, Inc. He also was affiliated with Shamrock Holdings, Inc., an investment company for the Roy E. Disney family. Shamrock Holdings, Inc., bought Central Soya company in 1985, turned it around, and sold the company two years later at a profit of about $125 million.

Mission

L.A. Gear defined its mission as follows:

> The Company's principal business activity involves the design, development, and marketing of a broad range of quality athletic and casual/lifestyle footwear. Since its inception, the Company has expanded its product line from its original concentration on fashionable women's footwear to diversified collections of footwear for men, women,

and children. The Company is organized into two primary marketing divisions: Athletic (including men's and women's basketball, fitness, walking, tennis, and aerobics) and Lifestyle (casual footwear styles intended for non-athletic use). All of the Company's footwear products are manufactured to its specifications by independent producers located primarily in South Korea, Indonesia, Taiwan and the People's Republic of China.[15]

Objectives and Strategies

L.A. Gear's short-term objective was to streamline its operations over the next two years. In the long-term, the company would attempt to achieve the following objectives:

- to provide a broad range of quality athletic and casual/lifestyle footwear, primarily in the "mid" price range (i.e., $30–$65 retail);
- to improve relations with, and increase shelf space at, full-margin retailers;
- to improve production and quality control practices; and
- to increase international sales and profitability.

In attaining these objectives, L.A. Gear adopted a retrenchment/turnaround strategy that involved a comprehensive restructuring of its operations. Thus in 1992, the company cut its staff by 613 employees, or about 45%. In addition, the company reduced its occupancy from about 200,000 square feet of leased office space in five buildings to about 116,000 square feet in two buildings. Further, it reduced general and administrative expenses in 1992 by $42.7 million, or 21.2%, to $158.7 million from $201.4 million. The company also discontinued its apparel marketing and design operations, which had a pre-tax operating loss of $14.2 million in 1991.

The company augmented restructuring with a product development strategy. This strategy involved developing a broad range of innovative new products for the athletic, lifestyle, and children's lines. Footwear industry analysts praised grouping the products into three well-identified divisions. Bob McAllister, West Coast market editor for *Footwear News,* said, "In the past, there was no rhyme or reason to L.A. Gear's different styles. Now, the company has introduced new lines that are cleanly divided into athletic, lifestyles and kids."[16]

The company also sought to differentiate its products from its competitors. Goldston was confident that L.A. Gear would increase its market share by using materials in a unique way to carve a specific niche for its products. According to Goldston, "L.A. Gear is committed to designing shoes that do not resemble its competition."[17] While pursuing retrenchment and product development strategies, L.A. Gear launched a marketing campaign that focused on projecting a consistent brand image across varying retail price points and distribution channels.

Production

L.A. Gear's footwear was manufactured to its specifications by independent producers located primarily in The People's Republic of China, Indonesia, South Korea, and Taiwan. In 1992, manufacturers in these countries supplied 34%,

32%, 30%, and 4%, respectively, of the total pairs of footwear purchased by the company.

The footwear products imported into the United States by the company were subject to customs duties, ranging from 6%–48% of production costs. Duty rates depended on the construction of the shoe and whether the principal component was leather or some other material.

The use of foreign manufacturing facilities subjected the company to the customary risks of doing business abroad, including fluctuations in currency values, export duties, import controls, trade barriers, restrictions on the transfer of funds, work stoppages, and political instability. These factors, however, seemingly have not adversely affected the company's operations.

Products

L.A. Gear's product lines were organized into three marketing categories: Athletic, Lifestyle, and Children's. Athletic footwear included fitness, walking, tennis, cross-training, and basketball shoes, and the recently introduced Light Gear Cross-Runner and Dance Training shoes. The company marketed these products under two brand names: L.A. Gear, with suggested domestic retail prices under $70; and the newly released L.A. Tech, which was a higher priced premium brand.

The Lifestyle lines comprised men's and women's casual footwear styles, including the Street Hiker, Vintage Series, and Fashion Athletic and Casual collections. The Children's footwear products incorporated features from the Athletic and Lifestyle lines and products specifically developed for children. L.A. Lights, lighted shoes for children introduced in June 1992, became one of the largest selling children's shoes in the company's history. The age ranges of the company's target markets were 14–35 years for adult products and 5–13 for children.[18] Some of L.A. Gear's products and the technologies incorporated in the Athletic, Lifestyle, and Children's lines are described in Exhibit 27.2.

Product Quality

In 1990, L.A. Gear committed a grave marketing blunder in the process of launching its new line of basketball shoes. In a scramble to launch the new shoes, the company outfitted the Marquette University team with handmade pairs because molds had not been completed for the large sizes the team members required. As TV cameras zeroed in on one player, the bottom of his sneaker peeled away from the top. This and other cases of poor quality served to tarnish seriously the company's brand image. In an effort to improve quality, L.A. Gear reduced the number of foreign manufacturers from 44 in 1991 to 29 in 1992, retaining only those known for their quality products. The company also engaged a "sourcing" agent with the responsibility of inspecting finished goods prior to shipment by the manufacturer, supervising production management, and facilitating the shipment of goods.

EXHIBIT 27.2 **Products and Their Technologies: L.A. Gear, Inc.**

Athletic	Description
Catapult	A midsole system consisting of a carbon graphite spring to provide cushioning and shock absorption
Encapsole Air	A cushioning system that uses air chambers built into the outsole to provide shock absorption
Light Gear	Shoes incorporating battery-powered lights in the outsole that flash upon impact
Lifestyle	**Description**
Street Hiker	A lightweight casual hiking shoe
Vintage Series	Footwear based on classic athletic styles
Children's	**Description**
L.A. Gear (Glactica for boys; L.A. Twilight for girls; Nightcrawlers for infants)	Shoes incorporating motion activated battery-powered lights in the outsole that flash with movement
Regulator	Shoes with an adjustable fit and support system using an air inflation device to cushion the foot over the midfoot area
Bendables	Flexible shoes for infants
Clear Gear	Shoes with a clear outsole in flexible plastic with an assortment of designs printed on the midsole

Source: L.A. Gear, *Form 10-K Report* (1992), p. 4.

Advertising

Sandy Saemann, Greenberg's second in command, was the architect of L.A. Gear's early advertising campaign. His success in signing celebrities such as Paula Abdul and Kareem Abdul-Jabbar was responsible for the phenomenal increase in the company's sales between 1985 and 1990. Saemann fit the image of the laid-back California executive perfectly—right down to the flashy necklace. And his flamboyant vision proved perfect for peddling flashy sneakers. Saemann represented L.A. Gear's brash, entrepreneurial roots by producing virtually all the company's ads and commercials himself without the help of Madison Avenue. However, L.A. Gear's tumble began, ironically, with its biggest advertising deal ever. In 1989, Saemann signed mega-star Michael Jackson to what was described as the largest endorsement contract ever: $20 million. L.A. Gear had hoped to time the release of a new line of shoes to an upcoming Michael Jackson greatest-hits album, but the album never materialized. Teenagers everywhere thumbed their noses at the black, buckle-laden shoes. The company eventually discontinued the entire line, taking a loss of several million dollars.

After the failure of the Michael Jackson advertising campaign, L.A. Gear stopped contracting for the endorsement of its products by entertainment celebrities. Instead, the company turned to endorsements by athletic stars such as Karl "The Mailman" Malone of the Utah Jazz, Hakeem Olajuwon of the Houston Rockets, and Joe Montana of the San Francisco Forty-Niners. The company used a new slogan, "Get in Gear," in the campaign.

Under the new management, L.A. Gear changed the focus of many of its advertising campaigns from promoting a fashionable shoe to promoting a performance shoe. It emphasized performance with the advertisement tag line for the Catapult performance shoe, "It's not just a shoe, it's a machine."[19] L.A. Gear's most successful commercial was the use of the tag line "Anything else is just hot air" to promote the Catapult shoe, with its high-tech, carbon-fiber soles. The ad was an indirect attack on Nike, which made the Air Jordan shoes, endorsed by Chicago Bull's star Michael Jordan. NBC refused to run the television ads, and the ensuing exposure received by coverage of NBC's refusal was worth millions to L.A. Gear.[20] In promoting the $110 Catapult shoe, the new management decided to drop the L.A. Gear logo, believing that the L.A. Gear name was a liability in marketing performance shoes.

The new management team subdivided the marketing of the company's products on the basis of price. Shoes costing less than $70 per pair retained the L.A. Gear name and logo, and shoes costing more than $70 per pair carried the L.A. Tech name. L.A. Gear's management believed that the L.A. Tech name would help establish the line as a high-technology, performance product. The lowest cost L.A. Gear shoe retailed for approximately $30 per pair, whereas the top of the line L.A. Tech shoe, the Catapult, topped out at about $150 per pair.[21] L.A. Gear's marketing budget amounted to 10%–15% of total sales.

Sales

The phenomenal rise in L.A. Gear's sales between 1985 and 1990 reflected Greenberg's ability to create a clear-cut image for the company with brightly colored shoes and sexy ads aimed at teenage girls. The company's spectacular success led Greenberg to set a higher objective for the company: $1 billion in sales. To achieve this objective, Greenberg decided to challenge Nike and Reebok directly by adding a line of men's performance shoes. The move was too much, too fast. Venturing into the men's performance shoes blurred L.A. Gear's image. According to one analyst, "When L.A. Gear moved into the performance side, it lost its way." Greenberg, however, was unwilling to blame the company's problems on the men's shoes. Instead, he maintained that "in any battle you're gonna get a little bruised or battered. And we're playing with a couple of billion-dollar companies that don't need us around."

The rapid growth also placed an enormous strain on the company. Employees had to push hard to attain the new growth objective. As a result, the company's internal controls failed. A shareholders' class-action lawsuit called those controls "chaotic and virtually nonexistent."

As a result of the relentless push for fast growth, product quality problems, and the attendant bad publicity, L.A. Gear saw its share of the overall athletic shoe

EXHIBIT 27.3

Net Sales: L.A. Gear, Inc.
(Dollar amounts in thousands)

	1992		1991		1990	
	Net Sales	Percentage of Total Net Sales	Net Sales	Percentage of Total Net Sales	Net Sales	Percentage of Total Net Sales
Domestic footwear						
Women's	$112,990	26%	$178,481	29%	$285,709	35%
Men's	104,593	24	176,238	28	196,969	24
Children's	90,997	21	134,485	22	174,486	21
Other	2,688	1	2,517	—	4,217	1
Total domestic net sales	311,268	72	491,721	79	661,381	81
International footwear	118,926	28	127,454	21	158,220	19
Total net sales	$430,194	100%	$619,175	100%	$819,601	100%

Source: L.A. Gear, *Form 10-K Report* (1992), p. 5.

market drop from a high of 12% in 1990 to 5% in 1992. Company net sales (see Exhibit 27.3) declined from $820 million in 1990 to $619 million in 1991 to $430 million in 1992. The 1992 sales figure represented a 31% decline from 1991. The company incurred losses of $72 million in 1992 and $45 million in 1991. Net international sales, which accounted for about 28% of the company's total net sales, declined by 6.7% from 1991.

According to management, the overall decline in net sales for 1992 was principally the result of a drop in the number of pairs sold worldwide owing to lower customer demand, and, to a lesser extent, to an average reduction of $1.52 in the selling price per pair. The decline reflected the continuing recession and price reductions by the company's principal competitors, which resulted in increased competition at lower prices.

Another factor that contributed to the drop in 1992 sales volume was delivery delays. As part of its restructuring program that year, the company changed manufacturers. These changes contributed to the company's difficulties in meeting its delivery deadlines on orders for its back-to-school season.

International Strategy

In recent years, sales of athletic and casual/lifestyle footwear in many international markets has grown faster than in the United States. However, L.A. Gear's own sales in the international market declined from $158 million in 1990 to $127 million in 1991 to $119 million in 1992.

In an effort to stem this decline in sales, L.A. Gear decided to increase its investment in the international market through joint ventures, acquisitions of distributors, and the creation of wholly owned foreign subsidiaries. By selling its products directly abroad (as opposed to the company's historical reliance on independent distributors in those markets), the company sought to increase sales by adopting more competitive marketing and distribution programs. In March 1992, the company established its first foreign subsidiary to conduct direct sales of its products in France.

L.A. Gear also began to focus on Asia for its potential as a retail sales market. "We see Asia as a huge market. You have basically got two billion pairs of feet out here," said Goldston. Consequently, the company began investigating promotional alliances and equity partnerships with Asian companies.

Distribution

L.A. Gear distributed its products from a one million square foot warehouse/distribution center in Ontario, California. In the United States, the company sold its products to about 4,000 distributors that included department, sporting goods, athletic footwear and shoe stores, and wholesale distributors.

In recent years, L.A. Gear has relied on extensive distribution through wholesale distributors who sold into deep-discount outlets. This policy tarnished the company's image and, as a result, several key retail accounts ceased or reduced their business with the company in 1991. To improve relations with full-margin retailers, the company began to distribute its products through specific channels, using what it called the "Gear Strategy Classification System." In line with this system, it grouped distribution channels in terms of "Image," "Mainstream," "Volume," and "Value." The company used the Image channels to market its most technologically advanced and expensive high-performance products, such as the L.A. Tech. It used the Mainstream and Volume channels to market "2nd Gear" and "1st Gear" products, which had fewer technological and aesthetic features. The Value channels were intended only for the distribution of inventory that could not be sold through the other channels. As part of the Value channels, the company planned to open a limited number of outlet stores.

Under Greenberg, the company maintained a next-day (at once) open stock system, whereby retailers could order products and have them shipped within 24 hours. This system made inventory expenses skyrocket. To mitigate this problem, the company also adopted a "futures" ordering system, which provided discounts to retailers who ordered products four to six months in advance of shipment. The company hoped that the new program would enable it to improve inventory management.

Internationally, L.A. Gear distributed its product in about 60 countries, primarily through agreements with independent distributors. The distribution agreements were intended to maintain a consistent product offering and brand image throughout the world. However, this arrangement afforded the company little or no control over the ultimate retail price of its footwear. It also restricted both profits and growth potential.

Research and Development

In designing its products, L.A. Gear conducted comprehensive market research, using a variety of conventional research techniques. Primarily, the company depended on focus groups, product testing, and interviews with consumers and retailers. These methods allowed the company to gauge accurately the image and reputation of L.A. Gear's products and to incorporate changes demanded by the public.

L.A. Gear maintained close ties with firms that conducted basic materials research. For example, L.A. Gear had an alliance with U.T.I. Chemicals Corporation of California. U.T.I. developed a new outsole material known as Z-thane, a patented plastic compound that outlasted similar materials already on the market.[22] L.A. Gear also applied older materials to its shoe lines, such as the innovative use of carbon-fiber heel protectors in its performance shoes. With the Catapult, L.A. Gear hoped to challenge the high-performance image of Nike and Reebok by luring the performance-oriented buyer away from these market leaders.

L.A. Gear, however, lagged behind its competitors in product innovation. For example, the company introduced a "pump" style shoe almost two years after Nike and Reebok introduced their versions of this technology. Ironically, former CEO Robert Greenberg once boasted that the company spent a fraction of what its competition spent on research and development.[23] The company's "catch-up" R&D practices damaged its relations with retailers. For example, one shoe buyer for a large department store chain said: "We saw Nike and Reebok 1993 spring lines in May or June of 1992 and started committing for product in July. We didn't see L.A. Gear's product until mid August."[24]

Human Resources

L.A. Gear has 753 full-time employees. In 1991, the company embarked on a restructuring program to reduce its work force. By 1992, 613 employees had been released, 152 of whom were associated with the company's discontinued apparel design and marketing operations. This cutback represented a 45% reduction in staff and reduced the company's monthly payroll expense from $4.8 million in 1991 to $3.4 million in 1992. The company's employees were not covered by any collective bargaining agreement, but management considered the company's relations with its employees to be satisfactory. The company offered its employees 401(k) retirement savings programs and provided an employee stock option plan (ESOP). The company instituted the ESOP program as an incentive program for employees and management alike.

Communication and Corporate Culture

As L.A. Gear grew, it had to hire more employees to handle new functions. In 1985, 50 people turned out the product; by 1992, that number had swelled to 1,200. As a result, the company, which was characterized by an informal communication system and corporate culture, splintered into departmental fiefdoms scattered in several buildings. The new structure eroded the informal relationships that existed among L.A. Gear's management and employees. In the early days, for instance, Greenberg and Saemann worked just across the hall from each other, and their basic form of communication was to yell back and forth. Greenberg, who had a passion for tropical fish and kept a large tank in his office, often would march across the hall to see Saemann with a dripping net in one hand and a new sneaker design in the other.

The new management brought with it buttoned-down seriousness. Coats and ties were now a regular sight at L.A. Gear. Gone were the days when Greenberg would slip each of his employees $100 bills in pink envelopes whenever the company turned a profit. Now, employees carried around black coffee mugs that read ATTACK BUSINESS COSTS.

Legal Issues

In 1990 and 1991, shareholders brought three class-action lawsuits against L.A. Gear. They claimed that the company had violated U.S. securities laws by inflating sales by tens of millions of dollars in 1990 when it counted as revenues the value of merchandise stored in L.A. Gear's warehouses and docks. In settling these lawsuits, the company recorded a $23 million pre-tax charge against its 1992 earnings.

In October 1992, L.A. Gear reached an agreement with the U.S. Attorney for the District of Massachusetts regarding the resolution of all customs claims arising from the importation of footwear from Taiwan in 1986 and 1987. Accordingly, L.A. Gear entered a guilty plea with respect to two counts charging underpayment of duties on such shipments. A sentencing hearing was scheduled in 1993. In addition, the company paid $1.3 million in settlement of all potential civil claims arising from underpayment of duties on the 1986 and 1987 shipments from Taiwan.

In November 1992, L.A. Gear settled a patent infringement lawsuit brought against it by Reebok International Ltd, alleging that certain footwear products marketed by the company infringed on a patent issued to Reebok covering "inflatable bladder" shoe technology. L.A. Gear paid Reebok $1 million to settle the lawsuit. As part of the settlement, L.A. Gear entered into a license agreement under which Reebok granted the company a four-year nonexclusive worldwide license to manufacture, use, and sell footwear utilizing the "inflatable bladder." The license agreement, however, did not grant L.A. Gear access to Reebok's technology.

Another legal issue involved L.A. Gear's relationship with entertainer Michael Jackson. In September 1992, the company filed a complaint against Jackson alleging, among other things, fraud, breach of contract, and breach of good faith. The company's claims arose from contracts between the company and the defendant that granted the company the exclusive right to use Jackson's name and likeness in advertising and promoting the company's shoes and apparel and the right to develop and market a Michael Jackson athletic shoe line. Michael Jackson countered with a lawsuit, alleging fraud and breach of good faith on the part of the company. This dispute has not been yet settled.

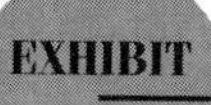
EXHIBIT 27.4

Consolidated Statements of Operations: L.A. Gear, Inc., and Subsidiaries
(Dollar amounts in thousands, except per share data)

Years Ending November 30	1992	1991	1990
Net sales	$430,194	$619,175	$819,601
Cost of sales	321,174	448,682	533,420
Gross profit	109,020	170,493	286,181
Selling, general and administrative expenses	171,169	225,280	225,662
Shareholder litigation settlements	23,075	—	—
Interest expense	1,421	13,156	18,615
Interest income	(1,159)	(220)	(100)
Income (loss) from continuing operations before income taxes	(85,486)	(67,723)	42,004
Income tax (benefit) provision	(13,585)	(22,727)	16,376
Income (loss) from continuing operations	(71,901)	(44,996)	25,628
Discontinued operations			
Income (loss) from discontinued operations (net of income tax provision (benefit) of $4,898 and $3,660)	—	(9,350)	5,710
Provision for estimated loss on disposal (net of income tax benefit of $6,146)	—	(11,854)	—
	—	(21,204)	5,710
Net income (loss)	$ (71,901)	$ (66,200)	$ 31,338
Dividends on mandatorily redeemable preferred stock	(7,746)	(1,625)	—
Income (loss) applicable to common stock	$ (79,647)	$ (67,825)	$ 31,338
Income (loss) per common share			
Continuing operations	$ (3.76)	$ (2.40)	$ 1.28
Discontinued operations	—	(1.09)	.28
Total	$ (3.76)	$ (3.49)	$ 1.56
Weighted average common shares outstanding	21,180	19,453	20,041

Source: L.A. Gear Inc., *1992 Annual Report,* p. 18.

Finance and Accounting

L.A. Gear's gross profit declined from $286 million in 1990 to $170 million in 1991 to $109 million in 1992. The company had a net income of $31 million in 1990, but it lost $66 million and $72 million in 1991 and 1992, respectively (see Exhibits 27.4 and 27.5).

Because of an imbalance between inventory purchases and sales, L.A. Gear accumulated excess inventory. As was the custom in the footwear industry, substantial changes in current product lines were made at least twice a year (i.e., for the spring and back-to-school seasons). As a result, certain styles usually were discontinued. However, the introduction of the company's new product lines also re-

EXHIBIT 27.5

Consolidated Balance Sheets: L.A. Gear, Inc., and Subsidiaries

(Dollar amounts in thousands)

Years Ending November 30	1992	1991
Assets		
Current assets		
Cash and cash equivalents	$ 55,027	$ 1,422
Collateralized cash	28,955	—
Accounts receivable, net	56,369	111,470
Inventories	61,923	141,115
Prepaid expenses and other current assets	2,557	8,506
Refundable income taxes	25,269	22,795
Deferred income taxes	—	11,763
Total current assets	230,100	297,071
Property and equipment, net	17,667	26,869
Other assets	1,735	1,631
Total assets	$249,502	$325,571
Liabilities, Mandatorily Redeemable Preferred Stock, and Shareholders' Equity		
Current liabilities		
Borrowings under line of credit	$ —	$ 20,000
Accounts payable and accrued liabilities	49,753	55,856
Dividends payable on mandatorily redeemable preferred stock	7,746	—
Costs related to discontinued operations	4,552	18,000
Total current liabilities	62,051	93,856
Mandatorily redeemable preferred stock		
7.5% Series A Cumulative Convertible Preferred Stock, $100 stated value; 1,000,000 shares authorized, issued and outstanding; redemption value of $100 per share	100,000	100,000
Shareholders' equity		
Common stock, no par value; 80,000,000 shares authorized; 22,898,182 shares issued and outstanding at November 30, 1992 (19,542,513 shares issued and outstanding at November 30, 1991)	127,714	92,331
Preferred stock, no stated value; 9,000,000 shares authorized; no shares issued	—	—
Retained earnings (accumulated deficit)	(40,263)	39,384
Total shareholders' equity	87,451	131,715
Commitments and contingencies	—	—
Total liabilities, mandatorily redeemable preferred stock, and shareholders' equity	$249,502	$325,571

Source: L.A. Gear, Inc., *1992 Annual Report,* p. 17.

sulted in a greater number of styles being discontinued than otherwise would have been the case. As part of an inventory reduction program, the company sold inventory at significant discounts, resulting in lower margins.

In September 1991, Trefoil Capital Investors L.P. invested $100 million in L.A. Gear in the form of a new issue of Series A Cumulative Convertible Preferred Stock, the net proceeds of which were used to repay indebtedness. In November 1992, the company had cash and cash equivalent balances of $84 million (see Exhibit 27.6). In addition, the company expected to receive income tax refunds in 1993 of about $25 million.

The Footwear Industry

The U.S. general footwear market was valued at about $12 billion, of which the athletic shoe market comprised about $6 billion. According to *Footwear News,* the domestic retail shoe market was expected to continue to grow at a rate of 5.5% at least until the year 2000.[25]

The *1987 Census of Manufacturers* conducted by the U.S. Bureau of the Census revealed that more than 100 companies participated in the footwear industry.[26] During 1992, two dozen companies competed in the U.S. branded footwear market.[27] Domestically, the two largest athletic shoe makers were Nike and Reebok, with a combined share of the market of 50%.[28] Although Nike and Reebok, along with L.A. Gear, were headquartered in the United States, most of their products were manufactured in Asia, Europe, and South America. A shoe that retailed for $100 cost the company between $20 and $25 if manufactured in foreign countries. Thus markups to both the retailer and consumer were nearly 100%.

The footwear industry was not cyclical but did show some seasonality with back-to-school sales in August and September. Although footwear company profitability and sales fluctuated, these fluctuations were attributed not to economic cycles but to changes in advertising expenditures, price, product quality, and overall market trends such as consumer preferences for fashion versus performance shoes.

Entry into the footwear industry was difficult. The reason was that success in this industry depended to a great extent on heavy advertising, brand awareness, and intensive research and development. In the high-performance athletic shoe market, advertising was essential in promoting new styles and creating brand awareness. Footwear companies spent vast sums to get popular athletes to endorse certain shoes. Nike and Reebok, for example, spent $200 million on advertising and promotion in 1992—a prohibitive cost for smaller firms whose revenues often were too small to mount effective marketing campaigns. Another barrier to entry was brand awareness. Consumers purchased shoes based either on how well they perceived a brand to perform or on its fashion characteristics. On average, when selecting a shoe, men tended to look at sole cushioning and how well an inner structure supported the foot—not fashion or style. However, women based their purchases more on the shoe design or style.[29]

An even greater entry barrier in the footwear industry was the excessive capital required for research and development. Nike, Reebok, and L.A. Gear had large

EXHIBIT 27.6

Consolidated Statements of Cash Flows: L.A. Gear, Inc., and Subsidiaries

(Dollar amounts in thousands)

Years Ending November 30	1992	1991	1990
Operating Activities			
Net income (loss)	$(71,901)	$(66,200)	$ 31,338
Adjustments to reconcile net income (loss) to net cash provided by (used in) operating activities			
Shareholder litigation settlements	17,075	—	—
Depreciation and amortization	7,107	7,182	3,394
Provision for loss on discontinued operations	—	18,000	—
Loss on sale or abandonment of property and equipment	1,871	4,146	—
Issuance of shares to employee stock savings plan	233	382	—
(Increase) decrease in			
Accounts receivable, net	55,101	44,431	(52,969)
Inventories	79,192	19,553	(21,152)
Prepaids and other assets	6,343	1,565	(998)
Refundable and deferred income taxes	8,791	(26,174)	(3,795)
Increase (decrease) in			
Accounts payable and accrued liabilities	(6,103)	(8,222)	3,143
Costs related to discontinued operations	(8,343)	—	—
Net cash provided by (used in) operating activities	89,366	(5,337)	(41,039)
Investing Activities–Capital Expenditures	(4,881)	(14,188)	(18,939)
Financing activities			
Net proceeds from issuance of mandatorily redeemable preferred stock	—	92,511	—
Payment of dividends on mandatorily redeemable preferred stock	—	(1,625)	—
Exercise of stock options and warrants	1,986	414	908
Tax benefits arising from the disposition/exercise of incentive stock options	2,089	356	5,408
Proceeds from issuance of common stock	14,000	—	—
Net borrowings (repayments) under line of credit agreement	(20,000)	(74,000)	56,600
Net cash provided by (used in) financing activities	(1,925)	17,656	62,916
Net increase (decrease) in cash and cash equivalents	82,560	(1,869)	2,938
Cash at beginning of year	1,422	3,291	353
Cash and cash equivalents at end of year, including collateralized cash	$ 83,982	$ 1,422	$ 3,291

Source: L.A. Gear, Inc., *1992 Annual Report*, p. 20.

R&D budgets. Each of the top three competitors had a highly advanced technology. Nike had its Air Jordan; Reebok had the Pump and Insta Pump; and L.A. Gear had its Catapult and Regulator, which incorporated high-tech carbon-fiber soles.

In the highly competitive discount athletic footwear market, barriers to entry were less formidable. Volume companies (mass producers) tended to carve out a niche through brands they licensed or created on their own. According to *Footwear News*, "the mass market usually followed where the better-grade merchandise had already beaten a path. Volume sources capitalized on the consumer appetite for branded-athletic footwear generated by the sophisticated marketing of companies such as Nike, Reebok, and L.A. Gear." According to the Sporting Good Manufacturers Association, discount stores commanded $3.4 billion of the athletic shoe market.[30]

The U.S. footwear industry was maturing, and analysts expected that consumers would purchase more nonathletic footwear than athletic footwear. With the domestic market maturing, many footwear companies began expanding overseas where the market was expected to grow at a rate of 23% a year during the next decade.[31]

The appeal of overseas markets to U.S. footwear companies stemmed not only from their sheer size but also from the inexpensive advertising common in such markets. Furthermore, a growing number of consumers overseas were becoming increasingly interested in U.S. sports generally and in basketball in particular. Actually, U.S. basketball was now a close second to soccer in worldwide popularity.[32] As a result, footwear companies discovered that their big endorsers, such as Michael Jordan for Nike, translated well across borders.

Competitors

The athletic and athletic style footwear industry was highly competitive both in the United States and worldwide. L.A. Gear's competitors included both specialized athletic shoe companies and companies with diversified footwear product lines. The company's primary competitors in the domestic athletic and athletic style markets were Nike and Reebok. These companies were more established than L.A. Gear and had greater financial, distribution, and marketing resources—and greater brand awareness, than the company. Internationally, L.A. Gear's major competitor was Adidas.

Nike

Nike was a publicly held sports and fitness company with a 26% share of the domestic market. Nike was the first company in the sports and fitness industry to exceed $2 billion in U.S. revenues and $3 billion worldwide. The company reached these levels in 1991. Nike's product lines were diverse. The company designed and marketed athletic footwear, apparel, and related items for competitive and recreational uses. To promote this breadth of product lines, Nike's advertisements featured high-profile athletes. Nike's impressive stable of endorsers included Michael

Jordan, Bo Jackson, David Robinson, and Andre Agassi. The success of these advertising campaigns enabled Nike to command a higher price for its shoes than its competitors could.

To add to its image as one of the premier athletic footwear companies, Nike began to open a series of high-tech, futuristic looking, company-owned outlets around the world called Nike Town. This outlet was a tribute to Nike's innovative flair and marketing genius.[33] The design concept represented sports, fitness, entertainment, history, and product innovation.

Nike spent more than its competitors on R&D, having learned the hard way to push its technology. In 1987, Reebok surpassed Nike as the number one domestic footwear company. At that time, Nike was concentrating on marketing its apparel and fashion shoes instead of promoting its air-cushioning system. Within 18 months of being surpassed by Reebok, Nike regained the number one spot by marketing its Nike Air Jordan shoes. Now, Nike's engineers—not its fashion designers—began to call the shots.

Reebok

Reebok International Ltd designed and marketed active lifestyle and performance products, including footwear and apparel, and held 24% of the domestic footwear market. According to industry sources, Reebok was the company best positioned to take advantage of the developing worldwide sneaker market.[34] Reebok announced in early 1992 that it had established a new worldwide sports marketing unit and that it would increase advertising spending by 25%. Moreover, international sales soared by 75% to $832.6 million from $475.2 million in 1990. The sports marketing unit worked in conjunction with the fitness and casual units to deliver the best products and programs to consumers and retailers worldwide.

In 1988, Reebok acquired Avia and Rockport, two fast-growing companies. Paul Fireman, Chairman and Chief Executive Officer, believed that Avia and Rockport exemplified a "sense of aliveness," which also was a characteristic of Reebok.[35] In 1991, Avia's sales rose by 4.3% to $161 million, and Rockport's sales grew by 8.5% to $251.3 million. Rockport produced products primarily for the walking shoe market, whereas Avia competed directly with Reebok in the athletic footwear market.

Reebok replaced its ineffective advertising with a cause-related campaign aimed at supporting philanthropic organizations while promoting its own products. In 1990, industry sources noted that Reebok lacked a winning advertising campaign when two consecutive advertising campaigns flopped. In 1991 and 1992, Reebok reversed this trend with its cause-related advertising. Practitioners maintained that such advertising could be risky but, when handled carefully, could supply the best of all promotional worlds: higher visibility, a unique image niche resulting from association with worthy projects, and stronger ties to the community.[36] As part of its cause-related marketing, Reebok gave financial support to Amnesty International's Human Rights Now tour. Angel Martinez, Vice-President of Business Development at Reebok's Los Angeles office, said that "the tour was an extension of our value system as a company. We believe in freedom of expression and wanted to do something of importance, beyond selling sneakers."[37]

Reebok's President, Joseph LaBonte, added, "We both believe very strongly in the freedom to do what you want."

To remain competitive with Nike, Reebok also planned to contract endorsements with high-profile athletes. Even though the Insta-Pump would not be available to consumers until January 1993, Reebok hoped to get a lot of promotional mileage by putting the shoes on several Olympic track and field stars at the 1992 summer games in Barcelona, Spain.

Adidas and Puma

A decade ago, Adidas or its smaller rival, Puma, made most of the athletic shoes sold in Europe. For years, the two German companies controlled about 75% of Europe's athletic shoe and apparel market, and they also were strong in the United States. However, the situation changed. Now, Nike and Reebok, and to a lesser degree L.A. Gear, made spectacular inroads in Europe. Although Adidas continued to be number one with $1.6 billion in revenues, Nike ranked second with $500 million, and Reebok ranked third with $380 million. L.A. Gear's sales were less than $119 million.

Both Nike and Reebok profited from long-term problems at Adidas and Puma. In the past five years, both German companies reported steady losses because of unfocused marketing, high costs, and product glut. At Adidas, the confusion was acute: In footwear alone, it had 1,200 different variations and styles. "We had everything," said Michel Perrauding, Adidas's manager for logistics, "even shoes for left-handed bowlers."

Adidas's poorly coordinated marketing in Europe angered many distributors, who started to defect to Nike and Reebok. And in the United States, where Adidas was once number one in athletic shoes, chronic delivery problems and a failure to spot the trend to more comfortable shoes led to huge losses and a dramatic drop in market share.

Nike and Reebok, however, might have to confront revitalized Adidas and Puma operations. A Swedish company took full control of Puma and planned to pump cash into it. At Adidas, a new French owner slashed its product range in shoes and apparel to several hundred from several thousand, retired hundreds of employees, and started a network of more efficient purchasing and production facilities in Asia. Adidas launched a new line, Equipment, featuring no-frills shoes for sports such as soccer, tennis, and track. Adidas also introduced a new Adidas series of hiking and outdoors shoes. Nevertheless, Adidas and Puma lacked the deep pockets of Nike and Reebok to enable them to spend as much on advertising as the two U.S. companies.

Customers

L.A. Gear sold to retail stores, specialty shoe stores, and sporting goods stores, but its ultimate customer was the individual retail consumer. L.A. Gear's customers historically were young fashion-minded girls. Under Greenberg, the company promoted the young southern California lifestyle. Its advertisements featured young blondes on the beach in stylish L.A. Gear shoes. Under the new management, the company repositioned itself. Former CEO Robert Greenberg said that the company knew that in order to grow it eventually would have to enter the men's market and that meant more technically oriented footwear.[38] Fashion athletics was now only a part of L.A. Gear.

Other External Factors

Government Regulations

In 1990, Congress passed the Textile, Apparel, and Footwear Trade Act (the "Textile Act"), which would have set highly restrictive global quotas on imported textile, apparel, and footwear products. However, President Bush vetoed this legislation, and the House of Representatives sustained the veto. Similar legislation could be proposed again in the future. If such a legislation were enacted into law, L.A. Gear could face restrictions on its ability to import its footwear products manufactured abroad.

In 1992, the U.S. government placed L.A. Gear's suppliers in Taiwan, China, Indonesia, and South Korea on a "priority watch list" for engaging in unfair trade practices. If proof could be obtained that these countries engaged in unfair trade practices, the United States might retaliate against them, which could result in increasing the cost or reducing the supply of footwear generally and L.A. Gear's footwear in particular.

Demographics

The U.S. population, which totaled 250 million in 1990, was expected to reach 283 million by 2010, an increase of about 13%. Perhaps more significant to the footwear industry was the size of the baby boom generation, born between 1946 and 1964. A prime target of footwear companies, this segment, which comprised 18% of the population in 1990, was expected to grow by about 9% by 2010.

Culture

Lifestyle changes in the United States, and in many other countries, were propitious for footwear producers. An increasing segment of the population was becoming more health conscious, engaging in athletic activities such as jogging and walking. Because of the increasing popularity of walking, the walking shoes market was expected to be the largest growth segment of the footwear industry. According to industry sources, 75% of the walking shoes market consisted of women in their mid 30s and older.[39]

Economy

In 1991 and 1992, the Federal Reserve Board laid the groundwork for an economic recovery by keeping prime interest rates low and gradually expanding the money supply. At the same time, the Fed was able to keep inflation at less than 4%. Depressed consumer confidence in economic recovery, however, continued to be a major obstacle to increased consumer and business spending. The slow start of President Clinton's economic program served only to slow a long-awaited growth in the nation's economy.

Technology

Counterfeiting is the perennial enemy of brand name producers in Asia. Recognizing the danger to his company's technology, Goldston, L.A. Gear's President, said, "The major focus of our agreements with new manufacturers is on integrity. Our technology innovation will be protected."[40] However, an L.A. Gear executive said the means available to foreign shoe manufacturers for protecting patents were limited. As a result, athletic–shoe makers could find that their most nagging competitors were not each other but the companies who filled their orders. Such companies as L.A. Gear "tend to stumble when faced with competition, and this time it will come from say, . . . a factory in Indonesia that has acquired the technology to make a good jogging shoe."[41]

Politics

With political changes occurring in Eastern Europe and the Soviet Union, markets that were previously closed to Western companies were now fairly wide open. The enactment of NAFTA (North American Free Trade Agreement) among the United States, Canada, and Mexico, was likely to strengthen U.S. exports. According to estimates made by the U.S. Trade Representative, tariff reductions alone, if undertaken by all countries, could raise U.S. real GNP by 3% by the year 2000.[42]

Notes

1. "L.A. Gear," *Los Angeles Magazine* (December 1991), p. 116.
2. "L.A. Gear Calls in a Cobbler," *Business Week* (September 16, 1991), p. 78.
3. "L.A. Gear +184.6%," *Institutional Investor* (March 1990), pp. 52, 53.
4. "L.A. Gear Co-Founder Saemann Quits in Wake of Firm's Deal with Trefoil," *Wall Street Journal* (June 13, 1991), p. B-1.
5. "The Best and Worst Stocks of 1989," *Fortune* (January 29, 1990), p. 114.
6. "L.A. Gear Inc.," *Wall Street Journal* (April 4, 1991), p. B-1.
7. "L.A. Gear Co-Founder Saemann Quits...," p. B-1.
8. "Stanley P. Gold, L.A. Gear Chairman & Chief Executive Officer," L.A. Gear, *Press Release* (January 24, 1992).
9. Ibid.
10. "L.A. Gear Inc. Investor Steps in with New Team," *Wall Street Journal* (January 27, 1992), pp. B-1, B-5.
11. Ibid.
12. Ibid.
13. Ibid.
14. "L.A. Gear, Several Changes at Senior Level," *Wall Street Journal* (September 17, 1991), p. A-22.
15. L.A. Gear, *Form 10-K Report* (1991), p. 2.
16. Ibid.
17. Ibid.
18. L.A. Gear, Inc., *1990 Annual Report,* p. 7.
19. B. Horivitz, "Some Companies Find They Get More," *Los Angeles Times* (February 5, 1991), p. D-6.
20. "L.A. Gear Says High Inventories May Affect 1992 Earnings," *Bloomberg News* (March 3, 1992).
21. Ibid., p. B-5.
22. L.A. Gear, Inc., *1990 Annual Report,* p. 8.
23. "The Goldston Prescription," *Footwear News* (January 27, 1992), pp. 11–12.
24. "L.A. Gear Still Looks Like an Also-Ran," *Business Week* (December 21, 1992), p. 37.
25. "Footwear (Men's, Women's, Boy's and Girl's)," *Fairchild Fact File* (1990), pp. 5–9.

26. Ibid.
27. F. Meeds, "The Sneaker Game," *Forbes* (October 22, 1990), p. 114.
28. J. Schlax, "The Shoe as Hero," *Forbes* (August 20, 1990), p. 77.
29. K. Kerwin, "L.A. Gear Is Going Where the Boys Are," *Business Week* (June 19, 1989), p. 54.
30. Ibid., p. 52.
31. M. Grimm, "To Munich and Back with Nike and L.A. Gear," *Adweek's Marketing Week* (February 18, 1991), p. 21.
32. Ibid., p. 22.
33. M. Wilson, "Nike Town Goes Back to the Future," *Chain Store Age Executive* (February 1991), pp. 82–83.
34. M. Tedeschi, "Reebok Splits U.S. Int'l Setups," *Footwear News* (November 26, 1990), p. 12.
35. S. Gannes, "America's Fastest-Growing Companies," *Fortune* (May 23, 1988), p. 37.
36. A. Shell, "Cause-Related Marketing: Big Risks, Big Potential," *Public Relations Journal* (July 1989), pp. 8, 13.
37. Ibid., p. 8.
38. M. Rottman, "L.A. Gear Catapults into Technology," *Footwear News* (February 18, 1991), pp. 12, 14.
39. D. McKay, "Walk This Way," *Footwear News* (September 9, 1991), pp. 14–15.
40. "L.A. Gear President Says Shoe Maker Will Recover and Will Focus on Asia," *Wall Street Journal* (October 16, 1992), p. B-7.
41. Ibid.
42. *OECD Economic Survey, United States, 1990/1991,* pp. 60–65.

Rykä, Inc.: The Athletic Shoe with a "Soul"

Valerie J. Porciello, Alan N. Hoffman, and Barbara Gottfried

> *"Rykä has a great story to tell. We are the only athletic footwear company that is exclusively for women, by women, and now supporting women."*
>
> [Sheri Poe]

It was the day after Christmas, 1990, and Sheri Poe, President and Chief Executive Officer of Rykä, Inc., knew that she was on the verge of the marketing break she'd been waiting for. During the past year, Poe had sent several free pairs of Rykä athletic shoes to Oprah Winfrey. Now Poe was going to be featured as a successful female entrepreneur on Winfrey's popular talk show, with a television viewing audience numbering in the tens of millions—almost entirely women. Rykä's new line of Ultra-Lite aerobic shoes had just begun to penetrate the retail market. Poe could not have planned for a better advertising spot than Winfrey tossing pairs of Rykä shoes into the studio audience and exclaiming, "Can you believe how light these are?"

After the "Oprah" broadcast, the Ultra-Lite line became an overnight success. Lady Foot Locker immediately put the Ultra-Lite shoe line in 200 stores, up from the 50 that had been carrying Rykä's regular line of athletic shoes. Consumers swamped retailers with requests for Rykä products, and the sharp upturn in consumer demand quickly exhausted inventories. Rykä needed more than three months to catch up with the orders. Many industry analysts believe that the shot in the arm provided by the Ultra-Lite sales literally saved the company.

Rykä, Inc., designs, develops and markets athletic footwear for women, including aerobic, aerobic/step, cross-training, walk–run, and walking shoes. Sporting goods, athletic footwear specialty, and department stores throughout the world sell the company's products.

As a new entrant in the highly competitive athletic footwear industry—an industry with very deep pockets—fledgling Rykä had no choice but to rely on low-budget, "guerilla marketing" tactics such as the "Oprah" show appearance. Since then, however, Rykä has turned to more traditional marketing techniques such as radio and glossy magazine advertising. Rykä print ads appear regularly in *City Sports, Shape, American Fitness, Elle,* and *IDEA Today*—magazines that target women aged 21–35, who care not just about how they look but are serious about physical fitness.

This case was prepared by Valerie J. Porciello, a student at Bentley College, and Professors Alan N. Hoffman and Barbara Gottfried of Bentley College. The case authors would like to thank Jeffrey Shuman, Mary Fandal, Christine Forkus, Holly Fowler, Liliana Prado, and Maura Riley for their valuable contributions to this case. This case was edited by T. L. Wheelen and J. D. Hunger for this book. Reprinted by permission of the authors.

Company Background

First organized in 1986 as ABE Corporation, the company changed its name to Rykä in February 1987 when it commenced operations. Martin P. Birrittella and his wife, Sheri Poe, co-founded the company. Prior to founding Rykä, Birrittella had worked at Matrix International Industries as Vice-President of Sales and Marketing from 1980 to 1986. At Matrix, he was responsible for developing and marketing footwear and health and fitness products and has two patents pending for shoe designs that have been assigned to Matrix. From 1982 to 1985, Poe was national sales manager for Matrix. She then moved to TMC Group, a $15 million a year giftware manufacturer based in New Hampshire, where she was national accounts manager from May 1986 to June 1987.

Sheri Poe, Rykä's current President and Chief Executive Officer, is one of only two women CEOs in the state of Massachusetts. Poe admits being an exercise fanatic who really knew nothing about making athletic shoes when she co-founded Rykä. In 1986 Poe had injured her back in an aerobics class and was convinced that the injury had been caused by her shoes, which had never fit properly. After an exhaustive search for footwear that would not stress her body, Poe realized that many other women probably were having the same trouble finding a shoe that really fit and decided to start her own women's athletic footwear company. Her conception was a distinctive company that would design and market athletic shoes especially suited for women's feet and bodies rather than adapting men's athletic shoes for women. Despite heavy odds, Poe realized her goal: Rykä introduced its first two styles of athletic shoes in September 1987 and began shipping the shoes in March 1988.

In 1987, Poe had considerable difficulty obtaining venture capital to start a women's athletic shoe company. Potential investors questioned her ability to compete with industry leaders such as Nike and Reebok because she had no money and no retail experience—then turned down her requests for loans. Ironically, some of those same venture capitalists now call Poe to ask how they can get in on her $8 million a year business.

When she couldn't get start-up money from venture capitalists, Poe mortgaged her own house, then turned to family and friends to help finance the company. She also continued to search for more open-minded commercial investors and eventually discovered a Denver investment banker who was willing to do an initial public offering. Poe got a $250,000 bridge loan before the initial public offering, which happened to be about the time the stock market crashed in October 1987. Nevertheless, Rykä went public on April 15, 1988, and despite the unstable market, four million shares in the company sold at $1 each in less than a week. The Denver firm completed a second offering before failing. Poe then turned to Paulson Capital Corporation in Oregon for a third offering in mid 1990.

Sheri Poe

Sheri Poe believes that the fact that Rykä's President is a woman inspires other women to buy the company's products. As she points out, "we're the only company that can tell women that the person running the company is a woman who works out every day." Even Nike doesn't have a woman making all its product decisions.

In fact, Poe's image and profile is the crucial component in Rykä's marketing strategy. Rather than using professional models, Rykä's print advertisements feature Poe working out; in the company's recent venture into television advertising spots, Poe is the company spokesperson. The caption on a 1992 ad for Rykä's 900-series aerobic shoes reads, "Our president knows that if you huff and puff, jump up and down, and throw your weight around you eventually get what you want," cleverly referring to Poe's own determination to succeed and including her audience as coconspirators who know how hard it is for a woman to make it in the business world because they have "been there" themselves.

As part of Rykä's unique marketing strategy, Poe appears on regional television and radio shows throughout the country and has been interviewed by numerous magazines and newspapers. Feature articles on Poe and Rykä have appeared in *Entrepreneurial Woman, Executive Female,* and *Working Woman.* Poe has successfully worked the woman angle: she particularly appeals to today's working women because, although she has become something of a celebrity, she considers herself a down-to-earth woman who also happens to be a successful executive, and a (divorced, and now remarried) mother. A *Boston Business Journal* article describes her as a CEO whose title "does not cramp [her] style . . . she eschews power suits for miniskirts and jeans, drives herself to work, and lets calls from her kids interrupt her meetings."

The Athletic Footwear Industry

The $11 billion a year athletic footwear industry is highly competitive. Three major firms control the market: Nike, Reebok, and L.A. Gear. Second-string competitors include Adidas, Avia, Asics, and Converse. All these companies have greater financial strength and more resources than Rykä. Rykä's sales were $12.1 million in 1992; Nike's were $3.4 billion, Reebok's $3.0 billion, and L.A. Gear's $430 million.

In 1987, the industry as a whole grew 20%, but by 1991 its annual growth rate had shrunk to approximately 4%. The athletic footwear market is now considered a mature market. Despite the subdued growth characteristics of the overall industry, however, several of its submarkets are expanding through high specialization, technological innovation, and image and fashion appeal.

Product Specialization

The athletic footwear industry is divided into various submarkets by specialization. Product use categories include basketball, tennis, running, aerobics, cross-training, walking, and so on. Rykä competes in only three markets: aerobics, walking, and cross-training shoes.

Aerobics Segment

The aerobics segment of the athletic shoe market accounts for approximately $500 million in annual sales. Reebok pioneered the segment and continues to be the industry leader. The market primarily consists of women and has grown rapidly in recent years. Rykä's number one market is aerobics; in 1991, 80% of Rykä's sales resulted from the Ultra-Lite and step aerobics lines.

Walking Segment

The walking segment of the athletic shoe market is now the fourth largest product category in the industry. In 1991, some 70 million people walked for exercise and sales reached $1.7 billion. Reebok leads this market and is concentrating its marketing efforts on young women. Although the number of male and younger female walkers has grown some, the walking segment primarily represents women 45–55 years old. Ten percent of Rykä's sales derive from its Series 500 walking shoe, and the company expects the walking shoe segment to be its greatest growth category.

Cross-Training Segment

Rykä also competes in the cross-training segment of the athletic shoe market. Cross-training shoes are popular because people can use them for a variety of activities. Nike created this segment and maintains the lead in market share. Overall sales for the segment are currently at $1.2 billion, and growth is strong. Rykä earns 10% of its revenues from its cross-training shoes.

Technological Innovation

Reebok and Nike are moving fast toward the goal of being the most technologically advanced producers of performance shoes. Rykä understands that it must keep up with research and development to survive. In October 1988, Rykä introduced its nitrogen footwear system, "Nitrogen/ES" (the "ES" stands for Energy Spheres). A design team with more than 35 patents in shoe design and state-of-the-art composite plastics developed the system over a two-year period. The idea is that the ES ambient air compression spheres contain nitrogen microballoons that provide significantly more energy return than do the systems of any of Rykä's major competitors. Consumer response to the Nitrogen/ES shoe was overwhelming, and in 1989 Rykä discontinued sales of several models that did not include this special feature.

Two patents were filed for the Nitrogen/ES System. One has been granted; the other is pending. Although the purpose of patents is to provide legal protection, the cost of defending patents can be quite high. Reebok or Nike, with their vast resources, could easily adopt Rykä's technology at little or no risk of an infringement suit. Rykä's limited financial resources would make it impossible for the company to enforce its rights should one of its competitors infringe on a patented design.

Fashion

Rykä has focused on performance rather than fashion because Poe believes that fashion athletic footwear is susceptible to trends and the economy, but performance shoes will not be affected because women always need to protect their bodies.

Nevertheless, a large segment of athletic footwear consumers purchase products based on looks rather than function. In fact, the fashion market is a mainstay of Rykä's major competitors, especially Reebok, the originators of the fashion aerobic shoe market; 80%–90% of fashion aerobics shoe buyers do not participate in the activity.

Although Rykä shoes are as technologically advanced as Reebok's, Nike's, or L.A. Gear's, fashion-conscious consumers unfamiliar with the Rykä name often overlook them. Despite the fact that Rykä's sales have grown even during the current recession, retailers haven't always carried Rykä shoes because they prefer to stock only easily recognizable brands. The lack of a nationally recognized name is a serious concern for any company; thus for Rykä, as for its competitors, expensive, leading-edge advertising campaigns have played an essential part in its marketing initiatives.

A Rocky Start

Because of the saturation of the athletic footwear market, athletic shoe companies need more than a good product to stay alive—they need powerful marketing and advertising. Rykä concentrates much of its energies on marketing. As a new manufacturer in an already crowded industry, Poe understands the possibility of being marketed right out of business by big competitors with deep pockets, such as Nike and Reebok. Rykä's approach is to offer similar products but to focus on the most cost-effective ways to reach a target market, thus carving out a niche that the industry giants have overlooked.

To protect a niche requires staying one step ahead of the competition. Unfortunately for Rykä, Poe had to learn this lesson the hard way. At first the company tried unsuccessfully to challenge the brand name manufacturers in all product categories, including running, tennis, aerobics, walking, and cross-training shoes. However, its limited capital and the huge advertising budgets of Reebok, Nike, and L.A. Gear kept Rykä from competing in all these different markets at the same time. Instead, Rykä cut back and chose to focus on aerobics shoes and secondarily to push its walking shoe line. Thus, in addition to limiting product line breadth, Rykä has designed its marketing approach to attract a specific set of customers rather than a broad audience. Poe doesn't believe that Rykä has to be a giant to succeed. Rather, she contends that Rykä needs to maximize its ability to perform in a particular niche within a large industry.

A New Direction

In the already crowded athletic footwear industry, the various competitors are continually jockeying for a better market position and competitive edge. Currently, women are, and probably will continue to be, the fastest growing segment of the athletic footwear market. Women's athletic footwear accounts for 55% of Reebok's sales, 60% of Avia's, 45% of L.A. Gear's, and 17% of Nike's $2.2

billion domestic sales. In recent years, Reebok and Nike have fought for the number one spot in the women's market, and Reebok initially prevailed; but in each of the past two years, Nike has posted a 30% growth in the market. This unparalleled growth in the women's athletic footwear market is the most important trend in the sporting goods industry today, and it is on this niche that Rykä is staking its future.

Rykä's crucial selling point is that its athletic shoes are designed specifically for women, with a patented design for better shock absorption and durability, whereas the big-name athletic shoe companies merely make smaller sizes of men's shoes for women. Rykä has a first-mover advantage in this segment of the market and maintains its edge because none of its competitors has a business strategy entirely focused on women; the competition has concentrated on other niches. Ultimately, however, it is the Ultra-Lite midsole, Rykä's most significant and successful product advancement, that keeps Rykä ahead of the competition in its market. The Rykä Ultra-Lite aerobics shoe weighs 7.7 ounces, or roughly 30% as much as a regular aerobics shoe. Within two months of its introduction in December 1990, the company had sold all its Ultra-Lites at a unit price of $70 a pair (wholesale). The company needed three months to fill additional shoe orders. Eventually, Rykä did lose some ground to Nike and Reebok—both of which quickly jumped into the lightweight aerobics shoe market. Some investment firms were concerned that Rykä might not be able to capitalize on the success of its new line owing to its difficulty with keeping retailers supplied with sufficient quantities. Despite the competition, however, Rykä's Ultra-Lite lines are a success, accounting for close to 90% of its total sales for 1991.

After establishing a solid foundation in the aerobics category, Rykä again turned its attention to product differentiation. Its current product line includes the Series 900 Aerobic/Step shoes, the Series 700 Aerobic shoes, the Series 800/Cross Training shoes, and the Series 500 Walking shoes. To make sure that its shoes were not perceived as "too specialized," Rykä designed the Aerobic Step 50/50 and a lightweight version of it, the Step-Lite 50/50, each of which can be worn for both high-impact and step aerobics. Rykä also designed a dual purpose walk–run shoe, the 570, for women who complement their walking routine with running, but don't want to own different shoes for each activity. Rykä is now considering entering the medical footwear market because an increasing number of podiatrists and chiropractors are recommending Rykä walking shoes to their patients.

The Rykä ROSE Foundation

The Rykä ROSE (Regaining One's Self Esteem) Foundation is a nonprofit organization that Sheri Poe created to help women who have been the victims of violent crimes. Poe launched the foundation in September 1992 with a personal pledge of $250,000. Poe set up the ROSE Foundation because she was raped at age 19 and for years suffered from bulimia as a result of the trauma. She sees herself as a survivor who needed to do something to help fellow victims: "For me, having a company that just made a product was not enough. I wanted to do something more."

Rykä has made a commitment to donate 7% of its pre-tax profits to the foundation and sponsor special fundraising events to help strengthen community prevention and treatment programs for women who are the victims of violent crimes. Rykä includes information on the foundation in brochures that are packaged with each box of shoes in the hope that its social conscience may favorably influence some consumers. But for Poe, it is more than a marketing ploy. She considers Rykä's financial commitment to the ROSE Foundation a natural extension of the company's commitment to women.

The foundation has created alliances with health clubs, nonprofit organizations, and corporations in an effort to reach women directly with educational materials and programs. In addition, the foundation funds a $25,000 grant program to encourage organizations to develop creative solutions to the widespread problem of violence against women. One of the foundation's beneficiaries, the National Victim Center, received an award of $10,000 to set up a toll-free (800) telephone number for victims and their families through which they can obtain immediate information, referrals, and other types of assistance.

Poe hopes that the foundation will act as a catalyst for coalition building to help stop violence against women. But she also envisions the foundation as a means of involving retailers in marketing socially responsible programs directly to women. Lady Foot Locker has taken advantage of this opportunity and became the first retailer to join forces with the ROSE Foundation. In October, Lady Foot Locker conducted a two-week promotional campaign in its 550 United States stores in conjunction with the ROSE Foundation. The retailer distributed free educational brochures and held a special sweepstakes contest to raise awareness about the issue of violence against women. Customer response was overwhelmingly positive, and Lady Foot Locker is considering a future partnership with the ROSE Foundation. Foot Locker, Champs, and Athletic X-press also have expressed interest in the foundation.

MVP Sports, a New England retailer, also has participated in Rykä's activities to help stop violence against women. The company, which operates eight stores in New England, sponsored a two-week informational campaign featuring Sheri Poe that included radio, TV, and newspaper advertisements. In addition, Doug Barron, President of MVP Sports, was so impressed with the concept and progressive thinking of the Rykä ROSE Foundation that he decided his company would donate $2 to the foundation for each pair of Rykä athletic shoes sold in his stores during the 1992 holiday season. Poe sees MVP Sports' support as an important first step toward actively involving retailers in Rykä's efforts to help prevent violence against women and is reaching out to other retailers who she hopes will follow suit.

Poe considers Rykä and its foundation unique. As she sees it, the company has a great story to tell. It is the only athletic footwear company that is exclusively for women, by women, and now supporting women: "the first athletic shoe with a 'soul.'" And Poe is banking on her hunch that the foundation will appeal to Rykä customers who appreciate the idea that their buying power is helping women who have been the victims of violent crimes.

Nevertheless, Poe's choice to make Rykä a socially responsible company right from the beginning, rather than waiting until the company is fully established, has affected its financial status. Some industry analysts have suggested that Rykä would be better off funneling any extra cash back into the company until it is completely solvent and recognition of its product lines and company name is automatic. Others argue that Rykä's reputation as an ethical company, concerned about social issues and not just the "bottom line," effectively appeals to many women consumers. For them, the ROSE Foundation is worth in "good press" whatever it has cost the company in dollars, because the company has effectively carved out a niche that speaks on many different levels to women's ethical and consumer concerns.

Marketing

Rykä's promotional strategy is aimed at creating both brand awareness and retail sales. By garnering the support of professional sports organizations early, Rykä acquired instant name recognition in a variety of key audiences. In 1988, Rykä entered into a six-figure, eight-year licensing agreement with the U.S. Ski Team that permitted Rykä to market its products as the official training shoes of the Team. Also in 1988, the American Aerobics Association International boosted Rykä's brand name recognition when it replaced Avia with Rykä as the association's preferred aerobics shoes. The next year, *Shape* magazine labeled Rykä number one in its aerobics shoe category.

Rykä has also begun sponsoring both aerobics teams and aerobics competitions. In July 1992, 25 countries competed in the World Aerobics championships in Las Vegas, Nevada. Rykä Athletic Footwear sponsored the Canadian team. In September 1992, Rykä was the premier sponsor and the official shoe of the Canadian National Aerobics championship held in Vancouver, B.C. To ensure the success of the event and build awareness for the sport of competitive aerobics, Rykä successfully promoted the nationals through retailers, athletic clubs, and individuals. Because Reebok had sponsored virtually every previous aerobics competition worldwide, Canada's selection of Rykä as its official sponsor was a company milestone, bringing it international recognition as a core brand in the women's athletic shoe market.

The Rykä Training Body

From the beginning, Sheri Poe determined that the most effective way to reach Rykä's female aerobics niche would be through marketing to aerobics instructors, and she targeted Rykä's advertising accordingly. In fact, Rykä spends almost as much as industry leaders on print advertisements in aerobics instructors' magazines and very little on print advertising elsewhere. Unlike its big competitors, Rykä doesn't use celebrity endorsements to sell its products because its marketing theory is that women will care more about what feels good on their feet than about what any particular celebrity has to say.

Beyond advertising in aerobics magazines, Rykä has used direct mail marketing techniques successfully to target aerobics instructors. The Rykä Training Body comprises more than 40,000 women employed as fitness instructors and personal trainers throughout the country. They receive product information four to six times per year, as well as discounts on shoes. Rykä also has tied a group of its instructors to specific local retailers. The instructors direct their students to those retailers, who then offer discounts to the students. Finally, Rykä-affiliated instructors offer demonstrations to educate consumers about what to look for in an aerobics shoe.

In addition to increasing sales, the relationship between Rykä and the aerobics profession has led to significant product design innovations. Basing their suggestions on their own experience and on feedback from their students, aerobics instructors' input has led to shoe improvements such as more effective cushioning and better arch support. Poe considers these teachers as the link to Rykä's customers. In fact, as a direct result of instructor feedback, Rykä was the first manufacturer to respond to the new step aerobics trend by developing and marketing lightweight shoes specifically designed to support up and down step motions.

Salespeople

Rykä's marketing efforts also are aimed at the people who sell Rykä products. In Rykä's early days, Poe and her advertising manager, Laurie Ruddy, personally visited retail stores to meet salespeople and "sell" them on Rykä products. Now, the Vice-President of Sales and Marketing maintains contact with retailers using incentive programs, give-aways, and small monetary bonuses to keep salespeople excited. The company also provides premiums, such as fanny packs or water bottles, for customers.

Advertising Budget

The highly competitive nature of the athletic footwear industry makes effective advertising crucial in distinguishing among brands and creating brand preference. As a two-year-old company in 1989, Rykä was particularly capital-intensive for a company trying to penetrate the athletic shoe market. Its $3.5 million loss that year is largely attributable to advertising spending of approximately $2.5 million, but that amount was negligible compared to Nike, Reebok, and L.A. Gear, whose combined advertising spending exceeded $100 million per year.

At that time, Rykä advertised only in trade publications, resulting in a lag of consumer recognition. Since then, Rykä ads have appeared in *Shape, City Sports, American Fitness, ELLE,* and *Idea Today* magazines. By 1992, Poe could claim that Rykä's brand recognition had grown dramatically, even though Rykä's advertising and marketing budget was only about 9% of sales. Poe attributes Rykä's marketing success to its direct marketing techniques, especially its targeting of certified aerobics instructors and getting them to wear Rykä shoes.

In October 1992, after three successive quarters of record sales and little profitability, Poe announced that Rykä was going to expand its direct marketing to consumers, even if it required increased spending to penetrate the marketplace beyond aerobics instructors. But Rykä is still in another league compared to the industry's giants. Rykä's total advertising budget is estimated at approximately $1.5 million, whereas Nike spent $20 million on a 1991 pan-European campaign to launch a single product, and Reebok is currently spending $28 million on its "I Believe . . ." ad campaign that specifically targets women.

Operations

As is common in the athletic footwear industry, Rykä's shoes are made according to Rykä's product specifications by independent manufacturers in Europe and the Far East, including south Korea and Taiwan. Rykä's first three years were rough, in large part because of the poor quality of the products provided by its manufacturer in Taiwan. Now, however, the shoes are made in South Korea under strict quality controls. The company relies on a Far Eastern buying agent, under its direction, to select suppliers, inspect goods prior to shipment, and ship finished goods.

Rykä's management believes that this sourcing of footwear products minimizes company investment in fixed assets and reduces cost and risk. Because of the underutilized manufacturing capacity in countries other than South Korea and Taiwan, Rykä's management believes that alternative manufacturing sources are readily available should the company need them. Because of the volatility of international and economic relations in today's global marketplace, and to protect itself from complete dependence on one supplier, Rykä remains free from any long-term contracts with manufacturers, that is, beyond the terms of purchase orders issued. Rykä places orders on a volume basis through its agent and receives finished products within 120 days of an order. To meet customer demand, Rykä may pay a premium to reduce the production time for finished goods.

The principal raw materials in Rykä shoes are leather, rubber, ethylvinyl acetate, polyurethane, cambrelle, and pigskin, all of which are readily available both in the United States and abroad. Even though Rykä could locate new sources of raw materials for its overseas manufacturers within a relatively short period of time, its business could be devastated by any interruption in operations. In contrast, Reebok and Nike have large stockpiles of inventory and would be less affected by difficulties with suppliers.

Distribution

Rykä products are sold in sporting goods stores, athletic footwear stores, selected high-end department stores, and sport specialty retailers, including Foot Locker, Lady Foot Locker, Athlete's Foot Store, Foot Action, US Athletics, Oshman's, and Nordstrom.

Rykä's major distribution relationship is with the 476 Lady Foot Locker stores in the United States and the 250 Lady Foot Locker stores in Canada. In November 1992, Rykä announced that, in early 1993, 400 Lady Foot Locker stores would display permanent Rykä signs, identifying Rykä as a brand especially promoted by Foot Locker. Both Sheri Poe and Amy Schecter, Vice-President of Retail Marketing for Lady Foot Locker, agree that Rykä shoe sales have been solid in Lady Foot Locker stores and that the Lady Foot Locker's display of permanent Rykä signs expresses the confidence Lady Foot Locker has in Rykä's future success.

During the spring of 1992, FOOTACTION USA, a division of the Melville Corporation and the second largest specialty footwear retailer in the country, began selling Rykä athletic shoes on a trial basis in 40 stores. The trial was so successful that FOOTACTION agreed to purchase five styles of Rykä shoes for its stores, and in September 1992, Rykä announced that 150 FOOTACTION stores would begin to carry its products nationally.

On November 3, 1992, Rykä announced that it had received orders from three large retail sporting goods chains, adding well over 200 store outlets to its distribution network. The twelfth largest sporting goods retailer in the country, MC Sporting Goods, based in Grand Rapids, Michigan, now carries five styles of Rykä athletic shoes in each of its 73 stores. In addition, Rykä has received orders from Tampa, Florida–based Sports and Recreation, which will sell four styles of Rykä athletic shoes in its 23 sporting goods stores. Charlie Burks, head footwear buyer for Sports and Recreation, based his decision to stock Rykä shoes on his sense that the chain's customers are looking for new, exciting styles of athletic shoes at affordable prices and that Rykä delivers on performance, fashion, and value. More than 135 Athletic Express stores also carry Rykä shoes.

In the competitive athletic footwear industry, distributors and retailers have considerable clout. In 1989, Lady Foot Locker and Foot Locker retailers accounted for 13% of Rykä's net sales, but the company realized that it needed a broader pool of retailers. More recently, Rykä has managed to control its customer base so that no single customer or group under common control accounts for more than 10% of its total revenue.

Human Resources

From the beginning, Poe set out to gain credibility through human resources. The company offered industry-standard salaries, stock options, and the opportunity for significant input into the company's day-to-day operations. In addition, Poe attracted four top executives from Reebok for positions in sales, advertising, and public relations. This high-powered team performed so effectively that sales doubled between Rykä's first and second years. But total executive compensation was too much for the young company. Poe realized that a change in strategy was necessary, and three of the four Reebok veterans have since left.

In 1988, Rykä had only four employees; it now employs 22 people at its Norwood (Massachusetts) headquarters and 35 sales representatives across the country. Rykä's small size gives it a certain flexibility, enabling the company to concentrate on continual streamlining and improvement and to implement new ideas and adjustments in stores within 120 days.

In November 1992, Rykä appointed Roy S. Kelvin as Vice-President and Chief Financial Officer to reinforce its commitment to the financial community. Poe sees Kelvin, a former New York investment banker, as instrumental to helping the company grow. In a sense, however, Poe's appointment of Kelvin is her acknowledgment of the fact that she's competing for funds in an "old-boy's" network and that having an "old boy" to help build her list of contacts is extremely valuable. Kelvin's main priorities are to secure domestic financing, reduce operating expenses, and improve profit margins.

Financial Position

Rykä originally financed its operations principally through public stock offerings, warrant exercises, and other private sales of its common stock, netting an aggregate of approximately $7.2 million. In July 1990, Rykä completed its public stock offering, which raised net proceeds of $3.5 million, allowing the company to market its products aggressively during the fall of 1990 and beyond. So far, Rykä has sold shares to private investors, who now control 65% of the shares.

In September 1992, Rykä extended the date for redemption of its outstanding common stock purchase warrant issues in the company's 1990 public offering another two weeks in response to requests from warrant holders. Poe was pleased with the response to the warrant solicitation and agreed to the extension to allow the maximum number of holders to exercise their warrants. If all public and underwriter warrants are exercised, the company will receive approximately $6.3 million in gross proceeds.

In 1991, Rykä signed an agreement with its South Korean trading company to increase its line of credit from $2.5 million to $3.5 million. In addition, working capital resources are available from a letter of credit financing agreement, coupled with an accounts receivable line to credit.

Rykä's product costs are higher than those of the industry leaders for several reasons. First, because Rykä is significantly smaller than the industry leaders, it cannot take advantage of volume production discounts. Second, the company has opted to pay somewhat higher prices for its products than other suppliers would charge in order to achieve and maintain high quality. Finally, higher production costs have resulted from Rykä's inventory financing arrangement with its South Korean trading company, which includes financing costs, commissions, and fees as part of cost of sales.

Rykä has taken on some formidable competition in the form of Nike and Reebok. For Rykä to prosper, Sheri Poe must successfully carve out a niche in the women's athletic shoe market before exhausting the company's supply of money. Time is rapidly running out.

Exhibits 28.1–28.4 provide selected financial information about the company.

EXHIBIT 28.1

Consolidated Statements of Operations: Rykä, Inc. and Subsidiary

Years Ending December 31	1992	1991	1990
Gross sales	$13,329,777	$8,838,911	$ 5,090,208
Less discounts, returns and allowances	1,136,134	860,986	388,670
Net sales	12,193,643	7,977,925	4,701,538
Cost of goods sold	8,867,375	5,231,346	3,688,093
Inventory write-down to lower of cost or market	—	—	906,557
Gross profit	3,326,268	2,746,579	106,888
Operating expenses			
General and administrative	1,239,245	1,287,925	1,614,773
Marketing	1,722,618	1,396,769	1,756,164
Research and development	148,958	155,576	227,791
Total operating expenses	3,110,821	2,840,270	3,598,728
Operating income (loss)	215,447	(93,691)	(3,491,840)
Other (income) expense			
Interest expense	516,455	418,469	272,797
Interest income	(4,195)	(12,648)	(53,980)
Expenses incurred in connection with termination of merger agreement	—	—	377,855
Total other (income) expense	512,260	405,821	596,672
Net loss	$ (296,813)	$ (499,512)	$(4,088,512)
Net loss per share	$ (0.01)	$ (0.03)	$ (0.27)
Weighted average shares outstanding	19,847,283	18,110,923	15,336,074

Note: Notes were deleted.

Source: Rykä, Inc.

EXHIBIT 28.2 Selected Financial Information, 1992–1988: Rykä, Inc.

Years Ending December 31	1992	1991	1990	1989	1988
Statement of Operations Data					
Net sales	$ 12,193,643	$ 7,977,925	$ 4,701,538	$ 4,916,542	$ 991,684
Gross profit before inventory write-down	3,326,288	2,746,579	1,013,445	1,364,340	308,901
Inventory write-down to lower of cost or market	—	—	906,557	—	—
Gross profit	3,326,268	2,746,579	106,888	1,364,340	308,901
Costs and expenses	3,110,821	2,840,270	3,598,728	4,368,774	1,687,806
Operating income (loss)	215,447	(93,691)	(3,491,840)	(3,004,434)	(1,378,905)
Interest expense, net	512,260	405,821	218,817	548,149	148,485
Expenses incurred in connection with termination of merger agreement	—	—	377,855	—	—
Net loss	$ (296,813)	$ (499,512)	$(4,088,512)	$(3,552,583)	$(1,527,390)
Net loss per share	$ (0.01)	$ (0.03)	$ (0.27)	$ (0.31)	$ (0.16)
Weighted average shares outstanding	19,847,283	18,110,923	15,336,074	11,616,088	9,397,360
Number of common shares outstanding	23,101,948	18,136,142	18,005,142	13,242,500	10,252,500
Balance Sheet Data					
Total assets	$ 8,319,229	$ 4,498,021	$ 2,711,713	$ 3,553,000	$ 2,073,058
Total debt	410,673	68,256	86,149	974,521	247,340
Net working capital	4,077,404	743,587	1,097,827	1,643,352	1,140,173
Stockholders' equity	4,166,377	834,902	1,299,264	1,848,059	1,341,858

Source: Rykä, Inc.

EXHIBIT 28.3

Consolidated Balance Sheets: Rykä Inc. and Subsidiary

Years Ending December 31	1992	1991
Assets		
Current assets		
Cash and cash equivalents	$1,029,161	$ 166,030
Accounts receivable, less allowance for doubtful accounts of $446,034 in 1992 and $389,000 in 1991	2,958,629	1,760,309
Inventory	3,260,617	2,244,159
Prepaid advertising	723,460	119,361
Prepaid expenses and other current assets	240,511	77,396
Total current assets	8,212,378	4,367,255
Security deposits and other assets	21,485	16,087
Equipment, furniture and fixtures, at cost less allowance for depreciation and amortization of $371,587 in 1992 and $308,876 in 1991	85,366	114,679
Total assets	$8,319,229	$4,498,021
Liabilities and Shareholders' Equity		
Current liabilities		
Accounts payable	$3,597,179	$3,469,856
Accrued expenses	145,000	125,007
Notes payable to shareholder	375,000	0
Current portion of capital lease obligations	17,795	28,805
Total current liabilities	4,134,974	3,623,668
Obligations under capital leases, less current portion	17,878	39,451
Shareholders' equity		
Preferred stock, $0.01 par value, 1,000,000 shares authorized; none issued or outstanding		
Common stock, $0.01 par value, 30,000,000 shares authorized; 23,101,948 and 18,136,142 shares issued and outstanding at December 31, 1992 and 1991, respectively	231,019	181,361
Additional paid-in capital	14,214,459	10,635,829
Accumulated deficit	(10,279,101)	(9,982,288)
Total shareholders' equity	4,166,377	834,902
Total liabilities and shareholders' equity	$8,319,229	$4,498,021

Note: Notes were deleted.

Source: Rykä, Inc.

EXHIBIT 28.4

Stock Prices, 1992 and 1991: Rykä, Inc.

Calendar Period	1992 High	1992 Low	1991 High	1991 Low
First quarter	$2.31	$ .53	$1.06	$ .22
Second quarter	2.44	1.19	.87	.50
Third quarter	1.69	1.19	.90	.56
Fourth quarter	1.89	.97	.78	.56

Notes:

1. Rykä's common stock is traded on NASDAQ.
2. The company does not pay dividends to its shareholders and does not plan to pay dividends in the foreseeable future.

References

Gene Colter, "On Target: Athletic Shoes Just for Women; Women's Awareness of Athletic Shoes; Special Super Show Athletics Issue," *Footwear News* (February 18, 1991).

Greg Dutter, "Making Strides," *Sporting Goods Business* (March 1992), 25(3), p. 34.

Suzy Fucini, "A Women's Game: Women Have Become the Hottest Focus of Today's Marketing," *Sporting Goods Dealer* (August 1992), p. 34.

Doug Goodman, "Reebok Chief Looks Beyond Nike," *Advertising Age* (January 29, 1990), 61(5), p. 57.

Matthew Grimm, "Nike Targets Women with Print Campaign," *Adweek's Marketing Week* (December 10, 1990), 33(12), p. 12.

Wendy Hower, "Gender Gap: The Executive Suite Is Still Wilderness for Women," *Boston Business Journal* (July 27, 1992), 12(23), p. 5.

Craig T. Kelly, "Fashion Sells Aerobics Shoes," (January 1990), 23(1), p. 39.

Sharon Lee, Robert McAllister, Ellen Rooney, and Mark Tedeschi, "Community Ties Nourish Growth of Aerobic Sales; Aerobic Programs Boost Sales of Aerobic Shoes," *Footwear News* (October 7, 1991), 31(33), p. 17.

Marcy Magiera, "Nike Again Registers No. 1 Performance," *Advertising Age* (May 7, 1990), 61(19), p. 4.

Marcy Magiera, "Nike Again Registers No. 1 Performance," *Advertising Age* (January 29, 1990), 61(5), p. 16.

"New England Retailer Joins Rykä in Fight Against Domestic Violence," *Business Wire* (November 13).

"Nike Takes Reebok's Edge; Advertising Expenditures of Top Sports Shoes Manufacturers," *Nexis Marketing* (April 16, 1992), p. 10.

Sheri Poe, "To Compete with Giants, Choose Your Niche," *Nation's Business* (July 1992), 80(7), p. 6.

Robert J. Powell, "Rykä Is Off and Running," *Boston Business Journal* (February 29, 1988), 8(1), p. 3.

"Rykä Adds 100 Stores to Distribution Network," *Business Wire* (November 3, 1992).

"Rykä Announces Extension for Warrant Redemption," *Business Wire* (September 11, 1992).

"Rykä Announces Record First Quarter 1991 Results," *Business Wire* (April 24, 1991).

"Rykä Completes $4.7 Million Offering," *Business Wire* (July 24, 1990).

Rykä, Inc., *1991 Annual Report.*

"Rykä to Expand Its Presence in Foot Locker Stores," *Business Wire* (June 4, 1992).

"Rykä Introduces New Nitrogen System," *Business Wire* (October 20, 1988).

"Rykä Launches ROSE Foundation to Help Stop Violence Against Women," Rykä, Inc., *News Release* (September 29, 1992).

"A Rykä Rose: Sheri Poe on Career, Family and Purpose," *Sporting Goods Dealer* (September 1992).

"Rykä Vaults to $8M in Its Lightweight Sneaks," *Boston Business Journal* (March 30, 1992), 12(6), p. 9.

Ruth Simon, "The No-P/E Stocks," *Forbes* (October 2, 1989), p. 40.

Laurel Allison Touby, "Creativity vs. Cash," *Working Woman* (November 1991), 16(11), p. 73.

Louise Witt, "Rykä Turns to Aerobics for Toehold in Market," *Boston Business Journal* (April 1, 1991), 11(6), p. 6.

Beth Wolfensberger, "Shoe Makers Have Itch to Enter Niche Markets," *Boston Business Journal* (March 19, 1990), 10(4), p. 7.

Johnson Products Company, Inc., 1993: Joan B. Johnson's Tenure as Chairman

Thomas L. Wheelen, David B. Croll, Laurence C. Pettit, Jr., and William G. Shenkir

Eric Johnson's Resignation

On March 9, 1992, a Johnson Products Company, Inc., representative announced that Eric G. Johnson had quit as President and CEO "to pursue personal business interests." Eric Johnson had served as CEO since October 28, 1989, and replaced his father, George E. Johnson, who had left the company.[1] George E. Johnson and Joan B. Johnson, Eric G. Johnson's parents, had co-founded the company in 1954. As part of their divorce settlement, Joan B. Johnson received George E. Johnson's 49.5% of Johnson Products Company, Inc., stock (valued at $5.5 million). She already owned 6.8% of the company's stock and was trustee of a stock trust, so she now controls approximately 61% of the company's stock. On October 2, 1989, she was elected Chairman of the Board of Directors with the resignation of George E. Johnson, who remained affiliated with the company as a consultant.[2]

Eric G. Johnson had overseen the turnaround strategy of the company for the past two and one-half years. During the decade of the 1980s the company had sustained losses of $14.0 million on sales of $344.7 million under the direction of George E. Johnson (see Exhibit 29.1).

Joan M. Johnson, age 27, Eric Johnson's sister, had joined the family business in 1991 as Director of Marketing Research. She had earned an MBA from Northwestern University. According to George Johnson: "He [Eric] underestimated the rancor of his sister and how far she would go to get revenge."[3]

On April 1, 1992, Thomas P. Polke, Vice-President, Finance, announced that the Company's Operations Committee (formed three years before) "will function as the 'Office of the President' and will consist of four executives. The committee, of which one member will be Joan M. Johnson, will be responsible for the day-to-day activities of the company."[4] George Johnson characterized the four-person Office of the President as "a joke."[5] Comer Cottrell, Chairman of a major competitor, Pro-Line Corporation, said, "Frankly, I think the timing may have been bad."[6] Concerning Eric Johnson, Cottrell said, "I've seen him definitely increase his shelf [display] and market share, but he has been very profitable in so doing."[7]

Commenting on her son's resignation, Chairman Joan B. Johnson said, "Eric Johnson has made a significant contribution at Johnson Products."[8] She went on to say, "I understand his decision and wish him well in his future endeavors." When asked if he had resigned or was ousted, she responded, "Whatever you're looking at is the will of the Chairman."[9]

Polke's announcement also included the appointment of Joan B. Johnson, Chairman, to the additional position of CEO as of March 31, 1992. She said, "Internally, it's back to business as usual at the company. This team has proven over the last years that they can produce solid results. Having seen them operate in the past, I am confident they will continue to prove this to the business community and to our stockholders."[10]

Timothy Elbright, a portfolio manager for Eagle Asset Management, who holds a 3.5% stake in the company, said about the events, "I will keep a very wary eye on the company for the next six months."[11] Comer Cottrell got to the heart of the issue: "Even if the company prospers after this latest management shakeup, the Johnson family may have 'fractured for good.' "[12]

The company made a $480,000 severance payment to Eric Johnson. In addition, the company is paying him $450,000 over one year for a two-year noncompetition agreement. He also received $30,000 for a one-year consulting agreement.[13]

Highlights of Eric Johnson's Management Tenure

In June 1988, Eric Johnson had been appointed Vice-President and Chief Operating Officer, and had been elected Director. His charge was "to take whatever operating measures necessary to put to the company on a consistent profitability footing."[14] He implemented a massive reorganization that cut the company's payroll by almost 50%, including seven of the company's ten officers, in order to reduce the firm's break-even point. He overhauled the Marketing and Sales departments, which he felt had been providing inadequate customer service.[15] He restructured the company's vendor relationships so that these managers dealt with 50 suppliers rather than 140 vendors.[16] In October 1989, Eric Johnson became CEO, replacing his father, George E. Johnson, who left the company.

On February 2, 1990, the company acquired four brands (Curly Perm, Sof-N-Free, Sta-Sof-Fro, and Moxie) and their inventories for $5 million from a competitor, M&M Products Company, Inc., of Atlanta. These four brands had total estimated sales of $12.5 million in 1989. The $5 million purchase consisted of $1.5 million in cash and two promissory notes of $2.4 million and $1.1 million. The notes are interest free, unless the company defaults.[17] In the event of default, the notes then become interest-bearing at the prime lending rate. After the sale, M&M Products announced that it was ceasing its operations. It ranked 36th on the 1989 BE (Black Enterprise) Industrial Services 100 with sales of approximately $20 million. According to analyst Sheila Poole, "the business [ethnic hair care companies] was perhaps damaged the most when mainstream companies began to make inroads into the ethnic hair-care market."[18]

In 1990, Johnson Products became the main sponsor of the Grambling Football Radio Network, which covered 40 markets nationwide. Management believed

EXHIBIT 29.1

Financial Performance Under Three CEOs: Johnson Products Company, Inc.
(Dollar amounts in thousands, except per share data, employees, and stock prices)

A. JOAN B. JOHNSON'S TENURE AS CEO (1992–)

Half Year	Net Sales	Cost of Sales	Selling General, and Administrative Costs	Advertising and Promotion	Research and Development	Income (Loss)
1993[2]	$19,370	$8,017	$8,026	$ NA	$ NA	$2,043
1992[3]	24,073	9,735	9,754	NA	NA	4,403

Notes:
1. Price from *Value Line.*
2. 1993 half fiscal year—September 1, 1992 to February 28, 1993.
3. 1992 half fiscal year—March 1, 1992 to August 31, 1992.

B. ERIC G. JOHNSON'S TENURE AS CEO (1990–1992)

Year[1]	Net Sales	Cost of Sales	Selling General,and Administrative Costs	Advertising and Promotion	Research and Development	Income (Loss
1992[4]	$17,907	$ 8,213	$ 7,941	$ NA	$ NA	$ 977
1991	38,406	18,167	12,166	3,999	332	1,894
1990	33,497	15,909	11,190	4,080	322	1,448

Notes:
1. Fiscal year ends August 31.
2. Price from *Value Line.*
3. Net income per share restated to reflect the two stock splits in December 1990. The 1990–1980 net incomes were factored by 3.36.
4. 1992 is for six months ending February 29, 1992.
5. Includes a one-time write-off of $480,000 to cover Eric Johnson's separation package, which was equivalent to $.40 per share.

that the sponsorship had been a "very successful promotion"[19] and renewed the company's sponsorship for 1991.

In September 1990, company management announced that it was considering moving its headquarters from Chicago's South Side, where it had been since 1954, to the suburbs. This move was to be another step in the company's ongoing cost-cutting efforts. The new site would offer the company lower taxes and the space required to expand or modernize, which would lower operating costs. Eric Johnson said, "The advantage of a new facility is that we can get better efficiencies and

Working Capital	Share-holder's Equity	Dividends per Share	Net Income per Share	Number of Employees	Stock Price[1]	
					High	Low
$ NA	$ NA	$ .17	$ .82	NA	$ 46	$NA
12,330	20,815	.14	3.68	219	$39½	$13½

Source: Johnson Products Company, Inc., *1992 Annual Report: Form 10-K Report* (August 31, 1992); *Form 10-Q Report* (February 28, 1993), p. 4.

Working Capital	Share-holder's Equity	Dividends per Share	Net Income per Share	Number of Employees	Stock Price[2]	
					High	Low
$ NA	$ NA	$ .28	$ .81[5]	NA	$21½	$13½
7,450	15,905	None	2.67	224	23¾	6
5,248	12,645	None	1.78	232	11⅝	4½

(continued)

Source: Johnson Products Company, Inc., 1992, 1991, and 1990.

upgrade the equipment."[20] Johnson noted that he was not committed to leaving the city or even its existing South Side site. He had been holding talks with Chicago's Department of Economic Development—which had offered the company several city sites and some tax incentives—and had explored economic development incentives offered by other municipalities. Finally, in April 1991, management announced that the company would remain at its present South Side location because of proximity to the firm's 232 employees, a downturn in real estate values, and management's continued focus on restructuring operations.[21]

Financial Performance Under Three CEOs: Johnson Products Company, Inc. *(continued)*
(Dollar amounts in thousands, except per share data, employees, and stock prices)

C. GEORGE E. JOHNSON'S TENURE AS CEO (1980–1989)

Year	Net Sales	Cost of Sales	Selling General,and Administrative Costs	Advertising and Promotion	Research and Development	Income (Loss)
1989	$29,368	$13,515	$10,564	$ 4,736	$362	$ 1,255
1988	29,104	13,292	11,657	6,496	542	(2,474)
1987	31,641	12,999	11,066	5,518	540	580
1986	29,811	13,178	12,134	5,384	693	(1,730)
1985	33,580	14,986	15,185	5,986	840	(3,571)
1984	35,589	15,419	21,055	10,031	818	(4,083)
1983	40,937	16,649	18,490	7,226	799	1,628
1982	39,177	18,191	19,122	7,467	868	(3,623)
1981	43,197	19,528	17,866	8,067	870	385
1980	32,294	15,250	16,773	7,243	782	(2,379)

Notes:

1. Net income per share restated to reflect two stock splits in December 1990.
   The 1989–1990 net incomes were factored by 3.36.
2. These figures are from Standard American Stock Exchange stock reports (January 9, 1992), p. 8259.

On May 29, 1991, a special committee of Eric Johnson and two outside directors—James H. Lowery, President of James H. Lowery & Associates (a consulting firm), and William G. Giles, Chairman of E.P.C. International, Inc.—proposed a $20.6 million leveraged buy-out (LBO) to take the company private. The group proposed to purchase the 39% of the company stock not owned by Joan B. Johnson for $17.25 a share or $8 million. The stock had closed the previous day at $15.37, up $.125. Initially, Joan B. Johnson would own the company, with senior management acquiring a "substantial stake" over time.[22] She favored any transaction that provided a fair price to shareholders and "satisfied my financial requirements."[23] She withheld any final determination until her advisors and the special committee (the takeover group) could fully review the offer. The LBO offer was subject to the procurement of financing, the negotiation of a definitive agreement, and, of course, Board and shareholder approval.

Cornelia Stanek, hair-care consultant, said about taking the company private that "they don't have to answer to stockholders or wait for them to vote," thereby allowing the company to make strategic decisions faster.[24] She went on to say, "Things like launching a new product can happen quickly." Eric Johnson said,

Working Capital	Share-holder's Equity	Dividends per Share	Net Income per Share[1]	Number of Employees	Stock Price[2]	
					High	Low
$ 4,883	$10,622	$ None	$ 1.18	190	$ 12½	$ 5 7/16
3,987	8,612	None	(3.16)	246	10	4 9/16
7,725	12,378	None	1.04	285	16 11/16	7 1/16
6,327	11,150	None	(1.18)	325	11¾	5 13/16
4,809	13,118	None	(3.80)	405	21 11/16	8 5/16
7,711	17,646	None	(3.46)	540	33 5/16	9 9/16
12,708	21,715	None	1.38	550	37 15/16	10 7/16
11,060	20,062	None	(3.06)	540	11 11/16	6 11/16
13,429	23,660	None	.34	568	17⅛	8¾
13,177	23,257	.18	2.02	563	NA	NA

Source: Johnson Products Company, Inc., 1991, 1990, 1987, 1984, 1983, 1982, 1981, and 1980.

"We haven't talked about changing directions but rather . . . what we have talked about is going from a public company to a private one."[25]

Two months after the initial LBO proposal, on June 25, 1991, the offer was withdrawn. The two principal reasons cited were that (1) the debt terms were too tough, and (2) Joan B. Johnson's personal risk was too great. The lenders were requiring the company to pledge the majority of its assets as collateral, which would choke off any access to future capital to sustain and expand the business. The proposed LBO also would hamper new product development (the life blood of this business) and advertising spending. Eric Johnson said, "More [LBOs] have done poorly in meeting their plans than have done well. So, it was better not to do it."[26] The other factor was that his mother would have become the sole shareholder and she would have been extremely vulnerable if the company were to suffer a downturn and the lenders were to gain control from management. Additionally, a class-action lawsuit had been filed in a Delaware court charging that the offer was a "grossly inadequate and unfair price."[27] The stock had closed at $14.50 on June 26, 1991.

In 1991, company management became a cosponsor (with Wrigley's Spearmint Gum) of the Singsation Gospel Competition, which was held in Atlanta,

Greensboro, and New York. Sponsorship allowed the company to reach an audience of at least 4,000 at each competition, thereby boosting the public's awareness of its products.

During the same year, management entered into a promotional agreement with *Upscale* magazine. Although in circulation for only one year, *Upscale* was the third largest African-American magazine, with 600,000 readers. Under the agreement Johnson Products flagged a subscription offer to *Upscale* on its hair relaxer (Ultra Sheen, Supreme Gentle-Treatment, and Sof-N-Free) cartons. In return, the company got a full-page monthly exposure for its brands and prime magazine positioning of its advertisements next to much read articles or features.[28]

In early 1992, Eric Johnson decided to implement a strategic marketing shift from price promotions to brand advertising. The company produced (in-house) three television commercials.

During Eric Johnson's tenure, the stock price had appreciated from a low of $1.63 at the end of 1989 to a high of $23.75. It closed at $19.50 the day after he resigned, off $.875 from the closing price of the previous day. On February 27, the stock closed at $15.25, a drop of $5.125, or 25.2%.

George E. Johnson's Thirty-five Years as an Entrepreneur

In 1954, George E. Johnson estimated that he would need $500 to get his new product, Ultra Wave Hair Culture, a hair straightener for black men, to the marketplace. The first loan officer he approached was not impressed with his new product, saying, "You've got a good job, you've been there ten years, why blow it? If your boss finds out that you are in business, you might lose your job and then you can't pay us back."[29] Johnson was disappointed, but he did not give up. He went to another bank and told the loan officer that he wanted to go to California on vacation and needed a $250 loan. The loan was granted. With this loan, Johnson, his wife, Joan, his brother, John, and a friend, Dr. Herbert Martini, a chemist, started Johnson Products on February 15, 1954. Originally organized as an Illinois corporation in 1957, the company became a publicly held corporation in 1969. On December 10, 1969, it became the first black-owned company to be publicly held.

George E. Johnson began his career as a door-to-door salesman in Chicago for Fuller Products, a black cosmetics company. Sometime later, he had an opportunity to work as an assistant chemist with Dr. Herbert Martini in the laboratory at Fuller Products. During the ten years Johnson worked with Martini, he learned what he needed to know to build his own cosmetics business.

Johnson started the Johnson Products Company after he became aware that blacks were unhappy with their naturally coarse, thick hair. Many blacks wanted their hair straightened to permit more flexibility in hair styling. The beginning of Johnson Products can be traced back to a particular day on which Johnson met a barber who had visited the managers at Fuller Products to seek help in formulating an improved hair straightener. Fuller Products wasn't interested, but Johnson was.

Johnson spoke with the barber, Orville Nelson, about his problem and later visited his shop to explore the matter further. At the shop, Johnson found customers standing in line to have their hair straightened, but the straightener being used simply did not work. Johnson and Nelson formed a short-lived partnership by putting up $250 each in capital, and Johnson sought the assistance of Dr. Martini in solving the problem with existing hair straighteners.

To obtain as much information as he could about the demand for hair straighteners, Johnson visited many owners of beauty shops with black clientele to learn "their perceptions of the market." He found that the problem was universal: blacks wanted a hair straightener that worked. Johnson was quoted as saying, "Black beauticians used a hot comb and grease on the hair of black women. Dr. Martini and I agreed that the smoke was bad for the health, and the grease was no good for the hair, so we worked on a process to eliminate the smoke and grease and came up with a creme press permanent, creme shampoo, and Ultra-Sheen that could be applied at home between visits to the beauty shop."[30] The hot comb technique required constant redoing of an individual's hair; rain or moisture would destroy the arrangement.

Although Johnson was not the first to enter the black hair care products market, his company became a leading firm because of his efforts to satisfy the needs of the black consumer. The "black revolution" of the 1960s brought the Afro and a dilemma. Johnson said, "I didn't know if it was a fad or not, so I took a wait-and-see attitude until I was sure it was a trend. Then we developed Afro-Sheen for the natural. But, I always felt the natural wouldn't last. It's too monotonous, and sure enough, women are moving from it."[31]

Historically, a vigorous, competitive hair care products and cosmetics manufacturing enterprise, Johnson Products was an important black institution and a growing American business. In 1971, Johnson Products Company, Inc., became the first black-owned firm to be listed on the American Stock Exchange. Through innovative product development and promotional techniques, it rapidly became one of the success stories of American business in the 1960s and early 1970s.

Growth of the company was steady but not spectacular until product innovations in 1965 spurred sales. In five years (1971–1975), gross sales increased from $14.4 million to $37.6 million, and market share reached an estimated 75%–80%. Companies such as Revlon and Alberto Culver then stepped up the competition, and after 1975, the firm experienced a series of setbacks.

Its first attempt to move beyond the ethnic market through an expensive men's cologne, Black Tie, was a disaster. This failure was attributed to improper distribution channels and poor shelf space and displays at retail establishments.[32] Coinciding with this setback was the mounting pressure exerted by major competing firms, primarily Revlon, which viewed the fast-growing ethnic market as an untapped well.

In February 1975, its public image suffered serious damage when the firm felt obligated to sign a consent order issued by the Federal Trade Commission requiring warning labels be placed on its best-selling hair straightener, Ultra-Sheen Permanent Creme Relaxer. Although its competitors also used the damaging chemical, sodium hydroxide, in their products, they were not compelled to take similar action until 20 months later. In the meantime, sales of the Johnson Products brand dropped significantly.

The late 1970s and early 1980s brought high inflation, generally poor economic conditions, fierce competition for customers and shelf space, and high black unemployment. The latter part of the 1980s brought low inflation, general prosperity, and low unemployment.

During the 1980s, the company sustained losses in six of the ten years: 1980 (the first year that the company had suffered a loss), 1982, 1984, 1985, 1986, and 1988. These net losses totaled $14.0 million on sales of $344.7 million for the ten-year period.[33] Net sales for the preceding decade (1970–1979) had been $278.5 million, with net profits of $29.0 million.[34] The company wrote down or off its investments in Johnson Products of Nigeria (1982) and Debbie's School of Beauty Culture, Inc. (1988). In 1989, the company sold land and one of its Chicago warehouses, using the cash from this sale to reduce debt. In 1989, Natalia Holynskyj, ethnic hair care consultant, estimated that the company's market share was 6%. This share put Johnson in third place in ethnic hair care sales behind Sof-Sheen Products, Inc., with 12.5% and World of Curls Products with 6.8%.[35]

George E. Johnson was an entrepreneur during his 35-year association with the company. His son stated that the company had been "mission driven [by an] entrepreneur."[36] Eric Johnson also noted that "the entrepreneur is not necessarily the most savvy in financial areas; he is simply the most creative."[37] Exhibit 29.2 shows key events in the evolution of Johnson Products.

Strategic Managers

Restructuring reduced the number of corporate officers during the years 1985–1993. In 1985, the company had ten officers. The number of corporate officers declined to eight in 1986, rose to nine in 1987, and declined again in 1988, 1989, and 1993 to five, three, and two officers, respectively. Joan B. Johnson is the only officer in 1993 who also had served in 1985.[38]

The present corporate officers are: Joan B. Johnson and Thomas P. Polke. Joan B. Johnson, 63, co-founded the company with her husband, George E. Johnson, in 1954 and since 1957 has served as Treasurer and Director. She was elected Chairman of the Board in October 1989 and Chief Executive Officer on March 31, 1992.

Thomas P. Polke, 30, joined the company in November 1988 as Vice-President, Finance, and Chief Financial Officer. Previously he had been with Arthur Andersen & Co. from 1984 until November 1988, where he was a senior consultant in its Financial Consulting Division. In 1990, he was elected Corporate Secretary and to the Board of Directors of Johnson Products Company, Inc.

The Board of Directors consists of the following individuals.

Joan B. Johnson (elected in 1957): Chairman of the Board, Treasurer, and Chief Executive Officer.

Thomas P. Polke (elected in 1990): Vice-President, Finance, Chief Financial Officer, and Corporate Secretary.

James J. Lowery (elected in 1989): President of James H. Lowery and Associates, Chicago (consulting firm).

William H. Giles (elected in 1990): Chairman of the Board of E.P.C. International, Inc.

Joan B. Johnson received George E. Johnson's 49.5% of Johnson Products Company, Inc., stock (valued at $5.5 million) as part of their divorce settlement. She already owned 6.8% of the company's stock and was trustee of a stock trust, so she now controls approximately 61% of the company's stock.[39]

Industry and Competition

The U.S. Commerce Department estimated that consumers spent $18.5 billion on cosmetics and toiletries in 1990. Exhibit 29.3 shows the breakdown of these personal health care product sales.[40]

Total hair care product sales increased by 8% in 1990 to an estimated $4.6 billion. Shampoos accounted for approximately 33% of this segment's sales, and tonics, conditioners, and rinses made up an additional 15%. The balance (approximately 52%) of sales consisted of hair colorings, fixatives, ethnic preparations, home permanents, mousses, and other products. Hair care imports were about $40 million and exports were about $210 million.[41]

The hair care segment is probably the most competitive of the home care products industry. It is also characterized by low brand loyalty, especially in shampoo and conditioner lines. Packaged Facts, a market research firm, estimated that hair care products, largely hair straighteners, accounted for about 73% of the $510 million in sales. It also estimated that total ethnic market product sales will be approximately $626 million in 1995. Skin care products accounted for an additional 14%, with cosmetics representing the remaining 13%. Good growth is predicted in all three segments of this market.[42] More than 75% of black women do their own hair at home versus the beauty parlor.[43] Revlon, Estée Lauder, Maybelline, and others have introduced new cosmetics for specific female minority target markets. Newcomers also are entering this market. Michael Ghafouri, former Max Factor executive, formed Kayla Cosmetics to market an upscale makeup line to Asians via direct response TV advertising.[44]

Products designed for ethnic minorities have provided another important source of growth for the hair care market. Sales of ethnic hair care products have increased in recent years, reflecting the above average population growth of blacks, Asians, Hispanics, and American Indians, and the increasing buying power of black women for hair care products and cosmetics (see Exhibit 29.4).[45] In the mid 1980s an estimated 30% of Johnson Products' sales were to minority consumers other than blacks.[46] Peter Francese, publisher of *American Demographics,* said that "projections are minorities will represent one of three people in this country in 20 years."

EXHIBIT 29.2

Historical Timetable: Johnson Products Company, Inc.

1954	Company founded with one product, Ultra Wave Hair Culture.
1957	Ultra Sheen Conditioner and Hair Dress introduced.
1958	Ultra Sheen line entered professional beauticians' market.
1960	Ultra Sheen line introduced in retail market.
1964	Fire destroys production facilities.
1965	Ultra Sheen No Base Creme Relaxer introduced.
1966	Completed first phase of new headquarters.
1968	Afro Sheen products introduced. Established the George E. Johnson Foundation.
1969	Sponsored its first nationwide TV special, ". . . & Beautiful."
1969	First black-owned company to become publicly held.
1970	Ultra Sheen cosmetics introduced.
1971	Began sponsorship of "Soul Train," a nationally syndicated TV show. First black-owned company listed on the American Stock Exchange.
1972	Established the George E. Johnson Educational Fund.
1973	Completed third phase of new headquarters.
1975	Entered men's fragrance market with "Black Tie" cologne and splash-on. Started exporting to Nigeria.
	Acquired the Debbie's School of Beauty Culture, Inc.—five salons.
1979	Reformulated cosmetics lines. Acquired Freedom Distributors, which distributed the company's and competitors' products on the Eastern seaboard.
1980	Established Johnson Products of Nigeria (JPN) as a manufacturing subsidiary, with a 40% interest.
	Introduced Ultra Sheen Precise, first of 42 innovative products. Suffered first loss—$4,240,000.
1981	Expanded overseas by establishing a sales and service center in Eastbourne, England. Introduced new products Gentle Treatment, Tender Treatment, and Bantu Curl.
1982	Established Debbie Howell Cosmetics, direct sales line in key black market areas.
	Introduced 19 new products.
1983	Formed Mello Touch Labs, Inc., to manufacture, market, and distribute a line of consumer products.
	Introduced two lines of cosmetics, Ultra Sheen and Moisture Formula.
	Sold Freedom Distributors.
1984	Introduced new line of hair products for men—Ultra Style.
1985	Ultra Style renamed Ultra Star.
	Signed Michael Jordan of the Chicago Bulls to a multiyear endorsement contract.
1986	Restructured the marketing and sales organization. Formed Excel Manufacturing Company, Inc., as a private-label subsidiary of the company.

(continued)

EXHIBIT 29.2 **Historical Timetable: Johnson Products Company, Inc.** *(continued)*

	Eric G. Johnson, son of founder, appointed President of Excel Manufacturing Company, Inc. Sold Debbie's School of Beauty Culture, Inc., and assets of Ultra Precise Boutiques, Inc., to their managers for $2,533,000. Implemented turnaround strategy.
1987	Excel Manufacturing Company, Inc., renamed Celex Corporation.
	Eric G. Johnson promoted to Senior Vice-President, Corporate Sales.
1988	Eric G. Johnson appointed Chief Operating Officer and elected to the Board of Directors.
	Sold warehouse and land in Chicago for $2,965,000 plus extension fees of $545,000 and carrying costs.
	Wrote down the balance ($1,293,000) in the promissory note due from sale of Debbie's School of Beauty Culture, Inc.
	Eric G. Johnson elected President.
	Company renewal program.
	Introduced Ultra Sheen Supreme and Soft Touch.
1989	George E. Johnson, Chairman, Chief Executive Officer, and Director, resigned from the company.
	Joan B. Johnson, Treasurer, appointed Chairman of the Board and granted George E. Johnson's stock interest (49.51%) as part of their divorce settlement.
	Eric Johnson, President, appointed Chief Executive Officer.
1990	February 2—Purchased four brands (Curly Perm, Sof-N-Free, Sta-Sof-Fro, and Moxie) from M&M Products Company, Inc., of Atlanta.
	Covered 40 markets nationwide as main sponsor of the Grambling Football Radio Network. Renewed in 1991.
	December 12—One-for-ten reverse stock split of company's common stock, both issued and outstanding, followed immediately by a three-for-one forward stock split.
1991	Leveraged buyout (LBO) proposed by Eric Johnson and two outside directors—James H. Lowery and William G. Giles—for $20.6 million. Offer withdrawn two months later.
	Cosponsored with Wrigley's Spearmint Gum the Singsation gospel competition.
	Promotion agreement with *Upscale* magazine. Strategic marketing shift from price promotion to emphasizing brand advertising.
1992	March 9—Eric G. Johnson resigned as President and CEO to pursue personal business interests.
	April 1—Chairman Joan B. Johnson appointed to the additional position of CEO.
	"Office of the President," formed three years ago, to have responsibility for day-to-day activities of the company. Joan M. Johnson, daughter, one of four members appointed to the office.

EXHIBIT 29.3

Personal Health Care Products
(1990 sales by category)

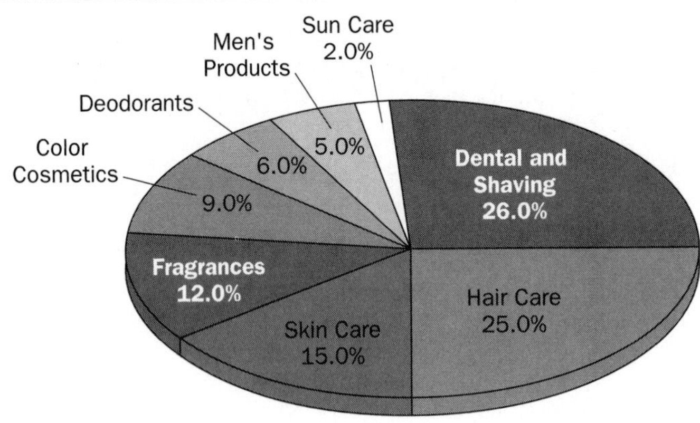

An *Essence* magazine writer stated that "styling trends in hair and makeup this spring [1992] offer something new for every sister. The trends are influenced by a broad spectrum of people and places. . . ."[47] The magazine writer went on to say, "There is so much happening now with our hair—everything from Afroesque (Afro styling on mildly relaxed hair) cuts to braids to locks, sometimes real, sometimes realistically fake (hair pieces with our texture)."[48] The writer cited, "Other hot trends [such as]: roller sets that give a softer look and are healthy for relaxed hair and twists . . . sculpted hair—braids, rolls, and twists . . . a mix of hair textures with one style, [and] adornments with combs and jeweled stickpins."[49] Stylist Jeffrey Woodley says, "Cropped hair is going to be the image that sets women free in the 90s."[50]

Value Line stated, "In the domestic marketplace, new product development is alive and well. It's true that the plethora of offerings introduced each year consists mainly of imitative items, many of which are short-lived. . . ."[51]

The early 1980s were characterized by the wet, Jheri-Curl style of Michael Jackson, which created multimillion dollar companies overnight. This fad has given way to dryer, shorter hair styles that require fewer gels and sprays. The industry is both highly competitive and fragmented. There are approximately 50 black-owned regional companies, which sell only one or two brands, and megacompanies such as Revlon, Avon, Gillette, and Alberto-Culver (see Exhibit 29.5). The black-owned companies once had as much as 80% of the market, but their share dropped to approximately 45% in the 1990s.

Johnson Products states that "the primary competitive factors affecting the company's sales are product quality, price, advertising, sales strategy, and availability of distribution and merchandising channels."[52] Johnson's nonmega competitors are Soft Sheen, World of Curls, Naomi Sims Beauty Products, and Gazelle International.

EXHIBIT 29.4

Ethnic Market Information

A. THE BLACK PROFILE

Slightly more than half the black population is between the ages of 18 and 34, according to a study done by Impact Resources, a consumer information company based in Columbus, Ohio, and Deloitte & Touche Trade, a retail and distribution services group in New York City. In contrast, slightly over 37% of the white population is in the same age bracket. The following facts should be of interest to retailers.

- Slightly more than half of all black consumers are single heads of household, either single/never been married, or divorced/separated.
- The majority of black consumers report having three or four persons per household. And more than 42% of black households include children under age 18, compared to 31% of white households.
- Among black working women who head households, there is a strong interest in such products and services as one-stop shopping, fast food, and wide selection at low prices.
- Watching TV, listening to radio, and shopping are the preferred indoor activities of black consumers.
- The black consumer purchases 19% of all health and beauty aids and 34% of all hair care products.

Source: Iris Rosenthal, "Ethnic Products Will Bloom into Substantial Market," *Drug Topics* (April 23, 1990), p. 64.

B. U.S. MINORITY POPULATION COMPOSITION: 1980–1990

The rate of increase for minorities in the United States during the 1980s was nearly twice as fast as in the 1970s. The breakdown of U.S. minority resident population is as follows.

- 29,986,000 blacks, an increase of 13.2%, about 12.0% of the population, and 1990 median household income of $18,676.
- 7,274,000 Asians, an increase of 107.8%, about 3% of the population, and 1989 median household income of $36,102.
- 1,959,000 American Indians, an increase of 37.9%, and about .78% of the population.
- 22,354,000 Hispanic origin, an increase of 53%, about 9.0% of the population, and a 1990 median household income of $22,330.

(continued)

Source: *1992 U.S. Statistical Abstract,* Table No. 695, p. 445, and Table 18, p. 18; Felicity Barringer, "U.S. Racial Composition Has Changed Dramatically," *St. Petersburg Times* (March 12, 1991), p. 10A.

EXHIBIT 29.4 **Ethnic Market Information** *(continued)*

C. PERCENTAGE OF SALES CONTRIBUTIONS PER GROUP PER SHOPPING TRIP (REGIONAL MALLS)

Store Type	White	Black	Asian	Hispanic
National department stores[1]	15.33%	12.07%	8.98%	15.11%
Conventional department stores	33.85	30.80	41.67	31.00
Specialty department stores	0.40	0.31	0.36	0.03
Discount department stores	2.27	2.08	0.09	1.61
Women's apparel	9.75	13.02	9.13	10.19
Men's apparel	2.70	6.80	4.36	2.94
Children's apparel	0.49	0.57	0.09	0.91
Shoes	4.93	10.27	4.17	6.01
Jewelry	4.49	9.18	2.65	4.39
All other[2]	25.80	8.09	28.61	27.89

Notes:
1. Sears Roebuck, J. C. Penney, and Montgomery Ward.
2. Because of rounding, numbers may not add up to 100%.

Source: 1992 Stillerman, Jones and Company National Benchmarks; Debra Hazel, "The Changing Faces of California," *Chain Store Age Executive* (May 1992), p. 55.

D. TIPS ON MARKETING TO MINORITIES

When they see advertising for a product or service aimed at their particular minority group, consumers "want to see a representation of their people in the message," says Peter Doherty, an analyst with Impact Resources, Inc., a Columbus, Ohio, consulting firm. He stresses sensitivity to cultural and language differences. "When you're trying to send a message to, say, the Cuban consumer in Miami, don't have a [non-Cuban] Hispanic that the Cubans cannot relate to," Doherty says. "You have to do your homework." If you don't do your homework, you can be sure that competing marketers will. The following are some further tips aimed at helping firms target ethnic markets.

- Never assume anything about your target audience; verify through research and interviews.
- Avoid stereotypes in profiling your target market and advertising to it.
- Just as all whites certainly don't act or think alike, neither do all African-Americans, Asians, or Hispanics. Each group is diverse, which creates challenges, but it also creates opportunities for marketers who spot the differences.
- Advertise locally. Advertisers trying to reach ethnic groups often achieve better results through community newspapers, radio stations, and cable TV than by using mainstream media.
- Keep the advertising message simple and friendly. Many minority consumers are immigrants who are not fully assimilated or conversant with U.S. commerce and consumerism.

Source: William Dunn, "The Move Toward Ethnic Marketing," *Nation's Business* (July 1992), p. 40.

EXHIBIT 29.5

Selected Financial Information on Competitors

(Dollar amounts in millions)

Company	Sales					Profits				
	1997–95	1993	1992	1991	1990	1997–95	1993	1992	1991	1990
Alberto-Culver	$ 1,660	$ 1,200	$ 1,091.3	$ 873.7	$ 795.7	$ 75	$ 45	$ 38.6	$ 30.1	$ 35
Avon Products	5,250	4,200	3,850	3,592.3	3,453	405	275	246	210.6	195.3
Gillette	7,650	5,825	5,130	4,683.9	4,344.6	960	600	510	427.4	367.9
Helene Curtis	1,865	1,325	1,170	1,019.9	867.3	40	26	23	19.2	6.5
Industry total	19,910	15,130	13,485	12,247	11,422	1,935	1,240	1,160	883	790.2

Company	Net Profit Margins					Operating Margins				
	1997–95	1993	1992	1991	1990	1997–95	1993	1992	1991	1990
Alberto-Culver	4.7%	3.8%	3.5%	3.4%	4.4%	9.0%	8.0%	8.2%	7.3%	8.9%
Avon Products	7.7	6.6	6.2	5.9	5.7	16.0	14.5	14.6	14.2	14.6
Gillette	12.6	10.3	9.9	9.1	8.5	25.5	23.5	23.0	22.5	21.9
Helene Curtis	4.1	1.9	1.9	1.9	0.7	6.5	6.4	6.3	6.3	4.8
Industry average	9.7	8.2	7.9	7.2	6.9	19.0	17.5	17.5	16.9	16.8

Note:
1. 1995–1997, 1993, and 1992 estimates by *Value Line*.

Source: *Value Line* (January 15, 1993), pp. 816–818, 821–822.

New products grabbed the spotlight at the 1992 National Association of Chain Drugstores Marketplace Conference. The new products ranged from alternative fragrances, ethnic hair care items, and novelties such as temporary tattoos. Pro-Line Corporation introduced a new Pro-Line Soft & Beautiful Just For Me No-Lye Conditioning Creme Relaxer in a children's formula. The manufacturer advertised this new product in *Essence* and *Ebony* and on national television in prime time sports, on children's shows, and on cable TV.[53]

Product Lines and Products

Johnson Products has both retail and professional product lines. The ten main product brands for the retail line are (1) Classy Curl, (2) Curly Perm, (3) Gentle-Treatment, (4) Moxie, (5) Sta-Sof-Fro, (6) Sof-N-Free, (7) Soft Touch, (8) Ultra Sheen, (9) Ultra Sheen Supreme, and (10) Ultra Star. The four main product brands for the professional line are (1) Bantu, (2) Sof-N-Free, (3) Ultra Sheen, and (4) Ultra Sheen Precise (see Exhibit 29.6). The professional line has constituted about 25% of the company's sales. Ultra Star is Johnson Products' second attempt to penetrate hair care products for men. In 1975, it introduced the Black Tie, a line of expensive men's fragrances and hair products, marketing the line to all men, not just ethnic minorities. The company quickly dropped the line when it failed to generate sales. The company produces more than 100 products, including those of its subsidiaries, Celex Corporation and Mellow Touch Laboratories, Inc. In the mid 1980s, an estimated 30% of Johnson's sales were to minorities other than blacks. The retail and professional lines account for approximately 95% of the company's consolidated revenues.

During the past two years, the company has continued to integrate the M&M Products Company brand lines into the company's business. Company brand management directed Sta-Sof-Fro brand advertising to a younger target market.

Bantu professional brand line sales increased significantly during the past year. Bantu brand, the company's top professional line, received a new, upscale package design.

Sales Promotion and Advertising

One of Eric Johnson's first priorities after accepting the position of Chief Operating Officer was to revamp the Marketing and Sales Department and its staff. Separate Marketing and Sales departments had been combined earlier in 1986 to reduce costs and increase coordination. Johnson believed that for a long time the company's sales organization had lacked the intensity and direction needed to sell Johnson products effectively.[54]

In reorienting the marketing/sales effort in 1989, he stated, "[The] marketing efforts will be coordinated and executed this year by an expanded staff of professionals. A main emphasis will be on in-store promotions designed to attract customers that may come in for other items."[55] He also stated, "Prudent budgets have to be established and expenditures for every promotional program are being carefully weighed against sales potential."[56]

EXHIBIT 29.6 **Main Product Brands: Johnson Products Company, Inc.**

I. Retail Brands

A. Classy Curl
B. Curly Perm[1]
C. Gentle-Treatment
D. Moxie[1]
E. Sta-Sof-Fro[1]
F. Sof N' Free[1]
G. Soft Touch
H. Ultra Sheen
I. Ultra Sheet Supreme
J. Ultra Star

II. Professional Brands

A. Bantu
B. Sof N' Free
C. Ultra Sheen
D. Ultra Sheen Supreme

Note:
1. These product brands were acquired from M & M Products for $5 million on February 2, 1990.

Source: Johnson Products Company, Inc., *1992 Annual Report,* inside front cover.

As President, Eric Johnson had implemented a "top down" sales approach by which the company's sales force established programs and promotion directly with top management of the company's accounts. He believed that this approach allowed the company's sales force to become more results-oriented, which was consistent with corporate objectives. These changes in the management of the Marketing and Sales Department allowed streamlining of the company's sales force while maintaining the potential to generate more sales. In recent years, the company has been more active in cultivating the professional beautician both through personalized incentive programs and participation in trade shows. The professional business accounts for approximately 25% of the company's sales.[57]

The advertising budget for 1992 was $5.5 million, which was an increase of $1.5 million (or 37.8%) over the previous year. Average yearly expenditure for the 1980s was $6.8 million.

In 1985, the company signed Michael Jordan of the Chicago Bulls to a multi-year endorsement campaign.

In January 1989, the company launched a major in-store promotion program, "Give to the Dream." In conjunction with Dr. Martin Luther King's birthday, Johnson Products donated $1 for each purchase of the company's hair care kit during the program to the King Center for Non-Violent Social Change. The company presented an initial check for $50,000 to Mrs. Coretta Scott King. According to Johnson Products' management, the program was successful and will be repeated.[58]

In 1992, the company conducted three major advertising campaigns that ran on billboards and buses in major markets. One campaign focused on Gentle-Treatment, which remains the company's leading retail sales product. The brand campaign for Ultra Sheen won the first-place award from the Eight Sheet Outdoor Advertising Association. The campaign theme was, "The workout for beautiful hair." The company's internally generated ad competed with advertising agencies and companies nationwide throughout the health and beauty aid industry.[59] The company's Creative Director coordinates all advertising efforts.

The company continued to use promotions to increase retail sales. Management has encouraged distributors to buy in volume and has provided buying incentives directly to consumers (bonus packs and cents-off coupons).

Marketing and Distribution

The company distributed its products directly to chain warehouses, wholesalers, retailers, and beauty and barber distributors. Retail stores sell directly to consumers and because convenience is foremost in the minds of the customer, the majority of sales occur in mass distribution outlets (supermarkets and drugstores). Shelf space allocation has become a more pressing problem, both for the manufacturer and the retailer, as more products compete for limited shelf space. Eric Johnson's solution to this problem was that "it is far easier to buy shelf space through a buy-out of another company product line. . . ."[60] The company also is more demanding regarding the trade-off between price and quality. This approach has led to a stream of products at the low-end price niche with characteristics hard to distinguish from the more expensive products.[61]

In the domestic marketplace, the expanded distribution system offers another way to increase sales. *Value Line* said, "We think the market-dominant companies under our review stand to benefit from the increasing popularity of mass merchandisers and warehouse clubs among today's cost-conscious public." *Value Line* went on to say, "These high-volume retailers deal with a limited number of suppliers, choosing among the manufacturers on the basis of their size, market position, and ability to provide service. Getting a foot in the door can mean exclusivity (and a reprieve from battling with rivals for shelf space)."[62]

International Operations

In November 1989, Johnson Products sold its interest in its Nigerian operation, Johnson Products of Nigeria (JPN), for $450,000. The company realized a $369,000 gain on the sale of JPN's common stock. Johnson Products of Nigeria was established in 1981, with Johnson Products owning a 40% interest in the venture with its Nigerian partners. Problems plagued the operation from the start, and it sustained losses of $1.1 million in the first three years of operations.

In 1981, Johnson Products opened a sales and service center in the United Kingdom and is now located in Felixstone, England. This is essentially a low-overhead central distribution center for the U.K. and Western European markets (primarily Belgium, France, Germany, and the Netherlands). In 1991, the company began to serve customers in these countries directly through its International Sales Division.

Also in 1981, Johnson Products entered into an agreement with a Jamaican manufacturer to produce some of Johnson's brands. This licensing agreement allows entry of Johnson's products to most of the West Indies. In June 1987, the company signed a similar licensing agreement with a Trinidadian manufacturer.

The company, through its military and international sales divisions, exports products to more than 20 countries, including Canada. Nevertheless, total exports generated less than 10% of the company's consolidated revenues for the past five years.[63]

In 1992, the company responded to the needs of its customers by introducing trilingual packaging for several of the company's top-selling products.

Facilities and Subsidiaries

Johnson Products' corporate headquarters and manufacturing facilities are located on 12.5 acres at 8522 South Lafayette Avenue in Chicago. The building contains approximately 64,000 square feet of office space and 176,000 square feet of warehousing and manufacturing space. The company also leased sales office space in Atlanta, Georgia, and Baltimore, Maryland. Management believes that its facilities are adequate to meet expected sales volume for the immediate future.

The company's two subsidiaries are Mellow Touch Laboratories, Inc., and Celex Corporation. Formed in 1983, Mellow Touch manufactures, distributes, and markets a line of consumer products. Formed in 1986 as Excel Manufacturing and renamed in 1987, Celex serves as the private-label arm of Johnson Products. It manufactures a wide variety of products—skin and baby care products and medicated gels and lotions for hair—to customer specifications. Celex shared common manufacturing, marketing, distribution facilities, and resources with Johnson Products. Management has shifted its focus from custom manufacturing to more profitable private-brand manufacturing and sales.

Research and Development

Johnson Products cut research and development expenditures by 38.6% from $542,000 to $333,000 between 1988 and 1992. The company spent $333,000, $332,000, and $322,000 on R&D in 1992, 1991, and 1990, respectively. Research and development expenditures have declined since 1980, with the average yearly expenditure during the 1980s being $711,400.

During the years 1980–1985, the company introduced more than 50 products and line extensions for both the retail and professional markets. The company then did not introduce any new products for several years. The company's recent introduction of some new products accounts for about 3% of total sales.

One significant aspect of the company is its capability to conduct scientific research, enabling it to develop unique technologies for producing a variety of beauty aid products. During the past several years, the company has received several patents for products presently on the market, but many of these patents will expire in the 1990s and early 2000s. Further patent applications are pending; if granted, they will extend well beyond 2000.

The Johnson Products Research Center is considered to be the largest laboratory of its kind devoted exclusively to R&D. Technicians and scientists representing a variety of disciplines work with the latest sophisticated equipment in a 7,000 square foot research laboratory. Approximately one-third of R&D employee hours are spent on quality control; the rest are spent on new product development and improvement of existing products. Outside consultants and technical services supplement in-house capabilities in developing concepts, designing packages, and researching the characteristics of ethnic skin and hair. Management has reduced the size of the R&D staff over the past ten years.

Human Resources Management

There have been several large reductions in force at Johnson Products over the past decade. The number of employees was 575 in 1980; 568 in 1981; 541 in 1982; 550 in 1983; 540 in 1984; 558 in 1985; 431 in 1986; 285 in 1987; 246 in 1988; 190 in 1989; 232 in 1990; 224 in 1991; and 219 in 1992. During Eric Johnson's tenure as Chief Operating Officer, he reduced the company's payroll by almost 50%. He overhauled the marketing and sales departments, which he felt were providing inadequate customer service. Sales per employee increased by 177% to $191,689 in 1992, compared to $69,167 in 1986 and $57,360 in 1980. Thus the reduction in employees has led to a leaner operation while maintaining approximately the same sales level over the past decade (see Exhibits 29.4 and 29.5).

Johnson made personnel cutbacks in both the employee ranks and executive positions. He said, "I found employees were content to see an effort made to stem the decline, when the example was set at the top."[64]

Finance

During the period 1980–1989, the company sustained losses in 21 of the 40 quarters, totaling $14.0 million on sales of $344.7 million. During the five-year period 1985–1989, the company's financial performance improved over the preceding five years. The company sustained losses in eight quarters during this period, compared to losses in 13 quarters for the period 1980–1984. Johnson Products lost more than $5.9 million on sales of $153.5 million during the five years 1985–1989, and lost $8.1 million on sales of $191.2 million during the five years 1980–1984.

Since 1990, the company has earned a profit in each of the 14 quarters. The company's total sales for this period were some $133.3 million, with total net income of about $12.1 million (see Exhibits 29.1 and 29.7–29.10). The price of the company's stock rose to $46 in the first quarter of 1993, a record high.

EXHIBIT 29.7

Five-Year Financial Review: Johnson Products Company, Inc.
(Dollar amounts in thousands, except per share data, percentages, and employee data)

Years Ending August 31	1992	1991	1990	1989	1988
Summary of Operations					
Net sales	$41,980	$38,406	$33,497	$29,368	$29,104
Cost of sales	17,948	18,167	15,909	13,515	13,292
Selling, general, and administrative expenses (exclusive of advertising and promotion)	12,006	12,166	11,190	10,564	11,657
Advertising and promotion	5,509	3,999	4,080	4,736	6,496
Nonrecurring operating expenses	480	—	—	—	—
Other income	—	—	638	2,200	451
Interest expense, net	304	810	797	719	584
Income (loss) before income taxes and extraordinary item	5,733	3,264	2,159	2,034	(2,474)
Income taxes	2,306	1,370	711	779	—
Income (loss) before extraordinary item	3,427	1,894	1,448	1,255	(2,474)
Income (loss) per share before extraordinary item	2.86	1.59	1.21	1.05	(2.07)
Other Financial Data					
Research and development expenses	$ 333	$ 332	$ 322	$ 362	$ 342
Current assets	15,923	15,233	16,663	14,395	12,829
Current liabilities	3,593	7,783	11,415	9,512	8,842
Working capital	12,330	7,450	5,248	4,883	3,987
Property, net	5,825	5,283	5,486	5,611	5,842
Total assets	25,061	24,788	26,060	20,322	18,956
Long-term debt	282	1,100	2,000	—	1,313
Shareholders' equity	20,815	15,905	12,645	10,621	8,612
Shareholders' equity per share	17.37	13.30	10.57	8.88	7.20
Cash dividends per share	.42	—	—	—	—
Capital expenditures	767	638	447	328	414
Ratios					
Income (loss) before income taxes and extraordinary item to net sales	13.7%	8.5%	6.5%	6.9%	(8.5%)
Income (loss) before extraordinary item to net sales	8.2%	4.9%	4.3%	4.3%	(8.5%)
Return on average shareholder's equity	18.7%	13.3%	12.5%	13.0%	(23.6%)
Advertising and promotion to net sales	13.1%	10.4%	12.2%	16.1%	22.3%
Average common and common equivalent shares outstanding	1,198	1,196	1,196	1,196	1,196
Number of employees	219	224	232	190	246

Source: Johnson Products Company, Inc., *1992 Annual Report,* p. 4.

EXHIBIT 29.8

Consolidated Balance Sheet: Johnson Products Company, Inc., and Subsidiaries[1]

(Dollar amounts in millions)

Years Ending August 31	1992	1991
Assets		
Current assets		
Cash	$ 1,873	$ 426
Accounts receivable less allowance for doubtful accounts of $822 in 1992 and $472 in 1991	8,827	8,439
Inventories	3,136	5,494
Prepaid expenses and other current assets	1,139	874
Prepaid taxes	948	—
Total current assets	15,923	15,233
Property, plant, and equipment	17,429	16,679
Less accumulated depreciation	11,604	11,096
	5,825	5,583
Intangibles, net	3,162	3,415
Other assets	151	557
Total assets	$25,061	$24,788
Liabilities and Shareholders' Equity		
Current liabilities		
Short-term loans	—	3,042
Current maturities of long-term debt	89	879
Accounts payable	1,989	3,193
Accrued expenses	346	386
Accrued payroll and employee benefits	632	283
Accrued taxes payable	537	—
Total current liabilities	3,593	7,783
Long-term debt	282	1,100
Deferred taxes	371	—
Shareholders' equity		
Capital stock: Preferred stock, no par; authorized 300,000 shares; none issued. Common stock, $.50 par; authorized 7,504,400 shares; issued 1,217,662 and 1,215,979 shares in 1979 and 1991, respectively	609	608
Additional paid-in capital	2,039	2,040
Retained earnings	18,519	13,638
Cumulative translation adjustment	—	(29)
Treasury stock, 19,578 shares, at cost	(352)	(352)
Total shareholders' equity	20,815	15,905
Total liabilities and shareholders' equity	$25,061	$24,788

Note:

1. Notes were deleted.

Source: Johnson Products Company, Inc., *1992 Annual Report*, p. 6.

EXHIBIT 29.9

Consolidated Statement of Operations: Johnson Products Company, Inc., and Subsidiaries[1]

(Dollar amounts in thousands, except per share data)

Years Ending August 31	1992	1991	1990
Net sales	$41,980	$38,406	$33,497
Costs and expenses			
Cost of sales	17,948	18,167	15,909
Selling, general, and administrative expenses	17,515	16,165	15,270
Nonrecurring operating expenses	480	—	—
Total costs and expenses	35,943	34,332	31,179
Income from operations	6,037	4,074	2,318
Other income (expense)			
Interest expense, net	(304)	(810)	(797)
Gain on sale of investment	—	—	369
Other income	—	—	269
Income before income taxes and extraordinary item	5,733	3,264	2,159
Income taxes	2,306	1,370	711
Income before extraordinary item	3,427	1,894	1,448
Extraordinary item			
Utilization of tax loss carry forward	1,953	1,294	677
Net income	$ 5,380	$ 3,188	$ 2,125
Net income per common and common equivalent share			
Income before extraordinary item	$ 2.86	$ 1.59	$ 1.21
Extraordinary item	1.63	1.08	.57
Net income per common and common equivalent share	$ 4.49	$ 2.67	$ 1.78

Note:
1. Notes were deleted.

Source: Johnson Products Company, Inc., *1992 Annual Report,* p. 7.

EXHIBIT 29.10

Quarterly Financial Statements, 1993–1990: Johnson Products Company, Inc.

(Dollar amounts in thousands, except per share data)

Quarters Ending	Nov. 30, (First)	Feb. 28, (Second)	May 31, (Third)	Aug. 31 (Fourth)	Totals for Year
1993					
Net sales	$8,842	$10,528	$ NA	$ NA	$19,370
Gross profit	3,974	4,043			8,017
Income before extraordinary item	801	1,179			1,980
Extraordinary item	21	42			63
Net income	822	1,221			2,043
Net income per share					
Continuing operations	.32	.48			.80
Extraordinary item	.01	.01			.02
Net income	.33	.49			.82
1992					
Net sales	$8,619	$ 9,288	$11,265	$12,808	$41,980
Gross profit	4,666	5,028	6,703	7,635	24,032
Income before extraordinary item	458	166	1,148	1,655	3,427
Extraordinary item	255	98	583	1,017	1,953
Net income	713	264	1,731	2,672	5,380
Net income per share					
Before extraordinary item	.38	.14	.96	1.38	2.86
Extraordinary item	.21	.08	.49	.85	1.63
Net income	.59	.22	1.45	2.23	4.49
1991					
Net sales	$7,223	$ 9,075	$11,375	$10,733	$38,406
Gross profit	4,069	4,669	5,988	5,513	20,239
Income before extraordinary item	386	413	717	378	1,894
Extraordinary item	174	184	310	626	1,294
Net income	560	597	1,027	1,004	3,188
Net income per share					
Before extraordinary item	.32	.35	.60	.32	1.59
Extraordinary item	.15	.15	.26	.52	1.08
Net income	.47	.50	.86	.84	2.67
1990					
Net sales	$6,146	$8,166	$9,652	$9,533	$33,497
Gross profit	3,187	4,423	5,209	4,769	17,588
Income before extraordinary item	259	136	482	571	1,448
Extraordinary item	161	72	277	167	677
Net income	420	208	759	738	2,125
Net income per share					
Before extraordinary item	.22	.11	.40	.48	1.21
Extraordinary item	.14	.06	.23	.14	.57
Net income	.36	.17	.63	.62	1.78

Source: Johnson Products Company, Inc., 1992, 1991, 1990, and 1989 annual reports and Form 10-Q reports.

On December 12, 1990, shareholders had approved a one-for-ten *reverse stock split* for the company's issued and outstanding stock. For every 100 shares, shareholders received 10 shares. Immediately following this reverse stock split, the company implemented a three-for-one *forward stock split* to attract more interest in its stock. The two splits combined to reduce the number of outstanding shares to about 1.2 million from nearly 4 million. The investor with 100 shares before the two splits ended up with 30 shares. The stock price increased from $4⅝ to $6¼ (adjusted for the split) in the week following the announcement.

As a result of its rapid financial turnaround, in December 1991, the company declared a dividend of $.28 per share, payable in January 1992. The company had not paid a dividend since 1980. Management's stated intention was to pay a regular quarterly dividend of $.07.

On March 23, 1993, the company's Board of Directors declared a two-for-one stock split in the form of a 100% stock dividend on its common stock to shareholders of record as of the close of business on April 6, 1993. The Board declared a $.05 per share dividend.

As of March 31, 1993, the company's sales had been more than $43.4 million and its net revenue more than $6.4 million (see Exhibit 29.1)—both records for the company. The stock price rose to $46 a share, also a record high. On April 6, 1993, the company entered into a $3 million unsecured bank revolving credit agreement bearing the bank's prime rate that runs through December 31, 1993. Effective February 1, 1993, the company increased the price of its products by approximately 4%. Sales of new products are not expected to materially affect overall company sales during this year.[65]

Notes

1. Jeff Bailey, "Chief of Johnson Products Quits; Row Is Reported," *Wall Street Journal* (March 10, 1992), p. B-8.
2. "Johnson Products Company, Inc., Announces Resignation of George E. Johnson," (October 2, 1989), pp. 1-2.
3. Karen Springer and Larry Reibstein, "So Much for Family Ties," *Newsweek* (March 23, 1992), p. 49.
4. Johnson Products Company, Inc., *Announcement* (April 1, 1992), p. 1.
5. Lois Therrien, "Brawl in the Family at Johnson Products," *Business Week* (March 22, 1992), p. 34.
6. Ibid.
7. Ibid.
8. Frank McCoy, "Johnson Products Regroups After Family Row," *Black Enterprise* (May 1992), p. 17.
9. Therrien, p. 34.
10. Johnson Products Company, Inc., *Announcement* (April 1, 1992), p. 1.
11. Therrien, p. 34.
12. Ibid.
13. Johnson Products Company, Inc., *1992 Annual Report,* p. 13.
14. Johnson Products Company, Inc., *1988 Annual Report,* p. 1.
15. Ibid.
16. Leslie Brokaw, "Putting the House in Order," *Inc.* (March 1991), p. 102.
17. Johnson Products Company, Inc., *Form 10-Q Report* (February 28, 1990), p. 7.
18. Sheila M. Poole, "M&M Products to Close Atlanta Operations After Selling Brands," *Atlanta Journal* (February 3, 1990).
19. Johnson Products Company, Inc., *1991 Annual Report,* p. 7.
20. *Crain's Chicago Business* (September 17, 1990), p. 4.

21. "Johnson Products Opts to Stay in City," *Crain's Chicago Business* (April 29, 1991), p. 70.
22. Charles Storch, "Johnson Family Sets Buy-Out Bid," *Chicago Tribune* (May 29, 1991), p. 3.
23. Ibid.
24. Jerry Thomas, "JPC Seeks Stock Buy-Back," *Black Enterprise* (September 1991), p. 18.
25. Ibid.
26. Judith Crown, "Why Johnson Deal Failed," *Crain's Chicago Business* (July 1, 1991), p. 80.
27. Ibid.
28. Johnson Products Company, Inc., *1991 Annual Report,* p. 8.
29. Thomas L. Wheelen, Charles E. Michaels, Jr., Robert L. Nixon, and Janiece L. Gallagher, "Johnson Products Company, Inc., A Turnaround Strategy," case in *Strategic Management and Business Policy,* 3rd ed. (Reading, Mass.: Addison-Wesley, 1989), p. 808.
30. Neil H. Snyder, "Johnson Products Company, Inc.," case in *Strategic Management and Business Policy* (Reading, Mass.: Addison-Wesley, 1983), p. 820.
31. Ibid.
32. Ibid.
33. Johnson Products Company, Inc., *1984 Annual Report; 1989 Annual Report.*
34. Johnson Products Company, Inc., *1980 Annual Report,* pp. 18–19.
35. Susan Chandler, "Divorce Triggers Change in Leadership at JPC," *Black Enterprise* (December 1989), p. 17.
36. "Johnson Products Turnaround," *Babson Bulletin* (Winter 1990), p. 14.
37. Ibid.
38. Johnson Products Company, Inc., 1984, 1985, 1986, 1988, and 1989 annual reports.
39. Chandler, p. 17.
40. "Health Care," *Industry Survey* (August 22, 1991), p. H-40.
41. Ibid., p. H-42.
42. Ibid.
43. *Essence* (March 1991), p. 6.
44. Christy Fisher, "Ethnics Gain Market Clout," *Advertising Age* (July 1, 1991), p. 10.
45. Ibid.
46. Chandler, p. 17.
47. *Essence* (April 1992), p. 12.
48. Ibid.
49. Ibid., p. 14.
50. Ibid.
51. "Toiletries/Cosmetics Industry," *Value Line* (January 15, 1993), p. 816.
52. Johnson Products Company, Inc., *Form 10-Q Report* (August 3, 1992), p. 3.
53. Iris Rosenthal, "New Products Showcased for Chain Drugstores," *Drug Topics* (August 3, 1992), p. 86.
54. Johnson Products Company, Inc., *1988 Annual Report,* p. 5.
55. Ibid.
56. Ibid.
57. Johnson Products Company, Inc., *1989 Annual Report,* p. 4.
58. Ibid., p. 5.
59. Johnson Products Company, Inc., *1992 Annual Report,* p. 3.
60. Chandler, p. 17.
61. "Toiletries/Cosmetics Industry," p. 807.
62. Ibid., p. 816.
63. Johnson Products Company, Inc., *Form 10-K Report* (1992), p. 3.
64. Chandler, p. 17.
65. Johnson Products Company, Inc., *Form 10-Q Report* (February 28, 1993), pp. 6–7.

Invacare Corporation

Walter E. Greene

Introduction

Looking ahead, A. Malachi Mixon III says that he wants Invacare to win the Malcolm Baldridge National Quality award, both for the prestige it would bring and as a way of attaining "world-class" quality status for the company's products.[1]

President, Chairman, and CEO Mixon has been taking a visible role in the industry's lobbying efforts to educate Congress about the home medical equipment industry. Despite the rhetoric, few people in Washington have the answers to health care issues says Mixon as he quotes a senior policymaker in the Health Care Financing Agency (HCFA) as saying, "You'll never convince me that taking a bath is a medical necessity."[2]

The question is: "Can Invacare continue its lobbying efforts and what does it need to do to win the Malcolm Baldridge National Quality Award?"

Background

Invacare goes back a long way—107 years to 1885—when the Worthington Company of Elyria, Ohio, began producing "vehicles" designed for the physically handicapped. The Worthington Company merged with a manufacturer of rubber tire wheels and casters in the early 1990s, at which time the company changed its name to the Colson Company. It became a major supplier of bicycles and paid little attention to wheelchairs. When the Colson Company moved its headquarters in 1952, three of its employees purchased the wheelchair operations and named their company Mobilaid, Inc.

By 1960, Mobilaid, Inc., had annual sales of $150,000 and 15 employees. It grew slowly during the 1960s and was acquired in 1970 by Technicare, Inc., which renamed it Invacare Corporation in 1971. Technicare focused most of its resources on medical diagnostic imaging and became a leading manufacturer of that type of equipment. Invacare continued to grow at a modest rate but with little direction and not much in the way of new products.

Medical giant Johnson & Johnson acquired Technicare in 1978. Management decided to sell off Invacare, at that time a relatively small and obscure part of Technicare.

This case was prepared by Professor Walter E. Greene of the University of Texas–Pan American. This case was prepared under a Department of Education Grant to the University of Tulsa International Management Center for case development. This case was presented at the *1993 World Association for Case Research and Case Method Applications* meeting (WACRA).

Invacare Under Mixon

Mal Mixon, then 39 and a manager at Technicare, was in charge of marketing CT scanners. Mixon became interested in acquiring Invacare, but the asking price for it was $7.8 million. Although he had only $10,000 to invest, Mixon was not dismayed. He knew that the growth potential for the home health care industry was strong. Mixon convinced two real estate brokers to purchase the facility for $2 million, thereby reducing the asking price to $5.8 million. Mixon assembled and convinced a group of Cleveland investors to purchase $1.3 million in both preferred and common shares. He then secured a commitment from First Chicago Bank to loan the company $4.3 million; the note was later transferred to National City Bank. Mixon invested his $10,000, borrowed $40,000 from two personal friends, and borrowed $100,000 from the company (paid off when the company went public five years later) to meet the asking price. Mixon's leveraged buyout created some problems, namely, the high cost of the debt and equity. The bank loan carried an interest rate of three percentage points over prime, which at that time in December 1979 meant a rate of about 25%.

The buy-out was structured so that Mixon retained a 15% interest in Invacare. In 1979, Invacare's sales were about $19 million and net earnings after acquisition costs were approximately $100,000.

Invacare then employed about 350 individuals. In the first year of operations under Mixon, the high cost of debt drained Invacare's profits of about $1.4 million. In addition, the company faced well-established competitors. The main competitor was Everest and Jennings, a California-based home health care company that had more than 80% of the wheelchair market.

Mixon's strategy was to concentrate first on the company's employees, who were demoralized and had little incentive to stay with a company that was going nowhere fast. Mixon focused on sales by making sales calls himself and accompanying sales personnel on their calls. Mixon often told his sales staff that the company someday would be number one in the industry. Mixon also brought in some experienced personnel to fill key positions, which enabled the company to begin slowly to grow.

Mixon studied Invacare's product lines and weeded out obsolete or unprofitable ones. In January 1981, Invacare entered the home care bed business with the acquisition of a small start-up company in Sanford, Florida. Also in 1981, Invacare broadened its product line by entering the respiratory equipment business with the acquisition of Prime Air, Inc., a manufacturer of oxygen concentrators in Hartford, Connecticut. Invacare moved this operation to the Cleveland Street facility in Elyria, Ohio, in 1985. Exhibit 30.1 contains a list of Invacare acquisitions. Sales and earnings continued to grow during the early 1980s, and by the end of 1983, Invacare had sales of $70 million and earnings of $2.8 million. Exhibits 30.2 and 30.3 show Invacare's latest financial data. At that time wheelchair sales still comprised almost 50% of Invacare's total sales. In the first quarter of 1984, Invacare announced its first public stock offering, which was successfully completed by the end of May 1984 and raised $15 million on the issuance of 1.5 million shares.

EXHIBIT 30.1 **Acquisitions: Invacare Corporation**

Date	Firm Acquired	Product	Sales (in millions)	Number of Employees
1979	Technicare (Invacare)	Wheelchairs	$19.5	350
1981	Home Bed Care	Home beds	—	—
1981	Prime Air, Inc.	Oxygen concentrators	—	—
1984	Carters Ltd	Wheelchairs	—	—
1984	Gunter and Meier	Wheelchairs	—	—
1988	Invamex	Wheelchairs	—	—
1991	Canadian Posture and Seating Centre, Inc.	—	1.2	—
1911	Canadian Wheelchair Manufacturing Ltd	—	6.0	50
1992	Hovis Medical Ltd	Home medical equipment	—	60
1992	Perry Oxygen Systems	Oxygen systems	—	—
1992	Poirier S.A.	Wheelchairs	55.0	—
1993	Top End	Athletic wheelchairs	—	—
1993	Dynamic Control Ltd, New Zealand	DC controls and power wheelchairs	305	150
1993	GSI, Inc.	Low air loss therapy systems	4–5	—

Source: Invacare Corporation reports.

Invacare Foreign Operations

In April 1984, Invacare acquired Carters (J&A) Ltd, a leading U.K. manufacturer of wheelchairs and other patient aids. Since 1850, Carters had manufactured and marketed durable medical equipment in Europe. Among Carters' principal products were a full line of manually operated standard wheelchairs, patient aids, and parts similar to those marketed by Invacare and its competition.

As part of the purchase, Invacare also acquired substantially all the assets and business of the U.S. affiliate of Carters—Rajowalt/Carters—located in Atwood, Indiana. Rajowalt produced splints and other types of orthopedic equipment used in the treatment of bone fractures.

Approximately 50% of Carters' sales were in the United Kingdom. The rest were in other European and worldwide markets.

In 1984, Invacare also acquired for $250,000 an 85% interest in Gunter Meier GMB II, a small West German manufacturer of durable medical equipment. Invacare purchased the remaining 15% in 1985.

The home health care market in Europe was different in several respects from that in the United States. In most European countries, socialized medicine was the norm; consequently, governments were the largest single customers of home

EXHIBIT 30.2

Consolidated Balance Sheet: Invacare Corporation and Subsidiaries
(Dollar amounts in thousands)

Years Ending December 31	1992	1991
Assets		
Current assets		
Cash and cash equivalents	$ 8,181	$ 1,472
Marketable securities	2,533	1,723
Trade receivables, net	66,293	51,006
Investment in installment receivables, net	18,606	13,972
Inventories	47,875	42,217
Other current assets	4,357	4,648
Deferred income taxes	4,089	4,776
Total current assets	151,934	119,814
Other assets	9,059	4,897
Property and equipment, net	51,040	35,260
Goodwill, net	50,379	2,378
Total assets	$262,412	$162,349
Liabilities and Shareholders' Equity		
Current liabilities		
Accounts payable	$ 30,836	$ 15,947
Accrued expenses	39,063	22,946
Accrued income taxes	2,065	2,267
Current maturities of long-term obligations	422	896
Total current liabilities	72,386	42,056
Long-term obligations	74,488	31,795
Deferred income taxes	1,538	1,788
Shareholders' equity		
Preferred shares	—	—
Common shares	5,004	4,522
Class B common shares	2,225	2,323
Additional paid-in capital	59,666	45,728
Retained earnings	51,132	33,393
Foreign currency translation adjustment	(1,671)	(1,294)
Treasury stock	(2,356)	(550)
Total shareholders' equity	114,000	86,710
Total liabilities and shareholders' equity	$262,412	$162,349

Source: Invacare Corporation reports.

health care products. The rental market in countries with socialized medicine was virtually nonexistent, with a resulting market oriented more toward price than durability. However, in some European countries (e.g., Germany), the market was geared strongly toward quality and durability.

Other significant differences between the European and U.S. markets were their sizes and the fragmentation of the European market. The European market—smaller and growing much less rapidly than the U.S. market—was dominated by several companies, each of which possessed particular strengths in one or more countries.

In Europe, the distribution network generally relied on direct government outlets and some independent medical equipment dealers. As the home health care equipment industry developed, the role of the medical equipment dealers was expected to strengthen.

Prior to its acquisition of the U.K. and German operations in 1984, Invacare's foreign sales were insignificant. In 1984, European operations accounted for 13% of net sales but lost $1.0 million. In 1985, these operations continued to show a loss ($803,000). In 1986, the loss declined to $529,000 when European sales accounted for 15% of net sales. In 1987, European operations accounted for approximately 13% of net sales and a pre-tax loss of more than $1.1 million.

Present foreign plant locations and products include Wales (patient aids and wheelchairs); Porta Germany, Gunter Meier GMB II (wheelchairs and patient aids); and Reynosa, Mexico (wheelchairs). Wheelchairs and orthopedic soft goods are manufactured in Rajowalt's Atwood, Indiana, facility. In January 1988, Invacare began operating its newly constructed maquiladora plant, a 78,000 square foot manufacturing facility in Reynosa, Mexico, just across the border from McAllen, Texas, named Invamex. This plant enabled Invacare to manufacture low-cost manual wheelchairs that can compete with competitors from the Far East. In October 1991, Invacare acquired Canadian Posture and Seating Centre, Inc., of Kitchner, Ontario, maker of seating and positioning products, with annual sales of about $1.2 million. Also in October 1991, Invacare acquired Canadian Wheelchair Manufacturing Ltd, which has annual sales of about $6 million. In August 1992, Invacare acquired Perry Oxygen Systems, a small manufacturer of liquid oxygen and oxygen delivery systems located in Port St. Lucie, Florida, and transferred its operations to the company's Sanford, Florida, facility. On October 15, 1992, Invacare completed the acquisition of Poirier S.A., France's largest manufacturer and distributor of wheelchairs and other home medical products. The acquisition involved a combination of cash and common stock in the total amount of approximately $55 million. Poirier's sales for the fiscal year 1992 were $45 million and its earnings exceeded $3 million[3] (see Exhibit 30.4).

Invamex

In the third quarter of 1988, Invamex shipped its first wheelchairs. Invamex paid its Mexican workers $3.70 per day, or slightly above the minimum wage in Mexico. Mandated benefits in Mexico were approximately 60% of pay. Invamex also

EXHIBIT 30.3

Income Statements and Other Selected Financial Information: Invacare Corporation[1]

(Dollar amounts in thousands, except per share data)

	1994[2]	1993[2]	1992	1991	1990	1989	1988	1987	1986
Domestic	$296,627	$257,937	$224,293	$204,078	$181,113	$152,353	$139,373	$113,332	$ 97,607
International (including Canada)	147,007	124,582	80,878	59,103	48,684	33,702	21,470	$ 17,424	13,923
Net sales	$443,634	$382,519	$305,171	$263,181	$229,797	$186,055	$160,843	130,756	$111,530
Cost of goods sold	297,235	258,776	207,788	178,621	159,717	134,174	111,886	91,070	77,567
Gross profit	146,399	123,741	97,383	84,560	70,080	51,881	48,957	39,686	33,963
Selling, general, and administrative	101,148	86,730	69,716	60,932	53,330	43,058	38,064	32,688	28,773
Goodwill amortization	1,250	1,240	100	—	—	—	—	—	—
Operating income	44,001	35,771	27,567	23,628	16,750	8,823	10,893	6,998	5,190
Interest income	4,000	5,504	4,601	3,589	2,771	1,636	1,175	941	1,079
Interest expense	(4,402)	(5,182)	(4,610)	(4,324)	(5,654)	(5,417)	(3,681)	(2,205)	(1,674)
Nonrecurring items	—	—	—	—	—	—	—	(899)	663
Pre-tax income	43,599	36,092	27,558	22,893	13,867	5,042	8,387	4,835	5,258
Income taxes	16,568	13,715	9,819	8,765	6,257	2,414	3,332	2,443	1,891
Net income	27,031	22,377	17,739	14,128	7,610	2,628	5,055	2,392	3,367
Earnings per share	$ 1.80	$ 1.50	$ 1.25	$ 1.06	$ .65	$ .23	$ .45	$ .21	$ .30
Average shares	15,000	14,960	14,237	13,382	11,666	11,544	11,256	11,198	11,198
Percentage Increase									
Domestic sales	15.0%	15.0%	9.9%	12.7%	18.9%	9.3%	23.0%	16.1%	—

International sales (including Canada)	18.0	54.0	36.8	21.4	44.5	57.0%	23.2	25.1	—
Sales	16.0%	25.3%	16.0%	14.5%	23.5%	15.7%	23.0%	17.2%	18.3%
Gross profit	18.3	27.1	15.2	20.7	35.1	6.0	23.4	16.9	34.9%
Selling, general, and administrative and goodwill amortization	16.4	26.0	14.6	14.3	23.9	13.1	16.4	13.6	15.0
Operating income	23.0	29.8	16.7	41.1	89.8	−19.0	55.7	34.8	NM
Pre-tax income	20.8	31.0	20.4	65.1	175.0	−39.9	73.5	−8.0	NM
Net income	20.8	26.1	25.6	85.7	189.6	−48.0	111.3	−29.0	NM
Earnings per share	20.5	20.0	18.0	61.8	186.5	−49.3	110.2	−29.0	NM
Gross margin	33.0	32.3	31.9	32.1	30.5	27.9	30.4	30.4	30.5
Selling, general, and administrative ratio	22.8	22.7	22.8	23.2	23.2	23.1	23.7	25.0	25.8
Operating margin	9.9	9.4	9.0	9.0	7.3	4.7	6.8	5.4	4.7
Net margin	6.1	5.8	5.8	5.4	3.3	1.4	3.1	1.8	3.0
Tax rate	38.0%	38.0%	35.6%	38.3%	45.1%	47.9%	39.7%	50.5%	36.0%
Percentage sales international	33.1%	32.6%	26.5%	22.5%	21.2%	18.1%	13.3%	13.3%	12.5%
Research and development				$ 4,518	$ 3,343	$ 3,322	$ 2,992	$ 2,603	$ 2,158
as percent of sales				1.7%	1.5%	1.8%	1.9%	2.0%	1.9%

Note:
1. Earnings Model, 1986–1994.
2. Estimated.

Source: Invacare Corporation reports.

EXHIBIT 30.4

International Sales and Earnings: Invacare Corporation

(Dollar amounts in thousands)

Year	Sales[1]	Percentage of Total	Pretax Profit	Percentage of Total
1992[2]	$79,000	26%	$1,400	5%
1991	59,103	22	1,010	4
1990	48,648	21	838	6
1989	33,702	18	461	9

Notes:

1. Excludes sales and earnings from Poirier in 1992.
2. Estimated.

Source: 1992 Invacare Corporation reports.

provided retirement, vacation, and health and life insurance benefits for its Mexican workers. In addition, it provided food stamps, uniforms, and transportation to and from work for its employees. A nurse and doctor were always available at the plant.

Highly dependent on an ample water supply, Invamex used approximately 68,000 gallons daily in its operations. It received other raw materials from Ohio. Plans called for enlargement of the plant from 78,000 square feet to twice that amount within a three to five year period.

In 1988, the facility produced some 150 wheelchairs per day and employed 136 workers. The company planned to increase production to 180 wheelchairs per day and employment to 200 workers by 1990.

A Major Setback

In 1984, Invacare suffered a major financial setback, posting a loss on sales of $91 million. The main reasons were (1) nonrecurring charges against income, which included an adjustment for inventory carried on the books that the company did not physically have on hand; and (2) recall of a defective product that cost the company an estimated $1.5 million. On the heels of the financial setback, the U.S. government changed its Medicare reimbursement policy, which essentially required wheelchair dealers to sell rather than lease more of their chairs. This change reduced dealers' income because many of the motorized wheelchairs were too expensive for Medicare recipients to buy and too costly for dealers to finance themselves.

By the end of 1985, Invacare had returned to profitability. It had cut costs by reorganizing its divisions and introducing new products that had begun to have an impact in the market. For example, in 1985, Invacare introduced the first power wheelchairs designed specifically for children's use. Until then the industry had offered children's seats fitted on an adult-sized base. Between 1986 and the end of

EXHIBIT 30.5

Executive Officers: Invacare Corporation

Name	Age	Position
A. Malachi Mixon III	51	Chairman of the Board, President, and Chief Executive Officer
Joseph B. Richey II	55	Senior Vice-President and General Manager—North American Operations and a Director
Gerald B. Blouch	45	Chief Financial Officer and Treasurer
A. Chace Anderson	39	Vice-President and General Manager—International Operations
Richard A. Sayers II	40	Vice-President—Human Resources
Louis F. J. Slangen	44	Vice-President—Sales and Marketing
M. Louis Tabickman	47	Vice-President and General Manager—Service and Distribution

Source: Invacare Corporation, *Form 10-K Report* (December 31, 1991).

1992, Invacare's sales grew from about $111 million to more than $305 million. At the same time its earnings increased from $3.4 million to about $17.7 million. Exhibit 30.3 provides comparative balance sheet data for the years 1991 and 1992. Exhibit 30.2 provides financial data for the seven-year period ending December 31, 1992, and estimated earnings for 1993 and 1994.

Structure

Invacare was highly centralized at its headquarters in Elyria, Ohio. The company planned to build a new headquarters office complex in nearby North Ridgeville, Ohio, with more than 300,000 square feet of office space, at an estimated cost of $30 million. The company planned to move to its new location no later than September 1993, when its current lease expired.[4]

The company's current executive officers are its Chief Executive Officer, Senior Vice-President and General Manager of North American Operations, Chief Financial Officer, Vice-President and General Manager of International Operations, Vice-President of Human Resources, Vice-President of Sales and Marketing, and Vice-President and General Manager of Service and Distribution. Exhibit 30.5 lists the executive officers.

Invacare's manufacturing plants were headed by a plant manager, and each plant's financial and cost accounting functions were headed by a local controller, who along with the plant manager was responsible for local budgeting. The distribution centers also were headed by a local manager. Inventory and distribution controls were the responsibility of both the manager and the local controller, who performed functions similar to those of the manufacturing plant controller in terms of budgeting. The company supposedly utilized just-in-time (JIT) inventory controls, but plants still maintained a 30–45 day inventory stock. As of December

31, 1991, the company had 11 manufacturing plants and 28 warehouse and distribution centers throughout the world. During 1992, the company reorganized its worldwide distribution centers to minimize costs, leaving it with 22 distribution centers as of December 31, 1992.

As of December 31, 1991, the company had 2,440 employees. Although Invacare had managed to work successfully with its employees and had no unions to contend with in the United States, its European labor force was well organized. Invacare had had little interference from European labor unions primarily because of the sluggish worldwide economy. However, future labor negotiations may determine how successfully Invacare can continue to perform in the European market.

Invacare issued annual audited consolidated financial statements in accordance with Securities and Exchange Commission (SEC) regulations. All accounting data were compiled through an on-line computer networking system, with current information provided to users as soon as the transmitted information was compiled. Consolidated financial statements included the accounts of Invacare Corporation and its subsidiaries, with European subsidiaries consolidated on a November 30 fiscal year end, and intracompany transactions eliminated. Substantially all the assets and liabilities of the company's foreign subsidiaries were translated to U.S. dollars at year-end exchange rates.[5]

Products

Invacare manufactures and distributes prescription power and manual wheelchairs, standard wheelchairs, respiratory equipment, hospital-type beds for the home, patient aids, motorized scooters, and other home health care and extended care equipment. It had manufacturing locations in Ohio, Florida, Texas, California, Canada, Mexico, the United Kingdom, Germany, and France. A worldwide network of more than 10,000 medical equipment dealers, including more than 3,500 domestic dealers, handled its products.

One key to Invacare's success over the past 12 years had been its commitment to product development and technological improvements. In 1991, the company introduced some 75 new products or enhancements of existing products in the United States. However, in 1992, Invacare introduced only 26 new products or enhancements owing to product design and manufacturing delays. Research and development (R&D) expenditures had been running at about 2% of sales, and in 1991, they totaled approximately $4.5 million. The number two manufacturer of home health care products was Sunrise Medical, with worldwide sales of about $185 million.

Wheelchairs represented about 61% of Invacare's total annual sales in 1992. Older people, who usually were reimbursed by Medicare, generally purchased standard wheelchairs. They were regarded as a commodity item and were therefore price-driven. In general, the price range was from about $350 to $1,000. Power wheelchairs were Invacare's most attractive product line, and the company led the U.S. market with more than a 50% share. People with severe disabilities purchased power wheelchairs. Typical users were quadrapalegics who had some motor skills in at least one arm and could manipulate a joystick to accelerate, turn, and stop the wheelchair. For those who didn't have enough arm control to operate a joystick, more sophisticated "sip and puff" breath controls were available. Invacare was the only manufacturer who designed and manufactured its own controllers (electronic microprocessors that control wheelchair movements). In May 1991, Invacare had begun manufacturing its ACTION line of wheelchairs. These ultralight wheelchairs were the second-fastest growing segment of the market. Ultralight wheelchairs were generally purchased by younger, active users with permanent disabilities who wanted to participate in sports or other types of social activities requiring great mobility. They generally were made of aluminum, but the latest advances in materials enabled the production of carbon composite frames, which were even lighter.

Invacare's home health beds accounted for about 12% of the company's total annual sales in 1992. They were specifically designed to aid persons with disabilities that prohibited or limited their movement. In this regard Invacare was utilizing the latest advances in seating and cushions of its Canadian subsidiary, Posture and Seating Centre, Inc.

Invacare's respiratory equipment accounted for about 16% of the company's total annual sales in 1992. Until then, Invacare had sold only oxygen concentrators, a $150 million market. During 1992, the company introduced an expanded line of respiratory equipment and accessories, including nebulizers and aspirators. With the acquisition of Perry Oxygen Systems, Invacare introduced its liquid oxygen line, placing it in a market of $450 million of annual sales. Most patients using respiratory products were elderly, so sales depended heavily on Medicare reimbursement.

Invacare's other products fell into a general category of patient aids, which accounted for about 14% of the company's total sales in 1992. These products included walkers, crutches, commodes, bath rails, patient lifts, traction equipment, standard and power recliner chairs, and other home health aids. Most patient aid products were regarded as commodities.[6] Exhibit 30.6 illustrates the sales mix by product line.

Distribution

Soon after the Mixon group acquired Invacare, marketing of its products became a priority. In a competitive field dominated by Everest and Jennings, Mixon's strategy was to become dealer-oriented. That is, in an industry influenced not so much by a doctor, but rather by a therapist or the dealer, Mixon began a strategy to win over dealers. In the early years, contact and product orientation was about all they could offer dealers because of the high costs of the leveraged buyout, so the company stockpiled inventory. In 1984, when the first public stock offering was completed successfully, Invacare had the capital needed to begin implementing its dealer strategy. The company aggressively offered dealers prepaid freight, 48-hour delivery, cheap financing, money for cooperative advertising, and volume discounts. Dealers quickly became familiar with and began offering Invacare's products because of these financing, discount, and other incentives. By 1992, Invacare had 22 distribu-

EXHIBIT 30.6 **Product Line and Sales Makeup: Invacare Corporation**

THEN AND NOW: A COMPARISON

A group of investors including Mr. Mixon and several board members purchased Invacare from Johnson & Johnson in 1979 and have expanded the company considerably since that time. The following chart details the company's remarkable progress. Invacare became a public company in 1984.

	1979	1991
Annual Sales	$19.5 million	$263.2 million
Shareholders' Equity	$1.5 million	$86.7 million
Product Offering	Standard wheelchairs, limited patient aids	World's broadest line of home medical equipment
International Business	None	22.5% of sales
Public Market Valuation at year-end, December 31	NA	$380.9 million

Sales Mix

- Rehabilitation wheelchairs, 1
- Standard wheelchairs, 2
- Patient aids and beds, 3
- Respiratory, 4
- International, 5
- Distributed products, 6
- Other, 7

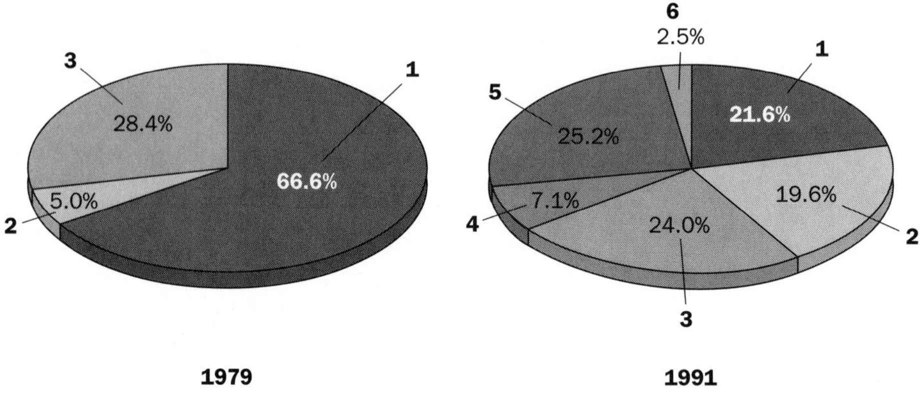

Source: 1992 Invacare Corporation reports.

tion centers worldwide, which were served by 150 company salespersons, 24 telemarketing employees, and four independent representative organizations.[7]

One-Stop Shopping Plus

Invacare's basic product strategy was simple: offer the most attractive products available to home medical equipment dealers. Invacare became known for its one-stop shopping marketing strategy. It was the only manufacturer committed to being the single source of supply for the approximately 3,500 home health care and medical equipment dealers in the United States. By 1992, Invacare distributed approximately 85% of what dealers needed. In 1992, it began its One-Stop Shopping Plus program, which provided discounts to dealers as sales of Invacare products exceed 65% of their total sales. As dealers move past the 65% break point, the program amounts to an exclusive distribution agreement with Invacare for that dealer in their market areas. The company soon had signed up 100 dealers for the program. By showing a concern for the dealers' bottom lines, Invacare had built and enjoyed a continued loyalty from many dealers. This strategy had pushed product lines that can be sold on the basis of value (standard wheelchairs, beds, etc.) rather than on the basis of premium price and quality (ultralight wheelchairs, highly complex motorized wheelchairs, etc.). Invacare also began an advertising campaign in 1992 to create a "pull" demand from end-users and clinical professionals such as therapists.

Competition

Domestic

The home health care industry was quickly becoming a sector of the haves and have nots. Former giants such as Everest and Jennings International, continued to struggle and lose market share, whereas small manufacturers suffered from lack of distribution as dealers remained cautious about dealing with companies they were not sure would survive.

A large portion of Invacare's market share success had come at the expense of Everest and Jennings, which once controlled about 85% of the total wheelchair market. Everest and Jennings continued to suffer operating losses, but its brand name retained a strong following, and its bed business (Smith and Davis) remained profitable. Everest and Jennings had recently restructured its debt, but financial difficulties continued to loom as it suffered losses of about $120 million in the period 1988–1991 (and about $8 million in 1992). Even though Everest and Jennings began matching Invacare's prices in 1985 and an all out price war erupted in 1989, Everest and Jennings's response to Invacare was late in coming. The price war drove Invacare's net margin to less than 1% in the wheelchair market in the second quarter of 1989, but its competitor was pushed to the verge of bankruptcy.

The most significant challenge facing Invacare over the next several years will come from the second largest manufacturer of wheelchairs: Sunrise Medical, a California-based subsidiary of Hoyer International, a Japanese manufacturer of home health care products. Sunrise had been very successful in the manual ultralight wheelchair market. Invacare itself entered this market in May of 1991 with the introduction of its ACTION wheelchair line. Sunrise Medical, in 1992, had over 60% of the ultralight wheelchair market in the United States. Sunrise also competed with Invacare on other home health care products (such as beds); but it concentrated primarily on the domestic market it then controlled—ultralight wheelchairs—and wasn't viewed as a serious competitor in areas other than wheelchairs and patient aids. Invacare had over 50% of the U.S. home health care market, with Sunrise holding a 30% domestic market share of patient aids (crutches, canes, walkers, commodes, patient lifts, etc.) compared to Invacare's approximately 20% share.

In the area of domestic respiratory equipment sales, Puritan-Bennett and DeVilbiss held over 40% of the market. Invacare was a relative newcomer and had only about 8% of the market. With the acquisition of Perry Oxygen Systems (See Exhibit 30.1, p. 1087), Invacare should be able to gain market share in a product line that had about $150 million in domestic sales.[8]

International

Invacare continued to make huge inroads into the European home health care industry. With the acquisition of Poirier S.A. in 1992, Invacare became the second largest competitor in the home health care industry behind German-based giant Meyra, a privately held company. Exhibit 30.4 summarizes Invacare's international sales and earnings for 1992, excluding those of Poirier, which was acquired that year. However, with the exception of Sunrise (about $100 million in 1992 sales in Europe), most of Invacare's European competition focused on their local markets. Invacare was establishing a manufacturing and distribution system that would allow it to compete across the continent. Sunrise Medical also was aggressively establishing itself in Europe by acquiring several European home health care manufacturers.

Poirier S.A., France's largest home health care product manufacturer, sold products similar to Invacare's. Poirier's sales mix was roughly 40% standard wheelchairs, 40% rehabilitation wheelchairs, and 20% patient aids, including beds. Invacare's German subsidiary (Gunter-Meier) also was capturing market shares from both Meyra and the second largest German home health care manufacturer, Ortopedia. Invacare had capitalized on Meyra's and Ortopedia's reluctance to manufacture low-cost wheelchairs and other patient aids. (Meyra recently acquired Ortopedia and will become an even more formidable competitor.)

In Canada, Invacare's competitors were small and generally operated regionally rather than nationally. It sold the wheelchair products manufactured in Mexico in both the United States and Canada. With the ability to manufacture low-cost wheelchairs in Mexico, Invacare should continue to dominate the standard wheelchair market, of which it had over a 60% domestic share. Exhibit 30.7 identifies the major wheelchair products by manufacturer.

Mixon recently stated that "he isn't about to let Quickie [a subsidiary of Sunrise] do to him [Invacare] what he did to Everest and Jennings." In a recent advertisement, Invacare pokes fun at its competitor by stating, "Why settle for a Quickie? Get Real ACTION!"[9]

Government Regulation

Invacare received no revenues directly from Medicare or Medicaid, but typical home medical equipment dealers generate 40%–50% of their revenues from Medicare and Medicaid sales. Changes in Medicare and Medicaid budgets would affect sales and Invacare's earnings. One of the proposed cuts in President Clin-

EXHIBIT 30.7

Wheelchair Competition

Invacare	Everest and Jennings	Hoyer	Theradyne	Gendron
World Chair (current)	Traveler	2000	Maxim "Max"	Regency Transporter 5825
1000 E	Vista	1000	Maxim "Mac"	Economy 8555
1000	Traveler	2000	Maxim "Max"	Regency Transporter 5825
1000 Hemi	Universal	NA	Maxim "Hemi"	Lowboy Hemi
World Chair (economy)	Vista	1000	Maxim "Mac"	Economy 8555
2000 Series	E-Z-Lite	(Sunrise) Quickie Breezy	Envoy	2058 QR
9000 Series	Premier 2	(Sunrise) Quickie RX	Venture	Sportlite 4000
2000 LT	Premier 2	(Sunrise) Quickie Breezy	Thunderbird	2058 QR
4000 Series	Universal	NA	Envoy	X2 Series

Source: 1992 Invacare Corporation reports.

ton's economic plan specified a $75 million cut in domestic home health care spending in 1994. However, the proposed cuts focus on perceived program abuses, as in home infusion therapy, parenteral and enteral equipment, prosthetics, and orthotics—all areas in which Invacare was not involved. The White House Task Force on Health Care Reform recently stated that a goal of the new long-term care program is to shift spending from nursing homes to community-based services that provide medical care and other types of assistance to people living in their own homes. This policy should certainly enhance the sales of home health care products. Furthermore, successfully extending health care benefits to the estimated 35 million working but uninsured people in the United States would greatly expand the market for home health care products.[10]

Outlook

One of the reasons for Invacare's success has been its strong emphasis on quality control, which began in earnest shortly after J. B. Richey joined the company. Sales representatives were asked to prepare monthly reports detailing complaints about Invacare's products. Armed with those results, management was able to begin correcting problems during the manufacturing process. At the same time, Invacare began to educate its employees in statistical process control methods, and

EXHIBIT 30.8

Products and Related Home Care Services: Invacare Corporation
(Dollar amounts in millions)

Market Segment	Revenue 1991	Revenue 1986	Average Annual Growth
Respiratory therapy, equipment and gas	$ 556	$ 350	10%
Durable medical equipment	435	285	9
Pressure sore products	95	58	10
Apnea monitors	21	12	12
Parenteral and enteral nutrition products	924	415	17
Home antibiotic and chemotherapy	181	46	32
Renal dialysis supplies and services	616	348	12
Incontinence products	425	311	6
Ostomy products	336	252	6
Transcutaneous electronic nerve stimulators	80	44	12
Total	$3,669	$2,123	9%

Source: 1992 Invacare Corporation reports.

its representatives regularly began to visit suppliers' plants to check their quality controls. Largely as a result of these measures, Invacare reduced the rejection rate of its parts to only 1%–2%. The goal, says Richey, is to be able to measure rejection rates in parts per million, as many Japanese companies now do.

Mixon recently stated in his annual report to shareholders:

> The long-term outlook for home health care is excellent. Recent meetings between industry representatives and the White House Task Force on Health Care Reform indicated that the Clinton administration views home care as a cost-effective alternative to institutional care. In fact, at his pre-inaugural economic summit, President Clinton said, "Let's keep in-home services. . . . We can serve more people at lower cost even if we have to cut back a little on what we're doing institutionally." Invacare will be a clear beneficiary of this policy.[11]

The company has enjoyed tremendous growth. In 1992, its sales exceeded 1991 sales by 16%, while its earnings rose more than 26%.[12] The National Association of Home Care projects that growth rates for products and related home care services will rise an average of 9% per year for the five years commencing in 1992. Exhibit 30.8 summarizes the projected growth rates for specific product lines. Baird Corporation estimates that revenue growth will continue at about 15%, with earnings growth at about 20% over the next several years.

Mixon believed that the company's success was the result of the strategy it had followed since 1979.

1. Offer the industry's broadest product line.
2. Provide the highest levels of customer service in the industry.

3. Enhance the industry's most extensive warehouse and distribution network and build supporting systems to increase its efficiency.
4. Continue to build on the dealer orientation policy as well as enhance consumer demand through marketing programs.
5. Maintain industry's most productive sales force.
6. Lead in product development.
7. Maintain costs at a minimum to yield the lowest cost to the consumer.
8. And above all, never lose touch with your customer.

Mixon stated in a recent *Forbes* article that "Everest and Jennings International had [had] over 80% of the wheelchair market, but they were arrogant and had lost touch with the customer." This is a failing that Mixon vows never to let happen to Invacare.

Mixon must fly to Washington, D.C., next week to give expert testimony before a congressional committee concerning the home medical equipment industry. What, he mused, should be his next move to win the Malcolm Baldridge National Quality Award as he continues his lobbying efforts?

Notes

1. Jeffrey Bendix, "Invacare Rolls to #1," *Cleveland Enterprise,* Case Western Reserve University (Spring 1991).
2. A. Malachi Mixon III, *Medical Industry Executive* (March 1993), p. 28.
3. Invacare Corporation, *1991 Annual Report;* Invacare Corporation, *1992 Consolidated Financial Statements.*
4. Chris Thomas, "Cities Courting Invacare to Win Headquarters," *Crain's Cleveland Business* (August 12, 1991), 12(32), p. 2.
5. Invacare Corporation, *1991 Annual Report.*
6. Peter H. Emch, "Health Care Research" (Milwaukee: Robert W. Baird & Company, Inc., March 10, 1993), p. 13.
7. Christopher Palmeri, "Wheel to Wheel Combat," *Forbes* (February 15, 1993), 51(4), pp. 62–64.
8. Emch, "Health Care Research."
9. Ibid.
10. Malachi A. Mixon, "A Partial Solution to the Nation's Problems with Health Care Costs," Speech given at Case Western University (October 23, 1992).
11. Invacare Corporation, *1991 Annual Report.*
12. "Invacare Reports Record Fourth Quarter Earnings on 24 Percent Sales Gain," *News from Invacare* (February 18, 1993), pp. 1–2.

References

Jerry H. Dombcik, "Invacare Corporation—Earnings Review and Estimate Revision." (Cleveland: McDonald & Company Securities, Inc., Equity Research Department, February 22, 1993), p. 5.

"Forbes Names Invacare to 200 Best Small Companies List," *News from Invacare* (Elyria, Ohio: Invacare Corporation, November 4, 1992), p. 1.

Brenda Hayslett, Human Resources, Invacare Corporation, Telephone interview (April 12, 1993).

"Invacare Acquires Canadian Firm," *Wall Street Journal* (November 5, 1991), p. A-20.

"Invacare Adds 'Top End' to Action Wheelchair Line," *News from Invacare* (Elyria, Ohio: Invacare Corporation, March 4, 1993), p. 2.

"Invacare Buys Canadian Concern," *Wall Street Journal* (October 11, 1991), p. B-6.

"Invacare Completes Poirier Acquisitions," *News from Invacare* (Elyria, Ohio: Invacare Corporation, October 15, 1992), p. 1.

"Invacare Corporation," *Wall Street Journal* (July 23, 1991), p. B-9.

Invacare Corporation, *Form 10-K Report* (February 20, 1992), p. 34.

Invacare Corporation, *Form 10-Q Report* (November 3, 1992), p. 9.

Invacare Corporation, 1992 Consolidated Financial Statements.

"Invacare Corporation—Perry Oxygen Systems," *Wall Street Journal* (August 10, 1992), p. C-6.

"Invacare's Support of Wheelchair Basketball Helps Slam-Dunk Outdated Perceptions," *News from Invacare* (Elyria, Ohio: Invacare Corporation, December 3, 1992), p. 2.

Javier Ledesma, Controller, Reynosa plant, Invacare Corporation, Personal interview (April 5, 1993).

Lynn D. Malkes, "Recommendation: Buy Progress Report" (Detroit: Roney & Co., Investment Research, March 10, 1993), p. 2.

Malachi A. Mixon, "The Invacare Story." (July 1989).

Ellen Paris, "The Perils of Being Too Successful." *Forbes* (February 9, 1987), 139(3), p. 2.

Dan Shingler, "Invacare's Record Earnings in '90 a 183% Boost from '89," *Crain's Cleveland Business* (March 4, 1991), 12(9), p. 23.

Dan Shingler, "It's the Midas Touch," *Crain's Cleveland Business* (October 21, 1991), 12(42), p. 17.

"Wheelchair Undergoes Streamline Makeover," *Wall Street Journal* (May 1, 1991), p. B-1.

McDonnell Douglas Corporation's Transport Aircraft Business: Focus on the Commercial Aircraft Industry

Michael De Luz

Introduction

John F. McDonnell liked to tell people that his favorite place in which to reflect was a 12-foot by 12-foot turret that he had built on the top of his St. Louis, Missouri, home. The glass-enclosed enclave's furnishings were but a single lawn chair and an $89 telescope, from which he could sit and gaze at the stars.[1] Away from the turret, many interested individuals hoped that John McDonnell's managerial vision would guide the firm he was leading—McDonnell Douglas Corporation (MDC)—toward an apogee of its own.

At the outset of 1991, as the second full year of his tenure as Chief Executive Officer came to a close, John McDonnell faced a major challenge. His corporation's basic objective was clear: to be the world's leading aerospace firm. From his corporate-level perspective, the long-term outlook for the firm's most lucrative products appeared to be extremely cloudy. The combat aircraft business historically had contributed approximately two-thirds of the corporation's total sales revenue, but the thawing of cold war tensions with the Soviet Union led analysts to forecast that demand for combat jets would decline throughout the upcoming decade.

In contrast, the second main business of McDonnell Douglas—commercial aircraft—had experienced surging demand for years. Total aircraft orders increased dramatically from the mid 1980s to the middle of 1990. The increase was so steep that production could not meet global demand, and an enormous backlog ensued. McDonnell Douglas's commercial aircraft backlog was $25.8 billion and the company's total backlog was $52.8 billion in 1990 (see Exhibit 31.1). The backlog figure was even higher for its chief rivals. Record commercial sales of $5.8 billion had been reached during 1990,[2] an increase of 29% from the previous year (see Exhibit 31.2). In addition, McDonnell Douglas's market share of aircraft deliveries had risen to 21%, in second place behind industry-leader Boeing (see Exhibit 31.3). However, concerning future orders that were placed during 1990, market share tumbled to just 14%, well behind that of Boeing and Europe's Airbus Industrie. Analysts wondered whether McDonnell Douglas had a coherent, stable strategy that would guide its efforts. A particularly crucial question involved McDonnell Douglas's ability to compete in the long run while addressing only a limited segment of potential aircraft buyers. Just months into his tenure as CEO, referring to the commercial aircraft business, John McDonnell had re-

This case was prepared by Michael De Luz, who is a doctoral student candidate at Florida International University. Copyright © 1992 by Michael De Luz. This case was edited by T. L. Wheelen and J. D. Hunger for this book. Reprinted by permission of the author.

EXHIBIT 31.1 MDC Commercial Aircraft Backlog

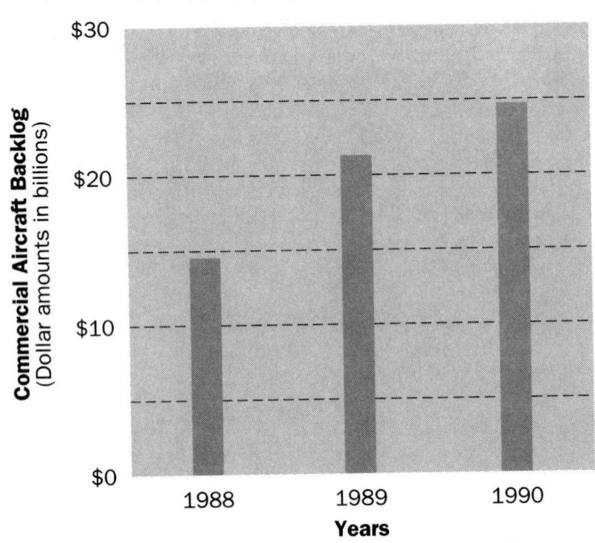

Source: McDonnell Douglas Corporation, *1990 Annual Report,* p. 30.

marked, "In the short-term I'm not worried about our business. But in the long run it's a tough strategic situation against much larger competitors with full product lines."[3]

To achieve its announced objectives, was it necessary for McDonnell Douglas to widen its product range to the same extent as its rivals? And to help meet this daunting challenge, would a partnership or joint venture with a foreign aerospace firm be necessary? Or would the enormous costs involved in such an expansion prohibit potential profits and thus force a dramatic downscaling of the McDonnell Douglas corporate mission?

As he contemplated his second full year as Chairman and CEO of the world's second largest commercial aircraft manufacturer, John McDonnell might well be reflecting in his turret, his eyes on the stars and his mind conceptualizing another vision, one oriented toward the long-term viability of his company.

History

McDonnell Douglas was born McDonnell Aircraft Corporation, the brainchild of James S. McDonnell. The year was 1939 and the city was St. Louis, Missouri, in the heartland of the United States. The key products manufactured in the beginning decades were combat aircraft—fighter jets especially—designed to pounce on enemy planes and deliver devastating missiles.

The company founder, known simply as "Mr. Mac," was a brilliant engineer with an autocratic leadership style. The catalyst of the firm's growth was the constant innovation in combat aircraft, due largely to his aerospace engineering ex-

EXHIBIT 31.2

Financial Highlights: McDonnell Douglas Corporation and Its Industrial Segments
(Dollar amounts in millions, except per share data)

Years Ending December 31	1990	1989
Revenues	$16,255	$14,589
Net earnings	$ 306[1]	$ 219[2]
Earnings per share	$ 7.99[1]	$ 5.72[2]
Dividends paid per share	$ 2.82	$ 2.755
As of December 31		
Debt-to-equity ratios		
Aerospace and other segments	.95	.88
Financial services segment	6.55	6.82
Firm backlog	$36,544	$32,531
Total backlog	$52,770	$50,230
Shareholders' equity per share	$ 91.72	$ 85.88
Personnel	121,190	127,926
Summary of Revenues by Industry Segment		
Combat aircraft	$ 5,830	$ 6,124[3]
Transport aircraft	5,812	4,511[3]
Missiles, space, and electronic systems	3,188	2,761[3]
Financial services	619	497
Other and nonoperating income	806	696
Total	$16,255	$14,589
Operating Earnings (Loss) from Continuing Operations		
Combat aircraft	$ 46	$ 207[3]
Transport aircraft	(177)	(167)[3]
Missiles, space, and electronic systems	167	116[3]
Financial services	100	77
Other	49	17
Total	$ 185	$ 250

Notes:
1. Includes $376 million, or $9.82 per share, from pension settlement.
2. Includes the cumulative effect of an accounting change of $179 million, or $4.68 per share.
3. Restated.

Source: McDonnell Douglas Corporation, *1990 Annual Report,* p. 1.

pertise. However, the rate of innovations eventually slowed considerably, and Mr. Mac looked toward a merger to expand the firm's product line.

This corporate expansion came in 1967 as McDonnell Aircraft merged with Douglas Aircraft to become McDonnell Douglas. Douglas Aircraft had been the leader of the then-fledgling commercial aircraft market until the Boeing Aircraft Corporation introduced the advanced technology passenger jet in 1952.[4] The

EXHIBIT 31.3 **Market Share of Commercial Aircraft Deliveries**

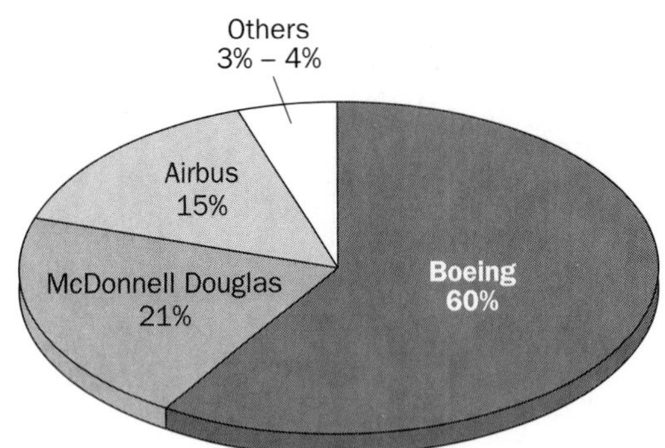

Source: McDonnell Douglas Corporation, *1990 Annual Report,* p. 13.

"Douglas Commercial" propeller-driven plane soon relinquished its industry-leader role and could not regain it. Eventually, Douglas Aircraft was unable to fill orders for new planes owing to inefficiency.

After the merger, the firm was restructured into five distinct sections. The largest was the original combat aircraft segment, which would account for approximately two-thirds to three-quarters of total corporate revenues. The newly acquired commercial aircraft section was second in size, in terms of sales volume. Also included in this strategic business unit were military transport aircraft built for specific noncombat missions; subsequently, the section became known as the "transport aircraft" division. A third strategic business unit focused on the manufacture of missiles carried by the combat jets and, later, the development of space systems. A fourth section, financial services, had been established prior to the merger and had grown steadily through the years. The fifth section was referred to as containing "other" operations, such as information systems and community service.

After the merger, Mr. Mac retained his CEO position and kept a tight grasp on decision making. Even after he promoted his nephew Sanford ("Sandy") McDonnell to Chief Executive Officer, he retained ultimate authority. Although the original combat aircraft section continued to produce the acknowledged world-premier fighter jet—the F-15 Eagle—and several others, the transport aircraft division did not introduce a single new aircraft.

In 1980, the year after Mr. Mac died at age 81, Sandy McDonnell faced his first crucial decision regarding the future of commercial aircraft production by the transport aircraft division. A dissident group of executives believed that commercial aircraft manufacturing should be abandoned; a price war with Lockheed in the early 1980s had forced Lockheed from the passenger aircraft market, but simultaneously had drastically reduced the profitability of McDonnell Douglas's commercial aircraft operation. Arguing in favor of remaining in the passenger aircraft industry, another set of executives sharply disagreed and proposed expanding the existing line. They proposed additional aircraft models to supplement the

EXHIBIT 31.4

Commercial Aircraft Top Management Team (Key Members): McDonnell Douglas Corporation

Executive	Age	Current Position
J. F. McDonnell	51	MDC Chairman and Chief Executive Officer since March 1988.
H. J. Lanese	44	MDC Senior Vice-President—Finance since December 1989.
J. S. McDonnell	53	Senior Vice-President since February, 1989. Background in Human Resources/Employee Relations.
R. H. Hood	57	President of Douglas Aircraft Company (DAC) since January 1989.
J. P. Capellupo	55	Deputy President of DAC since January 1990.

Source: McDonnell Douglas Corporation, *1990 Annual Report*, p. 49.

DC-9 medium-range planes and long-range DC-10s. To these managers, the objective of the McDonnell Douglas commercial aircraft section should have been to compete in all niches with industry-leader Boeing.

After weighing both sides of the issue, Sandy McDonnell resisted the divergent pressures and steered a conservative middle course that included retooling and modification of the two existing models. During his tenure, the company incrementally enhanced the process of commercial aircraft production. With his engineering orientation, McDonnell emphasized internal improvements; outside the plant door a series of threats loomed. In 1988, he shifted to the position of Chairman of the McDonnell Douglas Board of Directors (see Exhibit 31.4). As the CEO torch passed to 50-year-old John McDonnell—son of the late founder—the time had come for the top management team to scan the environment more closely, assess threats and opportunities, and develop effective responses.

John McDonnell was a 26-year veteran of McDonnell Douglas at the time of his promotion to CEO in March 1988. With an MBA from Washington University, and a solid aeronautical engineering education, his background was very similar to that of Boeing's CEO, Frank Schrontz. For McDonnell Douglas, going into what promised to be a turbulent new decade, insiders believed that MBA-style strategic thinking could be a catalyst toward sustained satisfactory performance.

Financial Data

After starting the decade with a loss of $144 million, McDonnell Douglas's transport aircraft business had recouped to post substantial earnings driven by a consistent increase in sales.[5] By 1990 revenues earned by the transport aircraft division exceeded $5.8 billion, by far a record for any year. However, 1990 net operating earnings declined to –$177 million (see Exhibit 31.5).

Further analysis revealed underlying threats to the profitability of the industry itself. At the corporate level, McDonnell Douglas's earnings as a percentage of revenue stood at a mere 1.9%. Exhibits 31.6, 31.7, and 31.8 show corporate financial performance. For a high-technology company employing expertly skilled

Earnings of the Transport Aircraft Division, 1984–1990: McDonnell Douglas Corporation

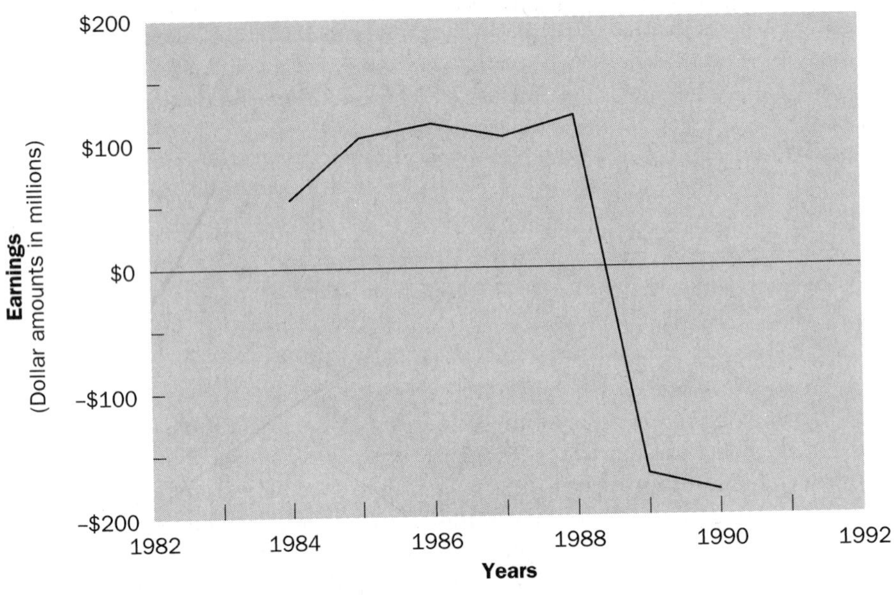

Source: *Aviation Week and Space Technology* (October 30, 1989), p. 17; McDonnell Douglas Corporation, *1990 Annual Report,* p. 1.

engineers and highly trained factory employees, this figure might have seemed low to some observers. Boeing's earnings margin was somewhat higher, or about 5% in 1990. (Both of these ratios include combat operations sections, typically more profitable than commercial divisions.) Although Airbus did not divulge its financial data, its own executives admitted that the consortium had yet to become profitable. Thus the earnings ratios for the entire commercial aircraft industry ranged from slim to none.

In a general discussion of the company's financial situation, the CEO stated that specific actions to remedy these problems had, in and of themselves, precluded immediate financial relief. He anticipated that costs of shifting and retraining assembly workers, upgrading and investing in the manufacturing process, and installing more sophisticated supplier communications networks would have a negative short-term impact on earnings for the commercial aircraft operation.

McDonnell Douglas's corporate debt continued to be a cause for concern as the company financed product development by increased borrowing. For example, corporate repayment of long-term debt, at $527 million, far exceeded the net earnings from continuing operations in 1989. The severity of the predicament caused Moody's Investor Service to lower its rating of McDonnell Douglas's long-term debt to just slightly above rock bottom.[6]

EXHIBIT 31.6

Five-Year Consolidated Financial Summary: McDonnell Douglas Corporation
(Dollar amounts in millions, except per share data)

Years Ending December 31	1990	1989	1988	1987	1986
A. SUMMARY OF OPERATIONS					
Revenues by industry segment					
Combat aircraft	$ 5,830	$ 6,124	$ 6,288	$ 6,190	$ 5,988
Transport aircraft	5,812	4,511	4,637	3,682	3,554
Missiles, space, and electronic systems	3,188	2,761	2,390	2,176	2,040
Financial services	619	497	449	377	31
Other	797	688	671	655	613
Operating revenues	16,246	14,581	14,435	13,080	12,505
Earnings (loss) from continuing operations	275	(37)	372	347	310
Per share	7.18	(.97)	9.70	8.59	7.66
Net earnings	306	219	350	313	277
Per share	7.99	5.72	9.13	7.75	6.86
As a percent of revenues	1.9%	1.5%	2.4%	2.4%	2.2%
As a percent of beginning equity	9.3%	6.9%	11.8%	11.0%	10.5%
Research and development	620	617	562	604	463
Interest expense					
Aerospace and other segments	380	366	194	129	102
Financial services segment	233	198	145	113	105
Income taxes (benefit)	127	(83)	167	162	233
Cash dividends declared	108	108	98	94	84
Per share	2.82	2.82	2.56	2.32	2.08
B. BALANCE SHEET INFORMATION					
Receivables and property on lease	$ 4,410	$ 4,623	$ 3,988	$ 3,513	$ 3,264
Contracts in process and inventories	6,201	5,128	4,244	3,712	3,210
Property, plant, and equipment	2,624	2,648	2,426	2,190	1,882
Total assets	14,965	13,397	11,783	10,523	9,423
Notes payable and long-term debt					
Aerospace and other segments	2,970	2,597	1,856	1,613	992
Financial services segment	2,614	2,338	1,770	1,464	1,096
Shareholders' equity	3,514	3,287	3,186	2,970	2,845
Per share	91.72	85.88	83.42	76.71	70.13
Debt-to-equity ratios					
Aerospace and other segments	.95	.88	.64	.60	.38
Financial services segment	6.55	6.82	5.92	5.25	4.72

(continued)

Five-Year Consolidated Financial Summary: McDonnell Douglas Corporation *(continued)*
(Dollar amounts in millions, except per share data)

Years Ending December 31	1990	1989	1988	1987	1986
C. GENERAL INFORMATION					
Shares outstanding (in millions)	38.3	38.3	38.2	38.7	40.6
Shareholders of record	37,662	33,237	34,310	35,354	37,525
Personnel	121,190	127,926	121,421	112,400	105,696
Salaries and wages	$ 5,300	$ 4,969	$ 4,399	$ 3,913	$ 3,561
Firm backlog	$36,544	$32,531	$26,351	$18,890	$16,512
Total backlog	$52,770	$50,230	$40,492	$33,102	$28,419

Source: McDonnell Douglas Corporation, *1990 Annual Report,* p. 48.

Much of the debt incurred financed technological developments for the new MD-11 tri-engine jet, estimated to have cost approximately $700 million. The company utilized other loans to expand production of the MD-80 model. McDonnell Douglas's top management pointed to operational investments such as these as the reason for the transport aircraft division's operating loss in 1990.

Key Products

McDonnell Douglas's combat aircraft models historically had earned substantially higher margins than those built by the transport aircraft division. Because of such performance differences, John McDonnell was frank about the potential effects of shifting the firm's emphasis from military to commercial production. Concerning the profitability of nonmilitary goods, in early 1990 he admitted:

> The shift from military to commercial in the McDonnell Douglas product mix does not favor our traditional strength. . . . We must learn to hit for a higher average in what has been, for many years, the weaker side of our business.[7]

McDonnell then reiterated his determination to ensure that the commercial aircraft manufactured by McDonnell Douglas would remain viable competitors. With operating earnings from combat aircraft falling and orders for commercial aircraft then accelerating, the CEO's statements appeared to reflect a realistic assessment of shifts in the external environment.

Transport Aircraft Division

The transport aircraft division had first become profitable in 1984, when it contributed 21% of McDonnell Douglas's total sales. By 1990, it accounted for 35.8% of the firm's sales volume. The product line eventually consisted of two commercial aircraft models and one military cargo plane.

Commercial Aircraft

The company's commercial aircraft products consisted of only two aircraft and targeted broad market segments. Each of the two was one generation more advanced than the earlier Douglas commercial aircraft.

MD-80/MD-90 Initially designed in 1983, the narrow-body MD-80 by 1990 competed head-to-head with certain versions of Boeing's 737 and the Airbus A-320. Demand was strong from the beginning for the $25 million plane, and the MD-80 was being produced at the rate of 3.0 aircraft per week. Unfortunately for McDonnell Douglas, this production rate left an enormous volume of orders unfilled. The backlog began to slow, however, as rising fuel costs and weakening passenger traffic caused airlines to restrain purchasing during the second half of 1990.

Company executives had not foreseen the huge increase in demand from 1985 to 1990. The throughput of assembly materials being transformed at the Long Beach, California, facility had increased 100% during a four-year period in the late 1980s. Internal as well as external production units were hard-pressed to fill the enormous volume of orders received. Although the MD-80 captured 15% of its market, McDonnell Douglas executives lamented that this figure could have been augmented substantially if the assembly process had been accelerated.[8] McDonnell Douglas's rivals guaranteed delivery of their aircraft before 1995, but McDonnell Douglas did not have matching production capabilities.

A derivative of the MD-80 prototype, the MD-90 design addressed airline purchasers' demands for improved fuel efficiency and reduced noise. In early 1990, a 50-plane order from Delta Airlines officially launched McDonnell Douglas's latest entry into the mid-sized commercial jet market. Several other buyers soon reserved substantial numbers of the MD-90. With only slight structural modifications in its direct predecessor, the 158-seat MD-90 also had begun competing in the same market as the Airbus A-320 and Boeing's 737.

MD-11 In 1988, the company introduced a 300-plus seat modified DC-10 wide-body, the MD-11, to an initially enthusiastic response. The first major customer, Delta Airlines, selected the $100 million MD-11 over its competitor from Airbus (the A-340). Once the door had been opened by this initial sale, American Airlines followed suit, placing a large order. American Airlines planned to use the long-range jets to serve its lucrative and expanding Pacific routes.

After a costly and time-consuming process, the MD-11 earned Federal Aviation Administration (FAA) certification in November 1990. Within weeks, the company had delivered MD-11s to customers in Finland, Japan, and the United States.

The MD-11 accommodated airline strategists' demands for planes that could travel long distances but carry fewer passengers than a Boeing 747. These "long thin" aircraft were narrower and thus were lighter, more fuel-efficient, and more economical. Airlines considered the planes to be ideal for routes such as New York

EXHIBIT 31.7

Consolidated Statement of Earnings: McDonnell Douglas Corporation

(Dollar amounts in millions, except per share data)

Years Ending December 31	1990	1989	1988
Revenues	$16,255	$14,589	$14,438
Costs and expenses			
Cost of products, services, and rentals	13,767	12,180	11,715
General and administrative expenses	1,453	1,348	1,283
Research and development	620	617	562
Pension settlement	(600)	—	—
Interest expense			
Aerospace and other segments	380	366	194
Financial services segment	233	198	145
Total costs and expenses	15,853	14,709	13,899
Earnings (loss) from continuing operations before income taxes and cumulative effect of accounting change	402	(120)	539
Income taxes (benefit)	127	(83)	167
Earnings (loss) from continuing operations before cumulative effect of accounting change	275	(37)	372
Discontinued operations			
Earnings (loss) from operations, net of income taxes	15	2	(52)
Gain on disposals, net of income taxes	16	75	30
	31	77	(22)
Earnings before cumulative effect of accounting change	306	40	350
Cumulative effect of initial application of new accounting standard for income taxes	—	179	—
Net earnings	$ 306	$ 219	$ 350
Earnings (loss) per share			
Continuing operations	$ 7.18	$ (.97)	$ 9.70
Discontinued operations			
Earnings (loss) from operations	.39	.05	(1.36)
Gain on disposals	.42	1.96	.79
Cumulative effect of accounting change	—	4.68	—
	$ 7.99	$ 5.72	$ 9.13
Dividends declared per share	$ 2.82	$ 2.82	$ 2.56

Source: McDonnell Douglas Corporation, *1990 Annual Report*, p. 32.

to Seoul, which were characterized by lighter traffic than, say, New York to Tokyo. Three slightly different versions of the MD-11 were eventually created: one standard version, a model built for cargo (marketed toward firms that specialized in the transportation of goods), and a combination prototype. All models had the capability of flying nearly 7,000 nautical miles without refueling.

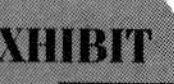

EXHIBIT 31.8

Consolidated Balance Sheet: McDonnell Douglas Corporation
(Dollar amounts in millions, except per share data)

Years Ending December 31	1990	1989
Assets		
Cash and cash equivalents	$ 226	$ 119
Accounts receivable	883	1,350
Finance receivables and property on lease	3,527	3,273
Contracts in process and inventories	6,201	5,128
Property, plant, and equipment	2,624	2,648
Other assets	1,504	879
Total assets	$14,965	$13,397
Liabilities and Shareholders' Equity		
Liabilities		
Accounts payable and accrued expenses	$ 2,818	$ 2,440
Income taxes	1,000	979
Advances and billings in excess of related costs	2,049	1,756
Notes payable and long-term debt		
Aerospace and other segments	2,970	2,597
Financial services segment	2,614	2,338
Total liabilities	11,451	10,110
Shareholders' equity		
Preferred stock—none issued		
Common stock—issued and outstanding 1990, 38.3 shares; 1989, 38.3 shares	38	38
Additional capital	283	281
Retained earnings	3,168	2,970
Translation of foreign currency statements	25	(2)
Total shareholders' equity	3,514	3,287
Total liabilities and shareholders' equity	$14,965	$13,397

Source: McDonnell Douglas Corporation, *1990 Annual Report,* p. 33.

Military Transports

For many years the military aircraft operation in the transport aircraft division had successfully won many government contracts. In fact, McDonnell Douglas boasted the highest market share among defense contractors in the military transport market. However, the changing tactical missions of the military branches called for modification of existing planes and, at times, entirely new models. McDonnell Douglas had two models in particular whose progress management highlighted in the company's *1990 Annual Report.*

C-17 Designed specifically for the U.S. Air Force, the gargantuan C-17 aircraft could transport massive amounts of cargo and troops. The same California facility housed assembly of both the C-17 and commercial aircraft. McDonnell Douglas had recently won a Department of Defense bid to provide 210 C-17 aircraft to the Air Force by the year 2000.

The C-17 was a year behind production schedule in 1990 when the Air Force decided to review the necessity for it. Fortunately for McDonnell Douglas, Congress later approved the purchase. The first C-17 was assembled in December of 1990, and its maiden flight was scheduled for mid 1991.

T-45 The T-45 addressed the Navy's need for pilot training, and the company had received several orders for it. In addition to the planes themselves, the Navy also contracted with McDonnell Douglas to provide the training system for the plane. This system included flight simulators, specialized instruction, and logistics support.

In a troubling development for McDonnell Douglas, military analysts had identified numerous mechanical problems in the T-45. McDonnell Douglas spent several months attempting to correct the flaws in the aircraft's aerodynamics and in October 1990 delivered the first two T-45s to the Navy.

Operations

McDonnell Douglas integrated a complex combination of manufacturing activities to transform raw materials and other inputs into high-technology aerospace products capable of providing substantial value to airline executives and military planners. Descriptions of McDonnell Douglas's operational situation at the onset of 1991 follow.

Buyer Relations

A dramatic increase in orders for commercial aircraft had boosted industry demand. Analysts identified several reasons for this phenomenon. First, inhabitants of newly industrialized countries in the Pacific Rim, with the world's fastest-growing economies, were taking advantage of new-found relative affluence to travel by air. In fact, Asian economists had forecasted that, during the 1990s, air traffic in the Asia–Pacific region would surge 100%[9] to account for fully 40% of all international passengers.

In addition, long-time airline customers in industrialized and developing nations were increasingly cost-conscious, purchasing planes that would help them reduce costs per flight. Finally, airplane leasing companies were expanding their models in an effort to provide increased flexibility to airlines during peak traffic periods.

Tailoring the design, manufacture, and service of commercial aircraft to the exact specifications of buyers was becoming a crucial focus for the industry's three main firms: Boeing, McDonnell Douglas, and Airbus. During the 1980s, airline executives made clear their desire for planes that could travel long, limited-traffic routes economically. The reason was that, in the United States, Congress had deregulated the airline industry, and competition had intensified. The essential objective for airlines, then, became the significant reduction of costs per flight, to thereby raise profit margins.

A second crucial factor in the buying decision was the manufacturer's ability to adhere to delivery schedules. To meet the demand for flights, airlines hoped to receive their ordered aircraft within reasonable periods of time. Owing to overwhelming demand, a five-year wait was common. This situation made some buyers furious and frustrated.

Boeing responded to customers' cost-cutting desires by initiating the design of its enhanced 767, and McDonnell Douglas countered by deciding to build the new MD-11. Airline executives reacted positively to the development of new aircraft, but could do little to shorten the waiting period.

Supplier Relations

As a group, commercial aircraft manufacturers depended on suppliers for nearly 50% of their components.[10] From engine manufacturers such as General Electric to lavatory builders such as JAMCO of Japan, this heavy dependence was an industrywide phenomenon. Part of the reason that the manufacturers had such a huge backlog of orders was that their suppliers had not been able to provide sufficient volumes of parts. Shortages of essential components had reached what insiders admitted were near-critical proportions in early 1990.

Assembly Operations

Suppliers were not the only link in the production chain who were unable to deliver parts in sufficient numbers. McDonnell Douglas's management criticized its own parts and components section for inability to fill internal demand for assembly of the MD-80 and MD-11 aircraft.

Assembly quality was another imposing challenge. Inspections had revealed striking and damaging procedural problems. Inspectors discovered more than 13,000 "open items"—incomplete tasks that were passed down the line—during one inspection period at the Long Beach, California, facility. This revealing quantitative measure of inadequate quality control pushed McDonnell Douglas top management to shift completely to a total quality management (TQM) system of human resource management.[11]

The new corporatewide TQM system, first implemented in the transport aircraft business, was based on the premise that employees have a basic desire to do high-quality work. Therefore management's role was to train, assist, and support personnel to the greatest extent possible. Middle- and upper-level management did not escape: the number of vice-president positions was cut from 245 to 80, and the layers of management were reduced from eight to five. Bureaucracy was streamlined and decision-making authority was decentralized as groups of team leaders and members conferred with department managers to solve problems more expediently. This shift may have had a drawback, however. The transition period lasted several months and may have diverted employees' attention from day-to-day concerns, temporarily lowering productivity.

A rapid increase in transport aircraft personnel augmented the manufacturing section's capabilities to address the surge in demand for the two commercial aircraft models. In fact, for the first time in the history of McDonnell Douglas, the transport aircraft division employed more workers than the combat aircraft division. Management shifted many new transport aircraft mechanics from the combat aircraft section as production there slackened. The major disadvantage to boosting the number of factory/assembly workers assigned to commercial aircraft production was the ensuing decline in productivity the division suffered. Expanded training was needed to bring the new employees' skills up to the level of seasoned workers.

Outbound Logistics

Upon completion of manufacturing, one additional step remained before an aircraft was considered flightworthy for passengers: an evaluation process mandated by the U.S. government to ensure that manufacturers maintained the highest safety standards possible. The FAA inspected the airworthiness of all new models of aircraft flown in the United States. McDonnell Douglas had received a substantial number of orders for the MD-11, which it proceeded to fill. It could not actually deliver the planes, though, until the FAA inspectors had flown the aircraft a predetermined number of hours and had measured the planes' performance against various criteria. Government regulators traditionally used three of the new aircraft to conduct the months-long inspection. McDonnell Douglas management was discussing ways to reduce this amount of time in order to deliver those aircraft to waiting airline executives more quickly.

Marketing and Sales

Historically, McDonnell Douglas had attributed much of its success to technological innovations by engineers in the combat aircraft section. On the civil aircraft side, the high barriers to entry that characterize this industry contributed to a stable, though small, market share for McDonnell Douglas. Market research—which included listening closely to airline executives, identifying needs, and then responding to those needs—traditionally was not a high priority for McDonnell Douglas. As John McDonnell stated:

> Culturally, McDonnell Douglas was a strong hierarchical organization of people with a fierce pride—bordering on arrogance—in their technical engineering excellence. We did not always listen to what the customer had to say before telling him what he wanted.[12]

To be sure, the financial services section had been created to help potential buyers facilitate the purchase of McDonnell Douglas aircraft, and salespeople considered it to be helpful in the closing of many sales. Aside from this effort, to many insiders, the lack of a customer-responsiveness attitude appeared to be embedded in the McDonnell Douglas corporate culture. The new CEO immediately tried to address this concern by setting a personal example.

John McDonnell embarked on a round of meetings, traveling to the Pacific Rim, Europe, and across the United States. He personally visited key airline purchasing executives. Some of them were previous McDonnell Douglas buyers; others were not. The CEO's travels visibly symbolized arrival of a new era of soliciting information from the buyer and acting on this feedback. He also initiated discussions concerning potential cooperative projects with Airbus Industrie. McDonnell Douglas sent signals that it was interested in producing an Airbus model aircraft from an American location.

Although these negotiations soon stalled and were later abandoned, by 1990 top management again explored the idea of a risk-sharing partnership with a foreign firm. Company engineers designed a stretched version of the MD-11, called the MD-12X, to break the Boeing 747 monopoly on huge, 400–450 seat passenger jets. Developmental costs were so imposing, however, that McDonnell Douglas could not initiate this potentially lucrative venture without a committed partner.

Recent Technological Developments

Airline executives were demanding aircraft that would reduce the cost per flight by 33%. Commercial aircraft manufacturers attempted to comply as rapidly as possible. They designed and began modeling new planes for future manufacture. In fact, they had already integrated certain innovations into recently introduced models. The four notable innovations that would characterize this proposed "next generation"[13] of aircraft were

1. state-of-the-art, more fuel-efficient engines;
2. drag-reducing aerodynamics improvements;
3. lighter weight construction materials; and
4. advanced avionics and controls (flight deck instruments, etc.).

Apart from these product innovations, major aerospace companies also implemented significant production process innovations. McDonnell Douglas integrated a costly method known as high-speed machine technology (HSM) into its manufacturing process.[14] Executives expected HSM to raise productivity levels in transforming large sheets of aluminum into various aircraft sections.

The Competitors

The intensity of the competition in the commercial aircraft industry had shifted substantially, and by 1990 consisted of several European firms in addition to the traditional American manufacturers. Two of the three foreign companies (Fokker of the Netherlands and British Aerospace of the United Kingdom) held small niches with tiny market shares. The third (Airbus) intended the opposite: an industrywide challenge to the world's largest aerospace firm.

The Industry Leader: Boeing

Boeing, the Seattle-based powerhouse of the commercial aircraft industry, occupied the lead position despite the presence of two rivals offering similar, more competitively priced products.[15] During its nearly four decades as an industry leader, Boeing built a reputation for superior quality and on-time delivery and operated with a higher earnings ratio (see Exhibits 31.9, 31.10, and 31.11) than McDonnell Douglas or, later, Airbus.[16]

Boeing constructed at least one aircraft model for each of the two medium-range segments and three long-range segments of the market. Most of these passenger planes were at the vanguard of technological innovation, with R&D facilitated by the billions in cash and little long-term debt that characterized Boeing's financial position. Boeing designed and produced aircraft such as the 767 and projected 767-X in response to buyers' specific recommendations for more fuel-efficient, thinner, long-range planes.

Technological innovations continued to emerge. Extensive redesign of the pilot control system supplanted more than 600 lights, gauges, and dials with nine clear computer displays. The commanding lead in market share and earnings that Boeing enjoyed was a product of acknowledged technological enhancements. However, certain insiders warned of clouds forming over Boeing's head. Potential problems were linked, to an extent, to the tremendous surge in demand.

Several complaints dealt with an area that Boeing had excelled in for decades: product quality. Feedback from key long-term buyers indicated that quality had slipped noticeably; that important safety equipment such as fire detection devices often were defective. One British Airways planning executive remarked, "Boeing has very, very, very big problems. But we believe them when they say they are correcting them."[17]

In addition, Boeing did not quickly respond to Airbus advances. Top executives admitted that they took the threat lightly, believing that the cooperative had been created primarily to provide jobs to unemployed Europeans. By 1990, Boeing's share of aircraft orders had fallen significantly, and Airbus had gained enough to reach a market share of 15% (see Exhibit 31.3). Still, Boeing controlled 60% of the industry, with commercial sales of nearly $22 billion (plus transport sales to the U.S. government of some $5 billion). The firm's number one position in commercial aircraft still appeared to be solid.

The New Industry Competitor: Airbus

Founded in 1970, Airbus Industrie was a consortium backed by four European governments. It failed to achieve a profit in its first 19 years of operation, but it succeeded in its primary objective: to gain substantial market share from its established rivals.

The four governments, and their respective share of the consortium, were Germany (38%), France (38%), the United Kingdom (20%), and Spain (4%). After being provided with an abundance of capital for investments and operations, Airbus attacked Boeing with a full-fledged "frontal assault."[18] This strategy required enormous resources in order to succeed, and Airbus received nearly $10 billion in direct subsidies during the 1974–1987 period, as estimated by the U.S. Department of Commerce.[19] The tactics were manifested in pricing policies that would be considered suicidal without the cash inflow that covered the resulting losses. For example, the Airbus A-340, competing in the long-range, thin-body market (the "long-thin" segment), was priced a full 25% below the MD-11, which itself was priced approximately 20% below Boeing's 767 model.

EXHIBIT 31.9

Four-Year Summary: Boeing Company and Subsidiaries

(Dollar amounts in millions, except per share data)

Years Ending December 31	1990	1989	1988	1987
Operations				
Sales (including other operating revenues)				
Commercial	$22,158	$14,994	$12,170	$10,623
U.S. government	5,437	5,282	4,792	4,882
Total sales	27,595	20,276	16,962	15,505
Net earnings	1,385	675[3]	614	480
Per share[1]	4.01	1.96[3]	1.79	1.38
Percent of sales	5.0%	3.3%	3.6%	3.1%
Cash dividends paid	$ 328	$ 269	$ 237	$ 217
Per share[1,4]	.95	.78	.69	.62
Other income, principally interest	448	347	378	308
Research and development expenses	827	754	751	824
General and administrative expenses[2]	1,246	1,066	954	891
Additions to plant and equipment	1,586	1,362	690	738
Depreciation of plant and equipment	636	584	541	486
Salaries and wages	6,487	6,082	5,404	5,028
Average employment	161,700	159,200	147,300	136,100
Financial Position at December 31				
Total assets	$14,591	$13,278	$12,608	$12,566
Working capital	1,638	1,987	1,856	2,246
Long-term customer financing	1,120	822	1,039	392
Cash and short-term investments	3,326	1,863	3,963	3,435
Total borrowings	315	280	258	270
Long-term debt	311	275	251	256
Long-term deferred taxes	161	174	205	189
Stockholders' equity	6,973	6,131	5,404	4,987
Per share	20.30	17.73	15.67	14.55
Common shares outstanding (in thousands)	343,573	345,834	344,774	342,614
Firm Backlog				
Commercial	$91,475	$73,974	$46,676	$26,963
U.S. government	5,719	6,589	6,925	6,241
Total firm backlog	$97,194	$80,563	$53,601	$33,204

Notes:

1. Share data restated for 1990 three-for-two stock split.
2. Prior years have been restated to conform with the presentation used in 1991.
3. Exclusive of the effect of adopting Statement of Financial Accounting Standards No. 96, Accounting for Income Taxes. Net earnings including the effect were $973 or $2.82 per share.
4. Cash dividends have been paid on common stock every year since 1942.

Source: Boeing Corporation, *1991 Annual Report,* p. 54.

Consolidated Balance Sheet: Boeing Company and Subsidiaries
(Dollar amounts in millions, except per share data)

Year Ending December 31	1990
Assets	
Current assets	
Cash and cash equivalents	$ 2,188
Short-term investments, at cost, which approximates market	1,138
Accounts receivable	2,044
Current portion of customer financing	13
Deferred federal taxes on income	55
Inventories	14,402
Less advances and progress billings	(11,070)
Total current assets	8,770
Customer financing	1,120
Property, plant, and equipment, at cost	8,991
Less accumulated depreciation	(4,543)
Investments and other assets	253
Total assets	$14,591
Liabilities and Shareholders' Equity	
Current liabilities	
Accounts payable and other liabilities	$ 5,566
Advances and progress billings in excess of related costs	1,083
Federal taxes on income ($0 deferred)	479
Current portion of long-term debt	4
Total current liabilities	7,132
Long-term debt	311
Deferred federal taxes on income	161
Deferred investment credit	14
Shareholders' equity	
Common shares, par value $5.00—600,000,000 shares authorized; 349,256,792 shares issued	1,746
Additional paid-in capital	581
Retained earnings	4,840
Less treasury shares, at cost—1990 - 5,683,314	(194)
Total shareholders' equity	6,973
Total liabilities and shareholders' equity	$14,591

Source: Boeing Corporation, *1991 Annual Report,* p. 39.

Reacting vigorously to what they perceived as unfair trading policies, the two American companies joined voices in condemning Airbus pricing practices. They accused the European cooperative of selling its goods below cost on the world market. Together, they highlighted the positive impact of the commercial aircraft industry on the U.S. balance of trade. The protests galvanized only a limited amount of support in Congress, however, as even U.S.-based airlines were purchasing the economical planes. In addition, Airbus executives argued that over one-third of their aircraft components were provided by American aerospace firms, such as Pratt & Whitney engines.

Airbus planes eventually won acclaim for providing certain innovations, such as avionics advances. One significant breakthrough that received much praise was Airbus's "fly by wire" flight deck control system, which allowed the pilot to direct the aircraft electronically, by computer. This system replaced the traditional process of cables and pulleys.[20]

A second advantage that Airbus exploited to win orders was accelerated delivery schedules. Both the long-range A-330 and the medium-range A-320 were set to fulfill their delivery contracts at least two years before competitors' new models rolled off the assembly line. The research and development and production head start again was attributed to the cash advantage Airbus enjoyed over McDonnell Douglas, as well as corporate responsiveness to buyers' specific needs.

On the other hand, by 1990 evidence existed to show that the spigot controlling the free flow of Airbus cash was being turned off, as the once-solid foundation of solidarity showed signs of wear. The German and British partners in the coalition were especially critical of the firm's estimated multimillion dollar annual losses. Representatives of these nations publicly announced an end to the subsidies if cost-cutting reforms were not implemented. In one notable reversal of policy, Airbus managers decided to raise development funds for the 200-seat A-321 from private investors rather than the usual government loans.[21]

Potential Entrants

By the early 1990s, what was once a two-horse, U.S.-dominated race had become a competitive threesome as the European competitor first gained technological respect and then significant market share. Analysts believed that Airbus Industrie was able to successfully join the fray because of two key factors: immense financial resources and sufficient national resolve.

These three corporations represented the efforts of only five of dozens of industrialized and newly industrialized nations. What other nations, if any, were on the horizon with the potential to forcefully enter the fight for a slice of the expanding commercial aircraft pie?

Japan

For years Japanese economists had expressed aspirations for their nation to become an active participant in the commercial aircraft production industry.[22] Analysts had noted that, although Japanese aerospace technology was several years behind that of the Europeans and Americans, the Japanese were laying the foundation required for success in the industry. By 1990, in fact, the three large commercial aircraft builders already were sourcing sophisticated components from Japanese aerospace firms.[23]

Many Japanese industries were strong financially, in part because of huge annual trade surpluses. And with the total investment required for developing a new model estimated at about $4 billion, such resources would be crucial. Manufactur-

EXHIBIT 31.11

Industry Segment Information: Boeing Company and Subsidiaries
(Dollar amounts in millions)

Military sales were approximately 10% and 8% of total sales in Europe for 1990 and 1989, respectively. Military sales were approximately 6% and 5% of total sales in Asia for 1990 and 1989, respectively. Exclusive of these amounts, sales of Military Transportation Products and Related Systems and Missiles and Space were principally to the U.S. government.

Financial information by segment for the two years (1990 and 1989) ending December 31 is summarized below. Revenues consist of sales plus other income applicable to the respective segments. Corporate income consists principally of interest income from corporate investments. Corporate expense consists of interest on debt and other general corporate expenses. Corporate assets consist principally of cash, cash equivalents, and short-term investments.

Years Ending December 31	1990	1989
Revenues		
Commercial transportation products and services	$21,230	$14,305
Military transportation products and related systems	4,123	3,962
Missiles and space	1,739	1,467
Other industries	503	542
Operating revenues	27,595	20,276
Corporate income	448	347
Total revenues	$28,043	$20,623
Operating Profit		
Commercial transportation products and services	$ 2,189	$ 1,165
Military transportation products and related systems	(299)	(559)
Missiles and space	(119)	85
Other industries	(66)	26
Operating profit	1,705	717

(continued)

ing operations' speed and quality—the aircraft industry's weak points for several models—was acknowledged as an area of competitive advantage for many Japanese companies. Finally, a nation had to exhibit sufficient resolve to invest heavily for years before receiving remuneration for a single aircraft. Observers believed that the Japanese could meet this challenge.

Republic of Korea

South Korea (Korea) had emulated the Japanese model with unquestionable success in certain manufacturing industries such as automobiles. However, Korean firms typically played a subcontracting role for aircraft manufacturers, providing components such as airframe parts. In 1990, Korea began a new push to extend into the major aircraft assembly industry.[24] Competitive advantages included lower

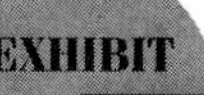
EXHIBIT 31.11

Industry Segment Information: Boeing Company and Subsidiaries *(continued)*
(Dollar amounts in millions)

Years Ending December 31	1990	1989
Corporate income	448	347
Corporate expense	(181)	(142)
Earnings before taxes	$ 1,972	$ 922
Identifiable Assets at December 31		
Commercial transportation products and services	$ 6,267	$ 6,675
Military transportation products and related systems	3,556	3,367
Missiles and space	940	911
Other industries	351	329
	11,114	11,282
Corporate	3,477	1,996
Consolidated assets	$14,591	$13,278
Depreciation		
Commercial transportation products and services	$ 349	$ 280
Military transportation products and related systems	197	208
Missiles and space	64	72
Other industries	62	62
Total depreciation	$ 672	$ 622
Capital Expenditures, Net		
Commercial transportation products and services	$ 1,001	$ 612
Military transportation products and related systems	407	506
Missiles and space	89	155
Other industries	89	89
Total capital expenditures, net	$ 1,586	$ 1,362

Source: Boeing Corporation, *1991 Annual Report,* p. 51.

employee wages, effective human resource management policies, and proximity to the fastest growing market for aircraft, the Pacific Rim.

Financial resources and a national determination to excel in science and high-technology industries were acknowledged plusses in Korea's feasibility equation. One glaring minus that needed to be addressed was the national shortage of qualified aerospace engineers.

McDonnell Douglas: Policy Directions

As January 1991 rolled around, picturing Chairman and CEO of McDonnell Douglas, John McDonnell, reflecting in his turret in the heartland of America and gazing out into a cloudy nighttime sky was not difficult. McDonnell would be making preparations to address McDonnell Douglas shareholders. He began his annual letter by articulating the rationale behind the turbulence of 1990:

> A six-year-long boom in orders for new commercial aircraft came to an end in the second half of 1990 as airlines grappled with higher fuel prices, reduced travel, and falling profits. . . . [W]e continue to face difficult challenges as a result of growing financial constraints and highly visible difficulties. . . . [A]t the same time we must continue to invest in new commercial aircraft. . . . [N]ew programs represent the future of the corporation.[25]

The transport aircraft division had already begun implementing innovations: installing a TQM system, soliciting additional information from airline executives, investing in the production of new models, contemplating joint ventures, and allocating more R&D for the proposed new generation of passenger aircraft.

Would measures such as these be sufficient to ensure continued success of the commercial aircraft operation? After all, 1990 sales far outdistanced the previous record, huge backorders showed that demand could be sustained for years, and McDonnell Douglas employed an abundance of talented engineers.

But warning signs were also flashing. At the start of 1991, airline executives were beginning to complain about unexpected difficulties with the engines powering the MD-11. Continuing problems with suppliers frustrated McDonnell Douglas operations executives, as did excessive "open items" on the assembly line. Most important, with McDonnell Douglas competing in only two of the five medium- and long-range aircraft market segments, analysts believed that the firm was bound to lose a share of the market to its two full-line competitors. But McDonnell Douglas already was deeply in long-term debt, and costs for developing new models were staggering.

Entering 1991, the commercial aircraft section, operating in an intensely competitive environment, clearly was accounting for an increasing share of McDonnell Douglas's total revenue. High corporate debt severely restricted McDonnell Douglas's ability to rapidly develop planned new models. Lucrative military contracts were drying up, and, simultaneously, the realization set in that the policy of competing on price for commercial aircraft market share no longer was feasible. The first two decades of the McDonnell Douglas merger had come to a close. A new, more turbulent era, with many looming threats and several potential opportunities, had dawned at McDonnell Douglas Corporation.

Notes

1. C. Leinster, "The Odd Couple at McDonnell Douglas," *Fortune* (June 22, 1987), p. 120.
2. McDonnell Douglas Corporation, *1990 Annual Report*, p. 2.
3. J. Ellis, "Tower to McDonnell: Turbulence Ahead," *Business Week* (May 23, 1988), p. 118.
4. A. Ramirez, "Boeing's Happy, Harrowing Times," *Fortune* (July 17, 1989), p. 43.
5. B. Smith, "Douglas Transport Losses Ease; Reorganization Issues Persist," *Aviation Week and Space Technology* (October 30, 1989), p. 19.
6. J. Rees, "Debt Keeps Douglas Hope Alive," *Long Beach Press* (June 11, 1990). Microfilm: TRN 33:B5.
7. McDonnell Douglas Corporation, *1989 Annual Report*, p. 3.

8. Ibid, p. 12.
9. "European Airframe Manufacturers Pursue Growing Asia/Pacific Market," *Aviation Week and Space Technology* (February 12, 1990), pp. 62–70.
10. McDonnell Douglas Corporation, *1989 Form 10-K Report,* p. 19.
11. Smith, p. 18.
12. McDonnell Douglas Corporation, *1988 Annual Report,* p. 2.
13. T. A. Heppenheimer, "New Commercial Aircraft Promise Efficiency," *High Technology* (February 1987), pp. 23–27.
14. A. Senia, "High Speed Machines Taking Wing in Aerospace," *Production* (February 1988), pp. 52–55.
15. Boeing Aircraft Corporation, *1988 Annual Report,* p. 33.
16. Ramirez, p. 44.
17. Ibid., p. 42.
18. H. Banks, "Airbus Comes of Age," *Forbes* (February 23, 1987), p. 36.
19. Ramirez, p. 43.
20. R. Evans, "An Embarrassment of Riches," *International Management* (June 1987) p. 35.
21. J. Lenorovitz, "Airbus Industrie Partners Approve Development of Stretched A-320,"*Aviation Week and Space Technology* (December 4, 1989), p. 31.
22. P. Proctor, "Asian Manufacturers Seek Aircraft Development Share," *Aviation Week and Space Technology* (March 19, 1990), pp. 88–90.
23. W. Offut, "Can Japan Take Off in Aerospace?" *Across the Board* (July/August 1989), p. 40.
24. J. Morrocco, "Korean Aerospace Firms Seek Greater Role in World Market," *Aviation Week and Space Technology* (June 12, 1989), p. 202.
25. McDonnell Douglas Corporation, *1990 Annual Report,* pp. 2–5.

The Morgan Motor Car Company: The Last of the Great Independents

Peter G. Goulet and Allen Rappaport

In the early 1900s, three young Englishmen left school and became apprentice engineers at the Great Western Railway Works in Swindon, Great Britain. These three talented men were Henry Royce, W. O. Bentley, and Henry Frederick Stanley Morgan (H. F. S. to his admirers). Each eventually founded a company to manufacture automobiles. W. O. Bentley was forced to sell out to his competitor, Henry Royce, in the worldwide depression of the 1930s. Although the Rolls-Royce and the Bentley became international symbols of sophistication and wealth, Rolls-Royce went bankrupt in the 1960s and was divided up at government insistence. Only the firm founded by H. F. S. Morgan, now run by his son Peter (semi-retired) and his grandson Charles, has survived. Not only has the firm survived, but it still operates in the same plant facilities it has occupied since 1919. There are cynics who would say that the reason the firm has used the same plant since 1919 is because the car hasn't changed much since then. However, in 1992, there was a *ten-year waiting list* of prospective purchasers awaiting delivery of a "mog," as the Morgan marque (like brand name) is affectionately referred to by those who see it as the last real sports car!

The Morgan Car

The Morgan car line consists of a small variety of quick, stiffly sprung, classic English sports cars. The smallest is a two-seat, four-cylinder, fuel-injected, five-speed, open sport model called the "Four Four." The middle model is a slightly larger, faster, more sophisticated four cylinder two-seater called the "Plus Four." The largest model is powered by a Rover V-8, which develops 200 horsepower. This car, the "Plus Eight," has tremendous acceleration, even when fitted with pollution control equipment (see Exhibit 32.1). All are open sports cars, although they do have soft tops and simple weather-control gear. All have direct handling and a classic hard, stiff ride. In U.S. dollars the 1992 Four Four sells for $35,000. The Plus Eight sells for $50,000. In contrast, sports cars with comparable reputations sell for $150,000 and up. For the person who wants a personalized car, the Morgan is available in 35,000 colors.

Although Morgans have state-of-the-art engines with fuel injection, electronic ignition, and pollution control devices, they get reasonably high gas mileage and

This case was prepared by Professors Peter G. Goulet and Allen Rappaport of the University of Northern Iowa. This case was presented to and accepted by the referred Midwest Society for Case Research Meeting, 1992. This case was edited by T. L. Wheelen and J. D. Hunger for this book. Reprinted by permission of the authors.

EXHIBIT 32.1 **Morgan PWS 8**

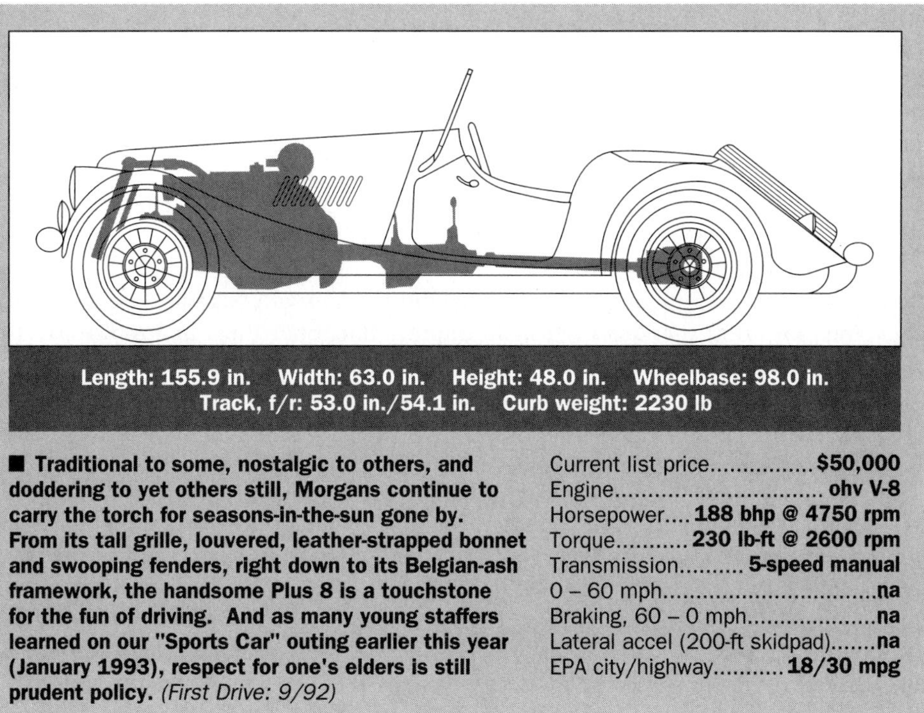

Length: 155.9 in. Width: 63.0 in. Height: 48.0 in. Wheelbase: 98.0 in.
Track, f/r: 53.0 in./54.1 in. Curb weight: 2230 lb

■ **Traditional to some, nostalgic to others, and doddering to yet others still, Morgans continue to carry the torch for seasons-in-the-sun gone by. From its tall grille, louvered, leather-strapped bonnet and swooping fenders, right down to its Belgian-ash framework, the handsome Plus 8 is a touchstone for the fun of driving. And as many young staffers learned on our "Sports Car" outing earlier this year (January 1993), respect for one's elders is still prudent policy.** *(First Drive: 9/92)*

Current list price................**$50,000**
Engine................................ **ohv V-8**
Horsepower.... **188 bhp @ 4750 rpm**
Torque........... **230 lb-ft @ 2600 rpm**
Transmission.......... **5-speed manual**
0 – 60 mph...............................**na**
Braking, 60 – 0 mph...................**na**
Lateral accel (200-ft skidpad).......**na**
EPA city/highway.......... **18/30 mpg**

Source: *Road & Track* (September 1993), p. 80.

are still relatively simple cars. In fact, the basic front-end suspension design has remained unchanged conceptually since H. F. S. Morgan built the first Morgan by hand in 1908. This suspension was probably the first workable independent front suspension system used on any car. Although the chassis is based on a simple steel frame, the body is still constructed on a hand-built *wooden* frame of specially aged ash. The Morgan's hand-cut body panels are different enough that parts must be individually fitted by hand. The Morgan "experience" is described by British writer Kevin Blick:

> The cockpit is cramped and noisy. Two occupants sit shoulder to shoulder, yet can converse only when halted at traffic lights. The seats are flat and formless. The footwell is cramped, the clutch is heavy, the unboosted brakes much heavier still, and the long-travel accelerator all but impossible to push to its far limit. The tiny gearstick shifts cogs with palm-bruising stiffness. . . . Instead of being a homely little runabout bought by retiring gents wanting to revisit their youth, here is a rip-snorting monster. . . . And in a chassis with the torsional rigidity of a banana. . . . [After a rain] sitting in that dank and steamy interior, on a wet leather seat, with soggy trousers, soaked coat, and frozen fingers, how I cursed the Morgan. . . . But all this is part of the fun.[1]

The first Morgan was a cycle car with three wheels (two up front) powered by a two cylinder Peugeot motorcycle engine. The company produced and sold that three-wheeled cycle car—in larger and faster versions with both two and four seats—until 1950! However, in 1936, sales of the original Morgan three-wheelers fell to 137 units, and the firm clearly needed to broaden its product line to include a more conventional four-wheeled model if it was to survive. In the following year, in an effort to save the company, Morgan introduced the first Four Four. This model has survived into the 1990s with only minor engineering modifications and technological advancements required by government regulations and the marketplace. Overall, Morgan built a total of nine models of the three-wheeler, including a small number of vans.

Although various engines have been used and other minor changes have been made over the years, the only four-wheeled models Morgan has built are the Four Four, the Plus Four, the Plus Eight, and the rare Plus Four Plus. In 1963, to overcome a public perception that the Morgan was an outmoded car, the company developed the Plus Four Plus. This aerodynamic coupe fitted a sleek, "Ferrari" style fiberglass body to a Morgan chassis and engine. The car retained the Morgan-style radiator grill and front bumper, but offered, for the first time, a curved windshield. Production of this car ended in 1967 after only 26 were produced and sold over four years. The Plus Four Plus had the desired effect, however. Its introduction stimulated demand for the more traditional Morgan models, once again saving the company.

During the 1960s, Morgan sponsored an extensive and successful racing and rallying program in Great Britain, Europe, and the United States—often competing successfully against more "modern" designs from its more famous competitors. One highlight of this program was a win in the 2-liter class at the 24-hour endurance race at Le Mans in 1962. The winning car, which placed thirteenth overall, was a specially strengthened Plus Four called the Super Sport. The win was ironic because race officials had prevented a similar car from racing the previous year because it "looked too old-fashioned." A Morgan had also won thirteenth place at Le Mans in 1938 with a woman co-driver, although it did not win its class that year.

Building the Morgan[2]

Morgan cars are built by hand in a factory established in 1919 in Malvern Link in the West Midlands of England. This plant has remained largely unchanged since that time. By current standards, industrial engineers would view the layout of this factory as a production nightmare. Workers wheel cars back and forth, by hand—outdoors and back in, and in and out of various sections of the plant. After being worked on in one place for a few days or weeks, the cars are moved again, occasionally retracing a prior route. The complete factory tour taken by each Morgan requires three months! The firm's Chief Development Engineer, Maurice Owen, would like to make major modifications to the plant layout to increase production efficiency.[3]

The assembly process has remained largely unchanged at Morgan since the 1930s. Each Monday morning two men place the chassis frames for the cars to be started that week on sawhorses. (Before 1990, nine cars were started each week. Since that time the number has fluctuated between nine and ten, depending on the number of workers in the chassis shop.) During the rest of the week an expert veteran assembles the chassis from its parts, such as the suspension, axles, brakes, and drive trains (including the engine), entirely by hand. Although workers use a hoist to lift the engine and transmission onto the chassis, even it is hand-powered. The last step in completing the chassis is the addition of the wheels so that the chassis can be rolled into the body shop at the end of the week.

Body-shop carpenters craft the basic underbody of a Morgan, a complex handmade birdcage, of seasoned ash. They hand-fit each door frame to the birdcage frame at this stage, and adjust its hinges just like those on a custom-built kitchen cabinet. When the subframe is finished it receives a three-hour bath in a chemical to prevent dry rot. This Cuprisol bath was an option until a few years ago, when the company made it standard to lengthen the life of the car. The Morgan now is the only car in the world for which a major worry of the owner is dry rot or attacks by wood-boring worms!

The completed subframe is attached to a completed chassis. Metal workers then finish the body in the sheet metal shop, covering the subframe with traditional sheet metal panels. These sheet metal parts include the bonnet (hood), boot (trunk), fenders, door panels, and quarter panels. Owners have a choice of steel or aluminum for most sheet-metal parts, another custom feature of the Morgan. Craftsmen fashion these parts largely on simple hand-operated sheet-metal tools. The hardest of these operations is punching the louvers in the two halves of the bonnet. Each is punched one at a time, based on locations penciled onto the part by the metal worker.

When the body is completed, workers wheel the Morgan outside to the paint shop. Here painters sand, fill, and give the car's surface several coats of paint. Between each coat they hand-rub the car to make sure that no bumps, even invisible ones, mar the top-coat finish. Several basic colors are standard on the Morgan, but for an extra $400 an owner can have any one of more than 35,000 custom colors.

From the paint shop the car proceeds to the wiring shop where workers install wiring, lights, gauges, and other electrical equipment. Although the Morgan has changed little in the last 55-odd years, an owner can get a cassette stereo for $800 (which the owner probably can't hear unless the car is stopped). Finishers install seats, carpets, and interior upholstery. Much of the interior is now the same Connolly leather used in a Rolls-Royce. Upholsterers cut, sew, and install it with the same care as that used on the rest of the car.

The last step in building the Morgan is the installation of the owner's steering wheel. (The real one has been protected from greasy hands until now, with a factory wheel used during production.) A 20-mile test is used to work out bugs, and the car is then certified for shipment. Symbolic of the attention to detail at the Morgan works is that the wall of the final finish department is adorned by two stuffed owls whose job is to scare away stray birds who might fly in the open doors and make unwelcome deposits on the nearly finished cars.

In addition to the departments of the factory just described, the factory also manufactures or finishes from purchased castings many of the car's parts, such as brake drums, wheel hubs, and other machined parts. These machined parts are used at various stages in the assembly process. A spare parts department makes and stocks "spares" (time permitting). Finally, a service department restores and repairs Morgans for their owners. At any one time several cars may be in this shop, in various stages of repair. Some of these cars have been here for months or even years. Time does not fly at the Morgan works. (Neither do the owls.)

Although the company produces most of the Morgan in its own factory, it obtains key parts (such as chassis frames, engines, transmissions, gauges, windscreens, wipers, and mass-produced electrical components) from outside suppliers. Various firms, including Buick, Fiat, Triumph, Ford of England, and Austin Rover, have supplied engines, Ford and Rover are currently the primary suppliers. Rear axles, chasses, transmissions, and electrical parts come from numerous large well-established suppliers. The company depends totally on the availability of these critical mass-produced parts, especially engines that fit without major engineering modifications to the car's chassis. If any of these components were discontinued or modified in a way that required Morgan to make major changes in one of its cars, the firm's survival could be threatened.

Although the true cost of building a Morgan in this precise handcrafted manner is unknown, the labor cost is an estimated 30%–40% of the total cost.[4] Most cars built today are assembled from numerous subassemblies. The ability to produce these subassemblies in quantity and install them as units reduces the amount of labor required in final assembly. One reason that Maurice Owen would like to change the Morgan plant layout is to support the restructuring of the assembly process to permit the firm to utilize this more modern approach. Owen also would like to introduce some simple production jigs and fixtures to speed up and standardize the hand operations used to make parts for the Morgan. Finally, Owen would like to use more simple power tools, such as air screwdrivers, to speed up the hand work. The use of subassemblies, jigs, and power tools need not detract from the handbuilt character of the car. Rather they should permit the more effective use of the firm's skilled labor, permitting an increase in productivity.[5]

Selling the Morgan[6]

The Morgan is just one marque in a broad array of British sports cars, which includes names such as MG, Triumph, Austin-Healey, Jaguar, and Aston Martin. Sales of these British sports cars were largely confined to the British Isles until after World War II, when the British government encouraged these companies to export their cars in exchange for the steel they needed to make them. (All steel was supplied by the government-owned steel company.) The various British sports car lines straddled all price brackets. The smaller manufacturers generally resembled Morgan in that they were primarily assemblers who bought their parts from larger manufacturers. The popularity of British sports cars in the United States peaked in the late 1950s and 1960s. Beginning in the 1970s, safety regulations, the need to increase fuel efficiency and control pollution, and the entry of Japanese competitors such as Nissan and Mazda with high-quality, luxury sports models, effectively forced the British out of the market. Consolidation of many of these classic auto marques (MG, Triumph, Austin-Healey, and Rover) into one company further reduced production efficiency. Ford now owns Jaguar and Aston Martin—and reportedly is losing a great deal of money on them annually.

A network of 42 dealers sell the Morgan in North America (3), Africa (1), Australia (1), Japan (1), Western Europe (17) and the United Kingdom (19). Until 1948, the Morgan was sold only in the United Kingdom. For a brief time after World War II, the company sold much of its output in the United States to stay afloat. However, each time the company sought to enter the U.S. market in earnest, the environment prevented its long-term exploitation. In the 1950s, the popularity of the imported MG, Triumph, Jaguar, and Austin Healey reduced Morgan's U.S. sales to nearly nothing. The image of the glass-bodied Plus Four Plus and the win at Le Mans helped revive Morgan and its U.S. sales temporarily. However, pollution regulations soon cut this trend short, and again Morgan had to cut back production and concentrate on Europe. A dealer who fitted Morgans to burn propane to satisfy environmental regulations reintroduced them in the United States during the 1970s. Although a few of those Morgans still burn propane, it was not a good long-term solution. U.S. sales did not rise again until the company put new state-of-the-art Ford and Rover engines in the car. Although current U.S. demand is unknown, it may be as high as 1,000 cars per year.

Perhaps the biggest issue facing Morgan Motor Car Company over the years is the level of real demand. Between 1920 and 1930, the company produced an average of 2,000 cars per year. During that time the firm also licensed a French firm to produce its cars, and that licensee produced an additional 2,000 cars a year. From 1982–1990, production averaged about eight cars per week, or about 400 per year. In 1991, this number rose to roughly 450. About half this production was exported, leaving about 200–250 cars per year to satisfy U.K. demand. At this level of supply each dealer in the United Kingdom has about one car per month to sell. Just one of these dealers has said he has orders for 450 cars, a 40-year backlog! New orders currently run about 600–800 cars per year, creating a waiting list. The waiting list is variously estimated to be 2,500–5,000 cars, averaging about 3,600, or about 10 years' production!

Morgan's waiting list is a mixed blessing. Some who order a Morgan never actually take delivery. Some get tired of waiting; others find that they can take delivery and "scalp" the car to someone farther down on the list at a tidy 15%–20% profit. (The company does not approve of this practice. In fact, Charles Morgan once said that a customer who sold his waiting list spot was probably not a suitable owner anyway, and the company would prefer not to sell to such people.) Still, in spite of the cushion it provides, Peter Morgan worries about the list. Some potential buyers, such as the Italians, are put off by it and simply don't order. Peter Morgan remembers that his father (H. F. S.) always told him to make sure that demand exceeds supply. Peter Morgan says:

> I am never complacent over orders—they change so much. At any point I can have 2000–3000 named orders; if I was to finish them in three months, I'd be lucky to collect the money for 10 percent! I've always tried to go for a spread of markets. The

> Japanese, for instance, would like more than their 10–20 cars per year, but we cannot commit ourselves to the detriment of others, when regulations and economics are constantly changing.[7]

Competition

Although all cars sold are effectively substitutes for one another, the Morgan has few real competitors. It is clearly a niche product with a very restricted supply. Many of the hard-top, two-seat sports cars available worldwide (such as the Ferrari, Aston Martin, Porsche, and 300ZX) have become high-performance, expensive luxury cars. Although many of these cars, especially the European models, retain much handcrafting, none is as "primitive" as the Morgan or provides the mystique of the Mog.

Perhaps the strongest competition for the Morgan is the Morgan itself. Someone who doesn't want to wait the 5–10 years required for a new Morgan can try to purchase a pre-owned model. Although hard to find, they are available, often at significant premiums over their original "sticker" prices. Still, part of the "Morgan experience" is knowing that your car is unique. You must wait a long time to be part of that small and exclusive group of original owners, which is like no other group of owners.

Financial Results

Overall, Morgan has enjoyed steady growth in sales and profits in recent years (see Exhibits 32.2 and 32.3).[8] From 1980–1991, sales increased at an average annual rate of 10.8%, and pre-tax profits grew at 12.7% per year. Pre-tax margins ranged from a low of about 1% to nearly 11%. Actual production figures in units ranged from 397 cars (about eight per week) to 456, (about nine per week), depending on the number of weeks worked. Morgan has no long-term debt, but current debt grew from roughly £647,000 in 1982 to £1.75 million in 1991.

To put Morgan's sales in perspective, *in dollar terms,* Morgan's 1989 sales were $8.75 million (£1 =$1.64), up from $8.6 million (£1 = $1.78) in 1988, based on production of just over 400 cars. In contrast, Ford, the English market share leader, sold 515,000 cars and trucks in Britain, 2.3 million units outside the United States, and 6.4 million worldwide out of a total of roughly 50 million vehicles sold worldwide by all manufacturers. Ford's car and truck sales were $82 billion in 1989, which translates into more than $9.4 million *per hour,* or more than Morgan's sales for an entire year!

Morgan Culture and Strategy

In 1980, the editor of *Thoroughbred & Classic Cars* interviewed Peter Morgan concerning the reason why the company did not mark its seventieth anniversary with a celebration. Morgan replied:

> Two reasons arise in my mind. Firstly, when discussing the future of the company with my father, HFS, before he died in 1959, neither of us felt we could stay the course and

> survive until the 80s. . . . The second reason was a somewhat more personal one of my own, in so far that after the 50th year event at Malvern I remember thinking that we will work towards reaching the 75th anniversary and mark that when it occurs.[9]

Thus a strong survival mentality influences Morgan's goals and strategies. In a discussion of the Morgan Company, British consultant Sir John Harvey-Jones reported a reminiscence of Peter Morgan's:

> As a small boy Peter Morgan can recall periodic bad times [sic], particularly in the mid-1920s. . . . He remembers walking through the factory when most of the cars were ticketed for stock, and wondering why Mr. Stock needed so many cars. These memories of bad times . . . appear to have affected the development of the company at the kind of psychological level which is rarely taken into account when the history of a company is told.[10]

The personnel at Morgan spend many years acquiring the skills required to build the firm's cars and are dedicated to their work. Although the proportion of labor cost in a Morgan is high by modern automotive standards, this cost is more a reflection of the methods the firm utilizes to build the car than poor productivity and work habits. The difficult plant layout creates numerous bottlenecks and movements of the partially finished car, further contributing to labor costs. Because of current space and flow limitations, speeding up certain parts of the process would be difficult. As Maurice Owen has noted, however, changes in the process and layout might lower these costs a good deal, without sacrificing the essential handbuilt character of the car.

Workers receive a basic wage and a production bonus, which often is as much as half of total weekly pay. Although this bonus may encourage some departments to step up production, the total output of cars does not increase much because plant bottlenecks hold up one or two operations. Further, foremen are not paid a bonus if their workers increase production, so they have little reason to encourage productivity.

The labor force at Morgan is unionized. As with most British manufacturing operations, the union has a great deal of control over process, and change is not always encouraged. As dedicated as the workers are to the firm, they are not dedicated to change. Every afternoon at the appointed hour, everyone still observes the best of British traditions and takes a tea break. This strict adherence to the status quo and tradition, too, may contribute to the cost and nature of the Morgan manufacturing process, although relations with the union are excellent.

The Morgan labor force is closely matched to its task. The firm employs just enough workers to build ten cars a week using present methods. However, British workers get longer vacations than U.S. workers, and with the small labor force employed by the company, the absence of even one or two key workers can significantly lower production. To raise production significantly would require a significant increase in the number of workers throughout the plant—or a change in process and layout. Management believes that to preserve its current methods and increase the work force significantly would require 4–6 years.

The executives at Morgan all perform a variety of duties. Mark Aston, the Works Manager, personally deals with the service department and warranty claims. The Sales Manager, Derek Day, personally writes to each new customer to

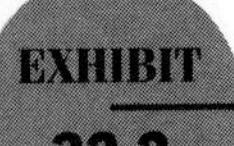

EXHIBIT 32.2

Income Statement and Production Volumes: Morgan Motor Company Limited

(Financial amounts in British pounds; production numbers in actual units)

Years Ending May 31	1991	1990	1989	1988
Sales	£7,054,669	£5,700,305	£5,330,549	£4,827,018
Cost of goods sold	5,176,687	4,193,767	4,001,900	3,682,910
Gross profit	1,877,982	1,506,538	1,328,649	1,144,108
Other expenses				
Plant expenses	371,615	347,097	290,564	296,246
Office and administrative expenses	716,877	612,290	565,032	568,685
Selling expenses	86,564	35,667	56,790	43,765
Total expenses	1,175,056	995,054	912,386	908,696
Other income	217,873	114,469	71,602	47,492
Operating income				
Before taxes	920,799	625,953	487,865	282,904
Income taxes	301,344	211,516	166,133	94,916
Net income	£ 619,455	£ 414,437	£ 321,732	£ 187,988
Production[1,2]	456	412	425	411

Notes:

1. Contains at least two models provided by the company.
2. 1992 production was 459 units.

Source: Companies Registration Office, Companies House, Cardiff CF4 3UZ, Great Britain.

ask how they would like their new car configured. With a ten-year waiting time, this task would not seem urgent, but there are 600 such letters a year to write and replies to process. When a customer's car is being built, he or she is notified and may come to the plant to view some or all of the car's construction. Many new owners pick up their cars in person. Because production is so limited, Derek Day may be considered a rationer of cars, rather than a sales manager. Production really dictates what will be sold.

The Troubleshooter Program

In the spring of 1989, an unexpected event disrupted what some might call the peaceful complacency of Morgan. British management consultant Sir John Harvey-Jones contacted the Morgan Company to inquire whether he could include them in a series of programs produced by the British television network BBC 2. This series, called "The Troubleshooter," was designed to go inside small firms and show a consultant evaluating the company and making suggestions for improving its operations. The Morgan show was to be the fifth in the series. Based on the success of the first four shows, expectations were high for the Morgan program. However, the Morgan show did not work out as planned. At first, Morgan welcomed the idea of an appraisal by a distinguished consultant. However, after the numerous

1987	1986	1985	1984	1983	1982
£ NA	£ NA	£ NA	£3,184,462	£3,001,942	£2,761,549
NA	NA	NA	2,515,429	2,429,968	NA
1,039,321	891,839	792,486	669,033	571,974	2,761,549
258,799	236,196	200,752	196,814	201,790	NA
517,860	486,689	335,558	433,377	295,181	NA
51,888	37,075	37,181	24,427	25,572	NA
828,547	759,960	573,491	654,618	522,543	—
82,414	46,695	32,459	19,427	71,097	NA
293,188	178,574	251,454	33,842	120,528	142,646
95,732	60,863	92,741	2,450	13,645	32,589
£197,456	£117,711	£158,713	£ 31,392	£ 106,883	£ 110,057
402	411	396	397	408	404

visits required to prepare the program, management's mood changed. The day before the program aired, Charles Morgan wrote an open letter to a newspaper that was previewing the program. Excerpts included the following:

> It is Sir John's view that we should double production in a short time-scale, paying for this by increasing the price of the car and investing in an expensive new plant. His methods would result in making many changes in the traditional way the Morgan is built.
>
> We disagree strongly with his solution, and believe the Morgan policy of gradual and carefully considered change will enable us to maintain the car's qualities, and unique appeal, and thereby ensure its survival for the foreseeable future.
>
> Sir John's criticisms have been noted, but they are unworthy of us.[11]

That wasn't all. Sir John had arrived at the Morgan factory in a chauffeur-driven Volvo. When he heard how management had reacted to his visit he responded, "but their pride seems to be in manufacturing from the furthest-back state they can. . . . I'm surprised they don't start with the tree itself." In response to Sir John, a Morgan employee said, "You would think that someone coming to tell a car company how to run a business would at least be able to drive himself." However, Sir John did test drive a Morgan on his first visit to the firm.

When Sir John saw the Morgan operation he came to several immediate conclusions. First, he felt that the car was a luxury good and, because of the wait-

EXHIBIT 32.3

Balance Sheet: Morgan Motor Company Limited
(Financial amounts in British pounds)

Years Ending May 31	1991	1990	1989	1988
Assets				
Current assets				
Cash	£2,010,823	£ 936,810	£ 734,496	£ 554,651
Accounts receivable	313,733	361,419	342,298	291,860
Stock	1,917,499	1,867,254	1,699,751	1,485,434
Total current assets	4,242,055	3,165,483	2,776,545	2,321,945
Fixed assets				
Property, plant, and equipment	356,970	343,380	346,968	320,307
Investments	163,761	168,701	167,154	166,707
Total fixed assets	520,731	512,081	514,122	487,014
Total assets	£4,762,786	£3,677,564	£3,290,667	£2,808,959
Liabilities and Shareholders' Equity				
Current liabilities				
Accounts payable	£1,351,349	£ 960,643	£ 982,436	£ 870,005
Taxes payable	352,491	247,430	223,177	145,632
Dividends payable	45,000	30,000	30,000	30,000
Total current liabilities	1,748,840	1,238,073	1,235,613	1,045,637
Deferred taxation	—	—	—	—
Total liabilities	1,748,840	1,238,073	1,235,613	1,045,637
Shareholders' equity				
Common stock (1 par, 100,000 issued and outstanding)	100,000	100,000	100,000	100,000
Retained earnings	2,913,946	2,339,491	1,955,054	1,663,322
Total shareholders' equity	3,013,946	2,439,491	2,055,054	1,763,322
Total liabilities and shareholders' equity	£4,762,786	£3,677,564	£3,290,667	£2,808,959

Source: Companies Registration Office, Companies House, Cardiff CF4 3UZ, Great Britain.

ing list, should command a higher price. Second, he felt that profits were too low to provide sufficient capital to cushion the company against the shock of changes in the environment. Accordingly, he recommended to the Morgans that they raise the car's price and increase production to at least 600 cars per year. Sir John felt that this level of production would allow the company to increase profits and still maintain its waiting list. Even so, he was not convinced of the value of the waiting list as insurance for Morgan's future. He viewed it as a problem, rather than a shield against hard times. The fact that people have paid more than market prices to acquire a Morgan seemed to be evidence of the ability to raise prices and the urgency of the demand. Sir John also felt that to change production and methods only incrementally would not have the desired outcome. He felt that the company would have to make major changes if it was to survive.

1987	1986	1985	1984	1983	1982
£ 482,798	£ 402,754	£ 481,701	£ 158,718	£ 258,409	£ 166,979
292,114	207,357	208,759	200,649	202,401	199,761
1,338,586	1,299,383	1,134,733	1,176,395	1,071,564	1,043,722
2,113,498	1,909,494	1,825,193	1,535,762	1,532,374	1,410,462
325,461	281,886	271,524	250,626	257,936	262,132
61,425	78,926	33,218	56,852	54,372	64,256
386,886	360,812	304,742	307,478	312,308	326,388
£2,500,384	£2,270,306	£2,129,935	£1,843,240	£1,844,682	£1,736,850
£ 737,350	£ 725,258	£ 632,687	£ 593,609	£ 596,632	£ 582,524
127,700	87,170	137,081	38,177	57,988	54,725
30,000	20,000	20,000	10,000	10,000	10,000
895,050	832,428	789,768	641,786	664,620	647,249
—	—	—	—	45,916	52,338
895,050	832,428	789,768	641,786	710,536	699,587
100,000	100,000	100,000	100,000	100,000	100,000
1,505,334	1,337,878	1,240,167	1,101,454	1,034,146	937,263
1,605,334	1,437,878	1,340,167	1,201,454	1,134,146	1,037,263
£2,500,384	£2,270,306	£2,129,935	£1,843,240	£1,844,682	£1,736,850

When Sir John visited the plant he seemed to find one ally, Maurice Owens, the Chief Development Engineer. Owens told Sir John that he felt the car could be made more efficiently. He said that he would like to see the plant rearranged and production be shifted to more of a modularized process. He expressed a desire to have the firm eliminate some minor differences between models that make production difficult. Because all the cars are handmade, these differences would seem to be immaterial, but some of them greatly slow production. Owens also would like to have the car redesigned by softening the suspension, for example, to make it more attractive to modern car buyers.

During his initial visit and later conferences with Peter and Charles Morgan, Sir John had the impression that the son would like for the firm do more to be successful (in an unspecified way). Charles Morgan also mentioned changing the car's suspension, incorporating power tools in production, using computerized stock control, and even doubling the size of the company. He even talked about trading on the Morgan name to produce and sell a line of accessories based on the marque (similar to the Wimbledon line of sports gear). He has been with the firm less than five years and initially seemed to be flexible. In spite of these attitudes, Charles Morgan's letter, written at the time the program aired, indicated that he has not yet made up his mind about change. Although the younger Morgan seemingly adopted a defensive position on the company, Sir John hoped that he would be willing to change things in the long run.

Six months after the initial program visit (in November 1989) Sir John met the Morgans at a car rally in Scotland. At this meeting he found out that the new clean-burn Rover engine would permit the car to be sold in the United States without having to be converted to propane. He also found out that Charles Morgan had enrolled in a local technical school to learn more about modern manufacturing and engineering techniques. Among other things, his schooling was to provide for a number of visits to regional factories with up-to-date manufacturing facilities.

When "The Troubleshooter" program aired in May 1990, Sir John remained concerned for the firm's survival. Moreover, Charles Morgan still remembers that the founder of the Porsche car company once said that generally the founder starts the company, the son consolidates the operation, and the grandson ruins it. Charles Morgan, the grandson, must decide if change will save the company or kill it.

Notes

1. K. Blick, "Rage On," *Sports Car International* (January 1991), pp. 34–40.
2. This description of the Morgan production process is based on information provided in B. A. Holm, *Famous Car Factories: Morgan* (Gothenburg, Sweden: AB Nordbook, 1991), pp. 56–113.
3. Sir John Harvey-Jones and Anthea Massey, "The Troubleshooter," BBC 2 television program (May 1990). (The authors obtained a transcript of the program, along with a tape of the program itself. A revised version of the transcript has been published by the authors above. Page numbers for this source refer to the transcript.)
4. Sir John Harvey-Jones, program tape.
5. Sir John Harvey-Jones, program transcript.
6. Ibid.
7. C. Harvey, *Morgan: The Last Survivor* (Somerset, England: Haynes Publishing Group, 1987), p. 246.
8. The authors obtained these financial data from copies of the firm's financial statements through a data service in England. Items marked NA were not reported by the firm or were not available on the statements received.
9. P. Morgan, "The Morgan Car: A Message from Peter Morgan," *Thoroughbred & Classic Cars* (November 1980), p. 3.
10. Sir John Harvey-Jones, program transcript, p. 4.
11. Holm, pp. 54–55

Crisis in Geneva

Rolf Hackmann

Business Background

At 9:00 A.M. Mr. Lansing, Vice-President Europe, is busy already in his Geneva, Switzerland, office, with its sweeping view of the lake and distant mountains. It is the European central office for the Allen Corporation of Chicago, a major producer of over the counter (OTC) pharmaceutical and nutritional products. He is preparing himself to call the Chicago headquarters at 4:00 P.M., which is the start of the business day in the Midwest.

Last week he had received an urgent call from Mr. Davidson, President and CEO of the Allen Corporation, who was concerned about the under-plan performance of his European operations for the first quarter. The profit shortfall for this period is estimated to reach $65,000 because of slower than expected sales, higher than planned operating expenses, and a constantly rising exchange rate for the dollar. The president seemed well briefed about business details. The rather one-sided conversation emphasized his deep concern for the present situation and its likely impact on the rest of the year. He accused Lansing of not having a viable business plan to reverse the under-plan performance of his major affiliates in local currency. Such a reversal would help minimize the exchange rate problem, which otherwise was accepted as being outside the sphere of influence of both executives.

Davidson had demanded a return call first thing this morning and specific answers to the following questions.

1. What accounted for the soft sales in almost all of the major affiliate markets, and why were sales 5%–9% under local budgets for France, the United Kingdom, and Germany, which together accounted for 72% of all European sales?
2. What was being done to reduce the operating expenses, which were both in excess of local budgets and, because of the low sales, far above approved company guidelines? Davidson had sarcastically accused Lansing of not being in control of his business at this point.
3. What were the new sales and profits forecasts for the next quarter and the rest of the year, following the first-quarter disaster? Could new product introductions, marketing strategies, or customer groups be expected to compensate for the loss of the first three months? If not, where was he proposing to cut expenses without further hurting business development?

Lansing had prepared himself well for the afternoon's teleconference with headquarters. In addition to Davidson, the corporate Vice-President of Finance, the

This case was prepared by Professor Rolf Hackmann of Western Illinois University. This case was presented at the 1986 Workshop of the Midwest Society for Case Research. It also appears in *Annual Advances in Business Cases,* 1986, pp. 77–87, edited by Phillip C. Fisher. This case was edited by T. L. Wheelen and J. D. Hunger for this book. Reprinted by permission.

Treasurer, and the Vice-President of Marketing most likely would attend the meeting and have an array of uncomfortable questions.

During the past week Lansing had called in the national managers, with their finance directors and marketing managers, for a business and budget review. After thorough discussions, he was confident that he could address the issues constructively.

He could handle the first two questions straightforwardly and factually to help to defuse the potentially explosive atmosphere. However, the last question had caused him some difficulty, not so much because he and his associates lacked ideas about the revival of the business, but because certain aspects of their implementation were delicate.

He hoped that against the background of his dismal profit record—actually, his first since he had been appointed to his present position—his proposal would be accepted even though it was rather innovative by the standards of the fundamentally conservative company. Actually, it presented the only workable solution to his present predicament as he saw it.

His response to the first question could be that the consensus in hindsight of his European colleagues was that the sales budget had been overly optimistic for the first quarter. Everybody, from public health authorities to industry sources and retailers, had anticipated a recurrence of the strong flu epidemic of three years ago. So far it had not materialized, and it was unlikely to occur this spring.

Allen's European sales thus were affected by the heavy stocking of cough and cold products with wholesalers and retailers at the end of last year, in anticipation of a strong first-quarter demand. This inventory had helped produce a record profit performance for the prior year but was now haunting the new budget period.

Another factor depressing to Lansing was the recent increase in interest rates throughout Europe, which led to tighter inventory policies by the trade. This tightening of inventories could actually provoke product returns, as the channels were grasping for any chance to improve their working capital situations. According to the affiliate managers, the likelihood of actual and sizable returns looked remote despite the company's liberal returns policy. However, they all agreed that the high inventories could not be worked off until the middle of the second quarter and again would lead to poor sales during the next three months. After June, sales were expected to return to normal and meet the plan for the rest of the year. The second quarter was expected to produce another profit shortfall, which, under the best of circumstances, could be as low as $40,000 and, in the worst case scenario, might go as high as $54,000.

He could defend expenses in excess of the first quarter's plan by citing the effects of the high sales expectations for that period. The overperformance was mainly the result of heavy advertising and promotion expenses. Sixty percent of the annual advertising and 45% of the promotion budget had been concentrated in the first three months, to give maximum push to all OTC (nonprescription) health products. The contracting policies of Europe's state-owned TV and radio stations required advertisers to prepay air time and did not grant them the right to quick cancellation as was done in the United States. These funds thus had been committed and were spent. The remaining advertising and promotion budgets offered very little room for significant expense cuts. An area that would allow immediate and substantial corrective action, though, was selling expenses.

The U.K. subsidiary had hired five new reps and one district manager the first of January at a total annual budgeted expense of £128,000 ($193,100), including salary, training, and operating expenses. The French subsidiary had added seven salespeople at the cost of FF1,840,000 ($241,630), and the German subsidiary had expanded its sales force by five reps and one district manager at a total of DM620,000 ($242,900). (All dollar figures are calculated at the budgeted exchange rates for each currency.) The other European subsidiaries also had increased their sales forces, but at a combined expense of only $150,000 for the full year. All positions had been approved in the budget.

In accordance with local labor laws, any or all of the new salespeople in the three big countries could be terminated without cause during a 90-day probation period. Sizable amounts of profit could be produced immediately by slashing sales-force budgets if headquarters really pressed for economy now. Compensating for the projected profit loss of the first half would require the termination of five or six salespeople. This action would represent only minor cosmetic surgery if the firings were distributed among the three markets, but Lansing disliked the idea of even such a small setback for his organizational development plans.

After four weeks of training and a six-month break-in period, these people would finally become productive. Within two years they should contribute average sales of $280,000 per year and a total of roughly $42,000 in operating profit.

Cutting personnel now, after only three months, not only would waste all the money invested so far, but also would make reversing the consequences of such a decision difficult if business improved later in the year. Most subsidiaries are on annual bonus plans that make salespeople reluctant to change jobs before year end and forfeit the accrued bonus. One way to overcome this obstacle would be to offer reimbursement of the lost bonus to potential recruits, but under present business conditions that didn't seem very practical.

Developing a New Business Plan

During the discussions with his managers, a line of action had surfaced that would allow Lansing to retain the sales-force expansion and still meet his profit goals for the year, should Davidson immediately approve the plan that he intended to submit this afternoon.

Over the past two years, Allen Corporation had successfully introduced a diet product under the trade name Figurella™ in most European markets except France. The French introduction was subject to government approval, a lengthy process required for all drugs and dietary products. Approval was not expected before the end of the year, which would be far too late for the all-important summer demand peak for this highly seasonal product. Thus it had not been included in the French budget for the year.

It was Mr. Dedieu, the French Manager of Laboratoires Berliot (the Allen subsidiary in Paris), who had come up with a novel and timely solution to the profit problem. He suggested that they proceed with the marketing of Figurella even before summer. In support of his proposal, he had pointed out that sales of the product as a simple food supplement or a quick meal would not require formal government registration procedures.

Although this was a welcome suggestion, he admitted that a problem could arise with trying to position the product in the dietary market without a clear-cut promotional message for weight control. That vital message would, under this plan, not be approved by the authorities. But, according to Dedieu, this problem was minor in view of the proposal's advantages and could be overcome if the product were sold only through pharmacies. Market research had shown that in France, as in other markets of Europe, pharmacists played a significant role in counseling people concerned about their weight but who were overwhelmed by the multitude of products in the market. This role was also the reason why pharmacies accounted for two-thirds of the sales of all diet products in France. Heavily promoting the weight-control aspect of Figurella to French pharmacists would help in overcoming or at least minimizing the lack of the diet theme in advertising and promotion. Marketing the product this way also would allow maintenance of better margins and higher retail prices than would result from mass-marketing outlets. These outlets were notoriously unsuited for direct and personal customer counseling. Besides, they tried to attract business strictly on price.

Excluding other channels from the marketing strategy would be unique in this very competitive market, but it would appeal strongly to the ultraconservative pharmacists who jealously protected their professional status and business interests. Obtaining their full support in the early phases of the marketing program made good business sense by also being consistent with Allen's overall business strategy. Over the years, Laboratoires Berliot had established close ties with the French pharmacies because of its health-related product lines, and this new product would certainly help to deepen the friendly relations.

Withdrawal of the application for product approval now before the French authorities would thus clear the way for immediate product introduction.

The plan delighted Lansing because it not only offered a seemingly perfect solution to his present profit crunch, but also presented a legitimate defense of his sales-force expansion in France.

Dedieu had come prepared with a complete marketing plan for Figurella. Proposing a May 15 introduction date, which would be right on time for the summer season, he was confident that he could sell 125,000 cans of 500 grams each for the season, as shown in the following list.

May	40,000 cans (initial stocking)
June	20,000
July	20,000
August	20,000
September–December	25,000
Total May–December	125,000

At a wholesale unit price of FF44.70 ($5.87), excluding the value added tax (VAT), this volume would generate sales of nearly FF5.6 million. Dedieu had not prepared a profit estimate because he did not have the details on laid-down costs for the

EXHIBIT 33.1

Figurella Product Specifications

	Grams/100g	
Protein	23.5	
Fat	3.5	
Carbohydrates	66.4	
Minerals (ash)	4.1	
Moisture	2.5	
	Grams/500g	**% of Total Content**
Milk powder[1]	287.5	57.5
Sucrose	212.5	42.5

Note:
1. Includes 119.5g of lactose.

product at his Paris warehouse. Germany and the United Kingdom would be potential supply sources because the product was manufactured in both countries. Assuming that production costs would be lower in the United Kingdom than in Germany, he had indicated a preference for U.K. supplies. He had further assumed transportation charges, based on truck delivery, London–Paris or Frankfurt–Paris, to be about the same. As members of the European Community, both countries were exempt from French import tariff levies.

Product Information

Figurella is basically a variation of a nutritional supplement developed by Allen Corporation for use by persons debilitated by inadequate food intake because of disease or other medical reasons. The original product is sold under a different trademark and provides accurately measured supplementation of daily nutritional requirements.

Figurella is supplied in 500-gram cans and three different flavors—chocolate, vanilla, and strawberry—to prevent product fatigue in users. Basically the product is a milk powder formula with added carbohydrates for taste improvement and nutritional balance. Data for the formula in each can are presented in Exhibit 33.1.

Two sugars provide the carbohydrates: lactose, naturally occurring in milk, and sucrose, added for taste and quick supply of energy. The sucrose content is maintained at 42.5 grams per 100 grams of final powder mixture, and the total carbohydrate content of the formula is 66.4 grams per 100 grams. Each 100 grams of powder mixed with about 7–8 ounces of water provides 390 calories. Although originally developed to provide additional caloric intake to cases of nutritional deficiencies, the concept of scientifically dosaged nutrition serves the market for weight-control products well.

The Allen Corporation thus modified the original product slightly and promoted the new Figurella product as a balanced formula for weight loss. The daily regimen consists of one glass of diluted powder each for breakfast and lunch (780 calories total) and one regular meal of the user's choice at night. Such a meal ordinarily should provide another 800 calories, for a daily total of about 1,600 calories—roughly half or even less of the amount that obese people tend to consume. If more rapid weight control is desired, the user may replace the regular meal with one glass of Figurella, for a daily count of 1,170 calories. Such a regimen induces a weight loss of about one pound per two days, as the caloric deficit is 1,800 calories per day for the average adult. (One pound of fat is 3,500 calories.)

One of the three variants presently on the market in the United Kingdom and Germany, the strawberry formula, cannot be sold in France. The European Community (EC) had banned the coloring agent FDC Red #2 for some time because of its potentially mutagenic properties.

Manufacturing Cost Information

According to data from the finance department, production costs for the chocolate and vanilla product in the United Kingdom amount to £0.981 per can ($1.48) for the chocolate and £0.884 per can ($1.34) for the vanilla flavor. Production costs are 2.5% higher in Germany than in the United Kingdom for both flavors.

Based on this information and a 50/50 sales split (number of cans) between the two flavors, the average cost per finished and French-labeled can is $1.41 from the United Kingdom and $1.445 from Germany. If there is an average net wholesale price of $5.87 per can in France, the gross margin amounts to $4.46 per can for U.K.-produced and $4.43 per can for German-produced material, before allocation of freight, handling, and storage charges. All three countries are EC members and therefore no import duties apply.

Transportation Charges

Transportation expenses for U.K.- and German-produced materials vary only slightly. Based on a standard shipment of 20,000 cans—3,333 cartons of six cans each—and a total estimated shipping weight of 15,000 kilograms, the following are the estimated total handling and freight charges supplied by freight forwarders, for carriage to Paris.

Inland freight (truck) from Frankfurt	DM3,060 ($1,199)
Barge and inland freight (truck) from London	£1,056 ($1,593)

The charges translate to $.06 per can for German supplies and $.08 per can for U.K. Figurella material.

Profitability Projections

The sales forecast of 125,000 cans for France looks realistic and in line with introductory sales volumes generated in other markets.

EXHIBIT 33.2

Figurella P&L Consolidation (Based on U.K. Production)
(Dollar amounts in U.S. dollars)

	Amount
Sales	$733,750
Cost of goods sold (COG)[1]	186,250
Gross margin (GM)	547,500
Total operating expenses[2]	63,750
Direct operating profit	483,750
Corporate taxes	
U.K. (50%)	8,125
France (50%)	—
Switzerland (22.96%)	107,338
Total tax liability	115,463
Other income	
EC export refund	38,348
Net profit adjusted	$406,635

Notes:

1. The transportation charges London–Paris have been charged to the COG.
2. French marketing, selling, overhead, and other operating expenses relating to the Figurella introduction have been assumed to be equal to the local gross profit generated by the transfer pricing for simplicity's sake. The purpose of Lansing's exercise is to demonstrate to top management in Chicago that these profits will at least offset the profit shortage of the first half of the year. This was estimated to range from $105,000 to $119,000.

Checking with pharmacists in major population centers indicated a high level of enthusiasm for the new product because of its exclusive sale through pharmacies and the good profit margin for this type of product. No big difficulties were anticipated for promotion of an official food supplement as a weight-control product.

The consolidated profit picture looks good and would allow Lansing to more than compensate for the expected shortfall in the first half. If U.K. supplies were used, unadjusted gross profits of $547,500 would be generated from the sale of 125,000 cans of Figurella (see Exhibit 33.2); German supplies would contribute the slightly lower amount of $545,625.

Tax Considerations

With an effective rate of 50% on reported profits, corporate taxes are practically identical for all three nations. (Germany's rate may go up to 56%, but that would apply to undistributed profits only and would not apply in this case.) Therefore, shifting profits among the three countries through intracorporate pricing manipulations ordinarily would not affect overall corporate tax liability. But Allen Corporation has honed its tax management skills during many years of transfer pricing, involving Swiss corporate intermediaries.

EXHIBIT 33.3

Local P&L Data for Figurella

(Dollar amounts in U.S. dollars)

	United Kingdom	Switzerland	France
Price per can	$ 1.54	$ 5.28	$ 5.87
Cost of good per can	1.41	1.54	5.36[1]
Gross margin per can	.13	3.74	.51
Gross margin per dollars	$16,250	$467,500	$63,750
Operating expenses	—	—	63,750
Direct operating profit	16,250	467,500	—
Taxes	8,125	107,338	—
Other income	38,348	—	—
Net profit	$46,473	$360,162	$ —

Note:
1. Includes handling/freight London–Paris: $.08 per can.

To minimize the impact of high taxes within some countries on consolidated corporate profits, the Allen Corporation has set up three trading companies in Switzerland. Each of them operates under a different name, is not readily identified with its owner, and is located in a different city with a different tax structure. The companies are practically one-person organizations (small offices, a manager, a secretary or two, telephones, Telex equipment) and serve the sole purpose of shifting profits among Allen Corporation and its subsidiaries. Some third-party business is occasionally added for window dressing.

For the purpose of selling Figurella to France, Lansing has selected Flueli GmbH. in Zug to act as the pro-forma purchaser of the U.K. product. After consulting with his financial director, Mr. Lombardi, he will propose to headquarters that the U.K. subsidiary sell a finished can of Figurella at £1.02 ($1.54) to Flueli who in turn will sell the can for $5.28 to the French subsidiary, with a profit of $3.74 per can going into the Swiss account (see Exhibit 33.3). Transportation and related charges do not affect this part of the transaction. The French gross profit of $.51 per can (adjusted for transportation charges) will have to cover product introduction and marketing expenses but is not expected to produce a profit for the French operation.

This tax maneuver is going to net $126,412 in extra profit because the maximum corporate tax rate in Zug is only 22.96%. That portion of the consolidated profits alone more than offsets the profit underperformance forecasted for the first half of the year for all European operations.

Lansing expects to get quick approval from headquarters for this part of his plan, partly because it promises a substantial and quick recovery of profits and partly because the payoff depends entirely on the introduction of the product by mid May, which is only two months away. It presents no unusual business risks, and his European associates unanimously support it.

Sourcing and transfer-pricing decisions invariably lead to resistance by his country's managers, who always are quick to suspect that they are getting an unfair deal. He thus is hearing complaints from the managers in the United Kingdom, Germany, and France. Their bonus plan rests on profit performance, and any over-plan operating results yield substantial payoffs over and above base salary.

The German manager resents not having been chosen at least as a partial supplier. His contention is that the minimal production-cost advantage of the U.K. material is more than offset by the stability of German labor relations—the U.K. plant has been the target of wildcat strikes in the past—and the lower transportation charges.

The U.K. manager wants to have an "arm's length" price equal to his average local net wholesale price of £3.12 ($4.71). Under the proposed pricing, he stands to lose a local profit of £2.1875 per can ($3.30) and claims that the arbitrarily low export price will lead to inquiries by the tax authorities, who are always suspecting tax evasion maneuvers by multinationals.

The French manager argues that his purchase price is too high to make the product profitable locally because of the high launching expenses required for sales-force training, distribution, selling, and promotion. He points to the corporate profit guidelines whereby no new product should be introduced with pre-tax profit margins of less than 25%, which in this case is not going to be realized initially or eventually, because of the high landed (delivered) cost in France.

Lansing will have to address the issue at some time in the near future because management unrest about bonus prospects can be disruptive. But he does not intend to raise the subject with Chicago today unless specifically asked. If asked, he is prepared to propose allocation of profits on a management basis by splitting the Swiss profits equally between France and the United Kingdom.

Profit Maximization Potential

While the Figurella plans for France were being discussed, an interesting and tempting piece of information came up. According to Dedieu, exports of agricultural surplus products from the EC are subsidized by Brussels (EC headquarters).

In the Figurella case, both the milk powder and the sucrose are eligible for export-support payments based on a rate of ECU85.86 per 100 kilograms of spray-dried milk powder and ECU37.78 per 100 kilograms of sugar. (ECU stands for European Currency Unit, comprising a currency basket of the ten-member currencies.)

The sale of 125,000 cans could thus result in subsidies amounting to

35.94 tons of milk powder	=	ECU30,858
26.56 tons of sugar	=	ECU10,034
Total subsidy payment	=	ECU40,892

Converted at the green (agricultural) rate of £0.618655 per ECU, this subsidy is equivalent to £25,298 ($38,348). This extra profit promises to expand with growing sales of Figurella, but there are some caveats.

In order for the sale to Flueli GmbH to qualify Allen Ltd for payment of the EC subsidy, the merchandise itself should become a bona fide EC export. But in order to save transportation and handling charges, and time, Allen Ltd sells the merchandise to Flueli GmbH, and in a simultaneous transaction Flueli sells the same shipment to Laboratoires Berliot. With two sets of the necessary shipping and insurance documents, commercial invoices, and certificates of origin prepared in the United Kingdom, the shipment does not need to be detoured to Switzerland but can go straight from London to Paris.

From many similar transactions between Allen Ltd and Flueli GmbH in the past, the company has developed an efficient order-handling procedure. It allows the use of Flueli GmbH letterhead stationery and invoice forms by Allen Ltd order-processing personnel in the London offices. This procedure avoids unnecessary mailing delays and transportation expenses. The blank forms are presigned by an authorized Flueli GmbH official, and copies of the entire process go to Zug for filing. Without violating any customs procedures, the documents will be processed and stamped at the respective border crossings and thus legitimize the merchandise so that the merchandise has both proof of export from the United Kingdom to Switzerland—which makes it eligible for the subsidies—and entry as Swiss-owned but EC-produced merchandise into France—which eliminates any import levies.

These "triangle" business transactions are widely practiced because the rewards are so tempting. But they obviously violate ethical and legal norms and are thus subject to the EC penal code. Nonetheless, Lansing intends to ask for headquarters' authorization for this particular aspect of the plan this afternoon, and he will plead that the chances for embarrassment are practically nil.

Profit Consolidation

For the afternoon's discussion Lansing has prepared a profit and loss consolidation, which summarizes the effect of the various transactions he will propose. The data look extremely favorable and should present a pleasant surprise even to Davidson. Above all, they are very realistic, and Lansing is confident that approval from Chicago will be forthcoming during the afternoon business review. After all, the realization of these figures rests entirely on top management's authorization today, as time for implementation of the plan is already running very short.

To be ready for any question that might come up during his presentation, Lansing also has prepared local P&L data for each country in support of the consolidated P&L figures. In addition he has Telexed a copy of all financial data to Chicago for review by the participants there.

Lansing deliberately set the French operating expenses at a level equal to the local gross margin of the product. This step neutralizes the tax aspects of the plan and simplifies the calculation, although it does not account for realistic levels of introductory expenses. Davidson probably would not be overly interested in precise data on this point, as the total package assures him of an extremely positive consolidated profit recovery for Europe. This outcome will hold even if he should not approve all parts of the plan as presented.

Uncoupling 50 Years of Soviet Central Planning: Case of a Privatized Lithuanian Manufacturer

Robert P. Vichas

For 20 years Leonas Karpalavičius (pronounced *Car-pe-lá-ve-chas*), Managing Director of the state-owned Šiauliai (pronounced *show-lay*) Factory of Nonwoven Fabrics, successfully dealt with a centralized bureaucracy. He had survived the German occupation during World War II, nearly 50 years of Soviet subjugation of Lithuania, a near-perilous encounter with a Communist Party chieftain, and a brush with the KGB. Now, in mid 1992, he focused on survival of the firm. Recent events weighed heavily on the 60-year-old director. On this Friday afternoon the staff had already left, but he remained in his office because he needed quiet time to think about the firm's future, including a possible international joint venture. However, one of five telephones on his desk demanded his attention: a man from Kazakhstan was trying to sell him wool.

"How much is it?" asked Karpalavičius.

"I don't know," answered the voice.

"What grade is it?"

"I don't know."

"How much of it do you have?"

"I don't know."

"Is it washed or unwashed? There are three types of washing."

"I don't know."

"I can't buy a cat in a sack." Karpalavičius abruptly terminated the conversation. "Amateurs," he said aloud. "They're all amateurs nowadays."

He had weathered independence from Moscow, breakup of the Soviet Union, and privatization. However, getting needed quantities and qualities of raw materials, Moscow to pay for exports to Russia, credit to finance slow-pay receivables and accumulate inventory, hard currency to pay for Western machinery and technology, new foreign customers—these knotty problems seemed nearly unsolvable. Early next month he would travel to Sweden to discuss a joint venture. He wasn't optimistic because nothing concrete had materialized from discussions with two other Western firms. In two weeks on the longest day of the year, the sun would set late, and complete darkness would not envelop the office until nearly midnight. He wondered whether the sun had set on his career as well. In August the Supervisory Board would vote on a slate of directors.

The author acknowledges the financial support of a U.S. Department of Education BEFEE (Business and Economics Fellowships in East Europe) grant administered by the Center for Russian and East European Studies, University of Pittsburgh, the cooperation and financial assistance of Leonas Karpalavičius, Managing Director of SFNF, and the continued help of Virginija Vaičekonienė, Coordinator of International Programs, Kaunas Technological University at Panevėžys, as interpreter, translator, and colleague. This case was prepared by Professor Robert P. Vichas of Texas A&M International University and Kaunas Technological University at Panevėžys. This case was edited by T. L. Wheelen and J. D. Hunger for this book. Reprinted by permission.

Setting and Background

At one time the largest country in Europe, Lithuania had stretched from the Baltic Sea to the Black Sea and nearly to Warsaw and Moscow. Having been occupied by Swedes, Germans, Russians, Poles, and others over the centuries, the country had been reduced to its current size (slightly larger than the state of West Virginia) after World War I. The geographical center of Europe lay only 15 miles from Vilnius, the capital city. Despite successive occupations, its 3.5 million inhabitants maintained purity of language (Lithuanian with ancient roots in Sanskrit), Aryan ethnicity (80% of the population was pure Lithuanian), and a unique culture (in song, dance, and theater). After dislodging the Germans during World War II, the Soviet Union annexed Lithuania in 1945, an annexation that the United States never recognized *de jure*. Nevertheless, the agriculturally rich economy was integrated into the Soviet empire, and virtually all trade was linked to the Eastern bloc. In 1990, Lithuania forged a bloody independence, but in mid-1992 more than 50,000 Russian troops remained in the country.

The fourth largest city, Šiauliai, remained closed to foreigners until 1988 because of military-sensitive, Soviet installations, which included a 15,000 foot long runway and radar equipment. A civilian airstrip served nonmilitary traffic. Šiauliai also boasted several high- and low-tech manufacturing plants crucial to the functioning of the Soviet economic system.

Established in 1937, the Šiauliai Factory of Nonwoven Fabrics produced linen products from domestically grown flax. When they occupied the city on June 25, 1941, the Germans ordered the factory to begin producing linen for flags. Although two-thirds of Šiauliai was destroyed in 1944 when the Soviets drove the Germans out, the plant (located at the edge of the city) suffered little damage. In 1964, under its present name, the Šiauliai Factory of Nonwoven Fabrics (SFNF) began producing nonwoven products, and, in 1966 it began producing yarns. When Karpalavičius joined the firm in 1971, the annual value of the firm's manufacturing output equalled 6 million Russian rubles (Rs); by the end of 1992 it would reach Rs500 million.*

Until May 1992, the Šiauliai Factory of Nonwoven Fabrics operated under state ownership. Although the Lithuanian government took over all Soviet-claimed property in 1990, it did not privatize the firm until 1992. Exclusive of land (land remained under state ownership), at the end of 1991, the operation was valued at Rs41 million which was essentially the historical value of buildings, equipment, rolling stock, and inventory. To ease the transition to a market economy and assist workers, Karpalavičius paid a substantial bonus from 1991 undistributed profits, which workers added to state-issued certificates of investment to purchase 67% of the firm's equity. The government retained ownership of 5% of

*During much of this period, the Soviet government maintained an artificial ruble rate of US$1.35. Toward the end of its empire days, a commercial ruble sold at a little less than one-half the official rate. Parallel market rates in Western Europe pegged the real value of the ruble at about US$0.20 in the 1970s. Although there is no accurate measure of Soviet inflation between 1970 and 1990, probably one-half of the 1990 production value was accounted for by inflation. In November 1991, the rate in Lithuania averaged Rs75 to the U.S. dollar; in June 1992, 120–130, with a continuing downward spiral. Lithuania continued to use the Russian ruble until September 1992.

equity as a contingency fund for historical claims. The other 28% comprised outside Lithuanian owners (i.e., not SFNF employees).

The Lithuanian government had issued certificates of investment to the entire population, according to age: Rs5,000 to those over age 30; Rs3,000 to adults under 30; and smaller amounts to children. At their option citizens could exchange these certificates for equity shares and match, up to 100%, the value of these certificates with personal savings. Foreigners could acquire equity in selected firms, based on book value, in U.S. dollars, at the artificial rate of US$1= Rs2.

The Ministry of Economy retained oversight of present and former state concerns and could issue or approve loans to them. Consequently, privatization of state firms proceeded at various levels of state ownership, ranging from temporary retention of complete government ownership (such as the microchip manufacturer in Šiauliai) to the minimum extent of government ownership (such as SFNF).

Centralized government planning had focused on volume of production more than any other functional activity. Even production costs, largely a matter of decree, were secondary to physical volume of output. Marketing and R&D had virtually no role under the communist system, and the Ministry of Economy controlled capital budget allocations. Although upper management controlled the personnel function, employee review and evaluation procedures were not standardized. Socialist accounting bore little resemblance to the profit and cost accounting of Western companies chiefly because all assets belonged to the state, which set prices and claimed year-end surpluses.

Organizational Structure

Based on the Soviet system of management, power theoretically resided in the hands of the workers who, through elected representatives, determined the management board with the approval of the Ministry of Economy. Quinquennially (every five years) workers elected a six-member supervisory board, the Council of Observers, who, in turn, annually reviewed performance and elected the Board of Directors (i.e., managers of the firm, who had to be approved by the Ministry of Economy). The Council functioned as an oversight committee. Meeting quarterly, it discussed and approved salaries, bonuses, plans, budgets, personnel policies, and reviewed the Managing Director's report. The Managing Director (chief operating officer), Commercial Director, and Technical Director comprised the executive team (see Exhibit 34.1).

On average, the current directors had 25 years of experience with the firm. The Commercial (Marketing) Director was responsible primarily for buying raw materials, shipping and receiving, and inventory management; he did little marketing of products.

At many factories, the Technical Director (comparable to an executive vice-president) was the second in command, to further signifying primacy of production in the Soviet system. However, at the Šiauliai Factory of Nonwoven Fabrics, the Technical Director, although part of the executive team, was not second in command. Nevertheless, he bore primary responsibility for all aspects of manufacturing. Exhibit 34.2 illustrates the scope of his responsibilities and direct involvement in operational details.

EXHIBIT 34.1 **Management Organization Chart: Šiauliai Factory of Nonwoven Fabrics**

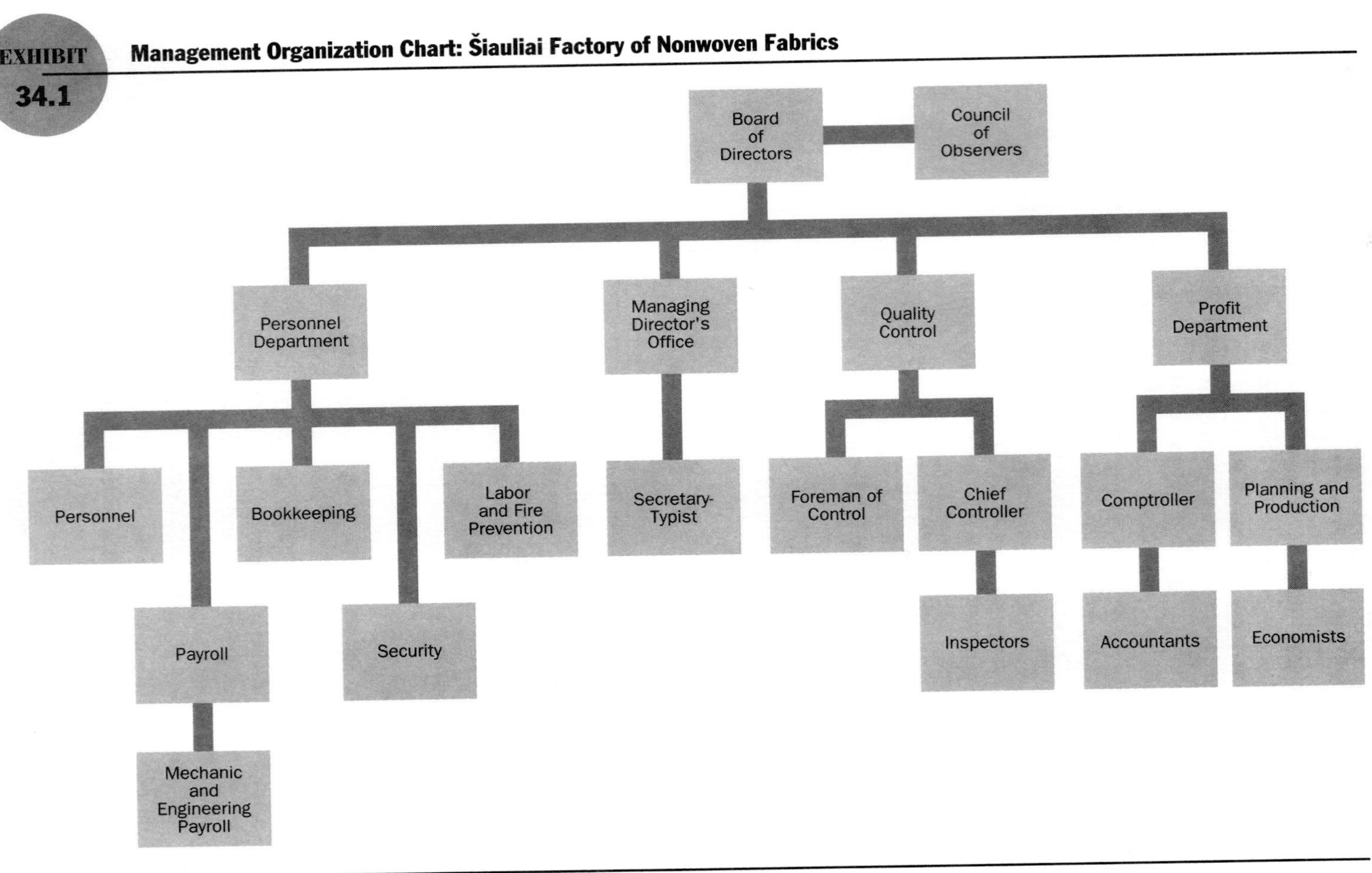

Source: Šiauliai Factory of Nonwoven Fabrics organizational charts. Translation by Virginija Vaičekonienė.

EXHIBIT 34.2

Organization Chart: Šiauliai Factory of Nonwoven Fabrics

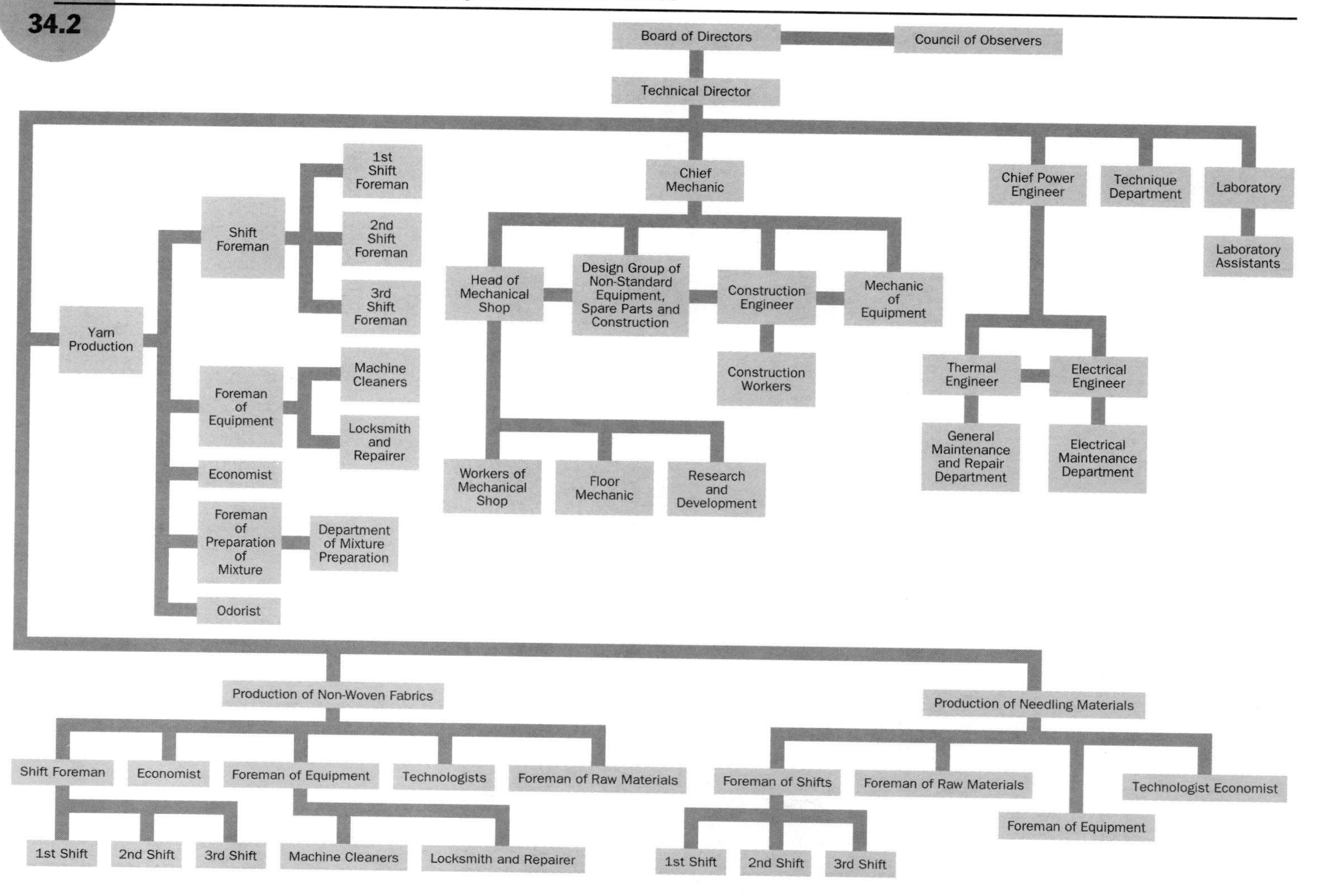

Source: Šiauliai Factory of Nonwoven Fabrics organizational charts. Translation by Virginija Vaičekonienė.

Following privatization, lines of authority became blurred. Accountability had been centered in the Managing Director but he had lost considerable power, and the Technical Director could now bypass his decisions and report directly to the Board of Directors (on which both men served). Adding to the confusion of who was in charge, the Council of Observers attempted to wrest power from the Managing Director. Thus the transition from a central planning environment to one resembling a market economy was beset by problems.

Leonas Karpalavičius, Managing Director for 20 years, was born in 1932 and grew up in Kaunas, Lithuania (second largest city and former Lithuanian capital). His father, a government employee, was "transferred" to Russia in 1941 and executed in 1942. (Not until 1991 did Karpalavičius learn the real truth because the KGB had said that his father had died of pneumonia. During the German occupation he once ran through fields for his life because the Germans mistook him for a Jew.) With two children to support, his mother became a seamstress, and Karpalavičius began work at age 16 at Patika, a curtain manufacturer, while attending night school. After completing night and extramural studies, he received his five-year university diploma, quickly rose to become a director in 1962, and earned the nickname "Quicksilver" because of his mercurial rise through the ranks. Soon thereafter he was appointed Managing Director of Spatolis, a wool products manufacturer.

Because of a minor indiscretion at a social event in Kaunas in 1971, a Communist Party chief ousted Karpalavičius from his directorship. Through a friend at party headquarters, he managed to secure a post in Šiauliai, considered at that time the boonies, as Managing Director of the Šiauliai Factory of Nonwoven Fabrics. Although he traveled to Poland and East Germany, Moscow never allowed him to travel beyond the Iron Curtain and severely limited his contacts with Western businesses. He also was President of the Association of Trade and Industry of Šiauliai, a regional organization formed in 1991. The association worked to promote products manufactured in Šiauliai, mostly by means of exhibits and by introducing them to visiting foreign business people.

Despite socialist training and party affiliations, Karpalavičius comprehended the need to westernize management techniques. After independence, for example, he wanted to introduce a merit system for workers, with severe penalties for nonperformers. His Personnel Manager, Regina Poškienė, grasped this new philosophy, but she had no concept of how to implement it as policy. A "manager by walking around," Karpalavičius toured the factory three times daily, inspecting production and stopping to chat with workers (most of whom he knew by name).

Karpalavičius said, "My problems start mainly with my assistants because they are the product of 50 years of the socialist system. They are particularly confused by the whole bargaining process between investors and the factory." He lamented:

> Things are different now. Before Lithuania's independence I could do things without consulting anyone else. Laws have changed. Now everyone's functions are different. The Chief Engineer and Deputy Director reported directly to me. Now the Chief Engineer is called the Technical Director, and the Deputy Director is now called the Com-

mercial Director. They are responsible for their own areas, and I am responsible for nothing. Higher levels of management have taken away many areas of my concern.

Products and Manufacturing Facilities

Outputs and Inputs

The Šiauliai Factory of Nonwoven Fabrics produced nearly 9 million square yards of the following products.

1. Nonwoven sewn material for heat- and sound-insulating gaskets.
2. Nonwoven sewn material for linoleum backing.
3. Nonwoven sewn material for lining heavy clothing.
4. Nonwoven sewn material for padding and softening.
5. Nonwoven sewn material for lining shoes.
6. Spongy fiber bonded synthetic material for lining overcoats.
7. Knitted stitched lining cloth for sportswear.
8. Knitted stitched wadding lined with gauze for lining overcoats.
9. Knitted stitched padding from production waste for furniture.

Imports of basic raw materials—polyvinyl chloride, polymeric amide, viscose, wool, cotton, and polyether fibers, along with capron and dacron—mostly from Latvia, Belarus, Kazakhstan, Ukraine, and Russia supplemented those available domestically. Availability, and quality, of scrap material, an important source of inputs, declined as prices jumped 12 to 20 times in less than two years.

The Commercial Director, Adomas Alfonas Navickas, was responsible for acquiring raw materials. He had bought 80% of the firm's inputs within the the Soviet Union before its break-up and it in turn had purchased about 80% of the firm's outputs. Following independence, his job became increasingly difficult, not only because of the erratic availability of raw materials, but also because of the widening gap between accounts receivable and accounts payable and the lack of short-term financing. Increasingly, he had to negotiate with diverse private, often unreliable vendors, who demanded cash up front, while Moscow delayed paying for products delivered to its state-owned factories. Navickas said that in the past they could barter for their needs, but:

> Now, many of our suppliers are out of business and the remaining want cash. In Bernova, where I come from, the Russian government ordered businesses to boycott the sale of goods to Lithuania. Two documents state that Lithuania could trade with no increase in customs duties for a period of three months; but further instuctions say not to sell certain items to Lithuania. Some Russian companies are not honoring the agreement. They have said that they will honor the agreement for one month. Our suppliers try to keep us informed. For example, formerly many of our raw materials were purchased from Russian factories, which had purchased from suppliers abroad. Now Russian companies are not buying their raw materials from abroad, which affected the dependability and availability of our supplies. We cannot forecast our sales from month-to-month because we depend upon the amount of raw material available.
>
> We heard rumors that some political developments would result in shortages of raw materials so we stockpiled inventory and manufactured for nine months without re-

ceiving additional raw material. We had to invest part of our 15 million ruble profit in anything so we began acquiring assets. This has been profitable because raw materials increased 200% this past year along with high import duties. Lithuania is in the process of forming a formal marketplace, which would allow us to hedge our position. All we can do now is raise the cost of the finished product.

In 1991, Karpalavičius estimated the percentage breakdown of direct manufacturing costs for wool and synthetic fibers: raw materials, 90%; wages, 3%; and other expenses, 7%. For production of all other output, he stated that direct costs were: raw materials, 65%–70%; wages, 12%–14%; and other expenses, 16%–23%. As the economy freed itself from the Soviet system, these cost relationships would change both relatively and absolutely, which complicated the development of a long-term pricing strategy.

Manufacturing Operations

Under Soviet rule, no quality standards prevailed for the industry. Nevertheless, the Šiauliai Factory of Nonwoven Fabrics created its own standards for quality, strength, and thickness of nonwoven fabrics. Although it could not meet European Community ISO 9000 standards in 1992, it entered into an agreement with an institute in Riga, Latvia, to receive information on international quality standards. The Šiauliai Factory of Nonwoven Fabrics had more than 40 control standards in place (e.g., rules based on caring for and maintaining machinery). Foremen bore responsibility for breakdowns resulting from poor employee performance. Plant supervisors requested repairs, replacement parts, and the like, from top management to establish an audit trail and accountability.

Although management attempted to implement a policy of 0% rejects, they bottomed out at 2%–4%, partly owing to problems with raw materials. Workers had to remove inferior fabrics and threads by hand. Because this labor-intensive effort increased input costs, management researched new products for the shoe industry and potential markets for products manufactured from cotton wastes. The Technical Director explained:

> About 20% of the raw materials are unacceptable and getting worse. We have also been forced to use some of our own labor to process the raw materials to improve the quality, which has added to our processing costs. Quality is directly proportional to labor costs and processing costs, and both have increased. We have absorbed some of the cost in our spinning department by creating two categories of production. The best go to one category, the seconds to another. We hope to continue to pass along the increased costs to our customers as we have done this year. We hope to increase the quality of raw materials by looking for a larger number of suppliers.

At mid-1992, the Šiauliai Factory of Nonwoven Fabrics operated at full capacity, defined as 23 hours a day, five days a week. Machines were maintained daily, and major overhauls were accomplished on a one and one-half year cycle. A six-month inventory of replacement parts was stockpiled. Despite the age of equipment, regular maintenance permitted a high level of output for the state of technology the equipment represented.

EXHIBIT 34.3 **Factory Layout: Šiauliai Factory of Nonwoven Fabrics**

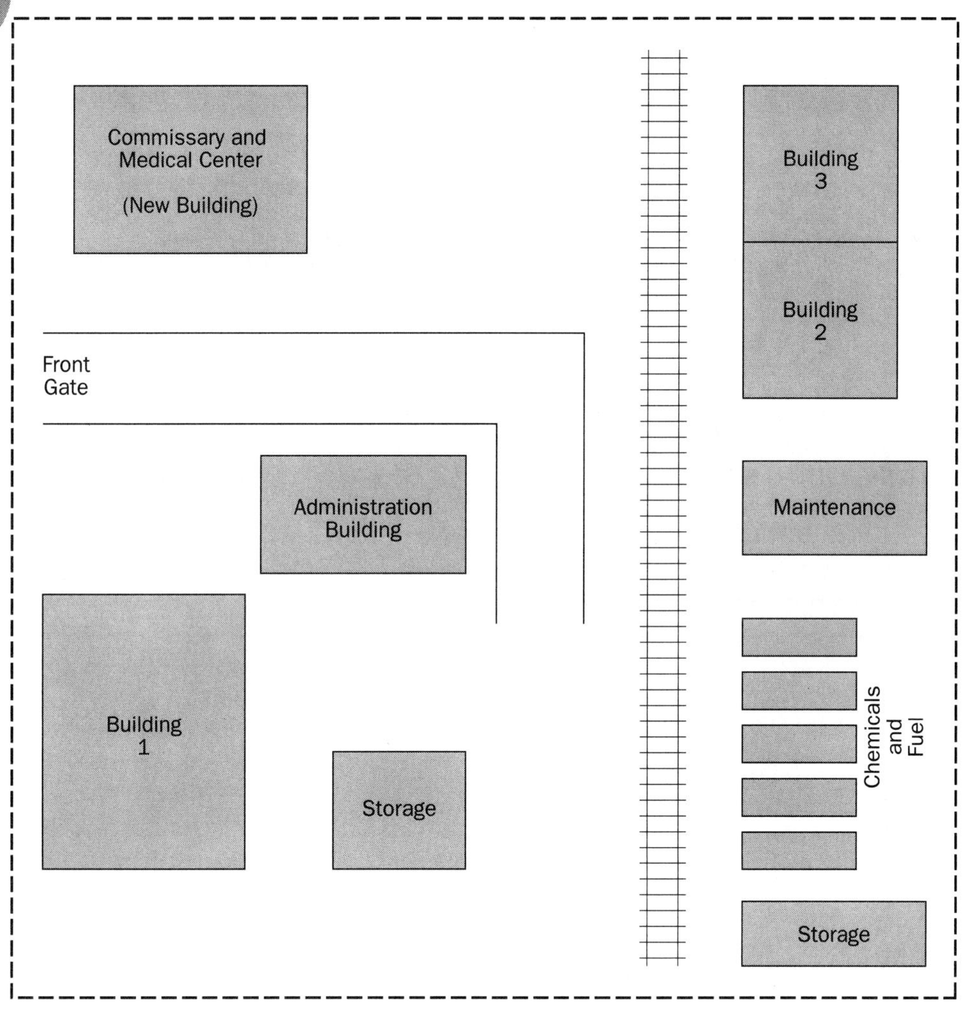

Exhibit 34.3 shows the general plant layout. A guard-controlled electric gate permitted vehicle access to the fenced property. Most buildings were two stories in height. A railroad spur allowed direct loading and unloading of materials, and, in 1991, about 100 carloads of material per month passed through the plant. To complete the manufacturing process, workers had to shift materials among various buildings. Even on a single floor of a building, materials and products did not flow continuously. Because of dwindling customer demand, the Šiauliai Factory of Nonwoven Fabrics had no backlog of orders for its products. Exhibit 34.4 shows the production sequence on one floor of one building, indicating a seriously dis-

EXHIBIT 34.4 **First Floor of Building 1: Šiauliai Factory of Nonwoven Fabrics**

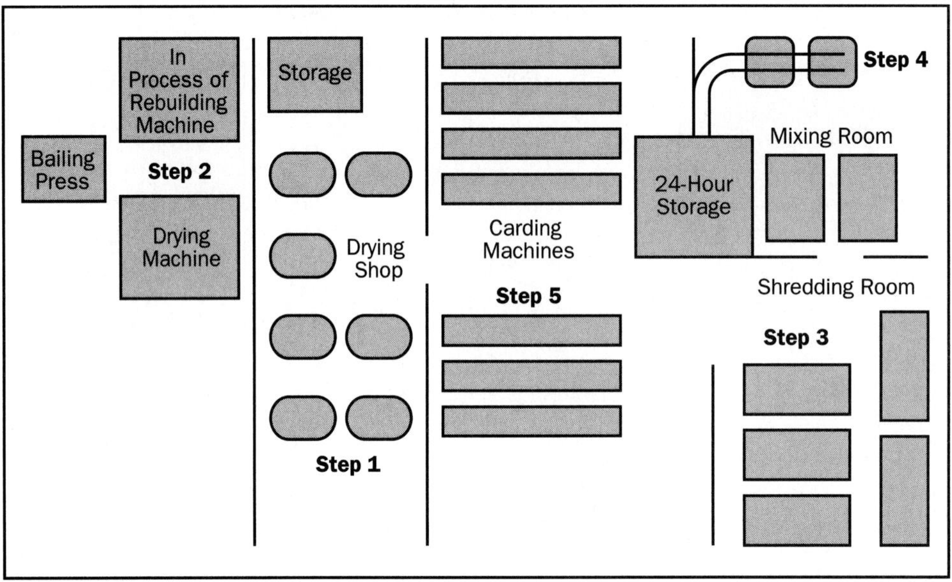

continuous process. In most instances workers loaded and carted materials by hand.

The factory complex comprised six departments: dying and drying, preparation, spinning, nonwovens, glued and synthetic fibers, and needling.

- **Dying and drying department.** This department could dye as many as 15 colors or shades of wool but only processed 3–5 daily in 25 dying vats. Wool, mixed with polymers and other synthetics, was dyed, dried, and baled. Dried fibers were sold as raw materials or sent to spinning. Rebuilding equipment, now some 30 years old, would cost Rs500,000 versus Rs2.5 million for new machinery.
- **Preparation department.** Wool, again cleaned, shredded, fluffed, stored for 24 hours, and transferred to seven carding machines (ten years old), became bolts of yarn. Material was stacked and loaded by hand. The department produced 810 tons annually.
- **Spinning department.** Eight machines spun yarn first onto small spools, and then onto large spools, which were shipped to carpet manufacturers. Production was 50% wool and 50% other fibers, including polymer and viscose. Delivery of replacement parts for the eight Soviet-built spinning machines, 35 years old, might take as long as six months.
- **Nonwovens department.** Purchased scrap fibers were processed in regenerate fiber machines, which mixed half wool and half chemical fibers from regener-

ated waste. Transferred to sewing, it became white nonwoven fibers for the apparel industry and gray fibers for the upholstery industry. Three 20-year-old Polish regenerate fiber machines produced 500–600 meters* of fabric every eight hours. Four 25-year-old Soviet machines produced 200–300 meters of fabric in eight hours; two were used for white fabrics and five for gray. The department also produced upholstery with twelve, 25-year-old Soviet machines at a rate of 88 meters per hour.

- **Glued synthetic fibers department.** Here, 100% polyester fiber first went through a carding machine; two sheets were glued together and returned to dryers at a density of 140 grams per 100 square meters. Material was rolled and readied for shipment at a rate of 4.8 meters per minute. Three Polish gluing machines, more than 10 years old on average, produced 70 rolls, each 30 meters long, per 23-hour day. Drying machines were Soviet-made.
- **Needling department.** The needling department uses scraps of wool and other fibers from textile factories and makes rolls of non-woven materials. Materials were shredded, processed, and then covered with an antirotting chemical and fiber backing. The automobile, apparel, land draining, and floor covering (i.e., linoleum) industries used huge rolls of this nonwoven material. Three German cutting and shredding machines and one Austrian webbing and sewing machine, acquired in 1987, produced 2,500 tons per year.

Personnel Management and Benefits

Some 350 workers and 100 managers, supervisors, and management trainees kept these departments functioning. Of these, 80% were women, including nearly 60% of the middle managers, such as Personnel Manager Regina Poškienė. Hourly workers comprised about 40% of the work force, whose wages ranged from Rs25–Rs70 hourly.

In each department a bulletin board proclaimed the names of the most efficient workers (those exceeding their quotas) in yellow. Names of least efficient workers (those failing to meet their quotas) appeared in red. "That is our incentive system," declared the Managing Director. Karpalavičius introduced differential pay to reward productivity. "Wages correspond to quality and quantity that each worker produces." Wages of less productive workers were lowered or raises discounted. The Šiauliai Factory of Nonwoven Fabrics workers did not have a trade union.

Karpalavičius received a daily report on absenteeism by employee name and also personally interviewed prospective employees. When interviewing, he would ask the interviewee why he or she wanted to work at the Šiauliai Factory of Nonwoven Fabrics and what each expected to contribute to the firm—a departure from the communist system popularly described by Russians as "we pretend to work, and they pretend to pay us."

Ranging as high as 20% in the past, turnover fell to 11% in 1991 (about 4% of whom were retirees), which partially reflected increasingly difficult economic

*A meter equals approximately one yard or, specifically, 39.37 inches.

times. Also, absenteeism per employee dropped from a previous 130 days lost per year to 79 days lost during 1991. Annual value of production per worker rose from Rs16,000 in 1971 to Rs48,000 in 1990, reflecting a 50% inflation-adjusted rise in productivity.

Employees received eight paid holidays and 28 paid vacation days annually. (When raw material shortages arose, some employees accepted vacation days in lieu of furlough. Also, about 50 employees were eligible for retirement, and their departure could delay layoffs of younger workers, if necessary.) For the first 30 days of sick leave, an employee received 80% of salary and then 100% for the next three months, after which the Šiauliai Factory of Nonwoven Fabrics could dismiss the employee. Under Lithuanian law, a child-bearing mother received full pay for the first year and reduced pay for as long as three years, at which time she had to return to her job. However, the firm provided a full subsidy for one and one-half years, permitted the employee to return to the same position at the end of three years, and guaranteed a job somewhere within the Šiauliai Factory of Nonwoven Fabrics for as long as eight years. In permanent disability cases, however, the government and firm shared the cost, which was indexed to inflation.

Most employees received both the thirteenth month bonus and a food allotment. The government set a 1992 minimum of Rs150 monthly; the firm paid employees Rs280 monthly when they ate meals in the company cafeteria. Karpalavičius believed that a positive correlation existed between the quality of food and productivity.

Even after independence, a housing shortage prevailed. The Municipal Council of the city of Šiauliai allocated a certain number of apartments to each factory and other legal entities (such as universities and hospitals) for a set price per unit. The organization then decided who would be permitted to buy an apartment and subsidized part of the purchase price. Even after marriage and having children, some couples waited years for private living quarters. (A typical one-bedroom apartment might measure 600 square feet.) While waiting assignment of living quarters couples might live with their parents or other relatives. Karpalavičius described the problem:

> We have been providing housing one-half mile from the factory. We have subsidized 70 apartments funded from our profits. The government has now started to tax the factory on profits before we pay for the apartments. We are paying double to provide this benefit to our employees. Most of our employees live an hour's bus ride south of town, away from central shopping. Our workers have to go farther to shop, which is why we are building the store here on the factory premises. Employees can order food from our new store, and it can be ready for delivery when they leave to go home. This will save them time and frustration since there have been some shortages of food.

The company store illustrated Karpalavičius's innovative approach to problem solving (shown in Exhibit 34.3 as the commissary and medical building, which was under construction). Principal shoppers were Lithuanian women, 90% of whom worked, raised children, and kept house without many of the conveniences and appliances taken for granted by Western women. Offering little variety, understocked grocery stores quickly sold out of quality merchandise. Women shopped at many stores several times a week, often after a full day's work, spending 10–15 hours per week seeking food, clothing, and other merchandise. They waited in long lines to be served by—at best—an indifferent or impolite employee. When the company store became operational, employees could request meat, vegetables, and other groceries in the morning and pick up their orders at the end of the shift. Store (i.e., SFNF) employees would shop for the highest quality products at the best price. Karpalavičius expected that, after the Šiauliai Factory of Nonwoven Fabrics store opened at the end of 1992, employee productivity would rise—that both the employee and the company would benefit from this added convenience.

Under the Soviet system, the state had prepared workers for specific jobs or a narrow specialty and had dictated where they lived and worked. After independence, Karpalavičius attended an American exhibition and discovered that employees needed to be trained in more than one specialty. Consequently, he initiated cross-training programs to improve employee productivity and mobility; the more training they received, the more they earned. Management also organized lectures on alcoholism and discouraged alcohol abuse by denying addicted workers their thirteenth month bonus or firing them; about four per year were dismissed.

The Market and Competition

Marketing represented a new experience for the Šiauliai Factory of Nonwoven Fabrics because under central planning the government had dictated output, sources of supply, costs, prices, and financing. "Today all departments are linked by the chain of quality," said the Technical Director. Under Soviet rule, supply contracts were drawn up for five years, but changing economic conditions made those old contracts virtually meaningless. Long-time customers, such as the shoe industry, bought less, so the firm had to develop new products and new markets simultaneously in a volatile environment.

When the demand for wool and some nonwoven products decreased, the Šiauliai Factory of Nonwoven Fabrics shifted to higher inputs of cotton waste, which were available in large quantities in Russia. Karpalavičius said, "We are experts in recycling waste from cotton fabrics and threads, and we think there is a market for recycled cotton waste products." However, inflation-driven prices meant that the Šiauliai Factory of Nonwoven Fabrics must allow customers to cancel orders as much as three months before the start of production. Karpalavičius added,

> We do our best to accommodate special orders from our customers. We can initiate production and be ready to ship an order in one or two days. Our chief problem is transportation. Everything depends upon who pays the transportation costs. We have our own trucks but no fuel for our fleet. Fuel prices have increased 300% during the past year. The railway between East and West is incompatible due to different rail gauges. Measures must be taken to standardize railways before the factory can hope to ship anywhere outside of the East.

The Šiauliai Factory of Nonwoven Fabrics spent nothing on advertising because it lacked the funds. However, the Managing Director envisioned an advertising budget of 12%–15% of revenue and thought that he should spend much of it on television advertising.

Russian competitors penetrated the Šiauliai Factory of Nonwoven Fabrics' markets through price-cutting, but Karpalavičius maintained that his firm produced goods of superior quality. Although it was the only Lithuanian producer, 27 competitors still operated in the former Soviet Union. He said, "Those competitors are having problems, and they are coming here for advice, but we are not telling them how to solve their problems. The time of helping other competitors is finished. Three years ago we would have told them how to solve their problems, but now we are not telling them anything."

The Šiauliai Factory of Nonwoven Fabrics held a virtual monopoly in supplying the apparel industry and was a chief manufacturer of insulation and soundproofing for the automobile industry. Recently, Ashilen (a factory in Gelisnogorsk, Russia) purchased three French production lines to produce similar goods and close substitutes. Klauses in Vilnius developed the Šiauliai Factory of Nonwoven Fabrics's present technology. Thirteen machines based on this design were manufactured; three remained at the Šiauliai Factory of Nonwoven Fabrics, and ten were shipped to Russia. The firm attempted to maintain its competitive edge in Eastern markets with high-quality products and low labor costs. However, some competitors established joint ventures with Western companies, thereby obtaining easier access to hard currency financing and better technology. To compete in Western markets, the Šiauliai Factory of Nonwoven Fabrics also sought joint venture partners.

Finances*

The objectives of Soviet socialist accounting were to (1) control performance, (2) use resources economically, (3) meet Central Committee production quotas, and (4) protect socialist property. In the system used at the Šiauliai Factory of Nonwoven Fabrics, total production costs were offset against sales revenue and recorded in a realization account. Against this balance, ordinary and nonrecurring gains and losses were charged, including losses resulting from natural disasters, bad debts, and profits or losses from housing and communal services. The residual was called profits.

Profits of state-owned entities belonged to the government. The distribution of profits required approval by the Ministries of Finance and Economy for the purpose of interest payments, transfers to an economic stimulation fund and a material incentives fund, sociocultural activities, housing construction, and (after privatization in 1992) payment of dividends to equity owners. Prior to 1992, the Šiauliai Factory of Nonwoven Fabrics could utilize two-thirds of its profits for capital expenditures and one-third for discretionary purposes. Management had

---

*Financial data under socialist accounting methods are not easily translated into financial statements recognizable under accounting board standards in a market-based economy. Thus the financial data presented for the Šiauliai Factory of Nonwoven Fabrics are not comparable to U.S. companies' and therefore cannot be subjected to the same type of financial analysis. Attempts to reconcile differences or to understand every entry are virtually impossible for those not expert in both systems because of the lack of common terminology and definitions.

EXHIBIT 34.5

Interim Income Statement, January 1–April 17, 1992: Šiauliai Factory of Nonwoven Fabrics
(Russian Ruble amounts in thousands)

Revenue	
Sales and other revenue	Rs87,658.0
Income attributable to inventory gains	574.0
	88,232.0
Costs and other deductions	
Excise taxes	36.0
Operating expenses	27,341.0
General expense	4,624.0
Total operating expenses	32,001.0
Net operating income	56,231.0
Less	
Interest on capital from the state	1,335.2
Cultural amenities	2,034.8
Addition to reserves	2,520.4
Charity	163.8
Other expenditures	18,142.2
Total	24,196.4
Net income before taxes	32,034.6
Less income tax	13,069.4
Net income	Rs18,965.2

Source: Compiled from Šiauliai Factory of Nonwoven Fabrics financial documents. Translation by Virginija Vaičekonienė.

to explain discrepancies. In 1991, the state charged the firm 7% for the use of long-term capital, 12%–14% for one-year working capital loans, and 29% in taxes on residual income.

The Šiauliai Factory of Nonwoven Fabrics' accounting records contained more than 100 separate items, which were combined in Exhibits 34.5 and 34.6 to produce something recognizable by Western standards. Plant and equipment values represented historical costs, with depreciation allowed at a rate established by the government (6%–7% for a state firm). Inventories and work in progress were carried at cost.

Through creative management, Karpalavičius retained "profits" for future company use instead of returning them to the government. An example was accumulation of materials over several years to build the commissary and medical center, now under construction. Compared to most other factories of its size, the firm's offices, including those of the directors, and other facilities were spartan; cafeteria fare even for managers was rather basic. The company maintained only three automobiles: a chauffeured Volga (a few years old) for the Managing Direc-

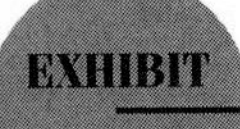

EXHIBIT 34.6

Estimated Financial Condition as of April 17, 1992: Šiauliai Factory of Nonwoven Fabrics
(Russian Ruble amounts in thousands)

Assets	
Current assets	
Cash and cash equivalents	Rs 790.0
Securities	2,830.0
Accounts receivable for exported goods	3,873.6
Receivables due from other debtors	66.1
Inventory	19,187.0
Total current assets	26,646.7
Plant and equipment	
Buildings	25,157.5
Less depreciation	5,022.6
Total	20,134.9
Unfinished buildings	2,168.1
Net property and equipment	22,303.0
Total assets	Rs49,049.7
Liabilities and Shareholders' Equity	
Current liabilities	
Due to bank	Rs 1,598.8
Accounts payable	1,670.2
Accrued wages	1,112.2
Total current liabilities	4,381.2
Long-term debt	—
Shareholders' equity	
Nominal state capital	24,792.4
Nominal stock capital	16,690.7
Retained earnings	3,185.4
Total shareholders' equity	44,668.5
Total liabilities and shareholders' equity	Rs49,049.7

Source: Compiled from Šiauliai Factory of Nonwoven Fabrics financial documents. Translation by Virginija Vaičekonienė.

tor, and two new, smaller Moskeviches purchased in May 1992 for approximately Rs300,000. (SFNF could purchase vehicles directly from Russian factories at courtesy prices of about one-third the retail price.)

Until recently, the government allocated capital expenditures from profits contributed by various state firms. Hence the central government played the dominant role of strategist, deciding when and where to expand and which businesses to be in, whereas local governments controlled the housing market. Therefore political influence and friends were crucial to the successful management of any state enterprise. After mid-1992, the Šiauliai Factory of Nonwoven Fabrics could seek working capital loans and funds for expansion from any source. However, interest rates were in the three-digit range (owing to risk plus inflation), and hard currency for technological upgrading and expansion virtually did not exist for firms such as this one that exported little to the West. Theoretically, short-term loans were available through the Ministry of Economy at a heavily subsidized rate of interest; however, the central government, nearly broke, rationed such funds severely. Because of his influence in the Ministry of Economy, Karpalavičius secured a working capital loan in May 1992, below market rates, from the Ministry to finance accounts receivable.

Russian customers, chiefly state firms, paid for imported products through the government bank in Moscow even after formation of the Confederation of Independent States (CIS). Partly because of its own credit problems and partly to punish Lithuania—the first Soviet republic to pursue independence aggressively—Moscow sometimes delayed payments to the Šiauliai Factory of Nonwoven Fabrics for more than a year and to other Lithuanian manufacturers for as long as three years. This created a countrywide credit crunch. Over the decades the Soviets had forged tightly controlled economic ties among its republics, whose manufacturers, in turn, became captive suppliers to Soviet industry. By necessity, these linkages continued after independence. The credit crunch was further exacerbated when both private and state CIS suppliers of raw materials and components demanded cash payments from Lithuanian importers. Furthermore, the real value of burgeoning accounts receivable deteriorated with inflation.

Although Karpalavičius had a reserve of funds to carry operations through 1992 (worst case scenario) or through 1993 (likely case scenario), he said that the firm's survival depended on his shrewdness and doubted that a new management team would be so clever. He anticipated a second quarter (1992) operating profit of Rs20 million and Rs14 million net after taxes and other deductions. He projected gross revenue in 1992 of Rs500 million compared to Rs250 million for 1991. Increased profits, he thought, should result from raising product prices while holding down labor costs. Instead of retaining and reinvesting those profits, he anticipated that shareholders would vote to increase dividends.

Strategic Planning

In this complex situation of old rules, new environmental parameters, and economic chaos, the Managing Director believed that the crucial decisions for the remainder of 1992 were to

- formulate a business plan,
- prepare a cash flow budget for 1993, and
- implement new production plans to improve efficiency and quality.

He further believed that several factors hampered planning and affected profits. They included privatization and restrictions placed on new shareholders; the ruble-linked economy and high inflation originating in Moscow; raw material shortages that disrupted production scheduling and caused the firm to overinvest in stockpiled inventory; political unrest, especially in parts of the CIS; slow payment of receivables from Moscow on products shipped to Russian state firms while Russian suppliers demanded cash up front; lack of both hard currency and ruble credits, which forced the Šiauliai Factory of Nonwoven Fabrics into barter and countertrade; and the government's continuing economic and political crises, involving changes in laws and the imposition of high tariffs, taxes, and license fees.

He identified the following intermediate term goals.

1. Increase profits.
2. Modernize production.
3. Establish training programs.
4. Budget for Western-style advertising.

Karpalavičius stressed that the Šiauliai Factory of Nonwoven Fabrics's strategic focus was first to survive and second to introduce its products to new, especially Western, markets. It included the following components.

- Research and develop new products made of synthetic fibers but remain with its core technology, the regeneration of waste materials into nonwoven fabrics.
- Differentiate its products from those of competitors especially in terms of quality.
- Continue to strive for 0% rejects by the end of 1992 and work toward developing products of world class quality and, in particular, meet the EC ISO 9000 quality standards.
- Pursue joint ventures with Western firms, not only to secure hard currency funding to update production technology, but also to enter such target markets as Sweden, Germany, the Netherlands, Belgium, Austria, and Australia.

Karpalavičius added, "We hope to reach countries interested in taking advantage of lower labor costs."

Karpalavičius's planned trip to Sweden in July 1992 was to discuss formation of a joint venture. He said, "The Swedes are very happy to do business with us, but they are worried whether the Lithuanian government will let them expatriate profits. We do not understand this problem. If the Swedes wish to buy Lithuanian products, the government should not be allowed to place currency controls on their profits." Although he had initiated preliminary discussions with an Austrian firm and an Italian firm, only the Swedish option held near-term prospects. Additionally, together with myriad management challenges, Karpalavičius would face his first post-privatization reelection. He predicted that under a new leadership the Šiauliai Factory of Nonwoven Fabrics would not survive through 1994.

A North American Free-Trade Agreement (Trading Blocs)

Suk H. Kim

The world is moving swiftly toward three trading blocs distinguished by the dollar, the mark, and the yen. Analysts describe the formation of a free-trade zone around the dollar as a practice run for turning North and South America into a patchwork unified regional trade group. Hence many consider the North American Free Trade Agreement (NAFTA) the first step toward "One America."

In 1990, President George Bush set a free-trade zone encompassing all the nations of the Americas as a goal of his trade policy. Its proponents argued that free trade throughout the Americas would channel investment and technology to Latin nations, radically restructure their economies, and give U.S. companies a head start in capturing business there. And free trade would gradually lift millions of people in those countries from poverty.

Regional groupings based primarily on economic cooperation have become the most debated topic in world trade. Although some world leaders are trying to suppress national in favor of regional interests, those groupings may reflect the difficulties in preserving the present global trading system under the General Agreement on Tariffs and Trade (GATT).

People have cooperated economically for centuries because they recognized the advantages of working together. More recently, intergovernmental cooperation has been directed at making member countries a single economic union. And, successful trading blocs historically have consisted of member countries with similar levels of per capita income, geographic proximity, compatible trading regimes, and political commitment to reorganization. As a result, five forms of economic integration have developed among countries: free-trade agreement, customs union, common market, economic union, and political union.

A Tripolar Economic System

Geography underlies the organization of most current trade agreements. Economists say that the global economy will become increasingly tripolar in the 1990s and beyond. They caution that this trend is likely to lead to less trade among the three groups—Europe, North America, and Asia—in favor of increased trade within individual blocs and regions. Moreover, they argue that this emergence of three giant trading blocs will make the GATT irrelevant. Most issues then may have to be negotiated bilaterally between blocs, with ways found to make multilateral the bilateral negotiations between the blocs.

Six European countries—Belgium, France, West Germany, Italy, Luxembourg, and the Netherlands—established the European Economic Community through the Treaty of Rome in March 1957 and thus removed trade barriers among the member countries. Since then, it added Denmark, Greece, Ireland, Portugal, Spain, and the United Kingdom, becoming, in the process, the European Community (EC). These 12 member countries created a single market in 1992 based on the Single European Act of 1987. The EC countries expect to have a single central bank with a single European currency by the end of the 1990s. At that time, 12 central banks would become regional banks, much like the 12 Federal Reserve banks in the U.S. Federal Reserve System. The EC countries could be the leader in the global economy because they agreed to reap the benefits of economic union. They are still separate countries politically, but they will become a single economic unit for all practical purposes by the end of this century. A worldwide integrated economy does not exist. Yet, economic integration probably can be approached in a free-market system.

The first steps toward NAFTA were taken with the U.S.–Canadian Free Trade Agreement (UCFTA), which went into effect January 1, 1989. The United States and Canada became each other's most important trading partners. The UCFTA liberalized the largest trading relationship in the world; in 1991, the U.S.–Canadian merchandise trade volume was $170 billion compared to the U.S.–Japanese trade volume of $140 billion. Throughout this decade, the UCFTA will phase out tariffs, liberalize investment laws, and grant "national treatment" to companies on both sides of the border. In August 1992, negotiators from Canada, Mexico, and the United States concluded a North American Free Trade Agreement (NAFTA). This proposed union would convert North America into the largest trading bloc in the world, with 360 million people and $6 trillion in purchasing power. The Bush administration hailed the proposal as an opportunity likely by 1996 to create 400,000 jobs in the United States.

Japanese and other Asian government officials loudly assail regional trading blocs that serve as protectionist trade umbrellas. Nevertheless, they concede that trading blocs may be an unfortunate but emerging trend. Development in Asia has been quite different from that in Europe and North America. Political will drives the European and North American arrangements, but market forces may cause the politicians in Asia to integrate more formally. Even though Japan is the dominant force in the area and is likely to be the leader in economic cooperation, neither the Japanese themselves nor other Asian nations want Japan to dominate any such arrangement. However, if Asian countries continue to compete in the world marketplace individually, they could lose their competitiveness. Consequently, Asian leaders view some sort of an informal trading bloc in Asia as a foregone conclusion. Japanese government and corporate strategists intend to shape and coordinate the economic development of the region. Other Asian countries intend to work with Japan to create an informal trading bloc around the Japanese yen.

Basic Elements of NAFTA

Mexico persuaded the United States to launch a two-nation trade pact in 1990. Canada, which had recently signed its own free-trade agreement with the United

States, subsequently entered the negotiations. These three countries agreed on a historic free-trade pact in the early hours of August 12, 1992.

To meet the implementation date—January 1, 1994—the legislatures of Canada, Mexico, and the United States must first ratify the pact. The political challenge of NAFTA is to develop a trinational nonpartisan consensus on competitiveness and free trade. Four requirements stand out. First, free traders should not sacrifice sensitivity and compassion for principle. Second, in exchange for attention to its concerns, labor should end its ostrich-like denial of global economic realities. Third, all three countries should set their sights on improved economic competitiveness and so define NAFTA in the public domain. Fourth, they should recognize that the cost of failure to achieve an agreement would be high.

As a free-trade type of agreement, NAFTA requires the three countries to remove all tariffs among themselves over 15 years, but they are allowed to have their own tariff arrangements with nonmember countries. Key provisions of the agreement include the following. First, tariffs on about half of most U.S. exports to Mexico will be removed immediately; remaining tariffs will be phased out entirely within 15 years. Second, Mexican tariffs on autos will be halved to 10% immediately and eliminated entirely in ten years. Third, cars and trucks must have 62.5% North American content to qualify for duty-free status. Fourth, Mexican trade and investment curbs on most energy and petrochemical products will be lifted. Mexico will allow U.S. and Canadian companies to sell goods to Pemex (the state oil monopoly) and Mexico's State Electric Commission. Fifth, U.S. and Canadian financial institutions will be permitted to open wholly owned subsidiaries in Mexico. All restrictions on services that they offer will be lifted by the year 2000. Sixth, Mexico will let U.S. and Canadian trucking companies carry international cargo into Mexican border states by 1995 and throughout Mexico by 1999. Finally, Mexico will increase its protection for pharmaceutical patents to international standards and will safeguard copyrights for North American movies, computer software, and records.

NAFTA is expected to enlarge possibilities for growth and control inflation in North America. Europe and Japan have two major concerns. First, North America's emerging continental marketplace will be formidable competition for European and Japanese goods and services. Second, Europeans and Japanese believe that NAFTA will give North America a stronger hand in future trade negotiations with Europe and Japan.

In addition, several interest groups of the United States have serious concerns about the impact of NAFTA on their welfare. For example, labor unions and their supporters believe that the trade agreement will hurt U.S. workers because most U.S. manufacturers will move some manufacturing facilities to Mexico. Environmentalists argue that the environment will suffer because free trade would lead companies to seek pollution havens in Mexico, deplete natural resources, and lead to the downgrading of standards. Some business executives are concerned about the so-called "Trojan Horse" effect, that is, foreign companies will use Mexico as an assembly site or distribution center from which their products will be exported to the U.S. market duty free.

Finally, Asian countries are wary of NAFTA for good reasons. Asia's continuing economic success still depends largely on easy access to North American markets, which account for more than 25% of annual export revenue for many Asian countries. Asia has neither any pan-Asian trading bloc nor does it expect to have one as counterweight to NAFTA or the EC. And if the Uruguay Round of the GATT global trade negotiations fails, regional protectionist groups might become a fact of life.

Movement Toward One America

After three failed tries this century, the United States and Canada signed a free-trade agreement that went into effect on January 1, 1989. North American free trade is expected to expand soon with the inclusion of Mexico under NAFTA. The morass of stagnation, inflation, and debt during the decade of 1980s led Latin America to discard its old model and look to free trade and free enterprise as its salvation. Recently, most Latin countries have attempted to meet the four essential criteria demanded by the United States as prerequisites for the formation of a One America free-trade zone: a democratic government, macroeconomic stability, market-oriented policies, and reduced tariffs. Some Latin countries have successfully met these criteria.

The Bush administration's goal of the formation of a hemispheric free-trade area was contained in its Enterprise for the Americas Initiative (EAI). This initiative is already taking form. Brazil, Argentina, Uruguay, and Paraguay are trying to establish a common market by the end of 1994. It would be called Mercosul in Portuguese and Mercosur in Spanish. The Andean nations of Bolivia, Colombia, Ecuador, Peru, and Venezuela also are talking free trade. Meanwhile, Chile, after signing a free-trade agreement with Mexico in 1991, wants a similar accord with the United States. Both Mexico and Venezuela are working on free-trade pacts with Central American nations, and Mexico, Venezuela, Chile, and Colombia are seeking to harmonize their trade.

Trading blocs discriminate explicitly and implicitly against outsiders by granting preferences only to member countries, and regional trade groups have the potential for protectionism. However, many trade analysts believe that completion of the Uruguay Round of trade talks, now in its sixth year, is the key to making the GATT relevant as a way to forestall protectionism. If not, regional groups may disown the GATT, thereby thrusting the post–Cold War world into economic confusion and regional trade wars.

Notes

1. Delal M. Baer, "North American Free Trade," *Foreign Affairs* (Fall 1991), pp. 132–149.
2. Amy Borrus, "A Free-Trade Milestone, with Many More Miles to Go," *Business Week* (August 24, 1992), pp. 30–31.
3. Jay Camillo, "Growth Through North American Trade: The Economic Facts," *Business America* (October 19, 1992), pp. 12–16.
4. Michael R. Czinkota and Masaaki Kotabe, "America's New World Trade Order," *Marketing Management* (Summer 1992), pp. 49–56.
5. Anne M. Driscoll, "Key Provisions of the North American Free Trade Agreement,"

Business America (October 19, 1992), pp. 3–11.

6. Norman S. Fieleke, "Europe in 1992," *New England Economic Review,* Federal Reserve Bank of Boston (May/June 1989), pp. 13–26.
7. Linda C. Hunter, "Europe 1992: An Overview," *Economic Review,* Federal Reserve Bank of Dallas (January 1991), pp. 17–27.
8. Daniel James, "Benefits of U.S.–Mexico Free Trade," *The Corporate Board* (January/February 1991), pp. 20–24.
9. Timothy Koechlin and Mehrene Larudee, "The High Cost of NAFTA," *The Challenge* (September–October 1992), pp. 19–26.
10. Paul Krugman, "A Global Economy Is Not the Wave of the Future," *Financial Executive* (March/April 1992), pp. 10–13.
11. Ingrid A. Mohn, "NAFTA and Jobs," *Business America* (October 19, 1992), pp. 17–21.
12. John S. McCleanaben, "Japan, Europe Take the NAFTA's Measure," *Industry Week* (September 1992), p. 79.
13. Rene Riely-Adams, "America Builds Its Single Market," *International Management* (November 1992), pp. 42–43.
14. Ilkka A. Ronkainen, "Trading Blocs: Opportunity or Demise for Trade?" *Multinational Business Review* (Spring 1993), pp. 1–9.
15. J. Jeffrey Schott, "Trading Blocs and the World Trading System," *World Economy* (March 1991), pp. 299–301.
16. Emily Thornton, "Will Japan Rule a New Trade Bloc?" *Fortune* (October 5, 1992), pp. 131–132.
17. U.S. International Trade Commission, *Rules of Origin Issues Related to NAFTA and the North American Automotive Industry,* Publication No. 2460 (Washington, D.C.: USITC, 1991), pp. 5–6.
18. "One America," *The Wall Street Reports* (September 24, 1992), pp. R1–R28.

CASE 36

Dinette Furniture Company, Inc.

Julius Brown and Brentt Eads

John Sedgewick had been with the Dinette Furniture Company for 30 years. The Joseph Kaneen family started the wood and metal furniture maker in Columbus, Ohio, during the 1930s. Now into the third generation of owners, the company employed some 800 people and had annual revenues exceeding $100 million.

Sedgewick began working at Dinette shortly after graduating from Ohio State in 1959 and progressed through the organization to become Vice-President of Manufacturing on the West Coast. His duties included overseeing the construction and maintenance of the manufacturing and distribution plants in the western United States. Although still family-owned, a committee of five equal managers, three in Los Angeles (Sedgewick being one) and two in Columbus, managed the firm.

In the early 1980s, Sedgewick began hearing rumors at social and business gatherings that competitors and other area businesses were finding it advantageous to relocate to the other side of the Mexican border. Intrigued, the Dinette official began investigating the advantages of building production and assembly plants ("maquiladora" operations) in Mexico and was amazed to find labor costs to be one-seventh of what they were in similar U.S. plants. Excited by the potential savings, Sedgewick continued researching the maquiladora industry.

Maquiladora Program

In 1965, the Mexican government established the maquiladora program to replace its predecessor, the bracero program. Under the bracero program, hundreds of thousands of Mexicans came to the United States for temporary farm work and returned home after their jobs ended. When Congress stopped the program in 1965, many U.S. companies lost tax and tariff breaks and suggested that the Mexican government implement a similar work-exchange program. It created the Border Industrialization Program to meet this request and also to introduce new jobs into the stagnant economy of Mexico's border states. Under the new system, foreign-owned plants would be allowed to manufacture or assemble goods with low-cost Mexican labor, and favorable U.S. tariffs would permit the companies to pay duty on only the value added to the products south of the border. A country foreign to Mexico could enter into the maquiladora program in one of three ways: as a 100% owned-and-managed subsidiary, as a "shelter" or subcontracted operation, where all work would be done for the investing company, or as a supplier to the maquiladora industry.

This case was prepared by Professor Julius Brown and Brentt Eads, M.B.A., of Loyola Marymount University. This case was edited by T. L. Wheelen and J. D. Hunger for this book. Reprinted by permission of the authors.

During the first few years, most of the maquiladora plants were small, labor intensive, low-skilled, and without advanced capital equipment. The first plants were regarded primarily as experiments. A major boost to the program came in 1968 when RCA leased a 120,000 square foot plant to produce components for color television sets. As competition and the U.S. dollar strengthened in the 1970s, more U.S. companies began building maquiladora plants. In the early 1980s, Mexico devalued the peso while the dollar grew stronger, bringing in even greater numbers. From 30,000 workers and 300 plants ten years ago, the industry reached 350,000 workers in 1,400 plants at the beginning of 1990. The number of plants was expected to exceed 1,900 by late 1990, with 400,000 workers expected by 1993.

Because of the maquiladora plants, Mexico became the third largest U.S. trading partner after Japan and Canada. The maquiladora operations surpassed tourism to rank second only to oil in generating foreign currency for Mexico. The plants assembled goods ranging from light manufacturing, including ceramics, toys, and sporting goods, to heavy industry such as cars, trucks, and engines. In 1987 alone, these types of imports into the United States from Mexico amounted to nearly $9 billion.

U.S. companies benefited from the agreement not only in cheaper labor and lower prices but also in increased output and employment. During 1987, U.S. firms employed more than 100,000 workers in U.S. plants and exported $4.2 billion in parts and components to the maquiladora assembly plants. In return, imports into the United States from Mexico topped $8 billion, of which approximately half was value added by the maquiladora plants.

San Diego, the closest California city to the border, was a major beneficiary as employment mushroomed when companies moved their support personnel into the area. Examples included Sherwood Medical, which built a 210,000 square foot plant to employ several hundred people, and Nypro, Inc., of Massachusetts, which opened a plastics plant in Chula Vista, California, to be closer to a major customer's manufacturing plant in Tijuana.

With the plant relocations, however, came criticisms that U.S. jobs were being lost in the process. In particular, U.S. labor groups complained that their members were being hurt the most. One fear was that, although maquiladora operations would make Mexico culturally more like the United States, firms pulling out of the United States would make it economically more like Mexico. Proponents of the programs argued that those jobs would have gone to other countries, especially to Third World countries, if they hadn't gone to Mexico. According to many U.S. government agencies, some low-technology jobs were lost, but retail, service, and high-technology jobs increased because of greater profits and interest in research and development.

Another criticism was that Mexicans coming to the northern cities of Mexico to work were forced to live in badly overcrowded slums where medical care and sanitation facilities were woefully inadequate. Many lived in houses made from cardboard boxes discarded by U.S. plants. Maquiladora proponents countered that, overall, workers in maquiladora plants fared better than their counterparts in manufacturing in other parts of Mexico.

In terms of the environment, maquiladora factories in Mexico were accused of emitting dangerous pollutants and toxic waste because Mexican officials allowed them to do so. In fact, a major attraction to building in northern Mexico was the lack of health, safety, and environmental regulations. Many opponents claimed that both workers and the environment were being exploited for the sake of cutting costs.

Despite the problems, the maquiladora plants continued to grow in ever-increasing numbers. Ciudad Juarez attracted 220 factories with 110,000 jobs to an area that previously had only a limited industrial base. In the 1980s General Motors became the largest private employer in Mexico after establishing automobile parts plants along the border. The Mexican work force at GM was expected to double in the near future. U.S. companies generally found that they could reduce labor problems, operating costs, and labor costs as much as $20,000 a year per worker by opening maquiladora plants.

Dinette Furniture

After speaking with companies that had installed maquiladora operations, John Sedgewick realized that there was more to setting up a plant than he had initially realized. He sat down and listed several areas of concern that he needed to address before making a decision: personnel problems, building and construction obstacles, transportation and shipping problems, competition, and the business environment.

Personnel Problems

An obvious obstacle for most companies would have been the language and cultural barriers, but this wasn't a major concern for Sedgewick. A large percentage of Dinette workers, including management, were already of Mexican heritage or were already fluent in Spanish. The Dinette Vice-President knew that a successful maquiladora would have to use the language of the people; that the company would need to be perceived as a Mexican company to gain the trust and respect of the Mexicans living where the plant would be built. One area of concern to Sedgewick were the few executives and managers nonfluent in Spanish who would be relocated or have contact with the maquiladora. These people would have to be trained in order for them to work and communicate adequately with the new work force.

If relocation was called for, Sedgewick didn't expect any problems from Los Angeles unions. Dinette workers in the United States were mostly unskilled Hispanics with little collective clout and were not expected to call on their unions for help. Company officials believed that if relocation jobs were offered first to existing employees and that if layoffs were gradually implemented, there would likely be little negative publicity. However, the number of unemployment and workers' compensation claims could go up. One competitor, Tableworks, had set up a maquiladora plant and, after closing the L.A. plant, had 270 unemployment, compensation, and stress claims. However, Sedgewick firmly believed that Dinette wouldn't be affected as dramatically because any layoffs would be gradual.

Another potential problem lay in the morale of Dinette employees: how would a move affect their attitudes? Workers relocating to Mexico would face less hospitable living and working conditions. Mexican plants weren't always as clean or safe as those that U.S. workers had become used to. The work week in Mexico was longer, about 47 hours a week, and it wasn't unusual for employees to work 9–9 1/2 hours each day. Also, Saturday work was common and frequently expected.

Many U.S. workers who worked in Tijuana, where Dinette's plant would likely be built, often commuted across the border from San Diego or its suburbs. Not only would travel distance and time be greater for those who preferred the American lifestyle, but border crossings could take anywhere from five minutes to two hours. An additional problem was that U.S. customs and Mexican customs closed at different times and for different holidays, which could prove inconvenient for those commuting between countries.

Sedgewick knew that hiring Mexican locals could present additional difficulties. The annual turnover of Mexican labor in maquiladora plants was reported to be as high as 90%. The reason was that many young workers would come to Mexican border states to work for a short time and return home after earning a few months' income. If the company employed 800 workers in Mexican plants and even 400 left each year, it would be like managing 1,200 workers. Among other things, such turnover would mean higher hiring and training costs and a less productive and stable work force. Sedgewick also estimated that the average age of his line workers would drop from 30 to 20, giving Dinette less sophisticated and skilled workers. He figured that 1½ Mexican workers rather than 1 U.S. worker would be required to do a job because of the native workers' lack of experience and training. Recruiting, training, and keeping good, young workers for any length of time seemed difficult.

Building and Construction

In speaking with experienced maquiladora managers, John Sedgewick became aware of several set-up problems that he would likely encounter. The main one seemed to be a shortage of water. To ensure water for a plant, the company would have to build its own cistern and pumping station. Water was so scarce in some areas that plants were constructed without water sprinklers to prevent fires.

Obtaining power was another difficulty. Because of huge demand, getting hooked up for power could take weeks or sometimes months. Maquiladora managers also told Sedgewick that commencing operations could be delayed indefinitely because of bureaucratic hassles and paperwork back-ups.

Another issue was whether to construct maquiladora plants in stages or to build all at once. One idea was to construct a 25,000–35,000 square foot building and monitor its effectiveness. If this operation was profitable, additional buildings could be constructed. This approach would allow Dinette to ease into the process without an absolute commitment to the maquiladora industry. If the company decided to pull out, losses would be minimal. The disadvantage to this approach would be the difficulty in evaluating whether the project was a success without "pulling out all the stops." Under this plan it would probably take four to five years to put a majority (75%–80%) of the manufacturing workers in Mexico.

The alternative would be to build one main plant where operations would be integrated under the same roof. This approach would allow a clearer evaluation of the effectiveness of using a maquiladora for assembling furniture. However, if the experiment proved unsuccessful, constructing a larger facility would mean greater losses.

Transportation and Shipping

Since opening the plant in Los Angeles, Dinette had always done its assembly and distribution from there. With a maquiladora, smaller items would be assembled in Mexico, and the larger, bulkier items would continue to be assembled in L.A. The reason was shipping costs: furniture freight was charged by volume, and larger shipments tended to waste a lot of space, thus being less cost-effective. The problem, as Sedgewick saw it, would be deciding whether building a plant in Mexico would be efficient if only smaller furniture products were assembled there.

Another question was whether products assembled in Mexico could be transported to Dinette's distribution center in L.A. in a timely manner for transshipment to retailers and customers. Congestion in and around San Diego was increasing, which would mean delays. Sedgewick concluded that these issues needed to be resolved, as distribution would not be possible from the maquiladora plant. With almost 3,000 cartons a day leaving the distribution plant, shipping north through San Diego would be nearly impossible. From L.A., furniture would be distributed in all directions. Finally, with Dinette's supplies coming from various locations—wood from the Northwest and East, fabric from the Eastern Seaboard, and glass from all over the world—Sedgewick was worried that transportation costs into and out of Mexico would increase.

Competition

U.S. industry had always been the dominant force in the growth of maquiladora operations, but this condition was changing. Far Eastern countries were scheduling plant openings because they wanted to be closer to the huge American market, especially with the dollar weakening and Mexico's low labor rates. Entries from Japan were Hitachi, Sony, and Sanyo; Korea was represented by Lucky, Goldstar, and Samsung.

In the furniture industry, U.S. companies feared the offshore competition from Taiwan. Taiwanese firms had come in with lower production costs and margins, forcing U.S. firms to change their strategies. Dinette had been affected, leading it to depend less on sales of metal products and more on those of wood furniture. Also, the U.S. company became almost exclusively dependent on sales of upholstered furniture and other higher priced and higher margin items. Sedgewick knew that Dinette would need to cut costs and prices to remain competitive or perhaps try to find a new position in the market. Whatever decisions Sedgewick made on investing in a maquiladora, he was certain the pressure from Asian-owned maquiladora plants would only increase.

Business Environment

Initially, John Sedgewick found the most appealing aspect of the maquiladora plants to be the potential $9 million savings per year on labor costs, based on a projected $1.50 hourly wage (generous compared to the average pay range of $.90 to $1.30). However, Sedgewick soon realized that the primary advantage to moving south would be the friendlier business environment. Many in the furniture industry, including Dinette, believed that the business climate in California was becoming increasingly hostile because of strict environmental regulations imposed by the South Coast Air Quality Management District (SCAQMD), EPA, and various other state and federal agencies. In an attempt to crack down on solvents polluting the air, the SCAQMD had ruled that certain paints, stains, and lacquers containing these solvents would be banned by 1996, if not filtered by special chambers costing $250,000 each and $50,000 a year to operate. Some estimated that these expenses could force furniture companies to raise prices as much as 30%, a cost that could be avoided by relocating to areas without such stringent regulations.

Moreover, Sedgewick believed that these agencies had a "we'll drive you out of California" mentality and that because regulations passed to clean up the big and powerful aerospace and automobile industries couldn't be enforced, the furniture industry, although a minor polluter by comparison, was viewed as an easy target. Dinette had already been forced to install a million-dollar powder sprayer to be used on metal products. Sedgewick felt that rules to cut back on sawdust levels would soon be forthcoming.

Sedgewick perceived Mexico as a country willing to work with foreign investors. Mexican officials indicated that they were flexible about pollution issues concerning maquiladora plants. Their standards were more relaxed, the political climate was more friendly, and the society was much less litigious.

As recently as 1989, the Southern California furniture industry was a $1.35 billion giant employing almost 70,000 people, and it ranked second only to North Carolina as a furniture producer. This situation changed when the pollution standards in California became the most stringent in the United States, driving many companies to states with lower standards—or to Mexico.

With the environment becoming an ever-increasing topic of debate, Sedgewick worried that the public would perceive a potential relocation as an opportunity to "dump trash in somebody else's backyard." He didn't feel that this perception was accurate because Mexican standards were not that far behind those in the United States. The SEDVE, the Mexican version of the EPA, had already closed down several maquiladora plants for environmental infractions and was expected to continue scrutinizing the border plants more closely. Sedgewick didn't believe that Mexican policy would change drastically within the next ten years and jeopardize possible Dinette investment in the maquiladora program. After that, he concluded, it was anybody's guess.

Now, in the spring of 1991, Sedgewick still had not made a decision and was, in fact, considering additional options. One was the possibility of opening manufacturing facilities in Asia instead of Mexico. He had made an exploratory trip to Taiwan, Korea, and Singapore, and was particularly impressed with the latter. The business climate was very favorable in Singapore. However, he saw two possible problems because of the distance: (1) despite cheaper manufacturing and shipping, quality, style, and delivery controls would be more difficult to maintain than in nearby Mexico; (2) the cost of longer term inventory financing.

Shifting his thoughts back to maquiladora plants, Sedgewick thought of two other possibilities. One would be to find a Mexican company from which he could subcontract the simplest and most basic manufacturing. This solution would cut costs, but he feared the control problem. Also, competition was driving Dinette more toward high-end, higher margin furniture, and he did not want to rely on Mexican production if that trend continued.

Sedgewick was thinking of sending a team to Tijuana for four to six months. He had in mind an Assistant Vice-President and two supervisors—all Mexican-Americans, fluent in Spanish, and thoroughly familiar with Dinette's operation. Sedgewick thought that such an approach would give him two things: first, a more accurate, perhaps quantified cost of some potential infrastructure problems, such as water, power, and phones, and second, over that time period his team could get a much better idea of some potential cross-cultural problems and how to solve them.

The Boston YWCA: 1991

Donna M. Gallo, Barbara Gottfried, and Alan N. Hoffman

In the summer of 1991, Mary Kinsell, Controller and Chief Financial Officer for the Boston YWCA, briefed her successor, Carolyn Rosen, and Marti Wilson-Taylor, the YWCA's new Executive Director. Deeply aware of the organization's financial crisis, Kinsell noted that changes during the past 20 years had created many difficulties for the once-predominant Boston YWCA. Especially pressing was the need to find new sources of funding because of significant cuts in federal funding to nonprofits, increased demand and competition in the fitness and day-care industries, and increased real estate costs. In addition, the YWCA faced questions about how to deal with several aging YWCA buildings, located in prime neighborhoods of Boston but unmodernized and slowly deteriorating. Kinsell warned, "The Boston YWCA is like a dowager from an old Boston family that has seen better days: it is 'building rich' and 'cash poor.' Leveraging equity from its buildings is difficult and making operations generate enough cash flow to maintain the buildings seems almost impossible." The YWCA must now meet these challenges, or it will be forced to cut back its activities and may even face bankruptcy.

The First 100 Years

The Young Women's Christian Association (YWCA) is a nonprofit organization whose original mission was "To provide for the physical, moral, and spiritual welfare of young women in Boston." For more than 12 decades it has done just that: meeting the changing needs of women in the community by providing services, opportunities, and support in an environment of shared sisterhood.

In 1866, a group of affluent women formed the Boston Young Women's Christian Association to rent rooms to women and children whom the Industrial Revolution had enticed to leave their farms for work in city factories. Not only were their working conditions deplorable, but their living conditions consisted almost entirely of unsafe slums and unsanitary tenements. The Boston YWCA offered a clean, safe alternative to these living conditions, as well as recreation, companionship, and an employment referral network for women. The success of the facility led to the opening of the Berkeley Residence (40 Berkeley Street, Boston) in 1884, with accommodations for 200 residents and an employment and training bureau. It also housed the first YWCA gymnasium in America, a crucial part of its mission to "empower women through fitness, health care, and independent employment opportunities." At this early date in the YWCA's history, most

This case was prepared by Donna M. Gallo of Boston College and Professors Barbara Gottfried and Alan N. Hoffman of Bentley College. This case was edited by T. L. Wheelen and J. D. Hunger for this book.

of the funding for the YWCA's facilities and services was raised by wealthy women patrons both through their family connections and from among their friends and acquaintances. From its inception, the YWCA, unlike the larger, more well-known, and more aggressive YMCA, which easily garnered bank loans and donations, had to struggle to fund its projects.

In the ensuing decades, the Boston YWCA opened *The School of Domestic Science* to train women as institutional housekeepers and managers, and started a secretarial training program and other training and educational programs for women. In 1911, the Boston YWCA became affiliated with the other YWCAs in the United States. By this time, the YWCA was no longer merely a philanthropic association run by upper class women for women of a lower class, but an association of working women meeting the needs of other working women in the home and in the marketplace. Nevertheless, the continued support of wealthy patrons was crucial to the YWCA's viability as a community resource.

In the early 1920s, the "Y" initiated a capital campaign under the slogan "Every Girl Needs the YWCA" to raise funds for another building. It received more than one million dollars in contributions by subscription from donors of both the middle and upper classes, and in 1927 ground was broken at the corner of Clarendon and Stuart Streets for the Boston YWCA's new headquarters. Dedicated in 1929, the new building, including recreational facilities, a swimming pool, classrooms, meeting rooms, and offices for the staff, has served as headquarters for the association ever since.

During World War II, the YWCA contributed to the war effort by sponsoring educational lectures and forums such as "Fix-It-Yourself" for the wives of servicemen, offering housing to women doing war work, and providing recreation and entertainment to men and women in the armed services. During this time the YWCA continued to be managed and funded primarily by women, for women.

After the war, YWCA administrators made a concerted effort to reach out to immigrant women. An interracial charter was adopted at the national convention, which called for the integration and participation of minority groups in every aspect of the association, the community, and the nation. In addition, rapid postwar population growth in the suburbs west of Boston led to the opening in 1964 of the West Suburban Branch of the "Y" in Natick, Massachusetts, 20 miles west of Boston. The Natick "Y" focused its energies on the needs and wants of suburban women and their children. Additionally, advocates formed a lobbying group, the YWCA Public Affairs Committee, to focus on housing and family planning, and to call attention to the needs of those women, especially mothers, that were not being met by traditional social service organizations.

Throughout its first 100 years, the Boston YWCA, staffed and funded almost entirely by women, worked to empower women by helping them take charge of their lives, plan for their futures, and become economically independent and self-supporting.

Recent History

In 1866, the Boston YWCA became the first YWCA in the nation. Today we are part of the oldest and largest women's organization in the world, serving all people regardless of sex, race, religion, or income. Our One Imperative is the elimination of racism.

Mary L. Reed—Former Executive Director, 1986

The 1960s were a time of social and cultural upheaval, especially with regard to civil rights, the movement whose goal was equality for all races. In support of the civil rights movement, the YWCA made a commitment to fight racism and integrate its programs and services at every level, initiating a special two-year action plan in 1963. The operating budget for the plan provided for two staff members and support services to become more involved with other community groups working in the areas of fair housing, voter registration, and literacy programs. In 1967, the YWCA's first black President, Mrs. Robert W. Clayton, was elected at the National Convention. In 1968 the Boston YWCA opened Aswalos House in Dorchester, Massachusetts, especially to meet the needs of women in the inner city. As a fitting ending to the 1960s, the *One Imperative* "to eliminate racism wherever it exists and by any means necessary" was adopted and added to the statement of purpose as the philosophical basis for the YWCA in coming years.

Although fighting racism remained important, in the 1970s the YWCA shifted its attention to issues raised by the changing roles of women in American society. The 1960s and 1970s were decades of the revival and growth of the feminist movement in the United States and throughout the world. The social and political arena in which the Boston and other YWCAs were operating was changing rapidly. More and more women were working outside the home while raising children. The number of women living at or near the poverty level was on the rise. Classes and programs at the YWCA had to be redesigned to meet changing demands. For instance, the "Y" offered instruction in survival skills for urban living; but more radically, because nontraditional jobs for women were on the rise, in 1977 the "Y" launched its first nontraditional training program, funded by the federal government, to train women to work in the construction industry. Thus, in the 1970s, federal, state, and local governments became increasingly involved in social welfare, whereas in the past these needs had been met by private charitable and voluntary organizations. At the same time that the YWCA began to rely more on government funding and less on private donations, in the 1960s and 1970s its Board of Directors changed to reflect the racial and class diversity of the women in the communities the "Y" served. Although the new Board members helped the YWCA respond effectively to the immediate needs of the inner city community, it lost touch with the monied constituency that formerly had been the YWCA's base of support. That monied constituency in turn shifted its attention and support to other causes. See Exhibit 37.1 for the YWCA's organization chart.

The Changing Environment

In the late 1970s, the number of unwed mothers, teen pregnancies, and teen parents rose dramatically. At the same time, more and more state and federal funds became available for social programs, and many nonprofits directed their energies to establishing themselves as vendors or service providers to win government contracts. The Boston YWCA became a major vendor in the areas of child care, employment training, teen services, and domestic abuse programming. As a result of

EXHIBIT 37.1

Organization Chart, 1991: Boston YWCA

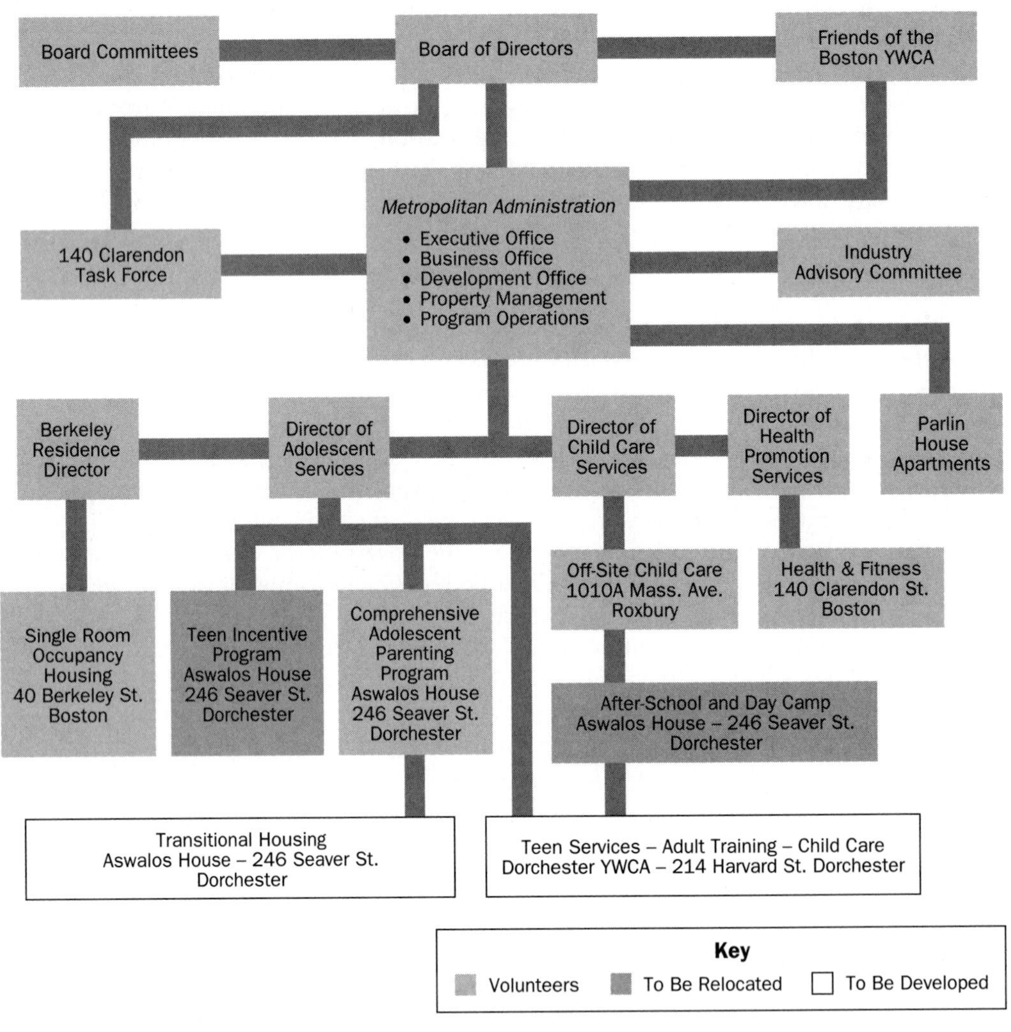

Source: Boston YWCA records.

its strong advocacy efforts, the YWCA received substantial federal and state contracts for further study of issues related to teen pregnancy. However, by redirecting its efforts toward securing government funding, the YWCA seriously eroded its base of private support, especially among those upper class women who had, for generations, been the primary source of funds for the YWCA in Boston. As a result, the YWCA, which had for a long time been one of a few nonprofits, became but one of many contending for the same funds.

As the decade came to a close, the outlook for the "Y" began to shift. Faced with the community's growing need for services and the Boston YWCA's aging facilities, the members of its management team realized that they would have to make some tough decisions about allocating funds that were becoming scarcer. If they were to decide that a major outlay of cash or large loans for facilities were necessary, they would have to pull funds from the programs and services the association provided to the community at a time when the need for community services was greater than ever and funds for these services were scarcer than they had been for some time. However, if the YWCA's management team continued to allocate funds for services and programs while making only minimal allocations for facility maintenance, it risked incurring the cost either of major repairs further down the line or the serious deterioration of major assets. Though the management team did not want to lose sight of the YWCA's commitment to the women and children in the community, the "Y's" financial crisis would require foresight, careful planning, and some hard choices.

The Economic Crunch

In the early 1980s the need for social services grew, increasing the number of nonprofit organizations competing for the same funds. At the same time the Reagan administration cut back federal funding, and nonprofits were forced to go back to raising funds through private donations, grants, bequests, and the United Way. The mid 1980s, however, were prosperous years, especially in the Boston area. Individuals and companies gave more generously than in past years to nonprofits, and in response to the limited availability of federal funds for social services during the Reagan years, nonprofits increasingly funded everything from homeless shelters and food pantries to drug and alcohol rehabilitation centers.

However, the economic downturn in late 1987 immediately cut into the flow of funds to nonprofits. Corporations and the general public became more discerning in making charitable contributions. Many people lost their jobs; a high-debt lifestyle caught up with others: in short, people's disposable income dropped. Raising the funds necessary to keep up the facilities and provide the services the community continued to demand became increasingly difficult. As the economy worsened, the need for services increased proportionately and more rapidly than the "Y" had ever witnessed. At the same time, the YWCA had to contend both with its old "mainstream" image in the face of the proliferation of more "chic" nonprofits such as homeless shelters, battered women's shelters, or "safe houses," and with the growing misperception of the YWCA as an organization run primarily by women of color for women of color.

The climate for the banking industry in Boston during the late 1980s also altered dramatically. Many banks were in financial trouble and those that had lent freely in the mid 1980s now scrutinized every loan request, especially those for capital improvements, and rejected a large majority of those they received. Money to fund new projects and large renovations became nearly impossible to obtain. These negative trends have only worsened so far in the 1990s, as the YWCA faces

EXHIBIT 37.2

Percentage Breakdown—Sources of Funding: Boston YWCA

Source of Funding	1990	1989	1988	1987	1986	1985
	Years					
Support funds	33%	24%	21%	23%	22%	22%
Operating revenue	54	63	67	65	66	67
Non-operating revenue	13	13	12	12	12	11

the absolute necessity of making some hard decisions regarding the allocation of its shrinking resources.

Sources of Funding

Revenue for the Boston YWCA comes from three sources:

1. **Support funds**—funds from the United Way of Massachusetts Bay, contributions, grants, legacies, and bequests.
2. **Operating revenue**—money from program fees, government-sponsored programs, membership dues, housing and food services.
3. **Non-operating revenue**—income from leasing of office space to outside concerns, investment income, and net realized gain on investments.

Exhibit 37.2 shows the percentage each has contributed to total revenue for the past five years.

From 1985 to 1989 the United Way accounted for 70–80% of the support funds revenue. But like all nonprofit organizations in the late 1980s, the United Way was under fire for its operational procedures and found itself in a fiercely competitive fundraising environment. The United Way anticipated a 30% drop in fundraising for 1991, which would affect all the agencies it funded, including the Boston YWCA (see Exhibit 37.3). At the same time, operating revenues for the YWCA dropped off in 1990 so that more, rather than less, support funding was needed to operate. Support funding is expected to continue to decline in the next three to five years, so the Boston YWCA must discover new sources of funding to maintain its services and meet its operational expenses. Exhibits 37.4 and 37.5 present the financial statements of the Boston YWCA.

Facilities

In 1987, the Boston YWCA was operating from four facilities in neighborhoods of Boston and one in Natick, a western suburb of the city. During 1987, the Boston Redevelopment Authority, which oversees all real estate development in the city, awarded a parcel of land to the YWCA for $1.00 on which to build a new facility as part of the city's redevelopment plan. The new facility would replace the old

EXHIBIT 37.3

Detailed Analysis of YWCA Funding Revenues, 1991: Boston YWCA

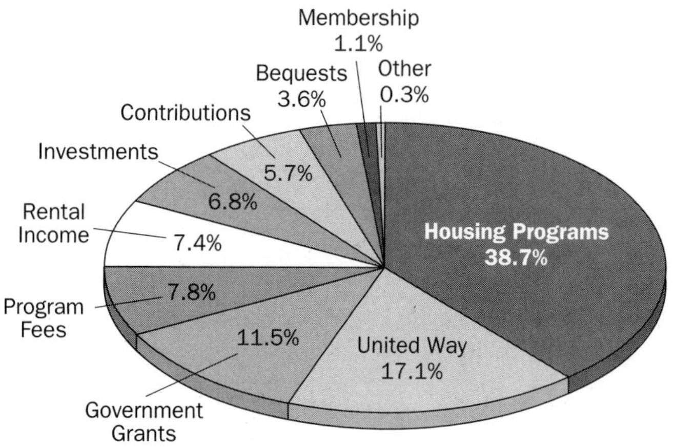

Source: Boston YWCA records.

Dorchester YWCA, Aswalos House, which a grant would then convert to transitional housing for unwed mothers and their children. The YWCA now had a new parcel of land, along with existing facilities in need of maintenance and repair. The management team embarked on a three-year study to analyze its programs and services, and its properties. Most importantly, it decided to implement an aggressive renovation schedule designed to modernize all facilities, to protect the value of the YWCA's major assets, its buildings.

As part of this renovation, repair, and maintenance program, the association's management team had to perform a thorough review of its programs and services. The programs most beneficial to the agency in terms of revenue and those the community had the greatest need for had to be assessed for future expectations of growth and space requirements. New programs would have to be accommodated, and those programs that were no longer financially feasible or in demand would have to be eliminated. The management team planned to complete its research and establish priorities before undertaking any expansion or renovation of the buildings.

West Suburban Program Center

When the YWCA expanded and opened a branch in Natick, Massachusetts, a suburb 20 miles west of Boston in 1964, it bought a building that quickly became inadequate to the YWCA's needs, and in 1981 the center moved to a new facility. This branch was designed to serve its suburban constituency, and resources included programs for women re-entering the job market after years of parenting, training programs for displaced workers, spousal and family abuse programs, divorce support groups, and counseling for women suffering from breast cancer.

Statement of Support and Revenue, Expenses, Capital Additions, and Changes in Fund Balances: Boston YWCA

Years Ending June 30	Current Fund	Plant Fund	Endowment Fund	1991 Totals	1990 Totals
Support and Revenue					
Support					
United Way	$ 703,643	—	—	$ 703,643	$ 713,500
Contributions and grants	233,264	—	—	233,264	197,700
Legacies and bequests	150,386	—	—	150,386	537,540
	1,087,293	—	—	1,087,293	1,448,740
Operating revenue					
Program fees	320,611	—	—	320,611	355,170
Government-sponsored programs	471,615	—	—	471,615	411,050
Membership	45,674	—	—	45,674	71,579
Housing and food service	1,589,587	—	—	1,589,587	1,586,553
	2,427,487	—	—	2,427,487	2,424,352
Non-operating revenue					
Rental income	302,641	—	—	302,641	298,036
Investment income	278,982	—	—	278,982	244,224
Net realized gain on investments	41,392	—	—	41,392	2,308
Other revenue	7,967	—	—	7,967	43,790
	630,982	—	—	630,982	588,358
Total support and revenue	$4,145,762	—	—	4,145,762	4,461,450
Expenses					
Program services					
Aswalos House	$ 250,621	14,782	—	265,403	384,776
Berkeley Residence	1,053,131	86,465	—	1,139,596	1,054,106
Cass Branch	1,216,544	128,673	—	1,345,217	1,394,075
Child Care	422,411	2,030	—	424,441	344,011
Harvard	6,132	—	—	6,132	—
	2,948,839	231,950	—	3,180,789	3,176,968

(continued)

However, in 1988, after much research and years of restructuring the services offered at the West Suburban Program Center, its inability to support itself financially through its operations led to a decision to close the facility.

Aswalos House

Aswalos House, located in Dorchester, Massachusetts, a neighborhood within the jurisdiction of the City of Boston, originally opened in 1968. Until 1989, it housed

EXHIBIT 37.4

Statement of Support and Revenue, Expenses, Capital Additions, and Changes in Fund Balances: Boston YWCA *(continued)*

Years Ending June 30	Current Fund	Plant Fund	Endowment Fund	1991 Totals	1990 Totals
Supporting services					
General and administration	632,657	15,364	—	648,021	793,861
Fundraising	287,448	6,981	—	294,429	135,978
	920,105	22,345	—	942,450	929,839
Total expenses	3,868,944	254,295	—	4,123,239	4,106,807
Excess (deficiency) of support and revenue over expenses before capital additions	$ 276,818	(254,295)	—	22,523	354,643
Capital Additions					
Grants and gifts	106,495	38,985	—	145,480	314,798
Investment income	—	5,529	65,598	71,127	68,018
Net realized gain on investment transactions	—	—	72,577	72,577	63,874
Write-off of deferred charges	—	—	—	—	(305,312)
Loss on sale of asset	—	—	—	—	(11,856)
Total capital additions	106,495	44,514	138,175	289,184	129,522
Excess (deficiency) of support and revenue over expenses after capital additions	$ 383,313	$ (209,781)	$ 138,175	$ 311,707	$ 484,165
Fund balances, beginning of year	$1,379,040	$1,486,053	$3,042,128	$5,907,221	$5,423,056
Transfers between funds					
Plant acquisition	(274,155)	274,155	—	—	—
Principal repayment on loan payable to endowment fund	(143,841)	143,841	—	—	—
Permanent fund transfer	346,908	(346,908)	—	—	—
	(71,088)	71,088	—	—	—
Fund balances, end of year	$1,691,265	$1,347,360	$3,180,303	$6,218,928	$5,907,221

Source: Boston YWCA, company records.

an After School Enrichment Program and a Teen Development Program that offered training for word processing and clerical work, and GED preparation courses. Later, Aswalos House added a program for teen mothers.

In 1989, the receipt of a $100,000 Department of Housing and Urban Development (HUD) grant transformed Aswalos House into transitional housing for teenage mothers and their children, and existing programs were transferred to other facilities. Originally the programs were to be transferred to the new Dorchester Branch planned for the parcel acquired from the Boston Redevelopment Au-

EXHIBIT 37.5

Balance Sheet: Boston YWCA

Years Ending June 30	Current Fund	Plant Fund	Endowment Fund	1991 Totals	1990 Totals
Assets					
Current assets					
Cash	$ 137,469	66,292	—	203,761	110,684
Cash in escrow and security deposits	40,642	—	—	40,642	37,932
Accounts receivable (less allowance for doubtful accounts of $3,500 in 1991 and $2,687 in 1990)	102,334	—	—	102,334	166,245
Supplies and prepaid expenses	54,452	—	—	54,452	73,613
Total current assets	334,897	66,292	—	401,189	388,474
Pooled investments	1,793,198	—	3,180,303	4,973,501	4,775,252
Land, buildings, and equipment, net	—	2,147,155	—	2,147,155	1,869,963
Deferred charges	—	349,638	—	349,638	349,638
	1,793,198	2,496,793	3,180,303	7,470,294	6,994,853
Total assets	$2,128,095	2,563,085	3,180,303	7,871,483	7,383,327
Liabilities and Fund Balances (Deficit)					
Current liabilities					
Current maturities of long-term notes payable	—	18,979	—	18,979	17,524
Accounts payable and accrued expenses	254,757	—	—	254,757	201,581
Deferred revenue	182,073	—	—	182,073	202,717
Total current liabilities	436,830	18,979	—	455,809	421,822
Long-term notes payable, less current maturities	—	1,196,746	—	1,196,746	910,443
Loan payable to endowment fund	—	—	—	—	143,841
Total liabilities	436,830	1,215,725	—	1,652,555	1,476,106
Fund balances (deficit)					
Unrestricted					
Designated by governing board to function as endowment	1,507,135	—	—	1,507,135	1,453,867
Undesignated	(101,933)	—	—	(101,933)	(354,084)
Total unrestricted	1,405,202	—	—	1,405,202	1,099,783
Restricted—nonexpendable	286,063	223,798	3,180,303	3,690,164	3,545,183
Net investment in plant	—	1,123,562	—	1,123,562	1,262,255
Total fund balances	1,691,265	1,347,360	3,180,303	6,218,928	5,907,221
Total liabilities and fund balances (deficit)	$2,128,095	2,563,085	3,180,303	7,871,483	7,383,327

Source: Boston YWCA records.

thority. However, the YWCA never developed that parcel because development costs were estimated at $1.5–$2 million, and the YWCA was able to raise only $300,000. Consequently, the parcel of land was returned to the authority.

The new Aswalos House for teen mothers opened in October 1990, and provided transitional housing for ten mothers and their children. Prospective occupants have to be between the ages of 16 and 20 and demonstrate severe financial need. Counseling services are provided, and a staff case worker arranges for schooling and job training for the teenagers. In addition, a staff housing advocate coordinates finding permanent housing for the mothers and their children.

Half the expense of running the facility is covered by a federal grant to the Boston YWCA. The remaining half is made up by fees paid by the teen mothers from their welfare income, United Way funds, and private donations.

YWCA Child Care Center

The YWCA Child Care Center is rather inconveniently located in downtown Boston on the fringe of the main commercial district and is rented rather than owned by the YWCA. To be licensed as a day-care center in the Commonwealth of Massachusetts, it had to undergo extensive renovations. The owner of the property contributed a substantial portion of the cost of the renovation work, and a private grant covered the balance so that no loans were necessary to complete the project.

The center, a licensed preschool, provides day care for 50 children at fees of $110 a week per toddler and $150 a week per child for children under three years of age. Some scholarships are available for families who are unable to pay. When the center first opened, many of its clients were on state-funded day-care vouchers. Participation has now dropped considerably, however, because a significant percentage of that program was cut from the state budget. To compensate for the loss of clients, the center went into the infant care business, caring for children from six months to two years of age, but it continues to run at less than capacity.

The Berkeley Residence

The Berkeley Residence opened in 1884 in downtown Boston to provide housing for women of all ages. Originally there was housing for 100 residents, an employment and training bureau, and a gymnasium, the first in the country for women. In 1907, 35 rooms and a meeting hall were added to the facility.

In 1985, the Boston Building Code Department cited the Berkeley Residence for not meeting current city and Commonwealth safety and fire codes. Major repairs and renovations estimated at $1 million were necessary to bring the building up to health and safety standards. In 1986, the YWCA obtained a construction loan for the full amount at 10% interest to be amortized over 25 years. After project completion, payments would be approximately $100,000 annually. Work began in 1988. Needed repairs included conversion from oil to gas heat, installation of a sprinkler system and smoke detector system throughout the building, new elevators, and many other less costly types of repairs and maintenance work. Tenants were not displaced during construction, a major concern at the beginning of the project's planning stage. The renovation work was completed in the spring of 1991.

The facility now rents 215 rooms, providing both long-term and short-term housing for women of all ages. The Berkeley Residence offers inexpensive rent and meals, an answering service, and maid service. Other services located at the facility include a referral network for jobs and services, social services, tourist information, and emergency services. The building is open and staffed 24 hours a day, 7 days a week, providing safe, secure housing at reasonable rates for single women in the city.

Boston YWCA Headquarters at 140 Clarendon Street

Constructed between 1927 and 1929, the headquarters for the Boston YWCA is advantageously located at the corner of Clarendon and Stuart Streets. It is located on the edge of one of the city's most prestigious retail districts, Newbury and Boylston Streets and Copley Place, in the heart of Boston's Back Bay business district. The area offers the finest in upscale retail stores and desirable office space, including the John Hancock Building and the Prudential Center. The Clarendon Headquarters, a 13-story brick and steel building, sits on approximately 13,860 square feet of land and includes approximately 167,400 square feet of space. It currently houses the YWCA administrative offices, the Parlin House Apartments, the Melnea Cass Branch of the YWCA, and several commercial tenants. The Melnea Cass Branch operates health and fitness facilities, which include a swimming pool and employment training programs. The Parlin House Apartments occupy floors 9–13 and comprise studio, one- and two-bedroom apartments rented at market rates.

The building has not been significantly renovated since its completion in 1929, and no longer complies with city and state building codes. In 1987, the building elevators desperately needed repairs at an estimated cost of $270,000. The building also now needs a new sprinkler system to ensure the safety of its residents and tenants and to bring the building up to code. The Parlin House Apartments also require major renovations to achieve an acceptable standard of safety, appearance, and comfort. The Apartments currently use common electric meters, and need to be rewired so that tenants can control the electricity to their individual units, and pay accordingly. The YWCA's administrative offices also require improvements and repairs.

The health and fitness facilities also require significant repairs, updating, and renovation. Old, dreary locker rooms are unattractive to current and potential members, and a larger men's locker room is needed to accommodate male members. In addition, to keep up with new trends in the fitness industry, the YWCA needs to refurbish its space for aerobics classes and purchase new weight training equipment. During this time, the YWCA also has been forced to close the pool for repairs, and the pool building itself needs substantial exterior work. Cost estimates for the work on the pool and pool building exceed $200,000. At the same time, decreased demand for health and fitness clubs and increased competition in both the day-care and health and fitness industries has had a negative impact on revenues for this facility.

Because it is in such a state of disrepair, maintaining and operating the building has become very costly. In years past, the Board of Directors has chosen to funnel their scarce available resources into programs rather than into general repairs and maintenance of facilities. As a result, the building at 140 Clarendon Street is currently running at a net loss of more than $200,000 a year.

In 1988, a certified appraiser valued the Clarendon property at $16 million. (However, the real estate market in the Boston area has since declined significantly.) The Boston YWCA's Board of Directors then sought a $7 million loan for the proposed renovations from several major Boston area banking and financial institutions, but most of these institutions did not respond favorably to the loan request. The banks had some valid reasons for refusing to loan the YWCA funds for the renovations, including the YWCA's own uncertainty about how the changes would affect revenues. However, the fact that the YWCA is a women's organization without connections in the "old-boy" network of the banking establishment contributed to the YWCA's lack of financial credibility. Finally, although the Clarendon building's excess value would cover the loan-to-value ratio, the banks raised serious questions about whether the YWCA's existing and potential cash flow could meet the debt service obligation.

The executive committee of the Boston YWCA is now faced with a serious dilemma. It must decide what to do with a deteriorating facility that not only serves as its headquarters, but also as a flagship of services offered by all the area YWCAs. After several years of study, review, and debate it is considering the following options for the Clarendon headquarters.

1. Sell the building with a guaranteed leaseback for its facilities and offices.
2. Sell the building to an interested local insurance company and rent space for the administrative offices in a nearby office building.
3. Bring in an equity partner to fund the renovations for a percentage of ownership in the facility.
4. Continue with minimal renovations and operate as in the past.

Increasing Competition in Fitness Services

In 1989, the management team of the Boston YWCA hired a consulting firm to review the Health Promotion Services division, housed at 140 Clarendon Street, one of the YWCA's primary sources of both operating revenue and expense, and to assist in finding ways to enhance these services. The consultants surveyed current, former, and potential members about the strengths and weaknesses of the YWCA's Health Promotion Services including appearance, cleanliness, scheduling, products (i.e., equipment, classes, swimming pool, etc.), and overall management of the facility. This study also noted considerable competition from the following vendors of health and fitness services:

- Bally's Holiday Fitness Centers
- Healthworks
- Fitcorp
- BostonSports

- SkyClub
- The Mount Auburn Club
- Nautilus Plus
- Fitness International
- Fitness First
- The Club at Charles River Park
- Mike's Gym
- Fitness Unlimited
- Gold's Gym

For the most part, the health club marketplace is a standardized industry in terms of the products and services offered at various facilities. Most clubs offer free weights, weight equipment, exercise and aerobics classes, locker rooms, and showers with towels available. During the 1980s, many new health clubs opened and the health club market became increasingly competitive. These clubs went to great expense to promote elaborate grand openings and fund extensive advertising campaigns to attract new members. The consultants' study found that 15 other health and fitness facilities within the city compete directly with the YWCA. However, the YWCA does fill a unique niche because it is affordable, strongly emphasizes fitness in a noncompetitive and noncommercial environment, appeals to a diverse cross section of people, and is conveniently located. Other clubs are perceived as more commercial and competitive than the YWCA, with a greater emphasis on social interaction and frills such as saunas, racquetball and squash courts, eating facilities, and the like. Comparing the YWCA's Health Promotion Services to other health clubs in the city shows the YWCA to be in a price range somewhere between the commercial clubs and the no-frills gymnasiums. The commercial clubs range from \$800–\$1,200 a year, plus a one-time initiation fee of from \$100–\$1,200; the no-frills gymnasiums range from \$300–\$400 per year; and the YWCA costs between \$420 and \$600 a year, plus an annual membership fee of \$35.

The YWCA is comparable in size to the competition, but its space is not as well laid out as that at other clubs. Most of the other clubs are air-conditioned, but the YWCA isn't. Its membership drops significantly during the summer months, whereas summer is the peak season for other clubs. The YWCA also ranks behind the top four clubs in cleanliness, and members noted that its dreary atmosphere contributes to their sense of its uncleanliness. The YWCA's weight-lifting equipment and weight machines are not quite up to the standards of the competition, and the YWCA lacks the staff and supervision other clubs provide. However, the YWCA does have a swimming pool, an indoor track, and day care. Only one other club has a pool that comes close in size to the YWCA's, and only two other clubs offer indoor tracks or day care.

According to the consultants' study, current users of the YWCA's Health Promotion Services joined because the "Y" is convenient, provides a caring environment that promotes interaction, and is relatively inexpensive. A current user profile revealed that members generally are seeking a health and fitness experience for themselves as individuals rather than a social atmosphere. Additionally, what mattered to them were sensible class schedules, adequate staff, good staff communication with members, timely information, affordable pricing, an atmosphere without pressure, and an open, caring, and diverse environment. The complaint most often cited among current users was the lack of communication with members with regard to scheduling changes for classes, changes in the hours of operation, class cancellations, pool closings, and changes in procedures and policies. Other factors that concerned current members were the lack of cleanliness, dreary appearance, small men's locker room, poor staff management, poor class capacity management, inadequate equipment maintenance, poor scheduling, poor facility layout, and the lack of public relations and advertising to attract new members.

The consultants also surveyed former members to determine why they did not renew. Their reasons mirrored the complaints of current members:

- Poor communication with members
- Equipment breakdowns
- Untimely equipment repairs
- Poor upkeep/cleanliness
- Poor ventilation
- Dreary appearance
- Dissatisfaction with staff (no personal attention)
- Rigid schedules
- Lack of air-conditioning
- Overall deterioration of the facility

The study also concluded that marketing and promotion of the Health Promotion Services are minimal, with little effort made to attract new members, making it nearly invisible in the community.

Marti Wilson-Taylor, the new Executive Director, and Carolyn Rosen, the new Chief Financial Officer, quickly realized as they took control of the Boston YWCA in 1991 that several major decisions concerning the YWCA's physical facilities and programs and services had to be made. However, first and foremost, they had to determine the strategic direction of the YWCA for the remainder of the decade. In an environment of increasing competition and shrinking resources, they face a great challenge.

Name Index

For Chapters 1–15 only.

For Chapters 1–15 only.